TOSCANINI

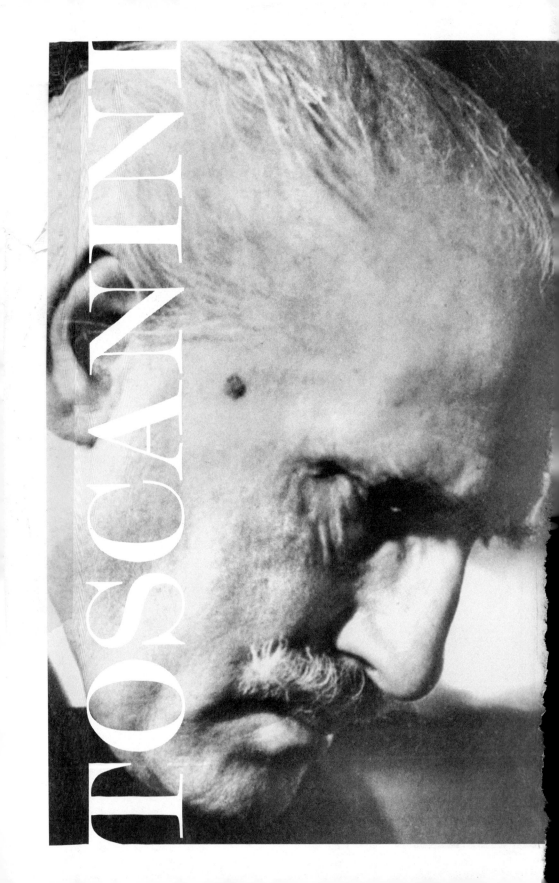

TOSCANINI

Harvey Sachs

TOSCANINI

Musician of Conscience

LIVERIGHT PUBLISHING CORPORATION

A Division of W. W. Norton & Company

INDEPENDENT PUBLISHERS SINCE 1923

NEW YORK | LONDON

For information about permission to reproduce selections from this book,
write to Permissions, Liveright Publishing Corporation, a division of W. W. Norton & Company, Inc.,
500 Fifth Avenue, New York, NY 10110

For information about special discounts for bulk purchases, please contact
W. W. Norton Special Sales at specialsales@wwnorton.com or 800-233-4830

Manufacturing by LSC Communications, Harrisonburg, VA
Book design by Barbara M. Bachman
Production manager: Anna Oler

Library of Congress Cataloging-in-Publication Data

Names: Sachs, Harvey, 1946– author.
Title: Toscanini : musician of conscience / Harvey Sachs.
Description: First edition. | New York : Liveright, [2017] | Includes bibliographical references and index.
Identifiers: LCCN 2017016654 | ISBN 9781631492716 (hardcover)
Subjects: LCSH: Toscanini, Arturo, 1867–1957. | Conductors (Music)—Biography.
Classification: LCC ML422.T67 S35 2017 | DDC 784.2092 [B] —dc23
LC record available at https://lccn.loc.gov/2017016654

Liveright Publishing Corporation
500 Fifth Avenue, New York, N.Y. 10110
www.wwnorton.com

W. W. Norton & Company Ltd.
15 Carlisle Street, London W1D 3BS

1 2 3 4 5 6 7 8 9 0

For Eve

CONTENTS

PREFACE

"IF I THOUGHT THAT MY LIFE COULD INTEREST ANYONE, I WOULD have a lot to tell," Arturo Toscanini remarked to some friends during a late-in-life conversation. The friends laughed in disbelief. At the time, tens of millions of people worldwide knew Toscanini's name, and many among them would certainly have been interested to hear or read his own account of his life. But writing a memoir would have been out of character for him; he never made the attempt.

There was a lot to tell. Toscanini was one of the most scrupulous and dynamic opera and concert conductors of all time, and the first-born among them to have made abundant use of the electronic media and to have left recordings of substantial portions of his repertoire. His work as an interpreter was so original and so powerful that it has influenced musicians down to our own day: generations of conductors, including those who disagreed or disagree with his interpretations, have been the beneficiaries of his reforms in the opera house and concert hall, and his insistence that the performer's job is to come as close as possible to revealing the composer's intentions, rather than to use the music as a vehicle for self-expression, remains a basic principle for many of today's outstanding performers. The intransigent personality that allowed him to accomplish his reforms and pursue his musical ideals also led him to stand up to Europe's fascist regimes in the 1930s; as a result, he became an example of nonpartisan political morality.

In the mid-1970s, when I was working on my first Toscanini biography (published in the United Kingdom and the United States in 1978 and subsequently in many other editions and translations), I was able to gather firsthand testimony from many of my subject's family members, colleagues, and friends, but primary source material from Toscanini himself was scarce, since he had rarely granted interviews or written about himself for publication. Then, in the mid-1990s, approximately fifteen hundred of his letters came to light—a discovery that culminated in the publication, in 2002, of *The Letters of Arturo Toscanini*, which I edited, translated, and annotated. In his letters, Toscanini revealed his thoughts about himself, his family, other people, the music he studied and performed, his work, travels, early life, tastes in literature and the visual arts, political beliefs and activities, and attitudes toward love and sex. Later, two of his grandchildren, Walfredo Toscanini and Emanuela Castelbarco, made available to me more than a hundred tape recordings of their grandfather in conversation with his family, friends, and colleagues during the last years of his life. These conversations—recorded without Toscanini's knowledge—shed even more light on his life and thoughts.

Much other significant material has emerged during the forty years since I was writing the early biography: the archives of many of the organizations with which Toscanini worked—La Scala's, for instance—have opened up, as have previously unexamined parts of the Metropolitan Opera's and the New York Philharmonic's archives and the Italian Fascist government's enormous dossier on Toscanini, who was considered one of the most prominent enemies of Mussolini's regime. Most important, the Toscanini family's vast official archive, the Toscanini Legacy, was acquired by the New York Public Library in 1986 and cataloged during the 1990s, and I supplemented my investigation of the material contained therein with the abundant documentation that belonged to the grandchildren. (Most of Walfredo Toscanini's material has since been united with the Toscanini Legacy collection, and Emanuela Castelbarco's has been acquired by the Archivio di Stato in Milan.) I was also able to travel to Buenos Aires to investigate documentation of the five substantial opera seasons that Toscanini conducted there between 1901 and 1912, and I have made use of many other sources as well.

In short, this book is a completely new biography, not a revision or an expanded version of the earlier book. Apart from quotations from other sources, I don't believe that a single entire sentence from the old book is to be found in this one. I have examined new sources, reexamined old ones, and produced what I hope is a close-to-definitive account of a long life filled with artistic, personal, and political drama. I have tried to probe my subject's complicated character and to describe his relationships—some of them deep, others casual—with the remarkable figures he knew firsthand, including composers (Verdi, Boito, Puccini, Mahler, Debussy, Richard Strauss, Ravel, Stravinsky, Kodály), conductors (Mengelberg, Walter, Beecham, Stokowski, Ansermet, Furtwängler, Erich Kleiber, Fritz Busch, De Sabata, Szell, and Cantelli), instrumentalists (Busoni, Huberman, Adolf Busch, Arthur Rubinstein, Heifetz, Horowitz, Piatigorsky, Menuhin), writers (Gabriele D'Annunzio, Stefan Zweig, Thomas Mann), Mussolini, Einstein, the historian Gaetano Salvemini, the philosopher Benedetto Croce, the descendants of Richard Wagner, and most of the well-known singers active from the 1870s through the 1950s and beyond, from Paul Lhérie—Bizet's first Don José—and Victor Maurel—Verdi's first Iago and Falstaff—through Enrico Caruso and Feodor Chaliapin, and on to Renata Tebaldi and Giuseppe Di Stefano.

Toscanini's was a ninety-year life that began before the invention of the phonograph and the incandescent light bulb and ended at the dawn of the space age; an eighty-year musical immersion that began before Wagner and Verdi had written their final masterpieces and that ended in the era of Boulez and Stockhausen; a sixty-eight-year career, carried out in twenty European, North and South American, and Middle Eastern countries; and a private existence that was torn between love of family and erotic recklessness.

There is, as Toscanini said, a lot to tell, and I have tried to tell it honestly, thoroughly, and engagingly.

ACKNOWLEDGMENTS

THIS BOOK WAS MADE POSSIBLE BY A FELLOWSHIP FROM THE National Endowment for the Humanities, Washington, DC.

A travel grant for research in Buenos Aires was provided by the Janet Levy Fund of the American Musicological Society.

I give very special thanks to Eve Wolf, whose love, encouragement, and advice have helped me throughout the six years that this project has required; to the late Walfredo Toscanini, Arturo Toscanini's grandson, who wanted this book to come into being and provided access to important materials and memories; to Emanuela di Castelbarco, Arturo Toscanini's granddaughter, whose materials and memories likewise contributed to this biography; to my editor, Robert Weil, at Liveright, and his staff, including his assistant, Marie Pantojan, anf the excellent copy editor, Otto Sonntag; and to my children, Julian Sachs and Lyuba Sachs, for their love and patience.

Special thanks also to the following individuals: Luciano Crivello, Luca Di Bari, the late Christopher Dyment, Jeffrey Karp, Corinne Salada, Pia Sebastiani, Allan Steckler, Cia Toscanini, Liana Toscanini.

My thanks to all of the following, in alphabetical order:

ARGENTINA: Sebastiano De Filippi; Gustavo Gabriel Otero; Daniel Varacalli Costa, Director of the Revista Teatro Colón; Inés Urdapilleta, Directora vocal del Ente Autárquico Teatro Colón.

CANADA: Richard Caniell, Immortal Performances; Michael Kater, York University; Philip A. Maxwell.

FRANCE: Fabian Gastellier, Notes de Nuit, Paris; Alain Hirsch; Bérengère de l'Epine, Bibliothèque Historique de la Ville de Paris; Rémy Louis; Georges Zeisel.

GERMANY: Peter Aistleitner; Thomas Blubacher; Uwe Kaiser.

ITALY: Massimo Ansbacher; Dino Belletti, Head of Institutional Relations, Teatro alla Scala, Milan; the late Gaetano Bonafini; Mariagrazia Carlone, Soprintendenza archivistica per la Lombardia, Milan; Diego Cescotti, Biblioteca Civica e Archivio Storico di Rovereto; Pier Filippo D'Acquarone; Paolo Dalla Sega and Maurizio Romano, Archivio Visconti di Modrone, Università Cattolica del Sacro Cuore, Milan; Duccio Dogheria, Archivio storico del Museo d'Arte Moderna e Contemporanea di Trento e Rovereto; Maria Pia Ferraris, Archivio Storico Ricordi, Milan; Renato Garavaglia, Museo Teatrale alla Scala, Milan; Giulia Giovani, Fondo Carlo Placci, Biblioteca Marucelliana di Firenze; Francesco Lombardi; Nicola Luberto, Museo Casa Toscanini, Parma; Carlo Marinelli Roscioni; Raffaella Nardini, Biblioteca Palatina, Parma; Fiamma Nicolodi, Università degli Studi di Firenze; Roberta Paganelli; Simonetta Puccini; Federica Riva, Librarian of the Conservatorio di Musica "A. Boito," Parma; Giuseppe Richichi; Susanna Rinaldi; Francesca Sgroi, Ufficio servizi stampa, Teatro Regio, Turin; Roberto Spocci, Archivio storico del Comune di Parma; Anna Tedesco, Università degli Studi di Palermo; Patrizia Veroli.

THE NETHERLANDS: Anton Haefeli, International Society for Contemporary Music.

NEW ZEALAND: Roger Flury, National Library of New Zealand, Wellington.

UK: James McCarthy, *Gramophone*, London.

USA: Sam Bodkin; Remi Castonguay, Irving S. Gilmore Library, Yale University; Herb Depke; Victor DeRenzi; Álvaro Domingo; Arthur Fierro; Mortimer Frank; John Freeman; Michael Gray; Barbara Haws, Archivist, New York Philharmonic; Deborah Hefling, Archivist, Cleveland Orchestra; David Kettler; Bob Kosovsky, New

York Public Library for the Performing Arts; Jonathan Kuhn, City of New York/Parks & Recreation; Steven Lacoste, Archivist, Los Angeles Philharmonic; Roberta Montemorra Marvin; Donald C. Meyer; Anthony Paterno; Suzanne Ryan; Alma Schwisberg; David Seubert and Daisy Muralles of Special Collections, University of California at Santa Barbara Library; Amanda Sewell; Elaine Toscanini; Maya Toscanini; the late Robert Tuggle and John Pennino, Metropolitan Opera Archives; Frank Villella, Chicago Symphony Orchestra Archives; Ann Ziff.

The author wishes to thank:

The Estate of Arturo Toscanini, represented by Allan Steckler, for permission to quote from documents and other materials

Archivio dello Stato, Roma, for permission to quote from documents in government files on Toscanini, 1923–1938

The New York Philharmonic Archives, represented by Barbara Haws, Archivist, for permission to quote from documents in the Archives

The New York Public Library for the Performing Arts, for permission to quote from writings by Bruno Walter and B. H. Haggin

Richard-Wagner Gedenkstätte, Bayreuth, for permission to quote from documents regarding Toscanini

Arthur Fierro, for permission to quote from *This Was Toscanini*, by Samuel Antek and Robert Hupka

Vera Leinsdorf, for permission to quote from *Cadenza*, by Erich Leinsdorf

Maria Grazia Paulucci delle Roncole, for permission to quote from the letters of Giulio Gatti-Casazza

Simonetta Puccini, for permission to quote from the letters of Giacomo Puccini

Richard Rodzinski, for permission to quote from *Our Two Lives*, by Halina Rodzinski (1976)

Corbo e Fiore Editori, Mestre-Venezia, for permission to quote from *Tullio Serafin, il patriarca del melodramma*, by Teodoro Celli and Giuseppe Pugliese

Edizioni Curci, Milano, for permission to quote from *Ricordi scaligeri*, by Enrico Minetti (1974)

Éditions Robert Laffont, Paris, for permission to quote from *Les Balcons du Ciel*, by Margarita Wallmann (1976)

AUTHOR'S NOTES

―――――

I.

IN ORDER TO AVOID LONG LISTS OF PERFORMANCES AND REPER-
toire within the body of the text, I am providing the following lists
online at https://www.scribd.com/document/342450854. The first is
a chronological list of all of Toscanini's known performances; the
second an alphabetical list, by composer, of all of the works in his
repertoire, with the dates of their performances.

These two lists can easily be cross-referenced. A third list provides
a select bibliography, and a fourth provides reference notes for all
quotations and much other material as well; these, too, have been
created in order to avoid encumbering the physical book.

II.

THE FOLLOWING INFORMATION IS PROVIDED TO ENABLE READERS
to convert fees, salaries, ticket prices, and the like into present-day
values.

HISTORIC EXCHANGE RATES (APPROXIMATE) IN TOSCANINI'S LIFETIME

US dollars (USD) to Italian lire (ITL) to British pounds (GBP)

Up to 1915:	1 USD	=	5.5 ITL	=	0.20 GBP
1920–1926:	1 USD	=	25 ITL	=	0.20 GBP
1927–1939:	1 USD	=	19 ITL	=	0.20 GBP

(Second World War and immediate postwar years: anomalous)

1950–1957:	1 USD	=	625 ITL	=	0.38 GBP

In average purchasing power:

1 USD in 1885–1908	=	25	USD in 2016
1 USD in 1926	=	13.40	USD in 2016
1 USD in 1932	=	17.30	USD in 2016
1 USD in 1937	=	16.50	USD in 2016
1 USD in 1945	=	13.20	USD in 2016
1 USD in 1954	=	8.81	USD in 2016

TOSCANINI

Arturo with his sister
Narcisa circa 1876, the
year the boy entered
Parma's Royal School
of Music.

INDETERMINATE AND DETERMINATE SOUNDS

Milan, 11 May 1946

THE WAR HAS BEEN OVER FOR A YEAR, BUT THE DEVASTATION and grief that it provoked have barely begun to fade. The city is still filled with rubble. Chunks of the historic Duomo and of the Galleria, the glass-roofed nineteenth-century arcade that connects the vast Piazza del Duomo to the smaller Piazza della Scala, are still missing. There is much poverty and even more near poverty; people have to scrounge for basic necessities, most homes lacked heat through the previous winter, and electric power still fails frequently.

But something unusual is in the air this evening. By eight o'clock, people are streaming into the Galleria and the Piazza del Duomo, where loudspeakers have been hung from buildings and lampposts; the Piazza della Scala, similarly festooned, is already crowded with onlookers, and the doors of the old Teatro alla Scala itself are about to open, to receive an audience for the first time in nearly three years. During several summer nights in 1943, bombs from Allied planes demolished large swaths of the city as part of a massive and ultimately successful attempt to force Italy's Fascist government to surrender, and on the night of 15–16 August a firebomb crashed through the roof of La Scala, leaving the stage and backstage areas intact but reducing much of the auditorium to ruins. Since war's end, the reconstruction of La Scala has been a high priority of the

Allied Military Government: more than any other building in the nation's commercial capital, La Scala is a symbol of secular Italian civilization, and funding its restoration is seen as a major gesture of goodwill toward a country that is still reeling from the disastrous effects of fascism and of Mussolini's ill-conceived and ill-fated alliance with Hitler.

The house is now ready, and its old master, who had not set foot in it for sixteen years and who had been living in exile for the last eight of those years, has returned to prepare and conduct the inaugural concert. An hour or so earlier, a crowd of Arturo Toscanini's admirers was hovering around the artists' entrance in Via Filodrammatici, hoping to catch a glimpse of the seventy-nine-year-old conductor, who is not only the most celebrated performing musician in the world but also a symbol of unwavering resistance to totalitarianism. Now the maestro and his family are inside the theater; he has made sure that the evening's soloists have arrived and are warming up, and he is trying to collect his thoughts as he paces nervously back and forth in his dressing room.

Sixty years have passed since he first entered La Scala, fifty since he first conducted here. This is where he observed Verdi rehearsing the first production of *Otello*; where he conducted the world premiere of Puccini's *Turandot* and the national premieres of *Siegfried, Eugene Onegin, Salome, Pelléas et Mélisande*, and many other works; where he coached and assisted and tormented three generations of singers, orchestra musicians, chorus members, and production staffs; and where he presided over groundbreaking organizational and technical reforms. For many years he dedicated himself to this institution, and even from afar he has never ceased to concern himself with its fortunes. Now he has come back as an old man to face *his* public, in *his* theater, in *his* adoptive city, in *his* beloved country.

At a few minutes to nine he picks up his baton and walks from the dressing room to the wings. Through an opening he sees the house lights go down, and he hears the audience become quiet. He fears that he may faint. At exactly nine o'clock the stage manager says, "Maestro, we're ready. Break a leg"—and opens the door for him.

Toscanini walks decisively onto the stage.

1.

PARMA IS ONE OF THE MOST BEAUTIFUL CITIES IN NORTHERN ITALY, and thanks to the global mania for Parma ham, Parmesan cheese, and other local culinary products, it is also among the most prosperous and well-looked-after ones. Banks and industries provide the wherewithal for restoring the old center's monuments; pedestrian-only zones have been thoughtfully laid out; and signs point the way to sites of historic, cultural, or purely practical interest.

If Toscanini, who was born in Parma in the third quarter of the nineteenth century and spent most of his childhood and adolescence there, could revisit his home town today, he would have no trouble finding his way around its center or recognizing most of the buildings in that area, but he would be astonished not only by the city's vastly expanded outskirts but also by the historic center's well-turned-out appearance. Photographs of Parma from the time of Toscanini's youth show shabbily dressed urchins in front of buildings with smoke-darkened, peeling façades. You can almost smell the poverty.

In the eighteenth century, Toscanini's paternal ancestors lived about fifty miles from Parma, in the remote mountain village of Bogli in the township of Ottone, in the Upper Trebbia valley of the Ligurian Apennines. Bogli di Ottone now lies in a corner of the *regione* (roughly equivalent to a US state) of Emilia-Romagna that converges with the *regioni* of Lombardy, Piedmont, and Liguria. The name Toscanini means "little Tuscans"; the family had evidently emigrated from what is today the *regione* of Tuscany, the northwesternmost reaches of which lie only about twenty-five miles from Bogli.

Of Simone and Maria Toscanini, the conductor's great-great-grandparents and earliest known ancestors, we have only the names, but their son Pietro, born in Bogli in 1769, is known to have migrated to the town of Cortemaggiore, fifty miles away in the Po valley, where he married one Domenica Alberici. Pietro and Domenica's son Angelo—Arturo's paternal grandfather (1790–1864)—eventually became the owner of a textile mill in Cortemaggiore and of a small shop there and another in Piacenza, the provincial capital, where he sold his products. Angelo had no known musical talent, but as a begetter of children his achievements rivaled those of the prolific Johann Sebastian Bach. His first wife, Giuseppa Zerbini (1795–1821), produced eight children, including two sets of twins, in eight years; twelve days after the birth of her second set of twins, she committed suicide by throwing herself down a well. Four months later, Angelo married Eligia Bombardi, Arturo's grandmother, who was born in Cortemaggiore in 1795 and was evidently made of stronger stuff than her predecessor: she gave birth twelve times and survived. But the infant mortality rate was so high that by the time Eligia's last child was born, the Cortemaggiore census registry listed only ten of Angelo Toscanini's eighteen offspring.

Claudio Toscanini, Arturo's father, was born on 25 January 1833, the third-youngest of Angelo and Eligia's children. At the age of twelve, he had an argument with his father, slapped Angelo's face with a handkerchief, left home, and walked thirty miles to Parma, where he was given lodging by a sister and began to work as a tailor. He was of a restless nature—and his restlessness dovetailed fortuitously with major political events that were unfolding when he was in his teens and twenties: Italy, splintered into city-states, duchies and foreign-run territories since the fall of the Roman Empire a millennium and a half earlier, was on the verge of becoming a nation.

By the 1850s, the Risorgimento movement, which had begun among middle- and upper-class radicals as an expression of discontent with foreign rule, had spread to vast numbers of Italians of all classes. In 1858, Count Cavour, prime minister of King Victor Emanuel II of Piedmont, Savoy, and Sardinia, plotted with France to provoke a war with Austria and create a kingdom of northern Italy that would annex the Austrian-dominated Lombardy, Veneto, and central Italian duchies to the king's other territories. Claudio Toscanini was among the many young volunteers who joined General Giuseppe Garibaldi's red-shirted irregular army to help the Piedmontese fight the Austrians, despite Garibaldi's aversion to monarchy. But after the combined Italian and French forces had won the battles of Magenta and Solferino and had triumphantly taken control of Milan, Napoleon III pulled France out of the agreement. An armistice with

Austria was signed, Piedmont and Lombardy remained weakly confederated, and Garibaldi's forces were disbanded. In 1860, however, the charismatic general reassembled his redshirts; Claudio enlisted and took part in the successful campaign to rid Sicily of Bourbon rule, then joined the Bersaglieri (sharpshooters), a division of the regular armed forces.

The following year, a plebiscite created the Kingdom of Italy under Victor Emanuel, with its capital in Turin, but Garibaldi, angry with the new national government for its unwillingness to wrest Rome from the control of Pope Pius IX, again began to gather a volunteer corps; Claudio, as hotheaded as ever, deserted the Bersaglieri to join his idol's irregular forces in Sicily in a campaign that was intended to sweep northward toward the ancient imperial capital. The attempt ended on 29 August 1862, when Garibaldi's 1,500 redshirts were confronted by the regular army, 3,500 strong, at Aspromonte in Calabria. There was a brief skirmish; Garibaldi was wounded, and the regular army took control. Claudio and his fellow deserters were imprisoned and sentenced to death; some were shot, but Claudio was among those resentenced to life in prison, where he contracted scurvy and lost some of his teeth but survived for three years, until a royal decree pardoned the surviving Aspromonte irregulars.

A young man, Giuseppe Montani, was among the volunteers from Parma who had taken part with Claudio Toscanini in Garibaldi's Sicilian expedition of 1860, and after Claudio's return from prison Giuseppe introduced him to his family. Before long Paolina (called Paola), one of Giuseppe's sisters, had become engaged to Claudio.

The Montani family hailed from Altare, a hill town west of Genoa, known for its master glassworkers. In 1827, the twenty-year-old Pietro Montani, Paola's father and the future conductor's maternal grandfather, made his way to Parma, where he was employed first by the Serventi and then by the better-known Bormioli glassworks. Pietro married Carolina Notari, born (1811) in nearby Reggio Emilia; Paola was the fourth of Pietro and Carolina's ten children.*

---

* Pietro was the son of Giuseppe Antonio and Anna Maria (née Granni or Grenni) Montani. Arturo Toscanini later described Grandpa Pietro as a handsome man who had such a beautiful beard that local artists used him as a model for Joseph in paintings of the Holy Family. Parma's Bormioli glassworks still exist in the twenty-first century.

Paola's family warned her about becoming attached to Claudio Toscanini, a womanizer and anything but a steady worker. She, however, was already in her midtwenties (Paola was born on 29 June 1840)—a spinster, by the standards of the day—and Claudio, seven years her senior, was an attractive fellow. They were married in Parma's Santo Spirito church on 7 June 1866. A few days later, Claudio learned that Garibaldi was once again gathering his Corpo Volontari Italiani to help in the imminent Third War of Independence; he said goodbye to his bride, and off he went, together with two of his brothers-in-law. One night toward the end of June, Claudio's troop train stopped in Parma, and the new husband slipped away to spend a few hours with his wife. "That night they manufactured me," their son said with a chuckle, many years later.*

In mid-July, Claudio fought in the successful battles of Castel Condino and Bezzecca, near Lake Garda. Austria won the brief war but ceded Venice to France as a token of gratitude for Napoleon III's intermediary efforts; France allowed Venice to become part of the Kingdom of Italy, but the Trentino would remain Austrian for another half century.

Claudio returned home, put away his red shirt, and went back to tailoring, albeit unenthusiastically. On 7 November 1866, a confidential political report from the Royal Prefecture of Parma, sent to the Ministry of the Interior in Florence, noted that "five or six citizens belonging to the radical party met [. . .] to discuss badly-needed assistance for the periodical *l'Unità italiana*. [. . .] A new assessment was made, and one Toscanini, Claudio, son of Angelo, 30 [*sic*] years old, tailor, and Ceresini, Augusto [. . .], both resident in Parma and both already compromised in the Aspromonte affair, were charged with collecting donations to that end. Their footsteps will be followed."

The radical party in question was the Associazione Unitaria Democratica, an antimonarchist group headed by the exiled Giuseppe Mazzini. Claudio was also a leader of the local branch of the similarly antimonarchist Alleanza Repubblicana Universale and a member of its fearful-sounding but in fact dormant Compagnia di

---

* These and many other direct Toscanini quotations (most of them translated from Italian) are taken from tapes of conversations recorded, unbeknownst to the maestro, in the 1950s.

Punizione Accoltellatrice (company of punishment by stabbing). One hothead more or less made little difference to the local authorities: Parma was known for its radicals—anarchists, communards, republicans, and anticlericalists—and sixty years later it would be the last northern Italian city to cede to Mussolini's Fascists, after a doomed battle at the barricades. Although Claudio's name appears again in some official correspondence, his political activities were not serious enough to be of real concern to Parma's police. And he had other things to think about.

2.

AT ABOUT THREE IN THE MORNING OF 25 MARCH 1867, FOUR OR five months after Claudio's return to Parma, Paola gave birth to a baby boy. Later that day, the new father carried the infant from the house at Borgo San Giacomo (now Borgo Rodolfo Tanzi, no. 13), in the working-class quarter known as Oltretorrente ("beyond the river"—the Parmesan equivalent of "the wrong side of the tracks"), to the town's tall, octagonal, thirteenth-century baptistery, one of the most striking buildings in northern Italy. "Infantulo imposui nomina Arturus Primus Alexander Secundus," reads the baptismal record. The next day, Claudio registered Arturo Alessandro Toscanini at the town hall; one of the two friends who acted as witnesses was a wrought-iron artisan, Francesco Campanini—a fellow radical and the father of two boys who, in their day, were nearly as famous in musical circles as Claudio's son was to become: the tenor Italo and the conductor Cleofonte Campanini.

Baby Arturo, nursed on his mother's milk, was thin, delicate, and frequently ill—so sickly that after he had been weaned he was kept on a strict diet of broth and mush. One day he saw a plate of beans in olive oil on the table and pointed at it. "That's all he needs!" said one of his aunts. But his grandma Montani replied, "If he wants beans, give them to him. He's going to die anyway, so it's better to make him happy." Almost immediately, the child's health began to improve.

Since 1967 Toscanini's birth house in Borgo Tanzi, which had once belonged to the Montani family, has been a museum filled with relics from its most celebrated resident's career, but, in fact, the three Toscaninis lived there only briefly, for within a few months of Arturo's arrival they had moved to an apartment in Borgo del Voltone (now Via Carducci). And in March 1869 they moved to Genoa, where Claudio, whose tailor shop in Parma had not prospered, hoped to open a more profitable establishment.

Arturo Toscanini's biographers—this one included—have heaped criticism on poor Claudio for his unreliability as husband, father, and breadwinner. But, as Gustavo Marchesi, another biographer, has pointed out, Claudio, like many other Italians, probably believed that Garibaldi, Cavour, and company had rid the peninsula not only of Austrians and Bourbons but also of its "chronic poverty." In reality, however, much of the nation found itself in worse economic shape than it had known before. Parma, for instance, had been the capital of a small but prosperous duchy prior to reunification; now it was nothing but a financially declining county seat. Genoa, on the other hand, was a regional capital and a thriving port, and Claudio believed that life would be better there. He and his wife and infant son lived on the sixth floor of a building at Salita agli Orti di Sant'Andrea no. 8, where Paola gave birth to a girl, Narcisa.

But the goddess Fortuna did not smile upon Claudio in Genoa any more than she had in Parma, to which the family soon returned so that Claudio could make another in what would become a long series of fresh starts and increasingly foolish business ventures. He was a good-natured fellow who preferred building castles in the air to making and mending clothes, and he missed the excitement of his years as a Garibaldino. The family had to move frequently: civic records show that they lived in some fifteen different dwellings in Parma during Arturo's childhood and teens. Claudio began to drink to excess, and he was anything but a faithful husband. "My father was a good-looking man," his son said of him. "Women went after him. And what's a young man to do? Some say yes, some say no." Claudio did not say no.

Arturo's father had good qualities, too—a sweet, undemanding nature, above all. Paola, on the other hand, was proud, harsh, and unaffectionate. She had to take care of her four children (Ada, Arturo's second sister, was born in 1875, and a third, Zina, came along two years later), look after the household, and run the tailor shop during her husband's not infrequent absences. Her son, even in old age, remembered that her threatening voice had frightened him and that she had spanked and slapped him frequently for minor infringements or for no reason at all, whereas his father "never gave me a whack," he recalled. As a child, Arturèn—the diminutive of Arturo in Parmesan dialect—sometimes thought that he had been adopted, because his mother always gave Narcisa one more lump of sugar for her *caffelatte* than she gave him for his. "These things make an impression on a child," he commented.

Arturèn was generally well behaved, although he indulged in the dangerous sport of jumping onto carts and carriages to get free rides. "Once, my mother sent me to buy some salt, and I [. . .] got myself onto the back of a carriage," he recalled. The carriage kept going, far beyond the boy's destination, and he was afraid to jump off while it was moving. It took him "to San Pancrazio, three kilometers from Parma. It finally stopped, and I walked home. They were waiting for the salt!"

Unsure though he was of his mother's feelings toward him, the boy recalled having had a fundamentally happy childhood, and he was considered bright and good-looking. He found great warmth among his Montani relations and was much fussed over by them— especially by his youngest aunts, Cesira and Esterina—although whenever he was about to visit them his mother would instruct him to say that he had already eaten, even if he had not: she did not want to hear her parents and siblings say, "We told you not to marry Claudio Toscanini." Arturo, for the rest of his life, remembered having always felt hungry during his childhood.

As an adult Toscanini was opposed to organized religion and refused to partake of the sacraments of the Roman Catholic Church, but as a child he enjoyed attending mass. He liked "seeing those colorful paintings, and I had fun listening to the music sung in church," he said. "My little voice would join in when they sang the benediction. After the benediction they would raise up the images that they passed to everyone to kiss—I would change places three or four times to be able to kiss them." He once served mass, and he had his first communion at the church of the Santissima Annunziata in Oltretorrente.

Arturo learned to read before he went to kindergarten: one of his earliest recollections was of a nighttime train ride to Genoa (the family moved there again, briefly, in one of his father's eternally doomed attempts to succeed in business) and of being able to read the name of the city of Alessandria when the train stopped at the station. He was not brought up in a cultural void. Despite the Toscaninis' impecunity, neither they nor the Montanis were considered lower or peasant class: they were lower-middle-class urban artisans. For both families, culture was not something to be carefully nurtured or regarded with awe; it was a natural part of daily life. Parma's residents were surrounded by masterpieces of architecture, painting, and sculpture of nearly every period from the Romanesque to the Neoclassical; throughout his life Toscanini particularly loved the *Deposition from the Cross*, a celebrated twelfth-century bas-relief by Benedetto Antelami in Parma's cathedral, but he was also familiar with the sixteenth-century paintings, in the cathedral's cupola and elsewhere in the city, by Correggio—who was from the nearby village of that name—as well as works by Correggio's younger contemporary known as Parmigianino. There was widespread enthusiasm for literature, too—especially for High Romantic poets and novelists—and workers at Claudio's shop often took turns reading aloud to each other. Toscanini was always grateful for having thus become acquainted not only with Italian literature but also with many foreign works, such as Sir Walter Scott's *Ivanhoe*, in translation, and he remained a voracious reader.

Parma's great passion, however, was opera. In the 1870s and 1880s, five theaters hosted opera seasons of varying length and quality, and two outdoor arenas provided summer opera performances—all in a town of only 47,000 inhabitants. The main venue for opera was the beautiful Teatro Regio (Royal Theater; originally Nuovo Teatro Ducale, or New Ducal Theater), built in 1829 at the command of Duchess Marie Louise, daughter of Emperor Francis II of Austria and widow of Napoleon I. During Toscanini's youth, the Regio was the focal point of social life for Parma's aristocracy and bourgeoisie, but artisan- and working-class people also poured into its upper galleries during the opera season. When the general program was posted every December, local citizens referred to it as *la gioia*, the joy. Popular productions received multiple performances, and many people came night after night to find out whether a certain singer would perform a certain aria as well or as poorly as the night before, to voice their approval or disapproval, to chat with friends, and perhaps to go to a café afterward to argue about the performance and trade the latest theater gossip.

Claudio Toscanini, who, according to his son, had a pleasant voice and "a good ear," sometimes sang in the Regio's chorus, and his shop assistants went to the theater every evening during the opera season to help dress the cast. The Montanis, too, were amateur singers and passionate opera fans, and it was either Grandpa Pietro or one of his sons who first took Arturèn to hear an opera—Verdi's *Un Ballo in Maschera*—in February 1871, a month before the boy's fourth birthday; he had already heard parts of the opera sung repeatedly around the shop, and at some point during the performance he chimed in, singing the inaccurate version he had learned and provoking laughter in the audience.

He attended a local kindergarten in which the boys were separated from the girls, but he would often sneak over to the girls' section because he had a crush on a pretty blonde. The teachers "always found us sitting on the floor, and we slept together, with our heads close together," he recalled. But the girl died, "and I cried a lot." Later, when he was at the conservatory, "sadness would come over me," he said, "because my sister [Narcisa] had [also] died, when she was eight years old, of diphtheria. I [. . .] would go to the window, I would look toward the poplar trees at the cemetery, and I would think of the little girl and of my sister."

Toscanini also remembered that a fifteen- or sixteen-year-old girl who worked for the family would sometimes have him sleep in her bed at night, when he was five or six, and that this upset his mother. The girl, Medea Massari, spent much time in the Toscanini household learning tailoring skills and recalled many years later that Arturèn was "like an old man"—quiet, serious, and stubborn—and did not enjoy playing with other children. He was fascinated by musical sounds, she said, and loved to play on a little two-stringed instrument that she had fashioned for him from a hollowed-out corncob.

There is a story that Medea's father had studied music and kept a piano at home, and that the girl taught Arturèn to play scales and pick out tunes, but Toscanini did not mention this in later conversations about his childhood. It was his elementary school teacher who, he said, first realized that the boy —whom she teasingly called Napoleon because he often had a stern look on his face—could memorize poems after a single reading, and she was surprised when he asked to visit her home because she had mentioned that she owned a piano. She played some notes; he sang them back to her correctly and then began to pick out the tunes of arias and songs that he had heard people sing. "She said to my father, 'Have this boy study, because he has a great capacity for music,'" Toscanini recalled, and she suggested that Arturo be enrolled at the local conservatory. The idea must have appealed to Claudio and Paola, since tuition was covered by the crown, and those students who were accepted as residents had their room and board completely subsidized. Many artisan-class children were apprenticed to masters who fed, clothed, and sheltered their young assistants but did not pay them; for poor parents of children who seemed to be musically inclined, the Regia Scuola di Musica (Royal School of Music) was a place where boys could learn a trade and where they could live most of the year at the expense of the state.

After Arturo had scored 90 percent on his final school examinations at the end of second grade, Claudio engaged a tuba player named Bonini—a member of the Teatro Regio's orchestra—to give the boy his first music lessons. "He began by hitting the table [and saying] 'Sing these notes!'" Toscanini later recalled, laughing.

"'I can't. I don't know how.'

"'Well you see, this is a noise, it's an indeterminate sound.' I had never heard the term. And then he sounded a note on a glass: 'And this is a determinate sound.'"

However much, or little, Arturo may have learned from Bonini, he did teach himself to "play the piano immediately, to get into my fingers all the songs that my father sang [. . .], to be together at Christmas, at Carnival." And on 9 September 1876 Claudio applied on his son's behalf to the music school's director, Giusto Dacci, with a grammatically and syntactically shaky letter.*

---

* Claudio had had little schooling, and for most Italians of the day "standard" Italian was learned at school but not spoken locally. Toscanini recalled, for instance, that his mother

Most Illustrious Director,

Toscanini Claudio of Parma resident in Strada dei Genovesi No. 65 profession tailor.

Having a son of his named Arturo of the age of about 9 and a half who seems very inclined toward Instrumental music, who knows how to read, and write, and instructed in music lessons.

It is for this that he presents to Your Most Illustrious Lordship his most fervent supplications in order to obtain the Favor that his son were admitted as a resident pupil in the Royal and Highly Honored Musical Institute, the influence of which the son having the necessary requisites to the purpose will certainly be able to call himself very fortunate one day together with his poor family.

And to further prove to Yr. Illus. L. the truth of what he has set forth above attaches to the present

    1st   The boy's birth certificate
    2nd   The vaccination certificate
    3rd   Certificate of Good behavior
    4th   The Certificate of promotion to the Municipal Elementary School of Parma in Via Caprazucca.

The writer trusting to obtain so high a Favor has the great honor of presenting in advance to Yr. Illus. L. his most heartfelt expressions of thanks in the act that with deep respect he has the pleasure of being

                Yr. Illus. L.'s
                Much obliged Servant
                Toscanini Claudio

Arturo was allowed to participate in the entrance examinations, which were held early in November—the very same week

---

never spoke to him in anything other than Parmesan dialect, even after they both had lived in Milan for many years.

in which Brahms's First Symphony had its premiere, in Karlsruhe, and only three months after Wagner's *Ring of the Nibelungen* had been heard in its entirety for the first time at the inaugural Bayreuth Festival. Twenty-three of the twenty-four available residence posts were already filled, and eighteen boys vied for the one remaining spot. Arturo did not obtain it, but he was the second of three boys who were accepted as nonresident students, with the understanding that they would become residents as soon as positions were open. For over a year, he spent his days at the conservatory but returned home every evening, and his parents struggled to pay for his school meals. In July 1877 he passed his first exams with 136 points out of 160, and on 1 February 1878, after another letter from Claudio to the director and another exam, Arturo was admitted as a resident student.

3.

PARMA'S MUSIC SCHOOL, OPENED BY DUCHESS MARIE LOUISE IN 1825, was originally intended only for the instruction of singers, but eleven years later the already legendary violinist Niccolò Paganini created a ducal orchestra in town, and the school's curriculum was broadened to include all the orchestral instruments. With the birth of the Kingdom of Italy, the institution was officially dubbed a Royal School of Music; during Arturo's first year as a student, the Council of State in Rome confirmed the school's status as a government-subsidized entity under the jurisdiction of the Ospizi Civili—a civic association that oversaw the town's hospitals, charitable institutions, and shelters.

The school occupied and still occupies a large deconsecrated Carmelite convent built in phases between the early fourteenth and the late seventeenth centuries. It was not a cozy place in Toscanini's day. Winters in the Po plain are damp and bitterly chilly, but the conservatory boys slept in two unheated halls, unfurnished except for the twelve cots in each of them. Straw for the mattresses was not replaced often enough, bed linen was changed so infrequently that the rooms usually stank, and bedbugs were common. There was a single water closet but no bathtub: baths were provided once a year at the Civic Hospital. Health regulations required students to have had smallpox vaccinations prior to admittance and to be given cholera vaccinations whenever outbreaks occurred in the country. Reports of gastritis, fever, and other ailments were common.

Each student had a daily allotment of 700 grams of bread, 33 centiliters of milk, 12 grams of cheese, 160 grams of soup, 300 grams of vegetables, and 210 grams of meat or, more often, fish on the verge of going bad; for the rest of his life Toscanini would hate fish. Students also received 60 centiliters of poor-quality wine each day, but the young Toscanini often sold his wine to other students in order to buy printed music. A few students complained about the food and even registered official protests; for most, however, and certainly for Arturo, the conservatory's living standard was no lower than what they had known at home: well-to-do parents did not want their children to become musicians.

All day every day and in all seasons, the students wore charcoal-colored, military-style uniforms: thigh-length, neck-high jackets with two vertical rows of yellow buttons and with gold lyres on either side of the collar; cuffless trousers; and black, button-up shoe-boots, of which each student was given two pairs. For outdoor wear they received calf-length coats and military caps adorned with royal insignias over the shiny brims. Each student also received six white shirts, two nightshirts, six pairs of underpants, twelve pairs of long socks, six starched collars, four knit shirts or sweaters, twelve handkerchiefs, a set of cutlery (each piece was numbered), a toothbrush, a comb, and a clothes brush.

According to Gaspare Nello Vetro, who did fundamental research on the Parma Conservatory's history and on the school years of the institution's most famous graduate, life for the resident students in Toscanini's day was "regular and monotonous: wake-up at seven, prayers, breakfast, lessons [from eight until noon, when lunch was served], a brief interval, lessons [from two until six], study, prayers, break, supper, study, lights-out. The students had few diversions: two weekly walks accompanied by the teacher-prefect, a few holidays, and mass on Sunday." The boys were allowed and perhaps even encouraged to get fresh air and exercise during the breaks, within the building complex's three spacious cloister courtyards. Attendance at mass was compulsory, and discipline was rigid. For the older students, smoking seems to have been tolerated, as were visits to a nearby brothel. Toscanini never became a smoker, but by his midteens he probably indulged in the other extracurricular activity. "I smoked my first cigarette and kissed my first woman on the same day," he is reported to have said, "and since then I've never had time for tobacco."

Although internal students could not visit their homes except during vacation periods, they were permitted to have visitors on Sunday. But Arturo's mother never came to see him "in the eight years that I was at the boarding school," he recalled. According to Toscanini's daughter Wally, Paola was ashamed of her shabby clothes: "It was a mixture of pride and ignorance," Wally said. "His aunts came but not his mother."

"I loved those aunts"—Cesira and Esterina, the youngest of his mother's siblings—"because they came every Sunday," Toscanini said, and in later years he helped to support them.

Despite the monastic conditions and the absence of his immediate family, the young Toscanini loved conservatory life. His initial curiosity about music soon turned into fascination and then into a complete, absorbing passion. During the first two years, he studied solfeggio (sightsinging), the rudiments of music theory, keyboard harmony, piano, choral singing, music history, and standard nonmusical subjects including Latin and catechism.* Conservatory students were required to learn proper Italian and to write brief essays in it. They also had to learn addition, subtraction, multiplication, division, and fractions; algebra and other more advanced forms of mathematics were not offered, nor were scientific subjects. A math problem dealing with areas and prices, correctly solved by Toscanini, is preserved in the conservatory's archives, as is a carefully wrought essay by him in epistolary form, based on a given, anodyne theme.

At the beginning of his second year, he was told that the cello would be his principal instrument. He liked the violin better, but

---

* Toscanini also learned French, although not at the school. His written French was defective and his spoken French worse, but he read widely in the language.

since students were obliged to play in the Teatro Regio's orchestra when they became more accomplished, certain proportions had to be followed when instruments were assigned. Leandro Carini, a nationally respected cellist and pedagogue, was Arturo's cello teacher throughout the boy's conservatory years. Carini did not allow his first-year pupils to practice on their own: he worked directly with them six days a week so that they would not develop bad technical habits. Even when they were proceeding properly, he gave them several lessons a week, and he produced a number of players who became section leaders in orchestras all over Italy. Toscanini, in old age, joyfully remembered the cello studies of Duport, Servais, and Grützmacher that he had learned as a boy, and he would sing parts of them when he chatted with cellist friends. In those days, cellos were not equipped with end pins; cellists gripped the instrument between their knees, and as a child Toscanini found this difficult— even with the half-size cello that he used at first—because his teacher insisted that he sit near the edge of his chair. Carini at one point threatened to hit him with his shoe, and child and cello tumbled onto the floor.

Once the young Toscanini had learned to read music fluently and had mastered the basics of music theory, he was able to memorize scores after a single reading, and he could do the same with poetry, plays, opera libretti—virtually anything. Teachers or fellow students would give him a piece of music to sight-read, then they would take the score away and have him play it again or copy it out. His memory was photographic—he himself said, in old age, that he didn't really understand how he memorized, that he often remembered in every detail even pieces of music that he could not recall having studied, and that he felt sorry for colleagues who had to spend many hours knocking the details of a score into their heads. Throughout his career, much of his score studying took place in his mind's eye, and evidently his extraordinary ability to internalize music was as much subconscious as conscious.

Many accounts of Toscanini's life state that he developed an exceptional memory because his vision was bad, and he later admitted that he had never bothered to deny the story, just as he rarely bothered to comment on anything else that people reported about him. He was slightly nearsighted in his youth, but his astonishing memory had nothing to do with his eyesight. He also developed an extraordinary aural memory that allowed him to remember in great detail pieces of music that he had heard but not seen in print, as well as the particulars of performances long past.

"I was a hard-working student because I liked music and did not have to force myself to study it," he said. But, like many other exceptionally gifted people, he did not care to devote much time to tasks that did not interest him. "I could never practice for four hours in a row," he recalled. He would play the cello for an hour and then go listen to other students' lessons on other instruments—an invaluable preparation for his future career. He even taught himself to play the violin and the double bass, not well, but enough to understand their techniques. And he became a completely unorthodox but fluent pianist. "I've never been able to play a scale twice with the same fingering," he laughed. "I was the despair of my teacher. I loved the piano only because it gave me the means for getting to know music." Indeed, he taught himself to play even the most complicated orchestra scores at the keyboard, at sight. "I practiced the cello, which I didn't love, and I studied it to make my teacher happy," Toscanini wrote, many decades later; "he saw *much more* in me than what I was, but I had an *inexhaustible thirst to familiarize myself with music,* to *get to know it—all music!*"

Arturo's fellow students teased him by calling him *Gèni,* the dialect word for "genius." "I enjoyed everyone's esteem, but it was of no importance to me," he recalled at the age of seventy. "Then as now, I tried to achieve the maximum, and I couldn't do it, and I still can't do it today." His modesty and loyalty made him well liked by his classmates. Dacci's diary contains numerous accounts of boys fighting with one another, but Toscanini was hardly ever involved in such incidents. Once, however, during an argument, an older boy hit Arturo on the head with a shoe brush. The cut bled; Arturo washed it but told no one what had happened; the wound suppurated and caused a fever, and a doctor had to treat it. Dacci, the director, asked Arturo who had hit him, but the boy stubbornly refused to tattle on a schoolmate—a refusal penalized by five days on bread and water in the school's "punishment room." Dacci never learned the culprit's name.

Notwithstanding the harshness of life at the conservatory and the financial ease that his career would eventually bring him, Toscanini always remembered his student days as the happiest period in his life, when he was discovering the musical repertoire and beginning to put his talent to work, but before he had chained that talent to an impossibly high artistic and professional ethic. "When I look back at the years of my adolescence, I don't remember a day without sunshine, because the sunshine was in my soul," he wrote half a century later. Several of his schoolmates remained lifelong friends, and he remembered the gifted ones from time to time during the following decades, when he needed to supply good musicians for the various orchestras that he conducted.

Count Stefano Sanvitale, a music-loving local aristocrat, amateur composer, and founder of Parma's Quartet Society, often invited faculty members and advanced students to the beautiful music room in his palace, to play chamber music together with capable amateurs among the nobility, and the young Toscanini gladly participated in the sessions. Otherwise, there was little in the way of public performing by the students, except when the older ones augmented the ranks of the Teatro Regio's orchestra, and when the conservatory opened its doors for an annual student recital. The latter events were usually performed only by pupils in the graduating class, but in the spring of 1882 the fifteen-year-old Toscanini was the piano accompanist in two chamber music pieces. Among themselves, however, the students played a great deal of orchestral and chamber music. Toscanini recalled that although Bach's music was little studied, "Beethoven, Mozart, Haydn, Mendelssohn, and a good deal of Schumann and Schubert were my usual repertoire." He remembered being among the students who played through Haydn's Symphony no. 98 in B-flat Major, "and it was a joy for us. I acquired my classical culture during my conservatory years." He arranged orchestral works for chamber ensembles and gathered together groups of his schoolmates to try the pieces out under his direction—his very first conducting experiences. His cutting comments, combined with the fact that he was a tailor's son, caused the other young musicians to give him a second nickname: *Forbsòn*, the dialect word for "shears."

Arturo's interest in the orchestra led him to study instrumentation by copying out scores by the masters. In a late-in-life conversation, he mentioned having written out Berlioz's "Rákóczy" March,
but he added that when he had studied the first movement of the
same composer's *Symphonie Fantastique*, he had been unable to
grasp its harmonic structure. Years later, in conversations with
Claude Debussy and Paul Dukas, he learned that they, too, had not
at first been able to come to terms with that score. He quoted
Debussy as having told him, "Later, when one grows up, one enjoys
this music."

Advanced composition studies were carried out under Dacci's
rigorous but conservative tutelage, and most of the songs and
other pieces that Toscanini wrote, approximately between the
ages of fifteen and twenty, stayed within a strict canon. Six of
Toscanini's songs and a berceuse for solo piano were published
between 1887 and 1889.* Yet Dacci's conservatism proved to be ben-
eficial in two ways: it gave Toscanini an ironclad grounding in harmony, counterpoint, and all the other materials of musical
composition, and it stirred the young musician's curiosity about
the forbidden fruit—more recent and more radical musical developments in Italy and abroad, especially the works of Richard Wagner, who was the most controversial representative of the European
musical avant-garde.

"The first impression I received of Wagner's music goes back to
1878–79, when I heard the *Tannhäuser* Overture at a concert of Parma's Quartet Society—and I was astonished," Toscanini wrote,
many years later. (He was eleven years old when that performance
took place; the sixty-five-year-old Wagner was then in Bayreuth, 450
miles to the north, working on *Parsifal*.) "My teacher brought a cello
part of this overture to school for me and made me study various
passages, which were very difficult for me at that time. In 1884
Parma was the first Italian city to present *Lohengrin* after its success
in Bologna and its failure in Milan. I was playing in the orchestra.
That was when I had the first great, sublime revelation of Wagner's
genius. At the first rehearsal the prelude, from the first bars, gave

---

* A collection of the published and unpublished songs was issued in print in 2010; see
www.subitomusic.com.

me magical, unearthly impressions—with those divinely celestial harmonies that revealed a new world to me, a world of whose existence no one had dreamed until Wagner's supernatural mind discovered it."

That 1883–84 opera season was the third of five during which the young Toscanini played cello in the orchestra of the Teatro Regio, at a pay of 1.50 lire per performance; he saved the money in order to buy a cello for himself, for 250 lire, after he graduated from the conservatory. The Regio presented only a *stagione di Carnevale* (Carnival season)—three or four operas that ran from Christmas until just before Lent—whereas seasons at La Scala in Milan and other major houses in big cities would produce six or seven operas during *stagioni di Carnevale-Quaresima* (Carnival-Lent seasons) that continued up to and sometimes even after Easter.

Opera life differed radically from its present-day incarnation: during the 2015–16 season at New York's Metropolitan Opera, for instance, the most recent of the twenty-five works performed was Alban Berg's eighty-year-old *Lulu*, whereas all of the twenty-one operas performed during Toscanini's five seasons (plus a brief extra season in September 1882) in the Regio's orchestra had been written within the previous half century, and several were altogether new. There was not a single work by Gluck, Mozart, Rossini, or Bellini; the oldest opera presented was Meyerbeer's *Les Huguenots* (1836). Five of the operas performed were by favorite son Giuseppe Verdi; Donizetti, Meyerbeer, Bizet, and Ponchielli were represented by two operas each; and single works by Wagner, Gounod, Ambroise Thomas, Antônio Carlos Gomes, Fromental Halévy, and the now forgotten Antonino Palminteri and Salvatore Auteri-Manzocchi (a singing teacher at the Parma Conservatory) were heard. Eight of these twelve composers were still alive when Toscanini was playing their works in the Regio's orchestra. Verdi, in particular, was living and working on his agricultural estate at Sant'Agata, about twenty-five miles from Parma; his late-in-life masterpieces, *Otello* and *Falstaff*, were still unborn.

In Italy, virtually all operas were sung in Italian, whatever their original languages may have been, just as in Germany operas were sung in German, and so on in most European countries: opera was theater, and the words were meant to be understood.

On the other hand, performance practices lacked the sort of single-mindedness that is generally applied to them today. A poster announcing a *Lohengrin* evening at the Regio on 2 March 1884, for instance, informed potential ticket buyers that "after the first act of the aforementioned Opera, the ORCHESTRA will play the OVERTURE to the Opera—DER FREISCHÜTZ—(The Free Shooter) by Maestro WEBER, and after the second act Madame BERTA PIERSON will perform AGATHE'S GRAND ARIA from the aforementioned Opera FREISCHÜTZ [. . . .] After the Performance [there will be a] GREAT MASKED BALL."* A few weeks earlier, on the first anniversary of Wagner's death, the *Tannhäuser* Overture and March and the Wedding March from *Lohengrin* were inserted, in memoriam but incongruously, into a performance of *Les Huguenots*.

The opera house was where the Parmigiani went to experience outsize emotions, however vicariously, and the young Toscanini's observations of people's reactions at the Regio formed one essential aspect of his later approach to his art. Seventy-one years after the fact, he described an 1883 performance of Auteri-Manzocchi's long-forgotten *Stella*, for which a tenor, Eugenio Mozzi, was called in at the last moment to replace a colleague. In the last act, Toscanini said, Mozzi stood still until the climactic, passionately sung words, "Non ti amo più!" (I don't love you anymore!), at which point he moved forward and put his hands in his hair, causing a sensation: people in the boxes wept with emotion. "The whole orchestra turned around," Toscanini recalled: it was as if "we were hearing new music." This was the sort of reaction that he later tried to teach, cajole, or browbeat singers into eliciting, because—he always told them—the emotion counted for more than the notes.

Giulio Ferrarini, secretary of Parma's Theater Commission, made notes—preserved in the Regio's archives—that provide vivid sketches

---

* Ground-floor seats were not stationary; they could quickly be removed after a performance and the theater converted into a grand ballroom. Pity the poor orchestra members! Although *Lohengrin* was given with substantial cuts, the added *Freischütz* excerpts and the postperformance ball meant that the musicians must have played from seven in the evening, when most performances began, until one or two in the morning.

of the rough-and-tumble Italian opera world of those days, when singers and even whole operas were switched around or replaced altogether on a moment's notice. For instance:

11 [JANUARY 1883]— [. . .] Miss Bernau declares that she can't go onstage because she is menstruating.—Her husband shouts and weeps!

20 JANUARY 1884—Big stir—thanks to Maestro Vittorio Vanzo's amorous doings with the prima donna Pierson under the auspices of her husband, who amuses himself by playing violin in the orchestra while the lover plays on his wife.

15 JANUARY [1885]—1st performance of [Bizet's] *La Jolie Fille de Perth*—The performance proceeded well enough [. . .]. The audience however was determined to get rid of the opera and besides having booed the ballet in the 2nd Act they booed the opera so insistently at the end that the Agency and the Administration were advised not to do further performances. [. . .] They'll do *Rigoletto* [instead].

21 JAN. 85—They want to open with *Rigoletto* tomorrow evening— without offstage band and without being sure that the costumes will arrive. The Agency says that since it's a repertoire opera rehearsals aren't needed! Poor art, poor Verdi!

This was the gritty, amoral, and catch-as-catch-can, yet thoroughly alive, musical world in which Arturo Toscanini grew up.

4.

IN MAY 1884, THE SEVENTEEN-YEAR-OLD TOSCANINI TOOK PART IN a public concert presented by conservatory students in the grand foyer of the Teatro Regio. The fifth of twelve items on the program was the Introduction and Polonaise, op. 24, for cello, by Emile Dunkler, played by Toscanini, and the sixth was Toscanini's own Andante and Scherzo for orchestra, "conducted by the composer"—his first public, albeit nonprofessional, podium appearance. Formal study of conducting did not exist in those days, but all composition students at the Parma Conservatory were instructed in instrumental coaching, which probably included rudimentary time beating. Toscanini recalled having been intimidated by the audience's applause following his cello solo: It was "the first applause I ever had [. . .], and I ran away with my cello [. . .] to the farthest room, and I didn't stop until there was a wall in front of me." The concert was reviewed in no fewer than ten newspapers and journals—four from Parma, three from Milan, and one each from Rome, Piacenza, and Ravenna; Toscanini's cello playing was lauded, and his composition was praised as the best of the four student works on the program, but no mention was made of his conducting.

That summer, the young musician had his first independent, paid job, as principal cello in an orchestra that accompanied an opera-ballet by Guglielmo Branca in the town of Carpi, about thirty miles from Parma. He earned a meager five lire a day, with which he had to pay for food and lodging. "I always ate soup and bread—never meat," he recalled; thus he never spent all of his money, and the local administrator had to remind him to pick up his remaining pay, since the young cellist did not keep track of earnings and expenditures. "Is there still some left?" he would ask his astonished interlocutor. This is the first known instance of Toscanini's lifelong financial insouciance. "I always had someone who looked after [money] for me," he admitted in old age. "If I had been obliged to think about these things, I would have been eaten alive." He did eventually learn to make fee requests, but as soon as he married he put that task in his wife's hands.

A month after his Carpi job, Toscanini was engaged to play in an ad hoc, 120-member orchestra made up of musicians from Parma and conducted by the twenty-four-year-old native son Cleofonte Campanini. Two potpourri programs were performed at home and then in the Great Hall of the National Exposition in Turin and at the Teatro Dal Verme in Milan—Toscanini's first, brief encounters with cities that would play major roles in his life.

These special orchestra concerts had been approved in advance by Dacci, who nevertheless reprimanded Toscanini for having breached the school's regulations by failing to ask him for permission to take the earlier, paying job in Carpi. Toscanini had already angered Dacci the previous spring for refusing, with some fellow students, to attend confession or take communion. By then, however, Toscanini was the school's star pupil; Dacci relented and made him an assistant instructor (*maestrino*) of harmony for 1884–85, Arturo's final year at the conservatory.

Dacci's diary reports that on Sunday, 11 January 1885, fifteen students, including Toscanini, once again refused to drag themselves out of bed to go to early mass, as required. When they finally got up, Dacci informed them that they would have to attend a later mass during the time reserved for the weekly family visit, and he ordered them to go immediately to their respective rooms and begin studying. They refused. Dacci, dumbfounded, told an assistant to take the names of the disobedient boys, which made the increasingly brazen Toscanini "declare that he wanted his name to be first on the list. [. . .] I had his father sent for at once and told him that if his son did not write a letter asking to be pardoned, he would certainly be expelled from the School. [. . .] The young Toscanini [. . .] walked out of the room in another disrespectful act. The same day I informed the Royal Commissioner of the occurrence."

The letter was not immediately forthcoming, and Dacci, worried about losing his best student only a few months before graduation, asked some of the professors to write the letter and to persuade Toscanini to copy and sign it. Toscanini eventually gave in.

He took his last examinations the following July. Seven decades later, he recalled that in preparing for his final cello exam he had played a sonata by Boccherini for his teacher. "My teacher was very happy. 'You play very well,' he said." But the pupil, as self-critical then as later in life, was of a different opinion: "'No, I play *badly*. I cannot play this piece.'" So he learned and played a different piece instead—despite which he received the maximum number of points and highest honors in cello and composition, and was awarded the special Barbacini Prize of 137.50 lire, presented annually to the outstanding graduate.

5.

AT EIGHTEEN, TOSCANINI WAS A FREELANCE ORCHESTRAL CELLIST who contributed toward his family's expenses when he lived at home and supported himself when jobs took him away from Parma. He grew a mustache, to give himself a more mature appearance, and his first job was as principal cello in productions of *La Favorita* and *Ernani* in Busseto during the summer of 1885. During an intermission in one performance, he accompanied the prima donna in a piece for soprano, cello, and piano. He then went to the town of Rovigo to play principal cello in a production of Ponchielli's *La Gioconda* conducted by his fellow Parmesan Giovanni Bolzoni, a well-known musician respected by Verdi. And he probably played again in Carpi that summer.

At the Regio in Parma during the 1885–86 Carnival season, Toscanini was the first-stand partner of Carini, his former teacher, and he often sat in as section leader. The conductor, Nicola Bassi, became annoyed by the young cellist's habit of playing while looking at what was happening onstage and in the orchestra without ever glancing at the music on his stand. "I never had to turn a page," Toscanini remembered with a chuckle, "and when we got to [Ponchielli's] *Marion Delorme*, which was a brand-new opera, Bassi came over to me and said, 'Now we'll see if you can play *this* by heart!' And I said, 'Why not? Isn't this music, too?'" But Toscanini admired Bassi for his controlled gestures and later emulated that aspect of Bassi's conducting style.

Carlo Superti, a violinist in the Regio's orchestra that season, was also co-impresario and assistant conductor of an opera company that Claudio Rossi, a theatrical scene painter from Carpi, was putting together to take to Brazil and, if the gods were merciful, to other South American countries. "One fine day," Toscanini recalled many years later, Superti "comes up to me and says, 'Wouldn't you go to [South] America with me?' I said, 'I can't go to America because I'm only eighteen. I need my family's permission.' 'Ask for permission; I'll take you to America as principal cello.'" The permission was forthcoming, and Toscanini was engaged not only as principal cello but also as assistant chorus master.

When the Regio's season ended, the young musician traveled to Genoa, where his family was living once again. On 20 March 1886, he packed his school uniform—the only formal set of clothes he owned—and a few other belongings, said goodbye to his parents and sisters, made his way to the port, and boarded the *Perseo*, a three-year-old Italian steamship, bound for Brazil. He was embarking on a journey that would transform his life forever.

Toscanini in
his twenties.

BEARDLESS MAESTRO

1.

———

ATRIP ACROSS THE WESTERN MEDITERRANEAN, THE ATLANTIC, and the equator must have been liberating for a youngster who had never left northern Italy and who was accustomed to living within either his parents' emotionally and economically bleak home or the well-defined routine of a boarding school.

The voyage took nineteen days, and Toscanini spent his nineteenth birthday, 25 March 1886, at Cádiz, the ship's last port of call before it headed across the ocean. He quickly discovered that, unlike many of his shipmates, he did not suffer from seasickness, even when the ocean was rough. When he was not busy rehearsing the chorus—a job that the chorus master, Aristide Venturi, happily turned over to him—or helping the solo singers to learn or refresh their roles, he spent hours on deck observing the ever-changing waves. The company was to perform twelve operas, of which eleven were popular favorites at the time: Verdi's *Rigoletto*, *Il Trovatore*, *La Traviata*, and *Aida*; Ponchielli's *La Gioconda* and *Marion Delorme*; Donizetti's *La Favorita*; Thomas's *Hamlet*; Meyerbeer's *Les Huguenots*; Gounod's *Faust*; and Gomes's *Salvator Rosa*. Only the Portuguese composer Augusto Machado's three-year-old French opera *Lauriane* was barely known, and all of these works except *Hamlet* and *Lauriane* had been performed at the Teatro Regio in Parma during Toscanini's five seasons in the orchestra's cello section.

Some of the company's singers were well known. The French-man Paul Lhérie had begun his career as a tenor and had sung the role of Don José at the world premiere of Bizet's *Carmen* in Paris in 1875; later, as a baritone, he had been chosen by Verdi as the first Rodrigo for the revised, four-act version of *Don Carlo*, at La Scala in 1884. Toscanini had heard the twenty-nine-year-old Russian Nicolai Figner, the ensemble's principal tenor, and his fiancée, the Florentine mezzo-soprano Medea Mei, twenty-seven, during the Regio's previous season; Mei was gradually switching to the soprano repertoire, and during the Rossi company's tour she sang the principal mezzo roles in four operas and the title soprano role in *Marion Delorme*.*

The twenty-six-year-old Russian soprano Nadine Boulichoff, a pupil of the celebrated Mathilde Marchesi, had already appeared successfully in Brussels, Madrid, and Naples, and the Italian contralto Eugenia Mantelli, also twenty-six, would soon become a regular at the Metropolitan Opera and in many major European houses. The tenors Tobia Bertini and Carlo Callioni, sopranos Carolina Buglione di Monale and Isabella Meyer, and baritone Napoleone Zardo were mainstays in various Italian theaters. The bass Napoleone Limonta would sing the role of Montano at the world premiere of Verdi's *Otello* at La Scala a few months later, and his fellow bass Gaetano Roveri would "create" the part of Roucher in Umberto Giordano's *Andrea Chénier* in 1896. All of them except Boulichoff and Bertini were aboard the *Perseo*, as were Superti and Venturi. The singers traveled first-class; Toscanini and the other orchestra and chorus members, many from Parma, were berthed in second-class cabins.

Not on board, however, was the designated conductor, Leopoldo Miguez, a thirty-five-year-old Brazilian known mainly as a composer; he met the troupe upon its arrival at São Paulo.† Miguez, an accomplished musician, exercised a positive influence on the devel-

---

* Four years later Tchaikovsky chose Mei as Liza and Figner as Gherman for the world premiere of *The Queen of Spades* in St. Petersburg, and in 1892 he chose them again to star in the premiere production of *Iolanta*.

† The *Perseo* docked at Rio de Janeiro on 8 April and presumably arrived at Santos, São Paulo's port, a day or two later.

opment of his country's musical life, but he was not a gifted conductor. At one rehearsal, Toscanini recalled, Roveri, onstage, shouted at the young principal cello, " 'Those cellos aren't keeping time!'

" 'I can't follow the conductor's beat,' I said.

" 'For heaven's sake, just don't look at him anymore!' "

The ensemble's two-month-long São Paulo season opened to lukewarm reviews on 17 April, and by the end of the run audience reactions were decidedly negative—sometimes violently so. The company then began a two-month engagement in Rio de Janeiro, at that time Brazil's political, economic, and cultural capital. Since 1870 the city's population had nearly doubled, to half a million, and it was continuing to grow rapidly thanks to a huge influx of immigrants from southern Europe, especially Italy. Emperor Dom Pedro II, a liberal ruler by the standards of his day, had abolished the country's slave trade—although not slavery itself—in 1850, and two years after the Rossi company's visit he would manage to pass a law that freed all the remaining slaves. Poverty was rampant in Rio, but there were also growing numbers of comfortable bureaucrats and successful merchants, an aspiring bourgeoisie hungry for imported European entertainments.

In an 1883 story called "Capítulo dos chapéus" (Chapter on Hats), the Brazilian writer Joaquim Maria Machado de Assis described one such bourgeois, who showed off for two lovely ladies by talking about opera performances he had attended: "In his opinion the opera company was excellent, except for the rather lame baritone. [. . .] The female leads, yes, indeed, both the soprano and the contralto, were first class. And he discussed their repertory, mentioned the finest passages of various operas, and praised the orchestra, most especially their rendition of Meyerbeer's *Les Huguenots*."* Those performances would have taken place at the Imperial Theatro Dom Pedro II, which had been inaugurated in 1871 precisely as a receptacle for musical events imported from the Old World. The Rossi ensemble opened there on 25 June 1886.

Perhaps because Rio was seen as a more important venue than

---

* Some of Machado de Assis's delightful writings are found in his *The Alienist and Other Stories of Nineteenth-Century Brazil*, ed. and trans. by John Charles Chasteen (Indianapolis: Hackett, 2013).

São Paulo, internal dissensions within Rossi's ensemble exploded immediately upon the artists' arrival in town. The singers called for Miguez to resign, and Miguez blamed his difficulties on his forces. "At our first performance of *Faust*, the stage band sounded as if it was at war with the orchestra in the pit," Toscanini said. "Miguez thought we had done it on purpose, to give Superti a chance to conduct *Aida*," which was indeed performed under Superti's baton on the twenty-seventh. Another *Aida* was scheduled for the evening of 30 June, and on that day Miguez sent Rossi a letter of resignation—for reasons of health, he said. Superti prepared to conduct. But news of Miguez's resignation spread quickly among local music lovers, many of whom saw the Brazilian maestro as a victim of Italian intrigue.

Toscanini dawdled at his boardinghouse that evening, "studying Schubert lieder with Eugenia Mantelli," the contralto. (This, at any rate, was his description of their activities, in a conversation with friends that was taped in 1955; according to what he had told others, their doings that evening were of a nonmusical nature.)* "At the last minute I remembered that I was first cello in *Aida*," he said. "I took the tram and arrived at the theater," where there was "a hell of an uproar! I went to my place, took out my instrument, and asked what was going on. 'The audience doesn't want Superti,'" who had been shouted off the podium, Toscanini's stand partner told him. "The ballet master, who spoke Portuguese, came out to tell the audience to quiet down and that there would be a different conductor," Toscanini continued. Venturi, the chorus master, attempted to conduct but had

no luck at all. The impresario spoke, too, but that didn't work, either. We orchestra players were saying to each other, "Now they'll close the theater." At that moment, it occurred to me

---

* Toscanini told Friedelind Wagner, the composer's granddaughter, that a beautiful young black woman had flirted with him in Rio, but something frightening about her behavior had kept him from taking advantage of her interest. He also told friends that once, during his Rio sojourn, he had eaten some pork that had made him ill, and he had decided to subsist mainly on a sort of broth during the rest of his stay. Although throughout his life Toscanini frequently ate salami, prosciutto, and other cured or smoked pork products, cooked pork dishes always made him ill—sometimes so violently that he would pass out.

that I'd forgotten, as usual, to pick up my pay on time and that I'd have to buy a ticket back to Italy—and that now the impresario wouldn't pay me. While all this stuff was running through my mind, a subscriber came over and said, "Isn't there anyone in the orchestra who can conduct *Aida*?" My second cellist turned to me, and I left my cello right then and there and ran onto the stage [behind the closed curtain] to save my soul.

But I'd gone from the frying pan into the fire. [. . .] On the stage I ran into all the women from the chorus who had studied with me. Everyone knew about my memory because the singers had all had lessons with me, and I had played the piano without ever looking at the music. There was a woman named Leoni from Parma, ugly as the devil, who started to cry, and who said [in Parmesan dialect], "Who knows if Toscanini can do it? Let him go out and conduct." Then the impresario [Rossi] came; everyone was imploring me. He even wanted to give me his frock coat, since we were the same height. I was barely out of school, and I was still wearing my military-style school uniform, with gold buttons. I said, "No, no, if I have to go and conduct, I'll go dressed as I am."

But the others persuaded him to change, and, said Toscanini, "I went to conduct in a stunned state, as if I were drunk."

It was 9:15 P.M.; members of the audience had protested loudly for an hour and a quarter and had had the satisfaction of chasing two conductors off the podium. But they had paid good money to hear an opera, and now a youngster was sitting down at the conductor's desk and preparing to start. The protest abated, and Toscanini, without looking at the score, began to conduct the Prelude to *Aida*.

"When I got up on the podium and saw the orchestra below me, it didn't disturb me at all," he recalled. "But when I saw the curtain go up and heard [the first words] 'Sì: corre voce'—well, singers aren't like an orchestra; you always hear them a little bit late, and that disturbed me. I was afraid that my arms couldn't go on. [. . .] My arms were used to playing the cello, not to conducting. But as soon as the chorus entered—'Ed osan tanto?'—I conducted. I really conducted. I didn't have the technique for conducting, but I conducted. I got used to it. As you can imagine, after the second act I don't know how many people rushed onto the stage—painters who wanted to do everyone's portrait, and what-not."

For the rest of his life, Toscanini would remember two errors that he made that evening: one wrong downbeat and one brief memory lapse. But by the end of the performance a near disaster had turned into a triumph and the company had been saved from ruin.* During the following days, reports of the remarkable debut appeared in the local newspapers.

> *A Evolução*: In the end [. . .] a young boy, a modest cellist, Mr. Toscanini, was designated to conduct. Bravo! to the inspired youth. This beardless maestro is a prodigy who communicated the sacred artistic fire to his baton and the energy and passion of a genuine artist to the orchestra. [. . .] After he took over the conductor's podium, the stamping dwindled away by itself and the stampers spoke only of the extraordinary turn of events.
>
> *Gazeta de Noticias*: Toscanini is a youth of nineteen who is said to be a musical prodigy. He knows sixty operas by heart— or perhaps 120. It is he who coaches the artists at home, accompanying them at the piano without looking at the score, which he knows even in his sleep. Lively, alert, enthusiastic, and courageous, Mr. Toscanini turned out at the last moment to be a sure-handed and secure conductor.

Further exchanges between Miguez and Rossi appeared in the press, but Miguez's continued participation in the ensemble's tour was out of the question. "Mr. Arturo Toscanini is definitely remaining at his post as conductor," stated an article in *O Pais*, "and we are convinced that he will carry it out worthily [. . .]. He brought off *Traviata* in the same way [as *Aida*] [. . .]; and according to report, although these are his first conducting experiences, he has been preparing himself for the task for some time, only wishing that it would happen later, in order to learn by heart the entire operatic repertoire and to acquire practical experience." Toscanini himself said, many

---

* The cast that evening consisted of Boulichoff (Aida), Mei (Amneris), Bertini (Radamès), Lhérie (Amonasro), and Roveri (Ramfis).

years later, "I thought about becoming a conductor at twenty-seven or twenty-eight, but not at nineteen."

He did not write home to let anyone know what had happened, but someone in the company informed Parma's newspapers. The most telling of the few articles that appeared in the young conductor's hometown was written by one Nando Vàlapuch, who knew Toscanini and described him as "a distinguished musician who has the good fortune of possessing uncommon artistic cultivation, brilliant intelligence, and exquisite artistic feeling [. . .] combined with a rare modesty that makes even the things he does that are greatly praised by everyone else seem like nothing special to him. [. . .] I wager that within a few years the name of this young man will be very favorably known in the world of the arts."

THE RESPONSIBILITY FOR THE TOUR'S SUCCESS now rested on Toscanini's barely postadolescent shoulders. "I had to continue, otherwise they would have had to close the theater," he recalled, and the ensemble would have been stranded. "They didn't increase my pay—I still got 920 lire a month"—presumably because he didn't think of asking for more and Rossi did not offer a raise.

From his first *Aida*, on 30 June, to the final performance of *Huguenots*, on 16 August, Toscanini conducted hundreds of rehearsals and twenty-six performances of twelve operas, all from memory. In those days, each of the principal singers and, sometimes, the conductor, was allowed a *serata d'onore* (literally, "evening of honor") each season: during an intermission, the singer in question would perform an aria or two with piano accompaniment and would receive gifts and, usually, a small percentage of the night's net profits from ticket sales, plus a laurel wreath or a similar token of esteem. Boulichoff received diamonds at her *serata d'onore* but immediately donated them to purchase the freedom of seven slaves—an act of support for the emperor's policies; years later she declared that this had been the proudest moment of her career.

Toscanini had not anticipated a *serata* for himself, but the ensemble's members felt such gratitude toward him that they scheduled one, on 5 August. "On the theater's portico there was a big poster with my name in big letters, and I stopped in my tracks when I saw it," he recalled. "I didn't want to conduct." His colleagues persuaded him to change his mind and to rehearse two extra orchestral pieces. According to a report in *O Pais*, during the intermission between Acts II and III of *Faust* "the orchestra, under the direction of the beneficiary, played the grandiose Overture to *Guarany* [by Gomes] quite perfectly. The public applauded [Toscanini] at length and called him to the stage; then the company's artists appeared, bringing him various gifts, and, after the presentations, they applauded him enthusiastically, joining in the acclamations of the whole theater. Following this ovation he led Bolzoni's Minuet [. . .]. It could not have been played with greater polish. The enthusiasm shown for this magnificent composition is indescribable. It was repeated, and so was the applause. His Majesty the Emperor sent to ask the name of the piece performed, and Mr. Toscanini went to the imperial loge in order to show him Bolzoni's score." According to another newspaper, *O Rio de Janeiro*, Toscanini was again applauded, "and the timid Maestro came onstage only to flee, frightened by his glory, which is already great and which will be immense."

The gifts from his singers included a cup, saucer, and silver spoon; a silver-framed blotter; a jeweled ring; and a gold pencil case. The sixty-year-old emperor, a sincere music lover who had attended the first Bayreuth Festival ten years earlier, gave Toscanini a diamond ring, among other items. He and his daughter, who was also present, spoke Italian with the young musician. "I went back to the hotel and put everything into a drawer, and someone stole everything, plundered it all. It's not that I was stupid, but I was still a schoolboy."

But the best gift that Toscanini received during his six and a half weeks as de facto music director of the Rossi ensemble was professional experience. He later spoke gratefully about what he had absorbed from working with Lhérie, especially the important art of when to lead and when to follow singers. "He used to tell me, 'Look, Toscanini, here I sing slowly, but you keep going and I'll follow you.' In fact, when he sang 'Vien Leonora' in *La Favorita* [. . .] I pressed forward and he followed."

The day after the company's last performance, the orchestra's concertmaster, Ferruccio Cattelani—a former classmate of Toscanini's—gave a recital at Rio's Beethoven Club, accompanied by Toscanini at the piano, playing pieces by Vieuxtemps and Wieniawski.* Rossi, in the meantime, had tried to organize a season in Buenos Aires, but when the project did not materialize he dissolved the company and departed, still owing money to everyone. Left with insufficient funds for their passage back to Europe, the performers organized a benefit concert for 23 August. At the piano, Toscanini accompanied several singers in short pieces, and he and Cattelani repeated the Vieuxtemps piece that they had played for the Beethoven Club; Toscanini then conducted the orchestra in six short pieces. Three days later, most of the ensemble boarded the French vessel *Savoie* for the return trip to Europe.

2.

IF A NINETEEN-YEAR-OLD MUSICIAN WERE TO DO TODAY WHAT Toscanini did in Rio de Janeiro in 1886, there would be an enormous amount of international fuss and publicity. But Toscanini returned to Genoa in mid-September, greeted his family, gave his mother whatever remained of his earnings, and prepared to return to anonymity. "I started to play the cello again," he said many years later. "I didn't feel important enough to think of myself as a conductor yet."

The Rossi ensemble's lead tenor, Nicolai Figner, thought otherwise. "Figner had studied many operas with me," Toscanini recalled, "even Russian operas like [Tchaikovsky's *Eugene*] *Onegin*"—which was only seven years old at the time and had never been performed in Italy. "When I didn't show up in Milan," the hub of Italian musical life, Figner wrote to him. "'What are you doing, playing the cello? After what you've done!' But what was I supposed to do—go around telling people I was a conductor? I was nineteen years old and looked even younger than my age. And whom was I supposed to tell? But then he called me to Milan, gave me the money I needed, and put me up at the Hotel San Michele."

Figner and his fiancée, Medea Mei, had Toscanini accompany

---

* Cattelani eventually settled in Buenos Aires and became a major force in local musical life as a player of solo and chamber music, composer, conductor, teacher, and founder of important musical organizations.

them when they auditioned at La Scala for the celebrated conductor Franco Faccio, the powerful music publisher Giulio Ricordi, and the well-known librettist, impresario, and critic Carlo D'Ormeville; neither singer was engaged, but Toscanini had set foot for the first time in Italy's most famous lyric theater. Figner then introduced Toscanini to various agents and to another important publisher, the seventy-two-year-old Giovannina Lucca.

Italian music publishers were omnipotent in those days, when opera was a lucrative business. They controlled the rights to the operas they published, and they often decided who would perform important productions of those works. Signora Lucca "had a beautiful villa above Cernobbio, on Lake Como, and she invited us to lunch," Toscanini said. "There, Figner began to extol my abilities, to talk about what I had done in [South] America." The tenor asked the publisher whether she knew of a possible opening for the young maestro. "There could be a theater—Turin," she said to Toscanini. "They want to do *The Flying Dutchman** and Catalani's *Edmea* this autumn." Figner was already under contract to sing in the Turin premiere of *Edmea*, the latest opera by the thirty-two-year-old Alfredo Catalani, an up-and-coming composer, and Signora Lucca held the rights to the work, which had had its world premiere at La Scala the preceding February.

There was nothing unusual, at the time, for a new production of a significant new opera to be organized at a major venue virtually at the last moment, since staging and sets were simple. Toscanini had returned to Italy from Brazil not earlier than mid-September, and his encounter with Signora Lucca cannot have taken place before early October, barely a month before *Edmea* was to be performed in Turin. Toscanini did not know *Edmea*, but Figner assured her that the young man could conduct it. And he hit on a trick, as Toscanini recalled:

One morning, I was in bed, and Figner called my room to say, "Come over immediately! They've sent me the score of *Edmea*. Let's start to study it." [. . .] There, in a ground-floor room of the

---

* In 1868, Signora Lucca's late husband, Francesco, had secured the Italian rights to all of Wagner's works.

[nearby] Hotel Leone, I started to play, and on and on I went. I used to sight-read very well [. . .]. I got to the finale of the second act—it was a grandiose finale, along the lines of that of the third act of *La Gioconda*—and I was sweating. And someone came up to me, looking at me through a monocle; he was following [the score]. It was the impresario from Turin [Giovanni Depanis]. When I had finished the second act he said, "You must have known this opera already!"

"No," I said, "I didn't know it. It just came this morning, and I'm reading it for the first time." Then he turned and motioned to another man to come forward. It was Catalani, and Catalani had been listening to me play.

On the basis of this unorthodox audition, Toscanini was engaged for Turin's Teatro Carignano. "So I owe Figner my career," he said, "because if he hadn't called me to Milan I would have continued to play the cello. Maybe I would have become a conductor [later]. I knew I could do it [. . .]; I had the ability to do it. But now, as I look back, [. . .] how could those people have taken me seriously?"

He made his way to the Piedmontese capital late in October and discovered that "all the orchestra musicians were members of Turin's Royal Chapel," as he later recalled. "I was rehearsing the opera"—he laughed as he told the story—

and there's a point in the first act, a short cello solo. The [principal] cello was out of tune, and I asked the musician, "Let's do it again." I repeated the same phrase two or three times. [. . .] He said, "Do we have to go on like this?"

"Sir, until you play in tune."

"Am I out of tune?"

"Yes."

"Get yourself [another] first cello"—and he left. [. . .] So when I think about it now I tell myself that I did have some authority. [. . .]

Maestro Bolzoni [. . .] was in Turin at that time to conduct [concerts with] the orchestra at the Teatro Regio, almost the same [personnel] as my orchestra, and there were a few cellos missing. [. . .] I went and played under his baton. [. . .] Then

Depanis summoned me. "Listen here, Toscanini, what are you, anyway?" [. . .]

"What do you mean?"

"I mean, are you playing the cello?"

"Yes, with Maestro Bolzoni I'd played *La Gioconda . . .*"

"Very well, but now you're a conductor."

"Yes, but so what? I can conduct and I can play the cello. Why not?"

"But your dignity . . ." Ah! I understood.

What he understood was that he could not play cello in what was virtually the same orchestra that he was conducting: it would diminish his authority—the more so because he was so young. After having played in two of Bolzoni's concerts, he withdrew from the series.

Initially, Toscanini was engaged to rehearse *Edmea* but not to conduct the performances. In nineteenth-century Italy, the more established conductors called themselves *direttori d'orchestra* (the term still used today), but many of them delegated the all-important responsibility for rehearsing to a *maestro concertatore*—often a barely competent time beater. The *direttore* would arrive for the final rehearsals, after the Augean stables had been cleansed, and lend the attraction of his name and presence to the proceedings. When Giovannina Lucca had engaged Toscanini, she had assumed that the well-known Alessandro Pomè would take over the performances, but Pomè decided to cede the *Edmea* performances to Toscanini, whose work had more than satisfied the cast and the orchestra.

Thus Toscanini made his professional Italian conducting debut at Turin's freshly restored eighteenth-century Teatro Carignano on 4 November 1886, with the famous soprano Virginia Ferni-Germano in the title role—which she had sung at the opera's premiere—and with Figner and Senatore Sparapani as, respectively, the lead tenor and baritone. The results exceeded everyone's hopes. There were twenty curtain calls for the artists and the composer, and the reviews were ecstatic. "*Edmea* had a truly enthusiastic success yesterday evening," wrote the critic for the *Gazzetta Musicale di Milano*, Ricordi's journal, which did not easily pay compliments to works published by the rival Lucca company. "The theater was full, overflowing; His Highness Prince Amedeo attended as did all the highest society [. . .]. [It was] not only a perfect, exceptional performance: It had been years since Turin had admired a more homogeneous, more secure company of artists. [. . .] The chorus was irreproachable; the orchestra, made up of Turin's finest musicians, exceptionally attentive and accurate. The debut of the *maestro concertatore* Toscanini was a triumph. It is a splendid dawn on the artistic horizon. [. . .] He conducted the score from memory with the sureness and energy of a seasoned maestro. The audience expressed all its admiration for him."

Pasquino, a journal, published a caricature of the overstuffed Ferni-Germano taking a bow onstage with the other cast members and the rail-thin Catalani; Toscanini—shown as an incongruously mustachioed little boy seated before the orchestra—wears knee breeches and has a fat tome, presumably the score, under his bottom and a table under his feet to make him tall enough to see and be seen. Most conspicuously, his music stand has no score on it.

Everyone—the participants as well as the critics—seemed to apprehend, immediately, that this boy was no mere shooting star that would quickly vanish but rather a thoroughly competent musician and a major talent. The *Gazzetta Piemontese*'s critic referred to Toscanini's "assurance, communicativeness, sangfroid, diligence, ironclad memory—this very young maestro has everything, and he seems destined to go a very long way." Carlo Brosovitch, the editor of *Il Trovatore*, a theater journal, wrote, "Arturo Toscanini, that beardless young thing, unknown until yesterday, [is] today one of the *best conductors*. He revealed *real genius*. [. . .] As conducted by Toscanini, the orchestra performed miracles." And a month later, Ricordi's *Gazzetta* reported that *Edmea* had been performed fifteen times "with ever-growing success," that it "cannot be better performed," and that Toscanini "has built a solid base for enduring fame." At the final *Edmea* performance, on 8 December, "after the second act, since the ovations wouldn't stop, the singers, thoughtfully interpreting the audience's wishes, pulled the young conductor Toscanini onto the stage."

During the month of *Edmea* performances, Toscanini rehearsed *The Flying Dutchman* for Pomè, who conducted the performances (this was the young man's first experience conducting Wagner), and he made a side trip to the nearby town of Asti to give a cello recital. At the end of Toscanini's stay in Turin, Catalani wrote to a friend, "I have found a very worthy, sincere, passionate conductor in young Maestro Toscanini [. . .], about whom one would think that this wasn't the first time he had climbed onto the conductor's stool, but that he had been doing so for twenty years! He is a real phenomenon. His career is assured."

3.

THE *EDMEA* EXPERIENCE INDUCED TOSCANINI TO SEEK FURTHER conducting engagements. He persuaded his family to move to Milan so that he could have a home there and so that the feckless Claudio could work at an already extant tailoring establishment instead of trying to run his own business. The Toscaninis' first dwelling was on the top floor of a boardinghouse in Via San Vito; the young maestro had a tiny room of his own, but his parents and sisters shared a large one. There was no kitchen—meals were taken with the two elderly owners—and when paying for board proved too onerous, a different apartment, with kitchen, was found in Via San Simone (now Via Cesare Correnti).

Before he began his life as an itinerant conductor, however, Toscanini took on a different job. The highlight of La Scala's 1886–87 season would be the world premiere of Verdi's *Otello*, his first new opera in sixteen years; the composer would supervise the rehearsals, Franco Faccio would conduct, and lead roles would be taken by well-known singers: the tenor Francesco Tamagno as the Moor of Venice, the baritone Victor Maurel as Iago, and the soprano Romilda Pantaleoni as Desdemona. In those days, opera orchestras were hired season by season, and Toscanini, determined to observe the *Otello* preparations, auditioned for and won the position of second cello in the Scala orchestra. In addition to *Otello*, he would play in productions of *Aida*, Donizetti's *Lucrezia Borgia*, Bizet's *Pêcheurs de Perles*, and the world premiere of *Flora Mirabilis* by the Greek composer Spyridon Samaras (known in Italy as Spiro Samara), all under Faccio's direction.*

---

* La Scala's principal singers that season included several artists (Buglione di Monale, Bertini, Limonta, et al.) who had worked with Toscanini in Rio de Janeiro.

For the rest of his life Toscanini referred to the *Otello* rehearsals and performances in January, February, and March 1887 as one of his greatest learning experiences. He later described how the seventy-three-year-old Verdi had sat on the stage and had set the tempo for Faccio at the first orchestra rehearsal by sharply and quickly counting off the first four beats before the tremendous *tutti* that opens the opera. But what fascinated Toscanini most about the whole process was the fact that at the first ensemble rehearsal—soloists and chorus in costume, singing and acting their roles; sets in place; full orchestra playing—"we went to the end of the first act without stopping, which means that they had rehearsed *in camera* [Verdi and Faccio rehearsing the singers with piano accompaniment] sufficiently, onstage sufficiently, and the orchestra [sufficiently]." In other words, maximum thoroughness was combined with maximum efficiency. What he had experienced as an orchestra member and conductor in second- and third-rate companies—and probably also in Turin, given the short rehearsal period—was a catch-as-catch-can system; the Scala experience made him understand, at the outset of his career, that detailed, separate rehearsals of each of the elements that go into an opera production saved time when all of those elements were put together: there was little or no need to stop and start over and over; minor errors could be corrected at the end of a run-through of a complete act.

The young conductor was curious about how closely Verdi's tempo and metronome indications would be followed: "I compared the tempi Faccio took with the marked tempi, and they were one and the same."* Toscanini described a staging rehearsal during which Verdi "made Tamagno fall I don't know how many times," presumably at the end of the third act; the tenor "almost became ill." Pantaleoni sometimes sang shrilly and out of tune, causing Toscanini to wince and grimace. But Pantaleoni was Faccio's mistress; when the conductor saw his young second cello making faces, he had him fined.

---

* When Toscanini was asked whether Faccio was a great conductor, he replied, "Yes, operas like *Gioconda*, *Aida*, he did well." He also said that he based his interpretation of *Aida* on that of Faccio, who had conducted the work's Italian premiere at La Scala in 1872 (the world premiere had taken place in Cairo), under Verdi's supervision, and was conducting it again in 1887, when Toscanini was in the orchestra.

Once, while Faccio was rehearsing the orchestra in the first-act love duet, which begins with a passage for four cellos alone, Verdi called out, "Second cello!" Toscanini's stand partner gave him a nudge and whispered to him to stand up. The young cellist sprang to his feet, and Verdi said to him, "You're playing too softly; play louder next time." The parts are marked *piano* and *pianissimo*, but Verdi wanted an expressive, vocal sound. This incident made a great impression on Toscanini, who took its ramifications to heart. In his recorded conversations, phrases like "Verdi never told us to play softly," "the orchestra must play naturally," "the life [of the work] is in the orchestra!" often recur; and he would tell his musicians that a *piano* marking in Verdi is not the same as a *piano* marking in Beethoven, Wagner, or even Mozart. The orchestra had to "sing" and sustain its sound.

At the *Otello* premiere, on 5 February 1887—one of the most memorable evenings in La Scala's history—"Verdi allowed three encores," Toscanini said. The first was the "Fuoco di gioia" chorus in Act I. A little later, at the end of Iago's drinking song, "the audience let off steam: 'Viva Verdi! Show yourself, Verdi!' and so on. But Verdi did not appear, we didn't do [that] encore," Toscanini said. Tamagno's high B-flat on "O gioia!" at the end of his third-act monologue "brought down the house," but there were no further encores until Act IV, when "the soprano had to repeat the 'Ave Maria.' She had gone to bed, [but] after that last note of the violins she [got up and] went back to kneel and sing. But that's nothing! Tamagno comes in with the [solo passage of the] double basses. When the double basses finished, we had to encore the solo," and Tamagno had to leave the stage and come back in again to kill Desdemona. This ridiculous, anti-theatrical interruption planted a seed in Toscanini's mind.

Toscanini was fined again—this time with many other orchestra members—for an act of protest that they had organized together. At La Scala as at most other Italian houses, operas were usually followed by ballets. Even after the world premiere of the first opera in sixteen years by Italy's most celebrated composer, and while throngs of Milanese were unhitching the horses from Verdi's carriage and pulling it to his hotel, the exhausted musicians had to accompany the dancers in scenes from Luigi Manzotti's ballet *Rolla*, in what must have been a nearly empty theater. They intentionally played badly, and they were fined.

Nevertheless, when the long evening had finally ended, an excited Toscanini ran home, woke his mother, and shouted, "Mamma, Verdi is a genius! Down on your knees to Verdi!"

4.

OTELLO HAD TO BE PERFORMED TWENTY-FIVE TIMES, SO GREAT was the public clamor to hear the new masterpiece. But once the season as a whole had ended, Toscanini, now twenty, left the relative glitter of La Scala and began to work as an itinerant conductor in provincial Italian theaters.

The journalist Filippo Sacchi, a Toscanini biographer who had grown up in the Italian provinces at the turn of the twentieth century, described the sort of existence that the young musician experienced during the early years of his career. There were the "little provincial hotels frequented by traveling salesmen," the "little daily struggles with props people who never have what's needed, or with the prima donna who wants to sing three arias for her *serata d'onore*, and the thousand vexations of small-time local politics: the mayor putting forward a singer for a minor part; the intellectual and influential lady who absolutely wants to have the conductor over for dinner; the garrison officers who trickle into the old theater clanking their swords." For eight years, this would be Toscanini's world.

His first stop was the Teatro Sociale in the Piedmontese town of Casale Monferrato, where, in June 1887, he was given only four orchestra rehearsals in which to prepare Meyerbeer's massive *L'Africaine*.* The local critic was amazed: "All intelligent people, first and foremost the members of the orchestra, are enthusiastic about

---

* Toscanini always remembered Almacinzia Magi-Trapani, who sang the lead female role of Sélika in Meyerbeer's opera, as a perfect example of a dramatic mezzo-soprano with a high extension who could bring off soprano roles like this one as well as such mezzo roles as Amneris in *Aida* and Leonora in *La Favorita*.

his talent." At his *serata d'onore*, Toscanini played a few cello pieces between two of the acts.

He was immediately invited back to Casale to conduct *La Gioconda* and Verdi's early *I Lombardi* from 24 October to 6 December, and he, in turn, invited three ex-schoolmates to reinforce the orchestra; one of them was the violinist Enrico Polo, who had recently graduated from the Parma Conservatory and was about to complete his studies in Berlin under the eminent Joseph Joachim. Toscanini successfully tempted Polo by reminding him of the virtuosic violin solo in the trio in Act III of the Verdi opera, and he composed an even more virtuosic cadenza for Polo to interpolate into the trio.

At the *serata d'onore* of Lola Peydro, the lead soprano in *La Gioconda*, Toscanini accompanied her in the song "Son Gelosa!!" (I'm Jealous!!), which he had written during his conservatory days. At another of the *Gioconda* performances, the audience shouted for the tenor's aria, "Cielo e mar," to be encored, but Toscanini refused to grant the request. Some members of the public were offended, and a military man in uniform shouted in Toscanini's direction, "You are an arrogant young conductor!" Toscanini turned around: "You are wrong, you dog!" He waited until the clamor died down and then continued the performance, without conceding the encore. Afterward, the soldier sent an intermediary to the conductor's dressing room and challenged him to a duel; Toscanini declined and the matter was dropped. This was the first skirmish in what would be a twenty-year, on-again, off-again encore war.

In Toscanini's youth, opera was hugely popular in Italy: in the northern half of the country and in many parts of the south virtually every town big enough to have a weekly farmers' market also had a theater. But quality was uneven, to put the matter mildly, and notwithstanding the battles that Verdi and some of his contemporaries had waged to make opera a convincing combination of music, poetry, and drama, the form remained, for the general public, essentially an arena for the display of vocal technique. Singers told the conductor how they wanted their arias done, although they might change their interpretations from one performance to another, and the orchestra was rehearsed just enough to ensure that the musicians would stay more or less together and play in the same key, since transpositions were frequent. Milan-based agents, some of them unscrupulous, sent singers, sets, and costumes to the provinces. Scenery and costumes were often used interchangeably from one opera to another, and acting as we know it barely existed. Sacchi described provincial opera performances in which emotions were represented by "a predetermined set of facial contortions and gestures: high notes were pre-announced by bringing a foot forward in a certain way; amorous tenderness was indicated by languidly inclining the head to a certain degree." Chorus members' basic task, apart from singing, was to stay out of the way of the solo singers, and orchestra musicians were gathered from the highways and hedges and given short-term contracts at low pay.

Toscanini, in his first three or four years as a conductor, could fight only a rearguard action against these practices. He needed to become familiar with all of the encrusted traditions before he could decide which ones seemed to him valid and logical and which ones did not. Besides, at the outset of his career he was anything but forward. "I felt uneasy saying that I was the conductor," he recalled, laughing, toward the end of his life. In those early years, "I would come into the [singers' rehearsal] room and sit down at the piano to make people understand that I was the conductor." He was not in a position to oppose, with any hope of success, established singers much older than himself, nor could he demand beautiful, virtuosic playing from orchestras that were incapable of it, or expect refined productions or efficient organization in towns in which only two operas were mounted in the course of a season.

And yet, Toscanini's formidable talents, his rigorous self-discipline, his lack of self-importance, and his seriousness at once attracted the admiration of perceptive singers and orchestra musicians. He not only *knew* every note and expression mark in every score that he conducted; he also *heard* every detail and could immediately pinpoint wrong notes, bad intonation, and incorrect rhythms. And he had a sense of theater, of the dramatic arc of an opera. These abilities obviated many of the problems that most young, inexperienced conductors confront at the outset of their careers.

5.

TOSCANINI MUST HAVE GONE DIRECTLY FROM CASALE TO VERONA, where, between late December 1887 and February 1888, he conducted *Carmen*, Donizetti's *Lucrezia Borgia*, and Thomas's *Mignon* at the beautiful eighteenth-century Teatro Filarmonico. The two French works went well, but a newspaper report of the first performance of *Lucrezia Borgia*—"a true, complete catastrophe"—gives an idea of how cruel Italian audiences could be. "The curtain was brought down at the beginning of the third scene of the first act, and the administration had to return tickets to the audience. [. . .] When Lucrezia (Madame Emma Wiziak) came out for her grand Aria, [. . .] the hurricane suddenly broke out violently and unstoppably. The artist, overcome with panic, was no longer able to get back on the right path; the audience was silent at first but then became impatient, then noisy, then began to shout, and so the prima donna, dismayed and lost, abandoned the stage. A devilish uproar ensued—whistles, laughs, and shouts of 'down with the Administration'—until the curtain came down and the conductor abandoned his place." In subsequent performances Wiziak was replaced. Yet Toscanini later recalled that the more he conducted *Lucrezia*, the more enthusiastic he became about the opera and about Donizetti.

At his *serata d'onore*, he conducted the local premiere of the *Tannhäuser* Overture; the critic for Verona's *Gazzettino* found the performance "stupendous" and hoped—in vain, as things turned out— that the young maestro would return to conduct the entire opera.

Toscanini had no other engagements for several months, and in May 1888 he may have received some basic military training, after which the Command of the Seventh District, Parma, of the Royal Italian Army granted him "unlimited leave" for having "completed instruction" as a "soldier in this unit." More likely, however, he had paid to be relieved of the obligation.

On 2 June, he was in Bologna to attend the Italian premiere of *Tristan und Isolde*, under the baton of the thirty-two-year-old composer-conductor-pianist Giuseppe Martucci. Martucci was a major figure in the campaign to bring the music of Wagner and the German symphonists into Italy, where influences from north of the Alps were regarded with suspicion. By the time the second act of *Tristan* had ended, an overwhelmed Toscanini—who until then had still dabbled at composition from time to time—had made up his mind to compose no more.*

In August he conducted *Aida* at the Teatro Rossi in the town of Macerata, in the Marches. Much more significant, however, was his Milan debut that fall, with a substantial engagement at the Teatro Dal Verme. The Lombard capital, which then counted about 400,000 inhabitants, was Italy's most important industrial and commercial center, and it boasted ten theaters that put on annual series of operas; La Scala was the most important of them, but the Dal Verme, built in 1864, ranked second. From 20 October to 9 December 1888, Toscanini conducted twenty-two performances of Verdi's *La Forza del Destino*, eight of Ponchielli's *I Promessi Sposi*, and nine of *Francesca da Rimini*, a ten-year-old opera by the now forgotten Antonio Cagnoni. At the end of the series, cast members, orchestra, and chorus presented the young conductor with a specially bound, gold-embossed full score of Beethoven overtures (published by Breitkopf & Härtel in Leipzig), signed by all of them, as a token of their esteem. He kept this gift much longer than the traditional laurel wreath given him by Cagnoni at the last performance of *Francesca*, and he filled it with penciled-in dynamic markings and other annotations.

Between late December 1888 and early March 1889, Toscanini conducted the inaugural season of the Teatro Coccia in the town of Novara; the repertoire consisted of *Les Huguenots*, *Aida*, and *La Forza del Destino*—"with only one [leading] tenor" for all the operas, Toscanini recalled. Legend has it that that tenor, one Eugenio Salto, was having such a passionate affair with Virginia Paltrinieri, the prima donna in *Huguenots*, that by the second performance he was exhausted and voiceless; Paltrinieri seems to have suffered no ill effects. Opening night, however, was a huge success, not least for the young conductor, about whom, according to the local critic, "any word of

---

* As late as 1891, however, he sent to Parma an arrangement for string quartet of a piece he had originally written for violin and piano; he suggested that Enrico Polo and some friends try the arrangement at one of Count Sanvitale's musical soirées and send him their impressions. But this seems to be his last reference to any of his compositions until, in old age, he wrote out (by heart) some of his juvenilia, to entertain friends and family.

praise is insufficient." Toscanini also found time to take his cello out of its case and, with three musicians from the orchestra, give a string quartet concert for Novara's Musical Circle. The program included Beethoven's Quartet in C minor, op. 18, no. 4, plus short pieces by Joachim Raff, Antonio Bazzini, Tchaikovsky, and Francesco Giaretta, and the audience was so enthusiastic that the program had to be repeated four days later.

Returning to Turin for the first time since his Italian debut more than two years earlier, Toscanini conducted *Carmen* at the Teatro Vittorio Emanuele in March and April 1889. Adele Borghi, a mezzo-soprano especially well-known for her interpretation of Bizet's heroine, was the star, and she also sang "Son Gelosa!!"—probably accompanied by Toscanini at the piano—at her *serata* on 13 April.* At the Carignano in May, he led a revival of *Edmea*, thanks, most likely, to Catalani, who had written to Toscanini that he would be "very happy if you could be the conductor."

Also at the Carignano, Toscanini again conducted *Carmen*, the same production that Friedrich Nietzsche had attended repeatedly and enthusiastically a year earlier, when the conductor was Leopoldo Mugnone. The German philosopher—at that time still barely known beyond a small circle of friends and admirers—had once been part of Wagner's circle and a propagandist for the Wagnerian aesthetic but had since turned against the composer; *Carmen* had come to symbolize, for Nietzsche, healthy, frank Mediterranean sensuality in music, as opposed to Wagnerian murkiness and pseudophilosophy. Nietzsche, who had been living in Turin, would almost certainly have heard Toscanini conduct *Carmen* there in the spring of 1889 had he not lost his sanity and collapsed on the city's streets the previous January. And Toscanini would soon become one of the most significant performing musicians to breach the gap between Mediterranean music and Wagnerism.

Returning to the great port city of Genoa, where he had spent

---

* Three days earlier, Toscanini had conducted two short orchestral pieces in a benefit concert for the Institute for Rickets Victims. During his stay in the Piedmontese capital, he also played the cello in two concerts of Bolzoni's chamber music: one at the Liceo Musicale, on 28 April, and the other at the Circolo degli Artisti, on 26 May. And on 14 June, at the Teatro Carignano, he played the piano accompaniment for some pieces for voice and/or solo instruments by the Neapolitan composer and pianist Gilda Ruta, a Liszt pupil.

part of his childhood, Toscanini made his local debut in July at the Politeama Genovese, a relatively minor theater, once again conducting Cagnoni's *Francesca*. After the second act, during one of the sixteen performances, the soprano Elena Boronat sang Toscanini's song "Nevrosi," with the composer at the piano, and at his own *serata d'onore* Toscanini conducted the overture to Verdi's *I Vespri Siciliani*.

Giulio Gatti-Casazza, a twenty-year-old student of nautical engineering who had inherited a fascination with the opera business from his father, an impresario, attended one of the Genoa performances and met its conductor afterward. "Toscanini was really a handsome young fellow," he recalled, "very elegant and affable indeed, a thing that surprised me, since I had heard that he was an extremely severe person with an inexpansive personality. In spite of the fact that the orchestra of the Politeama was rather mediocre, Toscanini had succeeded in obtaining a thoroughly fused and coherent performance, full of color and warmth. Everyone spoke of him as the most important factor in the entire performance." Within a decade, Toscanini and Gatti-Casazza would be working in tandem, with results that would have important repercussions in the opera world.

Following a two-month break, Toscanini made the brief journey from Milan to the Lombard town of Voghera to conduct *Aida* and Bellini's *Norma*, although the latter was canceled and replaced by *La Favorita*. According to contemporary documents, members of Voghera's town council, together with the influential citizens who made up the theater's administration, provided a Milanese impresario with 9,500 lire to put together the Teatro Sociale's autumn season. These meager funds had to suffice for eight solo singers, eight ballerinas, a chorus of twenty-four male and eighteen female voices, a forty-six-piece orchestra that would include fifteen out-of-town players, a stage band, and a conductor who was enjoined, in the contract, to conduct the scores "exactly as they are written, excepting the customary changes and deletions"—in other words, to chop them up as he and his singers saw fit—and to supervise the staging "as indicated in the respective texts." Rehearsals for *Aida* began only ten days before the first performance and did not always go smoothly—hardly surprising, given that forces twice as numerous and probably several times as competent would have been required to do the task well. At one rehearsal Toscanini turned to a double bass player, an unsuccessful local attorney who augmented his income by playing at dances, and said, "Mr. Lawyer, go burn that big box."

Both operas were well received, but the young conductor augmented his measly fee by playing a few pieces on the cello and conducting a small group in two short works at a soirée at the palace of a local nobleman. Likewise, during an intermission in the last performance of the season (*Aida*), which was also Toscanini's *serata d'onore*, he played two cello pieces and conducted two others. The "ovations aimed at him reached the point of rapture," wrote the local critic, and he received many gifts.

By mid-December, Toscanini was in Brescia, the largest city in Lombardy after Milan, with his mother in tow to keep house for him in rented rooms so that he could avoid spending money on hotels and restaurants. At the Teatro Grande he prepared and conducted *La Gioconda*, and, in January 1890, *Le Villi*, the first opera of a young composer named Giacomo Puccini, with whom Toscanini was not yet personally acquainted.

More significant was his second Genoese engagement, which took place in March at the Politeama Regina Margherita. Upon arriving in town, he had gone directly to the theater, where he found the impresario sweeping the floor in the lobby. Toscanini complained that he had been allotted only twenty-four choristers for his two operas, *Mignon* and *Carmen*; he needed forty-eight. "A heated argument ensued, up and down the hall, while the impresario continued to sweep the floor," according to the journalist Alfredo Segre, who heard the story from Toscanini many years later. " 'I'll give you thirty, is that all right?' "

" 'Then I'll return to Milan,' said Toscanini, walking away abruptly. He got the forty-eight choristers." And when, at the first rehearsal, Toscanini heard the orchestra, he demanded a substantial number of replacements in the personnel, thereby causing protests among the castoffs and further expenditures on the impresario's part.

The results were telling. "Maestro Toscanini, a little autocrat [. . .], demanded adequate time and adequate players; otherwise, he would have set down his baton and gone away," one journal reported. "If only there were many such conductors with conscience and energy! He postponed the first performance by three days, but at the *Mignon* opening the performance was so complete, so homogeneous, so well-proportioned, that the audience [. . .] was ecstatic over the perfect vocal interpretation and the most elegant orchestral conducting." The artists "sing and don't shout," another observer wrote; "they feel that they represent characters, not mannequins, on the stage.* [. . .] Finally we are seeing justice being done for the many crimes that have long been committed in the name of art."

6.

THE TWO GENOESE PRODUCTIONS WERE A TURNING POINT FOR THE twenty-three-year-old Toscanini. His career was still in its infancy, he was still working with second- or third-rate ensembles, and economic survival was a constant struggle, but he had already conducted some three dozen opera productions and had developed a clear idea of what was possible and what was not in any given situation. His goal was not to do the impossible—to convert minor ensembles into major ones—but rather to be uncompromising within whatever conditions obtained in order to make each company reach its highest level.

Many musicians who worked with Toscanini in later years remarked that he hated to fire musicians and would go to great lengths to keep players in his orchestras even if their approaches to music making diverged from his own. But that was when he was working with high-caliber, mid-twentieth-century orchestras that possessed substantial internal discipline. In *Memorie di un suggeritore* (A Prompter's Memoirs), a book published in 1902, the impresario and critic Gino Monaldi described what would often happen at a late nineteenth-century Italian opera orchestra's first rehearsal of the

---

* The famed French mezzo-soprano Lison Frandin sang the title role in *Carmen* and alternated in the role of Mignon with the Swedish soprano Georgina Sommelius Bottero. Toscanini later described Frandin—slender, with close-set eyes and cascading blond hair—as "a beautiful woman" who sang those two roles "as I've never [again] heard them, and I conducted [*Mignon*] many times with her. Aaahhhhh, that scene when she starts to cry, when she asks for alms from passersby—everyone wept! She was an artist."

season, "with players who were engaged one by one." There would be fights among the players over seating rank—fights "usually quelled by the conductor's moral authority—if he has any"; otherwise "police intervention is required." In orchestras like the one Toscanini confronted in Genoa in 1890, many of the players were poorly trained, yet they were accustomed to being reengaged from season to season, thanks in part to impresarios who did not want to pay higher fees to more competent musicians, but thanks also to conductors who did not want to upset the status quo.

Toscanini decided that the status quo was not good enough. By nature he was quiet, studious, and somewhat shy, but music was of such overriding importance to him that he would do whatever had to be done to alter the system within which he was condemned to operate. He could not understand how people who called themselves musicians could be lazy or halfhearted in their work. How could they feel whole and fulfilled if they were not putting body and soul into the great task—and the great privilege—that had been placed in their hands?

The more experience he gained, the less willing he was to accept complacency. He could rehearse patiently for hours if he sensed that his musicians and singers were working at maximum capacity, but if he suspected otherwise he would become a fury, breaking batons, screaming obscenities, tearing up scores, knocking over his music stand, and hurling insults at the offenders. Singers sometimes emerged from his coaching sessions in tears, and orchestra players left rehearsals wrung out from tension and exhaustion. Yet no one could convincingly accuse him of carrying on as he did purely out of self-interest or vanity. Here was a conductor who did not make exaggerated gestures to impress the public, who seemed to want to run away from applause, who spent his days in coaching sessions, staging rehearsals, chorus rehearsals, orchestra rehearsals, and ensemble rehearsals, and who stayed up nights absorbing new scores or trying to penetrate deeper into old ones. Many people resented, even detested, this superdemanding young conductor, but others realized that the tension and exhaustion of the struggle to achieve an artistic goal were far better than the anesthetizing boredom of mediocrity.

7.

AFTER HAVING CONDUCTED *MIGNON* AND *CARMEN* IN GENOA, Toscanini must have proceeded directly to Turin, where, at the Carignano, he conducted the same operas with essentially the same casts, plus five performances of *Faust*; at the time, all three of these French operas—*Faust* first and foremost—were among the most popular works in the repertoire. By the end of May or early June, he was back in Milan, with no further engagements in sight for four months, because, he said, he was considered too severe. But he seems to have enjoyed his free time at home. His family had moved to a larger apartment on the fifth floor of a building at 54 Corso (now Via) Torino, and Paola had taken in lodgers, including Enrico Polo and other young musicians from Parma. Sacchi, who knew some of these people in later years, said that they described the young Toscanini at home as "expansive and a prankster. He would arrive as hungry as a boy coming home from school and would burst into the kitchen. If a meal wasn't ready he would jokingly put on one of his mother's aprons and use a feather-fan to get the burners on the stove going." Sometimes he would show his friends how strong his mother was by climbing onto a table and insisting that she pick him up and carry him to his room. Mostly, however, he loved to tease his sisters, Ada—now fifteen, "lively, exuberant, and a bit flirtatious"—and Zina, thirteen, "shyer and quieter." Their brother would chase them, grab them, and spin them around like tops. Once, when Zina said that she thought kissing was disgusting, he tied her to a chair and kissed her over and over, while everyone laughed. The girls got back at him: when they heard him singing, they told him that he sounded like a priest—the worst possible insult for an anticlericalist.

Of his love life during his early years there are virtually no details. He was good-looking—slender and of average height (five feet five) for an Italian male of his day, with well-proportioned features and deep-set, black eyes—and he dressed fashionably, formally, and immaculately. His energetic character, his growing reputation as a brilliant musician, and his natural charm—off the podium—added to his attractiveness. Given the free-and-easy back-stage morals of the theater world and what is known about his erotic life in the following decades, there is no reason to believe that he was celibate in his twenties. He did once write to a lady friend that "as a young man, I stayed at home for months and months, working, without getting near a woman and without suffering from it," but this probably meant only that he did not visit prostitutes; he chose not to describe his sex life during the many months spent away from home.

One of the boarders from Parma told Sacchi that Toscanini played the piano constantly; even while he was chewing his food he would "play" on the dinner table. And when he was not studying music, he was reading literature. The poetry and prose of the early nineteenth-century poet and essayist Giacomo Leopardi and the still-living Giosuè Carducci particularly attracted him, but he was also reading other contemporary Italian poets, such as Olindo Guerrini (better known by his pseudonym, Lorenzo Stecchetti) and Enrico Panzacchi. He read Leopardi's letters aloud to his mother, and they wept together over the most desperate ones. Toscanini's readings would eventually extend to most classic and contemporary European literature, in French and, later, in English, as well as in Italian; German, Russian, and other works he read in translation. All of his children remembered him as a voracious reader of fiction as well as nonfiction books on many subjects.

Did the young Toscanini show any interest in Italian politics? Probably not. In those years, the country had moved from its earliest post-reunification phase into a period of *trasformismo*—liberal-conservative coalitions under Prime Ministers Francesco Crispi and Giovanni Giolitti, both of whom presided over economic crises and mostly ill-fated colonial adventures. But there is no evidence that the young Toscanini gave much thought to such matters. During the summer and early fall of 1890, he spent most of his waking hours devouring great quantities of music, at home and in the libraries of Milan's conservatory and its various music publishing houses. Two years earlier, Giovannina Lucca had sold her holdings to Ricordi, which meant that the latter now held the Italian rights to Wagner's works in addition to worldwide licensing rights to most of the significant operas by nineteenth-century

Italian composers. Edoardo Sonzogno, another intrepid publisher, was acquiring operas by many French composers and
showing even more curiosity than Giulio Ricordi—who was now
firmly in control of his family's company—for the works of several young Italian composers. Both publishers were interested in
Toscanini as a promising young purveyor of the music they were
promoting, and they were happy to provide him with any scores
he wished to examine.

During those free months, Toscanini was occasionally engaged
to play cello or piano in chamber groups at the home of Giovanni
Villa, a wealthy Milanese music lover and amateur violinist.
Between late April and early July, he participated in six of these
"Musical Evenings 1890," playing works by Haydn, Beethoven,
Mendelssohn, and others. Then, in October, Toscanini left Italy for
the first time since his return from South America four years ear-
lier, to spend a season as an assistant to Edoardo Mascheroni at
Barcelona's Teatro Liceo.

Spain in those years was a musical backwater in comparison with
Italy; perhaps Toscanini thought that he would profit from working
with Mascheroni, who was fifteen years his senior and whose
accomplishments included having conducted the first Italian production of Beethoven's *Fidelio*—seventy-two years after its world
premiere!—or perhaps he hoped that a job abroad would take him
away from the internecine strife of the Italian opera world. He
would have been wrong on both counts, because Mascheroni disliked having so gifted an assistant and tried to trip him up by assign-
ing to him, at the last moment, a new production of Bellini's *I
Capuleti e i Montecchi*, a work for virtuoso singers that was rarely
revived. To the older conductor's horror, however, under Toscanini's leadership the production, which opened on 14 November 1890,
was a success. Mascheroni countered by persuading the impresario
to cancel the opera after the third performance, and Toscanini
returned to Italy.*

In August 1891 he was in the town of Senigallia, on the Adriatic,

---

* Toscanini respected other senior Italian conductors of the day—Faccio and Luigi
Mancinelli, in particular—but he described Mascheroni as a cunning amateur who
obtained his positions by frequenting the ruling classes.

for what would today be described as a summer stock production of *Cavalleria Rusticana*, which had had its highly successful world premiere in Rome the preceding year: Pietro Mascagni, a composer not even four years older than Toscanini, had entered the work in the Sonzogno company's competition for a one-act opera, and within a year of its first performance the colorful score, with its clear-cut, violent emotions, had been performed all over Europe and the Americas, beginning what would prove to be a new phase in Italian opera. Toscanini conducted *Cavalleria* again in November, this time at the Carignano in Turin; the first performance was shaky, but from the second night on the production was a triumph—so popular, in fact, that it had to be performed seventeen times, whereas Verdi's beautiful but "old" *Luisa Miller* closed after only two performances.

The difficulties that Toscanini had confronted at Genoa's Politeama early in 1890 were trivial compared with those that he faced when he returned to the Ligurian capital at the end of 1891, to conduct a full season of five operas—his most important engagement to date—at the Teatro Carlo Felice, the city's principal opera house, under the auspices of the impresario Luigi Piontelli. The orchestra was in a parlous state; Toscanini's solution, once again, was to hold auditions, but his decision set off waves of recriminations that were reflected in the reviews of the first performance of Meyerbeer's grandiose *Le Prophète*: although some of the critics said that the young conductor had made the best of a bad situation (the singers weren't very good, they complained) and had obtained exceptional results from the orchestra, others declared that he had willfully distorted the work. The production was temporarily withdrawn, some cuts were made, the singers became more secure, and thirteen further performances were given.

The second opera, Verdi's *Simon Boccanegra*, set in Genoa, featured three star singers: the baritone Ramón Blanchart in the title role, the soprano Cesira Ferrani as Amelia/Maria, and the tenor Francisco Viñas as Gabriele Adorno. Critical opinion was favorable, but audiences were lukewarm at all nine performances—and indeed, this great musical canvas of political intrigue and personal upheaval began to be widely valued only in the late twentieth century. Toscanini loved it but never conducted it again. On the contrary, Mascagni's new *L'Amico Fritz* was a tremendous success at its local premiere, and Toscanini allowed four encores on opening night. According to one chronicler, at all ten performances "the attendance was extraordinary, with great applause for all the artists and the orchestra."

The last opera in the series was the new but now forgotten *Vindice* by the now equally forgotten Umberto Masetti; all four of its performances were poorly attended. It was preceded, however, by the Genoese premiere of Catalani's *Loreley*, a reworking of the composer's earlier *Elda*. Toscanini must have expressed a few qualms about the piece to Catalani, who wrote to him, "I believe that there is no one who *divines* me and interprets me as you do.—If you find anything too long in the 2nd act go ahead and cut. [. . .] I entrust myself completely to you for everything." And in another letter: "I think that in the 2nd act the *Waltz* or the *Epithalamium* must be cut, the choice is yours. [. . .] Anyway you'll do whatever you think best; I know that I'm in good hands, so I feel at peace and secure." Although *Loreley* received only four performances, the public liked it. "Yesterday evening's success was really splendid," Catalani wrote to Giulio Ricordi, the opera's publisher, after opening night. "Toscanini is a great and true artist; that is all there is to be said." Ricordi wired Toscanini, "Knowing the intelligent care you've taken over Loreley I send you my thanks [and] congratulations."

By mid-March 1892 Toscanini's Genoese season had come to an end, but his return to Milan was delayed, possibly by court order, as a result of a debt of three hundred lire incurred by his irresponsible father, who had used his son's name as security against a loan. Toscanini did not have that sum at his disposal; he sent desperate letters to Piontelli, saying that he did not know "which wall to bash my head against" and begging him to lend him the money to "get me out of this mess," which was the result of "too much goodness toward a family that is very ungrateful to me." The funds came through— Piontelli made him a gift of two-thirds of the amount, "for services rendered last season"—and the grateful Toscanini was able to return to Milan. For several years thereafter, Piontelli acted as the young conductor's agent and adviser.

8.

VERDI HAD BEEN HEARING GOOD THINGS, FROM VARIOUS SOURCES, about the young conductor from Parma and had recommended him to the famous baritone Victor Maurel, who had sung the role of Iago at the world premiere of *Otello*. Maurel had in turn recommended Toscanini to Edoardo Sonzogno, who engaged the conductor for a short season, at Milan's Teatro Dal Verme, that would include the world premiere of an opera by Ruggero Leoncavallo, a little-known thirty-five-year-old composer. Unlike Catalani, Puccini, and Mascagni—all Tuscans who had studied at the prestigious Milan Conservatory—Leoncavallo was a southerner, born in Naples and bred in Calabria; in a sense, the cards were stacked against his new opera, *Pagliacci*, but Maurel's interest in it gave the composer some advance prestige.

Toscanini took an instant liking to Leoncavallo, who was "a miserable wretch," he recalled. "He was a good man, too—a bit fat, but simpatico." The first-rate cast included Maurel as Tonio, the Austrian-born Adelina Stehle as Nedda, the young Parmesan tenor Fiorello Giraud as Canio, and Mario Ancona as Silvio. Even Francesco Daddi, the lyric tenor who sang the role of Beppe, had "a beautiful little voice," Toscanini said. The new work was unsophisticated but innovative; its characters were painted with broad brushstrokes but were full of life. A great deal of effort went into the production, not least because the opera hadn't yet been published: soloists, chorus members, and orchestra musicians were reading from hand-copied parts.

During the rehearsal period, Catalani once asked Toscanini what he thought of *Pagliacci*. "I said, 'It's an opera that will be liked, because it's melodic, it has a nice libretto,' and so on," Toscanini recalled.

" 'But what about the music?' " Catalani asked. "I couldn't speak ill of it."

At the premiere, on 21 May 1892, the opera "was an enormous success," Toscanini said. Nedda, Canio, and Beppe's arias had to be encored, and Maurel offended some audience members by refusing to encore any of Tonio's music. Afterward, Puccini and Mascagni went backstage to compliment Leoncavallo; Catalani came, too, "but he didn't go to pay compliments," Toscanini said. Instead, "he approached me, pinched me hard, and said, 'You pig!'" (Toscanini laughed in telling the story.) "Because he'd thought he was going to hear music that he would like. It really annoyed him." Toscanini, however, had been so exhausted by the difficult rehearsal process that after the first performance he went home, threw himself onto his bed, still wearing his starched shirt, tails, and shoes, and fell asleep.

Pagliacci was originally given as a single act, but "it was too long," Toscanini recalled. At the second performance they brought the curtain down after the tenor's "Vesti la giubba" and, after an intermission, began what is now Act II, with its trumpet-and-bass-drum introduction; Leoncavallo had not yet written the intermezzo that later became an integral part of the opera.* In its final form, *Pagliacci* quickly triumphed around the world. Leoncavallo's years of poverty were over.

Together with Mascagni's slightly older *Cavalleria Rusticana*, *Pagliacci* seemed to signal a new trend in opera—a trend that would be fostered also by other composers, including Umberto Giordano, Francesco Cilea, and to some extent Alberto Franchetti and even Puccini. By no means did these men create a formal group, much less a school, although the term *verismo* was soon applied to their output; they merely faced similar creative difficulties at the outset of their careers and found divergent but related solutions. The greatest difficulty was posed by their much older colleague Giuseppe Verdi, who had dominated the world of Italian opera for half a century, leaving every other composer of his nation and generation far behind him, and whose astonishing *Otello* and revolutionary *Falstaff* were confounding, or about to confound, his younger contemporaries. And then there was the question of the gradual internationalization of the repertoire: the music of Wagner, Gounod, Bizet, Massenet, and others was finding its way into Italy, and young Italian composers could not avoid the new influences.

One way for them to produce something different was to adopt

---

* Maurel did not initially sing what has since become a "traditional" high A-flat at the end of the phrase "al pari di voi." But in 1915 Leoncavallo wrote to Toscanini that the high note could be allowed, "for the sole reason that central voices like Maurel's no longer exist."

relatively realistic plots and texts, as opposed to the formulaic con-
coctions of their High Romantic Italian predecessors and the myth-
ological-philosophical, or pseudo-philosophical, inventions of
Wagner. According to these young Italian composers, all in their
twenties or thirties at the time of *Pagliacci*'s premiere, audiences
were ready for up-to-date stories that focused on everyday people
instead of gods, heroes, and royalty—lives like those that Emile Zola
and Giovanni Verga were presenting in their novels. In the prologue
to *Pagliacci*, Leoncavallo, who wrote his own libretto, had Tonio say,
"The author has sought to depict a slice of life for you. His only
maxim is that the artist is a man and that he must write for men.—
And he was inspired by the truth." Pompous but sincere.

Toscanini's attitude toward the *veristi* was ambivalent. Until he
reached middle age, his interest in new musical currents at home
and abroad was vast, and he wanted to do his best for the most gifted
composers among his compatriots and contemporaries. But, with
the partial exception of Puccini, he found much of their music
crude—which helps to explain his affinity for and friendship with
the more refined Catalani.

Catalani taught composition at the Milan Conservatory, and
whenever Toscanini was in town the two musicians would meet.
The tubercular composer would often climb, with difficulty, the
many stairs to the Toscanini family's apartment and ask Paola
whether Arturo was at home—so Toscanini recalled decades later. If
she said no, he would sit and wait. "My mother used to say, 'Those
eyes of his are always open; he seems to be looking into the distance,'" Toscanini remembered. Catalani often asked his younger
colleague to play his operas for him: "He would sit down in an armchair, with his legs over the chair's arm, and he would fall asleep."
Toscanini laughed in recalling those sessions: "Ah, he was a character," he said. He described Catalani as "the most simpatico composer" of his generation—"kind" and "well-mannered," and he "had
a heart." Toscanini felt the sort of affection and admiration for Catalani, his senior by thirteen years, that he might have had for an older
brother, and Catalani's faith in Toscanini was total. "He never played
an opera [of his] for me," Toscanini told friends, and "I'm not familiar
with his musical handwriting"—because Catalani never wrote anything in his young acolyte's scores.

Years later, Toscanini told the *New York American*'s music critic Charles Henry Meltzer that Catalani was "unhappy and unfortunate. [. . .] He lived apart from his contemporaries. They saw him seldom in the busy Galleria and in the Milan restaurants. [. . .] He was a dreamer and he was a poet, a man of singular modesty, misunderstood and wronged. He—and no other—was the chief of the Young Italian school. Puccini and Mascagni and the rest of them, who have grown famous, all—all—borrowed from Alfredo Catalani. There are echoes of his music—whole passages—in [Puccini's] 'Le Villi' and in 'Cavalleria Rusticana.' [. . .] The young composers who owed so much to him treated him unfeelingly. I could tell you of some among them who used even to drink to his failure when one of his works was produced. [. . .] He had a grace, a charm and a delicacy which were almost French." His music was "not cheerful," but it was "very strong, very poetic."

To the end of his life, Toscanini believed that Catalani's fellow Tuscans Puccini and Carlo Carignani (the latter made the Ricordi company's piano-vocal reductions of the operas of Catalani, Puccini, and others) had spread rumors that his music had the evil eye: so much of it was sad, in minor keys—the music of a sickly man, they said, according to Toscanini. Catalani was upset by these real or imagined innuendoes. "He would say, 'And Chopin? Isn't he, too, in minor a lot?'" Toscanini recalled, also pointing out, "Think of the third act of Puccini's *Manon*. It couldn't be more funereal than it is! If Catalani had done it . . ."

But Toscanini admitted that Catalani's indications regarding tempi and other interpretive details were often vague, which made life difficult for conductors, whereas Puccini, Mascagni, and Giordano were "very precise." Worse still, Catalani had made use of inferior libretti: "The only passable one is *La Wally*," but even that one left much to be desired, he said of the story of Catalani's last opera.

Unstated yet omnipresent in Toscanini's recorded comments about Catalani is his awareness that the composer, who died at the age of thirty-nine, never reached his full professional and artistic stride. He was convinced that Catalani was more gifted, especially as a melodist, than Puccini and their contemporaries, but he also knew that Puccini had learned to handle his musical materials more skillfully and to choose more attractive subjects and libretti. Yet Toscanini could never quite forgive Puccini and the *veristi* their success, accompanying as it did the near oblivion of his friend's work.

9.

JUNE AND JULY 1892 WERE CALM MONTHS FOR TOSCANINI, AFTER his exertions for *Pagliacci*, and he spent early August relaxing in Voghera, at the home of one of his adoring Montani uncles. But eight months of unrelenting activity awaited him. By late August, he was hard at work at the Teatro del Giglio in Lucca, the home-town of both Puccini and Catalani, rehearsing the local premiere of the latter's *La Wally*, which had had its world premiere at La Scala the preceding January.

Catalani, who saw or imagined enemies everywhere, was particu-larly overwrought in Lucca because he had convinced himself that the Puccini family was plotting against him. And the whole produc-tion nearly collapsed over a misunderstanding. Toscanini recalled that at one rehearsal he had said, "Let's go, chorus, holy God! You're *polentoni!*" But whereas in Parma, *polentoni* (literally, "big polenta eaters") merely meant "sluggards," in Lucca it meant "idiots." Laugh-ing as he told the story many years later, Toscanini said that the head chorister had told him, "We're not *polentoni*, God damn it!" and had threatened a strike. "Poor Catalani—he suffered," Toscanini com-mented. The matter was quickly settled, however, and after the first performance Catalani sent a telegram to a friend: "*Wally* success enthusiastic, indescribable. Audience deeply impressed. Six encores [. . .]. Toscanini's conducting admirable." Fourteen performances were given, not bad for a small town. But Toscanini must have turned the last few performances over to an assistant, because he had been sum-moned to Genoa in an emergency situation.

One of the great events of Italy's 1892–93 opera season was the world premiere of Franchetti's *Cristoforo Colombo*, commissioned by the Teatro Carlo Felice in Columbus's hometown to mark the four hundredth anniversary of the discovery of America. Luigi Manci-nelli, among the best-known conductors of the day, was to take the final rehearsals and the first two performances, but all the prepara-tory rehearsals and remaining performances—as well as the Geno-

ese premiere of *La Wally*—were to be conducted by Vittorio Maria
Vanzo, under whom Toscanini had played the cello in Parma's
orchestra a decade earlier. When Mancinelli arrived, he began to
alter many of the tempi; Vanzo protested that he had studied the
score with the composer, and when Mancinelli remained adamant
Vanzo left town, saying that Piontelli, the impresario, could find
someone else to take the performances that Mancinelli would not
conduct. Catalani had gone to Genoa to follow the *Colombo* rehearsals, and when the clash between Mancinelli and Vanzo occurred he
persuaded Piontelli and the theater's administrators to invite Toscanini to take Vanzo's place. In a letter to Toscanini (22 September),
Catalani exulted, "I'm happy, super-happy, that you'll [also] be the
one to conduct La Wally for me."

"I arrived for [Mancinelli's] final rehearsals," recalled Toscanini,
who had not yet seen the score of the vast, four-act *Colombo*, a work
that required a substantial cast, large orchestra, and large chorus. "I
liked the opera," Toscanini said, and the first two performances,
under Mancinelli, were successful, with first-rate singers, including
the famed Croatian baritone Giuseppe Kaschmann in the title role.
When the older maestro left, "they asked me, 'Do you need
rehearsals?'

"I said, 'Rehearse what?'

" 'With the singers.'

"I said, 'Listen, they've had so many rehearsals that they'll say,
'You're the one who should go study.' [. . .] I had no rehearsals, not
even with the orchestra."

At the first performance, Toscanini set the score of Act I on his
music stand and opened it to the first page: "I thought that I would
have to turn pages," he said. But he found that he was conducting
from memory. The orchestra players stared at him in astonishment,
and they stared even harder when the same thing happened in the
following acts. At the end of the massive opera, he realized that he
"had never looked at the score. I didn't know that I knew it by heart."

According to *Il Caffaro*, a Genoese newspaper, "Last evening Maestro Toscanini [. . .] conducted the difficult score by heart, and splendidly, bringing off a true tour de force. The orchestra members gave
him a real ovation, thereby showing him the esteem that they have
for his youthful, powerful intelligence." Following the final perfor-

mance, the same newspaper mentioned that "the leonine figure of Giuseppe Verdi sat enthroned" in Box 23 of the third tier, "admired by all, in the company of Camillo Sivori* and Giulio Ricordi. [. . .] I saw [Verdi], too, applaud with maximum enthusiasm," wrote the chronicler, who also noted that Franchetti and Toscanini were repeatedly called before the curtain "amid the warmest and sincerest applause." This was the only Toscanini performance that Verdi ever attended.

Toscanini had in the meantime been rehearsing *La Wally*, which opened on 17 October and received seven performances in all. The famous, and famously beautiful, Romanian soprano Hariclea Darclée sang the title role, as she had at the opera's world premiere at La Scala. There were twenty curtain calls on opening night, and Catalani wrote to a friend, "I am really happy with the success."

Toscanini must have put the last two or three performances of *La Wally* in the hands of an assistant in order to rush to Rome for some hurried rehearsals of *Carmen*, which opened on 30 October at the Teatro Costanzi, the city's main opera house. This was his debut in, and probably also his first visit to, the capital, which he found "not too *pleasant*—especially because of its agitated people," he recalled a few years later. "Above all, its climate is very unpleasant. I've never felt as ill as during the fall that I spent in that city."

While the performances of Bizet's opera were in progress, Toscanini prepared the world premiere of *Gualtiero Swarten*, by Andrea Gnaga, a thirty-two-year-old composer now remembered only for his mandolin music; Francesco Tamagno had made the production of this opera, of which he was the protagonist, a condition of his participation in the season's following production, Verdi's *La Forza del Destino*. Although he triumphed in *Swarten*, the opera did not survive, whereas *Forza* was an all-around success.

Toscanini must already have been rehearsing the Costanzi's orchestra in Mascagni's latest opera, *I Rantzau*, when the composer, thrilled with his work's wildly successful world premiere, which he himself had conducted in Florence, announced that he would take over the first Roman performances of the work and then hand the baton to Toscanini for the remaining ones. Toscanini was offended:

---

* Sivori, Paganini's only pupil, was Italy's most famous living violinist.

although he had taken over from Mancinelli to conduct later performances of *Cristoforo Colombo* in Genoa on a very special occasion, he
was, at twenty-five, already one of Italy's most established conductors and was unwilling to play the *maestro concertatore* (rehearser) to
Mascagni's *direttore d'orchestra* (conductor). When *Fanfulla*, a Rome
newspaper, stated that Toscanini had proposed the idea to Mascagni,
the younger maestro sent a denial to the paper. "Far from giving up
this honor, I would have liked to retain it," he wrote, "and I would
have felt equal to the task—and with no effort—*even given the limited
amount of time*; but Mascagni wanted to keep for himself the honor of
the first three performances . . . I, for my part, beg him to take the
remaining ones as well"—which is what happened. When Toscanini
took up the baton a day or two after the *Rantzau* premiere, to conduct another performance of *La Forza del Destino*, "the whole audience rose to its feet in a warm and impressive demonstration," an
eyewitness reported, "and he was presented with a laurel wreath, a
gift from Tamagno."

10.

HOWEVER UPSETTING THE ROMAN INCIDENT MAY HAVE BEEN TO
Toscanini, he must have looked back on it with nostalgia a month or
two later, when he was in the midst of a tumultuous first, and last,
professional engagement in Sicily. During a season that lasted from
late December 1892 to early May 1893, at Palermo's Politeama Garibaldi, there was more drama offstage than onstage.

The impresario, Carlo Di Giorgi, began badly by scheduling
opening night—the local premiere of *Pagliacci*—for Christmas Eve,
when Palermo's citizens traditionally stayed home with their families before attending midnight mass. The audience was sparse at the
underrehearsed first performance, but by the third—for which
Leoncavallo arrived to bask in his glory—the situation had improved,
and a lowering of ticket prices further reconciled people with
Pagliacci and with the impresario. Indeed, the new work became so
popular that it had to be given twenty times, and at one of the performances the audience demanded that Arlecchino's aria be encored
three times.

The second opera, *Loreley*, opened on 12 January, with Catalani present: the composer, now gravely ill, had nevertheless made the cold, turbulent winter boat trip across the Tyrrhenian Sea to Palermo. Oddly enough, *Loreley*, with its esoteric plot and frequently ethereal music, proved to be as popular with Palermo's audiences as the immediately accessible *Pagliacci*. Catalani received twenty-six curtain calls on opening night, and *Loreley* was performed seventeen times; its success provided the composer with one of the last savorable moments of his life.

Toscanini's honeymoon with the local public ended quickly, however. At one rehearsal, the exasperated conductor told the third-rate orchestra, "You people have a conservatory in Palermo, isn't that right? Turn it into a brothel!" The musicians walked out on him and made an official protest at city hall. The crisis passed, but at one performance of *Loreley*, Toscanini recalled, during the ballet scene the audience shouted, "Down with Maestro Toscanini!" To show his contempt, he conducted the rest of the opera sitting on his chair with his legs crossed. Before he managed to leave the orchestra at the end of the performance, a group of spectators shouted "Avanti!" and started to charge at him, with the intention of beating him up. But then "I felt four hands on me; they grabbed me, they carried me to the [theater] director's room." His saviors were local mafiosi who had admired his courage in insulting the audience. "'No one is going to attack Toscanini,'" they ordered. "The Mafia adored me," he recalled, laughing. "The next evening, there was [. . .] a tall, good-looking young man in a tailcoat, who was ready to silence me when he saw me come out [to conduct]." But when the poor fellow began to shout, the mafiosi appeared. "Madness!" said Toscanini. "And that guy—out!"

The next opera, *Cavalleria Rusticana*, had been successfully performed in Palermo two years earlier. As the opera is short, Toscanini preceded it with Foroni's Overture in C, Bolzoni's Minuet for strings, and Gillet's *Loin du bal*. Nevertheless, the singers, who included Ferni-Germano and contralto Alice Cucini, did not please the audience, or at least a powerful and vociferous segment thereof. On the second night, the pandemonium reached such levels that the curtain had to be brought down and the performance suspended, and the hostile demonstration continued outside the theater. One critic implied that the protests had less to do with the actual performance than with "old and new grudges and jealousies and more or less dishonest interests," and that the disturbance had been planned in advance "through the press and through gossip." In short, the Mafia had turned against Toscanini because he had refused to follow the brotherhood's orders as to which arias were to be encored—the result of a local boss's interest in one of the female singers. Representatives of the ensemble asked the mayor to suspend the rest of the season, but after a day or two the situation was cleared up, although *Cavalleria* had no further performances, and ticket buyers got their money back. Toscanini began to receive bloodied letters and drawings of hearts with knives stuck into them.

To fill the gap in the schedule, a production of Bellini's *Norma* was quickly arranged. Toscanini feared the worst: many years later he recalled having told Di Giorgi, "All the Sicilians will think that they wrote [*Norma*] themselves"—because Bellini was Sicilian—"and so anything could happen." Virginia Damerini was brought in to sing the notoriously difficult title role, which she had performed many times; Toscanini remembered her as good but too old for the part, and during rehearsals he feared that her exaggeratedly slow tempi would not be liked. On opening night, 13 February, the audience cheered her wildly during the first act, demanding that she encore "Oh non tremare, o perfido," but Damerini, fearing that she might not be able to get through the rest of the opera, did not concede the encore. Her refusal provoked the audience to boo her during the second act.

At the start of a subsequent *Norma* performance, some audience members began shouting, insistently, "The hymn! The hymn!" Toscanini didn't understand that people were demanding that the orchestra play the patriotic "Garibaldi Hymn" in the theater that was named after Italy's great Risorgimento hero. He left the orchestra and went backstage. "I can't stay in this theater!" he told Di Giorgi. "Release me, let me go back to Milan!"

The impresario begged Toscanini to finish the performance, after which he would release him from his contract. Toscanini tried to start again, but when the heckling continued he left the theater, returned to his hotel, and went to bed; the concertmaster, La Cara, had to conduct the rest of the performance. Toscanini wrote a formal letter asking to be released from his contract, and the following two performances of *Norma* were conducted by La Cara.

Toscanini rehearsed *The Flying Dutchman* for his replacement, whoever that might be, but when he went to Di Giorgi to take his leave the impresario said, " 'Do you seriously think [. . .] that I'm going to sign up another conductor so that you can do as you please?' " Toscanini later recalled. "He told me that I had overstepped my rights and that I wasn't fulfilling my duties—because, after all, the public is right." Di Giorgi made him address a letter to the theater's president, explaining what had happened; it was published in the *Giornale di Sicilia* of 21–22 February 1893. The young conductor stated that when he had taken his place in the orchestra on the evening of the "unpleasant incident,"

> part of the audience was clamoring for something; and, not knowing what they wanted, I began the overture, convinced that those noises had nothing to do with the orchestra and the production, which had been so greatly applauded the previous evening; but given that the persistent noises impeded me from continuing, I thought I ought to leave my post for a moment and return once calm was restored.
>
> I then learned that they were asking for the hymn; thus there was nothing for me to do except comply with that request, with which moreover I had complied on another occasion.
>
> But I found that the hymn had already been performed; and the audience, certainly believing that I had refused to grant its wish—which was not my intention—greeted me, on my return to the orchestra, in such a way that it was not possible for me to continue to conduct.

Toscanini conducted the six remaining performances of *Norma* and all ten performances of *The Flying Dutchman*—a local premiere and his first complete Wagner production—which opened on 2 March. "The orchestra performed it so well, with such energy and such richness of coloring, that the audience broke into long, warm applause, forcing Maestro Toscanini to stand and bow," wrote one critic.

Every evening, the audience called for an encore of the *Flying*

Dutchman Overture, but the "hymn" incident continued to rankle with Toscanini; instead of returning to the beginning of the piece, he told the orchestra to cut the encore short by going back only to the second statement of the sailors' chorus theme; people wouldn't know the difference, he figured. Someone spread the word, however, and at one performance the audience began to shout, "From the beginning, Maestro!" He turned to the auditorium and shouted back, "Ah—you're clever, eh? You've figured it out."

"I was a pig," Toscanini admitted. "I was a rascal. And that's where the break with the audience began again." Yet the next opera—*The Barber of Seville*, which opened on 13 March, with the young Polish soprano Regina Pinkert as Rosina—was well received, and Toscanini completed his Palermo engagement with five further performances of Rossini's opera in addition to an ill-received production of *Rigoletto* and a triumphant one of *La Gioconda*. At the end of the tempestuous season, during which Toscanini had conducted eighty performances of eight operas, a local critic summarized it as "unfortunate and wretched" and commented that Toscanini was "absolutely incompatible with the public, which, irritated more than once by his obstinacy, demonstrated its feelings by whistling. Did Toscanini believe he could veil his defects as a conductor by keeping the score closed on the music stand?"

Not until Di Giorgi accompanied Toscanini to the boat that would take him back to the mainland did the impresario reveal the real reason for his refusal to allow him to break his contract: the conductor Leopoldo Mugnone had learned of Toscanini's "disaster" and had offered to come to Palermo to fix the situation. Di Giorgi, who admired Toscanini, had made him stay for the good of the young conductor's reputation. "I had a nasty character," Toscanini said, "but I was simpatico because I was so spontaneous"—not a calculating careerist, in other words. Late in life Toscanini remarked that the difficulties of his Palermo season had faded into the past and that he had always loved Sicily. "I've kept what was good," he said: "that sun, that Mount Pellegrino, that beautiful country."*

---

* During Toscanini's Palermo season, both Johannes Brahms and Richard Strauss visited the city, but there is no record of any of the three musicians' encountering either of the others.

11.

VERDI'S *FALSTAFF* HAD HAD ITS WORLD PREMIERE AT LA SCALA
on 9 February 1893—six years after the *Otello* premiere—while
Toscanini was in Palermo, but after the performances in Milan the
original production, with the original cast and its conductor,
Mascheroni, toured other major Italian and foreign opera houses.
Toscanini traveled as quickly as he could from Palermo to Venice to
hear the opera performed at the Teatro La Fenice, and he followed
the ensemble to Trieste to hear further performances. Many years
later he recalled serious discrepancies between Verdi's score and
Mascheroni's performances; he mentioned, specifically, the opening of the second part of Act I, when the women greet each other in
a very fast (Allegro vivace) 6/8 tempo: "Alice" / "Meg" / "Nannetta."
Mascheroni had made a substantial pause after each name, Toscanini said, instead of keeping the pulse going, as Verdi had written it.
"If Verdi liked the way Mascheroni did *Falstaff*, he wouldn't have
liked the way I do it," Toscanini said. But he was later reassured by
the enthusiasm of the composer and poet Arrigo Boito, *Falstaff*'s
librettist, about his interpretation of the opera.

In Milan, Toscanini attended "a good performance," as he recalled,
of Berlioz's grand dramatic legend, *La Damnation de Faust*, in its version as an opera, recently created by the Romanian-born jack-of-all-
theatrical-trades Raoul Gunsbourg at the Monte Carlo Opera; and the
production was conducted in Milan by none other than Mugnone.
Afterward, Toscanini went to a beer parlor with Lison Frandin, who
was singing the part of Margarita, and the impresario Alessandro
Barilati, who, as Toscanini put it, "functioned as her husband." While
the three were chatting together, Mugnone came by, and Toscanini,
who had not forgiven his older colleague for having tried to supplant
him in Palermo and ruin his reputation, got up and left without greeting him. Toscanini laughed in telling the story many years later,
because ever afterward, he said, when Mugnone conducted in a theater in which Toscanini had recently worked, he would ostentatiously
dust off the "contaminated" conductor's stool before deigning to sit
down on it.

The partial disaster in Palermo may indeed have damaged Toscanini's reputation, because it was followed by a nine-month lacuna in his career. It was this period to which he was referring when he wrote, many years later, "I shut myself in the house for months and months, studying and reading a little of everything. At that time, *no one* wanted me as a conductor, and I spent many a month inactive, *by others' lights*. They didn't deny that I had a certain amount of talent, but they were frightened by my *nasty character* and my exacting demands." He spent time with his family and even went with his parents and sisters to a photography studio to pose for a joint portrait photo.

On one of the last days of July 1893, Toscanini and some other friends saw Catalani off at Milan's Central Station: the composer was hoping to obtain some relief from his tubercular condition by spending part of the summer at Airolo, in the Swiss Alps. But by the time the train reached the town of Chiasso, just inside the Swiss border, an hour north of Milan, Catalani was hemorrhaging seriously. He returned home with assistance and was put to bed. Three or four days later, Toscanini, walking across the cathedral square, bumped into Carlo Superti, who asked whether he knew that Catalani was in Milan and dying. Shocked, Toscanini rushed to his friend's apartment.

For several days, Toscanini was with Catalani and his doctor from nine in the morning until midnight, alongside the poet and librettist Luigi Illica—another of the composer's close friends—and some of Catalani's cousins. Toscanini sent a telegram to Switzerland to summon the composer's lover, Teresa Garbagnati, the wife of his composer friend Benedetto Junck. She came, but made such a scene that Catalani asked her to leave. On 6 August, Catalani's sufferings became so intense that Toscanini had to restrain him from throwing himself out the window. When Toscanini arrived the next morning, Illica let him in: Catalani had died during the night.

For Toscanini, Catalani's death at thirty-nine was not only the loss of a dear friend but a tragedy for post-Verdian Italian opera. Whether his hopes for Catalani would ever have been realized is impossible to say, but many years later he remarked, "The place he left will never be filled for me."

12.

LEONCAVALLO, THRILLED WITH THE SUCCESS OF *PAGLIACCI*, WANTED Toscanini to conduct the premiere of his new opera, *I Medici*, at the Teatro Dal Verme in November 1893, but Sonzogno, the work's publisher, had not forgiven the younger conductor for the uproar he had provoked over Mascagni's *I Rantzau* in Rome a year earlier. "If you are so fond of Toscanini, then go ahead," Sonzogno told Leoncavallo, "but I will not go to the theater that evening." The production was conducted by Rodolfo Ferrari.

According to the librettist, impresario, and critic Carlo D'Ormeville— one of the most influential figures in Milan's musical life—Toscanini was also to have conducted two recent operas, *Falstaff* and Puccini's *Manon Lescaut*, at the Teatro San Carlo in Naples during the 1893–94 winter season, but that engagement, like the Dal Verme job, did not materialize. D'Ormeville, however, in profiling Toscanini in the *Gazzetta dei Teatri*, referred not only to the young maestro's memory but also to his encyclopedic knowledge of the repertoire: "I always say that the only music he doesn't know is that which hasn't yet been written," D'Ormeville joked.

Toscanini did not take up his baton again until February 1894, when he conducted his first productions of *Otello* and *Manon Lescaut*, at Pisa's Teatro Nuovo. He had insisted on making some replacements in the local orchestra's personnel, which explains why, during a performance of Verdi's opera on 25 February, "a large explosive device was thrown onto the stage from a window that sheds light on the rear of the stage [. . .] making a huge din and breaking all the windows," according to one newspaper. The report continued, "Maestro Toscanini had the presence of mind to have the orchestra immediately play the Royal March, which was greeted by warm and enthusiastic applause. The ladies stood up in the boxes and waved their handkerchiefs. The Garibaldi Hymn was then played amid renewed acclamations. The theater was completely full and the explosion occurred during the duet between Otello and Iago" ("Sì, pel ciel," at the end of the second act). "The callboy came onto the proscenium and announced that a flare had gone off. But later the truth was known, and the audience demonstrated its great indignation at the cowardly attack, the perpetrator of which is unknown. The performance continued in the greatest calm, everyone from the artists to the audience having demonstrated the greatest sangfroid. General Tournon rushed to the scene." The culprit was never found.

Manon Lescaut, Puccini's third opera, had received its world premiere in Turin a year earlier, and Toscanini, who had studied the score while he was in Palermo, had sent the composer his compliments. During the intervening months they had evidently become more closely acquainted—by the time of Toscanini's Pisa engagement, they had switched, in their correspondence, from the formal *lei* to the familiar *tu*—but nothing else is known of their relationship at the time. In the midst of his *Manon* rehearsals, Toscanini wrote to Puccini that the tenor, Luigi Rosati, "*is a cretin*, but he makes up for this misfortune with a beautiful, warm, and expressive voice." He was not happy with the baritone, who was replaced, and he did not comment on the soprano, Emilia Corsi, who was also singing Desdemona in *Otello*. *Manon's* popularity grew so great that Puccini came to a performance and "had to take twenty bows amid all the enthusiasm," a newspaper reported. "The ending of the third act was repeated three times."

Often, in those early years, once the rehearsal period had ended and he had only to conduct performances in the evenings, Toscanini would borrow a cello and persuade some of the violinists and violists in his orchestras to play string quartets with him in the afternoon. At one such session in Pisa that year, he and three other musicians were playing through a Mendelssohn quartet in E-flat Major (presumably op. 44, no. 3), which Toscanini loved. They then decided to start reading through all the Beethoven quartets, beginning with op. 18, no. 1, in F Major, and Toscanini described the experience as "a revelation." His real, profound love of Beethoven, whom he came to consider the greatest of all composers, began on that day.

Documentation demonstrates that, in typical fashion, arrangements for a production of Massenet's *Le Roi de Lahore* in Ravenna in May and June were not completed until three weeks before opening night; these arrangements included the choice of impresario, singers, and conductor. The participants were required to arrive in town only eight days after the contract was signed and only twelve before the scheduled first performance, although the opening was eventually delayed by four days. Within just over two weeks, Toscanini organized and trained the orchestra, which was made up of both local and imported players; taught roles to those singers who had not previously sung the opera; coached the whole cast separately and jointly; oversaw the chorus master's work; directed the minimal staging; and coordinated cast, orchestra, chorus, and stage action, including the ballet. The town of Ravenna had never heard anything like it, fourteen performances were given, and the local critic declared that Toscanini was "predestined to occupy the conductor's chair at La Scala."

Toscanini was now working as if to make up for lost time. By the end of July he was in Brescia, preparing productions of Massenet's *Manon* in addition to Bellini's *I Puritani* and *La Traviata*; Verdi's opera was sung by the celebrated couple Gemma Bellincioni and Roberto Stagno as Violetta and Alfredo, respectively. The performances ran well into September, and by early October Toscanini had journeyed to Treviso, in the Veneto, to begin rehearsing his first production of *Falstaff*—which he would eventually conduct more than any other opera—as well as *Cristoforo Colombo*.

Falstaff, Colombo, and the world premiere of *Savitri,* by the now forgotten Natale Canti, were the works with which Toscanini made his debut at Bologna's beautiful and prestigious Teatro Comunale in November and December 1894. Most of the *Falstaff* cast, beginning with Ramón Blanchart in the title role, was the same as the one he had prepared in Treviso, and it remained basically the same in late December, when Toscanini opened a demanding two-month season at Genoa's Carlo Felice with the same opera. But Antonio Pini-Corsi, who had sung the role of Ford at the world premiere, now resumed the part under Toscanini's direction, and the baritone and the conductor had a disagreement over the passage that begins with "Quella crudel beltà," in the opera's second act: Toscanini wanted it sung at the speed indicated in the score (Allegro moderato, eighth note = 112), whereas Pini-Corsi insisted that Verdi had had him sing it twice as fast at the premiere. Verdi was spending the winter in Genoa, and Piontelli, the ensemble's impresario, had already arranged to have cast members present their Christmas greetings to the eighty-one-year-old master. Toscanini, whose natural timidity was intensified in the presence of the man who was not only Italy's most famous musician but the most famous living Italian, had to summon up all his nerve to ask Verdi to decide the issue. Verdi pronounced in Toscanini's favor, and when Pini-Corsi maintained that he was doing the part as he had done it with Verdi at La Scala not even two years earlier, Verdi raised his voice—as Toscanini recalled, "'[You] did it with me? And then where did you sing it—how many times?'" Pini-Corsi admitted that he had sung it many times since, and Verdi told them, "'That's the way it is in the theater. I put *Don Carlos* on stage in Paris'"—the world premiere, in 1867—and "'we had plenty of time'" to rehearse it. "'Well, when it opened, it was as I wanted it. After one month—one month, I say—not one tempo was left, and it was [with] the same conductor and the same singers. Think of what operas become after many years!'"

Unfortunately, *Falstaff* did not triumph with the Genoese public; indeed, a quarter century would go by before most opera lovers grasped the musical brilliance and autumnal wisdom of Verdi's last stage work. The old composer did not attend any of the local performances, but he kept himself informed of the situation. On 30 December 1894, he wrote to Giulio Ricordi, "*Falstaff* is a fiasco! But really a first-rate fiasco. Nobody goes to the theater! The beautiful part is that they say that never before has anyone heard an opera so perfectly performed and so well-blended! In that case it must be that the music is accursed!" He sarcastically suggested that Piontelli, the impresario, offer free tickets to the performances but set up a beer stand on the ground floor so that he could make some money on the drinks.

Audience reception notwithstanding, all the reviews were positive, for *Falstaff* as for the other works performed during that Genoa season; these included Toscanini's first production of *Tannhäuser*, a local premiere and a great success for cast and conductor. Altogether, Toscanini led fifty-nine performances of seven operas in sixty-five days, then rushed to Pisa to prepare and conduct the local premieres of *Falstaff* and *Colombo*. The casts were mainly the same as in Genoa, but the orchestra was local and of poor quality. Early in the first rehearsal, Toscanini stopped and told the long-suffering Piontelli that it was impossible to be ready by the date that had been set because many of the players were inadequate. A witness recalled that Piontelli asked the Maestro to choose the best and release the others. Toscanini chose twenty-six players who, however, declared their solidarity with those fired, and this led to a strike. [. . .] The uproar against Piontelli and against Toscanini was so great in and out of the theater that the Prefect had to intervene in person to reconcile the parties.

Since Toscanini was adamant about his choice, Piontelli—to please the Prefect—said that he would pay a fixed sum to those who had been fired, but only the musicians chosen by the Maestro could remain [. . .].

Toscanini then brought in the best musicians available in Milan and elsewhere and created a high-quality, seventy-piece orchestra. The productions triumphed, Toscanini was singled out for ovations, and the season was an artistic and financial success. "Piontelli left Pisa praised by all for having freed himself of so much dead weight!" recalled one observer.

The *Falstaff* and *Colombo* troupes moved on to Venice, where Toscanini worked alternately with the orchestras in two theaters. He made his local debut with *Falstaff* at the Teatro Malibran on 14 April 1895 and also conducted *La Forza del Destino* there, both operas part of a popular-priced series, with tickets averaging one lira each. *Colombo*, *Le Villi*, and a single performance of *Falstaff* were given at the more prestigious Teatro La Fenice, where Toscanini also prepared and conducted the world premiere of Antonio Lozzi's short-lived *Emma Liona* and presented a half-length concert on 4 May 1895, in honor of Italy's armed forces and with King Umberto and Queen Margherita in attendance; the program consisted of overtures by Verdi (*I Vespri Siciliani*), Wagner (*Tannhäuser*), Rossini (*William Tell*), and Francesco Giarda, a teacher at the Venice Conservatory. The royals also attended one of Toscanini's opera performances during their stay in Venice.

A production of *Colombo* at the Teatro Sociale in Trent (then still under Austrian rule) in June finally brought to an end an eleven-month season during which Toscanini had conducted at least 130 performances and twenty-two productions of twelve operas in seven cities. In October, he returned to Treviso for fifteen performances of *Tannhäuser* and six of *Loreley*; evidently worried about the quality of the orchestra, he begged Polo to come and serve as concertmaster: if other obligations required him to leave before the final performances, Toscanini wrote, "we could close an eye, and maybe both eyes."

In the meantime, however, Toscanini was preparing for a major change in his career. Giuseppe Depanis, the most influential organizer of Turin's musical life, had been following Toscanini's career with growing interest and admiration, and had devised a plan that could bring glory to both Turin and Toscanini. Nine years after the young maestro's debut in Rio de Janeiro, his journeyman days were about to come to an end.

*Playbill for the world premiere
of Puccini's* La Bohème, *which
Toscanini conducted at Turin's
Teatro Regio in 1896.*

III.

———

TURIN

1.

———

THE CITY OF TURIN, IN 1895, WAS POISED TO LEAD ITALIAN industry into the twentieth century. The ancient Romans' Augusta Taurinorum would soon become the home of FIAT* and of much of the rest of the nascent automobile trade, with all of its contiguous businesses. But Turin was also a pleasant city of 300,000 inhabitants, situated on the banks of the Po, flanked by Alps to the north and west, and endowed with beautiful piazzas, French-influenced architecture (the border with France lies only forty miles away), first-rate cafés and restaurants, and chocolatiers who had recently invented *gianduiotti*, the chocolate-hazelnut confections that remain one of the city's trademarks.

Turin had played an important role in Toscanini's career from its outset: thanks in part to the confidence shown in him by the local impresario Giovanni Depanis, the young man had made his Italian debut there in 1886, and he had returned many times since to conduct operas at the Teatro Carignano and the Teatro Vittorio Emanuele. But a new and much more significant enterprise awaited him in the Piedmontese capital.

Since Giovanni Depanis's death, in 1889, his son, Giuseppe, had become the most influential musical administrator in the city.

———

* FIAT is an acronym for Fabbrica Italiana Automobili Torino, or Italian Automobile Factory Turin.

Although he was a lawyer by profession, Giuseppe was a passionate music lover and an adherent of Richard Wagner's ideas about opera, or music drama, as a *Gesamtkunstwerk*—a total work of art. In 1895, at forty-two, Depanis became administrative director of the Teatro Regio, the city's foremost opera house, and he exerted his clout as a member of the town council to bring about drastic physical, artistic, and economic changes at the house. He believed that the artistic side of the revolution could be realized only by a gifted, determined conductor; and he had singled out the twenty-eight-year-old Toscanini as the best person to implement the reforms.

Depanis and Toscanini both believed in the importance of establishing conditions under which an opera ensemble made up of first-rate individuals could improve from season to season, rather than having to start virtually from scratch every year. They both wished to bring Wagner into Italy's mainstream opera repertoire, and they agreed that their country ran the risk of becoming a musical backwater if Italian composers, performers, and audiences did not open their ears, minds, and hearts to symphonic and chamber music. Opera could continue to dominate, but it could not be the only interest.

On 12 June 1895, Toscanini was officially appointed *maestro concertatore e direttore d'orchestra* of the Regio; in practical terms, he became the theater's artistic director and music director, and Depanis became its general manager. "It was necessary [. . .] to break with deep-rooted practices, to collide with personal interests, and nothing less than Toscanini's iron will was needed," Depanis later recalled. An impresario—Luigi Piontelli—was still employed to provide singers, but the orchestra was directly financed by the municipal government, and the instrumentalists, selected under Toscanini's supervision, became the backbone not only of the opera company but also of a music school and a concert society. A tremendous fuss broke out when the Regio's orchestra members were told that they would have to audition for their jobs—that they would not be engaged simply because they had previously played in the ensemble. Numerous players refused to comply, and many of their replacements came from other parts of Italy. In the end, the full orchestra numbered seventy musicians, but as many as twelve extra players could be drawn, as needed, from the local music school's best students. Toscanini engaged Enrico Polo as concertmaster, and as chorus master he chose Aristide Venturi, whom he had assisted during his life-changing trip to Brazil in 1886.

Plans also included a ban on encores, keeping the auditorium dark during performances (this reform was instituted only gradually), and a rule prohibiting audience members from moving in and out of the auditorium while performances were in progress. These changes, already in place in some major theaters outside of Italy, were meant only to allow audience members to focus their attention on what was happening musically and dramatically and to eliminate the corrida-like behavior of those who came to the opera house only for the pleasure of cheering for their favorite singers and booing the ones they disliked. But the rules were also, inadvertently, emblematic of the gradual transformation of opera from "entertainment" to "culture."

Felice Rignon, Turin's mayor, wrote to Toscanini to ask for advice about the organ that was being constructed for the Regio and to request a seating plan for the orchestra musicians, "so that we can provide for the proper diffusion of electric light." Since the organ cost much less than anticipated, the remaining money was used to create the house's first orchestra pit. At the Regio, as at La Scala and most other eighteenth-century Italian theaters, the orchestra had always played at ground-floor level, which worked reasonably well for lightly orchestrated eighteenth- and early nineteenth-century works but not for Wagner, late Verdi, and their successors: singers struggled to be heard over the forces at their feet. Toscanini also wanted to have a thin wooden wall constructed between the orchestra pit and the main-floor seats, to keep the orchestra members from walking into the ground-floor area and from being distracted every time a spectator walked in front of the pit. The council approved the additional expenditure.

Toscanini and Depanis boldly selected *Götterdämmerung* to inaugurate their first season; this was the first production by any Italian company of the last and most complex of Wagner's *Ring* operas, and the preparations for it attracted much attention. One of the participants—presumably an orchestra member—sent a report to a local newspaper.

"Very good, gentlemen. Oh, you understand, you feel this music, since you're playing it so well. [. . .]" Thus Toscanini, the dread Toscanini, spoke to his musicians during the rehearsal of *The Twilight of the Gods* the other evening. A great deal of lofty satisfaction and legitimate pride were revealed by the emotion in his voice and the broad and unusual expression of approval. [. . .] Because artists tremble before Toscanini but understand very well that some of his outbursts and the long, continuous rehearsals are necessary for achieving a good result, they willingly bend to the young conductor's wishes, because he demonstrates that he is worthy of the position entrusted to him, with his tenacious willpower and his high concept of the responsibility that he faces.

The production included only about three-quarters of Wagner's score: Toscanini and Depanis had evidently decided that audiences unfamiliar with Wagner's later musical idiom could not reasonably be expected to accept, at a first hearing, an opera twice as long as most standard Italian operas. Thus the Waltraute episode and several other parts were excised, which still left over three hours of new music. Although he rehearsed the individual singers and the staging in advance, Toscanini had only eleven days in which to rehearse the newly created orchestra and the ensemble as a whole—not much time for an exceedingly difficult work that few of the participants could have performed or even heard before.

The results were gratifying. The musicians and critics from all over Italy and beyond who gathered in Turin for the opening night, 22 December 1895, unanimously declared that the orchestra was already one of the best, possibly the very best, in the country, and praised the singers, the sets, and the production. "The success was full, complete, and uncontested," wrote Carlo Bersezio in *La Stampa*, Turin's most influential newspaper. To satisfy demand, *Götterdämmerung* had to be performed twenty-one times in six weeks—an average of once every two days.*

---

* Anyone who still believes the myth that singers today sing more often than they did in the "good old days" should note that in Turin's *Götterdämmerung* production only the roles of Brünnhilde and Gutrune were double-cast; Raffaele Grani (Siegfried) and all the others sang their demanding roles every other day, on the average, for six weeks, and some of them were rehearsing other parts at the same time. This was normal practice.

Three days after the premiere, a report sent to the *Song Journal*, printed in Detroit, contains the first known mention of Toscanini in any North American publication. "What a wonderful chef d'orchestre Toscanini is!" wrote the critic, Alma Dalma. She described "the superb manner in which Toscanini conducts. How sure, how calm he is; the best leader in Italy, and the only one in Italy capable of conducting Wagner's music in such a grand manner. [. . .] I will not be surprised to hear in the near future of his engagement with Abbey & Grau," the managers of New York's twelve-year-old Metropolitan Opera Company.

One of the *Götterdämmerung* performances was attended by Arrigo Boito, who was greatly impressed by what he heard and saw; thus began a friendly relationship between Boito and Toscanini that would have far-reaching consequences for both men. Boito returned to Turin for a performance of the Regio's next production—*Falstaff*, of which he was the librettist—and was delighted with the young conductor's interpretation of Verdi's last masterpiece for the stage.

It was during an ensemble rehearsal for the *Falstaff* production (which opened only six days after the *Götterdämmerung* premiere) that Toscanini stopped the orchestra, ran onto the stage, and said to the chorus members, "Let me see your shoes." The astonished singers stuck out their feet, and Toscanini said calmly to the stage manager, "You must have different shoes made for them." He described how the shoes should look, then returned to the orchestra and continued the rehearsal. This certainly was not the first time that Toscanini had turned his attention to the visual details of opera production, but it is the first such incident to have been preserved.

Canti's *Savitri*, the third opera, flopped miserably at its local premiere, but barely six weeks after the *Götterdämmerung* event the international press again flocked to Turin, this time for the world premiere of the much-anticipated fourth opera by the Ricordi company's great hope, Giacomo Puccini. The thirty-seven-year-old composer had initially opposed the choice of Turin for the initial production of *La Bohème*, "in the first place because the theater is acoustically dead, secondly because encores aren't allowed in the same, thirdly because the conductor is a nasty man, fourthly because it's too close to the waspish Milanese who will certainly 'make fun' of me."

Given the triumphant welcome that the Regio's audiences had bestowed on *Manon Lescaut* at its premiere in 1893, Puccini's opposition to the choice of Turin is hard to attribute to any cause other than sheer nervousness. His complaints about the Regio's acoustics can no longer be judged: the sound was altered by the installation of the orchestra pit, and the theater burned down in 1936. His dislike of the no-encore rule is comprehensible, because in those days one of the measures of an opera's success was how many musical numbers had to be repeated, and how many times—but the rule was rarely enforced. And Puccini's reference to Toscanini as a nasty man (*omaccio*) means merely that he had had, or had heard about, the sort of clashes with the sharp-tongued conductor that befell nearly everyone in the opera world sooner or later.

Puccini calmed down once he had arrived in town for the rehearsals. "I've found Toscanini very kind," he wrote on 8 January to Luigi Illica—co-librettist, with Giuseppe Giacosa, of *La Bohème* and, later, of *Tosca* and *Madama Butterfly*; Toscanini had been friendly with Illica since they had both looked after Catalani in his last days. And Puccini's diffidence soon turned to total admiration. "The orchestra! Toscanini! Extraordinary!" he wrote, adding that the conductor, his junior by over eight years, was "highly intelligent." He also described a typically grueling Toscanini rehearsal schedule: "today from eleven to 4:30 P.M. Tonight we rehearse from eight-thirty to midnight." Puccini was disappointed with the tenor Evan Gorga (Rodolfo), and he described the baritone Tieste Wilmant (Marcello) as "vile," but the soprano Cesira Ferrani (Mimì) was "excellent" and the rest of the cast ranged from acceptable to first-rate, the composer said. Ferrani, with whom Toscanini had worked before, had also been the first Manon Lescaut; rumor had it that Puccini was in love with her but that she was in love with Toscanini. Sets and costumes for the new opera were created by the already celebrated Adolfo Hohenstein, who would become one of the leading exponents of Italian Liberty style (Art Nouveau).

At its premiere on 1 February 1896, *La Bohème* was fairly successful with the audience but received mixed, and to some extent puzzled, reviews. "Boheme failure it won't make the rounds," read

D'Ormeville's famously shortsighted telegram to his associates in Milan. One journalist described the orchestral playing as "excellent, perfect"; others referred to Toscanini's "elect spirit," his "aristocratic temperament," and "the valor and artistic conscientiousness that make him one of today's best." But Tom—pseudonym of the writer Eugenio Checchi—said, in Rome's *Fanfulla*, that the orchestra sounded "feeble here and there." One would be hard put to find another review, however negative, of any Toscanini performance that makes use of the word "feeble," and one of Puccini's biographers theorized that "Tom" had misunderstood the "imperceptibly trembling" sound of Puccini's strings in *Bohème*—a sound that "imitates the violin of the *café-chantant*" and that Toscanini "was the first to reveal."

Bohème received twenty-three performances in February and March, with ever-growing success. It was followed by a curiosity—*Le Maître de Chapelle*, a comic opera dating from 1821 by the Parma-born Ferdinando Paer—and then, to close the season not with a bang but a whimper, by Lozzi's unfortunate *Emma Liona*. Altogether, Toscanini had conducted fifty-nine performances of six operas in about eighty days, and the reborn Regio's first season had been a resounding success.

Before he returned to Milan, which remained his base (in Turin he stayed at a hotel that also provided his meals), Toscanini gave his first full-length symphony concert. The program, performed at the Regio on 19 March 1896, consisted entirely of works virtually unknown in Italy at the time: Schubert's "Great" C Major Symphony, a suite from Tchaikovsky's four-year-old *Nutcracker* ballet, the Italian premiere of the "Tragic" Overture by Brahms, who was still alive, and the first performance by an Italian ensemble of the "Entrance of the Gods into Valhalla" from Wagner's *Das Rheingold*. The concert had originally been scheduled for a few days earlier, but since the Regio's stage was still cluttered with scenery, Toscanini had rehearsed the orchestra in the pit and had warned Piontelli that he needed at least one rehearsal on the stage, to work out proper balances. Piontelli had told him that this was not necessary. "I say I will not conduct concert," Toscanini told the American music critic B. H. Haggin more than fifty years later. "This man was like father to me; but when is time for concert I am in bed. Manager come to hotel; but I stay in bed." The audience was sent home and the concert postponed until Toscanini had had his rehearsal. Despite this inauspicious incident, the concert was a success and was attended by the Count of Turin (nephew of King Umberto) and Princess Letizia Bonaparte, the famously merry widow of King Amedeo of Spain.

2.

JUST AS TOSCANINI WAS CAPABLE OF SAYING, FROM THE OUTSET OF his career, "Verdi *and* Wagner" rather than "Verdi *or* Wagner," so he was able to say "Wagner *and* Brahms" rather than "Wagner *or* Brahms." The Alps were not a musical obstacle for him, and internecine strife among the composers of his own or any other nation or generation had no effect on his musical judgment, whether or not their aesthetic and philosophical arguments interested him. He had put these beliefs into practice at his Turin concert in March, and he did so again in April and May, when he finally made his debut at La Scala, Italy's temple of opera, conducting the house orchestra not in the lyric repertoire but in four symphony concerts. In addition to the four works that he had conducted on his Turin concert in March, his Milan programs included Haydn's "Clock" Symphony, Beethoven's First Symphony, excerpts from the *Götterdämmerung* Prologue, and short pieces by Wagner, Ponchielli, and living composers Verdi, Grieg, and Saint-Saëns, among others. Germany, Austria, Italy, Russia, France, and Norway were all represented.*

The reviews were ecstatic. "A theater such as we have never seen before: completely sold out," wrote Romeo Carugati, in *Lombardia*. "A success such as we have never seen before: great applause for all the pieces and an encore for Wagner's *Götterdämmerung*. A conductor such as we did not have, unfortunately, during the past season: Maestro Toscanini, a youth [. . .] on a level with the most glorious veterans." And Ricordi's powerful *Gazzetta Musicale di Milano* declared, "Maestro Toscanini surpassed the great expectations of the audience, which acclaimed him fervently over and over again."

---

* Toscanini and the orchestra repeated various pieces from these programs in Bergamo on 17 May.

Within a few days of his first Milan concert, Toscanini was asked to take command of La Scala, beginning with the forthcoming 1896–97 season, and at a higher salary than he was receiving in Turin: quite a show of faith in and esteem for a twenty-nine-year-old musician. He informed Depanis, who advised him to return to Turin for the "moral effect" of such a decision, a raise of 1,000 lire per season, the quality of the Regio's orchestra, the possibility (not realized, in the end) of mounting an entire *Ring* cycle, and the prospect of a series of concerts at an exposition to be held in Turin in 1898. "I realize that you're aiming at La Scala, and [. . .] I can't think of anyone who could compete with you in that regard," Depanis said. "But reflect, too, on the fact that another two or three years at the Regio—the Italian theater at which serious music is most likely to triumph and at which certain other kinds of music [i.e., the *verismo* operas] don't take root at all—will stand you in good stead at La Scala and certainly won't do you any harm."

After hesitating for several days, Toscanini wired Depanis, "If you agree pay eight thousand I accept contract." Depanis was shocked. Toscanini's salary the preceding year had been 5,000 lire, ridiculously little for the quantity and quality of the work he was doing, and for a young man who was supporting his parents and two sisters as well as himself. Although he had made it clear from the start that he considered the sum too low, this great, sudden leap was deemed excessive by the municipality, and Depanis tried to persuade Toscanini to accept either less money or a longer season. But Toscanini—presumably advised by Piontelli, his guide in all practical matters—would not bend on the money issue, and he could not begin his Turin season earlier, he said, because he had been invited to conduct in New York in the fall.

The minutes of a city council meeting on 25 May point out that Toscanini had not wanted to sign the previous year's low-paying contract; that he was "a conductor of exceptional worth," considered "the most important element in a production's success"; and that an attempt to find another conductor "would lead to an expense that would certainly not be lower than 8,000 lire"—the equivalent, in buying power, of about $50,000 in 2016—"while lacking the element of security provided in the person of Maestro Toscanini." Thus, "the Council has decided to grant the sum of 8,000 lire." For Depanis it was a bitter victory, but Toscanini telegraphed the next day, "I assure you that for Turin I gave up contract America five months thirty thousand lire[,] very happy however to have settled things."

The sources of the offers from New York and North or South America are not known, but Toscanini had decided to stay in Italy for two reasons: he was in charge of what was virtually his own opera company, and he was seriously courting a young woman.

Toscanini had met Carlotta—known simply as Carla—De Martini, a pretty, dark-haired, dark-eyed eighteen-year-old Milanese girl, in Treviso the previous October, when her older sister, Ida, had sung the parts of Anna in *Loreley* and the Shepherd in *Tannhäuser,* under Toscanini's direction; Ida had then been invited to take the roles of a Norn and Woglinde in the Turin *Götterdämmerung.* Like all proper young ladies in those days, Ida was accompanied by her mother, and what could Signora Francesca De Martini do with Carla except bring her along? Francesca's husband, a stockbroker, had died, and her son, Battista (called Batta), an adventurer, had gone off to South America. The De Martinis were not poor, but they had to be careful with money; Ida's artistic aspirations may have been perceived as a possible path toward economic improvement.

Toscanini found Carla vivacious, pretty, and amusingly bizarre in her views. He fell in love with her, and she was overwhelmed by the attentions of a man ten years older than herself (she was born on 7 August 1877) who was quickly becoming famous throughout the country. When the series of *Götterdämmerung* performances ended, the De Martini women returned to Milan; Toscanini arrived there soon afterward and began assiduously visiting them.* His first known letter to Carla, in which he used the formal *lei,* dates from 29 March 1896. "'Can it be true that she loves me?'" he asked, rhetorically. "This is the incessant thought, this is the doubt that pursues me ceaselessly, implacably. [. . .] If it's true that you have given me a little of your affection as I've given you my whole soul, write a few words to me. They will be very dear to me."

Carla's response must have been positive, because by the end of May, when he was about to set off for engagements in various north-

---

* He was living at no. 5 in Via Maddalena, a five-minute walk from the De Martinis' home at no. 8 in Via Speronari.

ern Italian cities and towns, he was sending presents to all three De Martini women (to Ida he sent one of the "Songbooks" of Heinrich Heine, a poet he particularly loved); he and Carla were already using the familiar *tu* form in letters and were as good as engaged. On 31 May, Carla wrote to Arturo, "Mamma, knowing that you're leaving this evening, begs you to come and dine with us along with that very nice Mr. Polo," who was courting Ida. "Come yourself to give us your answer so that at least I'll see you twice. Many little kisses."

This was the real beginning of a courtship correspondence that would continue until their marriage more than a year later and that Carla preserved for the rest of her life in two damask-covered coffers; the exchanges provide information about Toscanini's daily thoughts and activities throughout much of that period, in addition to a normal, decorous flow of lovers' longings, jealousies, and minor misunderstandings, mainly over questions of who owed a letter to whom. Francesca worried that Carla was "still a child" and of too "impetuous and capricious a nature" to be able to live in harmony with anyone, Carla wrote. "But when you love someone as I love you doesn't even your nature change, don't you submit to whatever the person you love wishes?!" Toscanini responded that even if Carla were impetuous and capricious, "this doesn't necessarily mean that you're not good and capable of creating the happiness of the person who loves you [. . .]. And then, I love and adore you just this way, as you are!"

3.

PIONTELLI AND GIULIO RICORDI CONSIDERED SENDING TOSCANINI and most of the original *Bohème* cast to Vienna, Berlin, and other European capitals late in June, but the plan was scrapped. Instead, they arranged for local premieres of the opera in several Italian towns, the first of which was Trent. Although Toscanini's Mimì, Musetta, Rodolfo, and Colline were the same as in Turin, he still had to prepare the Marcello and Schaunard as well as the orchestra, chorus, and staging. Initially, Carla complained that he wasn't writing to her often enough, and when Ida wrote to tell Toscanini that her sister was suffering from a lack of news, he wrote to his future sister-in-law, "No one's life is as embittered by this cursed theater as mine is! The worst of it is that I in turn embitter others' lives, unconsciously, through no fault of my own." On top of that, he did not like Trent, which was still under Austrian rule, and he was experiencing "nasty pains that take hold of my back and right arm, making it painful even to breathe!"

Once the premiere had taken place, however, Toscanini wrote frequently to Carla. *Bohème* "was accorded a truly enthusiastic success—much greater than in Turin," he told her. The opera "gained a lot" from being performed in a smaller theater, and he described Michele Wigley as "a very handsome, elegant Marcello—the voice *is what it is*, but he is good on stage and enunciates well," whereas Alessandro Guerras, the Schaunard, was "a real dog." He teased Carla by sending her the love letters that he was receiving from a Russian woman whom he had coached in some roles; he professed his absolute fidelity to his fiancée, and perhaps he was telling the truth.

In Trent, Toscanini also conducted his first performances of Verdi's *Un Ballo in Maschera*, with an entirely different set of singers, including the well-known soprano Elena Bianchini Cappelli and the tenor Giovanni Peirani. The latter's "grandiosely bestial ignorance frightened me," Toscanini joked, but he worried because "expectations are high" for *Ballo*, which hadn't been performed in Trent in twenty-seven years, "and I think those expectations will be disappointed." The baritone, Virgilio Bellatti, arrived not knowing his part, which caused Toscanini to comment, "You can imagine the work that's cut out for me, with so great a fool!" Besides, audiences of the day generally showed little enthusiasm for works as out of fashion as the thirty-seven-year-old *Ballo*. In the end, *Bohème* was performed twelve times, *Ballo* only four.

Before he left Trent, Toscanini wrote to Depanis about making improvements in the Turin orchestra. He wished to augment the first violins and to send warnings to two of the seconds: one of them had shown up drunk at some performances, and the other had sometimes not shown up at all, "with the aim of *carrying on behind his wife's back*." Toscanini asked for an additional viola and three replacements in the cello section, and he insisted that another cellist obtain a better instrument. A new principal flute was needed, and as to the piccolo player: "Instead of making Nizza change instruments, I would have him change brains—but since the operation would be painful and might not work, I advise you to change the whole person by replacing him with Prof. *Gennaro Giuliani* [. . .]." And so on, through the rest of the woodwinds and brass. His aim, he said, was "to bring Turin's orchestra to a level of perfection that has perhaps never before been achieved in Italy."

From 1 July, when Toscanini returned to Milan, he and Carla saw each other every day until 4 August, when the De Martinis, like all good middle-class Milanese families, left the torrid city for a vacation near a body of water—in this case, the village of Salò on Lake Garda. From time to time Toscanini sent Carla gifts, mostly books, including Antonio Fogazzaro's early novel *Miranda*. And he again visited his adoring Montani uncle in Voghera.

Ida was to sing the title role in *Manon Lescaut* in Voghera that fall, and Toscanini, who had coached her in the role the previous month, sent her, via Carla, some reminders—early examples of his overriding concern with the literary-dramatic-communicative quality of opera performances. "She must look hard at the words and try to become familiar with Abbé Prévost's novel," on which Puccini's work was based. "She must declaim her part. This will be an excellent exercise for learning to phrase well and, what's more important, to *recite warmly*."

He returned to Milan for two days and then proceeded to Brescia on 12 August to begin rehearsing another production of *La Bohème*, with the original Turin cast, except for a new Rodolfo and a fresh Schaunard; the latter replaced a Spaniard who, Toscanini said, had "a nice voice" and "may be intelligent," but lacked "the sort of comic talent that a part like this requires." The young maestro was suffering from a stiff neck and boredom: there was little to rehearse with most of the singers, and since many of the orchestra musicians had been imported from Turin or Milan, he was teaching the score only to the local players who had been engaged to fill in the ranks and who "would strike terror to the hearts of anyone who heard them," he told Carla. One of the ensemble rehearsals of the "damned second act" went so badly that it made him "curse the day I was born." When Franchi, Turin's stage manager, arrived to help Toscanini organize the *Bohème* mise-en-scène, Toscanini played the piano for the chorus's staging rehearsals: then, as in later years, no task was too small in the struggle to achieve the best-possible results.

Brescia is only about thirty miles from Salò, where Carla, Ida, and their mother were staying, but travel between the two, in those last years before the widespread appearance of the automobile, required transportation by boat, horse-drawn carriage, and train, and took several hours. The three women did manage to attend the first two or three *Bohème* performances, but, just as the series was ending, Toscanini learned that his youngest sister, Zina, not yet nineteen, was suffering from severe intestinal tuberculosis, and he rushed to Parma to be with her. He stayed until she was on the mend, then returned to Milan. Zina married shortly afterward, but she died ten days after her twenty-third birthday. Toscanini later expressed the unscientific opinion that his sisters Narcisa and Zina had died young because they had been breast-fed by a wet nurse whose milk wasn't good, whereas he and Ada—his other sister, who lived to old age—had been breast-fed by their mother.

With the exception of another short visit to Zina, Toscanini stayed in Milan from mid-September to late October 1896 and saw Carla daily until she and her mother accompanied Ida to Voghera on 10 October. He worried about Ida's performance in *Manon Lescaut* and continued to send advice via Carla: *"liven her up,"* he underlined; *"encourage her to look at the vocal score after the rehearsal"*; *"she can never know the opera well enough"*; *"above all she mustn't drag the tempi."* And then: "Advise Ida to sing out immediately the main items, such as, for example: *In quelle trine morbide, L'ora, o Tirsi,* the love duet from the second act, and the fourth act. Remind her above all that if one makes an honest mistake, one is only half a jackass; the other half is the listener who swallows it. [. . .] She must be straightforward on the stage [. . .]. She must support the voice and breathe calmly."

He was pleased that Ida was well received at the first performance, but in the meantime he was running around to various Milanese theatrical agencies, auditioning singers and new operas for Turin. "I leave home at 8:30 [A.M.] and get back at midnight," he wrote. Then he was off to Bologna, where he conducted the local premiere of *La Bohème* with a mostly new cast. His first rehearsals had left him "desperate" because Rebuffini, the soprano engaged to sing the role of Musetta, was "such a dog that it would be hard to find her equal. I'm

heartsick at having to send her away, but neither do I want to jeopar-
dize the production on her account, especially since the Bolognesi
aren't very easygoing—on the contrary, the public here is highly
intelligent." Rebuffini tried to forestall her removal from the production by inviting Toscanini to go over the part with her in her room,
but, Toscanini told Carla, "however wily she may be, I could buy her,
sell her, and buy her again." Carla was not reassured until Toscanini
sent her three letters from Rebuffini, to show her "how we took our
leave of each other"—angrily, one assumes.* But he further stirred
up Carla's jealousy by telling her about his private coaching sessions
with Ella Prossnitz, a twenty-four-year-old Viennese soprano to
whom he was teaching the Italian versions of Wagner roles—especially that of Isolde, which she was to perform with him in Turin a
few months later. "She isn't pretty," he reassured her. "I haven't seen
her since Thursday afternoon."

On 5 November he reported that the first performance of *Bohème*,
the previous evening, had been "a true, unanimous success at this
delightful Teatro Comunale"; there were nineteen more performances of the new opera. Giulio Ricordi was thrilled: "As to sending
you congratulations on the success of *Bohème*, they seem futile! With
you, I sleep peacefully on four pillows!—and everything goes marvelously," the publisher wrote. "Too bad I can't do like St. Anthony
and multiply you!" This was an extraordinary compliment from an
extraordinarily tough customer. On behalf of the Comunale's management, Toscanini had requested that Ricordi reduce the rental fee
for the season's second opera, Puccini's *Le Villi*, and Ricordi replied,
"Nothing is to be denied such an intermediary: thus it won't be a
rental but a *mini-rental* of 500 lire—and see to it that the Impresa
thanks you properly [because] without a word from you I would
have made them pay twice as much at the very least."

One of the *Bohème* performances was attended by King George I
of Greece and his family; Toscanini described the evening as "splendid" and said that the theater was "magnificent." He was often
invited to dinner by various local celebrities and officials, but in
those days such dinners were formal occasions; he disliked them and

---

* This was probably Bella Rebuffini, a soprano of exceptional beauty who had only a
minor career.

would sometimes feign illness to avoid having to attend. "Can you see me boring myself to death among people I barely know and [. . .] even wearing a tailcoat!" he wrote to Carla. He longed to be with his fiancée. "I'm working listlessly, contrary to my custom," he wrote; "it kills my spirit and makes me irritable. Oh my Carla, what have you done to this poor Arturo!"

Once he had begun to rehearse *Le Villi*, however, his listlessness turned to anger and frustration, which exploded at the dress rehearsal. He had spent the whole day at the theater to make sure that everything was ready, but in vain. "The stage manager didn't even know at which points the scene changes were to take place. I walked out halfway through the rehearsal, then I came back, only to leave for good toward the end, declaring explicitly to the organization and the management that I've never yet been anyone's marionette and didn't intend to start now [. . .]. I have 28 dancers who couldn't manage to dance a waltz. Compared to them, I'm Terpsichore." Most of the singers, too, were unsatisfactory, and the staging was "horrible, [. . .] unfinished, tawdry." Extra rehearsals were run, and *Le Villi* opened five days later than originally planned. Although it was performed "decently," Toscanini said, "it couldn't survive the comparison with La Bohème. The audience was bored to death. [. . .] For several days, members of the chorus and the corps de ballet have continued to melt away. [. . .] Yesterday evening a viola and a first violin ran off. At this point, I'm taking the whole thing as a joke. I'm tired of getting angry." *Le Villi* received only two performances.

From Bologna, Toscanini rushed to Milan, where he spent two or three days visiting Carla and fighting with his own family. Claudio Toscanini had evidently tried to embroil his son in yet another business scheme, and Arturo had had enough: he would continue to support his family, but he made up his mind to send them back to Parma. He told his landlord that he and his family would vacate their apartment by the end of March; if his family refused to move, they would have to pay the rent themselves. But he must have relented: his family continued to live in Milan. And he soon had to dash to Turin to begin his second season at the Regio.

A demanding season it was. He had never before conducted any of the five scheduled operas, and he began by leading his orchestra in two concerts, at the nearby Teatro Vittorio Emanuele, that included several pieces new to his repertoire, among which the most striking was the Adagio from the Seventh Symphony of Anton Bruckner, who had died two months earlier; it was "received coldly," Toscanini wrote to Carla. "It's beautiful but very hard to grasp at first blush." Toscanini had originally intended to conduct the *Rapsodie Cambodgienne* by Louis-Albert Bourgault-Ducoudray, one of the first European musicians to introduce Asian scale systems and instruments into Western music, but the piece was set aside at the final rehearsal, for reasons no longer known.

Rehearsals for the concerts ran contemporaneously with rehearsals for Giordano's *Andrea Chénier*, which had had its successful world premiere at La Scala the previous March. Toscanini would later describe Giordano as crude but simpatico and his works as theatrically trashy but well crafted. At the time, however, *Chénier* seemed to him so "unpleasant" that he hadn't taken the trouble to study it deeply in advance; thus "after each rehearsal I have to run home to study whichever act I have to coach at the following rehearsal." As a result, he "lost a rather remarkable amount of weight" and felt exhausted. His schedule was indeed frightening: he performed the second concert on a Sunday afternoon and then conducted "a very long orchestra rehearsal" of *Chénier* in the evening; the next day he ran a staging rehearsal for the singers at eleven, an orchestra rehearsal at one, another staging rehearsal at seven, and an ensemble rehearsal at nine; and no sooner had *Chénier* opened—successfully, with the composer present—than the difficult rehearsals for the local premiere of Saint-Saëns's *Samson et Dalila* began.

"I've had to order a French booklet that deals with this opera's staging and then explain it to Franchi, who didn't even know who Samson was," Toscanini told Carla. The booklet in question probably contained what the Italians called *disposizioni sceniche*, stage distributions. In the late nineteenth century, composers and/or librettists sometimes published diagrams, with accompanying descriptions, to explain where singers, chorus members, and supernumeraries were to position themselves during each of an opera's scenes, and they expected their instructions to be followed—although not rigidly—for as long as the opera survived. Franchi, the Regio's stage manager, had not taken the trouble to investigate the opera's stage distributions, so the responsibility was thrust upon

Toscanini. "I've not only had to attend all the staging rehearsals of Samson, as I do for all the operas," he wrote two days later, "but also to teach the chorus and extras where and how to move, point out the [singers'] various changes of position, and, last but not least, even deal with the ballet. [. . .] All in all, it seems to me that the opera ought to be liked. The music is pretty and has beautiful moments."

On opening night, however, Hector Dupeyron, the lead tenor "was such a dog that he would have [. . .] frightened a thousand wolves," Toscanini wrote. "But the audience, knowing that he sings at the Paris Opera, felt that he was someone who had to be applauded [. . .]." Cucini, the Dalila, "doesn't understand a thing about the character, but since she has a nice, even voice she made an excellent impression on the audience. [. . .] The orchestra [was] *awful, nerveless and inattentive.* The musicians had undoubtedly eaten too much focaccia." Subsequent performances went much better.

Boito's popular *Mefistofele* was next on the roster and was much applauded by the public, but the most demanding production of the season was *Tristan und Isolde*—the first production of the work in Italy since its national premiere in Bologna nine years earlier. "Tristan doesn't leave me time to breathe," Toscanini wrote to Carla. "I admit, however, that although working all day long—and part of the night—tires me, I'm working happily and don't feel the tiredness as much as I do with other operas. I'm driving those poor singers crazy. This is their rehearsal schedule every day. From one to four thirty, from nine to a quarter past midnight."

Toscanini persuaded the management to allow two innovations to coincide with the *Tristan* premiere. First, he had the Regio's traditional, vertically opening painted front-drop replaced with what *La Stampa* described, the next day, as "an elegant red curtain that separates and moves laterally toward the two sides of the forestage." This sort of curtain is common in opera houses today, but it was a novelty in Italian theaters in Toscanini's day. And then, he insisted on having the house lights turned out during the performance, another practice that became standard in the twentieth century (the theatrical illusion cannot be achieved if the lights in the auditorium are left on) but that nineteenth-century Italian audiences —accustomed to conversing, flirting, and even having meals during performances— found odd, even objectionable.

The premiere, on 14 February 1897, with Dupeyron and Ella Prossnitz in the title roles and with many aristocrats and the celebrated Belgian violinist Eugène Ysaÿe in attendance, was a grand event. "At 8:45 P.M.," continued the article in *La Stampa*, "Maestro Toscanini stepped onto the orchestra podium, and the hall became completely dark. There then arose, in the theater, a small battle between the lovers of light and the friends of darkness; the majority called for light, but it was not granted. [. . .] Once the little gale had subsided," the opera "was heard in religious silence and with the greatest attention, excepting some rare, isolated signs of agitation and impatience." Toscanini was hailed repeatedly after each act and was highly praised for the entire performance.

Unfortunately, two journalists transformed what had been the minor incident of the lights into a debate, in print, over basic principles, and at the second performance the protests against the darkened auditorium became so vociferous that Toscanini stopped conducting. When the management gave in and turned the house lights on, Toscanini lost his temper and smashed the light on his music stand. The remainder of the performance took place in half-light, but Toscanini was so disgusted that he conducted sitting on his chair, his right wrist resting on his knee, and barely moving his baton. Polo, the concertmaster, virtually had to lead the orchestra while the prompter tried to assist the singers.

"I thought my head was going to split from one moment to the next," Arturo wrote to Carla, "and yet I never for a moment stopped showing disrespect toward the audience. On the contrary, at the end of the 2nd act they were calling for me to take a bow, but I refused [. . .]. I won't even tell you what I shouted at the journalists [. . .] since all that pandemonium was their fault, a result of their asinine doings."

Toscanini lost the battle over the lights: from the third performance on, there was "a comfortable degree of light" in the theater, reported one newspaper, "not too strong but not too dim, either," so that "Wagner's opera could take place under excellent conditions in the presence of an elegant, numerous, and highly attentive audience." The incident left bitter feelings all around, and *Tristan* received only six performances.

———

TODAY'S MUSICIANS MAY WISH that they lived in an age in which audiences were passionately interested in serious new music, but performers like the young Toscanini, who had to work most of the time with unfamiliar material, were strained to the limit. "After the exertions for Tristan I now have to face this nasty new opera"— Arturo Buzzi-Peccia's *La Forza d'Amore*—"full of errors, which drives me crazy and puts me in a very bad mood," Toscanini wrote on 27 February. "To continue every day to rehearse from noon until five thirty or six and then to have a performance in the evening, and for months on end, is a little too much." A few days later, he reported that he had been up until 5 A.M. the previous two nights, "orchestrating bits of this new opera in order to help Maestro Buzzi-Peccia, who is very agitated and fearful these days over the forthcoming opera. I'll have to work tonight, too." The composer's fears were well founded: *La Forza d'Amore* received only three performances, and the second and third took place before nearly empty houses.*

Toscanini was eager to conduct more symphonic music, and Depanis and Piontelli arranged a series of five concerts at the Regio in March 1897, during the course of which the maestro conducted twenty-four different pieces, most of them for the first time and many by living composers—Grieg, Saint-Saëns, Dvořák, Bolzoni, Goldmark, and Verdi. Among the more important works programmed were Beethoven's Violin Concerto (with Ysaÿe, whose playing Toscanini did not like), Schumann's Second Symphony, excerpts from Berlioz's *Roméo et Juliette*, excerpts from *Die Walküre*, and Tchaikovsky's four-year-old "Pathétique" Symphony.

The fourth of these concerts took place on 25 March, Toscanini's thirtieth birthday, and on the same day Turin's city council approved his contract for the following season: 8,000 lire for a period of 102

---

* Arturo Buzzi-Peccia (Milan 1854–New York 1943) later thanked Toscanini for having conducted his opera "with the true patience of a friend." He immigrated to the United States and became a successful singing teacher. During Toscanini's various American sojourns, the two Arturos occasionally met, and Buzzi-Peccia, a born comedian, sent Toscanini doggerel poems and satirical, often scatological, comments on the world of music and its exponents. Since both men were anti-Fascists, Buzzi-Peccia would teasingly address Toscanini as "Mio Duce."

days, from 8 December 1897 to 20 March 1898. Three days later, about thirty of Toscanini's friends—including Depanis, Polo, and several other orchestra musicians—gave an end-of-season dinner in his honor at the Hôtel Trombetta & Angleterre, "for the year to come and [with] heartfelt good wishes for him and his bride," as Depanis wrote on the back of the menu: Arturo and Carla were planning to wed in June.

Leoncavallo had recently completed an opera called *La Bohème*, written in semifriendly rivalry with Puccini, and Sonzogno, Leoncavallo's publisher, had scheduled the premiere for Venice's Teatro La Fenice in the spring of 1897. Piontelli, probably in collusion with Ricordi, had arranged for Toscanini to conduct Puccini's *Bohème* at Venice's Teatro Rossini a few weeks earlier, with the Turin orchestra and with singers who, for the most part, had already worked with him on their respective parts. Sonzogno, fighting back, had bribed the Venetian critics to pan Puccini's opera; Toscanini expected the worst, but the first performance turned into "an astonishing success," he wrote to Carla, "so much so that it caused the entire Venetian press to record the event as a great triumph. [. . .] The theater was packed—the Venetian nobility all turned out, and so did the foreigners—and the applause was transformed into truly enthusiastic ovations."

Local audiences also liked Leoncavallo's opera, conducted by Alessandro Pomè, but it never gained the popularity of Puccini's work. And while Toscanini and his Turin musicians were in town, they gave a short concert of pieces that they had played together at home the previous month.

4.

ARTURO AND CARLA'S RELATIONSHIP HAD CONTINUED TO DEVELOP through the second half of 1896 and the early months of 1897, and they decided to marry as soon as possible. But some family problems arose. First, the groom-to-be discovered that his conniving parents had visited the concierge of a building owned by Carla's mother to find out whether their future daughter-in-law's family was wealthy. Then, one day, shortly after Arturo's return to Milan from Venice,

Carla's mother suddenly began to insult him "in the most horrible and at the same time the lowest way," he wrote to Polo; "in order to get away from that storm of injuries that poured forth from a worse than vulgar mouth, I was compelled to leave the house forever." The feud would eventually be resolved, but in the meantime, Toscanini, fed up with both families and determined to avoid the publicity that his wedding would have attracted had it taken place in Milan or Turin, arranged to marry Carla privately in the small town of Conegliano Veneto, Piontelli's principal residence.

As the story was later told to their daughters, Wally and Wanda, the couple left Milan "secretly by train," and "Mamma remembered that it was a beautiful trip. Papà was cheerful, calm, and very affectionate." But Piontelli "had not been able to keep the secret, and news of the wedding had spread through the town. There was a great crowd at the station, headed by a band waiting to greet the maestro. When our father looked out the window and saw those people, he became livid with rage. [. . .] He got off the train without saying a word, paying no attention to his fiancée, who was trying vainly to hold on to his arm." They went to the town hall, signed the marriage documents shortly after ten, and proceeded to the church, where Toscanini "went through the ceremony with a clouded face."

A week of festivities had been planned, during which Toscanini childishly refused to eat. In old age, he recalled with much laughter that at one of the meals there was "a piano dealer from Venice who made a speech. 'I wish for Maestro Toscanini the good luck that I've had: I've had three wives.' Ah, he was an idiot." When the newlyweds set out for their honeymoon, Toscanini was still in a bad mood. According to Wally, "Mamma always said, 'That was the worst trip of my life.' Toward evening Mamma started to cry. Then the gruff Toscanini tried to overcome his bad humor and with an effort started to break the silence he had kept up to that moment." They spent a night in the town of Vittorio Veneto, where Toscanini "ate a lot of risotto, to fill up the empty space," he remembered, and from there they went by carriage to Tai di Cadore, in the Dolomites. They ended their honeymoon at Vena d'Oro, a spa near the town of Belluno, because doctors had recommended that Toscanini take cold-water baths, probably for muscular problems. "The hydro-therapeutic cure is effective," he wrote to Polo. "Carla too has undertaken it and I hope it will do her good." By the time they returned to Milan, Carla was pregnant.

5.

THE LOMBARD TOWN OF BERGAMO AND ITS SURROUNDING *PROVINCIA* have given birth to several major figures, Caravaggio and Pope John XXIII among them. In the world of opera, Bergamo's favorite son was Gaetano Donizetti, whose centenary the town's leading citizens decided to celebrate in style in the summer and fall of 1897; they invited Toscanini to take charge of the most important musical events. But what ought to have been a joyful occasion turned into a disaster. The first production, *La Favorita*, was received tepidly: conductor and orchestra were liked, but most of the singers were not. "Toscanini couldn't get blood out of stones," remarked one commentator. When two of the principal singers for the second opera, *Lucia di Lammermoor*, became ill, Toscanini requested a postponement, but the impresario rejected the idea and ordered him to accept substitutes; the order was rejected.

According to a local newspaper, the audience at the first performance was "a little surprised, upon entering the theater, to see a printed notice in the foyer that announced that Maestro Toscanini, taken ill at the last moment, had had to leave the conducting of the performance to Maestro [Eraclio] Gerbella," the chorus master—one of Toscanini's teachers at the Parma Conservatory. "These notices always leave many skeptics, of course." At the end of the second act, the disappointed audience became so unruly that benches were thrown from the gallery onto the stage, and the police had to be called in to clear the house. A second performance, again without Toscanini, went no better than the first, and the tenor was so upset by the audience's hostility that he fled the city.

Toscanini's Bergamo contract also required him to conduct several symphony concerts. Dissatisfied with the orchestra's English horn player, he asked the impresario, Arturo Terzi, to engage the excellent Guido Zavadini, a former schoolmate from Parma who had moved to Bergamo. Terzi at first refused to cover the extra expense, but when Toscanini threatened to leave, Zavadini was engaged. During the poorly attended first concert, a group of the conductor's detractors began to scream, "Out with Toscanini! Out of the theater!" He turned to the audience, shouted, "Absurd!" and left the stage. He calmed down and returned to the podium, but his rage boiled over again and he conducted perfunctorily and rigidly. He refused to honor the rest of his contract and went to recuperate at Piontelli's home in Conegliano, where Carla awaited him. To a friend in Turin, he wrote that Terzi had "cheated me out of a cool thousand lire," and that he had "come to these delightful hills where I can forget about that unfortunate Bergamo season."

He enjoyed at least a taste of sweet revenge when *Lucia* became the centerpiece of a brief but particularly successful season that he conducted at the Teatro Dal Verme in Milan later that fall. The engagement, which would have far-reaching consequences, had been arranged by Giulio Ricordi, who was gloating over the fact that La Scala's previous season, under Edoardo Sonzogno's aegis, had been a disaster. Indeed, that season, led by the conductor Vittorio Maria Vanzo, had brought La Scala into the worst period of financial, administrative, and artistic chaos in its history, and an announcement had recently been made that the forthcoming 1897–98 season would be canceled. Toscanini's appearance at Milan's second-ranking opera house, under the auspices of Ricordi—with whom the maestro had had to fight for a decent fee—electrified the city's famished opera lovers.

Toscanini opened with a production of *La Bohème* that was compared favorably to the local premiere, which had taken place at La Scala the previous year under Mugnone's baton. During the first performance, an ecstatic Puccini was repeatedly called onto the stage with Toscanini and the singers, and he reported that the opera had been "splendidly performed." The reviewers concurred: Toscanini "was able to paint with maximum color effects while always maintaining a correct, refined, elevated interpretation," wrote one of them. "Nothing better has ever been heard or can be heard from our orchestras." Puccini returned for a *serata d'onore* for Toscanini at which the audience "suffocated" the conductor with "interminable applause, overwhelming ovations," said another reviewer. "The worthy maestro was obliged to appear innumerable times on the proscenium after each act of *La Bohème*, alone and with the singers. Toscanini deserved this imposing plebiscite of affection as well as the splendid gifts presented to him after the third act by Commendatore Ricordi and by Maestro Puccini [. . .] and the similarly magnificent ones from the orchestra and the management; this last consisted of a highly sought-after edition of *Parsifal*, artistically bound in blue velvet." At the end of that performance Toscanini thanked the audience by conducting Smetana's *Bartered Bride* Overture and the "Forest Murmurs" from *Siegfried*. Altogether, twenty-four performances of *Bohème*—in addition to two of *Lucia* and ten of *Manon Lescaut*—had to be given, to satisfy the local public.*

6.

TURIN'S CIVIC LEADERS, FORESEEING THAT LA SCALA WOULD SOON be knocking insistently at Toscanini's door, made him a munificent offer: 31,000 lire to take charge of a third and a fourth season at the Regio and, in between, to conduct a long and demanding series of concerts at the 1898 exposition. In mid-December 1897, he and his pregnant wife moved into an apartment at no. 17 in Turin's central Via Bogino; Enrico Polo, the Regio's concertmaster, had in the meantime married Carla's sister, Ida, and the two couples were able to "keep good company with each other," as Toscanini put it to his young wife.

The Regio's season opened on New Year's Day 1898 with the national premiere of Luigi Mancinelli's opera *Ero e Leandro*, a setting of a libretto by Boito. This was followed by revivals of *Bohème* and *Mefistofele*, which required relatively little preparation; thus Toscanini and the ensemble could devote themselves to rehearsing

---

* At Milan's Monumental Cemetery on the afternoon of 16 November, a few hours before the first *Manon* performance, Ricordi, Boito, Toscanini, Giordano, and the mayor of Milan, attended the burial of Giuseppina Strepponi Verdi, the composer's wife, who had died two days earlier, at the age of eighty-two; Verdi himself, now eighty-four, had been present at the funeral in Busseto that morning but had not had the emotional strength to make the journey to Milan.

a production of *Die Walküre*, still a rarity in Italy at that time. Wagner's opera was followed by the world premiere of *Camargo* by Enrico De Leva, a young composer better-known for his Neapolitan songs than for his theater works. Giulio Ricordi had placed considerable hopes on *Camargo* and had even sent his son, Tito, to help with the staging, but the opera survived for only two performances. One piece, however, an intermezzo between the first and second acts, pleased some audience members so much that they requested an encore. Toscanini felt so sorry for the composer that he signaled the orchestra to repeat the number, which caused other audience members to protest. Toscanini stopped the orchestra, motioned for the curtain to go up on Act II, and then softly told the orchestra to replay the intermezzo. The surprised protesters remained silent to the end. "Sorry negative result that certainly wasn't deserved," Giulio Ricordi wired Toscanini the next day. "I repeat to you my great thanks for all you did with the love of an artist and friend."

Toscanini and his Turin orchestra then performed four concerts; the first and third consisted of old-fashioned programs in which orchestral works alternated with pieces for voice or solo instruments accompanied by one or another local pianist. On the first of them—a benefit for an order of nuns dedicated to working for the poor—Toscanini gave his first performance of Dvořák's five-year-old "New World" Symphony. Afterward, Princess Elena, consort of Crown Prince Victor Emanuel, called Toscanini to her box, praised him for his conducting and charitable work, and awarded him, on behalf of the king, the title of Grand Master of the Order of the Crown of Italy. On the third concert, Toscanini and the orchestra accompanied the celebrated Spanish violinist Pablo de Sarasate in Heinrich Wilhelm Ernst's *Fantaisie brillante* on Rossini's *Otello*. *Norma*, which opened on 30 April 1898, brought the season to a close; Toscanini later described the production as "of no importance."

A few weeks earlier, on 21 March, Carla had given birth to a boy, named Walter after the hero of Catalani's *Loreley*. The proud father would amuse people for the rest of his life by pointing out that his first child was born nine months to the day after his own marriage to Carla—"in tempo, like a good conductor."

7.

THE INDUSTRIALIZED WORLD'S MANIA FOR NATIONAL AND INTER-national expositions in the latter half of the nineteenth century found enthusiastic support among Turin's civic leaders, who promoted major fairs in the city in 1858, 1884, and 1898. Although these events were created mainly to stimulate commerce and to demonstrate local pride, they all were adorned with cultural trappings: Toscanini, readers may recall, had first visited Turin during the 1884 exposition, when, as a conservatory student, he had played cello in Cleofonte Campanini's ad hoc Parmesan orchestra.

Turin's National Exposition of 1898—officially organized to mark the fiftieth anniversary of the Albertine Statute, the basis for Italian constitutional law—took place at a time of heightened economic, social, and political unrest in the country: Italy's liberal-conservative coalitions were being threatened by the growth of the Socialist Party on the left and the Catholic party on the right, and the Italian army's defeat at Adwa in Abyssinia two years earlier had become a matter of national shame. The 1898 exposition offered an occasion to try to bring the Catholics, if not the Socialists, into the fold, and to show off everything that was going well in the country.

One of the buildings created on the fairground was a 2,500-seat, domed concert hall with a pipe organ situated at its center and a painting representing the apotheosis of Giuseppe Verdi set in a prominent place. There, in two separate segments—from early May to mid-July and from late August to the end of October—Toscanini conducted the Regio's orchestra in a total of forty-three concerts that included 133 works by fifty-four composers; forty-eight of the compositions were being heard in Turin for the first time. Italian and German composers dominated the roster, but French, Russian, Bohemian, British, and Scandinavian works were also heard. Toscanini had wanted Saint-Saëns to play one of his piano concerti on one concert and Joseph Joachim as violin soloist on another, but neither was available.

The stellar event of the Turin exposition series, however, was the Italian premiere of three of Verdi's Four Sacred Pieces—the composer's final significant works—which had first been performed in Paris a month earlier.* In studying the *Te Deum*, Toscanini had dithered over some slight tempo modifications, particularly letups in the basic tempo, which he felt were implicit in the music at certain points but which Verdi had not indicated in the score. On Toscanini's behalf Depanis wrote to the composer, who was in Genoa, to request a meeting. Verdi replied on 18 April, saying, "Maestro Toscanini and Maestro Venturi [the chorus master] may come when they wish. I am always at home after midday. A chorus of 200 voices is too large, in my opinion. These great masses always have a fat, swollen color, and their pronunciation is too *unholy* (so to speak). . . . 120 voices would suffice . . . ."

Depanis, who was present at the encounter one or two days later, wrote that "Toscanini sat at the piano, and it didn't take long for the eighty-four-year-old Maestro and the young conductor to get on excellently. Verdi admired the quickness of Toscanini's perception. [. . .] [Verdi's] voice, husky at first, soon became clear and imperious; his eyes sparkled, and no detail of Toscanini's playing escaped him. He explained his ideas in short, precise, colorful phrases that said much more than a long commentary." (Toscanini later described Verdi's eyes as "phosphorescent.") At one point in the *Te Deum*, Toscanini made one of the *rallentandi* (tempo relaxations) that was not printed in the score. "Bravo," said Verdi, clapping him on the shoulder. Toscanini stopped playing and said, "Maestro, if only you knew how much this has been bothering me. Why didn't you write the *rallentando?*" Verdi replied: "If I had written it, a bad musician would have exaggerated it, but if one is a good musician one feels it and plays it, just as you've done, without the necessity of having it written down."

Verdi mentioned this encounter to Boito, who wrote to Toscanini, "I know that you went to Genoa to discuss the performance of the three sacred pieces with the Maestro and that the artistic understanding succeeded perfectly, and I am glad of that." Then, about ten days before the premiere of the three pieces, Toscanini received another letter from Boito: "I have a mad craving to hear a good

---

* The *Stabat Mater*, *Laudi alla Vergine Maria*, and *Te Deum* were presented; the *Ave Maria*, for unaccompanied chorus, was omitted.

rehearsal of the Maestro's three pieces; please tell me on what day and at what time I could satisfy this desire." Toscanini presumably replied, and a few days later he received yet another letter from Boito:

> You are too *intuitive* not to have guessed that my request to attend one of your rehearsals hid my intention of dragging the Maestro with me, to Turin, to bring him to you without anyone's knowing a thing (and thus to avoid any fuss for him), procuring for Him the intellectual joy of your interpretation, for you his great praise, and for myself this double satisfaction. But my whole strategy ended in naught. The Maestro is not to be moved, resists Giulio Ricordi's insistent pleas and my own, and doesn't give in. Perhaps he is afraid of exposing himself to some strong emotional reactions. His will be done. [. . .] But I plan to join a group of friends and attend the performance with them, and to admire you as I always do.

There was an ulterior motive behind Boito's invitation to Verdi. At the age of fifty-six, the poet-composer was one of the most prestigious figures in the world of Italian culture, and he had recently been named vice-president of La Scala's newly reconstituted governing board. He had wanted Verdi's moral support for his plan to make Arturo Toscanini, at the age of thirty-one, artistic director of Italy's greatest lyric theater.

Toscanini in his early thirties,
during his first mandate as
conductor of Milan's
Teatro alla Scala.

IV

LA SCALA
REFORMED

1.

———

THE REGIO DUCALE TEATRO, MILAN'S PRINCIPAL OPERA HOUSE through most of the eighteenth century, caught fire and burned down one night in February 1776. Within two weeks, a committee of ninety local aristocrats had produced plans for the construction of a new theater and had sent them to Vienna, since Austria ruled Lombardy at the time. Thanks to joint financial support from Empress Maria Theresa's treasury and the Milanese nobility, the ingenuity of the architect Giuseppe Piermarini, and the all-out efforts of three hundred workers, the new building was ready in just over two years. The old theater, for which Mozart had written three of his early operas, had been part of the Royal Ducal Palace, located across from Milan's monumental cathedral; the new one sat a few hundred yards to the north, on the site of the former church of Santa Maria della Scala, which explains why the New Royal Ducal Theater quickly became known to the Milanese as the Teatro della Scala or, as it is now called, the Teatro alla Scala.

The house's auditorium, with its broad ground floor, five tiers of boxes, and top gallery (the fifth tier of boxes was later transformed into another gallery), was one of the largest in Europe, and from the start it was meant to be a unique venue. A month before the theater opened, a newspaper reported, "It is intended that the enormous abuses that have permitted a performance style full of license within the Italian musical theater be reformed [. . .] by increasing movement and action in the dramas and by making the actors [i.e., singers] concentrate, and by showing greater verisimilitude, and consequently stimulating greater interest, in the performance as it unfolds."

According to Stendhal, the goals were achieved and surpassed. "I arrive [in Milan] at 7 in the evening, dead tired, and run to La Scala," he wrote in 1816. "This evening, I have seen everything that the most oriental of imaginations could dream up, the most singular, the most striking things, the richest in architectural beauty, [. . .] brilliant fabrics, characters who possess not only the costumes but also the physiognomies and gestures of the countries in which the action takes place. [. . .] I run to the leading theater in the world."

All four of Italy's great nineteenth-century *operisti*—Rossini, Donizetti, Bellini, and Verdi—premiered works at La Scala, and the most famous singers, dancers, choreographers, and scene painters were employed there. Opera houses elsewhere served as adjuncts to local society, but La Scala, during its early decades, simply *was* Milanese society—middle- and upper-class society, at any rate. "The Scala theater is the city's salon," Stendhal observed. "There is no society except there, not one open house. We'll see each other at La Scala, people say about every sort of matter."

From the start, and through the years of Napoleonic France's occupation of the city, La Scala was run entirely by its *palchettisti*, the noble families who owned and occupied the *palchi* (boxes) and subsidized the house. They licensed impresarios to organize the operas and ballets and, during various periods, to run a casino in the third-tier foyer, to help pay for the productions. But beginning in 1815, when the Austrians again occupied Lombardy, the government in Vienna provided a subsidy, and the casino was closed. After the birth of the Italian nation in 1861, the new government continued to provide an annual grant, but in 1897, during a period of austerity, the crown ceded its "property" (a euphemism, in this case, for "responsibility") to the city of Milan; given the abysmal state of the local economy and the disastrous artistic results of the 1896–97 season, the city councilors decided that what money remained in their coffers would be put to better use elsewhere, and they abolished the subsidy altogether. On 26 December 1897, which ought to have been the opening night of the new season, someone posted a sign on the theater's main doors: "Closed because of the death of artistic feeling, civic responsibility, and common sense." La Scala's 1897–98 season did not take place at all.

A committee was established to examine the problem, and a radical systemic change was devised. As part of an experimental, three-year plan, the city council agreed to an annual subsidy of 150,000 lire, with the proviso that the *palchettisti*—who by then included not only aristocrats but also members of the *haute bourgeoisie*—would raise their joint contribution to a total of at least 100,000 lire and that a society of shareholders would be formed to provide an operating capital of 300,000 lire. "The orchestra will be increased from eighty to a hundred members," reported one magazine. "Not only will the ballet school be revived, but the chorus school will be better regulated. We have learned, further, that the conductor (Toscanini?) will also be general artistic director of the productions. There will also be a capable stage manager, but no impresario, no speculator, given that the impresario system was what ruined the theater. All profits will benefit art."

These revolutionary changes were speedily accomplished. An eighteen-member board of directors was convened under the presidency of Duke Guido Visconti di Modrone, a former senator and one of Milan's best-known and most trusted noblemen, with Boito as vice-president; aristocrats, businessmen, and legal consultants made up most of the rest of the board. They accepted the city council's proposals, put up the necessary funds, and decided to hire a professional general manager (*direttore generale*) for the three-year experimental term. But a conductor also had to be found, and Boito firmly believed that Toscanini was the only person for the job.

At fifty-six, Boito—son of an Italian painter and a Polish countess—was a major figure and fixture in Milanese artistic life: composer of the ever-popular opera *Mefistofele*; librettist not only of his own work and of Verdi's *Otello* and *Falstaff* but also of Ponchielli's *La Gioconda* and of several other composers' operas; a close confidant of Verdi himself; a former lover of the actress Eleonora Duse; and an adherent of the avant-garde artistic movements of his youth. Boito had approached Toscanini on the Scala question as early as January 1898, and on 1 February he wrote to his favorite candidate, "Dear Maestro[,] I thank you warmly, also on behalf of my colleagues, for the favorable and much desired response that you have given us.

This encourages us to continue our work with greater fortitude and with more steadfast faith." Through the spring, Boito sent several board members to Turin to discuss details with Toscanini, and La Scala's board was soon able to announce officially that Arturo Toscanini had been appointed the ensemble's conductor and that Giulio Gatti-Casazza would become La Scala's general manager.

Not everyone was pleased. "The nomination of Arturo Toscanini as Conductor raised a hurricane of suspicions, not because of his artistic ability, which is undoubtedly great and beyond question, but because of his personality, which, according to some, is not well adapted to maintaining the tranquillity and the dignified severity that are necessary if productions are to proceed in the interests of the Administration"—this according to an article in a Milanese theatrical yearbook. Further, "the choice of Gatti-Casazza as general manager was also fought doggedly by some who felt that the young administrator was not sufficiently experienced for a Theater of such great importance." Gatti, twenty-nine, had been in charge of the city of Ferrara's much smaller opera house, and for only five years. "But it must be admitted that these little battles, fought on the sidelines and provoked more by personal ambition than by artistic or managerial considerations, did not make a breach in the spirits of those who, not mistakenly, based the most fervent hopes for and the surest guarantees of La Scala's good fortunes on the two young directors."

For Depanis, Toscanini's departure from Turin was sad but inevitable. "La Scala was worthy of Toscanini and Toscanini was worthy of La Scala," he wrote. "But it was a grave loss for Turin." Over half a century later Toscanini, typically, described the change in his life in less glorious terms: "I had gone up a step, you know. I had gone to La Scala."

2.

BEFORE HE MOVED BACK TO MILAN, TOSCANINI HAD TO COMPLETE his marathon concert series at Turin's National Exposition. During the one-month summer break between the two long blocks of concerts, he and Carla vacationed with baby Walter at Ceresole Reale, in the Italian Alps, where they were joined by Enrico and Ida Polo. Toscanini used the time to clear his head, study, do some mountain climbing—a new passion that would endure for several years—and begin to plan the forthcoming Scala season.

Boito wrote to him frequently. "Dear Maestro," begins one letter,

When you have filled out the list of orchestra Members, either in its entirety or even only in part, you can send a copy of it to Mr. Gatti-Casazza who will immediately proceed with the contracts. Gatti must already have sent you the list of singers, not yet entirely complete, but almost. In that list you will find artists chosen by joint agreement with you, and these have already been given regular contracts; the others are bound by letters of intent while awaiting your final decision on them. I would ask you moreover to be so good as to make any modifications that you see fit in the draft contract that I gave you in Milan, and to send it to me.

Toscanini stole Aristide Venturi from Turin to make him La Scala's choral chief, and the thirty-eight-year-old Pietro Sormani was brought on board as principal vocal coach and assistant conductor. The new music director also wrote to Romeo Orsi, a clarinetist in the Scala orchestra and head of the orchestra society—an embryonic musicians' union—to ask for a complete list of the current players and to enlist Orsi's support in persuading the current principal flute, whose playing Toscanini admired, not to retire from the ensemble. "It may well be that he suffers from nervousness, but this is nothing new, and still he has always played well," Toscanini said. "He says that he is old, but I would like to have an orchestra completely made up of old-timers like him." The flutist declined to return; to replace him Toscanini brought in Abelardo Albisi, a fellow Parma Conservatory graduate, whose brother, Giovanni, was already principal second violin in the Scala orchestra.

As his vacation was coming to an end, Toscanini wrote to Depanis, "I'm leaving Ceresole really unwillingly! If I had at least been able to reach the top of the [Gran] Paradiso! I had to give up the Levanna because my wife wouldn't hear of letting me go, since it is a more difficult ascent. [. . .] The day after tomorrow, I'll take up the baton again instead of the alpenstock, to climb the less dangerous mountains of eighth notes and sixteenth notes." Toscanini, who at that time was painfully thin, added, "I've gained weight. I always have a street musician's appetite."

The ever-generous Depanis helped the young maestro examine his new contract and request alterations to it. In its final version, it stipulated that "Signor Maestro Cavaliere Arturo Toscanini" was being engaged as conductor for three consecutive seasons at a fee of 12,000 lire (equal to about $55,000 in 2016 buying power) per season, payable in four monthly installments, from December through March. He was to be in Milan not later than the first of December each year to organize productions and begin rehearsing, and he was to remain at La Scala's disposal until approximately Easter Sunday. The contract included operas, concerts, oratorios, "and other musical performances that the Society may decide to give at La Scala even during the day, if there are no evening performances." Toscanini was to be responsible for "the entire artistic functioning of the theater season with respect to the performance of the operas," and he was entrusted with "supreme and incontestable authority over everything that concerns the execution of the art." He would have the final word on engaging or releasing singers, orchestra players, and (in consultation with the chorus master) members of the chorus. The recognition of his gifts implicit in this contract was great, but the responsibility laid upon him was even greater.

Plans for the new Scala administration's first season continued to be made while Toscanini was rehearsing and performing his remaining twenty-two concerts at the Turin exposition. La Scala "had been left in complete abandonment and had been closed for over sixteen months," Gatti-Casazza later recalled. "Nothing had been preserved of the old organization. It was, therefore, necessary to rebuild from the beginning. This took place amid a sea of difficulties," not the least of which was opposition to new ideas on the part of the older *palchettisti*. But the new bosses went ahead with their plans. "We decided to favor as much as possible the youthful element, in keeping with the youthfulness of Toscanini and myself," Gatti said.

The generational change applied even to the visual aspect of La Scala's productions. Carlo Ferrario, Verdi's favorite scene painter, who had been in charge of the house's scenery for nearly three decades, was now sixty-five and longing to stop. A team of Ferrario's star pupils—Angelo Parravicini, Vittorio Rota, Mario Sala, and Carlo

Songa—from Milan's celebrated Accademia di Brera, took over all the new productions, although some of Ferrario's sets were used in revivals of older productions. Luigi Zamperoni, head of the tailoring company that had long provided costumes for most of La Scala's productions, was also about to retire; costumes for new productions were gradually entrusted to the Chiappa family establishment. Functioning as *direttore di scena* (stage director)—a profession that, in those days, simply entailed working with the conductor to coordinate stage movement—was the veteran mime Rinaldo Rossi.

Early in October, Toscanini, together with Bolzoni, Martucci, and a few other musicians, judged a composition competition in Turin, and on the last day of the month he conducted the Turin exposition's final concert, attended by Queen Margherita, on an official royal visit from Rome. A day or two later, a dinner in Toscanini's honor was held at the Hôtel d'Angleterre, with many local dignitaries and celebrities in attendance. Toscanini did not make a speech, but Depanis did. "If the Milanese wanted a real conductor, they had to come to Turin to get him," he said. "In Turin, Toscanini leaves devoted friends who will remember his intelligence, zeal, and conscientiousness, which are rare today."

3.

FOR TOSCANINI, AS FOR STENDHAL THREE GENERATIONS EARLIER, Milan was a beautiful, energetic, and eminently livable city, adorned with architectural monuments spanning twenty centuries of Italian history and crisscrossed by a system of *navigli*—navigable man-made canals, the earliest of which dated back to pre–Roman Empire times. With a population of nearly half a million at the turn of the twentieth century, the city was Italy's financial capital and a major European industrial entrepôt, yet there was a coziness to Milanese life that Toscanini loved. He understood Milanese dialect and enjoyed reading the dialect poetry of Carlo Porta and, later, Delio Tessa. Now, a dozen years after he and his parents and sisters had moved into a primitive flat in the city, he was assuming a position of cultural power and prestige as the head of Milan's, and Italy's, greatest lyric theater.

Carla had found an apartment in Via San Vincenzino, an easy fifteen-minute amble from La Scala; by early November the family had settled into the new dwelling, and Toscanini was proceeding with his plans for the quickly approaching Scala season. These included the promulgation of some nonmusical regulations, such as forbidding women in the audience to wear hats (they blocked others' view of the stage) and keeping the auditorium dark during performances. For each change, Toscanini had to fight those who preferred the status quo. As at the Regio in Turin, so at La Scala he wanted to replace the painted, vertically opening front-drop with a laterally opening curtain. Boito was hesitant: he reminded Toscanini of how, during the soft tremolos of the violins at the end of the "Greek" act of his *Mefistofele*, the front-drop had slowly come down over the scene. Yes, what a beautiful view, Toscanini replied sarcastically: first it cut off Faust's and Helen's heads and then, gradually, their other body parts, until finally their feet disappeared. Wouldn't it be more beautiful if, instead, a curtain slowly came together from the sides of the stage, leaving only the two protagonists embracing at center stage and finally covering even them? Boito assented, but Toscanini then had to confront the rest of the board of directors, each of whom offered his own opinion. When one of them protested that the weight of the curtain would be too great for the overhead flies to sustain, Toscanini shouted, "Shut up!" The scenery that was constantly being raised and lowered weighed much more, he said. The curtain finally arrived, "and it's still there!" exclaimed Toscanini, more than half a century later. "That's why I got the reputation of having an impossible character. Because [there are] characters who always say yes, yes, yes, who always compromise. I never compromised, never, never! And I was right, wasn't I?"

Toscanini's first season at La Scala opened the day after Christmas 1898 with *Die Meistersinger*, which had been presented twice before in Italy, but with massive cuts; this was its first nearly complete Italian production. He had rehearsed long and hard with orchestra, chorus, and a cast that included the young Neapolitan baritone Antonio Scotti (Sachs), the soprano Angelica Pandolfini (Eva), and the tenor Emilio De Marchi (Stolzing). Scotti later recalled that he had learned his part with the cuts and had been shocked when Toscanini made him learn the rest of the role. Although most of the critics wished that the cuts had been maintained, there were few qualms about the quality of the performance. Giulio Ricordi, in his *Gazzetta Musicale di Milano*, summed up the opinion of the vast majority: "The overall applause with which all the acts were greeted was clear proof of admiration for the opera and for a performance of the highest order, such as we have never been able to sample in Vienna, Berlin, Paris, or even at Bayreuth, the Wagnerian temple. The orchestra was stupendous, well balanced, conducted with admirable assurance by Maestro Toscanini, whom the audience expressly called to the proscenium." The usually conservative Ricordi even approved of the new curtain. Many years later, Toscanini described the production, which was performed thirteen times, as "wonderful."

Toscanini's path to success seemed to have been cleared. But within a week of the season's opening, his position and reputation were in jeopardy. *Norma* was scheduled for the second production, and Toscanini had searched long and hard for a singer who, he hoped, would be capable of bringing off the taxing title role; he had eventually engaged Ines De Frate, a forty-four-year-old soprano who sang both bel canto and dramatic roles. During the rehearsals, Toscanini gradually became dissatisfied with De Frate and had a falling-out with the tenor, Augusto Brogi; he replaced the latter with Orazio Cosentino, who had been his Pollione in Turin's *Norma* production the previous spring. "Norma opens Wednesday—Thursday we'll know the outcome," a worried Toscanini wrote to Piontelli on or around 1 January 1899. "The public is so stupid that I don't know whether I should hope or despair."

The dress rehearsal seemed to proceed smoothly, but afterward—as Toscanini told the story many years later—he "turned to Maestro Boito and Giulio Ricordi" and asked,

"What's your impression of this production?" Boito didn't answer. Giulio Ricordi, who was more impudent and more practical about the theater, said, "Very good production. And then, you know, at La Scala we need a second production."

"What do you mean?"

"A production that's not as good as the first."

"I don't understand. I may be wrong, but I try to make all the productions equal." So the rehearsal ended and I went to Gatti-

Casazza and said, "Will you accept my spoken rejection [i.e., cancellation of the production] or do I have to give it in writing?"

"Oh, if you don't want to conduct it, let an assistant conduct it."

"Oh no. I'm the one who did wrong; I have to pay the price."

Even in those days, when staging and sets in major opera houses were far less complicated than they are today, a new production required considerable expenditures of time, energy, and money, and a cancellation after a dress rehearsal was extremely rare. Toscanini knew that his decision would raise doubts about his competence and would play into the hands of those who had opposed his appointment. But he refused to back down. "It was a *scandal* for Milan!" he remembered. "All the press said, 'Why is Mr. Toscanini rejecting the opera? *We* should reject it!' [I said,] 'No, my friends: the press [stands] behind my rear end. First I judge, then the press.'"

Gatti-Casazza, for his part, never forgave Toscanini for what he described, thirty years later, as the conductor's "crazy, ridiculous" behavior, "inimical to La Scala itself." He said that at the time "there was serious talk about replacing him." Indeed, Toscanini's detractors, who were numerous, promptly opened fire. One particularly colorful, defamatory article appeared under the headline "Bluebeard's Gallantries" in a theatrical gossip-sheet called *Il Corno* (The Horn), of no fixed address, written, edited, and probably also printed and distributed by one Pompeo Ferrari. "If La Scala is really to be saved, full powers must not be given to this abortion of Luciferian arrogance who was incautiously chosen to lead its artistic destiny," Ferrari said. "Toscanini, the famous Bluebeard, knows only how to conduct operas unknown to others, such as *Die Meistersinger*, to prove his superiority, and to cause repertoire operas like *Norma* to fail, so as not to reveal his own lack of knowledge."

Ferrari either did not know or pretended not to know that Toscanini had conducted *Norma* successfully, although not to his own satisfaction, in Palermo in 1893 and in Turin only a few months before the Scala debacle. In the 1950s, Toscanini told friends, "In fifty and more years I've never [again] conducted *Norma*, because I've never found a soprano who could sing Norma." When Walter Toscanini asked his father why he had conducted the earlier productions but not later ones, the maestro joked: "I made progress, intelligence-wise. Before, I was a bit stupid."

4.
———

LATE THE PREVIOUS NOVEMBER, WHILE HE WAS PREPARING THE Scala season, Toscanini had traveled to Rome to attend the world premiere of *Iris*, Mascagni's latest opera, conducted by the composer. The production was a failure, and when Toscanini met Mascagni at a café the next day, the composer of *Cavalleria Rusticana* blamed the disaster on the singers, whom he had allowed to make all sorts of transpositions and other changes. He asked Toscanini, who was to conduct the Milan premiere in January, to forbid the singers "to tear the music to shreds, and make them perform it as we [composers] have written it." Toscanini pointed out that most of the singers in the original cast would be repeating their roles at La Scala and would be able to argue that they had performed *Iris* under Mascagni himself, who had let them do as they pleased. The two musicians finally hit on an idea: Mascagni would send Toscanini a letter in which he would insist that the singers perform the music as written. Ricordi, *Iris*'s publisher, heard of the plan and asked that the letter be addressed to him so that it could be used for subsequent productions as well.

Early in January Toscanini began to rehearse the new opera, and Ricordi, familiar with Mascagni's unpredictable humors, decided to forbid the composer to attend the rehearsals and first performances in Milan. Mascagni was not pleased. "The 'absolute ban' imposed upon me by Signor Commendatore Ricordi [. . .] has justifiably made me a bit suspicious," he wrote to Toscanini three days before the scheduled opening. But he had heard "that you are putting your whole soul into the preparations and conducting of *Iris*. This is a great comfort to me. I thank you with all my heart."

Expectations for the new opera were high, and the gala opening-night audience "was reminiscent of the premieres of *Otello* and *Falstaff*," wrote one critic. The principal singers—the soprano Hariclea Darclée and tenor Fernando De Lucia—were praised, as were Toscanini and his orchestral and choral forces, but *Iris* was given a tepid reception. One reviewer remarked sarcastically that *Iris* "had the immediately positive effect of making La Scala's subscribers better appreciate the beauties of *Die Meistersinger*; indeed, the applause was never as lively as at the following performance of the Wagner opera, after the second *Iris* performance."

To make matters worse, from Mascagni's point of view, critics who had attended the Rome premiere judged Toscanini's interpretation "greatly superior to the composer's own performance." In a letter to Ricordi, the composer raged, "I alone knew how *Iris* should be done, but by some absurd quirk nobody thought that the author's ideas should and must be preferred." He changed his mind, however, after having attended a performance early in February, by which time the public had warmed to *Iris*. The *Gazzetta Musicale* reported that Mascagni, thanks to "the audience's insistent applause and the wishes of his valiant interpreters, presented himself, albeit reluctantly, before the curtain [. . .] and thus, together with the singers and Maestro Toscanini, was called out twice after the first act, three times after the second, and twice after the third." *Iris* received ten performances, which, for Toscanini, helped to mitigate the *Norma* disaster. And he developed a fondness for *Iris*, which he would conduct in several other venues.

As with *Meistersinger*, so with *Les Huguenots*, the season's third production: the Milanese critics took Toscanini to task for presenting Meyerbeer's old (1836) opera uncut, and in this case they also described the first performance as shaky. In subsequent performances, Toscanini cut the fifth act—a common practice at the time—and by the second performance the shakiness was gone. In its shorter form *Huguenots* became a hit with local audiences and had to be performed fourteen times. But the negative opening-night reviews gave a dangerous enemy a chance to open fire on Toscanini.

Giulio Ricordi had mixed feelings about La Scala's new musical boss. He recognized Toscanini's talent and reliability, but he did not appreciate the independence and determination of a conductor who was younger than his own son. The Ricordi company, at that time one of the world's largest and wealthiest music publishing firms, had already existed for nearly a century, and "Signor Giulio," as he was known, had inherited power from his father and grandfather. A strong-willed man with a Mephistophelian beard and a sardonic sense of humor, he was accustomed to being listened to and obeyed by everyone in the business, and he wanted to exercise a decisive influence in the operations of Italy's greatest lyric theater. Toscanini wished to bring Wagner, whose works Signor Giulio published but did not like, and the new European avant-garde into the repertoire; he would insist on presenting operas as musically, dramatically, and poetically viable works of art; and he would either make La Scala into a modern lyric theater, not merely a showcase for vocal display, or go down fighting.

Ricordi was not opposed to all of Toscanini's principles. Two years earlier, for instance, he had protested, in his *Gazzetta Musicale di Milano*, against excesses of vocal exhibitionism. Referring to a performance by Fernando De Lucia, Ricordi wrote, "Is it permitted to reduce many of *La Bohème*'s melodies and many of its notes to interminable adagios, to eternal fermatas? [. . .] These are big and small warts that disfigure the performance! [. . .] Should we not perhaps create a special *artistic police* force to watch over performances in order that they not deface works of art?" These were sentiments that Ricordi entirely shared with Toscanini—and with Verdi, Puccini, and most other composers.

Another, deeper problem existed, however. Ricordi occasionally turned his hand to composition, using the nom de plume Jules Burgmein, and the previous year he had composed an orchestral piece, *Pulcinella Innamorato* (Pulcinella in Love), which he had sent to Toscanini along with an ingratiating letter: "I am turning now not only to the true Maestro, but also to my friend, begging him to be so kind as to examine said work, and to tell me with complete frankness, without paying compliments, whether you think it possibly worthy of being conducted by you." But the request for "complete frankness" was followed by a not very subtly veiled threat: "There are great hopes for La Scala, and it seems that the City Council will meet soon to decide: I will keep you informed." In other words, if Toscanini, in his presumed aspiration to become La Scala's music director, wished to have Ricordi's support, he had better perform the piece by "Burgmein."

Before he even looked at the score, Toscanini had rashly decided to insert *Pulcinella Innamorato* into one of the Turin exposition concerts in October, much to Ricordi's delight. But once Toscanini had had a chance to study the score thoroughly, he removed it from the program. The official explanation, quoted in *La Stampa*, was that there was not sufficient rehearsal time for a new piece—"especially one in four movements like Burgmein's Suite"—but Ricordi wasn't fooled. The incident had grave consequences for Toscanini's early career at La Scala, and the fact that the Ricordi company's correspondence copybooks contain no further direct communications from Signor Giulio to Toscanini for the following thirteen years is no coincidence.

As Verdi's publisher, Ricordi had the ear of the aged composer; he hoped to undermine Toscanini's tenure at La Scala by turning Verdi against him, and the negative newspaper critiques of the first performance of *Les Huguenots* gave Ricordi his chance. He sent them to Verdi, who replied on 11 February 1899, "It is a result that allows one to foresee a considerable crescendo. I was surprised, however, by the comments made about the chorus, and even more by those regarding the orchestra! What the devil! You can't believe in anything anymore; but it's good to see clearly how things stand."

Ricordi evidently decided not to share with Verdi a quite different report, which appeared in his company's own magazine, on the second performance of *Huguenots*; it described "a more balanced and homogeneous performance" and said that the success was "splendid and at many points truly enthusiastic [. . .]. The orchestra was worthy of praise under the diligent direction of Maestro Toscanini."

Falstaff, the following production, was scheduled to open on 11 March, and well beforehand Ricordi tried to enlist Verdi in his anti-Toscanini campaign. On 27 February, a puzzled Verdi responded to what must have been an attack on Toscanini by Signor Giulio: "If Toscanini is not capable, the others are even less so," the composer wrote. "Soon comes the *Falstaff* revival. Everything is against it. Falstaff [Scotti] will be good (maybe!) but not Alice [Pandolfini]. [. . .] And take note that the protagonist of *Falstaff* is not Falstaff but Alice. What am I going around saying? Waste of time! Forget that I said it and *addio*."

Immediately after the opening performance, Boito wired Verdi an enthusiastic report; Verdi responded to Boito the next day: "I congratulate the valiant performers." And to Toscanini, the composer wired, simply, "Grazie Grazie Grazie"—a telegram that Toscanini carried with him as a talisman for the rest of his life. The production was performed ten times, and at least on the first night Scotti had to encore Falstaff's brief *arietta* "Quand'ero paggio" twice. Although most of the critics admired the performance, Ricordi declared that it had been too rigid: "the orchestra, very precise, did not have those delicate nuances, that gentleness of tone, that elasticity of movement that are all essential characteristics of Italian orchestras. [. . .] We see a serious danger for Italian art."

Verdi wrote to Ricordi on 18 March, "If things are as you say, it is better to return to the modest conductors of earlier times [. . .]. When I began scandalizing the musical world with my sins, there was the calamity of the 'rondos' of the prima donnas; today there is the tyranny of the conductors! Bad, bad! But the first is less bad!!" Verdi had not seen an article in the *Gazzetta Teatrale Italiana*, a rival of Ricordi's magazine, which stated, "One could almost say, reading between the lines of certain reviews, that a crusade is underway against Toscanini, who is under contract for three years at La Scala." Alfredo Colombani, writing in the *Corriere della Sera*, echoed some of Ricordi's criticisms but added that the performance was approved "by the person who could express the composer's intentions better than anyone else"—Boito.

Verdi was by then too detached from the day-to-day life of the theater to wish to observe, firsthand, Toscanini's struggle to implement reforms at La Scala, including many changes for which the composer himself had fought, largely unsuccessfully. Thirty years earlier, he had written to the same Giulio Ricordi, "So you see how important the Conductor is. In Parma, with four singers who were much liked, with the best orchestra members, with the finest scene painter in Italy, *Don Carlos* was only moderately successful [. . .] and it was above all and solely the fault of the conductor's spineless soul. Just about the same was true in Florence. In the end, I have only one answer to all the questions you pose: 'Find a man who knows how to mount and conduct an opera!'" And in another letter to Ricordi, regarding the premiere of *Otello*, Verdi had said, "Afterwards I regretted, and I still regret, not having been more severe and exacting in principle." Toscanini knew about Verdi's regrets, and he had long since decided that he would be as severe and exacting as necessary.

5.

MASSENET'S *LE ROI DE LAHORE*, ORIGINALLY SCHEDULED TO END the Scala season, was received apathetically and closed after only three performances. But something more was owed to the subscribers who had paid in advance to hear the canceled *Norma* production, and Toscanini and Gatti-Casazza engaged the celebrated tenor Francesco Tamagno to sing three performances of Rossini's rarely performed *William Tell*.

"Everyone was saying that I didn't conduct *Norma* because I didn't know how to conduct older music," Toscanini recalled. Before the first performance, "Tamagno became ill. There was a newspaper [*Lombardia*] that had it in for me—one Carugati. He started to publish [articles saying,] 'We knew that *William Tell* wouldn't open either,' because they said that I had argued with Tamagno about cuts and so on and so forth. And this pig [Carugati] got Tamagno to receive him. Upon entering he looked at him and said, 'Ha ha ha ha—you're no more ill than I am.' And [Tamagno] said: 'What do you think—that I would be stupid enough to lose 7,000 lire per performance if I weren't sick? I want to sing, and I will sing.'"

The first performance was postponed by two days. On the morning of the third day, Gatti-Casazza visited Tamagno and found him "sitting on his bed, his face in gloom," unsure whether he could perform that evening. Gatti told Tamagno that rumors were circulating to the effect that he was afraid of the role. "Tamagno uttered a roar such as to cause the room to resound. 'Me? Afraid!' Then changing his tone, 'But don't you hear it? The voice is clear! The nose is free! [. . .] I'll show these asses what I can do!'" The production opened that evening, and, Toscanini recalled, "The first night—an opera that hadn't been done at La Scala in years, precisely because of its difficulties—the success was such that even the third act, where there's no tenor, [. . .] was applauded as if Tamagno had been there. [. . .] [Boito] was *stunned* by the trio, with Tamagno, with that voice."

The critic of *L'Illustrazione Italiana* spoke for most of his colleagues in expressing great enthusiasm for the *Tell* production. "The public harked back with joy to a time of glorious memories for Milan's greatest theater, hoping that next year will begin at the point at which this year is leaving off." And so Toscanini's variable first season at La Scala ended well.

The series of five mixed-repertoire concerts that followed began with the Milanese premiere of the same three of Verdi's Four Sacred Pieces that Toscanini had conducted in Turin a year earlier. Verdi had initially opposed the idea, "first of all because I don't believe that [the pieces] will produce an effect there [. . .]; secondly because my name is too old and boring! Even I'm bored when I have to name myself. Add to this the critics' observations! It's true that I don't have to read them . . . ." But Verdi gave in, and Boito wrote to him, "The performance in the hands of Toscanini and Venturi, who learned the interpretation from you and who made such a striking impression in Turin, could only be outstanding, *and was outstanding.*"

6.

WHEN TOSCANINI HAD SUGGESTED OPENING HIS FIRST SCALA SEASON with *Die Meistersinger,* some members of the board of directors asked him whether he had ever heard the opera performed; they would not believe that he could interpret such a difficult work without having attended a performance of it. He lied and said that he had heard it in South America. Now, during the summer of 1899, many months *after* his own successful *Meistersinger* performances, Toscanini, accompanied by Gatti-Casazza, traveled to Bayreuth, where he heard Hans Richter, a Wagner disciple, conduct the opera, and he noticed that at one point Richter made a sudden *ritardando* on the last quarter beat of a bar, whereas he himself had made a gradual one. He later checked the score and was mortified to see that he had overlooked the detail in question and that Richter was right. Toscanini was impressed with the Bayreuth orchestra's playing of *Meistersinger,* "but I could only deplore the complete lack of good ensemble among orchestra, chorus, and singers," he wrote to Sormani, his assistant at La Scala. He described the singers as "dogs" and the performances in general as "a real hoax for people like me who are hoping to hear perfection."* The following

---

* After Richter had conducted the *Ring* at the first Bayreuth Festival, in 1876, Wagner commented that not one of the tempi was correct.

day he sent another message to Sormani: "Despite a deficient perfor-mance"—conducted by Franz Fischer—"*Parsifal* impressed me, espe-cially the 1st and 3rd acts. It is astoundingly sensational. Tomorrow I'll hear the 2nd performance too and then I'll leave for the moun-tains." He also heard the *Ring* conducted by Wagner's son, Siegfried, who by most accounts, was no baton virtuoso, but Toscanini's opin-ion on this subject has not been discovered. To Polo, he sent a picture postcard of Wagner's grave, and wrote on it, "Here is the tomb of the greatest musician of the century!"

Toscanini's biographers—this one included—have long assumed that 1899 was the year of his first visit to Bayreuth, because it is the first one that has been documented, and the tone of his messages in the previous paragraph seems to confirm this notion. But in conver-sations recorded toward the end of his life, Toscanini described, admiringly, the highly flexible *Parsifal* interpretation of Hermann Levi, who had conducted the work's premiere under Wagner's super-vision, and he chuckled gleefully over the fact that the rabidly anti-Semitic Wagner had had to turn to a Jew to conduct his most Christian opera: "those Jews have more talent than the Germans," he told the conductor Wilfrid Pelletier. He added that in Munich he had heard *Il Trovatore* conducted well by Levi, whom he character-ized as "a born conductor" and one of the few German-school con-ductors capable of performing Italian opera with proper sensitivity. In one conversation, Toscanini even sang a few phrases from *Parsifal* as Levi had conducted them, and he described the *Parsifal* interpreta-tions by other early Wagnerites as inferior to that of Levi. "I heard *Parsifal* by [Karl] Muck, and I heard it by [Felix] Mottl, and I heard it by [Franz] Fischer, but not as Levi did it, no. He had the elasticity." As a result of copyright law, until 1914 *Parsifal* could not be performed outside Bayreuth, where Levi conducted it for the last time in 1894 and Mottl in 1897; and by 1914 both Levi and Mottl were dead. Thus Toscanini had to have visited Bayreuth for the first time not later than 1894 and for the second time not later than 1897. He also called Anton Seidl a fine conductor, and the only place he would likely have observed him was Bayreuth, in 1897. In a 1937 letter to a friend, Tosca-nini mentioned having made his first trip to Germany in 1895—"the year of my first disappointment in those *German know-it-alls*"—but he could have been off by one year.

After his return from the 1899 Bayreuth Festival, Toscanini spent part of the summer at Groscavallo, in the Piedmontese Alps, where he was able to rest, study, and spend time with Carla, who was pregnant again, and with their young son, Walter. He had chosen to open his second Scala season with the first-ever Italian production of Wagner's massive *Siegfried*, third of the four *Ring* operas. And he had decided to mount two productions simultaneously, so that only one night after *Siegfried* opened, a new production of *Otello* would have its first performance. "This procedure [. . .] represented in those days a significant departure and a difficult one" for an Italian theater, Gatti recalled more than thirty years later.

"The two dress rehearsals went well," Carla wrote to her sister a few hours before the opening-night performance, and she added that Toscanini had been happy with them. He feared that there would be "conflict and many arguments" over the Wagner opera, but he hoped that the audience and critics would give it a fair hearing. Yet despite complaints about the opera's length, the production was a success and received twelve performances. Giuseppe Borgatti, who was becoming the most important Italian Wagner tenor of his generation, was much admired in the title role, and even the critics who did not like the work praised Toscanini's performance. An Italian correspondent for the *New York Times* reported that this premiere was "a complete victory" and that "the death-blow seems to have been struck at last against the opponents of the Wagnerian 'musik-drama' [*sic*] in this country."

Otello brought Toscanini headaches of a different nature. Tamagno was to sing the title role—opposite the soprano Emma Carelli and baritone Delfino Menotti—for the first time at La Scala since his triumph in the premiere production in 1887, but at other theaters during the intervening years he had begun adding ornamentation, singing soft passages too loudly, and insisting on transpositions. The love duet in the first act, for instance, he wanted Toscanini to transpose upward, and he claimed that Verdi had allowed this at the premiere. "I've always sung it a semitone higher," Tamagno insisted.

"And I'm telling you that you didn't," said Toscanini, who had been playing in the orchestra at the premiere, and who became even more upset when, during a rehearsal of the opera's final scene, at Otello's heartrending "Ah! morta! morta! morta!" on a descending series of seven notes, Tamagno took the second and third *morta*!s higher than the first one.

In despair, Toscanini asked to be received by Verdi, who was spending the winter in a suite at the Grand Hôtel et de Milan in Via Manzoni, a few blocks from La Scala. The composer assented; Toscanini recalled, "Verdi said, 'I did my best to set down the notes, the best ones I could, and he's no longer singing them?'"

"'No, he's no longer singing them, Maestro. He says that he always sang them this way. He no longer sings, he shouts! Send for him, Maestro, because I just don't know.'" Tamagno was staying at the same hotel; Verdi asked him, "'Did you sing it as it's written?' And [Tamagno] said, 'Conductors and composers never know what they want.'" Toscanini chuckled in remembering the scene. Caught between Verdi and Toscanini, Tamagno agreed to try to sing properly.

At the dress rehearsal, Boito "was so enthusiastic that he embraced [Toscanini]," Carla reported to Ida. Nevertheless, two days before the first performance, Toscanini "went to Verdi and played for him all of the tempi in Otello for fear that the Ricordi company would have something to criticize," Carla wrote the next day. "He was happy with how Verdi received him"—which means that Verdi either agreed with all of Toscanini's tempi or corrected those with which he did not agree.

In the end, all of the reviewers praised the overall performance and Toscanini's part in it, and they approved of the new sets and costumes, which were replacing those that had been created for the 1887 premiere and used in two subsequent Scala revivals. But several of them criticized Tamagno, who was again being paid 7,000 lire for each of the seven performances. "Why does he decorate his best phrases with those added high notes, with those outbursts that very much resemble terribly disgusting shouts?" asked Enrico Carozzi in the *Gazzetta Teatrale Italiana*. "I was assured last evening that at the rehearsals Maestro Toscanini pointed out to the great singer the futility of these outbursts. Why, then, did he insist on them?"

In later years, Toscanini commented that much of the role of Otello lay too low to be comfortable for Tamagno, and he recalled that although the tenor was only forty-nine years old at the time, he no longer had sufficient breath control: he "was breathing every moment" and even had to split up the phrase "Ora e per sempre addio sante memorie": "Ora e per sempre / addio / sante memorie." Nor did the audience give Tamagno the same sort of adoring reception that had overwhelmed him in *William Tell*. After the first performance, he summoned Toscanini and Gatti-Casazza to his dressing room and offered to withdraw from his contract, but they persuaded him to finish the series.

While Toscanini was in the midst of conducting *Siegfried* and *Otello* on alternate evenings, he was spending his days preparing a new production of *Lohengrin*, the only Wagner opera that was performed frequently in Italy in those years, although with massive cuts. Toscanini restored the work nearly to its original length. The rehearsals were fraught, and Tullio Serafin—at that time assistant principal violist in the Scala orchestra, later a famous opera conductor in his own right—described an incident at one ensemble rehearsal: "We had begun at 8 [P.M.], and at 1:30 A.M. we were at the beginning of the last act's [third] scene." The bass, Oreste Luppi, had just performed King Heinrich's line "Be thanked, dear subjects from Brabant," when "Toscanini's voice thundered: 'King of clubs! From the beginning, the whole act,'" Serafin recalled. "A tremor of revolt passed through the orchestra. But no one breathed a word."

Although Serafin described Toscanini as "unequalled, as man and artist," he added that he was "at times hard to put up with, especially in those years."

Toscanini's methods were really harsh, and they provoked endless grumblings and protests among my colleagues—under their breath, of course. But it didn't take me long to realize that he was right. Discipline in orchestras, even in La Scala's orchestra, was very slack in those years, although there were quite a few excellent musicians. But they didn't apply themselves. They didn't work at playing rhythmic figurations precisely and they almost completely neglected to observe dynamic indications, so that the results, with respect to interpretation, were often left to chance. And only rarely did it happen that the orchestra

struggled to obtain what Wagner, in his essay on the art of conducting, indicates as the most difficult thing: sustaining the
sound at length with equal intensity.

Against this [. . .] slackness, laziness, carelessness, and false
tradition, Toscanini fought like a lion. He wanted one thing
only: respect for art. But in his eagerness to achieve it, or rather
to impose it, he didn't control himself: he shouted, imprecated,
even insulted. [. . .] What he accomplished for musical interpretation and the good that he did for the art of performing was of
such great significance that even the excesses of his nature can
be understood. Understood, I say; not justified.

The most significant part of Serafin's statement concerns the long-
term psychological effect of Toscanini's tornado-like approach: "From
that time on, a special pride, a point of honor, something like an 'esprit
de corps' existed among La Scala's personnel," Serafin said. "Even the
least important stagehand or the most humble supernumerary felt
responsible for the success of the production." This effect would repeat
itself nearly everywhere Toscanini went for the rest of his career.

During an orchestra rehearsal of *Lohengrin*, on 16 January 1900,
someone rushed in with the news that Signora Toscanini had just
given birth to a girl. The musicians congratulated their maestro; he
tried to resume the rehearsal but, unable to concentrate, dismissed the
orchestra and ran home to see his daughter, who was so pretty that he
told Carla she must have sculpted the baby's face with her hands. They
named her Wally, after the heroine of Catalani's last opera.

7.

TWO NOVELTIES FOLLOWED *LOHENGRIN*: FIRST, THE WORLD PRE-
miere of *Anton* by Cesare Galeotti, a young composer who had studied in Paris with César Franck, and whose work was well received in
the short run but failed in the long run; and then, on 17 March, the
Milan premiere of *Tosca*, Puccini's brilliant story of passion, repres-
sion, corruption, and the struggle for freedom in Rome during the
Napoleonic Wars. Puccini had originally wanted Toscanini to conduct the opera's world premiere ("you must be the one to deflower

her," the composer had written to the conductor in 1898), and at about that time the two men had both been at a dinner at Giulio Ricordi's home, during which Puccini had first played the motifs that accompany the initial entrances of the sacristan and Cavaradossi. The composer had then declared that he was going to write a substantial prelude to the third act—a musical depiction of the Roman countryside—and a mad scene for Tosca when she discovers that Cavaradossi has really been killed. When the finished third act was turned in, with a subdued introduction and no mad scene, Ricordi wrote to Puccini that it was pallid, that it ruined the opera and would ruin the Ricordi company, which had invested heavily in its star composer's latest work. Toscanini, who visited Puccini at Torre del Lago on 11 October 1899—the day the composer received his publisher's letter—recalled that Puccini was so upset that he was tempted to call off the opera's premiere. Either during that visit or, more likely, at an earlier date, Puccini and Toscanini played through the opening of the last act—Puccini at the harmonium, Toscanini at the piano; Toscanini improvised a part for bells; Puccini liked it and incorporated it into the score.

Nevertheless, the world premiere went to Mugnone in Rome—in part, no doubt, because the opera is set there. But by October 1899 Puccini and Toscanini had selected the cast for Milan: the Tosca (Darclée) and the Scarpia (Eugenio Giraldoni) were the same as in Rome, but the original Cavaradossi, Emilio De Marchi, was replaced by Borgatti. "The performance will be *superb*," Puccini wrote to a friend three days before the Scala opening. "Toscanini, the sets, the chorus, the atmosphere—outstanding; and the singers come off better in this blessed theater than in other theaters." The reception was lukewarm on the first night, but with successive performances the opera's popularity grew, and on 3 April Puccini wrote, "*Tosca* has conquered the general affections here, filling the theater every evening [. . .]. The performance has been excellent because of Toscanini and a few others, especially Giraldoni."

Surprisingly little attention was paid to the final production of the season—another novelty. Toscanini had first studied Tchaikovsky's *Eugene Onegin* in 1886, when he was coaching Nicolai Figner and Medea Mei; now, fourteen years later and twenty-one years after the work's world premiere, he was able to conduct the first Italian production of what would eventually become a repertoire favorite. But the Milanese critics had difficulty pigeonholing it: Was it more Italianate than French, or vice versa? Did old-fashioned elements or modern ones dominate? Was Wagner's influence great or small? Were the specifically Russian motifs too strong or too weak? Was the story worth the telling? (Few, if any, of the reviewers had read the Pushkin masterpiece on which the opera was based.) The opening-night audience liked Tatiana's letter scene, sung by Emma Carelli, but as for the rest, one observer noted, there was "no hostility but, at the same time, no enthusiasm." The production* had to be dismantled after only three performances, as opposed to twelve for *Tosca* and seven even for the unfortunate *Anton*. Yet at the last *Onegin* performance, which was also the season's finale, the maestro received tremendous ovations from the audience—"an apotheosis," according to one newspaper—and was presented with gifts from La Scala's grateful board of directors as well as from Gatti-Casazza and the musical assistants Sormani and Centanini. His position at the helm of the ensemble was now secure.

In April and May, Toscanini and the Scala orchestra gave four concerts at home and toured eight northern Italian cities. While the orchestra was away, the Berlin Philharmonic under Hans Richter gave a concert in Milan, and the critic for *L'Illustrazione Italiana* wrote that although "admiration for the German orchestra was great," it was "not accompanied by the bitterness that we used to suffer in the face of such performances. We, too, can approach this. [. . .] Arturo Toscanini is the real victor today."

Toscanini was becoming involved in Milanese musical life outside as well as inside La Scala. In 1899, he had been a member of the examining committee for graduating composition students at the conservatory; now, in 1900, he again participated in the examinations and then rehearsed and conducted a student orchestra, enlarged by a few professionals, in new works by the twenty-one-year-old Arrigo Pedrollo and twenty-five-year-old Italo Montemezzi.

---

* The *Onegin* production was Toscanini's only production anywhere of a Tchaikovsky opera. *Onegin's* all-important dances were choreographed by Achille Coppini (1846–1912), one of the last significant members of a family that had played a distinguished role in Italian ballet since the mid-eighteenth century. Toscanini would bring him back during the following season to choreograph the ballet sequences in several other operas.

In June, Toscanini made what must have been his first visit to London, to hear Felix Mottl conduct *Götterdämmerung* at Covent Garden. His reactions to what was the world's most populous and wealthiest city at the beginning of the twentieth century are not known, but he was disappointed by what he heard at Covent Garden. The orchestra, he wrote five years later, "was sight-reading the opera's final scene before an audience. The audience noticed nothing, and the press found the performance superb. Of course! An eminent maestro was conducting, and he was German to boot." This was probably the London visit during which Toscanini met Paolo Tosti and Luigi Denza, Italy's famous song composers, both extremely popular in England, where they lived. Toscanini loved the songs of Tosti, Denza, and Augusto Rotoli, and even in extreme old age he remembered the music and words of many of Tosti's songs, which were "refined even in the accompaniments," he said.

Later in the summer, Toscanini and his family once again spent some weeks at Groscavallo; he did some more mountain climbing, and he became a lifetime member of the Italian Alpinists Club.

At Milan's Teatro Lirico on 10 November 1900, a few weeks before rehearsals for the Scala season began, Toscanini conducted the successful world premiere and twelve subsequent performances of Leoncavallo's opera *Zazà*, which became popular in the pre–World War I period but is rarely heard today. The role of the protagonist—a music hall singer who abandons Milio, her lover, when she discovers that he is married—was created by the soprano Rosina Storchio, an exceptionally sensitive, communicative, and intelligent musician, capable of singing both *verismo* and bel canto roles. At twenty-eight, she was also charming and pretty. During one rehearsal Toscanini exclaimed, "*This* is an artist!"—a rare compliment from him—and a spark was quickly ignited. Unlike Zazà vis-à-vis Milio, Storchio knew from the start that Toscanini was married. But the theater is a volatile place.

8.

THE LONG-AWAITED MILAN PREMIERE OF *TRISTAN UND ISOLDE* WAS scheduled to open the 1900–01 Scala season—the last of the three seasons stipulated in Toscanini's initial contract–on the traditional opening date of 26 December. A revival of *La Bohème* would be launched the following night. First, however, he conducted the Scala orchestra in a program, given twice, at the Milan Conservatory, under the auspices of the city's prestigious Società del Quartetto, which had been founded in 1864 by Boito, Faccio, and Tito Ricordi to bring chamber and symphonic music into the mainstream of Italian musical life. These concerts included the five-year-old tone poem *Till Eulenspiegel*, Toscanini's first performances of any music by his near-contemporary Richard Strauss.

Early in the *Bohème* rehearsals, Toscanini began to worry about the young tenor who was to make his house debut in the production. The maestro had heard and liked him two years earlier at the world premiere of Giordano's *Fedora* at the Teatro Lirico, but the tenor, who had already performed *Bohème* elsewhere, was now singing the high C in "Che gelida manina" in falsetto, which made Toscanini worry that the young fellow didn't have a reliable full-voice high C. He tried transposing the piece down a semitone, but the tenor then sang the B in falsetto.

The *Tristan* dress rehearsal took place on 23 or 24 December, and Toscanini probably planned to run the *Bohème* dress rehearsal on the evening of the twenty-fifth. Worried as he was about the new tenor, he called a brief extra rehearsal, probably on the afternoon of the twenty-fourth. Many details went wrong, and the "brief" session grew longer. Toscanini persuaded the tenor—a plump, mustachioed, nearly twenty-seven-year-old Neapolitan named Enrico Caruso—to sing all of "Che gelida manina," including the high C, full voice. "When I gave it without any vocal restraint Toscanini (and everybody else also) appeared relieved," Caruso recalled. By the end of the session, the entire opera had been rehearsed, although not sequentially. Just as the rehearsal was ending, Toscanini learned that Giuseppe Borgatti, who was to sing the role of Tristan two days later, was ill and that the season would have to open with *Bohème* instead of *Tristan*; thus there was no alternative but to tell the *Bohème* cast and orchestra to come back to the theater a few hours later: the *Bohème* dress rehearsal would have to take place that evening in order to leave forty-eight hours between the final rehearsal and the first performance.

La Scala's dress rehearsals were generally attended by an invited audience that included not only privileged patrons and important musicians but also those music critics who wished to have a foretaste of the performance, especially if the work in question was new or rare. By December 1900 *La Bohème* was well-known; most of the people who attended the dress rehearsal came mainly out of curiosity to hear Caruso. But the tenor, exhausted from the afternoon's rehearsal, did not sing out. Toscanini, exasperated with him, suspended the rehearsal, and only after Duke Guido had persuaded Caruso to sing full voice did the rehearsal resume; it did not end until one in the morning. Caruso developed a fever and did not want to sing the first performance, but Gatti-Casazza talked him into taking advantage of the much-desired opportunity to open the Scala season.

The results were disastrous. The audience, already disappointed by the postponement of the *Tristan* premiere, was doubly disappointed with the ailing Caruso, and the critics treated him cruelly. "He didn't show what he could do," Toscanini recalled, and Emma Carelli, the Mimì, "was a mess in the last act, when she comes in and faints—she looked like a charcoal-burner—her whole face was black. The audience laughed." Puccini was too upset to stay to the end, and the next day he wrote to tell Toscanini that he was going to spend two or three days in the country, "to breathe better air. [. . .] Tell [Carelli] to try to act the character a little [. . .] and not to slow down her whole part so 'tiredly.' I can only thank you for all the care you've taken with my opera. So I hope that the second performance will be livelier in every way, and that Caruso will show what he can do."

Subsequent performances went much better, but in the meantime the unrelenting Giulio Ricordi took advantage of the situation to attack Toscanini yet again. He accused him of caring only about Wagner, not about "minor" Italian music, and of not having the right feeling for *La Bohème*—an odd remark, given his earlier enthusiasm for Toscanini's interpretation of the opera.

Borgatti recovered and *Tristan* opened on 29 December, with the twenty-four-year-old Amelia Pinto as Isolde. At the end of the first act, "the audience members did not wait for the curtain to fall before they broke into immense, impetuous applause," wrote *La Perseveranza*'s critic. "The performers were greeted twice with uproarious acclamations, which were repeated three more times with triumphal ovations when Toscanini appeared with them before the curtain. It has become rare for the Scala audience to accord such honors to a production." At the end, Toscanini "was called before the curtain over and over." Some critics found the opera too long and prolix, but there were no qualms about the performance. "Maestro Toscanini swept his musicians along with marvelous impetus and precision," according to *Il Sole*'s critic. "Throughout, it is a production that does great honor to our greatest theater."

The production interested the theater world not only for its musical value but also for its technical and visual innovations. As the *New York Times* reported, "Toscanini has arranged a plan for lighting by which all the light can be thrown from one side of the stage, and yet with sufficient brilliancy given to prevent too heavy shadows. The German managers all sent representatives to observe [the system's] workings." The technology had been devised by Mariano Fortuny, a brilliant twenty-nine-year-old Spanish painter, inventor, and designer, who had been recommended to Toscanini by Giuseppe Giacosa. Fortuny, who also designed the production's sets and costumes, explained, by way of example, that he had "decided to make the tree transparent—the tree at the base of which Tristan dies—in order to obtain with gradual lighting a more intense sunset effect."

According to the *Times*, Siegfried Wagner, Richard and Cosima's thirty-one-year-old son, "told Toscanini that the production excelled even those of Munich and Berlin." And indeed, Siegfried wrote to his family,

> I have nice things to report from Milan, since the Tristan performance was truly, movingly outstanding. Charming sets designed by the young Fortuni [*sic*], especially the first act. Borgatti indescribably wop-ish, a [mime-like?] Isotta [Italian for Isolde], who, with moving innocence, got all of her positions wrong in the first act.* Gratifying, on the whole—and finally, it was not entirely without value to see that the house, filled to overflowing—this was the seventh performance—listened very

---

* I have used the word "wop" or variants thereof to translate Siegfried's word *Honol* and *its* variants. They were private, derogatory, racist terms used, within the notoriously racist Wagner family, to denote Italians. Siegfried evidently believed that there was only one "correct" set of positions for the singers to take in their performances—the ones prescribed by his father.

quietly and shushed energetically whenever there was any chat-
tering in the galleries. The work grips with such elemental force
that even the most frivolous idiots shut their traps. [. . .] Toscanini [is] an excellent conductor. [. . .] Toscanini was very nice—
Dettelchen [Cosima's nickname], if you have a moment's peace
it would be very good of you to send him a line. It would be a
beautiful reward for his sincere efforts (the house was even kept
dark during the acts). The letter will of course find its way into
the newspapers, but in the end that doesn't matter. Coming
from you it would have special value. Toscanini and the other
Wops spoke very humorously and wittily about Mascagni and
his colleagues and said with pride that in Milan their operas
have never been successful; ma in Germania [but in Germany]!

The suggested letter was written immediately, in French, by
Richard Wagner's widow, chief defender of the Wagnerian faith.

Berlin, 18 January 1901

Monsieur,

My son has described to me the performance of *Tristan* that he
attended in Milan, and he has had so many good things to say
about it that I am taking upon myself the duty of expressing to
you the contentment that I feel in knowing that a work of such
great difficulty was performed with care on a foreign stage.

My son has stressed the meticulous zeal that you brought to
the orchestra preparations and the excellent results obtained
through that zeal, together with your ability as a conductor.
He has also told me that the singers were in perfect command
of their roles and delivered them with warmth and
enthusiasm.

Lastly, he has spoken to me with great pleasure about the
sets owing to Mr. Fortuny's talent. And—to crown it all—he
has praised the audience's rapt attention and perceptive
liveliness.

All these indications of your respect for and intuitive understanding of the incomparable work to which you have dedi-

cated yourself, Monsieur, with so much ardor, have made my son very happy to have been a witness, and from afar I join in his satisfaction.

Please be so kind, Monsieur, as to communicate my sentiments to all the interpreters of *Tristan und Isolde* and accept for yourself my congratulations and my sincerest regards.

C. Wagner

9.

IN ADDITION TO THE NEW LIGHTING SYSTEM, ANOTHER REFORM that Toscanini accomplished at the beginning of his third Scala season was the elimination of the traditional postopera ballet on nights when especially long operas were performed. Although he did not conduct the ballets, he knew, as a former orchestra member, that making musicians play to the point of exhaustion was cruel as well as detrimental to both the opera and the ballet. Eventually ballet performances were scheduled for separate evenings.

The witty comments at Mascagni's expense that Siegfried Wagner had reported were connected with the exaggerated publicity for *Le Maschere*, which was to receive its world premiere simultaneously in seven Italian cities on 17 January, three nights after the *Tristan* performance that Siegfried attended. Mascagni was present at several rehearsals of La Scala's production and described Toscanini as "an insuperable conductor and interpreter, and the singers"—who included Caruso and Carelli—"were worthy of this champion." But in Milan, as in most of the other six cities, *Le Maschere* was a disaster. Toscanini was "unable to save *Le Maschere*, but not even the Lord in his infinite power could have done so," commented D'Ormeville in the *Gazzetta dei Teatri*.

Soon after the premiere, Toscanini paid another visit to Verdi, who was once again staying at the Hôtel Milan. The eighty-seven-year-old composer had heard about *Le Maschere* and asked Toscanini how Mascagni had treated the role of Tartaglia, a stutterer. "He has him sing with a stutter, like this"—and Toscanini sang a phrase or two. Verdi observed that most stutterers do not stutter when they sing. When Toscanini told him that the best-liked number in the opera had been the pavane—the slow dance in the second act—Verdi asked feebly, "What is a pavane?" Then, getting a grip on himself, he said, "Oh yes, now I understand." Toscanini told Gatti-Casazza that the conversation had then begun to drag and that he had felt heart-sick when he said goodbye to Verdi.

That visit took place on 19 or 20 January 1901. On the twenty-second, Verdi suffered a cerebral hemorrhage, and as the composer lay dying, the mayor of Milan ordered workers to put straw down on the winter-fog-bound Via Manzoni and other streets near the hotel so that Verdi would not be disturbed by the noise of passing horse-drawn carriages and trams.

When Giuseppe Verdi died, on 27 January 1901, La Scala closed its doors in mourning, but on 1 February Toscanini conducted a memorial program of excerpts from seven Verdi operas, with ten soloists, including the impressive tenor lineup of Tamagno, Borgatti, and Caruso ("How well Caruso sang then!" Toscanini recalled half a century later); the sopranos Carelli, Pinto, and Laura Brambilla; the mezzo-soprano Edvige Ghibaudo; the baritones Alessandro Arcangeli and Antonio Magini-Coletti; and the bass Oreste Luppi. "An unforgettable evening!" wrote the *Corriere della Sera*'s chronicler. "The auditorium looked imposing and solemn. The ladies were all dressed in black; on the proscenium a gigantic plaster bust of the great Master had been placed [. . .]. A black veil covered the velvet of the great curtains that close off the stage: the chorus and the solo artists were sitting in long rows at the sides of the bust. [. . .] I had never seen an audience more overwhelmed with enthusiasm."

Verdi, who disliked pomp, had left instructions forbidding a public funeral, and his wishes were respected. But on 27 February, exactly one month after the composer's death, his coffin and that of his wife, Giuseppina Strepponi, who had died in 1897, were transferred from Milan's Cimitero Monumentale to the Rest Home for Musicians that he had founded and funded, and this event occasioned a tremendous public display of affection and gratitude by tens of thousands of Milanese and visitors from all over Italy and abroad. Boito, Puccini, Mascagni, Giordano, and many dignitaries were present. At exactly 1:00 P.M. a herald sounded a trumpet, and Tosca-nini—so cold that he could barely move his arms—signaled a choral-orchestral ensemble of no fewer than nine hundred members, arrayed on the great outdoor staircase of the cemetery's chapel, to perform the chorus "Va, pensiero," from *Nabucco*. "The sad, impressive notes spread harmonically over the vast, crowded space," the *Corriere della Sera* reported; "and 'the thoughts on golden wings' flew from everyone's mind to the coffin that was being exposed to the sun for the last time."

Toscanini later recalled that Verdi's death, like that of the poet Giosuè Carducci six years later, made him feel that a whole world had come to an end. For the rest of his life, he regarded the composer as a model of artistic rigor and moral uprightness.

10.

VERDI—THE LAST REMAINING HERO OF ITALY'S RISORGIMENTO, the man who for half a century had dominated the world of Italian opera—was dead, but La Scala's day-to-day operations had to proceed. A major opera house is a "grande boutique," as Verdi himself had described Paris's Opéra; its denizens are, jointly, a mechanism that, once set in motion, presses forward on its own momentum; its musical, scenic, and technical staffs are always thinking about the next performance, the next production. Verdi's last opera, *Falstaff*, was already eight years old at the time of its composer's death; in the meantime, dozens upon dozens of new operas by younger composers had been performed in Italy, and dozens more were ready to be heard. The mechanism ground on.

Mascagni's *Le Maschere* closed after only three performances, leaving the ensemble in a bind. Karl Goldmark's opera *The Queen of Sheba*, popular at the time, went on the boards in February, and Toscanini and the cast, led by Pinto and Borgatti, were highly praised. But what to do next?

One evening Gatti-Casazza, Sormani, and Toscanini met to discuss the matter. Gatti mentioned *L'Elisir d'Amore*; Toscanini said that he would love to put together a production of Donizetti's seventy-year-old comic opera, which had not been produced at La Scala in forty-four years, but that he did not have a suitable bass for the comic role of Dulcamara. When Sormani recommended the well-known *basso buffo* Federico Carbonetti, Toscanini hesitated: Carbonetti's voice was said to be ragged. But they all agreed to try. They engaged the Polish soprano Regina Pinkert to take the part of Adina, and they persuaded Caruso to learn the role of Nemorino.

Many of La Scala's habitués considered themselves too sophisticated for Donizetti's "simple" and "old-fashioned" musical style; Gatti received letters from disgruntled subscribers who told him that he was turning the house into a tawdry provincial theater and who predicted a disaster. But the scene painters went to work, Duke Guido procured an old-fashioned carriage to be used for Dulcamara's entrance, and Carbonetti arrived "in the heart of the winter without an overcoat and carrying a little canvas valise tied up with a piece of string," Gatti recalled. The singer's voice proved to be in worse shape than the valise, and Toscanini began to anticipate trouble.

"Many times I have seen Toscanini in ill humor, but never in humor so forbidding as the morning of the day fixed for the premiere of *L'Elisir*," Gatti said. The audience that evening was small and initially hostile. But when Caruso sang Nemorino's reply ("Chiedi al rio perché gemente") to Adina in their magnificent duet, cheers exploded. An encore of the entire duet was demanded, and Toscanini granted it. Carbonetti's comic acting ability was so strong that the listeners laughed with pleasure. And Caruso's delivery of the celebrated *romanza*, "Una furtiva lagrima," was "interrupted at every phrase by exclamations of admiration" and had to be repeated, Gatti remembered. The performance was a great success, and a radiant Toscanini exclaimed to Gatti, "By God! If this Neapolitan continues to sing like this, he'll make the whole world talk about him!" Half a century later, Toscanini recalled that he had urged Boito to come hear him, because, he said, Caruso's voice and Donizetti's melodies were practically one and the same.

The production was performed ten more times to satisfy public demand, and *Sera*'s music critic commented that Toscanini, "who is today considered by everyone the greatest interpreter of Wagner, is now about to add the reputation of best interpreter of Donizetti." No one could continue, in good conscience, to accuse Toscanini of having no interest in or feeling for the pre-Verdian Italian repertoire.[*]

---

[*] Regarding Toscanini vis-à-vis so-called bel canto traditions, see p. 153.

Besides Caruso, another twenty-seven-year-old singer of astonishing ability made his Scala debut during the 1900–01 season. The
Russian basso Feodor Chaliapin—an outsize man with an outsize
personality and proportionately gigantic appetites for women and
drink—sang the title role in a new production of Boito's *Mefistofele*,
with Caruso as Faust, Carelli as Margherita, and Pinto as Elena.
There had been opposition in some quarters to the hiring of a foreigner to sing an important Italian role, and Toscanini was worried.
In Chaliapin's autobiography, produced a quarter century later in
collaboration with the Russian writer Maxim Gorky, the basso
recalled that, at the first rehearsal, Toscanini "looked quite ferocious
to me. A man of few words, unsmiling, he corrected the singers
harshly, and spared nobody."

After the first rehearsal, Toscanini asked Gatti to suspend the second one, scheduled for later the same day. He explained that Chaliapin had not sung full voice. "But, Maestro, did you tell him to sing
out?" Gatti asked, as he related the story twenty years post facto.
Toscanini replied, "I was afraid to intimidate him, and, strange to
say, I found myself embarrassed. After all we have heard about him,
I was almost afraid finally to hear his voice." They agreed that the
following day they would ask the basso to sing out, and Chaliapin
himself recalled that at the following rehearsal, Toscanini asked him
whether he intended to sing the opera half voice.

> "No. Certainly not," I said, embarrassed. "Well," he replied,
> "I have not had the honor of going to Russia and hearing you
> there. Thus I don't know your voice. Please be good enough to
> sing as you intend to do at the performance."
>
> I saw that he was right, and I sang in full voice. Often he
> would interrupt the other singers, offering advice, but he never
> said a word to me. I didn't know how to take this, and it left me
> with a feeling of uncertainty.
>
> Again the next day there was a rehearsal [. . .] [which] began
> with the Prologue. I gave it full voice, and when I had finished
> Toscanini paused for a moment, his hands lying on the piano
> keys, inclined his head a little, and uttered one single word in a
> very hoarse voice.
>
> "Bravo."

> It was quite unexpected, and had the effect of a pistol shot.
> [. . .] Elated by this success, I sang with tremendous enthusiasm,
> but Toscanini never uttered another word. [. . .]

Gatti heaved a sigh of relief and "mentally thanked all the saints of the Church, orthodox and unorthodox."

Chaliapin was born in the Russian provinces, but he had been befriended early on by such sophisticated musicians as Sergei Rachmaninoff—his exact contemporary—and had observed the work of Konstantin Stanislavsky and Vladimir Nemirovich-Danchenko, pioneers of naturalistic stage action. Early twentieth-century Italian notions of proper acting seemed to him old-fashioned.

> Toscanini [. . .] would come and watch me, order me to stand this way, that way, the other, sit like this, like that, walk that way, not this way. He would wind one of my legs round the other corkscrew-fashion, or make me fold my arms à la Napoleon. In fact what I was being instructed in was the technique of provincial tragedians, something with which I was already too well acquainted. If I asked him why he found this or that pose necessary, he replied with the utmost confidence: "Because this is a truly diabolic pose."

Chaliapin persuaded Toscanini to let him try to embody the role his own way, wearing a costume that made him look nearly nude and using relatively natural gestures. "The result was surprising," the basso recalled. "For the first time [Toscanini] smiled, a child-like open smile, slapped me on the shoulder, and then croaked: 'Let's not talk about it anymore.'" The results were magnificent: eleven performances had to be given, and Boito wrote to thank Chaliapin for the outstanding interpretation of his opera.

TAMAGNO HAD MADE HIS PARTICIPATION in *Otello* during the 1899–1900 season contingent on a promise from Gatti-Casazza to produce the French opera *Messaline* by the English composer Isidore De Lara during the following season. De Lara, *né* Cohen, was reputed to be the lover of Princess Alice of Monaco, and the opera's premiere had taken place at Monte Carlo in 1899, with Tamagno in the role of the Gladiator. In Milan, the celebrated tenor was to sing opposite the equally celebrated French soprano Emma Calvé, who had made a disastrous debut at La Scala fourteen years earlier and had not returned since.

According to De Lara, the odds were against him from the start. Boito had promised to finish his long-awaited second opera, *Nerone*, in time for La Scala's 1901–02 season, and Gatti-Casazza and the board of directors wanted to avoid staging two "ancient Roman" operas in as many years. They tried to persuade De Lara to move his opera's Italian premiere to Rome, but he refused. Calvé arrived and sang her part for Toscanini, accompanied by the composer, who told Toscanini that he was satisfied with Calvé's interpretation. The pretty soprano invited Toscanini to her hotel room to rehearse; Toscanini replied that rehearsals were held in the theater. Evidently offended, the diva left town the same day, after having sent a note to De Lara: "I have had an awful dream. Verdi's ghost appeared to me last night and told me that if I remained in Milan I should die." She was replaced by Renée Vidal, who had sung the role before but who was so frightened by the increasingly hostile audience on *Messaline's* turbulent opening night that she sang badly and contributed to what turned into a fiasco. There was no second performance. Still, De Lara recalled, "Toscanini conducted my score, which he knew by heart, magnificently; I have never heard a finer performance."

The Scala season ended with two more acclaimed performances of *Mefistofele*, and the theater's board presented Toscanini with a laurel wreath to mark the completion of his first triennial period with the ensemble; it was accompanied by a parchment document, the text of which had been written by Boito: "To Arturo Toscanini, Great Master of Art, who, thanks to his high-mindedness and the tenacity of his faith, knowledge, and love, triumphed—not without struggle—in guiding the new destinies of the Teatro alla Scala."

11.

NOTWITHSTANDING THE VINDICATION THAT HE MUST HAVE FELT at receiving expressions of praise and gratitude for his work at La Scala, Toscanini had practical considerations to face. Carla was pregnant again—a third child, Giorgio, would be born in September 1901—and her husband was still supporting his parents and probably also helping other family members. La Scala continued to pay him only 12,000 lire per season, whereas some of the company's singers earned that much in two weeks. At the invitation of the Italo-Argentine impresarios Attilio Bonetti and Achille Nardi, Toscanini agreed to take charge of the Teatro de la Ópera in Buenos Aires (the great Teatro Colón had not yet been built) for three months, at a total fee equal to 30,000 Italian lire.* Thus Toscanini became, intermittently, one of the many European opera performers who "never saw summer": as soon as their winter seasons at home had ended, they would travel to South America and take part in well-paid winter seasons on the other side of the equator.

Late in April 1901 Toscanini boarded the steamship *Orione* in Genoa and crossed the Atlantic for the first time since his life-altering trip to Brazil fifteen years earlier. This time, however, he was accompanied by a pregnant wife, two small children, two assistant conductors, and several Scala orchestra and chorus members who, like himself, could earn much more abroad than at home. Some of the principal singers, including Caruso, Darclée, Cucini, the Sicilian baritone Mario Sammarco, and the Spanish bass Andrés de Segurola, were also on board, and many sets that the Argentines had rented from La Scala were stowed in the ship's hold.

Segurola, who was meeting Toscanini for the first time, described him as a friendly and amusing shipboard companion, but noted that even when the young conductor was telling a funny story, his interlocutors experienced "the direct, strange, fascinating expression in the Maestro's eyes. Eyes that penetrated your soul and from which you could not turn." When the ship stopped in Barcelona, Segurola invited Toscanini and his wife to lunch and gave them a brief guided tour of the city, where Toscanini had worked a decade earlier but which Carla had never seen.

There were more than half a million Italian immigrants in Argentina by 1901, with more arriving every month, as were considerable

---

* In Argentina, Toscanini was paid in British gold coins. Walter Toscanini recalled that as a child he had seen bags of these coins at home; they bore the image of Queen Victoria, young and old, as well as that of King Edward VII, who ascended the throne in January 1901.

numbers of Germans, Austrians, and Central and Eastern European Jews. All were hoping to make their fortune in this southerly part of the New World, which was poised to equal or surpass the United States in wealth and opportunity, and many of them lived in Buenos Aires, where the appetite for European music was substantial and growing. "Today the great Nardi and Bonetti opera company will disembark," the Italian-language newspaper *La Patria degli Italiani* announced on Friday, 10 May, "and next Thursday the season at the Opera will begin with *Tosca* [. . .] conducted by the company's Divo, Maestro Arturo Toscanini, preceded by such curiosity among us as has never happened for any other conductor."

Within a few hours of the troupe's arrival in the capital, where the Toscaninis and several of the singers were lodged at the Hotel Americano, the workaholic maestro had begun rehearsing. "Preparations for the opening of the season are in full swing," the same newspaper stated four days later, and the report continued,

> Arturo Toscanini has already dominated the seventy-five-member orchestra, of whom twenty-four come from his regular Milan orchestra. [. . .] The local musicians were terrified by the reputation for severity that preceded the maestro. They believed in good faith that he would eat one instrumentalist in the morning and another in the evening. Instead, they found themselves under the baton of a very great artist, exigent, it is true, to an extreme degree, but polite, never [demanding] beyond human powers, always helping those in error by explaining and teaching.

On opening night, Toscanini had to take bows after each act of *Tosca*. *Tannhäuser* was the next opera, and Segurola recalled the "nervous excitement" with which he had anticipated his first piano rehearsal with Toscanini as well as the "inexpressible sensation" of the first ensemble rehearsal with orchestra: "I had sung *Tannhäuser* before in Lisbon under the baton of a celebrated conductor, but the Maestro's interpretation was a revelation." The critics agreed. "Maestro Arturo Toscanini, who perhaps is not accustomed to the habits of Buenos Aires's high society, which leaves the Opera's auditorium deserted until 9:30 or 10 o'clock, may not have been aware of the homage that the entire aristocracy paid him by being in its place—beginning with His Excellency the President of the Republic [General Julio Argentino Roca]—from the start of Wagner's very famous overture," one critic wrote.

On 25 May, Argentina's national holiday, Toscanini conducted a gala performance of *Tosca*. President Roca, the diplomatic corps, and the cream of local society filled the theater's boxes and parterre, which were festooned with roses and orchids. *Samson et Dalila* opened one night later and was followed by Goldmark's *The Queen of Sheba*. Before the first performance (4 June) of *Aida*, some of the critics complained about having to hear a thirty-year-old opera instead of more recent and challenging repertoire, but the following day *La Patria degli Italiani* declared that Toscanini "offers us performances that give new life to the most exploited operas" and that enable listeners "to procure the greatest enjoyment in the best-known pieces, toward which one no longer hoped to feel any attraction." Similar enthusiasm greeted *Rigoletto*, which was celebrating its fiftieth anniversary that year. In both Verdi operas, as indeed in virtually all of the season's productions, Toscanini conceded many encores; perhaps he felt that away from the "temple"—La Scala—he would rather not do battle with audiences. At the second performance of *Rigoletto*, Caruso sang "La donna è mobile" three times, "each time with different, extremely difficult cadenzas," one critic noted. Another performance of *Rigoletto*, on 26 June, was a gala event to mark the eightieth birthday of General Bartolomé Mitre, a former Argentine president, one of the central figures in the nation's history, as well as a historian, journalist, and translator of Dante into Spanish. Mitre appeared to be more enthusiastic about the beautiful Darclée, whom he observed through a spyglass, than about Verdi's opera.

The astonishment over Toscanini's prowess was such, Segurola said, that local "conductors, composers, and musicians flocked to witness ensemble rehearsals," to such an extent that Toscanini had to ask the management to keep people away. But *Patria*'s music critic was allowed to follow him around for a whole day during rehearsals for the Argentine premiere of Franchetti's *Asrael*—which was also Toscanini's first production of the opera—and the resulting article provides the most complete description extant of a typical working day for the young Toscanini.

Anyone who sees Maestro Arturo Toscanini on the street but doesn't know him will take him for a young student on his way to the University. He walks with short, hurried steps, in a straight line, at a vigorous pace. He wears a concert coat of indefinable color and a soft, broad-brimmed hat, and he proceeds without looking at anyone, simply because he [. . .] sees only in the theater—and how!

At 8:30 in the morning he enters the opera house. No one is there except the stage crew, the prop men, and the scene painter, with whom he has an appointment to go over the sets of *Asrael*. The [set] for the first scene—an infernal cave—has been set up. Toscanini goes into the main-floor seats, observes, corrects, and counsels: "Asrael has to go up those stairs. You have to glimpse a little patch of sky up high, through a small opening. Make the sky!"

He goes on to the change of scene from hell to Paradise. The change has to take place noiselessly before our eyes, but the canvases create a rustle, the hinges creak, and the trapdoors echo as they close. Toscanini, still calm, protests, arranges things, rushes over, and helps out.

And here we are in the clouds: a golden ladder leads up to the Lord's Throne. An ethereal light must predominate; there must be a pleasing, poetical pink and blue hue in the clouds and the air. Toscanini makes changes, modifies up there, removes things down here. "From high up on the golden ladder the stars must shine through. Make the stars!" And so it goes for all the sets of the six scenes that make up Franchetti's opera.

Now it's 10 A.M. [. . .] [The ballerinas] rehearse the [scene of] infernal mayhem; with their first steps they come alive, like old war horses at the sound of the trumpet. But the ballerinas' trumpet is a cane—the threatening, despotic cane of [Giacomo] Razzetto, the choreographer. Toscanini observes, tugging at his prickly mustache—a habitual gesture when he is not before the public. "Good! Very good! But you have to change this movement, Mr. Razzetto. The mayhem has to flow toward the right, making a spiral. And keep those arms out, young ladies, and do the splits in tempo, and hold on to them."

It's eleven. Toscanini moves on to the chorus room, where

Maestros Romei and Clivio [the chorus master] are running the last piano rehearsal. Toscanini has nothing to say; he is happy. The most difficult pieces—canons, fugatos, ensemble scenes—are going perfectly. "It's too bad that at the performances these choristers will be wrong." Clivio and Romei are surprised. "Not wrong when they sing, but when they're dressed as angels!"

It's 11:45. Toscanini runs to the Hotel Americano, where he is staying. His beautiful, elegant, intellectual wife is waiting for him, as are his two children—two lovely things, blond miniatures. The maestro hurriedly eats a mouthful and then runs back to the theater, where, at 12:30, the orchestra awaits him. He rehearses until 3, without a score and on his feet. If a musician makes a mistake, he corrects him courteously [. . .]. And he explains as he rehearses. Every musician knows exactly what he has to do, and why. The sole will of the maestro is infused into and shared by the 75 instrumentalists, who, with him, form a single person, a single soul, giving us those perfect, brilliant performances at which everyone marvels.

After having let the orchestra go, at 3 P.M., Toscanini rushed to the room in which Sormani was rehearsing the singers. Then, at 4,

Toscanini runs to the costume room, discusses the costumes, undergarments, everything. He makes changes, modifies, enriches. The singers consult with him on the details: "Maestro, hat with or without feathers?" "Curled wig?" "Beard or mustache or nothing?" "What shape should the shoes have?" "Gloves or no gloves?" And Toscanini explains, teaches.

At 5, stage rehearsal with the extras for the march in the second act; with the chorus for the battles, the figurations, the scenes, the apotheosis.

At 6 there is a lighting rehearsal—Lucifer's dark kingdom, the cloud with the angelic phalanx, the storm, nightfall, sunrise.

At 7 Toscanini runs to the Hotel Americano, where he [. . .] hurriedly eats a mouthful and runs to change clothes from head to toe, to put on his tailcoat. *The Queen of Sheba* is to be performed, and he has to conduct it.

At 8 he is on the stage, to see that everything is properly set up, after which he goes to visit the principal singers in their dressing rooms. He has a brief word with one, gives some advice to another, makes an observation to a third, reprimands a fourth.

At 8:30, there he is on the podium, conducting by heart, looking after everything, cuing all the singers, the chorus, the orchestra musicians—conducting that Teutonic piece of lead. The [first] act ends. "Maestro, maestro!" And Toscanini runs up the ladder in order to take a bow without making the audience wait too long.

He goes to his dressing room, fans himself with his handkerchief, waving it around his head; he changes his collar, which is drenched in sweat. And he rushes onto the stage, to check that everything is ready for the second act.

During the performance, the slightest error, an incorrect movement, a bit of bad intonation, a quarter beat too soon or too late—the inevitable blemishes that 99 percent of the audience won't notice during a performance—cause cruel suffering to Toscanini, like knives in his heart. The baton quivers in his nervous hand; his eyes are like lightning.

At 12:30 the long opera ends, thank God. Toscanini, fanning himself again, confers with the impresarios, with Rossi, the stage manager, and with the assistant conductors, giving orders for the following day. And at 1:30, he returns, running, to the Hotel Americano. He is exhausted, enervated. He eats reluctantly and finally goes to bed.

After all this work, Arturo Toscanini has earned a crumb of glory to add to his fame, and three hundred francs. A marvelous pay—the highest paid to a conductor to date. A star singer sings an aria or a few duet pieces and earns four to six thousand francs. And as they leave the theater you can hear them say, [. . .] "This Maestro Toscanini—how he makes us work! He kills us!"

Asrael, Franchetti's first opera, aroused public interest to an extent that seems like pure fantasy in the twenty-first century. Once again, President Roca and the diplomatic corps turned out for the first performance, as did the world-famous fencing master Agesilao Greco, who happened to be in town. Local aristocrats and the *haute bourgeoi-*

sie filled the remaining boxes, and the populace overflowed the main floor and galleries. In the president's box, there were arguments as to whether *Asrael* was inferior or superior to the same composer's *Cristoforo Colombo*, and so enthusiastic was the reception that six further performances had to be scheduled. Only *Tosca* was heard more times (eight, altogether) that season; the other operas received one to five performances each.

Local critics greeted *L'Elisir d'Amore* with disdain as unworthy of a modern audience but complimented Toscanini and the singers— including Darclée and Caruso—on the performance. Darclée had not wanted to sing either Adina in *Elisir* or Gilda in *Rigoletto*, and upon her arrival in Buenos Aires she had told Bonetti to inform the maestro that she would not attend the following day's rehearsal of *Elisir*. Toscanini recalled many years later that he had told Bonetti to " 'go back to Signora Darclée's lodging; tell the lady to come immediately to the rehearsal.' " She informed Toscanini that composers like Donizetti hadn't written real music but only outlines "to be fixed up as the singer wished. She wanted to do cadenzas and extra high notes. 'No, you sing what Donizetti wrote—you'll see that we'll do fine together,' " he replied, and indeed, Darclée was hailed in both roles. But, Toscanini added, in those days many singers complained: " 'The maestro is rude, the maestro asks for things that no one has ever asked for.' "

In fact, Toscanini not only allowed but often insisted on the interpolation of cadenzas and other unwritten material in early to mid-nineteenth-century Italian operas—the so-called bel canto repertoire—in which such interpolations would have been the norm in their composer's day. But he did not usually allow the insertion of elaborate, late nineteenth-century ornamentation,* nor did he usually permit singers to make willful changes in operas written in or near his own day—operas that, in some cases, he had worked on directly with their composers. Those were the interdictions that caused protests from some singers.

Toscanini also did not hesitate to suggest to contemporary composers, especially inexperienced ones, ways in which to improve

---

* For an intelligent discussion of this complex subject, see Philip Gossett, *Divas and Scholars: Performing Italian Opera* (Chicago: University of Chicago Press, 2006).

their works. During his stay in Buenos Aires, he agreed to conduct the Argentine premiere of *Medioevo Latino* by Héctor (Ettore) Panizza, a young Italo-Argentine composer who had been studying and working in Italy.* At Toscanini's request, Panizza made some cuts in the work, but when, at the first piano rehearsal with the singers, Toscanini asked for another cut, the twenty-six-year-old composer protested. Toscanini threw down the score, told Panizza to go to hell, and banned him from rehearsals. Panizza managed to sneak in anyway and was impressed with Toscanini's ability to bring the work to life. He and his family were invited to the dress rehearsal, and at the end of the first act the conductor called the composer onto the podium and embraced him.

The season proceeded with one success after another: *Otello, Iris, Lohengrin* (with Caruso in the title role), *La Traviata, Cristoforo Colombo,* and, most important, the South American premiere of *Tristan und Isolde* (with Borgatti and Pinto again in the title roles). In three months, Toscanini conducted fifty-eight performances—all in Italian—of fifteen operas by nine composers from five different countries, plus a special concert to mark the first anniversary of the assassination of Italy's King Umberto I, with an augmented orchestra and chorus and with Darclée, Cucini, Caruso, and Segurola as soloists.

12.

FOR MUSIC LOVERS IN ARGENTINA'S BOOMING CAPITAL, MONEY appeared to be no object, but their Milanese counterparts were in a less fortunate position. As the 1901–02 season approached, La Scala was once again facing serious financial difficulties. Two years earlier, the conservative party had lost a municipal election to the radicals, who had dithered over the question of extending the theater's municipal subsidy. In 1901, the city council granted a one-year subsidy of 150,000 lire, tied, however, to the promise of a 120,000-lira donation

---

* Toscanini's schedule in Buenos Aires was so tough that he had decided to conduct *Medioevo Latino* from the score, rather than learn it from memory. At the first orchestra rehearsal, however, he noticed that the concertmaster was looking at him as if to say, "What? You don't know this opera?" Toscanini felt so insulted that by the following day's rehearsal he had memorized the work completely.

by the boxholders; the donation was forthcoming, in anticipation of the world premiere of Boito's *Nerone* in 1902. But when the question of continuing the subsidy was put before the citizens via a referendum, in December 1901, the proposal was defeated.* Gatti-Casazza feared that La Scala would have to close, but Duke Guido and some of his friends continued to underwrite the theater's deficits. The ensemble's contracts with Toscanini and Gatti-Casazza were renewed through 1907, and since the city of Milan still owned La Scala, a legal cavil was found whereby the municipality continued to make an annual contribution, although at the reduced rate of 60,000 lire.

Economic issues notwithstanding, Toscanini plunged into preparations for his fourth Scala season immediately upon his return from South America. And even before opera rehearsals began, he conducted the world premiere of *Mosè*, an oratorio by the priest-composer Lorenzo Perosi, at Milan's church of Santa Maria della Pace; this was one of only three or four occasions on which the anticlerical Toscanini performed in a church. He then led two symphonic concerts with the Scala orchestra at the Milan Conservatory and set to work preparing *Die Walküre* to open La Scala on 26 December. Although in Italy *Walküre* was performed more than any of the other *Ring* operas, this was only its second production at La Scala and the first one without cuts. As usual, some of the critics raged at Toscanini for having presented the opera in its lengthy entirety but praised him for the quality of the performance. Although the audience was not as enthusiastic as it had been for *Tristan*, the production ran for the respectable number of eight performances.

The success of *L'Elisir d'Amore* the previous year had encouraged Toscanini to offer the Milanese another Donizetti opera. On 2 January 1902, *Linda di Chamounix*, which had not been heard at La Scala since 1855, opened, with Rosina Storchio in the title role. The successful production was presented ten times, and D'Ormeville, reviewing it in the *Gazzetta dei Teatri*, hazarded the guess that Toscanini, deep down, loved Donizetti even more than he loved Wagner. But Toscanini was also deeply in love with Storchio; their affair was

---

* Only about one-sixth of the city's adult population had the right to vote, and only one-third of those who had the right actually voted in the referendum, which was defeated by 11,240 to 7,214.

now at its height, and its consequences for the intense and gifted Rosina—"one of the best-rounded and perfect artists that I ever knew in the theatre [. . .] one of the glories of Italian lyric art," as Gatti-Casazza described her—would be much more devastating than the temporary insanity that afflicts Donizetti's Linda.

In La Scala's first production of Engelbert Humperdinck's *Hänsel und Gretel*, which opened sixteen days after *Linda*, Storchio took the part of Hänsel. She was "adorable, lively and funny," according to the *Corriere della Sera*, and "extremely graceful, full of verve, breeziness, roguish conviviality," as per *La Perseveranza*. The young French mezzo-soprano Jane Bathori was also much liked as Gretel,* and so was the mezzo-soprano Elisa Bruno as the Witch. Some of La Scala's patrons grumbled that the fairy-tale subject of the opera was not sufficiently dignified for so important a house, but the production became a popular success: thirteen performances were given, and Toscanini was once again acclaimed. Within a month, however, these and all the other acclamations that he had received so far would seem pale.

To begin: at La Scala on 27 January 1902, the first anniversary of Verdi's death, Toscanini conducted his first complete performance of the composer's *Requiem*. The critics waxed poetic over the performance and reported that at the end of the *Dies Irae* the audience had risen en masse, applauding, cheering, and shouting, "Toscanini! Toscanini!" But then came the real triumph.

Of the thirty different operas that Toscanini had conducted during his three seasons as artistic head of Turin's Teatro Regio and his first three seasons at La Scala, only two were by Giuseppe Verdi. And those two, *Otello* and *Falstaff*, were the septuagenarian Verdi's last works in the form—masterpieces, to be sure, but not the mainstream, popular operas of the composer's middle years. At other venues, Toscanini had conducted eight of Verdi's pre-*Otello* works, but in his two most important positions he had not presented any of the works that Verdi had created during his fertile thirties, forties, and fifties.

Toscanini's reluctance had many causes. He saw Wagner as the most influential figure in late nineteenth-century European music,

---

* The part of Hänsel is usually sung by a mezzo-soprano and Gretel by a soprano; Toscanini's reasons for turning them around for this production are not known.

and he understood that most of the significant new developments in music would derive either from Wagner's heirs or from composers who were reacting against Wagner's influence. In addition, the young Toscanini was probably unsure of his approach to Verdi's most popular works. He had grown up hearing them performed with interpolated notes and cadenzas, illogical key transpositions, arbitrary cuts, and tempo fluctuations that trespassed into the territory of gross distortion—what Verdi had described as "the rondos of the prima donnas." Expediency had become habit, habit custom, and custom tradition. Years went by before Toscanini decided that the investigative method that he applied to other music—the method of trying to discover what was both written and implied in the score instead of trying to adapt the score to his own or others' whims—was as just and logical in the older Italian repertoire as in Wagner's music dramas and in modern works. His successes with Donizetti encouraged him to continue to revive older operas, yet he needed a great deal of courage to schedule, at La Scala, the most battered of all the old repertoire operas: *Il Trovatore*.

Turn-of-the-twentieth-century audiences at major Italian theaters like the Regio and La Scala considered themselves too sophisticated for mid-nineteenth-century Verdi standards like *Rigoletto*, *Il Trovatore*, and *La Traviata*. Tunes from the old "stock operas" were played by street-corner hurdy-gurdy grinders, sung by drunks in taverns, and mimicked in vaudeville acts; catchphrases from their stilted libretti were used jokingly in everyday conversation; and forty or fifty years before the Marx Brothers wreaked havoc on *Il Trovatore* in *A Night at the Opera* (1935), the work was already an object of satire in Italy. Tullio Serafin, who, by 1902, had become Toscanini's second assistant, recalled that the celebrated comic actor Edoardo Ferravilla had done a *Trovatore* parody in Milanese dialect that had left Verdi himself "laughing until he cried." Serafin described Ferravilla donning "a big helmet with enormous, garishly colored ostrich feathers" for his imitation of Count di Luna. "When Toscanini decided to bring *Trovatore* back to La Scala, where it hadn't been done for some time, the great concern was to make sure that the audience didn't laugh."

Given the recent successes of *Elisir* and *Linda*, and given that the Ricordi company controlled the performing rights to *Il Trovatore*, Toscanini's decision ought to have pleased Giulio Ricordi. Instead, the sixty-one-year-old publisher became alarmed. On the one hand, he believed that the opera itself would be held up to public ridicule no matter who the performers might be; on the other, he did not want Toscanini to conduct it. Since the young maestro's accession to La Scala's throne, the attitude toward him on the part of most Milanese musicians and critics had changed from mistrust, or at best wait-and-see, to admiration, and then to enthusiasm. But Ricordi had hoped that Toscanini's whip-cracking approach to theater discipline—his insistence on unity of purpose in an art form in which egoism in its crudest form often reigned—would be self-defeating and would bring his reign to an end after one or at most two seasons; this had not happened, and the publisher had become an implacable enemy of the conductor who now enjoyed virtual carte blanche at the house, with respect to artistic policy. The idea that this insolent musician, this importer of Ostrogoth culture, was now going to "Wagnerize" and "metronomize" *Il Trovatore* made Ricordi overstep his mandate: he informed the Scala administration that his company would not permit *Il Trovatore* to be performed at La Scala.

Publishers of the day often denied a theater the performance rights to a new opera, if they wished to have it done first in a different venue or city. But to deny any theater, let alone La Scala, performance rights to the nearly fifty-year-old *Il Trovatore* was unheard of. Ricordi's resounding slap in Toscanini's face created a furor, and Toscanini's tactlessness exacerbated matters. Tito Ricordi, who was present during a heated argument between his father and Toscanini, commented, "You're both impossible characters." Toscanini replied, "Yes, but I keep to my own affairs, while your father insists on sticking his nose into everyone's business!" Only a well-timed diplomatic action by Boito persuaded Ricordi to relent, however ungraciously.

Gatti-Casazza recalled that Toscanini prepared the opera "with infinite care" and "forced every player and every singer to cast outworn tradition to the winds and restudy the score." But the maestro must have felt exceptionally nervous as he took his place before the orchestra on 9 February 1902 and raised his baton to begin the first performance. There were people twice his age in the audience who had heard *Il Trovatore* done every which way for decades, and there was a contingent of younger listeners and sophisticates, real and self-proclaimed, who believed that the opera was bereft of musical value and unworthy of La Scala. Yet Gatti noted that La Scala's notoriously difficult public, "which had come to the theatre rather ill-disposed, showed increasing surprise and manifested throughout the evening its great enthusiasm. At the end of the first scene, [. . .] with the basso and the chorus, there was a demonstration so overwhelming that it was long before Toscanini could proceed." By the end of the evening, the doubters had joined the rest of the audience in cheering, shouting, and applauding. Toscanini had won his greatest battle to date.

Carlo D'Ormeville's observations in the *Gazzetta dei Teatri* communicate the atmosphere of that remarkable occasion.

When the curtain fell on the last scene of the last act, I saw Maestro Toscanini radiant [. . .]. When one reaches the point of imagining such a brilliant reconstruction of an opera used and abused in the most ramshackle huts that claim for themselves the name of theater; when one has the talent to create (allow me the word) that first scene in such a way as to give it absolutely novel tone and coloration; when one succeeds in bringing into relief the tiniest details, in animating every scene, in enlivening every detail; when one obtains such marvelous fusion from the orchestra and such exquisite refinement from the chorus; when one encourages the set designers to create a real artistic revolution by indicating and explaining everything to them and practically guiding their pencils and paintbrushes with a steady hand; when one understands that only an artist like Pogliaghi* must be entrusted with the arduous task of banishing the customary old plumed helmets and capes with trains in order to reconstruct a completely new ensemble, harmonious in the elegance of its cut, in the correctness of its design; then it must be said that if Fortune smiles on audacity, she has shown, perhaps for the first time, that she is not blind.

Maestro Toscanini was able to will and to obtain all of this, and I think—may the intransigent Wagnerites not curse me!—that much greater talent and much greater authority were needed to will and obtain all of this than to prepare and conduct a *Tristan* or a *Walküre*.

---

* Lodovico Pogliaghi (1857–1950) was a much-admired Milanese sculptor and painter.

Most of the other reviewers expressed similar judgments. Gustavo Macchi declared, in the journal *Tempo*, that "a work of art largely unknown until now has been revealed to the public." The singers* were highly praised, but the success was not a result of "the tenor's high C or the bravura of individual artists," Macchi continued—although Toscanini did allow the tenor to sing most of his unwritten high notes. "No one, in the face of this interpretation of *Trovatore*, will again dare to doubt Toscanini's value, impartiality, or artistic honesty."

Toscanini's old foes Romeo Carugati and Giulio Ricordi did still doubt: Carugati, in *Lombardia*, praised the performance overall but described it as "precise and mathematical." And Ricordi wrote, in his *Gazzetta Musicale*, "For many, Toscanini is now as infallible as the Pope! He is actually superior to Verdi himself, the author of *Trovatore* —who, however, never prepared and conducted it like this!† My goodness gracious! One mustn't criticize the King!"

Whether Verdi himself would have approved or disapproved of Toscanini's overall interpretation of his opera cannot be known, but what can be known is that Verdi had a posthumous triumph. Many music historians consider the thirteen performances of La Scala's 1902 *Trovatore* production the beginning of the so-called Verdi Renaissance, which could more accurately be described as a Verdi Restoration: the reconditioning-restoration of a work of art, and the restoration of Verdi to his rightful position in the history of opera.

13.

ARRIGO BOITO ENJOYED LIVING AND WORKING MAINLY IN SOLI-tude, after having survived tempestuous affairs with Duchess Eugenia Litta (later the mistress of King Umberto I) and the actress Eleonora Duse (who threw him over in favor of the poet and playwright Gabriele D'Annunzio). But he would sometimes spend eve-

---

* Rosa Caligaris (Leonora), Elisa Bruno (Azucena), Julián Biel (Manrico), Antonio Magini-Coletti (Conte di Luna), Giovanni Gravina (Ferrando).

† So far as is known, Ricordi had never heard a performance of *Il Trovatore* prepared or conducted by Verdi.

nings at the Toscaninis' home, which was near his own, and Toscanini, in turn, often dropped in on the older man. Boito's projected opera, *Nerone*—a musical-historical fiction set in the time of the emperor Nero—was a frequent topic of discussion, and at some point, probably in 1900, the poet-composer had asked to read the libretto to Toscanini, who was flattered when Boito told him that the only other person to whom he had read it was Verdi. On reaching the scene with the death of Rubria, a sort of Mary Magdalene figure, in the last act, Boito began to weep; Toscanini had to read the rest himself. In 1901 Boito had the libretto printed, and by the time Toscanini left for Buenos Aires in April of that year costumes had already been designed, although not yet made, for a production of *Nerone* during the following Scala season, in keeping with the composer's promise to Duke Guido.

Toscanini did not doubt Boito's word, but the wilier Gatti-Casazza had been encouraging Alberto Franchetti to complete his opera *Germania*, on a libretto by Illica, in time to take *Nerone*'s place if need be—which is precisely what happened. Toscanini, in South America, received a telegram from Gatti, who informed him that *Nerone* would not be ready and that *Germania* would take its place. On returning to Italy, Toscanini visited Boito, and many years later he recalled that Boito had told him, "This opera has always fooled me. I realized that I don't know [enough] harmony." Boito subsequently promised Gatti that he would finish *Nerone* during the following three years, but that promise, too, was broken.

Franchetti's *Germania*—the story of a love triangle among Bavarian students during the Napoleonic Wars—has long since fallen out of the mainstream repertoire, but its premiere at La Scala, in March 1902, with a cast that included Caruso, Pinto, Bathori, and Sammarco, was one of the major events of the season. Serafin recalled that Toscanini had taken him aside before the rehearsals began and had warned him that Franchetti was a terrible complainer: if one of his operas wasn't liked, he blamed the failure on the conductor, and if it was liked, he said that it had succeeded despite the faulty performance. "Before starting the rehearsals," Serafin said, Toscanini "confronted the composer and told him: 'Alberto, beware: I know you. You're going to sit down at the piano and play your opera for me now. And I guarantee you that I'm going to photograph you [mentally] as you play, recording your tempi and your dynamics. But if you come and tell me later that my tempi aren't right or if you make other nasty comments, I'll bite your nose off.'"

During the rehearsals, Illica was constantly sowing discord between Franchetti and Tito Ricordi, Giulio's son, who had taken charge of the staging. "Toscanini observed all of these maneuvers, and for once he thoroughly enjoyed himself," Serafin said. The successful premiere was attended by, among others, Puccini, Mascagni, Giordano, and many leading German musicians, as well as by many of Italy's leading poets and playwrights, including D'Annunzio, Emilio Treves, Giuseppe Giacosa, and Marco Praga, and by various members of the royal family.

The following production, the last of the season, failed utterly, although it was dear to Toscanini's heart. Carl Maria von Weber's *Euryanthe*, written in 1823, had never been performed in Italy, but Toscanini, who saw it as a transitional work—even more than Weber's more popular *Der Freischütz*—between the *Singspiele* (operas that contained spoken dialogue) of Mozart and Beethoven and the music dramas of Wagner, believed that it deserved to be heard. Once again, he assembled a first-rate cast, including Storchio in the title role. At the opening performance the overture made a tremendous impact, so much so that many audience members called for an encore. Toscanini would not comply. "I had the curtain go up" on the first act, he recalled, "and they began to shout." The curtain closed again, and "two cowardly subscribers," thinking that it was Toscanini who now wanted to repeat the overture, shouted to him, in Milanese dialect, "Move it along!"

"I threw down my baton and left the orchestra," Toscanini recalled. In going backstage, "I wasn't paying attention to an exit; I didn't know there was a pane of glass. I broke the glass with my head, and I began to bleed."

Toscanini was about to leave the theater and go home when Duke Guido came backstage, calmed him down, and saw to it that the bleeding was stopped. Toscanini returned to the orchestra, repeated the overture, and went on with the opera. At this point, however, all of the performers were shaken. "It was as if the singers were drunk," Toscanini said. The audience remained cold, the whole evening went badly, and afterward Toscanini, who was superstitious, attributed the episode to the fact that earlier that day, while he was walking home after a rehearsal, a "famous *jettatore*"—a man with the evil eye—had greeted him and shaken his hand. After two more performances the production closed.

Richard Strauss's seven-year-old tone poem *Till Eulenspiegel* was the main attraction on the first of the four concerts that Toscanini conducted with the Scala orchestra at the end of the opera season; it made such a hit with the audience that Toscanini encored the entire piece, which outshone the program's novelty work, Leone Sinigaglia's Violin Concerto, with Arrigo Serato as soloist. The three remaining concerts, all received with great enthusiasm, centered on Beethoven's Ninth Symphony, which Toscanini was conducting in its entirety for the first time, although he had performed the second and third movements during a concert in Turin four years earlier.*

TOSCANINI DID NOT RETURN to Buenos Aires in 1902, but he did travel within Italy and beyond during the late spring, summer, and early fall. Walter Toscanini remembered that the family spent some days in Venice and then at Belluno, "where I cut off the left side of my father's mustache; he then had to proceed to amputate the right side." (The whole mustache soon grew back.) By late June the entire burgeoning family, joined by the similarly growing Polo family, was at Tai di Cadore in the Dolomites, where he and Carla had spent their honeymoon five years earlier. But the vacation turned into a nightmare for Toscanini when Gatti-Casazza dropped by and gave him a message from Rosina Storchio. What she had suspected before her lover had left Milan was correct: she was pregnant.

The news threw him "into consternation and pain," he wrote, in

---

* The Ninth had been performed in Milan on only three previous occasions in its seventy-eight-year history, and Toscanini had been in the audience at the last of the three, which was led by the well-known French conductor Charles Lamoureux, in 1896. Toscanini later described Lamoureux as "a good musician" but not a good conductor: he had buried his head in the score and had forgotten to cue in the trombones in the trio section of the symphony's scherzo. According to one critic, in 1902 Toscanini eliminated the bass drum and cymbals from the scoring of the *Alla marcia* section of the Ninth Symphony's finale, but other reports contest this statement. Those instruments are most definitely present in all of the recordings of Toscanini's performances of the work in his later years.

one of three extant letters that he sent her in July, and in which he affirmed that he loved her more and more. At the same time he felt *"more and more unworthy of you, because I have no idea what to do to save you either before the world or before my conscience, which fills me with remorse and tortures me."* He wanted to "react in a way that will help to alleviate your burden" but did not know how. He was "like a madman, pervaded by remorse that tears my heart to shreds. No, no! I can't be the cause of new, crueler sorrows in your life!"

Carla soon discovered that her husband was visiting the post office in a nearby village to pick up mail sent to him under the anagrammatic pseudonym Antonio Trascuri,* and Toscanini wrote to Rosina, "I even fear sleep now, because I'm spied on even then, and I talk continually."

Surely he saw Rosina again at some point during the summer, but we don't know when, where, or how. By late July he was staying at the Hotel Post in Bayreuth; Storchio may have followed him there. He heard the entire *Ring*, conducted by either Hans Richter or Siegfried Wagner, but once again his main interest was *Parsifal*, conducted this time by Karl Muck. From Bayreuth he went to Munich, probably to attend performances at the city's annual summer Wagner festival, after which he rejoined his family at Tai di Cadore and did some mountain climbing. Late in August, he traveled to the small town of Lugo in the Romagna to rehearse and conduct a production of *Aida*, most likely after a short stay in Milan to resolve casting issues for the coming Scala season. According to Filippo Sacchi, he had accepted the Lugo engagement at the suggestion of a double bass player friend who hailed from the town. Toscanini brought with him excellent singers "who had accepted Lugo's modest fees just in order to sing with him," Sacchi said.

Carla sent several letters to her husband while he was at Lugo. In one of them she combined quotidian details about the children— Giorgio was growing another tooth, Wally had fallen asleep in a meadow—with more emotionally revealing statements: "Write me lots of affectionate little things," she begged. "I feel alone and I'm very sad[.] I want to cry all day[.] My only joy is receiving your letters[.] You won't deprive me of your notes? I kiss your letters with emotion and I reread them continually[.] With all my affection and

---

* The Italian verb *trascurare* means "to neglect," thus *trascuri* = "you neglect."

the little kisses of your children, *Your Carla*." The tone of this and subsequent letters indicates that she suspected or even knew about Storchio, but believed, or wanted to believe, her husband's assurances that he loved only herself. On 5 October she wrote to him again, this time addressing the letter to a spa at Montecatini in Tuscany, where he had gone after the Lugo *Aidas* to try to alleviate pains in his right shoulder—a condition that would plague him intermittently for decades. "Have you found company?" Carla asked. "I, forever selfish, hope that you're alone, alone with your books, which don't make me jealous, so you'll think more about me and will want to come back soon." Carla began to receive anonymous letters about her husband, who had his share of detractors and envious colleagues in the poisonous theater world; she wrote to him, "I believe in you and I love you, I don't want to think about it and become nasty . . . why must I always be so tormented? . . . I don't believe [the letters] and yet they bother me and make me suffer."

At last he rejoined her and the children at Salò on Lake Garda and returned to Milan with them, but late in October he was back in Germany—Hamburg, this time—at the invitation of the impresario Raoul Gunsbourg. Toscanini had already seen Berlioz's "dramatic legend," *La Damnation de Faust*, performed under Mugnone's direction in Milan in 1893, in Gunsbourg's version of it as an opera, and he greatly admired the French composer's genius. But he wanted to make sure that the production would be effective enough to succeed at La Scala. The Hamburg version convinced him, and he decided to open the forthcoming Scala season with the work.

On his way back to Milan, he stopped briefly in Berlin ("This isn't a city but a whole state joined together!! What a marvel!" he wrote to Polo about Kaiser Wilhelm II's imperial capital) and made a pilgrimage to the town of Eisenach, to visit Bach's birthplace. Then he set to work preparing the Scala season, which opened with the Berlioz work, on 22 December. The production succeeded beyond his or anyone else's expectations: twenty-three performances were given—more than any of Toscanini's other pre–World War I Scala productions—and many years later he recalled those performances with particular pleasure.

D'Ormeville, in praising the *Damnation de Faust*, declared that La Scala, "thanks to its high priest, is no longer a theater but a temple."

Perhaps Milan would once again become not merely a place to hear decent performances of Italian operas but an important European musical and cultural center. In fact, Toscanini's services to the cause of music in Italy were now so widely recognized that on 28 December 1902 King Victor Emanuel III conferred on him the title of Grand Master of the Crown of Italy, similar to a knighthood. There was no ceremony: the document attesting to the honor was simply sent to Toscanini by the Chancellor of the Order. A similar honor (Merit Cross of the Crown of Italy) would be presented to him in 1905. But Toscanini seems never to have made reference to either title. Given his antimonarchic views, he probably ignored them entirely and may even have been embarrassed by them.

The Scala audiences' enthusiastic response to *Il Trovatore* the previous year had encouraged Toscanini to resurrect Verdi's *Luisa Miller*, one of its older sisters, which had not been performed at La Scala since 1851, two years after its premiere. The performers were much applauded, but the opera as a whole was received without much enthusiasm. It was followed by the world premiere of *Oceàna* by Antonio Smareglia, a forty-eight-year-old Italo-Croatian composer, one of whose earlier operas had been performed at Vienna's Court Opera thanks to Brahms's support for it. Toscanini perceived Smareglia, a poetic musician, as an antidote to the *veristi* and a potential successor to Catalani, but *Oceàna* never developed a substantial following.

Asrael, Franchetti's most popular opera, followed *Oceàna* and was succeded in turn by Verdi's *Un Ballo in Maschera*, which proved to be much more popular than *Luisa Miller*: even the anti-Toscaninian Carugati approved, and the production ran for thirteen performances, interspersed with unenthusiastically received performances of Ponichielli's *I Lituani* (The Lithuanians). The maestro paid a further tribute to Verdi on 19 March—the composer's name day—when he and members of the Scala orchestra opened and closed a brief program for the dedication of the crypt that contains the remains of Giuseppe and Giuseppina Strepponi Verdi. The crypt is located in a neo-Byzantine chapel on the grounds of the Rest Home for Musicians, which Verdi called his "best work."

The same month of March 1903 was a dramatic one for Storchio, who gave birth to a baby boy, Giovanni, called Giovannino, to whom she gave her own surname. "The child was beautiful," Sacchi recalled, "with huge black eyes, with his father's unmistakable eyebrows, but as he was being extracted with the forceps his brain was damaged, thus he was born ataxic and was never able to speak." In the religiously conservative Italy of the time, Storchio was the unmarried mother of a severely handicapped child whose father could not publicly acknowledge his paternity without risking the loss of his "legitimate" family and his position. He helped provide for the child's support, but how he and Storchio dealt with other aspects of the situation is not known. Their affair continued, however, and they continued to work together. And as at other emotionally difficult moments, Toscanini shunted the crisis onto a sidetrack and buried himself in his work, which, in this case, consisted above all in a pair of performances, in concert form, of Act III of *Parsifal*, preceded by the opera's Prelude.

14.

BAYREUTH HAD SOLE RIGHTS TO STAGED PERFORMANCES OF *PARSIFAL*, but Toscanini decided that a foretaste for the Scala audience would not constitute a sacrilege. The reception at the first performance, on Easter Sunday 1903, disappointed him: the Wagnerites complained about having to hear only part of the work and in an unstaged version, and the anti-Wagnerites complained of boredom. At the second performance, a handful of listeners called for an encore of the Prelude, and Toscanini granted it, as if to fling the music in the face of the majority of the audience: a sad dénouement to a season that had begun brilliantly with *La Damnation de Faust*.

The *Parsifal* outcome had made Toscanini angry with the Milanese audience and critics, but he was angrier still with La Scala's administration and board of directors. The previous November, Duke Guido Visconti di Modrone had died, and his eldest son, Uberto, had assumed both the dukedom and the theater's presidency. Toscanini always spoke respectfully and admiringly of Guido, but he considered Uberto a playboy and socialite who did not care profoundly about music in general or La Scala in particular. In addition, the old duke had died before Gatti-Casazza was able to approach him about a raise for Toscanini—an issue that the conductor had brought up with Gatti the preceding spring: Toscanini pointed out that the soprano Emma Carelli's salary had recently jumped from 12,000 lire to 36,000, although her workload at the house was only a fraction of his; he believed that he had the right to ask for 20,000 lire instead of his current 12,000. Gatti agreed to approach Duke Guido in the fall, but when, after Guido's death, Gatti mentioned the matter to Uberto, he did not receive an immediate response.

One evening, Count Giuseppe Visconti di Modrone, one of Uberto's younger brothers, happened to see Toscanini in a corridor at the theater and told him that the board had decided to give him a raise, to 18,000 lire. This was the wrong answer to give Toscanini, who did not enjoy bargaining. He felt that his request had been more than reasonable, and he knew that the difference of 2,000 lire was more or less what a medium-ranking singer received for a single performance. He turned his back on Giuseppe and walked away. As the 1902–03 season proceeded, the board's meanness continued to irritate Toscanini.

The season's last performance, a repetition of *Un Ballo in Maschera*, was to take place on 14 April, twenty-four hours after the second *Parsifal* evening. Toscanini had agreed to return to Buenos Aires that spring, again at the behest of the impresarios Nardi and Bonetti, and his ship was to depart from Genoa at noon on the fifteenth, which meant that he had to be on the 6 A.M. Milan–Genoa train. He asked to be excused from the last Scala performance—to have one of his competent assistants, Sormani or Serafin, take over for him on this sole occasion in five seasons—although at that time staff conductors rarely took over performances "unless the conductor died," as Toscanini himself put the matter. His request was denied, and he did conduct the performance, which went well until the end of the ensemble that begins with the tenor's words "È scherzo od è follia," in the second part of the first act. The audience clamored for an encore, but—as the newspapers reported the next day—Giovanni Zenatello, the tenor, "did not appear disposed to concede it," and "Maestro Toscanini signaled to proceed." Part of the audience continued to demand an encore, while the other part "noisily demanded that the performance go forward. The clamor for and against the encore went on thus for a long time. Finally the performance continued. After the act, however, a stage boy came out to inform the public that Maestro Toscanini had suddenly begun to hemorrhage and that Maestro Sormani would have to replace him."

In Toscanini's recollection of the incident, fifty years later, there was no mention of blood. He had said goodbye to the orchestra and left the theater through the nearest exit without going backstage, he said, "because I was afraid that they would not let me out." When he got home, "Carla looked at me—I was wearing my tails—and said, 'Where did you leave your coat?'

"'I left it at the theater.'"

La Scala's lawyer, Morpurgo, rushed to see him and asked whether he would go back to conduct the rest of the opera. "'*You* conduct it,'" Toscanini replied. "'I'm going to bed, and tomorrow I'm leaving for South America.'"

Particularly noteworthy about the *Ballo* incident is the fact that Zenatello, not Toscanini, "did not appear disposed" to grant the encore. Toscanini opposed encores because they interrupted the flow of the music and the drama—the theatrical illusion—but many singers hated encores for practical reasons. They enjoyed the audience's approval but not the extra wear on their vocal cords, especially in an age in which even singers of leading roles were often required to perform four times a week, many weeks in a row. For the protection of singers, there had been an anti-encore regulation on La Scala's books since 1793, but—to cite the Prince of Denmark— the regulation was "more honour'd in the breach than the observance." Toscanini, for all his severity, could not have put an end to so deep-rooted a tradition as the encore unless most of the singers had agreed with him.

Boito would sometimes pretend "to turn up by coincidence" on the morning after one of the conductor's encore-related run-ins with the audience, Toscanini recalled. While rolling a cigarette, he would ask what happened; Toscanini would reply, "Maestro, it's the same old story." Boito would object that even Verdi allowed singers to perform encores, and Toscanini would answer that although Verdi was a genius and he himself was not, Verdi was "a child of the era in which he was born. I am a child of my era. I'm a man who sees the theater in a modern way."

Gatti-Casazza believed that, had Toscanini not had to leave Milan immediately after the *Ballo* incident, his anger would have abated and a complete break with La Scala would have been avoided. Instead, Toscanini caught the early-morning train to Genoa, where, before he boarded the *Sicilia*, bound for Argentina, he sent a telegram to La Scala announcing that he would never again set foot in the house.

15.

THE ENCORE PROBLEM DID NOT EXIST FOR TOSCANINI IN ARGENtina: he simply allowed as many encores as the audience requested and as the singers were willing to perform. Besides, he had little time to worry about such ancillary matters, because his workload in Buenos Aires was even more crushing than what he was accustomed to in Milan. Between mid-May and mid-August, he rehearsed and conducted fifty performances of fifteen operas, including four Argentine premieres: Berlioz's *La Damnation de Faust*, Humperdinck's *Hänsel und Gretel*,* Francesco Cilea's *Adriana Lecouvreur* (an elegant work that had provided Caruso with a tremendous success at its world premiere the previous year and that Toscanini was conducting for the first time), and Massenet's *Grisélidis* (a first and last production for Toscanini). Sets and costumes were furnished by La Scala's designers, and all performances were in Italian.

As Buenos Aires's more cultivated citizens wanted to demonstrate that their sophistication was at least equal to that found in Europe's capital cities, they willingly paid astronomical fees to the artists they imported. Toscanini himself received 42,000 lire that year, and his stellar casts included, among others, the sopranos Darclée and Medea Mei Figner (who had participated in Toscanini's debut season in Rio de Janeiro seventeen years earlier); the tenors Caruso and Zenatello; and the baritones Eugenio Giraldoni and Giuseppe De Luca. Earlier in the year, Toscanini had invited De Luca to sing the role of Beckmesser in *Meistersinger*, and the twenty-six-year-old baritone had written to his agent, "Although unwillingly, I shall study

---

* Each of the three performances of *Hänsel* was followed by what the local newspapers described as a "Wagner concert"—presumably a performance of orchestral excerpts from Wagner's operas.

the role [. . .]. I say unwillingly because these are parts that ruin the voice; but to please Maestro Toscanini, what wouldn't I do?"

Following the last *Meistersinger* performance, the entire ensemble sailed to Montevideo, to stage ten of the season's operas at the Uruguayan capital's Teatro Solís. Like Buenos Aires, Montevideo was experiencing a rapid and ever-increasing influx of Spanish, Italian, and Central European emigrants (at the time of Toscanini's debut there, foreigners constituted about 25 percent of the population), and the anticipation for the opera company's arrival was great. "Today, in the early hours of a cold morning, the steamships 'Venus' and 'Paris' arrived from Buenos Aires," *La Razón*, a Montevideo newspaper, reported on 14 August. "Dozens of small rowboats began endless trips to carry people from the steamers to the docks. Soon there was pandemonium, with porters unloading hundreds of crates of furniture, scenery, huge boxes of scores, and thousands of pieces of luggage. The confusion was terrible, with people yelling and porters cursing loudly—while from the dock, the Teatro Solís's reception committee looked on helplessly." Toscanini, the reporter said, "looks amiable. Small of frame, he is slender, with an angular face and well-trimmed black mustache. Toscanini has small eyes—but the sharpest and most vivid I have ever seen. He looks natural, without the pose and mannerisms of many of his colleagues, but his voice sounds rough and husky, like someone in the habit of giving orders all the time."

Two days later, another newspaper, *El Día*, described Toscanini's appearance at the company's first performance: "From the moment he stepped onto the podium we could feel his authority: immediately all fell under the spell of his influence and strong magnetism." Each opera was given just once, except *Manon Lescaut*, which was heard twice; four of them, including *Die Meistersinger*, were receiving their Uruguayan premieres.

Toscanini earned enough during his three and a half months in Argentina and Uruguay to support his family for a while, but after a decade of virtually unrelenting activity—he had not had a substantial break in ten years—he must have felt odd, upon his return to Italy, having no season to plan and rehearse. In October he went to Montecatini for a cure, and Carla—worried, reasonably enough, that he might be there with a woman—sent him an affectionate letter right after his departure from Milan: "It's only a few hours since you've left me and it already seems a thousand years since I've had your kisses and caresses," she wrote, adding that she had slept in Wally's room because "sleeping alone without my darling in the big double bed made me melancholy." We do not know how Toscanini replied, but we do know that, brutally honest though he was in matters musical, in matters erotic he lied whenever his freedom of action was at stake.

Toscanini's only performances between late August 1903 and late May 1904 consisted of two concerts in Bologna and two more with his former orchestra in Turin. These programs included his first performances of four symphonic poems that would become staples of his concert repertoire—Sibelius's *The Swan of Tuonela* and *En Saga*, Dukas's *The Sorcerer's Apprentice*, and Smetana's *The Moldau*—as well as his first and last performances of Glazounov's Symphony no. 6. All of these pieces except *The Moldau* had been written within the previous dozen years, and, according to some sources, the *Swan* was the first public performance in Italy of any music by Sibelius.

Notwithstanding his ongoing relationship with Storchio and his many later affairs—or perhaps in part because of them—Toscanini was devoted to his family, and the break in his conducting activities allowed him to spend more time with his children. Wally Toscanini related that even when she and her siblings were infants, their father "very much enjoyed playing with us. Mamma said that when he was at home he took care of the babies himself. He bathed us, swaddled us, and gave us our pablum. He passed hour after hour reading pediatric and child-care books. I remember him as a very affectionate father. When he came home, he was greeted with shouts of joy." Carla worried that if the children made noise they would disturb their father when he was studying, but Wally said that he was so concentrated that he seemed not to notice when they were making a ruckus. "When we were small, he never shouted at us," she said. "Papà told Mamma what he wanted of us, and she passed it on. We always obeyed because we adored him."

Wally expressed only one regret: her father had not let his children study music, because none of them had talent and "he hated *dilettanti*," she said. As an adult, she came to believe that music should be taught "just like a language"—that it was important for one's general culture, whether or not one became a musician. Only Wanda, who was born later and spent much of her early childhood in Milan while her father was in New York, took piano lessons, at her mother's behest, and learned to read music.

For a while, Toscanini maintained his vow not to set foot inside La Scala, but his many friends and admirers there kept him informed of the house's activities. He later described his successor, Cleofonte Campanini, seven years his senior, as a musical fellow who played the violin and had "a certain amount of taste," and whose "orchestras always played well." But, Toscanini claimed, "he conducted from the piano score because he couldn't read an orchestra score." Toscanini felt that, "given our friendship," when Campanini was approached to replace him at La Scala "he ought to have asked me, 'What happened?' He accepted, period. But I didn't hold it against him [. . .]. It was enjoyable to be with him, because he was a Parmesan rascal who loved to talk. He was one of those theater people with all the vices, all the bad habits of the theater."

Upon being appointed to lead Italy's most important opera ensemble, Campanini had to prepare immediately for three major events that Toscanini had already planned: the first Italian production of *Das Rheingold* and the world premieres of Giordano's *Siberia* and Puccini's *Madama Butterfly*. The first two went well, but *Butterfly* did not.

Puccini, by now Italy's most popular living opera composer, had assumed that Toscanini would conduct the premiere of his sixth opera, *Butterfly*; this is clear from a note that the composer had sent to the conductor only days before the latter's rift with La Scala: "I wish you a good trip and a good stay in [South] America, hoping that upon your return my Butterfly will be finished and that she will begin to walk guided by you." But that was not to be. The story of the work's disastrous premiere has been told many times, but Toscanini, late in life, provided some additional information.

Early in 1896, when rehearsals for the premiere of *La Bohème* were beginning, and again in 1899, when *Tosca* was being completed, Puccini had played through his new operas for Toscanini, to communicate the score's tempi and nuances and to hear Toscanini's comments and suggestions. In March 1903, however, when *Butterfly* reached a satisfactory point, Puccini played only "a bit of the first act"—specifically, the extended love duet—Toscanini recalled. "Then he said, 'Here'—and he just gave me the piano-vocal score: 'You read through it.' I read through it. And I understood right away. I said [to myself], 'Puccini has lost his way.'"

Toscanini attributed much of the problem to the librettists, Illica and Giacosa, for having planned the opera in only two acts. But as he "felt sorry" for Puccini, who had broken a shin in a serious automobile accident (he loved new inventions and was one of the first people in his part of Italy to own a motorboat and a car) and was suffering from diabetes, he kept most of his criticisms to himself. Yet he couldn't resist criticizing Cio-Cio-San's reaction upon learning that Pinkerton's ship has returned and is in the harbor. "Weren't you thinking of Butterfly's heart?" Toscanini asked Puccini. "That moment, after she's been waiting for three years?" And, in a recorded conversation, Toscanini sings, intentionally anemically, Butterfly's little theme, and then sings full voice—by way of comparison—the driving, passionate music that accompanies Violetta's realization, toward the end of *La Traviata*, that Alfredo is about to arrive. But he does not say how Puccini responded.

Toscanini was so worried about the *Butterfly* premiere—probably more on account of Storchio, who was singing the title role, than on account of Puccini—that he gave the keys to his apartment to his friend and fellow Parmesan Mario Marchesi, La Scala's prompter, so that Marchesi could report back to him immediately after the performance without having to awaken the household. At the hour at which *Butterfly* was scheduled to begin, on the evening of 17 February 1904, Toscanini, alone in his studio, began to play through the opera, as if to give courage from afar to the performers, and he continued to the end. When Marchesi arrived, he asked Toscanini to guess at the outcome, and Toscanini replied that he thought *Butterfly* couldn't have been as successful as *Bohème* or *Tosca*. Not only had the opera not been a success, Marchesi reported: it had been "uno scandalo!" and the audience had actually laughed.

Toscanini was shocked. It was clear, he said, "that the opera was too long, that the second act was too long—but that they would laugh . . . !" The fiasco had in fact been prearranged in part by a claque hostile to Puccini and to Ricordi, his publisher; nevertheless, it was real—the worst episode in the mature Puccini's career.

There is no known comment by Toscanini on one of the evening's incidents: At some point, a draft from backstage had made Storchio's dress billow out, and someone in the audience had shouted, "Butter-fly is pregnant with Toscanini's child."[*]

Even after Puccini had thoroughly overhauled the opera—reshaping it into three acts, cutting here and there, adding an aria ("Addio, fiorito asil") for the tenor—Toscanini never developed a great liking for *Butterfly*, although he conducted it many times with much success. He maintained that it had become and remained pop-ular thanks only to the protagonist: "That little woman holds the hearts of the entire audience, but the music is rubbish," he said, although without explaining his drastic opinion. He claimed, too, that Puccini had stolen the opera's opening motif from *The Bartered Bride* Overture (see bar 8 et seq. of Smetana's piece), which he had heard Toscanini conduct in Milan in 1897, and that the music had been influenced further by the 1902 Scala production of Berlioz's *La Damnation de Faust*.[†] Toscanini also pointed out that in Italy *Butterfly* never became as popular as *Bohème* and *Tosca*; at La Scala it was not performed again during the remaining twenty years of Puccini's life.

16.

LA SCALA WAS OFF-LIMITS TO TOSCANINI, BUT SOUTH AMERICA remained a verdant musical pasture—and he had a family to sup-port. Between late May and late August 1904, he conducted fifty-five performances of fifteen operas in Buenos Aires and brought six of those productions (one performance each) to Montevideo. The rep-ertoire included the Argentine and Uruguayan premieres of *Madama Butterfly*, in the earliest of Puccini's revised, three-act versions, as well as of *La Wally* and Giordano's *Siberia*, and Toscanini's only per-formances anywhere of Weber's *Der Freischütz*.

The most popular singer in both capitals was Storchio, who appeared in five of the operas and moved audiences to tears. One of

---

[*] Many accounts state that this occurred when Storchio was in fact pregnant with Toscanini's child, but their son had been born nearly a year earlier.

[†] Mosco Carner, one of Puccini's biographers, also detected this connection to Smetana's piece. This writer hears, in the *Butterfly* opening, a resemblance to the *fugato* beginning of Berlioz's *Roméo et Juliette*; the *Damnation de Faust* connection seems more far-fetched.

her greatest successes was in *Butterfly*, which must have been particularly sweet for her, given the debacle of the previous winter. But the day-to-day situation must have been difficult: her affair with Toscanini was ongoing; she had had to leave their handicapped one-year-old son in Italy, in others' care; and Carla had accompanied her husband to Buenos Aires, probably also with six-year-old Walter.*

Pasquale Amato, a twenty-six-year-old Neapolitan baritone who was part of the Argentine ensemble, was frightened before his first encounter with Toscanini. He sang the part of Telramund in *Lohengrin* for the maestro, who said to him, as Amato later recalled, " 'This is not so bad, but, my boy, you come around early to-morrow morning, and I will show you something.' I came, of course, and he spent most of the morning working with me at the piano, as if it were the most important thing in the world. [. . .] This man, whom most people are afraid of, has the kindest heart in the world, and there is nothing he will not do for a young singer."

The Toscaninis had planned to take a ship to France rather than to Italy when the South American season ended late in August, and to spend time in Paris; instead they went directly to Genoa aboard an Italian vessel, because the maestro had accepted an invitation to conduct the Bolognese premiere of *Die Meistersinger* as well as what would remain his only production of Meyerbeer's *Dinorah*. Marco Enrico Bossi, an organist, composer, and head of the Bologna Conservatory, recalled that on *Meistersinger*'s opening night, as Toscanini raised his baton to begin the prelude, the terrified voice of someone in the gallery rang out: "Maestro, where's your music?" Some people, after all, had not heard about Toscanini's memory. Bossi also remembered "the laughs that would follow the funny stories that he would tell, wittily and picturesquely, in one or another Bolognese café, after rehearsals or performances at the Comunale. The hilarity would spread through the room; the circle of friends would expand and would further be surrounded by the waiters who, in order to be part of the general fun, would become deaf to the calls of the customers."

---

* Wally and Giorgio had been left in Milan with their nanny, Eugenia ("Nena") Rama. Nena "became our second mother," Wally said. "She always lived with our family and she is entombed next to Papà and Mamma."

After one *Meistersinger* performance, Toscanini received a visit from Pietro Suzzi, editor in chief of the Milanese newspaper *La Sera*, who brought him greetings from Gatti-Casazza. Toscanini immediately understood the subtext: Campanini was having trouble at La Scala. In fact, the orchestra members were complaining not only about the drop in quality but also about a lack of workplace consideration. Off the podium, Toscanini was famously kind to his musicians, and even on the podium he insisted on long rehearsals only when things were going badly and always allowed the players to take breaks, in an epoch in which barely nascent unions were powerless to rule on such matters. Campanini tended to rehearse at great length just for the sake of rehearsing, and he permitted breathing periods only when the spirit came over him.

But Toscanini could not be persuaded to return—at least not yet. "I wouldn't go back to La Scala if you paid me my weight in gold," he recalled having told Suzzi. In Milan, Toscanini did visit Gatti—at the manager's home, not at La Scala—but he remained adamant that the theater administration allow Campanini to complete his three-year term. His attitude was partly a gesture of fairness toward a colleague and partly a matter of pride: he no doubt felt that La Scala's administrators had not tried hard enough, the previous year, to keep him from leaving. Let them pay the full price for undervaluing him!

At the end of 1904, the Toscaninis moved temporarily to Rome, in order to explore the city's artistic and archaeological treasures. "I've begun the new year in full, sweet closeness with my family," the maestro wrote to Sormani on 1 January 1905. "Carla and I are happy with our new residence, we live very privately, travel all over Rome, which constantly sharpens our interest, and make ready to receive fresh impressions from our forthcoming trip to Sicily by reading books and pamphlets." The family visited Agrigento, Siracusa, Taormina, and other places of interest in Sicily, then returned to Rome.

During his restful weeks in the capital, Toscanini devoured large quantities of unfamiliar music, with a view toward future performances. Mahler's newly published Fifth Symphony he found lacking in both "personality" and "genius"; he did not grasp the composer's irony, and he compared his music unfavorably with that of Leoncavallo and minor Italian operetta composers. The work did not strike him as too radical; on the contrary, it seemed banal. But at the time, even most German-school conductors of Mahler and Toscanini's generation (Mahler was only seven years older than Toscanini) showed scant interest in Mahler's music; later, too, Otto Klemperer, a Mahler disciple nearly two decades younger than Toscanini, disliked most of the Fifth Symphony. Toscanini described Richard Strauss's *Symphonia Domestica*, also published in 1904, as "a formidable composition from a technical point of view, with flashes of brilliance, but highly debatable as an artistic path," a judgment with which most musicians today would agree. They would also agree with his view of a composer "of whose very name I was barely aware" but who "has won all my sympathy"—Claude Debussy, the forty-two-year-old Frenchman whose radical musical aesthetic, which made use of Eastern influences, pentatonic and whole-tone scales, and unorthodox harmonic progressions, was leading in an entirely different direction from that of the German post-Wagnerian avant-garde. Toscanini was studying *Pelléas et Mélisande*, which had first been performed three years earlier, in Paris. "His art overthrows everything that has been done up to now," Toscanini said. "He doesn't have Strauss's technique, but he is more brilliant, more elegant, and without a doubt bolder." Toscanini would soon begin to program Debussy's orchestral music, and he was already dreaming of conducting *Pelléas*, although he believed that "present-day audiences in all countries aren't yet ripe, I won't say for accepting it, but rather for making some sense of it!" Toscanini also had a look at Edward Elgar's "Enigma" Variations (published in 1899), which he began to conduct shortly thereafter, and at Tchaikovsky's Fifth Symphony and the recently deceased Dvořák's Sixth (D Major) Symphony, neither of which entered his repertoire.

In February, Toscanini led two concerts at Rome's Accademia di Santa Cecilia—his first professional appearances in the capital since 1892. He found the orchestra "horrid" but "good-hearted," and he told Count Enrico di San Martino Valperga, the Accademia's president, that he would need many rehearsals. But the count reported that despite advance warnings of the maestro's "terribly difficult character," he and his colleagues "always found Toscanini to be not only a most valuable artistic collaborator but also a wise and affectionate adviser on every problem."

In Rome, Toscanini received a letter from a Mr. Fano, who, it seems, was a concert agent with contacts in the British musical world, and who invited Toscanini to conduct two concerts with an unnamed London orchestra. Toscanini, recalling his dismay over the slapdash *Götterdämmerung* performance under Mottl's direction that he had heard at Covent Garden five years earlier, replied that he could not accept without first knowing "how many rehearsals would be granted me for [each concert], and of what length, and what criteria I would have to apply in working out the programs." He made the unusual declaration—typical, however, of his attitude—that he would "despair" were he to be accorded an enthusiastic reception for a performance that did not merit it. The proposed engagement never materialized.*

The Toscanini family's Roman idyll came to an end in mid-March: Carla and the children returned to Milan, while the maestro went to Bologna to prepare and conduct four concerts, in the course of which he added Elgar's "Enigma" Variations, Debussy's *Prelude to the Afternoon of a Faun*, and Strauss's *Death and Transfiguration* to his active repertoire. He then gave two concerts in Turin† and took the orchestra to the Milan Conservatory to give two performances—for the Società del Quartetto, at the conservatory—of a program that included Beethoven's "Eroica" Symphony, in honor of the one hundredth anniversary of the work's first public performance.

Early in June, he gave two more concerts with the Turin orchestra in Milan, but this time the venue was La Scala, despite his vow not to set foot again in the house. D'Ormeville reported that as the maestro walked onto the stage to begin the first concert, "the whole audience broke into a warm, spontaneous, affectionate, and prolonged ovation." And the *Corriere della Sera* published a sort of implicit, collective mea culpa, referring to Toscanini's "scrupulous sense of the highest artistic demands" and "unyielding intransigence with respect to certain production compromises," thanks to which "his glory seems more dazzling and pure: it is certain that also

---

* Two years later, the London Symphony Orchestra's board of directors "resolved to invite Signor Toscanini to conduct" during the 1907–08 season, alongside such celebrated older veterans as Hans Richter and Arthur Nikisch, although the board had turned down a request from Mahler to be invited. Toscanini did not accept the invitation. Subsequent LSO invitations to him were equally unsuccessful.

† Toscanini's fee in Bologna was 1,500 lire per concert, and in Turin, "as a special favor," 1,000 lire.

because of this his art grows ever greater and more beautiful." But the time was not quite ripe for a complete reconciliation.

17.

THE TOSCANINI FAMILY SPENT MUCH OF THE SUMMER OF 1905 thirty-three hundred feet above sea level at Pré-Saint-Didier, in the Aosta Valley, from which Toscanini made several mountain-climbing excursions in the company of a guide, a porter, and one of Carla's Milanese cousins.

The first expedition lasted three weeks and took him through nearby Courmayeur to the daunting peaks and glaciers of the Mont Blanc massif. En route, during a blizzard on the Col du Géant, Toscanini and his companions took refuge in a shelter, where they found two Swiss mountain climbers who had also been caught in the storm. One of them was the musicologist Aloys Mooser, who knew Toscanini's name and reputation. "Once the hot soup had been distributed," Mooser recalled, "Toscanini and I stretched out on the camp bed, where, curled up side by side under a wretched cover, the better to fight the cold, we began a spirited conversation that continued for the two and a half days during which the storm kept us prisoners [. . .]." When Mooser mentioned that he was living in St. Petersburg, he was

> surprised to hear him ask me point-blank: "So you have seen *Boris Godunov?*" I fell from the clouds. If at that time there weren't twenty people in the West who knew [Modest Mussorgsky's] opera, the situation was hardly more encouraging in Russia, where the official milieu, the court, the public, many professional musician s, and the majority of the press considered Mussorgsky a sort of failure nearly bereft of talent [. . .]. At that time none of his works was admitted on the imperial stages, and to get to know *Boris Godunov*—of which my teacher Mily Balakirev had spoken with delirious enthusiasm—I had had to read the full score at the piano. [. . .] And it was nearly 3,000 kilometers from there, in an ice-covered hut perched at an altitude of 3,350 meters, that a young Italian musician was talk-

ing to me about this work. I do not know how, but he had come to know it, he had studied it in great detail, and he had immediately perceived its moving grandeur and burned with a desire to see and hear it on the stage. "Someday I shall conduct it," he declared to me in a determined tone of voice.[*]

Toscanini refused to wear a balaclava or sunglasses during his mountaineering expeditions and always returned from them with red eyes and sunburn. Nor would he wear heavy gloves—and during the 1905 expedition, just a few meters below the summit of the Dente del Gigante, a 13,170-foot peak on the Mont Blanc massif, his hands became so numb that he had to call for help from Barmaz, the guide, "because he felt that with his stiff fingers he couldn't manage to grip the rock and the ropes that were rubbing against the wall [of rock]," Walter Toscanini wrote. "Barmaz urged him to hold out until he could find a more secure foothold, and when he was solidly supported, [Barmaz] told my father to let himself hang over the abyss and put his hands in his armpits. So my father dangled over the abyss for several minutes until his circulation was sufficiently reestablished to allow him to continue the climb."

Toscanini and his friends did eventually get to the highest peak in Western Europe, and as soon as they had returned to civilization he sent a postcard to Polo: "We reached the top of Mont Blanc. Dante, Beethoven, Wagner!!! Quivering with rapture." Instead of returning the way they had come, on the Italian side of the mountain, the group had descended the French side and gradually made its way back to Pré-Saint-Didier. After a rest, Toscanini and his friends undertook another lengthy excursion from the village of Degioz, at the foot of the Gran Paradiso in the Aosta Valley, and attempted to climb what he described as the "arduous and beautiful" Grivola, a Matterhorn-like peak. Later in August he wrote to Polo from the "very charming village" of Cogne, "Gave up the Grivola because of a blizzard; I'll try again today. Sunday I'll do the Herbetet and will

---

[*] Mooser believed that the year of his encounter with Toscanini was 1898, but Walter Toscanini was almost certainly correct in thinking that it took place in 1905, when Toscanini *père* made his only climb of Mont Blanc.

end my climbs for this year, seeing as the Matterhorn is impossible because of bad weather."

Climbing may have been arduous, but it was a trifle compared with the workload that Toscanini faced after having descended to the Po plain. Bologna was his first professional stop: in October, November, and December 1905, he conducted the local premieres of *Siegfried*, *Butterfly*, and *Hänsel und Gretel* plus the world premiere of an opera called *Cassandra* by one Vittorio Gnecchi, which received only two performances.*

Puccini, recovered from his physical and professional ills, was in London supervising a *Butterfly* production while Toscanini was preparing the same opera in Bologna. At first, the composer thought that he would not be able to attend the Bologna premiere, and he wrote to Toscanini, "I securely and tranquilly place the opera in your hands. Try to achieve the effect of the lamps that go out as if for lack of oil at the break of dawn, in the third act." There were other staging instructions as well, and in the end Puccini was so eager to hear Toscanini conduct *Butterfly* that he notified him that he would arrive two days before the Bologna premiere.

The first Bologna audience received the opera somewhat coldly, but Puccini was happy with the performance. "A million thanks for all the intelligence and heart that you transfused into my *Butterfly*," he wrote the next day. If the audiences warmed up, he said, he would return "to enjoy your stupendous interpretation." They did, and he did. Puccini made use of suggestions from Toscanini to further touch up his score and to complete what would become the third edition of *Butterfly*.

Cio-Cio-San in Bologna was Salomea Kruszelnicka (known in Italy as Krusceniski), a thirty-three-year-old Ukrainian soprano with a voice both powerful and expressive. Toscanini described her as "very beautiful" and reportedly told a friend that she was the only woman he had pursued who had said no to him—which was patently untrue.

At the time of his Turin concerts the previous spring, Toscanini had agreed to resume command of the Teatro Regio, which was about to reopen after renovations that had lasted several years. He

---

* Richard Strauss was later accused of having stolen bits of *Cassandra* when he wrote *Elektra*. The theory has been revived from time to time but has never diminished the popularity of *Elektra* or increased that of *Cassandra*.

rushed there from Bologna to prepare and conduct the local premieres of *Siegfried*, *Butterfly*, *La Damnation de Faust*, and Giordano's *Siberia*, plus a revival of *Loreley*. (Sonzogno, the publisher who owned the Italian rights to the Berlioz and Giordano works, had made the performance of the latter a condition for allowing the former to be performed as well.) The *Siegfried* production, with evocative sets by Ugo Gheduzzi—a well-known painter and enthusiastic Wagnerite— attracted an overflow audience. "Siegfried creates much interest," Toscanini wrote to Marchesi. "So far it's made an average of five thousand lire [per performance] and the public's interest is ever stronger." Fourteen performances of Wagner's opera were given to satisfy public demand.

In a conversation taped in his old age, Toscanini described to a younger colleague how much effort he had put into conducting *Siegfried* and other Wagner operas. "I conducted *Siegfried* a lot," until "I couldn't stand it any longer, I felt like throwing up." He would rehearse the winds alone, then the strings alone, then run twenty-one complete orchestra, ensemble, and dress rehearsals, because the orchestras weren't so good in those days, he said. "Wagner kills you." And he commented with a laugh that in performing *Die Meistersinger*, when he would get to the beginning of the grand final scene, "I felt as if I'd begun a week earlier."

Apart from *La Damnation de Faust*, Toscanini's original plan for Turin had been entirely different: it had included the Italian premiere of Strauss's *Salome*—but an Italian edition could not be prepared quickly enough (the world premiere, in Dresden, had just taken place); *La Wally*; the local premieres of Mascagni's latest opera, *Amica*, and of *Chopin* by Giacomo Orefice; and the entire *Ring* cycle!* A proposal to include *Iolanta*, Tchaikovsky's last opera, also came to naught. But in mid-March 1906, following his Turin opera season, Toscanini led the Regio orchestra in three concerts at home and a ten-day tour of seven northern Italian cities.

During the Turin season, Toscanini had made occasional brief visits to Milan, not only to be with Carla and the children but also to see his father. Claudio Toscanini, who turned seventy-three in January 1906,

---

* Toscanini never conducted a complete *Ring* cycle, nor did he ever perform *Das Rheingold*, except for some excerpts in concert form.

was seriously ill, probably with cancer. Late that month, Carla wrote to her husband that his father was "much thinner" but "recognized me right away and took a little marsala with me." Two days later, she wrote that Claudio was "still very weak and doesn't want to eat anything." The following day, 29 January, while his son was conducting the Turin orchestra in Como, Claudio died; he was buried, as he had wished, in the red shirt that he had worn in Garibaldi's army forty years earlier. Arturo, whose relations with his mercurial father had been uneasy at best, nevertheless valued Claudio's sweet nature and political idealism and would eventually allow the problems that Claudio's harebrained schemes had caused him to fade in his memory.

18.

BUENOS AIRES BECKONED ONCE AGAIN: FOR THE FOURTH TIME, Toscanini accepted a lucrative offer from the Nardi-Bonetti *impresa* to conduct an opera season in the Argentine capital.* On 26 April 1906, Arturo, Carla, and Giorgio embarked at Genoa (Walter and Wally remained in Milan in their nanny's care), together with Marchesi (the prompter), two musical assistants, the chorus director Giulio Setti, and at least twenty-six orchestra musicians: real Argentine music lovers as well as Eurocentric status seekers were willing to spend a great deal to secure Toscanini's services. As in his previous seasons at the Teatro de la Ópera, he faced a tremendous workload: there were sixteen operas to rehearse and perform in two and a half months, after which the whole ensemble went to Montevideo, where eleven of the operas were performed—one of them twice, the others once each—within fourteen days. The two South American capitals witnessed Toscanini's only performances anywhere of *Don Giovanni*, and in Buenos Aires he gave his sole performances—and the Argentine premiere—of Franchetti's *La Figlia di Jorio*.

In May a diphtheria epidemic broke out in Buenos Aires, and there was a shortage of serum to counter it. Giorgio became ill, and on 10 June 1906 he died, three months before his fifth birthday and less

---

* Toscanini was paid about 70,000 lire for the season, but he made a substantial donation to the survivors of an earthquake that destroyed much of Valparaiso, Chile.

than three months after Claudio Toscanini's death. "Heartbroken I announce death dear Giorgio diphtheria nephritis," Toscanini cabled Polo the next day. Many members of the company turned out for the boy's funeral and temporary interment at the cemetery in Buenos Aires's Recoleta quarter.

Before Giorgio became ill—according to one legend—he had taken the silent role of Cio-Cio-San's child in the Buenos Aires *Butterfly* production, and when Toscanini saw another child in the part at a performance after Giorgio's death he burst into tears—yet continued to conduct. But the only two performances of *Butterfly* that season took place on 5 and 9 June, when Giorgio was already ill but still alive, and even had the boy been well, Toscanini would never have allowed him to be seen as the child of Storchio, who was singing the title role. Another myth, which Wally claimed to have heard from her mother, was that Toscanini conducted a performance on the day after Giorgio's death: "He had a sense of duty to the point of exasperation, and he was embarrassed about showing his feelings," Wally said. It is true that Toscanini drowned his grief in work and probably continued to conduct rehearsals in the days following his son's death, but he did not conduct another public performance until nearly a week had gone by.

Carla, unlike her husband but like most other middle-class or wealthier women of her day, had no work outside the home; she had only her family. Besides, by this time she certainly knew about Arturo's affair with Storchio and about the child he had had with her. She was still in her twenties, still pretty, and completely devoted to him; she knew that in his way he was also devoted to her and to the children, and that he was good-hearted and generous, but she hated the easygoing, bed-hopping mores of the people who inhabited the theater world. In her grief over Giorgio's death, she made up her mind to leave her husband: she looked into ship departures and packed her trunks.

Toscanini begged her to stay. He wanted his children to have a more stable family life than he had had, and despite his dislike of organized religion in general and the Roman Catholic Church in particular he was categorically opposed to divorce, which, in any case, was not legal in Italy during Toscanini's lifetime. "I've always thought that the companion I chose in life [. . .] should never be replaced by any other woman," he once wrote to a lover. He regretted that he was "incapable of rebelling against old moral theories invented by abject, stupid, false men, not by nature, which binds two beings not by laws but by love!" And in another letter: "I see myself as a young man (30 years old), during the first year of my marriage, *already troubled* [. . .]—uncertain whether the fault was on my side or the other, but certain that matrimonial life didn't appear the way I'd wanted it, the way I'd believed it would be. I've been a good, honest, but unfaithful husband. C[arla] has never understood me"—a common excuse made by philandering men—"nor has she ever tried to improve, but she has always been good, honest, and faithful. In a life lived together, that's not everything [. . .]." In still another letter: "that dream of spiritual and sensual harmony that we all look for, from the threshold of adolescence to the eve of marriage, often dissolves the day after, or not much later, and forever. [. . .] Marriage has to be considered a sort of adventure, fortunate or tempestuous (glücklich oder stürmisch); at some point, we must find a modus vivendi if we want to make it to the end of the adventure."

With respect to himself as husband and father, and of ideal and real marriage, he said, "At home I am not—nor have I ever wished to be *authoritarian*. I've never understood the [idea of the] husband, the acting head of the household. [. . .] I believe everyone to be my equal, I think of life together as being in perfect, cordial friendship. In *life* as *in art* one must have exquisite sensitivity. Woe to those who lack it! [. . .] How many marriages are destroyed after only a few years for lack of reciprocal *self-respect!*"* It was a fine example of the double standard in action.

In the end, he persuaded his wife of nine years to stay with him, and they returned to Italy together. For the remaining forty-five years of her life, Carla was caught between love for and adoration of her husband and distress over his ongoing erotic restlessness.

19.

THE TOSCANINIS WERE EN ROUTE TO THEIR WRETCHED SOUTH American sojourn when, at the end of April 1906, the *Gazzetta Teatrale Italiana* reported that after long negotiations the maestro had

---

* Toscanini used the English term "self-respect," but he meant, simply, respect.

agreed to resume the artistic direction of La Scala beginning with the forthcoming 1906–07 season.

Cleofonte Campanini, Toscanini's successor at La Scala in 1903, had had "the misfortune of seeing always [. . .] the shadow of his illustrious predecessor," Gatti-Casazza would recall. In December 1905, at the start of the final season of Campanini's three-year contract, support for the conductor among the theater's musicians and administrators collapsed. During a rehearsal of Auber's *Fra Diavolo*, he kept the orchestra playing without a break for three hours and then said, "Let's go have a cigarette." The musicians rebelled: by the time Campanini returned after the break, the entire orchestra had deserted. He left the theater, packed his bags, and never went back to La Scala. Gatti-Casazza engaged Mugnone, who took over the rest of the season, but most of La Scala's personnel were clamoring for Toscanini.

Toscanini at first declared that he no longer wanted to lead opera seasons in Italy: he would conduct opera in South America, where he was paid handsomely, and would "give myself completely to concerts" in Italy, he said. Besides, in 1903, when Toscanini had left La Scala, Duke Uberto Visconti di Modrone, the president of the board, had sworn that Toscanini would never again be engaged there. The duke viewed the maestro as a demanding, annoying artist who did not understand that La Scala existed in the first place as a social venue for the upper and upper-middle classes; artistic standards were important but secondary. Thus, early in 1906, when Toscanini's name was resounding louder and louder through La Scala's corridors, the maestro insisted that the duke come to his home to ask him to return: "I wanted to make him swallow his words," Toscanini recalled, conveniently forgetting that he himself had vowed not to return to La Scala.

Even after the duke's visit, however, Toscanini dithered. He had been offered 50,000 lire to return to the Regio in Turin for the 1906–07 season and had been promised 100,000 for the following year. Such fees were possible because the Regio was still run by an impresario on a profit-and-loss basis, with guarantees from the municipality, whereas La Scala, despite its greater prestige, had to depend on the largesse of its board and subscribers. A letter from Leonardo Bistolfi, a well-known, Turin-based sculptor who had become one of Toscanini's best friends, helped him to make his decision. "I suffered in

Milan to see you tormented by the persistence of La Scala's directors," Bistolfi said, "but [. . .] I suffer even more at the thought that
you could manage to get yourself out of what I consider *your destiny!*
[. . .] God only knows what the cost will be for our poor intellectual
life in Turin—poor but not unworthy—not to have you here any
longer to raise it up. But I also know that your *right* is to support and
govern the greatest treasure in Italian musical life."

Toscanini agreed to return to La Scala at a fee of 30,000 lire per
season; the board tried to bargain him down to 28,000, but this time
he stood his ground.* And because his reputation had grown even
greater during the intervening years, he was able to impose some
noneconomic conditions before he accepted La Scala's offer: access
to the stage would be forbidden to anyone not involved in the production, thus eliminating the presence of well-heeled gentlemen
hunting for ballerina mistresses; La Scala's first orchestra pit would
be constructed during the summer of 1907; and encores would be
banned in reality, not merely in theory: the drama would not be
interrupted. "And so I returned to La Scala," Toscanini recalled, half
a century later, "not over Campanini's body but over that of my 'simpatico' Mugnone."

At his first performance—the opening of a new production of *Carmen*—Toscanini was greeted with great warmth by an audience that
included numerous aristocrats and Eleonora Duse, who, at forty-
eight, was the most celebrated actress in Europe, with the possible
exception of Sarah Bernhardt. The fiery Catalan mezzo-soprano
Maria Gay headed an all-star cast, with Zenatello as Don José and De
Luca as Escamillo.

Before beginning to prepare *Carmen*, however, and indeed immediately upon his return from South America, Toscanini had had to
resolve a pressing issue: the Italian premiere of *Salome*. He had
wanted to arrange the production for Turin the previous year, had
instructed the Regio's management to begin negotiations for the
rights, and had been in direct contact with Strauss on the matter
even before the score was complete: in July 1905, he had written—in

---

* The Visconti family's record books show that Toscanini was paid 7,500 lire on 1
December 1906 and the same amount on 1 January, 30 January, and 28 February 1907. As he
had done previously and would continue to do in the future, he did not accept free seats
for his family and friends but paid 200 lire per season for a box.

appalling French—to declare his "ardent desire to perform *Salome* in Turin," further stating that he would be "infinitely happy" to meet Strauss on that occasion, and mentioning that he had found a copy of Oscar Wilde's original French version of the text, which "could be of use for the Italian translation."

Strauss, then forty-one—only three years older than Toscanini—and one of Europe's most famous living composers, replied quickly, in almost equally awful French. "I greatly rejoice in your great interest in my works," he told Toscanini, and he said that an Italian translation was already underway. But when Strauss mentioned that "the piano score will be finished around 15 September, the orchestra score at the end of October"; that "the study of the vocal parts with the singers will require at least two months"; and that "the orchestra is very big and very difficult," Toscanini realized that he could not hope to program *Salome* for the 1905–06 season. In December 1905, he traveled to Dresden for the opera's world premiere, or one of its first performances; he probably met the composer on that occasion, and he later described the production's conductor, Ernst von Schuch, as *"molto bravo"* and *"simpaticissimo"*—although he noted with astonishment that the orchestra entered after the conductor's beat, as was and is the custom in many Central European countries, instead of on the beat, as elsewhere. And he laughed at the recollection of going to Schuch's dressing room after the performance and finding him "naked, because he had perspired, like me."

But a serious problem developed in the fall of 1906. Strauss and his Berlin-based publisher, Adolf Fürstner, had promised *Salome*'s Italian premiere to Turin, and since Toscanini was no longer there Strauss had agreed to conduct it himself. Toscanini was upset: the original idea and initial efforts had been his, and he now wanted to conduct the premiere at La Scala. He made up his mind to go to Berlin, to discuss the matter with Strauss and Fürstner, and he brought with him Carla, for moral support, and Polo, who spoke German, as interpreter. As they approached the composer's house in Potsdam, Toscanini suddenly turned and walked away, probably because he anticipated an unpleasant situation, but Carla and Polo caught up with him and persuaded him to complete the mission for which they had made the long trip. The tall, mustachioed, elegantly turned-out Strauss warmly welcomed the short, mustachioed, elegantly turned-out Toscanini and his entourage, but he reiterated that he and Fürstner had already given their word to Turin. Originally, La Scala had intended to present *Salome* the following February, by which time Toscanini would have had two full months to get his troops back in shape after their previous up-and-down season. Now, however, Toscanini proposed giving the opera simultaneously in both cities, to which Strauss responded that if Milan were willing to pay a fee equal to that being paid by Turin . . . . Toscanini stood up, said that Strauss's respect for his word of honor was evidently nothing but a question of money, and walked out.

Later that day, Strauss had a letter delivered to Toscanini at his hotel. "I am very sorry that you are angry with me; but really, this series of mistakes is not my fault," the composer wrote. He said that there had been correspondence on the issue throughout the summer; La Scala had offered him 3,000 francs for performance rights, but he had asked for 10,000—"more if Milan should give more than ten performances. Is it not true," Strauss continued, "that it is now a totally different thing when Mr. Gatti-Casazza asks for [performing rights for] four months, when he asks for the premiere on the same day as Turin, which is paying 15,000 francs?" Strauss expressed the hope that Toscanini would no longer be angry with him when they would meet again at Fürstner's office the next morning.

Toscanini replied immediately, assuring Strauss, "I am not at all angry with you: I am only very astonished that when I expressed my simple and more than natural personal wish to give *Salome* on [December] 26th in Milan you did not interpret this wish according to its true meaning but rather brought the matter onto commercial terrain." He still hoped that Strauss would reconsider; otherwise, the Milanese would have to present *Salome* at a later date, "because I cannot allow the administration of La Scala to make a [financial] sacrifice as a favor to me."

The meeting at Fürstner's changed nothing. Strauss saw the matter in terms of his legal right to earn a much larger sum of money and of Turin's legal right to present the *Salome* premiere, since it was paying more than the Milanese could pay; Toscanini, on the other hand, was disappointed—and angry, despite his protestations to the contrary—that he, as the earliest significant Italian champion of Strauss's then controversial music and the initiator of the proposal to bring *Salome* to Italy, would not be able to conduct the premiere, or at least the copremiere. The Toscaninis and Polo returned to Milan empty-handed.

Soon after Toscanini had begun to teach his singers their parts in *Salome*, he realized that he had been "perfectly stupid to settle on a date for the performance of an opera without having taken its difficulties into consideration," as he wrote (in Italian) to Strauss on 12 November; "consequently *Salome* cannot be performed before early January." In other words, the problem had resolved itself. "Please believe always in my admiration for your art, and accept my devoted greetings," Toscanini wrote.

"Admiration for your art," but not for *you*: the message was clear. Strauss already had a reputation—which he would maintain for the rest of his life—as a hard-nosed businessman, whereas Toscanini had no head at all for money. As the weeks went by, what the conductor saw as the composer's betrayal rankled increasingly. The *Salome* rehearsals began to go better and better, and at the first ensemble rehearsal they performed "the whole opera, straight through," Toscanini recalled; Puccini, who was present, could hardly believe that there had been no previous ensemble rehearsals. Thus Toscanini and the Scala administration decided to throw caution—and legality—to the winds and announce that their first *Salome* performance would take place on 26 December, the same night as the Turin premiere.

Strauss and the Teatro Regio's administrators made the next move by bringing their premiere forward to the twenty-third, and then to the twenty-second. The Scala people then took a different tack. "Not being able to give the premiere legally," Gatti-Casazza recalled, "I decided to invite to the dress rehearsal all the subscribers and, of course, the entire press. There were protests from Turin and from Strauss, but these were greeted by absolute indifference on my part. The dress rehearsal, with invitations, took place [on 21 December], constituting a real premiere. Thus it was we outwitted Turin."

D'Ormeville, whose interests, in this case, lay with Strauss and Fürstner, declared that Toscanini and Gatti's decision was based not so much on the desire to be first as on the belief that the Turin performance would be a fiasco and could therefore have a negative influence on the audience's reaction to the Milanese production.

"The Scala people are convinced, in their arrogant egotism, that nothing good can be done outside La Scala, just as the Pope is persuaded that no salvation is possible outside the bosom of the Holy Mother Church," he said.*

Whatever the motives may have been, Milan lost the official premiere to Turin. Strauss's tightly compressed and highly original *Salome*, closely based on Oscar Wilde's play of the same name—an extreme example of the fin-de-siècle and pre–World War I decadentism that had mesmerized entire segments of European culture—contains an explosive mix of near blasphemy, gore, and lurid sex. It was temporarily banned in Vienna, London, and New York, but if there were objections to it on the part of Italy's religious authorities, they were not allowed to prevail. At La Scala, the *Corriere della Sera* reported, the applause was warm and widespread, although "part of the audience looked around, uncertain, as if in a stupor. People didn't know what to think of what they had seen and heard. They knew only that a despotic, perhaps brutal, and certainly irresistible force had taken hold of them, penetrated them, and shocked them." The melodramatic violence of Italian *verismo* had been overtaken in a single leap by the refined violence of Germany's leading composer.

Two of the critics who heard both the Turin and the Milan productions declared a slight preference for Gemma Bellincioni's performance of the title role at the Regio over that of the appropriately named Salomea Kruszelnicka at La Scala,† but there were no significant criticisms of the performances at either house—and, as one reviewer pointed out, in Turin Strauss had the privilege of working with an orchestra that had been in Toscanini's hands until a few months earlier.

The fight over the premiere had infuriated Strauss, who did not attend any of La Scala's performances, but third parties convinced him that his own had been superior. "Toscanini, with a pitilessly raging orchestra, is said simply to have slaughtered the singers and the drama," he wrote to his wife. Thanks to Toscanini's insistence eleven

---

* Yet the Turin-based music historian Alberto Basso, in his history of the Teatro Regio, placed the blame for the Milan-Turin *Salome* fight squarely on Strauss, not on Toscanini.

† The Dance of the Seven Veils was performed by a ballerina, not by Kruszelnicka. And since *Salome* is short, each performance of it at La Scala was followed by a ballet.

years earlier, the Regio already had an orchestra pit, whereas the Scala orchestra was still performing at main-floor level during the 1906–07 season. Overpowering volume levels from the gigantic orchestra that *Salome* requires would have come as no surprise. But in more than a dozen published reviews of the Scala production, whether the reviewers were negatively or positively disposed toward the opera, there is not a single mention of the orchestra's outbalancing the singers. Toscanini remembered the performances as having been "very good," and so great was the demand for tickets that sixteen performances had to be given, not including the public dress rehearsal. Strauss's informants must have been telling him what he wanted to hear. And Strauss, himself an outstanding conductor, changed his mind about Toscanini when he eventually observed him at work. George Szell, the eminent conductor who, as a young man in the late 1910s, served as Strauss's assistant, heard that Strauss had said, "When you see that man conduct, you feel that there is only one thing for you to do: take your baton, break it in pieces, and never conduct again." Toscanini, for his part, would continue to conduct five of Strauss's symphonic poems, but he would never again perform *Salome*, and he disliked Strauss's subsequent operas.

Some time after the Milan-Turin episode, one of the singers from the Scala production bumped into a colleague from the Regio production and asked for a report. The answer, typically, had nothing to do with artistic matters: "Strauss went out to dinner with us every evening in Turin and never paid," the singer said. "Maestro Toscanini is different. He always pays."

20.

TOSCANINI WAS CONSISTENTLY PRAISED BY THE CRITICS AS THE 1906–07 season proceeded with demanding revivals of *La Gioconda*, *Tristan*, *Aida*, and *La Wally*. The season's seventh opera was a revival of Gluck's *Orfeo ed Euridice*, a work close to Toscanini's heart: like Berlioz and Wagner, he admired Gluck's pioneering originality in the musical theater. But the Milanese public was generally bored by what was considered an eighteenth-century relic, and one review sported the punning headline "Morpheus at La Scala." *Orfeo* received only two performances, as did the subsequent opera, Francesco Cilea's *Gloria*, in its world premiere. Cilea, whose posthumous international reputation rests almost entirely on his earlier *Adriana Lecouvreur*, had second thoughts about *Gloria*—a tale of passion and violence in fourteenth-century Siena—and asked to have it withdrawn, but Toscanini, tired of hearing the composer importune him to perform it, and after having studied and rehearsed the score, insisted on proceeding. Thus Cilea, like Mascagni at the time of *Iris* and *Le Maschere*, was subjected to the double indignity of witnessing the performance and performers praised but his opera damned. The audience received *Gloria* with indifference, and Toscanini never again conducted a note of Cilea's music.

The season was to have closed with the local premiere of Massenet's recent *Le Jongleur de Notre-Dame*; when this project collapsed, for reasons no longer known, a remounting of *Cavalleria Rusticana* was scheduled in its stead. The newspapers waxed ironic about a "millionth version" of "Mascagni's masterpiece," complained that the singers were not good enough, and claimed that Toscanini had not lived up to his usual high standards. This production, too, closed after only two performances.

Toscanini was having problems with his eyes for the first of many times in his life; after having brought the season to a close by conducting two pairs of concerts with the Scala orchestra, he spent two weeks in darkened rooms, on his doctor's orders, "like a ghost, without being able to read and without being able to keep busy in any way!" he wrote to a friend. Once he had reemerged into the light of day, he took his family to Giomein at Breuil-Cervinia, 6,560 feet above sea level on the Italian side of the Matterhorn, where he found a fellow spirit in the sixty-year-old Edmondo De Amicis, author of the perennially popular Italian novel *Cuore* (Heart), and a left-wing nationalist and Vatican baiter.

The maestro did some mountain climbing, but Carla relaxed: she was pregnant for the fourth time. Despite her distress over her husband's philandering, and despite, or perhaps because of, her grief over Giorgio's death, she wanted another child, and so, probably, did Arturo. But once she was pregnant, their sexual relations ended forever. Years later, Toscanini wrote to a friend that he hadn't been able to have "physical contact" with Carla since even before the last child's birth, but he did not say who rejected whom, or whether the cause was physiological or psychological, or both. Toscanini was forty at the time; Carla was only thirty, and as far as is known she had no sexual relations with anyone for the rest of her life.

The child, a girl, was born on 5 December 1907 and was named Wanda Giorgina: the first name was meant to continue the "lucky W" chain (as with Walter and Wally), related to the fact that the letter W does not exist in the Italian alphabet. Seventy years later, Wally hazarded the scientifically baseless but imaginative opinion that her younger sister's notoriously difficult character was the result of her having been conceived in bitterness rather than in love.

21.

BEFORE HE LEFT FOR THE ALPS, TOSCANINI HAD FACED A BATTLE over the construction of La Scala's orchestra pit. A committee made up of himself plus Boito, Puccini, and two others had been set up to deal with the matter, and Cesare Albertini, an engineer, had been sent to study the orchestra pits of the most important opera houses in Europe. But Boito opposed making any change to the theater, claiming that those who favored the installation of the pit were merely paying court to the Germans.

"I said, 'Maestro, no, I have never paid court to the Germans,'" Toscanini recalled. "'But here I understand why they're right at Bayreuth, not to see that clown conducting in the middle of the orchestra; not to see [. . .] the trumpet puffing to make a *forte*, the double basses sawing away [. . .]. In the midst of the drama's poetic zone, we see all these people working.'"

At the committee's final meeting, Boito read a letter of Verdi's in which the composer had expressed himself against the lowering of the orchestra. Toscanini reminded Boito that if one clapped one's hands behind the conductor's podium, an echo could be heard, and he promised that if at any point during the work on the pit the echo could no longer be heard, everything would be put back as before.

The pit did not harm La Scala's acoustics. And six years later, when a huge volume of Verdi's letters was published, Toscanini came across one (10 July 1871) in which he underlined an entire paragraph: "*. . . the* *invisible orchestra.* This is not my idea, it is Wagner's; and it is a very good one.—It seems impossible that in this day and age one still tolerates seeing our wretched frock-coats and white bowties, mixed together with an Egyptian, Assyrian, or Druid costume, etc., etc. . . ; and furthermore, to see the orchestra, *which is part of the fictitious world*, almost in the middle of the ground floor, in the world of the hissers or applauders. Add to all this the obscenity of seeing the harpists' heads, the double bass players' cuffs, and the conductor's windmill." Toscanini felt vindicated, and he wrote, in a marginal note, "Not at all Wagner's [idea], but that of the first Italian melodramatists."

He took full advantage of his new orchestra pit by opening La Scala's season, on 21 December 1907, with a production of *Götterdämmerung*, which demands large orchestral forces. About a revival of *Tosca* that followed the *Götterdämmerung* production, Puccini reported to Carlo Clausetti of the Ricordi company that there was "panic" at the first performance, "but as soon as the tummy butterflies disappeared there emerged a strong, incisive interpretation by Toscanini and a highly effective ensemble on stage." Toscanini then led a tepidly received reprise of Franchetti's *Cristoforo Colombo* and a production of Gustave Charpentier's *Louise*, a sort of French *verismo* opera that its composer called a "novel in four acts." *Louise* had been a great success in Paris since its premiere in 1900, and Toscanini, like Mahler—who was then chief conductor of the Vienna Court Opera— was fascinated by the intense and brilliantly scored work, which contains a Baroque viola d'amore and a modern sewing machine. It had failed miserably at its first Milanese performance, in 1901, with the composer conducting, incompetently by most extant accounts; Toscanini wanted to give the city's music lovers another chance to get to know the work, but his attempt failed: reviewers unanimously praised the performers but found the opera wanting, and the public's reaction was lukewarm.

For the title role, Toscanini had engaged Frances Alda (stage name of Fanny Jane Davis), a redheaded, twenty-eight-year-old, New Zealand–born, Australian-bred, Paris-trained soprano. She had sung recently in Parma, together with the celebrated baritone Mattia Battistini; Battistini had never worked with Toscanini, but Alda recalled that when she told her colleague that she would be working with the maestro, he "exploded in a volley of ecstatic praises." When she arrived at La Scala, Gatti-Casazza and Toscanini asked her whether she could sing various roles, and she replied yes to everything—at which "Toscanini's eyes twinkled and the corners of his mouth quirked into a smile," she later wrote.

At her first coaching session with Toscanini, in a rehearsal room at La Scala, "I sang the rôle straight through," she recalled. "[. . .] Toscanini leaned across the pianist's shoulder and closed the music book on the rack. Only then did he open his eyes and look at me. Blandly, in Italian, he asked: 'In what language were you singing?'" Although she was young and not yet well-known, Alda "marched out of the rehearsal room, out of the theatre and back to the Hotel Milan."

She eventually got over Toscanini's sarcasm, received careful coaching from him on her Italian diction, and scored a success with audiences and critics alike. Thirty years later, Alda wrote, "Now, recalling that childish fit of temper and hurt pride on my part, I think too of the innumerable times later on that Toscanini taught me the rôles I was to sing; his infinite patience and inspiring enthusiasm, and all that I owe him." And she commented to an American journalist, "I went to the Scala from the French theatres, where intrigue is always to the fore, and was astonished at the peace and quiet," she said. "It scarcely seemed like an opera house, everybody was so charming."

Most Italian opera houses operated and still operate on the *stagione* (season) system: the number of operas to be produced in a given season is established, and they are mounted one after another, with rarely more than two works alternating in any given week. Successful productions are set aside for a few years and then revived. But in many of the major foreign houses, successful productions were (and are) revived year after year, or after an interval of only a single season, and three or four different operas are presented in any given week. Toscanini began to consider the possibility of bringing this "repertoire system" to La Scala. If a production is thoroughly rehearsed, he reasoned, and if at least some of the principal cast members remain from one season to the next, a revival can be mounted with only a fraction of the rehearsal time required for a new production. During the 1907–08 Scala season, he experimented with this plan by reviving *La Gioconda* from the previous year, with three of the same leading singers. The press debated the pros and cons of the procedure, but it was a success with the public.

In the event, however, Toscanini would not be able to expand or even reattempt the experiment the following year; not in Milan, at any rate. The same articles that reviewed the *Gioconda* opening, which took place on 16 February, carried comments on recent news that had shocked the city's musical public: Toscanini and Gatti-Casazza would leave La Scala at the end of the season and would take up comparable positions with the Metropolitan Opera Company in New York City.

22.

TOSCANINI HAD FIRST BEEN APPROACHED BY THE METROPOLITAN in 1903, at the time of his break with La Scala, but he had rejected the proposal out of hand. Three years later, Heinrich Conried, the Metropolitan's general manager, and the financier Otto H. Kahn, a key member of the organization's board of directors, made him another offer through Count Enrico di San Martino Valperga, the president of Rome's Accademia di Santa Cecilia, and Toscanini asked Caruso for advice on the matter. The tenor—who, since his New York debut in 1903, had become what would soon be known as a matinee idol—answered (as Toscanini told some American friends many years later, in his Italian-laced English): "'No, Metropolitan is teatro per cantanti [theater for singers], not for conductors.'" Besides, Toscanini had just decided to return to La Scala on his own artistic terms, and all he knew about Conried was his reputation for authoritarianism and flamboyance. When Toscanini once again refused the Metropolitan's offer, Conried tried his luck with Gustav Mahler, who agreed to leave his position as head of Vienna's Court Opera and conduct in New York, beginning with the 1907–08 season.

In June 1907, Gatti-Casazza received a letter from an unnamed Metropolitan patroness, who informed him that Conried was seriously ill and inquired whether he would be interested in assuming the position of general manager. Gatti was invited to dinner at the Toscaninis' home that evening; he took the letter with him and showed it to Toscanini, who deemed the proposal worth considering. When Gatti protested that he did not know the United States or speak English, Toscanini replied, according to Gatti's recollection,

"If you care to consider the proposal that has been made to you and if you arrive at an agreement that is suitable to you, I will go to the Metropolitan willingly this time."

Early in July 1907, Gatti met Kahn in Paris. Kahn, a German Jew, had immigrated to the United States in 1893 at the age of twenty-six (he was one month older than Toscanini) and had quickly become a major figure in American finance and industry, and a patron of the arts. In his youth he had wanted to become a musician; he played several instruments, and music remained an important element in his life. At the Metropolitan, he was "as much concerned with the musical ideals of the opera as with the material," as the American writer and critic James Gibbons Huneker put it. Gatti and Kahn presumably discussed the terms of an agreement, and when Gatti suggested that Toscanini be re-invited, Kahn was delighted. During the following months, as negotiations proceeded by correspondence, Gatti and Toscanini learned that the Metropolitan's board of directors had come to the conclusion that major institutional changes were needed. Conried and his predecessors had been functioning not only as managers but also as impresarios: if the Metropolitan's earnings exceeded expenses, they made a profit. But a new rival, the Manhattan Opera Company, founded in 1906 by the Broadway impresario Oscar Hammerstein, was drawing famous performers—and many audience members—away from the Metropolitan, and Conried seemed incapable of fighting back. On 24 January 1908, the *New York American* reported that a final break with Conried was precipitated by no less a figure than J. Pierpont Morgan. "The securing by Oscar Hammerstein [. . .] of Mme. [Luisa] Tetrazzini, Miss Mary Garden and other stars made Mr. Morgan angry. 'Why should we,' remarked the eminent financier, 'be outdone by a private enterprise? Here we are, the leading organization of the country, subscribing during the last year upward of a million dollars to carry on our opera season, and a man [Hammerstein] with absolutely no guaranteed backing comes along and brings singers here who have taken the town by storm.'"

Speculation quickly swept through New York's newspapers. The *Times* reported that Toscanini "will come to America if [Gatti] accepts the invitation of the Metropolitan Directors." On 5 February, the *Times* announced that Toscanini "has been engaged as conductor at the Metropolitan Opera House in New York," and five days later the *New York Telegraph* informed its readers that Toscanini "is held by many to be one of the greatest of living conductors. For some years he has led the greatest orchestra of Italy. His reputation stands among the highest. His memory is the most comprehensive and encyclopedic. [. . .] With Italian clannishness M. Toscanini refused to come to New York unless M. Gatti-Casazza came with him." But Toscanini's refusal to come without Gatti had nothing to do with "clannishness" and everything to do with the assurance that Gatti would support, rather than interfere with, his artistic choices and demands.

Finally, on 11 February, the Metropolitan's board met in Pierpont Morgan's library, decided on technical changes in the company's legal status, and afterward announced that Conried's position would be filled jointly by Gatti-Casazza as general manager and Andreas Dippel, a forty-two-year-old German tenor on the Metropolitan's roster, as administrative manager. "The musical directors at the Opera House will be Gustav Mahler and Toscanini." According to *Musical America*, Kahn and William K. Vanderbilt now controlled the Metropolitan's stock, "by consent of their fellow directors, and both will give a large share of their time to the betterment of opera as an institution." Kahn, as president of the reorganized company, declared to the press, "We consider ourselves particularly fortunate in having secured the co-operation as equal and joint musical directors of the famous conductors, Messrs. Mahler and Toscanini, a combination which no opera house in the world can match." Or, one might add, had ever matched before or has ever matched since. In the following weeks, many articles appeared in various New York newspapers and magazines with tales about Toscanini's memory and the breadth of his repertoire.

Kahn had asked Gatti whether Toscanini would mind sharing the ensemble's music directorship with Mahler. Toscanini knew that the Metropolitan had a much longer and fuller season than La Scala's and that several conductors were required to carry out all of the company's responsibilities. Three years earlier, after having studied Mahler's Fifth Symphony, he had written, "If he conducts the way he writes, oh, what a trivial interpreter he must be!" But Toscanini was well aware of Mahler's reputation as an exigent conductor, similar in many ways to himself.* Late in life he explicitly and repeatedly declared that he had accepted the Metropolitan's invitation not despite Mahler's presence but because of it. In earlier years, he said, the Metropolitan had engaged conductors like Luigi Mancinelli and Anton Seidl, both of whom Toscanini respected, but subsequently the focus had been entirely on singers. Then Mahler went to the Metropolitan. "Look, I came to New York because Mahler came a year before me," Toscanini emphatically told a friend. "It was for Mahler's name that I accepted. Because I said, if Mahler is there, I, too, can go there." And Gatti-Casazza, in an interview that appeared in *Musical America* six months before Toscanini arrived in New York, said that Toscanini was "especially pleased that he is to work with Mahler."

Kahn sent Rawlins L. Cottenet, the board's secretary, to Milan, to present Gatti and Toscanini with preliminary contracts. Gatti, surprised that the contracts were for only three years and could be canceled at the end of each year by any of the parties involved, wondered whether he should change his mind and remain at La Scala, where he had a firm, nine-year contract. "Toscanini cut the thing short, saying [. . .] 'Neither you nor I are persons who can be sent away after a year of trial,'" Gatti recalled. "'I believe that we have the right to feel absolutely sure of our ability.'"

Toscanini's initial contract, dated 13 May 1908, gave him complete artistic control over "all that concerns the performing of the art" in the operas that he was to conduct. It stipulated that he was to arrive in New York between 15 October and 1 November each year and to remain at the Metropolitan's disposal until 30 April; that he would receive a salary of 25,000 lire per month, tax free;† that first-class travel by rail and by ship would be provided for him and his family; that he would be reimbursed for all hotel expenses "on account of preparing performances of the Metropolitan"; and that he and the manager would decide jointly on the distribution of repertoire.

---

* Among much else, they were alike in their suspicion of encrusted performing traditions in opera. "Tradition ist Schlamperei" (Tradition is slovenliness), said Mahler; "La tradizione è l'ultima brutta recita" (Tradition is the last bad performance), said Toscanini.

† The total of $31,200 for a six-and-a-half-month period was more than five times what he was earning at La Scala for a five-month period. The average American worker's total annual income at the time was about $700.

The Milanese press heaped vituperation on Toscanini. In Europe at the time, America was widely perceived as a destination for either the poorest of the poor or the greediest of the middle and artist-artisan classes. The maestro was accused of a lack of patriotism, of "acute dollaritis," of having provoked a "barbaric divorce" with La Scala, and of acting like the star singers whose behavior he so deplored. None of the articles raised the possibility that Toscanini might have had legitimate complaints about La Scala and its board of directors, or that others in comparable positions might have found the opportunity to work in a fresh environment on their own artistic terms with a world-class ensemble and at an unmatchable salary difficult to resist.

Under the circumstances, no one should have been surprised that *La Forza del Destino*—the first Scala production following the announcement of the imminent departure of Gatti and Toscanini—was an unmitigated disaster. Some critics asked why this old wreck of an opera was being performed at La Scala; they described Verdi's forty-six-year-old work as "overcome with age," "a mishmash," and a piece that could "no longer please" a sophisticated audience. The opening performance, too, turned into a catastrophe. Eugenia Burzio, originally scheduled to sing Leonora, the lead soprano role, had quarreled with Toscanini, and Ester Mazzoleni had to fill in. The tenor and baritone became ill late in the rehearsal process and were replaced by Icilio Calleja and Amato, respectively, both of whom had to scramble to learn their roles, and both of whom made serious mistakes on opening night. There was no second performance, and the shipwreck did not bode well for the season's next production—the riskiest of Toscanini's Scala projects and probably of his entire career.

His admiration for Debussy's *Pelléas et Mélisande* had continued to grow during the three years since he had first learned the score, and he had evidently decided that even if audiences were not yet ready to make sense of the mysteriously elusive music and plot, they deserved a chance to see and hear what seemed to him the most revolutionary opera of its day. The world premiere of an opera by Mancinelli had initially been scheduled for the Scala season, but Toscanini managed to cajole or bully the house's administrators into scheduling the Italian premiere of *Pelléas* instead.

The substitution automatically predisposed the more nationalistic segments of the press and public against Debussy's work. "At that time it was difficult just to *do Pelléas*," Toscanini recalled. But he was determined to forge ahead. He labored over this production even more intensively than on others, supervising every aspect of the proceedings with extreme care and going so far as to make the stagehands wrap cloths around their shoes to prevent extraneous noises during performances. For the role of Mélisande he chose Cesira Ferrani, one of his favorite singers from his Turin days—she had been Mimì at the premiere of *La Bohème*; Ferrani was now forty-five and on the verge of retiring from the stage, but Toscanini believed that her girlish voice and persona fit the part. Fiorello Giraud took the role of Pelléas, Amato that of Golaud. According to Gatti-Casazza, they and all the other singers were "perfect in their roles. To each of them Toscanini had transfused his entire being." Likewise for the orchestra: Toscanini believed that *Pelléas* was truly *lyrical*, that all of its lines, instrumental as well as vocal, had to be "sung." One oboist looked at him in amazement when he told him to "sing" out a melodic line that consisted of only a few notes. " 'Casta diva' isn't the only melody—this is, too," the conductor told him.

Toscanini tried to persuade Debussy to come to Milan from Paris during the rehearsal period. "You have already made a few little additions to the score here and there," he wrote to the forty-five-year-old composer on 8 March 1908; "it may be that, when you hear it performed in as big a theater as La Scala, you may feel a need to make a few other retouchings, and these retouchings, in an opera like Pelléas et Mélisande, can only be done by the author himself." The seating capacity of the Salle Favart, home of Paris's Opéra-Comique, where *Pelléas* had premiered in 1902, was barely more than half that of La Scala, thus Toscanini's reference to La Scala's size. And the "few little additions" to which he referred were fairly extensive changes in the vocal lines, handwritten by Debussy in a copy of the Italian-language edition of the piano-vocal score of *Pelléas* that the composer had sent to the conductor. In the same score Toscanini heavily altered the Italian translation of Maurice Maeterlinck's libretto, so that the words and the music would blend as seamlessly as possible.

Debussy replied that he would not be able to go to Milan, but, he said, "I put *Pelléas*'s fate in your hands, sure as I am that I could not wish for more loyal or more capable ones. For this reason as well I would have liked to work on it with you; it is a joy that one does not easily come across along the path of our art." Toscanini later admitted that he actually felt relieved that Debussy could not be present, because he feared that he had misunderstood the score.

An invited audience attended the dress rehearsal and, at the end, shouted *"Viva Toscanini!"* because—D'Ormeville commented—"if we have had the chance to hear a work that merits the esteem, attention, and respect of those who do not allow themselves to be misled by [. . .] ill-conceived chauvinism, we owe it to the high level of his ideals, to the firmness of his character, and to his apostolic faith." But Toscanini feared that the opening-night audience would be less indulgent. *Pelléas* broke all the rules of melodrama: much of the plot moves by implication rather than by outright statement, and at times the vocal lines have more in common with the *recitar cantando* style of early seventeenth-century opera than with the popular operas of the day. Toscanini called a brief brush-up orchestra rehearsal a few hours prior to the first performance, on 2 April, and, he recalled, "I told the orchestra, 'Gentlemen, this evening I don't know what will happen with the audience, but remember to be calm and to watch me [. . .]—we mustn't lose each other."

At the premiere, the first act was warmly applauded; some protesters tried to hush the applauders, but they were greatly outnumbered. The second act was more controversial: the "pro" and "anti" factions were equally balanced. During the third act's second scene (*les souterrains du château*), the protests became so loud that singers and orchestra couldn't hear themselves or each other and were able to proceed only by watching Toscanini, as he had foreseen. The critic for *La Perseveranza* reported that "the violence of the disapproval, of the whistles, and of the banal shouts of some hypercritical people who thought they were at the Arena instead of at La Scala, were animatedly disapproved by the assemblage, which reacted by decreeing a great success for the last scene of the same act, with four curtain calls for the singers."

That scene "brought down the house," Toscanini remembered.

And at the end of the fourth act, when the overall success was clear, he took a bow with the singers and applauded the audience, shouting, "Bravo! How intelligent the Scala public is!" The fifth act, according to *La Perseveranza*'s critic, "also ended amid unanimous applause that called the singers and Toscanini before the curtain several times." Late that night Toscanini wired Debussy, "I am happy Pelléas has won[.] It has won heroically[,] and despite an ignorant cowardly hostile part of the audience of subscribers provoking scandal [in the] grotto scene opera ended in a triumph for you [and] for your incomparable art." Debussy replied by sending Toscanini an autographed photograph with the inscription "To Maestro Toscanini, whom I shall never be able to thank enough." And on the back, the composer wrote the first bar of Act III, Scene 2 (*lourd et sombre*) with the comment ". . . at which point Toscanini came out victorious all the same."

With the exception of Carugati and one or two other ultraconservatives, the Milanese critics understood that *Pelléas*, with its sometimes nearly static action, its *apparently* uninflected vocal lines, and its elusive harmonic progressions that left first-time listeners wondering in which direction they were being led, represented a new and significant departure in the history of opera; their reviews ranged from respectful to enthusiastic. Most of them complained that the sets were too traditional for such an original work, but they praised the singers, the orchestra, and Toscanini, who vowed, however, that if he had further opportunities to conduct *Pelléas*, he would have it sung in French: if ever there was an opera in which words and music were inseparable, this was it.

In Paris two years later, Toscanini and Puccini attended a performance of *Pelléas* at the Opéra-Comique: Toscanini had wanted to find out whether his interpretation had strayed too far from the composer's intentions. What he heard—a slap-dash rendition in a noisy theater—horrified him. By that time he had made Debussy's acquaintance, and he told the composer that whereas in 1908 he had worried about not having understood the opera and that he might even have ruined it, he now felt doubly sorry that Debussy had not attended the Scala production. "I can say that the master never heard his opera," Toscanini declared many years later.

23.

CHALIAPIN RETURNED TO LA SCALA IN APRIL TO CLOSE THE SEASON
with a successful revival of *Mefistofele*, with Frances Alda as Margherita, after which Toscanini was to have conducted two pairs of concerts. Gaetano Coronaro, Catalani's successor as professor of
composition at the Milan Conservatory, had recently died, and
Toscanini had been asked by La Scala's Concert Society to include a
work by Coronaro on one of his programs; Toscanini replied that he
did not find any of Coronaro's music good enough to warrant a performance. When the society voted to take the second program away
from Toscanini and put it in the hands of young Ettore Panizza,
Toscanini's pride was wounded: he conducted two performances of
what was now his single program, which included his first go at
Strauss's *Ein Heldenleben* (deemed "madhouse music" by the local
critics), but he also sued the society, on the grounds that he had the
right to decide the content of his programs. A year later, the Milan
Tribunal decided the case in his favor, and the society's members
split among them the payment for the extra pair of concerts. Boito,
who was one of the members, wrote to one of his associates, "I do
not doubt that, after the storm, the rainbow of peace will rise
between us and the great artist, whom we admire and love."

24.

SOMETIME DURING THE SPRING OR EARLY SUMMER OF 1908, TOSCA-
nini began to take English lessons from a young Englishwoman,
although the nature of their studies drew ironic comments from
Carla's brother, Batta, who evidently had some inside information.
Then and later, Toscanini used a little notebook in which he wrote
numerous English words and phrases with their Italian equivalents.
He eventually became as voracious a reader in English as he already
was in Italian and French, but his spoken English remained shaky.

Toscanini and Gatti-Casazza knew that Puccini was working on
an opera set in gold rush–era California—*La Fanciulla del West*, based
on a play, *The Girl of the Golden West*, by the American author-director

David Belasco—and they thought that an opera with an American theme should have its premiere in the United States. When they visited the composer at his home at Torre del Lago, near the Tyrrhenian coast, he played them some nearly completed parts of the opera (Gatti recalled, in particular, Jake Wallace's aria about homesickness), and the three men agreed in principle that *Fanciulla*'s first production would take place at the Metropolitan. Puccini told the *New York Times* that the opera would be ready within a year, an overly optimistic prediction.

The Toscaninis spent much of the summer at Champex, in the Aosta Valley, where the maestro again went mountain climbing. But during one ascent his worsening myopia caused him to miscalculate a jump over a crevasse, and he found himself dangling from a rope over the abyss. "He realized then that he could no longer judge the force required by the distance, which he didn't see, and he didn't want to hamper and endanger his fellow climbers," Walter Toscanini recalled. For several more years, however, he continued to take long mountain hikes "and even rather difficult excursions."

Carla had decided that she would not accompany her husband to New York in the fall but would instead join him later in the Metropolitan's season, bringing baby Wanda along but leaving ten-year-old Walter and eight-year-old Wally in the care of Nena, their nanny, so that they could continue their schooling. Wally said that from that time on most of her father's life "was absorbed by his artistic activity and he no longer had much time for us" during the seven months each year that he spent in New York or traveling between continents.

Early in October 1908, Toscanini said goodbye to his family and traveled by train to Cherbourg, where, on the sixth, he boarded the White Star liner *Oceanic* for his first journey to North America. He was on his way to the city that would become his second home.

*Toscanini with the Metropolitan Opera's
ensemble in 1910 (left to right): tenor Enrico
Caruso, Toscanini, soprano Emmy Destinn;
(on the floor) General Manager Giulio Gatti-
Casazza, soprano Frances Alda.*

V.

———

THE
METROPOLITAN

1.

———

FOR TOSCANINI, HISTORY, EVEN MORE THAN PHYSICAL DISTANCE, separated Milan from New York. In 1778, when La Scala had first opened its doors in what was already a two-millennia-old city, New York was an outpost town of 25,000 inhabitants, under British occupation during the American Revolution. Once independence from Britain had been won, the town began to receive ever-increasing numbers of European emigrants, most of them poor ("The dukes don't emigrate," as the saying goes), dedicated to commerce in one form or another, and hoping to thrive in the New World. There was little room, initially, for imported European high culture—witness the rapid failure of New York's first opera company, founded in 1833 by no less a personage than the eighty-four-year-old Lorenzo Da Ponte, Mozart's librettist, who had immigrated to the United States to escape creditors in the Old World.

By the last quarter of the nineteenth century, however, two different strands of New York society had begun to view European culture as an important adjunct to local life. The first group consisted of several thousand affluent citizens, many of them descendants of the early Dutch and English settlers, who had amassed enough money to be able to dedicate part of their leisure time to "the finer things in life," in many cases merely because it seemed the thing to do, but in others out of sincere and growing interest in the arts. In 1883, when the Metropolitan Opera House first opened its doors on Broadway between West Thirty-Ninth and Fortieth Streets, it was, above all else, a meeting place for the wealthy: for several decades, reviews of new productions' opening nights gave as much coverage to the audience as to the music and its interpreters. "Mrs. Ogden Mills was in her accustomed box with Miss Beatrice Mills, who was in sapphire blue satin and silver spangled gauze," read part of a typical account of one such performance. "Mrs. Mills wore a gown of white brocade and lace, a diadem and collar of diamonds." This was Edith Wharton's New York—the New York of Fifth Avenue mansions, with their domestic staffs and carriage houses. But at the same time, increasing numbers of immigrants from Italy, Germany, and Central and Eastern Europe were flocking to the Metropolitan's upper galleries. These people had loved the lyric theater in their native countries and were eager to indulge that taste in their new environment.

These were the two audience elements that Toscanini confronted upon his arrival in New York in 1908. The forty-one-year-old maestro was assuming a position of authority with an ensemble that was only twenty-five years old and in a city that had hosted more or less regular opera seasons for not much longer than his own lifetime. Yet the Metropolitan was already a far bigger institution than any of those to which he had been attached in Italy. During his last season in Milan, La Scala had presented sixty-one performances of eight operas; during his first season in New York, the Metropolitan would present over two hundred performances of thirty-two operas, plus twenty-three concerts and gala events. At La Scala, he had been responsible for all of the performances of all of the operas; at the Metropolitan, three other conductors would share the burden with him.

The previous spring, the Metropolitan's board had announced that, owing to an increased demand for away-from-home performances, the orchestra would be enlarged from 75 to 130 players and the chorus's ranks would be doubled, from 100 to 200; thus half of the ensemble could tour while the other half was busy at home. The theater's pit would be enlarged and set on a hydraulic lift, so that the orchestra could be lowered for more massively orchestrated works and raised for lighter ones, and there would be improvements for the audience as well: elevators would be installed for patrons of the galleries; a platform would be built to improve the view of the stage for standees; the heating and ventilating systems were to be renovated; and the awnings and driveways at the entrances were to be extended, so that three carriages or automobiles could be unloaded or loaded simultaneously on each side.

Toscanini and Giulio Setti, the Metropolitan's new chorus master for Italian and French repertoire, were to help Gatti-Casazza engage singers from Italy for their half of the chorus, and Alfred Hertz, who shared much of the German repertoire with Mahler, would advise Andreas Dippel, Gatti's comanager, on the selection of new German-speaking chorus members for the other half. For the biggest productions, members of one chorus could be used to enlarge the other. And since the Metropolitan had become, in Otto Kahn's words, "an art institution of world-wide prestige," it would now be "administered without any thought to pecuniary benefit. If any season results in a surplus, such surplus will be devoted to the establishment of an endowment or pension fund, or to some similar purpose," Kahn stated. In short: Toscanini was arriving at the Metropolitan when it was undergoing major economic and physical transformations, just as he had arrived at the Regio in Turin and at La Scala under comparable circumstances.

Because the Metropolitan paid singers top fees in desirable US dollars, many world-famous artists performed regularly in New York. But not all of the company's stars had been pleased to learn of Toscanini's appointment. A report in the *New York Tribune* stated, "Signor Toscanini is an admirable conductor and an artist of strong and aggressive methods," and Caruso and a few other singers of Italian repertoire who had already worked with the maestro had probably told their colleagues that they could forget about resting on their laurels or having their every musical whim obeyed, once the demanding new boss arrived. In May, when Gatti-Casazza had made a preliminary visit to New York, he was immediately questioned about Toscanini. "Like Mahler, he has a very decided character and people are fond of saying that he is disagreeable," Gatti said, "but I notice that only the characterless people get a reputation for being agreeable."

Emma Eames, an American soprano admired for her broad repertoire and fine vocal technique, tried unsuccessfully to prevent Toscanini and Gatti-Casazza from taking command at the Metropolitan, because, she said, she had a "perfect understanding of Italian operatic ideals." She did not specify what she thought those ideals were—

certainly no one in Italy considered Toscanini's approach typical of the system as a whole—but there was considerable anti-Italian prejudice in America in those days. When the Toscanini-Gatti nomination was confirmed, the forty-three-year-old Eames, who had already been thinking about retiring, announced that their first season would be her last.

Further opposition came from the Metropolitan's German element, which did not welcome the announcement that the house's destiny would be entrusted to Italians after a decade under two Austrians—first Maurice Grau and then Heinrich Conried. The Metropolitan's press office took great pains to state that the arrival of Gatti and Toscanini did not mean that German opera would suffer a setback, and the journalists repeated what they were told. Toscanini "is quite as famous for his Wagnerian interpretations as for his conducting of Italian operas," the *Independent* assured its readers. "There need be no fear, therefore, that the preponderance of Italian performances, caused by the popularity of Caruso, will be still further emphasized."

Mahler's reaction to the Gatti-Toscanini appointment was wholly reasonable. From the start of the board's negotiations, he was kept informed, and on 20 January 1908 he wrote to Alfred Roller, who had been in charge of productions at the Vienna Opera, that there was a plan "to engage the present manager of the *Scala* as manager of the Metropolitan Opera and to appoint the highly praised conductor *Toscanini* to be in charge of Italian opera while German opera will be, so to speak, handed over to me.—But all this is for the future. On my part, I must wait and see how it all affects me." Upon Conried's resignation, Kahn had tentatively offered the Metropolitan's general managership to Mahler himself, but the majority of the board's members were either silently or openly against maintaining too strong a German and Jewish influence: Grau, Conried, Kahn, and Mahler were all Jews from Germanic countries. The board members may never have learned that Gatti-Casazza was part Jewish, on his mother's side.

Mahler was not interested in managing the Metropolitan. Although he was not yet forty-eight, he had learned the previous year that his heart was diseased; he was no longer physically able to take on the sort of burden expected of the principal conductor or general manager of a major opera house, let alone both positions combined. During his first Metropolitan season, 1907–08, the year before Toscanini's arrival, he conducted a total of only twenty-six performances of five different operas, roughly one-seventh of the workload.

Mahler found Gatti-Casazza to be a more enlightened administrator than either Conried or Dippel, which is not surprising, since Gatti had spent seven of the preceding ten years dealing with Toscanini's artistic demands. And just as Toscanini was aware of Mahler's high reputation, so Mahler knew of the esteem in which Toscanini was held. The only known clash between them stemmed from a misunderstanding: during the summer of 1908, Gatti-Casazza had rashly promised Toscanini that he could make his New York debut with *Tristan*, making use of the sets that had been created for his 1901 Scala production. Mahler was justifiably alarmed. "I find it incomprehensible, and cannot agree to the idea that *Tristan* [. . .] should be performed with new scenery without my being consulted in any way," he wrote to Dippel. "During the past season, I devoted particular efforts to it and can justifiably claim that the form in which the work now appears in New York is to some extent my artistic property. Without knowing him, I have the greatest respect for Toscanini and consider it an honor to call him my colleague. Should he undertake *Tristan* before my arrival it would, of course, bear an entirely different imprint, and it would be utterly impossible for me to take it over in the course of the season."

This was a compliment to Toscanini. During the 1907–08 season, Mahler had already ceded several performances of *Tristan* to Hertz, probably in the belief that Hertz did not have a strong enough artistic personality to alter his own imprint, whereas he knew that Toscanini would have his own clearly defined ideas about the work and would know exactly how to get his collaborators to realize them.

Contrary to Alma Mahler's often quoted story (her husband wearily relinquished *Tristan* to Toscanini, which the latter had made "his supreme object and an indispensable condition," she claimed), Toscanini, in fact, bowed to Mahler's request. Mahler conducted four Metropolitan performances of *Tristan* during Toscanini's first season there and gave two others to Hertz. Toscanini's only German opera that season was *Götterdämmerung*. According to contemporary newspaper reports, Toscanini had gone to see Mahler during the summer—in the Alps, according to some; in Vienna, according to others—and asked him whether he wished to add a French or Italian opera to his Metropolitan repertoire, since he (Toscanini) would also conduct some German works. Mahler replied that his burden was heavy enough already. If such an encounter took place, the *Tristan* issue was likely settled then and there.

The fable of Toscanini's forcing Mahler to leave the Metropolitan is precisely that—a fable—and it was largely constructed by Alma. Toscanini had agreed to be part of the organization only because Mahler was there: in conversations recorded in Toscanini's last years, he repeatedly made this clear. And as early as February 1908, barely a month after Mahler's Metropolitan debut and eight months before Toscanini disembarked in New York, Mahler wrote to Roller, "I do not intend to stay here long, but at least for next season, if I am still in good health." Mahler did not desire or intend to act as a general music director: he did not even arrive in New York for his first season until a month after the season's opening night. Toscanini, on the other hand, was engaged—according to the slightly revised contract that he signed in New York on 5 December 1908—specifically as "First Master of Concerts and First Director of Orchestra for the operas, concerts, and oratorios which will be executed in the Metropolitan Opera House of New York and in the theatres of the United States of America, in which the aforesaid Company will have their artists act." In other words, he was assuming those responsibilities that Mahler did not wish to take on and was no longer physically capable of taking on. This was done openly, not behind Mahler's back.

Mahler, already during his first Metropolitan season, had welcomed an offer from Mary Sheldon, a wealthy New York music lover, to put a symphony orchestra at his disposal. Alma wrote, "This came in very opportunely for Mahler. His relations with the Metropolitan were no longer very good. Conried was at death's door. Gatti-Casazza [. . .] had brought Toscanini over with him. The glorious days of German supremacy were over." But, as Jonathan Carr, one of Mahler's biographers, has pointed out, "Mahler had accepted the Sheldon committee's offer well before the Italians arrived on the scene," and although Mahler had also renewed his contract with the Metropolitan, "he certainly did not aim to go on doing both. That had not worked in Vienna, even before his doctors had warned him not to overstrain."

The silliness of the Mahler-versus-Toscanini postmortem fight is exemplified by a statement in Jens Malte Fischer's Mahler biography: "Toscanini's decision to slip in a performance of *Götterdämmerung* on 10 December with two of Mahler's *Tristan* singers, Erik Schmedes and Olive Fremstad, looks like an act of blatant provocation, even though Mahler had not yet conducted this work at the Met." As far as is known, Mahler never had any intention of conducting *Götterdämmerung* there, and either Fischer is being disingenuous or he simply does not know how major opera companies functioned in the days before easy air travel. During the Metropolitan's 1908–09 season—a typical one—principal singers performed as often as four times a week. Not only did Schmedes and Fremstad sing *Götterdämmerung* with Toscanini on 10 December, nearly two weeks before Mahler's first *Tristan* of the season: they sang *Götterdämmerung* again with Toscanini on 18 December, only five days before Mahler's first *Tristan*. But Mahler, Toscanini, and every other conductor of the day considered such a practice normal. Mahler himself gave the same two singers only two and a half days off between his second and third *Tristan* performances; by Fischer's lights, Mahler was blatantly provoking himself. The previous year, Hertz had conducted a performance of *Die Meistersinger* only four days before Mahler's American debut performance of *Tristan*, using the same leading tenor and bass-baritone, but Fischer does not accuse Hertz of having "slipped in a performance" to Mahler's detriment.

According to Fischer, by the end of Toscanini's first New York season, "the war had been won by the Italians." Some healthy rivalry certainly existed between the German and the Italian elements at the Metropolitan, but there was much crossover between the two camps—and no war. As Carr says, Mahler's departure "was due neither to the new Italian regime nor (another legend) to hostile critics. He went, as so often before, because he saw a more attractive post." Carr also demonstrates that Mahler's "second season at the Metropolitan proved to be a still bigger triumph than his first, Toscanini's presence notwithstanding."

Toscanini's often quoted description of Mahler as a "crazy man"— a statement made in the 1940s to the American music critic B. H.

Haggin—must be viewed in perspective. Mahler made a similar impression on other people with whom he came into contact in those years. The soprano Geraldine Farrar, for instance, described him, in a letter to a friend, as "very neurotic, and of uncertain temper and manner." But Toscanini, in private conversations recorded in 1953 and 1955, also said that "Mahler was a fine conductor" and "conducted operas well"—rare compliments from him—and he mentioned their shared contempt for early twentieth-century New York audiences, which were "more boorish than now." Wealthy subscribers tended to arrive at the theater only after an opera's first act, and Toscanini reported, with a chuckle, that when Mahler conducted Smetana's *The Bartered Bride* during the 1908–09 season, he inserted the overture before the second act instead of performing it at the beginning of the opera, so that "the audience could hear it and applaud." And, Toscanini added, the overture was played beautifully.

According to Howard Taubman, an early Toscanini biographer, Toscanini said that Mahler's *Tristan* interpretation had "no passion in it; but the poor man was tired and sick." This jibes with what Toscanini told the Canadian conductor Wilfrid Pelletier in one of the taped conversations. "I didn't find that Mahler had the character that they said he had in Vienna," he recalled. "It's clear that when they engaged him at the Metropolitan he had changed, because he did whatever the singers wanted." Toscanini witnessed some singers interrupting a full-ensemble rehearsal of *The Marriage of Figaro* to argue over whether a chair should be placed in one position or another, and Mahler "just stood there. He was ill," Toscanini said, and he added that his colleague even limped when he walked. Toscanini had nothing negative to say about Mahler's conducting, but only about specific musical matters, such as his nonuse of appoggiaturas (grace notes on the beat) in eighteenth- and early nineteenth-century music and his penchant for reorchestrating passages in works that Toscanini had either heard him conduct (trumpets blaring the main theme in the first-movement coda of the Schubert "Great" C Major Symphony; an E-flat clarinet doubling the flute on the first big chord in the introduction to Florestan's aria in *Fidelio*) or had seen in Mahler's scores (substantial changes in Beethoven's Seventh Symphony).

Alma Mahler, whose penchant for making trouble is well-known, declared that when she and her husband eventually heard a Toscanini performance of *Tristan* during the Italian conductor's second Metropolitan season, they found its nuances "distressing," but her statement was contradicted by Bruno Walter—a Mahler disciple—who reported that the master had told him: "'He conducts [*Tristan*] in a manner entirely different from ours, [. . .] but his way is magnificent.'" Julius Korngold, a Viennese music critic and friend of Mahler's, said that Mahler had described Toscanini as "really something," and Korngold himself, after having heard Toscanini's performances of various works many years later, wrote, "Like Mahler, Toscanini is an 'old-fashioned' conductor who wants to present the work and nothing but the work, which emerges sacrosanct through his individuality, through his subjectivity, through his temperament, although often as if newly discovered, newly thought out."

Shortly after Toscanini and Mahler had conducted their first Wagner operas of the season, the critic of New York's *Evening Globe* summed up then current opinion: "Fortunate indeed is the Metropolitan in possessing two conductors of the deservedly high rank of Mr. Toscanini and Mr. Mahler." Although Mahler and Toscanini had completely different artistic personalities, their rivalry is mainly a figment of the imaginations of their most fanatical adherents. And Mahler, whose compositions have endured and flourished, has long since beaten Toscanini with respect to posterity.

2.

THE *NEW YORK HERALD* REPORTED THAT WHEN ARTURO TOSCANINI disembarked from the *Oceanic* on 14 October 1908, he "positively declined to be interviewed, which so astounded the newspaper reporters that they expressed their admiration of the phenomenon in the one word 'Hooray!'" And the *Sun* reported, "Before he had been in New York an hour [Toscanini] had inspected the Metropolitan from top to bottom. He expressed himself as well satisfied with what he saw and the codirectors breathed a sigh of relief. The conductor has the reputation of being very exigent."

Theodore Roosevelt was president of the United States, Charles Evans Hughes was governor of the state of New York, and George B. McClellan Jr. (son of one of the Union's principal generals during the

Civil War) was mayor of New York City when Toscanini entered the country for the first time. What he saw upon his arrival was a city of 4.5 million inhabitants that was growing at the astonishing rate of approximately 100,000 a year. Tenement houses on Manhattan's Lower East Side and in other poor quarters of the city were being erected as quickly as possible. Yet in the New World as in the Old, Toscanini, like other sought-after artists, lived in a bubble—an environment in which his only real concern was his work and in which all practical matters were looked after by others. He was housed, at his own expense, in a suite in the four-year-old Beaux Arts–style Ansonia, one of the newest and most luxurious residential hotels in the world, located on Broadway between West Seventy-Third and Seventy-Fourth Streets in what was then a relatively quiet section of town. It contained tearooms, restaurants, a ballroom, Turkish baths, and a lobby fountain with live seals. Each apartment was high-ceilinged and elegantly turned out, with bay windows that provided grand views either along Broadway or across the Hudson River. There were several bedrooms, a parlor, a library, and a dining room in every suite, and each of the eighteen-story building's residential floors had a central kitchen with connecting "serving kitchens": the residents' personal cooks could use the central kitchen and then serve meals in their bosses' own apartments. Toscanini employed an Italian cook; his other daily needs were looked after by the hotel staff. The Ansonia's only negative aspect, from the maestro's point of view, was its distance from the Metropolitan Opera House, nearly two miles away; this may account for the fact that late in his Metropolitan tenure, probably in the fall of 1914, he moved to the almost equally modern and comfortable Hotel Astor in Times Square, just a five-minute walk from the theater. And he often took his meals at the similarly new and luxurious Knickerbocker Hotel, two blocks from the Metropolitan, where Caruso and several other Metropolitan regulars made their home.

Years later, Toscanini told Bruno Walter that he was so nervous before his first rehearsal with the Metropolitan orchestra that he had considered canceling his contract altogether. Much of his apprehensiveness must have been related to language: even in Argentina he had worked with orchestra musicians who spoke or at least understood Italian, whereas most of the New York orchestra's musicians were native German-, Russian-, or Yiddish-speakers who also spoke English to varying degrees. Toscanini had never yet conducted an opera in any language other than Italian, but at the Metropolitan each Italian, German, and French opera was performed in its original language. Memorizing French and German texts caused him little trouble, but he could not hone singers' pronunciation and enunciation in those languages as he could in Italian.

Toscanini boldly chose the Prologue and Act I of *Götterdämmerung* for his first orchestra rehearsal, on 19 October. He had uncharacteristically written out a little greeting, in English, in the same notebook that contained his English-language exercises; someone read it to the musicians on his behalf. "Gentlemen," it said, "I am very pleased at having the honour to conduct the orchestra of the Metropolitan Opera House—but I am sorry, that I do not speak either English or German to express myself as I would whish [*sic*]. Nevertheless I do not doubt, that, as music has a universal language, we shall understand each other very well[.]"

The players had heard stories about Toscanini's memory, but there was general astonishment when he began to rehearse Wagner's gigantic work in detail without consulting the score. And the astonishment grew as the new conductor began to hear and correct errors in the musicians' printed parts that well-known German conductors had never detected. Still more impressive was the way in which he immersed his co-workers in the very substance of the music; at one point, the orchestra spontaneously broke into applause, bravos, and a fanfare. The *New York Post* interviewed one of the musicians, who exclaimed, " 'Why, it is simply beyond understanding the way he knows his scores. We have often heard conductors direct without notes, but when it comes to knowing every mark and every instrument, to make every correction in expression as well as in everything else without once referring to the music, it shows an intimacy with the work and a self-confidence as inspiring as it is remarkable.' " The musicians were also surprised that Toscanini did not sit at rehearsals: "He conducts on his feet, and is the first man in charge of an orchestra here to do that since the days of Anton Seidl," the *Sun* reported. The first rehearsal "lasted for more than four hours, but the players were not too fatigued at the end of that period to give the new conductor another fanfare." Toscanini, even in old age, described the orchestra players as "magnificent!" And Gatti reported that "after a few rehearsals they understood his ideas exactly, although these ideas were new to them. He got along excellently from the start." *Götterdämmerung*, however, was not scheduled for performance until mid-December, and in the meantime he rehearsed *Aida*, *Madama Butterfly*, and *Carmen*, in addition to the Wagner work.

Toscanini made his North American debut—and opened the Metropolitan Opera House's season—on 16 November 1908, conducting *Aida* with an all-star cast that included the Czech soprano Emmy Destinn, making her American debut in the title role; Caruso as Radamès; the American mezzo-soprano Louise Homer as Amneris; Antonio Scotti as Amonasro; and the Polish basso Adamo Didur as Ramfis. The theater "was practically in a state of siege from half past 7 o'clock last night until an hour and a half later when the last of the unfortunates who hadn't got tickets in advance reluctantly abandoned their efforts to obtain admission," the *Sun* reported the next day. "There were 4,000 persons inside the opera house by the time the curtain fell on the first act. Long before that every seat had been sold and every standee had been admitted whom safety would allow to squeeze his way inside the swinging doors." Among those present were many of the Metropolitan's wealthiest patrons, including J. Pierpont Morgan and Henry Clay Frick.

The performance electrified the audience. "There were interruptions of the various scenes by applause, which may not be according to the strictest ethics of grand opera, but they showed an appreciation that must have flattered the artists," the *Herald* reported. The *Press* concurred: "Applause in measure that proved its sincerity was given to all the principals, but it was doubled when Toscanini appeared before the curtain. The conductor was greeted with bravos ardent as any that have been shouted at tenor idols."

Richard Aldrich, the *Times*'s critic, described Toscanini as

a strenuous force, a dominating power, a man of potent authority, a musician of infinite resource. He had the performance at every point firmly and directly under his hand. If it was a criterion of his musicianship, he is a man that insists on clear-cut outline, on abundant detail, on the strongest contrasts, on vivid color. [. . .] But there were other and finer points that could not have escaped the attention of the close observer: the fine modeling of phrase, the symmetry of the musical outline in many places where mere brute force was not in question. And the pulsing dramatic blood he sent coursing through [the] score was never allowed to stagnate.

Henry E. Krehbiel of the *Tribune* spoke of Toscanini as "a boon to Italian opera as great and as welcome as anything that has come out of Italy since Verdi laid down his pen." A review by the redoubtable Henry T. Finck in New York's *Evening Post* went even further: In Italian operas performed at the Metropolitan, "the conductor has been simply an accompanist when the singers are on the stage," he said.

Not so with Mr. Toscanini. Great as were the artists on the stage last night, he made them coordinate themselves to his general scheme [. . .]; in short, he proved himself one of the most masterful leaders of opera ever seen here, and the marvel of it was that his amazing memory enabled him to attend to every subtle accent and detail of phrasing without once looking at the score. [. . .] He made the whole score pulsate with life, warm with emotion. In a word, he lived up to his reputation. The Milanese are to be profoundly condoled for having lost this musician.

The German-language *New-Yorker Staats-Zeitung*'s reviewer summed up the general impressions in a single, Caesarian sentence: "Toscanini kam, ergriff den Taktstock und siegte"—Toscanini came, seized the baton, and conquered.

He would conduct thirteen performances of *Aida* in the course of the season, and he conducted fifteen performances of the following opera, *Butterfly*, which opened three days after *Aida*, with Geraldine Farrar and Caruso, the Metropolitan audience's two favorite singers.* Once again, listeners were enthralled. "Signor Arturo Toscanini performed a miracle at the Metropolitan last night," wrote Finck. "He added several inches to the artistic stature of Giacomo Puccini by an interpretation [. . .] which, for the first time, revealed

---

* Caruso was paid $2,000 per performance in 1908–09; Farrar, $1,200.

to New Yorkers all the poetry, beauty, and passion inherent in the orchestral score of that work. [. . .] We had not believed heretofore that Puccini would ever become a compeer of Verdi; but Toscanini last night converted us."

Despite the production's success, Toscanini and Farrar clashed almost immediately. The sensual, headstrong, twenty-six-year-old, Massachusetts-born soprano—daughter of a former infielder for the Philadelphia Athletics baseball team—later recalled her first impression of the conductor: "a bundle of concentrated quicksilver. [. . .] Portentous silence was broken by an occasional and solemn raven's croak. This was the result of long assault upon protesting vocal cords. We were to experience later—and often—the amazing crescendo to screams and expletives that rose to unparalleled dynamics in rehearsals. However, these tempests became less terrifying by reason of their frequency. We recognized the lightning's play, sure to be followed by disarming—if unstable—serenity."

The conflict between the soprano and the conductor began at a rehearsal of *Butterfly*, which Farrar had first sung early the previous year, during her debut season at the Metropolitan; Puccini, who had been visiting the United States, had complained about her interpretation and intonation. Now she and Toscanini disagreed over what must have been one or more particularly serious points, because Toscanini exploded. "We carried our differences to Mr. Gatti's office," Farrar said. "There ensued an exchange of heated words and retaliation—Italia versus New England—which Mr. Gatti vainly tried to stem."

The story created excellent grist for the newspapers' mills. According to the *New York American*,

the clashes of Toscanini and Miss Farrar have been much discussed about the Opera House, and the young singer is known to have openly defied the maestro on more than one occasion.

She was ordered to report for rehearsal on the morning following a performance. She sent word that she was indisposed and would not come.

Toscanini, who had been waiting the rehearsal of "Madama Butterfly," with a cast that had never sung the opera together before, rushed to the telephone when he received this message and implored, insisted and commanded that Miss Farrar should come to rehearsal.

He was told in a very cold and formal manner that Miss Farrar would not attend the rehearsal.

If the article is to be believed, Toscanini had the management cable Puccini, who cabled back that Farrar was to attend rehearsals and follow Toscanini's instructions. No sooner did Toscanini attempt to correct her, however, than Farrar answered back: "'I am a star,' she said. 'How dare you criticize me in that way?'

"'The stars are all in the heavens, mademoiselle,' retorted the conductor. 'You are but a plain artiste and you must obey my directions.'"

Farrar herself later wrote, "Outside influences fanned resentment to a white heat, at least on my part; I was in a fury. The papers gave space to stupid fabrications and stories purporting to emanate from those speaking with authority, whose names, however, one could never discover." Her recollection of the rest of the episode—that Toscanini then called on Destinn to sing Butterfly; that Destinn was unsuccessful; and that she herself had to take over for her—was incorrect. Farrar sang the first four performances of the opera that season, then Destinn sang one, Farrar another, Destinn two more, and so on. This alternation was planned on the basis of each soprano's responsibilities in other operas during any given week, as was customary. And the alternation continued in later seasons.

3.

TOSCANINI'S CLASH WITH FARRAR WAS SYMPTOMATIC OF NERVOUSness within the entire ensemble—nervousness, above all, over who was really in charge. Only nine days after the season had begun, Caruso, Eames, Farrar, Scotti, and Marcella Sembrich sent a joint letter to Kahn. They had heard of "a movement to grant Mr. Gatti-Casazza, the General Manager, and Mr. Toscanini, Conductor, a three years' binding contract," they said, and they expressed their wish, "in the protection of our artistic interests and the welfare of the Metropolitan Opera House, that Mr. Dippel be granted the same privileges under contract that may be accorded to the above-named gentlemen." According to an article in the *Times*, the letter was written at Dippel's request—a statement at first denied but later confirmed. The letter did not come from the company's German singers—Dippel's natural allies—but rather from two Italians, two Americans, and a Polish-American, all of whom sang mostly Italian and French repertoire.

The editors of Joseph Pulitzer's *New York World* asked one of their European correspondents to talk to people at La Scala, and the correspondent produced an article—with the headline "MILAN LOOKED FOR STORM AT METROPOLITAN"—that was severely critical of Gatti-Casazza and even more critical of Toscanini, including gossip about his relationship with Storchio and the (correct) implication that he had fathered her child. One orchestra musician praised Toscanini highly but said that "he unfortunately lacked tact in his method of reproof, and irritated artists unnecessarily. [. . .] Toscanini was almost always right in the object he aimed at, but nearly always wrong in the means he employed." But an unnamed Scala administrator also said, "Opera stars are the anarchists of the musical world—[. . .] leave them unchecked and they become incorrigible. If Geraldine Farrar and her companions complained [. . .] because they are stars who deem themselves beyond Toscanini's right of critical direction, then I say without hesitation they are wholly in the wrong."

The singers' letter to the Metropolitan's board of directors came as a serious challenge to the new administration, and the board's executives, Otto Kahn, William Vanderbilt, and F. Gray Griswold, were quick to reply, firmly, that "the greatest artistic success can only be accomplished if there exists a spirit of willing co-operation with, and submission to the Management, and a recognition of the necessity of centralized authority, together with mutual confidence and good will." Mr. Dippel, they said, would be treated fairly, "but there can be no divided artistic authority, and [. . .] his functions are and must be subordinate to those of the General Manager, Mr. Gatti-Casazza, who is the supreme executive head of the organization." No reference was made to Toscanini, but, by implication, he was to be the final authority in matters musical within his repertoire, just as Mahler and Hertz continued to exercise the same authority in their respective jurisdictions. Dippel was assigned to direct the smaller

New Theatre, which the Metropolitan opened the following season on Central Park West, between Sixty-First and Sixty-Second Streets, but after one year he left the ensemble altogether—and after another the Metropolitan sold the beautiful but acoustically flawed venue to the showman Florenz Ziegfeld.

Rumors that Toscanini had requested or even demanded a three-year contract were immediately countered by Griswold, who told the *Herald*, "Mr. Toscanini was asked by the directors to accept a three years' contract, and not until he had considered the matter for forty-eight hours did he finally agree to remain here that length of time." The end-of-each-year cancellation clause that the Metropolitan had stipulated in the original versions of its contracts with Gatti and Toscanini had been eliminated, just as Toscanini had predicted.

As soon as the singers realized that they had lost the battle, they came around, and within a year their misgivings about Toscanini would disappear. "No other conductor heard here in years and years plays such wonderful accompaniments for the singers," Krehbiel wrote in the *Herald*. "Ask the singers themselves, and the questioner will find that the orchestral support which this leader gives to them is simply unsurpassed by the leading of any other conductor." During one performance, Krehbiel said, the tenor Jacques Urlus "was taken ill, but continued to sing although suffering agony. The manner in which Mr. Toscanini helped ths singer was a wonder and a joy. He reduced the orchestral sound so much that a whisper could have been heard above it [. . .], and at other times, when he noticed that the singer was not able to 'deliver' [. . .], he let his orchestra soar, 'covering' the singer's voice so as not to make it necessary for him to force his tone and at the same time keeping complete Wagner's musical web."

Reviews indicate that Farrar's interpretation of Butterfly had been greatly altered, for the better, by Toscanini, and she later commented, "It would be difficult to estimate justly the influence Mr. Toscanini has had in the musical development of our opera, the artistic direction of which he rightly controls. Personally I am [. . .] far more indebted to him than I can properly place in words, certainly more than he, with a morbid dislike for any public attention to himself, would perhaps allow me to admit."

Whatever the artistic differences between Farrar and Toscanini may have been at the beginning, their personal relations were another matter. She fell in love with him; he responded at first by writing to her, and his letters "so delighted me," she later reminded him, "that I warned you, I should give every word its fullest meaning!" The twenty-six-year-old soprano, a classic beauty with almost sculpturally perfect features and intense blue eyes, and the fiery forty-one-year-old conductor became lovers; their affair would have serious consequences for both of them.

4.

"THE GATTI-TOSCANINI ADMINISTRATION IS GOING ADMIRABLY well here; more and more the Italian operas are magnificently successful and the others are falling apart." So Maria Gay wrote to her agent in Milan two weeks after Toscanini's New York debut. But the French and German repertoires recovered completely in December, when Toscanini conducted *Carmen* and *Götterdämmerung* and Mahler returned to conduct *Tristan*. Gay, in the title role in *Carmen*, was not liked by most of the critics; Caruso as Don José and Farrar as Micaëla fared much better, but for the *Times*'s critic Toscanini's interpretation was among "the most noteworthy features of the performance."

In *Götterdämmerung*, the Swedish-born, Norwegian- and American-bred soprano Olive Fremstad was Brünnhilde and the Danish tenor Erik Schmedes took the part of Siegfried. Toscanini cut the Waltraute episode, as he had done in Milan, but restored the Prologue and the Norn scene, which had long been omitted from Metropolitan performances. Aldrich described "a performance of remarkable energy and dramatic power, as well as one of great musical beauty." The city's Italian-language newspapers crowed, naturally, over their compatriot's success with Wagner. More remarkable were the ecstatic reports in the German-language press. "One must speak of a triumph for the great Italian conductor," declared the *Staats-Zeitung*. "With truly creative spirit, energy, and penetrating understanding, he gave us a greater portrait than we have ever before witnessed of the great closing tragedy of the Nibelung's Ring.

Let us be glad, as Germans, for this triumph of German opera, which a brilliant Italian yesterday led to victory."

Toscanini then conducted two US premieres: Puccini's *Le Villi* and Catalani's *La Wally*. The musical press found *Le Villi*—double-billed with *Cavalleria Rusticana*—not lacking in beautiful moments but barely worth the effort of a whole production. Toscanini prepared *La Wally* not only as a tribute to the dear friend of his youth but also to determine whether it would find a greater following in North America than it had captured elsewhere. Although most of the critics considered it better than *Le Villi*, the experiment did not have the results Toscanini had hoped for: Aldrich praised the whole production but noted that the "performance was received without great enthusiasm by an audience of moderate numbers." The three subsequent performances that Toscanini devoted to *La Wally* that season were the last he ever conducted of a complete Catalani opera.

One Sunday evening in January, some of the Metropolitan's leading members—including Mahler, Toscanini, Caruso, and Farrar—participated in a concert to benefit the victims of the catastrophic earthquake that had hit Sicily and Calabria six weeks earlier. In February, Toscanini conducted a benefit performance of *Aida* that garnered $7,000 for the Society for Italian Immigrants: the house was festooned with the American and the Italian colors; Italy's ambassador and consul general were present; and after the second act, Toscanini led the orchestra in the Italian and the American anthems.

At the Ansonia one evening, Toscanini bumped into the staff conductor Francesco Spetrino, who was about to go to the theater to conduct *Tosca*, but who looked ill. When Spetrino told him that he had a fever, Toscanini insisted that he go to bed: he himself would take over the performance, highly unusual though it was for a principal conductor to step in for a staff conductor. Toscanini walked into the pit with no rehearsal and conducted the whole performance by heart, with Eames in the title role, Caruso as Cavaradossi, and Scotti as Scarpia. Afterward, the concertmaster asked him whether he was satisfied with the orchestra's performance; Toscanini replied that the men had followed him perfectly and played wonderfully. The concertmaster was pleased, because, he said, not one of Toscanini's tempi was the same as Spetrino's.

5.

LATE IN LIFE, GIUSEPPE VERDI HAD PREDICTED THAT BY THE centenary of his birth, in 1913, his works would have fallen completely out of favor. But as that anniversary approached, the popularity of his music was increasing. A performance of the *Requiem* that Toscanini conducted at the Metropolitan on 21 February 1909 aroused such enthusiasm that three more performances had to be scheduled before the end of the season and two more the following year. Then came *Falstaff*, the opera Toscanini loved most, with Scotti in the title role and Destinn, Gay, Frances Alda (who had recently joined the Metropolitan's roster), and Didur among the other principals. The dress rehearsal was attended by Victor Maurel, who had taken the part of the fat knight in the original production under Verdi's supervision, and who was now teaching singing in New York. Before the season ended, Toscanini conducted three in-house *Falstaff* performances—"among the most enjoyable ones heard at the Metropolitan this season," according to the *Times*—and one tour performance. Alda later declared that "any performance of *Falstaff* without [Toscanini] is, for me, as flavorless as a salad without garlic."

The season's chronicles provide some remarkable examples of Toscaninian stamina. For instance, on the evening of 30 November 1908, the maestro conducted *Butterfly* in New York; the next evening he conducted the company in *Aida* in Philadelphia; two days later he gave his first *Carmen* performance back in New York; and the following evening he conducted *Tosca*. A matinee performance of *Carmen* on 12 December was followed by a *Tosca* that evening. Then there was the double bill of *Le Villi* and *Cavalleria Rusticana* on 17 December, *Götterdämmerung* on the eighteenth, and *Carmen* on the nineteenth; *Tosca* on 11 February, *Carmen* on the twelfth, and *Aida* on the thirteenth; the Verdi *Requiem* on the evening of 9 April, *Butterfly* the following afternoon, and *Götterdämmerung* that evening. On tour in Pittsburgh, a *Butterfly* matinee on 28 April was followed by an *Aida* in the evening—the last performance of his initial Metropolitan season.* Not to speak of the rehearsals needed for each performance,

---

* Eighteen of Toscanini's sixty-six opera performances during the 1908–09 season took

especially when one singer replaced another in a role, as was often the case: in *Aida*, for instance, the artists in three of the four principal roles had changed by the end of the season.

During his earliest years at the Metropolitan, Toscanini had only two major complaints. The first concerned the theater itself, which he considered mediocre acoustically and inadequate with respect to sight lines, stage depth (the stage was about eighteen feet shallower than that of La Scala), rehearsal spaces, and storage areas for scenery. In the mid-1950s, when the soprano Licia Albanese tried to enlist the aged Toscanini's support for a campaign to save the old house while plans for the new Metropolitan at Lincoln Center were being made, he turned her down, saying that the original theater ought to have been demolished decades earlier. Gatti-Casazza also found the house wanting from the first time he set foot in it. He was told that a new Metropolitan would be built within two or three years; in the event, the wait lasted nearly sixty years, thirty of them after Gatti's departure. Gatti, however, also made a promise that he did not fulfill: before coming to New York, he announced that he would learn English, but in 1935, when he retired from the Metropolitan, his English was still primitive, and even his French was awful. "Speaking foreign languages," he said disdainfully, "is a talent and job for waiters."

Toscanini's second major complaint concerned the visual blandness and backwardness of the Metropolitan's productions, which also appalled Mahler. Many years later, Toscanini recalled with horror that some of the company's scenery for *William Tell*, which takes place in thirteenth-century rural Switzerland, was also used for *The Barber of Seville*, which is set in a Spanish town five hundred years later. For their debut *Aida* production, he and Gatti had had the Metropolitan import sets and costumes created by their old Scala team, and even the normally cautious Richard Aldrich proclaimed in the *Times* that "nothing more gorgeous in the way of scenic effect" had been seen on the Metropolitan's stage in a very long time. In an interview in November 1908, Gatti predicted that within three or four years new productions would replace most or all of the old ones.

---

place away from the Metropolitan's home theater: six each in Philadelphia and Chicago, three in Brooklyn, two in Pittsburgh, and one in Baltimore.

Overall, however, the Metropolitan made Toscanini feel as satisfied as he was capable of feeling about his work. The singers, orchestra, and chorus were the best he had ever had at his disposal; by all accounts, including Gatti's, the company was much better organized than that of La Scala; and Otto Kahn was ready to make up deficits in the ensemble's finances, although he was ostracized by high society because he was Jewish. Toscanini, even in his last years, inveighed against the turn-of-the-century New York socialites who had been happy to have Kahn subsidize the theater for them but would not allow him to own a box in the house. "The Jews were treated very badly," Toscanini said.*

Toscanini was also beginning to feel comfortable in New York. He even joined Gatti, Caruso, Alessandro Bonci, Zenatello, J. P. Morgan, and various diplomats in paying for a monument to the Italian explorer Giovanni da Verrazzano, the first European to visit what is now New York Harbor; the statue, by the Sicilian artist Ettore Ximenes, was unveiled in Battery Park in October 1909. A little later in his Metropolitan tenure, Toscanini, along with other famous musicians, became a member of the Bohemians, a club dedicated to "giving assistance to musicians of New York City who, through illness or other misfortune, fall into temporary difficulties."

The Gatti-Toscanini team's first season in the United States had been a virtually unqualified success. "The artistic results obtained by the new management have unquestionably reached a higher level in many respects than has prevailed at the Metropolitan Opera House for years," according to the *Times*. "This has been especially noticeable in the matters of stage management, in the care and intelligence with which most of the performances were prepared, in the finish and competency with which they were set before the public, and in the effects of chorus and of orchestra. The acquisition of Mr. Toscanini has brought musical enjoyment of a high order in the Italian works that he has conducted as well as in the fine performances of 'Götterdämmerung' that are due to his labors."

In Milan, *Il Guerrin Meschino*, a satirical journal, took advantage of

---

* During the same taped conversation (7 December 1953), Toscanini remarked that although Jews were now treated better than they had been in turn-of-the-century America, blacks were still treated badly. "Abraham Lincoln—that was a real man," he said. "They killed him, and fundamentally they still have that mentality today."

the reports from New York to poke affectionate fun at La Scala's former conductor, in the form of a fake letter from him. "You ask me how things are going at the Metropolitan. How do you think they are going when I am there? Very well, God bless you!" said "Toscanini." "The millionaires do what I want them to, and if they failed to abide by my word I would send them quickly to ——."

6.

CARLA TOSCANINI HAD ARRIVED IN NEW YORK LATE IN JANUARY 1909, with one-year-old Wanda and a nursemaid, and remained for the rest of the season. On 4 May, the whole party boarded the *Kaiser Wilhelm II*, as did Gatti-Casazza and Frances Alda, who had become engaged and were returning together to Europe. In Milan, Toscanini expressed "the highest satisfaction with everybody and everything in America, especially the fact that Italian opera now occupies a prominent place," New York's *Sun* reported. "He praised [. . .] American audiences, who are not impulsive and do not rebel against deficient actors and bad execution. They merely do not applaud, he says, a course which is in contrast with the Italian custom of whistling and shouting."

Toscanini's American earnings allowed him, at last, to buy a home in Milan—an aristocratic, three-story seventeenth-century house in the central but tranquil (in those days) Via Durini, which runs southward from an extension of Piazza San Babila* to Largo Augusto. Count Alberto De Mojana sold the building to the Toscaninis for 160,000 lire, roughly what the maestro earned in one season at the Metropolitan. It has a courtyard, a quietly Baroque façade, and a street-side balcony adorned with a lovely wrought-iron enclosure. Santa Maria della Sanità, an early eighteenth-century church with a curved façade, stands next door to Casa Toscanini. For the rest of his life, Toscanini loved this house more than any of his other dwellings, and during all of his wanderings it was the place to which he longed to return. The family lived on the *piano nobile* (what Europeans call the first floor and Americans call the second); the ample living quar-

---

* The extension is now called Largo Arturo Toscanini.

ters were decorated in Art Nouveau style (called *Stile Liberty* in Italy) by the well-known architect Gaetano Moretti, and the basic decor remained unchanged until the house was sold, long after Toscanini's death. One of Leonardo Bistolfi's sculptures, acquired by Toscanini, still stands in the building's courtyard, and a doorway to a secondary staircase—the entrance used by maids, cooks, and delivery boys—bears a plaque with the words *Toscanini servizio.*

His American earnings also allowed Toscanini to contribute his services gratis to various events during this and subsequent stays in Italy. In June 1909, he conducted an orchestra made up of professors and advanced students at the Milan Conservatory in three concerts that raised money for furnishing the institution's new concert hall; the programs included his first performance of Debussy's *La Mer,* which would become one of Toscanini's favorite concert pieces. He also made a rare appearance in Naples, where he conducted—again without fee—a concert in memory of his revered friend Giuseppe Martucci, who had died in June, at the age of fifty-three. He spent much of the summer in the Alps with his family, but in September he went to Munich to attend a Brahms festival under the direction of Fritz Steinbach, a conductor greatly admired by Brahms himself. Steinbach's programs included all four symphonies, the "Haydn" Variations, the Violin Concerto, the *German Requiem,* and other choral-orchestral pieces. "I have enjoyed myself beyond words," he wrote to Polo. "Brahms is great—Steinbach marvelous." He fixed Steinbach's Brahms interpretations in his memory and thereafter made abundant use of his recollections.*

Around 10 October, Toscanini boarded the American Line steamer *Saint Louis* in Southampton, England, bound for New York, where he arrived on the seventeenth and immediately plunged into a heavy rehearsal schedule: the Metropolitan was initiating its busiest season to date, with 340 performances of forty-two operas to be presented in numerous venues, including its main home, the smaller New Theatre, the Brooklyn Academy of Music, and thirteen other cities—as far south as Atlanta, and as far north and west as St. Paul. The orches-

---

* For a detailed discussion of Steinbach's influence on Toscanini and other conductors, see Christopher Dyment, *Conducting the Brahms Symphonies: From Brahms to Boult* (Woodbridge, UK: Boydell Press, 2016).

tra had been increased to 160 players, who were paid a minimum of seven dollars per performance, although many received higher fees. The fees covered a fixed number of rehearsals; if a rehearsal exceeded four hours, the players were paid extra. Largely at Toscanini's insistence, the corps de ballet had been expanded to sixty-five members; young Michel Fokine became one of the company's six choreographers, and its étoiles included the twenty-eight-year-old Anna Pavlova in her American debut season and Mikhail Mordkin, who later founded what would become the American Ballet Theater. Members of the corps de ballet received a minimum of fifteen dollars per week. Running the Metropolitan cost an average of $80,000 per week during the opera season.

Mahler was now under contract with the New York Philharmonic; at the Metropolitan he conducted only the American premiere and three subsequent performances of Tchaikovsky's *Queen of Spades* (in German) during the 1909–10 season, and nothing thereafter. Spetrino and Setti had left the conducting staff (the latter would soon return) and were replaced by four other Italians. Hertz and several staff conductors led much of the German repertoire. But Toscanini's workload was enormous. During the season's first three weeks, he worked with twenty-eight solo singers on forty-five different roles in five operas—including three new productions—and conducted an average of one performance every two and a half days, plus countless rehearsals of every sort.

His season began in Philadelphia on 9 November with a reprise of the previous year's *Aida*; six days later, he opened the Metropolitan's home season with a new production of *La Gioconda*, with Destinn, Caruso, Homer, and Amato. Andrés de Segurola, who had not worked with Toscanini since 1901, sang the part of Alvise, and the Spanish basso's account of his first rehearsal conveys something of the atmosphere at these sessions, his sometimes unidiomatic English notwithstanding.

> Caruso and Destinn began by singing in full voice, Amato occasionally. I chose to start in full voice too [. . .]. [Toscanini] pointed his long finger at me and said: "Segurola, if I would not have known you before I would certainly have stopped you right after the first word 'Ribellion!' you sang. [. . .] Ponchielli wrote

the word in sixteenths. You sang it in slow eighths, thus depriving Alvise's inquisitive utterance of all the surprise and authoritative accent which the situation demands—look it over, caro Segurola," he said with a smile. [. . .] Caruso humorously interjected: "Experience has taught me that I don't know if I know a role until I sing it with the *Grande Omino* (great little man)!"

Caruso, who, only a year earlier, had been apprehensive about Toscanini's arrival at the Metropolitan, had in the meantime come to think of the conductor as a great boon. A few months later, a *Times* interviewer reported Caruso's praise for Toscanini, who, the tenor said, allowed "a certain license to the singer, but only on condition that the true musical line is never overstepped. 'We have all received his reproofs, but we none of us blame him.'" The results were telling: in 1907 Puccini had described Caruso as "indolent, a lazy man with an air of self-satisfaction"; by 1910 the composer was describing the tenor as "great."

An incident at the opening-night *Gioconda* performance must have reminded Toscanini of battles that he had had to fight at La Scala a few years earlier. After Caruso's aria "Cielo e mar," in the second act, "there was little short of a riot," the *Herald* reported. "The denizens of the upper gallery and the enthusiasts who stood shouted 'Bis' until they were hoarse. Mr. Toscanini [. . .] went right on conducting while Mr. Caruso bowed his gratitude. The applauders wanted to hear it again. Still the conductor refused. Hisses mingled with shouts and applause. [. . .] Mr. Toscanini stopped the orchestra. Then those that applauded and those that hissed waged emotional war for a second, but Mr. Toscanini won the day. He beckoned the orchestra to play, and the opera proceeded without an encore." The evening ended in triumph.

After just a year in the job, Toscanini was seen as a guarantor of musical excellence at America's largest performing arts organization. "With the exception of Mahler, Toscanini is the only conductor in the history of the Metropolitan Opera Company who has obtained consistently and without fail the highest artistic results," wrote Max Smith, a musically trained critic (for the *Press*) who spoke Italian and was becoming friendly with Toscanini. "He came to New York with eyes wide open, even if he failed to realize what a hornets' nest he would stir up [. . .]. [I]t is he, unquestionably, who compels the necessary number of rehearsals, he who is responsible for the results. The time has come when Toscanini's name on a programme means inevitably a performance of the highest standard."

The *Gioconda* production, like the previous season's productions of *Aida* and *La Wally*, had been created by Gatti and Toscanini's trusted scene painters in Milan, and so had the new production of *Otello* that opened two nights after *Gioconda*, with the Czech tenor Leo Slezak making his American debut in the title role, Alda as Desdemona, and Scotti as Iago—a role in which he alternated with Amato throughout the season. Slezak, a big man with a big voice and a big personality, had been a favorite of Mahler's in Vienna. He must have pleased Toscanini, because he sang all ten of the *Otello* performances that the maestro led that season, in New York and on tour, and many more performances of this and other operas under Toscanini's baton during the following three years.

"I got to know a personality of such paramount, gigantic importance that he remains unique," Slezak wrote late in life. "In private, he was one of the most charming and enchanting of men, but the moment he stood on the podium or led a rehearsal he became someone else. Truly terrifying in his conscientiousness, meticulousness, authority, and energy, he sought the same of everyone else. Without hesitation he ruthlessly demanded the utmost of each and every person. On this point he resembled Gustav Mahler. Woe to the artist who had not accurately studied his role exactly as it was written, and woe to those who did not obey his rather categorical wishes." But Slezak added, "There was no one among us who didn't give his best and blindly obey [Toscanini's] advice, because everything that he wanted made sense and led us to success."

Alda recalled that at the dress rehearsal of *Otello*'s final act,

when I came on the stage, Toscanini took one long look at me. [. . .] *"Senti, Aldina* [Listen, little Alda]," he said commandingly. "You will kneel and sing the 'Ave Maria.' Then you will get up, without turning your face to the audience. There will be not one smile. Not one bow. There will be no encores. You will not lift your eyes. You will just get into bed like a good pure virgin." We played and sang it that way, though after the "Ave

Maria," which ends on a tender high note, the audience burst into tremendous applause. But I felt Toscanini's eye upon me. I dared not look up. The scene went on with its poetry uninterrupted.

For Toscanini, however, the major event of the first half of the 1909–10 season took place in November, when he gave his first New York performances of *Tristan und Isolde* in a new production, with Carl Burrian and Johanna Gadski in the title roles. The conductor's interpretation "fully justified the enthusiasm in Italy and the warm praise awarded by the German critics" at the time of the 1900–01 Scala *Tristan*, wrote W. J. Henderson in the *Sun*. Toscanini "conceived the first act in a mood of restrained intensity and reserved the outpouring of thrilling passion for the second." Henderson, who had not liked Toscanini's *Götterdämmerung* interpretation the previous year, now said that the Italian maestro had "assumed his rightful position among the most interesting Wagner conductors known to this public." Aldrich, in the *Times*, wrote of the performance's "indescribable exaltation and intense passion" and said that Toscanini's "tempos were free and subtly modified always; at certain points somewhat slow, as in the second act; but he was able to gain through this an intensity of feeling that never lapsed."

Years later, after having heard many of the maestro's *Tristan* performances, James Gibbons Huneker, the best-known American writer on music of his generation, expressed some reservations. In this work "he does not achieve the ultimate heights," Huneker wrote. "It is a wonderfully worked-out musical picture that this Italian wizard evokes, but the surge and thunder and the elemental ground swell that Anton Seidl summoned from the vasty deep is missing. [. . .] And yet, with the single exception of Arthur Nikisch, there is no living conductor whose 'Tristan and Isolde' is so ravishing—in tone color, in poetic sentiment—as Toscanini's."

In the six subsequent *Tristan* performances that Toscanini conducted in the course of his second Metropolitan season, Gadski, Olive Fremstad, and Lillian Nordica alternated in the role of Isolde. Although Fremstad had sung the part under Mahler's direction during the two previous seasons, Aldrich wrote that with Toscanini she performed "with more power and more finished art than ever before." Mary Watkins Cushing, Fremstad's companion, described one unstaged ensemble rehearsal that was meant to be a mere run-through of an act of *Tristan* for the sake of a new singer who was being inserted into the production. On this occasion, however, the music rose from the pit "with electrifying sweep and power, catching up the soprano and carrying her to emotional heights even beyond herself," Cushing said. "Enkindled by Isolde's growing exaltation, the Maestro in his turn sent the flames of his own inspiration crackling higher and higher." The intensity grew to such a peak that Fremstad, fearing that nothing would be left for the evening's performance, "walked uncertainly toward the footlights, her face wet with tears," and begged Toscanini to "'go no further!'" He stopped the rehearsal, went up onto the stage, and began to point out something in Fremstad's score; before long, "incredibly, both were laughing. He kissed her hand and scurried off to his room." Fremstad's comment to Cushing: "'These things come rarely in any lifetime— for which I thank God!'"

Toscanini always remembered Fremstad as "a fine artist" who came to rehearsals thoroughly prepared. He described her as eccentric—she would dress and behave oddly during rehearsals, blurting out strange comments and assuming strange positions— but she had "an expressive face" and was "a beautiful Isolde," he said. According to Farrar, Fremstad's "dream wish" in later years was "to sing just once more Isolde, under the baton of Maestro Toscanini," and Fremstad sent Toscanini a letter to that effect when she was nearly eighty years old!

Undeterred by the lukewarm reception accorded his 1907 Scala production of Gluck's *Orfeo ed Euridice*, Toscanini led a new production of the work at the Metropolitan in December 1909. He eliminated Gluck's overture—following the opinion of Berlioz, a great admirer of Gluck, who had nevertheless described the opening piece as an "incredible bit of silliness"—and made several interpolations from other Gluck operas: the aria "Divinités du Styx" from *Alceste*, a trio from *Paride ed Elena*, and a chorus from *Echo et Narcisse*. Sets designed by Jacques Pacquereau for Paris's Opéra-Comique but remade to fit the Metropolitan's larger dimensions were imported from France, and the production dispensed with footlights and made use only of overhead and lateral lighting—a technique that had already been advocated not just by Fortuny in Milan but also by the avant-garde English theater director-designer Edward Gordon Craig.

Louise Homer, long eager to sing the part of Orfeo, had begun studying the role with Toscanini the preceding March, and he had blue-penciled his suggestions into her score: *agitato, con passione*, and so on. Toscanini later described Homer as "a fine artist," who "wasn't beautiful" but had "a theatrical bearing," he said. Gadski took the part of Euridice, and the twenty-five-year-old Romanian-born soprano Alma Gluck—no relation to the composer (she was born Reba Fiersohn)—made her house debut as the Blessed Spirit. Arturo Buzzi-Peccia, her voice teacher, had brought her to the attention of Toscanini, who later described her as "*very* beautiful—beautiful eyes, intelligent, and sly, with a smile for everyone, protected by everyone except Alda, who was jealous." He praised her pronunciation but said that her voice was too "milky" for his taste and that she had no acting ability. She was a prankster, too. During one of the Metropolitan's tours, Toscanini called a rehearsal for a certain morning, but when he got out of bed that day he discovered that he had no trousers to put on: Alma had bribed a hotel valet to remove the trousers from the room of every man in the company.

Krehbiel called the *Orfeo* production "the most interesting event of the operatic season thus far. [. . .] Mr. Toscanini's treatment of the music was reverential—more than reverential—it was loving." Milka Ternina, a former star soprano, went to hear *Orfeo* and declared that she had been "completely carried away by the performance. Such art! Such taste! Toscanini is in a large measure responsible for this. He is a musician with a soul—a great musician. [. . .] I have been told that he may go to the Boston Symphony Orchestra. I think that would be a great pity."

A rumor about Toscanini's going to Boston was indeed circulating; he had probably been approached by the orchestra's board, but he preferred to remain at the Metropolitan. A year earlier, Mahler had likewise been invited to take over the Boston ensemble but had opted to stay in New York.

During a brief break from work on the day after Christmas, Toscanini dined at Alda's Ansonia apartment with Gatti, Caruso, the soprano Lina Cavalieri (who was working at Oscar Hammerstein's

Manhattan Opera, the Metropolitan's rival), Amato and his wife, and his old friends Maurel and Buzzi-Peccia. A few days earlier, he had written to Carla to say that when he was not at the theater, he was either studying or reading—often reading in English, although he hadn't yet begun to speak it. He usually had Sunday dinner with Amato and his wife, who also lived at the Ansonia, and from time to time he would have a meal with other friends. Mario Marchesi, his Parmesan friend who had been a prompter at La Scala and now held the same position at the Metropolitan, often came to the maestro's suite for lunch or dinner, and various Italians from the conducting staff would sometimes join Toscanini there for a meal.

In January 1910, his usual frenzied schedule of rehearsals and performances—not to mention his Boston debut, conducting *Tristan* with the Metropolitan ensemble—was made even heavier by preparations for the North American premiere of Franchetti's *Germania*. Toscanini and the singers, including Caruso and Destinn, were much applauded, the opera less so: it received a few more performances that season and the next and has never been revived at the Metropolitan.

During a break in the *Germania* dress rehearsal, a *Times* reporter managed to corner Toscanini in a backstage corridor, tried to interview him, found him "courteous and pleasant," but got very little out of him. After the maestro had managed to escape, a stagehand told the reporter, "I don't know whether he's so modest because he's so great and can afford to be, or whether it is because he really has no desire to blow his own horn."

He conducted benefit performances, or parts thereof, for various causes (survivors of a flood in France, the Metropolitan's Pension and Endowment Fund, the Legal Aid Society) in February and March, but he was mainly preoccupied during those weeks with preparing his first Metropolitan production of *Die Meistersinger*, which opened late in March with Walter Soomer as Sachs, Gadski as Eva, and Slezak as Stolzing. Gadski recalled that at one of the rehearsals for this production, Toscanini suddenly stopped her and asked why her singing of a few phrases varied from the way he had heard her sing them at Bayreuth in 1899. "Such uncanny command of detail from memory astonished me and I replied that that was the way I felt it," she said. "Toscanini, like Mahler, treated singers like fellow artists, and that is one of the great qualities which make artistic association with him so memorable."

The *Meistersinger* sets were not new, but the staging was, and the musical performance, Aldrich said, "reached a pitch of perfection, of ravishing, intoxicating loveliness, of pure beauty of sound, of instrumental color, that was perhaps unique of its kind." Toscanini remembered the production as one that had given him particular satisfaction. But at one point in a subsequent performance Slezak committed some serious errors; he recalled that Toscanini

> came up during the intermission, beat his head in despair against the wall, and growled incessantly: *"Questo tenore è una bestia."* [This tenor is an animal.] Naturally I didn't go near him, and the whole evening he didn't deign to give me a glance from the podium. I sang as rapturously as I could—in vain. After the opera, while I was waiting for the elevator in my hotel, which was also his, he came over, his hat pulled down low over his forehead, without looking at me. I went up to him, stammered my apologies, and said that I would do everything to insure that such a thing would never happen again. He calmed down, murmured a lugubrious, *"Caro, era terribile"* [My dear, it was terrible], and everything was all right again.

Once again, the whole Metropolitan season had been an overwhelming success for the company. Toscanini had conducted sixty-six complete performances of nine operas, one single-act "gala" performance, and two performances of the Verdi *Requiem*. Forty-four of his regular opera performances had taken place at the Metropolitan Opera House, the remaining ones on tour. His season ended in Chicago, where, from 4 to 18 April, he conducted a total of nine performances of six operas. He then returned to New York and boarded ship, but his destination this time was France rather than Italy.

PARIS IN 1910 WAS THE CENTER OF THE EUROPEAN ARTISTIC AVANT-garde: Picasso, Braque, Matisse, Modigliani, Brâncuși, Chagall,

Proust, Apollinaire, Alain-Fournier, Cocteau, Gertrude Stein, Debussy, Ravel, and Sergei Diaghilev's Ballets Russes were all present at various times, all bent on revolutionizing their respective art forms.

One of the important organizers of performing events in the Ville Lumière was Gabriel Astruc, a Bordeaux-born rabbi's son who had transformed himself into an impresario, managing everyone from Mata Hari to Caruso to the young Arthur Rubinstein to Diaghilev's troupe. Astruc had joined forces with Gatti-Casazza to bring the Metropolitan Opera to the French capital, and thanks to $50,000 in financial guarantees from both sides of the Atlantic,* the ensemble, in its first venture outside North America, would give a total of twenty performances (six different Italian operas) at the Théâtre du Châtelet. All but three of the performances would be conducted by Toscanini, who, according to Gatti, had turned down an offer of $40,000 for a fourteen-week season in Buenos Aires in order to make his French debut with the American ensemble.†

Sets, costumes, solo singers, and most of the chorus were brought over from New York for the engagement, but the orchestra was not. Instead, Toscanini worked with the local Orchestre Colonne, strengthened by members of the Orchestre Lamoureux, and he quickly learned that these ensembles' standards were far below those of the Metropolitan and Scala orchestras. "I had asked for two reading rehearsals—one to read through all of *Aida*, the second because I had my Metropolitan chorus and all the solo singers, so I couldn't not have a[n ensemble] rehearsal," he recalled. "[But] at the first rehearsal, three hours long, I didn't finish the first act of *Aida*." He was shocked and frustrated by the orchestra's inadequacy, and no more tactful, let alone intimidated, in Paris than anywhere else. "In Italy we play *Carmen* by heart, and you aren't familiar with *Aida*!" he shouted.

---

* Sixty percent came from members of the Metropolitan's board, the remainder from Italians resident in Paris and from the patrons of Astruc's Société Musicale pour les Grandes Auditions de France.

† The staff conductor Vittorio Podesti was responsible for three performances of *Pagliacci*—double-billed with *Cavalleria*, which Toscanini conducted. Toscanini was probably paid for his work in Paris, but the Metropolitan's payroll books indicate nothing after the end of the home season. Toscanini could have made his Paris debut five years earlier: Tito Ricordi had invited him to present a concert of new Italian music with the Cercle de l'Union Artistique, but Toscanini had turned the offer down.

At the end of the session, Toscanini walked to Astruc's office, where he found a representative of the orchestra already complaining to the impresario. Astruc recalled, "The musicians' 'delegate' came to warn me that his colleagues would not tolerate either the comments or the sarcasm of the Italian conductor. Being responsible for receipts of 500,000 francs, I trembled at having to reimburse my subscribers." The delegate told Toscanini, "We've played with Mahler, we've played with Richter"—in other words, we were good enough for more famous conductors than you. Toscanini exploded: "But you haven't played with Toscanini!" He later spoke contemptuously of Richter's *laisser-aller* attitude: when Richter conducted in Paris or Rome, he would do a single rehearsal and then go sightseeing, Toscanini said, adding that he, too, loved to visit places of interest, but only when his work was done. "I had the habit of taking things seriously," he said.

During one frustrating orchestra rehearsal, Frances Alda, sitting in a parterre seat, saw Toscanini pull out a pocket watch and fling it hard into the auditorium. "The abandonment of despair conveyed by that gesture was sublime," she said. "For a moment it touched even the violins. They actually stopped sawing wood and began to play." Alda found the watch and returned it to Toscanini, who put it back in his pocket. But "it wasn't long before [the musicians] were out of tune and out of time. I saw Toscanini's hand steal toward his pocket. Out came the watch. Again it skimmed the tops of the orchestra seats and landed BIFF-BANG in a distant corner. Again the startled orchestra [. . .] paid sudden concentrated attention to their scores. I went quietly and retrieved the watch, [. . .] handed it to him, and gravely he replaced it in his pocket. This time it stayed there."

The stage of the fifty-year-old Châtelet presented a different problem. Its "broad, uneven, splintery boards, with wide-gaping cracks" reminded the *New York Press*'s correspondent of "an old, dilapidated country barn," and the "primitive" prompter's box was "sadly in need of a coating of paint." According to the *Times*'s Paris correspondent, Gatti had trouble with the Châtelet's stagehands, "but at last persuasion, both verbal and pecuniary, started them going."

The dress rehearsal of the first opera, *Aida*, took place on 19 May before an invited audience that included Prime Minister Aristide Briand, Chancellor (and future prime minister) Louis Barthou, the

American ambassador (and former secretary of state) Robert Bacon, the writers Edmond Rostand and Gabriele D'Annunzio, and many Parisian socialites. It was a de facto premiere, with crowds of attendees and onlookers jamming the Place du Châtelet beforehand and causing the curtain to go up forty-five minutes late. But the success exceeded Gatti's and Astruc's fondest hopes.

"One should not perhaps say anything after a dress rehearsal," wrote the critic Raoul Brévanne in the next day's edition of *Le Figaro*, but "I cannot resist [. . .], as it was so admirable in every way, so complete, so evocative, and so great was the enthusiasm that it aroused. They played *Aida*, but a new *Aida*, transformed as if by a miracle [. . .]." Brévanne singled out each of the principal singers for praise, as well as the chorus, the dancers, the staging, and the sets. "But he to whom much of the evening's honors were given [. . .] was the conductor, Arturo Toscanini. We knew that he is one of the best conductors in the world; we knew that there is something prodigious about his talents; but we did not yet know the extraordinary power that this great artist achieves; we did not know the power of suggestion that he exercises over musicians, singers, and audience. [. . .] Paris has immediately adopted him, admires him, and asks only to admire him again."

During one of the intermissions, Astruc brought a surprise visitor to Toscanini's dressing room. "When the door opened and he saw Debussy, Toscanini rose," Astruc recalled. The two men, who had never met before, "looked at each other for a long moment and, silent with emotion, fell into each other's arms." Astruc described Toscanini as a "Titan, a valiant zealot" on behalf of the music of Debussy and other French composers.

For Debussy, the evening was important in another way as well. "I still remember the astonished surprise of Claude Debussy 'discovering' Verdi one evening when Toscanini was conducting a performance of *Aida* in Paris," wrote the French musician and critic Emile Vuillermoz in 1935. "The author of *Pelléas* ingenuously shared current prejudices on the subject of Italian theater. For that matter, he was familiar only with the mediocre performances that can be heard in our theaters, which have neither the singers nor the traditions that are indispensable for understanding these works. For Debussy it was a true revelation, which he often liked to talk about." Debussy also attended a performance of *Falstaff*, and Gatti-Casazza later recalled, "At the end of each scene he would ask me the same question: 'But was Verdi really going on his eightieth year when he wrote music of this kind?' And at my affirmative answer he exclaimed: 'It is unbelievable! Prodigious! That old man must have made some pact with the devil, like Faust!' "

A single incident, however, nearly turned the Paris season into a disaster. The previous winter, Marie Delna, a well-known French contralto, had made her American debut at the Metropolitan in the role of Orfeo, replacing Louise Homer in the season's last two performances of the Gluck opera. She also sang in an opera and a concert not conducted by Toscanini and was to have sung in some of his *Gioconda* performances. In a statement to the press, she claimed that the maestro had not allowed her sufficient rehearsal time in *Orfeo*; this was probably the only such complaint from a singer in Toscanini's entire career—if anything, they complained about too many rehearsals. In addition, Delna said, he had accepted her tempi in piano rehearsals but tried to force her to speed up during the performances. After her second *Orfeo* performance, she declared, "Never again would I sing with Mr. Toscanini, and never again will I." She also accused the Metropolitan of unfair employment practices. "It is governed by Italians and run after the manner of Italian theatres. A German singer has little chance; a French singer even less." In a show of solidarity with Delna, the French tenor Edmond Clément announced that he would not return to the Metropolitan the following season, but he later changed his mind.

Delna's accusations were unfounded: of the fifty-eight female solo singers on the Metropolitan's roster that season, fewer than ten were Italian, and there was not one Italian among the female stars; all the rest were German, French, American, and of other nationalities. Among the male singers, stars and otherwise, the proportion of Italians was higher, but still only about one-third. Toscanini had often worked well with outstanding French singers: Lhérie, Maurel, Frandin, Dufriche, Dupeyron—the list was already long and would expand greatly in the years to come. Delna had also managed to antagonize several of her colleagues, including Caruso and the non-Italian Slezak, who were refusing to perform with her; their protests may have provoked the break more directly than any conflict with Toscanini. Nevertheless—and allowing for the fact that recordings of the period present only a pale image of singers' interpretive ideas—Delna's recording of Orfeo's aria "Che farò senza Euridice" is noteworthy not for its slow tempo (it is rather fast) but for the singer's waywardness, her illogical and unmusical pushing and pulling of tempi. If this is how she insisted on singing it with Toscanini, conflict would have been inevitable. She left New York in a huff after having given only ten of her fourteen scheduled Metropolitan performances.

Still seething over her unhappy American experience, she was almost certainly behind the publication in the Paris newspaper *Gil Blas* of a nasty article about Toscanini and Gatti-Casazza; it claimed, among other things, that "no one in New York pays any attention to [Toscanini]" and that his only friend and admirer at the Metropolitan was the prompter.

At the opening night performance in Paris, on 21 May, "a storm of hissing broke forth in the gallery as the curtain rose" on the second act of *Aida*, according to the *Times*'s correspondent. "Abusive epithets were hurled at Toscanini, the conductor, but he took no notice of them. Mme. Homer" (Delna's leading rival in New York) "was on the stage about to begin her solo. To quell or drown the hissing the people in the stalls and boxes applauded with all their might."

"My heart nearly stopped beating," Homer told a journalist. "Mr. Toscanini, white as chalk, [. . .] conducted inexorably. The chorus women seemed to be on the point of leaving the stage. Several near me asked what they should do. I answered, 'Sing!' They did sing, but you couldn't hear a note from the front, they tell me. The orchestra was not audible, even to us. My first notes are not supposed to be sung loudly, but I shouted them. [. . .] All I can say is that in one way and another we finished the scene, and when Mme. Destinn came on the hissing noise had ceased. From that time on we had nothing but success." There were no further incidents: Paris's music lovers had been conquered by the visiting troupe.

Toscanini always remembered Destinn's singing in Paris, especially in "the third act of *Aida*—she was adorable," he told his daughter Wanda in a recorded conversation. "She was more successful than Caruso—oh yes! She had those flute-like notes," he said, and she sang the phrase "O patria mia, mai più, mai più ti rivedrò!" in one breath, as Verdi had indicated and as "all" the Aidas in Toscanini's youth had done, he said, but as few did later on. He was also reported to have said of Destinn, "She looked like a cook but she sang like an angel."

During a benefit performance at the Opéra, Toscanini conducted the ensemble in the fourth act of *Otello* and the second act of *Tristan*—the first time in the forty years since the Franco-Prussian War that German had been sung at the Opéra; Podesti conducted other excerpts. The event raised 200,000 francs for the survivors of a recently sunk submarine.

The troupe also gave the first performance in Paris of Puccini's *Manon Lescaut*, which had become internationally popular since its world premiere seventeen years earlier but had been unofficially banned in France out of regard for Massenet's older *Manon*. The *Times* reported great enthusiasm for Puccini, who was present, and for all the performers. Caruso "acted with such vigor in the love scenes with Manon that he got his wig awry." And no wonder: the title role was sung by a pretty twenty-two-year-old Spanish soprano, Lucrezia Bori, who had auditioned for Puccini, Toscanini, and Gatti-Casazza in Milan the previous year and had immediately been engaged. A descendant of the notorious Borgia family—her real name was Lucrecia Borja y González de Riancho—she would soon become a favorite in New York.

Puccini, who had nervously been smoking one cigarette after another before the *Manon Lescaut* premiere and during the intermissions, was delighted with the outcome. As to the performance, he remarked, "I think I am the only composer who has never conducted his own work. I leave that to others, particularly to a man like Toscanini. He is marvelous in his understanding of the composer and the music." Puccini wrote to Giulio Ricordi, "A real and total triumph. Performance unique. I don't think I've ever had such an organic and perfect ensemble for *Manon*." With Puccini's encouragement, Toscanini had made some modifications in the orchestral score of the opera, and after the composer returned to Italy he wrote to Toscanini, "The Ricordi Company has finally decided to print the *Manon* score. You will be sent a copy, which you will want to edit. Believe me, you couldn't do me a bigger favor. Thus, with your corrections of colorings and effective bowings, etc. etc., I'll finally be able to have a definitive *Manon* and to free her from the anarchy that binds her. My soul is full of your performance and of the goodness of your spirit."

During Puccini's Paris visit, he and Toscanini attended performances of *Pelléas* and of Paul Dukas's *Ariane et Barbe-bleue* at the Opéra-Comique. Some of the singers were good, Toscanini recalled, but the performances as a whole were slap-dash, and the audience made so much noise that the music could barely be heard. "Puccini was satisfied," Toscanini said, but he himself was appalled.

Toscanini continued to be frustrated by the Paris orchestra, especially by the so-called deputy system: a musician who had a more lucrative job on any given day could ask an outsider to take his place at a rehearsal or performance. "The players were always changing, all of them!" Toscanini recalled. Yet by the end of the series, Toscanini had won over the musicians. A few days before the special season's end, the members of the orchestra invited him into the Châtelet's foyer and presented him with a bas-relief, *Truth*, by the nineteenth-century sculptor Henri Chapu. Alexandre Petit, the orchestra's first trumpet, read a brief speech in which he said, among other things, "The memory of the great master who was the performances' soul will remain imperishable for us. [. . .] In Paris you have a French orchestra that feels affectionate friendship and profound and sincere admiration for you, and [. . .] its dearest desire is to see you return promptly to Paris, to rediscover with you the intense artistic joys that we have experienced with you for a month and that, unfortunately, have vanished so quickly. Maestro Toscanini, do not forget your Paris musicians." Toscanini embraced Petit amid the huzzahs of the players and the singers who had crowded into the foyer. He also made a contribution to the Mutual Aid Association of Theater Artists, which presented him with a medallion and a laurel wreath.*

The American, Italian, and French supporters who had guaranteed the Paris venture received their money back, and the Metropolitan even made a profit of about $15,000. More significantly, the

---

* The Chapu work, the medallion, and the laurel wreath, along with hundreds of other pieces of memorabilia from Toscanini's career, are housed in the museum in his birth house in Parma.

Metropolitan's performances demonstrated to a European public that an American musical organization could equal and in many ways surpass the best that the Old World had to offer. And the ensemble's triumph put the last nail in the coffin of Oscar Hammerstein's Manhattan Opera Company, which could no longer compete with Gatti's well-oiled machine. To avoid bankruptcy, Hammerstein agreed to produce no operas in New York for at least ten years; the Metropolitan paid him $1,200,000 to get him out of the way.

The Paris success gave Gatti the idea of bringing the Metropolitan's artists and productions to the Drury Lane Theatre, London, the following year: by mid-July, he was negotiating a deal with one Thomas Beecham, a thirty-one-year-old English conductor and entrepreneur. But the plan was abandoned. Astruc, however, wanted Toscanini to return to Paris. He persuaded the senator and future prime minister Georges Clemenceau to recommend Toscanini—unbeknownst to the maestro—for the Cross of Knight of the Legion of Honor. The following February, Stephen Pichon, France's foreign minister, approved the proposal, and he and Astruc informed Toscanini that the French president, Armand Fallières, had signed an order that made the honor official. They probably thought that Toscanini would be thrilled, but so far as is known he never even mentioned the matter. Early in 1913 Astruc tried to engage Toscanini—together with Felix Weingartner, Arthur Nikisch, and the Russian Emil Cooper—to conduct regularly at the impresario's new Théâtre des Champs-Elysées, and a telegram from Tito Ricordi in the fall of that year indicates that Toscanini was seriously considering conducting a season of Italian opera there from mid-May to the end of June 1914. But neither proposal panned out. More than two decades would go by before the maestro agreed to conduct another French orchestra.

8.

CARLA, TWO-AND-A-HALF-YEAR-OLD WANDA, AND A NURSEMAID had joined Toscanini in Paris at the start of the Metropolitan's visit, and twelve-year-old Walter and ten-year-old Wally had joined the rest of the family in time for the last performance; they all stayed at the Hôtel Céramic in the Avenue de Wagram, and they spent some time visiting the sights of the Ville Lumière before returning to Milan. Did Toscanini attend the world premiere of *The Firebird* ballet, presented by Diaghilev and Astruc at the Opéra on 25 June, five days after the Metropolitan's final performance? The question is fascinating, since the performance launched the twenty-eight-year-old Igor Stravinsky's international career, but the answer is unknown.

Late in July, the maestro went to the Montecatini spa for a rest cure; Puccini wrote to him there on the twenty-eighth to say that he was about to complete his new opera, *La Fanciulla del West*: "I'm at the last scene and then God willing I'll have finished." One can almost hear the composer sigh with relief in his use of the expression "God willing": for over a year he had been caught up in serious domestic problems. Elvira, his wife, had accused Doria Manfredi, a pretty young housemaid, of having an affair with the maestro; Elvira had viciously slandered the girl, who had then committed suicide.* The horrific episode led to a court case, an international scandal, and a temporary separation and subsequent ongoing dissension between Giacomo and Elvira, whose relationship had been difficult enough even before the incident. As a result, *Fanciulla*'s completion was greatly delayed. But at a special meeting during Puccini's visit to Paris for the Metropolitan's *Manon Lescaut* performances, the composer, Gatti-Casazza, and George Maxwell, the Ricordi company's New York agent, signed a contract to have the new opera's world premiere given at the Metropolitan in December, and they decided that since the subject of the opera was American, the sets and costumes would be designed and created in New York, most of them by James Fox, the Metropolitan's chief scene painter. Some members of the company's board complained that Ricordi was charging the Metropolitan the exceptionally high fee of $5,000 for the privilege of giving *Fanciulla*'s premiere, but in the end the ensemble's benefactors paid up. Puccini put the finishing touches on his new opera on 6 August 1910, and within a few days Toscanini was visiting him in Viareggio. They went over the score together to settle the basic tempi and to examine other aspects of the work.

---

* An autopsy demonstrated that Doria had died a virgin, although some reports indicate that an incipient affair had existed. According to more recent speculation, however, Puccini was having or had had an affair with Doria's older sister.

Toscanini disembarked in New York on 15 October 1910, from the French ship *Lorraine* out of Le Havre, and immediately set to work rehearsing the season's opening production, the American premiere of Gluck's 133-year-old *Armide*. "'It is glorious, it is wonderful,'" Toscanini told the critic and dramatist Charles Henry Meltzer, who bumped into him in the Metropolitan's corridors after the first orchestra read-through.* "'I think it greater, nobler, purer, more dramatic than "Orfeo." [. . .] I question whether any of the composers who came after Gluck did more than he did to advance [operatic] music. Mozart? No. I love his "Nozze di Figaro." But "Don Giovanni"? Well—' With an expressive gesture the maestro hinted that he was not very fond of Mozart's most famous opera."

Some of the company's biggest stars—Fremstad, Caruso, Amato, Homer, and Alma Gluck, among others—were enlisted for the *Armide* production. Mary Cushing, Fremstad's companion, recalled that Toscanini "made an unusual number of excited invasions of the dressing room" before the opening-night performance, "and the atmosphere was electric within and without. But he and Fremstad usually saw eye to eye and the interviews were consultations rather than arguments. He worshiped her in the role and many years later sent her, on her eightieth birthday, a memento inscribed '*To my unforgettable Armida,*' which she kept beside her to the last hour of her life."

Toscanini "did not exercise vigorously the conductor's pruning knife in [the] long stretch of ballet music, for the most part antiquated," Aldrich complained, but, he continued, in the maestro's hands "*Armide* had freshness, vitality, delicacy and power." Henderson commented that "if the public fails to receive the opera with enthusiasm it will at least recognize the stupendous conception of genius," and he described the production as "a new laurel in the crown worn jointly by Messrs. Gatti-Casazza and Toscanini."

The next day, Toscanini and his troops traveled up the Hudson valley for a performance of *Butterfly* at Albany; two evenings later, the maestro was back on his New York podium, conducting *Aida*. By the end of the month, *Gioconda* and *Orfeo* had returned to his reper-

---

* Meltzer spoke Italian. These and other quotations from his conversations with Toscanini were almost certainly written down post facto and tidied up for publication. But they ring true.

toire. Destinn once again sang *Gioconda*'s title role; Toscanini considered it perfectly suited to her voice, but she admitted to the *Times* that she found the opera "odious and detestable [. . .]. I hate the music and I hate the action, all knives and murders and passion and corpses and what not!"

Toscanini, however, was already deep into his biggest task of the season: preparing the *Fanciulla del West* premiere, with a cast that included Destinn as Minnie, the good-hearted saloonkeeper;* Caruso as Johnson-Ramerrez, the good-hearted bad guy; Amato as the concupiscent Sheriff who lusts after Minnie and wants to get Johnson out of his way; and, in supporting roles, Didur, Pini-Corsi, Segurola, and the fine French baritone Dinh Gilly, Destinn's lover, who had made his Metropolitan debut the previous season. Destinn informed the press that she had not begun to study the score until she was able to go over it with Toscanini: "It is so much better to learn things right in the first place than to have to be compelled to re-learn them," she said. But once she had begun, "Four hours every day I worked alone and six hours with Mr. Toscanini—hard, serious study." The six-hour sessions included the other singers as well as Destinn.

The first orchestra rehearsals took place late in October; on the twenty-eighth, Puccini, in Milan, wrote to Toscanini, "You can't imagine how much pleasure your telegram for the good read-through of the opera gave me. I had been waiting for it for three or four days, and the wait gave me a bit of anguish. Now I'm at peace and satisfied."

Even before Toscanini had left Italy, he had been suggesting changes or alternate passages in the vocal line, which Puccini had accepted. When the composer arrived in New York, in mid-November, he found that Toscanini had already begun to sketch some possible alterations to the orchestra score, on the basis of the rehearsals that had so far taken place: the printer's proofs from which Toscanini had been working (the score had not yet been published) contain a "surprising number" of changes in the conductor's hand, according to the musicologist Gabriele Dotto, who made a thorough study of

---

* Farrar said that she ought to have been given the title role, that an American soprano should have played the part of an American girl. Toscanini, she claimed, had asked her to do the part, but she would not have had enough time to learn it. "Toscanini quite understood this [and] made no further insistence," but Puccini did not forgive her—or so she believed.

the material. There are alterations in phrasing, dynamics, tempi, and instrumentation, and they range "from light retouching of artic- ulations to general, albeit sporadic, rethinking of the orchestral sonority. Although most of the interventions have to do with techni- cal subtleties [. . .], there are others that entail changes in the orches- tration that may even seem heavy-handed within the score's overall sound 'texture.'" Dotto suggests that the more substantial changes may have had to do with the Metropolitan's great size and dull acous- tics. Puccini trusted Toscanini's judgment so completely that nearly all of the conductor's annotations were incorporated into the score as it was published seven months after the premiere, and here and there Puccini's own handwritten changes in the instrumentation seem to follow Toscanini's lead in the direction of denser textures.

Puccini also incorporated into the opera's final version some changes to the vocal parts that Toscanini had made on proofs of the piano-vocal score of the opera. Later, when the complete score was being prepared for publication, Puccini counted on Toscanini to cor- rect errors that he himself might not have detected. In referring to a cut that he was considering, he told Toscanini that he would decide on it only "after I've heard what you advise."

Dotto goes so far as to call *Fanciulla* "an opera, four hands," although Toscanini was responsible for none of the work's basic melodic, harmonic, rhythmic, or structural content; nevertheless, he did intervene much more substantially than was customary, and Puccini was grateful for his assistance.[*]

Puccini, who had already visited New York in 1907, for the North American premiere of *Madama Butterfly*, was greeted with great enthu- siasm when, at a performance of the same opera on 19 November 1910, he took a curtain call with Toscanini and the singers, and he was simi- larly received two nights later at the first of only two performances of

---

[*] For a fuller report on this subject, see Gabriele Dotto, "Opera, Four Hands: Collaborative Alterations in Puccini's *Fanciulla*," *Journal of the American Musicological Society* 42 (1989): 604–24; I have drawn upon a later, more complete Italian version of Dotto's essay, "Opera a quattro mani: Modifiche in collaborazione nella 'Fanciulla del West,'" in *Puccini*, ed. Virgilio Bernardoni (Bologna: Il Mulino, 1996), pp. 355–78. In 2016, La Scala staged an "original" version of *Fanciulla* that did not make use of the changes suggested by Toscanini or others. But since Puccini, who was no pushover, agreed to those changes, made some of them himself, and requested help with others, the attempt seemed ill advised.

La Bohème that Toscanini conducted during his entire Metropolitan tenure. The local critics raved over what Finck, in the *Evening Post*, described as "the first real 'Bohème' heard here." The orchestra produced "delicate nuances, details of loveliness unperceived before," he wrote. Toscanini's "hold on all his forces [. . .] was absolute, and yet he never drove the singers," he continued; "he upheld them with the most subtle feeling for their changes of mood." Several commentators pointed out that Toscanini took many passages at slower tempi than other conductors had done, and one critic noted that "of all the marvels, not the least was the influence Toscanini exerted over Geraldine Farrar, who gave an impersonation of Mimì [. . .] almost entirely free from disturbing affectations."*

Puccini's main purpose in coming to America, however, had been to participate in the rehearsals for *Fanciulla*, the first opera by a major European composer to receive its premiere west of the Atlantic. A well-known caricature drawing by Caruso depicts a moment in one of those long, exhausting sessions: in the Metropolitan's rehearsal area, crowded with singers, staff, and a few bystanders, the wasp-waisted Toscanini stands with outstretched arms while Puccini gestures, an assistant conductor sits at an upright piano, and David Belasco, author of the play *The Girl of the Golden West*, on which the opera is based, peers down from the stage.

A *Times* reporter was allowed into one such rehearsal and published an account of the proceedings five days before the eagerly anticipated opening:

> At the front of the stage at the left there is a piano, where a repetiteur [rehearsal pianist and vocal coach] plays [. . .]. In the centre at the front are two chairs in one of which Jules Speck, the stage director [stage manager, in today's terms], sits; in the other sits sometimes one person and sometimes another. Signor Toscanini goes from here to there making suggestions, and so does Signor Puccini.
>
> Somewhere in the darkened hall sits the man who is really

---

* The critics made similar, virtually unanimous comments later in the season, when Toscanini took charge of *Tosca*: the opera was darker, more dramatic, and better sung than previous *Tosca* performances in their experience, and Farrar was singing the title role more effectively and more intensely after having restudied it with Toscanini.

responsible for every movement, every situation in the play. He is the stage director to whom everybody comes [. . .]. This man, dressed in black, with flowing white hair, has given up every other duty for the time being. You may find David Belasco only at the Metropolitan Opera House these days.

[. . .] Mr. Puccini speaks in Italian and so does Mr. Toscanini. Mr. Belasco speaks in English, and yet there very seldom is any need for an interpreter. [. . .] Maestro Puccini and Maestro Toscanini lean forward to catch every word which falls from the lips of the "Wizard of the Theatre."

[. . .] Time and time again they go over the scene, while he makes suggestions. He shows Mr. Amato how to strike Johnson-Caruso across the face, and then he sets them to glare at each other. He shows Caruso-Johnson how to take in with one last despairing glance the whole range of mountains and forest as far as his eye can reach; one thing he cannot show to anybody, and that is how to throw a lasso so that it will knot on a tree limb. It is probable that this will not be done by an Italian on the opening night.

"The music of this opera is Italian, and that we understand," said Signor Toscanini [. . .], "but the play is American, and not only American but Mr. Belasco's. We want every detail to be correct because other theatres in the future must copy this production.* And Mr. Belasco is the man to initiate us into these details."

"I am more interested in this production," said Mr. Belasco, "and prouder to be connected with it, I think, than with almost anything else during my entire career. [. . .] Mr. Caruso is going to do the finest acting of his career, Mr. Amato is going to be a superb Sheriff, and I am absolutely pleased with Miss Destinn's conception of the girl. [. . .] I heard Mr. Toscanini rehearsing the orchestra the other day, and I feel that this music will make something very wonderful out of my play."

---

* Toscanini's statement exemplifies a practice generally accepted in those days: when the first production of a new opera was staged with care by one or more of the work's creators, that staging would serve as a model for future productions. Tito Ricordi, who had come to New York with Puccini, was responsible for several of *Fanciulla*'s subsequent productions and based his stagings very closely on the Belasco version.

Shortly before opening night, Puccini wrote to his wife, "The rehearsals are going very well. [. . .] Caruso is magnificent in his part, Destinn not bad but she needs more energy. Toscanini, the *zenith!* – *kind, good, adorable* [. . .]. But how tremendously difficult it is, this music and the staging!"

The premiere, on 10 December, became one of the great events in the Metropolitan's history. New York's upper classes were abundantly represented in the audience: the Astors, Vanderbilts, Belmonts, Harrimans, Juilliards, Baches, Flaglers, Choates, Goulds, Guggenheims, Morgans, Kahns, Mackays, and many more, filled the boxes. Celebrities from the music world also attended, among them the American conductor Walter Damrosch, the Polish pianist Josef Hofmann, and the German composer Engelbert Humperdinck, who was in town for the Metropolitan's forthcoming world premiere of his *Königskinder*, to be conducted by Hertz. Ticket prices had been doubled, and extraordinary measures to prevent scalping had been undertaken. The *Times* reported that "the house was filled to its utmost capacity and the audience was repeatedly wrought to a high pitch of enthusiasm and, as it seemed, could hardly give sufficient acclaim to those who were responsible for the production and those who participated in it." There were fourteen curtain calls at the end of the first act, nineteen after the second, and Puccini, behind the curtain, exclaimed, "'My heart is beating like the double basses in the card scene.'" By the end of the evening there had been fifty-two curtain calls.

Aldrich's comments on the score were lukewarm, but he described the performance as "one of Mr. Toscanini's masterpieces, so vitalizing, so full of detail, so broad in its outlines, so finished." Walfredo Toscanini remembered his grandfather's saying that he thought of *La Fanciulla del West* as a vast orchestral tone poem with voices. Much has been made of Debussy's influence on the work's harmony and orchestration; Toscanini's only known comment on the subject—"Just here and there, some chord or phrase reminds one vaguely of Debussy"—was made a few weeks before the premiere, during a conversation with Meltzer, to whom the maestro further observed, "The opera is flooded with melody. And the melody is of the kind with which Puccini has already won us. But there are new things—above all, exquisite new timbres, tones and colors—in the instrumentation. It has more vigor, more variety, more masculinity than the orchestration of the composer's earlier operas. It is more complex. In one word, it is more modern." Toscanini believed that *Fanciulla* was Puccini's most masterly opera to date, but he never came to love it as he loved *Manon Lescaut* and *La Bohème*, and after 1913 he never conducted it again. Nor has *Fanciulla* ever achieved the popularity that those two plus *Tosca* and *Butterfly* and, later, *Turandot* won for themselves.

At the time, however, Puccini was thrilled. En route back to Europe, he wrote to the Ricordi company's manager, Carlo Clausetti, "the success was great and it continues and, furthermore, it is growing. In my opinion, the whole opera comes off very well, strong, vigorous, and lovely. [. . .] Musical performance magnificent and staging surprising. Caruso great, Destinn very good, Amato excellent; Toscanini immense and good, a real angel."

Puccini also wrote a shipboard letter to Carla Toscanini, who had arrived in New York in time for *Fanciulla*'s first performance:

> Everything has now come to an end, but my great, strong good feelings for all of you are still there and will always be there! You [singular] were so good and kind to me, so sweetly attentive. Toscanini was so patient and so affectionately friendly! My thoughts are full of the two of you, and I envy you. I, too, would like to be like you, with your family together, with your children who love you so much, with the friends who surround you and believe in you. I, unfortunately, feel alone in the world, and I'm always sad as a result, and yet I've always tried to love and have never been understood, that is, I've always been misinterpreted. Now it's late, unfortunately I'm getting on, too far on. Keep your [plural] friendship for me, at least there will be good, intelligent people who tolerate me and who understand me.

The letter was typical of Puccini's morose reflections on his life, but it was also case-specific. He knew that Toscanini was anything but a monogamous husband and that the Arturo-Carla relationship was not all sweetness and light, yet he had also observed that the Toscaninis enjoyed a generally tolerable domestic situation, especially with respect to their children and in comparison with his own endless battle with Elvira. The month and a half that Puccini spent in close contact with Toscanini was one of the highest points in the two musicians' personal and professional relationship.

No sooner had the exertions for the *Fanciulla* premiere ended than Toscanini began to prepare revivals of six operas, all of which he conducted in January and February 1911, along with further performances of some of the works already in the season's repertoire. He led benefit performances for the Italian Benevolent Institute and Hospital and the Legal Aid Society, and he conducted the ensemble in one-night stands in Brooklyn and Philadelphia. But the maestro's biggest project during the second half of the season was the first North American production of Paul Dukas's *Ariane et Barbe-bleue*, on 29 March 1911.

Ariane, a forward-looking, brilliantly orchestrated work, had had its premiere in Paris four years earlier, and had since been performed in Vienna, conducted by Alexander Zemlinsky and admired by Arnold Schoenberg, Alban Berg, and Anton Webern, among others. Toscanini, even before his first New York season had begun, had persuaded Gatti-Casazza to reserve the American rights: he had read the score and had fallen in love with Dukas's music and with Maeterlinck's ambiguous, multilayered libretto. The composer, Toscanini now told Meltzer, "has much of Wagner in him. I am not prepared to say that he is always original or that he is as profound as Debussy. But his orchestration is rich, modern and ingenious. His music should be interpreted more delicately, I think, than it was in Paris," where Toscanini and Puccini had heard it the previous summer.

He worked even harder than usual on the preparations ("I haven't had news from you but I imagine you're rehearsing Ariane," Carla wrote to him from Milan in March), and there were heated discussions over the visual aspects of the production. The lighting for the original Paris version had been exceptionally subdued, sometimes almost nonexistent, in keeping with Maeterlinck's suggestions, but the Metropolitan's artistic team decided that at their theater, which was four times the size of the Opéra-Comique, too much darkness would not work. As Gatti put the matter, "it seems better to err on the side of having things seen than to have them not seen at all."

An invited audience attended the dress rehearsal, on the twenty-seventh. Farrar (Ariane), Léon Rothier (Bluebeard), and the other principals were much applauded, and when Toscanini took a bow from the pit before the final act, he received an ovation. The premiere, two nights later, took place before a full house. Aldrich extolled the production and the performance but added, presciently, that although *Ariane* would be admired by connoisseurs "it is hardly to be expected that the work will make a pronounced or a widely extended success." Dukas's opera received only four performances that season and three during the following one, has never again been performed at the Metropolitan, and is rarely revived elsewhere.

9.

OPERA, OR AT LEAST SOME OF THE METROPOLITAN'S STARS, HAD begun to interest sufficient numbers of New Yorkers to induce local reporters to hunt for backstage chitchat. One newspaper devoted an entire column to the story of how Toscanini had detected a mysterious, annoying overtone in the orchestra pit during a rehearsal of *Germania*. Another reported that Toscanini, with a salary of $30,000 per season, was "the highest priced conductor of grand opera in the world." Still another claimed to have received a statement from Toscanini on the question of performing operas in English. His answer amounted to this: it's a good idea, but I don't want to put it into practice.

Yet none of the newspapers paid much attention to Toscanini's encounters with a famous compatriot, the composer and pianist Ferruccio Busoni—his senior by one year—who was in the midst of an American tour during the early months of 1911. They knew each other by reputation but did not meet until 5 February, and the following day Busoni wrote to a friend and disciple, the pianist Egon Petri: "He is straightforward, sharp, and quick-witted.—Pleased me." On the twenty-first, the two musicians attended a Philharmonic concert at Carnegie Hall during which Mahler conducted Busoni's *Berceuse Elégiaque*. The *Times* reported that the piece was applauded "and Mr. Busoni, who sat in a box with Mr. Toscanini, rose to bow his thanks."* The following Sunday, Busoni dined with Toscanini at the Ansonia, and he described the encounter in a letter to his wife:

> It was the most pleasant evening I have spent since you left. The food was excellent and the conversation animated and interesting, right up to midnight.
>
> [The pianist Ernesto] Consolo was there. I played them the Sonatina, the Mephisto Waltz, the St. Francis legends.† [. . .] Toscanini is the most intelligent musician I have met up till now (with perhaps the exception of Strauss). Tremendously lively, quick, far-sighted, and artistic.
>
> He repeated whole pages out of my aesthetic. I mean, he spoke my thoughts and did not say one word which I could not corroborate with my whole heart. He seemed to have a particular sympathy for me, for (according to Consolo) it is seldom he is so communicative.
>
> He looks scarcely thirty years of age, but he is 44. [. . .] His memory is a phenomenon in the annals of physiology; but this does not impede his other faculties as is often the case with such abnormalities. He had just studied the very difficult score of Dukas's *Ariane et Barbe-bleue* and the next morning he was going to take the first rehearsal—from memory! But such achievements must wear him out; he is a bundle of nerves [. . .]. I hope with all my heart that life will bring me still more closely in touch with him.

Both men's professional commitments made frequent contact between them impossible, and however compatible their aesthetic points of view may have been, their attitudes to the art of musical interpretation differed sharply. Busoni's interpretation of Beethoven's "Waldstein" Sonata during one of his New York recitals so disturbed

---

* The event proved to be Mahler's last appearance as a conductor: he returned to Europe soon thereafter and died in May, at the age of fifty-one.

† Busoni's first Sonatina had been composed the previous year; the other two pieces were by Liszt.

Toscanini that he walked out before the end of the program. Some people were scandalized, but Busoni wrote to Toscanini to say that he would be happy to see him at his recital the following Sunday and that he promised to play "well" this time. Toscanini attended, remained to the end, and applauded enthusiastically.

What had disturbed Toscanini at the first recital was Busoni's tendency to take a composer's score as a point of departure for his own creative, and often witty, musical commentary, whereas Toscanini believed in the interpreter's sacrosanct obligation to try to represent a composer's expressive wishes as faithfully as possible. During the 1920s, the composer Alfredo Casella, in comparing Busoni's and Toscanini's interpretive philosophies, said that the pianist's performances were "so exaggeratedly personal [. . .] that every piece of music played by him seemed to become his own creation. [. . .] With Toscanini, precisely the contrary takes place. The composer's individuality expands before us in all its integrity."

Many years later, Toscanini stated categorically that he "did not agree with Busoni. As a performer he was a clown. Sometimes he played well, sometimes he played badly, on purpose. An artist doesn't do this. I may have conducted badly, but without knowing it and without wishing to do so. But I never tried to make people laugh. I never joked with my art."

The two musicians met again in May 1913, when Toscanini attended a recital by Busoni in Milan, and they saw each other at least one more time, in Rome in March 1916, when Busoni conducted a concert at the Augusteo concert hall; the program ended with the "Eroica" Symphony, and Toscanini was astonished that Busoni, who, he said, "played all Bach, all Chopin, all Beethoven by heart," conducted with his head in the score, barely looking at the orchestra. "It was ugly," he recalled, and reviews of the performance concur that it was a near disaster. Busoni had told Toscanini beforehand that he would be happy to have him in the audience, but afterward he admitted that his colleague's presence had made him terribly nervous. Toscanini, in replying, used typically Busonian wit on Busoni: "Di 'eroico' c'era solo il pubblico" (Only the audience was "heroic"). Busoni took the criticism good-humoredly, and the following year he asked Toscanini to allow him to dedicate his opera *Turandot* to him. Toscanini accepted the dedication but never conducted *Turandot* or any of the composer's other works except the *Berceuse Elégiaque* and *Rondò Arlecchinesco*. After Busoni's death, in 1924, Toscanini answered an appeal from Consolo and helped the late musician's widow pay her husband's substantial medical bills, and in 1937, in signing a broader appeal for financial aid for Gerda Busoni, Toscanini described her husband as "one of the greatest musicians of our time."

Nineteen eleven, the year in which Toscanini made Busoni's acquaintance, was a dramatic year in the annals of twentieth-century music: Igor Stravinsky completed *Petrushka* and did much of his work on *The Rite of Spring* that year; Béla Bartók composed *Bluebeard's Castle*, Arnold Schoenberg wrote his Six Little Piano Pieces, and Anton Webern began working on his Five Pieces for Orchestra, op. 10. These composers were shaking the very foundations of European art music, much as contemporary painters, sculptors, and poets were revolutionizing their respective arts. Had Toscanini been a decade or two younger, he might have ventured into the new repertoire, just as he had embraced the radical music of Debussy and Strauss a few years earlier. But he was now in his midforties and had been a professional conductor since Stravinsky, Bartók, Schoenberg, and Webern were children. His tastes were hardening in middle age. With the exception of Stravinsky, whose works in those years he considered brilliant, Toscanini rejected the young radicals. He continued to program new music for many years, but, with few exceptions, the new music that he performed was conservative.

10.

THE DIFFICULT *ARIANE ET BARBE-BLEUE* PREMIERE WAS TOSCANINI'S final new production of the 1910–11 season, which ended with tour performances in Montreal, Cleveland, Cincinnati, and Atlanta. Since opening night in New York through his final appearance in Atlanta, he had conducted seventy-eight performances of fourteen operas, an average of nearly one performance every other day. He departed from New York on 2 May aboard the *Kronprinzessin Cecilie* but was able to spend only a few days at home in Milan: he had to rush to Rome, where, at the Teatro Costanzi, he immediately began to rehearse *Falstaff* and the Italian premiere of *La Fanciulla del West*.

These productions were among the events programmed to mark the Kingdom of Italy's fiftieth anniversary.*

Putting together the *Fanciulla* cast was not easy. Of the New York production's three principals, only Amato was able to do the job. After much discussion, Eugenia Burzio was engaged to sing the title role; she and Toscanini had evidently made peace since their quarrel at La Scala three years earlier. "Beautiful voice" but "a wild woman"—thus Toscanini, decades later, described her. "She was so crazy that on the first night [of *Fanciulla*] she didn't sing one correct note!" he said. Burzio told him that she hadn't been feeling well, "so we engaged [Carmen] Melis, to have someone ready," since Melis had already sung the part in Boston. But Burzio "didn't let her sing—now she was feeling fine! Ah, what eyes she had—what a rascal, what a piece of work she was!" And yet, Toscanini added, "when she was on top form, oh yes, she had a voice that dominated [even] *La Gioconda*."

Problems also arose with *Fanciulla*'s leading tenor, Amedeo Bassi, who had taken over some performances of the part from the ailing Caruso during the Metropolitan season. Bassi sang only the first five of the nine Rome performances, then rushed to London to perform at the coronation of George V. His cover, Giovanni Martinelli, was a virtually unknown twenty-five-year-old singer from the Veneto whom Toscanini, Puccini, and Giulio Ricordi had auditioned during the conductor's brief stay in Milan. As the tenor told the story many years later, Toscanini, at a preliminary run-through with Martinelli,

> sat down at the piano and had me sing. Out of nervousness, [. . .] I didn't follow the Maestro at all. So all of a sudden he rudely interrupted me and shut the score. [. . .] Turning to his assistant, he said in Parmesan dialect, "This one is too green for me!"
>
> You can imagine how I felt at that moment; but I think that a good star was protecting me and supplied me with an answer: "Maestro, look, I'm so happy to have spent half an hour with you and to have seen Rome that I'll go away happy." Toscanini

---

* A production of *Aida* had also been planned but was canceled. According to some reports, the whole Metropolitan ensemble had been invited more than a year earlier to participate in these celebrations, but no such visit materialized.

smiled at me and said, turning to his assistant: "You take him; continue to study and rehearse, and we'll get it ready."

Toscanini must have been more than satisfied with the results: at the remaining four *Fanciulla* performances, he made an exception to his no-encore policy and allowed the boisterous, shaggy-haired Martinelli to repeat the short but important third-act aria "Ch'ella mi creda," and then engaged him for three Roman performances of the Verdi *Requiem*, which Toscanini conducted in July. In the fall of 1913 Martinelli joined the Metropolitan's roster, on Toscanini's recommendation, and he remained a company mainstay for over thirty years. "He could not sing *piano*," Toscanini said of him many years later, "*ma* [but] the voice was beautiful."

Toscanini's performances in Rome were the occasion of a sort of mea culpa on the part of Giulio Ricordi, who was gravely ill and must have regretted his attempts to ruin Toscanini's artistic reputation during the latter's early years at La Scala. Following the first *Falstaff* performance at the Costanzi, the publisher telegraphed Toscanini, "I join my enthusiastic applause to that of the Roman public, which recognized in you not only the great interpreter of every school but also the brilliant artist capable of bringing so much honor upon himself by bringing honor to Italian Art." And after the *Fanciulla* premiere, which was enthusiastically received by the Roman audience—less so by the critics—Ricordi wired, "I know how much is owed to you, who are now unmatchable as an artist [and as a] prodigious and admirable worker[.] I wish to express to you my liveliest admiration [and] my liveliest gratitude." The following April, only two months before his death, Ricordi sent Toscanini the new edition of the full score of *Falstaff*, with his handwritten salutations.

ACCORDING TO REPORTS in the *New York Times*, it was "probable" that Toscanini would conduct at the annual Wagner Festival in Munich's Prinzregententheater during that summer of 1911, and he had been approached to take over the direction of the Munich Court Opera following the recent death of Felix Mottl, the ensemble's previous music director. Neither engagement materialized.

Arturo, Carla, and the children spent much of the second half of July and the first half of August at Champoluc, in the Val d'Aosta, where they were visited by the civil engineer Cesare Albertini and his family—close friends of the Toscaninis—and by the poet Francesco Pastonchi. Walter, who was thirteen at the time, later remembered "declamations of whole cantos of Dante, poems of Carducci, and heated arguments about [the contemporary Italian poet Giovanni] Pascoli, whom my father loved but who was in disfavor, I think, with Pastonchi." Toscanini plus Albertini, Pastonchi, and the composer Leone Sinigaglia made long, difficult hiking excursions to the Teodulo pass, the Colli delle Cime Bianche, and Lago Bleu in the Valtournenche.

At Champoluc, Toscanini, whose myopia was worsening, met Dr. Gioachino Carlo Precerutti, a well-known ophthalmologist, and in mid-August he followed the doctor to a vacation spot at Moncenisio in the Piedmontese Alps, taking Walter with him. Precerutti "tortures me daily with rather painful eye injections," Toscanini wrote to Giuseppe Depanis, and he informed Carla, "My eyes bother me a little, of course, but I try not to tire them with any sort of reading. No music, no books in English, no newspapers. I spend as much time out of doors as I can, with my big glasses perched on my nose." But he found the resort too noisy: "Automobiles, bicycles, and motorcycles pound one's ears all day long. Not to speak of the children's racket. Walter is having the time of his life. He already made a hole in his new pants yesterday, by sliding down a hill behind the hotel." Walter had been having difficulties at school and had temporarily been put in a boarding establishment, which he hated and from which he wrote despairing letters. He was soon allowed to return home, and he would eventually become an even greater bookworm than his father.

To Toscanini's distress, Precerutti discovered that Walter, too, needed eyeglasses, but whereas Walter accepted his fate, Toscanini père stubbornly refused to wear glasses except in cases of dire necessity—partly out of vanity but mainly because he wanted to continue to make unimpeded eye contact with orchestra musicians and singers. He did not need glasses during rehearsals and performances because he was conducting from memory, and Carla would tell people that she always knew when her myopic husband was studying a new score: there would be printer's ink on the tip of his nose.

An emotionally trying event during the summer of 1911 was the transfer of the remains of Claudio and Giorgio Toscanini, both of whom had died five years earlier, to the Symbolist/Art Nouveau tomb that Leonardo Bistolfi and the architect Mario Labò had designed and recently completed in Milan's Cimitero Monumentale. This modern structure—much more modest than most of the hyper-ornate family vaults that stand near it—has no cross or other religious symbols on its exterior, but it was built with enough interior space to contain many more family members' bodies or ashes in the future.

At Depanis's invitation, Toscanini had agreed to conduct five concerts in Turin in September as part of the International Exposition of Industries and Labor, another celebration of united Italy's fiftieth anniversary. Other participating conductors included Debussy, Vincent d'Indy, Edward Elgar, Robert Kajanus, Willem Mengelberg, Tullio Serafin, and Fritz Steinbach. Steinbach, as previously mentioned, had reputedly been Brahms's favorite conductor; and Toscanini, who admired Steinbach, not only prerehearsed the orchestra for him in Brahms's Second Symphony but also performed it on one of his own programs. Steinbach, after having read straight through the piece with the orchestra, exclaimed, "I have nothing more to do!"

While Toscanini was in Turin, Gatti-Casazza visited Carla in Milan and learned, to his horror, that her husband was considering leaving the Metropolitan. The maestro had been invited to conduct a series of concerts in Germany and Russia the following winter, and he was constantly being invited to return to Buenos Aires, where he would be paid even more than in New York. Gatti wrote to Toscanini to ask that he not decide immediately, because he himself would also be "induced" to leave the Metropolitan if Toscanini left. Gatti had the ability and the strength to hold the company together, he said, "on condition that I have you as a co-worker." Although the Metropolitan "has gaps and drawbacks, it is still the only [and] most complete place in which your prodigious vitality and versatility and the totality of the gifts that set you apart can fittingly be used." In the end Toscanini decided to stay at the Metropolitan—for the time being.

Following his last Turin concert, he was able to spend two weeks at home in Milan, after which he traveled by train to Cherbourg, boarded the *Kaiser Wilhelm II*, and sailed for New York, where he arrived on 24 October 1911. His fourth Metropolitan season was originally to have included the world premiere of Giordano's *Madame Sans-Gêne* and the North American premiere of Mussorgsky's *Boris Godunov*, but both events were postponed—the former because the composer had not completed his opera; the latter owing to objections to Toscanini's choice of Didur for the title role. Thus his workload was somewhat lighter than he had anticipated: sixty-three performances, as opposed to seventy-eight during the previous season; one premiere, as opposed to three in 1910–11; and only one other opera that he had not already conducted in New York. According to Otto Kahn, Toscanini had also been "very favorably impressed" with *Mona*, a new opera by the American composer Horatio Parker (Charles Ives's teacher), and was expecting it "to meet with success" at its premiere at the Metropolitan in March, but he was leaving the job of conducting it to Hertz. The preceding spring, rumors had circulated to the effect that Toscanini would also conduct a series of symphonic concerts at the Metropolitan during the 1911–12 season, but no such events occurred.

The ensemble was at the height of its popularity. Much of the house, including nearly all ground-floor seats, had been sold out by subscription long before the season began, and on 9 November, in the hours before single tickets for the first week's performances went on sale, a long line formed along Broadway, with "three policemen and a special officer [. . .] on hand to prevent disorder," the *Times* reported. Toscanini opened the theater's season on 13 November with an *Aida* performance that marked Caruso's much-anticipated return after a voice-impairing illness. Destinn sang the title role; the thirty-year-old Austro-Hungarian mezzo-soprano Margarete Matzenauer made her New York debut as Amneris; and Amato appeared once again as Amonasro. The ballet sequences starred a twenty-three-year-old Milanese dancer, Lucia (later known simply as Cia) Fornaroli, who now led the house's corps de ballet, which she had joined the previous year; Toscanini and Gatti-Casazza had invited her to New York, and her story would later be entwined with that of the Toscanini family.

By the end of December, Toscanini had conducted seven more operas from his earlier Metropolitan repertoire, and in January 1912 he led the American premiere of *Le Donne Curiose* (The Inquisitive Women, based on a play by Goldoni), by the thirty-six-year-old Ermanno Wolf-Ferrari—an up-and-coming composer whose comic operas *I Quatro Rusteghi* (1906) and *Il Segreto di Susanna* (1909) had met with considerable success, more in Germany than in his native Italy. Toscanini's interest in Wolf-Ferrari's music was a result of its shunning of *verismo*'s excesses; the composer seemed to be following, instead, the path marked out by Verdi's *Falstaff,* by emphasizing well-crafted ensemble scenes that depended on the effective integration of sung recitation with orchestra. In New York, this was achieved thanks to a well-trained and well-coordinated cast that included Farrar and Scotti. The *Times* ranked the performance at the premiere—the first time the opera was performed anywhere in its original Italian version—among the conductor's "most consummate achievements."

Wolf-Ferrari, who arrived in New York in time to attend several performances of his work, was dumbfounded by what he heard. "Toscanini came to me last summer and asked me to play the music of 'Le Donne Curiose,' which I did gladly," the composer told the *Herald*. "He sat mutely by, listening to scene after scene and act after act, with nothing more than a nod. Not a single word of comment or encouragement could I drag from him, and my heart sank [. . .]. But now, after months, I come here to hear every single nuance, every bit of phrasing that I intended, expressed by this marvellous man." Wolf-Ferrari also thanked New York's musical press for not criticizing his avoidance of avant-garde techniques—quite different from the reactions that his music often provoked in Europe, he said.

While the performances of *Le Donne Curiose* were proceeding, the Metropolitan's board of directors unanimously approved the extension of Gatti and Toscanini's contracts for the following three seasons. Aldrich was overjoyed. "Each successive week of the seasons at the Opera House makes it plainer what a boon Mr. Toscanini is to the lovers of the lyric drama in this city," he wrote in the *Times*, "and he is the recipient of a continuous stream of admiration and gratitude on the part of the public. Some day a chapter ought to be written on what he has done for the singers of the company in the way of stimulation to the highest artistic impulses, of education to many things pertaining to style and technique in their art." Toscanini had been given a substantial raise, from $4,800 a month to $7,000—although two years later, when a small federal income tax was reintroduced in the United States, he had to begin to pay a 1 or 2 percent tax on his Metropolitan salary.

Yet despite his general satisfaction with the ensemble's artistic level and with the audiences' and the critics' appreciation of his work, Toscanini was showing signs of restlessness. Since he was paid by the month, he wanted to be able to determine his arrivals and departures—in other words, to make his New York seasons shorter if and when he so desired. And he was upset by what he perceived as Gatti's laziness and lack of understanding of the artists' difficulties. "Gatti would like to earn 150 thousand lire [a year] without having to raise himself for a moment from his horizontal position," Toscanini wrote to Carla. "We've worked like cart horses [on *Le Donne Curiose*]—one rehearsal after another, full steam ahead. Three or four staging rehearsals have lasted as long as six hours each. The singers and I, too, ate our lunches in the theater. And despite all this, dear Gatti and the beautiful Alda have had the nerve to complain." Accustomed as he had been, for over two decades, to the Italian practice of scheduling a new production's opening only when the performers deemed it ready, Toscanini disliked having to pile rehearsals on top of each other in order to meet prescheduled first nights.

He also charged that Alda, who had married Gatti, "gossips and intervenes in matters that are none of her business." The gossip must have involved him, since he did not reveal any specifics to Carla. Alda, a free spirit, had probably taken part in some bedroom activity with Toscanini and may have been jealous of his ongoing affair with Farrar, with whom she did not get along; she could easily have spread gossip about her stage rival's offstage doings. Toscanini, on his part, gossiped about Gatti's rumored sexual impotence, which he must have heard about from Alda. (Sex comedies in opera have never been limited to the public performance arena.) But he felt lifelong affection for Alda, and despite his opposition to divorce and remarriage, he refrained from ostracizing her when she eventually divorced Gatti and married the American advertising executive Ray Vir Den, ten years her junior.

At the center, Toscanini's maternal grandparents, Pietro and Carolina Montani; at the top right, Toscanini's parents, Claudio Toscanini and Paola Montani Toscanini.

Claudio Toscanini as a young man.

Arturo at age three.

(top) *Parma's Regia Scuola di Musica (Royal School of Music) in Toscanini's day.*

(middle) *Dormitory room at the Royal School of Music, where Arturo lived from 1878 to 1885.*

(left) *Cover of the young Toscanini's published song, "Son Gelosa!!" (I'm Jealous!!).*

Parma's Teatro Regio (on the right) in Toscanini's day.

Playbill from a performance at Parma's Teatro Regio in which Toscanini played cello in the orchestra.

Rio de Janeiro's Imperial Theatro Dom Pedro II, where Toscanini made his unanticipated conducting debut in June 1886.

Russian tenor Nikolai Figner, who helped to launch Toscanini's career in Italy.

The composer Alfredo Catalani, Toscanini's admired friend.

The soprano Cesira Ferrani, who sang Mimì in the world premiere of La Bohème *(1896) and Mélisande in the Italian premiere of* Pelléas et Mélisande *(1908), both under Toscanini's direction.*

The young maestro, circa 1890.

Carla De Martini, at about the time (1897) of her marriage to Toscanini.

The composer and librettist Arrigo Boito.

The Teatro alla Scala, Milan, in the 1890s.

*The tenor Francesco
Tamagno in the role of
Otello.*

*The soprano Rosina
Storchio as Leoncavallo's
Zazà (1900), at the time
of her encounter with
Toscanini.*

*February 1901: Toscanini in front of Milan's Cimitero Monumentale,
conducting "Va, pensiero" on the occasion of the transfer of Verdi's coffin
to the Rest Home for Musicians, founded by the composer.*

Playbill for a performance of Lohengrin, *with Toscanini conducting and Caruso in the title role, during Toscanini's first season (1901) at the Teatro de la Ópera in Buenos Aires.*

Toscanini during the first decade of the twentieth century.

1908: From left to right, eight-year-old Wally, thirty-one-year-old Carla, baby Wanda, and ten-year-old Walter Toscanini.

Toscanini with Giulio Gatti-Casazza in front of La Scala, circa 1908.

Toscanini in 1908, at the time of his arrival at the Metropolitan Opera House in New York.

The Metropolitan Opera House on Broadway, New York, circa 1908.

*Toscanini, Gatti-Casazza, and Geraldine Farrar
at the Metropolitan Opera House, circa 1910.*

*Caricature by Enrico Caruso of the first staging rehearsal (November 1910) for the
world premiere of Puccini's La Fanciulla del West. Identifiable, among others,
are David Belasco (No. 9, far left, on stage), Caruso himself (20, far right, on
stage), Puccini (11, below, center), Toscanini (15, arms outstretched),
Emmy Destinn (5, with hat), Pasquale Amato (17, at the far end of the piano),
and Gatti-Casazza (19, peeking from behind a door at the rear of the stage).*

*New York, 1910. In front, left to right: Puccini, Wanda Toscanini,
Toscanini; in back: Tonio Puccini (the composer's son), Carla Toscanini.*

(left) *Aboard ship with Czech tenor
Leo Slezak, May 1911.*

(below) *With Enrico Caruso.*

*Rehearsing a gigantic orchestra and chorus for a war benefit performance
at Milan's Arena, 26 July 1915.*

*With his military band on the Isonzo front,
August–October 1917.*

Segno di riconoscimento delle schede del
«Blocco Fascista»: un fascio di verghe
con in mezzo la scure.

I nostri candidati

1.° **MUSSOLINI BENITO** - Pubblicista -
combattente e ferito.

2.° **MARINETTI FILIPPO TOMASO** -
Pubblicista - volontario e ferito di
guerra, due proposte per medaglie
d'argento.

3.° **FERRARI ENZO** - Avvocato e Consigliere Provinciale - volontario di
guerra, decorato con una medaglia d'argento, una di bronzo, due
croci di guerra ed un encomio
solenne.

4.° **BASEGGIO CRISTOFORO** - Ingegnere - maggiore degli Arditi, volontario di guerra, fondatore della 1.ª
Compagnia degli Arditi che fu chia-
mata la «Compagnia della morte»,
due medaglie d'argento, una di
bronzo, due promozioni per merito
di guerra e tra altre proposte in
corso per medaglie d'argento.

5.° **BANFI ALFREDO** - Volontario di
guerra, una medaglia di bronzo,
croce di guerra, encomio solenne,
promosso a Capitano per merito di
guerra, proposto per due medaglie
d'argento; ferito cinque volte, rima-
se sempre in linea di combattimento.

6.° **TOSCANINI ARTURO** Maestro di
musica - decorato di medaglia di
argento.

7.° **PODRECCA GUIDO** - Pubblicista.

8.° **MACCHI GIACOMO** di Gallarate -
capitano aviatore, sottocomandante
della squadriglia di Gabriele d'Annunzio, tre medaglie d'argento, due
volte ferito, complessivamente decorato 12 volte.

9.° **ROMANINI ARTURO** - Ingegnere -
Consigliere Provinciale di S.t Angelo Lodigiano, capitano del genio alla
fronte, cadde prigioniero nell'offen-

*List of candidates for the Fasci Italiani di Combattimento,
Milan, 1919; Toscanini's name is sixth.*

The "Orchestra Toscanini" (future orchestra of La Scala)
at the Milan Conservatory in the fall of 1920.

With Gabriele D'Annunzio, Fiume,
November 1920.

Cover of souvenir booklet of the
Toscanini/La Scala Orchestra
American tour, 1920–1921.

Baritone Mariano Stabile as Falstaff.

Soprano Gilda Dalla Rizza
as Manon Lescaut.

Soprano Toti Dal Monte as Lucia di Lammermoor.

Mussolini's visit to La Scala, March 1923. Dal Monte is on Toscanini's right.

Most of all, however, Toscanini was unhappy being away from his children for such long periods. He had spent the entire day before Christmas alone, had had his Christmas Eve dinner alone, and "was already in bed at eleven, contrary to my custom," he told Carla. Living like this is terrible, believe me, and next year we absolutely must work things out differently. The greatest difficulty is for Walter. But if we could find a young teacher who would prepare him for his final exams and who would be thrilled to come to New York the problem would be resolved. Wally is much easier to deal with. We could find a magnificent apartment here and furnish it as the Amatos did, spending the same amount that I'm spending for myself, and having the home paid for year-round." Because, after all, "this theater remains the easiest to run, [. . .] inasmuch as the company is so large and the audience ideal." One may legitimately wonder, however, whether Toscanini really wanted Carla in New York with him all the time; if that had been his true desire, it probably would have been realized.

And despite the "ease" of running the Metropolitan, during one rehearsal Toscanini had a serious run-in with the house orchestra. On 29 January 1912, Gatti-Casazza received the following letter, signed by members of the Orchestra Committee:

> The common courtesy practiced in all public and private institutions by superiors to their subordinates has been grossly violated in the Metropolitan Opera House by the behavior of Mr. Toscanini, publicly using insulting language toward the Orchestra and otherwise reflecting on the efficiency of individual players as well as whole sections of the Orchestra, thereby creating a nervous tension unbearable in the course of time.
>
> The Orchestra as a body therefore demands an apology from Mr. Toscanini, and unless such is forthcoming at once will refuse to play under him any more.

"TOSCANINI CAUSES PLAYERS TO BALK," read a headline in the next day's *Press*, and the article, after referring to the letter, further explained,

> Giulio Gatti-Casazza is a [. . .] past master in throwing oil on troubled operatic waters, and forthwith began to draw on his

diplomatic resources. He asked what the grievances were. Evidently there was no dearth of complaints, for the question he put started a torrent of rhetoric, accompanied by much gesticulation. Why need Toscanini blow kisses to Hermann Basse, the first trumpet, when that unfortunate musician happens to make a few mistakes? Surely, such sarcasm was unbearable! Why need he act the suffering saint when things did not go exactly as he wanted them, wielding the baton in an irritatingly lifeless manner? What right had he to use vitriolic expletives, even in the excitement of his work? What license to apply horrible epithets which any good German American had to resent? Such indignities the musicians had borne long enough; their artistic pride had been deeply wounded; they did not propose to put up with the conductor's outbreaks any longer! [. . .]

At 1 o'clock Arturo Toscanini, with a storm brewing on his gloomy brow, passed out of the Thirty-ninth street door of the Metropolitan Opera House [. . .]. Gatti-Casazza's managerial diplomacy, however, had won a victory in the meantime. Quietly and with characteristic dignity he entered the room where the orchestra was assembled, bringing words of comfort and encouragement. That Toscanini was extremely sorry, he gave assurance [. . .].

The maestro himself provided a somewhat different version of the incident during a conversation with B. H. Haggin in the 1940s. At one rehearsal, "the Metropolitan orchestra 'play like pig' [Toscanini said] and he swore at it in Italian," Haggin related. "When, subsequently, the Italian was translated, the orchestra was offended and said it wouldn't play for him until he apologized. To the mediator who came to see him Toscanini explained that he couldn't apologize because 'orchestra play like pig.' But he proposed the solution that worked: 'I go to rehearsal and smile and say *Good* morning.'" Others who witnessed the incident reported that when the orchestra members told Gatti what Toscanini had said to them, the manager replied, "You should hear what he calls me!"

Generally, however, Toscanini got on well with the orchestra. "If you are in sympathy with the Metropolitan musicians [. . .] you can do almost anything with them," he told Meltzer. "Their technic is remarkable. They play even the most difficult scores with expression at first sight. I feel more at ease with them than with any orchestra I have directed, even in Milan." In 1932, a recently retired member of the orchestra commented to the press that the musicians had always considered "the tyrant Toscanini" a friend to whom they could speak. Toscanini's personal solicitude for his musicians would later become well-known.

During the remainder of the 1911–12 season, Toscanini conducted two more revivals and gave his first North American performances of Massenet's *Manon*, with Farrar, Caruso, Gilly, and Rothier. He had initially been scheduled to conduct *Manon* during his first Metropolitan season but had refused, owing either to insufficient rehearsal time or to a disagreement with Farrar—or, more likely, both. Thus Massenet's opera had been consigned to staff conductors for two seasons and then dropped altogether. Now, however, Gatti-Casazza begged Toscanini to revitalize *Manon* and save him from embarrassment with those subscribers who were disappointed over the postponement of the *Boris* premiere. Toscanini liked the opera; in particular, he found Massenet's handling of the last act better than the finale of Puccini's *Manon Lescaut*: the latter was "endless," he said, because Manon "never gets around to dying."* He agreed to conduct *Manon* on condition that the principal singers thoroughly restudy their parts with him: when he had heard them during his first two New York seasons, they had "shouted" shamelessly, he said. The entire ensemble worked very hard, and the aged Toscanini's recollection of "an enormous success" is corroborated by the reviews. Aldrich, for one, felt that Toscanini had demonstrated to New Yorkers for the first time "what there really is in the opera and what can be made of it" and said that the performance "revealed the master hand of Mr. Toscanini in every measure." The critic's objection to the cutting of the Cours-la-Reine scene did not prevent Toscanini from continuing to cut it in subsequent seasons.

---

* Puccini himself, in later years, told friends that he did not like the last act of his own *Manon*. On the other hand, Toscanini preferred the third act of Puccini's opera to the parallel fourth act of the Massenet work. "Compare them," he told a journalist in 1910, "and you will see how very much more dramatic Puccini's music is."

11.
———

THE PERIOD PRIOR TO WORLD WAR I HAS BEEN DESCRIBED AS THE golden age of ocean liners, and by 13 April 1912, when Toscanini boarded the *Olympic* in New York to return to Europe, he was about to complete his twelfth round-trip across the Atlantic. After two days at sea, the *Olympic*'s captain received a message via radio: the liner's sister ship, the *Titanic*, had hit an iceberg and was sinking off the coast of Newfoundland. The captain turned the *Olympic* toward the site of the disaster, three hundred miles away, to help with rescue efforts, but after having gone halfway he received word that the *Titanic* had gone down and that all the survivors had already been picked up. The *Olympic*, its passengers and crew in a somber mood—and many of them in mourning—turned back toward England.

And yet, Toscanini had to make another transatlantic voyage only a few days after he had returned home. On 24 April he boarded the *Principe Umberto* in Genoa and set out for Argentina. Since his previous engagement in Buenos Aires, six years earlier, the city had inaugurated a new opera house, the Teatro Colón, one of the world's largest and most impressive lyric theaters. Toscanini began rehearsing immediately upon his arrival in the city on 13 May, and his season opened only eight days later—with *Tristan*, no less. Between then and 28 August, he conducted a total of seventy-six performances—an average of more than five a week—of fifteen operas, including the Argentine premieres of Humperdinck's *Königskinder* (Toscanini's only production of this opera) and *Ariane et Barbe-bleue*. *Ariane* was sung in French; all of the other operas were sung in Italian. On nine occasions Toscanini conducted two operas in a day—a matinee and an evening performance—and on the last day of the season he led a gala performance that included the Prologue to *Mefistofele*, the second act of *Falstaff*, the third act of *Bohème*, and the second act of *Aida*.

The discipline required for bringing off such feats sometimes caused nerves to fray. At a piano rehearsal of Massenet's *Manon*, the tenor Giuseppe Anselmi began to berate the pianist: "That tempo goes faster!" he shouted. The pianist looked at Toscanini, who said, "No, go ahead at your tempo." The hotheaded Anselmi turned on Toscanini: "I knew that you didn't want me!"

"If I hadn't wanted you, you wouldn't be singing here now."

Anselmi became still angrier, at which point Toscanini said, "All right, you *won't* sing with me." He asked his young assistant, Bernardino Molinari, to take over the opera for him, but Anselmi soon apologized to Toscanini, who again took charge of *Manon*.

After Margarete Matzenauer botched the title female role at *Ariane*'s first performance, Toscanini persuaded Cecilia Gagliardi to learn it for subsequent performances. Matzenauer, however, was an accomplished musician who sight-read scores at the piano and learned roles quickly; Gagliardi, who had sung the Verdi *Requiem* with Toscanini in Rome the previous year, took a full month to learn her part. "She wasn't cut out for it," he later admitted; "she did it to please me." Gagliardi had a beautiful voice and was a beautiful woman, he said, but the role was too hard for her, and at the end of her first and only performance of the opera she passed out from the effort. A tremendous amount of work had gone into the production of Dukas's opera, but the local public received it coldly; it closed after the second performance. "My heart wept," Toscanini ruefully recalled more than forty years later.*

The Argentine season proved exceedingly burdensome for Toscanini; although, according to one source, the Colón paid him double, per month, what he received in New York—which means that for four months' work he earned $56,000—he never again conducted a complete opera in Buenos Aires or anywhere else in Latin America.†

Upon his return to Milan in mid-September, Toscanini consulted with Boito about the premiere of the composer's long-anticipated *Nerone*, which Boito once again claimed would soon be ready. He

---

* He also remembered the soprano Flora Perini, with whom he worked that season, as a similarly beautiful and lovely-voiced soprano, but thickheaded. He had a good laugh, in old age, when a colleague told him that he had heard Perini vocalize by singing do-re-mi-fa-sol-la-si-do, in that order, whether she was executing an ascending or a descending scale.

† Toscanini had gone to the Colón at the invitation of its impresario, Cesare Giaccio. In November 1913, Giaccio cabled Toscanini to invite him back to Buenos Aires the following year, but within two days of receiving the message Toscanini learned that Giaccio had died suddenly. This news may have influenced the superstitious maestro's decision not to return. According to a report by someone who knew him well, before or during 1914 Toscanini was offered $200,000 to conduct three four-month seasons in Buenos Aires during three successive years, but he likewise turned that offer down.

even gave Toscanini a letter to hand to Caruso in New York, inviting the tenor to sing the title role at La Scala in the fall of 1913, under Toscanini's baton. Tito Ricordi, however, had already told Toscanini of his doubts that *Nerone* would be completed in time, and those doubts were soon confirmed.

Toscanini joined and gave material support to the Milan-based Italian Society for Mutual Aid among Orchestral Musicians, and on 10 and 11 November he conducted, gratis, the Scala orchestra in a Beethoven-Wagner program at Milan's Teatro del Popolo—a new, 2,000-seat venue that belonged to the Humanitarian Society, with close ties to the Italian Socialist Party and its newspaper, *Avanti!* Boito and Polo were among the enterprise's enthusiastic supporters. Admission to the first performance cost less than half a lira and was strictly limited to workers and their families; the second performance was open to everyone at prices several times higher, with the receipts going to the theater's workers and staff.

Toscanini must have left for Rome immediately after the second concert, to rehearse the Santa Cecilia Orchestra in a program presented twice, on 17 and 20 November, at the Augusteo. He returned to Milan for a week or ten days, dealt as best he could with a cold or some other minor illness, and then departed for New York. Before he left, he had received a note from Boito, who had turned seventy earlier that year: "You are going once again to carry the divine light of Art to distant peoples. May heaven grant that you return soon among us with that light! It is the last remaining ray, everything else is darkness."

Toscanini arrived in New York aboard the *France* on 14 December 1912. This was the first time since his Metropolitan debut that he had not conducted an opening night in the main theater, and he had had to fight with Gatti-Casazza for the right to arrive later. "I don't want to do [Gatti] any harm," he had written to Carla the previous April. "I want only [. . .] to stick to the letter of my contract, thereby reminding him every once in a while that I'm worth something, after all, and that if he shines it's with light reflected from me."

Gatti, forced to find someone to take over many of the performances that Toscanini would normally have conducted, had settled on the Venetian-born Giorgio Polacco, who remained a sort of

second-in-command for the Italian repertoire for the rest of Toscanini's Metropolitan tenure. Toscanini had little respect for Polacco,
and when Polacco began telling people that Toscanini was pre-
venting him from conducting interesting operas, Toscanini told
him to his face that this was a lie and refused to have anything
further to do with him. The facts support Toscanini: during their
three shared Metropolitan seasons, Polacco conducted nineteen
operas, ranging from Gluck through the Romantic repertoire to
contemporary works, including many masterpieces.

Rumors had been circulating for some time to the effect that
Toscanini would quit the Metropolitan in favor of Buenos Aires,
thus New York's musical community heaved a collective sigh of
relief after his first performance—*Orfeo* on 19 December. "He was
warmly greeted with several handsome rounds of applause when he
came to the conductor's stand," Aldrich reported; "but the applause
did not come near to expressing the satisfaction that his return and
his activity in the performances at the Opera House will give to its
patrons." Toscanini was to have conducted *Tristan* the following evening, but the failure of Fremstad and Matzenauer to show up for a
scheduled rehearsal three days earlier had caused him to express his
dissatisfaction "rather violently," according to one report, and on the
day of the performance he declared that he was ill and "went home
and went to bed." *Götterdämmerung*, which had already been performed twice that season, was given instead, with Hertz conducting.
Toscanini's first *Tristan* of the season took place ten days later.

All eight of the operas that Toscanini conducted during the first
three months of his New York season were reprises of works already
in his Metropolitan repertoire. But during those same months he
was preparing the North American premiere of *Boris Godunov*—the
realization of the intention that he had expressed to Aloys Mooser
in 1905, in a refuge on the Mont Blanc massif. He was so enthusiastic
about the undertaking that he even spoke with, or issued a brief
statement to, the press: "'It is a very beautiful work,' he said, 'and
more genial than the operas by the other Russians, those of Tchaikovsky and Rimsky-Korsakov, for instance. Mussorgsky was an
innovator. He was several decades ahead of his time. He could not
be appreciated while he was alive. That remains for us and future

generations. Debussy owes much to him. You will find a great deal of Debussy in Mussorgsky, and he was writing when Debussy was a baby.'"*

Gatti-Casazza, parroting what Toscanini had told him and would later tell others, informed the press that Mussorgsky was a genius in the rough and that the opera would have remained unperformed outside Russia had Rimsky-Korsakov not revised and reorchestrated it. The last of these opinions has been disproved in recent decades, but it was widely accepted in Toscanini's day. When Haggin challenged Toscanini on the subject more than thirty years later, the maestro "conceded that Rimsky's correction of the consecutive fifths in the Simpleton's song had spoiled the passage, but insisted that the editing as a whole had made the work a success," Haggin said. "I cited Rimsky's own statement in *My Musical Life* that the Mussorgsky original had been a success when it had first been produced. 'Yes,' said Toscanini, 'but only in Russia.'" And yet, in 1913 Aldrich said that Toscanini was among those who claimed that Rimsky had sacrificed something of Mussorgsky's "original savage strength, strong lights and shadows, and pungent flavor."

The Metropolitan's scenery, which had originally been created by the Russian Symbolist Alexander Golovin for the Diaghilev ensemble's 1908 Paris premiere of *Boris*, contained "no building out," Gatti announced. "Everything is flat. Everything is simple as it can be, [. . .] quite unlike anything ever seen here." The decor for the Polish scene had been designed by the celebrated Alexandre Benois, and the sets for the Inn scene, which had been omitted in Paris, were created by the Metropolitan's own designers. The Paris production had been sung in Russian by Russians, but inasmuch as there were no Russian singers in the New York cast, the Metropolitan's *Boris* was sung in Italian, with the Pole Adamo Didur in the title role and an Italian, a Frenchman, a Spaniard, a German, and three Americans in the other principal solo parts. Toscanini had worked with the staff conductor Fernando Tanara to make an already extant Italian translation of the text more singable and more intelligible.

---

* "Genial" and "baby" are obvious mistranslations of the Italian words *geniale*, which means "brilliant"—full of genius—and *bambino*, which can mean "baby" but more commonly means "child." *Boris* cannot properly be described by the English word "genial," and Debussy was a child but not a baby when Mussorgsky composed *Boris*.

The first performance, on 19 March 1913, "had in every scene the impress of [Toscanini's] master hand and the certainty of his touch," Aldrich reported. "It was a superbly vigorous and at the same time finished performance of a score offering innumerable difficulties of an unaccustomed sort." The singers, orchestra, and, especially, chorus, directed by Giulio Setti, were all highly praised by all of the critics, but the overflow audience reacted with a mixture of enthusiasm and puzzlement to a work that was hard to pigeonhole. Many years later, Toscanini himself remembered the *Boris* premiere as "a beautiful performance," and he singled out the chorus for special praise.

Toscanini's last new production of the season was *Don Pasquale*; the New York critics almost unanimously expressed astonishment at the beauty, freshness, and comic spirit of what was generally considered an old trifle. But on 13 April 1913, only eight days after the opening of Donizetti's opera, the curiosity of the city's musicians and music lovers was piqued once again by Toscanini's first full-fledged concert in North America.

The six performances of the Verdi *Requiem* that Toscanini had conducted during his first two Metropolitan seasons were not counted as symphonic concerts, probably because the *Requiem* has no purely instrumental sections. His first official concert was entirely German: it began with *A Faust Overture* by Wagner, continued with Strauss's *Till Eulenspiegel*, and concluded with Beethoven's Ninth Symphony. Sixteen players from the New York Philharmonic and New York Symphony orchestras augmented half of the Metropolitan's house orchestra, and the chorus was augmented by thirty voices from the New York Oratorical Society as well as by some of the Metropolitan's staff singers. The circumstances under which the concert took place were inauspicious: Toscanini was suffering terrible pains in his right arm and had conducted a performance of *Butterfly* the previous evening using only his left; and the concertmaster, principal trumpet, and tuba player were all ill. Yet the quality of the concert—sold out long in advance—did not suffer, nor did its reception.

"It was a distinctly musical gathering, including conductors, composers, pianists and almost everyone prominently concerned with or interested in music," the *Herald* reported. "Many were eager to criticize the Italian for his conducting of Beethoven. [. . .] The answer of the critics and all was that they applauded each number, and after the final movement of Beethoven's Ninth Symphony, which ended the concert, they remained to cheer and cheer. The auditorium emptied so slowly that finally the lights were turned down, as the conductor would not appear again. [. . .] Mr. Toscanini's reading was not that of an Italian, but of a master of all schools, upholding his foreign reputation as a remarkable symphonic conductor." The concert was repeated five days later.

Many years later Toscanini told Haggin that the soloists in those performances—the German soprano Frieda Hempel in her Metropolitan debut season, Louise Homer, the Latvian tenor Karl Jörn, and the American bass Putnam Griswold*—were the "'best I ever have; and was good orchestra.'"

Toscanini's shorter than usual Metropolitan season (thirty-nine in-house opera performances, five on the road, and two concerts) ended on 26 April 1913 in Atlanta, where the ensemble took in $91,000 in a week. Three days later he sailed from New York aboard the *Kaiser Wilhelm II*, which also carried Farrar.

At some point during the season, he had had a serious falling-out with Gatti-Casazza for reasons no longer known, and rumors that he would leave the Metropolitan had once again been circulating. In June, Gatti sent Toscanini a conciliatory letter, saying, among other things, "The moment has come to put an end to this painful interval, which serves only to embitter us, to feed idiotic gossip, and to weaken the substance of the organization for which we are responsible. Knowing the nobility of your heart, I am convinced that I'm not making this appeal in vain." The rift was patched up, for a while.

12.

TOSCANINI DID NO CONDUCTING FOR FOUR MONTHS—HIS LONGEST break in five years. In July, he and his family vacationed for a while in the Alpine village of Schilpario (Bergamo province), then stopped at the town of Chiesa (Sondrio province) and proceeded from there

---

* Toscanini was among the many admirers of Griswold's singing and acting, but the basso died suddenly of appendicitis the following year, at the age of thirty-eight.

to the resort town of St. Moritz, in the Swiss Engadine. On a separate trip during the latter half of August, they visited the Republic of San Marino, presumably for another period of relaxation and a bit of tourism. But by early September, Toscanini was back at work.

The previous year, he had formulated an unusual plan for paying tribute to Verdi on the centenary of the composer's birth. Instead of undertaking a production or series of productions at a major Italian opera house, he would conduct—gratis—in the tiny theater that Verdi himself had had built in Busseto, his hometown. Toscanini remembered that Verdi had joked, twenty years earlier, that if he completed *Falstaff* he would present it at his villa at Sant'Agata rather than at La Scala. "I thought, not at Sant'Agata but at Busseto," Toscanini recalled, because "a prayer said in a little chapel or at St. Peter's in Rome has the same value."

The house seated a maximum of six hundred people, and the stage was proportionately small, but Toscanini proceeded with the project. He secured the services of Turin's impresario Alessandro Borioli to organize the event; chose the repertoire—*La Traviata* in addition to *Falstaff*; brought his engineer friend Cesare Albertini from Milan to design and supervise the construction of an orchestra pit; invited set painters from La Scala to create the scenery; commandeered furniture from his own home to be used as props; cajoled some of the finest singers of the day into participating for nominal fees;* and cherry-picked many of the players and singers for the reduced-size orchestra and chorus.

The brief season opened with *La Traviata* on 20 September 1913, with Bori in the title role. ("I taught *La Traviata* to Bori, who was young then," Toscanini recalled.)† Polo reported to a friend that it was

---

* The tiny municipality of Busseto laid out nearly 40 percent of the more than 50,000 lire that the brief season cost, but eventually recouped all of the season's profits, which amounted to nearly half of the investment. Toscanini recalled having conducted four performances of *Traviata* and six or seven of *Falstaff*; the Busseto theater's account book shows six of each, but another source indicates three of the former and only two of the latter.

† Bori was rumored to have had an affair with Toscanini and to have aborted a baby of which he was the father. There was certainly lifelong affection between the two of them, but Walfredo Toscanini, who was not reticent on the subject of his grandfather's dalliances, was surprised by the rumor, because, he said, "In our family Bori's reputation was rather virginal." And according to the late Robert Tuggle, the Metropolitan's longtime archivist, Bori was a lesbian.

"an unforgettable celebration; Toscanini was radiant with joy. Now they're preparing Falstaff, which will sparkle in all its prodigious beauty in this marvelous little frame." Public and press were beside themselves with enthusiasm over *Falstaff*, which featured Amato in the title role. Boito, the opera's librettist, wept with emotion. "A comic opera that's made me cry!" he exclaimed to Toscanini.

Toscanini was thrilled that in the little theater "every word, every expression" could be heard. But La Scala did not want to be left out. Not later than July, two months before the Busseto performances were to take place, Vittorio Mingardi, the Milanese theater's general manager, had gone to Toscanini's home to ask him to conduct the same operas at La Scala. Toscanini refused, because, he explained, when he had abandoned La Scala for the Metropolitan, Duke Uberto Visconti di Modrone had said that as long as he (Visconti) was chairman of the board of directors, Toscanini would not return to La Scala—a repetition of the vow he had made upon Toscanini's first departure, in 1903, and broken three years later. Mingardi then sent La Scala's music director, Tullio Serafin—Toscanini's former assistant—to persuade the maestro to relent. Toscanini gave Serafin a piece of his mind. "'With you, they need a[nother] conductor, but if I were there, I'd be enough,'" Toscanini told him. "I put on a haughty act. I really called him a jackass, and he left."

Enter Carla, who, unbeknownst to her husband, had allied herself with the Scala administrators; her reasons are unknown—perhaps she hoped that he would give up New York for Milan, although she certainly appreciated the extraordinary fees that he received from the American organization. One evening, Boito and Luigi Albertini, editor of the *Corriere della Sera*, came by to try yet again to persuade Toscanini to conduct *Falstaff* in Milan. "My wife came out of her room," Toscanini recalled, "and said, 'I'll bet that if Duke Visconti gives Smareglia's opera, Toscanini would conduct [*Falstaff*].'" Toscanini had been urging La Scala's administrators to present the world premiere of *Abisso*, Antonio Smareglia's latest opera, the following season, but many people at the theater had opposed the idea; Carla had simply taken advantage of the situation. "I said to Boito, 'At this point, my wife has backed me into a corner,'" Toscanini recalled.

Boito and Albertini went immediately to the duke, who wrote a humble, grateful letter to Toscanini; Serafin agreed to present *Abisso* at La Scala the following season; and Toscanini agreed to conduct not only three performances of *Falstaff*, with a somewhat different cast from the one he had had at Busseto, but also three performances of the Verdi *Requiem*, with an orchestra of 120 and a chorus of 360. He was greeted deliriously by public and critics alike, which cannot have been a pleasant experience for the good Serafin, however modest he was about his own gifts.

As part of the same Verdi minifestival, Serafin conducted *Aida* and *Otello*, and Mugnone conducted *Nabucco*. In agreeing to participate, Mugnone had declared to the management that his sole condition was to be paid ten cents more than Toscanini, whom he still detested. "At the end of the season, D'Ormeville"—Mugnone's agent—"went to him and put ten cents in his hand," Toscanini recalled.

" 'What's this?' " Mugnone asked. (Toscanini, in telling the story, imitated Mugnone's nasal voice.)

" 'We're giving you what you wanted: ten cents more than Toscanini. Toscanini didn't get anything.' Afterward they made it up, they gave him a fee," said Toscanini, laughing.

Late in October, Toscanini received a beautifully bound copy of Verdi's newly published correspondence, *I Copialettere*, with the inscription "To my very dear Arturo Toscanini, in remembrance of the immense intellectual joy he gave me with the *Falstaff* at Busseto and at La Scala—Arrigo Boito." Toscanini read the volume carefully and made some annotations in it. For instance, he wrote, "To be observed," next to the following statement in Verdi's letter of 11 April 1871, to Giulio Ricordi: "On the divining powers of Conductors . . . and *on creating at every performance*. . . . This is a principle that leads to the pompous and the false." And Toscanini underlined most of the following excerpts from the same letter:

> I want only one creator, and I'm satisfied if what is written is performed simply and exactly; the bad thing is that what is written is never performed. [. . .] You once referred with praise to an effect that [the conductor Angelo] Mariani obtained from the *Forza del Destino* overture, bringing in the *brass* in G with a fortissimo. Well then: I disapprove of this effect. Those brass [instruments], *mezza voce* according to my idea, had to express the Friar's religious Chant, and could express only that. Mari-

ani's *fortissimo* completely changes the character, and that fragment becomes a warlike fanfare, which has nothing to do with the subject of the drama, in which the warlike part is entirely episodic. And there we are on the road to the pompous and the false.

13.

"AH! HOW WE HAVE BEEN SPOILED IN NEW YORK!" COMMENTED James Huneker in a *New York Times* article about some Wagner performances he had heard in Berlin in the spring of 1913. The singers in the German capital had "screamed or bellowed, the band also playing at the top of its healthy lungs," he wrote. "Fancy Toscanini [. . .] whose every bar ambuscades emotional intensity, sitting through such a night; Toscanini, who spins the Wagner score into an iridescent web of fire, through which the vocal parts go and come as in a poet's vision. [. . .] But who believes all this? You tell a Berlin man that in New York Wagner has been, still is, better sung than in his native city, he will calmly reply—and there is no 'come back' at him, for he is both dogmatic and chauvinistic: 'With an Italian conductor?' You smile apoplectically and retire quite worsted."

Huneker's assessment reflected the esteem in which Toscanini was held by the vast majority of New York's musicians, critics, and music lovers as he entered upon his sixth Metropolitan season. Since Mahler's death, two years earlier, the New York Philharmonic had been working under the baton of the Czech conductor Josef Stránský, a mediocre maestro by most accounts (he eventually gave up music altogether and became an art dealer), and the New York Symphony was led by Walter Damrosch, an important pioneer in the city's musical life but, like Stránský, not a first-rate conductor. Toscanini had no podium rivals in the city.

He was to have reached New York on 11 November 1913, but he missed his boat and arrived four days later aboard the *Provence*; he went directly from the pier to a rehearsal of *La Gioconda*—a revival of the production that he had conducted during the previous four seasons, and with principal singers who had already sung their roles with him. Two nights later, *Gioconda* successfully opened the 1913–14 season, and on the twenty-second Toscanini conducted *Un Ballo in Maschera* for the first time at the Metropolitan. Just as the Milanese critics had found *La Forza del Destino* old-fashioned and barely presentable when Toscanini had revived it at La Scala in 1908, so the New York critics described *Ballo* as "out of its century," to quote Aldrich—which proves, once again, that a work that seems hopelessly passé half a century after its creation may later be loved and revered as a classic. Besides, no matter what the critics said, the new *Ballo* production, designed in Milan and with Caruso, Destinn, Hempel, Matzenauer, and Amato in the principal roles, was a popular success.

On 6 December, Toscanini led a special performance of *Tosca* for the benefit of the Italian Benevolent Institute and Hospital, and by the end of the month he had conducted revivals of five other operas. He did not like Strauss's latest stage work, *Der Rosenkavalier*, and did not conduct its American premiere, which took place under Hertz's baton on 9 December, but on 2 January 1914 he presented the US premiere of *L'Amore dei Tre Re* (The Love of Three Kings) by Italo Montemezzi, whose early *Cantico dei Cantici* (Song of Songs) he had conducted in Milan in 1900. Although the opera is well crafted—heavily influenced by both Wagner and Debussy yet Italianate in its melodic style—today one can only marvel at the fact that in pre–World War I New York it was much more successful than *Rosenkavalier*. It produced "a deep impression upon lovers of dramatic music, wholly unprepared for such a sensation," Aldrich reported, and he went on to describe the work as "one of the strongest and most original operatic productions that have come out of Italy since Verdi laid down his pen." Toscanini was astonished. The work "has been dazzlingly successful with the public and press," he wrote to Ida Polo less than a month after the premiere. "Like no other opera of any other modern composer. I'm still incredulous over it." Aldrich predicted that the opera was "certain to obtain an important place in the regular repertoire of the house," but it is now infrequently revived.

Toscanini was disappointed that Ida would not be accompanying Carla to New York that year, as she had done two years earlier: his sister-in-law's presence had made life in New York easier for Carla, thus also for Carla's husband. But this time Wally, who had just turned fourteen, was making the trip with her mother. "I can't tell you how happy I am and how strange it seems to me to be seeing

Wally here in New York!" Toscanini wrote in the same letter to Ida. And he joked, "If you see Walter and Wanda tell them not to study but hug them tenderly for me." Walter wrote to his father two months later to thank him for having persuaded Carla to buy him an expensive new bicycle for his sixteenth birthday: "I knew immediately that Papà must have pled in my favor, since Mamma isn't so generous by nature."

Carla and Wally remained in New York until late March, and Carla reported, in a letter to a family friend, that Wally had been having "a lot of fun" and was "enthusiastic about American life." The two of them sat in Gatti-Casazza's box at a Saturday afternoon performance of *Meistersinger*, on 31 January. "It was the first time little Miss Toscanini had seen her father conduct Wagner's great Comedy in Music—the first time, indeed, she had ever heard the opera at all, and she said, with becoming modesty, that she had enjoyed the experience 'quite well,'" the *Press* reported. "But to judge from her sparkling eyes, Signorina Wally, who much resembles her father, would have expressed her true feelings in superlatives." Carla was as usual "torn between the desire to come [back] to Italy to embrace the 2 dears whom I left so long ago already and sorrow at leaving my Tosca alone here!" she wrote to a friend. (Tosca was the nickname she had begun using for her husband.)

A FINGER INFECTION that had spread to his whole right arm forced Toscanini to wear a sling and to withdraw from single performances of three different operas in March 1914. These cancellations coincided with rumors to the effect that he would not return to the company the following season. In January, in the above-quoted letter to Ida Polo, Toscanini had written, "Kahn has offered me a *blank* contract for another three or five years but I won't make a decision about this for now." On 12 March, the *Times* reported that the renewal of Toscanini and Gatti-Casazza's contracts "was a mere formal matter," but not everyone was convinced. Aldrich expressed concern over the possibility of Toscanini's departure: "The thought of an opera season without his influence is not easy of acceptance," he wrote. "If Mr. Toscanini should leave the Metropolitan, it would be hard to come down to earth again."

Two days later, Max Smith confirmed, in the *Press*, that Toscanini would leave at the end of the 1914–15 season. Gatti had signed for a further three years, and Toscanini had felt obliged, at that point, to state that he would not sign such a contract. "In telling you I have decided not to continue my activities in the Metropolitan Opera House after next season and in giving you my reasons, I am answering simple questions simply and frankly," he said.

Viewed from the outside, Toscanini's situation at the Metropolitan seemed ideal: he had the best company of singers available anywhere in the world; his orchestra and chorus were outstanding and eager to please him; he was admired by the overwhelming majority of the public and press; he received a magnificent salary, and had he wished to increase it, the ensemble's board would have granted his request—thus Kahn's offer of a blank contract; and his duties in New York left him the time to spend nearly half of each year working elsewhere, or simply relaxing. Yet he was tired of his situation.

Smith, and probably even Toscanini, thought that the latter's decision might yet be reversed, although the journalist said that "the idea of conducting symphonic concerts is exerting a great attraction on Toscanini at present. The people of Berlin, Munich, Vienna and other musical centres of Europe are anxious to make his acquaintance. He is flooded with invitations from various musical organizations abroad." Sheer restlessness was the strongest reason for Toscanini's desire to leave New York, and by the end of the following season other factors would push him toward a final decision.

THE ILLNESSES OF TWO SINGERS caused the postponement of the American premiere of another Wolf-Ferrari opera, *L'Amore Medico* (Love, the Doctor), which took place under Toscanini's direction on 25 March 1914, his forty-seventh birthday. The critics referred to the work as an amusing, beautifully prepared trifle; following its four performances that season, it was never heard again at the Metropolitan.

The company's regular season closed on 25 April with a performance of *Tristan*; after the second act, "the applause rose to its climax when Mr. Toscanini made one of his rare appearances before the curtain," the *Times* reported. The next day the ensemble departed for Atlanta, where Toscanini ended his season by conducting single performances of three operas. In five and a half months, he had conducted sixty-one performances (eight of them on tour) of thirteen operas by ten composers and been paid $39,539.59. On 5 May, he boarded the *Kaiser Wilhelm II* in New York, together with Ignacy Paderewski, Josef Hofmann, Caruso, Farrar, the Scottish soprano Mary Garden, Scotti, Alda, and the Irish tenor John McCormack. According to the *Times*, Toscanini "is going to his home in Milan and says he will not do a thing but rest all summer."

Perhaps aboard ship Toscanini had a chance to talk with Paderewski. The celebrated Polish pianist and patriot had attended various Toscanini performances and later described him as the greatest of all conductors. "When all is said and done, there is nobody—nobody to be compared with Toscanini, for he is a transcendent genius—a genius of the first order," Padrewski wrote. "One cannot speak in any ordinary terms of Toscanini."

Toscanini and most of the other musicians on the ship disembarked at Cherbourg and made their way to Paris to attend the world premiere of Strauss's *Josephslegende* ballet, on 14 May. Toscanini's immediate reaction to the work is not known, but the fact that he never conducted it—or any of Strauss's other post-*Salome* compositions—speaks for itself.

14.

AMONG TOSCANINI'S PAPERS THERE IS A DRAFT, IN HIS HAND, OF AN undated English-language letter to an unnamed woman. Its contents, however, point directly to Geraldine Farrar as the intended recipient and to June 1914 as the date. Toscanini declares his love; he wishes for tranquillity but wonders how to achieve it; and he refers to the days that he had spent with the addressee in delicious intimacy. He realizes that even though they will be able to spend time together in the future, those days, too, will be "flying away sooner than ever and leaving us in this wretched solitude," he says. On a more mundane note, he mentions that he intends to "take a very pleasant villa at Viareggio for the summer months"—a statement that would not have filled Farrar with joy, because it meant that he would be with his family, from which she was hoping, even planning, to prize him away. She spent part of that summer at the spa at Salsomaggiore, near Parma, and Toscanini most likely visited her there; they could also have met at the Montecatini spa, in Tuscany, where he spent at least a few family-less days in late June and early July.

Farrar's extant letters to Toscanini from that period combine accounts of what she was doing at the time with high-flown (albeit at times ungrammatical) romantic sentiment and sexual innuendo. Before going to Salsomaggiore, she was performing at the Berlin Opera; she complained to Toscanini about the "long and tiring rehearsals and performances," yet "work is really my saving grace— did I pause to think, how long I must wait till you come, I should go mad!" She had decided, at least temporarily, to tell the Berliners that she would not return during the following two or three summers because of "my plans ahead!"—the implication being that she and Toscanini would be together. "I seem to see your dear incredulous smile . . . do you gently chide me? for such daydreams? Well, be it so! But nevertheless, I do my best to coax the Fates to continue a benevolent interest in our behalf!" She refers to her readings and to the readings they had done or would do together—a biography of Voltaire, Newton's *Elements of Philosophy*, and Pope's *Essay on Man*—but she then teases him about the distractions of Arethusa* and Amico, their code names for each other. Anyway, "remember, we are to read our favorites aloud in English. I shall love that, in quiet, close in your arms!" And she goes on, "Be of good cheer, and think of me, my beloved! I am waiting—not patiently, 'tis true, but *faithfully* which is better! You are my best and only—unique holder of heart! A thousand burning kisses *everywhere*, forever *Thine*."

Although Toscanini's letters to Farrar were probably destroyed, hers to him demonstrate that he wrote frequently to her. "I muse here over all thy cherished letters that lie before my delighted eyes!" she wrote to him on 8 July. He, however, spent much of the summer with his family at Viareggio, as planned, in a rented villa in Via Giotto, a two-minute walk from the Tyrrhenian shore. He preferred the mountains to the seashore—he hated the sight of bathing-suited

---

* In Greek mythology, Arethusa was a Nereid (sea nymph).

adults with bulging paunches and callused feet—but he believed that the beach and the sea air were good for his children. Even his mother came along: the young conductor Vittorio Gui, who saw the family there, later remembered the seventy-four-year-old Paola as having been "full of life, of energy, with her penetrating, commanding glance and her beautiful white hair." But her granddaughter Wally described her as "grumpy" and "always complaining."

Paola's son spent most of his waking hours studying, as usual. Schoenberg's *Gurrelieder* made up part of his summer fare that year, although he never conducted the piece. He was often in the company of Puccini, who lived nearby, and Wally recalled many years later that her father and Puccini "would discuss music and politics." Puccini, who came from a conservative family that had been in the employ of the church for generations, was a law-and-order man and strongly pro-German, "while Papà hated the Germans," Wally said. "I remember that on the eve of the First World War their arguments became very animated. One day Puccini complained that everything was going badly in Italy [. . .]. He ended his speech by saying, 'Let's hope that the Germans come to put things in order.' Papà went wild. He jumped to his feet and shut himself in the house. He said that he wouldn't go out again because if he were to see Puccini he would hit him. Some friends came to our house to try to make peace between the two, but Papà chased them out brusquely. [. . .] Friends came to the window and said, 'Puccini has repented, he asks you to forgive him. Come out, go visit him.' Papà shouted, 'If I meet him, I'll box his ears!' After a week, however, they were reconciled."

Archduke Franz Ferdinand of Austria was assassinated at Sarajevo on 28 June 1914; a month later, Austria invaded Serbia, and as a result of complicated international alliances this quickly led to war between the Austro-German powers, on one side, and Britain, France, and Russia, on the other. The Italian government dithered as to whether or not to join the hostilities, and on which side: Italy was formally allied with Germany and Austria, but Toscanini, like many other left-leaning Italians—with the exception of the officially pacifist Socialist Party—strongly favored intervention against the Germanic nations. They saw the war as, potentially, the final phase of the Risorgimento—a chance to wrest the "unredeemed" parts of the Italian peninsula, especially the Trentino and Friuli-Venezia Giulia regions, from the Austro-Hungarian Empire. For the time being, however, Italy remained neutral.

Toscanini had made arrangements to conduct in Russia early in the fall of 1914, but the outbreak of hostilities put an end to the plan. In Viareggio he was approached by municipal authorities from nearby Lucca, Catalani's hometown, about conducting *Loreley* there, but that proposal, too, came to naught. On 19 October, however, he participated in a special, mammoth performance at Rome's Teatro Costanzi for the benefit of Italian workers in northern Europe who had returned home from areas that had been or were in danger of being occupied by the various opposing armies. Mancinelli conducted the *William Tell* Overture and the third act of *Ernani* (with Battistini as Carlo); Toscanini conducted the second act of *Butterfly* (with Bori and De Luca) and all of *Pagliacci* (with the same plus Caruso).

The outbreak of war wreaked havoc on intercontinental shipping schedules. From Rome, Toscanini went to Naples to board the *Canopic*, one of the few ships that could get him to America on time; it also carried Gatti-Casazza and many of the singers, including Farrar, and it docked in Boston on 2 November. The company proceeded to New York by train the following day.

The United States remained hors de combat for the time being; thus despite the horrors of war in Europe, the new Metropolitan season opened on schedule with a remounting of the previous year's production of *Un Ballo in Maschera*. Upon entering the pit that evening, Toscanini "aroused a tumultuous demonstration," Smith reported in the *Press*. But the first week's main attraction came three nights later: a new production of *Carmen*, with Farrar singing the title role for the first time in her career, Caruso as Don José, Amato as Escamillo, and Alda as Micaëla. It was during the Atlantic crossing in October that Toscanini had "suggested the immediate preparation of *Carmen* for my first appearance of the season," Farrar recounted a few months later. "Here was indeed an occasion to refute many an unkind rumor that I had lost my voice and would never sing again. [. . .] Daily rehearsals were called, and I worked like a slave in the little stuffy dining-room of the ship."

Aldrich gave Toscanini the lion's share of the credit for "one of the most exquisite and musically perfect" performances of the opera he had ever heard. Toscanini commented, many years later, that Farrar's excellent French pronunciation was criticized in the New York press, whereas Mary Garden's terrible French was praised: Garden had been the original Mélisande in France, thus the critics had assumed that her pronunciation was good.*

Farrar recorded some excerpts from *Carmen* in the spring of 1915, with some surprising changes in the vocal line—changes that she presumably had not made during performances with Toscanini. (Singers tended to use the primitive recordings of the time as vehicles for vocal display rather than as more or less accurate evidence of their approaches to interpretation.) Later that year, she starred in a silent film based on the *Carmen* story, and her remarkable fight scene with the well-known screen actress Jeanie MacPherson demonstrates that not all singers of that generation were unable to do anything but stand and warble.

Within two weeks of the *Carmen* premiere, Toscanini had revived five of his prior productions and was busy preparing Weber's *Euryanthe*, which had not been heard at the Metropolitan in over a quarter century. As with his revivals of *Orfeo*, *Armide*, and even *Ballo*, so again now some observers doubted that the attempt to bring an old work back to life was worth the effort, but Toscanini's enthusiasm for the music had persuaded Gatti-Casazza to proceed with it. Many years later, the maestro declared that *Lohengrin* was *Euryanthe*'s offspring: he mentioned, in particular, the opening of the Prelude to Act III of *Lohengrin*, which is "the same" as the opening of the *Euryanthe* Overture, he said. Wagner was "like the pike that eats all the little fish. Weber was a little fish. [Wagner] ate him up, ingested him, and after that people talked about Wagner, not Weber." Musicians, however, could understand and demonstrate all the beauties that Weber's opera contains, Toscanini said.

In the end, the *Euryanthe* premiere (19 December) was a success. "All the singers found themselves buoyed up by Signor Toscanini's marvelous orchestra," Krehbiel wrote in the *Tribune*. The title role was the most substantial part that the young German soprano Frieda Hempel sang with Toscanini, and she "considered him to be one of

---

* Toscanini added that Farrar's German and Italian pronunciation were also very good, and—he said with a laugh—when she didn't know a word in Italian, she invented one.

the greatest conductors of all time," she wrote in her memoir; she also said that they were "good friends." Before the second act of an *Euryanthe* performance that was given for the benefit of the German Press Club (i.e., members of the German-language press in New York), the orchestra played "The Star-Spangled Banner" and "Heil Dir im Siegerkranz," a German national song, which Toscanini conducted while hoping that Italy would enter the European war against Germany and Austria.

Umberto Giordano's *Madame Sans-Gêne*—based on Victorien Sardou and Emile Moreau's play of that name, about a plain-speaking laundress who becomes a respected figure in Napoleon's court—received its world premiere under Toscanini's direction at the Metropolitan on 27 January 1915, with Farrar in the title role and Martinelli, Amato, and Segurola as costars. Aldrich praised the performance, but the work did not have the staying power of the composer's earlier *Andrea Chénier* or even *Fedora*; it is rarely performed today. Toscanini again chose Martinelli as the leading tenor in another new production: *Il Trovatore*, which opened late in February with Destinn, Margarethe Ober, and Amato in the other principal roles and with new sets based on authentic fifteenth-century Spanish architecture. Toscanini was "determined to present *Trovatore* as Verdi would have wanted it," Martinelli recalled:

> The result was a veritable revolution in thought on the opera. The first rehearsals [. . .] were called in October of 1914. We had a minimum of fifty rehearsals of two hours and more. [. . .] He staged the opera himself, since he wanted to be certain that at every point the stage action would not interfere with his direction and that his baton would be visible to the singers at all times. I remember that the first of these rehearsals was to set the chorus and the bass [Rothier] for the *"Abbietta zingara"* in Act I. This scene takes about five minutes to sing. Toscanini took more than two hours to arrange the singer and chorus, placing and moving them as he wanted.
>
> Certain cuts were restored, such as Leonora's *"Tu vedrai che amore in terra,"* [. . .] and other arias deleted. Toscanini allowed me the interpolated B-flat at the end of *"Deserto sulla terra"* and also in *"Ah! sì ben mio."* Toscanini pointed out that the two verses

of *"Ah! sì ben mio"* were identical, and for this reason the B-flat was allowed even by Verdi.*

Toscanini stressed the importance of the words in emphasizing the story of *Trovatore*. The recitative before the long lyric line for the tenor in the duet *"Mal reggendo"* [. . .] is a good case in point; and the final part of this duet, taken at a pace reminiscent of the galloping of a horse (but never must that horse slow down!), makes a tremendous effect because of the persistently quick and rhythmical tempos which continue to the very end.

Although the Metropolitan's *Trovatore* revival did not create as much of a stir as Toscanini's 1902 production of the opera had aroused at La Scala, observers nevertheless recognized that the conductor had rescued the work from the "banalities" that had gathered around it, as the *Times*'s critic put the matter. Pitts Sanborn wrote, in the *Evening Globe*, that the performance "must have made some hardened old opera-goers hammer their ears and pinch themselves black and blue to try to realize that the opera they were hearing was really 'Il Trovatore.'"

After having led two more revivals, Toscanini—encouraged, no doubt, by the success of *Boris Godunov* two years earlier—began to prepare the American premiere of Borodin's *Prince Igor*, but difficulties with the choral parts caused the production to be postponed; in the end, he would never conduct the work. In its place, he led a new production of Mascagni's *Iris*, for which he was listed as stage director as well as conductor. "For those who can distinguish between a dazzling performance and the merits of the work sung and played, 'Iris' remains a bore," said the *Evening Post*'s critic.

At an afternoon performance of *Carmen* on 18 March, Martinelli, replacing Caruso in the role of Don José and singing the part in French for the first time, became nervous and jumped several pages. Conductor and orchestra followed him, but Toscanini was furious—not so much with Martinelli as with the Metropolitan management,

---

* Toscanini also permitted Martinelli and other tenors to sing the two traditional but unwritten high Cs in the cabaletta, "Di quella pira."

which, he said, had not provided sufficient rehearsal time to allow the tenor to feel more secure.

Worse followed: on 13 April, at a *Carmen* matinee attended by Serafin, Maria Gay, the baritone Titta Ruffo, and other visiting opera celebrities, Martinelli was again insecure and Farrar was not at her best; Amato, who was ill, had been replaced at the last moment by a baritone who left much to be desired; the overworked orchestra was not alert; and at one point the stage band began to play ten bars early.

Some New York newspapers had reported two months earlier that Toscanini had decided not to abandon the Metropolitan after all and that, on the contrary, he would officially become the ensemble's music director and would take over much of the German repertoire from Alfred Hertz, who was leaving to become conductor of the San Francisco Symphony. And it was known that Toscanini had persuaded the Metropolitan's administration to schedule two concerts during the second half of April and then to send him with the orchestra and four vocal soloists on a tour, possibly all the way to the Pacific coast. Following the *Carmen* debacle, however, Toscanini informed Gatti-Casazza that he would conduct only the following evening's performance of *Iris*—because no replacement could be found in time—and that he was canceling all of his remaining obligations that season. The theater's administration gave out that the maestro was exhausted by overwork, and the *Times*, in announcing that Toscanini would sail for Genoa on 24 April aboard the Italian liner *Duca degli Abruzzi*, said only that he would "take a complete rest during the Summer at his home in Italy." Musical New York hoped that he would return.

15.

"LET ME ASK YOU, DEAR FRIEND, TO ACCEPT THIS EXPLICIT DECLA-ration of mine regarding my spontaneous withdrawal from the Metropolitan, and even to make it public if necessary," Toscanini wrote to Max Smith, probably during the summer or fall of 1915. "'I have given up my position at that theater because my artistic aspirations and ideals did not find the expression that I had dreamed of reaching when I entered it in 1908. Routine is that theater's ideal and foundation. This may suffice *for the artisan not for the artist*.* 'Renew yourself or die.' Voilà tout. This is the 'only' reason that distanced me from the Metropolitan. All the others that have circulated in the newspapers are false and unfounded."

A quarter century later, Toscanini was still sticking to this explanation as the sole reason for his departure. "My artistic views, which clashed with Gatti-Casazza's commercial ones, made me decide to leave the Metropolitan," he wrote to Edward Johnson, one of Gatti's successors, in 1939. But there were other reasons as well. For one thing, the star system that was operative at the house meant that conductors less brilliant than himself, and/or less severe than he in achieving their musical goals, often could not put together musically and dramatically unified performances. "Is no discipline," he told Haggin in the 1940s. "With me, yes; but with other conductors, no." The stars, including himself, were paid astronomical fees, but he recalled complaining to Kahn that the administration refused to spend small amounts of money on less eye-catching items: "When are performances of *Un Ballo in Maschera* and we must have five musicians to play on stage you say why we do not take five musicians from orchestra."

Further clarifications are to be found in a letter that Gatti-Casazza sent Kahn from Milan during the summer of 1915, shortly after Italy had entered the war against the German and Austro-Hungarian Empires. "Toscanini is tired and not in good health," Gatti wrote;

> his wife has enrolled in the Red Cross and his son is about to leave for the front, likewise enrolled in the Red Cross. He is a rabid nationalist and does not wish to abandon his country under present conditions in order to work in surroundings in which the German element is numerous. Furthermore, I am sure, as are his friends, that in this entire affair there is some great point of honor, for intimate reasons, that constitutes the principal reason for Toscanini's present behavior. He does not say this, however, and, not wanting to say it, he rehashes all the old accusations against the Metropolitan to justify his conduct.

---

* Italicized words in English in the original.

To these accusations I responded clearly: Excuse me, Maestro, what can you complain about, considering that everyone at the Metropolitan, from Mr. Kahn down to the lowest employee, is ready to do whatever you wish? Is it a question of [financial] conditions? We can always reach an understanding on that. Is it a question of a title? Then why did you refuse that of General Music Director? Is it a question of repertoire, artists, rehearsals, performances, etc.? But I wish for nothing better than to be in agreement with you, whom I consider not an employee but an associate whom I try to satisfy in everything possible. If I cannot always second your thoughts it is because you often do not state them. [. . .]

Toscanini was unable to respond seriously to these arguments, but he ended with the usual refrain that we do not value him as he deserves and that I think only about saving money for a Board of Millionaires.

I ask you, Mr. Kahn, how can one argue and make decisions under these conditions, while trying not to vex such an opponent? Not even Job in the Bible was put to such a test of patience. [. . .]

Gatti-Casazza then presented Kahn with a plan, including a sharing of administrative power between Gatti and Toscanini, for persuading the maestro to return to New York, and early in August negotiations made some headway; a letter from Kahn demonstrates that Toscanini was taking the proposal seriously. "I am happy to learn that you are considering Gatti-Casazza's proposal," Kahn said, "which has my full approval not only because it includes a public expression of our admiration and gratitude for all that the Metropolitan owes to your unique genius but also because it will give your great personality broader scope and effective power in the Metropolitan's artistic development. I express the sentiments of the Board, the New York public, and myself in expressing the sincere hope that we can continue to enjoy the inspiration of your splendid art. I assure you that I will gladly do everything possible to make your work here pleasant and satisfying."

On 15 September, the *Times* published an editorial under the simple heading "TOSCANINI."

The prolonged uncertainty about the return of Mr. TOSCA-
NINI to his post as conductor of the opera is wearing on the
nerves of the thousands of estimable persons who constitute
New York's musical public. The outlook for the opera season
would be dreary indeed without the magnetic inspirer of singers and instrumentalists whose "readings" of the great works in
the repertory have revealed new qualities. [. . .]

The progress of the world war may bring upon us many
afflictions, many even worse than the loss of TOSCANINI, but
until the Metropolitan Directorate makes formal announcement to that effect we shall refuse to believe that TOSCANINI
will not be here on Nov. 15. [. . .]

A *Times* article ten days later said that Toscanini "is very patriotic
and wishes to remain to help his country, and would have joined the
army, but was refused on account of his short-sightedness. Mr. Gatti-
Casazza may induce the maestro to change his mind." Finally, on 29
September, the Metropolitan issued a one-sentence statement: "Maestro Arturo Toscanini, owing to the war, has decided not to return
to America this year." At least sixteen New York newspapers carried
mournful articles on the subject.

Two decades later, Toscanini wrote that he had "felt *old, finished,*"
when he left the Metropolitan, and that he had "wanted to be done
with the theater, with music." But Gatti-Casazza had been correct in
his assumption that there was another, personal reason—in addition
to patriotism and to complaints, legitimate or otherwise, about the
Metropolitan—behind Toscanini's final decision. The reason was
Geraldine Farrar, who had made him an ultimatum: he must either
leave his family and marry her or lose her.

Just as he had done at the time of the Storchio affair a decade earlier, and as he would continue to do when he became involved with
other women, Toscanini opted to keep his marriage intact. Whether
or not this decision benefited any or all of the people concerned, he
made it over and over again. In leaving New York in April 1915, Toscanini left Farrar, who could not at first believe what had happened.
On 18 May she wrote him an overblown but despairing letter—
unsigned, of course—with many alluring sexual allusions:

Dearest,

I am anxiously waiting for your letter promised in the cable: this last message greatly relieved the tension of my mind, albeit my heart does not accustom itself to the loneliness it must now endure. [. . .]

If you knew the torments to which your absence condemns me! . I shall never again be the woman I was, before I met and loved you . . but I *cannot*, I *will not* believe you will not some day be sailing back to me . . That is the most hopeless and desperate of all depressing thoughts. Away with such a cloud! . . [. . .]

I have plunged into work, excitement, charity . . anything to kill the heavy hours, to numb the ache that tears at my heart; alas! do you think I can forget its inhabitant or deny his claim? I am not myself without you . . The mask of smiles but covers my soul, too sick for the absent one! Ah Darling, how insistent are the memories of our passion-fraught hours—the insatiable longings . . and their magic fulfillment . . . Dear yielding body of fragrant charm,—clamorous tongues of fire creeping over Arethusa, enveloping her All in divine Ecstasy! . . . When shall I behold again the superb pride of Amico? . . Oh hasten, dear one . . hasten, nor let me languish . . . alas! I must stem such tide, lest this fall into alien hands . . . But you must know after these years *all* I would say to you,—*give* you—! My hunger is unabated . . . nay, it grows, to feast upon you, to devour you, to slay you, perhaps. Yes, I can even rage at you in my wicked jealous moments . . that you should so infect my heart, poison my soul with the insidious honey of your love . . why must I love you to distraction, oh Cruel, inexorable yet ever uniquely Adored! .

Ah, wherever you may journey, whatever outward vision brushes your eyes, know however that you belong to *Me* that I claim you—You *can not*, you *must not* deny *US*!

Give me for a long, long while, the sweetness of those lips whose like I shall never find again. . Press their satin edges to mine. . *I love you, I hunger for you!* Send me word as often as you

can. . Oh God! What must I suffer till I see you again! Kisses. . .
You know well their power! . .

Thine

Ten days later, Farrar, pretending to be an unknown admirer—in
case Carla or others were intercepting her letters—wrote again to
Toscanini, from whom she had heard nothing; the language was the
same, but the sexual references were absent. Toscanini probably did
not respond to her letters: according to his way of thinking, she was
the one who had said either/or, thus the break had to be clean and
complete. Yet he, too, was deeply affected by the end of the affair.
More than twenty years later, he wrote to a friend, "Poor *Giovanni
Cena** said to me in 1915: 'My dear Toscanini, *one must dive deep into
one's sorrow until one touches the bottom*, if one is to *give a push with one's
feet and return* to the *surface.*' Golden words!! As long as there isn't
muck and mire at the bottom!" At the moment in question, Toscanini said, he had rebelled against his fate, "but then"—referring to
Carla—"someone else's suffering conquered my own and today I
continue to live out my tragedy."

Farrar spent part of the summer of 1915 in California, acting in
silent movies, and several months later she married Lou Tellegen, a
handsome Dutch-born actor. But her marriage on the rebound was
tempestuous; the couple soon separated, and Tellegen later committed suicide. Years later, Farrar and Toscanini would resume their
friendship; whether or not they became lovers again is not known.

In at least one respect, Toscanini's early departure for Italy was
undeniably fortunate for him and his future admirers: he had originally been booked to sail from New York on 1 May 1915 aboard the
Lusitania, which was bound on its fatal last voyage. Toscanini, who
had never learned to swim, would almost certainly have been one of
the nearly twelve hundred victims of the disaster; had that been the
case, his name would be known today to only a small number of
music historians and enthusiasts.

---

*   Giovanni Cena (1870–1917) was a poet, journalist, and ardent advocate for social reform
in turn-of-the-century Italy. Nothing beyond the quotation cited above is known of his
friendship with Toscanini.

16.

DURING HIS LAST METROPOLITAN SEASON, TOSCANINI CONDUCTED sixty-eight performances (one every 2.2 days, on the average) of fourteen operas by ten composers, and he was paid $39,900 plus, as usual, his travel expenses. Yet what counts much more than these and all the other impressive statistics of his first seven New York years is the high level to which Toscanini raised the quality of the Metropolitan's performances, according to nearly all contemporary observers.

"Toscanini is a superman," wrote Huneker in April 1915, before it was known that the maestro would not return. "In that frail frame is enough dynamic energy to assault Gehenna. [. . .] No hit or miss methods for him. Everything is thought out, every slur is recorded. [. . .] And despite this love of drill his musical imagination is never absent— it suffuses every bar." Giovanni Martinelli said, more succinctly, that Toscanini was "the heart and soul of the Metropolitan."

But world events were crowding in, and they would be followed by new developments in Toscanini's professional life. By May of 1915, the Metropolitan Opera Company belonged to his past.

World War I: at the front
near the Isonzo River in 1917.

VI.

———

INTERLUDE

1.

———

IN THE TWENTY-FIRST CENTURY, MUCH OF HUMANITY LIVES beyond the reach of reasonable optimism. We blunder our way toward catastrophe, through ecological insouciance, religious fundamentalism, and wars that give birth to more wars. Each new tack that politicians take leads all the more rapidly toward the precipice.

Arturo Toscanini was of a different time, a time before our species was capable of easily destroying itself. His first thirty-three years were contemporaneous with the last third of the nineteenth century—the heyday of progressivism and nationalism—and he imbibed his political beliefs from his father and other Risorgimento participants who had worked and fought for decades to rid the Italian peninsula of foreign domination and had striven to see their newborn country flourish. Claudio Toscanini often told his son how he had faced death at the battles of Condino and Bezzecca, in the unsuccessful attempt to bring the Trentino into the young Kingdom of Italy; he taught young Arturo that the Risorgimento would not be complete until the Trentino and Friuli-Venezia Giulia regions were wrested from Austrian control and officially annexed to Italy. By 1915, Claudio had been dead for nearly a decade, but the aged Austro-Hungarian emperor Franz Joseph was still clutching Trent and Trieste.

In the spring of 1915, Claudio's son was convinced that the war that had already engulfed much of Europe north of the Alps—the first continent-wide war in the Old World since the defeat of Napoleon a century earlier—provided an opportunity for Italy to "redeem" its "unredeemed" territories.* Yet, like every other rational being, he also knew that there was nothing worse than war. On 19 May, four days before the Italian government declared war, he wrote to a friend, "The events of these last days, which have turned all of Italy upside-down, the precipitate pressure toward the terrible yet ineluctable solution, have held me and continue to hold me in an unspeakable oscillation between trepidation and hope, so that all of my willpower is paralyzed by it."

Toscanini was a nationalist, but he was not an imperialist. He did not want Italy to conquer other nations, to establish colonies in Africa, or to dominate the Mediterranean, as several Italian governments had already tried to do and as another would attempt to do in the not so distant future. He believed, simply, that his country—one of the most productive centers of Western civilization—could pull itself together and assume a significant position in the modern world. And he felt certain that once Italy had annexed Trent, Trieste, and their surrounding territories, it would become a proud, vital, united whole. This commonly held notion helps to explain the widespread enthusiasm in Italy for the government's eventual decision to forswear the Triple Alliance with Germany and Austro-Hungary and enter what was expected to be a relatively short conflict on the side of Britain, France, and Russia.

The *New York Times*'s statement that Toscanini "would have joined the army, but was refused on account of his short-sightedness," is misleading: the Italian army did not accept recruits or volunteers over the age of forty, and in 1915 Toscanini was already forty-eight; his myopia merely made him unacceptable even for ancillary duties—otherwise, he might, for instance, have learned to drive an ambulance as Maurice Ravel was doing in France. Carla and seventeen-year-old Walter Toscanini enrolled in the Red Cross, and Walter later enlisted in the army: for him the war was a great adventure. Wally, who was fifteen in 1915, helped her mother with war-supply-related sewing and knitting at home and accompanied her to Milan's hospitals, to assist the wounded. Many years later, when she was asked what worthwhile instruction her mother had given her, Wally

---

* Italians who favored intervention in the war were called *irredentisti*—literally, "unredeemed-ists"; thus the English term "irredentism."

replied, "She sent me to hospitals instead of churches." Carla also organized other middle- and upper-class women into sewing and knitting brigades. And her husband, who had been feeling "old" and "finished" upon leaving New York only a few weeks earlier, now decided to do whatever lay within his power to help his country. "Our entry into the war was like a whiplash," he recalled two decades later. "I got back to work with real vigor."

First, he established a committee that provided financial support for a mammoth concert on 26 July at Milan's outdoor Arena, with a chorus of 1,500 and an orchestra of roughly 350; Toscanini himself contributed to the expenses. According to the *Corriere della Sera*, great applause greeted him when he entered the Arena, and 150 wounded Milanese soldiers, carried in on stretchers, were welcomed with enthusiastic gratitude. The all-Verdi program began with the Overture to *La Forza del Destino* and continued with vocal excerpts from six operas and with the *Hymn of the Nations*, a cantata for tenor, chorus, and orchestra, written in 1862 to thank Britain and France for their support for the Risorgimento. Twenty tenors sang the solo part in the *Hymn of the Nations* and fifty women sang Preziosilla's "Rataplàn," from *La Forza del Destino*. Boito, Gatti-Casazza, Cleofonte Campanini, Eva Tetrazzini, and Lucrezia Bori were present; Rosina Storchio distributed flowers to the wounded soldiers, and Wally Toscanini led a group of girls selling programs. Toscanini remembered the event as "truly memorable and moving. At the end of the concert I turned toward the audience, and I don't know how I managed to exert influence upon it, but [. . .] it began, under my direction, to sing the patriotic anthems as if with one voice, with infinite feeling and enthusiasm, and poor Boito came to embrace me, weeping like a child," he said. During the singing of the anthems, those audience members who had brought newspapers to use as cushions on the Arena's stone steps turned them into torches, which made a memorable visual impression.

The 40,000 people present in the Arena, augmented by some 60,000 crowding the surrounding streets, donated a total of 70,000 lire to the war effort. Toscanini received many letters of thanks, but also some protests, presumably from people who opposed Italy's participation in the war: at lunchtime on the day after the concert, a package was delivered to his home; when it was opened, it was found to contain horse excrement.

No sooner was the Arena concert over than Toscanini began to organize a special opera season to raise money for unemployed Milanese musicians: the mobilization of many thousands of men and of the nation's financial resources had caused most of the city's theaters to close. The series, which ran from mid-September to late November at the Teatro Dal Verme, included productions of *La Traviata, Tosca, Madame Sans-Gêne* (the Italian premiere of Giordano's opera), *Un Ballo in Maschera, Falstaff,* and a double bill of *Pagliacci* and Wolf-Ferrari's *Il Segreto di Susanna*—forty-two performances in all. The cast members, many of whom, like Toscanini, contributed their services gratis, included some of his previous collaborators in what proved to be their last professional encounters with him (Storchio, Caruso, and Bonci); some newcomers who would collaborate with him again in the future (Claudia Muzio, first and foremost); and one artist (Tito Schipa) with whom he was working for the first and only time. The season succeeded beyond all expectations: it netted over 211,000 lire, including a contribution of 5,000 lire from Otto Kahn, who had also sent Toscanini a letter in which he praised Italy's "Latin idealism." Before the series ended, Mayor Emilio Caldara and the entire city council awarded Toscanini a gold medal for his service to Milan.

Toscanini had cabled Caruso, who was in Buenos Aires, to persuade him to sing in *Pagliacci*, but when, in later years, he looked back on the Dal Verme series, his fondest memories were of the artistry of Bonci and Storchio. He remembered with special pleasure the tenor's musicality and vocal elegance as Riccardo in *Un Ballo in Maschera.* Caruso's voice was more beautiful, Toscanini said, but Bonci was better in this role; and Storchio, in *La Traviata*, was the only Violetta who ever made him weep—but perhaps his feelings of guilt toward her had helped the tears to flow.

The maestro and Carla involved themselves directly in dividing the funds into 3,527 parts and distributing them among 870 needy musicians—a job that dragged on for so long that Toscanini had to give up his plan to conduct a benefit opera season in Turin. He did manage to conduct three benefit concerts with the Santa Cecilia Orchestra in Rome, but without the originally programmed Beethoven Ninth: military conscription had decimated the male ranks of the city's choruses. The programs, which took place before overflow audiences at the Augusteo on 30 January and 6 and 9 February 1916, included three contemporary pieces new to Toscanini's repertoire: Busoni's *Berceuse Elégiaque*, Rachmaninoff's *The Isle of the Dead*, and excerpts from Stravinsky's *Petrushka*. The Busoni piece would show up many times in Toscanini's future concert seasons; the single performance of *The Isle of the Dead*, however, was his first and last venture with Rachmaninoff's music, although he admired Rachmaninoff as a pianist and musician and regretted, toward the end of his life, that he had never conducted the composer's Second Symphony.

Stravinsky regarded Toscanini's *Petrushka* performances as a turning point in his international career. "Can you imagine," he wrote to the Swiss conductor Ernest Ansermet, "that enormous room, seating an audience of thousands, was so full that to find a single seat was impossible! I do hope to go there. To hear Toscanini conduct my work would interest me immensely. He has stated that he plans to present the *Sacre* [*du Printemps*] next year, but we shall see what happens." Toscanini continued to conduct the *Petrushka* excerpts, albeit infrequently, until 1940, and he eventually added Stravinsky's early *Fireworks* and the "Infernal Dance" from *The Firebird* to his repertoire. But he never conducted *The Rite of Spring*, which—as he must have realized upon looking at the score—required specific, novel technical-rhythmic abilities that did not come naturally to him and that he did not wish to attempt.*

From Rome, Toscanini proceeded to Naples, where he prepared the local premiere of *Madame Sans-Gêne* at the Teatro San Carlo. Although the rehearsals were fraught, the dress rehearsal went well, but immediately afterward the orchestra and chorus called a strike: they claimed that Augusto Laganà, the San Carlo's impresario, had not carried out all of his contractual obligations to them. The following morning, Toscanini himself appeared at a union meeting, to everyone's surprise. He sympathized with the workers' protest, he said, but he asked that at least one performance be given, out of respect for art. Oreste Gentile, the union leader, not only rejected Toscanini's request but also called him an intruder, and he persuaded those assembled to proceed with the strike. Back at his hotel, Tosca-

---

* Although Pierre Monteux, who was Toscanini's junior by only eight years, conducted the premiere of *The Rite of Spring* and performed it brilliantly many times thereafter, most conductors of Toscanini's generation and many of the following one found its rhythmic complexities too difficult.

nini received a letter from Laganà, full of regrets and apologies, along with a check for 2,000 lire—the fee he was to have received for each of eight scheduled performances. But the angry maestro, who believed that the workers' accusations against Laganà were correct, returned the letter with the check and caught a train back to Milan.

The aborted production in Naples was the only engagement during the entire war for which Toscanini would have been paid. He refused to accept money even for what little work he was able to do, because he believed that as long as others were risking their lives for Italy, the least he could do was contribute his services wherever and however possible. He also donated a great deal of money to various war-related causes, and he and Carla eventually realized that their liquid assets were nearly gone.

"I didn't earn a cent from '15 to '21," he told a friend during a conversation recorded many years later. "I sold my house and got rid of my automobile.* I went by streetcar. I threw away a lot of money during the war. I had earned well, but I couldn't live on past income. For several years I paid rent for my apartment"—in other words, for the part of the house in Via Durini in which the family actually lived. After the war, however, "Carla had the good luck that the same people who had bought the house had to set up a bank and found themselves in bad shape; they re-sold [the house], and Carla took advantage, and so after just a few years"—when he had begun to earn well again—"we got the house back."

About Carla's "luck" in matters financial: Arturo thought of his wife as a paragon of practicality, as indeed she was in comparison with her economically clueless husband. The Milanese poet and journalist Delio Tessa observed that although Carla didn't actually conduct the orchestra, she did everything else. "There's a work proposal? 'Tosca' gives the preliminary approval, then the contract passes into Signora Carla's jurisdiction; she discusses it and arranges

---

* During his flush Metropolitan years, Toscanini had bought a car in Milan and had hired a driver, but he himself never learned to drive. He probably began to earn money again—although not much—in the fall of 1920 rather than in 1921, as he recalled. He also claimed that he had shamed Puccini and "the dukes"—presumably Visconti di Modrone and/or other Milanese aristocrats connected with La Scala—into giving money of their own for the war effort.

things." She seems to have run the household smoothly enough, too, and perhaps her husband figured that since her father had been a stockbroker she must have inherited or absorbed a knack for dealing with money. Certainly, she had become accustomed to looking after her husband's earnings, which were modest during the first few years of their marriage but much improved as a result of Arturo's first four Buenos Aires seasons, and outstanding thanks to his seven Metropolitan seasons and his final season in Argentina. Averaged out, Toscanini's annual income between 1908 and 1915 was well over a hundred times the annual income of an Italian worker.

How could most of that money have disappeared during the following three years? At a time when the British pound and the US dollar ruled the world, Carla always converted all of the pounds that her husband earned in Argentina and the dollars that he earned in the United States—except for the funds that he needed for his immediate living expenses—into Italian lire, and by the end of the First World War the lira had lost 80 percent of its prewar value. In other words, the Toscaninis' savings from Arturo's considerable prewar earnings in the Americas were worth less and less as the war dragged on, and most of the remainder was spent on day-to-day necessities and on contributions to the war effort. Nor did this disaster prevent Carla from following the same pattern—and with similar results—years later, when Toscanini again received extravagant fees in New York. Not until she was well into her sixties, when the family was living year-round in the United States, did she gradually turn financial responsibilities over to Walter, who found himself dealing with a colossal economic mess that took years to straighten out.

Many people who knew Carla told stories about her notions of how to save money: she would hear about a sale on a single grocery item or an article of clothing on the other side of town and would get the family's handyman-cum-chauffeur to drive her to wherever the sale was taking place, thereby spending more on fuel and on her employee's time than she could possibly have saved on her purchases. The expression "Penny wise, pound foolish" could have been invented for her. None of this reflects badly on Carla as a person, but it explains why her husband's earnings did not provide as they might otherwise have done.

2.

UNLIKE CARUSO AND OTHER ITALIAN OPERA CELEBRITIES WHO chose to remain in America, where they continued to earn large sums of money during the war years, Toscanini, by remaining in Italy for patriotic reasons, effectively brought his career to a standstill. So little musical activity was taking place in the war-mobilized country that, after he had led a single benefit concert in Rome in March 1916 and three benefit concerts in Turin in May, he did no conducting at all for five months. Perhaps the unaccustomed and undesired inactivity made him feel an occasional twinge of regret at having left the Metropolitan; what is certain is that observers of New York's musical life expressed plenty of regret over his absence. In summarizing the 1915–16 season, Richard Aldrich wrote in the *Times* that the maestro's "place was not filled" by Giorgio Polacco, who, although competent, could not "exercise the same authority, work the same magic, arrive at results of the same supreme distinction as the great master." By the end of 1917, New York's newspapers had been ordered not to compare other Metropolitan conductors with Toscanini or to mention any possibility of his returning to the organization, and as several newspaper owners were members of the Metropolitan's board, enforcing such an order was possible.

La Scala, in the meantime, limped along with makeshift seasons, but Toscanini refused to participate in them. Early in 1916 he learned that his old antagonist Duke Uberto Visconti di Modrone, who was still president of the theater's administration, had reached an agreement with the impresario Walter Mocchi to let the latter organize the house's 1916–17 season. Toscanini was shocked and angered. In the first place, the for-profit impresario system had been abolished at La Scala in 1898, when Toscanini and Gatti-Casazza had first taken responsibility for the house's fortunes; in the second, Mocchi was—in the opinion not only of Toscanini but also of Mascagni and many other important figures in the opera world—one of the most ruthless and untrustworthy of all the impresarios. A politically agile opportunist, Mocchi had started out as a socialist rabble-rouser but would end up, in the 1930s, as a Fascist spy and a propagandist for the regime's anti-Semitic "racial" policies.

"I am rising up to protest against you for violating a noble tradition of high moral significance, well established for years at La Scala, rooted in the conscience of the public and of the entire citizenry," Toscanini told the duke, in what was probably the longest letter he ever wrote. "The obviously secretive arrival on the scene of Mr. Walter Mocchi—the most singular exponent of theatrical speculation—to share with you the responsibility for La Scala's artistic decency, constitutes that violation [. . .]. You could not have been more badly advised, if you were advised at all in this rash act."

Toscanini went on to remind the duke that La Scala had previously been run in accordance with "the tradition begun and scrupulously maintained by your father," Duke Guido, and by others "who have given and who continue to give the best of themselves to Art, [. . .] and who cherish in their hearts the living flame of a religious love for all those institutions that, like La Scala, are the pride not only of the city but of the nation." He inveighed against the "municipality, box holders, and subscribers" for "not contesting the matter. Supine acquiescence is an outrage against the law." And he revealed that Mocchi had approached him to participate in the new venture—had stated that he was creating *"a new technical mechanism for operating the theater,"* a mechanism that *"ought to yield above-average artistic results."* Toscanini said that he had replied to Mocchi: "you cannot create anything, but only deform everything [. . .], moving from one theater to another, from one scandal to another, speculating one day on a singer's fame, the next on a composer's, without ever doing anything that was artistically beautiful." Toscanini concluded, "I have protested and I know that I have done so in vain. I have done it, however, to carry out a compelling but sad duty."

Luigi Illica urged Toscanini to prepare to take over La Scala in 1918, when Visconti's mandate would be up for renewal, but Toscanini was unresponsive to the idea. For reasons now unknown but probably connected with the Mocchi episode, in July 1916 the maestro had a violent altercation with Renzo Sonzogno, a nephew and one of the heirs of the music publisher Edoardo Sonzogno, and the younger Sonzogno challenged Toscanini to a duel. Toscanini turned down the challenge but presented "documents that can justify my behavior," he wrote. "So proceed, Mr. Renzo Sonzogno! Take heart: go ahead and choose your representatives, and we'll see whether I'll have to fight you." Several days of wrangling among the two parties' lawyers ensued, after which the matter was dropped. Illica heard about the incident and—reluctant to tackle the subject with Toscanini himself—wrote instead to Walter: "Your father wants at all costs to expect moral merits and virtues of the soul in an environment that has essentially remained what it was in the Middle Ages, when theater virtuosi who died couldn't be buried in consecrated ground [. . .]. He has the illness of Giuseppe Verdi, who wanted to feel the life of the conscience and also of the nation palpitating [. . .] in the life of art and of the Theater! [. . .] He'll have disappointments and unpleasantness."

No sooner had the Sonzogno incident been resolved than trouble of a different sort broke out. Toscanini returned to Rome in November 1916 for more benefit concerts at the Augusteo. The first half of the first concert, on the nineteenth, comprised Corelli's "Christmas" Concerto and Martucci's First Symphony, both of which were well received, as was the first piece after the intermission—*Chiari di Luna* by Vincenzo Tommasini, a local composer. Some Wagner excerpts and Sibelius's *Finlandia* were to conclude the program, but when Toscanini began to conduct the "Forest Murmurs" from *Siegfried*, a segment of the audience, led by adherents of the Futurist movement, protested vociferously. Augusto Rossi, a violinist in the orchestra, recalled that "Maestro Luigi Mancinelli, who was much loved by the Roman public and particularly by Toscanini, came down from his box [. . .], jumped onto the stage [. . .], and embraced the conductor in fraternal friendship, demonstrating his solidarity. This had the effect of calming the storm [. . .] and the concert resumed" with the Funeral Music from *Götterdämmerung*. Eight days earlier, the Austrians had carried out an aerial bombardment of Padua, and the incursion had claimed ninety-three civilian victims; as the piece began, someone in the auditorium shouted, "For the dead of Padua!" According to the composer Alfredo Casella, who was present, the phrase had been uttered by a music-loving soldier on leave, whose sole intention was to commemorate the victims of the bombardment through the performance of Wagner's funeral music, but it was interpreted as a protest. A huge uproar broke out, with pro and contra shouts back and forth. Sergei Diaghilev noted, in a letter to Stravinsky, that Vasily Khvoshchinsky, a Russian diplomat, "loudly defended the performance of Wagner."

Toscanini crossed his arms on his chest and waited for the noise to abate; when it did not, he left the hall and canceled his remaining concerts. A few days later an order was issued banning German music in Rome until the end of the war, and Toscanini did not conduct again in the city for the duration.

Filippo Tommaso Marinetti, the Futurists' leading poet and propagandist, noted later in his diary, "I compare conductors like Toscanini with prostitutes' vulvas [because] they adapt to various musical genres [. . .]. I declare Toscanini's sensibility as deaf as that of a rhinoceros for having imposed on the Augusteo a concert entirely [*sic*] of Wagner's music. I recall my article against Toscanini and the booing organized by the Roman Futurists, to the cry of *down with Wagner.*"

Although Toscanini always insisted that there was no place for musical exclusions on the basis of race, religion, nationality, or political beliefs, he claimed many years later that had the concerts' organizers warned him in advance, he would not have provoked the audience on that occasion by programming Wagner's music. Yet he must have known that many Italians frowned upon the performance of German music in general and Wagner's in particular during the war: as early as the fall of 1914, there had been an unofficial ban on the performance of *Parsifal* in Italy, and an editorial cartoon in the *New York Sun* had lampooned the ruling by showing a quizzical Richard Wagner up in the sky looking down on a gruff, bayonet-carrying Italian soldier who bore a more than passing resemblance to Giuseppe Verdi. The caption read, "Music (German) hath no charms to soothe the savage breast."

The following months were musically barren ones for Toscanini. On 18 January 1917, Puccini, writing to a friend, mentioned a plan to have Toscanini conduct the first performance of his newest opera, *Il Tabarro*, in Turin in the near future, "but I fear it will come to nothing. [. . .] The singers are lacking—they are at the front." Toscanini spent his fiftieth birthday, on 25 March, in forced withdrawal from his profession and in sorrow over the prolongation of the increasingly ghastly war. He followed the events of the conflict in great detail, mainly through the reports that appeared in each day's *Corriere della Sera*, and he marked the shifts in troop movements by moving little flagged pins around on a large map.

Several of Italy's leading generals had been presented to the mae-

stro at his various benefit appearances; he found most of them egocentric—they reminded him of singers, he joked—but he took a
liking to General Antonino Cascino, who, early in August 1917,
invited him to form a military band to perform for soldiers fighting
along the Isonzo River front. Toscanini had been spending the summer with Carla, Wally, and Wanda at Cantoniera della Presolana, a
pass 4,265 feet above sea level in the Lombard Alps, north of Bergamo and Lake Iseo, but he reacted with enthusiasm to Cascino's
proposal and immediately set about engaging musicians and select-
ing music. By mid-August all was ready.

One day, the nineteen-year-old Walter Toscanini, who was now
serving as an artillery officer on the Isonzo front, received an order
to go to headquarters, where he was astonished to see his father and
General Cascino himself come out to meet him, and even more
astonished to learn that a military band that he had heard playing in
the distance a day or two earlier had been led by his father. Later in
the afternoon, as the two Toscaninis walked together along a mountain path, they came to a water-filled shell hole and separated to walk
around it. At that instant a stray shell whizzed along the trail; the
pressure knocked them both to the ground. Fortunately, the shell
was a dud, but had they not separated to avoid the hole they would
have been decapitated.

Later that month, General Cascino asked Toscanini, who had
been transferred with his band to the village of Quisca (now Kojsko,
Slovenia), to go the following morning to Monte Santo (Sveta Gora),
which the Italians had just captured from the Austrians. On the
afternoon of the twenty-sixth, the maestro and his musicians, "carrying their instruments, struggled up the 2,250-foot-high mountain
while the 8th Division tried to fight its way to [Monte] San Gabriele
across the Dol saddle," according to the historian John R. Schindler.
"By the evening Toscanini's band was in place at the summit, beside
the ruins of Mt. Santo's monastery, in the open, protected only by a
rock." While the infantry fought, less than a mile away, the band
played. "The troops loved it," Schindler reports, "and responded
with euphoric shouts of approval, so the band kept playing long into
the night."

"I stayed there four days," Toscanini wrote to Walter on the thirty-
first. "We played in the Austrians' faces, and we sang our national

anthems. I observed several attacks on the San Gabriele, and I went [back] down to Quisca, sorry not to have seen this other conquest."*

To Carla, Toscanini wrote that the memory of what he had seen still made his heart beat wildly. "A month ago, among all of you there at the Cantoniera, at my piano, rejoicing in Pelléas's exquisite sweetness, I certainly couldn't have imagined that such a new, unprecedented chapter in my life was about to begin." And he told her that on the morning after the Monte Santo incident General Luigi Capello, commander of the Army of the Isonzo, awarded him a silver medal for military valor, in front of several thousand troops. "You can imagine my surprise and the violent emotion that followed!! I cried like a baby, and in the general's presence I was as stupid as a goose."† He felt that he didn't deserve the honor, and he naïvely hoped that the news would remain secret, since "no journalists were present," he told Carla. But the Italian war ministry took advantage of the propaganda opportunity, especially in order to send enormously inflated versions of the story to the United States, which had in the meantime entered the conflict. The *New York Times* reported that the Metropolitan's former conductor had been "decorated by the Italian Government for great bravery under fire. [. . .] In the midst of the fighting and at a time when the Austrian barrage fire was at its height Signor Toscanini led his band to one of the advanced positions where, sheltered only by a huge rock, he conducted a concert which did not stop until word had been brought to him that the Italian soldiers had stormed and taken the trenches of the Austrians to the music of his band."

A *Times* war correspondent reported, a few days later, from the headquarters of the Italian Supreme Command: "Wherever I have

---

* According to a book published in 2007 (*Grande guerra, piccoli generali*, by the historian Lorenzo Del Boca), the sound of Toscanini's band playing on Monte Santo caused the Austrians to fire toward it, which in turn caused the death of many Italian soldiers. But no such claim appears elsewhere, whether in positive or negative accounts made either at the time or by historians. As Toscanini and others present clearly stated, he and his band did not arrive on Monte Santo until the battle had ended; by then the Italian troops had left Monte Santo and moved toward Monte San Gabriele, which they conquered—temporarily—on 2 September.

† In the immediate post–World War I years, Toscanini sold a number of medals that had been awarded to him and contributed all of the money to a mutual aid fund for Milanese musicians.

been on the Italian front Toscanini had been there first. He climbed [. . .] Monte Santo just to lead the band on the day of its capture and he looked into the trenches at Volnik"—about thirty miles to the southeast, on what is now the Italian-Slovenian border—"just twenty-four hours before I arrived." As a result of such reports, a committee of American music lovers began a campaign to purchase an ambulance for Italy, in Toscanini's honor, and the French town of Verdun, which had suffered one of the worst and most prolonged battles of the war, with hundreds of thousands dead, sent him a sculpture of a fighting rooster titled "Verdun 1916."*

Toscanini wrote to Carla to request more music; she searched through his scores and in the Milan Conservatory's library to find what he wanted and sent him packages that included foodstuffs for Walter and for hospital attendants, plus stationery that had been requested by some nurses, and sweets for her husband—in the hope that he would think of her while he was eating them, she wrote.

The band continued to perform for the troops, giving informal concerts in makeshift venues but also playing in the trenches, at the funeral of General Achille Papa—a division commander who had been shot by an Austrian sniper—and wherever else they were sent. On 28 October, while the musicians were playing in the town of Cormons, which Italy had taken from Austria early in the war, they suddenly noticed that they were practically alone in the piazza: the Austrians were approaching, the army was withdrawing, and the General Command had forgotten about the band. Toscanini rushed to procure wagons and railroad cars to evacuate everyone to safety; he then found Walter, who had suffered a hand wound eight days earlier but had immediately returned to his battalion, and took him to the army hospital in the city of Udine.

These events occurred during the Battle of Caporetto, or Twelfth Battle of the Isonzo—a disaster for Italy. As the Austrians attacked, the Italians had to pull back southward and westward in order to regroup and establish resistance to the onslaught; some 10,000 Italian soldiers were killed, 30,000 wounded, and 265,000 taken prisoner. To

---

* Carla wrote to her husband that there was a proposal for him to go to Paris to conduct Berlioz's *La Damnation de Faust* at the Opéra for the benefit of French musicians, but the project never came to fruition.

this day, Caporetto—the Italian name of the village of Kobarid in Slovenia—is a synonym for "defeat" to Italian ears.

Toscanini, returning to Milan on a slow train, was haunted by the thought that Italy might actually lose some of the territory won from Austria fifty to sixty years earlier, instead of "redeeming" the ethnically Italian territories that had remained under Austrian control. "I still remember when he came into the house," Wally recalled more than half a century later. "He opened the service door; his face was ashen and dirty and his eyes swollen from crying. Mamma, thinking that something terrible had happened to Walter, jumped to her feet and screamed, 'Walter, Walter!' My father said, 'No. It's Italy. Italy is finished.' He embraced my mother and began to weep."

Resurrecting the band was out of the question, but Toscanini persuaded the Supreme Command to renew his safe-conduct pass so that he could return to the war zone, where he spent weeks trying to ascertain the whereabouts of his musicians, making sure that those he found were safe, and giving them money—this at a time when his own finances were plummeting. "I'm extremely uneasy because of the impossibility of getting information, if not precise at least approximate, of the movements of the troops on the march," he wrote to Carla from an undisclosed location. "No one here knows anything." In the town of Baone, he found one of his young musicians, "sad, desperate, penniless, and sorrowful over the loss of his double bass—a good instrument by a craftsman. I gave him fifty lire; he thanked me, in tears. [. . .] I've accumulated such sadness in my heart that I could cry every five minutes." Toscanini also searched, often successfully, for friends' sons who had no way of informing their families of their whereabouts, and he noted that the most important works of art in Venice and Padua were being dismounted and sent to Rome for safekeeping in case those northern cities were overrun by the enemy. "Doesn't all this make you want to cry?" he asked.

3.

WORKS OF ART—VISUAL ART—WERE AMONG TOSCANINI'S FEW consolations during those traumatic years. He had long had a strong interest in sculpture and painting: Leonardo Bistolfi, among the best-known Italian sculptors of his generation, had become one of Toscanini's closest friends during his Turin days, two decades earlier, and the Milan-based painter Arturo Tosi had also been befriended by Toscanini during the maestro's first years at La Scala: Toscanini sometimes accompanied Tosi on his landscape-painting excursions into the countryside. But this interest evolved into a real passion as a result of his friendship with the painter Vittore Grubicy de Dragon.

Grubicy, born in 1851 to a Hungarian nobleman and a Lombard noblewoman, traveled around Europe in his youth, familiarizing himself with the latest artistic movements, then worked as an art dealer, and eventually became a painter—an exponent of the Divisionist movement, related to French pointillism. He was associated with many leading Italian painters of the day, including Giovanni Segantini and Gaetano Previati. Toscanini had met Grubicy casually as early as 1904, but he first grew acquainted with the painter's works in 1911—and quickly became an admirer and acquirer of his paintings, of which he eventually owned more than sixty. Grubicy showed his gratitude by painting a photograph-based portrait of Giorgio Toscanini, and he persuaded Arturo and Carla to sit for photographs so that he could paint their portraits as well;* the maestro appears in a pensive pose—brow furrowed and left hand stroking his chin.

Toscanini and Grubicy could hardly have been more dissimilar. The conductor, healthy in mind and body, was a tremendous workhorse; the painter suffered from nervous and other disorders and had given up most of his painting activities by the age of fifty. Toscanini was seriously myopic but loved painting and sculpture; Grubicy was hard of hearing but loved music. Toscanini was short, slight, mustachioed but otherwise clean-shaven, and fastidiously neat; Grubicy was tall, burly, full-bearded, and careless about his appearance. When they were together, they looked like slender, energetic Charlie Chaplin next to big, clumsy Eric Campbell in the slapstick silent films of the day. The reference is not out of place: according to Filippo Sacchi, Grubicy would occasionally drag Toscanini with him to see a movie, and whereas Grubicy "enjoyed the film without hearing the music," poor Toscanini saw little "but had to suffer through the

---

* Those paintings now hang in the Parma Conservatory, where Toscanini's Milan study has been re-created in a special room.

banging" of the piano accompaniment. Yet the two men felt that they were kindred souls.

Throughout the war years, when Toscanini's musical activities were at their lowest ebb in decades, he would draw strength from Grubicy's paintings. "I spend many hours of each day in the most delightful corner of my home—made so precious *by you*," Toscanini wrote to his friend on one occasion. "It's a sweet way of detaching myself from life's material reality. . . Seated before your lovely song, 'Light Mists of October,' I live for the thought—for the ecstasy of the thought that is soul—vague, undefined ecstasy that lifts me up, high up amid the clouds, far, far away. [. . .] Lucky you, dear Vittore, who were able to make the voice of your beautiful soul sing!!"*

After the war, Grubicy became gravely ill; Toscanini spent as much time with him as he could and was with him when he died, on 4 August 1920, in his sixty-ninth year. The musician mourned his painter friend as he had mourned Catalani, and in the following years he helped the Divisionist painter Benvenuto Benvenuti, one of Grubicy's most fervent acolytes, and others, to preserve and find proper homes for the works of their deceased friend and master. He also helped, for a while, to keep Grubicy's studio intact, and in 1926 an Italian periodical reported that Toscanini would sometimes go there with Benvenuti and simply sit in contemplation.

Toscanini eventually owned over 150 paintings, drawings, and sculptures by Italian artists, including Mosè Bianchi, Umberto Boccioni, Giovanni Boldini, Giuseppe De Nittis, Silvestro Lega, Gaetano Previati, and Telemaco Signorini. In 1916, Arturo and Carla gave work to the academic painter Giacomo Grosso by sitting for portraits that now hang in the museum in Toscanini's birth house in Parma; Toscanini was so pleased with both of them that he wrote an enthusiastic note to Grosso, and he allowed his portrait to be displayed as part of that year's annual Christmas exhibition by the Turin Artists' Circle. Works by the Englishman Alfred East, the American George Innes, and the Russian Paul Troubetzkoy also became part of Toscanini's collection. Delio Tessa observed that

---

* In my edition of *The Letters of Arturo Toscanini*, I made use of an incorrect version of this letter, as it had been quoted by Sacchi. I have since been able to transcribe the original letter and other correspondence addressed to Grubicy and his disciples by Toscanini and members of his family.

"the works of art that surround [Toscanini] may not have a high commercial value, but one has the distinct impression that they are among his working tools"—in other words, that they stimulated his imagination. And Walfredo Toscanini used to joke that if his grandfather had bought French Impressionist paintings instead of works by their Italian contemporaries, he himself would never have had to do a day's work.

Many of the walls in the house in Via Durini were covered, up and down, with paintings and drawings, and Toscanini would periodically rehang them himself, so that he could better focus on those that most interested him at any given time. "He always had a hammer and nails, and he liked to change the position of the paintings," his daughter Wanda recalled. "Often he did this in the middle of the night when he couldn't sleep. He really adored paintings. When he would buy a new one he would take it to his bedroom, sit in bed, and look at it. Mother said that one night she woke up and found Father asleep with a painting in his hands. She was glad that she had awakened, or the painting would have fallen on his face." Family members also told of the time that Toscanini, in his later years, got stuck on a ladder during one of his late-night picture-hanging expeditions and wasn't rescued until someone in the house awoke in the morning. And in extreme old age, when his vision was so bad that he could no longer read, he would still gaze at his favorite paintings: by perceiving their general outlines he could remember their details.

4.

THE WAR RAGED ON FOR ANOTHER YEAR AFTER THE BATTLE OF Caporetto. Toscanini was near despair after his return from the combat zone late in November 1917, but toward the end of the year his old friend Giuseppe Gallignani, director of the Milan Conservatory, came up with a new plan to aid impoverished local musicians by organizing a dozen concerts in the school's auditorium. The two men sent out joint appeals to government ministries, banks, newspapers, and private individuals, and Toscanini himself contributed 1,000 lire to the undertaking—equal to the amount that some of the banks gave.

The concerts took place on successive Sunday afternoons, from 6 January to 24 March 1918, and two extra popular concerts were added at the end. Turnout was great, and 100,000 lire were raised. Gallignani and Toscanini also received letters of protest, some of them anonymous and nasty, others signed and civil, over the inclusion of works by German and Austrian composers—although nothing by Wagner or by living Germanic composers was scheduled; the programs were not altered, and no untoward incidents occurred. Several pieces new to Toscanini's repertoire appeared on the programs: *Ibéria* and *La Damoiselle Elue* by Debussy (who died that year on 25 March, Toscanini's fifty-first birthday), Franck's Symphony in D minor and excerpts from his *Psyché*, Ottorino Respighi's *Fountains of Rome*, Gian Francesco Malipiero's *Pause del Silenzio* (Pauses of Silence), Stravinsky's *Fireworks*, Mozart's "Prague" Symphony, and pieces by eleven other composers.

Fountains of Rome was the first work by Respighi to enter Toscanini's repertoire; the performance's success led to a contract between Respighi and Ricordi and from there to increasing good fortune for the composer. On the other hand, *Pause del Silenzio* by Malipiero, another significant twentieth-century Italian composer, failed miserably, and Toscanini did not like or perform any of Malipiero's subsequent works.

In May 1918, Toscanini returned to the war zone, but what he did there, beyond visiting Walter, is unknown. From Milan he sent books to his bibliophile son. "Have you received Emerson's Autobiography?" he wrote to Walter. "Reading it has given me much peace and enjoyment. I'm also sending you this book by [Giovanni] Papini on Carducci. I find it truthful and interesting." At the same time, however, Toscanini was worrying about Boito, whose health had been deteriorating since the previous winter. Four or five years earlier, Boito had finally shown Toscanini the score of the first act of his long-postponed *Nerone*, and Toscanini had been shocked to find the opera still in a primitive state; he must have expressed to others his doubts that Boito would ever finish *Nerone*, because some of the people nearest Boito turned Toscanini away when he tried to visit his old friend at the clinic.

On 6 February 1918, Eleonora Duse, Boito's ex-lover and once again friend, wrote to another friend,

It seems that they continue to mention [to Boito] neither the war, nor the battles, [. . .] nor Toscanini, nor the holy *manuscript of his opera*, which is the most *interior* part of his soul [. . .]. I cannot forget that during the days in which he realized that he was not yet ready *for his departure*, merely hearing *Toscanini* mentioned was [the cause of] copious weeping . . . because it reminded him of the Work, and the slow wait, and the promise of years and years, and the discouragement that Toscanini wouldn't believe and wouldn't see it in the right light! *"No one, no one can help me,"* he said, sobbing . . . —but, maybe, Toscanini could, and if *he were allowed to see him and talk to him, what a balm it would be!!*

Duse's letter may have worked: Toscanini managed to visit Boito, who was so weak that he spoke with difficulty, and Toscanini, in turn, was so upset over the older man's condition that when he returned home he shut himself in his study and refused to see anyone. Boito died on 10 June 1918, at the age of seventy-six, and Toscanini and a few other friends of the poet-librettist-composer spent the entire night before the funeral in a vigil beside the bier. Always aware of dates and anniversaries, Toscanini knew that exactly twenty years had gone by since he had been confirmed as conductor of La Scala, thanks above all to Boito's support for him. In the years to come, he would show his gratitude in several important ways.

His first tribute to Boito took place only five months after the latter's death: La Scala, which had been closed for over a year, for lack of money, housed a special season—organized by the Italian Society of Lyric Artists—for the benefit of unemployed opera artists, war invalids, and war orphans, and Toscanini participated in it by conducting nine performances of his deceased friend's *Mefistofele*, in a production that opened on 19 November; these were his only performances of complete operas between December 1915 and December 1921. Among his singers was the twenty-eight-year-old tenor Beniamino Gigli, whose stellar career was launched, in part, by this production. A nineteen-year-old American soldier named Ernest Hemingway, recuperating, in a Milan hospital, from his war wounds, attended one of Toscanini's performances of the opera; in a letter, he commented only that he would have preferred to hear *Carmen* or *La Bohème*.

Early in November 1918, during the *Mefistofele* rehearsals, the long-awaited announcement arrived: Germany and Austria had surrendered. The war was over. Toscanini copied out by hand a release from the Italian news agency, Stefani, which contained the Germanic countries' request for an armistice based on the US president Woodrow Wilson's Fourteen Points plan. The ninth of those points declared, "A readjustment of the frontiers of Italy should be effected along clearly recognizable lines of nationality." But how was "nationality" to be defined? Geographically? Ethnically? Linguistically? The triumphant allies were now free to fight among themselves.

ONE OF THE ALLIED NATIONS had offered Toscanini an important position even before the war had ended. Frederick P. Cabot, president of the Boston Symphony Orchestra, sent Toscanini a long letter in which he offered him the conductorship of what was at that time generally considered the finest symphonic ensemble in the United States. Although the orchestra's previous conductor, Karl Muck, was a citizen of Switzerland, a nonbelligerent nation, he was German born, and wartime patriotic hysteria had caused him to be fired from his post and interned in Georgia on trumped-up charges of espionage and other enemy-alien-like acts. Cabot's letter described the orchestra's seasons and offered Toscanini an annual salary of $25,000, much less than the Metropolitan had been paying him.

The offer quickly took on an extra shade of meaning. Sidney Sonnino, a former Italian prime minister who was then serving as foreign minister, sent a message to the minister of public education in which he transcribed a message that he had just received by cable from Italy's ambassador to the United States. "Various important personages, among them the influential Senator [Henry Cabot] Lodge of Massachusetts, ask me to request that the King's Government exert influence on the maestro so that he will accept," the ambassador had written.

In addition to the homage to Italian art through one of its illustrious representatives, this offer also has a political significance that we would be wrong to ignore. The conquest of musical primacy in the United States is sought by everyone, also and especially because it is an efficacious vehicle for penetration.

France strenuously contests this with us. The moment is favorable. By accepting, Maestro Toscanini would increase his patriotic merits and would render distinguished service to Italian influence in the United States. Any pressure upon him on the part of the R[oyal] Government would be amply justified, and I invoke it. I ask Your Excellency to be so kind as to telegraph [a] decision to me.

Olin Downes, the *Boston Post*'s music critic at the time, later claimed that Toscanini had "looked with favor on this plan" but that the orchestra's board had "at the last moment called off the Toscanini negotiations." This statement is unsubstantiated by documents. All that is known for sure is that Toscanini found himself in a generally depressed state, even though the war was nearing its end, and that the condition persisted after the armistice, in November 1918. "He was discouraged, and it seemed as if he had even lost his enthusiasm for music," Wally recalled. When she asked him for a photo of himself, he signed it, "your unemployed Papà."

Since his departure from the Metropolitan three and a half years earlier, Toscanini had worked less than he usually did in a single season, and the less he did, the more withered and useless he felt. There was little for him to do in Italy, yet how could he leave his country, which was now in incalculably worse condition than it had been before the war? Italy had "redeemed" its ethnic territories, but the enterprise had cost the lives of approximately 600,000 young Italian men and an outlay of 148 billion lire, double the sum of all prewar government expenditures since 1861, when Italy had become a nation. Of what use was a musician in the face of such catastrophes?

A trip to Rome in January 1919, to attend the Italian premiere of Puccini's *Trittico*—three one-act operas (*Il Tabarro*, *Suor Angelica*, and *Gianni Schicchi*) that are often performed together in a single evening—did nothing to raise Toscanini's spirits. A few years earlier, Puccini had told him of his intention to set *Il Tabarro* and of his hope that Toscanini would conduct its premiere. Toscanini read Giuseppe Adami's libretto and advised Puccini against the undertaking: "Why do you want to set it? The drama isn't worthy of you," he recalled having said, and he added that the text was *grand guignol*—lurid simply for the sake of being lurid. Puccini promised him that, after all, he would not write the opera, but he changed his mind again. The *Trittico*'s world premiere took place at the Metropolitan in December 1918, a month after the war's end; the first Italian production, in the presence of King Victor Emanuel III, was entrusted to the gifted young conductor Gino Marinuzzi and an excellent cast. Alberto Gasco, music critic of the Rome newspaper *La Tribuna*, was sitting near Toscanini. "It's a masterpiece," Gasco said at the end of *Il Tabarro*.

"For you," replied Toscanini, who found both the plot and the music low-class. "I'm leaving." As he was exiting the theater, Toscanini noticed the king's chamberlain accompanying Puccini to the royal box. Puccini had been trying to contact Toscanini for two or three days, and, Toscanini recalled, "I said to myself, 'should I say hello?' I didn't say hello. He passed near me, and I turned away." Toscanini's opinion of the work reached Puccini, who protested violently when he learned that the conductor had been invited to take charge of the *Trittico*'s British premiere, along with a production of Verdi's *Simon Boccanegra*, in London. "I've heard about Covent Garden," he wrote to his friend Sybil Seligman in London. "I protested to Ricordi because I don't want that *pig* of a Toscanini; he has said all sorts of nasty things about my operas and has tried to inspire certain journalists to run them down too." (Gasco had presumably made Toscanini's remarks known to others.) "I have already said that when a conductor thinks poorly of the operas he has to conduct, he can't interpret them properly." But there is no evidence that Toscanini ever gave serious consideration to the offer from London, if indeed it ever reached him; in any case, the British premiere did not take place until the following year, and Toscanini never conducted any of the *Trittico* operas.

The following December, during this rift in the Puccini-Toscanini friendship, the composer forgot to take Toscanini's name off the list of people to whom he sent a panettone, a traditional Milanese Christmas cake. When he discovered the mistake, he sent a telegram to Toscanini: "Panettone sent by mistake—Puccini." The answer came back: "Panettone eaten by mistake—Toscanini."

GRADUALLY AT FIRST, Toscanini began to emerge from his postwar funk. In May and June 1919, Turin's Teatro Regio was the site of his first concerts since the armistice; in one of them he added Mozart's

Symphony no. 39 in E-flat Major to his active repertoire. The Beethoven Ninth dominated three of the other concerts, and in June he repeated it four times in Milan; again, he took no fee for any of these performances. The solo singers—none of whom had worked with him before—were the young, later celebrated, soprano Toti Dal Monte (stage name of Antonietta Meneghel); the contralto Ida Bergamasco; the Canadian tenor Edoardo Di Giovanni (stage name of Edward Johnson); and the Czech bass Pavel Ludikar. Johnson, who later served for fifteen years as general manager of the Metropolitan Opera, recalled that at the singers' first piano rehearsal with Toscanini, Bergamasco was so nervous that she made a bad entrance. Toscanini began the passage again, but the same thing happened. *Da capo* yet again, but this time the contralto couldn't produce a sound and began to cry. Toscanini said nothing until she had regained her self-control. As they began again, Toscanini muttered, "And they say that I am impatient."

But he certainly could be impatient. During one of the orchestra rehearsals of the Ninth, the most violent incident in Toscanini's entire career took place and was observed by one Annibale Pastore, a professor of theoretical philosophy at the University of Turin, who, in preparing a book on the subject of enthusiasm, had obtained permission to observe the maestro at work. He reported,

> During the finale, when the tremendous outcry of the chorus must rise to maximum power [. . .] there were three dry taps of the baton [. . .]. The Maestro turned to one of the second violins, seated at the second stand, and shouted: "What kind of scratching is that? Two centimeters of bow!" And he threw his crumpled handkerchief, which he had been using to fan himself, at him. The violinist answered: "I'm playing, not scratching. And you? Why did you throw your handkerchief at me?" Toscanini, still trembling, responded: "I throw everything I have into it; and you—nothing. You ought to throw your bow into it." So saying, [. . .] he stepped involuntarily [sic] off the podium and approached the second stand of second violins.
>
> The violinist persisted: "I've always done what's possible, and you are impolite." Toscanini: "Ah, what's possible? And this?" And with a nervous motion of his baton he struck the

bow sidewise. It broke, and on the rebound hit the violinist on the forehead. The violinist was about to react; then players and soloists threw themselves in between and held them back [. . .]. The violinist was led away by a colleague. On leaving the stage he turned and shouted at Toscanini: "You aren't a maestro, you're a scoundrel."

Carla purchased a good new bow for the man, but his minor head injury was the cause of a lawsuit. Toscanini was acquitted on the basis of Pastore's ridiculous theories of "holy furor" and "the artist prey to the tyranny of the tragic (not individual) will." The judges decided that "a superman cannot be dealt with after the manner of ordinary mortals," reported the *New York Times*, "and that it would be a flagrant injustice to penalize a musical genius like Toscanini with even so much as the infliction of a fine." Fortunately, this is the only recorded case of physical violence in the history of Toscanini's often turbulent rehearsals. It is also the source of the false story that he once blinded one of his musicians.

5.

THE WAR'S CONCLUSION DID NOT PUT AN END TO UPHEAVALS, PERsonal or political. On 23 August 1919, the sixteen-year-old Giovannino Storchio, Toscanini's handicapped out-of-wedlock son, died. The maestro had gone secretly from time to time to visit Giovannino and Rosina at their home near Bergamo, but just how deeply the boy's death affected his father is not known. Then, in December, Luigi Illica died at the age of sixty-two. The librettist or colibrettist of operas by Puccini (*Manon Lescaut, La Bohème, Tosca, Madama Butterfly*), Catalani (*La Wally*), Giordano (*Andrea Chénier*), and others had been one of Toscanini's friends since the days when they had both tended the dying Catalani, and during the war Illica had written frequently to Toscanini on matters political as well as musico-theatrical. Toscanini attended Illica's funeral in Piacenza.

During the same period, postwar political and economic crises were making life difficult in Italy. By 1919, the traditional center-right governments of the five-time prime minister Giovanni Giolitti and his epigones were facing strenuous opposition from the left-wing Socialist Party and the centrist Catholic Popular Party, and the country was running amok: the lira had lost most of its prewar value, and unemployment was rampant among the millions of returning veterans, many of them infuriated by the government's inability to punish war profiteers.

Into the political breach stepped Benito Mussolini, ex-editor of *Avanti!*, the Socialist Party's newspaper; his enthusiasm for the war had caused his expulsion from the party, which had favored neutrality. In March 1919, the thirty-five-year-old propagandist—still a leftist firebrand—created a new party, which he called the Fasci Italiani di Combattimento (Italian Combat Groups), in reference and deference to the returning soldiers. Walter Toscanini, now a young veteran, brought the new formation to his father's attention, and together they attended some of the nascent party's semiclandestine meetings, probably in the early fall of that year. The maestro agreed with most of the principles of socialism but abhorred the Socialist Party for its unpatriotic (to his way of thinking) stand on the war. He was positively impressed by Mussolini's Bolshevik-like platform, which included, among many other radical objectives, the abolition of the monarchy and the proclamation of a republic; women's suffrage; the election of judges; international disarmament; the abolition of private banks and the closing of the stock exchange; the confiscation of unproductive capital, unoccupied houses, and ecclesiastical properties; land for the peasants; union participation in the management of industry and public services; an 80 percent tax on war profits; and the abolition of compulsory military service. Any honest discussion of Toscanini's initial support for Mussolini must begin with this platform, which was hailed by many future anti-Fascists.

A parliamentary election was to take place on 16 November 1919; Mussolini dithered as to whether or not his fledgling party ought to enter the fray, but at a meeting in a Milan gymnasium on 25 October, he quickly put together a slate that—according to Cesare Rossi, one of his leading supporters—was "made up of the first names that popped into his head." Toscanini's name "was included at the last moment, thanks to the insistence of Michelino Bianchi, who, as Secretary of the Orchestra Musicians' Union, [. . .] had deluded himself into believing that the name of the 'wizard of the baton' would guarantee [the musicians'] support." Rossi's testimony, which dates from 1960, is particularly significant because, as one of the people closest to Mussolini during the early years of the dictatorship—when Toscanini became an outspoken opponent of the regime—he had every reason to try to make Toscanini look like someone who had pursued political power through Mussolini, as Rossi himself had done. Instead, Rossi confirmed that Toscanini was "leaning on the parallel bars; [most of] those present hadn't noticed that he was there, and he was standing very still and very modestly, listening to some communications." His "designation as a candidate in the 'Fascist Block' happened unbeknownst to him." Rossi recalled Toscanini's "look of surprise when Bianchi, at the party's assembly, read the Maestro's name after that of Mussolini."

Marinetti—the very same Futurist leader who, only three years earlier, had said, "I compare conductors like Toscanini with prostitutes' vulvas," and who was now an ardent supporter of Mussolini—was present at the meeting and reported in his diary: "Laborious formation of the slate. Someone puts forward Toscanini. I greet the idea favorably. Voting[.] Mussolini abstains. I vote for Toscanini's candidacy. 4 in favor[,] 5 abstentions." Thereafter, Marinetti would always refer to Toscanini as "the illustrious conductor."

According to Rossi, when Bianchi "clearly pronounced the Maestro's name, the whole assemblage looked pleasantly shocked, and this was followed immediately by great acclamations; at that point [Toscanini] was surrounded by all 200 or 300 people, who were applauding. Toscanini, even more than the onlookers, was stupefied by this truly unanticipated designation, but he smiled, confused and pleased. Naturally," Rossi continued, the party's central committee "didn't expect any speech-making from so illustrious and so unusual a candidate. Toscanini would have scoffed at the idea, just as he would probably have scoffed at the idea of accepting the candidacy, had he been warned in advance; but, taken by surprise, he didn't feel able to react with a disdainful refusal."

At first, Toscanini did put up a mild protest: "My profession is that of a gypsy," he recalled telling Mussolini. "I travel all over. I can't be with you because I can't be in politics, because I can't stay put." But Marinetti put pressure on him to accept, after which Toscanini agreed to make the symbolic gesture, since everyone knew that at most only Mussolini, the first candidate on the list, could be elected. "Applause for Mussolini [and] for Toscanini," Marinetti reported. Toscanini signed a notarized document in which he declared that he had "all the prerequisites for eligibility indicated by the current electoral law" and that he accepted "the candidacy for the Milan area in the national elections that will take place on 16 November 1919 with the 'Fascist group.'"

Toscanini's name appeared sixth on the party's electoral list for Milan (Mussolini's was first, Marinetti's second), but the Fasci Italiani di Combattimento went down to an even more crushing defeat than the party's leaders had anticipated: they received just over 5,000 votes, in contrast to 170,000 for the Socialists. Not even Mussolini was elected; his political career was considered finished, whereas he had merely lost his taste for elections. Toscanini's unwanted political career was indeed finished, but he, like the other candidates, had pledged 30,000 lire toward the party's expenses, and, according to Cesare Rossi, he paid up without complaining. "He took it as a joke [. . .], saying: 'Of course, with a musician on the slate, there had to be a "resounding" defeat!'"

Toscanini could scarcely have imagined that within a short time Mussolini would make a U-turn from the extreme left to the extreme right, that his methods would change from persuasion to violence, and that many of his supporters would make the radical transition with him.

6.

NOTHING—NOT THE WAR, NOT THE ARMISTICE, NOT THE POSTWAR chaos, not politics, not musical activities or the lack thereof, and certainly not previous experience—could prevent Toscanini from becoming involved in another complicated erotic affair. In January 1918, on one of his concerts at the Milan Conservatory, he had conducted *Sortilegi*, a work for piano and orchestra by Riccardo Pick-Mangiagalli, a thirty-six-year-old, Milan-based Czech Italian composer, who also played the solo part. Toscanini gave the younger musician permission to attend all of his rehearsals, and Pick—as he was called—began to idolize Toscanini. "I felt that you were one of those blessed creatures whom an artist is fortunate to meet," Pick wrote to him in April of that year, and he felt that he had "vibrated in unison" with Toscanini.

Pick must have communicated his enthusiasm to his wife, Elsa, née Kurzbauer, a thirty-two-year-old native of Vienna, and he no doubt introduced her to his idol. Before long it was Elsa with whom Toscanini was "vibrating in unison." "*Sweetest* Elsa," begins Toscanini's first extant note (September 1918) to his new love. "My thoughts are saturated with you. I love you and I'm afraid of loving you. Why? And you, are you thinking of me? Do you love me? I give you a long kiss on the mouth. I hope to see you tomorrow." This message was in Italian, but he wrote subsequent letters to the multilingual Kurzbauer in English; perhaps her husband didn't speak the language. (Toscanini would have liked to have written to her in German, he said, "but to my shame I never endeavoured to succeed in learning your mother-tongue, sure of my failure.")

The affair went on for at least a year and a half, more likely for three years and possibly even for four, often with great logistical difficulties. Sometimes the lovers would meet in churches so that they could at least see each other and talk quietly, but clearly they did more than chat, and not in church. "Your kisses, your lips (oh! sweetness) your mouth inflame ever and evermore at the utmost my frenzy to have you under my libidinous caresses—kisses—suckings—lickings—bitings, all over your *girlisch* body," Toscanini wrote to Kurzbauer, probably in April 1920. His English was inconsistent, but his meanings were unmistakable. "I am dying and lusting for every part *nook—crevice—hole—holy hole* of *your lovely person.* [. . .] I will pass over all you like a river of fire! God! I am going crazy! I feel *something swelling and cooking*[.] Where is your hungry mouth, tongue—lips—hands? Where is that little doted spot of all raptures and deliriums?" In short, not much was left to Elsa's imagination.

Through all these months, Pick was unaware of what was happening. On 1 January 1920, Toscanini and a few other guests went to the Picks' home to audition Váša Příhoda, a nineteen-year-old Czech violinist who had gone to Italy to try to start a solo career but had ended up playing in a café orchestra in Milan; someone had told Toscanini about this gifted boy, and the maestro had arranged to have him give a private recital accompanied by his compatriot Pick.

Toscanini, impressed with what he heard, provided Příhoda with a warm recommendation that led within a few months to a major Italian and international career for the young violinist.

Not surprisingly, the Toscanini-Kurzbauer affair was eventually discovered. Years later, Toscanini speculated, in a letter to Elsa, that "we were tricked—betrayed—ignobly ambushed—Not knowing what had happened—we probably betrayed ourselves, too." Walfredo Toscanini, upon reading the letter many years later, commented that his grandfather had never completely grasped the fact that he was one of the most famous—thus also one of the most spied-upon and gossiped-about—figures in Italy. How could an affair like that have been kept secret?

Whether the lovers were actually caught in flagrante or were discovered by other means is not known. According to the most plausible version of the story's dénouement, Carla found out about the affair and informed Pick-Mangiagalli; the offended husband, unable to obtain a divorce in Italy, where divorce remained illegal until half a century later, applied for and received one in what was then the "free" city of Fiume. Elsa returned to Vienna, and the two lovers lost contact until 1933. Yet the maestro, in this case as in many others, separated the personal from the professional and artistic: he continued to perform Pick-Mangiagalli's music for several more years.

7.

ROME, PHYSICALLY UNTOUCHED BY THE WAR, BECKONED TO Toscanini for the first time since the dramatic anti-Wagner episode in 1916. In January 1920 he conducted five concerts in the capital; his programs incorporated several of the works that he had led for the first time in Milan two years earlier. He was to have gone to Prague, in the newly created Republic of Czechoslovakia, to conduct concerts and opera performances, but he came down with a severe influenza that left him debilitated for weeks; the engagement was canceled.

Four more Roman concerts in May were followed by six concerts at an international fair in Padua in June; these last were repeated in Ferrara at the invitation of none other than the town's former resident Giulio Gatti-Casazza, who had not seen Toscanini since 1916. In a letter to Otto Kahn, Gatti said that the events had taken place "with complete success and satisfaction of the Maestro," but that Toscanini had told him that "he now hates the theatre, the singers and scenic [i.e., stage] performances." Gatti also wrote to Edward Ziegler, his assistant at the Metropolitan, and expressed his impression that Toscanini's "character has remained the same as we knew it. Further, I have noticed in him a pessimism and a discouragement more accentuated than in the past. I attended his concerts and it is only justice to say that as an artist he is superior to any comparison."

Some of Toscanini's negative declarations about the theater were a defensive façade, put on to preempt any hard-to-resist invitations from Gatti to return to the Metropolitan. The previous fall, Milan's mayor, Emilio Caldara, one of the few Socialist Party exponents whom Toscanini respected, and the Liberal senator Luigi Albertini, editor of the *Corriere della Sera* and a man of great intelligence and broad culture, had begun to think about reopening La Scala, which had not had a regular season since 1916–17. Duke Uberto had given up the presidency of the theater, and no viable successor was forthcoming. Caldara, who, as a young firebrand in 1901, had strenuously opposed public funding for La Scala, had in the meantime come to the conclusion that a reorganized ensemble would be a boon to the entire city, and he and Albertini approached Toscanini.

Toscanini hesitated. The prospect of working at a theater run on the old impresario system or even on the newer managerial system, as it had evolved at La Scala since 1898 and at the Metropolitan since 1908, held no attraction for him. A new system was needed—a better artistic organization and a better method for financing the theater— and the realization of such a project would require forethought and commitment. Better to go step by step than to plunge into an incomplete project.

The three men discussed the matter at length and decided that step one might be the formation of a first-rate orchestra that would accumulate experience as an ensemble through an extended concert tour, first in Italy and then in North America, before it settled into La Scala's pit. The tour would also be a gesture of thanks to the United States for its part in the war effort and a demonstration abroad of Italy's artistic prowess. In October 1919, nine months before Gatti's above-cited messages to Kahn and Ziegler, Kahn had received a cablegram from an agent in Milan, offering the "Toscanini La Scala Orchestra" for an American tour of "three months or more" and an "unlimited number [of] concerts beginning January 15th, 1920," at a cost of $11,500 per week, including all fees and ancillary expenses, plus $30,000 for round-trip steamship transportation. Kahn's "interest and support will be greatly appreciated," the message said. But Kahn replied that it was too late to consider such a tour until the following season.

Caldara, Albertini, and Toscanini realized that the suggested postponement made sense: it would give them time to formulate more complete plans not only for the orchestra but also for La Scala as a whole. Over the following eight months they worked together on the project, and on 11 July 1920 the *Corriere* announced that thirty subscribers had jointly contributed six million lire toward the ten million or more needed for the modernization of the theater itself and the purchase of the house's boxes from their current owners, in order to make La Scala an independent body. None of the subscribers would retain any governing rights or privileges. "But now, the man, or rather, the artist-man, is needed," the article continued. "On this issue, the donors and public opinion are in perfect agreement: that person can only be Arturo Toscanini."

Four days later, a newly created executive committee—presided over by Caldara, and with a membership that included, among its better-known members, the socialist journalist Claudio Treves, the conservative businessman and politician Senatore Borletti, and the liberal journalist and entrepreneur Eugenio Balzan—nominated Toscanini plenipotentiary artistic director of La Scala. Angelo Scandiani, a former engineer for the Italian Edison Company and a fine bass who had sung the role of Gurnemanz in Toscanini's 1903 concert performances of *Parsifal* excerpts at La Scala, was named administrative director of the ensemble. Toscanini had not yet committed himself to conducting an actual opera season; his job, for the time being, was to advise the board on matters regarding the physical, financial, and artistic renovation of the theater and to create, prepare, and conduct its orchestra. He told Gatti-Casazza that his acceptance of these tasks meant only that he wished "to render a service to a great national institution." But the Scala project and the idea of the

Italian American tour galvanized him, and the pessimism and discouragement that Gatti had noted in him were shed in an instant.

The deciding factor was almost certainly the Americans' willingness to sponsor the new orchestra's tour; this came about thanks to the combined efforts of Ugo Ara (former violist of the famed Flonzaley Quartet, and a friend whom Toscanini later described as "a dear person"); the American banker André de Coppet; the Italian foreign minister, Count Carlo Sforza; the Italian ambassador to the United States, Baron Romano Avezzano; and the concert agent Loudon Charlton: they jointly persuaded a dozen patrons of the arts to guarantee the tour to a maximum of $250,000. Contracts were signed by all parties in May 1920. The orchestra's sea voyages from Italy to America and back would be paid for by the Italian government, and the musicians would receive diplomatic passports that would exonerate them from paying US income taxes. By 3 June 1920, American newspapers were able to announce that Toscanini and the Scala orchestra would tour the United States for ten weeks, beginning the following January.

The Metropolitan was also involved in the project, and shortly after the announcement was made, Ziegler informed Kahn that the total expenses would actually not exceed $180,000 and that there ought to be no trouble in raising that amount. Later, there were rumors that Kahn had profited from the orchestra's tour and that this had made Toscanini furious. Through the 1920s, however, and until Kahn's death in 1934, Toscanini often saw Kahn, and in recorded conversations he mentioned only Kahn's generosity. Given Toscanini's vehement reactions to opportunism and cheating and his unforgiving nature—not to mention his outstanding memory—the rumors must be considered unfounded.

Within days of his nomination as La Scala's plenipotentiary director, Toscanini was able to write to Carla, who was vacationing in the mountains, that Giuseppe Toeplitz, managing director of the Banca Commerciale Italiana, one of Italy's leading financial institutions, was seriously considering making a major contribution to the theater. He approached the task of forming the orchestra "with some misgivings," he later admitted. "It seemed that in Italy, which was in greater upheaval than ever in those days, it would have been impossible to put together an orchestral phalanx of ample proportions and made up of hand-picked members gathered from all over, to achieve solid discipline and a flexible, mobile organization." But he proceeded, attending to every detail in the attempt to create a high-quality symphonic body. For instance: during his years in New York, Toscanini had been impressed by the superiority of some American brass instruments over their Italian counterparts, and he now worked with various Italian players and local craftsmen to make improvements in domestic horns and trombones. As La Scala's legal status had not yet been completely formulated, the new ensemble was initially called the Orchestra Arturo Toscanini and financed by a society nominally headed by Carla Toscanini but in fact run by concert agencies and overseen by the nascent Scala administration. Not later than mid-September 1920, Toscanini had begun rehearsing his new, ninety-eight member orchestra in a substantial repertoire: thirty-one pieces by twenty composers. The often fraught sessions took place at the Milan Conservatory: La Scala's renovations were already underway.

Nuccio Fiorda, a young composer-conductor whom Toscanini had engaged as a musical assistant and extra percussion player, recounted that during a rehearsal of the most delicate part of Debussy's *Ibéria*, the sound of someone striking a match was heard. Toscanini stopped the orchestra "and started one of his well-known 'crescendos,'" exclaiming that although he didn't believe in religion, "'when I go into a church I take off my hat and make the sign of the cross. Who is the rascal who dares to smoke while I'm rehearsing?!?'" When no one responded, Toscanini walked out and threatened to cancel the entire tour unless the culprit confessed. The following day, a committee of orchestra players barged in on Toscanini at his home and told him the truth: the match had been struck by Walter Toscanini, who had been sitting in the balcony over the orchestra and had lit a cigarette on his way out. "Toscanini, after a moment of almost mysterious silence, said softly: 'I've always had little respect for men who wear monocles or gaiters—my son wears both.'" The rehearsals were resumed and the tour was saved.

What Fiorda did not know was that just at that moment Toscanini's twenty-two-year-old son was the source of more serious worries. In August, someone close to Walter had informed the maestro that his son was using cocaine. Arturo wrote immediately to Carla, say-

ing that for months he had been upset over their son's "half-extin-
guished, almost glassy gaze, the somnolence that very often seems
to take hold of him," but had attributed the condition to *amatory
overwork*," which "nature would have overcome and remedied later
on." Now, however, he had been "assured" that Walter "sniffs cocaine
very frequently." Toscanini suspected that Walter's "companion in
this misadventure" was Leopoldo Polo, the youngest of Enrico and
Ida's three children, who did indeed have an addiction problem and
who would die young. Walter, on the other hand, successfully kicked
the habit—if indeed the story communicated to his father was correct. The worry, in any case, was real, and it came at an already difficult moment: Toscanini was mourning Grubicy's recent death,
trying to keep his affair with Elsa Kurzbauer under wraps, disturbed
about his mother's health (the eighty-year-old Paola had been diag-
nosed with a cystic fibroma in her uterus, but she survived), and
upset over the ongoing existential and economic problems of Ada,
his only surviving sister.*

Regarding Toscanini's relations with his children during their
young adulthood, Wally commented that she was the only one who
confronted her father and argued with him if she disagreed with
him. "Wanda was very reserved, and Walter feared him," she said.
"He was never blinded by paternal love. He judged us and loved all
of us equally. I was closest to him. [. . .] Sure, we disappointed him.
Walter, educated or not educated by our mother, was the opposite of
what he would have wished." But that was before Walter found his
way—a difficult, sometimes impossible, process for the children of
famous people—and long before Walter became his aged father's
most trusted helper. Toscanini probably felt more at ease with Wally
than with Walter or Wanda, but Wally's lack of concentration sometimes irritated him. What the three children learned most from their
father, according to Wally, was "contempt for materialism." This
was true, but only to an extent: after all, they grew up without hav-

---

* Ada had married a Signor Riva but seems to have been permanently unhappy and to
have done something that made her brother refuse to have contact with her, although,
through Carla, he continued to support her. In 1922, at the age of forty-six, she
unsuccessfully attempted suicide in a Milan bar. In 1934, she was treated for cancer and
wrote to Toscanini to beg his forgiveness—for what, we do not know—but she survived
that illness, too.

ing to worry about money and lived well most of their lives. Walter eventually became responsible about money; Wally, however *simpatica*, had no economic sense whatsoever, as she freely admitted; and Wanda, in later years, was notoriously avaricious.

8.

ONLY AFTER MORE THAN A MONTH OF STRENUOUS REHEARSALS DID Toscanini deem his new orchestra ready to perform in public. The ensemble's first four concerts took place at the Milan Conservatory in late October and early November 1920; programs comprised classics (Vivaldi, Manfredini, Mozart, Beethoven, Rossini, Wagner, Verdi, and Brahms), music by Toscanini's contemporaries (Debussy, Strauss, Elgar, Sinigaglia, and Albert Roussel), and works by conservative representatives of the younger generation: the Swiss Ernest Bloch and the Italians Respighi, Ildebrando Pizzetti, Vincenzo Tommasini, and Adriano Lualdi. All four programs were repeated in mid-November, at popular prices, as part of an initiative by the Humanitarian Society. An article by the *Corriere della Sera*'s chief music critic, Gaetano Cesari, gave voice to what must also have been Toscanini's fondest hopes: the admirable orchestra, Cesari said, had been "entrusted with the task of revivifying, wherever it goes, faith in the fate of Italian art, and of holding high, abroad, the prestige of our musical energies."

Following the first Milan concerts, Toscanini and his troupe initiated what must still hold the record as the longest and most exhausting tour ever undertaken by a major orchestra—a tour that would not end until nearly eight months later, and that began with one or two performances each in twenty-one Italian cities, from Como in the north to Naples in the south, including the contested city of Fiume.

The Fiume concert was a political statement as well as a musical event. A year earlier, Gabriele D'Annunzio—who had enthusiastically participated as an air ace in the war effort and had lost the use of one eye during a flying accident—had led 2,600 irregular troops into the town, which had been part of the Austro-Hungarian Empire. The Treaty of Versailles declared Fiume to be a supranational city-state, but because the majority of the mixed Austro-Slavic-Italian population spoke a dialect related to Venetian, many Italians believed that Fiume belonged by right to Italy, as part of its war spoils. The Italian government had renounced its initial claim to the territory, but D'Annunzio, for reasons both patriotic and egocentric, decided to take matters into his own hands. In the charter that the poet, who dubbed himself *Comandante*, excogitated for his little realm, music was declared a "religious and social institution"; this fact plus disappointment over what many Italians referred to as the "mutilated victory" of the world war caused Toscanini to accept D'Annunzio's invitation to bring the orchestra to the occupied town. "The City of life awaits this sign from the man of life," D'Annunzio wrote to the conductor on 20 October 1920. And exactly one month later the ensemble arrived at Fiume's railroad station, greeted by the *Comandante* and a band playing patriotic anthems.

Like Byron in his Greek campaign a century earlier, D'Annunzio was as interested in the trappings of military glory as in the mission itself. He had arranged a banquet on the evening of the musicians' arrival and another the following evening, after a lengthy, enthusiastically received concert by the orchestra and Toscanini in the Italianate town's jam-packed Teatro Verdi. Various medals and ribbons were distributed, and D'Annunzio made fulsome toasts and magniloquent speeches in honor of what he called the Orphic Legion and its conductor, the Symphoniac. D'Annunzio also organized an onsite view of military maneuvers, complete with a battle-cry ("Eja, eja, eja, alalà") that he had fashioned out of an ancient Greek antecedent and that was later adopted by Mussolini. During the maneuvers, several soldiers were seriously wounded and one musician was slightly injured by shrapnel—as was Toscanini's hat. A month after the orchestra's departure, the *Comandante* and his troops would be routed by the Italian army, after Italy agreed to abide by the Treaty of Versailles. Fiume later became part of Yugoslavia and is now part of the Republic of Croatia; most of its Italian population is gone, and its name, in Croatian, is Rijeka.

In Naples on 30 November, Toscanini, Scandiani, and the orchestra boarded the Italian steamship *Presidente Wilson*. Two days later, when the ship docked briefly at Algiers, Toscanini wrote to Carla that his musicians were not suffering from the voyage—"not even

Serafin,* who has a lifelong subscription ticket to seasickness." But after the ship entered the Atlantic the seas became rougher, and Toscanini—who evidently shared the commonly held belief that certain fortified wines and liqueurs alleviate seasickness—had the bottles of *vin santo* that D'Annunzio had given him distributed to those men who were suffering from *mal di mare*. Toscanini himself, however, "didn't seem to suffer from anything," according to the orchestra violinist Ermanno Marchesi. During stormy weather, the maestro "would stay on the deck to enjoy the spectacle with the greatest enthusiasm. Throughout the crossing, the Maestro buoyed everyone up with his vitality."

On 14 December 1920, the *New York Times* announced that Toscanini and his orchestra had "arrived here yesterday," met at the pier by Gatti-Casazza and Alda, and that "the orchestra will give fifty-four concerts in ten weeks, commencing Dec. 28 at the Metropolitan Opera House. [. . .] Toscanini said that they had not come to make money, but to keep up friendly relations between Italy and the United States. In addition to the three concerts at the Metropolitan Opera House, the conductor said that an extra concert would be given at Carnegie Hall on Jan. 3 in aid of the Italian Welfare League."†

The musicians were feted at a banquet hosted by the local Italian American community and were then allowed two free days in New York. On 16 December they journeyed to Camden, New Jersey, where, over the following six days, they made a series of recordings for the Victor Talking Machine Company. Until then, Toscanini had resisted invitations to record, however lucrative his royalties might have been, but on this occasion he had had to agree to the proposal: Victor's payment of a $40,000 advance against royalties helped to finance the tour.

"The orchestra, reduced to its bare essentials, was stuffed and squashed into an enormous wooden niche," Fiorda recalled. "The agreement with the Victor Company stated that no record could be

---

* The orchestra's principal oboe, Leandro Serafin, younger brother of the conductor Tullio Serafin, was the best-known Italian oboist of his generation.

† The league had recently been founded by Lionello Perera, an Italian-born banker, and his wife, Carolyn; its aim was to assist impoverished immigrants. In later years, Toscanini continued to help the league, and he remained friendly with the Perera family.

marketed without the maestro's approval. The 'wax recording' technique did not allow for direct playback from the wax of a recorded piece of music; this would cause it to be destroyed irremediably. Consequently, once listened to, it was necessary to redo the whole thing! But unfortunately this 'redoing' happened rather frequently, given the maestro's dissatisfaction. One day the establishment's director said, 'If Toscanini comes back again, the company will go bankrupt!'" Many years later, Walter Toscanini asked his father how many players were used for the recordings. "Just a few," the maestro replied. The others "didn't fit. Only the first violin played into the [recording] horn; all the others were spread around. There weren't any double basses"—the tuba played the basses' line because the recording horn could not pick up the basses' frequencies. "But I was desperate because everyone played fortissimo," Toscanini recalled. "I said to myself, 'What do I do? What coloring can you do?' [. . .] I wanted to run away."

Nearly a week of arduous work yielded recordings of the third and fourth movements of the Mozart Symphony no. 39, Respighi's orchestration of a dance by Vincenzo Galilei, an excerpt from Pizzetti's La Pisanella, the "Rákóczy" March from Berlioz's Damnation de Faust, the Prelude to Act IV of Carmen, and the finale of Beethoven's Fifth Symphony—about thirty minutes of music in all. ("The Star-Spangled Banner" and the Overture to The Barber of Seville were also recorded but rejected, and the matrices were destroyed.) The sound quality is appalling by later standards, but the performances give at least a vague idea of Toscanini's approach, at the time, to tempi, phrasing, and articulation in the pieces in question.

Apart from the unpleasantness of the actual recording sessions, the stay in Philadelphia—across the Delaware River from Camden—provided the musicians with a chance to recover from the long ocean voyage and to gather strength for the long tour that stretched before them. Many of them enjoyed listening to an African American jazz trio that played at their hotel in the evenings, and Fiorda recalled that Toscanini was particularly delighted by a drummer who threw his sticks into the air and caught them behind his back. The Italians journeyed back to New York on Christmas Eve and were guests of the Metropolitan at that evening's performance of Halévy's La Juive, with Caruso and the young soprano Rosa Ponselle in the lead roles. This proved to be Caruso's last performance on any stage: the already ailing tenor died the following August, at the age of forty-eight.

Expectations were high for the Italians' debut concert. In *Musical Courier*, Guido M. Gatti, a young music critic who was becoming a key figure in the rejuvenation of Italian musical life, reported that even when the new orchestra was still in the planning stages, Toscanini had relished "the thought of the possible fulfillment of his dream—a vision of instrumentalists of the first rank, not only precise and reliable executants" but also as true artists who would bring "all their intelligence and all their enthusiasm" to their work. "That orchestra [. . .] has been formed from among the best and, at the same time, the youngest of Italy's instrumentalists." But the article's author, like most other Europeans of the day, did not know that the best American orchestras, with their fine discipline and their composite membership of excellent musicians from various cultures, were technically better than any of those that the Old World had to offer. Toscanini's new orchestra was no match for the domestic competition: even Richard Aldrich, who so greatly admired Toscanini, had to admit as much when he reviewed the first concert, which took place on 28 December before an audience that included such distinguished musicians as Rachmaninoff, Fritz Kreisler, Efrem Zimbalist, Mischa Elman, the Flonzaley Quartet, Eva and Luisa Tetrazzini, Frances Alda, and Margarete Matzenauer. "There was a tumult of welcome last evening for Arturo Toscanini when he appeared at the Metropolitan Opera House for the first time since he left it at the close of the operatic season of 1914–15," Aldrich wrote in the *Times*. He continued,

The welcome was given in applause and cheers by an audience that filled the Opera House to its utmost capacity behind the railings as well as in every seat on floor and galleries and in the boxes. [. . .] But the quality of the orchestra did not add much to the distinction of the occasion. [. . .] The strings seemed to lack not only brilliancy but amplitude and solidity. Nor were there unusual excellences at once apparent in most of the wood, wind [*sic*] and brass, though there were passages in which they did themselves credit.

Aldrich found the orchestra inadequate in Debussy's *Ibéria* and Respighi's *Fountains of Rome*, and he questioned Toscanini's great "freedom of tempo" in Beethoven's Fifth Symphony, "in the first movement especially; but the tempo was in part of a deliberateness that seemed alien to the character of the music; a tempo that weighed uncomfortably upon the effect." His comment jibes with Fiorda's description of Toscanini's treatment, at the time, of the Fifth Symphony's famous opening four-note motif in bars 1 and 2 and its various repetitions: Toscanini had his musicians accentuate each note, then take a quicker tempo for the body of the movement. Asked to comment on the matter, Fritz Kreisler said, "I don't believe Toscanini is wrong: but even if he were, I should rather hear it wrongly played by Toscanini than correctly by anyone else."

"At first, the press was a bit reserved, also because every big American city has its own orchestra," Toscanini told an Italian journalist after the tour had ended, "but later the general tone reached a higher, more ardent register."

"Ardent" may have been an exaggeration, but reactions did improve. The second New York concert, presented in aid of the Italian Welfare League, took place on 3 January 1921 at Carnegie Hall—Toscanini's debut in that venue—and it provided a much better acoustical environment for a symphonic ensemble than the Metropolitan Opera House could do. "The subtleties of Mr. Toscanini's nuances [. . .] were correspondingly more appreciable and more enjoyable," Aldrich wrote. Following the orchestra's Boston debut on 7 January, the *Daily Globe*'s unnamed critic described the ensemble as "second rate" but reported that the "large audience was stirred to almost unprecedented enthusiasm by Toscanini's individual and eloquent reading of classic and modern numbers."

A month into the Italians' tour, an unnamed critic in *Musical America* observed that the orchestra was simply different from American orchestras. "The strings have less sonority and greater purity, the winds are less delicate, the brass more vigorous. But it is wondrously homogeneous." And in another issue of the same magazine: "We have Toscanini back with us, the greatest maestro of his time, unquestionably the most distinguished conductor we have, and so we shall acclaim him, support him, and rejoice that he is with us again."

Most musicians who had rarely or never observed Toscanini before expressed unqualified admiration. A few seconded Artur Bodanzky, who was now in charge of German repertoire at the Metropolitan, and who described Toscanini as "simply the conductor's conductor." The thirty-eight-year-old Leopold Stokowski, music director of the Philadelphia Orchestra, said that he had been offered a free ticket to a performance but had insisted on paying because "everyone must pay to learn something." The Swiss composer Ernest Bloch was "astonished" when he "saw this little man come forward, with a sad air about him, seeming ill at ease before the crowd and with none of that repugnant obsequiousness of virtuosi who seek to flatter the public." A dissenting voice was that of the seventy-five-year-old violinist and pedagogue Leopold Auer, who had taught Jascha Heifetz, Mischa Elman, Nathan Milstein, and Efrem Zimbalist, among others. "I had not previously heard Signor Toscanini conduct the Wagnerian scores, and was unable to share the enthusiasm he roused here when he arrived with his Milan orchestra," he wrote in his memoirs. "He impressed me as rather pretentious, and his organization seemed to be inferior to the New York orchestras. His exaggerated conception of nuances was particularly distressing, inasmuch as he continually swayed from raging fortissimos to almost inaudible pianissimos. And although his reading of the 'Vorspiel und Liebestod' [Prelude and Love-Death from *Tristan*] was excellent, his accelerated tempos in the prelude to the 'Meistersinger' completely destroyed its solemn and pompous character. It was not in such fashion that I had heard Wagner's works conducted by Hans Richter, Felix Mottl, Gustav Mahler, and Arthur Nikisch."*

Just as Aldrich had implicitly disapproved of Toscanini's excessive tempo alterations in Beethoven's Fifth Symphony, so Auer, a German-school musician through and through, was criticizing Toscanini for excessive expressivity in other repertoire. Likewise, the *Boston Daily Globe*'s unnamed critic (presumably Olin Downes), who often expressed great admiration for Karl Muck, commented—

---

* According to the performance historian Christopher Dyment, "Wagner himself took eight minutes" for the *Meistersinger* Prelude, "as did Muck and Weingartner; Toscanini took nine minutes and was compared with Richter by Ferruccio Bonavia, who had played under the latter." Mottl took slower tempi in the piece. See also the letter from Richter's daughter, Maria Loeb, to Toscanini, cited in chapter 9.

approvingly, in this case—that Toscanini took more liberties than was customary in the works of Mozart, Beethoven, Wagner, and Debussy. Such observations, positive and negative, will surprise those who are familiar only with later criticisms of Toscanini's interpretations as insufficiently expressive and excessively rigid and fast.

The most telling comment, however, was offered by the Boston Symphony Orchestra's outstanding conductor Pierre Monteux, who had observed most of the significant conductors of all nationalities from the late 1880s onward, and who, in the immediate prewar years, had conducted the world premieres of Ravel's *Daphnis et Chloé* and Stravinsky's *Petrushka* and *The Rite of Spring*. "I had never seen the Maestro conduct until he came to America with his orchestra from Milan," Monteux wrote three years later. "My impression was that everything I had heard on the subject was very pale in comparison with the reality! I had before me, simply, a man of genius, a conductor such as I had never seen in my life, a true revelation in the art of conducting and interpretation. What is more, I feel that anything I could write would be unable to communicate my admiration for this great Master, who, in my opinion, is not only 'your' [i.e., the Italians'] greatest Maestro but 'the greatest of all.'"

THE ENTIRE NEW YORK SYMPHONY ORCHESTRA, headed by its conductor, Walter Damrosch, and its patron, Harry Harkness Flagler, honored Toscanini and his musicians with a reception at Enrico & Giolito's Italian restaurant after their New York debut concert, and Toscanini wired Damrosch the next day to thank him and his musicians for their "never to be forgotten brotherly reception." Intermittently throughout the tour the orchestra returned to New York for concerts at the Metropolitan (three, in all), Carnegie Hall (two), the Hippodrome (two), and the Brooklyn Academy of Music (one). In between, they traveled as far north, within the United States, as Portland, Maine; as far south as Richmond, Virginia; and as far west as Wichita, Kansas, and Tulsa, Oklahoma. They also performed in three Canadian cities: Montreal, Toronto, and Quebec City. Boston, Washington, Philadelphia, Providence, Chicago, and Montreal received two or more visits each, and in several of the other cities, as well, two or more concerts were given. In Washington, Edith Galt

Wilson, wife of an ailing President Woodrow Wilson, attended one of the orchestra's concerts. Altogether, the orchestra gave fifty-nine concerts in forty cities in twenty states plus the District of Columbia and two Canadian provinces.

Toscanini had steeled himself for the far from ideal conditions under which the orchestra had to rehearse and perform, since many of the venues had been chosen for their seating capacity rather than their acoustical properties; in addition to concert halls and opera houses, the sites included "circuses, Masonic lodges, warehouse entrance halls, cinemas, etc.," said Fiorda. "You can imagine the annoyances and worries in arranging the [players'] seating and putting everything in order before the Maestro arrived to rehearse the venue's acoustics and coordinate the program to be performed. [. . .] In one city in Canada the concert began at eleven in the evening, after the [movie] audience had cleared out of the hall." In Chicago, the orchestra played in the 10,000-seat Convention Hall, under what must have been horrendous acoustical conditions. One concert in New York's Hippodrome—"a huge theater built specifically for circus entertainments," Fiorda recalled—took place without the orchestra's third trombonist, who had been arrested for molesting a young woman in a city park. Gatti-Casazza and the Italian consul general had to intervene and pay a fine to get the man out of jail. "It's always the same thing with these Italians!" Toscanini shouted.

A valet traveled with Toscanini, who, however, was long acquainted with the hardships of travel and generally put up with them uncomplainingly. The maestro's only standing request was to have an apple waiting for him during each concert's intermission, so that he could quench his thirst. Aboard the special, sleeper-car-equipped train, Toscanini observed and at times participated in the musicians' teasing and practical jokes. Between the orchestra's two concerts in Buffalo, he and a few of his musicians visited Niagara Falls, and the maestro insisted on going up in a flimsy, shuddering biplane—his first known airplane flight—that allowed tourists to view the natural phenomenon from above; he even cajoled a reluctant Ermanno Marchesi to accompany him.

There were a few monumental outbursts at rehearsals, but Marchesi remembered above all "how much humanity there was in his behavior! And how he helped us!" In New York, "I had my eyes taken care of by his personal doctor and spent some time in a clinic, again for my vision; another [musician] had an appendicitis operation, and all at [Toscanini's] expense. And as long as the tour lasted he didn't fire anyone from the orchestra, even those who were unsatisfactory. He put up with the mistakes and kept quiet. Maybe he would ruffle up like a cat and sneer, but he wouldn't throw out the guilty party: he knew only too well what it meant to earn one's daily bread."

Scandiani left the tour at the end of January to return to Milan and deal with the Scala project. "Lucky man!" Toscanini commented, in a letter to Carla. "This is a great loss for me, because in addition to being pleasant company he has spared me many troubles." He had begun to realize, he said, that he had "taken on a responsibility, also toward myself, that's too great and too long-lasting. When will the end of June come? And what will my nerves be like? I'm more and more convinced that it would be madness to tie myself to La Scala for a long time." But he had "also enjoyed much satisfaction"—not least because the Americans were trying to persuade him to stay. "In Boston they again asked me, through the Consul General, to become Conductor of the Symphony." The invitation was turned down. "Yesterday, during a private encounter with Madame Kahn, I was invited to return to the Metropolitan for at least six or seven weeks. Naturally, I replied that conditions at the Metropolitan have worsened rather than improved since I was here and that I thought my coming back would be useless and perhaps downright harmful, because it would disrupt everyone's peace and quiet. At that point, Mrs. Kahn made me promise at least that if the [New York] Philharmonic orchestra is reorganized at the end of this season, I won't deny her the pleasure and honor of announcing to the public that I would accept to come for *a few weeks, when I please,* as *guest conductor.* I accepted but put off a final acceptance until I've arranged my situation at La Scala."*

In March 1921, the orchestra returned twice to Camden: from the eighth to the twelfth they recorded short pieces by Mendelssohn, Wolf-Ferrari, and Bizet, and from the twenty-ninth to the thirty-

---

* This was comparable to a statement attributed to Serge Koussevitzky: when invited to conduct a concert that he did not want to conduct, the Russian maestro reportedly telegraphed, "I accept with pleasure, but don't count on me."

first—following the final (Canadian) concerts—they committed to master discs the finale of Beethoven's First Symphony, and pieces by Donizetti and Massenet. Attempts to remake the *Barber of Seville* Overture, which had failed three months earlier, and to record the Prelude to *La Traviata*, were unsuccessful, and the matrices were destroyed. As in December, so in March: many hours of work yielded only half an hour of publishable recordings. All of the approved material from the combined sessions was eventually released on single- or double-sided ten- or twelve-inch seventy-eight rpm discs, and later reissued on long-playing records and compact discs. But "after this disastrous trial, the Maestro swore never to make another record," according to the violinist Enrico Minetti.

Notwithstanding the critics' qualms about the orchestra, the tour was so successful that it had to be extended to sixteen weeks from the ten originally planned, and it brought in a gross sum of $300,000. Toscanini himself was unusually happy with the tour, for its musical virtues but also as a propaganda vehicle for Italy at a time when the country appeared to be descending into political and economic anarchy. "Excepting some inconveniences having to do with travel, disembarking, and organization, nothing serious occurred to disturb our vertiginous rush—and that's the right term—across the States," he declared afterward. "Belief in what we were doing, stamina, and ardor aided us from the first concert to the last." There had been some complaints about the length of his programs, he said, but the concerts were listened to "attentively and calmly." Although some lighter repertoire was performed in smaller towns, where audiences were unaccustomed to symphony concerts, "the average cosmopolitan mentality in America seems not at all inferior to that of European cities," he said. "What was extremely heartwarming for me was the reception given to the most recent Italian music." He was gratified that "the best-known figures in politics, the arts, industry, and finance outdid each other in paying homage to Italy."

Toscanini and his orchestra boarded the *Argentina* in New York on 2 April 1921. "More than 2,000 persons, mostly Italians, assembled at the pier," *Musical America* reported. "Several hundred of them managed to get on the boat to bid a personal farewell to the conductor. A tug, the Mexpet, accompanied the ship a way and a band played the Italian national anthem. In response, Mr. Toscanini assembled his men and they played the 'Star-Spangled Banner' as the ship steamed out."

The exhausted musicians must have been relieved to learn that a proposed stop in England, to give four London concerts on four successive evenings, did not materialize. When the orchestra disembarked in Naples, Toscanini was met at the pier by Carla with Walter, now twenty-three; Wally, twenty-one; and Wanda, thirteen. In his room at the Hôtel Londres, the maestro—looking fresh, wearing a camellia in his buttonhole, and surrounded by his family—greeted members of the press and commented freely and proudly on the tour. But even before the musicians had regained their land legs, the marathon resumed, with two concerts at Naples's Teatro San Carlo.* Then it was onward to Rome—where Toscanini again spoke with journalists—and beyond: thirty-six concerts in nineteen Italian cities between 20 April and 16 June, with a two-week break in May.

BEFORE THE SCALA ORCHESTRA LEFT NEW YORK, the music critic W. J. Henderson had written that Toscanini ought to be kept in America at any price and on any condition, and, if necessary, kidnapped and prevented from leaving the country. But by the time the orchestra returned to Milan, to give the last performance of its eight-month, 127-concert tour, the maestro was laying the groundwork for the first season of a revivified La Scala. The crowning years of his life in the theater were about to begin.

---

* Toscanini also visited the studio of the Neapolitan sculptor Vincenzo Gemito, then in his late sixties, and bought one of the artist's own copies of his well-known bust of Verdi, made in 1873 when the composer was preparing the local premiere of *Aida*.

Playbill for the performance of
Verdi's Falstaff that opened the
newly reorganized La Scala's first
season, on 26 December 1921.

—

VII

LA SCALA
RE-CREATED

—

THE TEATRO ALLA SCALA OPENED ITS DOORS ON THE EVENING
of 26 December 1921, more than four years after the end of the house's
previous regular opera season. Gaetano Cesari, the *Corriere della
Sera*'s principal music critic, described the occasion—a performance
of Verdi's *Falstaff*—as a solemn yet joyful one; a ceremony and a
great musical-theatrical performance; an opportunity to observe
how the theater had been simultaneously resuscitated and rejuvenated; and a profoundly moving and artistically unforgettable experience. Many people also hoped that it would be seen as a harbinger
of Italy's ability to extract itself from postwar chaos. But that glorious evening was preceded by many months of intense preparations:
an institution that had ceased to exist as anything but a venerable
historic building had had to be re-created.

The previous spring, at the end of the long North American tour,
Toscanini had met with Emilio Caldara and Luigi Albertini, his principal interlocutors, to take stock of the ensemble's situation. Caldara
had relinquished the mayoralty to a fellow Socialist, but he remained
the most prominent member of the city council and would soon be
elected to parliament; and Albertini's *Corriere della Sera* had promoted the city council's successful campaign for donations to pay for
the renovation of La Scala's stage. On 1 May 1921, Toscanini partici-

pated in a meeting of the entire board of directors, and concrete plans for the forthcoming season were established.

Exactly a century earlier, in 1821, Angelo Petracchi, a former Scala administrator, had published a treatise, *On the Regulation of Public Theaters*, in which he suggested that governments subsidize theaters because "the promotion of industry and culture are the principal sources of public prosperity." Major opera houses attracted large numbers of monied people to the city, Petracchi reasoned, and caused many local residents as well to spend on fine clothes, expensive dinners, and carriages; thus governments would do well to view subsidization as an investment that would be recouped many times over. In Petracchi's day, some of La Scala's funding did indeed come from the crown in Vienna—Milan was then under Austrian rule—but the impresario system remained in force until 1898, after which a society of hereditary boxholders guaranteed the theater's solvency, sometimes with the city government's assistance. Duke Uberto Visconti di Modrone's decision, in 1916, to entrust La Scala to an impresario was a backward step, and the theater closed after only one season.

Now, in 1920 and 1921, the Albertini-Caldara-Toscanini troika devised a revolutionary new system—revolutionary not only for Milan and Italy but for theaters all over Europe. La Scala was reconstituted as an *ente autonomo* (autonomous society), although the mayor of Milan would automatically serve as president of its board of directors—a deft move that made La Scala's survival a matter of civic pride. The theater's operations were to be financed by a combination of subscription and single-ticket sales, donations (some thirty businesses and individuals made initial gifts of a total of 6,200,000 lire), a small annual municipal grant of 350,000 lire, and a 2 percent surtax on the admission prices of all the other theaters and all the cinemas, sports venues, and other places of public entertainment in Milan and its *provincia*. The old societies of boxholders and shareholders were dissolved, and the seats in La Scala's 155 boxes, like those on the ground floor and in the galleries, were made available to the general public. Each boxholder received a liquidation payment and was given a nine-year option to retain the family box, not through ownership but through subscription at the rate established for the general public; during that period the boxholders also received nominal interest payments on their expropriated property.*

As early as the summer of 1920, the Scala board sent Cesare Albertini, the engineer who had designed the house's first orchestra pit thirteen years earlier, on a tour of the most advanced theaters in Europe, and upon his return to Milan, he again performed surgery on the house. The roof over the stage was raised twenty-three feet; the pit was enlarged and put on a hydraulic lift, so that the orchestra could be raised or lowered in accordance with the acoustical exigencies of any given score; a new dome was installed to house an up-to-date lighting system invented by Mariano Fortuny, who had created the prior system twenty years earlier; and the forestage (proscenium) was shortened from approximately twenty-three feet to ten feet. This last operation was a necessary evil, Toscanini said many years later: in earlier times, singers had often sung on the forestage itself, near the footlights, but this wasn't feasible "with modern operas, in which a singer has to stand elsewhere," sometimes far behind the point at which the curtain comes down. The old system had placed the nearest singers fifty feet—an impossible distance—from the conductor; the shortened forestage plus the placing of much of the orchestra pit under the stage greatly improved the lines of communication between conductor and singers and the balance between singers and orchestra, although many singers were unhappy about being placed farther from the audience; and the alteration allowed three rows of seats to be added at the front of the main floor, bringing the downstairs capacity to eight hundred. Unfortunately, La Scala's acoustics, which had been "marvelous," were "lost, absolutely," Toscanini said.†

Toscanini had not initially committed himself to conducting an opera season; his job, as plenipotentiary director, was to advise the board on the artistic, physical, and financial renovation of the theater and to create and train the house orchestra and conduct it on its long tour. Not until 2 August 1921 was Caldara able to confirm that the

---

* La Scala's archives contain receipts for Carla Toscanini's annual full-price payment for Box 12, Left, in the third tier, for the family's use, because her husband believed that he and other well-paid performers should not receive complimentary tickets to performances.

† In 1945–46, during the hurried rebuilding of the bomb-damaged auditorium, the use of too much concrete and carpeting on the ground floor further deadened the sound, but the restoration of the theater in 2002–04 markedly improved it.

maestro had "responded to our desire—which is the desire of the citizenry—to collaborate in the first season of La Scala's resurrection, not only as artistic consultant, but also by personally conducting some productions." Toscanini's fee for the year would be 150,000 lire, less than he had been paid in a single month at the Metropolitan ten years earlier. But he wanted to do the right thing for his country, which was struggling to emerge from the postwar economic upheaval, and he relished the opportunity to reshape Italy's leading lyric theater in accordance with his ideas and ideals. Besides, he had agreed to take charge for only a single season; if things did not go as he wished, he would be free to leave without having to make a dramatic break.

Once the theater's new fiscal system was in place, Toscanini set about completing his staff. Fortunately, his musical and conductorial talents were complemented by striking organizational abilities, described by Cesare Albertini as "external manifestations of a very well-balanced and harmonious intellect. [. . .] A deep penetrator of people's hearts, Arturo Toscanini chooses his colleagues with shrewd prudence. He does not love those who adulate him or those who present themselves to him prostrate or dully submissive. [. . .] He wants colleagues who are intelligent, who know how to argue with him; he listens to their objections, and he trusts those who show that they really know something; he greatly appreciates those who spiritedly try new paths, even if those paths are full of difficulties."

For administrative matters, Toscanini relied on General Manager Angelo Scandiani; together, they chose Anita Colombo as chief administrative assistant and problem interceptor. Colombo, an intelligent, multilingual, indefatigable thirty-year-old violinist of part-German Jewish origin, had aided Toscanini in organizing some of his wartime benefit events. But the choice of administrators was the smallest of the problems that Toscanini had to confront. The *ente autonomo*'s first season would comprise ten new productions; to prepare and conduct all of them with a new ensemble would have been beyond even his powers. During the previous winter, Scandiani, at Toscanini's behest, had invited the Italo-Argentine Héctor (Ettore, in Italy) Panizza to become co-conductor. In the two decades since Toscanini had conducted Panizza's opera *Medioevo Latino* in Buenos

Aires, the composer had become an accomplished conductor, in demand at many of Italy's most important opera houses. He understood that becoming La Scala's number two conductor could be perceived as a backward step in his career, since he was already forty-six years old. But, as he wrote many years later, "so great was my enthusiasm, my passion, my pleasure at being able to work alongside a man like Arturo Toscanini, [. . .] that I didn't care at all what my friends and enemies would say about me."

Scandiani, Toscanini, and Panizza had to deal right away with the question that all opera directors have faced since the art form was born: Can we program the repertoire that we would like to present, given the singers available to us? And while they were dealing with that issue, they also had to put together a team of competent, hardworking musical assistants; select stage directors and set designers; choose a chorus director and take part in chorus auditions; oversee a few changes in the orchestra's personnel; and make their artistic choices fit within the organization's budget.

Panizza persuaded Toscanini to add Ferruccio Calusio, another Italo-Argentine, and Antonino Votto, an Italian who had assisted Panizza in Buenos Aires, to head the staff of *maestri sostituti* (assistant conductors who functioned as rehearsal pianists and coaches for the singers); both men would remain important figures at La Scala for decades, and Votto was later Riccardo Muti's conducting teacher at the Milan Conservatory. Completing the team were Sergio Failoni, who would enjoy a major conducting career in Hungary, and Mario Frigerio, who acted mainly as director of offstage ensembles.

The forty-three-year-old choral director Vittore Veneziani had collaborated with Toscanini at Bologna's Teatro Comunale in 1904 and had since been active in other major Italian venues; Toscanini liked his work and lured him to La Scala to instruct and direct a professional chorus initially made up of seventy men and fifty women, although it could be reinforced, when necessary, by as many as seventy capable members of La Scala's Choral Academy.

Vincenzo Dell'Agostino, a former primo ballerino at La Scala whom Toscanini had employed as choreographer as early as 1902, became the official choreographer of the corps de ballet, which numbered sixty dancers. During the first season, the corps performed only during those operas that included dance scenes, but Toscanini and Scandiani reopened the theater's once celebrated but recently defunct school of dance, initially under the direction of the Russian étoile and teacher Olga Preobrajenska, so that complete ballet evenings would be possible in subsequent seasons.

During the first season, four men collaborated with Toscanini and Panizza in directing stage movement. Toscanini personally examined and approved or rejected the maquettes (scale models) of sets for each season's productions; when the real sets were ready, he sat in the auditorium and looked at them as they were placed on the stage under an approximation of the correct lighting, and he maintained the prerogative to accept, suggest modifications to, or reject the designers' work at any point in the process. His visual artists described him as exceptionally supportive and knowledgeable, and he encouraged them to come up with fresh ideas. During the first season, he relied in part on the set designers and scene painters Vittorio Rota and Antonio Rovescalli, with whom he had worked before, but he also turned to the younger Edoardo Marchioro, Giovanni Battista Santoni, and Giovanni Grandi; Marchioro, in particular, would become one of his most important collaborators. Costumes were provided by the veteran Zamperoni and Chiappa companies, and stage construction and crews were directed by Giovanni Ansaldo, assisted and then succeeded by his son, Pericle. All of these people would contribute to making La Scala one of the wonders of the opera world in the 1920s.

Late in the summer of 1921, Toscanini and Scandiani went to Munich on opera business. Puccini's friend Riccardo Schnabl-Rossi saw Toscanini there and described him, in a letter to the composer, as "more tense than ever. I found him irritable and irritated against everything. It seems impossible, with his intelligence!" Toscanini proceeded to Vienna, where he met Franz Schalk, the Staatsoper's chief conductor, and he visited the Bösendorfer piano factory to determine whether he could get a good deal on pianos for La Scala: no detail was too small for his attention, where his theater was concerned. (But La Scala eventually bought four Bechsteins.) In the fall, Italy's secretary of state for the fine arts invited Toscanini to direct a Permanent Commission for Musical Art, but he turned down the offer: he belonged to La Scala.

2.

TOSCANINI HAD DECIDED TO INAUGURATE THE NEW ENTERPRISE with *Falstaff*, which he regarded as the crowning glory of Italian opera, but he was unhappy with the list of potential protagonists. Calusio had recently worked with a young Sicilian baritone who, he told Toscanini, was both musical and eager to learn; the thirty-three-year-old Mariano Stabile might be the man they needed.

Toscanini asked Calusio to teach Stabile the first part of Act I and the monologue at the beginning of Act III, but he told him not to mention either himself or La Scala to Stabile. Calusio informed Stabile that an impresario was looking for someone to sing the role of Falstaff in a town near Milan, and they began to work on the part. After two months' preparation, the unsuspecting Stabile was led into La Scala's main auditorium.

"La Scala was all a mess," Stabile recalled many years later. He mounted a temporary stand in the auditorium and, accompanied by Calusio, sang the parts he had prepared. Afterward, the baritone approached his auditioners. "At first, with one of those silences that killed people, [Toscanini] twirled his mustache between two fingers. Then finally he said to me, 'You sing too metronomically,'" Stabile related.

"'Maestro,' I said, 'I didn't come here to have you hear how I sing *Falstaff*; I came here to have you hear whether I have the potential to be able to sing *Falstaff* with you some day, if you tell me what I have to do.' This impressed him, of course. Another terrible silence. 'Well, come to La Scala tomorrow at six and I'll be able to tell you something.' Naturally, I didn't sleep that night; I was like a madman, waiting for six the following afternoon."

At their second encounter, Toscanini told Stabile only to come to his home at ten the following morning.

At exactly ten we began to go over the monologue from *Falstaff*'s third act, "Mondo ladro. Mondo rubaldo." And until 1:00 or 1:30, I repeated those words over and over, because he wanted me to bring out the regurgitation—that *oahhh* of the fat man, the drunkard, the glutton, the paunch. [. . .]

Naturally, another night went by with me having visions, and—well, after two or three days of going to him, I calmed down, he was already using *tu* with me, he began telling me stories—he told me about the scene between Verdi and Maurel, when Maurel couldn't manage to do that "Vado a farmi bello" with the pianissimo that Verdi wanted*—and there was also the "Alfin t'ho colta raggiante"—I couldn't do that F-sharp with the simplicity and naturalness that Toscanini wanted.

One day—it was two in the afternoon, and with Maestro Toscanini, who never got up from the piano, because he didn't smoke, didn't drink cocktails, didn't eat, wasn't hungry—at one point Signora Carla came in: "Arturo, don't you understand that Stabile has to go eat? It's two o'clock—won't you let up so that he can go home?" So then I went away, joking and laughing.

Finally, after seven days of this torture, he accompanied me to the door of his apartment and said, "Go to La Scala, go to Scandiani—I'll phone him—and he'll give you the contract for La Scala." You can imagine my joy!

Toscanini sent Stabile back to Calusio for further work, but "once or twice or three times a week we both went to the Maestro in Via Durini to have him hear what we had studied." Although Stabile would successfully take on many other roles as well, he eventually sang the part of Falstaff some twelve hundred times, and in many parts of the world his name became practically eponymous with the protagonist of Verdi's last opera. Since *stabile* means stable or permanent, a joke conflating two Verdi operas circulated among Milanese music lovers: "La donna è mobile, ma Falstaff è Stabile."

And not only Stabile was *stabile*: among the nine other solo singers chosen for the inaugural *Falstaff*, all but two sang the same roles with Toscanini during one or more of the following seasons, and many of the other artists chosen for the first season's operas would remain with the company for several years—even decades, in some cases. Toscanini needed this relative stability in order to create an ensem-

---

* Besides having heard early *Falstaff* performances by the original cast, Toscanini had also conferred with Verdi about various details in the opera, and on many occasions he had talked at length with Maurel. He learned of this incident from either the opera's composer or its first protagonist, if not both.

ble that would combine flexibility with high artistic quality. If he decided to stay with the company—he reasoned—he wanted to be able to revive operas, year after year, with minimal rehearsal time, as he had been able to do at the Metropolitan, but to carry out such a plan at La Scala, with its far more limited economic resources, he had to have at his disposal singers who could and would remain in situ for long stretches every year. Fortunately, his prestige was now so great that he was able to realize his goal: a singer who had been part of Toscanini's ensemble at La Scala could be engaged anywhere in the world.

3.

POSTWAR SOCIAL AND POLITICAL UNREST HAD REACHED INTOLER-able levels in Italy by 1921, with Mussolini's now violently right-wing Fascist *squadristi* on the rampage against their adversaries, some of whom met violence with violence. Cultural institutions and entertainment venues were by no means exempt from the turmoil: in March, anarchists had exploded a bomb in a small theater in Milan's Kursaal Diana, in an attempt to kill the city's police commissioner; the commissioner had emerged unscathed, but twenty-one people—including at least one child and two adolescents—had been killed, and eighty more were injured. Nine months later, on 26 December, a few hours before the newly renovated La Scala was to be inaugurated, rumors of a bomb in the theater began to circulate. Members of the public were searched as they entered the theater, which slowed down the seating process, but Toscanini stubbornly insisted on starting the performance precisely on time, which caused some of the blameless latecomers to complain vociferously. But everyone calmed down, the evening ended in triumph, and successive *Falstaff* performances—ten of them, after the premiere—were greeted with unadulterated enthusiasm. Among those present on opening night were the thirty-year-old German violinist Adolf Busch and his wife, Frieda, who introduced themselves to Toscanini afterward; Toscanini attended the Busch Quartet's concert at the Milan Conservatory the following evening and admired what he heard. Thus began a long friendship.

Toscanini had restudied *Falstaff* from the original manuscript, which belonged to the Ricordi company, and he had discovered a piece of paper on which the seventy-nine-year-old Verdi had written a brief, touching farewell to what he knew would be his last opera. "The last notes of *Falstaff*," it read. "All is over! Go on, go on, old John. . . Go along your way as long as you can. . . Amusing sort of rascal[.] Eternally true, under various guises, at all times, in all places!! Go along, go, go[.] Farewell!" Toscanini asked whether he might hold on to the note during his lifetime, and he received official, written permission to that effect from Ricordi's directors.

Parsifal, the season's second opera,* was conducted by Panizza, who was moved and proud because Toscanini had personally invited him to take charge of Wagner's final opera. Panizza recalled that the maestro "was always at my side" during his rehearsals. "On the night of my debut, before I began, Toscanini stayed by me like a father [. . .]; his behavior was truly that of a great artist and a great soul!"

Toscanini's next task was a new production of *Rigoletto*, with three excellent artists in the principal roles: Carlo Galeffi as Rigoletto, Toti Dal Monte as Gilda, and Giacomo Lauri-Volpi as the Duke. Dal Monte had sung in Beethoven's Ninth Symphony with Toscanini in Turin and Milan in 1919, but it was Carla Toscanini who, after having heard her in *Rigoletto* in Rome in April 1921, had indicated the twenty-eight-year-old soprano as a possible Gilda for La Scala.

"I shall always remember 'my' [first] rehearsal in La Scala's Red Room," Dal Monte wrote in her memoirs.

> I came to the famous "Caro nome." I was very worried; I tried to do my best. Toscanini stopped me, saying, "Listen, dear, you sing this aria technically perfectly, but holy God! You need more than that. First of all, let me tell you that Verdi's women all love the same way—Gilda like Aida, Leonora like Violetta—they all have the same heartbeat. Yet there are differences. Why do you think that Verdi wrote this 'Caro nome' in such a detached style? For fun? No no no. Verdi used this technique,

---

* As in earlier years, so in the 1920s and indeed up to and in some cases after the Second World War, in Italy foreign operas were performed in Italian, just as in Germany they were performed in German, and so on. Text comprehensibility was considered paramount.

with short rests, to make the girl's anxiety more tangible. She is experiencing love for the first time, and she feels almost breathless at the thought of her beloved, who has made her drunk with all his fine talk. That's why she breathes after every syllable [. . .]. If you keep thinking about Gilda's state of mind, your voice will certainly be able to express the anxiety that Verdi wanted."

[. . .] Another of Toscanini's precise observations came in the [final] act, in the death scene: "Lassù in cielo vicino alla madre." Toscanini said to me, "Remember that when Gilda utters these words of final farewell, *she is more up there* [in heaven] *than down here.* There is something unearthly in that aria. You need an 'angelicized' voice that speaks to heaven. If you can get into that state of mind, the voice will become ethereal on its own."

[. . .] After the first rehearsal, instead of all the anxiety I had felt beforehand, I felt great joy. Toscanini said nothing to me, but I understood that in his opinion I had overcome the difficult obstacle of that first, direct contact.

Lauri-Volpi noted that at one rehearsal Toscanini asked Dal Monte to sing "Caro nome" with a fuller, rounder tone, and that she replied, "'Maestro, I wouldn't make it to the end of the aria if I were to sing it as you would like.' Toscanini was silent and let her do it her way." Like several other observers, Lauri-Volpi noted the effectiveness of a segment that was usually cut but that Toscanini restored, in Gilda and Rigoletto's first, extended duet: "Quanto affetto! quali cure!" It was, according to the tenor, precisely at that moment that Dal Monte was at her best. "Whether it was because of the beauty of the music or the sweetness of the voice, one never knew, but the crowd certainly held its breath during the performance and, at the end, greeted the segment with enthusiastic applause."

Lauri-Volpi fared less well in his relations with Toscanini. He wanted to insert a "traditional" cadenza into "La donna è mobile" but Toscanini wouldn't hear of it. Votto, who was at the piano, recounted, "When Lauri-Volpi told him that even Caruso had done it, the Maestro replied that Caruso had done it, but with a different voice and in a different style. Then the dissension arose, because after the [three] subscription performances of *Rigoletto* the Duke's part was taken over by the house tenor Alessio De Paolis." Lauri-Volpi would remain on Toscanini's black list for years.

Galeffi, on the other hand, quickly became one of Toscanini's favorite singers. Dal Monte recalled how the maestro taught the baritone the opera's entire second act, "transforming himself into Rigoletto, showing him every gesture, every expression, every 'spoken' recitative, every anguished outbreak of anger. How infinite were the sensations that that man knew how to analyze in depth, and how capable he was of probing the music and the words of Verdi's creation!"

Although Toscanini disliked Puccini's *Trittico*, he knew that the latest completed work by Italy's most famous living composer could not be ignored by La Scala; thus the triptych's house premiere took place with Panizza on the podium. (Panizza also conducted *The Barber of Seville*, *La Wally*, and Wolf-Ferrari's *I Quatro Rusteghi* in the course of the season.) Toscanini, in the meantime, was busy preparing *Boris Godunov*, with Zygmunt Zalewski, a thirty-six-year-old Ukrainian-born, Italian-trained Polish bass, in the title part. *Mefistofele* was due after the successful *Boris* premiere, but Toscanini found several of the tenors under consideration for the role of Faust unsatisfactory and decided to try a thirty-six-year-old who, like Dal Monte, had been recommended by Carla: she had heard him sing the part at the Arena di Verona. Aureliano Pertile arrived at La Scala only a day before the first ensemble rehearsal and went onstage "full of doubt and anxiety, subjugated by the great Maestro's fame and authority. At the end of the first act, I had the unanticipated satisfaction of hearing the Maestro say, loudly, 'At last I've heard someone sing my way! That's the way to sing!'"

Pertile—a lyric tenor with a brilliant, powerful voice, although not an extraordinarily beautiful one—was an intelligent, dedicated worker: malleable, quick, and not egomaniacal. Toscanini turned him into one of the most subtly communicative vocal artists of his day and chose him to sing leading roles in no fewer than fourteen operas—operas as diverse as *Lucia* and *Meistersinger*—in addition to other works with other house conductors. Pertile, for his part, gladly admitted that he owed a great deal to Toscanini. "Imagine what help a good singer can get from such a teacher," he said. "There is always the chance of being told to go to the devil, but if you manage to do well and to overcome the awe that such a strong personality commands, you have everything to gain."

In terms of sheer size, *Meistersinger* was Toscanini's biggest enterprise of the season, and the production enjoyed a great success. Hans Sachs was sung by the French bass-baritone Marcel Journet, who would continue to perform the role in subsequent seasons; Stolzing was interpreted by Francesco Merli; and Juanita Caracciolo and Eva Didur—daughter of the basso Adamo Didur, who had worked with Toscanini at the Metropolitan—each took the part of Eva in three of the six performances. Like Pertile, the pretty, lively Caracciolo quickly won Toscanini's esteem for her intelligence, artistic flexibility, and vocal intensity; he entrusted several major roles to her the following year and was planning to give her others, but she died in childbirth in 1924, at the age of thirty-five.

A tall, sturdy-looking, twenty-nine-year-old Roman baritone named Ezio Pinza was given the role of Veit Pogner in *Meistersinger*, and he recalled the curious fact that

> instead of a routine audition, I was to take part in a rehearsal with the other singers, who had already worked with the Maestro for about a month. [. . .] [Toscanini] appeared exactly on time, looking much smaller than I had expected, but instantly filling the hall with his presence. [. . .] Without a nod, a smile or a word of salutation, Toscanini announced, "We will begin with the entrance of the Meistersingers."
>
> That meant he was starting with me. In fact, the major part of that rehearsal revolved around my role. I concentrated on what I was doing with such single-mindedness that I could form no idea of Toscanini's reaction, and impatiently waited for the rehearsal to end; then the Maestro would surely pronounce his verdict. He did nothing of the kind. Without as much as a glance in my direction, he said, "Rehearsal tomorrow at the same time." And he left the room.
>
> One of the baritones patted me on the shoulder. "Congratulations, Pinza, you're in!"
>
> "But the Maestro said nothing!" I remonstrated.
>
> "You can always tell by his face. Didn't you see it?"

Pinza went on to sing ten more roles at La Scala—seven of them with Toscanini—until 1924, when the Metropolitan lured him to New York.

Two *Meistersinger* performances brought the *ente autonomo*'s first, grandly successful season to a close. Many years later, Walter Toscanini reported that "each new production cost La Scala about 600,000 lire, and the first season's financial success allowed [the company] to pay off many of its debts." La Scala directly employed approximately 1,000 people, and during the opera season the ensemble provided full-time, part-time, or occasional work to another 2,000 to 3,000 tailors, shoemakers, painters, and the staffs of music publishing houses, printing presses, restaurants, hotels, taxi companies, and numerous other industries. "For Milan, La Scala represented business totaling about thirty to forty million [lire in the first year] at the very least," Walter said. Angelo Petracchi's calculations, a century earlier, about the benefits that opera brought to local economies, proved correct.

La Scala's board members, knowing that Toscanini's salary represented only a small fraction of what he could have earned abroad, presented him, at the end of the season, with a bonus of 100,000 lire, 60 percent above his actual salary. He returned the check, saying that he had been paid adequately. The perplexed directors sent the check back to him: the sum was but a token of their appreciation for his work, they said. This time, Toscanini accepted the gift but immediately donated the entire amount to the theater, anonymously. For the following season, however, the board fixed his salary at 250,000 lire, still only about one-eighth what he would have earned at the Metropolitan. But La Scala had become the place where he could at last realize his dreams for the lyric theater.

4.

THE SUCCESS OF THE *ENTE AUTONOMO'S* FIRST SEASON GALVANIZED Toscanini even more than the planning of the Scala orchestra's mammoth tour had done two years earlier, and he immediately began to prepare season two. When a reporter for the American *Musical Courier* buttonholed him at La Scala and asked about the veracity of rumors that the Chicago Opera Association had invited him to become its conductor—and that he had asked for $50,000 per season—Toscanini replied that he had indeed been invited but had not answered the letter. He had no intention of working ever again in a traditionally run theater anywhere in the world, he said.

In June and July 1922, Toscanini conducted the Scala orchestra in three concerts at La Scala itself and three more, with low-priced tickets, at the Socialist Party's Teatro del Popolo—thus repeating, with equal success, the experiment that he had carried out at the same venue ten years earlier. Late in July he visited Paris, for reasons no longer known, then spent much of August with his family in a rented house in Viareggio, near the Puccinis, and was visited a little later by Max Smith, his American journalist friend, and Smith's wife, Mary.

Toscanini and La Scala's other administrators decided that instead of opening their second season on the traditional date of 26 December, Saint Stephen's Day, and continuing for four and a half months, the ensemble would give its first performance on 2 December and continue for over six months; instead of ten operas, there would be seventeen—eleven new productions and six revivals from the previous season; instead of 91 performances, there would be 133; and instead of two conductors to share the burden, there would be four. Panizza, who had accepted a lucrative contract in the United States, conducted only 4 performances that year and none at all the following year; he would return with a full schedule in 1924–25. Instead, Toscanini engaged the well-established Antonio Guarnieri to take on the world premiere of Respighi's *Belfagor* plus other productions new and old. But Guarnieri and Toscanini clashed, musically and temperamentally, and Guarnieri was not invited back during Toscanini's reign.* Franco Ghione, a younger co-conductor, led one new production and miscellaneous other performances. According to Puccini, Toscanini had initially wanted the gifted thirty-year-old Victor De Sabata on his conducting staff but had decided otherwise after having attended and disliked a concert conducted by the young man. Toscanini made Giovacchino Forzano—a well-known Tuscan journalist, librettist, and man of the theater—responsible for the

---

* "He was a good cellist, but as a conductor I never heard more of a dog," Toscanini commented decades later. But many other musicians had a high opinion of Guarnieri. And the dislike was mutual.

staging of every new production that season, but, as Toti Dal Monte pointed out, the maestro himself played at least as big a role as Forzano in the theatrical aspect of every opera.

In 1922 as in 1921, *Falstaff* opened the season, and two weeks later Toscanini conducted the world premiere of Ildebrando Pizzetti's *Dèbora e Jaéle*. Toscanini had been aware of Pizzetti—a fellow Parmesan, thirteen years his junior—at least as early as 1903, when the aspiring composer had played part of his opera *Il Cid* for the conductor. Toscanini's comment on that occasion was "Are you really sure that you have something to say?" Nor was Toscanini attracted to a subsequent Pizzetti opera, *Fedra*, for which D'Annunzio provided the libretto. He did, however, conduct two of Pizzetti's orchestral pieces, and he hoped that something important would emerge from the composer's pen, because he had become deeply concerned about the state of contemporary opera in Italy.

Fewer and fewer new creations in the genre were demonstrating the combination of beauty, originality, and vitality that had given staying power to the works of the country's finest composers over the three previous centuries. Toscanini was not at all convinced that the more-recent works of Mascagni, Franchetti, Giordano, or even Puccini—all of whom were now in their fifties or sixties—possessed true musical and dramatic value, and most of the operas by younger Italian composers that had so far come to his attention left him cold. But in July 1921, Pizzetti visited Toscanini and played through all three acts of his new opera, *Dèbora e Jaéle*, for which he had also written the libretto—loosely based on the story of Deborah in the Book of Judges—and Toscanini was taken with what he heard. Less than a month later, the soprano Giulia Tess wrote to inform Pizzetti that Toscanini wanted her to learn the part of Jaéle, and "the Maestro told me that *Dèbora* is marvelous and that he had been impressed by the beauty of the music and the libretto," she said.

Toscanini threw himself wholeheartedly into preparing this complex, difficult work, and the audience at the premiere was enthusiastic enough to demand sixteen curtain calls; most of the reviews, however, were lukewarm. Puccini, whose curiosity had been piqued by Toscanini's enthusiasm for *Dèbora*, attended the third performance and wrote from Milan to Riccardo Schnabl-Rossi, "For me, it doesn't work—but certainly [. . .] there are things of the greatest interest—that abolition of melody is a great mistake because this opera will *never* be able to have a long life." He duly attended another performance and reported that the theater was largely empty, and that he was bored to death.

Puccini's remarks were prophetic: although Pizzetti wrote skillfully and sometimes even interestingly for the orchestra as well as for voices, *Dèbora* is fundamentally bland; it seems to occupy a desolate no-man's land between Italian melodrama and *Pelléas*: it lacks the energy of the one and the subtlety of the other. Its melodic lines follow the text but go nowhere in particular. After having been produced in a number of important venues and revived in subsequent Scala seasons by Toscanini, who continued to believe in it, *Dèbora* sank into oblivion.

Puccini, on the other hand, was thriving at La Scala. One of the grandest events of the 1922–23 season was a new production of *Manon Lescaut*, which had not been heard at the house in fourteen years. Although this was a peaceful period in the Puccini-Toscanini relationship, it came at the end of a long, rough patch that had begun with Toscanini's expressions of contempt for the *Trittico*, nearly four years earlier. As late as February 1921, when plans for the new *ente autonomo* were being revealed while Toscanini was in America with the Scala orchestra, Puccini had been pouring vitriol on the conductor. "Encores are no longer permitted," he complained to his friend Carlo Paladini. "Toscanini has settled it thus. I read bewildering things about him in today's *Corriere*. He who was so disinterested at first glance, with his eye fixed on Art, has had himself recorded along with his orchestra! This great animator of foreign things, so little sensitive to our music, [is the subject of] articles and exaltations, as if he, a new Guido d'Arezzo, had discovered the notes of St. Joseph's hymn!* As far as I'm concerned, he has a great, prodigious memory, but music has to make the soul vibrate. In his hands its physiognomy changes. [. . .] Toscanini is fine for concerts, especially if he is conducting Debussy's embroideries and cold and colorful things. For the rest, where the soul vibrates humanly—*nihil*—or little more."

---

* Puccini was referring ironically to the eleventh-century monk who is credited with the invention of modern musical notation, but he meant St. John's hymn, not St. Joseph's hymn.

But Toscanini's prestige was important to Puccini—and after all, maybe the fellow wasn't such an insensitive musician. Not even five months after penning the letter just quoted, Puccini wrote to Carlo Clausetti of the Ricordi company, complaining that the *Trittico* would receive its Scala premiere under Panizza's baton. "Without Toscanini, the opera would be presented in an inferior light." The tactic didn't work, and Puccini refused to believe that Toscanini simply did not like the *Trittico*. A few weeks later, he wrote to Riccardo Schnabl: "Toscanini is really a bad man—perfidious—and I deny that he has the soul of an artist—because those who really do are not so full of wickedness and also, I think, envy! At bottom, I couldn't care less"—how could anyone have imagined such a thing?—"but it bothers me for the Milanese, because with another conductor my opera won't be seen in the best light by the more or less intelligent public." In January 1922, Puccini heard *Rigoletto* at La Scala, and he admitted that it was "really well performed, without notes held too long or corrections of Verdi. Toti is excellent, Galeffi and Lauri-Volpi good. Toscanini's tempi are serene and right, third act excellent, even dramatically."

By August, when the Puccini and Toscanini families were both at Viareggio, the two musicians had mended their relationship. "Toscanini is here, two steps away from me," Puccini wrote to Schnabl. "He'll conduct my *Manon* at La Scala. I've done some substantial retouching on the score"—with Toscanini's suggestions, added to those he had made a dozen years earlier. Toscanini charged Marchioro with preparing new sets for the opera; for the costumes, he turned for the first time to the multitalented Count Luigi Sapelli (1865–1936), better-known by his pseudonym, Caramba, who had recently been appointed to oversee all the visual aspects of La Scala's productions.

Puccini attended Toscanini's *Manon* rehearsals, and a few hours before the first performance (26 December 1922)—with Caracciolo in the title role and Pertile as Des Grieux—he wrote to Schnabl: "This evening *Manon*, a great *Manon*, and if the audience isn't moved it will mean that we're living on Saturn instead of Earth. I assure you that Toscanini is a real miracle of feeling, of refinement, of sensitivity, of balance. What a pleasure the rehearsals were for me. Never, never have I so enjoyed hearing my music." The audience was not only moved; it was ecstatic. Seventeen performances had to be scheduled—more than for any other opera that season. On the day after the opening, Puccini sent a long letter to the *Corriere*, which published it in its entirety.

Your music critic states that I have retouched the instrumentation of *Manon*. "Especially in the second and fourth acts there are several retouchings, and others are evident even in the first act." He is referring to some trifling modifications of coloring, but the score printed by Ricordi can testify to the fact that I have not redone the opera's instrumentation. My *Manon* is exactly that of thirty years ago, only it has been conducted by Arturo Toscanini, which means conducted in a way that brings its composer the great and rare joy of seeing his music illuminated with the same brightness that he saw and dreamt at the moment of composing it and never saw thereafter. For too long it has been the custom in Italy to present the so-called repertoire operas— that is, those which have resisted time and unfaithful performances—in an indecent style: one orchestra rehearsal, none for staging, and off goes the worthless thing, deformed by the abuses with which it has become encrusted, little by little, owing to the bad habits of conductors and singers.

When Arturo Toscanini, with that conviction and love that are inflamed by his marvelous art, takes the scalpel in hand and clears away the filth, and brings the opera back to its natural state, revealing to the audience the true intentions of the composer, the old opera seems new to the listeners, and they say that it's something different. No, it is simply itself, enlivened by the greatest animator of which the art of music can boast.

At La Scala these miracles are happening frequently nowadays, and last night, when the emotion of the audience [. . .] took hold of me as well, and when I felt impelled to embrace our Toscanini, that embrace was not only a gesture of selfish gratitude for the performance of my *Manon*. No, it was the gratitude of one artist toward another artist, who had succeeded in making La Scala into a real temple for artistic consecrations and re-consecrations. What he has accomplished at La Scala is wonderful. I visit all the world's theaters, and I see and study what they do. This seems to me the moment to say that what is being done at La Scala today is not being done at any other theater. Toscanini has achieved here not only the work of organization: he has created an institution that is the pride of Italian art. [. . .] This nucleus of energy, guided and animated by Toscanini, yields results that, as happened last night, make *Manon* appear to be a new opera—to such an extent that even to me it seemed to be thirty years younger.

Puccini wasn't merely providing good publicity to the press. To Schnabl he wrote that *Manon* continued to move him: "Believe me, *never* has an opera been heard that is so well balanced and performed— [. . .] Toscanini is truly *now* the best man in the world as a conductor because he has everything—soul poetry suppleness order impetus dramatic finesse—in short, a real miracle." In January 1923, he complained to Schnabl about a performance of *Fanciulla* in Rome, and added, "Listen, after having heard my Manon at La Scala all the other theaters disgust me." And on 2 February, in Milan, Puccini wrote to Toscanini, "Dear Arturo, you have given me the greatest satisfaction of my life. *Manon*, in your interpretation, is beyond what I thought it to be in those distant days. You have done this music of mine with unapproachable poetry, suppleness, and passion. Yesterday evening I really felt your whole great spirit and the love you bear your old friend and companion of early days. I am happy because you, more than anyone else, were able to understand my youthful, passionate spirit of thirty years ago. Thanks, from the bottom of my heart!"

5.

TOSCANINI WAS NO LESS WORRIED THAN OTHER ITALIANS ABOUT the political, social, and economic chaos that reigned throughout the country, and he viewed with increasing alarm the rise of what was now officially known as the National Fascist Party. As the historian Denis Mack Smith wrote, in his biography of Mussolini, Toscanini and a few other early adherents of the movement had long since "left or lost interest on the grounds that fascism was becoming unprincipled, corrupt, authoritarian, and moving far away from its earlier left-wing idealism."

Late in October 1922, five weeks before the opening of the *ente autonomo*'s second season, the Fascists marched on Rome; Prime Minister Luigi Facta asked King Victor Emanuel III to declare the capital under siege, so that the army could arrest the Fascists. But the king, knowing that the Fascists had the support of the military, big business, and the conservatives, invited Mussolini to form a government. Toscanini told friends that if he were capable of killing a man, he would kill Mussolini.

In the early months of the Fascist administration, Italy remained a democratic country: Mussolini was far too canny a politician to try to make radical systemic changes immediately. Toscanini had an early run-in with some young Fascists at a gala performance of *Falstaff* on the feast day (7 December) of Milan's patron, Saint Ambrose, but the incident was merely the result of the excessive enthusiasm of some of Mussolini's youngest adherents. After the second intermission that evening, Toscanini conducted the Royal March in honor of various dignitaries who were present, but then, according to the *Corriere della Sera,*

> some Fascists, who were right behind the conductor's podium, requested the [Fascist Party's] anthem, *Giovinezza*. Maestro Toscanini turned to them and, smiling good-naturedly, said that he had never rehearsed the anthem and the orchestra didn't know it and thus couldn't play it.
>
> This reason, which ought to have been decisive for everyone, didn't seem so to a small group of very young black-shirted Fascists, who continued to demand the anthem, saying, "That's enough: one violin can play it alone." The idea [. . .] was not shared by Maestro Toscanini, who turned again to the most agitated of the youths, repeating courteously to them that it was not possible for a single violin to play the anthem! Then someone shouted, "We'll remember this refusal." The maestro, who had stayed calm until then, responded heatedly: "It's not a matter of refusing; it's a matter of material impossibility." The demands became increasingly heated; the maestro left his place until everything quickly calmed down, and, when calm had been restored, Toscanini, greeted by an ovation upon his return, began the third act.

According to the soprano Maria Labia, who was singing the role of Alice, Toscanini hadn't merely left his place calmly when the disrupters became more vociferous: he had broken his baton and exited from the orchestra pit, shouting and cursing. Scandiani had then announced to the audience that the anthem would be played at the end of the performance. "When the opera ended," Labia recalled, Scandiani "told us, 'Stay where you are, everyone. You'll sing the anthem, accompanied by the piano.' Toscanini intervened: 'They're not going to sing a damned thing. La Scala's artists aren't vaudeville singers. Go to your dressing rooms, all of you.'" With hindsight, the whole story seems a harbinger of worse things to come, but at the time it appeared to be nothing but a case of boorish behavior on the part of some overly enthusiastic youths.

During the first year of Mussolini's premiership, the chaos in Italy diminished considerably, since the Fascists themselves had caused much of it in their attempt to achieve power. Toscanini, like millions of other Italians, assumed at first that the movement's more obviously deplorable aspects—violent rhetoric, shifting pronouncements and policies, slandering of opponents—would fall away, and that the party would mature into yet another typically Italian middle-of-the-road force. Many people involved in artistic and intellectual endeavors admired Mussolini's intelligence and energy, and the fact that Mussolini sincerely liked music undoubtedly made La Scala's administrators hope that financial support from the national government would be forthcoming.

For about a year and a half, Toscanini probably regretted his initial wish for Mussolini's death. Throughout 1923, the maestro and La Scala's other authorities treated the prime minister respectfully during his official visits to Milan. Local elections in December 1922 had not only made Senator Luigi Mangiagalli, a Liberal (thus to the right of the previously dominant Socialists but to the left of the Fascists), the city's mayor and, automatically, La Scala's president, but had also put several Fascists on the city council, which gave one Fascist the right to sit on La Scala's board of directors. For a while, the board members from various parties got along with one another.

In January 1923, the new prime minister accepted the honorary presidency of a lottery that had been organized to continue to pay for the modernization of La Scala, and in February he attended part of a performance of *The Barber of Seville* (conducted by Guarnieri, who led the Royal March and "Giovinezza" in the special guest's honor). Then, at the end of March, he made an official visit to La Scala, where he was greeted by the board of directors, the artistic staff, journalists (including Margherita Sarfatti, Mussolini's Jewish mistress and future biographer), and many of the star performers. As the next day's *Corriere* reported, the directors presented the prime minister with a memorandum that requested a contribution from the state to help cover La Scala's expenses. Mussolini replied, "'The Fascist government certainly knows what La Scala signifies in the spiritual life of Italy [. . .]. Above all, the Fascist government admires the intentions of La Scala's life-giver, my companion from the electoral list of 1919: I refer to Arturo Toscanini.' The mention of Maestro Toscanini was greeted by those present with warm applause, after which the Honorable Mussolini continued, 'The Government will without a doubt do whatever is possible in order to facilitate La Scala's artistic functions as well as possible. But I must not hide the fact that the Treasury is empty.'"

On the stage, amid the workers and the scenery, Mussolini "stayed on, curious and interested, asking questions of and receiving explanations from Maestro Toscanini, Mr. Scandiani, and the head stagehands Giovanni and Pericle Ansaldo, about the work that had been carried out on the stage and about the mounting of productions."

On the same occasion, Mussolini was photographed, looking stiff and uncomfortable, with Toscanini, Mangiagalli, Toti Dal Monte, and dozens of other Scala artists and personnel. He thought that he had persuaded Toscanini to bring the company's *Falstaff* cast to Rome the following May for a special performance of the opera at the Teatro Costanzi, on the occasion of the visit of Britain's King George V. But on 23 April the *Corriere* reported that Toscanini was unwell and was therefore "greatly disappointed" to have had to cancel the Roman project. Although several sources indicate that he was indeed suffering from visual and gastric disturbances in the spring, he was well enough to conduct many rehearsals and performances at La Scala throughout that period.*

Despite Toscanini's initial moderate optimism about the new government, and his protestations—right to the end of 1923—of esteem and even affection for Mussolini, he was worried from the start about the prime minister's intentions. Early in 1923, Mussolini made the Fascist militia into a taxpayer-supported paramilitary force under his own control, and, as Wally Toscanini reported later, her father, upon learning of this, had said, "He is not interested in the country—he is interested in himself."

6.

KURT WEILL SAT IN THE AUDIENCE AT A PERFORMANCE OF CHARPEN-tier's *Louise*, Toscanini's first new production of 1923. Although the twenty-three-year-old German composer's fame as Bertolt Brecht's collaborator on *The Three-Penny Opera* lay five years in the future, his talents had been noted by Ferruccio Busoni, his former teacher. Weill wrote to Busoni about his Milanese experience: "Of all the theatrical [situations] that I have seen, this one comes closest to Mahler's ideal of an 'uncompromising' [musical theater]," he said. "Toscanini conducted, and that in itself was an event that made this whole trip worth the effort. I never knew that one could play 'on' an orchestra with such freedom, with such willful rubati. It was splendidly sung, the chorus was flabbergasting in the way it brought off its musical and dramatic tasks. I don't know whether the piece was so winning [only] as a result of the performance—I found it beautiful in places (such as the beginning of Act 4). You can imagine with what verve the great spectacular scene in Act 3 was brought off. I will remember this evening for a long time."

Weill's comments are noteworthy not only as a description of what he had heard but also because in Berlin, where he lived, he was

---

* "Poor guy, his stomach isn't well at all," Puccini had written to Schnabl-Rossi as early as the previous January. "May God protect him!" Toscanini had also claimed ill health as a reason for bowing out of a concert, scheduled for 23 February 1923, with the orchestra of London's Royal Philharmonic Society, although he conducted the dress rehearsal of Charpentier's *Louise* at La Scala that evening.

accustomed to hearing such outstanding German-school conductors as Arthur Nikisch (who had died the preceding year), Bruno Walter, Otto Klemperer, and Wilhelm Furtwängler—yet he found Toscanini's conducting freer than any he had previously observed. And the Scala ensemble seemed to him far superior to anything that Germany could offer at the time.

Toscanini had preceded the *Louise* production—with the Belgian soprano Fanny Heldy, whom Toscanini greatly admired, in the title role—with revivals of *Meistersinger* and *Rigoletto*, and he followed it with a revival of *Boris Godunov*. But his next major effort was a new production of *Lucia di Lammermoor*, which he had previously conducted in only two performances at the Teatro Dal Verme in 1897, for the centenary of Donizetti's birth. He was encouraged to schedule it now because of Toti Dal Monte, who, he felt, would make an ideal Lucia. This time, however, their collaboration got off to a rough start.

The previous fall, "La Toti," as her many fans called her, had sung *Rigoletto* in Bergamo, with Guarnieri on the podium, and Guarnieri had told her to forget about the cleaned-up version of the opera that she had sung with Toscanini a few months earlier. "Caro nome," for instance, was to be transposed down a semitone so that she could belt out some unwritten high notes, and various cadenza-like passages that Toscanini had removed were reinstated. Now, when Toscanini entered the room, he "responded to my greeting with a snarled *buon giorno*, and he sat down at the piano," she recalled.

> My heart was in my mouth for fear of an explosion. He banged out a few chords and then, in a fury, he exclaimed, "How could you have allowed yourself to sing *Rigoletto* differently than the way I taught it to you? And to think that I raised you up among the elect! You're a wretch, like all the others! You're a circus artiste, that's what you are! You're not going to sing with me anymore!" He violently slammed down the keyboard lid, got up, and left without even giving me a chance to defend myself. [. . .] I threw myself onto an armchair and cried all the tears of despair that were in my heart. [. . .]
>
> Little by little I recovered my tranquillity, so that when the Maestro came back, still very annoyed but less hostile, I was

able to go on with the rehearsal. The Maestro probably noticed that my eyes were red; in any case, sitting at the piano, he began the session.

It didn't escape me that little by little, as I sang with increasing courage, he became calmer. Thank you, Donizetti! When we got to "Verranno a te sull'aure," Toscanini stopped me: "You sing this phrase well," he said, "but there isn't enough air in your voice. You need more color, more sweetness, more expression." I tried and tried, and I found the color and sweetness and expression that he wanted. [. . .]

When we got to the "mad scene," I sang the cadenza with some trepidation. The Maestro asked me, "Who taught you this cadenza?"

"Paolantonio," I said, "like all the other ornaments in the score."*

"Yes, it's all good," he said at last, "but it's too short. You need to add a couple of bars. Tell him."

When the session was over, the Maestro got up from the piano and said, very affectionately, "Despite everything, you're still good, and you have a beautiful voice."

[. . .] It wasn't easy to satisfy Toscanini, who hated the extravagant exhibitions of certain singers very much in vogue at the time, and who wanted technique to be entirely at the service of expression.

[. . .] The *Lucia* rehearsals were detailed and enervating. [. . .] The "curse scene" alone had thirteen rehearsals. At one of the last ones, noticing that Toscanini had passed over [the staging of] the "mad scene" (my big moment!), I plucked up my courage and said, "Maestro, we haven't rehearsed the mad scene yet—how will we manage it?"

He looked me up and down and said, jokingly, "Come on, now! You've been acting crazy all your life—don't you think you'll be able to do it on stage?" I persisted. "All right," he said, "we'll rehearse it at the piano tomorrow at three."

The next day, [. . .] I made my entrance from the top of the

---

* Franco Paolantonio, an Italo-Argentine pianist and conductor, was Toti's regular coach.

stairs, trusting my intuition [. . .]. Toscanini stopped me immediately: "Remember," he admonished me, "that mad people
stare straight ahead of themselves before they speak." I repeated
the entrance with my eyes wide open and with an expression of
confusion. Toscanini followed me, moving backwards and
beating time without ever stopping me. I didn't even look at
him; I thought only of giving everything. [. . .] We got to the
famous phrase "Alfin son tua." At one point, Toscanini laid a
hand lightly on my shoulder and said very softly, "That's enough
. . . the rest is a concert piece . . . with the flute . . . ." I looked at
him. I saw two big tears running from his eyes. This is the most
beautiful memory of my career.

Toscanini never again conducted a performance of *Lucia* with
anyone but Dal Monte in the title role.

Pertile was asked practically at the last minute to take the role of
Edgardo, because Toscanini had not been happy with the tenor originally selected for the part. "I did not know the opera," Pertile
recalled. "I learned it with Toscanini in five days. However, I had
only one ensemble rehearsal [. . .]. I went fairly calmly to the first
performance, but I was nervous for fear of not having prepared well
enough. At the famous ensemble [the sextet in Act II] I got lost for a
moment [. . .]. After the performance, [. . .] I said to Maestro Toscanini, 'Forgive me for the involuntary error, Maestro. Please let me
have an orchestra rehearsal.' He clapped me on the shoulder, and,
with his characteristic, infrequent smile of encouragement, he said,
'Calm down, get some rest, and come to the next performance.'
That's what I did, and everything went well."

Toscanini's next new production, Giordano's *Madame Sans-Gêne*,
was warmly received, but once it had opened the maestro switched
his main focus to *The Magic Flute*, which had not been heard at La
Scala in over a century. He was determined to convince his public of
the work's greatness, but he failed. On the opening night, 12 May, not
even the overture was applauded. Cesari, the *Corriere*'s critic, offered
the explanation that the audience, "faced with the novelty of spoken
dialogue, perhaps felt a bit offended [. . .] by seeing the gags and bits
of grotesque dancing that used to delight the galleries in operetta
theaters repeated on its glorious stage." Only two performances were

given, but Toscanini, angered by the failure of his loving attempt, made *The Magic Flute* the first work that he conducted the following season, when it survived only four further performances.

There was more work, however, before the 1922–23 season came to an end. First, Toscanini revived the previous season's *Mefistofele* production; then, on 22 May, the fiftieth anniversary of the death of Alessandro Manzoni, he conducted the Verdi *Requiem*, which had been dedicated to the memory of the celebrated writer. But a new production of *La Bohème*—the season's last opera—was conducted by Ghione. When Toscanini asked Puccini to sit in on the final rehearsals, to make sure that things were going as the composer desired, Puccini sent an angry telegram: "If you don't conduct I don't feel interested in being present." Toscanini refrained from responding in kind, and the day after the first performance Puccini wrote to Schnabl, "I received a telegram reporting an excellent outcome: sixteen curtain calls. The God didn't conduct! Maestro Ghione conducted. This made me angry. [. . .] I know that he's ill, but a little friendship, a little thoughtfulness, and even good manners. Enough. I couldn't care less." All this barely five months after the joy of the *Manon* production. Thus the *ente autonomo*'s otherwise successful second season ended unpleasantly.

Toscanini conducted no concerts in the spring of 1923; instead, he invited a thirty-seven-year-old German conductor, Wilhelm Furtwängler, to make his Scala debut in a pair of concerts. Berta Geissmar, Furtwängler's secretary, recalled that during one rehearsal, "Toscanini, who had been sitting unnoticed at the back, suddenly rushed forward and shook him warmly by the hand; he and his family were extremely friendly to him during this whole visit. The year after, Furtwängler visited La Scala to attend some of Toscanini's own operatic productions." Geissmar did not reveal Furtwängler's opinions of Toscanini's performances; in general, however, the German conductor was even less tolerant than his Italian colleague of others' interpretations.

The Toscanini family spent most of the summer of 1923 in a villa in the hills above Lake Como, where the maestro prepared the *ente autonomo*'s third season, which was even more ambitious than the second: it would open in mid-November instead of in December; twenty-four operas were programmed; and 141 performances would be given in just over six months. Toscanini would conduct fourteen of the operas; eight would be entrusted to the thirty-eight-year-old Vittorio Gui, his second-in-command that year (and later an important conductor in his own right); and the remaining two were conducted by Arturo Lucon, recently returned to Italy after having established a career in Russia.

Something important was beginning to shift in Italy's opera world. A quarter century earlier, during Toscanini's three seasons as head of the Teatro Regio in Turin, ten of the fifteen operas performed were by living composers, and three of the remaining five were by Wagner, thus radical rarities in Italy at the time. After the First World War, however, Italian opera audiences, like their counterparts elsewhere, began to show less interest in the new and to become more attached to the old. Today, none of the world's major opera ensembles devotes 35 or 40 percent of a season's repertoire to works by living composers, as La Scala was still doing in the 1920s, but at the time several professional critics complained that the percentage was insufficient: the public was becoming lazy, they feared, and too few new works were being heard. Giulio Ciampelli, *La Sera*'s principal music critic, suggested that since other public entertainment venues were obliged to charge their patrons a surtax to help defray La Scala's expenses, the venerable institution ought to present at least ten significant new or recent works each year.

While these criticisms were starting to circulate among the radicals, some conservative newspapers began to grumble that La Scala had no right at all to receive tax-based contributions. Scandiani, alarmed by the attacks from both sides, suggested that Toscanini and one influential board member discuss the matter directly with Mussolini. Thus, early in November 1923 Toscanini and Senatore Borletti*—a powerful Milanese industrialist who had been a strong supporter of D'Annunzio's Fiume enterprise—made a quick visit to Rome.

Mussolini, who had been in office for just over a year, "listened attentively" to his two interlocutors, according to a statement released immediately afterward by the Agenzia Stefani—the official government press office—"and at the end of the conversation he declared his unchangeable fondness for and admiration of Arturo Toscanini and

---

* Borletti's first name was Senatore; he was not a senator.

his approval of the activities of the Administration of the Ente autonomo della Scala." The prime minister "expressed once again the wish to have the polemics cease, since the reopening of La Scala is imminent and the season is opening with excellent expectations."

Calm was restored, and Gui opened the season on 15 November with Strauss's *Salome*, paired with *I Compagnacci* by Primo Riccitelli, a Mascagni protégé. After reviving *The Magic Flute*, Toscanini turned to his first new production of the season: *Aida*. Benvenuto Franci, making his house debut as Amonasro, quickly became a company mainstay and one of Toscanini's favorite baritones. He had "one of the most beautiful voices that I can remember," said a colleague, the soprano Gilda Dalla Rizza, but, she recalled, he liked to sing full throttle all the time, which made Toscanini tease him: "'Away from here you can shout all you like, but with me you have to sing!'" A performance of *Aida* later in the season was attended by the king and queen, who, however, entered just before and left just after the "triumphal" scene in the second act. Toscanini, "turned halfway toward the orchestra seats, nervously started the Royal March" when they arrived and again when they departed, reported *La Sera* the next day.

Dalla Rizza—a creamy-complexioned, thirty-one-year-old lyric soprano who had made her name mainly in the *verismo* repertoire—sang for the first time with Toscanini in the season's following production, *La Traviata*, with Pertile as Alfredo and Luigi Montesanto alternating with Franci as Germont. She had not previously sung the role of Violetta, which requires coloratura-like agility in the first-act cabaletta, "Sempre libera." But Toscanini always wanted a Violetta who, like the recently retired Storchio, could not only bring off that piece but also convey the powerfully emotional and dramatic second and third acts. "He considered many voices, also better ones than mine, I believe, but as they were all 'light' they could not, in his opinion, be right for the character of Violetta," Dalla Rizza recalled.

> "Try Violetta's part a bit—in fact, let me hear a bit of your *agilità*." "Maestro," I replied, "I've never done *agilità*. What could I let you hear?" I sang, and he said, "Right now you sound like a double bass, but try to study it anyway."
>
> [. . .] I set out to study the first act of *La Traviata* for four months, twice a day with Maestro Calusio. [. . .] The character

of Violetta was sketched out for me by Forzano, but there wasn't a single staging rehearsal at which the Maestro wasn't present. I remember that during a staging rehearsal of the second act he kept telling me that I wasn't giving my maximum in the famous "Dite alla giovine." I tried and tried again, but I didn't manage to express all the emotion that Toscanini wanted. At one point, I put all of my willpower, all of my soul, my heart into it, so that I actually burst into tears.

"That's it, that's it!" he shouted from the podium. "*La Traviata* needs emotion!" "Yes, Maestro," I replied, "but if this happens to me on stage I don't know how it will all end."

Toscanini gave everything of himself when he conducted, and when I sang he would sing with me, to make me feel the expression, the *piano*, the *forte*.*

Mario Labroca, a composer, music critic, and, later, an important music administrator, recalled, years later, that at the first performance of the *Traviata* production he and his friends—typical young radicals who thought of Verdi's midperiod works as old-fashioned and uninteresting—made their way up to La Scala's top gallery with low expectations but left afterward feeling exalted. "It was as if all of a sudden a treasure that we could finally enjoy had fallen in our laps; everything that we had thought of until then as base stuff became a rare, precious thing."

The exaltation was contagious. H. E. Wortham, a British writer, visited Milan during the 1923–24 season and was struck by everything he saw and heard: the amount of time devoted to thorough rehearsals at La Scala, as compared with the paucity of rehearsal time at Covent Garden; "the extraordinary technical perfection of the lighting and scenic equipment"; the hyrdraulic lift under the orchestra pit; and, most of all, the orchestra and Toscanini. Wortham interviewed Gui, who told him, regarding the Maestro, "La Scala takes all of his energies and is his whole life. He is always here, no matter who is taking the rehearsals, making suggestions and experi-

---

* Both Puccini and Toscanini may have pursued Dalla Rizza, and some of their antagonism during that period may have resulted from this rivalry. Dalla Rizza, who died in 1975, is said to have destroyed letters that she received from Toscanini and some of Puccini's letters as well, although other letters that Puccini sent her have been published.

ments, throwing out new ideas, absorbed in every detail, and listening, listening." Everyone who worked within this institution took pride in being part of it.

7.

DURING THE FASCISTS' FIRST PERIOD IN POWER (1922–25), THEIR party made significant inroads into all of the cabinet ministries. Mussolini, an experienced journalist and propagandist, was keenly aware of the particular importance of the national public education system for shaping young minds to his way of thinking, and the man he chose as his first minister of public education was Giovanni Gentile, a fundamentally independent-minded philosopher who did not hesitate to engage non-Fascist or, at first, even anti-Fascist intellectuals for jobs for which they were exceptionally qualified. As fascism's principal intellectual apologist, however, he also did not hesitate to condone some of the party's more questionable methods of proselytization. In one of his speeches, Gentile, attempting to whitewash Fascist violence, remarked that distinctions between moral and material persuasion are naïve: "All force is moral force, because it is always addressed to the will," he said; "and whatever form of persuasion is adopted, from the sermon to the truncheon, its efficacy can only be that which in the end urges man internally and persuades him to consent."

In December 1923, Gentile's ministry made its first significant incursion into the area of music education by removing the seventy-two-year-old Giuseppe Gallignani from the directorship of the Milan Conservatory, a post he had held since 1897. Although Gallignani had been a highly regarded administrator, faculty members had recently complained that the white-bearded director had become disorganized and authoritarian; he had also shown no enthusiasm for fascism. Unaware of the attempts to unseat him, Gallignani received, one day, a brusque ministerial telegram announcing his dismissal. He read the communication, went home, and jumped to his death.

The story of the firing and the suicide was not made public, but Milan's artists and intellectuals quickly learned the real story. Gentile, who was making his first, tentative pronouncements about "regulating the study of music in Italian schools," must have been shocked to receive a brutal telegram from the nation's most celebrated performing musician, who had been a friend of Gallignani's. "Maestro Gallignani, who did what no Minister or Director-General was capable of doing for our Conservatory, has committed suicide," the message read. "Gentlemen of the Ministry of Public Education, Ministers, and Directors-General: I tell you that this suicide will weigh upon your consciences forever. Arturo Toscanini." And to Mussolini, Toscanini wired, "Maestro Gallignani[,] victim of a ferocious act of injustice on the part of the Minister of Education[,] committed suicide this morning[.] With broken heart and all my tears I protest against this Minister who did not have even the slightest respect for a man who gave all his marvelous activity for the Conservatory's welfare[.] Arturo Toscanini."

Toscanini and other leading Milanese personages attended Gallignani's funeral,* arrangements for which had been supervised by Gaetano Cesari, who, in addition to being a musicologist and the *Corriere's* music critic, was the Milan Conservatory's librarian. When Cesari noticed that a huge wreath from Gentile was to be placed on the hearse, he exclaimed to the attendants, "He makes people kill themselves and then expects to have his wreath attached to the hearse! Put it wherever you like, but not here." At that point, a professor who was believed to have been one of the instigators of Gallignani's removal stepped up to make a commemorative speech; Toscanini approached the man, grabbed his notes from his hand, threw them to the ground, stepped on them, and shouted, "No! You will not speak!" According to Filippo Sacchi, "even many years later the workers at the Monumental Cemetery remembered the funeral as the most exciting one they had ever seen."

Cesari's words were reported to the ministry, which promptly fired him from his post at the conservatory. Toscanini wrote at once to Mussolini: "His Excellency, Minister Gentile, is evidently unaware of Cesari's worth. I consider him the very, very best of Italy's musicologists and [. . .] I beg Your Excellency with great fervor to have the

---

* Gallignani's wife had predeceased him, and Arturo and Carla Toscanini became de facto guardians of his young daughter, Lalla; Carla looked after the distribution of funds for the girl's support, some of which derived from royalties accruing to the estate of Boito, who had been a close friend of Gallignani's.

measure revoked. It will be a true act of justice toward an artist. With unchangeable devotion and affection[,] Arturo Toscanini."

Cesari was reinstated. Pizzetti assumed the direction of the Milan Conservatory, but he and other astute Italian music administrators now understood how precarious their positions were. During the remaining twenty years of Mussolini's rule, most administrators who were not convinced Fascists took care to pay lip service to the regime and to praise its magnanimity toward the arts. But Toscanini's message on Cesari's behalf proved to be his last positive communication with Mussolini. Within a few months, the "unchangeable devotion and affection" would change forever.

8.

A RADICAL NEW PRODUCTION OF *TRISTAN UND ISOLDE*, DESIGNED BY the Swiss theatrical theorist Adolphe Appia, debuted at La Scala in December 1923, twenty-three years after Toscanini had conducted the work's Milan premiere. Appia, recognized today as one of the fathers of modern opera design, had come under the spell of Wagner's music early in life but had been repelled by the spectacle of Rhine Maidens being hoisted up and down on ropes, half-dead cart horses appearing onstage as Brünnhilde's mighty steed, and lovers trying to show their feelings through embarrassingly trite, unconvincing gestures. As early as 1896, he had presented some of his ideas for more symbolic stagings to Cosima Wagner, but she had dismissed most of his plans out of hand: the only sets and the only stage movements that could be taken seriously were those that had been approved by her husband, she declared.

Familiarity with Emile Jaques-Dalcroze's eurhythmics (rhythmical gymnastics) persuaded Appia that opera could best be served by singers with gymnastically trained, pliable bodies capable of symbolic action, which would replace unconvincing attempts at naturalistic action; these performers would be seen in spaces of simple design that would serve mainly as backdrops to inventive lighting effects and, secondarily, to color effects, in order to create the proper dramatic backgrounds to the works being interpreted. But such ideas were so far ahead of their time that Appia spent most of his life on the fringes of the theater world, little known and less esteemed.

Toscanini favored naturalistic stagings for operas like *La Traviata* or *Manon Lescaut*—purely human dramas. But attempts to produce naturalistic stagings of dramas that included mythological characters or characters whose lives were controlled by potions or spells, not to mention operas that took place partly in the air or underwater, inevitably produced absurd results. "Listen to *Siegfried*: you can imagine the leaves rustling in the trees," Toscanini said. "Then look at the stage: a tree painted on paper. It's ridiculous! You can't present these operas without murdering them!" He had learned of Appia's ideas as early as 1910, when he had read Jacques Rouché's book *L'Art théâtral moderne*. Why not present dream worlds in dream settings? Appia asked. Why not suggest rather than depict? More recently, in 1921, Appia had published *L'Oeuvre d'art vivant*, which included sketches of sets for several of Wagner's works; the simplicity of those sketches appealed to Toscanini, who—encouraged by Marquis Emanuele Ordoño de Rosales, a Milanese sculptor—invited Appia to Milan to design the new *Tristan* production for La Scala.

Appia must have thought he was dreaming. Never before had he been granted a chance to realize his ideas on a world-famous stage and with first-rate artists and competent collaborators at his disposal. In addition, Walter Toscanini, now twenty-five and a passionate bibliophile with a special interest in theater history and dance history, asked him to bring along a collection of his drawings and stage designs so that an exhibition could be presented at Bottega di Poesia (Poetry Boutique), a gallery *cum* small publishing house *cum* antiquarian book and manuscript shop that Walter and a friend, Count Emanuele di Castelbarco, had opened a year earlier in central Milan. Appia duly arrived in town, white-bearded, unkempt, wearing shorts and woolen socks as if for a hiking expedition, but full of hope. The entire Toscanini family took a liking to this gentleman, who looked much older than his sixty-one years yet seemed as dreamy as a teenager, and the affection was mutual. In November, Walter and Castelbarco inaugurated the promised exhibition and published one of Appia's essays, "Art vivant? ou nature morte?" (Living Art? or Still Life?). A lecture on Appia's work, with an accompanying slide show, was organized at Il Convegno, a club of which Walter was president and which also issued a translation of Appia's essay "La Mise en scène et son avenir" (Staging and Its Future). Appia seemed pleased, too, that there was "a press campaign in my behalf."

Caramba oversaw the entire production and, with Appia, designed the costumes, but the members of La Scala's technical staff were put off by Appia's ideas and by his lack of interest in the practical side of stagecraft. Toscanini would encourage him to persevere—"Speak up, Monsieur Appia!"—but the shy theoretician had little experience in dealing with the day-to-day realities of life in the theater. He later claimed that his ideas had not been entirely realized, and he even complained about the Viennese director Ernst Lert, who was responsible, together with Toscanini, for the stage action, although Lert was an admirer of Appia's theories. (Lert would continue to codirect most of La Scala's German repertoire for the duration of Toscanini's tenure.) But even if Appia's designs had been perfectly brought to life, he could hardly have expected the cast members, accustomed as they were to the stock operatic productions of the day, to move as easily and poetically as gymnastic dancers. One observer went so far as to describe the Swedish soprano Nanny Larsén-Todsen's emphatic gestures as more appropriate to Mascagni's Santuzza or Puccini's Tosca than to Wagner's Isolde. (The role of Tristan was sung by the Ukrainian-born Stepan Bielina.) In the end, Appia was so disappointed that he did not attend the first two performances of "his" *Tristan*, and he reserved his wholehearted praise only for Toscanini, the Toscanini family, and his own assistant, Jean Mercier.

Appia's extant drawings for Acts II and III of La Scala's *Tristan* are in no way radical even by conservative early twenty-first-century standards. For the second act, for instance, tall trees on either side of the stage, their branches touching high up over center stage, seem to shelter what appears to be a small, secondary entrance to King Marke's castle; only a minuscule part of the castle's lower area is visible, raised on a platform about ten feet over the stage, and a blazing torch juts out of a wall near the entrance. The general atmosphere is dark, not only in keeping with the nocturnal setting but also, as the Wagner scholar Philip A. Maxwell has written, "to play up the symbolism of the torch, which was supposed to have the sort of blinding impact on the audience that it had on the two lovers—the putting out of the torch was the signal that Tristan and Isolde could rush into each others' arms and surrender themselves to the vast expanse of eternal night." Two drawings—one dark, the other light (related, perhaps, to the sharply contrasting lighting in the German Expressionist films of the 1920s)—for Act III show a similar, semihidden small entrance to an old stone building, presumably Tristan's castle; the wooden door is shut in the lighter drawing but open in the darker one. To the viewer's left, a large, leafy tree stands near the entrance; to the right, there is an open area with a few stone steps and a low stone wall. "Appia intended to combine subtle lighting with simple, practicable scenery to mould the visual and the aural into one unified dramatic force," Maxwell writes. "The transfiguration of the scene by light corresponds to the trans-figuration of Isolde by undying love at the end of the opera."

Appia's designs cannot be called abstract: they are minimal but pictorial, and they were meant to focus the audience's attention on the music and the drama. The conductor Gianandrea Gavazzeni, who was a conservatory student in 1923, recalled much later that "we young people were very much taken with this new attempt and enthusiastic about it." But the enthusiasts were a tiny minority. Most of the reviewers praised Toscanini and the orchestra, declared the principal singers to be merely passable, and expressed perplexity and dismay over the production. The decor was "conceived and realized contrary to the original, customary one, and furthermore, in itself it has no beauty or pictorial justification," wrote the composer and critic Alceo Toni, who described Appia's sets as cold, shabby, and lacking in imagination. "Calvinist" was the epithet applied by some critics and audience members to Appia and his designs: many felt that La Scala's productions ought to be dazzling and opulent, no matter what the underlying nature of any given opera might be, and the ultraconservative Bayreuth acolytes in the audience were the spec-tacle's most outraged and outspoken opponents of all. Only six per-formances were given. Thirty years later, however, when Wieland Wagner and other creative theater people began to rethink opera staging, Appia's 1923 Scala production was seen as a milestone.

TOSCANINI HAD PRECEDED *TRISTAN* with reprises of *The Magic Flute* and *Manon Lescaut*, and he followed it by conducting new produc-tions of Mascagni's *Iris* and Gluck's *Orfeo ed Euridice*, the latter with two now legendary contraltos, the Mexican Fanny Anitúa and the Roman Gabriella Besanzoni, alternating as Orfeo, and the young Florentine soprano Ines Alfani Tellini as Euridice. He applied the same cuts and interpolations that he had used fifteen years earlier in his Metropolitan *Orfeo* production.

Toscanini usually attended his colleagues' rehearsals, helping, encouraging, and criticizing as each case required, in his view. Following a rehearsal of *The Barber of Seville* (conducted by Lucon), during which Toti Dal Monte had interpolated much ornamentation in the aria "Una voce poco fa" and in her duet with Figaro, "Toscanini hurtled into my dressing room like a comet and insulted me with filthy language," she recalled: "'superficial,' 'ham,' and 'circus-tent singer' were the most gracious of his epithets. When the outburst had ended, he left, slamming the door, and I, stupefied, was left crying."

She angrily withdrew from the first performance, which was canceled; the production opened three days late, after she had calmed down. Immediately thereafter, she began to rehearse *La Sonnambula* with Gui. "Toscanini was always present," she said, "generously advising [the tenor Dino] Borgioli, Pinza, and all the others. He didn't interest himself at all in me, or at least so I thought. I kept my mouth shut and watched." But at one of the last rehearsals she asked for his comments.

> He looked at me with a smile and answered, "For the last act I have nothing to tell you. I only wish that you would move the tempi along in the first. We all know that you sing well, but for pity's sake, don't amuse yourself by listening to yourself and move, move more, especially in the recitatives."
>
> The next evening, at the dress rehearsal, I had only one thought: speed up, move, and lighten up the interpretation.
>
> On opening night, while I was finishing getting dressed, Toscanini shouted through the door: "I listened to you yesterday evening. Sing as before, because you were no longer yourself yesterday evening." He, too, had heard that by speeding up the tempi the typically Bellinian pathos was lost.

During the early months of 1924, Toscanini rehearsed and conducted revivals of six different operas, but most of his attention throughout that period was focused on a new undertaking: the world premiere of Boito's *Nerone*.

9.

NERONE HAD REMAINED IN TOSCANINI'S CONSCIOUSNESS SINCE Boito's death in 1918, and preparing its premiere was the biggest single project that Toscanini ever undertook or would ever undertake. "Boito had announced to me many times the completion of *Nerone* and his wish to have it performed at La Scala under my direction," Toscanini explained to the music journalist Raffaello De Rensis.[*] "Every time, owing to his now legendary self-dissatisfaction, he would postpone his proposal, tearing up paper, changing or entirely redoing whole scenes and acts." The composer's "annotations concerning harmonization and orchestration were correct," Toscanini said, "since his intuition for sound hardly ever failed him, but as soon as he had to make them concrete, to realize them, he wandered away from his intuition and did not achieve the effects he had planned and wanted. At that point there would be second thoughts, discouragement, piles of paper in the wastebasket, and indefinite postponements."

According to the composer Antonio Smareglia, in 1914 Boito had shown Toscanini and himself a completed piano-vocal score as well as his ideas for the work's orchestration—ideas that were sketchy at best, impossible at worst. Smareglia and Toscanini had agreed that Boito needed to hear the truth, but neither of them had felt up to the task of facing their aging, infirm friend and running the risk of depressing him. Then came the war, during which Smareglia was confined to his home region in Austrian-held territory; by the time he was able to return to Milan, Boito had died.

Luigi Albertini, Boito's heir and executor, had put *Nerone* in Toscanini's hands, in the hope that the opera would be ready by the fall of 1921, in time to open the reborn Scala ensemble's first season. Indeed, seeing *Nerone* through to its premiere had been one of Toscanini's

---

[*] In a letter sent to Toscanini on 24 August 1902, Gatti-Casazza quoted Boito as having told him, "I count on [Toscanini] absolutely for the interpretation and conducting of *Nerone*; there is no one else who can realize what I desire and what must be achieved for the opera's victory."

main reasons for returning to the house: "It was a moral obligation," he said, many years later. Toscanini at first turned to Smareglia for help, and not later than the spring of 1920 the two men set to work on the project. But after they finished the first act, the collaboration ended, for reasons that Smareglia described as "sinister" and "mysterious" but that in all likelihood were purely practical: the blind composer needed a pianist to play each phrase over and over for him, which made the process extremely time-consuming. Perhaps Toscanini was dismayed by the time factor, or perhaps he simply disliked Smareglia's solutions to the myriad problems that the task posed. He engaged another composer, Vincenzo Tommasini, to collaborate with him on the score; Smareglia, who, only a short time earlier, had described Toscanini as "the only personality in Italy who warmly and affectionately worked for the popularization and recognition of my operas," now took the trouble to express, in a codicil to his will, his "bitterness" over Toscanini's "hateful hostility to my operas."

The immense task of preparing new productions for the *ente autonomo*'s first two seasons had pushed the *Nerone* project into the background, but by the end of the second season Toscanini decided that the opera had to be ready the following year. "I know that Toscanini and Tommasini will withdraw to some villa on Lake Como to manhandle *Nerone*," Puccini wrote sarcastically to Schnabl-Rossi in June 1923, and that is more or less what happened.

The many hundreds of work hours that Toscanini, Smareglia, and Tommasini spent on making *Nerone* performable were soon outnumbered by the tens of thousands of work hours that La Scala's forces began to put into designing and producing the sets and costumes, working out the staging and choreography, and carrying out the musical preparations. For the title role—which Boito had intended first for Tamagno and then for Caruso, both of whom had died in the meantime—Toscanini turned to Pertile, who "began an exhausting period of rehearsals with Forzano and Toscanini— whole days for about two months," the tenor recalled. The even more difficult lead soprano role, Asteria, was assigned to the thirty-one-year-old Rosa Raisa, with whom Toscanini was working for the first time.

Raisa—originally Raitza Burchstein—hailed from Bialystok but had immigrated to Italy at the age of thirteen, after having survived one of the worst anti-Jewish pogroms of the era. She had received vocal training in Naples from Barbara Marchisio, who was also Toti Dal Monte's teacher, and had quickly made a name for herself in many of the world's principal opera houses. According to Charles Mintzer, her biographer, Toscanini had first heard Raisa sing in New York in January 1921, in a somewhat rough-and-ready interpretation of *Norma* with the visiting Chicago Opera Company, and never forgot the power of her voice; he was said to have called her "the Tamagno of dramatic sopranos."* He wanted her for the *Nerone* premiere, and when he learned that her Chicago contract would keep her in America until the end of March 1924, he postponed the opera's premiere by over a month. He sent the score to Panizza, who was returning to Europe from a season in the States, to teach Raisa her tremendously difficult, high-lying part during the Atlantic crossing, and as soon as she arrived in Milan she presented herself to Toscanini at La Scala. "This was the first time that I had ever sung for this great Maestro," she wrote in a projected memoir that she did not live to publish. "I had heard so much about his being demanding, severe, temperamental, that when I entered the large rehearsal room I confess I was very nervous. But when I saw him come in with his beautiful, smiling, and penetrating eyes I felt at ease and confident. [. . .] I could hardly wait from one [rehearsal] to the next."

The production required 13 solo singers, a 100-piece orchestra, 120 choristers, 42 dancers, 108 mimes and movement people, 238 extras, and 55 stagehands, electricians, tailors, and backstage assistants. No wonder, then, that Toscanini and the house's entire administration were determined to make the premiere and subsequent performances a series of unforgettable events. Special publications about the opera and its origins were issued: not only a large, illustrated souvenir program, with a cover in color, but also books and booklets by at least five different authors about Boito and *Nerone*, and numerous printings of Boito's original text for *Nerone*. Publicity in the national and international press reached unprecedented levels. Forzano reported to Toscanini that in a Tuscan mountain village that did not yet have electricity or paved roads, the local schoolmistress

---

* A late-in-life comment by Toscanini indicates that he did not like Raisa in *Norma*: "I never found a soprano who could sing Norma for me. Raisa, no!"

had told him that her pupils had asked about *Nerone*, and that she had had to give two lessons on that bit of Roman history.

"We are on the eve of the greatest artistic event of the year," the British *Observer's* Milan correspondent wrote fully two months before the event. Musicians and critics from all over Europe arrived for the dress rehearsal and first performance, which were also attended by many European opera house managers as well as various countries' ambassadors and consuls general. Ticket sales for the first performance alone brought some 827,000 lire into La Scala's coffers, and the charged, anticipatory atmosphere was recounted the following day, with some irony, by a chronicler for *L'Ambrosiana*.

> The automobiles and carriages arrive, stop, and leave after having set down their overdressed human cargo. [. . .] In the meantime, at precisely 7 P.M., when the small lateral doors that lead to the upper regions are opened, crowds of undistinguished citizens—those who haven't paid the thousand pieces of gold necessary for inhabiting the best boxes and the orchestra seats, if not the podium itself—enter in spurts. The tumultuous crowd trots up the steps to conquer a tiny bit of decent room. [. . .]
>
> Eight-thirty comes. The wait has become tense. Late-arriving matrons and cavaliers and grave-looking senators, somewhat winded by the rush, are still entering. The matrons lift the trains of their dresses and the stairways resound with the rustle of silk.
>
> At exactly 8:40, while latecomers are still being pursued through the corridors and in the entrance hall, the auditorium's great chandelier slowly goes out and Maestro Toscanini enters rapidly from the little door to the left of the orchestra and quickly ascends the conductor's podium. Great applause breaks out on high, spreads, bursts out warmly, twice, three times. The maestro barely turns to show his thanks with a nod of his head, and gives the signal. The curtain opens silently, and the Appian Way is seen, barely visible in the first glow of dawn.

Nerone was praised by the great majority of the reviewers present at the opening, and Albertini expressed his particular gratitude and admiration for Toscanini's work in completing and performing the mammoth opera. Nevertheless, a few observers immediately noticed some of the flaws that would condemn the work to a position as an also-ran in the long history of opera: a plot that included a strong dose of the decadent, sentimentalized pseudo-Christianity typical of late nineteenth-century nonbelievers like Boito; the predominance of plot, text, and spectacle over musical substance; the stylistic bumps that resulted, at least in part, from the enormous time span during which the composer was haphazardly working on the piece; and the use of a melodic and harmonic language that would already have seemed antiquated a quarter century earlier. Much of *Nerone* sounds like an odd mixture of late Verdi (*Don Carlos*, *Aida*, *Otello*) and late Wagner (*Parsifal*, in particular). In a letter to a friend, Gatti-Casazza, who had been involved in the *Nerone* project at the turn of the century, now described the opera as a "dark-hued piece of ornate décor" that "wouldn't have survived two performances with the old public, and in the end it isn't even really by Boito! When one sees an Artist like Toscanini—who used to be so orthodox, intransigent, puritanical, and austere—become the champion of this falsification and spend his great authority to persuade the crowd that fireflies are beacon lights, what's left to hope for or to believe in? I'm ashamed for him and for our art."

Camille Bellaigue, a French critic who had been friendly with both Verdi and Boito, wrote, "With Boito gone, only Toscanini could be the all-powerful soul of this great body." This statement proved to be true in a sense unintended by Bellaigue: when Toscanini ceased to conduct the work, *Nerone* virtually disappeared. Yet he remained convinced of its superiority to Boito's earlier and more popular *Mefistofele*: there was a "huge difference" between the two, he said, during a late-in-life conversation with a fellow musician, and he singled out *Nerone*'s third act as being particularly masterly. "It has things that are so very beautiful!" he said. But, he admitted, *Nerone* "came along too late."

SO HIGHLY ANTICIPATED was the *Nerone* premiere that during the first intermission, "Mussolini himself telephoned General Manager Scandiani from Rome, asking for news of the outcome of the first act [and] expressing his happiness when he learned that it was triumphal," the *Corriere della Sera* reported. But the period of Toscanini's wait-and-see attitude toward Mussolini and his party had already ended.

As the 1923–24 season was drawing to a close, the Milanese Fascists announced that they intended to take control of La Scala's board of directors, and on 6 June Mayor Mangiagalli warned Mussolini of the possible consequences of such a move. The Scala question "may seem small but is not so," and "could seriously damage the structure of the Municipal Administration," Mangiagalli wrote to the prime minister.

> La Scala now has worldwide prestige and fame, thanks to Toscanini. Astronomic distances separate him from other conductors. He may have his faults, but he also has great moral virtues. His disinterestedness is total, as a result of which he has damaged himself by remaining at La Scala to ensure its primacy. He has turned down fabulous offers, and he would not accept the check for 100,000 lire that we offered him as a bonus payment. La Scala is his passion; it is the temple of art, and he does not want it profaned by selfish interests or party passions. [. . .] The Fascist Party wishes to have three Fascist municipal representatives [on the Scala board]; but besides disrupting the harmony among the various political groups, this would give Toscanini the impression of a political act. He won't hear of it. Can we allow Toscanini to leave and La Scala to lose its prestige?

Realizing that he was unable, at this early juncture, to risk damaging so great a cultural icon as La Scala, Mussolini acquiesced.

Four days after Mangiagalli sent his letter, Giacomo Matteotti, secretary of the Italian Socialist Party, was kidnapped and brutally murdered by Fascist thugs. Matteotti had discovered, exposed, and denounced evidence of the Fascist Party's fraudulent and often violent manipulation of a recent election campaign and of Mussolini's plans to create a dictatorship. The question of the budding dictator's knowledge or ignorance of the organization of this crime has never been settled, but at the time the country was convulsed with anti-Fascist protests, and there were demands that the king force his prime minister to step down. Victor Emanuel stood behind Mussolini.

Toscanini was appalled by both the increasingly authoritarian head of government and the pusillanimous head of state, and Mussolini, who was accustomed to bringing people into the fold by massaging their egos, evidently intended to soften Toscanini's increasingly harsh attitude toward fascism by offering him a senatorship: rumors to that effect began to circulate widely toward the end of 1924. After all, Puccini had been made a senator earlier that year and had joined the Fascist Party. Carla Toscanini, fearing that her husband would turn the offer down with a violently antigovernment statement, spoke in private to Ugo Ojetti, a journalist who had Mussolini's ear, and asked him to try to prevent the offer from being made. Ojetti did as requested, and a minor crisis was averted. A few months later, the government issued orders that photographs of the king and Mussolini had to be prominently displayed in every public venue, including theaters, but Toscanini refused to comply. As long as he was in charge at La Scala, neither portrait was hung there. A long and difficult standoff had begun.

10.

LIKE SO MANY OTHER ARTISTS OF BOUNDLESS ENERGY, TOSCANINI had an unusual way of reducing his workload. After having conducted eighty-two performances of fourteen operas—including *Nerone* and seven other new productions—during the 1923–24 season, he "relaxed" by rehearsing his orchestra for a two-week concert tour that began on 13 June in the Lombard town of Varese and continued in the Swiss cities of Zurich, Bern, Lausanne, Geneva, Basel, and St. Gallen. Adolf Busch heard the orchestra and wrote to his older brother, Fritz, already a well-known conductor: "Toscanini was wonderful in Zurich—in the Brahms second symphony, thank God, there was even something *happening* for a change."

Busch's recital partner and future son-in-law, the twenty-one-year-old pianist Rudolf Serkin, was also present and later recalled his impression of Brahms's Second Symphony. "It was an incredible revelation," he said. "It was architecture with passion. Afterwards, at a reception [. . .] Toscanini was there with the Busches and me and Furtwängler. And Furtwängler was shocked at some things in Toscanini['s Brahms performance]. It was so new! Embarrassingly and painfully, he told Toscanini in violent terms what he thought. Toscanini was like a little boy and then answered: 'Look, when Steinbach came to Turin and conducted the Brahms Second Symphony, after the first rehearsal he turned to the orchestra and said, 'I have nothing to do. Who is your conductor?' And the answer was Toscanini."

Toscanini spent much of the month of July with his family in Guello, a hamlet in the hills above Bellagio, on Lake Como, but he was summoned back to Milan in the middle of the month to be with his eighty-four-year-old mother, who was gravely ill. Paola Montani Toscanini died on the twenty-third, and her remains were placed next to those of her husband and her grandson in the family tomb in the Cimitero Monumentale. How Toscanini reacted to his mother's death is not known, but only a few days later he and Scandiani were in Paris to make plans—with Jacques Rouché, general manager of the Opéra—for bringing the Scala ensemble to the French capital between mid-May and mid-June of the following year. Financial and logistical problems arose, however, and the visit never materialized. Similar attempts to bring the Milanese company to London's Covent Garden the following year also failed.

At the same time, another Puccini-Toscanini crisis was in full bloom. During the weeks leading up to the *Nerone* premiere, Toscanini had heard rumors to the effect that some of Italy's most prominent living composers had predicted that the opera would prove to be worthless. As a result, he had banned Puccini, Mascagni, and company from *Nerone*'s dress rehearsal—although they did attend the premiere. Mascagni was so angry that he wrote to Mussolini to complain, and Puccini felt so deeply offended that he eventually wrote a long letter to Toscanini, in which he confessed that the incident had "collided violently with my sensitivity and my feelings as a friend and comrade. [. . .] [T]o see myself kept out of the dress rehearsal, by you of all people, was so painful for me that I left a few days later, full of bitterness, an ungreeted guest." Puccini was convinced that "someone near you in La Scala's circles, someone who bends with the wind, took it upon himself to create discord between us," and he believed that his "nonexistent opinions about *Nerone*" were "most likely attributed to me by the same unseen viper. [. . .] I can't accept the fact that such wretches can disrupt the friendship between two upright men connected through so many years of friendship, esteem, and memories!" He added that *Turandot*, his new opera, was near completion, "but I'm taking plenty of time, the more so as it's not my intention to present the opera this year."

Puccini's letter did not have the desired effect, but early in September, when Toscanini was in Bologna to plan the local premiere of *Nerone*, Forzano—who would direct the staging—suggested that they pay a visit to Puccini in Viareggio. Toscanini at first refused, but when Forzano told him that he had heard that Puccini was seriously ill, Toscanini relented. Puccini—sixty-five, gray-haired, but as elegant as ever—was delighted to see Toscanini, and he joked about his voice, which sounded strange. " 'Don't you hear it, Toscanini? I used to be a basso, now I'm a tenor—[. . .] I sound like Lucia's husband' "—the light tenor role of Arturo in *Lucia di Lammermoor*. They laughed and told him that "he would be able to sing *Turandot* himself—at least he would be satisfied" with the interpretation, Forzano recalled. " 'It's just a little grain of flesh, like the head of a pin,' " Puccini told them about his throat problem. " 'The doctor wants to see me again in a few days.' "

On 7 September, Puccini wrote to Schnabl, "Toscanini has just left and all the clouds have disappeared, and I am very, very happy about it. I'm sure that in his hands *Turandot* will have the ideal performance. And this will be in April, so I have all the time in the world to finish the bit that I still have to do. I showed him and played him some parts and I think he was very satisfied. And so the whole disagreeable situation has ended." Twelve days later, Carlo Clausetti of the Ricordi company wired Toscanini, who was relaxing at the Salsomaggiore spa, to apprise him of a meeting in Milan two days later with Puccini and with *Turandot*'s librettists, Renato Simoni and Giuseppe Adami, plus Forzano and Caramba. With Toscanini, they would begin serious planning for the *Turandot* premiere the following spring.

Nerone opened in Bologna in mid-October; while the series of twelve performances was in progress, Forzano and Toscanini learned that Puccini had seen a famous specialist and that the reports were not reassuring. "Maestro Toscanini was very agitated," Forzano recalled, and early in November they returned to Viareggio. "Puccini himself opened the gate for us. 'I'm leaving for Brussels. They've ordered me to leave immediately. It seems to be something very serious; not dangerous, but very serious.' " When Puccini asked Forzano for a cigarette, Elvira, the composer's wife, said, "'No, don't give it to him, for pity's sake. They've advised him not to smoke.'" But Tonio, Puccini's son, who was sitting behind his parents, gestured to Forzano as if to say, "'Let him smoke if it makes him happy; there's no hope, anyway.'" Forzano noticed that "the truth had been confided to Toscanini, too."

Puccini was delighted with Toscanini's quick perception of the new opera. "They were bent over the pages of *Turandot* together," Forzano said, "and when, from some short question or comment of Toscanini's, Puccini understood that without needing to speak, to explain, to play, all of his intentions, even the subtlest of them, had already been grasped with sure, rapid, and precise penetration, he would stand up straight behind Toscanini's back, look at us, and wink, and he would giggle, admiringly and happily; it was clear that he was tasting in advance the joy that he would have at the rehearsals in hearing his opera revealed by that great, generous artist." Until late at night, the three men discussed "the details of staging," including "the entrance of the masked characters." Forzano and Toscanini had to leave early the following morning in order to reach Bologna in time for a *Nerone* performance that evening, but they stopped first to say goodbye to Puccini, who was "still in bed, reading the newspapers, as was his custom; he had rested peacefully and felt better." They embraced Puccini, who was departing for Brussels later that day, and took their leave, saying, "See you in Milan at the rehearsals" for *Turandot*.

When Toscanini, in the midst of rehearsals at La Scala, learned that the operations to which Puccini had been subjected had failed to save him from throat cancer, and that he lay dying, he asked Carla to go to Brussels to help look after the composer in his last days, because the hyper-emotional Elvira had not accompanied her husband and had never been told of the gravity of his condition. On the afternoon of 29 November 1924, Adami entered La Scala's orchestra pit in the middle of a rehearsal and advanced toward Toscanini. "He turned to me, and he understood in a moment," Adami said.

"'Dead?'

"'Dead.' He dropped his baton, ran to his dressing room, threw himself face down on the sofa [. . .] and broke into tears."

Toscanini and another of Puccini's friends—probably Adami—took upon themselves the difficult task of breaking the news to Elvira, and they remained with her until nightfall. The composer's body was brought back to Milan by train, and on 3 December, at the funeral in the cathedral, Toscanini conducted the Scala orchestra in the Funeral Elegy from the composer's *Edgar*, just as he had conducted "Va, pensiero," from *Nabucco*, when Verdi's coffin had been taken to its final resting place nearly a quarter century earlier. Puccini's body was placed temporarily in the Toscanini family vault at the Monumentale while a tomb was being prepared for him at his home in Tuscany. On the afternoon of 29 December, exactly one month after Puccini's death, Toscanini conducted a student orchestra in a memorial concert at the Milan Conservatory, the composer's alma mater, and that evening, at La Scala, he led the house orchestra in some of the same repertoire and a special performance of *La Bohème*.

Toscanini would pay several important tributes to Puccini in the years that followed, but his attitude toward the composer, postmortem, remained as complicated as it had been during Puccini's lifetime. In the first place, Toscanini never forgave Puccini for the latter's alleged intrigues against Catalani; although Toscanini did not blame Puccini for the lack of staying power of Catalani's operas, he could never quite reconcile Puccini's ascent to worldwide success with Catalani's fall into virtual oblivion. Then there were the political differences between the left-leaning Toscanini and the right-leaning Puccini (who, shortly before his death, had accepted a senatorship from Mussolini), and—if rumors are to be believed—their rivalry for the attentions of Cesira Ferrani in the 1890s and Gilda Dalla Rizza in the 1920s. In late-in-life conversations, Toscanini often spoke scornfully about Puccini, accusing him of stinginess, lack of patriotism, and even a lack of true melodic talent. Yet musicians who worked with him in the 1940s saw him weeping with emotion when he conducted *La Bohème* and excerpts from *Manon Lescaut*. In the end, Puccini and Toscanini were like two brothers who differed in almost every area but who also felt respect and affection for each other. After Toscanini's death, one person close to both musicians commented, with wry humor, that maybe in heaven they would manage to stop arguing.*

---

* The comment was made by Elvira Leonardi, Puccini's step-granddaughter, who, as "Biki," became one of the first famous Milanese stylists.

11.

NEWS OF PUCCINI'S ILLNESS WAS NOT THE ONLY EMOTIONAL UPSET for Toscanini during his stay in Bologna in the autumn of 1924. The wife of Count Emanuele di Castelbarco, Walter Toscanini's partner at the Bottega di Poesia, arrived from Milan one day to inform the maestro that her husband was seeking a foreign divorce (divorce was illegal in Italy) so that he could marry Wally.

Emanuele, scion of one of the oldest noble families in Europe (his full name was Emanuele Giuseppe, Count Castelbarco Visconti Simonetta Pindemonte Rezzonico) had married Ercolina (Lina) Erba, in 1906, when he was twenty-two. Lina, two years his senior, was a member of a prominent Lombard family that included scientists, artists, and aristocrats, and the couple had two sons and a daughter. In 1917, Emanuele, then thirty-three, had met and fallen in love with the seventeen-year-old Wally Toscanini, and a serious affair began; Walter Toscanini must have known about it early on, and Carla certainly found out at some point, but no one had the courage to tell the paterfamilias until Lina informed him that his daughter was destroying her marriage and family.

From her earliest childhood, Wally had enjoyed being praised for her beauty—at the age of six she would watch herself in the mirror as she ate—and she later admitted to having been vain and spoiled; by the time Castelbarco met her, the dark-haired, dark-eyed Wally was considered one of the most beautiful young women in Milan. Toscanini halfheartedly tried to rid her of her capriciousness and vanity, but deep down he was amused by Wally and doted on her more than on his other children. For the most part, however, Toscanini was consumed by his work and paid attention to his children's doings only by fits and starts, especially once they were grown up. But after his encounter with Countess Castelbarco, he returned to Milan in a fury. "Glasses, dishes, and everything else he could put his hands on went flying," Wally recalled half a century later. "He said terrible things to me"—he called her a *traviata* (a woman who has strayed—a prostitute, in other words)—"and he slapped me. It was the first time he had ever lifted a hand against one of his children. He did it with great sorrow, and he later asked me to forgive him." He even ordered his daughter to leave home, but when she began to pack her things, he changed his mind and told her to stay.

Notwithstanding his rejection of the Christian concept of heaven and hell (he considered his daughter's behavior rash but not sinful), Toscanini opposed divorce and second marriages, although he described his position on these matters as "stupid." Besides, he had a visceral disdain for the Italian aristocracy and irrationally considered blond men to be unserious, and Castelbarco was a blond count who also happened to be sixteen years older than Wally. Castelbarco's position vis-à-vis Lina and Wally was in some ways the same as Toscanini's position vis-à-vis his own wife and lovers. In addition to the recent scandal over the maestro's affair with Elsa Kurzbauer, rumors abounded throughout the 1920s regarding his affairs or brief sexual liaisons with many attractive singers and ballerinas; with Anita Colombo; with Irene (nicknamed Rirì) Campiglio, the woman who would become Pizzetti's second wife; and with women involved in artistic and intellectual circles. No doubt some of the rumors were accurate. According to one usually reliable source, Toscanini, in old age, told Antonio Ghiringhelli, who was then La Scala's general manager, that in earlier years he had been so overwhelmed with work that he had sometimes had sex with women without having had enough time to remove his trousers completely. Yet Toscanini never denied a role to a singer because she had refused to go to bed with him and never awarded roles to a singer merely because she had acquiesced. Dalliance was one thing; artistic standards were another.*

No one could deny that women flocked to him. His fame was worldwide, and his good looks seemed to increase as he aged. He may not have been as overtly vain as his daughter, but, as Wally observed, "he went to the best tailor, always wore highly polished shoes, and used eau de cologne d'Orsay—even on his mustache. He had many lovers and was unfaithful to all of them. He would even have affairs with two or three of them at a time. [. . .] If he became aware that they were taking things seriously, he abandoned them. He was cruel. [. . .] It didn't bother us [children] at all. On the contrary,

---

* By today's standards, Toscanini would be considered a sexual predator: some women probably acquiesced in the hope that he would advance their careers, even though his professional attitude toward them in fact remained neutral. By the standards of his own day, he was merely promiscuous.

we found Mamma tiresome about this. 'You would have to turn all your lady friends out of the house,' we used to tell her. She wouldn't confront him; she would become rude and ill-humored.'"

Toscanini had certainly experienced the combination of love and sexual gratification, probably with Carla early in their marriage and then with Storchio and possibly with Farrar, Kurzbauer, and others, but the two phenomena more often existed separately for him. He saw a clear connection between sexual energy and general energy levels, and he was acquainted with the theory, attributed to the celebrated physician Augusto Murri, that the best way for a man to remain healthy was to have at least one orgasm every day; the fact that Murri lived to be ninety-one no doubt lent some authority to the hypothesis, in Toscanini's mind. Walfredo Toscanini said that the only serious argument he ever witnessed between his grandparents took place in the 1940s, when Carla remonstrated with Arturo for one of his erotic escapades. "You think that morality is something we have between our legs!" he shouted at her. And he did, consciously, separate sexual behavior from other forms of morality. "Judge the man and the artist," he once wrote, referring to Verdi, "his life, as honest and upright as his art—but for pity's sake, stop short of the bedroom threshold." He knew that his attitude toward Wally and Castelbarco was hypocritical, but in this case emotion trumped reason.

In the event, obtaining a foreign divorce proved to be a much more complicated matter than Castelbarco had anticipated. For seven more years, Wally would continue to live in her parents' home, and she and her fiancé would continue to meet when and where they could.

Yet another family drama took place in 1924. Walter Toscanini and Castelbarco had been giving jobs at their Bottega di Poesia to well-known anti-Fascists who couldn't find work elsewhere; these employees—all of them watched by the police—included Ettore Albini, who had been drama critic for the Socialist newspaper *Avanti!*, and Guido Picelli, a leading Socialist, later an anti-Stalinist Communist, who would die leading an anti-Franco brigade during the Spanish Civil War. When Walter made a public protest over the Italian government's proposed law limiting freedom of the press, he was arrested, tried on a trumped-up charge of public indecency, and given a suspended five-month prison sentence. Not wishing to damage the Bottega di Poesia, he resigned from it and opened an anti-quarian bookshop, the Antiquariato Toscanini, first in the central Galleria De Cristoforis, then in Via Cerva, near his parents' home, where he was still living. Walter anonymously authored and published a book on historic bookbinding techniques and another on La Scala's history, and he coedited a collection of previously unpublished Verdi letters, while continuing to develop his expertise on the history of ballet and to help other anti-Fascists.

12.

TOSCANINI'S 1924–25 SCALA SEASON INCLUDED TWO WORLD PRE-mieres: Umberto Giordano's *La Cena delle Beffe* and Riccardo Zandonai's *I Cavalieri di Ekebù*. Cesari, writing in the *Corriere della Sera*, remarked that several parts of Giordano's opera that had "appeared in an unfavorable light" when viewed in print "benefited greatly from the reading that Toscanini gave them." In other words, the fine performance made the work sound better than it really was. The same critic was even more oblique in his comments regarding *I Cavalieri di Ekebù*. Toscanini, he said, "withheld nothing that his scrupu-lousness and his strong, well-tested musical mind could have thought up for the benefit of the opera." For those who could read between the lines, this signified that Zandonai's work (based on the Nobel laureate Selma Lagerlöf's novel *Gösta Berling's Saga*) was not a master-piece but had been effectively performed. Unfair remarks, perhaps, but neither opera has often been revived.

At Turin's Teatro Regio, Toscanini conducted a production of *Nerone* in the course of the season, and at La Scala he led revivals of *Nerone* and nine other operas. In the spring of 1925 he brought new productions of *Il Trovatore* and *Pelléas et Mélisande* before the Milanese public. Toscanini invited Rosa Raisa to sing Leonora in *Trovatore* but later regretted his choice: "I can't tell you what she made my ears suf-fer," he later observed, adding that she was fine for roles that required vocal power and good stage presence but implying that she was not right for those that needed pure lyric beauty. He also regretted his initial choice for the role of Manrico, but in this case he fixed the problem by postponing the opening of the opera and asking Pertile to take the part. Pertile hesitated at first, but Toscanini told him, *"Il Trovatore* isn't meant to be shouted, it's meant to be sung!"* Pertile recalled. "If you can sing *Aida*, you can sing *Trovatore* even better."

Franci was chosen for the role of the Conte di Luna, despite a rough audition. "Toscanini said, 'You're a bit of a screamer [. . .], a bit of a shrieker!'" the baritone recalled. "'I heard, for instance, that when you sang "Leonora mia!" you threw in a G. [. . .] This is a count talking, not a ragpicker.' And in playing the composer's version for me, he said to me, 'Hear how beautiful it is?'"

Alfredo Casella, a leading campaigner for new music, Italian and otherwise, attended the dress rehearsal of Verdi's anything-but-avant-garde opera and was amazed. Toscanini "resuscitated" *Il Trovatore*, he wrote in an article for the American *Christian Science Monitor*: "each note, each accent, remain[s] so deeply engraved in [the] memory that, afterward, in rereading the score at home, each bar, each detail, however unimportant, comes back stamped by the great interpreter."

Pelléas was Toscanini's biggest undertaking of the Scala season, and whereas his groundbreaking 1908 Italian premiere production of Debussy's lyric masterpiece had been sung in Italian, this version was performed in the original French and with a cast made up mainly of native French-speakers—in particular, the French tenor Alfred Legrand and the Belgian soprano Fanny Heldy in the title roles. It was the only opera production that Toscanini ever conducted in Italy in a language other than Italian, and Casella reported that this choice had "provoked a violent press campaign on the part of certain ultranationalist newspapers." Casella, who had attended the opera's world premiere in Paris, had feared that Toscanini's love of clarity and his passionate forcefulness would be out of place in this opera; instead, his "extraordinary pliancy has again made possible one of those tours de force of which he alone possesses the secret." Although the "element of mystery [. . .] was probably more profound" in the original version, Toscanini's interpretation achieved much greater dramatic intensity, Casella said.

The season's other operas had been split between Panizza and Gui, with Votto stepping in to lead some late-in-the-season perfor-mances of works that had initially been conducted by Toscanini. The maestro's collegial interest in his conducting staff's work occasionally led to trouble, and the most notorious incident occurred that season. Gui was preparing the world premiere of Adriano Lualdi's opera *Il Diavolo nel Campanile* (The Devil in the Belfry), which, at one point, contains a sort of proto-aleatoric passage: the orchestra musicians are instructed to play whatever they please—free improvisation. At one of the early rehearsals, some of the comedians in the orchestra added rude oral noises to the mix, and Gui let them have their fun. But when the same thing happened at the dress rehearsal he put his foot down, literally: the cloud of dust that went up from the podium after he had angrily stamped on it caused further noises—of protest, this time—from the musicians. "Gui, beside himself, left the podium and ran to tell Toscanini," recalled Enrico Minetti, who had become the associate concertmaster,

> and the orchestra left the pit commenting excitedly on what had happened. [. . .] The Maestro suddenly came down the steps leading into our anteroom [. . .] like an avalanche, screaming as I had never heard him scream. There was a thick, very heavy table in the middle of the room. Toscanini grabbed it by one side and started to shake it and to make it dance, while continuing to scream and challenging us to fight with him. He looked like one of the Furies. [. . .] My colleagues, pressed against the walls all around the room, their faces livid, sought to disappear. One, creeping along next to the wall, tried to get to the lavatory; others tried to flee to the next room. [. . .] The principal double bass, poor fellow, had the nerve to defend himself since, [. . .] justifiably, he did not want to be considered guilty. Toscanini, in his anger, said everything in his vocabulary to him, too; then, still challenging us to fight, raving and threatening, he departed, having injured his wrist during the gymnastic exercise with the table. He left us pale with fear.

The musicians decided to demand an apology from Toscanini, and the next morning "he came down into our room to make peace," Minetti said. "The lights weren't working in the basement room. Somehow, one guy managed to find a candle and light it; others lit matches. Toscanini gave a shadow of a greeting in a soft voice. Everyone present was a bit embarrassed. It was at that point that our old, half-crazy bass clarinet player—the one who lived in an attic with a chicken [. . .]—spoke the famous phrase about the 'sun and the candles,' in a clear allusion"—Toscanini being the sun as opposed to the others as mere candles—"after which the Maestro muttered, 'Imbecile!' in a half-gruff tone, and left. Peace had been made!"*

TOSCANINI'S FINAL *PELLÉAS* PERFORMANCE, on 21 May 1925, was also the last of his seventy-four Scala appearances that season and the end of the *ente autonomo*'s highly successful fourth season. In June, he once again took the Scala orchestra on a Swiss tour, which included concerts in Lausanne, Geneva, Basel, and Zurich, in repertoire that ranged from Haydn to Stravinsky. More concerts had been scheduled, but the tour's Swiss impresario, Ernst Stamm, could not pay the orchestra its promised fee, and the Italians walked out after the first Zurich concert. One promoter tried to recoup the losses he had sustained as a result of the orchestra's no-show by having the players' instruments impounded at the Swiss-Italian border, but the mayor of Zurich cleared the matter up, had Stamm arrested for fraud, and apologized to Toscanini, who was able to return to Milan together with his orchestra.

Knowing that his musicians had counted on their fees from the Swiss concerts to help get them through the barren summer and early fall months,† Toscanini had the Scala administration arrange two special performances in Milan, with the same programs that had been prepared for Switzerland; he conducted the concerts without a fee, insisting that all the proceeds be turned over to the players. Although he could be terribly hard on his musicians in matters musical, he was a soft touch in matters financial. Gianandrea Gavazzeni recalled that orchestra members who overspent their salaries or were in need of extra money in emergency situations knew that they could ask Carla Toscanini for "loans" and that she had instructions

---

* During that same period, Toscanini and Gui had a heated argument that led to a permanent rupture in their relations. Gui later sent Toscanini a long letter in which he attempted to excuse himself, but to no avail.

† Orchestra musicians in those days and for many years thereafter were paid per week or month of service, not for an entire calendar year.

from her husband to satisfy their requests, with no questions asked. During the last week before monthly salary payments were due, many musicians would be seen ringing the doorbell at the house in Via Durini.

Toscanini spent part of the summer of 1925 in the Piedmontese village of Alpino—known for its luxuriant vegetation and its panoramic views of Lake Maggiore far below—relaxing with his family and preparing for the forthcoming season. Early in September, he went to Venice to attend a festival sponsored by the International Society for Contemporary Music, at the Teatro La Fenice; other prominent musicians in attendance included Strauss, Schoenberg, Stravinsky, Leoš Janáček, Paul Hindemith, the cellist Gaspar Cassadó, and the pianist Artur Schnabel—all of them except Janáček and Strauss younger than Toscanini. His opinion of much of what he heard was negative, and at the end of the series he told the music historian Edward J. Dent, the society's president, "Now that the festival is over, we must have the theater disinfected." Years later, when Toscanini met Schnabel, who had attended the festival not as a pianist but as the composer of a complex piano sonata, Toscanini asked, with his usual lack of tact on musical issues, "Are you really the same Schnabel who wrote that horrible music I heard ten years ago in Venice?" Schnabel admitted to being the guilty party, and he recalled with amusement that Toscanini "seemed still to suffer" in remembering the piece.*

In mid-October, Toscanini and his orchestra gave three concerts at La Scala, then plunged into rehearsals for the *ente autonomo*'s fifth opera season, which opened in mid-November 1925 with an enthusiastically received new production of *Un Ballo in Maschera*. During the following five weeks, Toscanini conducted new productions of *Faust* and *Madama Butterfly* and revivals of five other operas. The *Butterfly* production, which opened on the first anniversary of Puccini's death, was the first presentation of the opera at La Scala since its disastrous premiere there twenty-one years earlier.

The season continued with a revival of Zandonai's *I Cavalieri di*

---

* Toscanini did not generally like Schnabel's playing, either, and, as the music critic B. H. Haggin pointed out, "the antipathy was mutual: 'He thinks only *he* is pure!' Schnabel once exclaimed to me scornfully."

Ekebù; the composer had sent Toscanini some cuts that he thought might improve the overall effect, but he had also given the conductor full authority to use them or not, or to make others, as he saw fit. Some saw this revival as further proof that the maestro wanted to make sure that the public had a chance to absorb a new work before passing judgment on it, but Gavazzeni recalled that as Toscanini was leaving the pit at the end of the second (and last) performance (27 December), several people in the orchestra heard him mutter, "Thank God I'll never have to conduct this ugly opera again."

The following day, Toscanini set out on a trip that would once again change the course of his life.

13.

"MAESTRO COMING FOR PERIOD BEGINNING JANUARY 14TH." THESE words—the beginning of a cablegram, dated 5 April 1925, from Max Smith, Toscanini's Italian-speaking journalist friend from his Metropolitan days, to Clarence Hungerford Mackay, multimillionaire chairman of the New York Philharmonic's board of directors—signaled the start of a new era in Toscanini's life and in the musical life of America's largest city.

As early as January 1921, Toscanini, then in the midst of the Scala orchestra's North American tour, had told Otto Kahn's wife that he would consider the possibility of an engagement with the Philharmonic, and in the summer of 1922 Loudon Charlton, who had managed the Scala orchestra's North American tour, approached the maestro directly on the subject. But, Charlton reported, Toscanini "could not consider conducting so many concerts as the Philharmonic schedule seemed to call for." In addition, Toscanini said that he "must have at least two weeks before the season in which to prepare the orchestra," and he set "other conditions financially and otherwise quite beyond the power of the Society." Renewed efforts were made through the well-known Dutch conductor Willem Mengelberg, who had become one of the Philharmonic's regular conductors, and through Mengelberg's manager, but to no avail.

Then, in the spring of 1925, Mackay dispatched Smith to Milan, to negotiate directly with the maestro, and Smith succeeded where others had failed. "Decision just communicated cost him tremendous struggle because unanticipated troubles and difficulties here placed him in cruel dilemma," Smith's cable to Mackay continued. "Strain on me also great. Inasmuch as till now remuneration has not been mentioned or even touched upon directly or indirectly, may I ask without being misconstrued whether offer by you to assume cost of American tax and ocean expense would not be noble gesture by you towards this man of incomparable genius. Hope I am justified in having offered six preparatory rehearsals including day of first concert and further rehearsals on every other open day of engagement, but realized importance of avoiding all obstacles to acceptance. Moreover wife advised me six preparatory were essential to success." Carla had probably also "advised" Smith that the payment of income tax and travel expenses, over and above her husband's fee, would be expected.

The "cruel dilemma" was caused by La Scala's administrators, who feared the negative box office consequences of a seven-week Toscanini-less gap in midseason. Toscanini, however, now had sufficient confidence in his ensemble to feel fairly comfortable leaving it in the hands of his colleagues for a while, and he must have thought that after having dedicated six years of his life almost exclusively to La Scala he deserved, and needed, a change, however brief. Only two months earlier, he had turned down a lucrative offer of the artistic directorship of the Teatro Colón in Buenos Aires, and during the same period a proposal for him to lead a season of Italian opera in Vienna was similarly rejected. But the Philharmonic's offer had worked because he was willing to conduct symphonic music—which he loved as much as opera and which required far less complicated arrangements—with first-rate ensembles abroad.

Mackay cabled a delighted response to Smith, and news of Toscanini's engagement was quickly released to the press, creating a "furor," according to Arthur Judson, the orchestra's manager. Toscanini's initial Philharmonic contract stipulated a fee of $20,000 for conducting eleven performances, payment of his income tax, and reimbursement of up to $1,500 for travel expenses. A few months later he agreed to expand the series to fifteen concerts, with an additional $2,000 for two of the extra performances; he would also conduct without fee one benefit concert and one performance before an audience of students.

On the morning of 28 December 1925, a few hours before his departure for America, Toscanini was summoned to a meeting with Mussolini at the Milan prefecture. One of the prime minister's more ambitious plans was the creation of a modern Roman empire, and in 1924 he had decided to resurrect the ancient holiday commemorating the Birth of Rome. Since this fell on 21 April, it gave him an excuse for eliminating the left-inspired Workers' Day on the first of May: he claimed that he was combining the latter with the former. And he gave the order that on the new-old holiday all places of public entertainment were to begin their performances with the Royal March and "Giovinezza," the Fascist anthem. The first year, Toscanini circumvented the issue at La Scala by scheduling a rehearsal rather than a performance on 21 April; in 1925, Gui conducted a performance on 21 April, but Toscanini instructed him to ignore the government's order. Mussolini was furious.

Toscanini later told friends that at the prefecture Mussolini kept him standing while subjecting him to a long harangue in which he upbraided him for his bad behavior and warned of possible negative consequences for La Scala should that behavior continue. Toscanini remained silent, staring at a spot on the wall over Mussolini's bald pate, and left when the lecture had ended.

The *Corriere della Sera*—which, one month earlier, had been taken out of the Liberal senator Luigi Albertini's hands and muzzled by the regime—reported that Mussolini had shown "great interest in the proceedings at La Scala and in [Toscanini's] imminent trip to America." Indeed, that very afternoon the maestro, together with Carla and Wally, boarded a train to Cherbourg, where they embarked on the Cunard liner *Berengaria*. The unpleasant encounter with Mussolini must have given Toscanini much to think about during the ocean voyage: perhaps reestablishing a close relationship with the United States would be wise, given the political climate at home. A few months earlier, the historian Gaetano Salvemini had clandestinely left Italy for France after having been briefly incarcerated for anti-Fascist activities, and other important figures in Italian cultural life were finding the atmosphere in their country increasingly stifling.

Upon disembarking in New York on 7 January 1926, and even before checking into the Hotel Astor at Times Square, Toscanini was distressed to learn that his name had been mentioned, together with the names of Guglielmo Marconi, the philosopher Benedetto Croce, the literati Gabriele D'Annunzio, Luigi Pirandello, Salvatore Di Giacomo, Sem Benelli, and several others, as a charter member of Mussolini's latest brainchild, the Accademia Italiana. "If it is true, I have not been informed of it," Toscanini said, according to the *New York Times*. It was true, but, like Croce and Benelli, Toscanini turned down the nomination, and he later heaped scorn on those who had accepted: he considered the new Italian Academy to be a shabby imitation of the Académie Française and, worse, bait offered to famous Italians who, by swallowing it, would automatically become beholden to the regime.

14.

THE NEW YORK PHILHARMONIC, FOUNDED IN 1842, WAS THE OLDEST extant professional symphonic ensemble in the United States. Its chief conductors had included such luminaries as Anton Seidl and Gustav Mahler; Willem Mengelberg, principal conductor of Amsterdam's Concertgebouw Orchestra, was now also the Philharmonic's principal conductor in all but name, with Wilhelm Furtwängler as his co-conductor. Mengelberg, Toscanini's junior by four years, was a great orchestra trainer and an early champion of the music of Mahler and Richard Strauss; the forty-year-old Furtwängler, principal conductor of the Berlin Philharmonic and Leipzig's Gewandhaus Orchestra, was already one of the most respected members of his profession in Europe.

The orchestra's management had cleared the entire week prior to Toscanini's first concert—14 January—for his rehearsals, with one exception: on Sunday afternoon, the tenth, Mengelberg conducted a repetition of a program that he had done with the orchestra eight days earlier.* That evening, Steinway & Sons gave a reception for Toscanini and Respighi, who happened to be in town, at the company's new headquarters on West Fifty-Seventh Street; the many

---

* Toscanini probably attended Mengelberg's concert; the previous evening he had heard the Boston Symphony Orchestra under Serge Koussevitzky, who was then in his second season as that ensemble's conductor.

prominent guests included Otto Kahn, Alfredo Casella, Leopold Auer, the pianist Alexander Siloti, the harpsichordist Wanda Landowska, the singers Elisabeth Rethberg and Beniamino Gigli, as well as the music critics Henry Krehbiel and Olin Downes. Downes, who had replaced Richard Aldrich as the *Times*'s chief music critic, was as great a Toscanini admirer as Aldrich had been, but whereas Aldrich's articles were well written and calmly reasoned, Downes's tended to be ornate, fulsome, and laced with pseudo-intellectual gobbledygook. For instance: shortly before Toscanini's Philharmonic debut, Downes wrote that the maestro was a manifestation of "the Italian mind—the racial mind that has the finest feature of any in the world; the genius which, at its height, combines marvelously the qualities of analysis and perception, the objectivity of form"—whatever that may be—"and the consuming fire of creative passion." Mussolini couldn't have put the matter better!

Toscanini's first Philharmonic rehearsals made him "very happy"—so Carla informed Scandiani in a cable—and New York's musical public was ecstatic over the results. "The concert of the Philharmonic Society last night in Carnegie Hall was one of those musical events which might well be turned over to the star descriptive reporter," W. J. Henderson declared in the *Sun* after the first performance. "It was not a concert at all; it was the return of the hero, a Roman triumph staged in New York and in modern dress. The hero was Arturo Toscanini, one time conductor at the Metropolitan and now lord high admiral of La Scala in Milan. [. . .] That Mr. Toscanini will engage the interest of music lovers is beyond question. He appeared last evening in a light vastly different from that which dimly fell upon him when last he conducted symphonic music here"—a jab at the Scala orchestra. "He had a magnificent machine with which to work. He did great things with it and will do more. His audience was moved to unusual demonstrations."

The program began with Haydn's Symphony no. 101 in D Major ("Clock") and continued with Respighi's *Pines of Rome*, Sibelius's *The Swan of Tuonela*, "Siegfried's Death" and Funeral Music from *Götterdämmerung*, and Weber's *Euryanthe* Overture. Afterward, Mackay honored Toscanini with a reception at the board chairman's Upper East Side home. The program was repeated on the following evening at Carnegie Hall and then again on the sixteenth as a benefit event, under the patronage of the US vice-president, Charles G. Dawes, at the Mecca Temple (later renamed as the New York City Center); the proceeds went to the Italian Welfare League. Giacomo De Martino, Italy's amabassador to the United States, came from Washington specifically for what amounted to a Toscanini Week in New York, and Consul General Emilio Axerio was also present. There were several more receptions during the remainder of Toscanini's stay.*

In the meantime, Toscanini had been preparing the Philharmonic musicians in a second program, which they presented for the first time on Sunday afternoon, 17 January. They then traveled to Philadelphia, to repeat the previous week's program at the Academy of Music. The next evening they were back at Carnegie Hall, performing a program that concluded with the first and fourth tableaux from *Petrushka*, at the end of which the orchestra as well as the audience cheered Toscanini. On the thirtieth, Toscanini conducted the Philharmonic in a full-length student concert that was broadcast live on the local radio station WJZ—the first time, as far as is known, that a Toscanini performance was heard over the airwaves—and the following evening they performed at the Brooklyn Academy of Music. Four days later, Toscanini made his first "electrical" recordings— recordings made with a microphone instead of the acoustic horn, which had been rendered obsolete. The session or sessions, for the Brunswick company, took place in the fifth-floor Chapter Room of the Carnegie Hall building, and the repertoire consisted of the *Midsummer Night's Dream* Nocturne and Scherzo, which he and the Philharmonic had performed on two of their concerts; these were the only authorized recordings he would ever make for a company other than RCA Victor or one of its predecessors, affiliates, or associated companies. The quality is incalculably better than that of the Scala orchestra recordings, made five years earlier, and the performances demonstrate the beauty of the Philharmonic's playing at the time, but the results did not convert Toscanini to the cause of recording: what he heard coming out of the playback equipment of the day bore little resemblance to what he heard in the concert hall.

---

* Also during his New York stay, Toscanini acquired a Steinway B piano (no. 237878) for $1,925 and had it shipped to Milan.

"TOSCANINI CHEERED AT HIS FAREWELL," proclaimed a headline in the *Times* on 8 February, the morning after his last concert. "It was obvious that the gentlemen of the orchestra shared the enthusiasm of the public," Downes reported. "Mr. Toscanini appeared again and again on the stage, evidently touched by the demonstration, conveying by gestures his gratitude to the audience, and in turn applauding the orchestra." Afterward, the musicians gave a party in his honor.

In New York, Toscanini was the man of the hour, as popular among the city's music lovers as Babe Ruth was among fans of the Yankees' baseball team. All fifteen of his concerts were sold out, and many people paid scalpers double the original ticket prices. His photo appeared on the cover of the 25 January issue of *Time* magazine, and there was great clamor inside and outside the organization for him to return the following year. On 2 February, Mackay formally rebutted reports that the Philharmonic had offered a five-year contract to Toscanini, but a week later the chairman announced "the completion of negotiations lately pending for the return of Arturo Toscanini [. . .] for a like number of performances during January and February of 1927," according to the *Times*.

On the day of his first Philharmonic concert, Toscanini had cabled Scandiani to reassure him: "My thoughts follow all of you constantly." But when the *New York World* printed the rumor that Toscanini would become the orchestra's music director if he could find a worthy successor at La Scala, an alarmed Scandiani cabled him to make sure that it wasn't true. (It wasn't.) The general manager had been sending cablegrams regarding the outcome of each production staged during Toscanini's absence: Gabriele Santini conducted *Carmen* successfully; there was a good *Aida* performance; and so on. Forzano, too, wrote to reassure Toscanini about the progress of various productions that were in rehearsal. The maestro, in turn, reassured everyone that he was returning to La Scala.

And yet, he had been exceptionally pleased with his work in New York and with the devotion shown him. Although he had rehearsed and performed twenty-two pieces by seventeen composers on fifteen concerts in four different venues within a single month, the Philharmonic series had seemed like a vacation in comparison with the stress of putting opera productions on the stage. On 10 February, en route to the dock and then aboard the *Conte Rosso* before it departed, the maestro and Edward Ervin, the Philharmonic's assistant manager, began to plan some of the details of the concerts that Toscanini would give the following year. When Ervin handed him a check for a concert that had been added to the original schedule, Toscanini thanked him but turned it down.

Upon disembarking in Naples, Toscanini received welcoming telegrams from Scandiani and Mayor Mangiagalli of Milan, and he publicly "expressed great admiration" for the New York Philharmonic. A new plan was beginning to take shape in his mind.

15.

_____

A DAUNTING, NOT TO SAY TERRIFYING, WORK SCHEDULE AWAITED Toscanini at La Scala. He could not have reached Milan before 20 February 1926; on the twenty-seventh he conducted the first of four performances of *Orfeo*—a revival of the production that he had led during the two previous seasons—and five nights later he led the Italian premiere of *Le Martyre de Saint-Sébastien*, a five-act "mystery play" by Gabriele D'Annunzio with incidental music by Debussy.

Debussy and D'Annunzio had wanted Toscanini to conduct *Saint-Sébastien*'s world premiere in Paris in 1911, but he had been unable to accept the task at the time. D'Annunzio then campaigned unsuccessfully to have the anomalous work performed at La Scala during the house's first postwar season, but such a project was considered too risky at the time. Now, with the sense of relative security that the *ente autonomo*'s manifold successes had created, Toscanini felt that he could put *Saint-Sébastien* on the stage, with the forty-two-year-old, Ukrainian-born Ida Rubinstein reciting and dancing the title role, as she had done in Paris fifteen years earlier. Like the Paris archdiocese in 1910, so now the Milan archdiocese protested in advance over the decadent, erotic dramatization of Christian lore and, specifically, over the impersonation of Saint Sebastian by a sensually beautiful woman, who also happened to be Jewish and bisexual. But the show went on.

D'Annunzio, dressed in his bemedaled air marshall's uniform, sat in a box near the stage on opening night and gave the Fascist salute when he was hailed by the elegantly turned-out audience between the first and second acts; he later told the French musicologist Henry

Prunières that Toscanini's performance of *Le Martyre* had far surpassed the world premiere performances in Paris under André
Caplet. The critics praised the performers as well as the sets by Léon
Bakst, and they were in general agreement that Debussy's music was
ravishing, but also that there wasn't enough of it: most of the evening was taken up by recitation in French, and the proceedings
seemed to drag on and on, although one whole scene had been cut.
When the curtain closed on the first night, the participants were all
warmly applauded, and D'Annunzio embraced Toscanini on stage.
But the production closed after only three more performances and
was never revived.

Toscanini conducted the first two performances of a new production of Montemezzi's *L'Amore dei Tre Re*—the opera that had been
widely hailed when the maestro had conducted its American premiere in New York in 1914—but he turned the remaining ones over
to Votto. Although he was on the brink of complete exhaustion,
owing to preparations for the forthcoming world premiere of *Turandot*, the season's most highly anticipated event, he nevertheless managed, during the four intervening weeks, to conduct revivals of
Nerone, *Pelléas*, and *La Traviata* (with the now legendary diva Claudia
Muzio in the title role). He felt that he had to work even harder than
usual to make up for the time he had spent in America.

PUCCINI DIED BEFORE HE COULD COMPLETE *Turandot*'s final scene.
According to some sources, when the Ricordi company's executives
asked Toscanini to recommend the composer who could best finish
the task, he suggested Riccardo Zandonai, but Tonio Puccini, Giacomo's son, opposed the choice on the grounds that Zandonai was
too well-known in his own right. Tito Ricordi, who no longer
directed the company, recommended young Franco Vittadini for the
job, and the names of Mascagni and Franz Lehár, the famed Austro-
Hungarian composer of *The Merry Widow* and other operettas, were
put forward. The final choice, made with Toscanini's halfhearted
acquiescence, fell on Franco Alfano, a fifty-year-old Neapolitan
whose early opera *Risurrezione* had enjoyed a measure of success and
whose more recent *La Leggenda di Sakùntala* had again brought his
name before the public. Puccini's twenty-two pages of extant

sketches for the scene were entrusted to Alfano, who produced 377 bars of music to bring *Turandot* to a close. According to Votto, "Toscanini was very angry when Alfano brought him the finished product," which he found too long and too divergent from Puccini's style*—although Alfano later claimed that he had originally provided a shorter version and that Toscanini himself had insisted that he expand it. In the end, Alfano produced a 268-bar version; some of the details of this more or less final revision are clear from a letter that Clausetti sent Toscanini during the latter's New York sojourn.

> Puccini's 2nd excerpt (Che mai osi, o straniero?) has been tidied up; another—which was entirely Alfano's material—has been eliminated and replaced by a short passage on a theme by Puccini; the aria is now entirely new and its first part is built on that agitated theme by Puccini himself (Del primo pianto, sì, stranier, quando sei giunto), and the second on the other theme, which, in the notes left by Puccini, is in *D flat*; etc., with a return, after that, to the *mosso* [moving along] of the first tempo.
>
> Finally, the full phrase of the opera's finale, which Alfano had at first given to the tenor and soprano, has now been shifted to the chorus. [. . .] Alfano is now working on the orchestration.

In the end, Toscanini unenthusiastically accepted Alfano's third version. According to contemporary accounts, after the dress rehearsal Alfano approached Toscanini and asked him, "What do you have to say, maestro?" Toscanini replied, "I say that I saw Puccini approaching from the rear of the stage to clout me."

Almost as controversial as Alfano's ending, and even harder to disentangle, is the matter of the original cast for *Turandot*'s three principal roles. A telegram that Scandiani had sent—undoubtedly under instructions from Puccini and Toscanini—to Herbert Johnson, the Chicago Opera's general manager, on 8 October 1924, clears up part of the enigma: "Glad to announce you that Maestro Puccini and Toscanini selected Raisa and [Edith] Mason for the creation of

---

* Various circumstances converge to indicate that this must have happened at the end of December 1925, before Toscanini left for America, and not at the end of January 1926, as Julian Budden states in his excellent book *Puccini: His Life and Works* (Oxford: Oxford University Press, 2002).

the two female roles of Turandot which will have the world premiere next April at La Scala stop For the baritone role [Giacomo] Rimini stop [. . .]." Raisa and Rimini, her husband, did indeed sing the roles of Turandot and Ping, respectively, at the world premiere. Nevertheless, Maria Jeritza, a star at the Vienna State Opera, always claimed that Puccini had promised the role to her; he had, in fact, offered her that hope, but contractual reasons had given Raisa the edge. Gavazzeni, who attended the dress rehearsal, later described Raisa as an "absolutely ideal" Turandot, and Casella, who was at the premiere, wrote that Raisa's "interpretation of the extraordinarily difficult role" was "one of her finest achievements."

Mason, a well-known American soprano, would have sung the part of Liù had the *Turandot* premiere taken place in 1925, as originally planned, but in the spring of 1926 she was pregnant, and she withdrew from the production. The "Liù Question," however, is further complicated by the fact that Gilda Dalla Rizza and Toti Dal Monte each declared that Puccini had wanted her for the role. But neither soprano was on La Scala's 1925–26 roster, thus Toscanini's choice fell on Maria Zamboni, who had already sung important roles at the house. "Zamboni, for the quality of her sound, was highly suited to the part," Gavazzeni said.

Scandiani's telegram to Johnson did not mention who the leading tenor was to be. Giacomo Lauri-Volpi, Beniamino Gigli, and Giovanni Martinelli each claimed that Puccini had wanted him to take the part of Calaf, but all three were on the Metropolitan's roster at the time; Martinelli had been warned by Gatti-Casazza that if he sang at the Milan premiere he would not be reengaged in New York, where his earnings were much greater than what La Scala could have offered him, and similar warnings were probably issued to his two colleagues. Besides, Toscanini had not yet forgiven Lauri-Volpi for their dispute over *Rigoletto* four years earlier, and Gigli felt that the role of Calaf was unsuited to his voice. Toscanini opted for the Spanish tenor Miguel Fleta. Some historians have claimed that Puccini disliked Fleta's voice, whereas the composer merely objected to the tenor's taste for hanging on to high notes. Gavazzeni recalled that although Fleta had some trouble in Alfano's final duet, the rest of his interpretation was superb. In the event, Fleta sang only the first three performances, after which he was replaced.

Raisa recalled that Toscanini worked tirelessly on every detail of the production, and she commented approvingly on the fact that he required the singers to sing their parts full voice—to get the roles into their throats, in opera parlance. She remembered his giving particular attention to the Ping-Pang-Pong scenes, during the ensemble rehearsals, in order to achieve an ideal balance between music and stage action. "He undertook this task as a sacred duty" and "plunged into the Puccini score [. . .], integrating the many contrasting elements of both the comedy and tragedy of this unique opera," she said.

Turandot did not require the sort of public relations campaign that *Nerone* had needed two years earlier: the simple announcement of the premiere of the last opera by the most popular contemporary opera composer was sufficient to attract much of the musical world to Milan. Many of these personages attended the dress rehearsal, which took place on Friday, 23 April, and then eagerly awaited the *prima rappresentazione assoluta* two nights later. Long lines of people hoping to buy standing-room tickets formed under La Scala's porticos on the rainy afternoon of the twenty-fifth, and an hour before curtain time the galleries were alarmingly overcrowded. By nine o'clock, curtain time, the rest of the auditorium overflowed with spectators, including "composers, singers, writers, major impresarios, conductors, publishers—the whole Olympus of the theater and opera worlds," the *Corriere della Sera* reported, plus "a multitude of journalists and critics who had gathered from all over Europe." According to *Il Secolo*, "When the lights went out and Arturo Toscanini emerged from the orchestra's door and proceeded toward the podium, the great conductor was not greeted with the usual applause. There was a minute of deep silence," a tribute to Puccini.

Each act was followed by tremendous ovations, but toward the end of the third act, following the death of Liù, something extraordinary happened. "The audience is overcome with emotion, and the cortège carrying the victim's light body dissolves into the dawn," the *Corriere* reported.

The music gives a final sob, a slight lament . . . Then, nothing more: silence. The cortège has disappeared; on the stage, Calaf and Princess Turandot freeze into an appearance of sorrow; the orchestra stops. And then we see Toscanini turn to the audience: he remains undecided for a moment, as if unable to conquer the emotion that is gripping him, then, in a strangled voice, he says [. . .], "Here ends the opera, left incomplete by the Maestro at his death." The audience is undecided for a moment. People knew that the first performance would be interrupted here, but all of a sudden they are thrown off by the exceptional scene and by the fact that Toscanini personally carried out this act. Then the curtain slowly closes. Toscanini descends [from the podium] and disappears, and then a cry rises out of the silence in the hall: "Viva Puccini!" Then everyone rises. And the cry is repeated, and the singers are called before the curtain five times, and Toscanini is acclaimed in the name of the Maestro who died and who has returned to us.

Two nights after the premiere, Toscanini again conducted *Turandot*, this time with Alfano's ending, and he led the third performance as well. But he put the remaining five performances of the opera that season and all of the *Turandot* performances during the following three seasons in Panizza's hands. He had dedicated himself to the task of realizing the final work of his old companion at arms, but he found *Turandot* impossible to love, and he never conducted it again.

Thanks to the special perspective that hindsight offers, we now know that among the seven operas that had their world premieres under Toscanini's direction at La Scala during the 1920s, *Turandot* was the only one to take hold, and that it remains the last Italian opera to have assumed an important place in the international repertoire.

16.

THE *CORRIERE*'S REVIEW OF THE *TURANDOT* PREMIERE REVEALED that during the first intermission, "the audience awaited the previously announced arrival of Mussolini. But the Prime Minister did not wish to attend, and he explained the reason [. . .]: he did not want his presence to distract the audience in any way: attention had to be devoted entirely to Puccini."

The truth of the matter was quite different. Mussolini, still angry over Toscanini's refusal to perform the Royal March and "Giovine-zza" on the Birth of Rome holiday in 1924 and 1925, had informed La Scala's administrators that this was not to happen again in 1926. But Toscanini had again ignored the rule and had scheduled only rehears-als on 21 April. Mussolini was in Milan that week; he sent for La Scala's administrators and informed them that if they could not con-trol Toscanini they would either have to get rid of the maestro or never again see Mussolini in their theater. He wished to attend the *Turandot* premiere on the twenty-fifth, and "Giovinezza" would have to be played upon his arrival.

Scandiani and his associates were navigating treacherous waters between the Scylla of Mussolini's wrath and the Charybdis of Tosca-nini's principles. When they communicated the prime minister's orders to the maestro, he replied that "Giovinezza" could be played if they found someone else to conduct it—and *Turandot*, and every-thing else, because he would leave La Scala. In 1926, Toscanini was more important than Mussolini to La Scala's well-being; thus the administrators sailed into Charybdis's arms. *Turandot*'s premiere took place without the presence of the head of government.

The Fascist press immediately circulated a rumor that Toscanini was quitting La Scala—he would be replaced by Panizza—because he objected to a new law that created a national corporation of opera house managers and a union among three theaters: La Scala, the Costanzi in Rome, and the San Carlo in Naples. In effect, Mussolini was giving La Scala a chance to dump Toscanini and Toscanini a chance to withdraw without hurting his pride. According to a *New York Times* report on 5 May, Toscanini openly denied the rumor, and three days later an Italian newspaper article written by someone close to the maestro or to La Scala, or both, declared that the mae-stro's absence from the later *Turandot* performances was "to be attrib-uted solely to reasons of health"—visual problems and sheer exhaustion; the latter had even caused him to have several memory lapses during the second *Turandot* performance.

Even after having ceded most of the *Turandot* performances to Panizza, Toscanini still faced revivals of *Tristan* and *Falstaff* in addi-tion to a double bill of Stravinsky's *Petrushka*, parts of which he had previously conducted, with the same composer's opera *The Nightin-gale*, which was entirely new to him. The *Tristan* rehearsals proceeded for a while, but the Dutch soprano Elisabeth Ohms, who had been engaged for the role of Isolde, recalled that her first piano rehearsal with Toscanini and her colleagues ended abruptly; Toscanini evidently was not well. "Next day we were informed that the scheduled performances of *Tristan* would not take place," she said. "The maestro was said to be suffering from nervous pains in the right arm."

Toscanini did conduct four performances of *Falstaff,* a less physically demanding work than *Tristan,* but he asked Stravinsky to conduct his own works. He had met the Russian-born, French-based composer in Venice the previous fall, during the contemporary music festival, and the two musicians had worked out plans for the Scala performances. Toscanini had begun rehearsing *The Nightingale* early in March, and at the end of the month or early in April Stravinsky—who was then nearly forty-four and in the early phases of his so-called neoclassical compositional period—went to Milan, where "Toscanini received me in the most charming fashion," he later recounted. "He called the choruses and asked me to accompany them on the piano in order to give them such instructions as I might think necessary. I was struck by the deep knowledge he had of the score in its smallest details, and by his meticulous study of every work which he undertook to conduct. This quality of his is universally recognized, but this was the first time that I had a chance of seeing it applied to one of my own compositions. [. . .] I have never encountered in a conductor of such world repute such a degree of self-effacement, conscientiousness, and artistic honesty."

The admiration was not entirely mutual: years later, Toscanini told his colleague Ernest Ansermet that he had "lost all confidence in [Stravinsky's] musicality when he heard him count the time out loud as he played through part of [*The Nightingale*] on the piano"—a peremptory judgment, to be sure. Nevertheless, Toscanini proceeded with the rehearsals until his near collapse caused him to ask Stravinsky to return to Milan and conduct the final rehearsals and all four performances. The composer readily complied and was "astounded by the high standards and rigorous discipline of the Scala orchestra."

Several commentators have suggested that Toscanini, unaccustomed as he was to dealing with radical early twentieth-century music, felt so uneasy with *The Nightingale's* complicated rhythms and frequently changing meters that he was unable to undertake the performances. Those difficulties may have strengthened his decision to absent himself from La Scala at the end of the season, but his exhaustion and eye and shoulder pains were real.

To make matters worse, as the season was drawing to a close, Toscanini was sued for defamation by a member of the Scala orchestra's violin section. Giovanni Licari had a number of nervous tics that some of his colleagues—and Toscanini—found annoying: he would make a series of exaggerated preparatory motions before picking up his instrument to begin a passage, and often his violin and bow would not be ready until the last possible instant—sometimes not even then. One day, according to Sacchi, the maestro turned to Licari and said, " 'You always prepare at the last moment. I want to see the violins in position two bars before the attack. I don't want to see any sluggards. You are a sluggard.' [. . .] Uncertain at first, Licari turned to his stand partner: 'Who is he talking to?' [. . .]

" 'I'm talking precisely to you. You're a sluggard, you don't know how to play the violin, and next year you won't be back in this orchestra.'

" 'I couldn't care less,' Licari replied facetiously." This infuriated Toscanini, who then said—according to a document in La Scala's archives—"Given your way of playing, you can only cheat your students," to which Licari replied, "And you, who have cheated the whole world?" At that, the violinist stood up and left the hall, and Toscanini—according to Sacchi—shouted, " 'Finally that creep is gone. I've been sick of him for five years!' "

Licari contended that these remarks constituted abuse and defamation; he sued Toscanini for damages. But the case proceeded no further. In camera, the judge gave his opinion that Toscanini had the right to unrestricted "artistic censure." Toscanini stated formally that he had not intended any personal offense against Licari—who could have imagined such a thing?—and Licari signed a declaration withdrawing the charges. While the violinist was signing, Toscanini exclaimed, "What an imbecile!" His lawyers pounced on him and begged him not to ruin everything, to which he replied, "I said it because if I were he, I would never sign!" Licari's name did not appear on the Scala orchestra's roster the following season.

17.

THE FALSE RUMORS ABOUT TOSCANINI'S RIFT WITH LA SCALA
reached the New York Philharmonic's administrators, who saw the
conflict as an opportunity to obtain the maestro's services for more
extended periods, perhaps even to make him the orchestra's chief
conductor. Mackay, Judson, and Maurice Van Praag—a Philharmonic horn player who served as the orchestra's personnel manager—agreed that if they could get Toscanini they wouldn't worry
about offending Mengelberg, Furtwängler, or anyone else. Judson
and Van Praag were dispatched to Milan for discussions with Toscanini—ostensibly, and to some extent truly, to work out programs for
the coming season, but with the main objective of luring him to
New York on a more stable basis. After the two men had returned
home, Van Praag sent Mackay a detailed report. Toscanini, he said,

told me [. . .] how happy he was with the Philharmonic; but
when he came back to La Scala he could not stand to hear their
terrible playing. I then asked him why it was he bothered with
them at all, when you Mr. Mackay were willing to give him the
best Orchestra in the world to conduct without any friction or
discontent on the part of the musicians, as he has in Italy. I told
him it was impossible for him to think of retiring as he is the
only great conductor living today. This touched him and his
answer was, "My dear Van Praag, Mr. Mackay, you and all my
friends in America are very kind, but I am nearly sixty years of
age, why should I keep on[?]" [. . .] Judson then spoke to him
about taking the Philharmonic for a tour in Europe, maybe in
1928. This interested him very much, and Judson pressed on by
saying you would like to have him next season as your regular
conductor. [. . .] Next day [Toscanini] spoke to me alone saying
he was interested but an entire season was too much. Then we
spoke of our plan for him to conduct ten weeks, then have an
associate conductor conduct the Orchestra for six weeks, while
he went to Palm Beach for a vacation, then to come back to us
and conduct eight weeks. This pleased him I could see [. . .].

Rumors, already rife, now began to run wild: Toscanini would leave Italy altogether and would guest conduct four American orchestras before returning to the New York Philharmonic; Toscanini would take over the Teatro Costanzi in Rome and Bernardino Molinari would replace him at La Scala; Mascagni or Mugnone would replace Molinari with the Santa Cecilia Orchestra in Rome; Mascagni would take over Toscanini's position at La Scala. None of these rumors was true, but together they demonstrated how volatile Toscanini's situation in Milan seemed, and indeed was.

Toscanini himself was of two minds. Date conscious as he was, he had surely noted, on 30 June 1926, the fortieth anniversary of his debut in Rio de Janeiro; he was indeed nearing sixty, and dedicating himself to conducting operas weighed more heavily on him with every passing year. On the other hand, he still wanted to realize several major projects in the opera house before he withdrew from it. Besides, he had devoted a tremendous amount of time, energy, expertise, and, above all, love, to creating the opera ensemble of his dreams, and in his own country, which was important to him. Despite the artistically and financially tempting offer from New York, the Fascists breathing down his neck at home, and the battles that had to be fought day after day in the opera house, he could not yet make up his mind to leave.

IN JUNE, SHORTLY AFTER THE DEPARTURE of Judson and Van Praag, Bruno Walter arrived in Milan for a pair of concerts with the Scala orchestra; this was the occasion of Toscanini's first encounter with the renowned German conductor, who was about to turn fifty. Walter had been one of Mahler's leading disciples and was, in 1926, chief conductor of Berlin's Städtische Oper as well as the German opera season at Covent Garden. "The meeting, casual though it was, made a deep and lasting impression on me," Walter wrote in his memoir, *Theme and Variations.* "I wished I could come to know the man better and fathom the secret of so exceptional a being. My wish was to be fulfilled later." Walter would become one of the few conductors whom Toscanini respected, even when he disagreed with his musical ideas.

During the spring Toscanini relaxed briefly on the Ligurian coast, and in the summer he took a cruise on the North Sea and traveled in Norway, accompanied by Vincenzo Tommasini; they explored fjords and stayed in village inns. It was a complete change of pace, and Toscanini returned to Milan feeling refreshed. On 4 September, after more than three performance-free months, he conducted *Falstaff* at Busseto's tiny Teatro Verdi to mark—more than half a year late—the twenty-fifth anniversary of the composer's death. As he had done in 1913 for the centenary of Verdi's birth, so now again Toscanini worked with a reduced, fifty-piece orchestra, made up mainly of players from La Scala; the cast included Stabile in the title role, the Spanish soprano Mercedes Llopart as Alice, Ernesto Badini as Ford, and the twenty-three-year-old Ebe Stignani, a future Scala mainstay, as Mistress Quickly. He had also wanted to present a number of performances of the last act of *Rigoletto*, with Beniamino Gigli as the Duke, but Gigli had replied to the Scala management that he would do only three performances, as a favor to Maestro Toscanini. "So I said [to Scandiani], 'Don't reply to this letter, because I don't want favors from anyone,'" Toscanini recalled many years later. "[It's for] Verdi and *Rigoletto*, it's not Toscanini."

Orio Vergani, a reporter for the *Corriere della Sera*, heard Toscanini tell the musicians, at one rehearsal, "Here you must play better than anywhere else," and "I would give anything if Verdi could hear *Falstaff* performed here!" Casella reported to the *Christian Science Monitor* that "no performance elsewhere in the world could take place in an atmosphere such as this, so essentially Verdian by the memories which fill every part of the theater—and also by the force of the interpretation of Toscanini who was visibly affected by conducting in this place." According to the *New York Times*, "hardly a tenth of those who have arrived from Italy and other countries will be able to crowd into the tiny theatre which Toscanini hopes to transform into a permanent musical institution, doing for the memory of Verdi what Bayreuth does for that of Wagner." His hope remained, and remains, unrealized.

One morning, Toscanini, his assistants, and the cast visited the humble inn in which Verdi had been born, in the nearby village of Le Roncole. They inscribed their names in the guest book and were photographed together in front of the birthplace. Toscanini entered

Le Roncole's little church to look at the organ on which Verdi had studied; the others left him alone there, but Vergani followed him in for the sake of his article for the *Corriere*. The parish priest asked Toscanini to play something on the organ; the Maestro replied, "Believe me—I would never dare."

18.

AN AMPLY ILLUSTRATED PROSPECTUS, IN THE FORM OF A 128-PAGE soft-cover booklet, provides a glimpse not only into La Scala's plans for the 1926–27 season but also into its status in Milanese life. The front cover, in color, shows an enthroned muse, or perhaps Orpheus, playing a lyre, and the back displays a lively advertisement, also in color, for Isotta Fraschini automobiles. Throughout, there are ads—aimed at a well-heeled clientele—for banks, insurance companies, radios, phonographs, player pianos, perfumes, furs, luxurious home accessories, Alfa Romeos, and liqueurs.

Chapters of text are dedicated to La Scala's history, its current operating system, and the forthcoming season's works, composers, and performers, but the booklet also indicates, without stating the matter explicitly, that by the fall of 1926 La Scala's board of directors was changing political orientation. Mayor Luigi Mangiagalli, a Liberal, had ceded his position to the pro-Fascist Ernesto Belloni, who automatically became La Scala's president; vice-president was Senator Giovanni Silvestri, a pro-Fascist industrialist; and members included, among others, four prominent Fascists. Unless the regime collapsed, it was only a matter of time until Toscanini would either have to accept an entirely Fascist board of directors or leave.

During the first half of October 1926, Toscanini conducted his first complete cycle of Beethoven's symphonies in four concerts at La Scala, in anticipation of the hundredth anniversary, the following March, of the composer's death. The French conductor Louis Fourestier attended some of the rehearsals for the cycle and later told how Toscanini had worked at balancing the oboes, clarinets, bassoons, and horns in the sustained opening chord of the Seventh Symphony's second movement. "His ear for balance was astounding and exquisite," Fourestier said, "but after all, that is a physiological phenomenon more than anything else. After he had reached his goal and had achieved the *diminuendo* in the same gradation from each player, he said to the first oboe, 'Your note—your E—make it sing! It's a melody!' *One* note, a melody . . . *That* was genius!"

During some of the rehearsals, the recording pioneer Fred Gaisberg, with the complicity of Walter Toscanini, hid recording equipment in a box at La Scala, and some of the results still exist. But the maestro discovered the ruse and had the equipment removed.

Following the Milan Beethoven performances, Toscanini and the orchestra repeated the entire cycle in Turin; then, again in Milan, performed the First and Ninth Symphonies on a special concert at popular prices.

Toscanini had always loved the vast theatrical canvas that is Verdi's *Don Carlo*—the personal, political, and religious conflicts that it contains as well as its great music—but he had never wanted to conduct it under less than ideal circumstances. Now, at last, he determined to present it in the five-act form (without ballet) that Verdi had approved in the 1880s. The outstanding cast included Antonin Trantoul in the title role, Galeffi as Rodrigo, Tancredi Pasero (in his Scala debut) as Filippo, Bianca Scacciati as Elisabetta, and Giuseppina Cobelli as Eboli. This was Toscanini's first professional encounter with Scacciati, and he engaged her for several other operas in all of his remaining Scala seasons. He admired Cobelli, too, and wanted her to sing Eboli with him again the following season, but she refused because—as he recounted with a laugh, many years later— Eboli is given lower billing than Elisabetta.*

Don Carlo was received enthusiastically on the season's opening night, 14 November 1926, but Toscanini had once again overworked himself during rehearsals. He relapsed into the state of exhaustion, with accompanying shoulder pains, that had overwhelmed him in the spring, and he had to put the second and third performances of the opera in Votto's hands. Toscanini then managed to lead *Don Carlo* five more times between 27 November and 22 December, and during the same period he conducted three performances of *Dèbora e Jaéle*, which

---

* Toscanini also invited Cobelli to sing the lead role in *La Favorita*, which he hadn't conducted in nearly four decades, but she turned down that proposal as well. The production did not take place.

had not been in the house's repertoire during the two previous seasons. But that was as much as he could handle during the first two and a half months of the season: two operas, nine performances—minuscule figures, by his standards. Mascagni was called in to conduct a double bill of *Cavalleria Rusticana* and *Pagliacci*—new productions that Toscanini had originally been scheduled to lead—and a planned revival of *Faust* was replaced by Mascagni's *Iris*, also conducted by the composer. All of the other operas during the first four months of the season were conducted by Panizza, Votto, and Santini.

Despite the warning signals regarding his health, Toscanini, together with Carla, Wally, and Wanda, left Milan by train on 28 December, immediately after his last performance of *Dèbora*; at Cherbourg they embarked for New York, where they arrived on 4 January 1927. At first, all proceeded well: the Philharmonic announced Toscanini's repertoire for his sixteen concerts, and the maestro—whose first rehearsal was to take place on Monday, 10 January—attended Mengelberg's final scheduled concert of the season on the previous afternoon. But almost immediately after Mengelberg's concert, Toscanini came down with what the *Times* described as a "severe bronchial attack," and he canceled his first four concerts. When his condition did not improve, further concerts were canceled (replacements were found for all of them), and Dr. Hubert Howe, who was looking after the maestro—and would remain his physician whenever Toscanini was in the United States—advised him to return to Italy and take a long rest. The maestro tentatively booked passage back to Europe for the end of the month.

All sorts of rumors began to circulate: Toscanini was suffering from depression; his nerves were "ripped by the resumption of an old artistic feud"; he had been advised to "retire from the musical world for a year"; he had "begun to lose his musical memory"; and he would retire altogether "from his directorship of La Scala Opera House in Milan and spend a year of quiet in his villa overlooking Lake Como" (he owned no such villa). But even before the rumors could be denied, the *Times* and other newspapers announced that Toscanini had recovered sufficiently to conduct his final week of Philharmonic concerts—two different programs, both devoted to Beethoven, as part of the centennial commemorations.

The first performance, which took place at the Metropolitan

Opera House on 1 February, presented the "Eroica" and Fifth Symphonies, both of which he had conducted in New York the preceding year. He was greeted with tremendous enthusiasm throughout the evening, and the following evening he and the orchestra repeated the program in Philadelphia. His remaining concerts, at Carnegie Hall on the fifth and sixth, consisted of Beethoven's First and Ninth Symphonies; both performances were to be aired on WJZ, but contractual impediments with three of the four singers led to the broadcasts' being cut off, absurdly, just before the soloists' entry in the finale.

"Every seat had been sold days ago," the *New York World* reported after the first of the Ninth Symphony concerts. "At 6:30 an excited crowd of disappointed music lovers stormed the doors of Carnegie Hall in an effort to obtain at least the standing room slips which were not to be put on sale before 7:30. The onslaught became so alarming the management sent in a hurried call for the police and soon a squad of thirty were [*sic*] rushed to Carnegie Hall. These drove the crowds back to the sidewalk, after which they took up their station at the outside doors and challenged each person who entered to produce a ticket of admission." At the end, the audience "rose to its feet with barbaric shouts and cried itself hoarse until the exhausted Toscanini retired from sheer weariness." The phenomenon repeated itself the following night.

On 11 February, Toscanini and family boarded the *Olympic* to begin their homeward journey. Two days earlier he had signed a contract to conduct "approximately 42 concerts" with the Philharmonic the following season, for a fee of $75,000 after taxes, plus travel expenses. Not until early in the spring, however, was it revealed that Toscanini would no longer be a guest conductor, but rather co-conductor, with Mengelberg. A few weeks later, a further announcement was made: Toscanini had been engaged as the Philharmonic's "regular conductor" for five years—in other words, through the 1931–32 season. "There is no doubt that the past season was the high-water mark" for the orchestra, Mackay declared on 23 May, "not only in artistic excellence [. . .]. The demand for seats has increased 25 per cent over last year," and the Philharmonic was now playing to 98 percent of Carnegie Hall's seating capacity.

Not everyone was happy with Toscanini's ascent to the Philharmonic's throne. Furtwängler, in particular, saw himself as a casualty of the orchestra's new arrangement with Mengelberg and Toscanini. And since the lunatic fringes among Toscanini and Furtwängler admirers—like warring fans of this or that opera singer—tend to invent conspiracy theories, each group painting the other's hero as a devil with horns and cloven hooves, let it be stated immediately that documentation in the Philharmonic's files demonstrates conclusively that there was no conspiracy involved in the Philharmonic administration's decision not to reengage Furtwängler.

First, a specific incident: Furtwängler claimed—or, more likely, his most fanatical defenders claimed on his behalf—that he had been upset by the Philharmonic's decision to let Toscanini conduct Beethoven's Ninth Symphony in 1927, because he had originally been told that the privilege would be his. But a cablegram dated 3 March 1926, from Toscanini to the Philharmonic, clearly indicates that Toscanini had arranged even before that date to conduct the Ninth the following year; at that time Furtwängler had not yet submitted even a tentative repertoire list for his 1927 concerts. It is possible that when Toscanini became ill, the Philharmonic management asked Furtwängler to take over the performances of the Ninth, in which case Furtwängler would have been disappointed when Toscanini recovered sufficiently to conduct his last four concerts, two of which included the Ninth, but it is not true that Toscanini had only pretended to be ill and had threatened to return to Italy unless the Ninth was snatched from Furtwängler's hands and put into his own.

More generally, although Furtwängler had enjoyed public and critical success in January 1925, when he first worked with the Philharmonic as a guest conductor, and had been engaged as Mengelberg's co-conductor during the two subsequent seasons, in the second of those seasons, 1926–27, the orchestra, several of the critics, and significant portions of the audience cooled toward him, and ticket sales to his concerts dropped considerably. So far as can be determined from contemporary reviews, this state of affairs was not a result of comparisons, invidious or otherwise, with either Toscanini or Mengelberg, but rather of comparisons with the German conductor's own previous work in New York. It is a matter of record that Furtwängler made appointments with the city's critics, attempting to win them over, and even tried, unsuccessfully, to have influential people exert their power to remove recalcitrant critics from their positions.

The forty-one-year-old Furtwängler was understandably hurt, but neither Toscanini nor Mengelberg was involved in the board of directors' decision. American arts organizations, unlike their European counterparts, receive little or no funding from municipal, regional, or national governments; they depend on donors and box office sales, and, as Mackay stated frankly, for Toscanini's concerts the Philharmonic received "two or three times the number of requests for tickets than could be taken care of." Many of the orchestra's board members were sincere music lovers, but their responsibilities to the orchestra were financial. If Toscanini and Mengelberg generated much greater ticket sales than Furtwängler, the choice to be made was clear.

Furtwängler made a last-ditch effort, a few months later, to turn matters around: Arthur Judson received two letters from Berta Geissmar, the conductor's secretary, in which she spread rumors that Toscanini was seriously ill and suffering from nerves owing to family troubles. There was no truth to the rumors of serious illness, and if family troubles existed they were nothing out of the ordinary. The tactic did not work.

Even some of Furtwängler's most ardent champions stated that he was envious—often irrationally so—of other conductors' successes. Toscanini, on the other hand, was disdainful rather than envious: the idea did not occur to him that any living conductor could reach his level in the repertoire in which he felt most at home. He considered himself barely adequate for the sacred task of bringing to life the works of the genius-composers whose music he performed, but better than any of his colleagues at making the attempt. And yet, when he heard other conductors' performances that impressed him as being as good as or better than his own, he would enthusiastically praise their achievements and recommend them for engagements or positions. In 1929, for instance, he made a point of telling the Italian music critic Raffaello De Rensis that he considered Furtwängler's Wagner performances absolutely as valid as his own (one can hardly imagine Furtwängler returning the compliment), and the fact that he thought well of Furtwängler's abilities would be made dramatically manifest a few years later.

Louise Varèse, wife of the French composer Edgard Varèse, who was living in the United States during Toscanini's Philharmonic years, noted that Furtwängler was "very bitter" over Toscanini's Philharmonic success and, even though the German conductor was no more partial to Varèse's music than was his Italian colleague, "Varèse had the pleasure of joining [Furtwängler] in flaying Toscanini alive, blood dripping from every word." The composer's dislike of Toscanini was a result of an encounter in New York: Respighi had taken the maestro to a concert of the International Composers' Guild, of which Varèse was a cofounder and major promoter; Toscanini hated most of what he heard and said so in no uncertain terms. "Like Varèse, Toscanini was notorious for his uncontrollable temper, and when he shouted at Varèse that it was a disgrace to make people listen to the kind of music he not only sponsored but wrote, Varèse met him temper to temper, insult for insult," Louise Varèse recalled. "It was quite a spectacle. From then on, the slightest mention of Toscanini was like the *muleta* to a bull; Varèse charged. [. . .] Varèse insisted that Toscanini was incapable of conducting anything better than Italian opera and that he had the mentality of a coiffeur and looked like one. Salzedo, who was an admirer and friend of Toscanini, argued with Varèse in vain."[*]

19.

LA SCALA'S ADMINISTRATORS COULD NOT HELP NOTICING THAT house attendance fell when Toscanini was away, and they tried to contain the damage by lowering ticket prices during his absences. But even before that problem emerged, Toscanini, on his own initiative, had reduced his annual Scala salary in proportion to the number of days he spent away. Scandiani wrote a letter urging him to accept an annual salary, "since you are occupied with our Theater

---

[*] The famed harpist Carlos Salzedo (1885–1961) was friendly with both Varèse and Toscanini; the latter had brought him to America in 1909 to become the Metropolitan's principal harp, and Salzedo always described Toscanini as the greatest of all conductors, musically and technically. He said that the "immortal maestro" was the only conductor in his experience who "never distorted or nullified the sound of the harp (or of any other instrument)."

not only for the season but also during the so-called vacation months. It would be much more logical for La Scala to pay you an over-all salary for the whole year, and not only, as is now the case, for the period of your actual presence at the Theater, thereby avoiding the exact daily computation every time you go away." But Toscanini insisted on doing things his way, and he maintained the practice for the duration of his tenure, making complicated computations and deducting money from his pay.

He returned to Milan not later than 20 February 1927 and immediately resumed his usual, mad work rhythms. But when he realized that he had not completely recovered from his illness, he took a brief vacation, with Carla, in the Roman campagna and attended the world premiere, in Rome, of Pick-Mangiagalli's opera *Basi e Bote*—which he did not like. Upon returning to La Scala, the maestro brought *Lucia* back into the house repertoire after a four-year absence; every available seat and standing position was sold out for the first performance, and a crowd, gathered outside the artists' entrance, cheered Toscanini upon his arrival at the theater. Within the following two months, he had rehearsed and conducted four new productions and five more revivals: his health had evidently returned to normal. But he carefully avoided scheduling a performance on 25 March, his sixtieth birthday, and once again kept the house dark on 21 April—the Birth of Rome holiday—contrary to Mussolini's orders.

One of the new productions, *La Gioconda*, marked the fiftieth anniversary of the world premiere—which had taken place at La Scala— of Ponchielli's best-known work. Beethoven's *Fidelio*, on the other hand, had never before been presented at La Scala because, like *The Magic Flute*, it mixed musical numbers with spoken dialogue, thus the more conservative elements of the Milanese public considered it beneath the dignity of the Temple of Opera. But Toscanini was determined to continue his commemoration of the Beethoven centenary with this masterpiece. The Dutch soprano Elisabeth Ohms, who had been disappointed by the cancellation of the previous season's *Tristan* revival, was now engaged to sing the role of Leonore. About the first rehearsal, of the vocal quartet, "Mir ist so wunderbar," she recalled,

Every bar was worked through with such patience and love for the music that I felt very happy to experience this way of rehearsing. Here I could learn enormously and I greedily grasped the rare opportunity.

We rehearsed for about two hours and every now and then he shook his head and muttered, "atrocious translation." We had not yet finished when Toscanini suddenly said, "I shall make another translation, and also change these miserable *parlandi* [spoken dialogues] into recitatives." My heart stopped, I remembered my newly learned text in that strange language, and the *première* was to take place in a fortnight.

To understand my state of mind, one must realize what rehearsing with Toscanini meant. Not the slightest nuance is left to chance and the piano rehearsals were legion, to say nothing of the stage rehearsals. Generally we worked from 12 to 3 P.M., and from 8 to 12 in the evening; would I find the spare time necessary to learn another new text? Toscanini must have read in my face how I felt, for he laughed and said: *"La Ohms la farà"* [Ohms will manage it]. [. . .] The recitatives were tried, did not suit him, were dropped and Toscanini returned to the *parlandi* [. . .], but with new words.

In spite of all this work I made it possible to attend many orchestral rehearsals. To see this great man at work was such bliss that I could not miss going to the theatre every time, even when it meant skipping my dinner or sleep. [. . .]

Every evening prior to the start of the performance he came to see me in my dressing room and asked me: *"Come sta Ohms?"* [. . .] Without saying another word he walked to and fro until the stage manager came to fetch him. He left me, saying with a deep sigh: *"Mah . . . cominciamo"* (Well, let's begin).

Ohms felt that the performances "were a great triumph for all of us and especially for Toscanini," and the reviews were positive. The public as a whole, however, was unenthusiastic about *Fidelio*: only three performances were given that season and four the following year.*

Similarly, Dukas's *Ariane et Barbe-bleue*—one of the season's major

---

* During his Metropolitan days, Toscanini had noted that Mahler used the *Leonore* Overture no. 3 as a curtain-raiser to the second part of *Fidelio*'s relatively short second act, and he decided to do the same.

efforts—was given only three performances: Toscanini was no more successful in persuading the Milanese public of its value than he had been with audiences in New York and Buenos Aires fifteen years earlier. Not surprisingly, a new production of *Tosca* was much more popular. But according to the *Chicago Tribune*, during one of the *Tosca* evenings "some one on the stage got tangled in his signals and lowered the curtain too soon in the second act, just about the time that Tosca was placing the candles around the recently deceased Scarpia. As soon as he could leave the orchestra, Toscanini, blazing with wrath, started for the back of the stage, but by the time he got there that particular curtain man had left the theater; and he [. . .] has not been seen around Milan since. At last accounts he was down in the heel of Italy and prepared to swim further south across the Mediterranean if necessary."

Honest mistakes usually elicited only a calm correction from Toscanini, but errors resulting from a lack of concentration were almost guaranteed to set off one of his volcanic explosions. According to Enrico Minetti, the Scala orchestra musicians referred to the maestro's annual visits to New York as their "winter vacation. [. . .] No afflictions of the spirit, no anxiety, no terror—everything ran as smoothly as oil; a little too smoothly, alas! But then, when he returned, he made us pay for our 'vacation'—and with interest! He was capable of running four dress rehearsals and opening as many productions in one week (to make up for lost time, he said). [. . .] Gritting our teeth and grumbling in muted tones, we gave everything we had to satisfy him, and on rare occasions we succeeded! And then, seeing him happy, we would forget the torture and the fear, the insults and the bad language, because although he maltreated us, we loved him."

The sort of schedule that Minetti described functioned because Toscanini had honed a repertoire system in which everything was prepared so meticulously that previous seasons' productions could be reassembled with a minimum of rehearsal time. Thinking back on that system half a century later, Gavazzeni recalled that

> it was an altogether new way of working for the Italian operatic tradition, because he instituted a custom, a method—a tyranny, one could say. [. . .] Before Toscanini, yes, there were good performances, there were great conductors, there were great

singers, but not yet a method for a complete realization from the aesthetic and even moral points of view. La Scala was completely reorganized for Toscanini, with respect to its rehearsal habits, to the way of conceiving its program, to the method of making singers study, and also with respect to educating the public. The public with Toscanini, during that era, was educated to consider the theater not as something for amusement but as something with a moral and aesthetic function that enters into the life of a society, into the life of a culture.

20.

AFTER A SUMMERTIME STAY IN THE VILLAGE OF ALPINO, HIGH ABOVE Lake Maggiore's western shore, Toscanini initiated his 1927–28 season with three October concerts that included three pieces new to his repertoire: *Pastorale d'Eté* and *Pacific 231*, by the thirty-five-year-old Swiss composer Arthur Honegger, and the "Infernal Dance" from Stravinsky's *The Firebird*. On 10 October—Verdi's presumed birthday, and the twenty-fifth anniversary of the opening of the Rest Home for Musicians, which the composer had founded—Toscanini brought a Scala ensemble to the home and conducted several pieces for the residents. He opened the opera season in mid-November with three revivals and a new production of *Otello*—his first performance of the opera in over fourteen years—with the complete third-act *concertato* (rarely done, in those days), and with Trantoul in the title role, Stabile as Iago, and Scacciati as Desdemona; Marchioro was responsible for the sets, and Forzano dealt with the staging, under Toscanini's watchful eye.

In December, Toscanini took over the double bill of *Cavalleria Rusticana* and *Pagliacci* that Mascagni had conducted in his stead the previous year, and on New Year's Day 1928 he conducted a revival of *Nerone*. Eight days later he left for New York. During his absence, which, this time, lasted over three months, the repertoire was entrusted not only to Panizza, Santini, and Votto but also to Richard Strauss, who conducted *The Marriage of Figaro* in addition to his own *Der Rosenkavalier* and *Salome* and the Italian premiere of his *Josephslegende* ballet.

Shortly before leaving Milan, Toscanini had met with Ernesto Belloni, the city's mayor and La Scala's president, who had told him of plans for the improvement of the theater's status and of Milanese musical life in general. The carrot dangled before Toscanini consisted of the stabilization of the orchestra's financial situation and the realization of renovations to the house itself. But there was a stick: all of the city's other musical organizations, with the possible exception of the conservatory, would be incorporated into a plan for direct government financing of La Scala. Toscanini knew that economic support from Rome was becoming a necessity for Italy's opera houses, including La Scala, but he also knew that accepting such support under the then current political circumstances would mean that Mussolini's regime could impose its will on the Scala administration. His immediate reaction to Belloni's declaration was not reported—perhaps not even printable—but in all likelihood this conversation was precisely what made Toscanini decide to leave La Scala after the following season. For eight more months, however, he kept silent.

Carla, Wally, and Wanda again accompanied him to America, but he did not know, then or later, that Count Castelbarco, not yet divorced, would also cross the Atlantic and stay at the Hotel Astor during the Toscanini family's annual sojourns there, in order to be with Wally as much as possible. Since Toscanini was busy with rehearsals and concerts, there were plenty of opportunities for the lovers to be together, presumably with the complicity of Wanda, who had turned twenty the previous December, and probably also with Carla's knowledge. The family arrived in New York aboard the White Star liner *Homeric* on 20 January 1928, and the *Times* reported that Toscanini's first concert, on Thursday the twenty-sixth, would be "radiated over WOR's wave length at 8:25 o'clock."

The radio was becoming increasingly important in American musical life, and most or all of Toscanini's Thursday evening concerts that season—as well as some of those of Mengelberg and of the guest conductor Sir Thomas Beecham—were broadcast "from the stage of Carnegie Hall through ten microphones," not only in the New York area but in many other parts of the country. One of the broadcasts was sent via shortwave to Italy, "at the request of the conductor, [. . .] who is anxious to have his son Walter in Italy hear one of his concerts," a representative of the WRNY transmitting company told the *Times*. Unfortunately, these concert broadcasts were not recorded.

A few days before his first concert, Toscanini—together with Rachmaninoff, the violinists Fritz Kreisler and Joseph Szigeti, the soprano Elisabeth Rethberg, and the cream of New York society—attended the Russian inventor Leon Theremin's demonstration-performance of his eponymous early electronic instrument, in the grand ballroom of the Plaza Hotel. Although "the novelty wore off" quickly and "about half the audience left before the program was over," most of those present "professed themselves deeply impressed" with the theremin, the *Times* reported. "Toscanini expressed eagerness to experiment with the apparatus," but this never happened.

During the forty-four concerts that Toscanini conducted that fall, most of them at Carnegie Hall but several on tour, he added to his repertoire Mozart's Symphony no. 32 (known at the time as "Overture in the Italian Style"), "Spring" from Vivaldi's 200-year-old *The Four Seasons* (with the concertmaster, Scipione Guidi, as soloist; this was the piece's American premiere—the Vivaldi revival had barely begun at the time), Saint-Saëns's Cello Concerto no. 1 (with the principal cellist, Leo Schulz), Ravel's *Daphnis et Chloé* Suite no. 2, Manuel de Falla's *El Amor Brujo* (with the contralto Sophie Braslau), Tommasini's *The Good-Humored Ladies* (orchestrations of keyboard music by Domenico Scarlatti), and an arrangement by Bernardino Molinari of Monteverdi's *Sonata sopra Sancta Maria* (with the Schola Cantorum). In the course of his New York visit, Toscanini led benefit concerts for the Neighborhood Music School (raising enough money for the institution to pay off its mortgage) and for the Philharmonic musicians' pension fund, and on 27 March he shared the Carnegie Hall podium with the Austrian Artur Bodanzky, the Englishman Eugene Goossens, the American Walter Damrosch, and the Spaniard Enrique Fernández Arbós, to raise funds for the National Music League of New York and the American Academy in Rome.

So many people had been unable to obtain tickets to Toscanini's two performances of Beethoven's Ninth Symphony the preceding year that the Philharmonic's administration asked him to conclude his 1928 New York stay—and the orchestra's season—with three more performances of the work. "The audience was of immense proportions," the *Times* reported of the last concert, which took place at the Metropolitan on 1 April. "Every one that the law allowed, and some who evaded the law, filled the seats and choked the standing space in the theatre. They attempted to force doors and climb fire escapes, and some who attempted to enter without right were caught and turned out." The fuss made over Toscanini at the end of the concert was so great, and the floral tributes onstage so cloying, that he escaped after only one or two bows and did not return to acknowledge the ongoing cheers.

A FEW DAYS BEFORE THOSE PERFORMANCES of the Ninth took place, New York's newspapers had published stories that seized the attention of all of the city's music lovers. "SYMPHONY MERGED WITH PHIL-HARMONIC; TOSCANINI TO DIRECT," read the headline in the *Times*, and the accompanying article said that Mackay, the Philharmonic board's chairman, and Harry Harkness Flagler, president of the New York Symphony Society, had jointly announced that the new ensemble would be called the Philharmonic-Symphony Orchestra of New York. The Symphony, which had recently worked under such outstanding guest conductors as Otto Klemperer and Fritz Busch, was experiencing financial difficulties, and Flagler, who carried much of its economic burden, could no longer cope with the situation. The idea, Mackay said, was "to place the consolidated orchestra upon a sound basis as a permanent, self-supporting institution" that would not be dependent on periodical fund-raising campaigns.

Flagler was to be president and Mackay chairman of the board of the new entity; Toscanini would be chief conductor and would choose those musicians from the Symphony to absorb into the Philharmonic's ranks; Mengelberg would be listed as "conductor," the same as Toscanini, but he was now clearly second-in-command. Walter Damrosch—whose father, Leopold, had founded the Symphony, and who had been that organization's principal conductor since Leopold's death, in 1885—would be the new ensemble's associate conductor, but the position was more symbolic than real: Damrosch had long since announced his impending retirement.

The pros and cons of the merger were debated in the press during the following days and weeks. Although the new ensemble's concert season would last longer than either of the two separate orchestra's previous seasons, there would be roughly forty fewer symphony concerts per year than the total number that the two orchestras had previously offered, and a significant number of good musicians would inevitably lose their jobs. Why could a wealthy city of seven million inhabitants not support two major symphony orchestras?

But the new arrangement was a fait accompli. Less than a week after the announcement was made, the New York Symphony played the last concert of its last season as an independent organism. Flagler presented each member with a pair of solid gold cufflinks, and one wit among the players referred to the occasion as "the day we got the cufflinks and lost our shirts."

21.

DURING HIS STAY IN NEW YORK, TOSCANINI AGREED TO AN INFOR-mal chat with the journalist S. J. Woolf, a frequent contributor to the *Times*, and even allowed his interlocutor to attend a rehearsal. Woolf published his substantial article—"Toscanini's Ideas on Music Old and New"—in April 1928, at the height of public interest in the about-to-be-formed Philharmonic-Symphony and its new chief conductor.

Toscanini said that he saw "many advantages" in the merger, especially an enlarged wind section, a reinforced pension fund for the musicians, a somewhat longer season that would be shared by various conductors, and the construction of a new hall—which, however, did not happen within his lifetime. Woolf observed that Toscanini "has built around himself a wall of reserve that few can scale. He feels that he should be judged by the music that he produces, and that his personality can be of no concern to the public."

Toscanini declared his indebtedness to Wagner's writings on music and the theater. "'I can honestly say that whatever I am today as a conductor I owe largely to what I learned from him.'" Verdi, however, "'represents the highest point in the development of the music drama in his native country. But aside from his musical genius he stands for everything that is fine and noble in man. Italy could well be proud of him as a citizen had he not written one bar of music.'" Toscanini's "veneration" for Wagner and Verdi, however, "is exceeded by his worship of Beethoven," Woolf said. "To Toscanini the nine symphonies are the apotheosis of all music. In conducting them he feels that in such works man approaches the divine, and that in them is the essence of all religions."

On the subject of musical nationalism, Toscanini remarked that music

"may be written by a German, an Italian, a Frenchman or an American, but to me that is unimportant. It is either good music or bad music. [. . .] The same thing may be said about classical as opposed to modern music. Music is not like wine; it does not improve with age. Nor, on the other hand, is it like an egg that can be spoiled by being kept too long. Occasionally, of course, the true worth of music is not appreciated until years after it is written. There is good old music, and there is bad old music, just as there is good or bad new music. The most essential requisite in listening to music is an open mind. When I hear a composition for the first time I try to put myself in the position of the average untrained listener. After all, music is not written for the enjoyment of professional musicians, but for cultivated lovers of music. I know many musicians who, while hearing a piece for the first time, analyze it in every minute detail. This is a mistake."

One of Toscanini's comments surprised Woolf: "'I am interested in jazz—as a matter of fact I have been from its very beginning. [. . .] The unexpected in it appeals to me. But there is a great deal of jazz music that is absolutely worthless. I have a number of gramophone recordings of an excellent jazz band, and I have just bought a number of new disks.'" His attitude on this subject was very different from that of his younger colleague Bruno Walter, who, even twenty years later, was describing jazz as detrimental to Western civilization. Toscanini also told Woolf that the mix of peoples and cultures in America gave it a musical advantage over Europe, because "'there is no one single dominating element at work.'" The fact that American orchestras could draw on talent from all over the world was a positive factor, as was the nature of the audience, which "'is so conglomerate in its make-up that no one type of music will satisfy it.

This makes for varied programs, which in turn tend toward creating a cosmopolitan taste.'"

Another journalist, Earl Sparling of the *New York Telegram*, somehow obtained secondhand but accurate information about Toscanini and was able to feed the growing public appetite for details of the maestro's daily life. Sparling noted that Toscanini "keeps a piano in his suite at the Astor Hotel" and that he "almost always dines in his suite. He eats very little, preferring Italian dishes. [. . .] When he visits a friend's home he likes to discuss books, paintings—and music, if the discussion is profound. [. . .] He has a Brussels Griffon dog named Pitciu [*sic*; Picciù], a gift from Mme. Frances Alda. He often takes Pitciu in his arms and sometimes tosses him into the air. Pitciu sleeps in a basket near his bed." Toscanini's "suits and shirts are tailored in Italy," Sparling continued. "If shopping must be done in New York Mrs. Toscanini usually attends to it." Toscanini "does not smoke and sleeps about five hours a night. At 61 his complexion is almost as clear as a boy's."

ON 3 APRIL 1928, when the Toscaninis boarded the *Berengaria* in New York and sailed for Cherbourg, Mussolini was planning to make the Grand Council of Fascism Italy's main governing body, thereby further tightening his control on the country. But the maestro, upon returning to Milan, concentrated on his work. He spent the remainder of the Scala season conducting three revivals and preparing the world premiere of Pizzetti's *Fra Gherardo*, which opened in May. The press praised Toscanini for the splendor of the performance, but the opera was heard only four times that spring and four the following season; like the composer's previous *Dèbora e Jaéle*, *Fra Gherardo* made the rounds of several major ensembles worldwide, then virtually disappeared from the repertoire.

The Toscaninis spent part of the summer of 1928 in a hotel on Isola dei Pescatori (Fishermen's Island) on Lake Maggiore; late in August, from the town of Baveno on the lake's western shore, the maestro cabled Judson, "After next season I take leave definitely from theatre. You may rely upon my cooperation for carrying out [European] tour spring of 1930." Although the news was not made public, La Scala's administrators either had been or were about to be similarly informed. They were not surprised, but they hoped that Toscanini would be persuaded to return, even if on a more limited basis.

Two of the four concerts that Toscanini conducted with the Scala orchestra in October were dominated by the first performances in Italy of Zoltán Kodály's *Psalmus Hungaricus*, for tenor, chorus, and orchestra. The forty-six-year-old composer—who, together with Béla Bartók, was one of the moving forces in twentieth-century Hungarian music—came to Milan for the occasion and was heartily applauded by the audience. Another program was devoted entirely to music of Schubert, to mark the centenary of the composer's death; at the end of the evening, "the occupants of galleries, boxes and main floor alike rose to their feet [. . .] and tarried as one man to acclaim [Toscanini] enthusiastically, not satisfied until 'Il Mago' (The Wizard), as he is affectionately dubbed, had returned three times, visibly affected, to acknowledge the demonstration," the *New York Times*'s correspondent reported.

Toscanini revived the previous year's successful *Otello* production to open La Scala's 1928–29 opera season, but two nights later he presented a new production, designed by Marchioro, of *La Forza del Destino*. As he entered the pit that evening, he must have recalled the disastrous Scala *Forza* of 1908, when the critics had described the opera as "overcome with age" and "a mish-mash"; that production had closed after a single performance. But what had seemed old and creaky two decades earlier now resurfaced as a classic: the reviews were ecstatic, and thirteen performances had to be given to satisfy public demand.*

Toscanini devoted exceptional care to his first production of *Parsifal*, which opened on 16 December. Ohms, in the role of Kundry, enjoyed her rehearsals with the maestro "with every bit of my being," she recalled. During a solo rehearsal of the second act, "We worked together about two hours, when he suddenly began to explain this music to me. Without realizing it, we soon were in the midst of the third act. Toscanini explained, sang every part, with his hoarse broken voice, up to the very end. He had so much love for this music

---

* The last four performances of *Forza* were conducted by Votto while Toscanini was in America.

that he forgot everything around [him]." Five sold-out performances of *Parsifal* were given.

Of the three further operas that Toscanini revived during November and December, the most significant was *Die Meistersinger*, which opened on 26 December 1928, the exact thirtieth anniversary of Toscanini's first performance (with the same opera) as La Scala's music director. It was the occasion for an outpouring of public affection and gratitude. "To find a similar occurrence in La Scala's annals one has to go back to Verdi's last appearances there," the next day's *Corriere* commented. "The applause that greeted the maestro when he first appeared on the podium went on for about ten minutes in a succession of frenzied waves, which he vainly tried to quell several times by motioning to begin the Prelude [. . .] and there were numerous curtain calls at the end of the second and third acts." At the conclusion of the performance, "all the artists of La Scala, the members of the chorus and the members of the orchestra, nearly 500 altogether, rushed onto the stage, surrounded the maestro and gave him an ovation, the spontaneity of which seemed to move the famous conductor deeply," the *Times* of London reported. The audience, which included members of Italy's royal family, foreign aristocrats, and Education Minister Giuseppe Belluzzo, "did not even seem satisfied after the lights had been turned off to put an end to the affectionate insistence."

La Scala's administrators and the city's officials had wanted to honor Toscanini in a special way, but they knew that a monetary gift would have offended him and that he would not have put up with a ceremony. They eventually hit on the idea of creating a Toscanini Foundation—a fund that would offer medical assistance and fresh-air summer camps for ailing children of members of the Scala orchestra, chorus, stage crew, and administration. Toscanini gladly accepted this tribute, and a sum of 680,000 lire was quickly raised among his admirers in Italy and the United States. The maestro himself contributed 100,000 lire, and he would repeat the gesture in the years to come.

An unanticipated problem had cropped up at La Scala in November 1928, when the seventy-eight-year-old Enrico Cecchetti, who headed the theater's ballet school, died suddenly. Cecchetti, one of the most famous dancers and ballet masters in history, had performed all over Europe and the Americas; among many other achievements, he created the role of Carabosse at the world premiere of Tchaikovsky's *Sleeping Beauty* in St. Petersburg in 1890 and that of the old magician in Stravinsky's *Petrushka* with Sergei Diaghilev's Ballets Russes in Paris in 1911, and he taught such luminaries of the dance as Vaslav Nijinsky, Anna Pavlova, and Serge Lifar. In 1925, Toscanini persuaded Cecchetti to come out of retirement and take charge of La Scala's school, and the old master, during his three years at the helm, helped make the institution into a leading training center. In the summer of 1928, however, he told Toscanini of his intention to retire; according to newspaper reports, Toscanini's first choice as Cecchetti's successor was Pavlova, but the famous ballerina turned down the honor to continue her dancing career. Then Cecchetti died, and the school needed a new leader immediately.

The choice fell upon Cia Fornaroli, whom Toscanini and Gatti-Casazza had engaged in 1910 as a *première danseuse* at the Metropolitan, where she first appeared in this story. After her return to Italy, in 1913, she danced with various companies, and by the end of the decade she was generally considered the finest Italian ballerina of her generation. Since 1922 she had been prima ballerina of La Scala's corps de ballet.

Three years earlier, in Rome, the slender, elegant Cia had starred in the world premiere production of a ballet with music by Riccardo Pick-Mangiagalli, who introduced her to Walter Toscanini. Although Walter was ten years her junior, they were immediately attracted to each other and soon became lovers. Cia believed that Walter, a serial womanizer like his father, would soon tire of her—she called him a *teppista* (hooligan)—and at her request the relationship was kept secret: she refused even to be seen at a café with him. But her move back to Milan in 1922 facilitated their encounters.

Under the direction of the elder Toscanini, who thought highly of her as a dancer and as a person, Fornaroli appeared in *Louise, Orfeo, Nerone, La Traviata*, and *Aida*, and she participated in many Scala operas and ballets conducted by Stravinsky, Richard Strauss, and others, as well as choreographing several productions. Toscanini may or may not have been aware of Cia's relationship with his son: despite the gossip on the subject that undoubtedly circulated in the city's artistic circles, he was oblivious to much of what went on in his family because people tended not to tell him things that they thought would displease him—as in the case of Wally's much-gossiped-about affair with Castelbarco, which had gone on for seven years without her father's knowledge.

Fornaroli had become pregnant twice during the mid-1920s but had miscarried both times; in January 1929, when she officially became head of the ballet school, she was pregnant again, and in August 1929, Walfredo Toscanini, the maestro's first grandchild, was born—an event of which the new grandfather was certainly apprised. A few years earlier, Cia had not wanted to be seen with Walter, but now the dynamic of the situation was reversed: although Walter was very much attached to his infant son, he was involved with other women and did not want to marry Cia or even to live with her, despite her pleas to cohabitate for the child's sake. In January 1932, Cia wrote to him that the maestro "is suffering from this ambiguous state and would like you to be more resolute, more decisive. He also fears that you don't love Dedè"—Walfredo's childhood nickname—"enough, otherwise you would try to normalize his life even if you had to fight [with the elder Toscanini]. This would never happen because he would never oppose you with respect to your responsibilities toward Dedè."

Toward the end of 1933 or early in 1934, Cia, Walter, and Walfredo moved, together, into an apartment that Carla had bought, and by 1936 they had moved to another apartment, also owned by Walter's parents, who contributed generously to their support. Dedè spent much of his time with his grandparents, except when they were away from Milan. In 1938, after a nineteen-year relationship, Walter and Cia finally married—at city hall, not in church. By then all passion was spent, but their marriage seems to have remained mutually respectful and not unhappy; one observer described Cia's attitude toward her husband as "maternal." Dedè was much loved by both of his parents and doted on by his grandparents.

22.

UMBERTO GIORDANO'S *IL RE* (THE KING), A BRIEF OPERA BILLED AS a "short story in three scenes," proved to be the last of the twenty-four opera world premieres that Toscanini conducted during his entire career.* His view of the contemporary opera scene was becoming increasingly negative: later that year, when the music critic Raffaello De Rensis asked him whether what was beginning to be perceived as a crisis was a result of the scarcity of new operas, Toscanini replied,

"Scarcity? No, it is rather the congestion of novelties that is disturbing the balance of our opera seasons. [. . .] And the unfortunate part is that composers insist on blaming the publishers and conductors for the lack of vitality in their operas. Now that's really not so. At present one cannot talk about thrown-away artworks. The publishers acquire new works, the theaters put them on, we conduct them, and the public comes. Whose fault is it if the opera folds its wings and falls after a short flight? I'll go further: Where is it written that all operas by modern composers must be liked? Didn't even Verdi and Rossini produce scores that have justly been laid to rest?"

Toscanini also made the curious comment that "composers today can't stand and don't love their own operas; therefore, the public can't stand or love them either." No doubt he was thinking of some of the more radical works being produced at the time. One may justifiably describe this attitude as conservative, and yet, as mentioned above, since *Turandot* not a single Italian opera has achieved worldwide popularity. In his day, Toscanini did what he could—a great deal, in fact—for composers, but by the time he reached his sixties he had passed that particular baton to younger conductors.

Toscanini's workload during the first months of the 1928–29 Scala season had once again put too great a strain on him. He was suffering from severe insomnia and acute pain in his shoulder and back, which were X-rayed in November. The X-rays showed only slight abnormalities, nothing was done about the problem, and the pains continued.†

---

* The number includes Mascagni's *Le Maschere* (1901), which was premiered simultaneously in several Italian cities. On *Il Re*'s opening night, 12 January 1929, Toscanini followed Giordano's opera with a performance of *Pagliacci*, but at the two remaining performances under his baton, other conductors completed the evening with other works.

† This may have been the occasion on which he was examined by the well-known physician Augusto Murri, who told him, "You were born well." "But my shoulder hurts," Toscanini complained. Murri replied, "Conduct with the other one!"

Since he could not bring himself even to finish deciding on his forth-coming Philharmonic programs, Carla wired Judson that her husband would not arrive in New York until mid-February, a month later than originally planned. Judson and the orchestra's board had to scramble to find guest conductors for the thirteen concerts (six programs) that Toscanini would miss. At last, on 13 February 1929 Toscanini and his family—this time including Walter—disembarked in Manhattan from the French liner *Paris*.

Five days later, the maestro held his first rehearsal with the regrouped Philharmonic-Symphony Orchestra. Before leaving the city the previous spring, he had auditioned those members of the New York Symphony who wished to join the renamed ensemble; approximately twenty of them were engaged, and since the old Philharmonic's personnel was being increased from about a hundred to a hundred and ten—and since at least a few Philharmonic players retired each year—this meant that probably five or six Philharmonic players lost their jobs.

When asked his opinion of American orchestras, Toscanini would jokingly ask, in turn, "What is an American orchestra?" And he would point to the Philharmonic's roster: among the fifteen string section leaders and principal wind, percussion, and harp players, only two were born in the United States—to foreign-born parents—and the rest of the orchestra was similarly populated. The personnel list in those years showed only four or five Anglo-Saxon names, as against considerable numbers of Eastern European Jews, Germans, and Italians, and a smattering of French and Dutch-Flemish names. The melding of all these different schools of playing into an outstanding, unified whole was among the tasks of conductors like Mengelberg and Toscanini in New York, Monteux and Koussevitzky in Boston, and Stokowski in Philadelphia, as they brought their respective orchestras to peaks of achievement during the 1920s and 1930s.

Toscanini's first concert, at Carnegie Hall on 21 February, included the world premiere of Respighi's *Feste Romane* (Roman Festivals), the final part of the "Roman Trilogy," which had begun with *Fountains of Rome* and continued with *Pines of Rome*. He also conducted the world premiere of Pizzetti's *Concerto dell'Estate* (Summer Concerto) and gave his first performances of Ernest Schelling's *Impressions from an*

Artist's Life, with the composer as piano soloist, and Sergei Prokofiev's "Classical" Symphony.*

At the concert of 28 February, as the orchestra was about to begin
the second movement of Pizzetti's piece, several latecomers made
their way to the front rows of Carnegie Hall and sat down noisily.
Toscanini turned around on the podium, "crossed his arms in a
Napoleonic gesture and fixed his brilliant, deep-set eyes on them,"
the next day's *Herald-Tribune* reported. "'You are late!' said Mr.
Toscanini sternly. The words could be heard all over the hall. That
was all, as he then turned to the orchestra, rapped loudly and vigorously on the cello stand before him and continued the concert." A
month later, nearly a hundred concertgoers who arrived after the
first movement of Schubert's "Great" C Major Symphony had begun
learned that Toscanini had given orders not to seat latecomers until
the entire symphony was finished. "Many departed homeward,
since the remainder of the program following the intermission
comprised only three short works," said the *Times*. "There were
many murmurs of dissatisfaction from those who waited, but no
open demonstration."

Toscanini's Philharmonic season included tour concerts, a benefit concert for the orchestra's pension fund, four concerts broadcast via radio, reduced-price tickets for students to Saturday
evening concerts, and—most important for posterity—four days
of recording sessions under the auspices of the newly formed RCA
Victor Company (the young and ever more powerful Radio Corporation of America had recently acquired the Victrola Company).
These 78 rpm discs comprised *The Sorcerer's Apprentice*, the Preludes to Acts I and III of *La Traviata* (which Toscanini and the
orchestra had not performed in his Philharmonic concerts),
Haydn's "Clock" and Mozart's "Haffner" Symphonies, and the
Scherzo from *A Midsummer Night's Dream*; all remain classic examples of Toscanini's work at the time and of the beauty of the Phil-

---

* Schelling, a composer, conductor, and pianist, was in charge of conducting the
Philharmonic's children's concerts. During the preceding Philharmonic season, Prokofiev
and his wife, the singer Lina Codina, had attended a Toscanini rehearsal, and the couple
had been shocked to see him lose his temper at the orchestra. "It already seemed flawless
to us," Lina recalled, many years later. Toscanini told them, at the time, that he was
planning to schedule the "Classical" Symphony the following year.

harmonic's playing. But Toscanini later confessed that when the technicians told him that *The Sorcerer's Apprentice*, as recorded the first time through, wouldn't quite fit onto two sides of a twelve-inch disc, he rerecorded the piece at a slightly faster tempo than he normally adopted.

He was delighted with the quality of the amalgamated orchestra, as Van Praag, the personnel manager, revealed in a memorandum to Judson. Toscanini said that "the string sections were excellent," and he "could not understand why I insisted on making a change in the first oboe, first bassoon and the flute," Van Praag related. "He admitted that at times Mr. Amans [the principal flute] was a bit dense [. . .] but [said] that he liked his tone and could see no reason for changing him for someone else." The players in question remained in their positions—and so much for the incorrect legend of a Toscanini who fired musicians on the slightest pretext. The only musician in the orchestra whom he wished to replace, at the time, was the second trumpet, who, he said, was not bad, but not good enough to sit next to the first trumpet, Harry Glantz—"such a fine artist," Toscanini remarked. The second trumpet was duly replaced, the following season, by Nathan Prager, who remained in that position for thirty-three years.

Another incorrect legend is that Toscanini wanted the Philharmonic to have nothing more to do with Mengelberg. Various documents in the orchestra's archives demonstrate that Toscanini stated emphatically and repeatedly that Mengelberg should be reengaged as a guest conductor, and the pianist Mieczyslaw Horszowski recalled spending an evening at Toscanini's home in Milan during those years with Mengelberg as an honored guest. As early as 1927, Toscanini had told Adolf Busch that he was *very unhappy* with Mengelberg, but "only on account of the crazinesses"—the erratic behavior, in other words, not the conducting. Toscanini, poles apart though he was from Mengelberg as an interpretive artist, knew how to distinguish fool's gold from the real thing, and Mengelberg was the real thing. Not surprisingly, however, the red-haired Dutchman did not care to return to what had been "his" orchestra as a mere second-stringer or guest, and he must have been offended that he was not invited to conduct any of the concerts that were being planned for the Philharmonic's first European tour. But the orches-

tra was now Toscanini's ensemble, and the Philharmonic management and board wanted to display their band and its conductor
together, everywhere.

Mengelberg's self-inflicted coup de grâce came in December
1929, when he returned to New York for eight weeks of concerts
with the orchestra. During rehearsals, he "expressed his disapproval of the present condition of the orchestra" and "ascribed this
condition in part to the changed personnel of the orchestra and in
part to the effect of Mr. Toscanini's rehearsing," the *Times* reported.
Mengelberg's remarks "reached the ears of Mr. Toscanini," who
"expressed doubt as to whether he would care to return as conductor of the Philharmonic Orchestra next season if his work should
be subjected to such criticism by his colleague." On 19 January 1930,
Mengelberg conducted his last concert with the Philharmonic. He
fired a parting shot by inviting two of the city's leading music critics to dinner and telling them that Toscanini conducted symphonic
music as if it were *Il Trovatore*, and then he sailed for Europe, never
to return to America.

For the people responsible for the orchestra's survival, however,
dealing with Toscanini was not the easiest task. After a lifetime
spent in the Italian lyric theater, the new chief conductor was accustomed to a system in which individual performances or even entire
productions could be rescheduled at will if more time was needed
for rehearsals or if a key artist took ill. For instance, Mackay was
"very much disturbed" to learn, in February 1929, that Toscanini
had only the vaguest notion as to which part or parts of the following season he wished to conduct. If Judson or Mackay or Van Praag
had sat down with Toscanini and asked him to help them by making concrete plans as far in advance as possible and sticking to them,
he would certainly have grasped the problem and might even have
mended his ways. But they were afraid of him—afraid that he
would abandon the Philharmonic and take his talents, fame, and
box office draw elsewhere. Thus he blithely continued to act as he
always had, changing his mind about his New York arrival and
departure dates, about which concerts he would conduct during
which part or parts of each season, and about shifting this piece to
that program and that piece to this program. Much of the Philhar-

monic's correspondence with or about Toscanini evokes the image of an unarmed zookeeper trying to coax a tiger back into its cage by smiling nicely at it.

A case in point: Toscanini had planned to close the season in mid-April 1929 with his first performance of Beethoven's *Missa Solemnis*, but he subsequently decided to return to Italy earlier than planned, to complete his tenure at La Scala. The Austrian conductor Clemens Krauss would take over what were to have been Toscanini's last two weeks of concerts, and Toscanini postponed for five more years his first attempt to scale the *Missa*'s daunting peaks. His last concert—another pension fund event—took place on 1 April, with Leo Schulz, the Philharmonic's longtime principal cellist, as soloist in Schumann's Cello Concerto. Schulz was retiring at the end of the season, and after the intermission several speeches were made in his honor while Toscanini stood aside on the stage. Before coming to the United States, the German-born-and-trained Schulz had been principal cello of the Berlin Philharmonic and the Leipzig Gewandhaus Orchestras and had played under Brahms, Liszt, Hans von Bülow, Nikisch, Weingartner, and Richard Strauss; in America he had worked with Mahler, Mengelberg, Furtwängler, and many others. But, he remarked—in responding to the speeches in his honor—Toscanini was "the master of them all." Toscanini, upon hearing this statement, "fled from the stage," the *Times* reported. "Mr. Schulz remarked that he knew the conductor did not like public praise, but he had to speak his mind." After all, he was retiring and couldn't be harmed by any of Toscanini's living colleagues, he said.

The previous evening, the Toscaninis had attended a postconcert dinner at the Upper East Side home of Malcolm Whitman, a textile manufacturer and amateur sportsman and poet, and his wife, Lucilla Mara De Vescovi Whitman, a onetime aspiring singer from Rome, who soon became one of the Toscanini family's best friends in New York and who later created a high-end line of men's neckties that she designed under the name of Countess Mara. Other guests at the dinner included the poet Lauro De Bosis, who would die two years later, before his thirtieth birthday, when the plane he was flying ran out of fuel over the Mediterranean after he had dropped anti-Fascist leaflets over Rome; and Margherita De Vecchi, an Italian merchant's San

Francisco–born daughter who began to act as a sort of amanuensis for the Toscaninis.*

On 5 April, the day after his final recording session, Toscanini was taken to see radio broadcasting equipment and sound amplification systems at the Roxy Theater, and the *Times* reported that he "showed a keen interest and understanding as the staff explained their permanent installations" for broadcasts such as his own Philharmonic transmissions. Interest, perhaps; understanding, unlikely: Toscanini was notoriously incapable of dealing with things mechanical or electrical. A few hours after the excursion to the Roxy, the maestro and his family boarded the *Paris* for their return trip to Europe.

A desire among American music lovers to find out more about the man who was playing so important a role in the country's musical life led to the publication of a biography of Toscanini, during his 1929 stay in the country. The author, Tobia Nicotra, wrote his book in Italian, but it was published only in an English translation.† It is superficial and full of errors and invented conversations. Nicotra's posthumous claim to fame, however, is as a forger of manuscripts, including a song by "Mozart," a poem by "Torquato Tasso," and letters purported to have been penned by Christopher Columbus, George Washington, Michelangelo, and many others. The forgeries were so brilliantly done, on blank pages that Nicotra had torn out of authentic old manuscripts, that experts at the Library of Congress and other major institutions were taken in, and, according to contemporary reports, with the money that he made from these fraudulent activities Nicotra was able to rent seven apartments in Milan for seven beautiful young mistresses. Walter Toscanini, who had become an authority on antiquarian manuscripts, began to suspect Nicotra after he had bought a "Mozart" manuscript from him; he had him investigated, and in 1934 Nicotra was arrested in Milan, tried, fined, and sentenced to two years in prison. But he was paroled

---

* De Vecchi, who spoke absolutely idiomatic Italian with a heavy American accent, was a leading member of the Italian Welfare League, which had been founded by Toscanini's friends Lionello and Carolyn Perera.

† Irma Brandeis, one of the book's two translators, later became the lover and muse of the Italian poet Eugenio Montale, who would win the Nobel Prize in Literature in 1975.

early: the Fascists needed him to forge their enemies' signatures on incriminating documents.

23.

NOT EVERYONE IN MILAN THOUGHT THAT TOSCANINI'S SCALA WAS operatic heaven. There were plenty of complaints, for instance, about the dearth of star singers. According to one observer, this was because many of La Scala's "old stand-bys [. . .] in their declining years" were engaged "on long-term contracts and held at the constant disposal of the management of this institution, which places more importance on well-routined, dependable and adaptable artists, willing to follow instructions absolutely, than on beauty and freshness of voice. It is well known that Toscanini is an enemy of the star system, or even of star artists who detract or distract from the conductor and his ensemble." Toscanini, however, did not object at all to "star artists," as is clear from his delight in the array of marvelous singers at his disposal during his Metropolitan years. La Scala simply could not offer top fees to the singers who were most in demand and who therefore preferred to spend their time working with the wealthy ensembles of North and South America.

Upon his return to Milan in the spring of 1929, Toscanini led dozens of rehearsals and fourteen performances of six operas in twenty-two days. He had chosen the German soprano Elisabeth Rethberg to sing the title role in an *Aida* revival, and before the first performance he asked her how she was feeling. "A bit nervous," she said. "*Cara mia*," he replied, "I am nervous before every performance—for the orchestra, for the chorus, and for myself."

A new production of *Don Giovanni*—an opera that Toscanini had conducted in only one previous version, in Buenos Aires in 1906—was on his spring schedule, but, to the dismay of everyone involved, he canceled the production after one of the final ensemble rehearsals. He was dissatisfied with the soprano who was to have sung the part of Donna Anna, and he was probably unhappy with himself as well. The production was salvaged the following season, but Toscanini did not conduct it.

Although no official statement had been published, most audience members knew that Toscanini's last performance of the season—*Aida*, on 14 May 1929—was likely to be his final appearance as La Scala's director. Labroca reported that after the second act, Toscanini, "despite the storm of applause and the shouts from the audience, did not appear for bows with the singers. This already appeared to be the first sign of his departure. Only at the beginning of the third act, when, upon his entry into the orchestra pit, the demonstration became even more enthusiastic and emotional, was he forced to turn around to greet the audience." But there was no time for valedictory celebrations. Not even twenty hours after the last notes of the last performance had faded away, Toscanini and the entire Scala ensemble converged at Milan's Stazione Centrale and boarded a special overnight train to Vienna.

A few months earlier, a vague proposal to take the company to Paris had been bandied about, but it had given way to a more concrete plan for the Milanese to participate in a spring music festival in Berlin. And no sooner did planning for the Berlin performances begin than the Viennese invited the Italians to stop first in the Austrian capital. Anita Colombo and a member of the stage crew were dispatched to the two cities to check whether La Scala's scenery would fit into the foreign opera houses; arrangements were duly made, repertoire selected, and the huge troupe departed, amid the cheers of a horde of well-wishers. Marquis Senator Giuseppe De Capitani d'Arzago, who had replaced Belloni as mayor of Milan, came along to represent his city and the theater over which he presided, and so did various Scala board members, as well as Carla, Walter, Wally, Wanda, Ida Polo, and a number of the Toscaninis' friends. The family's baggage must have been substantial: Arnaldo Fraccaroli, a reporter for the *Corriere della Sera*, noted that Carla had packed some sixty of her husband's starched shirts—one for each act of each opera, plus some extras.

The train had barely left Milan when Fraccaroli observed the normally abstemious Toscanini devouring noteworthy quantities of food; the journalist evidently teased the maestro on the subject, because Toscanini replied, in self-justification, "When I travel my appetite is always rather good." Planning sessions took place during the overnight trip, and upon arriving in Vienna the ensemble was greeted by Austrian government officials and by Italy's ambassador to Austria. Not later than nine thirty the following morning, Toscanini was at the ornate, sixty-year-old Staatsoper to oversee the stage installations and to test the acoustics with his orchestra and chorus; he seemed satisfied, Fraccaroli observed.

The Austrian Republic—the small, politically chaotic entity that had been carved out of the vast, defeated Austro-Hungarian Empire at the end of World War I—was a riven state in 1929, caught up in struggles between the right-wing Christian Social Party and the left-wing Social Democratic Party, with the extreme right-wing National Socialists (Nazis) gradually gaining in strength. In "Red Vienna," however, some of the prewar joie de vivre had resurfaced, and cultural life flourished. Fraccaroli noted that for the Scala ensemble, the Staatsoper was "sold out at prices that at first made the Viennese think there were typographical errors on the playbills," but by 2 A.M. on the night before the first performance groups of young people were camping out next to the theater, hoping to secure standing-room positions. Some of the young ticket seekers actually came to blows, and the police had to intervene.

One of the youngsters present at the opening performance—*Falstaff*, on 18 May, with Stabile in the title role and Mercedes Llopart as Alice—was the twenty-one-year-old Herbert von Karajan, who had managed to procure a seat in the fourth gallery. "From the first bar, it was as if I had been struck a blow," Karajan later recalled. "I was completely disconcerted by the perfection that had been achieved." He was impressed not only by the musical performance but by the unity of the entire production. "For the first time I grasped what 'direction' means," he said. "To be sure, Toscanini had employed a stage director, but basically, the essential concept came from him. The agreement between the music and the stage performance was something totally inconceivable for us: instead of people senselessly standing around, here everything had its place and its purpose. I do not believe at all that the Viennese understood then how great a service La Scala had performed in coming to Vienna and showing us young people, for once, what one can make of an interpretation if everything is in its right place."

Julius Korngold—the *Neue Freie Presse*'s critic, Mahler's old friend, and the father of the composer Erich Wolfgang Korngold—commented, "The fusion on stage is perfect, and the marvelous vivacity of *Falstaff* [. . .] has an incomparable and frankly stupefying interpreter in Maestro Toscanini." According to the *Neues Wiener Tagblatt*'s critic, "It is not easy to conquer the Viennese musical public, but the Italian artists succeeded; and when the Maestro attacked the first chord of *Falstaff*, no one could extract himself from the conquering force of his personality."

The following evening, the Scala ensemble presented *Lucia di Lammermoor*, with Toti Dal Monte, Pertile, and Franci. Karajan recalled that he, like many others, had been surprised to learn that Toscanini had chosen to bring this downtrodden old "stock opera" to Vienna; even after having played through the piano-vocal score, Karajan had wondered what it was all about. But he soon came to a different conclusion. "And it is astonishing that this music, which, in a normal 'repertoire performance' or, for instance, at the piano, sounds truly banal, was made to sound not at all banal," he said. "It was simply another type of music. [. . .] When one heard it under Toscanini, it had infinite significance." Korngold declared that this was the first time that *Lucia* had "appeared in all its beauty," and he used his review to castigate local conductors: "The appearance of someone like Toscanini is rare in the history of art; but the orchestra, soloists, and chorus of the Vienna Opera could well compete with those of La Scala if they were instructed and conducted according to the methods of the great Italian Maestro."

Paul Stefan, a former Schoenberg pupil and a well-known Austrian music historian, wrote, in *Die Stunde*, "Only an ensemble like that of La Scala and a conductor like Toscanini could reach absolute perfection in the *Falstaff* performance and also disinter *Lucia* from the musical cemetery and return her to us more flourishingly alive than before. Everyone in the theater had the sensation of being a witness to an unrepeatable artistic event."

Fraccaroli described "newspapers that dedicated whole pages to the event with words of stupefied admiration; [. . .] the President of the Republic and the Chancellor who came to the theater and then to a banquet in honor of Toscanini and the singers; groups of spectators who, after the opening with *Falstaff*, remained on the theater's steps in order to secure places for themselves at *Lucia* the following evening; and, in the auditorium at the end of each performance, the whole audience on its feet shouting and waving handkerchiefs."

Toscanini had initially refused to allow either performance to be broadcast on the radio, despite having allowed many of his New York concerts to be transmitted; he told the *Times* that "in America the quality of radio transmission is incomparably higher than in Europe" and that "radio can transmit only half of an opera performance, with nothing of the acting, stage setting and stage direction." But in the end he relented: an Austrian broadcasting company was allowed to transmit *Lucia*. So great was the power of opera in general and the Scala ensemble in particular that when the troupe prepared to depart the following morning, a huge crowd of radio listeners gathered at the station to applaud the performers, and as the train passed through the city, people stood on overpasses and at apartment windows to wave handkerchiefs.

As the troupe approached Berlin, on 21 May, "the bridges in the suburbs [. . .] were full of people awaiting our train's arrival," "La Toti" recalled. Over an eight-day period, the Scala-ites gave single performances of six operas—four of them at the Staatsoper Unter den Linden and two at the Städtische Oper in Charlottenburg. The complications were enormous, and Fraccaroli described the foyer of the Hotel Esplanade, where much of the ensemble was housed, as looking like "a branch office of the stage," with La Scala's personnel running here and there. The quietly efficient Scandiani had his hands more than full, and Anita Colombo, doing the work of ten people, according to the journalist, "must have slept fifteen hours in fifteen days." Fraccaroli also observed the foibles of star singers like Dal Monte, who ate all the time while claiming to be on a diet, and Pertile, who took long walks every day, whatever the weather, and whether or not he had to sing that evening. He also noted that the orchestra and chorus members were shocked by the high cost of living in Berlin but managed to make do with their allowances.

As in Vienna, so in Berlin: the opening work was *Falstaff*, but it was followed by *Rigoletto* and then by *Lucia*, *Il Trovatore*, *Manon Lescaut*, and *Aida*. No doubt impressed by the success of the *Lucia* broadcast from Vienna, Toscanini gave his permission for the *Aida* performance to be transmitted from Berlin. At La Scala, Pertile had sung in all of these operas except *Falstaff*, but since one tenor could not sing five operas in a single week, Toscanini had invited Beniamino Gigli—whose career he had helped to launch eleven years earlier and who was now one of the most popular singers in the world—to take the principal tenor roles in *Rigoletto* and *Trovatore*. Gigli, however, had asked for $2,000 per performance, far more than La Scala could afford, and Toscanini later recalled that he told the tenor's agent, "The theater in Berlin is already all sold out and they don't know yet which operas and which singers [there will be]. Why should [La Scala] spend $2,000 for Mr. Gigli? I'll do without him." Trantoul, too, asked for more money than the ensemble could pay him. Instead, Toscanini made his peace with Lauri-Volpi, seven years after their fight over *Rigoletto* at La Scala, and the tenor enjoyed considerable success in the German capital. "In 1922 Toscanini forbade me to sing the Masini cadenza* in 'La donna è mobile' because it wasn't written in the text, because it was ugly, vulgar, scandalous!" Lauri-Volpi commented a few years later. Now, however, Toscanini "advised me to include the 'ignoble' cadenza, and not only that, but also to crown the second-act duet in Rigoletto with the unwritten D-flat. So go figure." Perhaps Toscanini had more faith in the Milanese public than in foreign audiences to appreciate Verdi's operas without their "traditional" encrustations.

These were the twilight years of the Weimar Republic; Berlin was accustomed to welcoming and judging the greatest musical talents of the age, but the impression made by the Scala ensemble seemed to overshadow everyone and everything else. In Germany as in Austria, the responses to the Scala performances ranged from admiration to awe. Toti always remembered the "full, jam-packed Staatsoper" and the "enormous, moving success" of the operas. Among those who attended some or all of the performances were Artur Schnabel; Siegfried Wagner; the theater director Max Reinhardt; the musicologist Paul Bekker; and the conductors Bruno Walter (music director of the Städtische Oper), Leo Blech (Staatsoper), Wilhelm Furtwängler (Berlin Philharmonic), Fritz Busch (Dresden Staatsoper), Otto Klemperer (Kroll Oper), Erich Kleiber (also with the Berlin Staatsoper), Karl Elmendorff (Bayreuth Festival), Max von Schillings (former general director of the Berlin Staatsoper), and

---

* The reference is to a cadenza (ornamental passage) that had been interpolated by the tenor Angelo Masini (1844–1926).

George Szell (newly appointed music director of the German Opera and Philharmonic in Prague).

Berlin's fractious political newspapers were in agreement about the Italians' performances. *"Falstaff* surpassed all expectations and was a very great artistic event,"* declared the critic for the Social Democratic Party's *Vorwärts*. In the liberal *Vossische Zeitung*, the composer and critic Max Marschalk wrote, concerning the ensemble's discipline: "It is not true that this prevents the singers from bringing out their talents: on the contrary, Toscanini sets them on the best path and makes it possible for them to develop their true qualities individually." H. R. Gail, in the conservative *Bayerischer Courier*, reported that "all of Germany seemed like one single megaphone that echoed one single name: Toscanini. In Berlin, the excitement rose to such a fever pitch that it actually made us fear for German art, for the prestige of German musical culture. We ask ourselves whether a Blech, a Kleiber, or a Klemperer would have aroused similarly delirious enthusiasm in Italy, had he gone there at the head of the Berlin Opera. No! Because these three conductors put together do not make one Toscanini."

This was an unfair slur against Toscanini's colleagues, who must have been equally displeased by what the authoritative musicologist and critic Alfred Einstein wrote in the *Berliner Tagblatt*: "Let us hope that the German artists who attended this performance have learned something; in any case, the Italian opera company has given us a delightful but dangerous measuring stick for judging German art." Nevertheless, Heinz Tietjen, director of the Prussian State Theaters, told Fraccaroli that Toscanini had "elicited the most miraculous of all miracles, and precisely that of making all the [German] conductors agree in their enthusiasm for their Italian colleague." Blech concurred: "Such greatness makes an impression on me that is actually crushing," he said. Bruno Walter later recalled that Toscanini's "masterly performances conveyed to the German public a higher conception of the older Italian operas, [. . .] and the very highest conception of Italian operatic culture generally. [. . .] Every detail of the performances I witnessed spoke of the lifework and the imperative moral feeling of responsibility of an eminent musician. The perfection and stylistic sureness of his performances edified and refreshed me."

Even more indicative of this esteem was an article that Klemperer contributed to *Das Tagebuch*, a Berlin newspaper. "One says very little about Toscanini when one says that he can conduct everything by heart," Klemperer wrote. "It is more important to say that, in the truest sense, he knows how to conduct everything from the heart.* If we wish to distinguish between legitimate and illegitimate manifestations in art, Toscanini is legitimacy personified: he is the king of conductors. His performances are more than beautiful, they are right."

Klemperer went on to say that there was nothing eccentric about Toscanini's interpretations, nothing done for the sake of a startling effect:

> In 1923 at La Scala in Milan I heard a performance of *Die Meistersinger* under his direction, and I can only say that I have never heard so consummate a presentation of this work in any other theater in the world. In New York I heard Toscanini's concerts with the Philharmonic Orchestra, comprising the entire literature from Haydn to Stravinsky. [There was] always the same delightful impression of uncalculated rightness.
>
> Toscanini not only works with the orchestra to the last detail but also rehearses [. . .] the most subtle shades of expression, which, as he himself says, "can no longer be grasped through words." No one makes greater demands on the orchestra. Nevertheless, I never noticed in his rehearsals [. . .] any weariness or resistance in the orchestra. Any resentment would ricochet off his unassailable personality, for it stands above everything. Over and above the great musician there is a wholly integrated character, and to that we owe the rebuilding of La Scala, which, with exemplary musical performances, stands at the summit of opera companies.
>
> [. . .] We expect a great victory [of La Scala in Berlin]. No one can be happier about this victory than Toscanini's German colleagues, because we, too, who are living through opera crises, ought to learn from this victory how to be victorious.

---

* Klemperer used the words *auswendig*, "from memory," and *inwendig*, "internal, interior."

(above) *Tenor Aureliano Pertile in the title role in Boito's* Nerone *(world premiere).*

(right) *Soprano Rosa Raisa in the title role of* Turandot *(world premiere).*

La Scala's prima ballerina Cia Fornaroli, who married Walter Toscanini.

Carla, Arturo, and Wally Toscanini arriving in New York in January 1926 for the maestro's first appearances with the New York Philharmonic.

Accompanied by Maurice Van Praag, the Philharmonic's personnel manager, and Elsa Muschenheim, wife of the owner of the Hotel Astor, Toscanini avoids photographers in New York.

With fellow Philharmonic conductor Willem Mengelberg, Lake Maggiore, late 1920s.

With the Busseto Falstaff *cast and other participants,*
in front of Le Roncole, *the inn where Verdi was born,*
September 1926.

Caricature of Toscanini leading the Scala ensemble
to Vienna and Berlin, May 1929.

Left to right: Bruno Walter, Toscanini, Erich Kleiber, Otto Klemperer, and Wilhelm Furtwängler at a reception following one of Toscanini's Berlin concerts with the New York Philharmonic, May 1930.

St. MORITZ 20 Giugno 1930

446

Nel pomeriggio del 12 corrente è qui giunto il maestro Arturo Toscanini reduce dal giro d'Europa fatto con l'orchestra sinfonica americana.

Ha preso alloggio alla Villa "Chantarella" che dipende dall'Hotel Chantarella e dista da questo circa cento metri.

Conta di fermarsi un mese per riposare e per intraprendere poi un altro giro.

Sul conto del Toscanini vennero già segnalate in diverse riprese le dicerie che correvano sul suo conto, ora ne è una di carattere più grave che fa il giro di tutti i circoli e viene fortemente commentato negli ambienti antifascisti.

Durante la sua permanenza in Germania e precisamente a Berlino, essendo stato ripetutamente invitato a partecipare ad un ricevimento che si organizzava in suo onore nella sede di quel Fascio, il maestro rispose sempre che non poteva partecipare perchè stanco. Messo alle strette e richiestogli se autorizzava a spedire a suo nome un telegramma al Duce nel quale dichiarava che non aderiva alla manifestazione solamente perchè era stanco, rispondeva seccamente "che non interveniva perchè era antifascista, che detestava il Fascismo, che reputava Mussolini come un tiranno ed un'oppressore dell'Italia e che piuttosto che venir meno a queste sue convinzioni era pronto a non ritornare mai più in Italia."

Possiamo assicurare che fino ad oggi non ha avuto contatti con gente notoriamente antifascista e che vive ritiratissimo nella villa che ha preso in affitto.

Informant's report (20 June 1930) on Toscanini's anti-Fascist statements, with Mussolini's handwritten comment to contact Foreign Minister Dino Grandi.

With Siegfried Wagner, Bayreuth, June or July 1930.

With the cast of Tristan und Isolde, *Bayreuth, July 1930.*

Rehearsing the orchestra in the pit of the Bayreuth Festspielhaus.

Poster for the Martucci concert in Bologna (14 May 1931) that never took place.

Hitler's letter (3 April 1933) inviting Toscanini to return to Bayreuth that summer.

Ada Colleoni Mainardi.

Vladimir Horowitz and Wanda Toscanini at Milan's city hall on their wedding day, 21 December 1933.

On the Isolino, Lake Maggiore, mid-1930s.

Some of the five thousand people who lined up to try to buy the few standing-room tickets to Toscanini's final concert as music director of the New York Philharmonic, 29 April 1936.

Toscanini poses for a photographer at the train station in Vienna, mid-1930s.

Rehearsing the staging of Fidelio *with Erich Leinsdorf and Lotte Lehmann, Salzburg, mid-1930s.*

(top) *With Bruno Walter and Thomas Mann, Salzburg, mid-1930s.*

(middle) *With Stefan Zweig in Nice, January 1936.*

(left) *Toscanini between Luciana Frassati Gawronska and Eleonora von Mendelssohn, Kammer am Attersee, Austria, mid-1930s.*

Czech soprano Jarmila Novotná between Max Reinhardt and Toscanini.

With Adolf Busch and Rudolf Serkin at Neumarkt, near Salzburg, 1936.

*With Bronislaw Huberman and the Palestine Orchestra, Tel Aviv,
25 December 1936, at the end of the dress rehearsal for the new
orchestra's inaugural concert.*

At the Dead Sea,
January 1937.

Tourist in Egypt,
January 1937.

With David Sarnoff, chairman of the board of the
Radio Corporation of America, 1937.

THE NATIONAL BROADCASTING COMPANY

Presents

ARTURO TOSCANINI

Conducting

THE NBC SYMPHONY ORCHESTRA

CHRISTMAS NIGHT
Saturday, December 25, 1937
10:00 to 11:30 P.M., EST.
In NBC Studio 8-H—Radio City

Program

Concerto Grosso in D Minor, Opus 3, No. 11 . . . . Vivaldi
Symphony in G Minor . . . . Mozart
Symphony No. 1, in C Minor . . . . Brahms

These programs are broadcast over the
combined NBC Blue and Red Networks.

Since the modern microphone is extremely sensitive, your co-operation
in maintaining strict silence during the music is urgently requested.

PROGRAM FOR NEW YEAR'S NIGHT
JANUARY 1, 1938

Symphony in C Major . . . . Schubert
Two Movements from String Quartet in F Major, Opus 135 . . . . Beethoven
  (a) Lento Assai, Cantante e tranquillo
  (b) Vivace
"Death and Transfiguration" . . . . Richard Strauss

Toscanini's inaugural NBC
Symphony concert program
(25 December 1937),
printed on silk.

WESTERN UNION

R. B. WHITE
PRESIDENT

NEWCOMB CARLTON
CHAIRMAN OF THE BOARD

J. C. WILLEVER
FIRST VICE-PRESIDENT

Send the following message, subject to the terms on back hereof, which are hereby agreed to

To DUKTOR KERBER   19

Street and No. STAATSOPER   WIEN.

Place

GLI ODIERNI AVVENIMENTI

POLITICI IN AUSTRIA MI OBBLIGANO

RINUNZIARE MIA PARTECIPAZIONE

FESTIVALI SALZBURG. SALUTI.

TOSCANINI

Telegraph!
BIRTHDAY GREETINGS

WESTERN UNION
Birthday Telegrams

25¢   35¢
ANYWHERE
LOCALLY 20¢
Now its inexpensive to be smart

Sender's address for reference

THE QUICKEST, SUREST AND SAFEST WAY TO SEND MONEY IS BY TELEGRAPH OR CABLE

Sender's telephone number

*Toscanini's copy of his cablegram (16 February 1938) to Erwin Kerber,
head of the Vienna Staatsoper, saying that "the current political events
in Austria"—Chancellor Schuschnigg's first compromises with
Hitler—"oblige me to renounce my Salzburg Festival participation."*

*In Palestine, April 1938, with (from left) Bronislaw Huberman,
Chaim Weizmann, and NBC Vice-President John F. Royal.*

This was an astonishing testimonial from a German conductor who had worked under Mahler, and it expressed the general feeling among Klemperer's colleagues. The exception was Furtwängler, whose comments to Fraccaroli were only apparently positive. "The secret of the precision that Toscanini obtains with his ensemble [and] the mechanism that animates his work have not yet been discovered," he said. "We can all learn. Toscanini is an Italian who shows us not only his country's blue sky, but also his country's work." The words "precision," "mechanism," and "work" are the key to Furtwängler's real thoughts about Toscanini; a year later, he would set down those thoughts.

A sort of Toscanini mania swept over Berlin's music lovers. Everyone wanted his autograph, Fraccaroli reported, and people waited for hours in the hallway outside his hotel suite; "at night they waited for him in the lobby as he returned, and [they waited] at the theater's stage door all the time, and when he got into his car, and when he got out of it. The maestro adapted graciously to the situation, signing beyond all limits. But one day, terrified by the crowd in the corridor, he exclaimed, 'I'm going to have to put on a false beard, to save myself [and pass] unobserved.'" Some visitors, however, were welcome: an amateur, fifty-year-old violinist named Albert Einstein, for instance, was enthralled by the performances and wanted to meet Toscanini. The celebrated physicist, who had spent part of his youth in Milan and Pavia and still remembered some Italian, conversed with the maestro and gave an autographed photo to Wally (whom he found attractive), dedicating it to "the daughter of the beloved Maestro."

After performances, Toscanini often felt like staying up into the wee hours. Carla would tend to give up by three in the morning, but her husband, together with other stalwarts, would set out in cars, searching for an open Italian trattoria. "We finally found one near the Anhalt station," Fraccaroli reported; "it's run by a man from Piacenza who, when he recognized Toscanini, at first almost fell over from the shock, then tried to make us believe that he was from Parma," which is about forty miles from Piacenza. "But he was unmasked. 'Forgive me—I did it to feel closer to the maestro.'" While Toscanini was eating risotto, his daughter Wanda, now twenty-one, was visiting, and becoming fascinated by, Berlin's gay cabarets.

Toscanini managed to attend Erich Kleiber's dress rehearsal of *Don Pasquale* at Frederick the Great's little theater in Potsdam, and he was impressed with what he saw and heard. "At one point, before the third act began, Toscanini went toward the orchestra and publicly embraced Maestro Kleiber amid overwhelming applause," the *Giornale degli Artisti* reported. This was a rare sign of enthusiastic approval from Toscanini, and the Staatsoper's gifted thirty-nine-year-old co-conductor would soon be invited to become one of the New York Philharmonic's guest conductors. Kleiber and Toscanini remained on friendly terms to the end of their lives.

According to the various newspapers, La Scala's performances set box office records for Berlin. Most of the singers were deemed fine but unexceptional, and there were some negative remarks about the visual aspect of the productions, which reminded at least one reviewer of sets seen in Germany forty years earlier—although *Falstaff* and *Manon Lescaut* were generally exempted from these criticisms. Nevertheless, as Alfred Einstein declared at the end of the series, "For us it has been much more than an extraordinary operatic event. It has been an example; it has been the discovery of an infinitely simple secret: that the exceptional can be reached only by means of the absolute will of a man possessed by music, fanatically dedicated only to music and to nothing else, and that the basis for achieving the unusual consists in working, in serving the cause, and nothing else."

Karl Holl, the *Frankfurter Zeitung*'s critic, wrote a long, analytical piece about what he had heard. He pointed out, among much else, that for Toscanini virtuosity was only a means toward an end. "La Scala's performances moved and shook the public and sent it into ecstasy," he said. "Even granting that some part of the enthusiasm was owing to the attraction of the name and to the sensational effect of that which is foreign, it remains a success without precedent in the modern history of opera in Germany."

At the close of *Aida*, the final Berlin performance, "the audience members couldn't face leaving the theater and stayed on their feet shouting," Fraccaroli reported, "even after having made Toscanini and his colleagues appear innumerable times before the curtain, and even after the iron barrier had been lowered—a final sign that the curtain would not be opened again. But the acclamations were so insistent that Toscanini had to go down into the orchestra pit and present himself again on the podium amid a delirium of applause." In short, Fraccaroli said, "no one who didn't experience the atmosphere of those two weeks can have an exact idea of the intensity of the enthusiasm aroused by La Scala's performances in Vienna and Berlin."

Toscanini and the entire ensemble were welcomed joyously on their return journey to Italy on 30 May 1929. At every train stop from the border onward, civic officials, children carrying flowers, and people who had heard the *Lucia* broadcast from Vienna or *Aida* from Berlin greeted them and shouted their gratitude. As the train approached Milan, Toscanini walked through its corridors, stopping in every compartment to thank each of the singers, players, workers, and staff. The previous day, immediately after the company's final Berlin performance, he had made the official announcement that everyone had known was coming—he was retiring from regular opera conducting—and Fraccaroli described a great outpouring of mutual affection aboard the train. Toscanini's voice trembled with emotion as he embraced or shook hands with the members of his artistic army, and many of his collaborators wept openly. As the maestro made his way back toward his compartment, great shouts went up from everyone.

La Scala was now on its own.

24.

UPON THE ENSEMBLE'S RETURN HOME, TOSCANINI RECEIVED A telegram from Mussolini. "La Scala's performances made known not only the great historic virtues of an artistic organization, but also the new spirit of Contemporary Italy, which unites to its will to power the necessary harmonious discipline required in every field of human activity," the Duce proclaimed.

Toscanini understood the implications: by "harmonious discipline" Mussolini meant "dictatorship," and in contributing to La Scala's glory the maestro was also contributing, however involuntarily, to the glory of Mussolini's Italy. He did not want to reply, but the theater's administrators must have pointed out that they needed the government's economic assistance in the future—a future that would not have his name as its main box office attraction. Walter Toscanini, despite his own rabid antifascism, helped his father draft an answer (the original document is in Walter's hand), in which the maestro declared, "Today, as yesterday and as always, I am serving and shall serve my Art with humility but with intense love, certain that in so doing I am serving and honoring my Country."

He must have thought, when he agreed to send the message, that he performed such services wherever he was working, whether within Italy or beyond its borders. The fact that his reply made no reference to Mussolini's boastful statement did not pass unnoticed. "Since, in these times in which we're living, it is probable that few people grasped the noble feelings of *true* Italian-ness that inspired [your statement]," read one letter that he received shortly after his reply was published, "we wish to show you all our satisfaction, all our admiration, in noting that your gifts as a great Maestro are well matched with those of a great Italian." The letter was signed by "A group of admirers," because to give one's name in a declaration of this sort had become dangerous in Mussolini's Italy.

"La Scala weeps for Toscanini, her great conductor, who will lead her to victory no more," wrote a correspondent for the *Manchester Guardian*. But Toscanini's separation from La Scala caused him as much pain as it caused the ensemble. The preceding February, even before his resignation became official, he had told Maurice Van Praag that he was thinking of conducting "a few performances" at the theater the following December and January before returning to New York to complete the Philharmonic's forthcoming season. Four months later, Scandiani asked Lauri-Volpi to prepare the role of Arnoldo in Rossini's *William Tell*, because, he said, "After the triumphal outcome of the tour in Austria and Germany and after the demonstrations given [Toscanini] on our return home, I am hoping that he will withdraw his proposal and will again dedicate part of his activity to La Scala next season." In July, however, Scandiani informed Lauri-Volpi that "Maestro Toscanini has decided not to conduct at La Scala next

season because of the excessive work resulting from the preparations and conducting of his American concerts."

Toscanini eventually convinced himself that one of his reasons for
leaving La Scala had been the assumption of more and more performances each season by other conductors. "Then I feel I cannot take
responsibility for season, and I resign," he would tell B. H. Haggin in
1949. But he was the one who had made the decision to conduct fewer
performances and to spend part of each season in New York; the
theater's administration would happily have had him lead all the performances, had he so wished and had he been capable of such a feat.
The reasons for his departure lay elsewhere.

During a conversation with Raffaello De Rensis late in 1929,
Toscanini took pains to state that he had not left La Scala because of
any differences with the ensemble but because he was tired of devoting himself to the lyric theater in general. "It's conducting operas
that wears me out," he said, "and I must repeat that the only reason
for my departure from La Scala is the need for a less turbulent life. I
roamed the world's theaters for thirty-nine years, leaving fragments
of my existence everywhere, until I decided to leave the theater as
soon as I had brought Boito's *Nerone* to the stage. For me, that was a
debt of esteem and friendship."

Yet behind his decision there also lay grave political factors. The
Fascist Party was extending its reach into every sector of public life,
creating "corporations" that were loosely equivalent to labor unions
for workers and guilds for professional people, but with an extra
requirement that Toscanini found unacceptable: membership in the
National Fascist Party. For-profit and not-for-profit enterprises, too,
were grouped into categories and subjected to government control,
which, in this case, meant control by a single political party. Mussolini, having observed how well La Scala's *ente autonomo* system was
working, began to coerce all of Italy's major opera companies and
some of the minor ones to adopt similar organizational plans, and he
used the promise of government subsidies as a blandishment to
those who would have preferred independence. The irony of the
situation must have struck many observers: Caldara, Albertini, and
Toscanini, the inventors of the *ente autonomo* system, were now all
firmly in the ever-diminishing anti-Fascist camp, and all three had

been removed from or had quit their prominent positions in Italian public life.

Even a democratically elected Italian government, however, would have had to deal with the crisis caused by the decline of opera as a popular art form. The situation was attributable to many factors, especially the rapidly increasing enthusiasm for the cinema. As early as 1927, the mayor of Thiene, a town in the Veneto, had ordered local movie houses to remain closed on days when operas were being performed—a futile and short-lived measure for supporting opera. After 1930, the year in which Italy began to produce sound films, the crisis intensified. Major opera houses in big cities began to shorten their seasons, and in the provinces, where few forms of potentially enjoyable public entertainment other than opera had previously been available, companies found themselves struggling to survive. Even in small, isolated towns, people could now see and hear famous Italian actors and actresses in feature films; as a result, traditional summer opera seasons had to be canceled in fourteen towns in 1931 alone, and by 1936 Italians were spending over seventeen times as much money on movies as on opera performances. If opera, a significant element in Italian culture for three centuries, was to survive, the government would have to act, and the fact that all subsidies had to be approved by one sole party meant, once again, that survival depended on Mussolini.

Although Toscanini had managed to keep Mussolini out of La Scala after 1923, by 1929 the theater's board of directors was dominated by Fascists. The specific Fascists in question recognized Toscanini's importance to La Scala and behaved circumspectly toward him, but he knew that all of the house's orchestra and chorus members, stagehands, technicians, and other groups of employees were being herded—some willingly, others not—into Mussolini's corporations, and that these Fascist-dominated corporations would inevitably retain decision-making powers. Although he believed that all of the ensemble's employees ought to be well paid and should enjoy decent social benefits, he also believed that artistic decisions had to be made solely by himself and his coadministrators; he was convinced that if all the various corporations were to become involved in that process, chaos would ensue.

During the autumn of 1929, some Italian newspapers and journals expressed the wish that Toscanini would return to La Scala, but others began to denigrate him, in the hope of currying favor with the regime. The maestro had left La Scala, one of the latter publications declared, "to accede to more desirable and worthy economic recompense and to arrive very soon at his well-earned retirement." Then, on 13 November, during the first week of La Scala's season, word came from Rome that Mussolini's government had approved a substantial grant for La Scala: about 1.5 million lire per annum. Toscanini, who by then was well into his New York season, understood that the grant meant that "his" theater was now squarely under Fascist control.

Toscanini's career would last another quarter century, but he would never again conduct a complete opera in Italy. And the next time he would give a public performance with any Italian ensemble, Mussolini and his regime would be dead.

*Toscanini in the mid-1930s. This photo
was used on the cover of the program
of his final concert as principal
conductor of the Philharmonic-
Symphony Orchestra of New York,
29 April 1936.*

VIII.

———

THE NEW YORK
PHILHARMONIC
AND NEW HORIZONS

1.

———

TOSCANINI DID NOT LIKE THE NOISE OF MIDTOWN MANHATTAN— the ongoing sounds of construction, the honking of car horns, the screaming sirens—but he loved the energy that the ever-expanding city of New York exuded, and he felt free in the American metropolis in a way that was no longer possible in Milan or elsewhere in Italy. When he and Carla arrived in town on 23 September 1929, aboard the *Vulcania* out of Naples, the Wall Street stock market crash that would set off the worst economic depression in the nation's history lay barely five weeks in the future, but the United States in general and New York in particular still appeared to be in the midst of a boom that looked as if it would never end.

Throughout the 1920s, Toscanini had fulfilled his dreams for the lyric theater by creating an opera ensemble in his own image and bringing it to the highest level of achievement. Now, to realize his musical ideals as a symphonic conductor, he had at his disposal one of the world's great orchestras, honed to a peak of virtuosity and malleability by Mengelberg and himself. And now that he had liberated himself from the responsibility of running a major lyric theater, he would gradually begin to discover and respond to a desire to extend his activities to previously unexplored parts of the world. One remarkable period in his life had closed; another was opening.

When Toscanini walked onto the Carnegie Hall stage at the season's first concert, on 3 October, the audience gave him a standing ovation, and the entire program—Schumann's "Manfred" Overture, Strauss's *Don Quixote* (with the Philharmonic's new principal cellist, Alfred Wallenstein, as soloist), and Beethoven's Seventh Symphony—was greeted enthusiastically by the public and, the next day, by the press. The third of four performances of the program took place before a student audience, and the fourth, on a Sunday afternoon, was broadcast by WOR; similar patterns were followed through most of that season and on into the following ones.

During his initial eight-week stay in New York, Toscanini conducted twenty-nine concerts—eight different programs, with some overlap. They included several contemporary works, albeit conservative ones: Kodály's *Psalmus Hungaricus* (composed in 1923; US premiere), Ravel's *Boléro* (1928; US premiere), Adolf Busch's Variations on a Theme of Mozart (1928; US premiere), Vincenzo Tommasini's *Carnevale di Venezia* (1928; world premiere); and the German-born American Hermann Hans Wetzler's Symphonic Dance from *The Basque Venus* (1928; world premiere). Toscanini also presented, for the first time in America, his own arrangement of "Dawn" and "Siegfried's Rhine Journey" from *Götterdämmerung*—a version that bridged the two excerpts, and that many observers described as more effective than Engelbert Humperdinck's more familiar arrangement of the same pieces. Surprisingly new to Toscanini's repertoire were Brahms's Third Symphony and Double Concerto, the latter with the concertmaster, Scipione Guidi, and Wallenstein as soloists. Stravinsky's *Fireworks*, Berlioz's *Harold in Italy* (featuring the principal viola, René Pollain), Haydn's Symphony no. 88 in G Major (played, unusually for the time, with a reduced-size orchestra), Mozart's "Jupiter" Symphony, Strauss's *Ein Heldenleben*, and Beethoven's Eighth Symphony and *Coriolanus* Overture were new to his New York repertoire. The critics commented positively on the breadth of the offerings. And to complete the series of recordings begun the previous spring, on 21 November Toscanini and his musicians committed to disc the "Dance of the Blessed Spirits" from Gluck's *Orfeo ed Euridice* and a memorable version of the *Barber of Seville* Overture.

The great surprise of the season was the phenomenal success of Ravel's new work, at its premiere on 14 November. "TOSCANINI CAUSES FUROR WITH 'BOLERO,'" ran the headline in the next day's *Times*. The hypnotically sensuous piece, originally written as a short ballet for Ida Rubinstein, "brought shouts and cheers from the audience and delayed the performance by the prolonged applause." People stamped their feet, banged on their chairs, and all but tore the hall to pieces, and *Boléro* fever struck again during three subsequent performances.

Arturo and Carla sailed for Italy on 29 November aboard the Italian liner *Augustus* and arrived in Naples on 10 December. They visited Sorrento and stopped in Rome before returning to Milan for the holidays, after which they spent some time at a spa at St. Moritz, in the Swiss Engadine. By mid-February 1930, they were again on the high seas—this time aboard the *Paris* out of Le Havre, and with Wally and Wanda accompanying them—en route back to New York, where they disembarked on the nineteenth. The country's economic slide seemed, at the time, to have leveled off, and a small degree of optimism had returned, although in fact what would come to be known as the Great Depression had barely begun. Toscanini, in any case, focused on his work, as usual. Between 27 February and 20 April, he conducted the Philharmonic in thirty-three concerts that included new or recent pieces by Pizzetti (*Rondò Veneziano*; 1930, world premiere, in the presence of the composer),* Eugene Goossens (Sinfonietta; 1922, New York premiere), Kodály (*Summer Evening*, written in 1929–30 at Toscanini's request; world premiere); Mario Castelnuovo-Tedesco (Symphonic Variations for violin and orchestra, with Guidi as soloist; 1928, US premiere); and Arthur Honegger (*Pastorale d'Eté* and *Pacific 231*; 1920 and 1923, respectively), in addition to Toscanini's first performances of Ravel's orchestration of Mussorgsky's *Pictures at an Exhibition* and Respighi's orchestration of Bach's Passacaglia and Fugue in C minor. The rest of his repertoire ranged from Haydn through Debussy. On 7 March, he led a benefit concert that raised $8,000 for the orchestra's pension fund, and during the

---

* Toscanini attended other initiatives connected with Pizzetti's American visit: a concert and reception at Columbia University's Casa Italiana; a lecture-concert by the composer at the home of Anna de Koven, widow of the composer Reginald de Koven; and a concert of Pizzetti's chamber music at the home of Lionello and Carolyn Perera.

concerts of 3 and 4 April he conducted the Funeral Music from *Göt-terdämmerung* in memory of Cosima Wagner, who had died on the first day of the month, at the age of ninety-two.

In the course of the 1929–30 Philharmonic season, Toscanini featured Wallenstein, his new, thirty-one-year-old principal cello, as soloist not only in the two works mentioned above but also in Boccherini's Cello Concerto in C Major. He admired Wallenstein's playing and musicianship and encouraged his ambition to become a conductor. He also looked favorably upon the conducting aspirations of Léon Barzin, a young Belgian-born violist in the Philharmonic; thanks to the maestro's recommendation, Barzin became conductor of the National Orchestral Association, a New York–based training orchestra, through which he would influence generations of young American musicians.

As usual, the orchestra gave a number of guest performances in other East Coast cities. One of Toscanini's Washington concerts was attended by Lou Hoover, wife of President Herbert Hoover, whose laissez-faire economics were plunging the country ever deeper into depression, and by the writer Paul Claudel, who was also France's ambassador to the United States. The Italian ambassador, Giacomo De Martino, gave a reception for the Toscaninis: the maestro was not yet in official disgrace at home, and the embassy had orders from Mussolini to encourage all manifestations of Italian excellence.

The Philharmonic's series of children's concerts, conducted by Schelling, stirred Toscanini's enthusiasm, and toward the end of the last one of the season, on 22 March, he came on stage to distribute ribbons and medals to the forty youngsters who had shown the most interest in music. To the surprise of everyone who knew him, Carla included, he made a brief, sentimental speech—in English!—in which he thanked Schelling for giving him the opportunity to hand out the prizes, and then said, "I love and always have loved children. [. . .] In the heart of children there is always some music to be called out by a touch of sympathy and love. Therefore I have accepted today this very sweet task." Schelling pinned a red prize ribbon on Toscanini's lapel, and the *Times* reported that "of the many decorations he has received, it is the only one, according to friends, which he ever wore in public." He concluded the event by conducting the orchestra in the *Meistersinger* Prelude.

He was in an unusually easygoing mood. On his sixty-third birthday, three days after his oratorical debut at the children's concert, he went to Washington, accompanied by Clarence Mackay in the Philharmonic board chairman's car, to be honored, together with Paul Claudel, at Georgetown University, a Jesuit institution. The ambassadors of more than forty countries and dozens of other diplomats were present at the event, during which Toscanini was ridiculously and hyperbolically described as "the greatest master of music of modern times." He had been begged to accept these honors as a favor to Mackay, a devout Catholic.

Ridiculous hyperbole about Toscanini was getting out of hand. A few days after the Washington ceremony, the *Times* reported that the Reverend Harry Emerson Fosdick, an influential Protestant pastor, had mentioned the maestro in a sermon delivered at the impressive new, neo-Gothic, interdenominational Riverside Church, which was supported by John D. Rockefeller Jr. In comparing the religious life to music rather than science, Fosdick said, "You can abstract Copernicus's ideas from Copernicus, but you cannot abstract Toscanini's art from Toscanini. Toscanini's art is Toscanini. So you cannot abstract Jesus' truth from Jesus. Jesus' truth is His light [*sic*; presumably for "life"]." Toscanini considered his art to be purely interpretive, not creative, and not of lasting significance. To hear himself compared to Jesus Christ would have made him cringe or laugh, or both.* Perhaps as an antidote to Fosdick's comment and certainly as a reaction to the mindless Toscanini-can-do-no-wrong attitude then widespread, the American composer Deems Taylor is said to have commented, "I'm willing to admit that Toscanini was present at the Last Supper, but not that he was sitting at the head of the table."

Toscanini clashed with the audience at the Philharmonic's penultimate concert of the season, on 19 April 1930: some of the people in attendance wouldn't stop applauding after a seriously flawed performance of the "Forest Murmurs" from *Siegfried*, and when silence was finally established and Toscanini raised his baton to begin the following piece, some troublemakers applauded again. He left the

---

* A few years later, Fosdick compared Toscanini to Saint Paul, several notches down from Jesus himself. In a number of the conversation tapes recorded in Toscanini's last years, he mentioned Saint Francis of Assisi admiringly but never referred to Jesus, and he always spoke disdainfully of the pope and the Roman Catholic Church hierarchy.

stage, returned after a few minutes, conducted the final piece—
Elgar's "Enigma" Variations—and departed without acknowledging
the applause or returning to take a bow. He was visibly nervous at
the start of the final concert, on the twentieth, but the performance
went well, and afterward he attended a reception for the orchestra at
the home of Helen Huntington Astor, the wife of the philanthropist
Vincent Astor.* Three days later, the Toscaninis and the orchestra's
musicians departed for the Philharmonic's first European tour.

2.

THE AGE OF JET AIRPLANE TRAVEL BEGAN JUST AFTER TOSCANINI'S
career ended, and within a few years successful conductors were
able to make guest appearances all over the world—one week in one
country, the next week in another. Until Toscanini was well past his
sixtieth birthday, he had worked for substantial periods in only three
countries—Italy, the United States, and Argentina—and had
appeared briefly in only six others: Brazil and Spain at the outset of
his career, Uruguay in his thirties, France and Canada in his forties,
and Switzerland in his fifties. The 1929 Scala tour added Austria and
Germany to the latter list; the 1930 New York Philharmonic tour
would bring him before audiences in four more countries and in six
more major cities.

The prospect of demonstrating the New York orchestra's prowess
to audiences in fifteen major European cities stimulated Toscanini's
energies. It also stimulated the Philharmonic's board of directors to
underwrite the tour at a cost of $200,000, the economic crisis not-
withstanding. Had the tour been planned for 1931 instead of 1930, it
would likely have been canceled.

Toscanini insisted that the ensemble travel aboard the French
liner *De Grasse*—although it was not one of the newer or faster ves-
sels available—because it did not have class divisions: all passengers
could mix freely on all decks, and Toscanini could spend time with

---

* Toscanini did not generally enjoy receptions of this sort, but he understood the
importance of donors in American musical life and usually put in an appearance when
requested to do so.

the 114 members of the orchestra and its staff, many of whom had brought their wives and children along. "At sea, the orchestra musicians got to know a new Toscanini: no longer the nobly severe conductor, but an affable, smiling, even joking traveling companion," the *Corriere della Sera* reported shortly after the ship docked at Le Havre. Toscanini claimed to have done "nothing" during the crossing, and his musicians confirmed that he had sunned himself and taken many walks on the deck, watched his fellow passengers playing games and exercising, and stayed up till all hours observing them dancing to the music of the on-board jazz band—to which many of his musicians had contributed their services. As Prohibition was still law in the United States, many of the travelers had been delighted to partake legally of alcoholic beverages as soon as the ship had left the country's territorial waters. Arthur Judson claimed that the musicians had drunk the ship dry after two days at sea, but evidently some reserves remained: on the final evening of the voyage Toscanini offered champagne to everyone. The Russian members of the ensemble even sang toasts to Picciù, the Toscaninis' dog, who, however, "began to bark and energetically refused to initiate the whistle-wetting," the *Corriere* reported.

Upon disembarking at Le Havre, on 2 May, the maestro looked ruddy-cheeked and smiling, and he had even gained a little weight. "It's the sea air that always does me a lot of good," he told the *Corriere*. The Toscaninis were met at the pier by their son/brother Walter as well as by the wife of Carlo Clausetti of the Ricordi company and by Anita Colombo, to whom Judson had entrusted the coordination of the tour. The entire ensemble immediately boarded a train to Paris's Gare St.-Lazare.

A program of German classics opened the tour at the Opéra the following evening. "For the first time in history a complete American orchestra has been heard in Paris," the musicologist and critic Henry Prunières reported. "And let it be said at the outset that it was a signal musical victory. Never within my memory has such a perfect orchestra been heard in Paris or even in Europe. All critics and musicians of the capital who thronged to this concert are unanimous on this point." Prunières described Toscanini, who had not conducted in France in twenty years, as "the greatest leader in the world today," who "combines most extraordinary technique with the finest qualities of emotion, intelligence and sensitiveness. [. . .] The ovations were prolonged after each selection and I cannot remember ever witnessing such a triumph for a symphony orchestra."

In a subsequent article, Prunières quoted several French conductors, who concurred that they had never before really "heard" *La Mer*—the main piece on the second concert—and he mentioned that Debussy's widow had told Toscanini the same thing. Prunières recalled wonderful performances of varied repertoire that he had heard with the greatest European orchestras under Nikisch, Mahler, Mengelberg, Furtwängler, and others, but none of them could be compared to what he had experienced with the New York Philharmonic under Toscanini, he said. He added, "Never have I seen the Parisian public so intoxicated with joy."

Emile Vuillermoz, another authoritative French critic, reported that Toscanini had "crossed Paris like a meteor, like a shooting star, like a magical comet. Here, truly, is the master, not only of the orchestra, but of all conductors."

The Paris concerts were attended by a remarkable array of musicians: among others, the composers Rachmaninoff, Ravel, Gustave Charpentier, Alexander Glazunov, Alexandre Tansman, and Gabriel Pierné; the conductors Monteux, Ansermet, Désiré-Emile Inghelbrecht, Philippe Gaubert, Rhené-Baton, and Hans Kindler; the pianists José Iturbi and Alfred Cortot; the violinist Joseph Szigeti; the retired soprano Nellie Melba; the former French prime minister Paul Painlevé; and the writer Paul Morand. After the performance of *La Mer*, at the second Paris concert, Ravel, who was sitting with his friend Eva Gauthier, told her, "You know, even though it is not Debussy's best work, it is the one that opened the way to all of us, and that work needs all the interpretation that Toscanini can give it. But my 'Bolero' must not be interpreted." Then, amid the deafening applause for *Boléro*, the small (five-foot-three), dapper Ravel "bowed gracefully but refused to stand, and waved his hand at Maestro Toscanini as a gesture of recognition," the New York Times's correspondent noted. Afterward, however, the composer complained to Toscanini about the tempo. "People were upset that I had the audacity to tell the great virtuoso that it was twice too fast," he wrote the next day to a friend, "[. . .] but he is a marvelous virtuoso, all the same—as marvelous as his orchestra." And to another friend: "If I was seen at the Opéra it was only because I knew that Toscanini was taking a ridiculous tempo in the *Boléro* and I wanted to tell him so, which upset everyone, starting with the great virtuoso."

The incident had a strange sequel four months later, when Ravel wrote disingenuously to Toscanini:

> My dear friend, I have recently learned that there was a Toscanini-Ravel "affair." You yourself are undoubtedly unaware of it, although I have been assured that the newspapers have spoken of it: it seems that I refused to stand during the applause at the Opéra in order to punish you for not having taken the correct tempo in the *Boléro.*
>
> I have always felt that if the composer does not take part in a performance of his work, he must not receive the ovations, which must thus be directed only at the performer or the work, or both. Unfortunately, I was badly—or too well—placed to have my abstention pass unnoticed. Therefore, in order that my attitude not be misunderstood, I tried, in turning toward you, to applaud and thank you. But—wouldn't you know it—maliciousness lends itself to "sensational" news better than does the truth [. . .].

The composer had written this unsolicited letter because he wanted Toscanini to conduct the first performance of his recently completed Concerto for Piano (left hand) and Orchestra, commissioned by the pianist Paul Wittgenstein, whose right arm had been amputated during the First World War. Ten days after having sent off his first letter to Toscanini, Ravel wrote to him again: "This is only to tell you that I would very much wish to have the world premiere of the Concerto that I have written for Wittgenstein given by you and the admirable orchestra that you have shaped. And I am sure that Wittgenstein will not feel differently." So far as is known, Toscanini did not reply to Ravel's letters. He never conducted the concerto, but he continued to perform other pieces by the composer.

Ravel's reservations notwithstanding, the Philharmonic and Toscanini elicited paeans of praise everywhere. Works by nine living composers and fifteen others were performed as the musicians made their way across much of Western and Central Europe. During some of the long, overnight train rides between cities, Carla Toscanini went from compartment to compartment, making sure that the musicians were as comfortable as possible. Judson noted that the maestro himself never got to bed before five in the morning, whether aboard the train or in hotels, and that he seemed "the youngest man in the orchestra."

At the Tonhalle in pretty but normally businesslike Zurich—the first stop after Paris—"serious-looking men began to stand up and cheer" following *Pictures at an Exhibition*; "an almost unanimous 'Oh!' swelled up from the audience at the end of the gossamer Scherzo from *A Midsummer Night's Dream*"; and the members of the public "remained standing for twenty minutes after the concert, applauding, cheering joyfully, gratefully, and forcing Toscanini to call the orchestra members to their feet." In Milan, at La Scala, the maestro was greeted as a returning hero, and his orchestra was hailed as a marvel. Before the first of two concerts, the members of La Scala's orchestra gave a reception for Toscanini and their colleagues from New York in the theater's upstairs foyer, and many well-known musicians attended a postconcert reception.

In Turin, now the center of Italy's burgeoning automobile industry, the Teatro Regio had been sold out long in advance, fifty extra seats were squeezed into its galleries, and early in the afternoon of the concert day long lines of people hoping to acquire standing-room posts were bivouacked outside on the grass. When Toscanini finally appeared on the stage that evening, there was "an interminable ovation," *La Stampa* reported. But an untoward incident occurred: the presence of Crown Prince Umberto and his recently wedded consort, the music-loving Princess Marie José of Belgium, meant that the Royal March had to be performed, and, by law, the Royal March had to be followed by "Giovinezza," the Fascist Party's anthem. Toscanini, despite his antimonarchic beliefs, had always gamely conducted the Royal March when a member of the reigning family was present, but as he refused to conduct "Giovinezza" he made it clear that he would conduct neither piece.

How was the impasse resolved? Winthrop Sargeant—later a music critic for the *New Yorker* but at that time a last-stand player in the Philharmonic's second violin section—recalled that while the orchestra "waited on the stage, formal and stiff in evening dress, a ragged-looking local brass band, dressed in what looked like street cleaners' uniforms, filed out furtively in front of the footlights and gave both the Italian anthem [*sic*] and Mussolini's *Giovinezza* performances that sounded almost homicidal. During the whole proceeding Toscanini, with a perfectly straight face, stood with folded arms before the orchestra. When the anthems were over and the scared-looking band had filed out again, the concert began." The muzzled Italian newspapers did not report the incident, but they did mention that at the end of the concert the audience applauded and cheered for half an hour and that Umberto and Marie José went backstage to thank Toscanini and some of the orchestra's principal players.

Queen Elena herself wished to attend one of the Philharmonic's Rome performances, and when she learned that Toscanini would not conduct "Giovinezza," she "excused the orchestra from playing the Royal March upon her arrival," as an informer's report in the Fascist police files indicates. (Elena, much more popular than her husband, King Victor Emanuel III, never publicly expressed her political opinions.) Mussolini did not even attempt to attend, and no anthems were performed. After the first concert at the Augusteo, the US ambassador, John W. Garrett, and his wife gave a reception at the seventeenth-century Palazzo Rospigliosi, and the following afternoon they were cohosts, with Prince Boncompagni Ludovisi, the governor of Rome, of a reception at the Capitol. Nearly all of Rome's music critics declared that they had never heard anything even remotely comparable to this ensemble's playing; the only significant dissenting voice was that of Bruno Barilli, a composer and conductor manqué whose musical talents Toscanini had failed to recognize, and who expressed the opinion that Toscanini was unmusical and that his success was a result of the public's snobbery. Barilli's comments appeared in *Il Tevere*, an extreme right-wing (even by Mussolini's standards) and overtly anti-Semitic newspaper; at that time over one-third of the Philharmonic's personnel was Jewish.

The enthusiastic audience at Florence's Politeama included the anti-Fascist jurist Piero Calamandrei as well as a leading Fascist exponent, Roberto Farinacci, who would become one of Toscanini's most vociferous antagonists. The music critics who attended the Philharmonic's concert at Munich's Tonhalle agreed that the orchestra outranked all the major European ensembles. In Vienna, where Austrian and foreign political leaders joined royalty from Romania and Greece in applauding Toscanini and his players at the Staatsoper, several critics expressed the opinion that their own Philharmonic produced a warmer sound than their American colleagues could evoke but that "neither Vienna nor the rest of the Old World could better this orchestra." The Wiener Philharmoniker's members gave a reception for their New York counterparts in the great hall of the Stadtpark.

Admiral Miklós Horthy, the controversial regent of Hungary, and his prime minister, István Bethlen, attended the New Yorkers' Budapest performance at the Városi Színház (Municipal Theater), as did Kodály, in whose honor the ensemble played his *Summer Evening*.* After the concert, Toscanini and some friends sat in a café until three in the morning, listening to a group of gypsies perform their traditional music. In Prague, during a brief rehearsal in the 7,000-seat, underground Lucerna Hall, the maestro expressed worry over the acoustics, but when the hall was full the sound was excellent. The audience that evening included the Czech president, Tomáš Masaryk, and foreign minister, Edvard Beneš.

Bruno Walter was among the thousands who created a storm of applause in Leipzig, where the Philharmonic presented works by native son Wagner and former local resident Mendelssohn, among others; Toscanini later told Walter that the classic atmosphere of the historic Gewandhaus concert hall had made a strong impression on him, and many orchestra musicians described the Leipzig performance as the finest of the tour. After the following night's concert at the Dresden Staatsoper, Fritz Busch, that ensemble's chief conductor, threw a beer party for Toscanini and the whole Philharmonic.

When Toscanini presented works by the great German masters at Berlin's famed Philharmonie, the audiences—which included the Nobel Prize–winning playwright and novelist Gerhart Hauptmann, diplomats from all over the world, and the entire Prussian cabinet— "stood for more than thirty minutes cheering and applauding before

---

* Toscanini's service to Hungarian music, however limited it was in reality, earned him an honorary professorship in the Hungarian Academy of Music, at the instigation of the celebrated violinist Jenö Hubay.

they would leave the theatre," reported Leopold Stokowski, the Philadelphia Orchestra's conductor. A year earlier, all of the major conductors present in Berlin had turned out to pay tribute to Toscanini and his Scala ensemble; this year they paid homage to Toscanini and his New York Philharmonic. A photograph, taken after one of the concerts, shows the maestro with four of his colleagues: Kleiber, Walter, Klemperer, and Furtwängler. Sixteen years later, Walter wrote, in referring to those concerts, that a "splendid performance of Debussy's *La Mer* still sounds in my ear."

Even Richard Strauss, who evidently attended at least one of the Philharmonic's tour performances, later singled out Toscanini's Beethoven interpretations as "a praiseworthy exception" to those of most other conductors, who "impose personal conceptions on their performances before—as Bülow put it—they are able to read the score properly." He did, however, find Toscanini "somewhat rigid where the 'romantic' side of interpretation is concerned." Strauss's statement about imposing personal conceptions on Beethoven may have been intended, in part, as a dig at Furtwängler, the Berlin Philharmonic's conductor, with whom the composer had an uneasy relationship. Certainly Strauss's own interpretations of the classical Germanic repertoire that have been preserved in recordings are conceptually closer to Toscanini's than to Furtwängler's, although—unlike either Toscanini's or Furtwängler's—they often seem perfunctory.

Furtwängler himself, far from demonstrating the admiration that Strauss and other German conductors were exhibiting toward Toscanini, was dismayed by the maestro's success. In one of his notebooks, he wrote a disparaging essay about Toscanini, attributing to him barely any authentic musical talent and implying that all of the German musicians and critics who had been stimulated by and praiseful of the Philharmonic's performances had been fooled by the Italian conductor's strong personality and by the virtuosic playing that he obtained from his orchestra. Toscanini's interpretations of works by Haydn, Debussy, Mendelssohn, and Beethoven differed radically from Furtwängler's; thus, Furtwängler believed, they were fundamentally wrong.

The undercurrent that flows throughout the essay is Furtwängler's sense of alarm and revulsion at the positive reception that

Toscanini's performances had received in Germany and Austria—
Furtwängler's territory. He even attempted to attribute Toscanini's
success to the fact that the maestro was a foreigner, which endeared
him to the left-wing press, but not a Jew, which made him acceptable
to right-wing commentators as well. These observations say far
more about Furtwängler's feelings of insecurity and envy than about
any aspect of Toscanini's work, and, as the British critic Peter Hey-
worth remarked, they reveal Furtwängler's "alarming inability to
comprehend any culture other than his own."

IN ADDITION TO RECEPTIONS HOSTED IN BERLIN by the American and
Italian ambassadors, Toscanini was invited to a reception in his
honor at the local headquarters of the Italian Fascist Party's representatives. At first, according to an anonymous informant's report,
"the maestro kept replying that he could not participate because he
was tired. When pressed, and when asked whether he would autho-
rize the sending of a telegram in his name to the Duce, in which he
would state that he did not agree to the function only *because he was
tired, he replied sharply that he was not attending because he was an anti-
Fascist, because he held Mussolini to be a tyrant and oppressor of Italy, and
that rather than break with these convictions he was prepared never to return
again to Italy.*"

The Italian political police forwarded this typewritten statement
to Mussolini, who underlined the words reproduced above in italics
and forwarded the document to Foreign Minister Dino Grandi. The
report is one of the earliest significant documents in what would
grow into an enormous police file on Toscanini. The maestro had
become someone to be watched, but for another year he would
remain unaware of the latent danger.

THE FAMED BELGIAN VIOLINIST Eugène Ysaÿe could not be present
at the Philharmonic's performance at Brussels' Palais des Arts—he
was suffering from acute diabetes and had had his left foot amputated—so Toscanini accompanied Belgium's elegant, music-loving
Queen Elisabeth to visit Ysaÿe at his home. (Ysaÿe died the following
year.) The queen, together with King Albert, did attend the concert,

as did the US ambassador, Hugh Gibson. The event was yet another triumph for Toscanini and his musicians, but it was only a prelude to what awaited them two nights later, at their first London concert.

For a quarter century, various British musical organizations had tried unsuccessfully to secure Toscanini's services for London, but, fearing the slap-dash rehearsal methods for which the city's orchestras were infamous, he had always refused. (The English composer Ralph Vaughan Williams is said to have described his fellow citizens' approach to music making with the motto "Anything that's worth doing is worth doing badly.") Now Toscanini's long-delayed debut would at last take place—but with an imported ensemble. Lionel Powell, the London impresario who put up the guarantees for the Philharmonic's visit, had insisted that the New Yorkers give four concerts rather than the two that Judson and Colombo had originally proposed: two performances at the cavernous Royal Albert Hall, with its 7,000 seats, would automatically provide sufficient ticket sales to protect Powell against possible losses, and the other pair, at the acoustically excellent, 2,500-seat Queen's Hall, would allow the orchestra to be heard to better advantage.

Powell, along with numerous friends and fans of Toscanini and his musicians, greeted the Philharmonic's train when it pulled into Victoria Station on 31 May, and on the afternoon of the following day—a Sunday—the orchestra and its conductor made their joint British debut at the Albert Hall, playing a mixed program: Rossini, Brahms, Wagner, and Beethoven. When Toscanini appeared on the stage, he "received an ovation the like of which is usually reserved for popular heroes," reported Robin H. Legge, the *Daily Telegraph*'s longtime critic. "Again and again the great man bowed to the storm of applause," and when King George V and Queen Mary, followed by various other aristocrats, entered, the maestro conducted "God Save the King" and "The Star-Spangled Banner." The *Manchester Guardian* noted that the queen "frequently put up her opera glasses to watch the movements of the great conductor," as did Sir Henry Wood, the conductor who had created London's famous Promenade concerts (the Proms). Charles G. Dawes, a former US vice-president, now ambassador to Great Britain, was sitting in the box next to that of the monarchs.

A former music critic named George Bernard Shaw attended the first concert, wrapped in his raincoat, and "beamed with happiness after the Brahms [Second] symphony," according to one reporter. The nearly seventy-four-year-old writer commented afterward that he had heard "'a good concert,'" and at a postconcert reception Shaw regaled Toscanini and some of his musicians with the story of how he had come to like Wagner's music. He had originally hated it, after having heard one piece "'badly played by a brass band,'" he said, but one day someone had given him a copy of the piano score of *Lohengrin*. "'I sat at a piano, played the first two bars, and immediately realized that Wagner was a great man.'" This corresponded to the young Toscanini's first recognition of Wagner's genius, in the same *Lohengrin* Prelude. Shaw then explained that to most English listeners, the theme of the Wedding March from *Lohengrin* sounded like an incorrect version of a popular ballad, and he sang the theme both ways. "Toscanini raised his eyebrows in a supreme effort to remain serious," the correspondent reported, "but finally joined the laughter and nodded approvingly. 'Che tipo,' he said in Shaw's direction, meaning, 'Some character, that.'" As Shaw was leaving the reception, a journalist asked him how he liked Toscanini. His reply was typical of a lifelong freelance writer: "'An article by me on Toscanini would be worth £5,000.'"

Legge and London's other main critics—W. J. Turner in the *New Statesman*, H. C. Colles in the *Times* of London and in reports to the *New York Times*, Francis Toye in the *London Morning Post*, Eric Blom in the *Guardian*, and Ernest Newman in the *Sunday Times*—were as stunned by and enthusiastic over the Philharmonic's concerts as their counterparts on the Continent had been. Newman, a respected musicologist as well as Britain's most authoritative music critic, wrote, "That this has been the greatest week that the present generation of English music lovers can remember will be disputed by no one who heard the four concerts [. . .]. Those who expected to see and hear the usual star conductor must have been slightly astonished at first. There is nothing whatever of the prima donna about him. [. . .] The great thing about him is the perfect *musicality* of his mind; he never does anything that outrages our sense of music as an art devoted to the creation of beauty. [. . .] It would be difficult to find a conductor of the same strong personality who plays fewer tricks with a score."

Newman and several other local critics found parts of Toscanini's interpretation of Elgar's "Enigma" Variations insufficiently "English," and some of them had harsh words for Respighi's orchestration of Bach's Passacaglia and Fugue in C minor; otherwise, however, the reactions of London musicians, critics, and audiences alike were virtually a chorus of hosannas.

Sir Thomas Beecham, though no fan of Toscanini's then or later, nevertheless came backstage to congratulate the maestro after the first concert, and the goateed, fifty-one-year-old conductor-impresario told various orchestra members that "they had now surpassed the Boston and Philadelphia orchestras and were the best in the world." Serge Koussevitzky, the Boston Symphony's conductor, was also present in London at the time and described Toscanini as "formidable, formidable! He is a wonder." The most telling compliment, however, came from Sir George Henschel, a Polish-Jewish-German-English baritone-pianist-conductor who had been a close friend of Brahms's, had observed every major conductor from Wagner, Bülow, and Richter onward, and had been the Boston Symphony's first conductor. "Dear Maestro," he wrote to Toscanini following the Philharmonic's third concert, "May the old conductor of the Boston Symphony Orchestra be permitted to express to you his profound admiration? Never in my life (and I am past eighty) have I heard such marvellous orchestral playing as yours last night. It was simply perfect, and in spirit I grasp your hand and thank you for the supreme pleasure you have given me." Toscanini was so moved by this message that he sent Henschel a friendly reply and a signed photograph, and Henschel wrote back to thank Toscanini again.

Toscanini wrote out a little speech in English to give to the orchestra at a reception thrown by Mackay at the Carlton Hotel after the final concert, but five minutes before he was to deliver it he became nervous and asked Van Praag to read it for him. "The thought that this evening we will give the last concert of a successful tour and that tomorrow we will have to separate after seven weeks spent in affectionate, familylike cordiality moves me profoundly," the maestro said. He referred to the tour as "a magnificent artistic statement" and expressed his "great joy [. . .] in becoming more aware every day of the enthusiasm and the faith that you've brought to making every concert turn out better than the previous one, and you have never given the slightest sign of tiredness! You have really been marvelous, and I thank you and tell you that today not only am I proud of you but I love you as faithful friends." He was also overheard telling friends that the Philharmonic was "the most intelligent orchestra" in his experience, and that he was especially happy that there had been no personal conflicts among the players during the tiring trek across Europe.

The next day, while the orchestra members began the long voyage back to New York, their maestro flew from London to Paris and then took the overnight Orient Express to Milan. But the euphoria of the tour quickly passed. Toscanini began to suffer from insomnia, and he soon fled to St. Moritz, where he tried to rest and to prepare himself for another major new undertaking.

3.

"THE WELL-KNOWN ITALIAN CONDUCTOR TOSCANINI IS SAID TO have been won for Bayreuth by Frau Cosima Wagner." Thus read a brief notice in a 1903 issue of Germany's usually reliable *Neue Zeitschrift für Musik*. No such engagement took place, and, given the xenophobia of Richard Wagner's acolytes, including his redoubtable widow, the report must have been unfounded. As late as 1924, Siegfried Wagner, who was by then in charge of the Bayreuth Festival and who had wanted Toscanini to conduct a new production of *Tannhäuser*, was warned that the most conservative Wagnerites would have denied him the money for continuing the festival had he engaged the Italian maestro to perform at the sanctum sanctorum.

Siegfried and his English-born wife, Winifred Williams, initiated a fund-raising campaign of their own, and by 1929 they were able to schedule the long-delayed new *Tannhäuser* production (to be designed by Kurt Söhnlein and staged by Siegfried himself) for the following year and to offer it, as well as an already extant production of *Tristan*, to Toscanini. They discussed their proposal with him in Berlin in the spring of 1929, at the time of the Scala ensemble's visit, and in the fall they visited him in Milan with a final plan, which he accepted. When the matter of his fee was raised, Toscanini said that he would accept no payment for his participation because, as he later declared, he approached Bayreuth's Festspielhaus as if he were entering a temple.

The temple, however, faced artistic problems similar to those confronted by normal opera companies, and some of its problems were exacerbated by its nonpermanent status. The festival's participants gathered together for several weeks each summer and then dispersed, and the orchestra, in particular, was made up of players from a number of German orchestras, which meant not only that there was a high rate of year-to-year personnel turnover but also that individual players might not blend well within a section. In addition, the Bayreuth pit is exceptionally deep and mostly covered by the stage; players had to adjust to its unusual acoustic conditions. Finally, because most of Wagner's operas are exceptionally long and physically tiring, the Bayreuth orchestra was a nearly double-sized ensemble, each half of which performed roughly half of the season's repertoire. In 1930, the senior conductor at Bayreuth was the autocratic Karl Muck, who had been responsible for the festival's *Parsifal* performances since 1901 but who also served as a rallying flag for the festival's most conservative supporters. Muck envied Toscanini his worldwide success, and for nationalistic as well as professional reasons he was not pleased that Toscanini had been invited to Bayreuth. He made sure that the best players would work with himself and the weaker ones with Toscanini.

Toscanini had returned to Milan from St. Moritz not later than 23 June 1930 (the day on which he signed a will, leaving all of his possessions to Carla), and had then traveled most of the way to Bayreuth by air, to avoid a long rail or road journey; Carla followed later, in the family car driven by the Toscaninis' Swiss chauffeur and handyman, Emilio Monier. At the beginning of the first orchestra rehearsal, Siegfried presented the new guest to the orchestra, and Toscanini told the players of his long-standing desire to conduct at Bayreuth. But when the orchestra began to play, the maestro was dumbfounded. At the end of the first session, he told Siegfried that he had decided to leave, and only when Siegfried assured him that replacements for the weaker players would be found did Toscanini agree to continue. As he was determined to get the ensemble into the best possible shape in the relatively short amount of time available, the musicians were subjected to the Toscanini shock therapy at its worst. They had never experienced anything like it, and they were no less astonished when the Italian maestro, rehearsing from memory, as always, began to hear and correct mistakes in the printed parts that had gone undetected for decades by Bayreuth's celebrated conductors.

The Bayreuth chorus, on the other hand, greatly pleased Toscanini: he recalled, in old age, that the voices were "beautiful," that even when the choristers sang loud, "they didn't shout," and that the chorus master, Hugo Rüdel, a former horn player, was "extraordinary," "simpatico!" and "a treasure!" And yet, the only recorded instance of international interpretive incompatibility between Toscanini and his German forces took place precisely at the choral entrance of the guests in *Tannhäuser*'s second act, during the first fully staged ensemble rehearsal. The maestro took the famous march, marked Allegro, at a faster than usual tempo and sped it up still more during the latter half, according to Söhnlein:

> The chorus members stumble over each other. Interruptions, repetitions, two, three times—five, six times! Toscanini rages and shouts all his renowned Italian invective. The chorus members look for help from [. . .] Rüdel, who is standing at the right front of the proscenium. He shrugs his shoulders in resignation, makes a small backward movement with his head in the direction of the conductor's podium. Embarrassed silence for several long seconds.
>
> Then Siegfried, who is standing at the left of the proscenium, walks slowly to the center of the stage, until he is right out on the apron. He raises his hand a little and says very calmly [in Italian], in a gentle, muted tone of voice, "Dear Maestro, a little slower, please! There's a difference between singing in the flexible Italian language and in rough German! And we Germans feel this music in another way—than you!" [. . .]
>
> The angry man stares in silence, his arms folded, for three, five, ten, fifteen, maybe twenty seconds. Deathly silence. Finally, without saying a word, he picks up the baton, raises it, and begins at a slightly slower tempo. Siegfried bows his head a little in thanks, gives an obliging little smile, and goes back to his place. Now all the entrances click perfectly.

Siegfried's sunny personality and his status as the Master's son worked to his advantage, and Toscanini appreciated his diplomatic skills. Years later he told Friedelind Wagner, Siegfried's elder daughter, "You're just like your father. No matter what happens, you always laugh." But on 17 July, while Toscanini's rehearsals were in their final phase, Siegfried suffered a massive heart attack. Few outside his immediate family knew of the seriousness of his condition, and from his hospital bed he explicitly requested that the festival's preparations and performances proceed normally.

Other members of the Wagner clan sat in on Toscanini's rehearsals. Siegfried's sister, Eva Chamberlain, and his two half sisters, Daniela Thode and Blandine Gravina—Cosima's daughters by her first husband, the conductor and pianist Hans von Bülow—also attended, at first with curiosity, then with astonishment, and finally with nearly religious devotion. Blandine summed up their impressions in a letter: "For eight days we have been totally caught up in Toscanini's orchestra rehearsals for *Tannhäuser* and *Tristan*," she said. "It is the most incredible thing we have ever experienced. Eva, usually impassive, is completely overwhelmed by his greatness." They were amazed not only by his prowess as a conductor and his powers of persuasion—volcanic or pacific—but also by his deep devotion to Wagner's work and his attention to detail. Daniela, who had designed the costumes for *Tannhäuser* on the basis of illustrations in the fourteenth-century Manesse Codex, treasured for the rest of her life a two-page, handwritten note that Toscanini had sent her regarding the lighting change after the opening Tannhäuser-Venus scene in the first act: Siegfried, who was in charge of the staging, had decided to let the light increase gradually, but Toscanini wanted an immediate light change, in accordance with Wagner's instructions.

As the hospitalized Siegfried had requested, the series began on schedule—*Tristan* on 20 July and *Tannhäuser* two evenings later. Toscanini's *Tristan* cast included Lauritz Melchior and Nanny Larsén-Todsen in the title roles, Rudolf Bockelmann as Kurwenal, Alexander Kipnis as Marke, and Anny Helm as Brangäne. Larsén-Todsen had sung Isolde with Toscanini at La Scala, but the other principals were all working with him for the first time. Melchior, a gigantic Dane who was already the most sought-after heldentenor of the day, later recalled, "It was a thrill to work under the guidance of this brilliant conductor, and all the piano rehearsals—which he for the most part accompanied or conducted himself—were hours of great value as far as music was concerned. Toscanini could be charming and cordiality personified; at other times, when things did not go his way [. . .] he could be a devil. Everyone was afraid of him, and his will prevailed in all ways. [. . .] I can only say that I got along fine with Maestro Toscanini." Melchior was notoriously unreliable with respect to rhythm and tempo ("Once he learns a mistake he never forgets it," Fritz Busch was said to have remarked about him), but Toscanini admired the power and beauty of Melchior's voice, worked long and hard with him on his role, and called him "Tristanissimo," a nickname that stuck.

Bockelmann recalled that during rehearsals Toscanini would tap the score and say, "Hier steht, hier steht" (It's here, it's here). "The singer who didn't remember Toscanini's observations was treated roughly," Bockelmann said. "But if everything was in order, if he was happy with us, he would chat in a friendly way, he would tell us about Verdi and talk about Richard Wagner. 'C'est mon grand maître,' he would say." (In describing Wagner the man, however, as opposed to Wagner the musician, Toscanini used the word *farabutto*—which translates as "scoundrel," "crook," or "swindler.")

Kipnis, a highly expressive singer with an especially beautiful bass voice, had no trouble with the maestro. "When King Marke says: 'MIR dies? Dies, Tristan, MIR?'—in this quasi-*parlando* outcry I diminished the tone on *mir*, going over to a slightly breathy quality; and Toscanini looked up, but he didn't say anything. He insisted on the *rhythm* being the way he wanted it; but [. . .] he never said anything about the phrasing or accents which represented my feelings." Kipnis particularly loved the lyricism of Toscanini's approach to *Tristan*, "which I heard many times from other conductors, but never in such a degree as from Toscanini."

About the performances, Hans Schmidt-Isserstedt, a young German conductor, recalled that the first act "was a little disappointing to me: very slow, the rests calculated with absolute precision, and nothing that was not written in the score. Then came the second act: another world! I have never again heard it done as beautifully as that—so fluently; one could almost hear the Italian melody. Then came the third act: grandiose, ecstatic, and completely free."

In *Tannhäuser*, Toscanini was generally happy with his singers, all in their late twenties or thirties: Sigismund Pilinsky (Tannhäuser), Maria Müller (Elisabeth), Ruth Jost-Arden (Venus), Herbert Janssen (Wolfram), and Erna Berger (Shepherdess). The German critics, too, praised the *Tannhäuser* cast, although a few did not like Pilinsky, and lauded Toscanini for having "given us a wholly new work" instead of a "sight-read repertoire opera" and for bringing out shadings that "distinguished him from a thousand other *Tannhäuser* conductors."

Arthur Brooks, managing director of the Columbia Gramophone Company in Britain, attempted to persuade Toscanini to record *Tannhäuser*, but the maestro refused on the dual grounds of having his "nerves stretched to the breaking point" on account of the difficult rehearsals, and his general "aversion" to making recordings. He asked Blandine Gravina to "persuade the gentleman not to persist further with his request."

The profound impression that Toscanini had made on Siegfried's siblings during rehearsals was repeated at the performances. "Only an artist who, along with his Genius, possesses a soul of marvelous *human goodness* can stir such a heavenly breeze in the souls of others," Blandine wrote to Carla Toscanini.* Even more overblown statements would be forthcoming from Wagner's daughters and stepdaughters in the months and years to come. But it is important to remember that they had heard Wagner's music conducted by Wagner himself as well as by his celebrated disciples Bülow, Levi, Richter, Mottl, and Seidl. Their measuring stick was an extraordinary one.

Toscanini's own main delight at Bayreuth was the structure of the Festspielhaus itself: orchestra and conductor were hidden from the audience's view, and neither the singers nor the conductor took bows: the work was all that counted. But these factors did not prevent audiences from regaling Toscanini and his casts with tumultuous ovations at the end of every act of both operas.

---

* The letters of Wagner's daughters and stepdaughters to Toscanini were written in Italian, with occasional lapses into French, English, and German. Blandine's Italian was excellent—she had lived much of her life in Italy—but Daniela and Eva wrote it less correctly. In translating excerpts from their letters, I have not reproduced their mistakes or indicated where they switched from one language to another. All three addressed Toscanini with the formal *Lei*, even in their friendliest or most worshipful letters.

———

THE ARTISTIC SUCCESS OF Toscanini's productions was dampened by growing worry over Siegfried Wagner, whose initial heart attack was followed by others and complicated by pneumonia. On 4 August, Richard and Cosima Wagner's sixty-one-year-old son died, barely four months after his mother's death. The twelve-year-old Friedelind Wagner, the second of Siegfried and Winifred's four children (Wieland was the eldest; Wolfgang and Verena were younger), had been spending the summer in England but had been called home when her father's condition had begun to deteriorate. Immediately after his death, she went to be with her aunt, Eva Chamberlain. "A moment later the door opened," she recalled years later; "a slight man with deep, gentle eyes and fine sensitive face took Eva in his arms, then me, the child whom he did not know. This was my first meeting with the man who thereafter came nearer than any other to taking my father's place. Toscanini!"

"The festival must take no notice of my death," Siegfried had told his wife when he realized that the end was imminent. On the afternoon of 5 August, Winifred, her sisters-in-law, the children, Toscanini, Muck, and a few other friends attended a brief service next to the coffin, but that evening Toscanini conducted a performance of *Tannhäuser*, with Winifred in attendance. Siegfried was buried on the eighth, and at the Festspielhaus in the evening Toscanini led the *Siegfried Idyll*—which Wagner had written after his son's birth—at the start of a memorial concert that was completed under Karl Elmendorff and Muck.

Ernest Newman, who was attending the festival, wondered where the conjunction of Toscanini's Bayreuth debut with Siegfried's death might lead. The maestro's "performances have been so extraordinary that already people are saying that next year they will want only to hear him—supposing him to be there," he wrote in the *Sunday Times*. "The best thing that could be done would be to give Toscanini supreme control; but to hand over this greatest of all German national art-works to a foreigner would inevitably provoke an outburst of Chauvinism in Germany, to say nothing of the trouble Toscanini would meet with." Soon, rumors were circulating to the effect that the famed stage and film director Max Reinhardt would be put in charge of the festival, with Toscanini as music director. A Jew and an Italian as high priests in the Wagnerian shrine? Highly unlikely! Still, the maestro's presence had helped to bring a record number of 10,000 visitors (including 1,000 Americans) to the 1930 festival and to sell some 35,000 tickets for a total of nearly $250,000. The *New York Times* reported not only that Toscanini would assume the direction of the festival but also that he would make Bayreuth his home; Max Smith denied these rumors on his friend's behalf, but not before various observers had rushed to applaud the presumed development. Walter Damrosch, for instance, felt that Toscanini was the man who could return Bayreuth "to the level which Wagner dreamed and which he had begun to realize."

Toscanini, however, had no desire at all to take control of Bayreuth or of any other opera ensemble. The last of his ten Bayreuth performances (five of each opera) took place on 20 August, and Winifred, who—in accordance with instructions in Siegfried's will but much to the horror of her sisters-in-law—was assuming the direction of the festival, gave him a check for 10,000 marks, as the dying Siegfried had asked her to do. Toscanini returned it, but he accepted Winifred's invitation to return the following summer, to conduct *Tannhäuser* and *Parsifal*. Karl Muck was told that his services would no longer be needed; in a face-saving letter to Winifred, he said that following Siegfried's death he did not have the strength needed to undertake new responsibilities.* In effect, however, he had been replaced.

4.

———

A MONTH BEFORE HIS BAYREUTH DEBUT, TOSCANINI WAS SHOCKED to learn that Angelo Scandiani, La Scala's general manager, had died suddenly, at the age of fifty-eight. Senatore Borletti, the theater's liaison with the government, put forward the name of Anita Colombo

———

* Friedelind Wagner believed that her father's struggle to counteract Muck's machinations against Toscanini had exacerbated the heart condition that led to Siegfried's death.

as a replacement: she knew more about the internal workings of the ensemble than anyone living except Toscanini himself, and her efficiency was legendary. But some people did not approve. "I think I should tell you that the news has not made a good impression in various circles," the prefect of Milan wired to the Ministry of the Interior in Rome. "Various circles" meant the Milanese Fascists, who had looked upon Toscanini's departure and Scandiani's death as a double miracle that opened the path to untroubled party domination of La Scala. Piero Bottini, the Fascist federal secretary of Milan, informed Alessandro Chiavolini, Mussolini's principal secretary, that "Signora Colombo is not only Maestro Toscanini's ex-secretary but the person who is said to have received an explicit mandate from Toscanini himself to run La Scala according to his orders." But the nomination was approved, even by Mussolini, and Toscanini, in Bayreuth, wired his congratulations to Colombo and to La Scala.

Although Toscanini was not issuing orders as such, Colombo was indeed determined to remain faithful to his policy of minimal political intervention in the running of the theater. She had sufficiently high political connections to enable her to qualify for the job; on the other hand, Fascist policy generally favored limiting women's activities to the kitchen, laundry room, and bedroom, and only one party newspaper, *Il Regime Fascista*, is known to have supported Colombo's appointment. In a letter dated 24 July 1930, Colombo asked Walter Toscanini to obtain his father's advice on where to position this or that opera in the course of the forthcoming season, but she requested no assistance on any matter that could possibly have been considered controversial. The sole documented instance of a request by Colombo for real intervention on Toscanini's part came some months later, when Victor De Sabata, who had become La Scala's principal conductor, resigned his post after having had a dispute with the orchestra: Colombo cabled Toscanini, who was in New York, asking him to persuade De Sabata to return. Toscanini did not approve of De Sabata's conducting style or of most of his interpretations, but he respected his musicianship and believed him to be the best person available to guide La Scala's destinies. He immediately cabled his younger colleague, "Affection that binds me to you makes me insist asking you revoke your decision because damaging to you [and] to theater. Listen to my advice."

De Sabata returned to La Scala the following season. By then, however, Colombo had been removed as general manager, owing both to her sex and to her Toscanini connection; the Scala administration quickly became a battleground for intraparty and municipal-provincial rivalries, and so it would remain for the duration of Mussolini's regime.

5.

FROM BAYREUTH, TOSCANINI TRAVELED TO SALZBURG, WHERE HE was a guest of Max Reinhardt and his fiancée, the actress Helene Thimig, at Leopoldskron, the eighteenth-century palace that Reinhardt had bought and was gradually restoring. Reinhardt, one of the most influential theater directors in Europe, was a cofounder of the Salzburg Festival, and he invited Toscanini to conduct there in 1931. Toscanini liked the town and accepted the invitation.

He spent most of September and October 1930 between his home in Milan and a vacation spot on Lake Maggiore, preparing for his forthcoming New York season, but he also relaxed for a time at the spa at Salsomaggiore and was in Zurich on 20 and 21 October to attend the final rehearsal and first performance of Adolf Busch's Concerto for Large Orchestra, op. 43, with the Tonhalle Orchestra conducted by Volkmar Andreae. The work was dedicated to Toscanini, who promised to conduct it with the New York Philharmonic, but the promise was never fulfilled. After the rehearsal, he stayed up until two in the morning chatting with Adolf, Frieda, and their future son-in-law, Rudolf Serkin, at the home of Hermann and Lilly Reiff, their hosts. The next morning, he sat in on the Busch Quartet's rehearsal of Beethoven's Quartet op. 130, and after the Cavatina movement he "burst into tears, embracing Busch and saying that this day and the previous one had been the most beautiful in his life," according to Tully Potter, Busch's biographer. That afternoon, as Serkin drove Toscanini with Adolf and Frieda to visit Lake Zug, the maestro continued to exclaim over the beauty of the Cavatina.

He returned to Milan on the twenty-second, and one week later he boarded the *Vulcania* in Naples and set sail for New York. Carla did not accompany her husband on this trip: she had broken her leg in Bayreuth; it had not yet healed, and she seemed to be suffering from a form of depression as well. In her stead she sent Luigi, their jack-of-all-trades domestic helper, to make sure that her husband's day-to-day needs were looked after. During his time away, Toscanini—evidently worried about Carla's mental state—wrote to her frequently, affectionately, and in detail. Even during the ocean voyage he penned letters about his mixed feelings over Wally's forthcoming marriage to Castelbarco, about his terror at the amount of work he had taken on, and about his fellow passengers, including Count Giuseppe Volpi di Misurata, a leading financier and former Fascist finance minister, who was suffering from seasickness: Volpi was "very good at turning his sails to the prevailing wind on dry land but demonstrated less ability at sea," Toscanini wryly commented. And he demonstrated his usual reluctance to begin a new series of tasks: "I studied the new scores, but so far I don't feel a great desire to encounter my orchestra and begin to work!! I would gladly stay on this same ship and go back home. I hope that this state of mind will change tomorrow, on contact with that marvelous instrument."

Many friends, members of the orchestra, and Erich Kleiber were at the pier to meet Toscanini when he disembarked in New York early on the morning of Sunday, 9 November, and that afternoon he attended the final concert of Kleiber's six-week Philharmonic guest engagement, which Toscanini himself had encouraged. "Not bad at all," he commented to Carla—and since Kleiber had also made a positive impression on orchestra, audiences, and critics, Toscanini easily persuaded Judson to invite him back for seven weeks the following season.

Also at the pier was the forty-six-year-old Bruno Zirato, who, as a young man, had immigrated to America from his native Calabria, become fluent in English, worked as Caruso's secretary, and married the Italian American soprano Nina Morgana. Thanks to Toscanini, Zirato had been hired as a part-time Philharmonic employee, to act as a sort of "Minister in Charge of Maestro"—paid directly out of Mackay's pocket. Toscanini found Zirato simpatico, intelligent, and capable, and the maestro, on the day of his arrival in New York that fall, suggested to Mackay that Zirato replace Edward Ervin, who had just retired as the orchestra's assistant manager. Mackay engaged

Zirato on the spot; for the orchestra, the acquisition proved fruitful: in later years he and Judson were comanagers of the Philharmonic, and upon Judson's retirement Zirato became sole managing director, a position he held until his own retirement in 1959.*

Toscanini began his rehearsals on the morning following his arrival in New York and opened his portion of the season three days later with the world premiere of Respighi's orchestration of three Bach chorale preludes, followed by Beethoven's First Symphony, and, after the intermission, his first performance anywhere of Brahms's First Symphony, which elicited enthusiasm from public and press.†

Unusual works within Toscanini's repertoire during the first half of the Philharmonic's season were three pieces by Liszt (with the Russian pianist Alexander Siloti as soloist),‡ Kodály's *Dances of Marosszék*, Roussel's *The Spider's Feast*, and the Verdi *Requiem*, which he had not conducted in New York since his early Metropolitan days. As in previous seasons, there were again weekly radio broadcasts of the Philharmonic's concerts, but on WABC instead of WOR.

Within two days of Toscanini's arrival in New York, he was experiencing pain in his right arm; a doctor was summoned to massage the ailing spots, but Toscanini, writing to Carla on the day after his first concert, asked her to excuse his poor penmanship: his hand was shaking. It was a harbinger of troubles to come. For the time being, however, he forged ahead, and after having conducted approximately a dozen rehearsals and seven concerts (three different programs) within two weeks, he departed for Philadelphia, where he was to debut with that city's orchestra, while Leopold Stokowski, the Philadelphia Orchestra's conductor, would debut with the Philharmonic.

---

* The Toscaninis paid Zirato privately for various errands, and in 1931 they paid his passage to Calabria, to visit his dying mother. His letters to them demonstrate almost filial affection and solicitude, but without a hint of servility.

† Why Toscanini, who had already conducted the composer's Second and Fourth Symphonies for many years, waited until 1929 and 1930 to perform the Third and First Symphonies, respectively, remains an open question. But they soon became mainstays of his repertoire, along with their even-numbered sisters.

‡ Siloti, who had studied with Nikolai Rubinstein and Liszt, was only four years older than Toscanini, but he described the maestro as "a young man with a future!"

The exchange with Stokowski had been worked out the previous spring by Arthur Judson, who managed both ensembles. A few days before the two conductors temporarily traded cities, Stokowski's wife, Evangeline, née Johnson (of the Johnson & Johnson pharmaceutical company family), wrote to Toscanini to invite him to stand as godfather to their second child. Toscanini politely refused—he never accepted such requests, he said—but he offered his best wishes to "little Sadja and her lovely mother." At roughly the same time, Stokowski wrote a few paragraphs about Toscanini that appeared in the *Times* on 21 November. He had been "so moved with the beauty and magnificence" of Toscanini's conducting during the Philharmonic's two Berlin concerts the preceding spring that he had "tried to make an analysis of his mastery as a conductor," he said. He was struck by Toscanini's

> compelling rhythm—so subtle and flexible and vibrant. His beat breaks every academic rule, yet is always clear and eloquent. But it is between the beats that happens something almost magical. One can always tell when he has reached the half-beat or quarter-beat or three-quarter-beat, even when he does not divide his beats, and it is this certainty and clarity of beat which create such a perfect ensemble when he conducts [. . .]. His sense of harmonic balance is extraordinary. [. . .] His mastery of every score he conducts is complete. He always approaches the score from a fresh and new angle, but his originality of conception comes from his expressing the essence and soul of the score, instead of merely the literal notes. His command over the orchestra is so great that perhaps only other conductors can fully realize how powerful it is. [. . .] It is the divine fire in him which elevates all he expresses through tone.

Stokowski's remarks, however florid, were for the most part perceptive, but Toscanini was convinced that they, as well as the wife's letter, were a publicity stunt—and Stokowski did have a reputation for loving publicity. "Great charlatans, both of them," Toscanini said of Maestro and Mrs. Stokowski, in a letter to Carla. "And all this happened one or two days before I came to lead his orchestra and he mine." No coincidence, in other words.

On the evening before he left New York for Philadelphia, Toscanini spoke for the first time via transatlantic telephone to his family
in Milan. "It was a real joy for my soul to have heard your voices," he
wrote to Carla afterward. "Too bad that you were so nervous that
you couldn't talk a little more. I'm happy to know that you are well
again and sleeping better than before." In Philadelphia, he stayed at
the Ritz-Carlton Hotel, and he confessed to Carla that he was breathing easier there, away from their New York friends who, in his wife's
absence, were being overly solicitous. He didn't want to offend them,
he said, but he wished that they understood the Latin proverb *Beata
solitudo—sola beatitudo* (O blessed solitude, sole bliss). Yet he did need
help, for he was incapable of looking after the details of everyday life,
and Luigi was proving to be nearly as impractical as the maestro
himself. "He's very nice but a bit of a goose," Toscanini told Carla.
"In fact, I'd say he's quite a goose."

Toscanini did not generally like guest engagements, but he had
long referred to the Philadelphia ensemble as "a Stradivarius orchestra," and he evidently relished the challenge of working with it. He
conducted three different programs in a total of seven performances
in ten days; although two of the three programs were identical to
programs that he had just conducted with the Philharmonic, they
had to be rehearsed anew. "That damned Heldenleben of Strauss
kills me," he wrote to Carla. "I've already conducted it six times
between here and New York, and I can't stand it anymore!"

Enthusiasm on the part of Philadelphia's audiences and press
alike reached almost hysterical levels. Toscanini's final concert—
an all-Wagner program—brought nearly $10,000 to the orches-
tra's pension fund (a substantial sum in the Depression-era
economy), and many members of the orchestra expressed their
sadness at his departure: they told him "that they had spent two
heavenly weeks playing good music in a way that they had never
known," he reported to Carla. "They're already inviting me to
come back to Philadelphia next year, and not only that, but also
to do a California tour after the regular season. These people
think I'm eternal!" He agreed, however, to return for a pair of
concerts the following year.

Philadelphia's orchestra and public may have been thrilled, but
Stokowski must have been far less so. The Philharmonic had not

reacted well to his reseating of the orchestra in a nontraditional way or to his disciplinary action against some recalcitrant players. The orchestra refused to have him back, and he himself vowed never to conduct the New York ensemble again; he kept the vow for sixteen years.

A nighttime trip after his final Philadelphia concert brought Toscanini back to New York, and the following morning he began to rehearse his upcoming Philharmonic programs. "The orchestra welcomed me with shouts of joy," he told Carla. "I was really moved." Not that his relations with the players were always easygoing! On that subject, the Philharmonic double bassist Fred Zimmermann told B. H. Haggin,

> I remember a solo wind-player getting exasperated by Toscanini's prolonged shouting at the man next to him, and saying to the Old Man: "Oh, be quiet!" Toscanini turned to him and said: "I wasn't talking to you, you jackass!" The player answered: "Yes, I am a jackass—*I* am a young jackass, and *you* are an old jackass. *I* can still learn; *you* cannot"; and he packed his instrument and walked out. Afterwards Toscanini sent for him, and there was a reconciliation. Then there was the incident with the harpist [Theodore] Cella, whom Toscanini ordered out after an argument. "I will get *another* harpist!" Toscanini called after him; and Cella, at the door, turned and shot back: "He'll be one of my pupils!" [. . .] Cella was back the next day. On the other hand there was the incident with a solo wind-player who got angry and walked out. At the door he turned and said *"Good-by!"* "Good-by!" said Toscanini, adding: "When the Pope dies they elect a new one." This time it was not Toscanini but the player who was given something to think about (he was back the next day).

Despite Toscanini's reluctance to fire musicians, his Philadelphia engagement had given him a jolt. He had scant respect for Stokowski's musicianship, but he must have recognized that his younger colleague had shaped an orchestra of great beauty, with players who, in a few instances, outclassed their New York counterparts. There can be little doubt that his unusual request, in February 1931, to improve the Philharmonic by changing some of its personnel for the following season was directly connected to his recent Philadelphia experience. The concertmaster, Scipione Guidi, was replaced the following season by the San Francisco Symphony's departing concertmaster, the Russian-born Mishel Piastro, a former star pupil of Leopold Auer's. Toscanini also wanted to re-audition all of the first violin section's members; he refused to renew the contracts of two new second violins; and he asked to have one violist, the second oboe, the E-flat clarinet, and one percussionist removed from the orchestra—most of them on the grounds that they showed little interest in their work, but one of them because guest conductors had complained about the man's playing, and another for his unseemly behavior during the orchestra's European tour. Toscanini also wanted a new fourth oboe who could double on English horn; asked to have a fourth trombone engaged on a permanent basis; and requested to speak with two of the cellists with whose playing he was dissatisfied, before he made a decision about reengaging them.

Exaggerated rumors reached the press: Toscanini would re-audition a third of the orchestra; the Philharmonic would become a nonunion orchestra; youngsters fresh out of music schools would be engaged at low salary levels, to save money; and players were rebelling against administrative tyranny. Judson had to state formally that personnel changes would not exceed the yearly average of five to eight players; that there had in fact been no changes at all between the previous season and the current one; that the Philharmonic would continue its present close ties to the musicians' union; and that maintaining the orchestra's high performance standards was the only criterion involved. In the end, six players were fired, two others retired, and eight new players, including Piastro, were engaged, all in accordance with the union rules of the day. In addition, at Toscanini's request, Hans Lange, who had functioned as both assistant concertmaster and assistant conductor, was made full-time assistant conductor for the following season; this relieved Toscanini of some preliminary rehearsal duties.

6.

TO THE DELIGHT OF THE PHILHARMONIC'S BOARD, THE 1930–31 SEA-
son proceeded with one success after another, in New York and
with performances in Philadelphia and Washington. Following a
concert at the Metropolitan Opera House, on 14 December, Albert
Einstein and his wife went to greet Toscanini in his dressing room,
and on both Christmas Day and New Year's Day the maestro, in
the absence of any family members, dined with the Muschenheim
family, who owned the Hotel Astor. He developed a cough during
the holidays, and on New Year's Eve he evidently took too strong a
dose of the medicine that Dr. Howe had given him, because at the
following evening's concert he could barely wend his way to the
podium. But within a day or two he was busy rehearsing the soloists for his midmonth Verdi *Requiem* performances. Of the celebrated German soprano Elisabeth Rethberg—his Aida at La Scala
two years earlier—he wrote to Carla that she "has a nice voice but
is a potato dumpling,"* whereas the mezzo-soprano Margarete
Matzenauer, with whom he had worked at the Metropolitan and in
Buenos Aires, was "old, painted up, and a dog." The American
tenor Mario Chamlee was "not bad," and no comment was made
about the basso Ezio Pinza, who, following his successes under
Toscanini at La Scala, had become one of the Metropolitan's best-
loved artists, and whom Toscanini liked personally as well as for
his vocal virtues.

The maestro's last concert, on Sunday afternoon, 18 January 1931,
was transmitted via shortwave to Italy, where Carla and Wanda
were able to hear it. William S. Paley, president of the Columbia
Broadcasting System, was in the audience at Carnegie Hall, and the
Times reported that "as the concert was nearing its close he called
WABC and directed officials there to put in a transatlantic call to
the Toscanini home in Milan to determine if the concert was coming in clearly there." At the very end, Toscanini "was summoned
from the platform and talked for about two minutes with his wife

---

* Rethberg, thirty-six at the time, was one of the finest lyric sopranos of her day and was
good-looking. But Toscanini was writing to his wife.

and daughter, who informed him that the reception of his concert had been excellent."

He had hoped to have at least some of his family members with him in New York and to spend the month between the first and second parts of his Philharmonic season with them in Florida, but since Carla was still laid up and depressed, he boarded the Cherbourg-bound *Bremen* on 21 January. During his brief stay in Milan, Winifred Wagner visited him to conclude plans for the forthcoming Bayreuth Festival; he and Carla also spent some time on the Isola dei Pescatori on Lake Maggiore. Before long, however, he was back on the *Bremen*, this time with Wanda and Carla, whose leg had healed sufficiently.

The ship docked in New York on 24 February, and Toscanini immediately began another round of rehearsals and concerts. Works new to his repertoire included Dvořák's "Otello" Overture, Bruckner's Seventh Symphony—Toscanini's first performance of anything by Bruckner since 1896, when he had conducted the Adagio from the Seventh shortly after the composer's death—Sibelius's Fourth Symphony, Shostakovich's First Symphony (Toscanini's first performance of music written in the Soviet Union), and pieces by Johann Christian Bach, Rimsky-Korsakov, Pizzetti, Abram Chasins, and, surprisingly, Mozart's Symphony no. 40 in G minor.

Flirtation in a Chinese Garden and *Parade* by the twenty-seven-year-old, New York–born Chasins, constituted one of Toscanini's earliest concessions to a growing call for him to perform music by American composers. The previous year, there had been a debate in the *Times*'s Letters to the Editor column: Should outstanding artists like Toscanini have complete freedom in their choice of repertoire, or did they have a responsibility to perform music by composers native to the countries in which they were working? Supporters of the latter opinion had particularly deplored the fact that not a single piece by an American composer had been performed during the Philharmonic's European tour. In principle, Toscanini agreed with his critics, but he had found little American music that interested him. His American repertoire before 1931 had consisted of a single piece by Ernest Schelling and another by the German American Hermann Hans Wetzler, but he eventually conducted music by sixteen American composers, not counting those like the native Dutchman Bernard Wagenaar, the German-born Charles Martin Loeffler, the Swiss

Ernest Bloch, or the Italian Mario Castelnuovo-Tedesco, all of whom were already professional musicians before they immigrated to the United States.

A number of American composers detested Toscanini for his lack of interest in avant-garde music, American or otherwise. Charles Ives, in particular, reviled "Toscaninny" for his conservatism, although, oddly, the cantankerous New England modernist—whose works were largely ignored in his lifetime—also found the maestro's interpretations of nineteenth-century repertoire too modern, insufficiently Romantic. Virgil Thomson considered Toscanini a reactionary and his influence pernicious, and later on, from his pulpit as music critic of the *New York Herald-Tribune*, he castigated the maestro on many an occasion. But other prominent American composers took a broader view. Roger Sessions, for instance, stated clearly, at a gathering of his colleagues in 1933, that he could not blame Toscanini for not playing music if he did not believe in it, and others whose works Toscanini did not perform expressed their awareness of the value of his contribution to the country's musical life through his outstanding performances of the works to which he brought his passion and expertise. Young New York–based composers—Marc Blitzstein and William Schuman, for instance—drew some of their earliest impressions of live music from Toscanini's Philharmonic performances and remained grateful to him, just as later generations of American composers, including Philip Glass and John Adams, would become familiar with some of the classics through Toscanini's widely disseminated recordings.

The New York newspapers of the early 1930s carried a vast array of opinions on the subject of the Philharmonic's programming. Some critics and many audience members and radio listeners did not appreciate hearing *any* contemporary scores, American or otherwise; others simply wanted more classics and fewer contemporary pieces; still others wanted the opposite. One letter writer considered Rossini's overtures too trivial for concert performance, whereas another disliked Saint-Saëns because he wasn't as good as Beethoven and Wagner. Toscanini's philosophy was to do the best he could for music that he loved or at least found interesting. As he wrote to an intimate friend a few years later, "If the power of suggestion that I project over others is of uncommon strength, that which works on me is even greater. And that's why I can interpret with the same ardor Pagliacci and the 'Pastoral' Symphony of Beethoven."

Among the fifty-six composers represented in the Philharmonic's 1930–31 season, twenty-three—over 40 percent—were living, and Toscanini, who was the oldest and most musically conservative of the season's conductors (his colleagues that year were Molinari, Kleiber, Stokowski, and Lange), performed works by thirteen living composers (nine of them younger than himself) out of a total of twenty-six—50 percent! Often, the living composer in question was represented by only one or two pieces, as opposed to half a dozen or more by Mozart, Beethoven, or Brahms; nevertheless, no music director of any of the world's top symphony orchestras in the first quarter of the twenty-first century can claim that 40 to 50 percent of the composers represented in an entire season's subscription concerts are currently alive.

The Toscaninis departed for Europe aboard the *Berengaria* on 22 April, three days after the Philharmonic's final concert of the season, and were back in Milan by the end of the month. The maestro's plan was to conduct two concerts in Bologna in the middle of May, to commemorate Giuseppe Martucci, whose seventy-fifth birthday would have occurred that year. He would then go to Vienna, to conduct two concerts with the Vienna Philharmonic—his debut with that famed ensemble. After another period at home, he would proceed to Bayreuth, and finally he would go to Salzburg, to repeat with the Viennese orchestra one of the programs that he had conducted in Vienna. But his plans would soon be dramatically altered.

7.

DURING HIS STAY AT SALSOMAGGIORE THE PREVIOUS FALL, Toscanini had been approached by Giuseppe Lipparini, a poet, journalist, literary critic, and, at the time, deputy mayor of Bologna. Toscanini declined Lipparini's invitation to conduct the inaugural production of the city's newly restored Teatro Comunale, but when Lipparini told him of plans to honor the memory of Martucci, who had headed Bologna's Liceo Musicale for many years, Toscanini said that he would conduct not one but two concerts—two different programs—and that he would accept no payment for his work.

He arrived in Bologna—the town known to Italians as *la dotta* (the erudite), because it is the home of the world's first university—on 7 May, ready to begin an arduous series of rehearsals with an orchestra that he knew would be far below the level of his New York ensemble, and determined to do the right thing for the memory of Martucci, his esteemed friend and quasi-mentor. After the first few minutes of the first rehearsal, he called out to the orchestra's manager: "Where did you find these guys? At the morgue?" Aldo Pais, a cellist in the orchestra, later a well-known pedagogue and chamber music player, recalled that Toscanini "seemed like a furious storm [. . .]. He had a team of workers come in to raise the woodwinds, because they couldn't be heard from the podium. He broke at least ten batons that evening, with his hands and with his teeth," but he "got them into shape," Pais said.

Toscanini had not been told that his concerts would coincide with the opening of a national trade fair in Bologna, much less that part of the fair included festivities organized by the local Fascist Party. When he found out, he warned Lipparini, who had invited him, "I haven't come here for any tomfoolery." On the day of the first performance, Lipparini informed him that Costanzo Ciano, minister of communications, and Leandro Arpinati, undersecretary of the interior, would be in the theater; Toscanini would have to begin the concert with the Royal March and "Giovinezza."

"This happened a few minutes after the last rehearsal," Toscanini later wrote, "at which I had warmly exhorted the members of the orchestra to take their places only two minutes before the performance, with a maximum of concentration, conscious of the reverent and loving demonstration that they had been called to participate in—in order that no sounds other than Martucci's music should make contact with the public. I concluded, 'Gentlemen, be democrats in life but aristocrats in art.'" (This was an open provocation on Toscanini's part, since Mussolini often inveighed against the "feeble democracies" and touted the virtues of totalitarianism.) "I could not, therefore, accommodate Professor Lipparini's request—as unexpected as it was out of place—and allow the concert suddenly to take on a gala or political character [. . .]. Instead, I very gladly accepted the conciliatory proposal later formulated by the prefect of Bologna together with the deputy mayor, which they communicated to me at five in the afternoon [. . .]: when the ministers entered the theater, a band would play the national anthems in the lobby of the Comunale." This was similar to the solution used in Turin the previous year, at the time of the Philharmonic's concert there; Toscanini knew that it would again make his opinion clear. But "the conciliatory formula did not satisfy the ministers, and we were back at the earlier order; and I remained more steadfast than ever in my conviction about maintaining the commemorative character of the evening. At nine-thirty, Mr. Brianzi of the municipal administration telephoned that I could go to the theater, advising me that Their Excellencies would refrain from attending the concert. And I fell right into the ambush."

Toscanini arrived by car at the theater's stage door, together with Carla, Wanda, and Enrico Muggiani, a lawyer and family friend; Walter Toscanini had been assigned to accompany Martucci's widow to the Comunale and had already entered the theater. The maestro, on emerging from his car, found himself surrounded by a group of about twenty Fascist youths. One of them—Leo Longanesi, a young journalist and future author, editor, caricaturist, and publisher, who had coined the mindless but widely quoted phrase "Mussolini is always right"—asked Toscanini whether he would play "Giovinezza."

"No, no anthems," Toscanini replied. The Fascists began to imprecate against him; Toscanini told them to go to hell; and Longanesi hit him in the face and neck and shouted insults, including "A morte!" (Kill!), that were echoed by others in the crowd. Emilio, the chauffeur, extracted Toscanini and Muggiani from the crowd and got everyone back into the car, and two *carabinieri* (national policemen) who had been standing by in their plumed ceremonial hats, watching what was happening without intervening, finally walked over to the car and told Emilio to get going. He took his passengers back to the Hotel Brun, where they were staying.

Rumors of the attack quickly circulated inside the packed theater, where the long delay had already made the audience impatient. A functionary finally announced that the concert was being postponed because the maestro was indisposed, but many people in the auditorium began to shout, "It's not true!" Armed black-shirted guards shut the exits but were then ordered to reopen them, and the audience surged into the surrounding streets. One orchestra musician reported that there was so much commotion in the center of Bologna that a revolution seemed to have broken out.

Respighi and his wife, Elsa, were in the audience that evening; they had heard about the "Giovinezza" dispute and realized that something untoward must have happened. The alarmed couple, together with Mary Molinari, Bernardino's wife, drove to the Hotel Brun and found the maestro nursing cuts on his face and neck. He had no serious injuries (Muggiani had been somewhat more seriously hurt), but Elsa Respighi described him as like "a caged beast." Worse followed: some two hundred Fascists quickly gathered beneath Toscanini's windows, shouting insults and obscenities and threatening to hurl objects as well. Mario Ghinelli, the local party secretary, came to the hotel and asked to speak with a member of the Toscanini party. Arturo and Walter—the latter had since rejoined his family—were ruled out as negotiators because of their quick tempers; Carla went instead, but the Fascists refused to deal with a woman. Respighi then volunteered to represent the family and was told that the Toscaninis were to leave the city before sunrise, otherwise their safety could not be guaranteed. Elsa and Mary helped with the hasty packing, and the Toscaninis departed at 1:20 A.M. They arrived in Milan at sunrise.

Arpinati had phoned Mussolini immediately after the attack, and Gaetano Cesari, who was in town to report on the concerts for the *Corriere della Sera*, bribed a telephone operator to report what had been said. Cesari learned that Mussolini had said to Arpinati, "I am really happy. It will teach a good lesson to these boorish musicians." Mussolini then ordered the Milan prefecture to take away the Toscaninis' passports and to place their home under surveillance, wiretap their telephone calls, copy incoming and outgoing telegrams, and open their mail.

On the day after the Bologna incident, Toscanini sent a telegram to Mussolini:

Last evening, while going with my family to Bologna's
Teatro Comunale to carry out a kind act of friendship and
love in memory of Giuseppe Martucci (having been invited
there by the mayor of the city for a religious and artistic
commemoration, not for a gala evening), I was attacked,
injured, and repeatedly struck in the face by a contemptible
gang. The undersecretary of the interior was present in
Bologna. Not fully satisfied with this, the gang, its ranks
swollen, stood threateningly under the windows of the
Hotel Brun, where I was staying, uttering every sort of
insult and threat against me. Not only that: one of its leaders enjoined me, through Maestro Respighi, to leave the
city by six A.M., not being able to guarantee my safety otherwise. I am communicating this to Your Excellency so
that, despite the silence of the press or false information,
Your Excellency will be able to have precise news of the
deed, and so that the deed be remembered.

> *Salutations*
> *Arturo Toscanini*

Mussolini did not reply, and the Italian newspapers, all under
Fascist control, either refrained from mentioning the incident or
blamed Toscanini for it. Longanesi wrote an article for *Assalto*
(Assault), the appropriately named official newspaper of the Bologna Fascist Federation; the piece was reprinted in several papers
throughout the country. He accused Toscanini of refusing to conduct the Royal March but did not mention that the refusal grew out
of the law that the March had to be followed by "Giovinezza"; and
he claimed that Toscanini did this for reasons of musical and aesthetic purity. "As the news reports have stated, our little musician
replied to the authorities' and Fascists' invitations with a repeated,
insolent No. This was followed by a few slaps, some heckling, and
the end of an aesthetic."

Less sarcastic but equally misleading was the report in the Fascists' national daily, *Il Popolo d'Italia*:

Maestro Toscanini's inexplicable behavior met with just retaliation from the Bolognese Fascists. For some time the Maestro, like a god angry with everyone, had been showing off his attitude. Not even for the sake of propriety and courtesy could he conquer his contempt for logic and common sense. The belief that playing the national anthems would have been an offense against art is an outrage to the sensibilities of Fascists and of the Italian people. The reaction was therefore legitimate.

Libri e Moschetti (Books and Muskets), the national Fascist students' newspaper, declared that Toscanini was a "monster, not a genius," and said that the people who had attacked him ought to have "spat in his face." And according to *La Tribuna*, "A slap at the right time and place can sometimes have a salutary effect—above all, that of reconfirming, and sonorously, that the old formula of art for art's sake is not very suitable *today*."

But Toscanini was not interested in art for art's sake; he cared about art for humanity's sake. "The lesson they wanted to teach me," he wrote, "was to no avail, nor will it be to any avail in the future, for I would repeat tomorrow what I did yesterday if the same conditions prevailed in Italy or in any other part of the world."

I know perfectly well how great is the moral, political, and patriotic value of a national anthem played at the right time— and I have never refused to play that of the nation to which I belong, in any situation, so long as its moral and patriotic meaning was unmistakable. [. . .]

Am I, then, to take newspapers like the *Resto del Carlino* [Bologna] or the *Corriere della Sera* [Milan] seriously when, overnight, they replace the Hosannas to Toscanini with the Crucifixus? When they, like the *Popolo d'Italia* [Mussolini's newspaper], even find my person unsuitable for commemorating Giuseppe Martucci? And all the others that have actually called me unpatriotic? How tiny are these people, and of what little value is all this business, barely deserving of my compassion!

"The spine bends when the soul is bent." It is true. But the conduct of my life has been, is, and always will be the echo and reflection of my conscience, which does not know dissimulation or deviations of any type—reinforced, I admit, by a proud and scornful character, but clear as crystal and just as cutting—always and everywhere ready to shout the truth loudly—that truth which, as Emerson so rightly says, always comes into the world in a manger, but is rewarded by having to live until it is completely enslaved by mankind.*

The day after the incident, Toscanini received a telegram from the Bologna musicians' union, stigmatizing him for his behavior, but on the same day Adriano Ariani, a pianist and composer who had participated in the Bologna rehearsals, wrote to tell him that the message had been "sent unbeknownst to the musicians themselves, who very much want to express to you their endless devotion and their deep sorrow at not having been able to play before an audience under your direction." Ariani also mentioned that "there is general indignation among the townspeople. The financial and commercial damage is also huge. Bologna looks deserted and desolate today."

Artists and intellectuals throughout the country soon began to learn something of the incident, and the foreign press carried detailed although not always accurate accounts. Letters and telegrams of solidarity reached Toscanini from all over the world; one informer for the regime's political police estimated that the conductor received fifteen thousand such communications and stated that an extra postman had been taken on to deal with the overload. "10,000 Italians of the Paris Assembly applaud your gesture," read a message from anti-Fascist exiles in France. From Germany: "It is one year since you brought the city of Leipzig the fortune of hearing your sublime art. The Gewandhaus, always open to you, wishes to express its great affection, along with the hope of seeing you again before long." Karl

---

* Toscanini gave this handwritten account of the events of 14 May 1931 to his daughter Wally in St. Moritz, about a month after the incident had taken place; when she was about to return to Milan, he asked her to give it to a foreign newspaper correspondent there. As soon as she had reached home, however, her father phoned to tell her that he had changed his mind about having the message published. Forty years later, she allowed the musicologist Guglielmo Barblan to publish a photographic reproduction of the manuscript in his book *Toscanini e la Scala*. This proved to be fortunate: in the mid-1980s, the letter, which Wally kept in a plastic wrapper, caught fire, and nothing remains of it but tiny crumbs of scorched paper.

Kraus, the brilliant, much-feared Austrian essayist and satirist, protested the Fascists' treatment of Toscanini in his writings and in a song in which he adapted verses from Offenbach to contrast the conductor's baton with the ruffian's bludgeon. The *Manchester Guardian* commented, sardonically, that the treatment of Toscanini provided "a measure of the civilising influence of Fascism" and suggested that Toscanini's musical skill was so great that "Signor Mussolini may be afraid that he is capable of playing a certain tune which was played before the walls of Jericho."

Béla Bartók, rapidly gaining recognition as one of the most significant composers of the day, presented a protest resolution at a meeting of the UMZE (New Hungarian Music Society), expressing shock and indignation over "the grave assault that has been made on Arturo Toscanini. The Society wishes to assure him of its most wholehearted sympathy and solidarity, and salutes him with the utmost admiration." Serge Koussevitzky, who had agreed to conduct concerts at La Scala in June, canceled his engagement in protest over the affair and declared that "Maestro Toscanini does not belong only to Italy but to the whole world."

The Russian-born pianist and conductor Ossip Gabrilowitsch also canceled a scheduled conducting engagement at La Scala. He and his wife, Clara Clemens, Mark Twain's daughter, took a train from Zurich to Milan as soon as they had heard of the Bologna incident, to learn firsthand whether Toscanini was all right. They found him at work in his study, where he "greeted us most cordially and seemed spontaneously inclined to describe the entire Bologna experience," Gabrilowitsch wrote soon afterward. "He did so with undisguised indignation against the Fascist factions, which, he said, had set the trap for him. [. . .] 'I have said to our Fascisti time and again, you can kill me if you wish, but as long as I am living I shall say what I think.' [. . .] He was in no way the broken man one might have expected to see. On the contrary, he was full of dynamic energy."

Mussolini, sitting at his desk in Rome's Palazzo Venezia, was inundated with informers' reports. The following telegram is typical of those kept in his file on Toscanini; it had been sent in cipher from Milan's prefect, Fornaciari, to the Ministry of the Interior in Rome on 19 May:

Yesterday Maestro Toscanini did not leave own home stop During day telegrams and letters [were] brought to him [. . .] Following people went to visit Maestro Toscanini Dr. Ravagio family doctor, Maestro [Vittorio] Vanzo [a conductor under whom Toscanini had played in Parma nearly fifty years earlier], Maestro Mario Castelnuovo Tedesco, Signor [Raffaele] Calzini [journalist and friend], Maestro Giordano [. . .] stop Inform that [the following] have been identified and have confessed having taken part in group that shouted "Viva Toscanini" the other evening in front of the same's residence Giovanni Bodrone, Ernesto; Missiroli, Roberto; Gilli, Carlo; Ferticucci, Carlo; Giovanardi, Eugenio; Arienti, Lodovico; and Valcarenghi, Aldo,* all students [. . .] stop Yesterday evening during symphony concert Teatro alla Scala at end of the first part several youths in top Gallery shouted "Viva Toscanini" greeted by long applause noteworthy part of public filling theater stop Through prearranged [police] forces nine individuals were quickly stopped [and] identified as those responsible stop These for the most part confessed [and] are being held pending further checks stop Meanwhile several hundred Fascists gathered before said theater [and] with singing of "Giovinezza" headed toward [Toscanini's house in] Via Durini where they put on demonstration hostile toward Maestro Toscanini stop Prearranged forces [of] public order were able to avert attempted invasion building stop [. . .]

A dossier held by the chief of the political police in Rome demonstrates the extent of the government's worry over the Bologna incident's repercussions. The file preserves over one hundred reports, all unsigned, from informers in ten Italian cities and in France, Germany, and Switzerland, as well as requests from the Interior Ministry to local prefects for information on individuals known to have been politically sympathetic toward Toscanini.

---

* Aldo, an ardent anti-Fascist, was the son of Renzo Valcarenghi, codirector of the Ricordi company. He was given a three-year prison sentence for participating in pro-Toscanini demonstrations and for distributing literature published by Giustizia e Libertà, an underground organization of the noncommunist left. The Germans sent him to Mauthausen concentration camp during the war, but he survived.

[ROME, 15 MAY] This morning a rumor has been spread [. . .], especially in foreign press circles, that Maestro Toscanini has been
manhandled by the Fascists. The wildest conjectures have been
made [. . .].

[MILAN, 16 MAY] [Toscanini] has always had everything from his
country: awards, honors, celebrations, offerings, praise from the
press. If Toscanini acts this way, what should those people do
who have suffered injustice, sorrow, slander, never an act of recognition? [. . .] Those responsible will do what is necessary, so that
the Maestro will talk about us [Fascists] as little as possible.

Another report from Milan, also on 16 May, noted that the Toscanini incident was the only thing people were talking about. A Fascist
general, Carlo Porro, opined that Toscanini's refusal was "more the
cowardly deed of a thoroughly cowardly person than a political
action. But that's not how it is seen in the city's cafés," the informer
continued. "At the Campari, [one man] told me that we need 100
Toscaninis in Italy, or rather in Milan, and that there are thousands
and thousands who see things Toscanini's way but don't have the
courage to say so." And another unsuspecting person told the
informer that "Toscanini's action in Bologna was an occasion for
great jubilation, because it is interpreted as a big-gun intellectual's
show of contempt toward the Regime. In reality, [he said], the intellectuals are all against the Regime [. . .] but they are fearful, like the
bourgeoisie. The fact that Toscanini actually said NO to Ciano and
Arpinati emboldens vast numbers of people who hope that others
will repeat the gesture."

The following day, various Fascist leaders, including the popular
air marshal Italo Balbo,* surrounded Arpinati in Italy's parliament
building, to hear more details. Arpinati said that he had wanted to
have Toscanini arrested, but "the Duce, reached by telephone,
replied that the matter should be dropped." In Naples, another
informer reported, the Bologna incident "has aroused unanimous
disdain and disapproval in all circles, even in the most markedly Fascist circles. The slap given the great, elderly conductor by an anony-

---

* Seven years later, Balbo would be the only high-ranking Fascist to oppose, openly,
Mussolini's anti-Semitic "Racial Laws" and the alliance with Nazi Germany.

mous, third-rate hero is considered a mad, reprehensible gesture, and the solidarity of *Popolo d'Italia* with so vulgar an act of hooliganism is spoken of with unanimous harshness."

And the reports continued to flow:

[MILAN, 21 MAY] From now on, the cries of Viva Toscanini! will have to be understood as Down with Fascism! This is absolutely not the moment for either slaps or beatings. It is urgent that many leaders in Milan be changed in order to attempt a Fascist reconstruction; otherwise (in Milan) there may be some nasty surprises.

[PARIS, 23 MAY] Newspapers of every political leaning have given [. . .] prominence to the act of the Bolognese Fascists. There have been many comments in Parisian artistic circles, which, of course, side with the musician.

[MILAN, 27 MAY] [. . .] a demonstration [at La Scala] of solidarity with Maestro Toscanini [. . .] provoked some reaction in the souls of many Fascists, especially the students who belong to the GUF [Fascist University Groups]. Thus, on the evening of Friday 22 May, seventy of them trickled in [to La Scala]. Their admission was paid by the [Fascist] Federation and the GUF. [. . .] I have just learned that the GUF's Directorate has met to discuss initiating a series of punitive expeditions, because the spread of anti-Fascist propaganda, which is carried out especially in the bosom of certain intellectual circles, can no longer be tolerated.

[MILAN, 27 MAY] Anti-Fascists are indignant toward the perpetrators who manhandled Toscanini and friends in Bologna, and toward Prof. Bruno [of the Milanese police headquarters] for having caused terror and despair in many Milanese families as a result of the arrests he ordered for students from the Liceo Berchet. [. . .] Those of our young people who committed the grave crime of applauding Arturo Toscanini on his return from Bologna, in a moment of fanatical enthusiasm for him, ought at most to have been given a spanking [. . .]; but to have turned our houses upside down, searching for documents attesting to a criminal organization against the Fascist State and the Duce, and then to have taken these young people away from us, and even to have sent some of them to prison—believe me, this is the best system for creating real anti-Fascism and for creating martyrs cheaply. [. . .] [Regarding a demonstration against Toscanini:] When the demonstration had moved into Piazza della Scala, the most hot-headed participants shouted, "What does Toscanini do? He makes us sick! What is Toscanini? A pederast! What is Toscanini's wife? A whore! What is Toscanini's daughter? A whore!" This dialogue caused real indignation among those present. Many asked themselves whether this is the Fascist style of the new generations.

On 22 May, one day before his scheduled debut with the Vienna Philharmonic, Toscanini officially canceled the engagement "for reasons of health." In the meantime, more reports reached Mussolini's police, especially from Germany, where Toscanini had become a musical hero. "The Scala in Milan as a Police Detention Camp," read a headline in the *Berliner Zeitung am Mittag*, with the subhead, in quotation marks: "'Those who are for Toscanini will be arrested.'" The Ullstein News Agency in Berlin reported that students at the Bologna Conservatory had staged a demonstration in Toscanini's favor, and that a group of Fascists had attacked them; the police had arrested the anti-Fascist students. A Leipzig newspaper, the *Neueste Nachrichten*, published a resolution by the Association of German Stagecrafts Workers, stating that its members were honored "to belong to the same field of endeavor as this great Italian and citizen of the world, and wish to express the hope that Toscanini may soon be free to pursue his work, which belongs to the greatest gifts of our age."

In New York, the attack against Toscanini was front-page news day after day, and there were widespread declarations of solidarity. "I know I am expressing the sentiments of the great masses of labor when I state that they resent the humiliating treatment to which Toscanini was subjected by misguided individuals who [. . .] had been influenced by the philosophy of the autocratic political authority which controls Italy," said William Green, president of the American Federation of Labor. Similar statements were issued by Joseph Schlossberg, general secretary of the Amalgamated Clothing Workers of America; the presidents of Yale and Harvard Universities and the University of Chicago; and by the philosopher and educational reformer John Dewey, who said, simply, "The Toscanini episode is a disgrace."

Worst of all for Mussolini, who cared a great deal about how his policies were perceived abroad, was an editorial that appeared in the *New York Times* on 16 June, a full month after the Bologna incident, under the headline "TOSCANINI OUT OF ITALY." The editorial stated that "a trap was laid to punish the conductor for his obstinacy" and that Toscanini was "made virtually a prisoner" in Milan. It continued,

> Italian officials near MUSSOLINI, doubtless realizing the embarrassing position into which they had put themselves, attempted to extort from the conductor a statement apologetic to the Fascist Government. It was also intimated that to get his passports back TOSCANINI had only to say that he intended no offense toward the Fascists, though from the beginning he had made every effort to avoid the political issue [. . .]. In the end the authorities gave in.
>
> TOSCANINI has been too independent to please the existing régime. It may be said that he might have been more tactful. But if he had, he would not have been TOSCANINI. The Fascists chose to forget that TOSCANINI played the Marcia Reale at the front, during the war, and received from the Italian Government the silver medal for valor in the zone of battle. They forget or do not know that TOSCANINI'S espousal of the cause of Italian composers in America has caused him to be much criticized for giving them an excessive share of his programs. But the world does not forget, and there are millions of Italians who must remain silent and ashamed at this violation of a long and proud artistic tradition.

What was Mussolini to do? To allow Toscanini to express himself freely made fascism look bad, but to have him killed would have made the regime look even worse. The prime minister decided to let the incident's repercussions wane on their own.

8.

ARTURO AND CARLA HAD ALREADY LEFT ITALY AND WERE RESTING at the Villa Chantarella, above St. Moritz, in the Swiss Engadine, by the time the *New York Times* editorial appeared. They had arrived on 10 June, and they spent two weeks at the resort, trying to put the previous month's events behind them. Even at 6,000 feet above sea level, and in the shadow of the 13,000-foot Piz Bernina, Toscanini was observed by an informer, who sent utterly inconsequential information to Rome. The maestro took long walks in the flower-filled meadows, enjoyed the views of the snow-capped Alps, received visits from Pizzetti and the writer Emil Ludwig, and studied, often at the piano, until two or three o'clock in the morning, preparing for the huge task that awaited him in Germany.

The Toscaninis arrived in Bayreuth by car on the evening of 23 June. Winifred Wagner greeted them and took them to their rooms in Villa Wahnfried. "The whole musical world is listening and waiting for *Parsival* [sic], which will blossom in newfound beauty under Toscanini's baton," the *Berliner Montagspost* declared. "A legion of music directors, singers, and various musicians already find themselves in Bayreuth and will be eavesdropping on the rehearsals, which form the most instructive part of the festival." A few days later, Carla wrote to Elsa Respighi that "in a few rehearsals he has already read through both operas"—*Tannhäuser* as well as *Parsifal*. "He is very happy with the orchestra, which is much improved this year, and he has found serenity and tranquillity in his work."

Carla soon departed for a spa at Marienbad, across the border in Czechoslovakia, while Toscanini moved into what the Wagner family called the "bachelor house." Friedelind, thirteen at the time and nicknamed Mausi, later recalled, "Every morning [Toscanini] took his breakfast on the little glass-enclosed balcony which got the full sun and was so hot that Wieland"—her fifteen-year-old brother—"named it 'Toscanini's Turkish bath.' But the Maestro loved the sun. He was one of the most pleasant guests we ever entertained, the maids adored him because he liked his meals and gave them no trouble. He kept his own car and chauffeur and never upset the household routine with demands for service. Toscanini was amused by my candid remarks. 'You are so fonnee,' he used to tell me between chuckles." (Friedelind already spoke fluent English.) "On days when there were no rehearsals or performances we sometimes drove to inns up in the mountains for tea, visited the beauty spots of Franconia or just drove about in the pleasant summer afternoons."

Despite the good start to rehearsals and the delightful times that Toscanini spent with Friedelind and her siblings, the 1931 festival would prove to be exceedingly difficult. Winifred, hoping to strengthen her position as head of the organization, the opposition of her sisters-in-law notwithstanding, had engaged Heinz Tietjen, a powerful Berlin-based theater administrator, as Bayreuth's artistic director, and Furtwängler as music director. To Toscanini, Tietjen was a largely unknown quantity; about Furtwängler, Toscanini was puzzled that he had not been informed in advance of the appointment but pleased by the appointment itself, because he knew Furtwängler to be capable. The German conductor was responsible for *Tristan* that summer and had arrived in Bayreuth about a week prior to Toscanini, who had sent him a telegram: "Before you begin your first rehearsal in Bayreuth I feel a warm impulse to send my friendly greetings to you and my best regards to the gentlemen of the orchestra." Liselotte Schmidt, Winifred's young secretary, wrote to her parents, on 18 June, that Toscanini's message had been a noble gesture toward Furtwängler, and since, in addition, the entire Wagner clan was positively impressed with Furtwängler's approach to *Tristan*, "Wini is happy that the first days have been so promising and are proceeding so harmoniously!" Schmidt also described Furtwängler as "very simple, natural, without pose and presumption (one can only hold against him that he brought along the loathsome Geissmar [his secretary-manager], a devilishly shrewd and clever 100 percent Jewess!")—which demonstrates one of the prevailing attitudes in Wagnerian Bayreuth.

Schmidt attended Toscanini's first rehearsal and was present "at the moment when he entered the rehearsal room and was festively greeted and applauded by the orchestra. He cannot be compared with any other musician at Bayreuth, so high does he stand above the others, despite their masterly performances. One can only say he is a saint, or as Frau [Eva] Chamberlain put it, 'a priest of art.'" On

1 July, however, Schmidt wrote that although Toscanini was "a love, a real angel," he was also "making a lot of difficulties over the cast."

These were not whims on his part. "The disaster here is that one can never have a whole ensemble for the rehearsals," he wrote to Carla. "The singers come when they please [. . .]. I was supposed to have had my first ensemble rehearsal for Parsifal today, but I vehemently declined, since I haven't heard the singers *even individually.*" When he finally heard Henny Trundt, who was to have sung the part of Kundry, he refused to accept her and had Elisabeth Ohms—his Scala Kundry—brought in to replace her. Herbert Janssen and Gotthold Ditter, who were to sing Amfortas and Klingsor, respectively, "haven't yet arrived," he said. "I'll probably agree to rehearse the third act tomorrow, Monday, afternoon, because the lady [Kundry] doesn't sing in it* [. . .], and I'll make do with *that French woman,*" Marcelle Bunlet, who alternated in the role with Ohms and Maria Rösler-Keuschnigg. Bunlet "seems very intelligent and a quick learner. I rehearsed Tannhäuser, too, without [Maria] Müller and [Sigismund] Pilinsky, who was ill"—both had sung their roles with him the previous year—"and while awaiting Melchior. In short, much patience is needed, and that's not precisely my forte. The other evening I was at dinner when they came to announce the first Parsifal ensemble rehearsal; that was the end of the dinner, of course, and I relieved my hunger by taking an automobile ride to calm my nerves."

There were compensations. Liselotte Schmidt wrote, on 7 July, that as the space in Winifred's car "was somewhat tight, I had to ride home all alone with Tosca"—which is what the Wagners called Toscanini among themselves; to his face they called him Maestro. The ride with Liselotte "made him as happy as a lark," she continued. He complimented her beautiful eyes, and when she said the same words ("*begli occhi*") to him, he "caressed me very gently," she said. Some days later, reporting on a dinner at the festival restaurant: "The Maestro and I again frequently 'made eyes' at each other!!" This was Fräulein Schmidt's last reference to her flirtation with Toscanini, which means that it either ended or became a matter that she chose not to write home about.

---

* Kundry is onstage for much of the third act, but she sings only "Dienen, dienen" (To serve, to serve), early in the act, and is then silent.

Tannhäuser opened on 16 July, and six days later Toscanini conducted his first Bayreuth performance of *Parsifal*. Melchior found Toscanini's *Parsifal* interpretation "too slow and dull." In fact, the maestro's performance of the first act clocked in at a little over two hours, the slowest in Bayreuth history. But the *New York Times* critic Herbert F. Peyser hyperbolically declared that Toscanini's approach "makes history" and "is perhaps the most intimate and unsparingly searching revelation of Toscanini's soul that any music has ever made." Eva Chamberlain, deeply moved by Toscanini's interpretation, gave the maestro Wagner's manuscript of the "Porazzi Theme," which was connected to both *Tristan* and *Parsifal*.

The eighty-three-year-old Baron Hans Paul von Wolzogen, a Wagner disciple who had been present at the premiere of *Parsifal* under Hermann Levi's baton and Wagner's direct supervision, wrote an emotional letter to Toscanini, praising his performance of Wagner's final opera. Toscanini replied, "No word of praise could be dearer and more desirable than yours. If my interpretation has been able to reawaken in you an echo of that memorable one of 1882, it is the most I could aspire to in the fulfillment of my ideal dream—that is, to come as close as possible to expressing the composer's thoughts. You, friend of that Great Man and faithful and wise popularizer of his ideas, could not give me a greater reward.—Your praise has moved me deeply and I thank you with all my heart."

Toscanini's right shoulder, however, which had been bothering him intermittently since the previous fall, now began to cause serious pain.* At times the agony of conducting caused tears to run down his face, and he often had to resort to using only his left arm. During performance intermissions a heat lamp was beamed onto the shoulder, and a friend who visited him in his dressing room witnessed him "screaming with pain." Late in life, Toscanini recalled that he had never in his life suffered comparable physical agony; the march in *Tannhäuser* during one performance was the worst moment, he said. He underwent daily therapy at a local hospital, and he wrote to Carla that every day "the doctor asks me whether I feel any

---

* He had been X-rayed in Milan after the Bologna incident and had undergone some sort of treatment, but to no avail.

improvement (it's clear that he thinks there should be some after even a few days), and he is surprised that this isn't the case."

Toscanini's physical pain was only one among many problems within the festival that summer. Tietjen, who was quickly becoming de facto director, did not like to share power with Furtwängler and did everything he could to create dissension between the conductor and Siegfried's widow.* Toscanini was not involved in the festival's administration, but since he was Bayreuth's "star" he undoubtedly had some notion of what was going on behind the scenes. He did not dislike Winifred—Friedelind believed that he found her buxom mother, who was thirty-three at the time, physically attractive—and he got along well with Furtwängler: the two conductors attended each other's rehearsals and met frequently to discuss musical and technical issues, on which they generally agreed. Furtwängler's *Tristan* interpretation, although very different from Toscanini's of the preceding year, was by all accounts hugely successful, and no trace of any negative reaction from Toscanini has been discovered. They also agreed that Tietjen was a master of intrigue and a creator of discord.

Another of the festival's difficulties that year was financial—a result of the deepening worldwide economic depression. Many foreign visitors, including American Wagnerites and Toscanini admirers, canceled their reservations, and inns, restaurants, and tourist attractions in the area cut their prices in the hope of attracting more people. There were swaths of empty seats at Elmendorff's performances of the *Ring*; fortunately, however, Furtwängler's and Toscanini's performances sold out, and by the end of the festival overall attendance had actually increased by more than 8 percent over the previous year.

A memorial concert for Siegfried Wagner, scheduled for 4 August—the first anniversary of his death—caused yet more trouble. The plans called for Toscanini to begin with Wagner's "Faust" Overture, Elmendorff to continue with the *Siegfried Idyll* and music by Liszt, and Furtwängler to conclude with the "Eroica" Symphony. But the program was communicated to Toscanini as a fait accompli;

---

* By the terms of Siegfried's will, Winifred would lose her directorship of the festival if she remarried; she and Tietjen became lovers but never married.

he believed that he, as the senior conductor (he was nineteen years older than Furtwängler and twenty-four years older than Elmendorff), ought to have been part of the selection process, but he was too proud to complain.

Of the several extant accounts of the ensuing episode, Furtwängler's—written in the third person—rings truest. At the prearranged time for Toscanini's working rehearsal of the overture, the orchestra parts

could not be found; and, typical of the prevailing atmosphere, two highly agitated répétiteurs [music coaches] appeared at Furtwängler's apartment, with the singular contention that he must have the parts. Only later were the parts found, in a cupboard in Toscanini's Bayreuth apartment, where his servant had stowed them. For this reason, Toscanini's rehearsal could only begin 35 minutes later than scheduled. After Toscanini had rehearsed the Faust Overture for 5/4 [sic] of an hour, Furtwängler spoke with him again and emphasized that both he and Elmendorf[f] would gladly schedule all their pieces after him, and that above all he should not feel that he had to rush his rehearsal in any way. At the final rehearsal, too—to which only the artists' friends and relatives were admitted—he would be able to stop and to rehearse as much as he liked. Shortly after the beginning of the final rehearsal, the regrettable incident occurred: Toscanini lost his temper because of a small error in the cellos, who declared that he had been beating in eight at the previous rehearsal but was now beating in four. He broke his baton and left the podium in a huff. All the pains that Furtwängler took thereafter to persuade him to continue the rehearsal were fruitless; and in the evening, too, he did not appear on the podium.

The result of this incident was a serious rebellion on the orchestra's part, and only with great difficulty did Furtwängler then manage, in the end, to induce the orchestra to play the rest of Toscanini's performances.

After having told Furtwängler, who had run after him, that he would not participate in the performance, Toscanini had Emilio drive him into the mountains, where he spent the afternoon. In the evening, while the concert was taking place without him, he placed flowers on Siegfried's grave.

Yet by all published accounts, Toscanini's remaining Bayreuth performances were as magnificent as the previous ones—so much so that the music critics of Germany's right-wing newspapers found themselves having to excogitate addenda to claptrap Nazi racial theories to explain how an Italian could conduct Wagner so well. According to the *Chemnitzer Tageblatt und Anzeiger*'s Paul Pretzsch, for instance, Toscanini's conducting was "echt wagnerisch," authentically Wagnerian, to such a degree that an unsuspecting listener would never have realized that the conductor was not German. "No one has ever surpassed Toscanini in depth of respect for Richard Wagner's work and in the accuracy and beauty of the performance of these scores." Pretzsch hypothesized that this was because Toscanini was a northern Italian and pointed out that "the great intermixing of Nordic blood in northern Italy has often been stressed by race researchers even in our own day." It therefore followed that . . . and so on and so forth. Where this article and Germany were going was quite clear.

The atmosphere had changed since Siegfried's death. In taking leave of Daniela Thode and Eva Chamberlain on 20 August, the day after his last performance, Toscanini said that he had sent back, unread, a letter that Winifred had had delivered to him, as well as her gift of a Wagner manuscript—a draft of the Flower Maiden scene from *Parsifal*. He had written to thank her for her hospitality, he said, but he had added that he was deeply disillusioned with Bayreuth and would not return in 1933.* He had come to Bayreuth as if to a temple, he remarked, but had found himself in an ordinary theater.

Bayreuth was both: a temple to Wagner's family and his most fervent followers, who believed that the composer's work and weltanschauung had a world-historical significance similar to that of a major religion; an ordinary theater insofar as its day-to-day artistic, financial, and organizational life resembled that of other opera houses. The combination had always been potentially explosive, but the explosion had been postponed as long as Richard, Cosima, and

---

* Nineteen thirty-two was to be a sabbatical year for the festival.

Siegfried Wagner had reigned. With all three gone, and with the oldest of Siegfried's children only fifteen, the Festspielhaus had no obvious heir apparent. Frau Thode and Frau Chamberlain could not forgive Winifred for excluding them from the festival's administration after Siegfried's death, and they saw Toscanini's withdrawal not only as a disaster in itself but also as a direct result of their sister-in-law's newfangled, if not downright sacrilegious, methods.

Frau Chamberlain sent Tietjen a list of complaints that she claimed to have heard Toscanini make during the festival—a list that, to her way of thinking, was nothing less than a *j'accuse* against Winifred and Tietjen himself. But in her attempt to discredit their management, she blurred the line between Toscanini's reasonable demands and his whims. The festival administration had not consulted with him regarding the choice of other conductors to be engaged, she said; the announcement that Furtwängler would be made music director was ill timed; Toscanini had not been notified that Frieda Leider had canceled her participation; he had not been informed that the Ullstein news agency's photographer had been given permission to enter a private rehearsal at his residence; his remarks to Alexander Spring, the stage manager, about "mistakes" in the staging had gone unheeded; the program of the memorial concert had been determined without his participation; he had not been given enough time to rehearse the "Faust" Overture and had been offended when no "objective clarifications" about the event were offered by the administration in response to the subsequent "slanderous" press attacks against him. Finally, Frau Chamberlain noted that "Toscanini was profoundly hurt that my sister-in-law *never* said a word to him during an intermission or after a performance, [and] he especially and most crucially regretted the lack of this personal touch after the last performance of *Parsifal*. He said bitterly, 'Even if there was no spontaneous impulse to do so, courtesy at least demanded it.'"

Tietjen admitted that mistakes had been made by all concerned, but he added that despite his "boundless admiration for the Maestro," Toscanini was partly to blame. By sending back Winifred's letter and gift, he said, Toscanini had "deeply wounded" Winifred's honor. Frau Thode answered that she already knew perfectly well what had happened to Winifred on the last day of Toscanini's stay, and she implied that she didn't care a rap.

Furtwängler claimed innocence in the entire matter—and he was probably right, except that he never mentioned the exclusion of Toscanini from the selection of the memorial concert program. He wrote that personal relations between himself and Toscanini were "always as good as they could imaginably have been," that Toscanini had been satisfied with Furtwängler's choice of orchestra musicians, and that he (Furtwängler) repeatedly attempted to change Toscanini's mind about returning to Bayreuth, even going so far as to visit him in Switzerland, but "unfortunately to no avail."

Winifred was just as determined as her sisters-in-law to bring Toscanini back to Bayreuth, especially since Furtwängler, the festival's other star, was likewise threatening to withdraw as a result of his antipathy to Tietjen. Tietjen, too, had a great deal of prestige to gain by persuading Toscanini to return—and nothing to lose, because Toscanini, unlike Furtwängler, represented no threat to Tietjen's potential administrative sovereignty. All of the Bayreuth factions concurred that it was best to leave Toscanini alone until he returned to Europe from his forthcoming season with the New York Philharmonic.

In October, however, before Toscanini left for America, the Bayreuthers found themselves locked in public combat with him. First, Max Smith, Toscanini's American journalist friend, made public (with the maestro's approval) the conductor's remark to Winifred Wagner about having left an "ordinary theater." Then the German newspapers picked up a report in the English-language press, according to which Toscanini had declared that he would never again conduct at Bayreuth, where "Wagner was degraded by Hitler's propagandists." This was an extremely controversial statement in Germany in 1931.

Tietjen begged Frau Thode to ask Toscanini to make a public denial of the statements. Toscanini, however, had indeed made the remarks that the press had picked up, although the political comment had been leaked without his approval. Most of the "Bayreuth Wagners" had been Nazis or at least pro-Nazi virtually from the party's inception, and Hitler had written part of *Mein Kampf* on Bayreuth stationery that Winifred had given to the future Führer when he was incarcerated following the unsuccessful Munich beer hall putsch in 1923.

Through Smith, Toscanini made another press statement, in which he said that he was sorry that his remark had been published, but did not deny having made it. "I must stress that I never tie art to politics, which don't concern me at all, either in my own country or in foreign countries," he said; "for I feel that every person has the freedom to believe as he will. When I left Bayreuth, I only expressed to Frau Wagner, in a letter, my deep bitterness over the artistic disillusionment I experienced in the theater that I had believed to be a temple of art."

This may have mollified the unobservant, but Tietjen, for one, was not satisfied. Such was the power that Toscanini's name wielded in the musical world of the day that, in October, Tietjen dispatched Frau Thode to Milan, in the hope that she would persuade Toscanini to provide a written retraction of his earlier statements. But, as she wrote afterward to Tietjen, "I did not achieve what you so much wanted."

9.

THE SHOULDER PROBLEM WAS BECOMING INCREASINGLY ACUTE IN the late summer of 1931. From Bayreuth, Toscanini had gone home to Milan and then to the Istituto Codivilla at Belluno, where Dr. Vittorio Putti, a famous orthopedic surgeon, examined him and made an elastic frame that allowed Toscanini to use the arm when he needed it but let it relax at other times. The doctor also advised him to undergo a mud bath cure at the thermal springs in Baden, Switzerland, which, he said, had helped the similarly afflicted Richard Strauss. Toscanini made the journey, and at first the cure, together with rest, seemed to have the desired effect. He also spent about a week with the Busches at their home in Riehen, near Basel, to go over the Bach A minor and the Beethoven Violin Concertos with Adolf, who would be his soloist in New York the following month. And he attended a concert in Zurich in which Busch played the same Bach concerto with Volkmar Andreae and the Tonhalle Orchestra.

In Milan, Toscanini studied for his forthcoming American season, which was to begin with a two-week guest engagement with the

Philadelphia Orchestra, continue with eight weeks of New York Philharmonic concerts, and conclude, after a winter break, with eight more weeks in New York. According to the terms of the contract that he had signed the previous March, he would be paid $110,000* for a maximum of sixty concerts, and the Philharmonic would continue to pay his income tax and two round-trip first-class steamship fares.

By mid-October, however, Toscanini had realized that his arm was not yet ready to resume its task. He canceled his Philadelphia engagement, which gave a wonderful opportunity to Jenö Blau, a thirty-one-year-old Hungarian-born violinist-conductor who had changed his name, in the United States, to Eugene Ormandy, and who took over Toscanini's concerts, thereby initiating a long and fruitful relationship with the orchestra. Toscanini then decided to postpone his New York duties as well, if only by a week, and Kleiber, who was leading the first part of the Philharmonic's season, arranged to prolong his stay in order to fill in for his older colleague. Toscanini finally arrived in New York on 16 November, aboard the *Europa* out of Cherbourg. "Disembarked very late yesterday evening," he cabled Carla; she was in Paris with Wally and Emanuele Castelbarco, who had finally been able to marry earlier that year. "Arm still painful. Affectionately Arturo."

Carla had written to Zirato to ask that he and the Philharmonic do everything possible to ensure that Toscanini would not be subjected to political demonstrations, whether pro- or anti-Fascist; Zirato, who had friends across the Italian American political spectrum, reported to Judson that "both parties were absolutely absent from the pier" when Toscanini arrived. Dino Grandi, Italy's minister of foreign affairs, was visiting New York at the time, and during a performance at the Metropolitan Opera he—along with thousands of others in the auditorium—was showered with slips of paper that carried the message, "Mussolini and his black shirts do not represent the spirit of Italy. Viva ARTURO TOSCANINI." Zirato saw to it that no demonstration would take place in Carnegie Hall before, during, or after Toscanini's first concert, on 26 November. The maestro was

---

* Counted on a per-service (rehearsal or performance) basis, $110,000 amounted to roughly eighty times the average Philharmonic musician's earnings at the time.

taken into the building through a door on Seventh Avenue rather than the stage entrance on West Fifty-Sixth Street, and "three plain clothes men mingled with the standees on the parquet floor and six in the Dress Circle and Balcony," Zirato reported. "No incident whatsoever happened either at the arrival or during the concert, but at the end of the concert when Maestro was called out to respond to the acclaims of the public, a couple of thousand slips were thrown from the Balcony into the Parquet floor." Some of them bore the same message as the one that had been thrown at Grandi; others said simply, "Long Live the Great Maestro ARTURO TOSCANINI." The detectives caught two of the slip throwers and brought them to Judson, who let them go with a reprimand. "Maestro Toscanini received his friends and admirers in his dressing-room after the concert, and we had three detectives standing at the landing on the first floor just before his dressing-room. [. . .] I was particularly careful not to have him understand we took such preventive measures of protection, and I am glad to report that he did not notice last night either the detectives around him or at the entrance doors."

Before his first week of rehearsals and concerts, Toscanini had allowed himself a week to acclimatize and relax, dining with friends and even attending—together with Kleiber, Schelling, Adolf and Frieda Busch, and Busch's accompanist Hubert Giesen—a Town Hall recital by a fifteen-year-old violin prodigy named Guila Bustabo. He also attended a recital given by Busch and Giesen at the Pereras' home and a Carnegie Hall recital by Fritz Kreisler, at the end of which Toscanini and Rachmaninoff both remained to hear all four of Kreisler's encores.

Toscanini's first program included the Bach and Beethoven violin concertos that he and Busch had studied together in Basel. Afterward, Busch wrote to Rudolf Serkin,

I haven't felt so terrific as I do now for a long time. [. . .] The maestro projects a tremendous calm, because he doesn't make any "fuss" at all—I think that is probably the main reason for it, shows incredible concentration even in rehearsals. [. . .] He always makes music as though he were performing in a concert. [. . .] You play with the proper dynamics because you understand immediately what he wants. The only thing that has to be "studied"—paradoxical as it seems—is the "expression"—and *that* to his extreme annoyance. He doesn't want anything written in the parts, preferring that you play it out of your own feeling. He certainly doesn't *tell* you how. But he curses when someone doesn't understand and feel what he wants from his movements. "It seems to me you don't like this music! Don't play, *sing!*"—and everybody freezes. All of this work is wonderful. And something altogether extraordinary.

In mid-December, Busch, Toscanini, and the Philharmonic took the same program on tour to Philadelphia, Washington, and Baltimore. Not only did First Lady Lou Hoover and Supreme Court Chief Justice Charles Evans Hughes attend Toscanini's Washington concert; Italy's Ambassador De Martino and his wife once again hosted a dinner for him after that performance, notwithstanding the Bologna incident and its aftermath. Yet on the day following that concert Toscanini drafted a cable message to Senator Francesco Ruffini, a leading Italian jurist and a law professor at the University of Turin: "Deeply moved I embrace you and your illustrious university colleagues for your proud and noble behavior stop the backbone bends when the soul is bent. Greetings. Arturo Toscanini." Ruffini was one of only twelve university professors in all of Italy who had refused to sign the oath of fidelity to fascism that Mussolini had recently demanded. Toscanini wanted to show his solidarity with Ruffini, but he was advised that by sending his message he might endanger the senator's already precarious position; he refrained.

New intercontinental radio hookups allowed Toscanini's family in Italy to hear some of his broadcast performances. After one of them, he cabled Carla that he was "overjoyed" to know that she could listen, but he felt it was "impossible" for him to continue his work with his arm "in such bad condition." And indeed by early December he found that he had to conduct portions of his rehearsals and concerts using only his left arm, which did not bode well for the rest of the season. At Mackay's insistence, he visited a doctor at the Rockefeller Institute and was given a number of unsuccessful diathermy treatments. The pain became so intolerable that on 8 December the Philharmonic announced that Toscanini would end his engagement three weeks early in order to continue treatments on his arm in Italy and then return at the end of February. On 23 December, Toscanini, together with Adolf and Frieda Busch and their daughter, Irene, sailed for Europe aboard the *Albert Ballin*.

Before Toscanini's departure, someone had brought to his attention a letter published in *Il Progresso*, a New York–based Italian-language newspaper: a woman who had been suffering from a debilitating form of arthritis claimed to have been cured by a Dr. Alberto Rinaldi in a tiny Tuscan village. By then, Toscanini was willing to try anything, and so, in January 1932, after having seen a doctor in Rome and a radiologist in Florence, he had Emilio drive him to Piazze, in the southeastern corner of the province of Siena, where he stayed in a small room in a village inn. This *pensione*, according to another Rinaldi patient, was a three-story building "with a sometimes workable toilet on each floor and washbasins in the bedrooms that could only be filled with a pitcher of cold water"— a setup quite different from Toscanini's suite at the Astor in New York. But he accepted it uncomplainingly, made friends with the Salvadori family, who owned the inn, and flirted with the owners' pretty young daughters.

Dr. G. Valerio, the radiologist in Florence, had informed Rinaldi that the maestro's right shoulder "shows significant signs of old periostitis"—inflammation of the tissue near a bone—"at the humeral connections of the deltoid muscle, and of progressive arthritis of the clavicular acromion joint." Rinaldi examined Toscanini, prescribed daily injections of a special serum, and predicted a complete recovery. "It seems a very bestial cure to everybody, but Toscanini is doing it with great enthusiasm," Carla wrote to Zirato on 23 January. To his amazement, Toscanini began to feel some improvement almost immediately; nevertheless, he warned the Philharmonic that he would not be able to return in time for the first concerts of his second series. He got along famously with Rinaldi, a firm anti-Fascist, and he liked the fact that Rinaldi did not give him preferential treatment but continued to treat his poor patients exactly the same as the rich and famous ones who, upon learning that Toscanini was taking the country doctor seriously, flocked to Piazze.

In the end, the treatments lasted three months and prevented Toscanini from fulfilling his Philharmonic obligations for the rest of the season. He had intended to conduct the world premiere of *Maria Egiziaca*, Respighi's new opera, in a concert version with the Philharmonic in March; that task was now left to Respighi himself. Judson, Zirato, and the orchestra's board feared that Toscanini's prolonged absence would harm their subscription campaign for the following season, because rumors that the maestro's condition was incurable were rife, and because a chain of calamities was besetting the Philharmonic: the guest conductor Bruno Walter was in a state of depression because one of his daughters had had to undergo an operation for a stomach tumor; Sir Thomas Beecham, who was taking over some of Toscanini's concerts, fell off the podium during a rehearsal, fracturing a bone in his foot; the concertmaster, Mishel Piastro, who earlier in the season had fallen onstage and injured his hands, now broke two ribs in an automobile accident; and the worsening economic depression was throwing the very existence of the Philharmonic into doubt.

Toscanini, whose arm and shoulder were feeling better and better, and who was aware of the crisis caused by his absence, decided to make an extraordinary gesture: he would undertake the long voyage to America, at his own expense and with no fee, to conduct a single concert for the benefit of musicians who had lost their jobs in the Depression. He had already sent a gift of $1,000 to the Musicians' Emergency Aid organization, and on 20 March he cabled the Philharmonic's board, "With all my heart I am at the disposal of the board of directors of the Philharmonic-Symphony Society for this good cause. I will sail on the *Ile-de-France* April 19. I have just completed my cure with wonderful results."

He arrived on the twenty-fifth in a New York reeling from the effects of the Depression; he affably said hello—but not much more—to the reporters who came aboard in the hope of interviewing him, and he held his first rehearsal that afternoon. The following day, he wrote to Judson that he had learned that the entire orchestra and administrative staff had agreed to "make a donation," in the form of 10 percent pay cuts, to help alleviate the crisis, and he gave orders to have $10,000 deducted from his salary of $110,000 for the following season; if he conducted concerts beyond the contractual number of sixty, the per-concert payment would be reduced proportionally. He was not paid for the part of the current season that he had missed.

The special concert, which took place at Carnegie Hall on 28 April 1932, comprised the Prelude and "Good Friday Spell" from *Parsifal* and Beethoven's Ninth Symphony, with the Schola Cantorum and soloists Rethberg, Matzenauer, Martinelli, and Pinza singing "in various degrees of German," as Downes put it. The ovations at the beginning and end of the evening were overwhelming, and $24,522 was raised for the fund.* "Concert obtained triumphal artistic and material results," he cabled Carla afterward. "Am very pleased arm very well."

Before attending a postconcert dinner, Toscanini had a private conversation with Giulio Gatti-Casazza at the latter's suite at the Savoy-Plaza Hotel. The two ex-colleagues had not been on speaking terms for over a decade, and the reconciliation—arranged by Margherita De Vecchi, Zirato, and the ballerina Rosina Galli, Gatti's second wife—surprised and delighted everyone concerned. The following day, Gatti was Toscanini's guest at lunch at the Astor, while Margherita and other friends packed the maestro's bags: he was due to depart aboard the *Ile-de-France* later that afternoon. Gatti accompanied Toscanini to the ship, where the two men even posed, shaking hands, for photographers, and from aboard ship Toscanini sent a friendly radiogram to his old comrade-in-arms. The newspapers immediately began to invent reports that Toscanini would once again conduct operas at the Metropolitan, but that never happened.

Toscanini underwent further treatments in Piazze with remarkable results: on 28 May, after new X-rays had been taken in Florence, Dr. Valerio, the radiologist, wrote to Rinaldi, "I am truly happy to let you know that Maestro Toscanini may consider himself cured, even anatomically." During the following three years, Toscanini would return to Piazze from time to time for further treatment. He continued to have shoulder and arm pain now and then for the rest of his

---

* Harry Harkness Flagler, the fund's chairman, used some of the money—which became known as the Toscanini Fund—to pay for twelve free concerts for students, to be held in several different venues in the city during the following summer; these events provided paid employment for otherwise unemployed musicians, and the fund was increased as the Depression continued, thanks to the ongoing contributions of Toscanini and other well-known musicians. Toscanini also contributed to New York's Lighthouse Music School, which provided music lessons for the blind.

life, but rarely as severe as before. "I send you my affectionate greetings and a hearty embrace," he wrote on a postcard to Rinaldi, and he signed it "Arturo Toscanini anti-Fascist."

10.

ALL THROUGH THE PREVIOUS WINTER AND ON INTO THE SPRING, the two Wagner factions had sparred bitterly over the Toscanini-Bayreuth Question, with Winifred and Tietjen in one corner and Daniela and Eva in the other. The latter maintained their friendly contacts with Toscanini, and on 25 March 1932, his sixty-fifth birthday, Eva wrote to him that her soul was "filled with an ardent prayer: 'O kehr' zurück, Du kühner Sänger'" (O turn back, thou bold singer)—a quotation from *Tannhäuser*.

At about the same time, he received a questionnaire from a German newspaper, the *Berliner Börsen-Zeitung*, and—probably because he had some free time—he responded to it. "I love and admire all the works that I conduct, symphonic or operatic, because—I conduct only those which I love," he wrote.

My preferences in the symphonic field are for the greats, Haydn, Mozart, and Beethoven. In recent years I have thoroughly studied Bruckner's monumental symphonies. I gladly leave modern works to other conductors. Among operas, I value those of Wagner and Verdi above all. It is difficult to state a preference for one of Wagner's operas. I have noticed that if I am conducting one or another of Wagner's operas, or playing it at the piano, whichever one it happens to be takes possession of my heart. And yet, every time I glance at the score of *Parsifal*, I say to myself: This is the sublime one. In Verdi's operas, I appreciate not only the richness of the melodies but also the effective and sure power of the musical drama. When I conduct *Falstaff* at Busseto I think about the possibility of a Verdian Bayreuth, along the lines of Wagner's Festspielhaus. These two masters are the real representatives of German and Italian national music.

Perhaps it was this publication that caused the Wagners to take action. On 19 May 1932, Winifred visited Toscanini in Italy; they had a frank exchange of opinions, and in the end he agreed to return to Bayreuth in the summer of 1933 to conduct *Parsifal* and *Die Meistersinger*. While Winifred was flying back to Germany that same evening, Toscanini wired Daniela, "Winifred come and gone[,] the sky is beautifully clear again."

Winifred had played her cards well: she had not told Furtwängler that she was working on Toscanini to return—a fact that might have induced the German conductor to continue as music director, which she and Tietjen wanted to avoid. And when she went to Italy to lure Toscanini back to Bayreuth, she did not tell him that Furtwängler had in the meantime resigned as music director (that news was made public only a month later) and that she and Tietjen were now solely in charge of the festival.

AT THE TIME OF TOSCANINI'S BREAK with the Wagners the previous fall, the tightly controlled Italian press had used the news against him. An article in *Il Popolo di Roma*, for instance, bore the headline "The Man Who Fights with Everyone" and the subheadline "Toscanini is even dissatisfied with Beyrut [*sic*] and is telegraphing nasty statements about the Widow Wagner and the Hitlerites." Throughout the following months, he was closely watched, whenever he was in Italy, as were the people with whom he came in direct or indirect contact. On 29 March 1932, during a break in his treatment at Piazze, he had attended a concert at the Milan Conservatory, and the prefecture had promptly informed the Ministry of the Interior that "as soon as his presence was noted, a part of the public directed continuous applause toward him, opposed by some whistling. After the performance, while some Conservatory students were again paying tribute to the maestro with their applause, again opposed by whistling, an individual, approaching his car, clapped his hands fervently, shouting, '*Viva Maestro*' and then trying to disappear from the area. Stopped by the police, he was identified as Dr. Gino Fanoli, Socialist, and is being held pending further information." But Toscanini carefully avoided acknowledging positive or negative public displays toward him.

A few months later, he let it be known that he would be willing to conduct a benefit concert for the poor in Milan the following winter, but local musicians were afraid of negative consequences if they accepted his offer. Through various party functionaries—and unbeknownst to Toscanini—they asked to obtain an act of clemency for him, "from the Duce's enlightened goodness," they wrote—although, since Toscanini had never been formally accused of anything, there was nothing for which clemency could have been granted. Mussolini saw the request and either responded negatively or did not respond at all; no such concert ever took place. Toscanini received other requests as well, and there is some evidence that he agreed to conduct Beethoven's *Missa Solemnis* in Turin, but only if he would not have to conduct the national anthems. Once again, nothing happened.

He hated the idea of not being able to contribute anything to his country's musical life, but he would not act against his convictions. And since every newspaper-reading Italian knew what those convictions were, Italy's most famous musician was unofficially but effectively banned from making music in Italy. As he himself put it, the politicians "created a vacuum" around him. His country had become an area in which he could rest, study, and spend time with friends and family, but not work. For the time being, he entered and left Italy as if Mussolini and his regime did not exist, although he knew that informers spied on him constantly.

Early in 1932, he rented the Isolino San Giovanni, the tiniest (about 425 feet in diameter) of the inhabitable Borromean Islands in Lake Maggiore, only about 130 feet across the water from the town of Pallanza. The noble Milanese Borromeo family, which had produced a saint and a famous cardinal, among other noteworthy personages, had acquired the property in the seventeenth century and had built a villa and created gardens on it. Through much of the first half of the twentieth century, it was rented to various wealthy people, including Vittoria Colonna di Sermoneta, the estranged wife of Leone Caetani, Prince of Teano; she had a passionate affair there with the painter Umberto Boccioni.

Toscanini adored the Isolino and particularly enjoyed the privacy that it afforded. He began to spend time on it whenever possible, often with various family members and friends but occasionally with only minimal domestic help. Walter Toscanini, always fascinated by new gadgets, bought an early model home-movie camera and often shot footage of gatherings on the Isolino, including snippets that show his father playing with Walfredo and, later, with his two granddaughters; guiding various guests through the island's wooded areas; throwing sticks for his dog to bring back; and just generally at ease. In one film, Walter captured a group of mostly young visitors in bathing suits doing a parody—choreographed by Cia—of a Fascist Youth military drill, complete with the Fascist salute at the end. On the mainland, they would have been jailed for such a disrespectful act, but on the Isolino no prying eyes could see them.

11.

TWENTY-TWO YEARS AFTER HIS FIRST, NERVE-RACKING EXPERIENCE of working with Parisian orchestra musicians, Toscanini finally accepted another invitation to conduct an ensemble in the French capital. The occasion was a concert at the Théâtre des Champs-Elysées, in the presence of President Albert Lebrun, on 17 June 1932, to celebrate the unveiling of two monuments to Debussy, and the orchestra was made up of top players from the Opéra, Opéra-Comique, and the major local symphonic ensembles. Toscanini conducted only *La Mer*; other pieces were led by Gaubert, Inghelbrecht, and—via a live radio hookup with Basel—Felix Weingartner. Toscanini was "the hero of the festival," Prunières reported; "by contrast the rest of the concert was all the more mediocre."*

Winifred Wagner wanted to attend the concert and then have Toscanini fly to Berlin with her, to audition a singer for the following year's Bayreuth *Meistersinger* and to discuss other matters with Tietjen. Her letter to Toscanini was openly flirtatious: "If I came [to Paris], would you allow me to live in the same Hotel as you do? and which is it? I hate to be *quite* alone in a strange town—which you will

---

* One statue, situated on the Boulevard Lannes, near what had been the composer's home in the Square de l'Avenue du Bois de Boulogne (now Avenue Foch), was the work of the twin brothers Jan and Joël Martel; the other, in Debussy's hometown of Saint-Germain-en-Laye, was by Aristide Maillol.

surely understand." Toscanini's reply is not known, but he did not make the trip to Berlin at that time.

The single New York concert in April 1932 and the performance of *La Mer* in Paris in June reassured Toscanini that his arm and shoulder were in satisfactory condition. In September, he traveled to New York aboard the *Bremen*; when the ship docked, on the twenty-ninth, he was in excellent health, full of energy, and ready to set to work. A reporter who had managed to scramble aboard asked him whether he had any objections to answering a few questions. "I certainly do," Toscanini good-humoredly replied. "You know how I am."

During that first part of his season, Toscanini conducted the world premiere of the Dutch American composer Bernard Wagenaar's Symphony no. 2; the US premiere of Four Polish Dances by the Polish French composer Alexandre Tansman; the local premiere of Schoenberg's arrangement of Bach's "St. Anne" Prelude and Fugue in E-flat Major; and his own first performances of works by Mozart (Symphony no. 28 in C Major), Mendelssohn (the "Italian" Symphony), Bruckner (the Fourth Symphony, given "almost without cuts," according to the *Times*); and short pieces by Franck, Marco Enrico Bossi, Georges Enesco, Giovanni Battista Viotti, and Vivaldi. Another feature was an unstaged performance of Act I, Scene 3, of *Die Walküre*, sung by the German soprano Elsa Alsen and the American tenor Paul Althouse.

In a cable to Carla after his first concert, Toscanini said that his arm was "responding perfectly," but a month later he complained to her that he was "tired, very tired. This work is no longer tolerable for me," he said. "Having a rehearsal and often two rehearsals every day, four concerts a week—rarely three—isn't the sort of life for someone my age, the more so when one gives a hundred percent at every rehearsal as at every concert. I can never go out for a breath of air. Only once did I go with Zirato, Nina [Zirato's wife], and Margherita [De Vecchi] for an automobile ride outside New York, but since then I've always been holed up in these rooms at the Astor, working." At last, however, on 29 November, after having been applauded and bravoed at every one of his concerts, in town and on tour, Toscanini reboarded the *Bremen* to sail for Europe and begin a three-month break.

Apart from a brief visit to Winifred and Tietjen in Berlin, to discuss details of the following summer's Bayreuth Festival, he spent most of his time in Milan. In January 1933, he attended two Brahms evenings performed at the conservatory by the Busch Quartet and Serkin, and on both occasions he and Carla gave postconcert dinners in their honor in Via Durini. One evening, the Toscaninis dined at the Pizzettis' home with Kodály and his wife, Emma. And once, when Miecio (Mieczyslaw) Horszowski and the Milanese dialect poet Delio Tessa paid him a visit, he showed them the portrait of himself that Arturo Rietti had just completed and that remains the best-known of all the Toscanini portrait paintings.*

When the weather permitted, he spent time on the Isolino, and he returned to Piazze for a follow-up treatment from Dr. Rinaldi. The two Salvadori girls, from the local *pensione*, had begun writing to him from time to time, always addressing him with the formal *Lei*, and he would respond with teasing, amusing letters, at first with *Lei* but later with the informal *tu*. No doubt his enchantment with Piazze and the Salvadoris resulted in part from their distance from his world of endless work and travel, but it also had to do with his lifelong enjoyment of the sound of the Italian language as it is spoken in Tuscany, its homeland, and of the typically Tuscan gift of the gab that the Salvadoris embodied for him.

Carla often accompanied her husband to the village, and he once wrote to Lavinia that "we frequently sigh as we think of Piazze's heart, *which is that of our delightful friends Gelsa and Lavinia.*" Gelsa developed a serious crush on Toscanini; she never married, and she carried a torch for the maestro for the rest of her life, even long after his death. There was much gossipy speculation in Piazze about the nature of their relationship, but the tone and content of his letters to her demonstrate that although he was curious about her feelings toward him, and even led her on, he never allowed the situation to get out of hand. In one of them he told her, "You have a head that *works very well*, that *can reason* and is therefore capable of self-control and of overcoming life's harshness. Just think, dear Gelsina, that more or less all those who want life to be tolerable must make a little

---

* Like Toscanini, Rietti—one of the finest Italian portraitists of his generation—had been opposed to Mussolini's regime almost from its inception. Wally Toscanini inherited the portrait and donated it to the Museo Teatrale alla Scala.

effort to pick themselves up and distance themselves from the banality and mediocrity of human society." In another, in response to a letter in which she made her feelings for him more or less explicit, he told her that she was "a *dear girl* who wins everyone's liking, affection, and tenderness. I love you like one of my daughters—*too bad I was born too early*; you understand me, right?" And he joked, "I don't want to say more so as not to compromise my seriousness. Seriousness is the cross I bear."

TOSCANINI ARRIVED BACK IN NEW YORK on 22 February 1933, aboard the Norddeutscher Lloyd liner *Columbus*; this time Carla and Wanda accompanied him. Four days later, he attended a gala performance at the Metropolitan to honor Gatti-Casazza on the manager's quarter century at the company's helm. Luckily, Toscanini did not stay to the end; if he had remained, he would have been shocked and angry to hear the program end not only with "The Star-Spangled Banner" and Italy's Royal March but also with "Giovinezza," and to see Gatti come to the front of his box and give the Fascist salute.

Toscanini devoted most of the rehearsal time for his first program to Howard Hanson's Symphony no. 2—a "lyrical" piece, "romantic in temperament," as its composer described it. As this was the first time that the maestro had grappled with a full-length work by a native-born American composer, he made sure that the rest of the program consisted of pieces that he had already performed with the orchestra: Wagner's "Faust" Overture and Strauss's *Ein Heldenleben*.

This time around, Toscanini added to his active repertoire—among other pieces—Tchaikovsky's "Manfred" Symphony (his first performance of any music by Tchaikovsky in thirty-three years); two pieces by young composers from the Soviet Union (the Jewish-themed *Dances and Songs of the Ghetto*, by Alexander Weprik, and the machine-age-inspired *Iron Foundry*, by Alexander Mossolov); Bach's Sixth "Brandenburg" Concerto; Brahms's Violin Concerto (with Jascha Heifetz);* the world premiere of Castelnuovo-Tedesco's Violin

---

* A few years earlier, Heifetz had written to Arthur Judson, "There is just one ambition which every artist visiting America has and that is at some time in his career to play under the conductorship of Maestro Toscanini." Now the thirty-two-year-old violinist had his wish fulfilled.

Concerto no. 2 ("The Prophets," again with Heifetz, who had commissioned the work); and three works by Beethoven: the "Triple" Concerto (with Maria Carreras, Piastro, and Wallenstein), the "King Stephen" Overture, and the "Emperor" Concerto (with Vladimir Horowitz). These last were part of a five-concert Beethoven cycle that also presented two more overtures and all of the symphonies except the Ninth, which Toscanini had conducted with the Philharmonic the previous spring.

This segment of Toscanini's eighth consecutive Philharmonic season included four out-of-town concerts. In the audience at the Washington concert—a Beethoven and Wagner program on 7 March—was Eleanor Roosevelt, whose husband, Franklin, had been sworn in three days earlier as president of the United States; the Philharmonic's performance was referred to in the press, albeit unofficially, as the "inauguration concert."

Musically, the Philharmonic was at its peak, but its financial situation was increasingly dire: the Depression was causing a decrease in income from all sources. Although the orchestra's 1933–34 season would be expanded from twenty-nine to thirty weeks, there would be no more concerts away from Carnegie Hall. Various other budget-trimming plans were being prepared, and the directors warned that if the situation did not improve, there might not be a 1934–35 season.

12.

WINIFRED WAGNER HAD SAID SHE WAS "BESIDE HERSELF WITH happiness" the preceding May, when she persuaded Toscanini to return to the festival to conduct *Parsifal* and *Die Meistersinger* during the summer of 1933, but she must have been even happier on 30 January 1933, when her close friend Adolf Hitler became chancellor of Germany. As a result, however, Toscanini's Bayreuth plans were once again becoming uncertain.

Hitler and his National Socialist Party quickly instituted a policy of *Gleichschaltung* (coordination) in order to bring all nonmilitary and nonreligious organizations under their direct control. The Nazis then claimed that a fire that destroyed the Reichstag (parliament) building late in February had been set by a communist, and they used this as an excuse for suspending civil liberties and for jailing their opponents. In March, parliament passed a constitutional amendment that allowed the government to do virtually anything it pleased, such as enacting legislation that restricted the rights of groups that the regime deemed undesirable, especially the Jews. Germany had quickly become a dictatorship.

Musicians everywhere learned that many of their German colleagues, including the conductors Bruno Walter, Otto Klemperer, and Fritz Busch, in addition to many opera singers and orchestra musicians, had lost or were about to lose their jobs and, in some cases, were fleeing the country, either because they were of Jewish origin or because they were outspokenly anti-Nazi, or both. In mid-February, the mayor and town council of Bayreuth had made Toscanini an honorary citizen of their city, on the occasion of the fiftieth anniversary of Wagner's death, but in mid-March, the international press reported that the persecution of Jewish musicians was making him reconsider his decision to return to Bayreuth that summer.

Artur Bodanzky, an Austrian Jew who had headed the German wing of the Metropolitan Opera's conducting staff since 1915, approached Berthold Neuer, vice-president of the Knabe Piano Company in New York on 22 March, and asked him to draft a letter to prominent musicians in America, requesting that they sign a protest cable to Hitler. Toscanini was among the musicians approached, and he almost simultaneously received a letter from Gabrilowitsch urging him to join his colleagues. "All these protests [. . .] will not impress the German rulers or the German nation," Gabrilowitsch wrote. "There is only one man who could protest effectively. That is you, Maestro Arturo Toscanini. [. . .] A decisive protest from you at this time would amount to a great historic fact. The world has a right to expect this noble gesture from you."

Toscanini did not need Gabrilowitsch's urging: he had already decided. On 31 March, he wrote to Neuer, "Not only can you use my name but if there is no objection and if it is possible I would like to have my name put at the *head* of *the subscribers* [*sic*; signatories] of this message." And the next day, a polite but clearly worded message was sent to Hitler in Berlin:

Your Excellency:

The undersigned artists who live, and execute their art, in the United States of America feel the moral obligation to appeal to your excellency to put a stop to the persecutions of their colleagues in Germany, for political or religious reasons. We beg you to consider that the artist all over the world is estimated for his talent alone and not for his national or religious convictions.

We are convinced that such persecutions as take place in Germany at present are not based on your instructions, and that it cannot possibly be your desire to damage the high cultural esteem Germany, until now, has been enjoying in the eyes of the whole civilized world.

Hoping that our appeal in behalf of our colleagues will not be allowed to pass unheard, we are

Respectfully yours, [. . .]

There followed the signatures of the conductors Toscanini, Damrosch, Koussevitzky, Bodanzky, Gabrilowitsch, Hertz, Fritz Reiner, and Frederick Stock; the educator Frank Damrosch (Walter's brother); the pianist Harold Bauer; and the composers Charles Martin Loeffler and Rubin Goldmark. Toscanini, Stock, and Loeffler were the only signatories who were not Jewish or part-Jewish.

The *New York Times* and newspapers around the world carried the text of the message the following day, a Sunday, and when Toscanini appeared on the Carnegie Hall stage to conduct a concert that afternoon, "the audience gave him a prolonged ovation, the response apparently to Mr. Toscanini's heading the signers of the appeal to Hitler," the *Times* reported. But Germany's musical world in general and Bayreuth in particular were thrown into a state of confusion. On 4 April, the head radio commissioner in Berlin issued a statement: "According to newspaper reports, several conductors and musicians in the United States—Arturo Toscanini [et al.]—have lodged a complaint with the Chancellor because of the rejection of certain Jewish and Marxist fellow musicians in Germany. Pending clarification of this matter, I direct that the compositions and recordings of the aforementioned gentlemen shall no longer find a place on the programs of German broadcasters and also that no musical performance in which they in any wise have a part shall be received from concert halls or other broadcasting sources."

Winifred Wagner dined with Hitler in Berlin that evening, to continue the discussion of the Toscanini question that she had begun with him by telephone two days earlier. The fifteen-year-old Friedelind was with her mother in their Berlin hotel suite, and she later recalled, "From the half of the [telephone] conversation that I heard, I gathered that [Hitler] felt very badly treated after he had generously permitted Mother to keep her Jewish artists" for the 1933 Bayreuth Festival. "On further thought he must have realized what it would mean to have such a powerful voice as that of Toscanini openly denouncing Nazi Germany, for his aides rushed back and forth from the Chancellery to the hotel all day long. Finally it was decided to send a wire in Hitler's name, urging Toscanini to reconsider [. . .]." If this is so, Toscanini must already have warned Winifred that unless policies changed in Germany he would not return, but there is no record of any cable from Hitler to Toscanini. Friedelind was correct, however, in her recollection that Hitler then sent a personal letter to Toscanini. Dated 3 April 1933, the letter (in German) read,

Most Honored Master.

As a longtime friend of the House of Wahnfried I have always seen the Bayreuth Festival as the fulfillment of a high artistic mission. That you yourself, honored Master, have helped this great work to flourish through the strength of your personality has filled me with deepest joy, even if my own difficult life's struggle has, to my sorrow, made it impossible for me to participate in the most recent festivals.

Today, as Chancellor of the German Reich, I am sincerely happy for the hour when I shall personally be able, in Bayreuth, to thank you, the great representative of art and of a people friendly to Germany, for your participation in the great Master's work.

> *With sincere admiration,*
> *Your devoted*
> A. Hitler

When Friedelind heard her mother read the letter aloud, she "couldn't keep still," she recalled. "'It would be crazy to send such a letter,' I protested. 'This is the surest way to drive Toscanini away forever. If you really want him to come, don't send it, because he comes to Bayreuth for Wagner, not for Hitler. It will be sure to make him furious.' Mother glared at me and her temper flared. In an angry voice she reminded me that I was speaking like a child, and advised me to leave the operating of the festival to her [. . .]."

Max Smith, who was urging Toscanini to return to Bayreuth, cabled Daniela Thode on 11 April to say that the maestro's "loyalty and good sense have been exercised by efforts of interested elements to influence him," the implication being that the interested elements were his many Jewish friends—as if anyone had ever been able to sway him on matters of principle! The following day, however, Smith again cabled Frau Thode: "receipt today by our dear friend of beautiful letter from Berlin [i.e., from Hitler] has entirely relieved my misgivings."

But Toscanini's reply to Hitler, however politely phrased, made clear his intention not to return to Bayreuth if conditions in Germany did not change. "Your *Excellency*," he wrote, in English, on 29 April—the day of his departure from New York, with Carla and Wanda, aboard the *Ile-de-France*—"For your very friendly writing I want to thank you heartily, only I greatly regret that I could not answer it sooner. You know how closely I feel attached to Bayreuth and what deep pleasure it gives me to consecrate my 'something' to a genius like Wagner whom I love so boundlessly. Therefore it would be a bitter disappointment to me if any circumstances should interfere with my purpose to take part in the coming Festival Plays and I hope that my strength, which the last weeks here taxed severely, will hold out. Expressing once more my thanks for your kind expressions of thought I subscribe [*sic*; sign] myself as your Excellency's sincere Arturo Toscanini[.]"

His final decision came three and a half weeks later, in the aftermath of an apparently unrelated event. Not long after his return to Italy, Toscanini was asked by Elizabeth Sprague Coolidge, an American patroness of contemporary composers, whether he would host the European premiere of Pizzetti's String Quartet no. 2—which she had commissioned—on the Isolino, and the event, with reception, was arranged for 23 May; the Busch Quartet performed, and various German neo-exiles, including the writers Emil Ludwig and Erich Maria Remarque, attended; Horszowski, Castelnuovo-Tedesco, the guitarist Andrés Segovia, and numerous other guests were also present. Before the performance, the German visitors gave Toscanini firsthand accounts of what was happening in their country, and Toscanini told Fritz Busch, who was also present, that he wanted to talk to him after the other guests had left.

"I felt that he was much preoccupied," Busch said. When they were alone, Toscanini showed him the letter from Hitler. Busch continued,

> What was depressing Toscanini, from his youth closely attached to the art of Richard Wagner, and its greatest interpreter, was anxiety for the future of the Bayreuth Festival. Feeling thus he asked me, "What will Bayreuth do if I refuse?" "Then they will invite me, Maestro," I said. Toscanini was speechless. "That is to say, they *have* invited me. Tietjen, who expects your refusal, has already taken steps."
>
> I was delighted at his astonishment and added with a laugh, "Of course, I will refuse, like you." Toscanini shut his mouth, which had remained open from astonishment, and purred, in his warm, melancholy voice, *"Eh, caro amico!"* We were both silent, and a feeling of great sorrow came over us.

Toscanini then telegraphed his resignation to Winifred Wagner, who, since March, had been denying reports that he would not return to the festival. She dispatched Daniela Thode to Milan, to try to make him change his mind, but, after a day and a half of diplomatic efforts, Frau Thode declared herself beaten. On 28 May, Toscanini sent a handwritten message to Winifred: "The sorrowful events that have wounded my feelings as a man and as an artist have not yet undergone any change, contrary to my every hope. It is therefore my duty today to break the silence I had imposed upon myself for two months and to inform you that for my peace of mind, for yours, and for everyone's, it is better not to think any longer about my coming to Bayreuth. With unchangeable friendship for the House of Wagner, Arturo Toscanini."

News of Toscanini's decision was made public on 5 June, and three days later the *Times* summarized reactions within Germany:

> Most Nazi organs thus far ignore Signor Toscanini's action, but the National Socialist Militant League for German Culture issued a statement saying Signor Toscanini "apparently had been unable to withstand the influence of large-scale anti-German propaganda" [. . .]. The *Börsen Zeitung* said: "[. . .] We may hope he will come to Bayreuth after all, for this much is beyond doubt: the participation of Signor Toscanini was the greatest attraction of the Bayreuth festival. He guaranteed the high artistic level that the festival must have [. . .]. He also was the only guarantee for its financial success." [. . .] The *Vossische Zeitung* was more obstreperous: "The great musician with incorruptible ears, suspicious, pedantically insisting on the last semiquaver, has heard only the discordant tone of the great orchestra that is Germany."

In a final attempt—presumably by Hitler—to persuade Toscanini to change his mind, the ban on broadcasting his performances and recordings in Germany was lifted; when the attempt proved futile, it was reinstated. Toscanini's recordings were eventually withdrawn from the market, and, according to Friedelind Wagner, Hitler used to "see red whenever the Maestro's name was mentioned"—a syndrome he shared with Mussolini.

Richard Strauss, never a Nazi but always an opportunist, informed Winifred Wagner that he would be glad to take over Toscanini's *Parsifal* performances at Bayreuth, just as he had taken over Bruno Walter's Leipzig Gewandhaus concerts when Walter had been forced to leave Germany; these gestures increased Toscanini's already strong personal antipathy toward Strauss. *Meistersinger* was conducted by Elmendorff in what one critic described as a "lumbering, uninspired and dull" interpretation. But the real star of the 1933 festival was neither Strauss nor even Wagner, but Hitler himself, who was greeted with joy by the throngs and the whole Wagner family. On the other hand, as the *Manchester Guardian*'s correspondent wrote, Toscanini's withdrawal "undoubtedly gave Hitler unpleasant food for thought. I am informed that the publication of the news practically stopped foreign bookings, and was followed by hundreds of cancellations from all parts of the world."

Toscanini would never again conduct in Germany, but his decision vis-à-vis Bayreuth wounded him as deeply as it wounded the festival. "Today, [July] 21st, first performance at Bayreuth, with Meistersinger," he wrote to a friend. "My thoughts rush there nostalgically and sorrowfully. [. . .] Oh, this cursed, nasty muscle of ours called the heart. How unforgiving it is toward those who violate it, and how it makes them suffer!" Four years later, in a note to Friedelind, he summed up his feelings: "Bayreuth! The deepest sorrow of my life."

13.

THE STUDY OF BACH'S MASS IN B MINOR AND BEETHOVEN'S *MISSA Solemnis* combined with the Isolino's peaceful beauty to bring respite to Toscanini's mind and spirit during the summer of 1933. "The deep emotion aroused by [Bach's] Kyrie has equaled and surpassed what I felt the first time I heard it," he wrote to a friend. "The Kyrie, the Qui tollis, the Incarnatus, and the Crucifixus are among the most divine things ever conceived and realized by the human mind. Beethoven, in the same numbers of the Mass in D [*Missa Solemnis*], is a long way behind. [. . .] Never has a more profound and desperate human cry been raised up to God than in Bach's Kyrie!" He would conduct the Kyrie from Bach's mass and the entire Beethoven mass for the first time in his life during the forthcoming Philharmonic season.

Eventually, however, he "put Beethoven and Bach to rest" and was "up to my neck in Chopin's études, nocturnes, mazurkas, waltzes—and I'm *obsessed* with one mazurka [in A minor, op. 17, no. 4]. Its sadness is consonant with mine. In the middle, there is a bit of joy darkened by a bit of regret, and then the infinite sadness comes back!" And so on, as he studied week after week, sometimes at the keyboard and sometimes away from it. He also spent much time reading, including two recent biographies: Emil Ludwig's life of Goethe, given to him by its author, and a life of Mary Stuart by Stefan Zweig.

Early in August, he rushed to Milan to visit a dying friend, a schoolmate from conservatory days, and in September another old friend, Leonardo Bistolfi, Italy's leading Symbolist sculptor, died at the age of seventy-four; Toscanini went to Turin for Bistolfi's funeral. To another friend, he described Bistolfi as "a poet in marble" who "spoke with his own voice. Despite fifty years of strenuous work, he died poor!" Toscanini accused modernist sculptors of having "created a vacuum around him and his name," just as the politicians had done to himself, he said. Bistolfi "was very much distressed by this, because he was a very weak man [. . .] a slave to and victim of publicity and superficial appearances. I laugh at them and will continue to laugh, because I've always been happy to swim against the current and to do battle for my spiritual and moral independence."

The Polos visited the Isolino frequently, as did the Pizzettis and Ugo Ara, the Flonzaley Quartet's former violist, who had helped to arrange the Scala orchestra's postwar American tour, and who lived on one of the other Borromean Islands. The violinist Joseph Szigeti's wife and daughter also arrived and stayed for a while. Miecio Horszowski came to dinner one evening and noted in his diary that afterward, as he and Toscanini were about to listen to a radio broadcast of the opera *Ruy Blas* by the nineteenth-century composer Filippo Marchetti, the maestro, who had never conducted any of Marchetti's music, recited the opera's entire libretto by heart. Walter and Cia brought Walfredo to the Isolino and celebrated the boy's fourth birthday there in August. Toscanini considered going to Salzburg to see Max Reinhardt's staging of Goethe's *Faust*, but he changed his mind: he preferred to stay on his little island.

Two young composers, the twenty-two-year-old Gian Carlo Menotti and twenty-one-year-old Samuel Barber, also dropped by in

August. Several years earlier, Menotti's mother had shown Tosca-nini some of her son's compositions, and Toscanini had recom-mended that the boy study composition with Rosario Scalero at the Curtis Institute of Music, in Philadelphia—just as he had done for another young Italian composer, Nino Rota, later known above all as a composer of film scores for Federico Fellini, Luchino Visconti, and other major directors. At Curtis, Menotti met Barber, a fellow Scalero student, who also had a Toscanini connection: he was a nephew of the mezzo-soprano Louise Homer, one of the maestro's principal singers at the Metropolitan. Menotti and Barber eventually became life partners.

And twice—once at the end of July and once toward the end of September—there was a visit from a thirty-six-year-old woman who, within days of Toscanini's decision to renounce Bayreuth, had opened a new subplot in his life's story.

TO BREAK UP ONE OF HIS VISITS to Dr. Rinaldi at Piazze, early in June 1933, Toscanini had made a day trip to Rome to visit the Respighis at their home, where he encountered one Ada Colleoni Mainardi. Ada had studied piano at the Milan Conservatory, where she was gener-ally considered talented but not brilliant, and where she had met Enrico Mainardi, who would come to be regarded as the finest Ital-ian cellist of his generation. They fell in love, married, often per-formed as a duo—although by 1933 her public appearances had become rare—and lived the typical life of itinerant concert artists.

Toscanini had met both of them not later than 1917, when he was fifty and they were twenty, and he later told Ada that even then he had considered her the most attractive young woman of her genera-tion—so much so that he had been envious, not so much of Enrico himself as of Enrico's presumed happiness. Milan was where the Toscaninis and the Mainardis spent more time than anywhere else during the 1920s, and Ada was friendly with both of Toscanini's daughters. The maestro was already a towering figure in the musical world by the time the young Mainardis began to take their place in that world, and Ada seems to have regarded him with something approaching awe. But their relationship changed dramatically after their chance meeting in Rome, where they spoke of private matters, including their unsatisfactory marriages. Enrico had multiple extramarital affairs, Ada said, and she took revenge by acting likewise. After hearing such a confession, Toscanini no doubt sympathized with Ada and told her that he was attracted to her.

The story might have gone no further had Ada not made a bold move: on 9 June 1933, she sent Toscanini a telegram—no longer extant—in which she evidently communicated feelings for him that went beyond friendship. "It was a sweet and pleasant surprise," he responded in a letter written at Piazze the same day. "Your telegram's few words were good, very good, for my soul." But, he added, "It was like pouring gasoline onto a fire."

Ada wrote back, implying—one may infer—that her feelings for him were strong; he wrote again, raising the voltage; and after a few exchanges, love was declared on both sides. "I had thought that my age had gently laid its hand upon my heart, like a harpist placing a hand on the strings to extinguish the vibrations, but you are working a miracle!" he said, in a letter dated 10 July. "There is still much unexpressed music in my heart, and you are making it sing melodies that have never yet been heard. Do you remember Keats's marvelous verse: 'Heard melodies are sweet, but those unheard are sweeter'?[*] And again I ask you, why have you appeared upon my path—this path that the sun illuminates with the reflected light of dusk?"

These were among the earliest of nearly a thousand letters, telegrams, and postcards that Toscanini would send Ada Mainardi over seven years and in which he would express not only his sometimes obsessive passion for her but also much about what was going on in the private, professional, and involuntarily political segments of his life during that particularly turbulent period. Both of them traveled constantly, thus they rarely saw each other, even more rarely had sexual relations, and were afraid to phone each other except when each could be sure that the other's spouse was away. Ada saved Toscanini's letters, which, as a group, constitute the best extant window on his inner being.

---

[*] Toscanini wrote the quotation from "Ode on a Grecian Urn" in English; Mainardi spoke English, French, and German, in addition to her native Italian.

14.

EVER SINCE HE HAD TAKEN CHARGE OF LA SCALA IN 1898, TOSCANINI had happily given up his life as a wandering minstrel of the podium and had concentrated, for the most part, on long-term musical relationships. Now, in his midsixties, his attitude began to change. Perhaps his happy encounter with the Philadelphia Orchestra in 1930 had shown him that his reputation now stood so high that he could count on cooperation and enthusiasm even in short-term engagements. But his growing desire to conduct outside his customary venues also had political origins: because the dictatorial regimes in Italy and Germany had put those two great musical centers off-limits for him, he gradually drew a musical border around them. If any of their citizens wanted to experience his art, they would have to cross their respective countries' frontiers. Thus yet another subchapter opened in Toscanini's life in 1933.

First, in October 1933, he went to Paris to conduct the fine Orchestre des Concerts Walther-Straram in two concerts—an Italian-French program and an all-Wagner program—at the Théâtre des Champs-Elysées; by public demand, a third concert was hastily scheduled. "The orchestra behaved well," Toscanini wrote to Ada Mainardi after his first work session. "I rehearsed the Ravel piece [the Second Suite from *Daphnis et Chloé*] in a detailed enough way and gave a good shake to Berlioz's Queen Mab. My nightmare is over, God willing. I'm getting back into my skin. But what suffering, my dear! It's ridiculous, but I don't know how to get the better of myself, nor have I ever known how. At times, I'm so unhappy that I'd like to quit once and for all."

After hearing Toscanini's performance of the Prelude to *Die Meistersinger*, Henry Prunières asked the maestro whether he would give listeners the opportunity to hear him conduct the whole opera again; Toscanini replied, "with melancholy and emotion: 'The opera is finished for me.'" He might conduct Verdi's operas at Busseto, or *Pelléas* at a projected opera house at Saint-Germain-en-Laye, Debussy's birthplace, but "'never again!'" would he perform operas under normal circumstances, he said.

From Paris, Toscanini traveled directly to Vienna, where a more momentous engagement awaited him: his debut with the famed Vienna Philharmonic. The orchestra had courted him for many years and had succeeded in engaging him for concerts in May 1931, but the engagement had been canceled in the aftermath of the Bologna incident. When Toscanini's withdrawal from Bayreuth was announced, Hugo Burghauser, principal bassoon and president of the self-governing Wiener Philharmoniker, renewed the invitation to the maestro; the fact that Burghauser was half Italian and had been educated in Italy facilitated communication about the proposal. At roughly the same time, Toscanini was approached on the subject by the renowned Polish violinist Bronislaw Huberman, who, like most other Jewish musicians, was grateful to Toscanini for his anti-Nazi stand. In June, Huberman had written to him, "An artist can only give what he possesses as a man. Your action, with the artistic solidarity and moving words which accompanied it, has given an example to the world, which will understand from now on where the sources of Arturo Toscanini's inspiration come from: the depth of the human heart." Late in July, Huberman was vacationing at Caldè on Lake Maggiore, a short boat ride from Toscanini's Isolino; he came "to show me his letter in reply to an invitation from Furtwängler for concerts in Germany," Toscanini wrote to Ada Mainardi. "A very nice, dignified, humane letter—of refusal, naturally." At that time, Furtwängler still believed that the Nazis might listen to reason, and he had made a brave but ultimately futile attempt to allow all musicians, regardless of their "racial" origins, to perform in Germany.

Huberman then came up with an idea: the maestro could make his anti-Nazi protest even more meaningful by conducting in Austria, Germany's "free" neighbor. The country's foreign minister told him that the government was already trying to extract a commitment from Toscanini. And in the end, Toscanini agreed to conduct the Vienna Philharmonic in the fall of 1933. The Viennese could afford to pay him only 5,000 Austrian schillings per concert—not even one-sixth of his per-concert fee in New York—plus 2,500 schillings for permission to broadcast one of his concerts on the radio, and his Austrian income tax, but he was keen to go anyway. "I have an indomitable desire to work," he wrote to Ada in August. "I need to work, otherwise I would die."

Viennese music lovers had already heard Toscanini's interpretations of some Austro-German classics during the New York Philharmonic's visit to the city, yet he wished to confront the hometown orchestra on its own turf: for his first program, he chose Mozart's "Haffner" Symphony, Brahms's "Haydn" Variations, Beethoven's Seventh Symphony, and Wagner's *Meistersinger* Prelude. He arrived in Vienna on the morning of 20 October, following a sleepless overnight rail trip, and, after having checked into the Hotel Bristol, he asked Burghauser to postpone the first rehearsal; Burghauser, fearing that the postponement would create rumors of trouble between Toscanini and the orchestra, persuaded him to rehearse at least briefly. Two days later, Toscanini commented to Ada, "The orchestra is good—not excellent, like mine in New York, and above all not as disciplined. You can tell that it's not accustomed to being in good hands. However, it's flexible, because at the first rehearsal it immediately modified itself so as to maintain the rhythm strictly, and it has responded perfectly to all of my demands."

In the end, he was satisfied—and the orchestra members were astonished. Years later, Burghauser, who had been part of the famed ensemble for fifteen years before Toscanini's arrival, described the maestro's impact. "I never had lived through the phenomenon of such a superhuman concentration as [the musicians] showed at these rehearsals," he said. "The orchestra, which had been day in, day out with Strauss, Weingartner, Bruno Walter, by then also Klemperer, with this ensemble of the greatest talent of the world—the orchestra, with Toscanini, realized this was the climax of every musician's experience. Not only because he was superior to other conductors— which was taken for granted; but because he made us *superior to ourselves*—which was the phenomenon that was practically unexplainable." Even in this repertoire, "which every one of us knew in his sleep," it seemed as if each piece was *"as newly created for us."*

The violinist Felix Galimir, a conservatory student at the time, sneaked into one of Toscanini's rehearsals and noted that *"before* the rehearsal—this was the historic event—all the violinists of the Vienna Philharmonic were actually practicing their part—which had never happened since Gustav Mahler left!" Toscanini was pleased by the reactions of the musicians: "The other conductors, they tell me, conduct differently and demand nothing at rehearsal; then they clown around at the performance, in front of the audience." He was tired, he admitted, but he also confessed, "It is a dear thing to me to note, from the demonstrations shown me by the whole orchestra, Rosé first and foremost, that I haven't yet started to go soft." Arnold Rosé, the orchestra's longtime concertmaster, was married to Mahler's sister and had played under most of the conductors of his day, from Brahms, the various Wagner disciples, and Mahler to the younger generation.

"It was the great Italian artist who honored our German masters and brought the Philharmonic musicians to a hitherto unachieved triumph," wrote Ernst Décsey, the city's leading critic, in the *Neues Wiener Tagblatt* after the first concert (24 October). "Their season began in the most auspicious way; only it will be rather hard for Toscanini's successors on the Philharmonic podium, since everyone will be measured against his vastness, everyone will be compared to what is incomparable."

At the end of the first concert, Margarete Wallmann—dancer, ballet mistress of the Vienna State Opera, future opera stage director, and Burghauser's wife at the time—was sitting at the side of the stage, applauding furiously, and as Toscanini walked off the stage, he kissed her on the forehead. At the postconcert reception, he joked, "I kissed his wife in public, now Burghauser won't sign my contract!" According to several normally reliable sources, Burghauser was homosexual; his relationship with the pretty, thirtyish Wallmann (who sometimes spelled her first name as Margarethe, Margarita, or Margherita) was a marriage of convenience: in the mid-1930s they were a force to be reckoned with in Vienna's musical world. According to Friedelind Wagner, Wallmann later became one of Toscanini's lovers,[*] and there are several not-so-subtle hints in that regard in Wallmann's memoir, *Les Balcons du Ciel*, concerning travels and other encounters with the maestro.

For his second Viennese concert (29 October), Toscanini offered an international program: Cherubini, Brahms, Debussy, and Respighi. "I had plenty to do to make [*La Mer*] clear and comprehen-

---

[*] When this writer asked Friedelind how she knew about the relationship, she said that Margarete had once told her that she had accidentally left her earrings next to Toscanini's bed and was afraid that Carla would find them.

sible," he wrote; "I think I succeeded. The whole orchestra broke into a great ovation. I was happy." And in another letter: "I can't begin to tell you what an enthusiastic and affectionate welcome I was given by the Viennese audience! Yesterday—I'm telling you this in confidence and a little shamefacedly—I wept a bit. But I managed not to show it. [. . .] And the orchestra players demonstrated that they adore me, and they're happy that I've promised to conduct two concerts with them in Salzburg next August."

But the usual negativity set in: despite the success, he was "bored," "not enjoying myself. Even the applause, the articles full of enthusiastic praise, don't make me want to continue." Furthermore, he had no privacy: "Photographers on the streets, at my arrival at the station, autographs, people who follow you down the street, who barge into your bedroom—it's enough to drive you crazy. I must have signed hundreds of albums and photographs! I'm rabid, and if I don't go home quickly I'll go mad."

During his stay in Vienna, Toscanini attended the Viennese premiere of *Arabella*, Richard Strauss's latest opera, in the composer's presence and with Clemens Krauss conducting an all-star cast that included Lotte Lehmann in the title role. "What desolation!" Toscanini commented to Ada, about Strauss's comedy of manners. "What wretched stuff! What a shame for an artist like Strauss to sink so low!!! I didn't have the nerve to go see him." He did not, however, tell his new love that he *had* gone to see Lehmann, with whose artistry and personality he had been favorably impressed; he had even stood to applaud her at the end of the opera's second act. But he did report that he had seen his former lover Elsa Kurzbauer: "At this moment she's out shopping with Carla and Wanda," he wrote to Ada. (Carla often befriended her husband's former paramours.) He did not subsequently mention that he had resumed writing to Elsa, telling her that he still loved her and that she was as beautiful and adorable as ever.

A family breakthrough took place in Vienna, when Toscanini bumped into Wally with her husband, whom he had refused to see in the nine years since he had first learned of their affair. Four months earlier, on 19 June 1933, Wally had given birth to a baby girl, Emanuela, whom Toscanini loved, but his obstinacy toward the child's father had continued. One day, "while I was walking all by myself in Vienna, wandering into the shops—an unusual thing for me—I heard Wally calling me," he wrote to Ada; "she was with her husband, Wanda, Tonio Puccini, and his wife, and she sort of pointed to Castelbarco. We greeted each other. I shook his hand, because it would have been terrible not to do so, but . . . I can't change the feeling of repulsion that I have for him. This saddens me for Wally, whom I love to distraction, but I can't get the better of myself!!! I have a nasty character, which makes me suffer a lot and makes others suffer." Wally later said that "from that moment on my husband was welcomed into the family," and Castelbarco was now able to come along when Wally brought little Emanuela to visit her grandparents.

Toscanini and the orchestra went to Budapest, where they repeated the program of their first Viennese concert, but, he told Ada, "On my arrival yesterday evening, I was surrounded by more than twenty cameras. Kodály and his wife were waiting for me. I ran off, swearing like a longshoreman. I jumped into a taxi, leaving behind everyone, including Carla, who caught up with me later, and I came directly to this hotel [the Grand Hôtel Hungaria], although I'd reserved an apartment in another—in order to shake those cursed pests!" But the success of the concert made him feel better, and he promised Burghauser that he would conduct concerts with the Vienna Philharmonic at the following summer's Salzburg Festival.

Immediately following his Austro-Hungarian adventure, Toscanini spent about three weeks studying and relaxing at home. Then, in mid-November, he and Carla set out for previously unexplored territory: Sweden. Tullio Voghera, one of Toscanini's assistant conductors at the Metropolitan, had been living and working in Stockholm, most recently as conductor of the Royal Opera's chorus, and had married the singer Iwa Aulin, whose father, Tor Aulin, was a founder of Stockholm's Konsertföreningens Orkester (Concert Society Orchestra, now the Stockholm Philharmonic). Tullio and Iwa had visited Toscanini on the Isolino during the summer, in the hope of persuading him to conduct their orchestra, and the maestro, after inquiring about the size and quality of the ensemble, had agreed to go.[*]

---

[*] Carla later worked out the contract with the orchestra's administration: Toscanini was paid 30,000 lire for two concerts, and presumably received half that amount again when a third concert was added.

The Toscaninis traveled by train across Germany and stopped in Berlin for a few hours to attend a recital by Enrico Mainardi, Ada's husband. "What a tragedy, what suffering, what humiliation!!" he wrote afterward to Ada. But he was not referring to the political situation in what was now Hitler's capital. "I listened to the music *he* was playing, I didn't dare to touch you, I felt the warmth of your adored body, but I didn't dare think of you, I wanted to be near *his* mind and not betray him."

Upon arriving in Stockholm, the maestro and Carla settled into a suite at the Grand Hôtel, in the Old City. His visit was producing enormous excitement: the newspapers printed articles about him day after day; he was mentioned in popular theatrical revues; and NK, Stockholm's largest department store, carried window displays about him. Rehearsals went smoothly, but after the second one "a shadow came over the Maestro's face," Iwa Aulin Voghera recalled, "and he hesitantly came out with a question: 'Do all Swedes have such uninterested looks on their faces? I wonder if they understand me. Their faces show so little reaction.' We laughed and explained [. . .] that that is just a part of the Nordic temperament: people don't show what they feel."

Toscanini had been warned by several musician friends that the orchestra was not an excellent one, but, he joked with Ada, "perhaps because of the immense pride of these players, who understood that they would have to play under a musician whose reputation is *almost* that of a *pestiferous ball-breaker*, they have certainly given the best of themselves." The first concert took place on 29 November, and "the public was extremely kind and enthusiastic," Toscanini wrote four days later. "It means that simplicity and truth still have value and power over the masses. One doesn't always need rifles or violent means to make one's worth felt."

A reporter for *Vecko-Journalen*, a Swedish weekly, managed to interview Carla during a rehearsal, presumably with Mrs. Voghera as interpreter. He asked Carla whether her husband was shy. "No, not if one understands how to approach him in the right way," she said. "He lives only for his art. If he has the public with him, he feels it in the air; but he doesn't value applause very highly, still less empty flattery and false opinions." When she mentioned that her husband loved children, Mrs. Voghera concurred: "Last evening, who but

Toscanini was sitting at our place, pasting postage stamps with the children and telling fairy tales!"

Toscanini conducted the Stockholm orchestra in two different programs, and they repeated the first program in Copenhagen—Toscanini's only appearance in Denmark. He was to have left for the United States immediately afterward, to conduct four concerts with the San Francisco Symphony between 15 and 19 December, but he postponed the engagement to the following spring. (He would eventually cancel it altogether.) Instead, he and Carla returned to Milan for a family event: Wanda's marriage to Vladimir Horowitz.

15.

TOSCANINI HAD RECEIVED GOOD REPORTS ABOUT HOROWITZ FROM Adolf Busch, and he had engaged the twenty-nine-year-old keyboard firebrand as his soloist in the "Emperor" Concerto during the Philharmonic's 1933 Beethoven cycle. When he mentioned to Wanda that Horowitz would perform with him, she gave a start: she had met the Russian-born and -trained virtuoso at a party in Milan the previous year, when she was twenty-four, and had then heard him play a recital that had impressed her deeply. As usual, Toscanini wanted to go over the score with his solo artist before rehearsing the concerto with the orchestra, and he arranged for Horowitz to come to the Astor. As Wanda recounted the story many years later, "Busch and other friends were continually warning [Horowitz], 'Be careful not to arrive late; if he starts to shout, don't be frightened; if he insults you, don't reply,' and things of that sort. Horowitz, who is shy and reserved by nature, was very frightened." He arrived too early and paced around outside the hotel; Wanda, afraid that her father would not like Horowitz's playing, had already gone out. "When the prearranged hour struck he introduced himself to my father," she said. "He expected a tempestuous welcome, but Papà was very gentle."

Issay Dobrowen had played a trick on Horowitz by telling him that Toscanini tended to conduct everything at excessively slow tempi, and Horowitz—who had never performed the "Emperor"—prepared it at tempi slower than seemed right to him. "I started to play—the Dobrowen tempo," Horowitz recalled. "'No, no,' said

Maestro. 'It should go faster, like this.' And he sang the theme fast, the way I had felt it should go. 'That's right!' I nearly yelled. I was so happy. We went through it and he liked it very much right away." The performance went well, and, unbeknownst to Toscanini, an understanding began to develop between Wanda and Volodya, as Horowitz was called.*

Each of Toscanini's children inherited some of their father's traits. Walter had his ability to concentrate but not his passion for any single profession. Wally had her father's liveliness and attractiveness but nothing of his ability to concentrate. Wanda, the youngest, was intelligent and had a keener ear for music than either of her siblings, but she shared neither her brother's wide-ranging interests nor her sister's social graces. Undiplomatic and with somewhat masculine features (Friedelind Wagner described her, cruelly, as looking like a death mask of her father), Wanda seemed to have been born into a lifelong losing competition with the beautiful Wally, her senior by nearly eight years, who was accustomed to, and expected, the admiration of men. Wanda always seemed to have a chip on her shoulder: the world owed her something, but what it was she didn't quite know. One close relative used to make an odd but telling analogy: "You can have the finest ingredients for a wonderful mayonnaise, but somehow the mayonnaise turns out badly. That was Wanda."

At least one and possibly both of Horowitz's two closest musician friends—the violinist Nathan Milstein and the cellist Gregor Piatigorsky—warned Wanda about Volodya's eccentric and egocentric nature and about the fact that he was bisexual, with a preference for men, but either she didn't care or, like many other women of her day, she thought that she could cure him of his same-sex attraction; the fact that she had been fascinated by Berlin's gay cabaret culture during the Scala ensemble's visit to the city in 1929 may indicate that she was naturally attracted to gay men. Perhaps the birth of her niece, Emanuela Castelbarco, Wally and Emanuele's daughter, in June 1933, encouraged her to move events along quickly: Wanda was at that

---

* The couple's main language of communication, then and later, was French, although they became fluent in English. With the maestro or at Toscanini family events, Horowitz spoke mainly French and English, alternating with a sort of pidgin Italian. Wanda never learned much Russian.

point the only one of Arturo and Carla's three children who was not in a steady relationship and had not produced a child.

Was Volodya as keen about marrying Wanda as she was about marrying him? One may be permitted a large measure of doubt, not only because of Horowitz's sexual preferences but also because he was narcissistic to an exceptional degree, even by celebrity standards. He was also timid, whereas Wanda was domineering. Whatever the truth of the matter may be, in September Horowitz asked Toscanini for his daughter's hand in marriage.

"What an idea—a foreigner, and of a different religion!!" Toscanini wrote to Ada. "What should I do? Continue to suffer! My children certainly don't fill my life with joy!!" But Horowitz was no more a practicing Jew than Toscanini and his children were practicing Catholics, and Wanda later said that her father's only comment to her on the subject was to quote an Italian proverb, "Moglie e buoi dei paesi tuoi" (Wife and cattle from your own village—in other words, keep to your own kind), although he also cautioned her, "You know very well that life with an artist is very difficult." But Toscanini, who knew nothing of his future son-in-law's sexual orientation,* soon changed his mind about the forthcoming marriage. "Wanda is radiant—she seems to be in a state of grace," he wrote to Ada. "I've never seen her so happy. May God protect her and preserve for her the [marital] happiness that has always been denied to me."

Sleek, stylish Volodya and plain, harsh Wanda were married in a civil ceremony on 21 December 1933 at Milan's city hall, in the presence of the bride's family and several friends;† the groom's family was not allowed to leave the Soviet Union, and Horowitz's father eventually died in one of Stalin's prison camps.

A daughter, Sonia, was born on 2 October 1934; she would remain

---

* Toscanini occasionally made mildly disparaging remarks about homosexuals, but in the world of the performing arts he inevitably worked with many gay men and lesbians, and he cared about his colleagues' sexual activities, whatever they were, only for their gossip value. The theory has been advanced that Horowitz became involved with Wanda because he had developed a crush on her father and Wanda was as close as he could get to Toscanini himself. This seems far-fetched but is not impossible.

† Toscanini gave the newlyweds an ivory carving of Saint Francis of Assisi—with his birds—that had belonged to Liszt and then to Liszt's daughter, Cosima Wagner. Horowitz kept it near his bedside for the rest of his life.

the Horowitz couple's only child, and she would have a difficult life, with two parents embroiled in a long, negatively symbiotic marriage.

WHEN ARTURO AND CARLA BOARDED THE *REX* in Genoa on 28 December 1933, for the trip to New York, their fellow passengers included Volodya and Wanda, Bernardino and Mary Molinari, Nathan and Rita Milstein, Gregor Piatigorsky, and the seventeen-year-old violinist Yehudi Menuhin with his family. This was probably the trip during which Piatigorsky tried to get Toscanini to play the cello for him. "I finally succeeded in luring him to my cabin," the famed Russian cellist recalled many years later. "My cello, with the pin out, waited for him. He sat on a chair but when I handed him the cello he said, 'No—no pin—it's a modern invention.' He pushed the pin back inside. I gave him the bow and he began tuning. 'The A is too high; the G is too low,' he grumbled. Fifteen minutes passed and he was still tuning. I hoped he would start playing. 'O bestia, stupido, now the D is too high!' He continued tuning until it was time to go to lunch. I never heard him play the cello."

Toscanini, now approaching his sixty-seventh birthday, had asked the Philharmonic's management to let him reduce his workload from sixty-plus concerts to forty-five during the 1933–34 season and to allow him to conduct all of his concerts during a single period in America, rather than in two separate trips. The administration, beset by Depression-related budget crises, pounced on the idea. The maestro's per-concert fee remained the same, but the total would reduce his $100,000 salary by more than 25 percent—with a parallel reduction in his income taxes, which the Philharmonic paid—and instead of reimbursing two of his round-trip transatlantic voyages, the orchestra would now have to pay for only one per year. This pattern would be maintained during the two following seasons as well.

Yet the reduced load made Toscanini all the more eager to get to work—for a while, at least. On 6 January 1934, two days after the *Rex* reached New York, he wrote to Ada, "I can't wait to begin rehearsals," and three days later he described his second working session: "After having re-rehearsed the last movement of the Brahms 4th (the marvelous Passacaglia) and having given a once-over to Tchaikovsky's Romeo and Juliet overture-fantasy, I rehearsed the *Lento assai* from Beethoven's last quartet, which I intend to play with string orchestra at the first concert, together with the *Vivace* from the same quartet. I can't begin to describe the emotion! [. . .] I hope to achieve something decent. But it's very difficult for us mortals to achieve divinity, and in this case we are really beyond seventh heaven." Following the second performance of the quartet excerpts, he wrote, "The orchestra is marvelous. I wasn't happy with myself in the Lento from the Quartet. Too little time for concretely expressing what there is spiritually in this sublime music, and which I feel that I possess only in my spirit, so far. I'll repeat it later, and maybe I'll be able to realize it as I feel it."

The excerpts were part of another Beethoven cycle that the Philharmonic's management had asked Toscanini to present: economic problems were continuing to worsen, and the previous season's five-concert cycle had netted nearly $17,000. He was only too happy to comply. Six different programs—twelve of his forty-five concerts that season (for which he was paid a total of $72,500.22)—were entirely dedicated to Beethoven, and ten of the remaining thirty-three concerts each contained at least one Beethoven piece.[*] At the end of the first concert, Toscanini received a visit from Fiorello La Guardia, who had been a patron of classical music in the city for two decades and had been installed as New York's mayor on New Year's Day. Toscanini liked the energetic little populist politician, whose father was from a small town in southern Italy and whose mother descended from a family of rabbinical scholars in Trieste; during the following years, the two men and their families would occasionally get together.

As soloist in the Beethoven Violin Concerto, Toscanini engaged Yehudi Menuhin. Four years earlier, the maestro, on Adolf Busch's recommendation, had attended a Carnegie Hall recital by the then thirteen-year-old prodigy, during which "the conductor kept his eyes glued on the youthful performer," the following day's *Times* reported. "After the last note, he went back stage, greeted him with enthusiastic exclamations, such as 'Divine!' and kissed him. The boy, who later told friends he felt this tribute more deeply than any other he

---

[*] At a performance of the "Eroica" Symphony on 1 April 1934, Toscanini dedicated the Funeral March to the memory of Otto Kahn, who had died three days earlier.

had received, said to the conductor he desired, above all things, to play a concerto like the Bach, Beethoven or Brahms under the conductor's baton. 'That will be a pleasure. We must arrange it,' replied Mr. Toscanini."

It did not happen immediately. But in the spring of 1932, when Toscanini was returning to Europe aboard the *Ile-de-France* after his single Philharmonic benefit performance of the Beethoven Ninth, Yehudi and his father were fellow passengers. "Yehudi's life-dream has come true," Moshe Menuhin wrote to a friend in England. "They have decided to make music daily from 11 A.M. to 1 or 2 o'clock. Occasionally Yehudi's accompanist [the Polish-born Artur Balsam] has been called in to assist [. . .]. From the beginning the boy insisted, 'Please, maestro, criticize me right and left, without hesitation. These will be my most precious lessons.' [. . .] After Yehudi had finished Beethoven's 'Kreutzer' Sonata, Toscanini burst out, 'Yehudi caro, bravo! Bravissimo! This is perfect, this is real music. How you have grown since I heard you three years ago; your heart, your mind! Oh, how little good music I hear in my life. . . Come, my child, play, play! Go on and on!'" Six months later, when Yehudi made his Milan debut in a recital at the conservatory, Toscanini gave the Menuhin family a guided tour of the city, during which he loudly bad-mouthed the Fascists, and he persuaded Moshe to let him "be Papa" during the recital, which meant acting as Yehudi's valet and moral support. Afterward, he hosted a party at his home in Yehudi's honor. Now, thirteen months later, he made good his promise to have the young violinist perform with him.

A day before the first concert, Yehudi went to the Astor to go over the concerto with Toscanini. The maestro had left orders at the hotel desk that telephone calls were not to be sent through, but just as they reached the most serene moment in the second movement, with Toscanini at the piano, the phone rang. They continued to play, but after the third ring Toscanini got up from the piano bench, strode over to the telephone, and ripped it out of the wall, plaster and all. Then, as if nothing had happened, Toscanini returned to the piano, and the two musicians calmly began where they had left off.

"He was always so respectful of the score," Menuhin recalled many years later. Beethoven wrote a strange indication in bar 45 of the second movement: two half notes—the G and B above middle

C—with a slur joining them, but with the words "*sul G e D*" (on the G and D strings) written over them. "We discussed it at great length when we rehearsed together, and I said, 'Well, I'll try taking it in one bow on the G string.' And the next day, the very afternoon of the concert, I got a message from him, handwritten, saying, 'After all, I think you'd better take it in two bows on the D string.' He was very conscientious, very meticulous about every detail." The performances were a success, but Menuhin never again performed with Toscanini.

Toscanini's soloists in his very first performances anywhere of the *Missa Solemnis* were Rethberg, the Swedish-born contralto Sigrid Onégin, Paul Althouse, and Pinza. "Ah, Rethberg, she was not good," he told an American friend many years later. Onégin, on the other hand, was a "beautiful woman, only she had the habit to sing flat. She asked me: 'I sing flat?'

"'Yes, Madame, yes—is not my fault.'"

In addition to the Beethoven cycle, Toscanini's repertoire that season ranged from Bach to Stravinsky. Each highly praised performance was followed by another, and yet the orchestra's economic prospects were bleak. Many major donors had suffered serious financial setbacks; even Mackay's empire was facing a crisis, and he ceded to Flagler much of his role in the orchestra's organization. When the board asked Toscanini whether he would be willing to participate in a public fund-raising campaign, he agreed to do whatever he could.* On 6 February, the Philharmonic-Symphony Society announced a plan to create a $500,000 "guarantee fund." To each person who sent a contribution of any size to the orchestra, Toscanini would send an autographed card. The Philharmonic's statement quoted Toscanini as having said that the city "owes it to itself to respond immediately and generously to the first call for help the orchestra has ever issued in its ninety-two years of existence." Requests for assistance were made from the stage by board members during concert intermissions and by important personages during breaks in the orchestra's radio broadcasts.

---

* He later suggested to La Guardia that entertainment and radio licensing taxes be instituted in America, as had been or was about to be done in many European countries, to subsidize arts organizations, but the concept never took hold in the United States.

Although a few people complained in the press that the Philharmonic was paying a huge salary to a conductor who did little to advance the cause of American composers, the plan worked. Within two days, $150,000 had been raised, mostly by a women's committee headed by Helen Astor and a men's committee led by Flagler, and within two weeks a national committee had been formed to aid the drive. On 25 February, during the intermission in the orchestra's Sunday afternoon concert, Eleanor Roosevelt addressed the nationwide audience directly from the White House; other broadcast appeals came from La Guardia, Geraldine Farrar—who had resumed contact with Toscanini—and the composer Deems Taylor, among others. On 25 March, Toscanini's sixty-seventh birthday, President Roosevelt and New York's governor, Herbert H. Lehman, sent him congratulatory telegrams, which the fund-raising committee had solicited and then published. A portrait drawing of Toscanini appeared on the cover of the 2 April issue of *Time* magazine, and the accompanying two-page article on the maestro and his orchestra mentioned that approximately nine million people—over 7 percent of the entire population of the country—were listening to the Philharmonic's concert broadcasts. On 30 April, the Philharmonic-Symphony Society was able to announce that the goal of half a million dollars had been met and surpassed.

The orchestra's board and the various donors, major and minor, would have been shocked to know that Toscanini was contemplating taking a year's sabbatical. "This fourth week is a little bit too much for me," he had written to Ada on 30 January, "and I'm more and more convinced that I ought to take a year off. As you see, I'm talking as if I still had a long enough life ahead of me to be able to subtract years from my work. Still, next year I don't want to come back." He would not mention this while the fund-raising campaign was underway, he said, but "once the thing has succeeded, I'll see to it that my point of view is understood. My hide, too, ought to be worth something!" But he was merely voicing one side of his eternal, internal struggle: on the one hand, he felt that he was working too hard, always trying to achieve what was unachievable; on the other, he felt completely alive only when he was making the attempt. Other unrealized plans to take a complete sabbatical or to retire altogether would recur over two further active decades.

16.

THE *MEISTERSINGER* PERFORMANCES THAT TOSCANINI WAS TO HAVE conducted at Bayreuth the previous summer would have featured Lotte Lehmann in the role of Eva. Widely considered one of the greatest singers of her generation, the German soprano was admired by audiences and musicians alike. Puccini and others had praised her to Toscanini for many years, and he had invited her to sing Eva with him at La Scala a decade earlier. "My refusal was one of the great blunders in life that can never be made good," she later admitted. "I had always heard of the impatience, ruthlessness and self-will of the Maestro, and it was simply fear of him that kept me from Milan. . . . So I foolishly threw away the artistic experience of making music with him."

After hearing her in *Arabella* in Vienna in the fall of 1933, Toscanini invited Lehmann to sing with him in the Ninth Symphony in New York the following winter; this time she refused because she felt that her voice was not right for the part. Now, on 11 February 1934, she finally collaborated with Toscanini, taking part in his first commercial radio broadcast. This half-length program, called *The Cadillac Hour*, made use of the Philharmonic's musicians under the name of General Motors Symphony Orchestra, for contractual as well as public relations reasons; the event was broadcast over station WJZ's network and took place before an audience of fourteen hundred in an auditorium in the RCA Building, a new skyscraper in Midtown Manhattan's burgeoning Rockefeller Center. The orchestra played pieces by Beethoven, Verdi, Wagner, and Mendelssohn and accompanied Lehmann in "Dich, teure Halle" from *Tannhäuser* and Leonore's great scene from Act I of *Fidelio*.

Lehmann recalled, in regard to the beginning of her piano rehearsal with Toscanini, "I trembled so much that I could scarcely sing," but "the object of my terror seemed so mild and friendly that my fears vanished and I sang with my usual freedom." The performance went well, to her great relief. A few days later, she sang some lieder as part of a Town Hall program for the Beethoven Association, and as she was about to walk onto the stage she told her accompanist that she felt relaxed: "An easy program, a nice appreciative audience, and no Toscanini there to be frightened of. . . .' And—my first glance at my audience fell on the Maestro. . . . My voice and my breath completely deserted me."

She wrote to him afterward, and he replied with a note written in French on the back of a picture postcard—a photograph of himself studying at the piano. "My dear *Lotte*. I am writing to you in haste. . . . I am very tired. . . . Six rehearsals and four concerts a week are too much for old maestro Toscanini. . . . Your letters are adorable. . . . Thank you[.] I hope to see you tomorrow at Carnegie"—where he was conducting the Ninth Symphony. "At the *Beethoven Association* you sang *very well dear—dearest Lotte*—believe me."

"Toscanini means to me a very special chapter in my life," Lehmann wrote to her close friend Viola Westervelt. "This man, before whom everyone that sings or plays for him trembles, is so *wonderful* to me, that I am quite speechless. After the recital he said to me that absolutely no one compares to me ('une artiste sans égale') and that no superlative would be too high to tell me how delighted he is. I am so proud—I almost wept for happiness. [. . .] He inscribed his picture to me: 'alla cara Lotte con affetto, amicizia e grande ammirazione' [to dear Lotte with affection, friendship, and great admiration] . . . ."

Toscanini was again in the audience at a Metropolitan matinee on 24 February, three days before Lehmann's forty-sixth birthday, to hear her sing Elisabeth in *Tannhäuser*, although he had to conduct a Philharmonic concert that evening. Sitting with him was Geraldine Farrar, now fifty-two and retired from the stage, and the maestro and Farrar were together again at another Lehmann recital at Town Hall, on 4 March; they stayed from the beginning to the end.

Toscanini's admiration for Lehmann was beginning to grow into something more complicated, notwithstanding his passionate correspondence with Ada Mainardi (which, however, abated between early February and late March 1934, owing, apparently, to the discovery of their secret by Carla or someone else close to him) and his resumed contacts with Elsa Kurzbauer and Farrar. As with Ada, so now with Lotte: *she* lit the flame. She had evidently written, late in February, that she feared bringing *Missklang* (discord) into Toscanini's life, because he wrote back to assure her that she brought him only *Gleichklang* (harmony).* She sent him an "avalanche of questions," he said, and she was thrilled but worried by his increasingly ardent replies. "I had a wonderful letter," she wrote on 6 March to her friend Mia Hecht. "He wrote that he was suffering 'comme un chien' [like a dog] and 'je vous aime, oui, oui, je vous aime . . . .' well, I am totally out of my mind."

"Have pity on me!!" he wrote to her the following day. "You are going to kill me with your blazing letters full of unbridled desires." But he enjoyed being killed. "Last night, lust tormented me to the point of madness," he continued, claiming that he had had "a sort of *hallucination* that made me dizzy. . . . I was looking at you in my bed *completely naked* and I, I was kneeling and caressing, with my expert hands, your breasts, which I don't know yet, while my mouth, my lips were engulfed in the *Divine source of all pleasure*. [. . .] It's a fact that this terrible distance which separates us only reinforces the chain that magically binds me to you—but what suffering must be endured!" And she replied, "When will you know my kisses?" (He quoted her words, in German, in answering her.)

"Mia, I am half crazy," Lehmann wrote a few days later. "These ever more intense letters are killing me. I gave him two postcard-sized pictures of me . . . and he wrote me, quite *madly*, that he keeps them next to his heart at night and kisses them like a madman and is dying of desire for me, etc., and laments that there is no chance to be alone together! [. . .] It is good that we are sailing soon; my nerves are destroyed." She worried—perhaps with good reason—that he had taken up again with Farrar: in one of his letters he protested that "no Geraldine could turn me away from you." To even the score, he said that he was jealous of her husband, who "*can possess you* when the caprice comes upon him," and of Bruno Walter, who "always accompanies you in your concerts!!"

Lehmann, who was married and also had romantic relationships with women, was falling in love with Toscanini. But was

---

* Toscanini kept at least some of Lehmann's letters to him; after his death they were returned to her, and she destroyed them. She intended to destroy his letters to her as well, but they were saved by Frances Holden, her longtime companion. In 1934, she wrote to him in German; he replied mainly in error-ridden French. Their later correspondence was mostly in English.

Toscanini falling in love with Lehmann? More likely this was merely another manifestation of his hyperactive libido—or of his desire to keep his libido as active as possible—combined with authentic admiration for Lehmann's art. His requests for photos of her and his protestations of suffering and desire could have been copied verbatim from his letters to several other women. (She was nearly a decade older and considerably heftier, at that stage in her life, than Ada Mainardi.) Toscanini attended another of her recitals, at Columbia University on 17 March, and they became lovers that night. "The thing between T. and me has taken on unforeseen and unwanted dimensions," she wrote four days later, again to Mia Hecht. "It is good that I am leaving—I can't take any more, I am at the end of my strength, my nerves are finished." Her husband was sad, she continued: "he feels everything, he said yesterday that I no longer seem to be living at his side, but rather in some other world, since I met T. . . . I could not even deny it. . . . Now I don't know what will happen."

Naturally, nothing happened—nothing, at least, of long duration. At first the affair continued by correspondence, after Lotte's departure for Europe. The lovers managed to tryst in Paris in June, and afterward she wrote to him (as he quoted her): "You transform this primitivity into such long, refined bliss that I feel an amazing longing immediately afterward." Two months later, they would meet secretly in Salzburg. By the following spring, however, the love story had reached its dénouement. "The flame is extinguished, no longer can I pretend," Lotte wrote to Mia in March 1935. She continued to write passionately to him ("My mouth belongs to you alone, I kiss no one as I kiss you," he quoted from a letter that she had sent him in May), and he lied to her ("you are the *only* woman in my heart—the *only* woman I love"). But he was gradually extricating himself from the affair. In July 1935, he denied her accusation that he was cold to her, and he hoped, or pretended to hope, that they would meet at his hotel in Salzburg. As late as March 1936, he was writing, with his usual blandishments, "I love you and adore you and owe my greatest happiness to you," along with typical descriptions of what he meant to do with her. One way or another, Lehmann and Toscanini remained artistic collaborators for a while and friends and mutual admirers until his death.

17.

SURPRISES CHARACTERIZED THE LAST MONTH AND A HALF OF THE Philharmonic's 1933–34 season. On the first half of one program, Toscanini conducted two Mozart piano concerti—no. 21 in C Major, K. 467, followed by no. 20 in D minor, K. 466—with José Iturbi as soloist; these were Toscanini's only performances anywhere of the two masterpieces, and his only collaborations with Iturbi. A few days later, he conducted a Town Hall benefit concert for the Beethoven Association, with an ensemble of twenty-seven players handpicked from the Philharmonic's ranks to play Mozart's Symphony no. 29 in A Major, K. 201; Wagner's *Siegfried Idyll*; and Beethoven's Septet. Even more unusual, in the annals of Toscanini's concerts, was an all-Bach program that included the Suite no. 3 in D Major; the Concerto for Two Violins in D minor (with the concertmaster Piastro and assistant concertmaster Remo Bolognini); the Kyrie from the Mass in B minor (with the Schola Cantorum), which he had been studying the previous summer; the Cantata no. 209 ("Non sa che sia dolore," with Rethberg); and the final chorus from the *St. Matthew Passion* (Schola Cantorum). Toscanini loved Bach's music, studied it thoroughly, and was familiar with all the available treatises on Baroque performance practices, yet he felt uncertain about the interpretation of this repertoire. He would have been attracted to the discoveries of the early music movement that began to gain momentum not many years after his death—and repelled by its orthodoxies—but his own Bach performances were few and far between. All of the pieces on this program were firsts for him, and, with the exception of the Suite and the chorus from the *Passion*, they were also lasts.

A more popular series—encouraged, like the Beethoven cycle, by the management, to increase the orchestra's earnings—consisted of three all-Wagner concerts on successive Sunday afternoons; each one included not only orchestral excerpts but also one or two substantial unstaged opera scenes: the love scene from Act II of *Tristan* on the first, excerpts from Act III of *Parsifal* on the second, and, on the last, the final scene of *Die Walküre*'s first act and the "Immolation" scene from *Götterdämmerung*.

In the course of the season, Toscanini received two awards: the Bruckner Society Medal, for his performances of two of that composer's symphonies, at a time when Bruckner was still infrequently performed in America; and a certificate of inscription in the Golden Book of the Jewish National Fund, presented by a group of leaders of the New York Jewish community "in recognition of [Toscanini's] magnificent act in refusing to direct the 1933 Wagner Festival at Bayreuth." Toscanini said that he was "deeply touched" by the latter honor, that he had "acted according to the dictates of his own conscience," and that "until the persecution in Germany of innocent people ceased, he would continue to refuse to participate in any musical activities in that country."

He was in the audience at several musical events, in addition to Lehmann's recitals, during his 1934 New York stay: the premiere of a new *Salome* production at the Metropolitan on 13 January; Horowitz's Carnegie Hall recital on 30 January; Milstein's performance of the Tchaikovsky Violin Concerto with the Philharmonic under Lange on 7 April; and, probably, a performance by Uday Shankar's Indian music and dance ensemble at Carnegie Hall on 21 February.*

At the Astor on 3 April, the orchestra and its board gave a belated birthday dinner in Toscanini's honor; the players had all signed a scroll as a "pledge of cooperation to your ideals in art" and a symbol of "respect, loyalty and love." The maestro, together with Carla and their niece Anna Polo, boarded the *Ile-de-France* on 5 May, six days after his last Philharmonic concert of the season. Toscanini shouted "No!" at press photographers on the ship's gangway but posed, smiling, for two schoolboys, shook hands with them, and gave them autographs. He had told the orchestra's administration that he would return in January 1935, but he would conduct only about thirty concerts—two-thirds the number he had conducted during the season just ended and only half as many as he had led in several previous seasons.

After disembarking at Cherbourg, Toscanini went directly to Paris and checked into the Hôtel Prince de Galles, near the Théâtre des Champs-Elysées, where he began to rehearse for his forthcom-

---

* Toscanini, Eleanor Roosevelt, and other notables were on the sponsoring committee of this last event—a benefit for the Child Health Center in Calcutta.

ing concerts with the Orchestre Walther-Straram: two performances each of a French program and a mainly German program. "I work and work," he wrote to Ada. "It's the only way to make life possible and to forget its miseries. And I'll work continuously. Always, until I draw my last breath. I still have a great deal of vitality. And the work doesn't weigh me down. This morning I rehearsed for three full hours, Wagner and the Bach[-Respighi] Passacaglia. I was very tired, but after a few hours I was as fresh as at the start, ready to begin all over again."

Désiré-Emile Inghelbrecht, recently engaged to create and conduct the French National Radio Orchestra, attended Toscanini's rehearsals and later wrote about the experience:

He knows, of course, that an orchestra will not go all out at rehearsals, giving its best only when in front of the public, like the majority of conductors. So he harasses them. *He* would *never* do that—spare himself! "You always do things *one-half . . .* ! Don't play *as if it were a habit . . .* !" [. . .] He threw his score down with a burst of anger which caused a grumbling in the orchestra. But this did not make him feel put out. [. . .] [He] roared: "And I'll always behave like this!" Another time after long attempts at getting what he wanted by persuasion, and not having been very successful, he calmly closed his score and said: "It isn't what I wanted, I did not enjoy it, but my conscience is easy." [. . .]

[In the Funeral March from *Götterdämmerung*:] So long as he does not achieve the same tone-value for the two harsh chords at the beginning, he will persevere. He will explain that they had been wrong in *always* playing the second chord of the first beat and the chord preceding the third beat less strong. Then he will proceed to the fourth beat of the *same* bar, dwelling on the chromatic triplet-figure of the [violas, cellos, and] basses, which he will take neatly to pieces, because it is being hurried, and this always and everywhere, in the attempt of somehow patching it up. "I have given this triplet lesson in vain all over the world," he says. [. . .]

Hardly has he left the orchestra, dripping even more with perspiration after a rehearsal than after a concert, his voice husky from continual comment and explanation, he will still talk of music as he moves away. If anything could be more striking than his unequalled mastery of conducting and his prodigious memory, it would be this constant fervor of his [. . .].

This may have been the occasion on which Margarete Wallmann heard Toscanini tell a Parisian orchestra, "It's bad to play 'so-so.' Better to play badly!" But the results were worth the effort. "One will never end praising the technical mastery of Toscanini," Prunières wrote of the Paris concerts, "but what is still more important is the way in which, in him, the musician transcends the conductor. He excels in conveying to us the profound sense of the symbols in the music of a Bach, a Beethoven, a Wagner, a Debussy. Behind the external musical form the mystery of thought and emotion emerge."

Toscanini returned to Milan after the Paris concerts, but by mid-June he was in Piazze for more of Dr. Rinaldi's treatments. Artur Rodzinski, music director of the Cleveland Orchestra, was there, too: he suffered from shoulder ailments and had learned of Rinaldi's successful therapies from Toscanini. The older maestro was pleased that Rodzinski's thirty-year-old bride, Halina, spoke Italian. "He immediately broke into a smile," she wrote in her memoirs, but she also recalled that the maestro "was no less a purist in his own language than in the musical languages of the composers he performed. He let no mistake go by, and every day in every conversation he would set right some grammatical construction. No woman ever had so august a tutor, I used to think [. . .]. 'I love your face,' he said, 'because I love women with big mouths.' Those teeth of mine, the subject of cruel teases by my brother Antek, had run the gamut from gross liability to invaluable asset. [. . .] Maestro had a wandering eye that, although myopic, ranged farther than broad smiles." She said no more on that subject, but years later Toscanini recalled with amusement that Artur and Halina had escaped to the nearby town of Chiusi when they were warned that the conductor's first wife was about to descend like a fury on Piazze.

While at Piazze, Toscanini developed a painful swelling in his gums but refused to see a dentist: "I've never gone to dentists," he told Ada. His home remedy—a combination of hot compresses and rinsing—worked. He managed to see Ada in Rome late in June, at the home of the Finzis, Roman Jewish music lovers who were friends of both of them, and he returned to the capital, again from Piazze, on 1 July, to visit the Finzis again, pick up a new tailcoat from a tailor* and some music from Molinari, and catch a plane to Milan.

"I'm sorry to say it, but coming back to my family is always depressing, oppressive," he wrote to Ada three days later. "It gives me the impression of entering a penitentiary! I feel that my every glance, my every gesture, my every movement are looked at, spied upon, discussed, weighed. It makes me want to leave again." He was probably exaggerating, to make Ada feel sorry for him; in any case, he closed himself up "in my nice study all day long," although the weather was extremely hot.

Both Arturo and Walter Toscanini spent a weekend in mid-July at Luigi Albertini's home at Gressoney-Saint-Jean, in the Val d'Aosta. They enjoyed the company of fellow anti-Fascists—Albertini himself, but also the poet Delio Tessa and the publisher Luigi Rusca of the Milan-based Mondadori house; Rusca had provided a job for Walter, who had given up running a business of his own. The maestro then went to the Isolino to enjoy the company of Emanuela Castelbarco, his one-year-old granddaughter, whom he found "bursting with health and cheerfulness."

As usual, however, he continued to be restless: "I would like to learn a bit of *peace*—but in my life it's always been like a language that's foreign to my learning ability!" he wrote to Ada. Internal agitation was both the bane of his existence and the source of his ongoing desire to probe more deeply into his art. Nietzsche's Zarathustra could have been referring to Toscanini in his well-known statement "One must have chaos in oneself to be able to give birth to a dancing star."

On 20 July, Toscanini traveled to Sils Maria, in the Swiss Engadine, to drop Carla off for a cure; there he received a message from Frau Thode and Frau Chamberlain in Bayreuth, who complained about the low artistic level of that summer's festival. He replied, sympathizing with them and inveighing against the "Pharisees" (Winifred and Tietjen) and the "perjurer Richard Strauss," who,

---

* Normally he bought his formal clothes from the Prandoni establishment in Milan. In 1931, for instance, he—or, more likely, Carla—paid Prandoni 6,250 lire for various suits of tails, other dress clothing, and accessories.

once again, was taking over what had been Toscanini's *Parsifal* production. By the twenty-third, he was back in Italy, but this time at an
eye clinic in or near Trent, where he underwent a three-week irriga-
tion of the conjunctival sacs. As he had to restrict the time that he
could dedicate to using his eyes for reading and writing, he often felt
bored. Yet the relaxation probably did him good, because after leaving Trent and spending three or four days in Milan, he set out for
Salzburg, to fulfill his promise to make his debut at the festival in
Mozart's hometown by conducting the Vienna Philharmonic in
three concerts.

The Viennese musicians had feared that he would not show up.
On 25 July, the Austrian chancellor, Engelbert Dollfuss, was assassinated by a group of Austrian Nazis in an ultimately unsuccessful
coup d'état, about which Toscanini commented, in a letter to Lehmann, "Oh! you accursed Mussolini and Hitler, you are the cause of
this storm of barbarism!! A spirit of violence is submerging old
Europe." The German-Austrian border is only three miles from the
center of Salzburg; there were reports of fighting and casualties in
the surrounding countryside; and a 10 P.M. curfew had been imposed
in the city—although it did not last long. During a performance of
Tristan under the baton of the Jewish-born Bruno Walter, a bomb
went off across the nearby Salzach River. Many visitors returned
their festival tickets and fled the area; other people who had planned
to attend simply stayed away. Neither Burghauser, the orchestra's
president, nor his colleagues in the orchestra believed that Toscanini
would appear in Salzburg in the midst of such instability. But the
maestro wrote to Lehmann that he had "never dreamed of not going
to Salzburg."

On 20 August, en route from Italy to Austria, he barely escaped
injury when his car, driven by Emilio, collided with another in the
treacherous Brenner Pass. Three days later, however, Toscanini
made his Salzburg debut conducting the Vienna Philharmonic in a
repetition of the program (Mozart, Brahms, Beethoven, and Wagner) with which he had introduced himself to the orchestra the preceding fall. Alfredo Amman, a friend and a driving force behind
Milan's prestigious Società del Quartetto, attended the final rehearsal,
during which Brahms's Third Symphony was played so remarkably,
from beginning to end, that "at the end, the musicians, transfigured,

jumped to their feet and gave vent to their exaltation with long, affectionate applause for Toscanini," Amman said. "In an encounter that same afternoon, Toscanini—who usually said that rehearsals were always a cruel torture for him—admitted that that morning's rehearsal had been an exceptional delight, also for him." As for the concert itself, the critic Herbert F. Peyser wrote, "Even he, to whom triumphs are as commonplaces in the daily lives of ordinary men, must have been shaken by the intensity of the demonstration with which a frenzied gathering acclaimed him." Afterward, Arnold Rosé, the Philharmonic's concertmaster, came to the maestro's dressing room and told him that he (Toscanini) had conducted Brahms's Third Symphony as Brahms himself had conducted it; Rosé, who was born in 1863, had worked closely with Brahms.

Three nights later, Toscanini led the orchestra in an all-Wagner program—proceeds donated to the orchestra's welfare fund—with Lehmann as soloist in "Dich, teure Halle" from *Tannhäuser* and three of the *Wesendonck-Lieder*: "Schmerzen," "Träume," and "Im Triebhaus"; this concert elicited similarly ecstatic reactions, although Lehmann was not at her best, vocally, and caused Toscanini to have to restart the introduction to one of the *Wesendonck* songs when she got the order of them wrong. But Blandine Gravina, Hans von Bülow's daughter and Wagner's stepdaughter, who had gone to Salzburg to try to persuade Toscanini to return to Bayreuth for the 1936 festival (he declined, saying that as long as there was discrimination against his colleagues he would not perform in Germany), declared after Toscanini's Wagner concert that in order to hear "the correct Wagnerian tempi" one now had to go to Salzburg rather than to Bayreuth.

On 30 August 1934, Toscanini conducted a final, mixed program (Cherubini, Brahms, Debussy, Berlioz, and Bach-Respighi), and, yet again, "an immense audience acclaimed the conductor with an enthusiasm bordering at times on hysteria," Peyser reported; that audience included Bruno Walter, Otto Klemperer, and Eugene Ormandy, as well as Kurt Schuschnigg, Austria's new chancellor, who, on behalf of the government, presented Toscanini with a facsimile copy of Leopold Mozart's *Violin-Schule*, emblazoned with the crest of the city of Salzburg.

A young, music-loving Russo-British philosopher, Isaiah Berlin, attended Toscanini's first Salzburg concert and wrote to his parents that it was "the greatest experience of my whole life. Toscanini is an enormous genius." Within a year, Berlin would "unhesitatingly" describe the maestro as "the greatest man in the world." Also profoundly impressed and moved by Toscanini's Salzburg performances was Stefan Zweig, one of the most popular writers in Europe at the time and a great music lover and collector of music manuscripts and autographs. Zweig, fifty-three, had a home on Salzburg's Kapuzinerberg; the previous October, after having been subjected to a house search by police (Zweig was Jewish, and the Nazis were gaining strength in Austria), he had made London his principal residence, but he occasionally returned to Salzburg, especially at festival time. Through his friend Bruno Walter, he made Toscanini's acquaintance, and he was able to attend rehearsals and concerts and to host both maestri at his home.

"This Toscanini is a wonder," Zweig wrote to the renowned French writer and Nobel laureate Romain Rolland. "I hadn't wanted to believe it. Now I am convinced! And what a man, what a rebel!! I spoke with him for five hours, and he filled my soul with a new glow, I felt like a twenty-year-old. Never has a man grasped music as he does; he is a genius of holy meticulousness and unbendingness in art. I would have rented an airplane to have you in my room with him and Bruno Walter!"* In a subsequent letter, Zweig told Rolland, "Nothing in the world gives me such an example of creative strength, of holy energy, as Toscanini's rehearsals (a thousand times more than the concerts), and I would undertake a three-day journey to be there. It is an *unforgettable* lesson for a musician: I saw Mahler, I saw them all, but nothing, I assure you, can be compared to this experience."

Zweig, who spoke Italian well enough to converse easily with Toscanini, developed an esteem for the maestro that bordered on idolatry; Toscanini, for his part, had already read and admired at least one of Zweig's many books, which had been translated into

---

* Rolland, however, had heard the radio broadcast of Toscanini's first Salzburg concert and had been shocked by the maestro's way with Beethoven's Seventh Symphony. "What remained of the broadly painted German dream in the depths of the woods?" he asked Zweig, and "why does this admirable Italian conductor do so much German music, which (in my opinion) he doesn't understand properly, and so little Italian [music], where he would have no rivals?" Rolland, a musical conservative, was equally critical of Walter's interpretation of *Don Giovanni*.

various languages, and he found the writer's company so congenial that he even offered Zweig the use of his home on the Isolino while he himself was in America.

Lehmann noted that "Toscanini was greatly taken with the [. . .] festival atmosphere of the old Mozartian town [. . .]. So he left Salzburg with the promise that the following year he would conduct *Fidelio* and *Falstaff*." The latter, she said, "would certainly introduce a new note in this Festival hitherto almost exclusively devoted to German works." Baron Heinrich Puthon, the festival's president, and Erwin Kerber, the general manager of both the festival and the Vienna State Opera, had persuaded Toscanini to make this commitment; at first they tried to change his mind about *Falstaff*, in part because Clemens Krauss, the Vienna Staatsoper's music director, had already planned a new *Falstaff* production for the forthcoming Vienna season and intended to bring it to Salzburg, under his own baton, the following summer. But Toscanini made his decision clear: No *Falstaff*, no Toscanini. The administration asked Chancellor Schuschnigg to decide, and the head of the Austrian government chose Toscanini over Krauss. Toscanini also agreed to return to Vienna in October for further concerts with the Philharmonic.

18.

AT HOME IN MILAN EARLY IN SEPTEMBER, TOSCANINI WROTE TO Ada Mainardi, castigating her for failing to appear there but of course not mentioning his Salzburg trysts with Lehmann. Relative epistolary peace soon returned, however. He spent a week on the Isolino but went to Venice on the twelfth to hear a performance of the Verdi *Requiem*, conducted by Serafin, in Piazza San Marco; his reason for attending is not known, but it gave him a chance to hear Maria Caniglia, the soprano soloist—an unintended audition that would prove useful the following summer. He left immediately after the concert, traveling through the night to the Trent area, to resume his eye treatment, and there he remained almost to the end of the month. He would often take his meals at a spa on the shore of nearby Lake Levico, and on one occasion he happened to meet Luisa Baccara, a former pianist and D'Annunzio's longtime companion. He found her "quite aged," he told Ada—Baccara was forty-two at the time—and he "wouldn't have recognized her if she hadn't been the first to rush over enthusiastically to greet me." But after a day or two they were dining together, and Toscanini was "beginning to discover the person I knew."

Baccara told D'Annunzio of their encounters, and the poet invited the maestro to visit him at the Vittoriale on Lake Garda, where he was a "kept man," as he described himself: his exploits at the time of the Fiume occupation had been an early inspiration to Mussolini and his followers, and the Duce, out of a combination of gratitude and caution, now had his government maintain the poet in high style, with the understanding that D'Annunzio would obey and praise the regime. Perhaps sincerely, perhaps ironically—or both—D'Annunzio wrote to Toscanini, "It is beautiful and infinitely rare that you stand erect in your glory, with such firmness and purity." Toscanini replied, "Not in glory, my dearest D'Annunzio, but in my disdain and contempt for mankind!" On 29 September, after his final ophthalmological appointment, he made his way to the Vittoriale, for lunch and a conversation with D'Annunzio; this would prove to be their final meeting. By nightfall, Toscanini was back in Milan, and the next day Emilio drove him to the Isolino, where he spent a few days studying for his forthcoming concerts in Vienna.

"If only you could make a quick trip to the lake!" Toscanini wrote to Ada on 1 October. "Divine days—the Isolino is bewitching! Just think, if we could be alone in this oasis kissed by God!" But four days later he left, first for Venice, where Wanda and newborn baby Sonia were staying with the Castelbarcos, and then for Vienna. "I'm fed up, my Ada, I'm exhausted—I no longer wish to be a good, reasonable person!" he wrote on the seventh. "Help me to stop being one—lose control of yourself, too." And a few days later: "Tell me you love me—even if it's not true." This last sentence reveals a great deal, not only about Toscanini's desire to be loved but also about his sharp awareness that women might think of him—a celebrity—as a "trophy lover" rather than as someone they truly loved.

As usual, however, work rescued him from himself. On 10 October, he and the Vienna Philharmonic, with Lehmann as soloist, gave an all-Wagner concert at the Musikvereinssaal, repeating, for the most part, the program they had presented at Salzburg a month and a half earlier; but instead of "Dich, teure Halle," Lehmann sang Isolde's "Liebestod" from *Tristan*. She was nervous about finding her first note after the orchestra finished the Prelude; Toscanini told her that he would hum it softly for her, but she had a hard time figuring out just what note his croaking voice was producing. Somehow, she managed, and, she recalled, "To the end of his days he was happy that he had helped me to sing right."* Four days later, Toscanini and the orchestra performed a mixed program, with Brahms's Fourth Symphony as the main work, and the following day they traveled to Prague, where their program combined some works from each of the two Vienna concerts. On the twenty-first, they presented a highly demanding program—Kodály's *Psalmus Hungaricus* and Beethoven's Ninth Symphony—in Vienna, and the next evening they repeated the program in Budapest.

After the Budapest performance, the maestro's arm was causing him so much pain that he was afraid of going to bed and then waking up feeling even worse; so the Toscaninis and various friends followed the postconcert dinner with visits to two nightclubs. The friends then dispersed, and "even the indefatigable Donna Carla's resistance began to flag," Margarete Wallmann recalled: "she put the Maestro in my hands for the rest of our 'Budapest by night' rounds. The final stop was a cabaret with a couple of contorsionists as its attraction. Fascinated and intrigued, Toscanini approached the tiny stage in order to see better. 'Margherita, where are their legs? Where are their heads?' Then, returning to our table: 'Go ask them to do their number again: you are such a famous choreographer that they won't turn you down!' But I suggested to the Maestro that we go instead to have breakfast: there wasn't much time until he had to get to work again—which he did, by the way, as fresh as a daisy."

The preparations for the Kodály-Beethoven program had given an important break to Erich Leinsdorf, a twenty-two-year-old Viennese opera coach and aspiring conductor. A day before Toscanini's first rehearsal with the solo singers, Burghauser was searching frantically for a pianist who could accompany both pieces, but none of the State

---

* There is something odd about this story, which Lehmann told many times over the years. Even for a neophyte, let alone so experienced a singer as Lehmann, thinking down a major third or up a minor sixth, from the final G natural of the Prelude to the first E-flat of the "Liebestod," would not normally pose a problem.

Opera's coaches knew the *Psalmus Hungaricus*—and they were all afraid of Toscanini. Leinsdorf had played the *Psalmus* two years earlier as rehearsal pianist for a choral society under the direction of Anton Webern, and he informed Burghauser that he could take the rehearsal. Having no viable alternative at hand, Burghauser told him to be at the Musikverein's rehearsal room at ten the following morning. The young musician arrived early, only to find the legendary bass-baritone Richard Mayr, a great favorite with the Viennese public, "already present, obviously tense and nervous," Leinsdorf recalled. Mayr worried that Toscanini would want him to go against his normal way of performing his part in the Beethoven Ninth. But "as soon as Mayr had finished the main part, Toscanini tapped him gently on his arm and said very simply but with much conviction, 'Bene, bravo.' [. . .] Toscanini had understood what caliber artist Mayr was." Leinsdorf continued,

I had this same experience time and time again: Maestro left well enough alone, never fussing over minutiae when the overall concept was there. Used as I was to the tempi of German conductors, it was also most astounding to me how fluently he took the tempo of the fearsomely difficult final quartet portion. Toscanini, perhaps because of his Italian background, was most keenly aware of vocal problems, and his way with that passage eliminated all terror for the singers. Nobody ran out of breath.

The Ninth was over fairly soon, three singers left, and only [the tenor Andreas von] Rösler, Maestro, and I remained for the raison d'être of my presence, Kodály's *Psalmus*. Toscanini once again simply sat and listened, at times making an ever so slight gesture to correct a tempo, but not stopping us at all. After we finished, he complimented the tenor and I got "bene" several times for the rendition of the difficult accompaniment. A few phrases were discussed and repeated and by eleven o'clock the rehearsal was over.

[. . .] When the Hungarian chorus arrived, it was immediately arranged that I must play the piano for the chorus rehearsal. Burghauser had one single idea: to keep any upset away from Toscanini. Having seen that I did nothing to upset him, he pushed me into every conceivable spot where trouble might develop.

Leinsdorf was then engaged to assist both Toscanini and Bruno Walter at Salzburg the following summer, and Toscanini suggested that Wallmann let Leinsdorf conduct one of the Staatsoper's ballets. " 'Maestro!' " she recalled protesting, " 'he has never conducted anything at all! How can I take such a risk?' 'But I, too, had to begin once!' he insisted. 'Yes, but you are Toscanini.' 'And he is Leinsdorf.' "

One person who was not at all pleased by Toscanini's Austrian successes was the pro-Nazi Clemens Krauss, the Vienna State Opera's music director, who did not hesitate to use every tactic at his disposal to make life as uncomfortable as possible, not only for Toscanini but also for Bruno Walter, whom Krauss saw as a potential rival for his position. Toscanini, before setting out for Vienna that fall, had received a request from the Austrian government to conduct a special performance of the Verdi *Requiem*, to commemorate the slain Chancellor Dollfuss. "Of course I've accepted," he told Ada, although he grumbled to Carla that the "Viennese seem to me like sandaled friars. They're always looking for handouts." When the government announced that, on 28 October, Toscanini would conduct the *Requiem* at the Staatsoper under official authority, Krauss could not openly object, but when Toscanini arrived at the theater for the first rehearsal he was turned away by a doorman who claimed not to have recognized him. Toscanini returned to his hotel, not in the best frame of mind. The problem was eventually resolved, but when the first rehearsal finally did take place, no pianist showed up to accompany the singers. B. H. Haggin reported the story of what then happened, as Burghauser, who was present, told it to him.

> Toscanini himself had to sit down at the piano, put his pince-nez on his nose, and begin to play for the soprano [Mária Németh, one of the State Opera's star singers]. Soon after they began, Toscanini stopped and asked her to sing a phrase in one breath, instead of breaking it to take breath; and she answered that she was accustomed to doing it her way, and showed him her score in which Bruno Walter had marked it to be sung that way. Toscanini, still quiet, told her she would have to sing it as

he asked. There were a few more exchanges, increasing the danger of a storm; and then an abrupt movement of Toscanini's head caused his pince-nez to fall off his nose to the floor. Before Burghauser could get there, Toscanini was on the floor, groping nearsightedly for the pince-nez, which he found; and sitting down again he put it back on his nose, only to discover that he could see nothing because the lenses had fallen out. In exasperation and fury he jumped up and stamped his feet; and at the terrible sound of the lenses being crushed, the soprano burst into tears and fled from the room.

The upshot of this Chaplinesque scene was that Németh refused to continue; Anna Báthy, the leading dramatic soprano at the Budapest Opera, was brought in to replace her, but the performance had to be postponed to 1 November, "as a result of a sort of plot here against the commemoration, instigated perhaps by Maestro Krauss," Toscanini wrote to Ada. In the meantime, he was feeling suffocated by Carla, Elsa Kurzbauer, Schnabl-Rossi, the journalist Italo Zingarelli—all of them seemingly with him "at all hours, at all meals, at all the rehearsals!!!" And he was convinced that Carla, or someone at her behest, was stealing his private correspondence. "From now on I'll travel alone, alone, completely alone, I no longer want to be surrounded by spies, thieves, people who aren't ashamed of stealing others' things," he said. But his anger dissipated: he needed other people to help him, and he wanted to be alone only some of the time.

The *Requiem* was performed at last before a packed audience that included Austria's president, chancellor, and various other dignitaries, and afterward Chancellor Schuschnigg presented Toscanini with a first edition piano-vocal score of *Fidelio* that contained Beethoven's handwritten dedication to his landlord, Baron Pasqualati, as well as some corrections, also in the composer's hand.

While the performance was taking place, Austrian Nazis were holding a demonstration at the grave of Dollfuss's assassin, where they laid wreaths bearing the inscriptions "Heil Hitler!" and "Long Live the Third Reich!" At the same time, various socialist groups were holding demonstrations at the graves of party members who had been killed by government forces the previous February. Dollfuss, during his two years in office, had created a homegrown form of fascism: he had abolished parliament, abrogated the constitution, governed by emergency decree, allied Austria with Mussolini's Italy, savagely put down a rebellion by Social Democrats and workers, declared the Social Democratic Party illegal, and, in short, governed as a dictator. Schuschnigg, his successor, continued his predecessor's policies. Dollfuss and Schuschnigg could hardly have been seen as upholders of democracy, but Toscanini—like most of his anti-Nazi colleagues—regarded them as bulwarks against Hitler and as politicians who had at least refused to adopt officially racist policies.

Barely a month after Toscanini left Vienna, Clemens Krauss left, too, to replace Furtwängler as director of the Berlin State Opera. Furtwängler had resigned in protest over the Nazi government's cancellation of the premiere of Paul Hindemith's opera *Mathis der Maler*, which was considered too radical for the spirit of the "new Germany"; besides, Hindemith's wife was Jewish. For the pro-Nazi Krauss, Prussian grass looked greener than the Austrian variety.

19.

TOSCANINI RETURNED TO MILAN JUST LONG ENOUGH TO REGISTER a complaint: La Scala was wasting tax money by commissioning Respighi to do a worthless adaptation of Monteverdi's *Orfeo*, he said.* By 8 November, he was in Paris to prepare four concerts with the Orchestre Walther-Straram at the Théâtre des Champs-Elysées, after which he took the ensemble to Brussels for two concerts at the Palais des Beaux-Arts.

Ada arrived in Paris while Carla was away. The lovers spent a day or two together and finally managed to consummate their affair, nearly a year and a half after their intense correspondence had begun. "Those Paris days were the dearest, most beautiful, most divine of my life," he wrote her from Brussels. "Love me, and forever. Be my last, supreme love." Was he being sincere? Certainly the

---

* According to some sources, Toscanini was considering giving a performance of the Monteverdi opera (probably in the musicologist Giacomo Benvenuti's realization) at Salzburg the following summer. But no such project materialized.

Ada story seemed more intense, and would prove longer-lasting, than most of his extramarital affairs, but, in reading his letters to her, one cannot always distinguish reality from wishful thinking or wishful thinking from pure invention.

From Paris, Toscanini proceeded directly to Stockholm—his second visit to the Swedish capital, where he conducted two different programs (28 November and 2 December). For each concert, people queued all night in the hope of obtaining tickets. But upper-arm pain was afflicting him once again; he was given an electrocardiogram and his shoulder was X-rayed (the doctor framed the X-ray and mounted it on his office wall), but to no avail. Rehearsals were tense, and Mrs. Voghera saw him pacing back and forth in his dressing room, complaining, "My arm no longer speaks." Gereon Brodin, a violinist in the orchestra, recalled that although it was sometimes "enormously stressful to play under Toscanini with his great demands and the high tension [. . .] he was normally patient and friendly, and then we loved him." The performances went well, and Toscanini promised to make a third trip to Sweden.

By 8 December—barely five days after his return to Milan—he was back at Piazze for further treatments by Dr. Rinaldi. There he remained for most of the month, although he managed to make an excursion to Florence on the sixteenth, ostensibly to attend a concert but in fact to enjoy what he described as a "divine night" with Ada. He spent Christmas with Carla in Rome, where, on the twenty-sixth, they attended the opening night performance of Monteverdi's *Orfeo* in the Benvenuti realization; Serafin conducted.

Around 1 January 1935, Toscanini returned to Milan and began working "like one of the damned, but with joy," in anticipation of his forthcoming New York season. One evening, a number of "very dear friends" came to dinner; they included Camillo Giussani, a financier and man of letters, author of Italian translations of Lucretius and Tacitus; Giulio Foligno, a Jewish industrialist who was among the Toscanini family's closest friends; and the poet Delio Tessa. After dinner, the Polos, Miecio Horszowski, Cesare Albertini, and the music-loving Count Giovanni Ascanio Cicogna dropped in, and "Tessa recited, magnificently, several poems by Porta and some of his [own] best ones—surprising for their poetic beauty, the

beauty of their new, unanticipated, and above all musical movements and rhythms."*

On the tenth day of 1935, Toscanini and Carla boarded the *Conte di
Savoia* at Genoa, together with Burghauser and Wallmann. At Ville-
franche (Nice), Stefan Zweig, his wife, and the Yiddish novelist
Sholem Asch also came aboard. The recently constructed ship was
famous for its giant gyroscopes, which were supposed to prevent
excessive bobbing on the ocean, and the captain gave Toscanini and
a few others a tour of the *sala macchina*. But the crossing was a particularly rough one all the same, Wallmann said. "Everyone got sick,
the gangways were deserted, the dining hall empty, with the exception of one passenger, who regularly took his meals with Olympian
calm: Toscanini. He called me in my stateroom so that I could better
contemplate, through the main hall's great bay windows, the colossal waves that made our ocean liner dance like a nutshell on the
rebellious sea. [. . .] '*Che meraviglia! Guarda, guarda!*' exclaimed the
Maestro, clearly in his element. But for me, a quick glance was
enough to send me back to my stateroom. [. . .] When the tempest
had ended, we all resumed the habit of getting together until very
late at night in the bar, where not even the jazz band, which made a
lot of noise paraphrasing themes from *Tristan*, could make the Maestro indignant enough to go to bed at last."

Although Zweig was among those who suffered from seasickness,
he and Toscanini managed to spend many hours conversing, and
Toscanini commented to Ada, "This writer is a lovely person, interesting to the greatest degree as a human being. He gave me his life
of Erasmus of Rotterdam in Mazzucchetti's translation,† which is
still in galleys. I've read it with the greatest interest. Magnificent! It's
about the eternal struggle of the spirit against brute force. Erasmus

---

*   Carlo Porta (1775–1821) remains the most famous of Milanese dialect poets. Delio Tessa
(1886–1939) is generally considered the best of the modern poets in that dialect; he was also
a strong anti-Fascist.

†   The Milanese literary scholar Lavinia Mazzucchetti (1889–1965)—a remarkable human
being, by all accounts—translated into Italian much of the most significant nineteenth-
and twentieth-century German literature. She was a close friend of Thomas Mann's and
several other major German writers, but she was unable to obtain a teaching position in
an Italian university because she refused to join the Fascist Party.

and Luther. The latter wins, of course. I don't know whether they'll let him publish it without creating difficulties."

The ship hove into the Port of New York on 17 January; Zweig, Asch, Burghauser, and Wallmann all spoke with the reporters who came aboard at the pier, but Toscanini "waved his hands above his head, cried 'andate via' or 'go away' and dashed down the hall-way," the *Times* reported. Among the friends on hand to greet Toscanini when he disembarked was Bruno Walter, one of the conductors responsible for the first half of the Philharmonic's 1934–35 season; the others were Klemperer, who had been recom-mended by Toscanini, plus Lange, Rodzinski, and Werner Jans-sen—the first American-born musician to lead part of the ensemble's subscription series. To Ada, Toscanini described Walter as "in good health and with an unusually animated expression for him, who always seems to me a *weeping willow*. He doesn't have his wife with him, and this explains everything."

The Philharmonic had come close to losing Toscanini during the eight months of his absence from New York. Although the previous spring's fund-raising drive had been a success, the Philharmonic's board still feared long-term financial disaster. At the same time, the Metropolitan Opera found itself in an even worse situation—so bad, in fact, that Gatti-Casazza decided to resign, after twenty-seven years at the company's helm, and retire to Italy at the end of the 1934–35 season. The two organizations' boards formulated a plan to merge, so that the Philharmonic would become the Metro-politan's house orchestra: the thinking was that although this would drastically reduce the number of both opera performances and symphony concerts in New York, it would also make Toscanini and the Philharmonic's other conductors available to conduct operas as well as concerts.

The proposal was widely debated within the respective organiza-tions, in the press, and by the public. For the Philharmonic's board, the decision hinged on Toscanini's reaction, and in December—a month before the maestro's next scheduled trip to New York—Zirato had been dispatched to Italy to present the matter to him. Even before Zirato's arrival, however, Toscanini had authorized his son to speak to the Associated Press. After having stated his father's com-plaints about the inadequacies of the Metropolitan Opera House,

Walter said, categorically, "It is absolutely to be excluded that my father would ever resume direction in the Metropolitan." And indeed, Zirato soon cabled Judson,

[Toscanini] believes the merger would not help either organization artistically. Giving concerts at the Metropolitan, the Philharmonic would lower its standards achieved so far. He believes it impossible that only forty performances of ten operas would satisfy the public. [. . .] The Maestro, however, wishes you to tell the members of the board that this honest opinion should not carry any weight in their minds, or arrest any negotiations if they still consider advantageous a merger with the Metropolitan.

The Philharmonic's board members did not fail to understand that such an amalgamation would cause Toscanini to resign. The plan was scrapped.

BEFORE A WEEK OF REHEARSALS for his first program of 1935 had gone by, Toscanini had begun to feel his usual internal conflict. On the one hand, "the orchestra is still magnificent—it plays with surprising enthusiasm and ability," he wrote to Ada, and "everyone—*orchestra, audience, friends*—says that life has begun with my arrival." But on the other, he felt overwhelmed: "It's a task for the young. [. . .] I feel the fatigue even if I don't show it. I always spend more than I take in; it's been this way all my life, but when one is thirty years old one can go into debt, certain of paying it off; but at nearly sixty-eight one may become a *defaulting payer!*" He said that he had mentioned to Judson the possibility that he would not return to the Philharmonic the following season; Judson's "eyes opened so wide that I thought they were going to pop out of his head. He told me that, on the contrary, he would like to make do with only two conductors, Furtwängler and me, plus one other to replace us in case of illness. I let him talk, but in my heart I know perfectly well that I'll make whatever decision is best for me." Toscanini feared a decline in his powers, and feared being unaware of the decline when it came. "I would be mortified to learn that people were saying, poor Toscanini [. . .], he's no longer his old self!!" he said. "I would like to end my career next year, once I've finished my fiftieth year of conducting, and I would like to end it full of enthusiasm and still more refined."

For the time being, however, the season proceeded normally. Between 24 January and 29 April 1935, Toscanini conducted the Philharmonic in thirty-seven concerts—thirteen basic programs, with forty-two pieces by thirteen composers, from Baroque masters to Castelnuovo-Tedesco, whose Cello Concerto, with Piatigorsky as soloist, received its world premiere on the season's second program. In his memoirs, Piatigorsky recalled that he had just arrived at his New York hotel after a terrible Atlantic crossing, with seasickness complicating a cold and fever, when he received a telephone call from Toscanini.

"What have you been doing all this time?" he said impatiently. "Your boat landed hours ago. Hurry, I am waiting for you." Soon I faced Maestro at the Astor Hotel, where he lived. [. . .]

Maestro at the piano, we began the concerto. Glancing at his score, I noticed that the cello part was virtually covered with penciled fingerings and bowings. No cellist except me had seen the concerto. Surprised, I asked who had made the markings. "I did," said Maestro. "Why?" "Did you forget I was a cellist?" he said, smiling. "One does hear fingerings and bowings, and I wanted to know if yours would be the same as mine."

Maestro banged on the piano in a true *Kapellmeister* manner. He spoke and he sang, and his spontaneity and vigor carried me away. By the end of our long and exhilarating session I had miraculously regained my strength, and I returned to the hotel in an exuberant frame of mind.

Piatigorsky, a nervous performer, also recalled that, before one of the concerts, Toscanini

paced the dressing room in which I practiced, warming up for the concert. His quick steps, his grunting and swearing to himself did little for my morale. I tried not to pay attention to him and to concentrate on my fingers and cello, but who could ignore Maestro? For a moment I stopped playing. Toscanini stopped, too. He looked at me and said, "You are no good; I am no good," took a deep breath, and began pacing again. I practiced, repeating passages frantically, and wished that I had died as a baby. After a while there was his terrible verdict again.

"Please, Maestro," I begged. "I will be a complete wreck." He was called to begin the concert and after the short [opening piece] he said to me in the wings just before we walked onstage, "We *are* no good, but the others are worse. Come on, *caro*, let's go."

Piatigorsky ridiculed the widespread notion that Toscanini believed in strict adherence to the score—whatever that might mean. "He would not trade a musical thought for the dot over a note," the cellist said. And as to the equally silly idea that Toscanini's performances of a given work never changed, "I once asked him if he ever misunderstood a composer. 'Yesterday, today, every day,' he shouted. 'Every time I conduct the same piece I think how stupid I was the last time I did it.'"

Six of Toscanini's Philharmonic programs were dedicated entirely to Brahms—a popular cycle that grew out of the success of the Beethoven cycles of the previous two seasons, and that included all four symphonies, three of the four concerti, most of the other purely orchestral pieces, the *Liebeslieder* Waltzes (with the Schola Cantorum and the pianists Coenraad V. Bos and Pierre Luboschutz), four choral-orchestral pieces, and *A German Requiem*. "Monday [11 February] I'll begin the rehearsals for the Brahms cycle," he wrote to Ada. "I'm conducting much of the music for the first time. [. . .] I'm behind [in studying], but I hope to make it through." Make it through he did, and two weeks later he wrote, "The Brahms cycle is going full steam. Never have there been such sold-out houses, not even, I think, with Beethoven and Wagner. It's stupefying when you think that only ten or fifteen years ago Brahms was [considered] hard to digest. The Requiem was given a magnificent performance. I think I understood it and made it understood. I didn't much like it formerly, but having had to study it in depth I realized that I had been an ass to judge it so lightly, just from the notes, superficially. It's been a good lesson for me."

One of Toscanini's non-Brahms programs, given twice, included two short, popular-influenced pieces—*Il Negro* (with cello solo, played by Wallenstein) and *Tango*—by Giulio Cesare Sonzogno, a young Italian composer, son of Renzo Sonzogno, the publisher who had challenged Toscanini to a duel in 1916. "Sonzogno had a great success with the audience," Toscanini told Ada, but "the *press is sour*." Indeed Downes, in the *Times*, described the pieces as "trash" and complained that "the serious works of young American composers have been passed by in favor of unworthy material from outside." Although eleven American composers were represented in the Philharmonic's 1934–35 programs—a distant second to composers from the German-speaking countries (twenty-two) but ahead of the Russians (ten), French and Italians (seven each), British (four), and representatives of four other nations—Toscanini himself conducted no American music that season. The previously described controversy over this issue had diminished but not completely gone away. In his seventies, Toscanini would try harder in this area, but the problem was that most American music was contemporary music, and most contemporary music, American or otherwise, did not appeal to him.

The program that included Sonzogno's "trash" also contained three Debussy pieces, and on the day of the first concert Toscanini "imprudently had an injection" of Dr. Rinaldi's serum administered to him after lunch. As a result, "just as I was about to begin to conduct the concert I felt as if I were going to faint. I didn't say a word to anyone. But while I was conducting '*Nuages*' I felt dizzy. So much so that when I had finished the Nocturnes, I gave the cue to begin *La Mer*," which was not the work scheduled next; "to my great surprise the Flutist, whom I hadn't looked at, began L'Après-midi d'un faune. Imagine how I felt!"

The incident exacerbated his feeling that he was working too hard. Three weeks earlier, he had written to Ada that "more is demanded of me than I can give" and that he was "terrified" at the prospect of having to conduct, as he had promised, concerts in London in June and operas plus concerts at Salzburg later in the summer. "I hope that God makes me take ill. This could still be a lifesaver for me!!" But he forged ahead.

As usual, he attended several musical and social events during his New York stay, most notably the local premiere, on 5 February, of Shostakovich's *Lady Macbeth of Mzensk*, a year after the opera's premiere in Leningrad and a year before Stalin virtually banned it in the

USSR; it was performed at the Metropolitan by the Cleveland Orchestra under Rodzinski's baton and with a Russian cast. Toscanini's opinion of the work is not known, but he continued to be curious, if generally unenthusiastic, about Shostakovich's compositions. Another Russian, Feodor Chaliapin—now sixty-two and nearing the end of his singing career—persuaded the maestro to come to a tea at the Hotel Plaza, to launch an exhibit of paintings and drawings by the basso's son Boris, later a well-known cover artist for *Time* magazine. And Toscanini was present at a mid-April gala performance at the Metropolitan to honor the about-to-retire Gatti-Casazza and at a send-off lunch for Gatti.

He had conducted an all-Wagner concert for the orchestra's pension fund on 13 February, and since the demand for tickets had greatly exceeded Carnegie Hall's capacity, he led a slightly shorter version of the program on 21 April. In between, and in the midst of the Brahms cycle, he conducted a commercial, one-hour radio broadcast on 24 March with the General Motors Symphony Orchestra, as he had done the preceding year. Instead of Lehmann, his soloist was Rethberg, who sang two Verdi arias as part of a mixed program. He concluded his New York season with three performances of the *Missa Solemnis*, after the first of which he went back to the Astor and took to bed with a medium-grade fever—but he conducted the remaining performances two and three nights later. In addition, his arm was "in a completely disastrous condition," he wrote to Ada.

On 2 May, Arturo and Carla departed aboard the Cunard White Star liner *Majestic*, and for the first four days Toscanini did not leave his stateroom. "I slept profoundly for the first two, and I made up for the sleepless nights in New York," he told Ada. "I stayed in bed to rest my painful and tired shoulder and arm, too. Then Carla came down with a [. . .] high fever and pains all over her body. So I never for a moment stopped helping her and keeping her company." They disembarked at Cherbourg on the eighth and spent two days in Paris, from which Toscanini flew to Milan via Zurich. He went to Piazze for treatments and remained there until the twenty-fifth—minus one excursion to Florence, to spend a night with Ada; and he spent another night with her there at the end of his stay in Piazze, when he was en route back to Milan. But more travel was around the corner: another significant segment of Toscanini's musical life was about to begin.

20.

FOR THIRTY YEARS, VARIOUS LONDON MUSICAL ORGANIZATIONS had tried to engage Toscanini, but his only professional appearances in Britain had been with the touring New York Philharmonic, in 1930. He had always feared that English orchestras were even less likely than their French counterparts to provide conditions that would allow for serious work. But the situation had changed.

In 1934, Horowitz had performed with the BBC Symphony Orchestra—the five-year-old ensemble that the British Broadcasting Corporation had put together under the direction of Adrian (soon to be Sir Adrian) Boult. Volodya had been impressed with the group's caliber and work ethic, and he had communicated his enthusiasm to his father-in-law, who had then accepted an invitation from the organization. Toscanini would conduct four concerts—two programs, each repeated once, with some variants—at the Queen's Hall during the London Music Festival in June 1935; he would have a maximum of twelve rehearsals in all and would receive a total fee of £2,000.

Arturo and Carla arrived in London on 29 May, just as Prime Minister Ramsay MacDonald was preparing to turn the reins of the national government over to Stanley Baldwin, amid serious concerns about German rearmament and how to counter it. The next day, Boult took the maestro to the first rehearsal, introducing him to the orchestra by saying "something about our achieving the desire of every one of us, using the word 'greatest,'" Boult recalled. "At this the Maestro gave me a hearty thump on the shoulders: 'No, no, no, no, no. Not that at all: just an honest musician.' So we all laughed and I left them to it, chose a seat in the circle and waited for the first explosion, wondering what on earth to do when it came."

It didn't come. "In fact, the two middle movements of the Brahms [Fourth Symphony] went through without interruption," Boult continued. "'Bene, bene, bene,' he said, 'just three things.' He then found three passages, put them right, and went straight on. [. . .] Needless to say, the orchestra worshipped the Maestro from that first rehearsal."

At the end of that session, "the maestro expressed his satisfaction," the *Manchester Guardian*'s special correspondent wrote. "The orchestra gasped and sent their leader* to make sure that the great conductor was really pleased. Back came Mr. Catterall with the answer, 'You would have known if I had not been pleased.' "

Toscanini's first BBC program, on 3 June, began with Cherubini's *Anacréon* Overture, continued with the Brahms symphony, and concluded with the "Enigma" Variations and the Funeral Music from *Götterdämmerung.* As in 1930, when the Elgar piece had been on one of the Philharmonic's London programs, so again now some of the critics found Toscanini's interpretation insufficiently "English," but Sir Landon Ronald, a well-known conductor and a friend of Elgar's— who had died the previous year—wrote to the *Times* of London: "This great conductor rendered the work exactly as Elgar intended, and the composer's idiom has obviously no secret for Toscanini. Some of the best performances I have ever heard were from the composer himself, but Toscanini excelled because he has a genius for conducting and Elgar had not." Boult agreed with Ronald, and said, further, that so great an artist as Toscanini "seems to have the power of grasping the essence of the style of any music he touches."

John Barbirolli, the thirty-five-year-old Italo-English conductor of the Scottish Orchestra, attended a rehearsal and the concert and, in a letter to his fiancée, the oboist Evelyn Rothwell, he said that he was "much moved by [Toscanini's] attitude to music, which is one of the greatest sincerity, humility and ideal of service. It is extraordinary how a man of such individual power can yet create the illusion that there is nothing coming between you and the music. A lovely tone quality he gets, and such endless lines of phrase, and all with such impeccable taste and dignity. The orchestra played well for him, strings especially, but the intonation was frankly *bad.* I really cannot understand it."

Barbirolli had a "Toscanini connection"—his father and grandfather had both played violin in the Scala orchestra with the future maestro at the world premiere of *Otello* in 1887—thus he managed to meet and chat with the maestro. "The two hours spent with Toscanini were lovely," he told Rothwell.

He talked much of Father and their times together, also I was able to ask him many things about the licence permissible in

---

* "Leader" in the UK = "concertmaster" in the United States.

Verdi operas, and very relieved to find I was perfectly right in the stand I had taken in this matter. On telling him of some of the things I had heard at C[ovent] G[arden] under so-called distinguished Italian conductors he proceeded to describe them as men who are not only ignorant, but traitors to music. [. . .] But the most revealing thing of all was the man's great *simplicity* and burning sincerity in his love of music. [. . .] He was so sweet to me, and to hear him call me "Caro Maestro" tickled me to death. [. . .] The orchestra played better last night. . . . The Brahms and Wagner were unforgettable. Such nobility of music-making becomes a great inspiration and I feel very secure about my methods of work. A great man should do this to his young contemporaries.

In addition to the works on his first program, Toscanini's London repertoire included works by Debussy, Beethoven, Mozart, Wagner (again), Geminiani, Rossini, and Mendelssohn. He was happy with the "excellent, intelligent orchestra that immediately showed me liking and affection," he told Ada—so much so that he cut several rehearsals short and canceled at least one and probably several of them. But there were the usual personal ups and downs: Wanda and Volodya were staying in an adjoining suite at Claridge's for the first ten days of Toscanini's stay, which made privacy difficult. Although he was pleased to be visited by Stefan Zweig, Rudolf and Irene Serkin (the pianist had recently married Adolf and Frieda Busch's daughter), Tonio Puccini, Vincenzo Tommasini, Luigi Albertini, and Giuseppe Emanuele Modigliani,* he complained that he was rarely alone long enough to be able to write to Ada or phone her. Yet when visitors left he complained that "every departure increases my sadness." Worse, he learned that the American journalist Max Smith, "my old and very affectionate friend," had died on 7 June: "I am terribly saddened, although I was expecting the sorrowful news from one moment to another," he wrote to Ada.

In the midst of all this, he received an upsetting message from the New York Philharmonic: Local 802 of the American Federation of

---

* The older brother of the painter Amedeo Modigliani, Giuseppe Emanuele was a former Italian Socialist Party leader; he was living in Paris, in self-imposed exile from Fascist Italy.

Musicians was making demands—presumably regarding an increase in salary and/or benefits for the orchestra's musicians—and this had caused the board of directors to consider reducing the ensemble's personnel from 110 to 95. Hans Lange was sent to London to try to persuade Toscanini that such a reduction would not lower the orchestra's artistic level, but Toscanini rejected the idea at once. "It is his opinion that if the Board of Directors cannot raise the money to comply with the demands of the Union they should rather disband the whole orchestra than reduce it," Lange wrote to Zirato. Toscanini considered the proposal "inartistic," especially with respect to letting go of "the 4th wind instruments." He reminded his interlocutors that there had been much sickness the previous year and that it would be "impossible" to have outside replacements "jump in at the last minute without a rehearsal. [. . .] Besides all this, is Maestro [*sic*] of the opinion that letting out of so many musicians is a very *inhuman* and unjust action, to which he never will agree," especially "in times like these, where there is no hope for them to get other engagements." In short, "If the Board of Directors finds ways and means to keep the orchestra at its full strength, he will come and conduct next season." Otherwise, "he would prefer to stay in Europe."

In a private letter to Zirato, sent along with the official one just cited, Lange wrote that Toscanini "seems to like now guest conducting and hates a steady position. He is tired and he wants a change. The [BBC Symphony] concerts have been an unbelievable success. The audience is just crazy. London tries to get him for a longer time, he likes the orchestra and they pay him more than N.Y. (at least the papers say so)."* Lange also let Zirato know that Toscanini wanted to keep all of the Philharmonic's current players, replacing only those who were retiring. Four days later, Toscanini backed up his comments to Lange with a strongly worded cablegram to the Philharmonic.

Zirato replied to Lange that he didn't understand "how Maestro can speak of 'humanity'" when he was contemplating disbanding the entire orchestra. But Toscanini knew exactly how his world functioned: "One must always threaten in order to get what one

---

* He was paid roughly 25 percent more per concert in London than in New York, but for a much shorter engagement.

wants!" he explained to Ada, on a later occasion. The Philharmonic's size remained stable as long as Toscanini was in charge.

The London concerts were indeed an "unbelievable success," as Lange had said. The critic Neville Cardus, writing in the *Guardian*, described them as "the most important events that have occurred for years in the musical life of this country." He said that although many musicians try, like Toscanini, to "follow the score faithfully," the "understanding of style is knowledge plus imagination. [. . .] Toscanini's art combines knowledge and vision." And a twenty-one-year-old composer named Benjamin Britten wrote in his diary, after Toscanini's final concert, "of course the crowd went mad" and "of course they were right, he is a great man."

During his stay in England, Toscanini found time to attend Fritz Busch's performance of *The Magic Flute* at Glyndebourne, a small opera festival created the preceding year by John Christie and his wife, the soprano Audrey Mildmay, in a 300-seat theater on their estate in East Sussex. "Toscanini and his wife and daughter and her husband Horowitz arrived and sat in our box and dined," Mildmay wrote in her diary. "Toscanini crept in at high speed into the back row of the box. Didn't speak, but at dinner he expanded, but did not say one word to me about the performance. He has enormous charm." He was to have returned to hear *Così Fan Tutte*, but something—probably his arm troubles—prevented the visit. He also attended a lunch given in his honor at Claridge's by the BBC's governors, and he told Sir John Reith, the organization's director general, that there was no better orchestra in Europe than the BBC Symphony.

Most surprising was Toscanini's willingness to answer questions at a press conference on 13 June—the only event of its kind in which he ever participated. He praised the orchestra and said that he had not previously conducted English orchestras, because they "had this reputation amongst foreign conductors, that their powers of sight-reading were so remarkable that at a first rehearsal they promised marvellous things," the *Guardian*'s correspondent reported—in his own words, not Toscanini's; "at subsequent rehearsals, however, they proved incapable of a process of polishing. Now it is precisely that process of polishing which Toscanini conceives to be his job, and he holds that the B.B.C. orchestra has proved itself amenable to the process." The maestro was asked whether he would return the following year. " 'Yes, if you wish,' he answered, turning to Dr. Boult. Dr. Boult was willing to make an engagement of it on the spot, and asked if Toscanini would conduct a choral work—Verdi's Requiem or the Beethoven Mass. Yes, Toscanini would."

About broadcasting, the maestro said, "If my concerts are heard by millions of listeners, then I am glad. It does not worry me to think of the microphones." But he declared that he would not make any more records, because "after I hear my own records once, I hate them."

Throughout the press conference, he "remained urbane, but only just, even when one member of the company, greatly daring, submitted for consideration an alternative to the Toscanini rendering of certain appoggiaturas in Beethoven's Seventh Symphony. But the hypnotic eyes flashed and a quick hand swept past the maestro's ear as though to brush away all memory of it." And at the end: " 'I am not happy being questioned like this. . . . Still, good day, gentlemen.' "

Toscanini's last London concert took place on the evening of 14 June, and the following day he returned to Milan by air. He spent most of the rest of that month and parts of the first half of July on the Isolino, occasionally alone with the domestic help but more often among family and friends. On one occasion, Artur and Halina Rodzinski observed Wally and Wanda "haranguing Maestro for not demanding greater royalties for his recordings, and generally ignoring anything he had to say in reply," Halina wrote. She continued,

> Artur was genuinely shocked. He had placed Maestro on so high a pedestal that he thought the man far above such family scenes, and with a subject that impinged on his rights as an artist. Royalties and fees were subjects that Artur never discussed with me.
>
> Finally the family went off for its siesta, leaving Maestro to Artur and me for what was an unforgettable afternoon. [. . .] Artur left us for a moment and I [. . .] expressed my concern over Artur's continuing discontent with his work despite his success.
>
> "*Cara*," Toscanini said, "in all my artistic life I have never had one moment of complete satisfaction." I was thunderstruck. "I cannot believe you, Maestro," I told him bluntly. Here, before me, was the most beloved and famous conductor in the world [. . .]. "*Cara*," he replied, "the people who love and

make a conductor famous are a crowd, and crowds know nothing. No true musician can be satisfied with his performance, even though an audience is driven to a frenzy." [. . .]

Artur returned just then to hear Maestro say "I am tired, and soon I will stop conducting."

"Maestro," Artur broke in, "you cannot be serious. You still have tens of years to make music."

"No, Rodzinski," he murmured, "I am tired, and I have already done enough. *Sono stufo, e sono stanco!*" [I am fed up, and I am tired!] [. . .] [He said] that already he had it in mind to resign as director of the New York Philharmonic.

On the last point, however, Toscanini was still of two minds.

21.

IN LONDON, JOHN BARBIROLLI HAD TOLD TOSCANINI THAT HE WAS looking well. The reply: "'My boy, five years *without* opera!'"

Since his last Bayreuth performance four years earlier, Toscanini had not set foot in an orchestra pit. But he was about to go back to his first love, if only temporarily. By early July, he was making trips from the Isolino to Milan nearly every day, to rehearse the singers for his forthcoming Salzburg production of *Falstaff*. He had invited Ezio Pinza to take the title role, but Pinza—already engaged to sing the title role in *Don Giovanni*, with Bruno Walter conducting—declined. Toscanini then turned to Mariano Stabile, his favorite fat knight during the 1920s, and he engaged several other members of his Scala *Falstaff* casts to resume their former parts: Giuseppe Nessi as Bardolfo, Fernando Autori as Pistola, Mita Vasari as Meg, and Angelo Badà as Cajus.*

Toscanini flew to Salzburg on 17 July and was pleased by "the great good fortune of having a house" at his disposal, in the adjacent village of Liefering. "It's really comfortable, delightful, in the midst of greenery with a magnificent mountain range all around," he

---

* The Russian-born Angelica Cravcenco (in the role of Quickly) and the American Edith Mason (Nannetta) had also sung with him at La Scala, although not in those roles. Piero Biasini (Ford), Dino Borgioli (Fenton), and the Italian American soprano Dusolina Giannini (Alice) were working with him for the first time.

wrote to Ada. Liefering was "far enough that I don't feel the burden" of being in town "but not so far as to make one feel totally isolated." Nevertheless, as Lotte Lehmann observed, people "crowd around him," and "he is pursued and persecuted by curiosity wherever he goes. When his fine big Cadillac draws up outside the Opera House, photographers, whom he particularly detests, are waiting for him, autograph-hunters fall on him and are furiously rebuffed."

But work proceeded on schedule. Lehmann, singing the title role in *Fidelio,** described the rehearsals as "a perpetual 'shaking and quaking in anguish and pain,'" although Toscanini was "full of consideration" and "advised vocal restraint when all of us were overexerting ourselves too lavishly during the rehearsals." He wrote out for her a description he had found of the legendary Maria Malibran's singing and acting in the role of Leonore a century earlier, and Lehmann was delighted to discover that Toscanini "belongs to the theater to his fingertips." Although he spoke hardly any German, "he has such a fine ear for German pronunciation that he constantly corrects words if the diction is not clear enough for him," she said. "It amazed me to find how a pure musician like him works from the dramatic text. A vividly acted performance is as important to him as a complete realization of the music. Through his sharp eyeglass he notices everything, nothing escapes that keen relentless eye." The stress level was high, but "what a compensation that *Fidelio* was!"

During the *Falstaff* rehearsals, Toscanini's "famous temper tantrums were in ample evidence," Leinsdorf recalled, "as if he had an authentic mandate" from Verdi himself. One reason for those outbursts concerned the set for the opening scene of Act III. The production, created by Robert Kautsky, the Staatsoper's chief set designer, had been undertaken for Clemens Krauss in Vienna the previous fall, and Toscanini, at the time of his rehearsals there for the Verdi *Requiem*, had noticed that in the scene in question Falstaff was not drying himself in front of the Garter Inn, as the instructions in the score indicate, but lying in bed, under a pile of blankets. He had informed Burghauser on the spot that if the same set were to

---

* The rest of the cast included Andreas von Rösler (Florestan), Alfred Jerger (Don Pizarro), Anton Baumann (Rocco), Luise Helletsgruber (Marzelline), Hermann Gallos (Jaquino), and Emanuel List (Don Fernando).

appear in Salzburg he would abandon the production.* Now, when Toscanini saw that the change had not been made, he walked out of the theater, and only a frantically produced new set brought him back to the Festspielhaus the following day.

Three days before the first performance, Dusolina Giannini came down with an inflamed larynx and was ordered to rest her voice for two weeks. Toscanini wired Maria Caniglia, a thirty-year-old Italian soprano who had already sung the all-important role of Alice and whom he had heard in the Verdi *Requiem* in Venice the preceding September; she caught an overnight train from Milan to Salzburg, arrived the following morning, and was driven immediately to the dress rehearsal, which took place before a full, invited house. By the time she had put on her costume, the first, all-male part of Act I was already ending; she was hustled onto the stage and saw Toscanini, on the podium, ready to begin the following scene, in which Alice is among the protagonists. "I crossed myself and began to sing," she recalled. "At the end of the first act I was shaking with fear; on my way to my dressing room I encountered the Maestro, who said to me: 'Pleased to meet you, signorina. It's fine, onward we go.'" To Ada, Toscanini commented, "Caniglia isn't better than Dusolina Giannini (the latter is more musical and intelligent), but she has a good voice and looks good." The dress rehearsal aroused enthusiasm, Toscanini said, "starting with the orchestra players, who, at the end, stood up and gave a warm, affectionate display, and the chorus on stage joined with the audience in the auditorium, increasing the enthusiasm."

The *Falstaff* premiere was "a performance of unmatchable perfection," Leinsdorf recalled, and Burghauser said that after the first act, the seventy-two-year-old Felix Weingartner, who had succeeded Krauss as head of the Vienna State Opera, "leapt" into the pit and exclaimed to the orchestra, "Such perfection I have never experienced or dreamed of."

"What a day!" Stefan Zweig exclaimed, in a letter to Romain Rol-

---

* By twenty-first-century standards of opera staging, Kautsky's infraction seems minor. But according to the printed instructions, Alice, Ford, and other characters in the story are hiding near the entrance to the inn, listening as Quickly begins to trick Falstaff into believing that Alice really loves him. Quickly and Falstaff then go into the Garter together, and the eavesdroppers emerge. If Falstaff is already inside the inn at the beginning of the scene, the plot's mechanics don't function.

land. "A supreme performance of 'Falstaff' with Tosc." Even Toscanini himself reported to Ada, "Falstaff was accorded a truly sincere and enthusiastic success. All the singers were calm and assured; they seemed to be singing a last performance, rather than a first one."

On the day before the second *Falstaff* performance, Leinsdorf was told to assemble the cast for a brush-up rehearsal at the piano, at which Toscanini and the singers "just sat around while old stories were swapped [. . .] until Toscanini with the kindest greetings all around dismissed the *Falstaff* cast." Leinsdorf asked what the purpose of the "rehearsal" had been, and Toscanini explained: it was important to remind the singers to "'set a schedule of rest and of refreshing the memory for the 24 hours preceding the performance according to their needs,' he said. 'Since all went well at the premiere there was nothing for us to rehearse or correct.'" Leinsdorf was surprised to discover the falsity of the legend that Toscanini required more rehearsal time than anyone else. Like Puccini and many others who had observed the maestro's rehearsal methods in the past, the young Austrian musician noticed "the incredible efficiency of his preparatory work." At piano rehearsals, Toscanini anticipated the tempi that he was planning to take with the orchestra, so that the singers didn't find themselves at sea when the full ensemble rehearsals began. This was because Toscanini's "mental image of the complete work was so clear," Leinsdorf said.

Caniglia sang the first two performances and always remembered Toscanini's guiding hand, which made her feel secure. She also recalled going to his dressing room after her final performance and saying, "'Maestro, this evening I could even end my career, because I've reached the highest of my aspirations,' and he, in saying goodbye, replied: 'Signorina, you did very well and can rest easy! But I want to tell you one thing: [. . .] every evening, in the scene with the laundry basket, instead of *"cavolo"* [cabbage] you said *"cavoli"* [cabbages]'"—which did not rhyme with *trisavolo* (ancestor) in the corresponding line of verse. "So the maestro picked up the score, we looked for the phrase together, and we found that he was right."

Toscanini's interpretation of *Fidelio* met with even greater success than the *Falstaff* production, not only with the public and press but also with the performers. At one orchestra rehearsal, "when I reached the end of the first act," Toscanini wrote to Ada, "Rosé, the concertmaster, stood up and said, in front of the whole orchestra, 'Maestro, this is the first time that I've heard this finale at the right tempo. I've played Fidelio with Richter, Mahler, Strauss, Schalk, etc., but I've never heard it like this.' The praise of this old musician gave me great pleasure." Peyser reported that at the close of one rehearsal, the entire Vienna Philharmonic "burst into a spontaneous ovation for the conductor," and he described the first public performance, on 7 August, as "probably the most spiritualized, ecstatic and sheerly beautiful 'Fidelio' that has ever been experienced."

At the first performance, Lehmann encountered trouble with the high notes in Leonore's terrifyingly difficult aria "Komm, Hoffnung," and particularly in its cabaletta, "Ich folg' dem innern Triebe." Toscanini transposed the whole scene down a semitone for the second performance, but he found that the lower key made the lead-in recitative, "Abscheulicher! wo eilst du hin!" sound too bland. "To remedy this and still help Lotte," Leinsdorf recalled, Toscanini "devised a clever transitory harmony that left the entire recitative in the original key and yet transposed the aria" and the cabaletta from E Major to E-flat Major. A shortwave broadcast of the first part of the opera during either the 1935 or the 1936 festival, from the overture through Leonore's great scene, was recorded, and despite the bad sound of the recording, the transition reported by Leinsdorf is all too clearly audible. For anyone who knows *Fidelio* well, the key change is grating, however "clever" Toscanini's new modulation may have been. But as Leinsdorf pointed out, the episode clearly demonstrated that Toscanini was willing to go to great lengths "to accommodate an artist whom he admired and appreciated."

Once *Falstaff* and *Fidelio* were underway, Toscanini rehearsed and conducted three concerts with the Vienna Philharmonic—the final one scheduled at the last minute, at Toscanini's suggestion, to benefit the orchestra. He attended most of the six operas and five concerts conducted by his colleagues Walter, Weingartner, Kleiber, Boult, and Josef Krips.* At one of Walter's *Tristan* rehearsals, during the long love scene in the second act, Toscanini turned to Margarete Wallmann, who was sitting next to him, and commented, "If they

---

* Of Krips, Toscanini reportedly said to Bruno Walter, "He is terrible—and so proud of himself!"

were Italians they would already have seven children! But there we are—they're Germans: they're still talking!"

Walter and Toscanini attended the thirty-eight-year-old Marian Anderson's recital before three hundred invited guests in the grand ballroom of Salzburg's Hôtel de l'Europe. "What I heard today one is privileged to hear only once in a hundred years," Toscanini told the African American contralto afterward, and his words were quoted wherever that magnificent singer appeared during the rest of her long career. This incident took place four years before Anderson's historic appearance at the Lincoln Memorial, at Eleanor Roosevelt's behest, after the Daughters of the American Revolution had denied the singer the use of Washington's Constitution Hall, on the grounds of her race.

Walter Toscanini, together with Cia and six-year-old Walfredo, arrived before the second *Falstaff* performance. This was the first time that Walfredo saw his grandfather at work (Toscanini had not conducted in Italy since Walfredo was a baby), but his strongest memory was of his mother's nervousness as their car was about to cross through a piece of German territory, en route to Salzburg: she feared that the name Toscanini on her husband's and son's passports would cause problems. The German border guard, however, handed back the passports and gave the Nazi salute, with a "Heil Hitler!"— to which the hotheaded Walter replied with an exaggerated Fascist salute and a shout of "Cupit!" which means "Drop dead!" in Milanese/Parmesan dialect. The guard smiled and waved them on.

At tea at Bruno Walter's home one day, Toscanini met Thomas Mann, who also attended the maestro's "wonderful" performance of *Fidelio*, and, as he wrote in his diary, was "seized by the enthusiastic spirit of the work." But Mann utterly misunderstood *Falstaff*, which he heard two days later and described as "a mocking, cool work of old age, the 'last word,' unsettled—it is nothing, joke, game, deception. Pale dance of elves."* He had no feeling at all for the warmth,

---

* Two months earlier, Mann, at his home in Küsnacht, Switzerland—where he was living in exile from Nazi Germany—had picked up Toscanini's first BBC Symphony broadcast and had remarked, in his diary, on the "magnificent sound" of the performance. It is curious that then and later, in America, whenever Mann heard Toscanini's performances live or on the radio, he liked them, but he generally described some of Toscanini's studio recordings as "extremely precise and somewhat dry."

wittiness, lightness, and graceful majesty of one of the greatest masterpieces in the opera literature.

The Toscaninis' house at Liefering was usually "full to bursting," Toscanini wrote to Ada. "What with relatives and friends it was like a carnival here day and night. [. . .] You alone were missing," he complained. Still . . . in Salzburg that summer he met Eleonora von Mendelssohn, a thirty-five-year-old actress with an unusual pedigree: she was a great-grandniece of the composer, a goddaughter of Eleonora Duse, a former wife of the Swiss pianist Edwin Fischer, and the current lover of Max Reinhardt and rival of Reinhardt's longtime fiancée, the actress Helene Thimig. Owing to their part-Jewish ancestry, Eleonora and her brother, Francesco—one of Horowitz's lovers— had left Germany and were spending much of their time in the United States, but they also had a home in Austria. Eleonora was "very simpatica," Toscanini told Ada, "an admirer of mine for years, who attends a great many of my concerts in New York but whom I'd never seen." Eleonora's parents, the banker Robert von Mendelssohn and the pianist Giulietta Gordigiani, were art collectors, and Eleonora gave Toscanini what he described as "a magnificent little painting" by Guardi. But he did not tell Ada that Eleonora had given him the painting when he was visiting her at her family's home at Kammer am Attersee, more than forty miles from Salzburg. A new dalliance was taking shape for the maestro.

Another event of the festival season was the publication of a short biography of Toscanini by the Austrian music critic Paul Stefan—a biographer of Mahler, a student of and propagandist for Schoenberg, and a founding member of the International Society for Contemporary Music—with an essay by Stefan Zweig as its preface; Italian and English translations would appear within a few months. Toscanini seemed pleased about the publication, for he procured a copy of it for Ada, although he claimed that he had not read it. Zweig told Romain Rolland, "I hope you have read my essay on [Toscanini]. Yet it does not say enough! He is *afire* with suppressed forces, it is impossible to escape him."

The book is an improvement over Nicotra's ridiculous Toscanini biography of six years earlier, but it is narrow in scope and contains many errors—no surprise, since the book's subject contributed nothing to it and few significant documents were available at the time. It is more a panegyric than a serious examination of Toscanini's life and work, and even at the time some readers found much of the writing cloying. In reviewing the English-language version, Richard Aldrich, the *Times*'s former chief music critic, quoted a passage on one Toscanini performance: "The genius of mankind came into its own, producing a rare sense of liberation. The Word descended upon us, and we had only to listen." Aldrich commented, wryly, "This is getting very near to St. John, and it is time to stop."

22.

"YOU SHOULD SEE ME—I'M AS TAN AS IF I'D BEEN AT THE BEACH OR high up in the mountains," Toscanini wrote to Ada on 1 September, the day after his last Salzburg performance. His family members and friends had already left for Italy, by car or train, but he had stayed an extra day so that he could enjoy some hours alone on the Liefering house's sunny terrace and fly back to Milan the following day.

For over two months, he stayed mainly in Italy—on the Isolino, weather permitting, otherwise in Milan. But on 21 September, he flew to Basel to hear a chamber orchestra perform Bach's "Brandenburg" Concerti under Adolf Busch's direction. Instead of staying with Adolf and Frieda, as he had done before, he checked into the Hotel Schweizerhof, where Ada had planned to visit him; but their tryst did not materialize. He was back home by the twenty-fifth, and one or two days later he went to Piazze for further treatment. On the morning of the twenty-eighth, he received a terrible shock: during the previous night the sixty-six-year-old Dr. Rinaldi had been bludgeoned to death outside his home. Rumors immediately began to circulate: the crime had been committed by someone in the pay of a group of doctors, envious of the success of his therapies; or of the Fascists, because Rinaldi was an anti-Fascist; or of both, or neither. The case has never been resolved. Toscanini remained in Piazze for the doctor's funeral, then returned home.

On the Isolino, a stream of guests came and went. Carla asked Margarete Wallmann, one of the visitors, to help her read and answer several suitcase-loads of letters in several languages. "And what did I find? A month-old invitation for an official dinner with the President of

Austria!" Wallmann recalled. "And many other 'Urgent' messages that remained unknown to Carla and Tosca, who lived and traveled without a secretary! Among the suitcases there was a briefcase: when it was opened, yellowed bank notes from every country flowed out of it."

Toscanini fretted over not being able to see Ada; occasionally they met in her apartment in Milan, when her husband was away, and for a while she rented, at Toscanini's expense, a convenient pied-à-terre, where they met whenever they were both in the city. But he was becoming increasingly upset over the political situation in Italy. "When I work, I don't have time to think about my country's sad, tragic current condition," he wrote to Ada in mid-September. "I've always thought that preaching peace and building up arms at the same time was absurd and monstrous! [. . .] What's certain is that we're in the hands and at the mercy of a man who is mad, delinquent, paranoid, syphilitic—and I'll put a period here, but the list could go on." Three weeks later, on 3 October, Mussolini announced that Italy had invaded Ethiopia, in an attempt to found a colony, and on the eighth Toscanini wrote, "My heart is grieving over the news coming in from Africa. [. . .] This is the proof of how dictatorships govern countries. As soon as they can't hide their terrible and no longer disguisable internal difficulties, they distract attention with foreign war adventures."

Ever since the incident of the attack on Toscanini at Bologna four years earlier, his telephone conversations had been routinely wiretapped, and on 19 October a part of one of his calls to Ada was transcribed and sent to Mussolini's office.

A[DA]: Have you noticed that they've forbidden the sale of all foreign newspapers?

T[OSCANINI]: It's a really dirty piece of work to put a country in this situation! It's unheard of that a person can't read the paper he wants and has to believe everything that they print! It's unbelievable stuff! And it isn't even clever, because it will generate still more doubts. To force a people this way . . . ,* with a slipknot at its throat! . . . [. . .] You have to read and know only what they want. . . . There must be only one mind! This is no longer living!

---

* Unbracketed ellipses are present in the original Italian transcript.

A: It's frightful! Worse than in Russia! For the previous few days the newsvendors had already had orders not to display foreign papers. . . .

T: And then, certain measures against our friends' newspapers.*

A: You can see that they're plotting something.

T: No, it's only this: the people must be kept in complete ignorance. . . [. . .] I can't wait to leave, because I can't stand it any longer! These things jar me. . . To see people enslaved this way! [. . .] I would even leave my home and I would go away to breathe freer air. Here they grab you by the throat, they choke you! You have to think the way that mind [Mussolini's] thinks. . . And I will never think the way he thinks. . . I never have thought that way! I was weak only for a moment, and now I'm ashamed.† You can read only their newspaper! . . . Because you can say that in Italy there exists only one newspaper.

A: They ought to let foreign newspapers in.

T: Of course; it would be the most politic thing to do. With certain methods they put our [i.e., Italy's] position in an even worse light. People will believe that they are telling lies and that the others are telling the truth. And people still have a thinking brain. . . They can't put thoughts in prison. Today, with all the means available, with the radio, etc., they can never imprison thought. They haven't yet invented a method for jailing thought.

A: But in Russia they block or disrupt all the news that they don't want to be heard.

T: We've reached the bottom of the ladder of the. . . And yet there are people who feel nothing, who live like this. . . For me, though, it's a distress that annihilates me.

Many sentences in the transcript were underlined, and a notation—not in Mussolini's hand, but read by him—says, "Which proves what we already knew, that Toscanini is untamable."

---

* Toscanini was referring to the recent arrests of people who had been caught importing and/or distributing the newspaper of the outlawed, left-wing (but noncommunist) *Giustizia e Libertà* movement; its leaders were living in exile in France. Toscanini gave money to *GL*.

† The reference is to Toscanini's support for the leftist firebrand Mussolini in 1919.

23.

TOSCANINI'S WEEKS OF RESPITE FROM WORK ENDED IN MID-NOVEMBER 1935: Paris and Vienna awaited him. In the French capital, he conducted two concerts at the Opéra with the National Orchestra of the State Radio;* both programs comprised mixed repertoire and were broadcast all over Europe. He then traveled directly to Vienna to conduct three programs with the Philharmonic. Among that visit's features were a performance of Brahms's *German Requiem* and another tour concert in Budapest.

Toscanini had become so popular in Vienna that, as one reporter put it, if he had run for mayor he would have won. But he unwittingly fed the Viennese opera world's unquenchable thirst for *Klatsch*—gossip. Since he was to conduct *Meistersinger* in Salzburg the following summer, he decided to attend a performance of the opera which was being given in Vienna, to have a look at the sets that would be used at the festival. When his intention to drop in was announced, only a few hours in advance, terror swept through the Staatsoper. Krips, the conductor, and Lothar Wallerstein, the stage director, called emergency rehearsals, in the hope of breathing new life into a half-dead production. "Before the performance had been fifteen minutes under way Toscanini was fuming and frothing, and the atmosphere of the box he occupied had grown sulphurous," Peyser reported. "Next day some of the papers carried the story with ill-concealed glee. But they did not tell about a supper afterward at which Toscanini spoke his mind to Herr Wallerstein so forcibly that peace-making friends had, it is whispered, to separate them." Toscanini had worked successfully with Wallerstein on the *Fidelio* production, but he insisted on a different collaborator for *Meistersinger*.

Horowitz gave a recital in Vienna while Toscanini was in town, and afterward Toscanini took his son-in-law to task for playing insignificant music on his program. When Adolf Busch, who was present, heard the maestro upbraiding his son-in-law, he spoke up: Castelnuovo-Tedesco's Overture to *A Winter's Tale* and Sibelius's *En Saga*, which Toscanini was performing in Vienna, were also junk,

---

* The Orchestre Walther-Straram had ceased to exist.

he said (although Castelnuovo was standing nearby), and he should not criticize others for not playing only great music. "The upshot was that Tosca stood there in the little corner, deathly pale and almost crying, like a boy forced to stay after school," Irene Busch Serkin, who was nearby, wrote to her mother. "But when we left they embraced each other anyway, and I hope that all is well." All *was* well: Toscanini held Busch in such high regard that a difference of opinion could not break their mutual trust; besides, Toscanini respected people who did not bow down before his reputation.

He attended a concert in which Busch played with the Vienna Symphony, conducted by Oswald Kabasta, and afterward he went to a party at the home of Karl Gombrich, a cultivated Viennese lawyer, and his wife, Leonie Hock, a brilliant musician who had been a teaching assistant to Theodor Leschetizky, the famed piano pedagogue. Also present was their son, Ernst, who would become one of the most respected cultural historians of the century and a lifelong admirer of Toscanini the musician and the man.

Accounts of Italian atrocities in Ethiopia were spreading around the world, and just before Toscanini left Vienna he wrote to Ada, "Never in my life have I gone through a sadder period! [. . .] To see to what point the Italians' conscience or *lack of conscience* has reached inspires terror. If I didn't love my country, my home, and the Italians themselves madly, I swear to you that I would go off to China, to Japan,* where I would be mute, and I wouldn't want to have any contact with the human race!"

He spent Christmas at home, but two days later he was on the road again. In Monaco, he prepared the Monte Carlo Orchestra for a concert on New Year's Day 1936; the mixed program was then repeated in Marseille and Nice. Although he was paid well for these concerts, his main reason for accepting the engagement was undoubtedly the locations' proximity to Italy: friends from Milan could easily come to hear him, and he could simultaneously thumb his nose at Mussolini and company across the border.†

---

* For Toscanini, China and Japan were simply places of nearly unfathomable cultural remoteness. In fact, in 1935 Japan had already occupied Manchuria and was preparing to invade China itself.

† Toscanini was paid 20,000 francs (about $1,500 at the time), minus 1,200 in taxes, for the

Also present at Toscanini's Monte Carlo rehearsals and concert was Ernest Newman, who finally had the opportunity to meet and talk with the maestro. "What a brain!" the English music historian and critic told his wife afterward. "What a fascinating man! I wish I had known him years ago. *There* is someone I can listen to and talk to with pleasure." Stefan Zweig attended the performance in Nice, and he wrote to Romain Rolland, "No other conductor can stand up next to him, and yesterday I experienced the wonder of how he was able to transform as mediocre an orchestra as Monte Carlo's into a masterly one."

After the Nice concert, Arturo and Carla traveled by train to Le Havre, where they boarded the *Lafayette* on 8 January; they arrived in New York on the sixteenth. The maestro was welcomed with nervousness by the Philharmonic's board of directors: the previous fall, while he was suffering again from shoulder pains and wondering about his future with the orchestra, the administrators had notified him that Sir Thomas Beecham had been engaged as a guest conductor for the season that was just about to begin. Toscanini, as the orchestra's music director, had been justifiably angry about not having been consulted on the matter and had cabled Zirato to protest the engagement, adding, "Please inform the Board of Directors not to count on me for season after next."

Toscanini's opinion of his British colleague was ambivalent: even many years later he described him as "a dilettante—who has talent, oh yes!" But at that moment, he would have used any irritant as an excuse for leaving the Philharmonic; the Beecham engagement was the proverbial straw that broke the camel's back.

Shortly after his arrival in New York, Toscanini reconsidered his decision to resign from the Philharmonic, and he discussed with Zirato the possibility of leading a reduced series of four to six weeks during the 1936–37 season. By early February, however, the orchestra's grueling schedule had tired him so much that he informed the management that he would not return. Attempts to persuade him to change his mind proved futile, and on 12 February 1936 Mackay made the announcement to the board of directors; the news was made public the following day. The orchestra was once again in dif-

---

performance in Nice and, presumably, similar amounts for the other two concerts.

ficult financial straits, but no new public funding drive was undertaken: the board members believed that without the allure of Toscanini's name, such an effort was doomed. Within a few days, the board revealed that the following season would be reduced from thirty weeks to twenty-four, although the players' minimum weekly wage scale would be maintained at ninety dollars.

Fatigue notwithstanding, Toscanini continued to work at his usual high energy level and was as pleased as ever with the Philharmonic's excellence. He conducted thirty-six Carnegie Hall concerts; two tour concerts in Boston—after one of which he and Carla attended a dinner party hosted by Koussevitzky and his wife—and one in Hartford; and a General Motors broadcast concert, with Dusolina Giannini as soloist. His repertoire, which ranged from Vivaldi, Bach, and Handel to Albert Roussel's new Fourth Symphony, comprised sixty-four works by thirty-two composers, and the season's special events included Rudolf Serkin's New York debut playing Beethoven's Fourth Piano Concerto and Mozart's Concerto in B-flat Major, K. 595; the Mendelssohn Violin Concerto with Nathan Milstein as soloist; three performances of the Beethoven Ninth; an all-Wagner pension fund concert on Toscanini's sixty-ninth birthday—after which the entire orchestra presented him with a platinum watch; and three performances of an all-Debussy program.

Under Adolf Busch's influence, Toscanini conducted Bach's Second "Brandenburg" Concerto with a small ensemble, but since the high-registered Baroque trumpet had not yet come back into common use, he replaced it with an E-flat clarinet, a decidedly "un-Bachian" instrument. There were a few welcome oddities, too, in the season's programming: an arrangement for string orchestra of two movements from a quartet by the eighteenth-century Bohemian composer Leopold Kozeluch, for instance, and two rarely performed Debussy pieces: "La Cour de Lys" (the introductory music from *Le Martyre de Saint-Sébastien*) and the early cantata, *La Damoiselle Elue*, with the Brazilian soprano Bidu Sayão, the American mezzo-soprano (later soprano) Rose Bampton, and the Schola Cantorum.

For the first time in seven years, Toscanini overcame his antipathy to making studio recordings: on 8 February and 9 and 10 April 1936, he and the Philharmonic committed to disc "Dawn" and "Siegfried's Rhine Journey" from *Götterdämmerung*, the Preludes to Acts I and III of *Lohengrin*, the *Siegfried Idyll*, Beethoven's Seventh Symphony, Brahms's "Haydn" Variations, and two Rossini overtures—*L'Italiana in Algeri* and *Semiramide*. All rank among the finest of the maestro's commercial recordings and bear witness to the results of ten years' work of a great orchestra with a great conductor.

Despite his intention to resign, Toscanini carried out all of his duties as music director, including the auditioning of potential new orchestra members. When William Vacchiano auditioned for the position of third trumpet, Toscanini asked him to play only three notes—but what notes!—the F-sharp, G-sharp, A-sharp sequence ("*pp et très lointain*," followed by a diminuendo) five to seven bars after no. 52, in the finale of *La Mer*. He played them well "and was told to wait upstairs," he recalled. Toscanini then "called me down to play the same thing again, and also a third time. I was completely baffled at this point until [Van Praag] told me this was considered a good test, to see if I could play it three times in a row. When he told me [. . .] I was engaged to play with the New York Philharmonic, I was thunder-struck." Six years later, Vacchiano became the orchestra's principal trumpet, a position he held for over three decades.

During Toscanini's stay in Vienna the previous December, he had spent many of his free hours at the Albertina Gallery, examining some of the forty thousand pages of music manuscripts that the institution had been microfilming over several years. News of this collection's existence spurred the New York Public Library to make a similar attempt, as a result of which Countess Marie Mercati—a patroness of the arts and a member of the Philharmonic's board—agreed to cosponsor the enterprise with New York's Beethoven Association if Toscanini would allow the collection to be named for him. He readily accepted the honor, and early in April he attended a private screening, at the library, of some of the microfilms.

He also managed to attend a performance on Broadway of the popular play *Victoria Regina*, by the British socialist and pacifist writer Laurence Housman, and afterward he went backstage to tell its star, the thirty-five-year-old Helen Hayes, that she was a great artist. She wept in appreciation. But his main non-music-related occupation during his entire New York stay consisted of fretting over and writing to Ada. He had heard rumors that she had gone back to a former lover, he told her; she promised to write to him but then didn't follow through; and when she did write, he asked her to use less restraint and to express herself as passionately as he did. Stormy periods alternated with calmer ones, and it is impossible to distinguish the deeply felt utterances in his letters from those that were intended simply to stir up Ada's senses, and probably his own as well. He declared himself her slave and said that he wished to live only a year with her and then die. He sometimes wrote a few lines using blood from his own finger as ink, and in some of his letters he crosses the border from eroticism into pornography. But, as he often said of himself, and as Ada surely knew by then, he was *sempre eccessivo* in all things.

THE PHILHARMONIC'S ADMINISTRATORS quickly initiated a search for Toscanini's successor and asked the maestro to advise them. He recommended Furtwängler as principal conductor, with Rodzinski to share the season with him. Toscanini's prestigious vote in Furtwängler's favor was cast not only because he valued his German colleague as a musician but also because he wished to give him the best possible chance to make a clean break with the Nazi regime. The board followed Toscanini's suggestion, and Furtwängler accepted at once. But Joseph Goebbels, the Nazis' propaganda minister and a Furtwängler admirer, outflanked the New Yorkers, and probably Furtwängler himself, by announcing that the German conductor was about to be reinstated as general music director of the Berlin State Opera—a position from which he had resigned in 1934 over the Nazis' cultural policies.

Furtwängler never joined the Nazi Party; he helped so many Jewish musicians and their families that Georg Gerullis, the Nazis' undersecretary of culture, wrote, disgustedly, to another functionary, "Can you give me the name of a Jew who is not backed by Furtwängler?" Nevertheless, Furtwängler had led Beethoven's *Egmont* Overture as a prelude to a speech by Goebbels at the opening of the Reich's Chamber of Culture in November 1933; he had accepted a decoration from Mussolini during his 1934 Italian tour with the Berlin Philharmonic; he had conducted a winter aid concert in Berlin in 1935, during which he was photographed shaking hands with Hitler; and in February of the same year, he had signed a statement, prepared for him by Goebbels, in which he recognized Hitler and his ministers as "entirely and solely responsible for cultural policy" in Germany. More recently, he had agreed to return to the thoroughly Nazified Bayreuth Festival, after a five-year absence.

Furtwängler's appointment, followed by the announcement of his reinstatement at the Staatsoper, caused immediate protests from New York's substantial and influential Jewish community, members of which made up a noteworthy portion of the Philharmonic's audience and donors. Letters pro and con poured into the city's newspapers, and the Philharmonic's administrators, trying desperately to chart a course of action, must have heaved a collective sigh of relief when, after two weeks in limbo, they received a cablegram from Furtwängler, who was vacationing in Egypt and would not know all the details of the situation until he returned to Germany. "Political controversies disagreeable to me," he wrote. "Am not politican but exponent of German music, which belongs to all humanity regardless of politics. I propose postpone my season in the interests of Philharmonic Society and music until the public realizes that politics and music are apart."

Furtwängler, for all his intelligence and intellectual preparation, seemed unable or unwilling to understand that Hitler and his regime were not garden-variety politicians, nor would he follow the lead of other non-Jewish, nonpolitical German artists—the Busch brothers, for instance, or Erich Kleiber and Thomas Mann—who had found the compromises involved in living in a racist dictatorship unbearable. As far as Toscanini was concerned, Furtwängler's refusal to use the magnificent offer from New York in order to take an unequivocal stand against Nazism made him persona non grata forever.

An editorial in the *Times*, following the termination of Furtwängler's candidacy, concluded with a single sentence: "The happiest outcome would be that Mr. TOSCANINI should reconsider and remain where he is unanimously wanted." But that was not to be. Toscanini subsequently recommended Fritz Busch to succeed him: Busch's anti-Nazi credentials were impeccable, although the Philharmonic's board worried, under the circumstances, about nominating another German. But Busch was happy with his position as conductor of the Danish National Symphony Orchestra in Copenhagen and the Teatro Colón in Buenos Aires, and he, like most of his colleagues, must have understood that following Toscanini would be at best an ungrateful task, a suicidal one at worst. He turned down the Philharmonic's offer. John Barbirolli, whom Toscanini had encountered in London the previous year, and Artur Rodzinski were engaged to split the bulk of the 1936–37 season, with neither of them named as principal conductor; the composers Stravinsky, Georges Enesco, and Carlos Chávez would each conduct programs of their own and others' works.

"TWO WEEKS' WORK REMAINS, THEN—all is done," Toscanini wrote to Ada on 10 April. "I'll leave my orchestra forever, with a sorrow that words cannot tell but that you can understand. Is this perhaps the beginning of the end?"

In the meantime, however, rehearsals and performances proceeded normally. For his penultimate subscription concerts, Toscanini repeated the program with which he had made his Philharmonic debut ten years earlier: Weber's *Euryanthe* Overture, Haydn's "Clock" Symphony, Sibelius's *The Swan of Tuonela*, Wagner's "Siegfried's Death" and Funeral Music from *Götterdämmerung*, and Respighi's *Pines of Rome*. A few days earlier, on 18 April, Respighi had died of heart failure, at the age of fifty-six; Toscanini dedicated to his memory the Wagner piece (with a request, in the printed program, for no applause afterward) as well as Respighi's own work.

At the end of the final subscription concert, on 26 April, the audience "stood and refused to move for about a quarter of an hour," according to the *Times*. "Mr. Toscanini, obviously overcome, was helpless. Under no circumstances would he have made a speech, but if he had attempted such a thing it would have been impossible. He could only come back and forth from the wings, bow, wave his arms in a futile attempt to express his appreciation and return back stage and come out again and again."

Even this event would pale, however, beside the special "farewell" concert—a benefit program that Toscanini had proposed, with the proceeds to be divided among the orchestra's musicians and staff, including doormen, ushers, and office workers, plus the Musicians' Emergency Fund. On 29 April, the day of the performance, numerous board members and even members of the orchestra's secretarial staff presented Toscanini with gifts. Vivacious little Dorle Jarmel, who was in charge of the orchestra's public relations office, and with whom Toscanini had flirted for several years, sent him a note with a quotation from a Shakespeare sonnet: "Farewell, thou art too dear for my possessing." He must have laughed to himself as he wrote back to her, "Farewell, thou art too young for my possessing."*

The first half of the special program consisted of Beethoven's *Leonore* Overture no. 1 and Violin Concerto (with Heifetz); Wagner's *Meistersinger* Prelude, *Siegfried Idyll*, Prelude and "Liebestod" from *Tristan*, and "Ride of the Valkyries" from *Die Walküre* occupied the second half. Tickets had all been bought within minutes of having gone on sale, and $23,841.50 was raised. Before seven thirty on the morning of the concert, people began to arrive at Carnegie Hall, in the hope of acquiring the 140 standing-room positions. By late afternoon, approximately 5,000 ticket seekers had formed a line several blocks long, choking some Midtown Manhattan streets, and when the doors opened an hour before the nine o'clock curtain time, pandemonium broke out. Five policemen on horseback, six officers, and some sixty patrolmen tried to keep the unruly crowd under control. Four of the people who managed to procure standing positions opened a fire-escape door and let in an additional 150 people before the police were able to plug the leak; the four culprits were arrested and jailed overnight.

George Gershwin and everyone else who counted in New York's musical life applauded Toscanini before and after each piece on the program. At the very end of the concert, an unauthorized photographer charged up to the stage and snapped a picture of the maestro; the flash dazed his weak eyes, and he staggered from the stage, not to return. The photographer was hauled away by a house detective, and Van Praag eventually went before the audience and apologized for Toscanini: "He is sorry. He asks me to say that he loves you all." But Toscanini recovered quickly backstage, where the board presented him with an original Beethoven letter and other gifts. He then returned to the Astor, where Carla had organized a party for the orchestra members and their spouses. "No other conductor

---

* In 1942, Dorle married Dario Soria, who had immigrated to the United States in the aftermath of Italy's 1938 anti-Semitic laws, and the couple became successful record producers in New York. Dario died in 1980; Dorle, in 2002, at the age of nearly 102. Some of the research materials used in this book were given to the author by Dorle.

showered such attention on the men," the trumpeter Bill Vacchiano recalled. "He moved from table to table spreading cheer and friendliness." Yet much as they liked Toscanini personally, some orchestra members were relieved by his departure: "No more stomach aches," one of them was heard to say.

The following day, Toscanini received a telegram of regret and appreciation from President Roosevelt, to whom he replied gratefully. To Ada, he sent a cablegram: "It was a unique unforgettable profoundly moving evening and I feel deeply the sadness of an epoch ended never to return." On 2 May, after having issued a press statement in which he thanked the orchestra, its board, and its public, he and Carla boarded the SS *Champlain*, bound for France. An editorial in the *Times*, praising Toscanini on the day after his final Philharmonic concert, began with these words: "ARTURO TOSCANINI ended last night his career as conductor in America."

The statement proved to be premature.

Toscanini studying a poster,
Salzburg, mid-1930s.

IX

CLEAR AS CRYSTAL
AND JUST AS CUTTING

1.

———

WHEN ARTURO TOSCANINI BOARDED THE *CHAMPLAIN* IN NEW YORK on 2 May 1936 and departed for Europe, he was a free man. For the first time in fifteen years, since the reopening of La Scala, he had no ongoing obligations with any musical organization. Some concerts in Paris were coming up, as was a demanding, six-week engagement in Salzburg, and a few other events had been arranged here and there. But he had entered his seventieth year; he wanted to decide for himself when, where, and how much to work, and he was determined to continue his musical protest against the Nazis and Fascists.

Invitations poured in from everywhere, but he either turned them down or did not respond. He had previously agreed to return to London for eight concerts with the BBC Symphony Orchestra after his final New York season, but a combination of contractual confusion and worry, on Toscanini's part, that he "wouldn't have had time to rest before Salzburg," made him withdraw from the undertaking—which caused the cancellation of the entire London Music Festival for that year: there was insufficient time "to secure the services of any other eminent conductor for this important task," the *Manchester Guardian* reported.

Upon his arrival in Europe, Toscanini went directly to Paris, where he conducted a special, all-French concert at the Salle Pleyel on 22

May, to raise money for the creation of a monument to Saint-Saëns. Toscanini admired Saint-Saëns's music, especially the Third Symphony, which he felt was not performed as often as it merited; he blamed its relative neglect on anti-Semitism: like many others at the time, he believed that Saint-Saëns was of part-Jewish descent, whereas the composer had merely contributed to the defense fund at the time of the Dreyfus Affair and had therefore been dubbed a Jew by France's right-wing press. Toscanini returned to Italy for a few days, then went back to Paris for a second Salle Pleyel concert, on 15 June. ("The orchestra is good and obedient," he wrote to Ada Mainardi. "I'm hoping for a good performance.") Afterward, family and friends feted him on the approaching fiftieth anniversary of his conducting debut.

Two problems made Toscanini threaten not to return to Salzburg that summer: the German government warned that it might not allow certain singers to leave Germany and perform in Austria with Toscanini and other politically or "racially" unacceptable artists, and Toscanini insisted on renting the house in Liefering that he had rented the previous year, although it had been sold and the new owners did not want to leave during the summer. Erwin Kerber, the festival's director, apprised Bruno Walter of the situation, and Walter immediately assured Toscanini that everything possible would be done to adjust matters favorably. "I can no longer imagine Salzburg without you," Walter wrote. Kerber, on behalf of the government, eventually bribed the house's owners to vacate it for a month and a half, and Walter, at the request of Austria's minister of education, interrupted his vacation to go to Italy and intercede with Toscanini on the other matter. Toscanini later wrote to thank his colleague, also for having auditioned many singers and providing him with "a detailed account of them. [. . .] Without your friendly intervention, I would never, ever have returned to Salzburg!" he said.

Another crisis developed when the Austrian government announced that it had reached an agreement with Hitler's government to have performances by Toscanini and Weingartner—but not by Walter, who was of Jewish origin—broadcast over the German radio network. Toscanini promptly informed the Austrians that if any of his performances were transmitted by the German network, he would leave Salzburg immediately and never return; equally promptly, the Austrian government withdrew from the agreement with Germany.

In the end, the thought that he would soon be returning to Salzburg made Toscanini happy, not so much owing to the beauty of the Baroque city on the Salzach River as because he could not tolerate long stretches of idleness. "I can't wait to get back to work," he wrote to Ada from the Isolino late in June. "It's still the best distraction and occupation." Another distraction was Ada herself, with whom he managed to spend 8 July at a hotel in Baveno, on Lake Maggiore's western shore. Two days later, his entire *Falstaff* cast came to the Isolino and worked with him through most of the day; four members of the ensemble—Franca Somigli (Alice), Augusta Oltrabella (Nannetta), Alfredo Tedeschi (Cajus), and Virgilio Lazzari (Pistola)— were singing their respective parts with him for the first time, and he considered at least the first three of them better than their predecessors. (He did not comment on Lazzari.) On 15 July, he flew to Salzburg; he stayed at the Österreichischer Hof in town until his family arrived, then moved to Liefering.

Fidelio opened the festival on 25 July, to less enthusiastic reviews than it had had the preceding year—a result of some nervousness and mediocre singing at the first performance. Most of the principal singers were the same, although Koloman von Pataky replaced Rösler as Florestan, and in one of the four performances Anny Konetzni stood in for Lehmann, who was ill. Toscanini had fretted once again over the modulation for Lehmann in Leonore's recitative: before leaving Italy, he had consulted with Horszowski, who proposed a different solution, which the maestro adopted.

Falstaff, which went onstage five nights after *Fidelio*, was received even more ecstatically this year than in 1935. Toscanini's biggest challenge, however, and the most eagerly anticipated event of the 1936 festival, was the new *Meistersinger* production. Rehearsals had begun immediately upon the maestro's arrival in town, and so had his usual doubts. "Every time I go back to work, my lack of confidence in myself comes over me, and it seems to become greater and greater," he had written to Ada at the time. "I put too much faith in myself and my strength." But the strength was there: on a single day, for instance, he conducted two long, grueling orchestra rehearsals of *Meistersinger* (about six hours, in total) and held a lengthy piano rehearsal with the *Falstaff* cast—altogether, enough to floor a man half his age.

Meistersinger requires orchestral forces that could barely squeeze into the old Festspielhaus's pit and choral forces that had worse problems fitting onto the shallow, ill-equipped stage; Walter Toscanini described the theater as a "shoebox." But the maestro had chosen *Meistersinger* not only because he loved it (although he agreed with Adolf Busch's comment that it had "too much C Major" in it) but also because it was the work that he would have added to his Bayreuth repertoire in 1933, had the Nazis not come to power. Now, three years later, German Wagnerites who wanted to hear his much admired interpretation of the work would have to cross into Austria, first paying the 1,000-mark visa fee that Hitler's government had imposed on citizens who wished to visit the neighboring country. Bruno Walter described the Salzburg Festival as "perhaps the last non-political place where art still has a roof over its head," but the truth is that the strong presence of Jewish, anti-Nazi, and anti-Fascist artists made the Salzburg of the mid-1930s Europe's most highly politicized musical venue. Situated only two miles from the German border and a half-hour drive from Berchtesgaden, Hitler's favorite getaway spot in the Bavarian Alps, the town and its festival were thorns in the Führer's side.

The thirty-three-year-old American writer Marcia Davenport—Alma Gluck's daughter and a friend of the Toscaninis—observed the maestro at work during the *Meistersinger* rehearsals. "There was no detail of the production that did not get his minute attention," she recalled in her memoir, *Too Strong for Fantasy*. "He stayed in his pit so long as the work went to his satisfaction. If not, if he wanted a change on the stage in action, lighting, setting, business (the riot in the second act!) he was up on the stage. Sometimes we heard his hoarse voice call 'Graf!' from the dark back of the theatre where he had run to see how the scene looked in perspective [. . .]. Herbert Graf, the stage director, and all the company slaved for him."* During one

---

* By the time of his Salzburg collaboration with Toscanini, the Vienna-born Graf—who was the "Little Hans" in Freud's famous *Analysis of a Phobia in a Five-Year-Old Boy* (1909)—had been fired, for "racial" reasons, from his positions in Germany, but hired as a stage director at the Metropolitan, where he began to work the following winter, and where he would remain for many years.

ensemble rehearsal Toscanini had shouted from the pit at Charles Kullmann, the American tenor who was singing the part of Stolzing: "Stand up straight! You're playing a nobleman!" Kullmann, pulling himself up, was heard to mutter, "I thought he was nearsighted."*

Meistersinger presented Toscanini with musical as well as logistical problems: "Everyone sings and plays in a humdrum way," he wrote to Ada. "And then I'm worried about the singer who's taking the role of *Sachs*, the *Bar[itone] Schorr.*" Friedrich Schorr, a famous Wagnerian bass-baritone, was not yet forty-eight at the time; he had sung leading roles in many major German venues, including Bayreuth, until the Nazis kicked him out because he was Jewish, and under Toscanini he had sung in Brahms's *German Requiem* in New York the previous year. "[H]e seems a bit old, and he's hoarse and breathless on the high notes," Toscanini said. "He always sings softly, and when I called on him to sing full voice like the others, he said that he had a cold." According to Erich Leinsdorf, "As soon as we began to rehearse with Schorr it became obvious that Toscanini disliked everything the singer did. Schorr, set in his ways, did not give an inch, or could not fall in with the conductor's suggestions, and the atmosphere became heavy with tension." In the end, Toscanini gently asked Schorr to withdraw, which left the singer no other option. "But it all caused me great pain," Toscanini told Ada. Hans-Hermann Nissen, engaged to replace Schorr, was not as well-known as his predecessor but was no less experienced in the role.

The dress rehearsal took place on 7 August, with a two-and-a-half-hour break between the second and third acts. A greatly relieved Toscanini reported to Ada: "Everything came off well. [. . .] The enthusiasm in all of us spread to the numerous audience members who attended the rehearsal." Lehmann said, "For me it was an unforgettable day—one of life's precious gifts," and Davenport recalled that at the end, "Maestro himself stood motionless in his place with his right hand covering his eyes." The production opened the following evening, to great acclaim, although there was criticism of Lehmann, who, at forty-eight, seemed to some not right, physically or vocally, for the role of Eva. Kullmann, too, seemed a dull Stolzing to some observers.

---

* Kullmann later changed the spelling of his last name to Kullman.

Special praise was lavished on Graf and on the set designer Robert Kautsky for having produced a delightful visual spectacle despite the house's spatial and technical limitations. But the highest praise, from the participants as well as the press, was reserved for Toscanini. "Free from all ponderousness or sentimentality, he made it a sparkling comedy—breath-taking from beginning to end," Lehmann said. Burghauser particularly recalled the second act: "those subtle modifications of tempo! In the dialogue of Sachs and Eva the subtlety, the tender polyphony in the orchestra! By then I had heard *Die Meistersinger* for twenty-five years; but this second act was an entirely new experience for me." Toscanini told Ada, "I don't think I've ever obtained a better performance of Meistersinger. Can you imagine that the singers were crying at the end of the opera? Bruno Walter came back after the 2nd act; he told me that we had brought off a miracle!" For two days after the first performance he was "in a daze" from exhaustion, he wrote, but he recovered and compared himself "to a good American car—my Cadillac, for instance—I have a *good, ready pickup.*"

He conducted the Vienna Philharmonic in two concerts, one of which centered on Brahms's *German Requiem*, which they had performed together in Vienna the preceding December with the same soloists. Afterward, Toscanini told Ada that he hoped she had heard the performance on the radio, and he admitted that "humility and vanity were combined in me. I think I did well."

Bebe Baslini, a magazine illustrator who was the daughter of friends of the Toscaninis and whose company the maestro usually enjoyed, made the mistake of telling him, after a *Meistersinger* performance, that he must have felt great joy at having been able to communicate joy to others. "I would have liked to slap her," Toscanini wrote to Ada. "No: when I'm working I don't have time to feel joy; on the contrary, I suffer without interruption, and I feel that I'm going through all the pain and suffering of a woman giving birth." Other postperformance visitors included the Hungarian-born actress Elisabeth de Paulay and her husband, Vittorio Cerruti, Italy's ambassador to France; Toscanini observed that "la Cerruti" had not dared to visit him in Paris, where her husband represented Mussolini's government, but now "threw her arms around my neck, kissed me effusively, and spoke most exaggeratedly. [. . .] *All the world's a farce,*" he remarked. He was pleased, however, that Adolf Busch and family had attended "three Meistersingers, two Falstaffs, and one Fidelio," as well as the Brahms concert.

Together with various family members, Toscanini attended a peasant wedding at Lehmann's rented home at St. Gilgen on Lake Wolfgang, "and he got on so well and was so pleased with all the merriment and so delighted with the marvelous old peasant costumes and customs that I have never seen him so gay," Lehmann recalled. Toscanini also attended many of his Salzburg colleagues' rehearsals and performances. He had been instrumental in obtaining an engagement for Artur Rodzinski, and he applauded enthusiastically during the younger conductor's concert, which consisted entirely of twentieth-century music. Afterward, he told some of the orchestra musicians, "You don't need me any longer—you have him!" When Rodzinski asked Toscanini for advice on the interpretation of the Verdi *Requiem*, the maestro played the entire score at the piano for him, singing and suggesting. Toscanini was also observed listening intently to Bruno Walter's performance of Mahler's Third Symphony.

After having conducted the festival's final performance—*Fidelio*, on 31 August—Toscanini repaired to the Kaiserhof Hotel at Bad Gastein, an Alpine spa about sixty miles south of Salzburg. There he remained for two weeks, taking thermal baths, undergoing diathermy treatment on his shoulder, hiking in the woods, and socializing with fellow musicians Fritz Kreisler, Joseph Szigeti, Emil Sauer, Moritz Rosenthal, and Bronislaw Huberman. Wanda and Volodya and granddaughters Emanuela and Sonia were also there. ("They're real loves!" he commented to Ada about the two little girls.) He had been "afraid of all the work that awaited me at Salzburg," he wrote to Ada, "but now that it's all finished I feel as if I hadn't worked at all! [. . .] When my work stops my life is empty," he admitted.

More work awaited: on 15 September, Toscanini traveled to Vienna, where he conducted, at the Staatsoper, two performances of *Fidelio* with his Salzburg forces, as a token of solidarity with Bruno Walter, who had recently become the ensemble's music director. *Fidelio* "was quite another thing from Salzburg," he reported to Ada. "The acoustics here are noble. So everything was better blended, nobler, more musical." Leinsdorf noted that Toscanini's tempi in Vienna "were from start to finish a tiny bit broader" than they had been in Salzburg, and he asked the maestro whether he was aware of the influence of acoustics on tempi. "He thought for some time until he allowed that this was not only possible but probable and that he was not conscious of any voluntary slowing down."

During his stay in Vienna, Toscanini suggested to the Staatsoper's administrators that they put Leinsdorf on their conducting staff, but not even the maestro's influence was enough to change the ensemble's policy toward unconverted Jews. (Bruno Walter, like Mahler and others, had converted to Christianity.) Toscanini then recommended Leinsdorf to Artur Bodanzky, who had visited Toscanini in Salzburg and had complained about his coaches at the Metropolitan. "Since Leinsdorf is a *magnificent* coach, [. . .] I said, 'Take him in New York'—and he took him, and he thanked me," Toscanini recalled. "*He* [Leinsdorf] ought to thank *me*, otherwise he would still be going hungry in Vienna!" More likely, he would have died in a concentration camp during the war.

With Kerber and Walter, Toscanini discussed plans for the following year's Salzburg season. He agreed to add *The Magic Flute* to his other three operas, and he suggested that a new Festspielhaus, larger and better equipped than the present one, and worthy of the festival's growing international reputation, be constructed. He was willing to become involved in fund-raising efforts, he said, and he even intimated to Lotte Lehmann that he would consider returning to New York to conduct a benefit concert for the enterprise.

Toscanini returned home on 23 September and stayed in Italy for almost seven weeks, dividing his time between Milan and the Isolino. In the city, he spent his days at home, studying and reading, but toward seven in the evening he would walk to the Baldini & Castoldi bookshop, in the central Galleria, peruse and often buy books, and discuss politics with fellow subversives, all of them well-known to local police informers. He visited Luigi Albertini and his family at Parella, near Asti, and saw the Riboldis—family friends—at Brunate, a village perched on a hilltop above Lake Como. Toscanini made sure to be on the Isolino during the last days of October and first days of November, when a major Fascist Party festival took place in Milan: his house in Via Durini was in the city's center, and he could not bear the thought of having to witness "the carnival of *that cowardly flock of ill-born slaves*," as he wrote to Ada. When several friends and family members joined him on the lake, he compared them and himself to the characters in Boccaccio's *Decameron*, who had abandoned Florence to avoid a different plague. "I'll stay until Milan has been *cleansed* of its *pestilential Mussolinian atmosphere*. Then," he joked with Ada, "I'll go back, after having touched the *specifically male features of my anatomy*, a great and highly efficacious remedy against the evil eye."

And apropos sexual matters, Toscanini told Ada that when Albertini and the musicologist Carlo Gatti had asked his advice about publishing some of the Verdi-Boito correspondence, they had referred to Verdi's presumed affair with the soprano Teresa Stolz. "I gave Gatti my frank opinion," Toscanini said. "Judge the man and the artist—his life, as honest and upright as his art—but for pity's sake, stop short of the bedroom threshold." Toscanini's attitude on this matter was typical of a man of his time: it was all right, he believed, for *him* to know the intimate details of Verdi's life and to gossip about them with his friends, but such information ought to be denied to people he did not know, because they could not be trusted to put it into the proper perspective. Today, the withholding of such information about long-dead subjects of biographies, including the subject of this biography, would be considered censorship. At the very time that he was casting his vote in favor of keeping Verdi's halo intact, Toscanini was tormenting Ada with letters of real or feigned jealousy, and he had begun to send her a fresh handkerchief each month, with increasingly insistent requests that she stain it with her menstrual blood and send it back to him so that he could suck it—or so he claimed—"since I can't quench my thirst directly at the *delightful fount*." She often complied, and he gleefully and blasphemously described each handkerchief as the Holy Shroud. She also gave him, at his request, samples of her pubic hair, which he referred to as "tiny flowers from Ada's little garden." In his seventieth year, his sexual energies seemed as unabated as his need to make music.

2.

Thousands of times we have been told that Beethoven could not write for the voice, and we know from painful experience that most conductors and singers believe this to be so. But when the Staatsoper choristers sang the [*Missa Solemnis's*] Gloria and the Credo (with its tremendous B-flat double fugue), [there was] never a trace of straining, of screaming, of hit-or-miss, of riotous pitch—just flowing and luminous tone, incomparable precision and a rhythm past belief. Anybody who may ever want an illustration of what plasticity in music means has only to hear Toscanini conduct the Vienna Staatsoper chorus in the "Et vitam venturi" fugue.

—Herbert Peyser, in the *New York Times*

For three weeks in November 1936, Toscanini once again dominated musical Vienna, this time in repertoire that included, in addition to the *Missa Solemnis*, ten works ranging from Cherubini's Symphony in D to Shostakovich's Symphony no. 1. And much of the repertoire was repeated when he and the Philharmoniker gave two concerts in Budapest.

At one piano rehearsal for the *Missa*, the solo basso failed to show up, and Alexander Kipnis—who had worked with Toscanini at Bayreuth—was rushed over to the Musikvereinssaal from the Staatsoper, where he had been rehearsing an opera. "Here and there he corrected a tempo," Kipnis recalled, "and I remember that he was very dramatic about the *Crucifixus*: he said he wanted it to be like hammering—'*CRU—CI—FI—XUS!*'—as if Christ were being nailed to the cross. After the rehearsal, as soon as I got to my hotel, I received a telephone call from the Director of the Opera: 'Toscanini wants you to sing in the performance; he doesn't want the other man. Could you do it?' I said, '*Could I?!*'"

Kipnis described Toscanini's approach to the *Missa* as "the burning of a volcano" and said that his own "real feeling" for the work "came to me only when I sang in it with Toscanini"—the "fanaticism—burning—expression—drama. The powerful rhythm of the opening chords of the *Kyrie!* And later, the *crescendo* to the *Christe*: the drive of this *Christe* I never experienced with any other conductor."

Toscanini also attended a performance of *The Magic Flute*, but he left the Staatsoper before it was over, "breathing fire and slaughter," said Peyser. "'Una caricatura!' he stormed." On 2 December, he flew from Vienna to Paris, where he gave what would prove to be his last three concerts in France and where Ada spent a night with him. Then, after a brief stop in Milan, he departed with Carla on an altogether new adventure.

Ten months earlier, in New York, Toscanini had received a letter from Bronislaw Huberman, with a request: Would the maestro be willing to discuss "a constructive idea in the artistic field" with which the Polish violinist had become "obsessed"? When the two musicians met, Huberman told Toscanini of his plan to organize in Palestine—which was then a British mandate—a first-rate orchestra made up mainly of Jewish musicians who were fleeing Germany or, presciently, leaving Poland, the Netherlands, Hungary, and other countries. He had been seeking financial support, particularly among American Jews, and he wondered whether Toscanini might be willing to renew his protest against persecution by conducting the new ensemble's inaugural concerts. Toscanini immediately declared his enthusiasm for the project, and when Huberman mentioned the word "fee," Toscanini said that he would accept no payment and would travel to Palestine at his own expense.

Huberman made the news public on 22 February 1936, stating that Toscanini's decision "would constitute a historical mark both in the struggle against Nazism and in the upbuilding of Palestine," and Toscanini declared that "it is the duty of everyone to fight and help in this sort of cause according to one's means."*

His support gave a tremendous boost to the project. An American-Palestine Music Foundation was created under the honorary presidency of Albert Einstein, the best-known of all German Jewish exiles in America; on 1 March, the physicist wrote to Toscanini,

---

* The suggestion that Huberman approach Toscanini on this matter had originated with John F. Royal, an executive with the National Broadcasting Company in New York.

Honored Master!

I feel the need to tell you for once how much I admire and honor you. You are not only the unmatchable interpreter of the world's musical literature, whose forms deserve the highest admiration. In the fight against the Fascist criminals, too, you have shown yourself to be a man of the greatest dignity. I also feel most deeply thankful because you have given the soon-to-be-founded Palestine Orchestra a push forward of inestimable significance.

The fact that such a contemporary exists cancels many of the delusions one must continually experience from the *species minorum gentium!*

> *With love and greatest respect, cordial greetings from your Albert Einstein.*

Late in March, Huberman informed Toscanini that most of the money needed for the first three years of the orchestra's existence had already been raised. The inaugural concerts were scheduled for October, but various logistical and political problems caused a postponement to the end of the year.

Arturo and Carla traveled to Brindisi on 18 December, but instead of flying immediately on to Alexandria, Egypt, as they had planned, a delay caused them to fly first to Athens, where, from the descending plane, Toscanini "enjoyed a truly fantastic spectacle," he wrote to Ada. "The Acropolis was illuminated by the dying sun, and in the last rays *the divine* Parthenon was the color of old marble." From Athens they flew to Alexandria, and on the twentieth they landed in Tel Aviv, where Toscanini "immediately received the most enthusiastic of welcomes," he wrote to Ada, and he joked, "It was as if their Messiah had finally arrived!"

In 1936, Tel Aviv—founded in 1909 on sand dunes near the ancient port of Jaffa—was already a substantial town of 150,000, an important center for Palestine's Jews, who were arriving in ever greater numbers from Germany. One of those refugees, Hans Wilhelm

Steinberg (later known as William Steinberg), a former conductor of the Frankfurt Opera, had been rehearsing the orchestra, with help from Michael Taube, formerly of the Berlin Municipal Opera, and the Russian-born Issay Dobrowen. Toscanini was pleased with what he found. "I got to work the very same day," he wrote. "The orchestra had been well prepared by Maestro Steinberg. With little effort, I got it to do what I wanted."

One of the musicians described the first rehearsals to a journalist. "You can well believe that we were all in an extraordinary state." Toscanini "stepped onto the podium and simply said: 'The Brahms Symphony.' Everything went excellently and the Maestro declared that he was satisfied. At the second rehearsal we felt that we had not worked as well as the first time. Toscanini said nothing. We were very unhappy, thinking he didn't take us seriously. At the following rehearsal, he bawled us out terribly; we were delighted. [. . .] You lose all nervousness, because his baton is so sure. With him, you can never miss your entrance. [. . .] He demands that every musician hear the whole work, and not just his own part. [. . .] He says that the orchestra is so good because many of its members were chamber music players."

"There are two rehearsals a day" for six days, Carla wrote to Wanda, "but they are short and not tiring. [. . .] They put us in a lovely little villa on the outskirts of town. As far as beauty and comfort go, it is everything one can desire, and we have at our disposal a car, a valet, and cook-maid. We are treated as if we were royalty. But at night we are isolated, and the villa, being modern, has enormous windows on the ground floor, and for the first time in my life I am uneasy. I'm afraid—afraid of everything. Papà laughs at me, but I gave up my beautiful big room, and we are sleeping in a smaller one together."

The first program began with Rossini's Overture to *La Scala di Seta* and proceeded with Brahms's Second Symphony, Schubert's "Unfinished" Symphony, the Nocturne and Scherzo from Mendelssohn's *A Midsummer Night's Dream*, and the Overture to Weber's *Oberon*. Free tickets were distributed to artists and workers for the final rehearsal, which took place on 25 December in the Great Hall of Tel Aviv's Exhibition Grounds, and the response was not only enthusiastic but also emotional: the significance of Toscanini's visit was not lost on those present, and many people, including David L. Magnes, the president of the Hebrew University, wept openly. The maestro insisted that Huberman appear on stage to share the ovations.

The Palestine Orchestra's first official concert, the following night, was attended by Sir Arthur Grenfell Wauchope, Britain's high commissioner for Palestine and Transjordan, as well as the future State of Israel's first president, Dr. Chaim Weizmann, and first prime minister, David Ben-Gurion. The hall was packed, and people who could not obtain tickets filled the surrounding area and even climbed onto the roof in the hope of hearing something. A salvo of applause lasting several minutes greeted Toscanini as he made his way onto the stage; as at his final New York concert the previous April, the explosion of a flashbulb before his weak eyes caused an upset at the end of the evening, but all was soon forgiven. Huberman described the concert as "divine" and thanked Toscanini on behalf of all the Jews of Palestine. The following evening the program was repeated for over twenty-five hundred workers—members of the Histadrut (General Federation of Labor)—and it was "amazing to observe the intensity with which they followed the music," London's *Observer* reported. Toscanini wrote to Ada, "I can't begin to tell you the enthusiasm the two concerts, given on the 26th and 27th, aroused."

The program was then performed at the Edison Theater in Jerusalem and the Armon Theater in Haifa, on 30 and 31 December, respectively. The Edison was a cinema; Toscanini invited five hundred workers to a rehearsal, to test the acoustics, and he helped move the music stands and double basses to different positions. "Such a thing I had never witnessed from a conductor," Jaap Stotijn, the principal oboe, reported. In Haifa, a tiny but glaring mistake made by an inattentive trumpet player at the start of the Brahms Second's third movement caused the maestro to conduct the rest of the piece in a barely concealed fury. But the following morning, when the poor musician went to the conductor's dressing room to apologize, Toscanini smiled and gave him an autographed photo. Apart from that incident, the series went well.

Following the first Jerusalem concert—the second half of which was broadcast to America—Toscanini told a *New York Times* correspondent, "This has been the happiest moment of my life. Just think, to have been able to conduct a modern first-class orchestra in the

Holy City, the cradle of three great religions of the world. Conducting an orchestra in Jerusalem was one of the highest points of my career." A second program—all-Beethoven—was likewise performed in all three cities during the first week in January and elicited similar enthusiasm and gratitude from overflowing audiences. Not only Jewish settlers and authorities attended the Haifa concerts: the city's Muslim mayor, Hassan Bey Shukry, was also present. According to the *Observer*'s correspondent, the maestro was "already convinced that if the training is continued, the orchestra can become one of the best in the world." And he told one of Tel Aviv's political leaders, "Several great countries of music lovers have been lost to me; I have found a new country to replace them, Palestine. Tell the people that I want to come back to this country every year."

Toscanini was eager to see not only the country's biblical and other historical sites but also its potash plants and agricultural settlements, and to observe the daily life of the people. He was impressed by a Hebrew-language performance of *The Merchant of Venice* presented by the Habimah Theater in Tel Aviv; he was greeted with thunderous applause when he entered a hall at the Hebrew University of Jerusalem to attend a lecture on Hebrew literature, which was translated into English for him; he attended several receptions; and he was taken to visit different types of collective and experimental farms.

Toscanini and Huberman were out for a drive one day when a rainstorm overtook them; their driver pulled into the nearby moshav (cooperative village) of Ramot-Hashavim, just north of Tel Aviv, and they entered the main building, to the surprise of the residents. The settlement had been founded by German Jews in 1933, the year of Hitler's accession to power, and one of its administrators recalled, years later, that nearly all of these farmers had been professors, doctors, and lawyers in Europe. They had been

raised in the world of German culture; they were all music lovers and, like the whole country, were full of love and gratitude for Toscanini and Huberman, who had brought such unexpected musical events to their new country. They had a lively conversation that afternoon, and Toscanini was so impressed by these people that he said he would come back soon. A few days later, he returned [. . .] with his wife, and they passed several hours of animated conversation at the house of one of the directors. The farmers were overjoyed to be able to present Mrs. Toscanini with a basket of eggs from their henhouses. There were more visits. As a token of gratitude for Toscanini's action toward the Jewish people [. . .] the village dedicated a piece of land to him.

He and Huberman planted trees on this piece of land at a special ceremony on 3 January 1937. Schoolchildren sang folk songs and children's songs for them, and a boy and a girl offered baskets of citrus fruits, honey, and eggs to the guests. Afterward, they went to the cottage of the moshav's leader and, over a glass of wine, they heard the story of the young settlement which had given shelter to sixty refugee families. Toscanini told Huberman, "I never before saw a country as small as this where there was so much culture as among the Jewish labor and farmer classes." Carla wrote to Wanda that in this "magnificent farm of fifty houses [. . .] the young people have adapted themselves, but for those who are fifty and over, it is very sad. There was one man who spoke beautiful French, and it was so sad that we were in anguish. But he did not utter one word of rebellion. One sensed only an infinite sadness, and when we left we were both crying. If you stop to think what they have achieved through sheer labor, it is nothing short of miraculous."

Toscanini wrote to Ada, "From the moment I set foot in Palestine I've been living in a continuous exaltation of the soul. [. . .] I'll say only that even today, Palestine continues to be the land of miracles, and that the Jews will eventually have to *thank Hitler* for having made them leave Germany." (This, of course, was long before the "Final Solution" was implemented.) "A beautiful German girl told me yesterday, in one of these settlements, 'My dear Maestro, my mother and I wept, we were in despair at having to leave Germany; now we're a hundred percent happy, and we noticed that there are seven pianos in our settlement. Music remains, still, our spiritual bread.'"

One of the Jerusalem concerts was broadcast, and traffic in the country came nearly to a halt as people listened to the program in their homes or in cafés. Toscanini was so moved by the people's thirst for music that he opened another final rehearsal to the public, to accommodate some of those who had been unable to obtain concert tickets. As he arrived outside the hall, half an hour early, he saw no one entering and thought that perhaps interest was not so great, after all. Once inside, however, he discovered that the entire audience had already arrived and that every seat was taken. The very fact that he allowed people to attend the rehearsal "proved two things," the *Observer*'s correspondent wrote: "his satisfaction with the new orchestra, and his understanding of the special conditions of the event."

As had already been planned, Toscanini then took the orchestra to Egypt, which was technically independent but still well within the sphere of influence of Great Britain (which controlled the Suez Canal). From 7 to 12 January 1937, the new ensemble gave two concerts each at Cairo's Ewart Memorial Hall (part of the American University) and Alexandria's Al-Hambra Theater. Lorand Fenyves, an eighteen-year-old Hungarian-born-and-trained member of the violin section, visited the pyramids with Toscanini and several other orchestra members and was impressed by the maestro's questioning of the guides—how he "sought a real knowledge and understanding of things that interested him."

Toscanini became so fascinated by Egypt that he readily accepted an invitation to prolong his stay and travel up the Nile. He and Carla set off by train for Aswan, with the intention of taking a rest at "the magnificent *Cataract Hotel* on the Nile," he wrote to Ada, but after only two and a half days, "the mania for familiarizing myself with and visiting temples, tombs, and all the antiquities of Upper Egypt took hold of me." They went by steamship up the Nile to Luxor, where they stayed for six days and even met Egypt's sixteen-year-old, recently crowned King Farouk. Mostly, however, they walked and walked, visiting the site's "colossal marvels." They then returned to Cairo to attend a recital by Adolf Busch, but the violinist had taken ill. Instead, they made "a quick trip [. . .] to Lakkara to see the Step Pyramid" and the site of the ancient city of Memphis. Toscanini learned that Pharaoh Ramses II had "lived to be 85, reigned for 67 years, and as a pastime fathered 162 children—111 males and 51 females," he related to Ada. "And among his many wives were three of his sisters and two of his daughters. Not bad! Were morals better back then or today? Who knows!!!"

About the trip as a whole, he reported feeling "tired in my head and in my legs" but added, "My mind has been enriched by so many things that I had known only in embryonic form, but my heart has been enriched by so very much affection! If only you knew how much good my presence did in Palestine! Modesty doesn't allow me to elaborate, but I can assure you that I won and was enriched by much love."

Arturo and Carla flew from Cairo to Benghazi on 26 January and from there to Rome the following day. "Cursed Rome," he later imprecated. *"Mussolini, the Emperor-King, and the Pope. Pigs, all of them."* By the thirtieth, he was back in Milan, where, as he had written to Ada from Egypt, he was to meet "a friend who's coming from New York, sent by someone or other, to present a plan for me to go back there."

3.

"SOMEONE OR OTHER" WAS DAVID SARNOFF, A RUSSIAN-BORN JEW-ish New Yorker who had left school at the age of fifteen to support his family. After having worked his way up through the ranks of the Marconi Wireless Telegraph Company, he became an early advocate of radio broadcasting, and by the late 1920s he was at the helm of the Radio Corporation of America (RCA) and its subsidiaries, including RCA Victor (the former Victor Talking Machine Company), which produced Toscanini's American recordings, and the National Broadcasting Company (NBC). By 1936, at the age of forty-five, the forward-looking Sarnoff had become the most powerful figure in the quickly expanding field of electronic media.

Sarnoff liked classical music in a casual way, but his initial interest in Toscanini came about through the New York Philharmonic: the maestro, before he had left New York the previous April, had told Bruno Zirato that he would consider returning for a tour with the orchestra, and Zirato and Arthur Judson had persuaded RCA Victor, through Sarnoff, to sponsor a five-week transcontinental tour, beginning in April 1937; Toscanini would be paid up to $50,000 to conduct twenty-four or twenty-five of the tour's concerts. Zirato suggested that someone be sent to Europe to present the plan to Toscanini, who was more likely to be persuaded by personal contact than by correspondence, but Sarnoff vetoed the idea. Instead, a cable was sent to Toscanini, who did not answer. To a second cable he replied (14 December), "For this year impossible. Only possibility April recordings, benefit concerts." Sarnoff expressed the hope that the tour could take place the following year: "We should like to have the entire country hear and see the Philharmonic-Symphony under Mr. Toscanini's direction," he told the *Times*. At the end of December, Toscanini, in Tel Aviv, received another cable: if he wished to make recordings he would be paid either his full concert fee (approximately $2,000) for each recording session or a 5 percent royalty on record sales, he was told. Carla replied from Aswan, "Toscanini will absolutely not make records. Sorry. Thanks." In a subsequent letter, she explained that His Master's Voice (HMV), RCA's London-based sister company, had offered her husband a 12.5 percent royalty on recordings. Out of fairness to the Philharmonic, she said, Toscanini would accept neither proposal.

The maestro's warm feelings toward the Philharmonic began to cool, however, when the orchestra's management announced that John Barbirolli would be engaged as principal conductor for the following three seasons. Toscanini may or may not have had first-hand experience of Barbirolli's conducting, but he had been favorably impressed by Rodzinski, who would be conducting most of the second half of the orchestra's 1936–37 season. "Maestro did not think it was right to announce the engagement of Barbirolli [. . .] before the other conductors started their terms," Zirato wrote to Judson, summarizing a letter he had received from Carla. Rodzinski and the season's other conductors (Stravinsky, Georges Enesco, and Carlos Chávez), "whose terms follow Mr. Barbirolli's meet the public under unfavorable conditions." Toscanini also wondered why he had not been consulted on or, at the very least, officially informed of the choice before it was made public, since he had previously assisted in the selection process. And at the very moment at which his attitude toward the Philharmonic was beginning to harden, an entirely new and alluring offer came his way from Sarnoff's organization.

When Toscanini turned down the joint RCA-Philharmonic tour offer, John F. Royal, NBC's vice-president in charge of programming, suggested to Sarnoff that the network could attempt to bring the world's most famous classical performing musician back to the United States under their company's aegis. Given NBC's huge and growing corporate resources, the network could afford to transform its already substantial, high-quality house orchestra into a first-rate symphonic radio orchestra, on a par with or better than the BBC Symphony in London, with Toscanini as its conductor. Furthermore, NBC and the powerful American Federation of Musicians would soon be negotiating an increase in network spending for live music—and indeed, not many months later, NBC had to agree to raise the number of its New York staff musicians from 74 to 115 and to increase its annual expenditure on live music by $500,000. Last but not least, surveys demonstrated that growing numbers of Americans, especially young Americans, were becoming interested in classical music.

Sarnoff liked Royal's idea, and since he also believed that increasing public support for great music was a good thing, he excogitated a preliminary plan. First, he asked Marcia Davenport, whom he knew to be a friend of the Toscanini family, to recommend someone whom he could send as an emissary to Toscanini and who might have a chance of persuading the maestro to return to New York; she introduced Sarnoff to Samuel Chotzinoff, who was promptly dispatched to Milan.

Like Sarnoff, Chotzinoff was a Russian-born Jew who had immigrated to the United States. During the 1910s, he had served as a piano accompanist to Efrem Zimbalist, Jascha Heifetz, and Alma Gluck (Davenport's mother), among others, and he later worked as a music critic for the *New York World* and *New York Evening Post*. Chotzinoff had married Pauline Heifetz, Jascha's sister, and Davenport described the couple as the "high priest and priestess" of a sort of "Toscanini Cult" that sprang up during the maestro's Philharmonic years. Whenever possible, the Chotzinoffs invited Toscanini and his family to dinner at their home, and they followed him to his European engagements at La Scala, Bayreuth, and Salzburg. In a conversation with Toscanini recorded in the 1950s, Chotzinoff sounds almost like an enamored suitor, but it was Pauline who became one of the maestro's lovers: her husband had admitted to Toscanini that

he had become impotent—so Toscanini told Friedelind Wagner—
and Toscanini had taken over.*

Chotzinoff had cabled Toscanini in Aswan, saying that "unexpected musical developments in America present a situation of tremendous possibilities stop I have all the facts and would like to lay
them before you personally so you may decide whether you are
interested stop If you can see me I will sail for Europe immediately
and meet you at any place convenient to you stop My visit would be
personal and confidential and involves neither you nor me in any
responsibility or commitment please telegraph me collect[.]" Toscanini replied, "Think to my age[.] Tell me if it is worth while to accept
new engagements." But Chotzinoff rebutted, "You are younger than
anyone I know and proposal I will submit very much worth while
your earnest consideration[.]"

Upon arriving in Milan, Chotzinoff presented Sarnoff's proposal
for a new radio orchestra; Toscanini indicated interest and examined
various alternate contract drafts that Chotzinoff had brought with
him. In the end, he opted for the briefest commitment: ten broadcast
concerts in a ten-week period, to begin the following December, at a
fee of $4,000 per concert (more than double what the Philharmonic
had been paying him), with his income tax and round-trip, first-class
travel to be paid by NBC. There would be no commercial interruptions in the broadcasts, and the orchestra would be of the highest
possible quality.

From Via Durini, Chotzinoff phoned Sarnoff with the news of
Toscanini's acceptance; within a day or two, Sarnoff cabled back the
terms of the agreement, and Toscanini immediately signed. There
was an exchange of formal messages for the press, and on 5 February
1937 Sarnoff declared that the arrangement with Toscanini had given
him "more gratification, perhaps, than any other single agreement
to which I have been a party."

The world quickly learned not only the basic fact—that Toscanini
would return to the United States to conduct a new orchestra—but

---

* Pauline (born in 1903) had dated George Gershwin when she was in her early twenties,
but since the young composer had shown no inclination to marry, she had married
Chotzinoff—to spite Gershwin, according to some sources. The Chotzinoffs had two
children, Blair and Anne ("Cookie").

also the financial details: the Fascists tapped Toscanini's telephone and read incoming and outgoing cables and wires, thus the information was passed to the *Corriere della Sera* and was picked up by the foreign press as well, and eventually confirmed by Sarnoff. But the news leak did not upset Toscanini enough to break the contract—if it upset him at all. The new situation was ideal for him. He would have to conduct only three to five rehearsals and a single performance each week for a small portion of the year, with an outstanding group of musicians, and at an unparalleled fee: each broadcast would earn him more than twice the average American family's annual income and more than five times the average Italian family's annual income. In addition, the schedule would allow him to continue to spend most of the year in Europe, working or not working there, as he saw fit. If he did not like the orchestra or anything else about the situation, he could leave after the first season.*

Despite NBC's assurances that only nonpaying, invited audiences would attend the new orchestra's concerts and that every attempt would be made to avoid conflicts or even the appearance of competition with the New York Philharmonic over dates and repertoire, the Philharmonic's managers and board members were shocked and dismayed by the news. "Very surprised acceptance radio proposal," Zirato cabled Carla on 8 February. He asked whether Toscanini had considered the bad effect the NBC Symphony's concerts would have on the Philharmonic's season if a live audience were allowed to attend and/or if the NBC broadcasts were to take place at the same time as those of the other orchestra.

Toscanini himself cabled back, "Was surprised at your surprise my acceptance radio proposal (stop) I feel no obligation to be courteous toward the Board of the Philharmonic and that boorish individual [Arthur Judson]† who advises it (stop) I won't say a word either

---

* Koussevitzky cabled Toscanini almost immediately upon learning the news, inviting him to guest conduct the Boston Symphony during his forthcoming visit to the United States, but Toscanini politely declined, citing his obligation to the new orchestra as the reason: his contract with NBC stipulated "no other engagements in United States" between February 1937 and March 1938.

† Judson (1881–1975) managed not only the New York Philharmonic and, until 1935, the Philadelphia Orchestra but also a number of first-rate conductors, singers, and instrumentalists; he was also paid to advise several other major American musical organizations and was, initially, the largest stockholder in the Columbia Broadcasting

for or against the Philharmonic to Mr Sarnoff who will act in accordance with his interests as the Philharmonic has always done and continues to do." Although Zirato heavily censored his English translation of this message when he communicated it to Judson, Toscanini's response angered him. There was another blunt exchange of cables, and then silence.

At a time when many millions of Americans listened to the radio most evenings, the NBC broadcasts were set for Saturday evenings from 10 to 11:30. They did not conflict with the Philharmonic's broadcasts, although they did overlap with its Saturday evening performances, which began at 8:30 and usually lasted until about 10:30, and they very much overlapped with the Saturday evening concerts of some orchestras in time zones farther west. But some conflicts would have arisen no matter which day of the week and time of day had been chosen. Tickets would be distributed free of charge, but RCA/NBC assured the Philharmonic's executives that players would not be poached from their orchestra's ranks; as far as can be determined, only Sol Klass, the Philharmonic's fourth trumpet, became a charter member of the NBC Symphony.

As soon as Rodzinski heard about the new orchestra, he cabled Toscanini to say that he would be the "happiest man in the world if you would wish to designate me" to organize and train the ensemble; this would be the greatest recompense "for the terrible injustice inflicted on me by the Philharmonic and Judson." Toscanini readily invited Rodzinski to choose the orchestra's personnel and begin the training, and Cia Fornaroli Toscanini wrote to Rodzinski's wife to say that the whole Toscanini family had been outraged by what they considered the Philharmonic's brush-off of Rodzinski. One of Toscanini's reasons for accepting the NBC proposal had been to teach a lesson to his former organization, Cia said.

Toscanini eventually patched up his relationship with the Philharmonic and apologized to Barbirolli and his wife for having "behaved like a pig" and spread unkind assessments of his succes-

---

System (CBS). He did not like Toscanini, over whom he had no control, and the choice of Barbirolli over Rodzinski to succeed the maestro had a great deal to do with the fact that the former was managed by Judson and the latter was not. Judson's organization later became known as Columbia Artists Management Association and was, in its day, one of the wealthiest and most powerful forces in classical music.

sor. In the meantime, however, he worried about how the new ensemble was to be formed. He wrote to Sarnoff to express his "great happiness" over the new project, but also to underline "how hard and difficult [it] must be to put together a very fine orchestra worthy to rival with those of Newyork [*sic*]—Philadelphia and Boston. Your undertaking is not a commercial but an artistic one [. . .]." He listed his requirements for the size of the orchestra: twelve first violins, twelve seconds, ten violas, eight cellos, seven basses, twelve woodwinds, eleven brasses, one or two harps, one timpanist, and two percussionists, for a modest total of seventy-seven or seventy-eight players. Not even two years earlier, he had threatened to quit the Philharmonic if its personnel had been reduced from a hundred ten to ninety-five; perhaps he felt that he didn't need as large a force in a small auditorium: Studio 8H in Rockefeller Center's four-year-old, seventy-story RCA Building, where the new orchestra would perform, seated only 1,250 people (soon expanded to 1,400), as opposed to 2,800 in Carnegie Hall. Or perhaps in February 1937 he was looking forward to beginning a new enterprise, whereas in June 1935 he had been seeking additional excuses for leaving the Philharmonic.

"Did you find the first horn?" Toscanini wrote to Chotzinoff on 14 May. "Is the *horns quartet* quite first *rate*? Who is the concertmaster? the first cellist? [. . .] Do you think the orchestra will be a wonderful one? It must be so—otherwise we shall make a *colossal fiasco* and everybody *will laugh at our expenses!*" Within two weeks, he had received a list of the orchestra's members, and, he wrote to Ada, "It seems to me to be made up of the best individuals to be found there. Money is no object. They're paying astonishing salaries!" Members of the new orchestra would be paid a minimum of $150 (compared with the Philharmonic's $90) to a maximum of $450 per week and would be given forty- to fifty-two-week contracts—unique among symphonic ensembles at the time: most professional American orchestras had twenty- to thirty-week seasons. Rodzinski damaged his own Cleveland Orchestra by bringing several of its best members to NBC, and outstanding players left the orchestras of Chicago, Detroit, Minneapolis, Cincinnati, Rochester, and the Metropolitan Opera, among others, to play under Toscanini. There were complaints that some of those orchestras were being raided by NBC; NBC countered, truthfully, that "men from many orchestras contacted us as soon as the announcement of the Toscanini coming was made."

But more than ten months separated the maestro's signing of the NBC contract from his actual return to America. In the interim, he had much work to do in Europe.

4.

BEFORE TOSCANINI'S ARRIVAL IN TEL AVIV THE PREVIOUS DECEMber, the Palestine Orchestra's two oboists had had a disagreement, and Huberman had wired Jaap Stotijn, first oboe of the Residentie Orkest in The Hague, asking him to assume the principal part during the maestro's tenure. The Dutch orchestra's administrators gave Stotijn a leave of absence, but they also asked him to "engage Toscanini at any cost to conduct a few concerts in The Hague," the oboist recalled.

> How I was to handle this request was not very clear to me, but luck was on my side.
>
> During the intermission of a concert in Cairo, I was standing behind the stage. All of a sudden Toscanini stood beside me. I summoned all my courage and introduced myself to him [in English]: "My name is Stotijn. I'm oboeplayer [sic] in Residence Orchestra in The Hague in Holland. It's a very good orchestra but I'm not the best player of it." Toscanini clapped me on the shoulder and said, "You are a great artist." That was the most beautiful compliment I received in my whole life. Then I asked him if he wanted to conduct in the Netherlands and how many concerts he wanted to give. He left that to me. How many rehearsals? Four before every concert.

After Toscanini returned to Milan, the Dutch orchestra's manager went to visit the maestro, who agreed to conduct the ensemble in two performances of a single program—once in Rotterdam and then in The Hague itself. And so, after having spent most of February in Milan, where he studied and read* but also visited with friends and family (and where, on the twentieth, the Busch Quartet got him "drunk on music," by playing, in his home, works of Haydn and Mozart plus Beethoven's op. 59, no. 2), he and Carla traveled by train to The Hague, where they arrived on the last day of the month.

The Residentie Orchestra ran a distant second, in the Netherlands, behind Amsterdam's Concertgebouw Orchestra, Mengelberg's fiefdom for over forty years. Toscanini may or may not have been curious about working with a Dutch orchestra; what is certain is that he was eager to perform in yet another country that bordered on Nazi Germany, as he had already done in France, Belgium, Austria, Czechoslovakia, Denmark, and—counting the Baltic Sea as a border—Sweden.

At his first rehearsal, on the day following his arrival, Toscanini seemed content with the orchestra. One of the players reported that the musicians, during their coffee break, couldn't stop talking about "this unique event. You hear the words 'magnificent,' 'unique,' 'unbelievable' in every corner of the room. It is best to be silent and to be grateful that we are permitted to witness this event." But at the second rehearsal Toscanini became increasingly unhappy, until some printing errors in the horns' parts in the *Tannhäuser* Overture caused an explosion. "This morning, at the height of exasperation, I walked out of the rehearsal, just like that, with my mind made up to leave The Hague this very evening," he wrote to Ada. "The orchestra is *crude*, lacking in discipline, and accustomed to playing as heavily as a millstone." Stotijn tried to explain to Toscanini that there must have been a mistake in the parts, "but Toscanini reacted with: 'What mistake, there is no discipline in the orchestra. . . . Go away!'"

"I spent a ghastly day, besieged by everyone trying to persuade me to resume the rehearsals and not to give a moral slap to the orchestra and to the city that supports it," Toscanini said. "And then there is a

---

* Of particular interest to him was a translation that Lavinia Mazzucchetti had made for him of Thomas Mann's published exchange of letters with the dean of the University of Bonn: Mann had recently been stripped of his German citizenship and then of his honorary doctorate at the university, and he had attacked the Nazis' dehumanizing, warmongering policies. Toscanini wrote to Mazzucchetti that he had found Mann's statement "magnificent—moving—profound—humane"; Mazzucchetti had had Toscanini's declaration photographed and had sent it to Mann, who noted the fact in his diary, with evident pleasure.

terrible rivalry with Amsterdam, so that this would be a sort of victory for Mengelberg, whose invitations to conduct his orchestra I've always refused. I couldn't resist these gentlemen's pleas. They've postponed the concert to Monday the 8th, and tomorrow I'll resume the rehearsals somehow or other."

Two players were replaced, new parts were flown in from Milan, and Toscanini resumed rehearsals, during the first of which he tore up the old horn parts and threw them over his shoulder into the auditorium. "There was intense joy in the orchestra and we embraced each other and played like madmen to please the maestro," Stotijn recalled. Toscanini reported to Ada: "The orchestra was transformed. Fear of losing me made them decidedly better." Evidently he was satisfied enough to maintain the scheduled date—6 March—of the Rotterdam concert, and in the end, he was "very happy to have made this orchestra happy," he said. The program was repeated in The Hague on the eighth, and Toscanini even agreed to return the following year.

During his stay in Cairo, Toscanini had had Carla write to the Vogheras, to let them know that he was willing to give two concerts—two different programs—in March in Stockholm, if there was room in the schedule; the organization promptly turned its programming upside down, and on 10 March Arturo and Carla flew from The Hague to Stockholm. But on the day after the first concert Toscanini decided to cancel the second. To Iwa Voghera he wrote an apologetic letter, claiming great tiredness and lack of both "the courage" and "the strength" to resume rehearsals the following day, and promising to return in a subsequent season—a promise that was not kept. To Ada, however, he wrote that he had been "disgusted" with the first concert: "Every day I become more impossible toward others and even more so toward myself. Art for me is a *lot of sorrow* and *little joy*. I didn't feel up to the task of getting this orchestra to play Mozart and Debussy well in a few hurried rehearsals. I'm sad and upset."

The Toscaninis flew back to Milan on 20 March, in time for Carla to prepare some surprises for her husband's seventieth birthday. At eight o'clock on the morning of the twenty-fifth, Toscanini was puzzled to hear the sounds of a Haydn serenade floating up from the courtyard of the house in Via Durini; he looked out the window and discovered the Busch Quartet below. As the day progressed, family members and friends from all over began to arrive; the Busch ensemble gave a full-fledged concert that included Beethoven's String Quartets opp. 74 and 130, interspersed with performances, by Serkin and Horowitz,* of Mozart piano duets. Toscanini "received telegrams and letters from all over the world," he told Ada; "the Austrian, Romanian, and Czechoslovakian radio networks referred to my *70th birthday* (aren't you afraid, Ada?), [but] the Italian radio and official Italy were silent—which makes me feel highly honored! *Thomas Mann, Stefan Zweig,* and *Benedetto Croce* were thoughtful enough to send me messages. Zweig wrote me a magnificent letter, accompanied by a Schubert autograph." Zweig's message: "After the good wishes one more wish *for us*—that you always remain the same—the highest example of artistic perfection in our poor times and a hero of moral independence in the midst of universal weariness."

Dinner for 120 was served at small tables that had been set up on two floors of the house. Perhaps not without a certain malicious pleasure, Carla put a number of her husband's ex-flames at his table, and, as Margarete Wallmann recalled, "Toscanini grumbled: 'These are all singers from bygone days, much older than I! If I had had all the girlfriends attributed to me, I wouldn't be here this evening.'" Not many months later, Eleonora von Mendelssohn wrote to a friend that Carla had told her how difficult Arturo's dalliances often were for her, "but one thing she always knew, that he loves her and that he needs her and that he would always come back to her, and so she always let him go, and now she is very happy. He has always done what he wanted on the side, but she has this serenity."

Burghauser, representing the Vienna Philharmonic at the party, heard Toscanini say, "'I am now an old man. And who knows: every new day is a gift of heaven, which I cannot even expect and hope for. I am not sick, but after seventy where are you? Should I even go out and conduct?" But in a letter to Chotzinoff a few weeks later Toscanini wrote that "the *old maestro* is still alive and thinks to be so for

---

* Horowitz was in the midst of the first of what would become a series of withdrawals from the concert platform; he had not played in public since the previous year and would not do so for two more years.

many years to come! *Don't laugh!!!*" And to Ada, who expressed worry about his travels by air: "My hour has not yet come"—a statement consistent with Walfredo Toscanini's description of his grandfather as a fatalist who firmly believed that one's allotted lifetime is virtually predetermined, and that until that time is up one can live as one wishes. "I've never feared death," Toscanini told Ada—especially since his children were grown up, he said; "on the contrary, one could say that I think of it every day with a certain indifference."

THE BIRTHDAY GREETINGS from Benedetto Croce, the best-known Italian philosopher of the twentieth century, had a special significance. Within Italy, although not internationally, Croce—Toscanini's senior by one year—was as famous an anti-Fascist as the maestro. In 1925 Toscanini had refused to sign Croce's "Manifesto of Anti-Fascist Intellectuals" because he had not wanted to make his personal political beliefs public and thereby risk losing financial support for La Scala while he was in charge of its destinies. Also, the radically leftist Toscanini of the post–World War I years would have considered Croce's liberal idealism too weak to provide serious opposition to Mussolini's ever-growing totalitarianism. A dozen years later, however, the two men realized that they were in some ways kindred spirits, and Toscanini was no doubt amused by the neologism that the philosopher had invented for Mussolinian government: *onagrocrazia*—literally, jackassocracy.

Two weeks after his birthday party, Toscanini "spent a delightful evening at Count Casati's in a peaceful and cordial atmosphere," he wrote to Ada.* "Benedetto Croce and many male and female friends, all *right-thinking*, were there. I found Croce rather low in spirits, and this made me feel bad. I know that times are discouraging, *almost* without a hope for seeing change, for those of us of advanced age! But that word *almost* leaves a fissure of light, a breath of faith that mustn't be suffocated [. . .]. I'm incapable, completely incapable, of becoming discouraged; I hate and I curse."

Yet he was becoming more and more "agitated, restless," as he

---

* Alessandro Casati, a Crocean liberal, had been Mussolini's minister of education in 1924–25 but had since become an outspoken opponent of the regime.

wrote to Ada: "the atmosphere in our country is infected, men are disgusting worms, the few whom I love and esteem are dispersed hither and thither. Some days I *am capable* of putting up with this stench, this plague-bearing rot. Other days—today, for instance—I would like to spit poison in the face of all mankind." The Spanish Civil War was raging, with extra troops being supplied by Germany and Italy to the Fascists and by the Soviet Union to the Communists. "I think of those poor young men who are going off, fooled or forced, to get themselves killed in Spain—and for whom? Not for their country, but for scoundrels named *Mussolini, Hitler, Stalin.*"

Despite his bleak mood, which matched the overall mood in Europe as the dictatorships moved toward a collision with the democracies, Toscanini longed to hear good music. During the first half of April, he attended the Busch Quartet's two performances, in one day, of Haydn's *The Seven Last Words of Christ*, at Milan's church of San Paolo Converso, and a recital by Rachmaninoff at the conservatory, which "interested me greatly, and I enjoyed it. Bach, Beethoven, and Chopin were interpreted by an elect artist. The second part of the program was much less interesting, musically [. . .] but the pianist's virtuosity was a success."

Later that month, Toscanini flew to Vienna to discuss with Herbert Graf the staging of the forthcoming *Magic Flute* production that he was to conduct in Salzburg, and to attend part of another performance of that work at the Staatsoper, with three of the leading singers (the Czech soprano Jarmila Novotná, Danish tenor Helge Roswaenge, and Russian bass Alexander Kipnis) who were scheduled to work with him in the same opera at Salzburg that summer. He detested Josef Krips's interpretation of the work, but he accepted all of the singers. He also went to three other opera performances and sat near the organ, out of public view, on the stage of the Musikvereinssaal, to listen to Bruno Walter's performance of Kurt Weill's Second Symphony, among other pieces.

He had intended to fly back to Milan on the twentieth, but when Burghauser hesitantly asked whether he would like to stay a few more days and give a concert with the Vienna Philharmonic the following weekend, Toscanini immediately accepted the proposal. "The rest was easy," Peyser reported. "Front-page stories in the next day's papers sent half the town scurrying to the Philharmonic box office, the more so as ticket prices were not raised."

As usual, Toscanini complained about being surrounded by people: he *"practically lived* with" Luciana Frassati Gawronska, who wouldn't leave him alone, he said;* he saw Elsa Kurzbauer, "who looked rather aged, and badly so," or so he told Ada; and he saw the Piatigorskys and had lunch with young Maria Salata, daughter of Italy's ambassador to Austria, and a female friend of hers from Budapest. "I'm like a deluxe object, a rare, precious item that *arouses others' vanity*," he wrote. On the other hand, he admitted to Ada that there were "many women who have a hard time behaving themselves," although he professed that he didn't "know what to do with them; on the contrary, they don't interest me! It's you for whom I'm *slowly dying* of *voluptuous passion*"—a declaration that must be taken with many grains of salt: Carla was not with him, and Margarete Wallmann plus the above-mentioned Luciana, Elsa, Maria, and Maria's friend were all hovering.

The Popular Front government of Léon Blum, France's Jewish Socialist prime minister, wanted Toscanini to conduct *Pelléas et Mélisande, Falstaff,* and some concerts in Paris in October 1937, as part of the city's great exposition; to that end, Paul Landormy, head of the exposition's music division, and Maurice Lehmann, an administrator of the Théâtre des Champs-Elysées, had visited him in Milan before his trip to Vienna. The proposal interested him, and on 1 May, five days after his flight back to Milan from Vienna, he went to Florence to attend a performance of *Pelléas* conducted by Albert Wolff, with the baritone André Gaudin and soprano Janine Micheau in the title roles and the baritone Claude Got as Golaud. "Most of the tempi seemed right, and the tone colors, too, but taken as a whole—*boredom!!!*" he wrote to Ada. "The music was lacking." (He refrained from mentioning that Margarete Wallmann had accompanied him

---

* Luciana was the daughter of Alfredo Frassati, a founder of the Turin-based newspaper *La Stampa*, and she was married to Jas Gawronski, Poland's ambassador to Austria. Like her brother Pier Giorgio Frassati, who was beatified by Pope John Paul II, Luciana was a liberal Catholic and an ardent anti-Fascist. In 1967, she published *Il Maestro*, a richly illustrated book on Toscanini that contained so many factual errors and so much chronological confusion that Walter Toscanini nearly had an apoplectic fit when it appeared. She died in 2007, at the age of 105.

on the trip.) A week later, he flew to Paris to listen to other potential singers for *Pelléas* and to visit Fanny Heldy, the Belgian-born soprano who had sung Mélisande with him at La Scala a dozen years earlier, and whom he greatly admired. Would she still be able to bring off the role? he wondered. But technical problems with the Champs-Elysées and probably a bit of intrigue on the part of Jacques Rouché, the head of the Opéra, caused Toscanini to abandon the project. This is especially unfortunate inasmuch as the performances would almost certainly have been broadcast and probably recorded.*

On 11 May, he flew to London—thrilled to be traveling at a speed of nearly 250 miles per hour—and checked into Claridge's. The previous year's problem with the BBC's accounting department had been cleared up, thanks to some diplomatic work by Owen Mase, who became a sort of Minister in Charge of Maestro for the BBC Symphony—more or less what Zirato had been for the New York Philharmonic. Toscanini had agreed to return to the orchestra to conduct six concerts at Queen's Hall for a total fee of £3,000.† As soon as the concerts were announced, the BBC received so many ticket requests that its administrators devised a lottery system for meting them out: over seventeen thousand applications were received, and all tickets were sold out on the day they went on sale.

While waiting to begin rehearsals, Toscanini attended several performances, including *Pelléas* and *Tosca* at Covent Garden, the latter conducted by Barbirolli, with whom he had by then made peace. And he visited with Stefan Zweig, who was living in exile in London and who "kept me at his home all last Saturday [12 June] with [the composer Vincenzo] Tommasini, to show me autographs of truly exceptional importance: Mozart, Beethoven, Wagner, Bach, Goethe, etc., etc." Zweig, depressed over the darkening political situation, wrote to Romain Rolland, "Only the hours with Toscanini here were pure delight. This man is so great and so pure and of such

---

* Toscanini had offered to conduct a concert at the Opéra on 9 May, with one of the Paris orchestras that he had already conducted, but the house orchestra's musicians had protested: if he wanted to conduct *them* at the Opéra, they would be honored to participate, but they felt offended that he wanted to perform there with a different orchestra. The concert did not take place.

† Sir Adrian Boult's annual salary, as the BBC Symphony's music director and principal conductor, was £3,500.

incomparable goodness. [. . .] His music and above all his rehearsals are moral lessons for me." Four months earlier, Zweig had written to Rolland, "I saw Freud in Vienna, very courageous, and Toscanini in Milan, very vehement—the old men are now the only ones who fight with spirit."

Once Toscanini had begun to rehearse the British orchestra, he found it "excellent—better than two years ago," and his enthusiasm increased after the first two concerts, which consisted of works ranging from Corelli to Ravel. "If only you knew how happy I am with this orchestra!" he told Ada. "It's a real joy to be working!" Most of his musicians would have said the same. "There have always been in every orchestra players ready to murmur and complain if a rehearsal is called unexpectedly," the *Daily Telegraph*'s critic Ferruccio Bonavia wrote in a correspondence to the *New York Times*: "now the orchestra is dissatisfied when a rehearsal is canceled; they resent missing a rehearsal with Toscanini." The Trieste-born Bonavia, who had played violin under Hans Richter for ten years in Manchester's Hallé Orchestra and who knew many of the BBC Symphony's musicians, said that Toscanini, like Richter, "seemed to obtain just a little more than others" from the orchestra, and that Toscanini resembled Richter "in the considered tempos and in the climaxes which retain the right balance between different families of instruments at their loudest." By coincidence, three months later Richter's daughter, Mrs. Maria Loeb, wrote to Toscanini, "Having heard your 'Meistersinger' Overture in London I at once felt you must have heard [Richter] which has now been confirmed. You are the only conductor whom I really love and enjoy since my Father [. . .]."

In a book called *The Orchestra Speaks*, published in 1938 but based on Toscanini's 1935 and 1937 London appearances, Bernard Shore, the BBC Symphony's principal viola, wrote perceptively about his experiences of playing under various conductors, and he began his chapter on Toscanini by saying, "How rare is the artist of whom we can truly say, 'He is supreme!'" Not even the names of great conductors of the past could be used against Toscanini, "the one living conductor whom every single member of the orchestra approves."

According to Shore, the boredom that players experience at rehearsals under most conductors was replaced by "sheer physical fatigue" under Toscanini, because "he stimulates his men, refreshes their minds," and because there was "no wasting a moment. Rehearsals finish as soon as he feels there is no more to be done. He is never satisfied, but he seems to have an exact picture of the utmost any orchestra can achieve. [. . .] If he cannot please himself he does not allow the players to feel they are to blame. [. . .] After running through Berlioz's 'Queen Mab,' he remarked with a winning smile: 'Bene! You play it bene! But me, no.' "

Shore believed that Toscanini's intense concentration was "very near the root of his greatness" and enabled him to "live and think the music he is recreating so deeply and intensely that all who are working with him feel drawn to the composer's very heart. It is a state of mind which blots out everything save the subject desired; he enters into another world, taking the orchestra with him."

Like most other observers, Shore was astonished by Toscanini's extraordinary memory, but he also remarked on the logical inevitability of his beat, so that "the most difficult change of tempo becomes, even to those farthest from him, clear and unmistakable just at the right moment." Personal magnetism, Shore said, "radiates from the man and holds each of us, not in a grip of iron, but with a power at once irresistible and intensely human and sympathetic." And he described a peculiarity of the maestro's modus operandi: "He collects himself, and in so doing compels all to do the same," Shore said. "He names the piece to be played; and there, as for a few moments he stands still, he seems to be presented with the whole picture of the work in his mind's eye."

About the habit of remaining frozen in concentration for a few seconds before he began a piece, then raising his baton and expecting the orchestra to be ready to start at once, Lorand Fenyves had questioned Toscanini in Palestine a few months earlier. Toscanini had explained that before he could set the music in motion, he had to think through the components of the work's structure: the phrase within the period, the period within the section, the section within the whole piece or movement, and the movement within the entire work—all compressed into a few seconds. Like the nesting boxes with which children play, Toscanini said, the smallest part fits into a slightly larger one, and so on. "I have to feel that I contain all the parts of a work in my mind before I can begin to conduct, and when I do contain them, I *must* begin immediately."

——

PRIOR TO ONE OF TOSCANINI'S REHEARSALS, Boult had entered his esteemed colleague's dressing room and "found John Barbirolli there with the Maestro who was pouring out a torrent of Italian fury and thumping a table with a folded newspaper. When the Maestro had left to start rehearsing I asked what it was all about. One of the fascist Spanish generals had that morning crashed from his plane and been killed. 'And Mussolini goes on flying and flying; and *nothing* will kill him!' was the comment."*

An attempt to make Mussolini look foolish, at least, had almost— but not quite—caused Toscanini to accept a public honor during his stay in England. Earlier in the spring, the University of Oxford had offered the maestro an honorary doctorate in music; Benedetto Croce and Count Casati wanted him to accept, he told Ada, "especially inasmuch as at this very moment the *great Scoundrel* [Mussolini] has received the same honor from the University of—Lausanne!"— a less exalted institution. He briefly considered the proposal but then rejected it, knowing that it would inevitably lead to similar invitations from other institutions. "I would begin to feel awful, living an agitated and unhappy life! Better to say no!"

In gracefully turning down the invitation, however, he offered to conduct the BBC Symphony gratis in a benefit concert for the university, and the BBC made its orchestra available for the event, which took place between the fourth and the fifth London concerts. Toscanini was pleased that the concert—the only performance he ever gave in Britain outside of London—raised more than £1,000 for the University Appeal Fund; according to the *Observer*, "The number of people who failed to get seats certainly broke a record." Afterward, Toscanini, his family, and several friends were taken on a drive through Windsor Park, and the following day Arturo and Carla visited Ernest and Vera Newman at their home in the village of Tadworth, Surrey, where the two men conversed for hours about Wagner, Monteverdi's *L'Incoronazione di Poppea*, and other musical matters. At Glyndebourne that evening, the Toscaninis heard a per-

---

* The general in question was Emilio Mola, one of Francisco Franco's co-commanders in the Spanish Civil War. Mola died in a plane crash on 3 June 1937.

formance of *The Magic Flute* under Fritz Busch's direction, then had dinner with the Christies and returned to London.

Happy though he was with his work, Toscanini resumed his usual litany of complaints—about never being alone, not having enough privacy to be able to write to Ada, and so on. Conversing and looking at composers' manuscripts with Stefan Zweig was fine, but then there was a lunch with the Holt sisters—presumably related to Harold Holt, a London concert agent; there were the heiresses Yvonne Rothschild (née Cahen d'Anvers) and Sybil (née Sassoon), Marchioness Cholmondeley, whose mother was a Rothschild; and there were members of the family of Giuseppe Toeplitz. "I've become a victim *of the Jews,*" he joked to Ada.

Sybil Cholmondeley had often befriended musicians, including Arthur Rubinstein, whose wedding to Aniela Młynarska had taken place at her home in 1932; she was also friendly with Horowitz, through whom she had met Wanda and Wally Toscanini. But with the maestro, her senior by twenty-seven years, the heiress had fallen deeply in love upon getting to know him, in 1935, and she had traveled to his performances in Paris, Vienna, and Salzburg. Now, two years later, she went by car to Glyndebourne with Arturo and Carla, and she wrote to him afterward, to reveal her love. He wrote back, trying to extricate himself gently, but to no avail. She wrote again, telling him that her love had grown increasingly intense, beautiful, and hopeless. Few people could ever have felt such powerful love as she felt for him, she said, but she feared causing him worry or becoming burdensome. She would never act in a way that he would not want; she asked only to be able to see him sometimes. She knew that others would be with him all the time in Salzburg that summer, but she would attend the last week of his performances so that she could be near him.

Sending Toscanini this agonized declaration must have cost a great deal to this proud, highly intelligent woman. Toscanini evidently was not attracted to her; he told Ada that he was "deeply disturbed" in addition to being "astounded [and] surprised" that this "English friend lost control of herself," because the person in question was "not at all a *vulgar woman*—on the contrary—she is very refined and well-mannered." Lady Cholmondeley eventually calmed down, and she and Toscanini remained friends.

While in London, he was delighted to encounter Friedelind ("Mausi") Wagner, Siegfried and Winifred's daughter, who was in England to perfect her English. She wrote to Toscanini "with so much friendly feeling that it makes me marvel," given his break with her mother four years earlier. She "stayed through my last week, attended several rehearsals of the Wagner program and the concert," he told Ada. "I can't begin to describe how affectionate she was. The last time I'd seen her, in '31, she was a little girl; now she's a young lady of 19, still a bit enormous, as she was then, but tall and with a pretty, smiling face!" And to Mausi herself he wrote charmingly and affectionately, in English, that he was "able to read in your eyes the goodness that your heart conceal[s]. This I wanted to say and nothing else. [. . .] Don't believe Mausi, I can understand *everything*[.] I am sometimes *short-minded* as I am *short-sighted!*" He asked whether she was going to spend part of the summer at Bayreuth, and he also asked, "Are you *aware* of the reason which *compelled* me not to go there in 1933?" Toscanini's political stand would soon exert a life-changing influence on Mausi.

On his last day in London, 17 June, Toscanini recorded the first two movements of the "Pastoral" Symphony with the BBC Symphony, "to see whether they make *records* well," he explained to Ada. He wondered whether he would find the results of HMV's recording process preferable to those of RCA's in New York. Owen Mase subsequently brought the test pressings to the Isolino; Toscanini was reasonably happy with them and promised to complete the set and to make other recordings when he returned to London in the fall. This caused temporary friction between HMV and RCA because the latter, through its NBC subsidiary, was about to employ Toscanini as conductor of its new orchestra and fully intended to make recordings with him. In the end, the problem was resolved to the satisfaction of both companies, which had intertwining business interests.*

All in all, the London concerts were "a triumph with respect to audience and even performance," he declared to Ada. This was a typically Toscaninian statement: the fact that the audience liked the

---

*   For further details about this and subsequent Toscanini-BBC Symphony recordings, as well as other aspects of Toscanini's relationship to the UK, see Christopher Dyment's book *Toscanini in Britain* (Woodbridge, UK: Boydell Press, 2012).

concerts was one thing; the fact that even he had found the performances good was more important. And yet, "I couldn't wait to leave London and the English," he said. The weather had been rainy and foggy through most of his stay, and he had hated being fawned over by admirers, however well meaning. Despite the political situation in Italy, "I couldn't wait to go back to my beautiful country. Oh, how I adore Italy, my Ada, and how I suffer because I adore it so!"

5.

"THE DAY AFTER TOMORROW, 21 JUNE, 40 YEARS OF MARRIAGE!" HE wrote to Ada from Milan. "How many lost illusions. How much emptiness! How much solitude!" he lamented. But since the anniversary itself was "a day of divine sky and blazing sun," with many friends on hand to help the family celebrate, all went well. Then, to Toscanini's great delight, he was left relatively alone for a few days. Carla's nerves were in an "abnormal state," he said, and, at his request, Wally had persuaded her to go to a spa by herself and to let her husband be on his own for a while.

He described to Ada the beauty of his surroundings on the Isolino, and he commented, "If we lived a little more in contact with nature, how much better we would be. [. . .] I feel so calm and tranquil this way! My brain is rested, although I keep it active all the time." He did have occasional visitors, but spread out over a three-week period; they included Owen Mase; the Polos; Lucilla De Vescovi Whitman; son Walter and grandson Walfredo; and, accompanied by her nanny, his not yet three-year-old granddaughter Sonia, whom he described as "a dream of a child—adorable!" and possessing a fine musical ear. He often listened to concert and opera broadcasts on the radio, and one evening he heard a "scandalous" performance of *Aida* by the Scala ensemble and De Sabata, given in Hitler's presence in Berlin. (The fact that De Sabata was half Jewish seems to have remained unknown to the Nazis; De Sabata's willingness to perform for Hitler, and even to conduct at Bayreuth as late as 1939, is another matter.) Toscanini raged over both the musical and the political aspects of the broadcast: "I blushed for everyone," he wrote to Ada. "The chorus was barking instead of singing.

And the singers? Everyone went off in a different direction. Poor art! But why talk about art? It's politics that count today. Everything is the slave of damned, dirty politics!"

Damned, dirty politics would disturb him more directly a few days later, on 2 July 1937, when he received an upsetting telegram from Erwin Kerber. The German government was again denying permission to German singers, as well as to non-German singers employed at German opera houses, to perform under Toscanini in Salzburg, and Wilhelm Furtwängler had successfully campaigned to conduct Beethoven's Ninth Symphony in Salzburg that summer.

No sooner had Toscanini received Kerber's message than he wired back, "I'm surprised that the Austrian government keeps you at the head of the State opera. Find a conductor to replace me in Salzburg." The following day, he sent Bruno Walter a detailed letter in which he described Kerber as "a boorish peasant who doesn't know what it means to live uprightly among people who always act by the light of day!" And he continued,

I believed the inclusion of Furtwängler in the Salzburg program, which was done unbeknownst to me, to be a clever move in order to obtain more easily those German singers who are needed for the festival. Only in such a case could that inclusion have been excused and accepted. But this was not at all what happened. We are navigating in very difficult waters, today, to complete the casts for the Meistersinger and Zauberflöte operas. But if the government and administrators of the German theaters deny their singers permission to come to Salzburg, why are the *Austrian government* and the *director* of the *Vienna Staatsoper* inviting this *most humble servant* [Furtwängler] of Messrs. Hitler, Goebbels, and company? It's a mystery! *Artistically*, there was no need! There were *three* of us capable of giving the cosmopolitan Salzburg audience a performance of the 9th Sym.* And so? These Austrian gentlemen ought to be

---

* The third Salzburg conductor that year was Hans Knappertsbusch, second-in-command after Walter at the Vienna Staatsoper. Then, and again after the war, Knappertsbusch passed himself off as an anti-Nazi, but documents uncovered after his death demonstrate that although he was not a party member he was an ultraconservative, anti-Semitic, opportunistic nationalist who, among other things, helped to run Thomas

sincere, for once—they must not continue to do conjuring tricks. Either in or out. Either for or against Nazism! Either the devil or the holy water. As for me, I am withdrawing forever from the theater. Its atmosphere makes me suffocate!

Despite their widely divergent musical viewpoints, Toscanini had always favored Furtwängler's career: his recommendation, only a year earlier, that Furtwängler succeed him as the New York Philharmonic's principal conductor is the most outstanding example of Toscanini's respect for his colleague's musicianship. But when Furtwängler's desire to continue to work in Nazi Germany caused an uproar that ended with his rejection of the Philharmonic position, Toscanini turned against him for reasons that were neither musical nor personal but ethical. Two years earlier, he would have welcomed Furtwängler's presence at Salzburg, but now he found his colleague's political opportunism, which included a return to completely Nazified, "Jew-free" Bayreuth in 1936, reprehensible. A few weeks later, Toscanini would begin to suspect that Furtwängler—whose erotic exploits were at least as wide-ranging as his own—was paying court to Ada Mainardi, but at the time of the Salzburg crisis this additional cause for antipathy had not emerged.

Toscanini was by no means alone among famous musicians in his accusations against Furtwängler and other "non-Nazis." Huberman, for instance, had published an open letter to German intellectuals in the *Manchester Guardian*, in which, after having described Furtwängler as "one of the most representative leaders of spiritual Germany," the celebrated violinist pointed out that in 1933 Furtwängler had clearly expressed the opinion of "all 'real Germans' concerning the shamefulness of the so-called race-ravishing pillories; and I have not the slightest doubt of the genuineness of his consternation." But, Huberman now demanded to know, "what have you, the 'real Germans,' done to rid conscience and Germany and humanity of this ignominy . . . ? Before the whole world I accuse

---

Mann out of Germany in 1933. See Michael H. Kater, *The Twisted Muse: Musicians and Their Music in the Third Reich* (New York: Oxford University Press, 1997), pp. 40–46. Why, then, did he not hold a top position under the Nazis? Probably because Hitler found his performances boring, according to various sources, and because Eva Braun, Hitler's mistress, told the Führer that the tall, blond Knappertsbusch was an attractive man.

you, German intellectuals, you non-Nazis, as those truly guilty of all these Nazi crimes."

Toscanini's thinking on this subject was the same as Huberman's, and his protest over Furtwängler's proposed Salzburg engagement was the logical consequence of that thought process. He wired the Austrian education minister, Hans Pernter, "German government [and] director Tietjen in Berlin refuse German artists for Salzburg out of hatred myself. Thus I judge inclusion *German* conductor Furt-wängler [in] Salzburg program a weakness, an error, a lack of respect toward me against which I rebel. Mr. Kerber had obligation to let me know."

Toscanini's statement about the German government's "hatred" of him was correct: on 1 June 1937, during one of the secret "Cultural Press Conferences" that Goebbels's Ministry of Propaganda had created the previous summer to instruct German arts journalists what they could and could not publish, writers were ordered to mention Toscanini's participation as little as possible, as he was "an enemy of the regime."

Since Toscanini had become the axis around which the Salzburg machine rotated, Pernter, together with Kerber, Walter, and Franz Rehrl, the governor of Salzburg's *Land* (province), all went into over-drive to try to resolve the situation. Pernter sent a letter that Tosca-nini described as "good" and "kind," and Toscanini replied, in another telegram, that he had "nothing personally against colleague Furtwaengler" but that the German conductor's "inclusion Salzburg Festival was mistake weakness and lack of respect toward me against which I protest. [. . .] Under these conditions to my great sorrow I must give up Salzburg."

Governor Rehrl offered to come in person to the Isolino to explain the situation to Toscanini, but the maestro, in thanking him for his courtesy, added that such a visit would be "futile [. . .] because I can confirm my departure for Salzburg as soon as I am assured [of the administration's] giving up conductor 9th Symphony[.]" Toscanini asked his, and Puccini's, old friend Riccardo Schnabl-Rossi, who was living in Vienna and knew what was happening in Austria's musical life, for advice on the situation. Schnabl told him that he was wrong to have criticized Kerber, who simply did what the politicians told him to do; he named a number of singers who were not beholden to

Germany and might have been available, but he advised Toscanini to eliminate the problem altogether by canceling *Meistersinger*, since there were enough singers capable of bringing off the remaining operas well, even without those who required permission from the Nazis. Toscanini ignored the advice.

While this tug-of-war was in progress, Toscanini was further disturbed by an attempt on the part of Guido Pesenti, the mayor of Milan, to persuade him to conduct again in Italy. "I'm so agitated and restless that I can barely hold the pen to write!" the maestro told Ada. "Why don't they let me live with my beliefs, be they good or bad? Do I ever try to persuade others to change their values in politics, in art, or in life?" He learned a little later that Crown Prince Umberto, too, had asked Wally whether her father would talk to him and perhaps be persuaded to conduct in Italy; that Wally had told Umberto that such an attempt would be to no avail; that she had shown Umberto and his consort, Marie José, Toscanini's lengthy, unpublished explanation of the Bologna incident; and that the royals had told Wally that her father was in the right.

And yet, just as Toscanini knew that he would not give in to his compatriots, he also knew that he would have to give in to the Austrians, if they met him halfway—otherwise the entire 1937 festival would collapse, and at a time when every liberal element in the country was struggling to prevent a Nazi takeover. "I wish it were all over," he confessed to Ada. "But that won't be the case—unfortunately! Clowns, all those Austrians! Hitler will do well to swallow them up—then he'll croak from indigestion!" On 13 July, only eleven days before Toscanini was to open the festival, Pernter informed him that Salzburg had obtained the German singers. Toscanini would still "have liked to let everything go to the Devil," he told Ada, since Kerber remained in situ and Furtwängler would conduct the Ninth Symphony, but "I felt what a disaster my absence would have created." Off he went.

As usual, once he was in working mode his state of mind improved. The preliminary work on what would be the reconstructed Festspielhaus pleased him immensely: Rehrl had personally taken charge, "and he wants everything done in keeping with my criteria," Toscanini wrote to Ada. "I'm open-mouthed over the speed of the work." In the meantime, rehearsals for the new production of *The*

Magic Flute began, and so did brush-up preparations for *Fidelio* and *Falstaff.* The Mozart cast was "excellent, of the highest order," he wrote to Ada; in addition to Novotná, Roswaenge, and Kipnis there were Willi Domgraf-Fassbaender as Papageno, Julie Osváth as the Queen of the Night, and first-rate singers even in the secondary roles—including the twenty-seven-year-old Anton Dermota as the First Armed Man.

The *Falstaff* cast was the same as in 1936, but in *Fidelio* three of the major roles had different interpreters: Roswaenge as Florestan, Kipnis as Rocco, and the American Harriet Henders as Marzelline; Toscanini preferred all three of them to their predecessors. Henders recalled sitting on a staircase in the Festspielhaus, trying to absorb the overwhelming experience of her first rehearsal with Toscanini, when the maestro, passing nearby, came over and kissed her on the forehead. She didn't wash her forehead for three days, she later told her daughter. Kipnis said that Toscanini was "completely absorbed" in *Fidelio*, which was scheduled to open the festival. "I think he was not *there*, actually. He was like a high priest of this work: in what he did, it was as if he felt Beethoven was present [. . .]. At the first rehearsal with piano we started from the very beginning; and after each number we stopped and waited for corrections from Toscanini. He was brief and to the point; and we understood him very well, speaking some Italian, some German, and also some English." Kipnis recalled that after he and Lehmann had finished singing the dark, dramatic "digging" duet in Act II, "Toscanini sat with his head bent down deep in his hands, and didn't say a word. After a few minutes he looked up at us and said, 'What music!' At that moment [Lehmann] went over to Toscanini and embraced him and kissed him on the mouth; and he was so embarrassed that he said loudly: 'If you do that again I will not transpose your aria!' " After a rehearsal that had gone particularly well, Kipnis "came out of the *Festspielhaus* and saw Toscanini sitting in his car. When he saw me he beckoned to me; and when I came to him he didn't say a word but only patted my cheek!"

"Everything went marvelously," Toscanini reported to Ada after the first performance, on 24 July, although according to other sources Lehmann had had some serious vocal problems. Two nights later, *Falstaff* triumphed once again. Then, on the thirtieth, came *The*

Magic Flute—the only one among Toscanini's Salzburg opera productions that did not meet with overwhelmingly positive reactions.

Even before the festival began, he had been "coming to the conclusion that the interpretation of the Magic Flute that I'll give at Salzburg will arouse outcries of either scandal or enthusiasm. There will be no middle of the road," he had written to Ada. Why? A partial explanation is to be found in his comments on Fritz Busch's performance of the work at Glyndebourne the previous month. His "impression was of boredom, as in Vienna!" where he had heard the opera earlier that year. "The tempi were slow where they should be moderati or andante, very slow in the Larghetti, and enough to asphyxiate you where they are Adagio. And then the interpretation of the embellishments was all wrong. [. . .] I'm more and more convinced that good musicians are rare, and sometimes even the good ones forget the art of knowing how to *go back to the beginning*, of looking at music they already know with innocent, pure eyes, like a child who is seeing things for the first time."

In the Romantic era and through the first half of the twentieth century—and in some cases even beyond—many of the numbers in *The Magic Flute* were often performed at slower tempi than the composer's written indications suggest. A recording of the first of Toscanini's Salzburg performances of the work reveals that he was ahead of his time. Indeed, the only tempi in that recording that seem seriously wrongheaded, by twenty-first-century standards, are those that are exceptionally slow—in particular, the march that opens Act II, and Sarastro's subsequent aria, "O Isis und Osiris." Basically, however, the mix of comedy, drama, and warm serenity is impressive in this performance.

Toscanini told Ada that certain details "seemed to me still unready!"—and the recording betrays some rough playing here and there, not to mention some terrible errors by Osváth in the Queen of the Night's first aria. One wonders in vain whether the bumps were ironed out at subsequent performances and whether the interpretation as a whole settled down, yet the comments by Kipnis and various other singers, as well as some orchestra musicians and outside observers, about the shock and overall failure of Toscanini's interpretation of *The Magic Flute*, seem nearly incomprehensible today. Toscanini had "brushed clean every particle of the score, and missed its fundamental character," wrote the London *Observer*'s correspondent. "It is a 'Zauberflöte' without religion and without longing. The singers are held in subjection." Comments of this sort underline the great changes in notions of Mozart interpretation that have taken place since the 1930s. But according to Burghauser, the critics of the day "forgot about [Richard] Strauss, whose tempi in *The Magic Flute* were like Toscanini's." These people were "used to the great Walter, who [. . .] made it so emotionally gripping that it was even sentimental. With Toscanini it was *not* sentimental; and people were not mature enough for this."[*]

There is, however, another element in this story. Toscanini, a child of the Romantic century, was an outstanding interpreter of *chiaro* and *scuro* (light and dark) in music but was not usually at his best with *chiaroscuro*—music in which the two elements occur almost simultaneously. Of all the masters of musical *chiaroscuro*, Mozart was the greatest, and Toscanini often did not understand him. In several late-in-life conversations, Toscanini inveighed against Mozart, whose *Requiem*, he said, lacked the power and drama of Verdi's *Requiem*; whose opera overtures lacked the cheerfulness (*allegria*) of Rossini's overtures; whose grasp of human destiny lacked the depth that permeates Beethoven's works; and so on. He seemed to consider Mozart a sort of idiot savant—a childlike creature gifted with adult genius, like the Mozart of Peter Shaffer's *Amadeus*. Toscanini succeeded in *The Magic Flute*—a fable that presents *chiaro* and *scuro* elements consecutively rather than in compound layers (he even preferred its overture to any of Mozart's other opera overtures)—

---

[*] Walter was moved by Toscanini's performance, although he disagreed with many of its details. As a true musician, he was "most interested in all the ways in which my interpretation differed from the usual ones," Toscanini told Ada. Toscanini's fascination with *The Magic Flute*, Mozart's "Masonic" opera, has occasionally been offered as evidence that the maestro was a Freemason, a "fact" that was held against him in Italy, where the Masonic Order, banned by the Roman Catholic Church, has been considered a subversive organization. (The para-Masonic P2 Lodge of the 1970s and 1980s—an illegal, secret society—was in fact implicated in numerous political crimes and plots.) Some Fascists branded Toscanini as a Mason, and in Mario Monicelli's prizewinning 1977 film, *Un borghese piccolo piccolo*, there are references to Toscanini as a Mason. But in over half a century of reading and writing about Toscanini, this writer has never come across any evidence, however tenuous, to suggest that Toscanini belonged to the Masonic order. In one of his letters to Ada Mainardi (18 March 1938), he mentioned that he had never belonged to any sort of society and had "always been a loner."

and he did equally well in the brilliant and often playful "Haffner" Symphony, the primarily dark-hued G minor Symphony, the mainly joyful "Jupiter" Symphony, and several other Mozart works. But he probably would not have done justice to the first-act finale of *Così Fan Tutte*, for instance, or the sextet in the second act of *Don Giovanni*, or either of the Countess's arias in *The Marriage of Figaro*, or the Clarinet Concerto—all of them dominated by psychological ambiguity, by a constant superimposition of dark upon light and light upon dark.

ONE OF TOSCANINI'S REHEARSAL PIANISTS during the summer of 1937 was a twenty-five-year-old Hungarian named György (later Georg) Solti, who was employed at the time as a repetiteur at the State Opera in Budapest. Solti had attended some of the previous year's Salzburg performances, been exhilarated by what he heard, and had returned this year hoping to sit in on some of Toscanini's rehearsals. The flu had knocked out a number of the festival's participants; when Solti arrived with a letter of recommendation for Baron Puthon, the festival's president, Puthon immediately asked him to play the piano at a staging rehearsal of *The Magic Flute* that afternoon. "I arrived at the appointed hour," Solti recalled nearly sixty years later.

> I entered the pit, went over to the piano, and discovered that the singers were ready, onstage, but that there was no assistant conductor around. I never dreamed that the great Toscanini would attend a mere staging rehearsal, so I started in, giving cues with one hand, just as I had been accustomed to doing in Budapest. Suddenly, out of the corner of my eye, I saw a little man enter from the right side of the stage. My heart stopped. It was Toscanini. [. . .] He peered into the pit a little suspiciously, because he was very near-sighted and didn't know who was playing. Without stopping me, he began to conduct—very small, simple, but clear indications of tempo and dynamics. I followed him as if my life depended on it. After an hour or so he called a break, turned to me and said, softly, *"Bene."* I do not think that any compliment I have ever received has given me as much joy as that one word from Toscanini.

Solti—future music director of London's Royal Opera and the Chicago Symphony Orchestra, to name only two among several exalted organizations—"played many other *Magic Flute* rehearsals for Toscanini, several *Fidelio* rehearsals and one or two *Falstaff* rehearsals," he remembered. "The level of concentration could not have been higher. I quickly became one of his assistants and ended up playing the glockenspiel for the *Magic Flute* performances." At the end of the festival, Toscanini invited Solti to help coach four of the five operas that he was to conduct at Salzburg the following summer.

NOTWITHSTANDING THE LUKEWARM RECEPTION of *The Magic Flute*, Toscanini remained the central figure in the 1937 festival. "More and more obviously, Salzburg is becoming Arturo Toscanini's fief," wrote the French critic Emile Vuillermoz in a dispatch to Paris. "Mozart's town is henceforth entirely in the powerful hands of the great magician." An enterprising businessperson created souvenir "Toscanini pins" to attach to scarves or lapels; they were snatched up as curiosities in local shops, and for the second year in a row the festival's administrators scheduled a Toscanini performance to open the festival and another to close it, in the hope that his myriad fans would want to stay for the entire duration.

Not everyone was happy about the Italian maestro's impact. According to Stephen Gallup, in his history of the festival, the annual event had become "Toscanini's anti-Fascist and anti-Nazi showcase," as opposed to the relaxed, summertime artistic-intellectual oasis intended by its founders, who included Max Reinhardt (a Toscanini admirer), Richard Strauss, the poet and librettist Hugo von Hofmannsthal, the stage designer Alfred Roller, and the conductor Franz Schalk—the last three deceased before Toscanini had conducted his first opera performance in the town. The anti-Nazi stance in itself was "laudable," Gallup said, as was the high quality of the performances, which attracted sincere music lovers from all over Europe and beyond. But Toscanini's name and fame also drew vast numbers of celebrities and snobs to Salzburg. In 1936, the controversial king Edward VIII of England had been present, incognito, with his even more controversial fiancée, Wallis Warfield Simpson; in 1937, following Edward's abdication the preceding December, the couple returned openly as the Duke and Duchess of Windsor. The Hungarian regent Miklós Horthy and Italy's Crown Prince Umberto and consort, Princess Marie José, had attended the 1936 festival, and Marie José, a real music lover, returned in 1937, when President Roosevelt's mother and his son John were also present, as was the seventy-three-year-old Margot Asquith, widow of the former British prime minister H. H. Asquith. (Lady Asquith had developed a crush on the maestro.) Marlene Dietrich—an anti-Nazi German who was already a Hollywood star—"caused a small scandal by dressing as a man in *Lederhosen*," Gallup reported, and "the Salzburg newspapers resembled extended social columns and described who ate with whom, the latest fashions and recreational habits of the famous." Color movies that Walter Toscanini shot in the town show crowds of local people gathered across the street from the Festspielhaus, gawking at the fancy cars that unloaded their well-heeled passengers.

Despite the constant threat of a Nazi takeover of Austria, attendance at the festival as a whole rose from 53 percent of seating capacity in 1934—the year before Toscanini's first opera performances there—to 89 percent in 1937. All of the opera and concert performances that Toscanini conducted at Salzburg during the summers of 1935, 1936, and 1937 were sold out, except one, at which a mere 98 percent of the seats were sold.

On 5 August came the revival of the previous year's *Meistersinger* production—again with Nissen as Sachs, but this time with the Dutch tenor Henk Noort in the role of Stolzing and the Austrian soprano Maria Reining as Eva. Preparations for the production had been so thorough in 1936 that Toscanini needed only two ensemble rehearsals to put it back into shape, and the first performance engendered an enthusiasm that nearly equaled the riot in the opera's second act: ovations, cheers, and stamping of feet took place at the end of each act, and as the maestro was about to begin Act III, someone—probably an Italian anti-Fascist—shouted, "Evviva Toscanini!" He "ground his teeth, made a furious grimace and struck his desk with his baton in the violence of unconcealed irritation," Peyser reported. Apart from that incident, however, the performance took place in "an infinitely poetic atmosphere," Toscanini told Ada, and after the first act, Eva Chamberlain, Wagner's daughter, who had hoped in vain to hear Toscanini conduct the work at

Bayreuth in 1933, came to him "with tears in her eyes and said to me, 'My dear friend, I feel as if I were hearing Die Meistersinger for the first time. Never, not even in Bayreuth's early days, has it made so great an impression as this evening.' And she kissed my hands, bathing them with her tears, which seemed unending." Daniela Thode, Eva's half sister, wrote that this performance "was for me the fullest revelation of this divine work." Toscanini felt exhausted afterward, "but tranquil enough for having once again done my duty as an honest artist."

After the final *Falstaff* performance, Toscanini described "the orchestra musicians, afire with sacred enthusiasm, showing me their joy through their applause. I, who had *pressed* them *implacably* morning, noon, and night, received their joy and gratitude in exchange. [. . .] This evening, all the performers—singers, chorus, orchestra, and the old maestro who kept them in line—seemed to me to have brought off wonders. We all had the Devil in us, as Verdi often said when he was happy with a performance."

Altogether, during that Salzburg season Toscanini conducted twelve opera performances and three concerts: a performance of the Verdi *Requiem*, a mixed Rossini-Beethoven-Strauss program, and an all-Brahms program. The last event went particularly well: his musician friends told him that it was "the best of all those I've conducted here during these years! Bruno Walter, Polo, Bruno Walter's family, many Italian and foreign friends, were moved to tears." There was, perhaps, a sense of "last things," of the ineluctable approach of a gigantic catastrophe, that created an especially intense emotional atmosphere throughout that summer's festival.

In the Verdi *Requiem*, Toscanini worked for the first time with the Croatian soprano Zinka Kunc, who would soon adopt her husband's surname, Milanov, and become one of the star singers of her generation; she replaced the originally scheduled German soprano Ria Ginster, whom the German government had refused to allow to sing with the Jewish basso Kipnis. Toscanini demonstrated to the thirty-one-year-old Milanov—known for her lovely, lyric voice but also for her limited adaptability and diva-like behavior—how to sing certain phrases. Kipnis wondered "how she would do them, because even with [Toscanini's] hoarse voice and his piano-playing the music sounded as if it were created at that moment. Milanov said: 'I cannot do it because I haven't the breath support'; and Toscanini was very kind and smiled. I don't remember him being irritable or shouting at any time."

As usual, however, Toscanini complained. Elsa Kurzbauer, who was living in reduced economic circumstances, was with the Toscaninis *"every day* and at *every meal* and at *every rehearsal,"* thanks to an open invitation from Carla; he felt that he was "to blame for her current state," yet her frequent presence bothered him—or so he told Ada. Then there were the fans and autograph hounds who surrounded him whenever he left the house in Liefering to go into town. "I can't stand being looked at any longer. Yesterday I wanted to attend the dress rehearsal of the Marriage of Figaro, out of respect for Bruno Walter. I couldn't hold out—I rushed home out of despair, before the rehearsal began." Then he learned that Ada and her husband had gone to the Bayreuth Festival, which left him "saturated in rage." And on 15 August he had to attend "a sort of concert of early music played on old instruments, given in the town hall, and as I *read* the *program* I realized that it was given in honor of Bruno *Walter, Knappertsbusch,* and myself. You can imagine my state. I refused to sit in the chair of honor that had been reserved for me, to avoid being exposed to curious glances; then at supper I didn't eat or drink anything, nor even open my mouth! The whole government was there, from [Chancellor] Schuschnigg on down. [. . .] Everyone was so *bandaged* with decorations that it was actually funny to see them!"

To his surprise and delight, however, Ada herself came, alone, to Salzburg, on 16 August, and attended single performances of each of the four operas as well as his last two concerts. He had been looking forward to spending the eighteenth, a free day, with the Busches at Eleonora von Mendelssohn's home at Kammer, but now he hated the visit, he said, because it kept him from Ada; and after having attended that evening's performance of *Euryanthe* conducted by Walter ("noblesse oblige," he told her), the Busches had come to dinner at his home—a further impediment. He also attended Walter's performance of Bruckner's Eighth Symphony on the twentieth and was seen following the performance with a score. But he managed to spend some private time with Ada. She had begun calling him Artù (in Italian, King Arthur is Re Artù), and he now began to combine their two names into Adartù.

Ada's presence no doubt added to Toscanini's overall relative satisfaction with his work in Salzburg, and so did the progress of construction work at the Festspielhaus, to which he was contributing his fees for the broadcasting of some of his performances in addition to the fee for his last Salzburg concert. He promised to assist further by conducting a benefit concert with his NBC Symphony in New York during its forthcoming inaugural season. And, in agreement with Kerber, Walter, and Rehrl, he made plans to add *Tannhäuser* to his festival repertoire in 1938, with Graf to be in charge of the staging. For subsequent seasons he was thinking about *Boris Godunov; The Barber of Seville*, which he had not conducted since 1906; and Gluck's *Iphigenia in Aulis*, which he had never conducted. Prospects for at least the following three years seemed excellent.

SANDWICHED BETWEEN Toscanini's last two concerts was Furtwängler's controversial Salzburg debut, which Toscanini had so strenuously opposed. Furtwängler attended at least one of Toscanini's concerts and a *Meistersinger* performance, but Toscanini was not present at Furtwängler's performance of Beethoven's Ninth Symphony, which received mainly tepid reviews. Furtwängler, however, insisted on seeing Toscanini and barged into his dressing room. According to Burghauser, the tall, lanky Furtwängler, who towered over Toscanini, told his colleague that he wanted to conduct *Der Freischütz* at the following year's festival, and Toscanini replied that he could do as he pleased, because he himself would not return. But sources close to both conductors reported that Toscanini had said, simply, "You conduct at Bayreuth, I conduct at Salzburg." In other words, each of them had made a choice and had to live with the consequences.

The encounter soon became known. Joseph Roth, the Austrian novelist and journalist—then living in exile in Paris and gradually succumbing to the alcoholism that would kill him in 1939—wrote to his friend Zweig about the "splendidly furious outburst of the old man against Furtwängler" and the maestro's opposition to "meanness, dilution, cowardice." But Furtwängler published a letter proclaiming the separation of art and politics. To Ada, Toscanini wrote that "the letter could be considered absolutely right and right-thinking if Furtwängler himself hadn't been the one to impose a political character on his artistic activity by accepting (at a pay of 10 or 12 thousand marks a year)"—from Hitler's government— "an inevitably political *state position*. Thus the letter is meant only to throw dust in the eyes of simpletons, of which the world is full. I, however, shall be as silent as the tomb. I don't want to fuel gossip. I told him what I needed to tell him. Enough!"

From then on, Toscanini would have nothing to do with Furtwängler, and he joked that even writing "fur" twice in Ada's Berlin address—Pension Fürstenhaus, 69 Kurfürstendamm—bothered him. Furtwängler, for his part, canceled the performances with the Vienna Philharmonic and Staatsoper that he had been scheduled to conduct in October, presumably because Toscanini would be conducting concerts in the city at about the same time.

Berta Geissmar, the German conductor's former secretary— forced to leave Germany because she was Jewish—"has let Dr. Kerber know that next year [Furtwängler] won't conduct in Bayreuth," Toscanini told Ada, late in October; in other words, he had decided to interpret Toscanini's statement to him literally, rather than accepting their intended meaning: You conduct in a racist dictatorship; I do not. And in January, Toscanini informed Ada that Furtwängler was again campaigning with the Austrians. "Can you imagine that after our conversation on 27 August, when I very clearly defined our situation in Salzburg, he's shamelessly resumed begging for a concert for the coming season? And the Viennese and Minister Pernter are again daring to take the subject up and trying to persuade me to allow him that concert? But what are men made of these days? Certainly not of the courage of lions. Oh, what a bad race we are!"

A few days later, Bruno Walter wrote to Toscanini in the hope that the maestro's attitude toward Furtwängler had not changed, because, Walter said, Furtwängler's "atmosphere is—at least for me—politically, personally, and artistically—intolerable; and particularly at Salzburg. [. . .] Furtwängler has one sole idea: himself, his glory, his success; he is a man of talent, of personal weight but badhearted, which expresses itself even in his music making." Walter said that if Furtwängler were to be allowed to conduct even a single concert or opera performance at Salzburg during the coming season, "I would have to say good-bye."

Hitler and the Austrian people would decide the matter for all concerned before long, and Toscanini may have had a foreboding when he wrote to Ada—immediately after he had closed the 1937 Salzburg Festival with a performance of *The Magic Flute*: "Sadness over things coming to an end is a tragedy for me! I don't know how to rid myself of it." Yet he could hardly have imagined just how final this particular ending was: he would never again conduct a complete, staged opera performance anywhere, and he would never again see Salzburg.

6.

TOSCANINI MADE THE SHORT JOURNEY TO BAD GASTEIN ON THE DAY after his last Salzburg performance and immediately dashed off a note to Ada, inviting her to join him there and urging her to spend as little time as possible in Germany: "Until when will you stay among those louts? Aren't you afraid of losing all your beauty, of becoming like Freia in Das Rheingold?" he teased her. Yet he was delighted to be alone for a while ("I need solitude more than I need air," he wrote), since the family members who had been with him during the last festival week had gone off in various directions. A few people he knew came to the spa but stayed only long enough to be pleasant company. He took the baths as prescribed by the spa's doctor, who found him in excellent condition: the maestro's arm and shoulder felt better than they had the previous year, and his blood pressure averaged around 125/80. "With a heart like that," the doctor told him, "you can live to be 120 years old!" This made Toscanini joke with Ada that by then she would be ninety and that they "would still be head over heels in love," although perhaps no longer capable of making love.

He came to the spa armed with books, and he had others sent to him from Milan. Above all, he reread the prose *Zibaldone* and the poetry of his old favorite Leopardi—"the poet I love best after Dante!" he said. Toscanini disagreed with Leopardi's observation that physical love was never as fulfilling as one hoped it would be ("poor L. must always have paid for those [favors] he received," he commented), but he agreed that the "soft, sweet melancholy" after lovemaking constituted the "best moments." He transcribed verses and other passages for Ada, and he mused over the poetry of Shakespeare and Byron, much of which he knew by heart in English, and of Carducci and D'Annunzio as well. He was enjoying his readings so much that he wished he could just go on with them; instead, "everyone wants me, unfortunately, and they steal from me what ought to be my life—*to work for myself, study, learn* the many things that I don't know and that interest me so very much, since I don't have *much more time* before me."

When he was not reading, or seeing his occasional visitors, he fretted. "I'd like to turn my back on everything and retire for good, so as not to have that endless *nightmare* that kills me every time I have to face an audience or an orchestra," he wrote. "The more time passes, the worse I get." And his vow not to conduct in Italy was a constant thorn in his side. "I can't tell you how homesick I am for my country! It *kills* me! [. . .] I am the *only Italian artist, truly* and *wholly Italian* musician, who must, who is obliged to remain *outside* his country!!!" He railed against the low artistic quality of most of the operas and concerts on the radio and about feeling ashamed of being "part of this gang of *commonplace* and *humdrum* musicians, *still,* at my age!" He had no desire to start working again, he said, and yet he had agreed to conduct concerts in Vienna, London, and Palestine before departing for America, and others in London and The Hague upon his return to Europe.

He bombarded Ada with questions and comments. Why hadn't she taken full advantage of her talents? he asked. "Do you think that I knew, when I was fifteen or sixteen years old, what sort of intellectual development I would undergo, or how, via what route, and toward which goal my future would be directed?" Whereas she had had "only one pressing aim: *to Get Married!*" he said. He held up as an example the Milanese actress Vera Vergani, whom he considered not particularly gifted but who had "at least tried to get away from the *humdrum,* monotonous life without a goal that nearly all women accept whether they want to or not. [. . .] I am absolutely certain that you have betrayed yourself, if not out of laziness then out of apathy!" Nor did he let her off the hook when she protested that her talents were insignificant. "Have you sacrificed (note well, *sacrificed*) *hours, days, months, years* to continuous, unremitting, wearying study at your piano, and of music in general?" But he stopped the harangue when Ada visited him at Bad Gastein, where they spent two days and two nights together. "Never were our bodies so united, never had we known each other so intimately," he wrote to her afterward.

But family matters, politics, and even the weather soon conspired to change his state of mind radically. Rainstorms and car problems caused what would normally have been a seven-hour trip from Bad Gastein to Milan, on 20 September, to last over fifteen hours, and the following day more rain prevented Toscanini from reaching the Isolino. Once there, he inveighed against Carla, who had used some of his earnings to buy a farm at Ripalta Guerina, near the town of Crema, southeast of Milan, and was having it fixed up; and he was fed up with Wally, who was "being a *countess* and lives among those *highly placed* and *overrated* scoundrels." He refused to go to Venice, where the family would celebrate Horowitz's birthday on 1 October, because he couldn't bear to face Wally's "*entourage! The Volpis*, the *Cinis*, and the *old Morosini woman* bring me to the point of *vomiting*." His mood was so dark that he "even avoided a visit from Zweig here [. . .], although he is very dear to me!" And the news that D'Annunzio had accepted the presidency of the Accademia d'Italia, following the death, two months earlier, of Marconi, its first president, further revolted Toscanini: he detested the academy, which Mussolini had founded, and he recalled that D'Annunzio, like himself, had originally refused to participate in it. "*Stinking old wreck!!!*" he exploded. "He already has one foot in the grave"—the poet was four years older than Toscanini— "but he can't stop being an obscene, repulsive clown."

He was angered by the not unwarranted suspicion that his letters to Ada in Berlin were being opened by the German censors, but the same notion made him joyfully redouble his violent descriptions of Hitler, "the *Madman*, the *Teutonic criminal*," who was preparing to receive Mussolini, "the Great *Scoundrel*," in Germany at the end of September. A year earlier, the two dictators had signed a military alliance, the so-called Rome–Berlin Axis; Mussolini's visit to Munich and Berlin was meant to seal the agreement. "And we look on, impotent, at the loosening and lowering of nearly the whole world's moral forces!" Toscanini wrote. "It's frightening! The *coalitions* that were created in the past against imperialism and dictatorships seem unrealizable today! How will we be judged fifty years from now?"

One day, Toscanini, in a black mood, told Ada that he would cancel his scheduled performances in Vienna, but two days later he changed his mind: "I'll get back to work," he wrote. "I'll toil, I'll kill myself, but there's nothing except work that can give me back a little peace." Once he had resumed studying scores, he was "a completely different man." But after two more days had passed, he was again "cursing the moment when I made this decision. I'm a wretch, an unhappy, dissatisfied man who ought to put an end to it once and for all, retire to private life, forget and be forgotten." A week later, within a few hours of having checked into Vienna's Hotel Bristol, he was rehearsing the Vienna Philharmonic and feeling just fine.

The first program was given twice in Vienna and repeated, with one program change, in Budapest. During the latter performance of the Ravel orchestration of Mussorgsky's *Pictures at an Exhibition*, Toscanini made a potentially serious error: after one of the piece's "Promenades," instead of giving the downbeat for the "Tuileries" section, which is quick and light, he indicated the start of the slower, heavier "Bydlo" section. Burghauser recalled that "a phenomenon occurred which not one of us, and hardly Toscanini himself, ever experienced: *not one musician started to play!* It was ghost-like, a little like a nightmare: [. . .] Toscanini, for a tenth of a second, was flabbergasted and stony-faced: how come nobody plays?" But he quickly realized what had happened, and "with an almost undiscernible nod, he gave the right dynamic sign for the beginning of 'Tuileries,' and then the orchestra, most harmoniously, as if nothing had happened, started to play. Afterwards he said: 'This is the greatest compliment an orchestra can pay me: *I* make a mistake, and the orchestra at once realizes I am wrong.' Why? Because [. . .] his gesture for communication and conducting is so unmistakable in its one possible meaning that you cannot take it as meaning anything else [. . .]. But that a *hundred people* should have this immediate mental contact—this happened with no other conductor in my fifty years of playing."

Two rapturously received performances of an all-Brahms program in Vienna concluded Toscanini's engagement with the Philharmoniker—permanently, as things turned out. When Arturo and Carla departed politically agitated Vienna aboard a plane bound for relatively tranquil London, they were leaving Austria forever.

7.

THE TOSCANINIS SETTLED INTO THE ENORMOUS BUT LUXURIOUS Langham Hotel, opposite Queen's Hall, and the maestro began to prepare for a series of recording sessions and two demanding concerts with the BBC Symphony Orchestra. Late in October, he completed his recording of the "Pastoral" Symphony (new versions of the first two movements, which they had recorded the previous spring, but the older version of the second movement was eventually released) and added Beethoven's First Symphony and Brahms's "Tragic" Overture to their recorded repertoire.* "These recording sessions are killers for me!" he wrote to Ada. "I even end up with a headache—an illness virtually unknown to me."

Once again, a lottery system was instituted for tickets to Toscanini's concerts (14,000 people tried to get into the 2,500-seat auditorium), the first of which, on 30 October, was dominated by Brahms's *German Requiem*; the second, four days later, centered on the Beethoven Ninth. He told Ada that he found the orchestra "superior to all others, at least for its magnificent discipline," yet he became upset during a rehearsal of the Ninth and "stopped after three-quarters of an hour. That first movement [. . .] always makes me despair." Still, the pianist Alfred Cortot, "who attended the rehearsal with his young mistress and Stefan Zweig, came to me with tears in his eyes and couldn't speak for the emotion!" the maestro wrote to Ada. "Too bad that the state of my nerves didn't allow me to resume the rehearsal." That state had been exacerbated by a cold or flu, and he was eating and sleeping even less than usual.

Toscanini had been restudying the Ninth Symphony, as was his custom before he began to rehearse any work in his repertoire. "I'll have to *surpass myself* again, hop up a bit higher in order to stay at the same level," he had written to Ada.

The Adagio! Elysian Fields, Paradise—I feel what is inexpressible. It lifts me off the earth, removes me from the field of gravity, makes me weightless; one becomes *all soul.* One ought to

---

* For these discs Toscanini was paid a 7.5 percent royalty, worldwide.

conduct it on one's *knees*. [. . .] Do you know that at the modulation to E-flat I always conduct with my eyes closed? I see extremely bright lights far, far away; I see shadows moving around, penetrated by rays that make them even more disembodied; I see flowers of the most charming shapes and colors. And the very music I'm conducting seems to descend from up there—I don't know where! It's all a mysterious spell that wraps around me during those sixteen bars, and it changes at the next modulation into the main key, when the second *divine* variation begins.

The evening before he began to rehearse the symphony in London, he wrote to her,

I'm already all full of dread at the thought of confronting that *colossal, marvelous first movement*. I always feel that I'm doing it for the first time, and that I've never understood it well enough! In the score, [at the opening of] the last 35 bars, where there begins a sort of march that concludes that tragic movement, I've written in pencil: Per me si va nella città dolente. / Per me si va nell'eterno dolore / Per me si va tra la perduta gente.* Every time that I play or conduct those bars, the well-known Dantean terzina rings in my brain. Dante and Beethoven! It's enough to make you quake!

Toscanini's uncompromisingly tragic, even harsh interpretation of that first movement shocked several British critics. But Bonavia, who had played the Ninth under Richter, pointed out that "stress and storm [. . .] inspired Toscanini's conception of the movement, his rapid tempo being wholly consistent with the idea of a contest from which there is neither rest nor respite." And he mentioned the slight slackening of pace here and there, "in order to give a rapid passage time to make its full effect felt," as well as the maestro's "meticulous observance of pauses." The finale was sung in English by the soloists

---

* Toscanini used modern Italian spelling in his quotation from the third canto of *The Divine Comedy*, but his recollection of the passage was otherwise exact. The words are those over the Gate to Hell: "Through me one goes into the sorrowing city, / Through me one goes into eternal sorrow, / Through me one goes among the lost people."

Isobel Baillie, Mary Jarred, Parry Jones, and Harold Williams, with the BBC Choral Society prepared by Leslie Woodgate. Among the audience members was Prime Minister Neville Chamberlain, who, within a few months, would become one of Toscanini's bêtes noires.

The maestro was politely pursued by Sybil Cholmondeley and Yvonne Rothschild during his stay in town, somewhat more insistently by Margot Asquith, but he managed to avoid giving any of them cause for hope—or so he told Ada. He again saw Zweig, who brought his attention to the exiled Italian anti-Fascist novelist Ignazio Silone; at Zweig's behest, Silone sent Toscanini copies of his *Fontamara* and *Pane e Vino* (Bread and Wine), which the maestro read immediately and enthusiastically.* During a luncheon organized by the Royal Philharmonic Society—which had commissioned Beethoven to write the work that became the Ninth Symphony—he accepted the organization's Gold Medal, and at the British Museum he examined several musical manuscripts, including the copyist's score of the Ninth Symphony that Beethoven had annotated and sent to the Philharmonic Society for the work's London premiere. He attended the opening of an exhibition of the paintings of his son-in-law Emanuele Castelbarco, as well as "a magnificent performance of Shakespeare's Richard the Second," he reported to Ada, with John Gielgud in the title role and Peggy Ashcroft as the Queen.

The Toscaninis traveled home by plane and train on 4 and 5 November; they were to have departed three days later for Palestine, but news of skirmishes between the Arab population and Jewish settlers had caused Wanda to contact Chaim Weizmann and ask for advice. "I'm a fatalist, and I won't hesitate to leave when the moment comes," the maestro told Ada, but Weizmann, who visited him in London, "told me that for the moment I mustn't make a move, that I absolutely must postpone going to Palestine until things there have been resolved or at least improved." Huberman, the Palestine Orchestra's founder, had been injured in a plane crash, thus concern over Toscanini's well-being was redoubled.

The postponement meant that Toscanini was able to spend five

---

* Silone's anti-Fascist credentials were later tainted by allegations of his having been an informer for the Fascists and, after the war, for the American OSS (predecessor of the CIA). But the novels retain their immediacy.

performance-free weeks at home, but within a day of his return to Milan he was anticipating future distress. "The thought of going to New York in a month drives me crazy! I'd like to say goodbye to everything—withdraw from every activity! I'm fed up with music, with orchestras, with audiences, and with myself!" And he was upset over not having heard from Ada in too many days; she was in Belgrade with her husband, who was giving a concert there. Once he had had word from her, however, he calmed down. "I'm studying Sibelius's 2nd Symphony, which I've never performed, and the Tchaikovsky 4th, which I've never wanted to conduct because I like it very little, but which I've promised to perform in America." (That promise was never fulfilled.) A suggestion from Vuillermoz to mark the twentieth anniversary of Debussy's death, the following year, with a Salzburg Festival concert dedicated entirely to the French composer's music, elicited his enthusiasm: he wrote to Bruno Walter to propose the program, and the proposal was accepted. Toscanini's other Salzburg concert was to be devoted to the *Missa Solemnis*.

Friends and family members visited frequently, and his former Scala assistant conductors Calusio and Votto and some of his former orchestra members also came to see him. One Saturday evening, late in November, several of his old friends from Parma—most of them schoolmates from the conservatory—came to Via Durini for dinner. Toscanini was delighted that not one of them had become a Fascist—except for Enrico Polo, his own brother-in-law, with whom he was growing increasingly impatient. "My God, how empty he is," Toscanini told Ada. Some months later, he said that he envied Polo, who had retired from his teaching position at the Milan Conservatory and who "sleeps from *ten* in the evening until *nine* in the morning, and *after* lunch until *four* in the aft[ernoon]. He admires Mussolini's genius and maybe Hitler's, too, and he doesn't give a damn about [. . .] anything in life that gives signs of movement!" Toscanini would have been even more upset to learn about Polo's correspondence with Daniela Thode, who, after having learned that the maestro's trip to Palestine had been postponed, wrote to his brother-in-law, "For me, it was an intolerable idea that the Maestro should again be in that land and among those people who crucified Our Lord."

In mid-November, Toscanini was about to go to the Isolino, but bad weather and several dinner invitations in Milan made him decide to stay in the city, where he remained until the evening of 5 December, when he and Carla left for Genoa. The following morning, they boarded the *Conte di Savoia*, bound for New York. At seventy, the maestro was about to begin the longest professional relationship of his life.

8.

BARELY TWO MONTHS EARLIER, THE ENTIRE NBC SYMPHONY PROJECT had teetered on the brink of collapse. During his stay in London, Toscanini received a radiogram from Kendal E. Davis, vice-president of the Broadcast Division of the American Radio Telegraphists Association (ARTA), who asserted that NBC was "discharging numerous employees citing cost of your engagment necessitates budget slash stop this organization confident that you as an artist and a liberal will not tolerate this misuse of your name." Chotzinoff and Royal immediately sent Toscanini an explanatory cable, and Toscanini, uncertain which of his interlocutors to believe, cabled Chotzinoff to cancel the engagement.

Lenox Lohr, NBC's president, then cabled Toscanini. ARTA's statements were "entirely false and seem to be caused by internal controversy between rival unions," Lohr said. "[. . .] To the contrary your engagement has resulted in employment of fiftyfive additional union musicians stop the few people released some weeks ago were in no way connected with your engagement [. . .] stop that there were any antilabor activities involved in this is preposterous and we deplore this unjustifiable annoyance to you."

As far as can be determined, some half-truths were told Toscanini by both NBC and the union. He had initially requested only seventy-seven or seventy-eight players for the new orchestra, but the basic number was eventually expanded to ninety-two, presumably for internal reasons: NBC's "classical" instrumentalists were needed not only for symphonic concerts but also for other broadcasts, thus some flexibility within the ranks was required. Before the new orchestra was formed, NBC had already employed a seventy-four-member house orchestra plus forty-one other musicians; only thirty-one of the seventy-four orchestra members were retained for the NBC Symphony, which means that sixty-one new instrumentalists were engaged and as many as forty-three members of the old house orchestra may have lost their jobs. It seems unlikely, however, that members of the telegraphists' union would have lost their jobs as a direct result of the creation of the NBC Symphony.

The tempest in a teapot blew over quickly; Toscanini accepted NBC's explanations. Rodzinski had been rehearsing the new orchestra since early October, and a sort of dress rehearsal had been broadcast before the ensemble was turned over to Pierre Monteux for three weeks of rehearsals and highly successful broadcast concerts, in repertoire that ranged from Bach and Handel to Stravinsky and Germaine Tailleferre. Rodzinski then returned for three more weeks of concerts in a similarly broad repertoire.

Although America, in the late fall of 1937, had not yet emerged from the Depression, to visitors from Europe the country seemed blessedly removed from the Old World's political convulsions. When the Toscaninis disembarked on 13 December, they were greeted by masses of "friends, acquaintances—even enemies, I think," he joked in a letter to Ada. Interspersed among all the melodramatic declarations of love and despair, complaints about the infrequency of Ada's letters to him, and accusations of infidelity, there are indications in this and subsequent letters that he was enjoying himself. "My love, how I would like you to get to know this marvelous, fantastic New York!" he wrote. "It seems to me even more marvelous than before." He adored the city's energy, its ethnic mix, and its positive, forward-march feeling, the economic crisis notwithstanding. And he was greeted as a returning hero. "I can't describe the welcome I've received. The entire personnel of the NBC, from President Sarnoff (a truly exceptional man) and the board of directors down to the doorman, are enchanted with me and treat me like their God. If I weren't the wretched creature that you know me to be, I would swell up with vanity, like a Lucifer."

Toscanini began his first rehearsal with no introductory speeches by himself or anyone else. Samuel Antek, a young member of the new orchestra's first violin section, later described how, before the maestro entered, the musicians had sat nervously rigid, scarcely breathing. Suddenly, from a door on the right side of the stage, a small, solidly built man emerged. Immediately discernible were the crowning white hair and the impassive, square, high-cheekboned, bemustached face. He was dressed in a severely cut black alpaca jacket, with a high clerical collar, formal striped trousers, and pointed, slipperlike shoes. [. . .]

As he stepped up to the podium, by prearranged signal we all rose [. . .]. He looked around, apparently bewildered by our unexpected action, and gestured a faint greeting with both arms, a mechanical smile lighting his pale face for an instant. Somewhat embarrassed, we sat down again. Then, in a rough, hoarse voice, he called out, "Brahms!" He looked at us piercingly for the briefest moment, then raised his arms. In one smashing stroke, the baton came down. [. . .]

With each heart-pounding timpani stroke in the opening bars of the Brahms First Symphony his baton beat became more powerfully insistent, his shoulders strained and hunched as though buffeting a giant wind. His outstretched left arm spasmodically flailed the air, the cupped fingers pleading [. . .]. His face reddened, muscles tightened, eyes and eyebrows constantly moving.

As we in the violin section tore with our bows against our strings, I felt I was being sucked into a roaring maelstrom of sound—every bit of strength and skill called upon and strained into being. Bits of breath, muscle, and blood, never before used, were being drained from me. I sensed, more than I heard, with near disbelief, the new sounds around me. Was this the same music we had been practicing so assiduously for days? [. . .] With what a new fierce joy we played!

"The orchestra is of the highest order," Toscanini reported to Ada. "Their manner of playing together is already magnificent. The strings are first class, beyond any description! Working is a delight." The string section was indeed remarkable. Mischa Mischakoff, the concertmaster, had been a gold medalist at the St. Petersburg Conservatory and, after having immigrated to the United States, had served as concertmaster with the New York Symphony, the Philadelphia Orchestra, and, most recently, the Chicago Symphony Orchestra. Other well-known string players among the orchestra's original personnel included the violinists Henri Nosco, Remo Bolognini, Josef Gingold, and Edwin Bachmann (principal second violin); the violists Carlton Cooley (principal) and William Primrose (second chair); and the cellists Alan Shulman and German émigré Ernst Silberstein (former member of the famed Klingler Quartet). Musicians of Jewish origin accounted for over 80 percent of the string section. Among the principal wind players, John Wummer (flute), Robert Bloom (oboe), William Polisi (bassoon), Bernard Baker (trumpet), Armand Ruta (trombone), and William Bell (tuba) were American-born, although most of them were first-generation Americans, as was Edward Vito (harp); Augustin Duques (clarinet) was born in France, Albert Stagliano (French horn) in Italy, and Karl Glassman (timpani) in Poland.

"I work with the new orchestra—which is truly exceptional—with great pleasure and satisfaction," Toscanini wrote, again during his first week of rehearsals. "I can't describe the enthusiasm of the musicians and of all the members of the NBC board." Not to mention the public, whose interest rivaled and then surpassed that of London's music lovers: for the first concert alone, NBC received 23,000 ticket requests for the 1,400 available seats in Studio 8H, which would be the orchestra's main home for most of its existence.

That concert, which took place on Christmas night, consisted of three minor-key pieces in falling fifths: Vivaldi's Concerto Grosso in D minor, from *L'Estro Armonico*; Mozart's Symphony no. 40 in G minor, K. 550; and Brahms's First Symphony in C minor. "I hardly need to tell you, but you can imagine how nervous I am," Toscanini wrote to Ada a few hours beforehand. "I'm the eternal beginner, perhaps the only person who doesn't hold me in esteem." This and subsequent programs were broadcast on 143 stations of NBC's transcontinental Blue and Red networks, thirty-three stations of the Canadian Broadcasting Corporation, and six shortwave outlets that transmitted to Europe and other parts of the globe. Programs distributed to the house audience (which included New York's governor, Herbert H. Lehman, the financier and presidential adviser Bernard Baruch, Adolf and Frieda Busch, Rudolf Serkin, and Geraldine Farrar) were printed on pieces of silk, so that the sound of rustling paper would not cause any disturbance over the air; the program bore the admonition: "Since the modern microphone is extremely sensitive, your cooperation in maintaining strict silence during the music is urgently requested."* There was no intermission: the pieces were separated by a radio announcer's brief comments—but at the first concert, the audience, unfamiliar with the Vivaldi piece, did not applaud at the end, which caused Toscanini to proceed immediately with the Mozart symphony.

At six o'clock the following morning, he wrote to Ada that he was "just this moment getting home. After the concert, which ended at eleven-thirty, I went to the home of the President of NBC, *David Sarnoff*, who had invited a great many people in my honor, and I stayed until five in the morning. [. . .] The concert went off very beautifully. There was much enthusiasm. Back at home I found a great many congratulatory telegrams. Many of them were sent by radio listeners (my son in Milan among them), and many by people who attended the concert." The musicians "played marvelously well. You ought to hear what a noble sonority this orchestra produces! It is truly made up of members of the highest order. In Italy, we could never put together an orchestra of this sort."

The ten concerts that Toscanini was under contract to conduct took place every Saturday evening from 25 December 1937 through 26 February 1938; only Sibelius's Second Symphony was new to his repertoire, but he was also preparing, for the first time with the new orchestra, thirty-eight other works by twenty-eight composers. Prokofiev, visiting New York for what would prove to be the last time, before Stalin decided to confine him within the USSR's borders, attended the concert of 5 February 1938 and wrote to thank Toscanini for it—especially the "magnificent performance" of Rossini's *Semiramide* Overture, he said. He had heard that Toscanini was

---

* Programs for subsequent concerts were printed on oilcloth or thin cardboard, for the same reason. One wag sent a letter to the *New York Times*, to the effect that he had mailed Toscanini a baton that could double as a poison-dart blowgun, so that if anyone applauded at the wrong time the maestro could turn around, blow into the baton, and kill the offender. As far as is known, however, Toscanini himself had never objected to spontaneous, enthusiastic applause between movements, just as he did not object to—and indeed expected—applause after well-sung arias in opera performances. Only now, when his NBC broadcasts had to remain within the ninety-minute time slot, did he occasionally gesture to stop inter-movement applause from the audience.

thinking about performing the "Russian" Overture that Prokofiev had composed two years earlier, and he offered to go over the score with the "dear Master," but in the end neither the encounter nor the performance took place. To his friend and colleague Nikolai Miaskovsky, Prokofiev wrote, "I heard Toscanini, who played trash, but how he played it!" What Prokofiev described as "trash" included not only the Rossini overture and Tommasini's Scarlatti arrangement, *The Good-Humored Ladies*, but also Mendelssohn's "Italian" Symphony and the "Queen Mab" Scherzo from Berlioz's *Roméo et Juliette*.

Toscanini suggested adding an eleventh concert to his broadcast series—one of his popular Wagner potpourris—and NBC gladly accepted the idea; this program added seven more pieces to his first-season repertoire. And three more pieces, plus one more composer, were tacked on, thanks to his two benefit concerts with the orchestra at Carnegie Hall. The first event, on 6 February, comprised Beethoven's First and Ninth Symphonies, and netted $22,000 for New York's Italian Welfare League. "I conducted, I believe, as never before in my very long career," he wrote to Ada. "I had *quicksilver* in my blood, in my veins [. . .]. The orchestra did wonders. The chorus, the solo singers, everyone was at one with me." The Schola Cantorum, directed by Hugh Ross, participated in the event, and the vocal soloists were the Belgian soprano Vina Bovy, the Swedish mezzo-soprano Kerstin Thorborg, the basso Ezio Pinza, and a thirty-three-year-old New York–born tenor, Jan Peerce.

Toscanini had heard Peerce (whose name was originally Joshua Perelmuth) singing on the radio, had asked him to audition, had chosen him for the vocal part in Busoni's *Rondò Arlecchinesco* on his fourth NBC concert and then for the Ninth, and he would select him for many other performances during the following years. He appreciated not only Peerce's voice and excellent intonation but also his musicianship, intelligence, flexibility, reliability, and good pronunciation of foreign languages.

The second benefit concert, on 4 March, featured the Verdi *Requiem* (again with the Schola Cantorum, but this time with the soloists Milanov, Castagna, Kullman, and Nicola Moscona—a thirty-year-old Greek bass who had recently made his Metropolitan debut); it was to have raised money for the new Salzburg Festspiel-haus. Mozart's hometown was anticipating its most financially successful summer to date: advance ticket sales had already doubled those of the previous year, which had broken all earlier records. But on 12 February, Chancellor Schuschnigg of Austria had met with Hitler and had bowed to some of the latter's demands, including the aligning of Austrian foreign and economic policies with those of Germany and the installation of Artur Seyss-Inquart, a leading Austrian Nazi, as minister of the interior, thus head of the national police force.

No sooner had Schuschnigg's concessions to Hitler become known than Max Reinhardt, in California, cabled Wally Toscanini (who spoke German), asking for her father's take on the situation. Two days later, Lotte Lehmann wired the Toscanini family's confidante Margherita De Vecchi to ask "what Maestro thinks about Salzburg[.] Will he come there now or shall he cancel[?] Am very excited and worried[.] Please give him my love[.]"

Toscanini's opinion became clear on 16 February. "The current political events in Austria oblige me to renounce my Salzburg Festival participation," he cabled Erwin Kerber. He sent a similar message to Salzburg's governor, Franz Rehrl, and issued an official statement, through NBC, that made the front pages of newspapers around the world the following morning:

> Owing to the unsettled conditions in Austria as reported in the American press this week, I have decided to abandon my plans to go to Salzburg for this year's music festival. In order to provide those in charge of the festival in Salzburg ample opportunity to make other arrangements, I have today telegraphed them of my decision. The benefit concert at Carnegie Hall, scheduled for March 4, will be held as previously announced, except that the net proceeds from the concert will be donated by me in the proportion of 75 per cent to the unemployed musicians of the New York local of the American Federation of Musicians and 25 per cent to the Verdi Rest Home for aged and destitute musicians in Milan.

Any ticket holders who objected to the new destinations of the proceeds could have their money refunded.

Many people, even among those who agreed with Toscanini's

political ideas, believed that he had overreacted or reacted too quickly. Governor Rehrl cabled that the situation had not changed and that he should return to Salzburg; Toscanini did not answer him. On 19 February, a day after Lotte Lehmann had told the press that she still hoped to return to Salzburg that summer, she wired Toscanini from San Francisco, "Do not be angry with me[.] I do not believe everything that is said in the newspapers[.] I do not think that the situation is clear enough[.] I do not want to lose my second country unless it is absolutely necessary but I would sing there only if art remains free[.]" Even Huberman, at the request of Schuschnigg's chief of staff, promised to try to persuade Toscanini to go back on his decision. And Elsa Kurzbauer, herself Jewish, had sent Carla a cable from Vienna: "Everyone very desperate because of Maestro's renunciation which is unfounded [. . .]. You probably heard greatly exaggerated newspaper reports[.] Salzburg Festspielhaus and season would be ruined[.]" At the bottom of Kurzbauer's cable, Toscanini drew three bold exclamation points.

Burghauser cabled his hope that Schuschnigg's latest, reassuring speech would bring Toscanini back to Salzburg, and Daniela Thode, torn between her irreconcilable idols, Toscanini and Hitler, cabled from Bayreuth, "Desolate I beg you not to abandon us[.]" In a letter to Polo, she expanded on her ideas: "He, the enemy—but why!—of Fascist Italy and Fascist Germany, cannot conduct in a Fascist Austria; it is a consequence of his principled stand. But why take this stand? Why not render unto Caesar what is Caesar's, with Christian wisdom, and withdraw into the realm where he is the sovereign, absolute king, completely independent and incomparable?"

Bruno Walter, who, like Kurzbauer and Burghauser, was "on site" in Vienna, bombarded Toscanini with cablegrams, including the following (19 February): "Continuation Austrian cultural program convincingly and unequivocally assured to me by very authoritative source[.] I have signed new contract with Staatsoper stop Please support from your side as well contribution to Salzburg[.]" He asked Toscanini to await an explanatory letter that he would send the following day—a letter that said, among other things, "If Austria either becomes united with Germany or accepts German orders for her policies, please do not doubt that I too would leave here immediately"—as if Hitler would have allowed a Jewish-born conductor to choose to retain his position! "I only want to ask this: wait, dearest friend, until the development of events can prove in clarity where Austria's course is going. [. . .] [I]f developments should prove that Austria is not changing important principles, please return to Salzburg which can no longer live without you and don't leave me there alone, because your absence would mean Furtwängler's activity, intolerable for me and I too would therefore leave Salzburg."

But Toscanini had already answered Walter by cable: "Futile to await your letter [stop] my decision however painful is final stop. I have only one way of thinking and acting. I hate compromise. I walk and I shall always walk on the straight path that I have traced for myself in life."

Italian officialdom heaped vituperation on Toscanini. Most telling was an article in *Regime Fascista*, a newspaper edited by Roberto Farinacci, a former secretary of the National Fascist Party and one of the most physically violent and virulently racist members of the hierarchy. "We have always hoped that Toscanini would admit his faults and be reconciled to the Fatherland which made him famous," reads the article. "But no, he allows no opportunity to pass for insulting his country by his behavior. After the recent political developments in Austria he hastened to announce that he would go no more to Salzburg. Toscanini makes use of his art to conduct his idiotic anti-Fascist propaganda. We ask the Government how long he is to be allowed to enter or leave Italy as he pleases. The time has come to say that we have the right to strike him as he deserves."

From other sources, however, Toscanini received a flood of messages of congratulations and thanks for his uncompromising stand. Most moving was a letter from Gaetano Salvemini, twentieth-century Italy's most influential historian, who had escaped from Mussolini's regime, first to France and then to the United States, where he had joined the faculty of Harvard University. "In these Borgia-like years, you are the only person whose moral light remains steady amid the universal baseness," Salvemini wrote, on 18 February. "You are the only one who, at those important moments when we were lost in the darkness of despair, shouted words of faith, duty, and hope at us. [. . .] Fate has not been so adverse today as may seem, at first glance, to be the case, to those of us who have been scattered through the world by the tempest. To those cowards who bow down before the Great Beast, taking it to be Italy, we can teach that Italy is today represented not by Mussolini but by Toscanini. [. . .] May our Italy live forever—the Italy of Mazzini, which still continues, through you, dear Maestro, to speak to the world in terms worthy of its history and its nobility."

On 2 March, the Salzburg Festival's administrators, apparently in a state of collective denial, cabled Toscanini to request that he communicate by the tenth of the month whether he had gone back on his decision—"Otherwise we are forced to consider your renunciation final." Toscanini replied, "I am surprised by your insulting telegram and I am surprised that the finality of my decision was not already understood from my first cable."

Hitler's forces marched into Austria on 11–12 March 1938, and in April an overwhelming majority of the Austrian people voted in favor of unification with the German Reich. That summer, in Nazified Salzburg—the only Austrian city in which book burnings took place—Furtwängler opened the swastika-bedecked festival, replacing Toscanini in *Meistersinger,* and with Goebbels prominently in attendance. The other operas that Toscanini was to have conducted were taken instead by Knappertsbusch (*Tannhäuser* and *Fidelio*) and Vittorio Gui (*Falstaff*).* Walter's productions were led by the pro-Nazi Karl Böhm and Knappertsbusch, and the concerts were conducted by all four of the above "replacements" as well as by Edwin Fischer, Eleonora von Mendelssohn's former husband. Productions that had been created by Lothar Wallerstein, Herbert Graf, and Margarete Wallmann—all "non-Aryans"—were replaced by "racially pure" versions presented in the newly reconstructed Festspielhaus for which Toscanini had campaigned and which he had helped to finance. Walter, Reinhardt, Lehmann, Wallerstein, Graf, Burghauser, and Kurzbauer all found refuge in the United States—the last two with the moral and financial assistance of Toscanini and his family and friends—and Wallmann became chief choreographer at the Teatro Colón in Buenos Aires.

Among Toscanini's three principal Austrian interlocutors, Kerber

---

* After the war, Gui passed himself off as an anti-Fascist merely because he had never joined the Fascist Party.

continued for a while as head of the Vienna Staatsoper and implemented the Nazis' orders: under his watch more than two hundred Jewish and "mixed race" artists lost their positions, although he helped a few of them flee the country; he died in 1943. The Nazis threw Minister of Culture Hans Pernter out of office and into Mauthausen concentration camp, and Salzburg's Governor Franz Rehrl was also imprisoned; both survived the war.

9.

A FEW DAYS BEFORE HIS WITHDRAWAL FROM THE SALZBURG FESTIval, Toscanini was awarded the American Hebrew Medal "for the promotion of better understanding between Christian and Jew in America." At the same time, a testimonial fund drive in his honor was underway in New York to support the Palestine Orchestra. Kurt Lehmann, a music lover, presented Toscanini with memorabilia from the rehearsals and first performances of *Parsifal* at Bayreuth in 1882, as a token of his admiration.

The Toscaninis attended various events during their American stay: they spent an evening with Thomas Mann (who was still living mainly in Switzerland but would soon immigrate to the United States) and the Muschenheims at the Astor; dined with the Pereras and other friends; and went to a revue from which the maestro returned home "with my head spinning from the devilish din of the two orchestras, mainly brass, of that Broadway theater!" he reported to Ada. "The supper was magnificent, just as the entertainment was magnificent. Very beautiful creatures, very beautiful young bodies, mainly naked. Extremely sumptuous costumes in good taste, but a devilish din. I wouldn't go back."

All three of Arturo and Carla's children joined them in New York at various times during the course of the first NBC Symphony season. On the day after his final concert, the maestro—accompanied by Walter Toscanini, Sarnoff, Sarnoff's son Robert, and Olin Downes—toured the site of the forthcoming 1939 New York World's Fair, at Flushing Meadows, then being converted from a dumping ground for trash and horse manure; he examined plans, offered suggestions for the 2,500-seat polyvalent theater that was being planned there, and expressed his enthusiasm for the initiative. He would have been willing to conduct an opera or two there, but sufficient funding was not available.

Early in March, NBC announced that Toscanini had signed a contract for three more seasons with the ensemble; the company published a souvenir book about the new orchestra; and the maestro led his first recording sessions with the group. He and Carla set sail for Europe on 9 March aboard the *Queen Mary*, and shortly after their departure the Associated Musicians of New York, Local 802, announced that by a unanimous resolution, lifetime honorary membership was being conferred on Toscanini for "having achieved outstanding distinction as libertarian and defender of the civil liberties and rights of mankind."

The Toscaninis arrived in Paris on the fourteenth, spent a day there with the Horowitzes and Castelbarcos, then proceeded to The Hague, where Toscanini found the Residentie Orchestra much improved over the previous year—and no wonder: a forty-year-old conductor named Georg (later George) Szell had been working with the orchestra in the meantime. Within eight days, Toscanini had rehearsed two complete programs: the first was given at The Hague, Rotterdam, and the VARA Broadcasting studios in Hilversum; the second was performed only once, at The Hague, on the maestro's seventy-first birthday.

His relief at having found the orchestra in good condition did not relieve his distress over the Nazi takeover of Austria, which had occurred during his transatlantic crossing. "What has happened during these last weeks has made me lose every hope for the slightest improvement in humanity," he wrote to Ada on 17 March. "I am ashamed of belonging to the human race. The *scoundrels* who govern the people are beneath all imagining, however low." Referring to Mussolini, who had promised to act as a guarantor of Austrian independence but had backed down, Toscanini commented, "*Prostitutes*, the ones who do it for five lire a night or even less, care more about their honor and are more likely to keep their word." And with regard to his own attitude: "I've never been and will never be involved in politics; that is, I became involved only once, in '19, and for Mussolini, and I repented even before he came to power in '22. Of course I think and act as my conscience tells me. [. . .] Everyone ought to express his own opinion honestly and courageously—then dictators, criminals, wouldn't last so long."

Arturo and Carla returned to Paris the day after his final concert in The Hague, but by 29 March they were back in Milan, where "a whole battle of feelings is taking place in me, and it's torturing me," he wrote to Ada. "I love and hate my country and [hate] the men who are *dishonoring* it. I don't know what to do, how to live anymore. And everyone tortures me, they praise me, they admire me, and they continue to be *cowards*." Exasperated by news vendors in the streets announcing one of Mussolini's speeches to the senate, he left the city for a day's respite at the Ripalta Guerina farmhouse that Carla had bought and that Wally was busy furnishing. He had initially criticized the purchase, but now he appreciated the "divine peace that that magnificent green countryside exudes. A religious silence. [. . .] The Isolino is more romantic, more poetic, but not more restful—you still feel life too much around you, and the presence of people! *Disgust!*"

There was further respite on 2 April, when Count Casati brought the embattled philosopher Benedetto Croce to Via Durini for a visit. "I spent half an hour that did me good, like pure morning air in the Alps," he reported to Ada.

I found Croce much better in health and, I must say, in spirit than the last time I'd seen him, and this gave me much pleasure, because at that time he left me feeling very upset. That time it was I who was encouraging him; this time it was the opposite. But he lives such a different life from mine [. . .]. A philosopher is a little like an astronomer. [. . .] Both are perfectly able to withdraw from normal life and, if they so wish, to avoid any contact with the cowardly human race. But I, with my artist's life, haven't been able to avoid carrying out my activity among people. It's very difficult, my dear Croce, I told him, the other day, to find the serenity necessary to put up with everything horrible, grotesque, and tragic that the world has to offer today, when you're obliged to live in the midst of it, and *every day*!

Toscanini's intention to leave for Palestine just over a week after his return to Italy seemed to change when he received a telegram from Huberman, suggesting that he not go after all, and he contemplated meeting Ada on Capri instead. But the situation in Palestine changed once again. He and Carla traveled from Milan to Rome on 7 April, stayed overnight at the Hotel Quirinale, then flew onward, arriving in Haifa on the ninth. They were driven immediately to Ramot-Hashavim, where they were presented with oranges and orange blossoms from the grove that had been dedicated to the maestro the preceding year. Then onward to Tel Aviv, where they were guests of the poet Malka Locker and her husband, Berl, one of the Jewish Agency's administrators.

Toscanini began to rehearse his first program on the day after his arrival, and, according to the *Manchester Guardian*'s correspondent, he "expressed his delight. Three-fourths of the orchestra, he declared, were equal to any in Europe or America. [. . .] The concerts of Toscanini play a part in the Jewish national life like that which the tragedies in the theatre of Dionysus played in the life of the Athenians." For the dress rehearsal, in Haifa on the thirteenth, he and Carla traveled in Weizmann's armored car. "*It wasn't necessary,*" he stressed, in a letter to Ada. "But they are taking every precaution. In front of my auto and Huberman's there was another one, full of *police*. I felt like laughing, and I think that I could go around all by myself and that no one would touch a hair on my head."

The dress rehearsal impressed Toscanini even more than it impressed the audience: "*2,500 workers*, men, women, *children*, [. . .] shouted like mad people in the most affectionate excitement, their eyes full of tears! The rehearsal was scheduled for 8. At seven-thirty the hall was already packed. I began at seven forty-five." The first concert took place in Haifa the following evening; it was repeated in Tel Aviv on 16 and 17 April (the second time, for workers) and in Jerusalem on the twentieth (for a combined audience of subscribers and workers). Before the first Tel Aviv concert, the city's buses and taxis were swamped not only with the 3,000 people who had tickets to the event but by another 10,000 who wanted only to catch a glimpse of and applaud Toscanini,whose concrete demonstration of solidarity with the victims of persecution gave the immigrant population a sense of hope.

Bombs exploded in Jerusalem on the day of his first concert there; he and Carla had lunch at Weizmann's home in Rehovot and were driven to Jerusalem in the armored car—"and not only that, but with a rifle between me and the chauffeur," he commented. The concert took place as scheduled, with audience members arriving not only from various parts of Palestine but also from Egypt and Syria.

In the meantime, he had begun to rehearse his second program, which, in addition to music by Rossini, Beethoven, Saint-Saëns, and Tchaikovsky, included the preludes to the first and third acts of *Lohengrin*—the first, and among the very last, pieces by the notoriously anti-Semitic Wagner to be performed by the ensemble either under its original name, the Palestine Orchestra, or its later one, the Israel Philharmonic. "Nothing should interfere with music," Toscanini commented.

One afternoon, his young driver, Morris Ziatopolsky, arrived two minutes late to drive him to a rehearsal. Toscanini, a bear for punctuality, had already set out on foot; the driver soon caught up with him, but Toscanini refused to get into the car, which followed him at a walking pace. When they reached their destination, Toscanini smiled at the driver, said, *"Shalom,"* and entered the hall. On another occasion, when Ziatopolsky told Toscanini how sad he was that his wife could not attend a concert because she was expecting a baby from one day to the next, the maestro and Carla visited the young couple at their home. They also spent hours walking along the streets of rapidly growing Tel Aviv, stopping in shops, and watching children at play. When Toscanini expressed a desire to see some of the country's social welfare institutions, he and Carla were taken to a women's agricultural training farm in Petach Tikva, east of Tel Aviv, where they were offered strawberries and a basketful of newly hatched chicks; they accepted the fruit, but Toscanini joked that he would come back for the chicks when they were old enough to provide him with fresh eggs.

While he was showing his solidarity with what he described as "this marvelous people persecuted by the modern *Nero*," he was also reading about what had been taking place in Austria in the six weeks since Hitler's troops had marched in: Jews had been expelled from all positions of cultural or intellectual significance, and many were required to perform humiliating tasks. "My heart is torn in bits and pieces," Toscanini wrote to Ada. "When you think about this tragic destruction of the Jewish population of Austria, it makes your blood turn cold. Think of what a prominent part they've played in Vienna's life for two centuries! And remember that when Maria Theresa tried to expel them, Great Britain and other nations protested through diplomatic interventions. Today, with all the great progress of our civilization, none of the so-called liberal nations is making a move. England, France, and the United States are silent!"

When Toscanini learned that on 27 April the NBC Symphony, with Rodzinski conducting and Heifetz as soloist, would give a concert to aid refugees from Austria, he sent a message of support and made a contribution. At almost the same time, the Nazified Austrian press turned against Toscanini, just as the Italian and German media had done in 1931 and 1933, respectively. "One thing must be said openly—we spit, if we may respectfully say so, on Toscanini and on his Jewish boosters and express our preference for Hans Knappertsbusch," one Viennese newspaper declared. "Joyously do we renounce Toscanini's baton prima donna business and delight in the performance of a real German conductor." Another paper referred to Toscanini as "the champion of Jewish art in German countries."

Toscanini conducted his second program in Tel Aviv (where the mayor, Israel Rokach, made him a Freeman of the city), Jerusalem, and Haifa on three successive evenings. On 27 April, the day after the final concert, Arturo and Carla boarded a plane that took them from Haifa Bay to Rhodes; they stayed one night on the Greek island, then flew to Rome and traveled onward to Milan. "In these sad days of trial, when everything appears so black for Jews, Toscanini's friendly gesture in making the journey to Palestine is appreciated beyond words," Huberman commented. "But his tireless energy and generosity in conducting so frequently, sometimes two or three nights in succession, traveling from one city to another with almost no rest between to bring joy to music-loving people, brighten the hearts of Jews here, who know that in this great genius they have a true and sincere friend."

10.

TOSCANINI SPENT MOST OF THE FIRST HALF OF MAY 1938 IN INCREAS-ingly anxious and politically fraught Italy, partly in Milan, where he saw Ada several times, and partly on the Isolino. On the fifteenth, he traveled to London and began to prepare the first of six concerts (five different programs) with the BBC Symphony, all given in the Queen's Hall as part of the London Music Festival. He was once again experiencing shoulder pains, but this time they were manageable.

His soloist in Strauss's *Don Quixote* was the extraordinary thirty-five-year-old, Polish-born, Austrian- and German-trained cellist Emanuel Feuermann. The preceding spring, Feuermann had been at a dinner at the Muschenheims' in New York, together with the Toscaninis and Thomas Mann. "Maestro, I am very much ashamed," Feuermann had told Toscanini. "Eleven years ago, I played miserably in your presence." Toscanini replied, "Nonsense, nonsense. I never heard you play except on the radio." "Yes, you did, Maestro. It was in Switzerland." Toscanini laughed: "You mean to say that you are that rotten cellist I heard in Zurich?"—playing a concerto by C. P. E. Bach at the Tonhalle. "T'nini of course remembers Zürich very well," Feuermann wrote, "and he had a fit of laughter because I still think about it." But Feuermann, who had previously enjoyed only lukewarm success in England, now "created such a sensation that the Queen's Hall audience—Toscanini leading the applause—went wild with enthusiasm," commented the pianist Gerald Moore.

On 2 June, HMV made studio recordings of the finale of Beethoven's First Symphony (to complete the entire work), Rossini's *La Scala di Seta* Overture, Mozart's *Magic Flute* Overture, and the Berlioz-Weber *Invitation to the Dance*. The Brahms Second Symphony was also to have been recorded, but Toscanini walked out of the session because he was both tired and dissatisfied with the acoustical arrangements at the Abbey Road studios—thus all of his "official" London recordings were made at Queen's Hall. Fortunately, many of the live performances were also recorded and have been released.

Toscanini returned to Glyndebourne, this time to observe—and heartily approve—a production of Verdi's *Macbeth* conducted by Fritz Busch and staged by Carl Ebert.* Furtwängler was present at the same performance, but he and Toscanini did not meet, nor did Toscanini attend any of Furtwängler's performances of the *Ring* at

---

* At the outset of the Nazi regime, Goering had invited Ebert to take control of all of Berlin's opera houses; instead, Ebert left the country.

Covent Garden. He did, however, attend and enjoy a performance of *Boris Godunov* at Sadler's Wells.

Joseph P. Kennedy, the United States' ambassador to Britain and—despite his right-wing sympathies—a Toscanini admirer, attended some of the maestro's rehearsals, and he and his wife, Rose, took the American secretary of the interior, Harold L. Ickes, and his new bride, Jane Dahlman, to the BBC Symphony concert. Arturo and Carla, during their stay in England, dined at Sybil Cholmondeley's, where Anthony Eden—a future prime minister, who had recently resigned his position as Chamberlain's foreign minister, in protest over the government's policy of appeasing Hitler—was among the other guests; Toscanini found him "very simpatico and very natural." The maestro and Carla also visited Owen and Georgina Mase at their cottage in Buckinghamshire.

Stefan Zweig wrote to Romain Rolland that "the only joys" of his stay in London "were the hours with Toscanini and now with old Freud," who, at the age of eighty-two, had had to escape from Vienna following the Anschluss and had settled in the British capital.*

Toscanini returned to Italy the day after his final London concert, which took place on 10 June; for the following four months, he spent most of his time in Milan or on the Isolino, where his many house-guests once again included the young composers Samuel Barber and Gian Carlo Menotti, in addition to Nino Rota. Herbert Graf, who visited with his family, was surprised when Toscanini called one of his own grandchildren and Graf's five-year-old son over to the piano and played music from the Disney film *Snow White and the Seven Dwarfs*, which had come out the previous year. (The maestro also enjoyed playing "Happy Birthday" at his grandchildren's birthday parties: he would have fun improvising various versions of it, including a Charles Ives–like pastiche in which he combined the tune with the "Garibaldi Hymn.")

He fretted over the fact that Anita Colombo, his former administrative assistant at La Scala and later the theater's general manager, had adapted to fascism: she had even tried to persuade him to con-

***

* Did Freud, who disliked most music, and Toscanini, who knew nothing of psychiatry, ever meet? In the spring of 1938 Toscanini told Zweig that he would like to meet Freud, and the following spring Zweig expressed interest in organizing an encounter, but it probably never happened. Freud died in September 1939.

duct again in Italy. He also fretted over a swollen left foot, fretted over concert broadcasts by performers whose work he did not like, and fretted over unrealizable plans to meet Ada. But he spent as much time as possible reading: "I go from Shelley [and] Keats to the Bible (Job and Ecclesiastes), Dante, and Croce's latest book,"* he told Ada. Then he began rereading Dante and Virgil side by side, then Byron and Carducci side by side, then Shakespeare. The English poets he read in English, Virgil in Latin; and in his letters to Ada he analyzed and gave his opinions of some of his readings.

He tried not to think about what was going on in the outside world, but then "Walter, that jackass, brought a friend of his here to me [. . .]—*Alfredo Segre*, a writer of novels that are said to be rather good†—and I had to put up with him at lunch, at supper, during an outing to the Isola dei Pescatori, and always touching on the same subjects: politics, fascism, persecution of the Jews, and on and on with these subjects that poison me and embitter my existence! My soul is upside-down."

TOSCANINI MAY HAVE WISHED to avoid knowing what was going on in the world, yet he felt a responsibility to do what little he could to demonstrate that not all artists considered their careers more important than their humanity. No sooner had he withdrawn from Salzburg than invitations began to arrive from The Hague, Paris, Versailles, Fontainebleau, Saint-Germain-en-Laye, Orange, Prague, Glyndebourne,‡ and elsewhere—invitations to create new festivals or bring greater glory to already extant ones. Max Reinhardt sent him a long telegram in which he proposed organizing "a new Salzburg" under California's "better climatic and political circumstances and probably with vaster means." Toscanini replied with thanks "for your high esteem which honors me[.] I have reflected on your proposal but my age no longer allows me to embark upon a new theatri-

---

* Croce's *La storia come pensiero e come azione* (History as Thought and as Action) had just been published.

† Segre, who was Jewish, would eventually immigrate to America.

‡ See, in particular, Dyment's *Toscanini in Britain*, pp. 135–41 and 174–76, for a detailed account of the pro- and contra-Toscanini debates at Glyndebourne in 1938 and 1939.

cal undertaking." Queen Elisabeth of Belgium sent him a handwritten letter, inviting him to preside over a 1939 conducting competition, named in memory of Eugène Ysaÿe, but Toscanini, who opposed such competitions, turned the proposal down.

On 11 March 1938, just as the German army had begun to enter Austria, and while Toscanini was still sailing back to Europe, Jakob Zimmerli, the mayor of Lucerne, sent the maestro a letter on behalf of the Swiss town's entire administration, inviting him to conduct the inaugural concerts of a brief festival that would be dominated by artists who could not or would not work in Germany or Austria; Toscanini's first concert would be given on the grounds of the villa at Tribschen, on Lake Lucerne, where Richard and Cosima Wagner had lived. Zimmerli asked Daniela Thode, Cosima's daughter, who spent summers in the villa with Eva Chamberlain, her half sister, to encourage Toscanini to accept the invitation, and she agreed to write to the "colossal artist and equally great—although also sometimes misled—man"—misled by the Jews and others who did not appreciate Hitler as she did.

In the five years since the Nazis' accession to power in Germany, Toscanini had conducted in six of the nine countries that shared borders with Germany; the exceptions were Poland, Luxembourg, and Switzerland. The idea of bringing his art to Switzerland, where he had previously performed only with the visiting Scala and New York Philharmonic orchestras, evidently appealed to him, especially since the borders of both Germany and Italy were only two or three hours by train from Lucerne, arguably the most picturesque town in Switzerland. And Tribschen was where Wagner had "created Die Meistersinger, the Siegfried Idyll, etc., etc., in addition to two children, Eva and Siegfried," Toscanini told Ada. "So far, so good: there's a certain sort of poetry in the idea of this concert in that setting—but that's not enough—the good Swiss want to *exploit* something, that rare animal, Maestro Toscanini, and they immediately propose a concert with a *big orchestra*, and I waver, or rather rebel." He wondered, too, whether a decent orchestra could be formed in so short a time.

Enter Adolf Busch, who had been living in Switzerland since well before the Nazi takeover of his native Germany. In May, the outstanding violinist went to Milan and promised Toscanini that the string section of the ad hoc Lucerne orchestra would be made up of his own quartet, several of the best Swiss quartets, and various other outstanding string players. For the rest of the orchestra, Ernest Ansermet, who had created the Orchestre de la Suisse Romande in 1918, would secure the services of the country's best players. Toscanini, who held both Busch and Ansermet in high esteem,* agreed to participate without fee in the project, after which Fritz Busch, Bruno Walter, Mengelberg, Ansermet, and Count Gilbert Gravina (a grandson of Cosima and Hans von Bülow) were enlisted for further concerts; Cortot and Feuermann for concertos with orchestra; and the soprano Dusolina Giannini and the Busch-Serkin duo for recitals.

By early July, Toscanini had sent Busch—who was "bombarding me with telephone calls"—the orchestra parts for his program,

> because he wants to start making the players (strings) whom he has gathered together in addition to the quartet, practice. I don't know, for that matter, what he wants to make them practice! It's easy music that they know, that will quickly be ready with very few rehearsals. But the Busches are maniacal! And now they have the occasion to play under my direction! They're jumping out of their skin. The program is made up thus: Rossini—La scala di seta [overture]; Mozart—Symphony in G minor (which Wagner loved so much); Prelude to the 3rd act of Die Meistersinger; Siegfried Idyll; and Beethoven's 2nd Symphony. The concert will take place on August 25th (Cosima and Wagner's wedding day) in the park of the villa at Tribschen. Since the place is big enough for barely more than 500 people, I've given in to the entreaties of those Swiss fellows to repeat the concert [. . .] in a bigger venue.

Toscanini went to Lucerne late in July to consult with the Busches and the local authorities on the concert details, but also to spend time with Ada, who joined him there. When Toscanini arrived at Tribschen, Daniela was upset to see a "pretty young woman" sitting next to him in his car, and she later had the villa-museum's concierge

---

* Some years later, after having heard Ansermet's recording of Ravel's *La Valse*, Toscanini refused to allow his own recording of the piece to be released: Ansermet's was better, he said.

check the guest list at Toscanini's hotel to discover who the woman was. The concierge later commented, wryly, that giving Daniela a hug evidently had not consumed all of the maestro's energies. But something happened during this encounter between Ada and "Artù" that set off a gradual decline in their passionate but fraught relationship. What it was cannot be determined from his letters, but "the *days in Lucerne poisoned me,*" he wrote to her afterward. "*I can't get rid of the nightmare of them.* And to think that I have to go back there[;] I wish that God would send me the worst of illnesses." The situation was patched up, and for another year the correspondence continued as before. But something had changed.

After having spent nearly three more weeks on the Isolino, much of the time with his grandchildren Walfredo and Emanuela—and with Elsa Kurzbauer, whose presence, he claimed, weighed heavily on him—Toscanini returned to Lucerne on 19 August and checked into the Grand Hôtel National. "I have two rehearsals every day and many b . . . breakers," Toscanini wrote to Ada a few days later. Several of the string players were accustomed to performing only solo and chamber repertoire, not as members of an orchestra. "I am so scared of Toscanini, I have never played a Beethoven symphony before; he mustn't see me," Stefi Geyer (to whom the enamored young Bartók had dedicated his First Violin Concerto thirty years earlier) told Joachim Röntgen (who later created one of Holland's finest string quartets). Anna Hegner, a well-known Swiss violinist, played so loudly at first that Toscanini whispered to Busch, "She really needs two violins to play on." Polo, who had arrived from Milan, must also have been nervous playing under his brother-in-law's baton for the first time in decades and after having been retired for several years.

But the crafty maestro knew how to handle every situation. "You are not an orchestra," he said calmly, after the first few minutes of the first rehearsal, which took place at Lucerne's Kunsthaus; the musicians understood the problem and adapted quickly. At the first rehearsal on the specially constructed outdoor platform, Toscanini turned the baton over to Adolf Busch so that he could listen from the seats, and he immediately realized that no one beyond the first rows would be able to hear the music—thus Zimmerli had to call in workmen to redo the platform to the maestro's specifications.

For the afternoon of the concert, the town council ordered that steamships on the lake were not to toot their horns, motorboats were not to run anywhere in the vicinity, airplanes were not to fly overhead, police were to prevent automobile traffic from passing nearby, factory sirens and church bells would not be sounded, children and dogs would not be allowed in the area, and bells were to be removed from the cows on nearby farms.

Philipp Etter, president of the Swiss Federal Council, and several other members of the Swiss government turned out for the event, as did Daniela Thode, Eva Chamberlain, and their twenty-year-old niece, Friedelind Wagner, who had defied her mother, Winifred—now Toscanini's enemy—to accept the maestro's personal invitation to the concert; Carla, Wally, Wanda, and Volodya Horowitz; Bruno Walter, Ernest Schelling, Rachmaninoff, Huberman, Milstein, and a slew of Toscanini's fans from Milan; and, most noted by the audience and the press, Italy's Crown Princess Marie José. The weather, which had been rainy until the preceding day, turned beautiful for the occasion, and all went well until the end, when Frieda Busch, unaware of Toscanini's aversion to floral tributes, had two little girls present him with a basket of flowers; he left the stage and refused to return for further bows. Later, he apologized to Frieda for his behavior, and he laughed when Daniela told him that her father, Hans von Bülow, used to receive floral offerings or laurel wreaths with the comment "But I'm not a vegetarian!" As at Salzburg in previous years, Marie José tried unsuccessfully to greet Toscanini after the performance: although she was believed to harbor strong anti-Fascist sympathies, she was nevertheless the daughter-in-law of King Victor Emanuel III, thus, officially, a representative of the man who continued to collude in keeping Mussolini in power, and therefore persona non grata to Toscanini.

Two days later, in the Great Hall of the Kongresshaus, Toscanini conducted a second concert, as he had promised, but instead of repeating the Tribschen program he led entirely different repertoire with a larger orchestra—and, as if to underline the fact that this was not simply a Wagner-related undertaking, much less one that hewed to Nazi cultural dictates, he began with Cherubini (Overture to Anacréon), proceeded with Brahms (Third Symphony) and Mendelssohn ("Italian" Symphony), and only concluded with Wagner (Prelude to Act I of Die Meistersinger).

The Toscaninis and Busches had lunch one day with Rachmaninoff and his wife at the composer's Villa Senar at Hertenstein, across the lake from Lucerne; Milstein, Serkin, and (presumably) Horowitz were also present. The musicians all agreed that the Luzerner Festwochen (Lucerne Festival Weeks) had to be continued the following year, not only for their musical value but also to demonstrate that there was still a corner of the German-speaking world in which respected musicians could perform, regardless of their ethnicities or nationalities.

11.

THE LUCERNE CONCERTS HAD PROVOKED THE ITALIAN FASCIST hierarchs' anger—against Toscanini, but even more against the many Italian music lovers and socialites who had rushed across the Swiss border to attend his performances. As early as three weeks before the Tribschen concert, one Italian police informer had noted that of the 1,000 seats—"already completely sold out"—for Toscanini's first concert, 350 had been taken by "Italians from Milan, Genoa, Turin, and Rome. I don't believe that the purchase of these tickets on the part of some of them has been made only out of great love of art. It is surprising that among those who have reserved a place we find Signora Alfieri, wife of the Minister of Popular Culture." Italy's ambassador to Switzerland had assured the informer that he had "given instructions that no official Italian representative [. . .] attend the concert," and the ambassador himself left the country during the days in question.

Before departing for Switzerland, Toscanini had had to apply to police headquarters in Milan to have his passport renewed; the local chief telephoned the Interior Ministry in Rome for permission to grant the request, and the matter was referred directly to Mussolini, who made the authorization. At the same time, however, Mussolini ordered that Italians returning by car from Switzerland on the evening following the concert be stopped—although he later decided that it was sufficient for their license plate numbers to be noted. The Duce evidently thought that he could use Toscanini to discover the identities of some of the people who sympathized with Toscanini's political beliefs.

Several paid informers were dispatched to Lucerne. "I won't let [Toscanini] out of my sight for even an instant," Enrico Gerri, one spy, wrote to an unnamed official in Italy the day before the maestro's arrival; Gerri also persuaded people who worked at the local tourism bureau to provide information about those Italians who would be present at the concert—"naturally purely out of curiosity, inasmuch as everyone thinks I'm here as a tourist." After the Tribschen event, one informer reported that, in addition to Mrs. Alfieri, the concert was attended by such Italian notables as Countess Volpi di Misurata, wife of a leading Fascist financier and former government minister; Remigio Paone, director of Italian theaters; Marchioness Marconi, widow of the physicist and inventor; the composers Montemezzi and Tommasini; members of the Puccini family; the publishers Luigi Rusca (of the Mondadori company) and Leo Olschki; dozens of other artists, intellectuals, and aristocrats; possibly (the informer wasn't certain) the former prime minister Ivanoe Bonomi; and, most alarming of all, Marie José.

The Lucerne episode led to scores of Italian intragovernmental telegrams and telephone calls and hundreds of pages of reports to and from the political police regarding the "moral and political status" of the Italians whose cars' license plates had been noted at the border. The government seems to have gleaned no useful information from these costly efforts, but, once again, the party boss Roberto Farinacci's newspaper, *Il Regime Fascista*, published a libelous article—"The Honorary Jew"—against the conductor and those who admired him. Although Toscanini had conducted without a fee, he had asked for many tickets and hotel rooms "for himself and his family, and the same for the numerous Jews who accompanied him," the article said. "Since Toscanini is doing all this in a purely anti-Fascist spirit, we would like to know who those Italians were who went there." And he incited "comrades" in Milan, Florence, and Rome to seek out—and, by implication, to punish—the owners of cars that had been seen recrossing the border that evening; he even listed a few of the license plate numbers. *Il Nuovo Avanti*, the newspaper of Italian Socialist exiles in Paris, replied in an article: "Farinacci's punches do great honor to Toscanini. They don't dishonor fascist journalism, because fascist journalism is beneath contempt. But alas! they dishonor our country, which allows such a hooligan to insult one of the purest glories of Italian intelligence."

Upon returning to Italy, Toscanini learned the details of the new, anti-Semitic "racial" laws that the formerly antiracist Mussolini had prepared, in imitation of the Nazis, and that the rubber-stamp parliament—and the rubber-stamp king—would soon make official. This legislation declared that the Italians were now "Aryans," and it prohibited Italy's 47,000 Jews (slightly over one-tenth of one percent of the nation's population) from belonging to the Italian armed forces, teaching at universities or public schools, tutoring private students (with the exception of Jewish students), running businesses connected with the military, owning land or buildings, employing "Aryan" domestic help, being employed by civilian or military government agencies, participating in government at any level, belonging to the National Fascist Party, or owning or being employed by banks or insurance companies. In addition, Jews were not allowed to enroll in public schools or universities, and foreign Jews resident in Italy—many of them refugees from Nazi Germany and Austria— were to be expelled.

Given the tiny percentage of Jews in Italy, the Toscanini family's Italian friends included a surprisingly large number of people who were Jewish or part-Jewish—not only the previously mentioned Anita Colombo and Giulio Foligno but also Maria Da Zara, daughter of a well-known financier, and her daughter Amalia "Maly," who had married Giovanni Falck, scion of a part-Jewish family of steel barons; the music-loving lawyers Luigi Ansbacher and Alfredo Amman; and many others. On 3 September, a telephone call from Toscanini to Ada Mainardi was intercepted by the prefecture in Milan, and a transcript of the following parts of the conversation was sent to Mussolini. (The underlining, shown here in italics, was done either by Mussolini or by someone who prepared the document for him to read; the ellipses in square brackets are mine; the others are in the original transcript.)

[. . .] TOS.= Did you see *how they stepped back for Falck. They call him "comrade" . . . For comrades any position they want is okay!* They don't

even have the common sense to say, "at least let's disguise things."
They want people to be stupid.

ADA.= In fact, they're reducing them to that, little by little!

TOS.= *As a Jew he wasn't right for those positions, but as a "comrade" now, it's okay! . . . I'm going to the Isolino within the next few days and I'm going to do everything to have things moved out . . . because I don't know what could happen next. [. . .] There's no limit now. Tomorrow they'll say, "Give me your money, do this. . . ." They're capable of anything. Promises no longer exist; they don't remember today what they said yesterday. It's shameful! As long as it was a matter of [the laws regulating] foreigners, all right; but now there are people who have worked for many years, who have done so much! . . . The children mustn't go to school. . . . This is medieval stuff!*

The bottom of the transcript bears these words: "by order *of the Duce* take away Toscanini's passport."

On 6 September 1938, Arturo Bocchini, the much-feared chief of Italy's political police, communicated the confiscation order and ordered the nation's prefects to "give immediate instructions to border offices that [Toscanini] be prohibited from expatriation." A few hours later, Giuseppe Marzano, the prefect of Milan, wired the Ministry of the Interior, "I assure having withdrawn passport of Maestro Arturo Toscanini."

The next day, Wally went to see Foreign Minister Galeazzo Ciano,* who noted in his diary, "I received Countess Castelbarco Toscanini who cried over the withdrawal of her father's passport and worried over reaction in America, where he has to conduct concerts soon. The Duce is annoyed because many Italians, and above all the Princess of Piedmont [Marie José], went to Lucerne for the Wagner-

---

* Galeazzo was the son of Count Costanzo Ciano, whose presence in Bologna on 14 May 1931, when he was minister of communications, had helped spark the "Giovinezza" crisis, the resulting attack on Toscanini, and Toscanini's withdrawal from Italian musical life. At the age of twenty-seven, Galeazzo had married Mussolini's daughter Edda, and three years later, in 1933, Mussolini appointed him foreign minister. In June 1940, knowing that Italy was militarily ill-prepared, Ciano disagreed with his father-in-law's decision to declare war on France, and in July 1943, at a crucial meeting of the Fascist Grand Council, he voted to have Mussolini removed from office. A year later, Mussolini, as puppet dictator of the so-called Salò Republic, had his son-in-law shot. Ciano's diaries, which Edda preserved, constitute an important source of information about the Fascist regime.

ian concert. But the withdrawal of the passport is related to a wire-tap, from which it seems that Toscanini attacked the Duce for his anti-Semitic policy, terming it 'medieval stuff.' "

Toscanini or someone close to him managed to inform NBC of the passport predicament, and on 12 and 15 September, Sarnoff, in London, sent him telegrams that were clearly intended to alert the Italian government to the fact that Toscanini's situation was becoming known abroad. "Impressions in America would be most unfortunate if you did not come and serious consequences would have to be feared," one telegram stated. "Also would be impossible avoid unfavorable publicity stop please let me have your early reply stop [. . .] warmest greetings david Sarnoff president radio corporation of America and chairman national broadcasting company." Sarnoff had included his titles in the telegram to make sure that the Italian police, who read Toscanini's telegrams and mail, would understand who he was.

On 16 September, Carla wrote to the chief of the political police to warn that there could be "unpleasant interpretations and comments on the part of the foreign press" if the passport were not returned. Eight days later, the Milan prefecture reported to the ministry in Rome that Toscanini had left the Isolino and was at home in the city. On the twenty-seventh: "No news regarding my freedom of movement," Toscanini wrote to Ada. In a subsequent letter: "I am followed and spied on as never before. [. . .] I learned this morning at Baldini and Castoldi's that a *Commissar of public safety* recently inspected the bookshop and mentioned the names of people who from now on must *never again* meet as before in that shop. My name is among them. In fact, if I happened to be there at the same time as one Baroni (the head of a pasta company), Baldini and Castoldi have to *denounce me.*"

He considered escaping from the Isolino in a hydroplane that would take him to the northern end of Lake Maggiore, in Swiss territory; this appealed to his sense of adventure, but he feared that there might be reprisals against his family and friends. "[N]ever have I felt so *impeded* by family ties as I do now," he wrote to Ada. "You know and understand what *I'm alluding to.* One false step on my part could involve *everyone. God, God, what have we come to!*" And the next day: "I wish only that my family, all of it, adults and children, would take refuge in Switzerland, because [. . .] if I'm not alone, you understand, I can't *do absolutely any* of what I have in mind!"

During those same days, the Munich Conference—with Hitler, Mussolini, Chamberlain, and Prime Minister Edouard Daladier of France—was taking place; the fate of Czechoslovakia and possibly of all of Europe was hanging in the balance; the fate of Toscanini's passport was not a high priority even for the publicity-conscious Mussolini, and the maestro knew it: "At this *tragically difficult moment*, with these threats of war, of a European conflagration, even the *Great Criminals* have other things on their mind," he said. He hoped that the Rome–Berlin Axis would fall apart, because, he said, "I still have faith in the Italians' hearts!"

That faith was shaken by the Italians' willingness to obey the "racial" edicts. "They've forced Giulio Foligno to resign, and *he himself* signed his resignation," Toscanini told Ada. "I would have done the opposite. I would have forced them to fire me. The offense would have been entirely the government's responsibility. [. . .] Did you know that they want to deprive the Jews of their *citizenship* and to allow them only to be *subjects*? The *Inquisition* was less of a torture. And everything will be taken away—taxes, taxes, and more taxes will be imposed on them. Thieves!!!"

Toscanini understood that once he managed to leave Italy, he would not be able to risk returning to it, and he prepared himself psychologically for what would probably be a permanent separation, given his age and the regime's apparent durability. He made final visits to the Isolino and the farmhouse at Ripalta Guerina; he went to the Milan cemetery ("I wanted to say goodbye to my dead relatives, also a few friends—among them the painter Grubicy"); and he had Walter and nine-year-old Walfredo go with him to Parma, where he bade what must have been a deeply emotional farewell to the conservatory and to his beloved aunt Cesira Montani, now eighty-eight, who had always visited him at the school on Sundays and whom he had continued to support.

On 27 September, hoping "to pull the wool over the eyes of you know who," as he told Ada, he sent a telegram to NBC: "At this point it is futile to hope[.] I think it is more prudent to replace me." The tactic didn't work. Wally had in the meantime approached Fulvio Suvich, Italy's ambassador to the United States, who happened to be in Italy and who, in turn, contacted Ciano for advice. The foreign minister warned him not to become involved in the matter: "The Duce flies into a rage if you talk to him about Toscanini," he said. But since Suvich had to meet with Mussolini anyway, he broached the issue; he then told Wally that he had informed Mussolini of the scandal that would ensue when the facts became known in America and elsewhere. Toscanini, reporting to Ada what Wally had told him, said that the *"monstrous beast* replied that after the scandal he will give back the *passport.* Or else they must come up with some new factor to make *said beast* change its mind. A new factor? What could it be? The *princess* of Piedmont [Marie José], for instance, could make a personal request. That's all we need! I don't want either princes or princesses helping out. Tomorrow Carla will go to the prefect to find out how I'm supposed to answer the American telegram. [. . .] I don't sleep, I don't work, I rack up kilometers in my study, my brain hurts because of the thousands of mad, sad, senseless thoughts—*all of them*—that besiege it."

Walter Toscanini at last figured out how to unblock the situation. He alerted an acquaintance, Carlo Franquinet de Saint-Rémy, one of the United Press's correspondents in Italy, who then "innocently" contacted the political police in Rome, saying that the American press agency was bombarding him with urgent requests for information about Maestro Toscanini: Was it true that he had been arrested? Was it true that he was under house arrest, guarded by police agents? Was it true that his passport had been confiscated? Franquinet didn't want to say anything that might harm the Fascists—so he told the police—but how, he wondered, should he respond to his interlocutors from the other side of the Atlantic?

Sure enough, wild rumors—perhaps circulated by Franquinet himself—began to appear in print. "Toscanini Disappears," read a headline in London's *Sunday Referee* on 2 October, and the *Daily Telegraph* reported, incorrectly, that Toscanini was staying at a villa in Stresa while waiting to have his passport "renewed." On the third, a reporter phoned Carla to ask about her husband's whereabouts, and she cleverly referred the man to Milan's police headquarters. That same day, Bocchini forwarded Franquinet's request to Mussolini, who, evidently fearing further bad publicity, wrote across it "return the passport / M." But on the fourth Mussolini was informed,

in a brief note from his secretary, that Bocchini—who apparently
had not received the Duce's message—was asking whether to return
the passport. At the top of the page, the exasperated Mussolini
scrawled "Sì."

Toscanini had gone, that morning, to a village about twenty-five
miles from Milan, for the funeral of Giulio Setti, one of his chorus
masters and assistant conductors at the Metropolitan. "When I got
back home, around one, to my surprise joy was gleaming in everyone's eyes and I found that my passport had been returned," he wrote
to Ada.

> In less time than it takes to tell the story, two suitcases with
> basic necessities were packed, a phone call was made to Paris
> for the cabin [on a passenger liner], seats were reserved on the
> 5 P.M. train, and at 5 P.M. Carla and I left for Paris. [. . .] To flee, to
> flee—that was the consuming thought! To flee in order to
> breathe freedom, life!

At Domodossola, the last Italian town before the Swiss border, a
police commissar boarded the train,

> took my passport, and requested that I follow him, with my
> suitcases. [. . .] I got off with Carla, and we went to a sort of bar-
> racks where some creatures with mugs more like those of life-
> sentence servers than of cops had congregated. I asked whether
> my passport was going to be taken away again or whether some
> formality hadn't been looked after, and I was told that the office
> hadn't been advised to let me leave and that only a telegram
> from the Milan Police Headquarters could cancel their orders.
> I asked them to phone at my expense. They phoned. The reply
> was favorable, but it wasn't enough; a confirmation in *code* was
> required. I couldn't resist saying: That's why Napoleon lost at
> Waterloo: *Grouchy's* excessive zeal *screwed him.* But so be it!
> After all, I wasn't about to lose a battle—nothing but a train
> and, at worst, a steamship. My wife was on tenterhooks; her
> fear that I would compromise myself was making her blood
> pressure suffocate her. They *searched* the suitcases. *In great
> detail!!!* Even the little secret one. The *three* packets of your

letters, each fastened with a rubber band, were looked at; they separated letter from letter, maybe trying to see whether there was money. I was on the verge of exploding with indignation. Then I said to myself: *I'm cleverer than you talentless spies. There is money, I have it*, but not amidst those adored letters, *but rather at my feet*. And in fact, I could feel something between my socks and my skin that seemed to be laughing at those *scoundrels*.

[. . .] At last the telegram arrived. Luckily, we were able to catch the deluxe train. I informed Wanda, [who was] in Paris, to spare me the trouble of changing the embarkation ticket so that I could proceed from one station to the other. And that's what happened.

In a letter to Miecio Horszowski, Wanda wrote that her father, whom she had seen at the train station, "was very shaken in morale as I've rarely seen him. [. . .] I feel that our family is being dispersed in the world and for the time being we will not see our country again."

As he prepared to board the French steamship *Normandie*, Toscanini was asked by journalists whether he had experienced difficulties in leaving Italy. His family had yet to expatriate, thus his reply was evasive: "It is the newspapers that have been printing these reports," he said. "They know more about it than I do." But to Ada he wrote, "And here I am alone—alone and with death in my heart. Carla left [for Milan, from Paris] yesterday evening to prepare everything for the *real* departure for America. She'll leave aboard the Savoia on the 12th, with Walter, his wife, and their little son. The house, or rather the houses, will be *empty*! For how long?"

John Barbirolli was a fellow passenger on the *Normandie*, the largest and most luxurious liner built during the 1930s, and Toscanini had many music-related chats with him. Also on board were the tenor Giovanni Martinelli and his lover Colette d'Arville, a would-be singer and actress, who was involved with the American composer Deems Taylor as well. During the Atlantic crossing, she tried to add Toscanini to her list of celebrity conquests; he was tempted, he admitted to Ada, but for some reason she disgusted him, "and when you feel nausea *every other appetite goes away*."

NBC had arranged with the *Normandie's* chief steward to have Toscanini disembark in New York—on 10 October—"via the staff's exit, with *sailors, cabin boys, scullery boys,* etc.," he wrote, in order to "avoid encounters with journalists." While the ship was stopped in quarantine, reporters managed to send written questions to the maestro's cabin: Had he had trouble with his passport? Had he fled Italy because of the persecution of the Jews? Did he intend to become an American citizen? The questions were all sent back unanswered. Sarnoff, Lohr, Lohr's assistant Clay Morgan, Royal, and Chotzinoff met Toscanini at the pier and whisked him across town to the Astor.

He appreciated their solicitude. But something had happened that made this New York arrival different, and much sadder, than his two dozen previous disembarkations in the city: there was no return home in view. At the age of seventy-one, Arturo Toscanini had become an exile.

A portrait photo of
Toscanini circa 1940.

X.

————

EXILE AND RETURN

————

1.

————

"I AM IN AN ABNORMAL STATE. I WORK BUT I DON'T EAT, NOR do I sleep. I could—I should be content with the affection, the esteem, the veneration with which I am surrounded, and instead I have only bitterness and unhappiness in my heart. I'm living like a bear, shut into the two rooms that are mine—*study* and *bedroom*. Excepting the few rehearsal hours, I stay here, a prisoner, with no other desire than to remain undisturbed in my thoughts."

The negativity of this and other letters that Toscanini dispatched to Ada Mainardi in the early days and weeks after his departure from Italy in October 1938 far exceeded his usual bouts of self-commiseration. If there was a constant love in his life, apart from music, it was Italy, and he felt that in tearing himself out of his home-land he had torn something essential out of his being. His messages during this period are a seething cauldron of frustrations: over the dire European situation in general and the Italian one in particular; over his wish for solitude and his need to communicate; and over the realization that seeing Ada—always a rare occurrence—had now become virtually impossible. Gone, temporarily, was the ambiva-lence that had crept into his correspondence with her since their dis-appointing encounter in Lucerne in September; now, once again, he saw her, or persuaded himself to see her, or pretended to see her, as the most beloved woman in his life, and he alternately raged at her and begged her to continue to love him.

He particularly upbraided her for having expressed satisfaction that Prime Minister Neville Chamberlain had bowed to Hitler's demands in Munich. He quoted a letter in which she had written to him, "Over a question that was of only indirect interest and prestige for most of the nations, Europe was on the verge of catching fire."

"Oh, if only it had caught fire," he replied, "and if only the fire had burned away forever those two wild beasts," Hitler and Mussolini. Sybil Cholmondeley had written to Toscanini to express her shame over the Munich compromise, and he asked Ada to "tell me that you, too, think and feel as I do, [. . .] that you would give everything, give up your personal well-being for freedom, justice, the rights of the world's peoples!" But he was beginning to understand that she did not think and feel as he did.

One day after his arrival in New York, Toscanini walked onto the stage of Studio 8H for his first NBC Symphony rehearsal of the season; the orchestra members, aware of the ordeal that he had faced in Italy, "rose to their feet in his honor, tapping bows against music stands, knocking the sides of brass instruments, cheering and applauding," the *New York Times* reported. "This continued for about three minutes—even after the conductor's first signal—while Mr. Toscanini, obviously deeply moved, faced his men in eloquent silence."

Some twenty new faces were to be seen in the NBC Symphony a year after its founding—a larger annual turnover than that of an average orchestra, caused, at least in part, by a professional situation that some distinguished musicians found unappealing. By joining the orchestra, players became part of the National Broadcasting Company's musical staff, and, with the exception of section principals and a few others, they had to play whatever jobs were assigned to them. During the 1938–39 season, for instance, they would perform sixteen weeks of broadcasts with Toscanini, four with Rodzinski, one with Steinberg,* five with Bruno Walter, one with Hans Lange—who had been Toscanini's assistant conductor with the New York Philharmonic—and one with a young Italian, Alberto Erede,

---

* NBC had brought Hans Wilhelm Steinberg (who had not yet changed his name to William Steinberg) from Palestine to act as Toscanini's assistant. Some months later, Toscanini recommended Steinberg to Edward Johnson, the Metropolitan Opera's general manager, to replace the recently deceased Artur Bodanzky as chief conductor of the company's German wing. This did not happen, for reasons no longer known.

who had served as Fritz Busch's assistant. For the remaining twenty-four weeks of the year, the musicians performed various other functions—sometimes as an anonymous "Symphony Orchestra," "Summer Symphony," or simply "orchestra"—often in programs of light classics, with conductors ranging from Steinberg, Erich Leinsdorf, the young Americans Izler Solomon and Edwin MacArthur, and the composer Howard Hanson, to the chief staff conductor Frank Black. At other times, they played for the "Cities Service Show Variety Concerts," usually with Black; the "Voice of Firestone" series, under the baton of Alfred Wallenstein; and the "Magic Key Variety Hour," conducted by Nathaniel Shilkret, a former child prodigy clarinetist. Some of these programs were broadcast only locally, others nationally, a few also internationally; many contained commercial announcements from sponsors, whereas the NBC Symphony, as such, was a noncommercial, public service enterprise. In a country that had not yet fully emerged from the Depression, NBC's musicians were privileged to have year-round employment at much better than average pay, but musical standards were not always high during the five and a half months of the year when the NBC Symphony was not the NBC Symphony.

Toscanini is not known to have requested any of the personnel changes, which were probably arranged by H. Leopold Spitalny, NBC's director of music, possibly in agreement with Chotzinoff, who had recently been made a full-time NBC music executive, and/or with Rodzinski. Toscanini himself, even more now than earlier in his career, was loath to fire musicians. Robert Bloom, the principal oboe, said that he himself would gladly have fired the principal clarinet, Augustin Duques, who, in Bloom's opinion, was technically accomplished but musically insensitive. But Toscanini worked hard, albeit not always patiently, with Duques, who retained his position for twelve years.* Whatever the reasons for the changes may have been, Toscanini reported that the orchestra was "better still than last year. Improved in the horn and trombone sections. The balance is magnificent."

---

* At one rehearsal, an exasperated Toscanini commented that when Duques was born, his mother had been pleased to see that he was normal—two eyes, two ears, two arms, two legs, and so on. The only thing lacking was musical taste.

Highlights of Toscanini's first eight weeks of broadcast concerts included Strauss's *Don Quixote*, with Emanuel Feuermann and Carlton Cooley as soloists, and—to the maestro's and everyone else's surprise—Tchaikovsky's Sixth Symphony ("Pathétique"), which he had conducted for the first time in Turin in 1897 and never again since (except for a performance of the second movement in 1898). "I was afraid of not being able to do it, of not being capable of getting anything out of that music!" he wrote to Ada immediately afterward. "As always, after the first few bars, my nervousness, uncertainty, and fear disappeared." But "while I was conducting it this evening, I wept like a *man in despair*. At the phrase in D Major [bars 38–42 of the Finale] I couldn't contain myself. Tears flooded my face and mixed with my sweat, luckily, because the stupefied musicians were looking at me. But what could I do? As the whole orchestra little by little took over that phrase in its powerful crescendo, I was at the peak of despair. [. . .] I won't return to Italy ever again as long as the present regime lasts."

Soon after the performance, Mischa Mischakoff, the concertmaster, happened to meet Rachmaninoff on a Manhattan street; the composer, who had known Tchaikovsky and his milieu personally, raved about the interpretation.

The same program had also included Bach's Second "Brandenburg" Concerto and Haydn's Symphony no. 31 ("Hornsignal"), both done with what were, for the time, reduced ensembles and exceptionally light textures. Special features of the concert of 5 November were the world premieres of two pieces by the twenty-eight-year-old Samuel Barber: the Adagio for Strings (an arrangement for string orchestra of the second movement of the composer's String Quartet, op. 11) and the Essay for Orchestra, op. 12. By performing the elegiac Adagio, which quickly became a modern classic, Toscanini helped to launch the international career of a significant twentieth-century American composer. On another fall program, Toscanini inserted the Prelude to the third act of *Die Meistersinger* in memory of the New York Philharmonic's former patron Clarence H. Mackay, who had just died; this gesture began the process of reconciliation between the maestro and his former ensemble. And following his last broadcast of 1938, on 3 December, Toscanini conducted the NBC Symphony's first out-of-town concerts, in Newark—where Thomas Mann was in the audience—and Baltimore.

WHEN CARLA, WALTER, CIA, AND WALFREDO arrived, in mid-October, Toscanini was "pleased on the one hand," he told Ada, but upset by Carla's messiness. "For *41 years* I've suffered from this disorder of hers!!!" Carla's disorganization was attested to by many who knew her, but what really annoyed Toscanini was living *en deux* in a relatively small space. At home, he could have privacy whenever he wanted it; at the Astor, he could not. Margherita De Vecchi and other friends tried to keep Carla busy with shopping and diversions, but they could do only so much.

Walter and family had had little choice but to follow the elder Toscaninis to America: although Walter had done excellent work for Mondadori's advertising department, the Fascists had forced the publishing company to fire him for his outspoken antifascism and his family name. Starting over at forty and in a new country was not easy; he had at first hoped to find a job as a librarian in the Italian division of the New York Public Library or the Columbia University Library, but after having spoken with Sarnoff in Lucerne the previous summer he accepted a job in the Press Division of RCA Victor's headquarters in Camden, New Jersey, where he began to work in December 1938. His English, passable even before his immigration, quickly improved.

At first, he stayed in hotels in Camden and nearby Philadelphia and returned to New York on weekends to be with Cia and Walfredo, who were living at the Ansonia Hotel, where the maestro had resided during his Metropolitan years. The arrangement was inconvenient, but Walter appreciated not being always at his parents' beck and call. "How are people's nerves at the home of the senior Toscaninis?" he asked Margherita, in a half-joking letter in March 1939. "Is it better to keep one's distance for fear of a short circuit, or can one come to N.Y.?" Eventually, Walter and family moved to a house in Haddonfield, New Jersey, near Camden.

On 21 November 1938, Arturo and Carla attended the opening performance (*Otello*) of the Metropolitan Opera's season, sharing a box with the future US secretary of state Edward Stettinius Jr., among others. Early in December, Toscanini, along with Einstein, Thomas Mann, and other celebrities, contributed autograph manuscripts to

an auction held at the Hotel Plaza by joint Christian and Jewish char-
ities, for the benefit of refugees from Europe. The maestro's contribution was a surprising one: the two-page manuscript of an original,
sixteen-bar composition by himself! The minipiece, for violin and
piano, in E-flat minor, bears the inscription "Cade lento la pioggia e
s'addormenta il cuore nel dolore" (The rain falls slowly and the heart
falls asleep in sorrow), which reflected his state of mind; the manuscript bears his signature and the date of the auction, and it was sold
for $1,200.

Among other marginalia: An informal survey indicated that thousands of amateur and professional musicians across the country
attempted to play along with the NBC Symphony during its broadcasts; the popular entertainer Jimmy Durante had added a skit,
"Toscanini, Stokowski and Me," to his nightclub routine; and Toscanini was said to have been approached by Warner Brothers to conduct the soundtrack of, and perhaps appear in, a movie, "The Life of
Beethoven," that would star Paul Muni. The film was never made,
because, as Jack Warner famously told Muni, "Nobody wants to see
a movie about a blind composer." Toscanini later showed interest in
a proposal from the Hollywood producer Joseph Pasternak to conduct in a film for which he would be paid the munificent sum of
$150,000; this plan was never realized, nor was a later one, also from
Pasternak, for him to conduct music by Tchaikovsky in a movie,
"Scorched Earth" (later called "Song of Russia"), about the Russo-
German war.

Also in the fall of 1938, Farrar & Rinehart in New York published
Toscanini and Great Music, by Lawrence Gilman, the *New York Herald-
Tribune*'s music critic. The book is a combination of program notes
and panegyrics, in high-flown prose; like Paul Stefan's biography of
Toscanini, it is valuable today mainly as a cultural artifact. When
Gilman died, a year later, Toscanini dedicated a performance of the
"Good Friday Spell" from *Parsifal* to his memory, and late in life he
referred to Gilman as a "dear person" and said that he preferred his
book to "that imbecile" Howard Taubman's later book about him—
because Gilman's book concerned musical interpretation, for better
or for worse, whereas Taubman's was a biography, and the book's
subject did not approve of biographies of himself.

Rodzinski conducted four weeks of broadcast concerts during the holiday period, but his cordial relationship with his mentor was about to end. When he told Toscanini that NBC had not paid him for his work, the outraged maestro registered his protest with an NBC executive, who promptly sent Toscanini a photograph of a $6,000 check endorsed by Rodzinski. During the same period, Toscanini attended Rodzinski's final rehearsal of Scriabin's *Divine Poem*, a work that he himself had never studied. He complimented Rodzinski, who, however, complained that he had been forced to make do with four horns instead of the six that the score demanded. Toscanini summoned Spitalny and told him that this was shameful—other conductors were to be treated exactly as he himself was treated; Spitalny then showed him the sheet of paper on which Rodzinski had written a list of the instruments required: it indicated four horns, not six, for the Scriabin piece. "So I said [to Rodzinski], 'Listen here, my friend, you're the one who wrote this!'" Toscanini recalled. "He began to cry, and he went home, and a half hour later a doctor called me. 'I'm at Mr. Rodzinski's, I don't think he'll be able to conduct.' 'Let him go to the devil!' I said." Rodzinski did conduct the concert, but it was his last appearance with the NBC Symphony. He continued to have an outstanding career elsewhere, and Toscanini later described him as a fine conductor but "crazy."

During January and February 1939, Toscanini conducted eight more Saturday evening programs. New to his repertoire were *Memories of My Childhood*, by the German American composer Charles Martin Loeffler; Manuel de Falla's *El Amor Brujo*, with the contralto Josefina Burzio as soloist; and Edmund Rubbra's recently completed orchestration of Brahms's Variations on a Theme of Handel. Single-composer concerts were dedicated to Brahms, Wagner, and Sibelius.

In his seventies, Toscanini was still conducting a great deal of music that, from his point of view, was contemporary. Of the thirty-four composers represented during his 1938–39 NBC season, nineteen were active within his own conducting career and seven—from Ravel to Shostakovich and Barber—were his juniors. Nevertheless, the radical new music of the 1930s held little appeal for him. Two years earlier, when Rodzinski had shown him a score of Bartók's newly published Music for Strings, Percussion, and Celesta, he had "raised his shoulders in a shrug of doubt," according to Rodzinski's wife. "'If *that* is music, I leave it to you, the younger generation. *Non mi dice nulla*,' he said. 'It says nothing to me.'"* Now, he admitted to Ada, "I can't get modern music to enter either my head or my heart! I'm too old, and my faculties have *calcified*." Younger musicians could deal with new trends, he believed, just as he had done in his day; he would "keep conducting the *same music!*" and would try to deepen his understanding of it.

Miecio Horszowski was in New York early in 1939 and often dined with the Toscaninis and their other guests, including Bruno Walter, Jascha Heifetz and his wife, and the Italian actress Emma Gramatica. Horszowski was amazed by the excellence of the NBC Symphony, which he was hearing for the first time. "I have the impression that the Maestro has never reached such a level of perfection as with this orchestra in the [Brahms] Fourth," he wrote in his diary, and he received an "extraordinary impression" of the Sibelius Second, "as if I were hearing its song and the flow of its sounds for the first time."

On eight different days in February, March, and April 1939, Toscanini and the orchestra recorded Beethoven's Fifth and Eighth Symphonies, Rossini's *William Tell* Overture, and an arrangement of Paganini's *Moto Perpetuo*†—a showpiece for the NBC's violins—and they completed the recording they had begun a year earlier of Mozart's Symphony no. 40 in G minor. Ernst Silberstein, a member of the cello section, later recalled that Toscanini had become agitated upon listening to the playback of the first movement of the Beethoven Eighth. "This is not my tempo! It's too slow!" he shouted. The record producer asked him, "Maestro, is the pitch correct?" "Yes, the pitch is correct." "If the pitch is correct, this is your tempo." "It's not my tempo!" He insisted on rerecording the movement at what was indeed a breakneck tempo.

When Toscanini performed and recorded in Studio 8H—which George Szell and other musicians described as acoustically "dry as dust"—his tempi were often faster than they had been with the Philharmonic or than they would continue to be when he worked with the NBC Symphony or other orchestras at Carnegie Hall or in other

---

* Rodzinski, twenty-five years younger than Toscanini, was surprised by the maestro's reaction, but by the 1950s he was reacting similarly to the new music that was then being written, his wife said.

† According to some sources, the arrangement was by Toscanini; others attribute it to Molinari.

venues. Since the majority of his commercial recordings, including those made during live concerts, took place in 8H, the perception of many listeners unfamiliar with his other recordings is that Toscanini "took fast tempi." This is a gross, indeed grotesque, distortion of the truth, but, like so many other handed-down opinions, it has endured.

Apart from those few recording sessions and an NBC Symphony performance in Washington (14 March), Toscanini had little work to keep him occupied during the seven weeks that separated his final NBC broadcast of the season from his departure for Europe. He wrote often to Ada, but his opinion of her dropped dramatically when he realized that she was afraid to write to him from Rome because the regime's censors tried to read anything addressed to or from him. "You avenge all those unfortunate women who believed in me," he wrote to her. "I love you desperately, although I would like to hate you for your lack of blood, life, enthusiasm, passion, which makes you able to stand more than I can." Worse still, she had expressed indifference over what was happening to Italy's Jews. "Never say again that you don't love the Jews!" he exclaimed. "In what way do they differ from us Catholics? Not [worse] in coward-ice—the proof is overwhelming. *Look at the Italians of today.* Their leader hasn't yet come to the point of requiring that they put holes in the seat of their pants, but if he requests it, all the tailors will imme-diately adapt to *that style.*"*

If she had told him that she no longer loved him, it would have caused him much less sorrow, he said, "than to hear that you were afraid of *communicating* with me, afraid that the Fascist government would discover our friendship, our intimacy." Her reticence meant that she was losing herself "in the company of people whom I *despise* as men of no faith or moral principles, like the Pizzettis, Molinaris, Panizzas,† and the whole mob of bad and good artists who infest

---

* Ada would have known that this was a reference to the vulgar expression that translates as "Go do it up the ass," more or less equivalent to "Go fuck yourself" in English.

† All three of these musicians continued to accept whatever positions and honors the Fascist and Nazi regimes offered them. Pizzetti and Molinari were enthusiastic fans of Mussolini; Toscanini described Pizzetti, in particular, as "one of the greatest disappointments of my life!" and refused to speak to him for the rest of his days. Panizza conducted not only in Fascist Italy but also, from 1937 to 1939, at Berlin's thoroughly "Jew-free" Städtische Oper.

Italy and the world. Artists who don't deserve to be counted as men, but rather as slaves. [. . .] Because you, too, are the victim of the *entourage* in which you live, the victim of general human cowardice." Nevertheless, for the time being the correspondence continued.

2.

AFTER MORE THAN SIX MONTHS IN AMERICA—THE LONGEST SINGLE stretch he had spent west of the Atlantic since his departure from the Metropolitan twenty-four years earlier—Toscanini, together with Carla, boarded the *Queen Mary* on 21 April 1939, bound for England. He had promised to conduct the BBC Symphony in a seven-concert Beethoven cycle, the centerpiece of that year's London Music Festival. Also aboard ship was the matinee idol Spencer Tracy, and when the boat train from Liverpool disgorged its passengers at London's Waterloo Station on the twenty-sixth, a horde of the popular Hollywood actor's female fans stampeded toward him, shoving Toscanini against some baggage. Owen Mase, on hand to meet the maestro and Carla, was able to shield them from the worst of the onslaught. Tracy, quickly spirited away to his hotel, expressed to the press only "anxiety about Toscanini," who, however, was unharmed.

There can be little doubt that the likelihood of a European war in the near future was one of Toscanini's reasons for focusing on Beethoven in 1939. Beethoven was not only the greatest of all composers, in Toscanini's opinion, but also a symbol of courage in the face of adversity and of humanity's eternal quest for freedom— political, artistic, and spiritual. "The pope and those old men [the cardinals] don't understand a thing," Toscanini exclaimed on more than one occasion. "There's no one who's more of a saint than Beethoven." British music lovers evidently agreed: some 75,000 of them applied to the BBC in the hope of receiving 1 or 2 of the roughly 17,500 tickets available for the entire cycle. Toscanini conducted all nine symphonies, six overtures, and the *Missa Solemnis*, and he was paid a total of £3,675.

At nine o'clock one morning, before a rehearsal of the "Pastoral" Symphony, Mase came by to have breakfast with Toscanini and found him "hard at work on the score. He had been working on it since six. As always, he was faithful to his own creed: 'Every time you play anything it must be for the first time.'" And Mase recalled Toscanini's words to a young colleague: "'You must not conduct a piece until the notes have marched off the paper and come alive in your head and heart.'" The principal viola, Bernard Shore, thinking back on the series ten years later, felt as if the musicians had made "contact with Beethoven's very mind. The conductor's intensity and his relentless power and rhythm carried us through the colossal cycle with no intervention of an alien idiosyncrasy between composer and orchestra," Shore said, and the whole cycle "became a steady crescendo of interest and power."

King George VI, together with the queen, the queen mother, and the Duke of Kent, attended the first concert and respected Toscanini's request not to visit or be visited by them, although the maestro began the performance with "God Save the King" and, together with the audience, applauded the royals when they departed. For the most part, he enjoyed his time in London: the BBC's administrators gave him an informal lunch at Pagani's restaurant; he attended Callender's Massed Bands' performance at Kenwood of Handel's *Music for the Royal Fireworks*—and he canceled a rehearsal in order to watch the actual fireworks; he heard the London Singers and the folksinger John Goss perform a program of sea shanties and other folk music at the Prince's Galleries in Piccadilly; he visited a small exhibition of music-related manuscripts at the Bumpus bookshop in Oxford Street and even lent Bumpus one of his prized possessions: a portrait of the young Beethoven made by the composer's friend Franz Wegeler; and he chatted with the BBC Symphony's musicians at a party given for him by the orchestra members in the small Queen's Hall—"a unique occasion afforded no other conductor and a measure of the affection and respect in which the orchestra by now held him," according to Dyment. The maestro also listened to the twenty-eight-year-old Swedish tenor Jussi Björling sing the title role in *Il Trovatore* at Covent Garden and immediately invited him to sing in the Verdi *Requiem* in Lucerne that summer.

Toscanini enjoyed a performance of the ballet *Checkmate* at Sadler's Wells, with Arthur Bliss's music conducted by Constant Lambert, and he invited Bliss to visit him at the Langham Hotel. While Carla prepared tea, Toscanini led Bliss to a sofa and, "settling me down by him, he said 'Tell me, Mr. Bliss—do *you*, as an English musician, think that *I*, as an Italian, take the slow movements of Beethoven rather fast?' "* This, Bliss said, was "an example of how courteously to put a humbler musician at his ease. [. . .] I have at times in my life suffered from the arrogant manner assumed by some famous conductors, so I like to recall this hour with Toscanini as a signal proof of my contention that a great man is usually also a modest one."

At Queen's Hall on 1 June, Toscanini led the orchestra in a marathon recording session that yielded three Beethoven overtures (*Leonore* no. 1, *Coriolan*, and *Prometheus*) and the Fourth Symphony; he eventually approved all of them except *Coriolan* for release. The symphony and *Leonore* were issued by the end of the year. *Prometheus* was not released at the time, because there was no proper coupling for the other side of a 78 rpm disc; it was first issued in 1986.

Plans were laid for Toscanini to conduct six concerts during the 1940 London Music Festival, with a varied repertoire that would include his first performance of Ralph Vaughan Williams's Third Symphony. But world events would intervene. When, on 5 June 1939, Toscanini boarded the plane that would take him from London to Basel, he was leaving England for a very long time.

THE VILLA ALTHAUS is situated in the lakeside village of Kastanienbaum, just outside the city of Lucerne. Arturo and Carla rented the house from June through September, so that their two daughters, two sons-in-law, and two granddaughters could spend time with them there; Walter, Cia, and Walfredo had stayed in America.

Emilio picked the maestro up in Basel and drove him to his new, temporary residence, which was "comfortable, large, well furnished, far enough from Lucerne not to have b——breakers here often but not so far as not to be able to reach the city in a few minutes by automobile," he wrote to Ada. "But it's not my Isolino, it's not my lake,

---

* Toscanini had been criticized by the *Manchester Guardian*'s critic Neville Cardus for doing what today is considered common practice: taking andante movements as true andantes, not as adagios, for instance, and using Beethoven's metronome marks as guidelines, although Toscanini never adhered to those indications rigidly and sometimes ignored them completely.

my sky, my mountains—in short, it's not my country, and my homesickness is profound."

Exile had weighed less heavily on him when he was across the Atlantic in New York than it did here, with Italy so near and yet so maddeningly far. Even before he left London, he had been raging about Mussolini, "who martyrs my country with injustice, with cynicism, with ancient barbarity," he wrote. Now, his country—and Mussolini—were all but staring him in the face, and in addition he had to deal with a nearly two-month-long hiatus in his professional activity, which, "however necessary it may be, allows tempests to gather in my restless spirit! Those two or three hours of sleep that I manage are upset by *nightmares* that destroy me. I keep dreaming that I'm conducting music that I don't know, and that I don't have enough rehearsals."

Jakob Zimmerli, no longer mayor of Lucerne but still head of the festival, invited Toscanini to have a look at the local Stadttheater (Municipal Theater), in the hope of persuading him to conduct an opera or two there the following year. The venue had room for only six hundred spectators and its pit held only thirty-five musicians, but an acoustical test provided by frightened members of the local casino's house orchestra and their terrified young conductor, Walter Ducloux, led Toscanini to agree to conduct something there the following year—if the pit could be sufficiently enlarged in the meantime. He also smiled appreciatively at the musicians and told Ducloux that his tempi in the *Oberon* Overture had been just right. "The spirit of the music matters more than the number of violins!" he exclaimed.

Arturo and Carla made a day trip to visit the Horowitzes at Gstaad, in the Berner Oberland. Back in Kastanienbaum, the Polos stayed with them from mid-July through early August, after which they would be alone—or so Carla wrote enthusiastically to Horszowski. She did not mention that, around 20 June, Eleonora von Mendelssohn had checked into a small, nearby hotel, and "morning and evening *she eats at our place*," Toscanini wrote to Ada. Eleonora remained for the duration of the Toscaninis' stay and even received telephone calls at their home. One evening, "Carla lost her self-control," Toscanini reported. "*Nothing* was left unsaid [. . .]. Leonora [*sic*] wept floods of tears. The dramatic scene took place before supper, while I was working in my study. But she sat with us *imperturbably* at supper, and stayed with us until eleven, like every other evening!" Carla's nervous outburst was at least in part a result of jealousy, which Toscanini would not have mentioned to Ada: Eleonora was staying nearby because she and Toscanini were having an affair. The ivory-complexioned, fascinating actress, thirty-three years younger than the maestro, even made a drawing, at about this time, of herself in his embrace.

He spent a week at a spa at Vermala-sur-Sierre, in the Valais canton, then returned to Lucerne to begin to rehearse the ninety-piece "Elite-Orchester" that Adolf Busch and Ansermet had put together. It was a bigger and better ensemble than the one hastily assembled the previous year, and this time Toscanini accepted a fee for his services. During three and a half weeks in August, he conducted four different programs of purely instrumental music in the Kunsthaus and two performances of the Verdi *Requiem* in the seventeenth-century Jesuit Church—the last of only three or four occasions in his career on which he performed in a church. Jussi Björling, singing with Toscanini for the first time, reported afterward that the maestro's "musical instruction was wonderful" in the *Requiem*, "and when he conducts, he keeps his eyes on the soloist the entire time. I don't understand how he does it, but he is able to hold all the performers in this magic circle—it is like hypnotism." His comment jibes with the remarks of many of Toscanini's orchestra musicians, who said that they always felt that he was watching them, although they knew that this wasn't possible.

Thomas Mann and members of his family attended the first performance of the *Requiem*, as did Bruno Walter and his family, who were now living in exile in Switzerland. The following day, Walter, his wife, and their two daughters visited the Toscaninis in Kastanienbaum. Margarete (known as Gretel or Grete), the younger daughter, had separated from her husband, Robert Neppach, a German architect and film director: she refused to return to Germany because she was half Jewish and because she was involved with Ezio Pinza, who was divorcing his wife. Toscanini teased Gretel about how silly Pinza looked when he wore tights to sing the title role in *Don Giovanni*: "I said, as a joke, 'How can you women fall in love with Pinza, with those stupid-looking legs?' " That same afternoon, Gretel took a train to Zurich, an hour away, to meet her husband and work out the terms of their divorce, but Neppach, psychologically incapable of accepting her decision, shot and killed her and then himself.

Carla and Wally, among the first to be informed of the tragedy, took upon themselves the grim task of communicating the news to Walter and his family. The Toscaninis and Busches went to Zurich to be near the devastated Walters and Pinza for Gretel's cremation, and Walter asked Toscanini to conduct the concert that he was to have led in Lucerne a few days later. Toscanini quickly rehearsed an all-Beethoven program, including the Violin Concerto with Busch as soloist, but the Walter family's calamity cast a pall over the rest of the festival. "I'm still under the extremely sorrowful impression of Grete Walter's tragic passing," Toscanini wrote to Ada on the twenty-fifth, from a spa at Rigi-Kaltbad, high above Lake Lucerne, where he had gone to try—unsuccessfully—to relax. "I see her in my study at Kastanienbaum with her beautiful smile, and it seems to me unreal that only three hours later she had ceased to exist."

An even heavier pall was being cast over the festival by the inexorable approach of a much vaster tragedy. On 23 August, Germany and the Soviet Union signed a nonaggression pact that paved the way for a German invasion of Poland, and military mobilization began across Europe. Many foreign visitors fled Lucerne; the Chotzinoffs, who were present, tried to persuade the Toscaninis to leave immediately, and the festival's administrators considered canceling the remaining concerts. But the maestro, though aware of the danger, was determined to conduct his remaining performances and did not want the administrators to yield to the general panic. The festival continued as programmed.

Toscanini attended most of the other festival concerts, all given by first-rate artists, including Ansermet, Rachmaninoff, Fritz Busch, Huberman, Boult, Pablo Casals, Kipnis, the Busch Quartet, and the English clarinetist Reginald Kell. Ada Mainardi attended two or three of Toscanini's concerts and congratulated him afterward, but they had no opportunity to be alone together. They would never meet again.

Young György (Georg) Solti, whose work opportunities in his native Hungary were disappearing as a result of the country's increasingly severe anti-Semitic legislation, had traveled from Budapest to Lucerne to ask Toscanini for help in finding work in the

United States. Solti attended his idol's concerts but hesitated at first to seek him out. "Several times I had the opportunity to approach him, but I was too timid and in awe," Solti recalled.

> Finally, one morning, I summoned up enough courage to walk up to him as he was about to leave the Kunsthaus. He was very nearsighted, so I asked him whether he recognized me. *"Maestro, mi riconosce? Solti? Salisburgo?"*
>
> *"Oh sì, sì, sì, sì!"* He was very friendly, very nice. In fact, he was always good to musicians—always.
>
> I said, "Maestro, I must go to America." I described the situation in Budapest, and he listened to me quietly and seriously.
>
> "All right," he said, when I had finished. "I live in New York. When you come over, contact me, and I'll try to help."
>
> I was as happy as a little bird, because I thought that this was all I needed. [. . .] What I didn't know, until I was told by an [American] official, was that the quota for Hungarian immigrants to the United States was full for the following fifty years.

Solti ended up stranded in Switzerland for seven difficult years, but the fact that he had traveled there to see Toscanini probably saved his life, given the dire fate that awaited 70 percent of Hungary's 800,000 Jews.

ON 27 AUGUST, Toscanini conducted a small group of musicians in a performance of the *Siegfried Idyll* at the villa at Tribschen, where Wagner had written it and had first performed it as a surprise for Cosima, seventy years earlier. The miniconcert was attended by Daniela Thode, Eva Chamberlain, Friedelind Wagner, Zimmerli, Carla, Wally with daughter Emanuela, Wanda with daughter Sonia, and a few friends.

Two nights later, Horowitz, who had emerged from a long period of ill health and depression, played Brahms's Second Piano Concerto with Toscanini at the festival's final concert. German troops were massing on Poland's western border, and the mood around Europe, even in as tranquil an enclave as Lucerne, was grim. The Italian journalist Camilla Cederna attended Toscanini's last rehearsal and observed several of the maestro's friends and acquaintances in tears: there were two celebrated Hollywood actresses, Luise Rainer and Madeleine Carroll; an aged granddaughter of Wagner's beloved Mathilde Wesendonck; and Renato Levi, who owned a much-frequented record shop near La Scala and who would die five years later in a German concentration camp. Yet the concert itself ended in a blaze of C Major joy—the *Leonore* Overture no. 3—and there was a lovely reception afterward at the Hotel Schweizerhof, with the Toscaninis, the Busches, Ansermet, Horszowski, and others.

The following day, in the office of the Italian consul general in Lucerne, Arturo and Carla gave Wally power of attorney over all of their possessions in Italy, and they said goodbye to her and to Emanuela, who returned home. Two days later Germany invaded Poland, and on 3 September Britain and France declared war on Germany.

Toscanini had hoped to spend some time by the sea, at Cannes or Cap-Martin, in the south of France, immediately after having completed his work in Lucerne, and he had planned to fly, in October, on Pan American's luxurious new Boeing 314 Yankee Clipper seaplane service from Southampton harbor to New York. With the outbreak of war, however, the Mediterranean vacation idea was scrapped and the transatlantic airline service canceled. Arturo and Carla decided to remain in Kastanienbaum until late September, when they would make their way to Rotterdam and sail from there, but they were warned that mines could be placed in Rotterdam's harbor, which would prevent the ship from departing. Instead, they left Lucerne by train on the morning of 12 September, probably with Eleonora, and made their way to Bordeaux, where thousands upon thousands of people were trying to arrange passage to America before the war heated up.

They booked their voyage on the overstuffed liner *Manhattan*, which was scheduled to depart on the sixteenth but was held in port at nearby La Verdon for eight days; other passengers, besides Eleonora, included Stravinsky, the Canadian press mogul Lord Beaverbrook, and Joseph and Rose Kennedy's three youngest children, including the future senator Edward (Ted). Aboard ship, Carla had to share a cabin with four other women, and her husband had to share one with four other men. Rumor had it that Toscanini refused to stay in his crowded stateroom and instead remained on deck, sleeping in a deck chair, but when the ship docked in New York on 30 September the maestro, unusually affable with reporters and photographers, said that his roommates "were very charming and everybody was very nice."

Volodya, Wanda, and Sonia arrived two days later aboard the *Vulcania* out of Genoa, which meant that two of Arturo and Carla's three children and two of their three grandchildren were now in America, probably for the duration of the war, however long it might last. But the Toscaninis would not see Wally and Emanuela, or Europe, for a long time.

3.

THE WAR NOTWITHSTANDING, TOSCANINI WAS COMMITTED TO CON-tinuing his work with the NBC Symphony, and the work helped him to keep his mind from fixating entirely on the events that were beginning to unfold in Europe. "Impossible though it seems, I can tell you that the orchestra has improved even more," Toscanini wrote to Ada after his arrival in New York. He had increased the number of cellos to twelve, he said, and he described the playing of his new principal cello, the twenty-seven-year-old Frank Miller, as "magnificent." He would conduct eight complete concert programs on consecutive Saturday evenings, beginning on 14 October. Two weeks later, just before he conducted the first concert in the NBC Symphony's first, six-part Beethoven cycle,* he wrote, "Oh, how hard it is to repeat the same music after a short lapse and to find a way to make new life flow into all of it! I can still bring off this miracle! At least *I think so*!!!"

The cycle included all nine symphonies and many of the other pieces that he had conducted in London in May, but also his only performance anywhere of the Choral Fantasy and one of his rare readings of the composer's early Septet, performed "with six Violins, 5 violas, 4 Cellos, and two Double basses," he told Ada—"because I

---

* One concert in the cycle was attended by Helen Keller, the famed deaf-blind activist, who thanked Toscanini afterward for letting her "feel the spirit of Beethoven" and who was "overcome with joy" in his presence, she said. "You are just as I always pictured you." Toscanini kissed her hand and thanked her for having been present.

never loved this marvelous, youthful music as played by seven instruments. I think that the Clarinet, Horn, and Bassoon are *better balanced* over a large base of strings!" The Choral Fantasy, with the pianist Ania Dorfman (a friend of Horowitz's), was played before the Ninth Symphony on the last concert of the series—a benefit event for the Junior League's Welfare Fund. That performance took place at Carnegie Hall, and Toscanini was so pleased with the orchestra's sound that he considered switching all of the NBC Symphony's concerts to that venue; unfortunately for the maestro's posthumous reputation, NBC's executives persuaded him that the dry acoustics of Studio 8H were better for broadcasting purposes.

Knowing that they might be living full-time in New York for many months or even years, Arturo and Carla decided to leave the Hotel Astor for a larger home, preferably away from Manhattan's noise and bustle. Someone among their acquaintances had discovered a large house for rent at 655 West 254th Street, at the corner of Independence Avenue, in the elegant Riverdale section of the Bronx; the rent, initially, was $600 a month, and the decision and move were quickly made. The three-story, twenty-eight-room, half-timbered imitation Tudor Villa Pauline, built in 1907, had a large living room, large parlor (where Toscanini kept a Steinway concert grand), dining room, kitchen, and other spaces on the ground floor; a central staircase led from the living room to the second floor, where Toscanini's study and his and Carla's bedrooms were located; and a third floor, too, was fully inhabitable. The five-acre estate on which the house was built included gardens and a greenhouse. "It's situated in an enchanting position, facing the *Hudson*, with a magnificent park abounding in big trees and terraces where I can enjoy the *sun* and the *silence*!!" Toscanini informed Ada. The Hudson River is so broad at that point in its course that, as he looked across it toward the New Jersey Palisades, he could imagine that he was on Lake Maggiore. "It makes me think of the Isolino," he noted, wistfully.

In his new home, Toscanini's domestic habits continued more or less unchanged. He usually went to bed in the early hours of the morning and awoke by six thirty, and he sometimes took pills to help him sleep even four or five hours. The maid would serve him a cup of espresso coffee while he was still in bed, and he would read or study until eight, when he would go downstairs and have another espresso and bread rolls with Carla. (He took his espressos with four lumps of sugar but no milk.) There would be more study through the morning, often interspersed with walks on the property and visits to the greenhouse to look at the flowers. Lunch, at one thirty, began with a minestrone or other thick soup, or else with a small portion of risotto, polenta, or pasta. Veal often constituted the main course, which was followed by cheese, another espresso or two, perhaps fruit, but no sweets—although the multiple lumps of refined sugar in the multiple daily espressos may have had the same effect as a dessert. Supper was lighter than lunch. Wine was served with both lunch and supper, but Toscanini never drank more than one or, occasionally, two glasses at a meal; likewise, after concerts he drank champagne, but never more than two glasses: his throat closed up, he said, if he even tried to drink more. He also liked high-quality cognac but rarely drank it. His granddaughter Emanuela joked that water, in the Toscanini household, was used strictly for ablutions, but her grandfather told friends that he had never in his life been drunk.

Unless he had to go out in the morning, Toscanini would remain in pajamas and dressing gown until long after breakfast, while working in his study. Otherwise, he dressed formally. Carla usually cut his hair, but he shaved himself with a straight razor and without looking in the mirror, and he used an old-fashioned, fire-heated mustache iron to keep his mustache bristly.

He surprised friends and family by saying yes to a request from *Life* magazine to let a photographer shoot pictures of him studying at his piano and playing with five-year-old Sonia Horowitz, for a feature article that appeared in the publication's issue of 27 November 1939. He did not agree to be interviewed, but the pictures were so charming that *Life*'s editors used one of them as the issue's cover. "I was in *good humor that day*," he wrote to Ada. "How could one not be with that dear, adorable creature?" About Sonia's parents, however, he commented, "They have a daughter, and she almost always lives with her grandparents! They're really funny, the *two* of them!" Although he later referred to Horowitz as an "egoist," he seems to have had little notion of just how "funny" his daughter and son-in-law were or of how difficult Sonia's life was when her grandparents were not available to look after her, whether she was living with her self-absorbed, unloving father and her moody, self-pitying mother, or with governesses. That same month, during one of her stays with her grandparents, Sonia cut off her curls; Toscanini pretended to be angry with her but was actually amused, and "when she came to excuse herself, I can't tell you how many kisses I gave her," he wrote. "As far as I'm concerned, she looks better now than when her hair was long. She looks like a little boy, and she says that she wants to be a *boy* and not a *girl*."

Toscanini loved being a grandfather. "It's a real joy to have her with us, and it goes a long way toward filling our lives! Walfredo [. . .] comes to us here on Friday evening and stays until Sunday evening. [. . .] He, too, is very intelligent and has an excellent character." The boy had arrived in America a year earlier speaking no English; now, at age ten, he spoke it better than his parents and grandparents.

Not that Toscanini was devoting all of his nonworking time to being Grandpa. He was dallying at various times with Eleonora Mendelssohn, Pauline Heifetz Chotzinoff, and Marcia Davenport, all in their thirties. And enter, or rather reenter, Elsa Kurzbauer, who, at fifty-three, was more or less midway in age between the maestro and his other occasional loves. With the Toscaninis' help, Elsa had escaped from Vienna to New York and had found work as a music copyist and as a German and Italian language coach for opera singers. By the fall of 1939, Toscanini was sending Elsa the same sort of letters—indeed, virtually the same letters—that he had written to her twenty years earlier and that he was still writing to other women, including Ada. "I love you as I never loved you before, and you delight me more than any other woman," he told Elsa. "You drive me crazy with desire and make me do absurd things that are inconceivable for an old man like me!"

Elsa, who had been there before, took his protestations with many grains of salt, but she evidently wanted to enjoy herself as much as he did—and the tone of his letters to her quickly changed. Most of the surviving ones from this period (there are about forty of them, written between 1939 and 1947) are not primarily erotic: they are joyfully pornographic—a tangle of descriptions of what Arturo and Elsa had done together, were going to do together, or would like to do together. And the handwritten drafts of several of her letters to him show that she could match him in hard-core descriptive language. In his letters to Elsa, Toscanini seems a sort of septuagenarian teenager, pretending to discover the joys of sex for the first time but simultaneously aware that time was running out. "Don't *lose time*," he wrote, in one of the letters. "Maybe *before long* God will take away even the *little bit* of *virility* that's left me. And then? What misery!" He continued to believe that prolonging his sex life would help him to prolong his artistic life as well, and he was delighted to be able to put this belief into practice as often as time and increasing age allowed.

When he had too much free time on his hands, Toscanini felt his age creeping up on him. "I have days when I feel *all* of my 72 years on my shoulders and I think that I should not live much longer on this old planet of ours," he wrote to Ada. "And I think about it tranquilly and with true stoicism." But then he would become intensely interested in his work or the world situation or a woman, and he would feel strong and energetic again.

The question naturally arises as to how he managed to see Kurzbauer or Chotzinoff or Mendelssohn or Davenport—all of whom lived in Manhattan—without arousing excessive suspicion. Sometimes, when Carla was out, they would visit him in Riverdale; sometimes his chauffeur would bring him to them; and once in a while, when the driver was taking Carla into Manhattan for one reason or another, her husband would go along and have himself dropped off at the building in which Edwin Bachmann, the NBC Symphony's principal second violin, lived: in theory, Toscanini was going to examine some of the musical manuscripts of which Bachmann was an assiduous collector, but instead he would hail a taxi and visit one of his lovers. A 1940 receipt found among Margherita De Vecchi's papers demonstrates, further, that for the modest fee of $2.50 per year, one "Antonio Trascuri"—Toscanini's longtime favorite anagrammatic pseudonym—was able to receive letters sent to him at the Hotel Astor as well as telegrams sent to the registered wire address "GERALDY," which he had used for communications from Farrar twenty-five years earlier.

What emerges most clearly in the letters to Elsa, as indeed in all of Toscanini's correspondence with lovers, friends, or family, is his seemingly limitless capacity for experiencing a whole panoply of emotions and states of mind as if they were raw, fresh, new. This capacity to do whatever he was doing as if for the first time, no matter how many times he had done it before, was also the hallmark of his work as an interpreter of music.

"COME L'ITALIA MA SENZA ANIMA" (like Italy but without a soul): this is how Toscanini was reported to have described California when, in December 1939, he and Carla first visited the western United States. They traveled to Los Angeles and San Francisco, then to the Grand Canyon, where the maestro wrote to Ada that he was "drunk with beauty." They returned to Riverdale in time to celebrate Christmas and New Year's with their family.

In between the two holidays, Toscanini participated in an unusual fund-raising event for the Chatham Square Music School, where poor but talented children on Manhattan's Lower East Side were given music lessons. He described the program in a letter to Ada:

> This evening I'll conduct a little orchestra made up of players from [the NBC Symphony], plus Heifetz, Busch, Milstein, Feuermann, and Wallenstein. I'm doing a sort of *café-chantant* program. A Moment musical of Schubert with Loin du bal by Gillet, for strings, Strauss's Pizzicato Polka with a polka by Shostakovich that's *all dissonances*, Ries's Moto perpetuo played by all the violins accompanied by [the rest of] the orchestra, and a Mozart Divertimento [*A Musical Joke*] for strings and two horns, full of wrong-note passages. [. . .] I [. . .] will come out not made up but dressed in a long overcoat, an 1830s-style collar, a huge necktie with stickpin, and old-fashioned dark glasses. [. . .] All the musicians will be dressed like children, in shorts, some with long stockings, others bare-legged. Can you imagine Adolf Busch?

No one involved was surprised that Toscanini carefully rehearsed every number in the show and even persuaded the celebrity members of what was dubbed "Toscanini's Children's Orchestra" to rise gradually out of their seats and lower themselves down again in crescendo-decrescendo passages in the Mozart piece. A *Times* reporter suggested in vain that the program be repeated at Madison Square Garden, where a vast amount of money could be raised.

A hiatus of nearly three and a half months separated the last of Toscanini's fall 1939 broadcasts from the first broadcast of his spring 1940 series. In the interim, he conducted only a single concert with his orchestra, in Newark, and recorded the Beethoven Violin Concerto with Heifetz. According to the pianist Eugene Istomin, Adolf Busch was "terribly disappointed" that Toscanini had not chosen him for that recording: "He felt that as a player of that music he was better." But Toscanini, a sincere admirer of Busch's musicianship, was also a sincere admirer of the Russian school of violin playing, with Heifetz at the top. He spoke, in one late-in-life conversation, of the first time he had heard Heifetz, in a recital at the Milan Conservatory; he had played Saint-Saëns's Introduction and Rondo Capriccioso "with such assurance—not a note is sharp or flat! He plays the highest harmonics, and notes come out! They're not whistles—they're notes!" Heifetz had played an arrangement of Schubert's "Ave Maria" as an encore, and in one passage in octaves the two notes were so perfectly in tune that they seemed to be a single sound, Toscanini recalled.

During his nonworking periods, the maestro, assisted by Carla, sometimes also by Eleonora, and always by Margherita De Vecchi—their constant, good-hearted, highly efficient amanuensis—continued to help refugees to secure American entry visas, jobs, and homes. As non-US citizens, the Toscaninis could not sponsor European émigrés to enter the country, but they provided financial aid to many people and persuaded fellow musicians who held US citizenship to vouch for their colleagues. Among the Italian Jews whom the Toscaninis aided were Roberto Foligno, their old friend Giulio's son, who, for "racial" reasons, had lost his commission in the Italian Army Air Corps and had immigrated to America; and the composers Mario Castelnuovo-Tedesco and his brother-in-law, Fernando Liuzzi. They also helped Ida and Enrico Polo's daughter Anna and her Jewish husband, Walter Marx, to settle in New York.* The ledgers and lists that Margherita kept for many years—entries of expenses that she

---

* The senior Polos had long since lost their youngest child, Leopoldo, to drugs. Anna, the middle child, now in her midthirties, had had to leave Italy for America for her husband's sake, and Riccardo, the oldest, who had already done military service during the First World War, would soon be called to arms again and would die on the Russian front.

incurred on behalf of the Toscaninis and of their repayments to her, plus copies of telegrams and cablegrams that she sent and received for them—also show that the maestro sent money to Arnold Rosé, the Vienna Philharmonic's concertmaster (and Mahler's brother-in-law), then in his late seventies, who had been forced to flee Austria for "racial" reasons and was living in straitened circumstances in London. Dozens of other people, none of them well-known, received checks from the Toscaninis, who never requested repayment or spoke publicly about their gifts.

Both Arturo and Walter Toscanini became involved in the newly formed Mazzini Society, a group of liberal and socialist Italian expatriates who favored the establishment of a republic in their native country after the downfall of fascism, for which they all ardently strove as best they could from abroad. Members included the historians Gaetano Salvemini and Giorgio La Piana, both professors at Harvard University; the art historian Lionello Venturi, at Johns Hopkins University; the writer Giuseppe Antonio Borgese, at the University of Chicago; Colonel Randolfo Pacciardi, a First World War veteran who had commanded an anti-Fascist battalion in Spain; and Count Carlo Sforza, a pre-Fascist-era foreign minister. Max Ascoli, professor of political philosophy at the New School for Social Research in New York, became president, and the journalist and diplomat Alberto Tarchiani was elected secretary. Walter Toscanini also tried to organize an Italian news service in New York, in opposition to the pro-Fascist *Il Progresso*, the main Italian-language newspaper in America—although *Il Progresso*'s publisher, Generoso Pope, would switch to the Allied side once the United States entered the war against Germany and Italy.

4.

THE MIDDLE FOURTEEN WEEKS OF NBC SYMPHONY CONCERTS WERE conducted by the Belgian Désiré Defauw (a future conductor of the Chicago Symphony), Bernardino Molinari, and Bruno Walter. Toscanini sometimes attended the other conductors' rehearsals, but not too often, he told Ada, "so as not to upset myself." When he did go, however, his presence upset the other conductors far more than it

upset him. His rehearsal method, especially when he was conducting an unfamiliar orchestra or a new piece, was to begin by going
through an entire movement or a similarly long segment of a work,
so that he and the orchestra would become familiar with each other
or so that the orchestra would develop a general sense of the piece
being studied; then he would go back and work on the details. He
complained that many conductors immediately began to make
detailed corrections, which seemed to him counterproductive for
the conductor and humiliating and boring for first-rate orchestra
musicians. Molinari, he told Ada, "stops the orchestra every three or
four bars, and he does so not only at the first reading but at the last
rehearsal. Whether the orchestra is good or bad, it's all the same—
just like Bruno Walter, he can't go on, he has to stop every moment."

There was probably much truth in this assessment, but most conductors—frightened out of their wits knowing that Arturo Toscanini
was sitting behind them in an otherwise empty auditorium—
presumably felt that if they did not immediately correct errors or
request changes in phrasing and the like, the maestro might consider them inattentive at best, incompetent at worst.

Bruno Walter was not afraid of Toscanini, but he could not have
been pleased when, at one of his rehearsals during the previous season, he had heard the maestro grunting with disgust at his (Walter's)
interpretation of the first movement of Mozart's Symphony in G
minor. Yet Walter always excused Toscanini: *"Er ist ein Heiliger"* (He
is a saint), he would say, knowing that in matters musical his older
colleague could not control himself. Toscanini's behavior probably
reminded Walter of his own uncompromising mentor, the irascible
Mahler—and indeed, in speaking of having come "into personal
touch with greatness" upon getting to know Mahler in 1894, Walter
added, "Later, I once again was to know true greatness—in Arturo
Toscanini." Within days of the unpleasant rehearsal incident (which
was unknown to the public at the time), Walter told a *Times* reporter,
"Toscanini's merits for music in America are tremendous. [. . .] He
lives for music. The NBC Symphony which has felt his master touch
is marvelous. [. . .] Toscanini has taken great music to the masses;
they might never have heard Beethoven, Brahms and Mozart speak
so directly to their hearts." Nor was Walter merely trying to ingrati-
ate himself with Toscanini: the Columbia Records producer John T.

McClure reported that he "once created a brief frost by making a negative remark about [Toscanini]" during a conversation with Walter—and this was after Toscanini's death.

Toscanini resumed his broadcasts on 16 March 1940. On the first of his eight programs, he conducted the American composer Roy Harris's Third Symphony, which Koussevitzky and the Boston Symphony had premiered the preceding year; Toscanini brought Harris onto the stage afterward to receive the audience's enthusiastic applause. The third program included the world premiere of Verdi's unpublished *Aida* Overture, which the composer had written subsequent to the opera's premiere but had then set aside in favor of the original, shorter prelude.* Single-composer programs were dedicated to Tchaikovsky, Debussy, and Brahms, and other composers represented in Toscanini's concerts ranged, chronologically, from Mozart to Castelnuovo-Tedesco and Harris. New to his active repertoire was Ravel's *La Valse*.

During the same period, plans were being laid for the NBC Symphony to give a series of concerts in South America during June and July 1940. The orchestra's broadcasts were already heard in Latin America via shortwave, with commentary in Spanish and Portuguese, and the idea of a tour had been raised as early as the spring of 1939, when Norbert A. Bogdan, a music-loving American financier resident in Brazil, had suggested that NBC send the orchestra to Rio de Janeiro. But the plan moved forward thanks mainly to Floro Ugarte, an Argentine composer who managed the Teatro Colón in Buenos Aires. Although Argentina was no longer the musicians' El Dorado that it had been before the First World War, it still enjoyed an intense musical life, enhanced by the presence of numerous European exiles, including the conductors Fritz Busch and Erich Kleiber.

---

* In 1926, Angelo Carrara Verdi, son of the composer's adopted daughter (and sole heir), had let him borrow the original manuscript of the overture and—Toscanini claimed—had told him to perform it or not, as he saw fit. Toscanini had held on to the score until 1935, when Carrara Verdi wrote to Walter Toscanini to request that it be returned to him and to ask whether the maestro thought that the overture ought to be published. (It was not published.) In October 1939, Toscanini had Elsa Kurzbauer copy the instrumental parts from a full score. He then read through the piece with the NBC Symphony and decided to conduct it on the concert of 30 March 1940. Carrara Verdi protested upon learning that Toscanini planned to perform the overture, but Toscanini performed it anyway—once but never again.

Ugarte flew north early in January 1940 to sign up some of the New York–based opera singers who had previously gravitated toward Europe each summer, but his main quarry was Toscanini.

RCA's and NBC's executives were interested in the proposal. There could be no direct monetary gains: proceeds from the concerts, even if they all sold out, would not even cover expenses. But Sarnoff and some of his fellow executives took genuine pride in what their expensive orchestra was doing for musical culture in the United States, and the idea of displaying it abroad pleased them. They also pointed out to skeptics on the board of directors that RCA was seeking to expand radio, phonograph, and record sales in the Southern Hemisphere, thus the tour would serve as a publicity tool.

There were political reasons, too, for undertaking the tour. RCA/NBC needed to demonstrate readiness to cooperate with the government, which controlled the airwaves—at least de jure—and a tour would provide an excellent opportunity for contributing to the United States' "Good Neighbor" policy toward Latin America. Moreover, by the late 1930s, American diplomats, like their counterparts in the Western European democracies, had begun to worry about the increasingly massive propaganda barrage aimed at Latin America from Nazi Germany and Fascist Italy. Sending a virtuoso orchestra to South America together with the world's most famous conductor—who also happened to be one of the world's most famous anti-Fascists, sheltered in the United States—would be a fine propaganda tool for the Americans and a positive gesture toward Washington from RCA/NBC.

The tour proposal delighted Toscanini. From Lucerne he had received a cable asking whether he could be counted on to return to Switzerland that summer, but Europe was at war. "How do they have the nerve to think about what will happen in August?" he asked Ada. On the other hand, concerts in South America would "keep my spirit and nerves occupied."

Leopold Stokowski, who had not renewed his contract with the Philadelphia Orchestra, was also beginning to plan a South American tour with an All-American Youth Orchestra, and the press immediately pounced on the "rivalry between the two conductors"—neither of whom saw the situation as anything of the sort: Toscanini would have scoffed at the notion of Stokowski as a rival, and Stokowski told the *Times* that "a tour by Toscanini will be a splendid thing for music and for South America." Stokowski initially believed that NBC had come up with the idea of sending its orchestra southward only after word of his own enterprise had been circulated, but in fact NBC's initial negotiations predated his own. And his tour, which began after the NBC Symphony's had ended, was enthusiastically received.

By mid-April, NBC's tour had been planned, thanks to the encouragement of the various governments involved, a massive effort on the part of RCA/NBC's executives and their staffs, and the cooperation of the American Federation of Musicians as well as local administrations and impresarios in the cities that the orchestra was to visit. Toscanini would be paid $28,500, about 45 percent of his regular fee, calculated on a per-concert basis; the hundred musicians (including five extra players, as required by the AFM) would be paid a total of $65,000, or about 80 percent of their usual salaries; and the Moore-McCormack steamship line would transport the orchestra, staff, and equipment to and from all ports of call at a greatly discounted rate of $35,000, in exchange for free publicity on NBC. In the end, NBC lost only about $9,000—less than anticipated—on the whole venture.

Before the troupe set out, however, the orchestra's home season had to be completed. The last regular broadcast—a benefit event for the Greater New York Fund, with Horowitz as soloist in Brahms's Second Piano Concerto—took place at Carnegie Hall on Monday, 6 May, rather than during the usual Saturday-night time slot, and three days later the same performers recorded the concerto. Horowitz would say, late in life, that he had felt constrained by his father-in-law's highly structural concept of the piece and that he hated the recording. When Toscanini was asked what he thought of the recording, he responded, "I don't know, I'm afraid to listen to it."

In anticipation of the tour, Toscanini and the orchestra gave a concert at Washington's Constitution Hall on 14 May, before an audience that included eight hundred North and South American delegates to the Eighth American Scientific Congress. Back in New York, the musicians boarded the SS *Brazil* on 31 May and set sail the following morning. In addition to the players, other orchestra personnel, the maestro, and Carla, a number of orchestra wives came along, as did John Royal and the Chotzinoffs. Several trunks full of printed music were also loaded onto the ship: the tour repertoire would comprise forty-seven pieces by twenty-seven composers—enough music for eight different programs. Toscanini included in the tour repertoire pieces by three Brazilian and two Argentine composers.

The weather was fine throughout the voyage, and the maestro spent most of his days on deck, chatting with his musicians and enjoying their jokes and games. But on 10 June, as the German Wehrmacht prepared to enter Paris, Mussolini ordered Italian troops to cross the border into France and attack Italy's World War I ally. Toscanini, upon hearing the news, was beside himself with grief, rage, and shame over his country's treachery. He shut himself into his cabin and refused to come out until the ship docked in Rio de Janeiro, two days later.

TOSCANINI HAD NOT CONDUCTED in Rio since his unanticipated debut season, in 1886. At the time, the astonished local music critics had described the nineteen-year-old maestro as a prodigy with a great future ahead. Now the prodigy was back—staying at the Hotel Copacabana Palace instead of the backstreet rooming house that he had lived in fifty-four years earlier—and local music lovers received him not only with enthusiasm but also with pride. A *New York Times* correspondent described the ovations in the overcrowded Teatro Municipal on 13 and 14 June as "unparalleled in the history of Rio de Janeiro's musical life," and local critics expressed astonishment at the beauty and power of the interpretations, the restrained control and energy of Toscanini's conducting, and the virtuosity of the orchestra.

After the second concert, the company traveled by overnight train to São Paulo, gave a concert that evening, then departed from the port of Santos, bound for Buenos Aires, the main city on the tour. All eight NBC Symphony programs were presented to vast, enthusiastic crowds at the Teatro Colón, where Toscanini had last appeared twenty-eight years earlier. Norman Armour, the American ambassador, described the NBC Symphony as "the United States' fifth column."

Pro-Nazi demonstrations had been anticipated in Montevideo, the orchestra's fourth port of call, but nothing of the sort occurred. At the first performance, held at the Uruguayan national radio headquarters on 3 July, the applause and cheering were so long, intense, and loud that, after having taken repeated bows with the orchestra, a smiling Toscanini waved to the audience, clapped his hands over his ears, and signaled the musicians to follow him off the stage. The following morning, the musicians appeared in the hall at eleven o'clock, puzzled as to why a rehearsal had been called—until they saw the US ambassador, Edwin C. Wilson, sitting in the auditorium and the music for "The Star-Spangled Banner" on their stands. Toscanini appeared, conducted his players in the anthem, wished the men a happy Fourth of July, and let them go.

That afternoon, more than one thousand people stood in the rain for up to six hours hoping to get standing-room tickets to the second concert, which had been sold out for weeks. A quarter hour of applause and cheering followed the last piece on the program, with Toscanini's name shouted in unison by the audience. Afterward, "hundreds stood in the rain at the theatre entrance, at the hotel and at the port to applaud the conductor as he passed," the *Times*'s correspondent reported. "The NBC executives who have accompanied Toscanini on the trip said nothing in other cities approached the enthusiasm accorded here." For decades afterward, many orchestra members would recall the Montevideo concerts as the high point of the tour.

Immediately after the second concert, the musicians reboarded the SS *Uruguay*, which had brought them from Buenos Aires to Montevideo and would take them on the remainder of their journey. They played another concert in São Paulo and two more in Rio de Janeiro—the final performances of the tour.

Aboard ship on 22 July, the day before they ended their seven-week, 18,000-mile journey, Toscanini sent a letter to his musicians, in which he wrote, in his own brand of English, "I wish I could express my feelings and my thanks personally to you . . . but it is impossible—My throbbing heart would raise up to the throarth chocking my poor voice. . . Mr. Chotzinoff will be so kind as to read these few lines to you. [. . .] I can't say which of these concerts has been the best! I only know that the next to the first was better, and so on. I hope you will never forget them."

But the journey ended sadly. In Rio on the day of the last concert, Jacques Tuschinsky, a charter member of the orchestra's viola section, had been hit and killed by a bus. Toscanini had not noticed his absence at the concert, and a decision was made not to tell him what had happened until the last day of the return voyage home. When the maestro finally heard the story, he wept and blamed himself for the man's death, saying that if he had not undertaken the tour Tuschinsky would not have died. In New York, he sent $1,000 to the musician's widow and three children; Sarnoff made a similar contribution, as did the orchestra members as a group.

Despite the tour's unfortunate dénouement, the US government, Sarnoff, and even the maestro were satisfied with the results. "The tour went magnificently," Toscanini later wrote to Ada. "The orchestra was beyond all praise. Never had it played better. Every concert was a revelation!"

5.

ARTURO AND CARLA WERE ABLE TO RELAX THROUGH THE REST OF the summer and most of the fall of 1940. Early in August, they were in the Berkshire Hills of Massachusetts, visiting Herbert Graf, the director who had collaborated with Toscanini on the Salzburg *Meistersinger* production and was now a fellow exile, staging operas at the Metropolitan and teaching at the Tanglewood Music School. The elder Toscaninis also went by car with Walter and Cia to visit Walfredo in Maine: the boy had been sent to Camp Kohut for a month of athletic activity, which he loved, and so that he would gain some independence from his family. But, as he laughingly recalled years later, "after all, we're Italian, so the entire family came up to visit me, and Grandfather became the center of attention for photo-ops."

At home, however, Toscanini frequently slid into a state of near despair over the war in Europe. "For some months my life has no goal," he wrote to Ada. "While millions and millions of people are being swept away by the most fearful tragedy that the world has ever known, I sit here, a ridiculous spectator, with my hands folded, sighing, hating, but an inert and useless tool." In another letter: "What sorrow, what sad suffering it is *not to be able to love* one's own country any longer, and to feel contempt for all the Italians—the good ones because *they're cowards*, the perfidious ones because they're evil."

On 16 May 1941, Toscanini brought his already nearly extinguished relationship with Ada Mainardi to an end by sending her a violent letter in which he denounced her as a coward for not having answered his previous messages. "You are too poisoned by the atmosphere that surrounds you," he wrote; "you are all now living too much amid shame and dishonor, without showing any sign of rebellion, to be able to value people like me, who have remained and will remain above the mud, not to give it a worse name, that is drowning the Italians!!! [. . .] I feel disgust at belonging to the family of artists, who, with a few exceptions, are not men, but poor creatures, full of vanity. Life no longer holds any interest for me, and I would pray God to take it from me if it weren't for my firm, *never diminished hope* to see the *scoundrels* swept off the face of the earth before I go." To Toscanini, Mainardi herself had come to represent Italy's complete moral collapse.

In a letter to Sybil Cholmondeley, who was working for the Admiralty in London, he quoted Garibaldi: ". . . if ever England should be so circumstanced as to require the help of an ally, cursed be the Italian who would not step forward in her defense." She replied, "I showed your quotation [. . .] to Winston [Churchill]—of course he knew it well but he seemed pleased to see it again *and* from you." Toscanini later became furious with Sir Thomas Beecham, who, instead of staying in Britain and conducting benefit events, as Toscanini had done in Italy during the First World War, was earning money in the United States. Beecham had earlier defended Furtwängler's political position and had recorded *The Magic Flute* in Hitler's Berlin in 1938, and these facts led Toscanini to the incorrect assumption that the English maestro was a Nazi sympathizer. He complained to Olin Downes that Beecham "lives here, in America protected, adulated and honoured by critics"—including Downes—"and American public. . . Truly, it is a very *farcical* and *deploring thing*, but so is life."

At last, after Steinberg had conducted the first six weekly concerts of the NBC Symphony's 1940–41 season, Toscanini returned to the orchestra, opening with an all-Verdi program: the *Te Deum* from the Four Sacred Pieces, followed by the *Requiem*. The performance, at Carnegie Hall on 23 November, was a fund-raising event for the construction of an Alma Gluck Zimbalist Memorial building as part of

New York's Roosevelt Hospital complex.* But exhaustion from the *Requiem* preparations plus news of the death, in Parma, of Cesira Montani, his beloved aunt and surrogate mother, caused him to withdraw from the following week's concert, which Steinberg conducted in his stead.

Toscanini returned to the airwaves on 7 December with an all-Sibelius program, on the eve of the composer's seventy-fifth birthday; it was recorded and rebroadcast to Finland the following morning for the composer and his compatriots. Two mixed programs followed, and on 28 December Toscanini conducted a magnificent performance of Beethoven's *Missa Solemnis*; this concert, like the Verdi *Requiem*, was given at Carnegie Hall as a benefit event for the National Conference of Christians and Jews. But preparations for the performance had led to trouble.

A rehearsal had been scheduled from 5:00 to 7:30 P.M. on the day before the concert, but since another orchestra had performed in the hall that afternoon, Carnegie's stagehands needed more time than anticipated to set up the chorus's risers for Toscanini's rehearsal, which then began half an hour late. He assumed that it would run until 8:00 instead of 7:30, but, as the cellist Alan Shulman told B. H. Haggin, "thirty-five men of the orchestra had to play with Frank Black in the Cities Service program in Studio 8H [at Rockefeller Center, nearly a mile away] at 8; and they had to leave at 7:30 [. . .]. So 7:30 came, and he kept right on working; then it was 7:32, and 7:33; and at that point the personnel manager [Spitalny] stood behind Maestro and signaled to the men one by one to sneak out." When Toscanini realized what was happening, he became "so infuriated that he threw down his stand and walked out," Shulman said.

Toscanini conducted the performance, but he felt that he had been betrayed. And he was further angered to learn that despite his having recommended Hugo Burghauser, who had fled Austria, for a position in the NBC Symphony, Spitalny and Chotzinoff had turned down the Vienna Philharmonic's former principal bassoon, telling

---

* The soprano Alma Gluck, with whom Toscanini had worked at the Metropolitan, and whose second husband was the violinist Efrem Zimbalist, had died at the age of fifty-four in 1938.

(above) *Inaugural concert of the Lucerne Festival, 25 August 1938.*

With Sergei Rachmaninoff, Lucerne, 1938.

Dall'apparecchio N...X.... Telefona il maestro Arturo Toscanini.
Dall'apparecchio.N.72943 (Hotel de la Ville) Telefona la signora Ada.

(A proposito dei recenti provvedimenti sugli ebrei:)

TOS.= Sono delle cose per cui non si sa dove si andrà a finire. Si può tutto pensare!

ADA.= Quello che spinge e fa vedere rosso è la bugia, la mala fede...

TOS.= Hai visto come si sono ritrattati per Falck. Lo chiamano "camerata"... Per i camerati vanno bene tutti i posti che vogliono! Non hanno nemmeno il buon senso di dire: "almeno mascheriamo". Vogliono che la gente sia stupida.

ADA.= Infatti, poco a poco la riducono così!

TOS.= Da ebreo aveva torto ad avere tutti questi posti; ma come "camerata", adesso, va bene!... In questi giorni andrò all'Isolino e cercherò di fare tutto per portar via... perchè non so domani che potrà succedere.

ADA.= Sì, è meglio. Credo, però, che non potranno andare tanto in là...

TOS.= Ormai, non c'è più limite. Domani diranno: "Datemi i vostri soldi, fate questo,...". A tutto si potrà arrivare. Non c'è più parola; non ricordano quello che hanno detto ieri. E' una vergogna! Finchè, poi, si è trattato per gli stranieri, bene; ma adesso c'è della gente che da tanti anni ha lavorato, ha fatto tante cose!... I bambini non devono andare a scuola.... Ma questa è roba da Medio Evo!

ADA.= Sì, precisamente.

Transcript of wiretapped telephone conversation between Toscanini and Ada Mainardi, 3 September 1938, with Toscanini's biting criticisms of Mussolini's new anti-Semitic racial laws, and the handwritten comment at the bottom: "by order of the Duce take away Toscanini's passport."

Photographs taken by Robert Hupka during
NBC Symphony rehearsals in the 1940s.

With grandchildren Walfredo Toscanini and Sonia Horowitz, as the senior Toscaninis prepare to depart for Buenos Aires, 5 June 1941.

With Friedelind Wagner, Buenos Aires, June or July 1941.

*"Jamming" in the 1940s, in New York, with singers Lillian Raimondi
(bending forward), Frances Alda (dark hair), Giuseppe De Luca (his hand
on Raimondi's shoulder), Maria Jeritza (behind Alda), and
Giovanni Martinelli, plus Mrs. De Luca (behind her husband)
and Carla Toscanini.*

Posters ("Toscanini return" and "Long live Toscanini") plastered on La Scala's walls immediately after Mussolini's fall, late July 1943.

Return to Italy and La Scala: end of the inaugural concert, 11 May 1946.

With son Walter during the NBC Symphony's Spring 1950 US tour.

In his dressing room before his last concert at La Scala, 19 September 1952, with Guido Cantelli and Emanuela Castelbarco, Toscanini's granddaughter.

*Overcome with emotion at his last concert, with the
NBC Symphony Orchestra, 4 April 1954.*

*With granddaughter
Emanuela, 1956.*

him—as Burghauser recounted the incident—that although Toscanini had the right to veto players whom they had engaged, they alone had the right to select them.

The three-year contract that Toscanini had signed in March 1938, at the end of his first NBC season, was about to expire, and rumors that he would not sign a new one began to circulate. Robert Bloom claimed that Spitalny and some of NBC's other administrative personnel did not want the maestro to return and asked him to write a letter of resignation; extant correspondence on the subject suggests that Sarnoff himself wished to have Toscanini remain at the orchestra's helm but also needed to clarify a complicated situation: Did Toscanini really want to leave the orchestra, or did he not? As late as May 1941, Toscanini declared that he would resign, but wasn't quite sure. "My old age tells me it is high time to withdraw from the militant scene of Art," he wrote to Sarnoff.

> I am tired and a little exhausted. The tragedy which tears apart this unhappy humanity saddens me so and makes me crazy and restless; how can I find heart, will and strength in order to meet with new responsabilities [sic] and new work? For me it is impossible, so that my dear David, don't be hesitating any longer and make up your plans at once, for next season.
>
> Later on, if my state of mind, health and rest will be improved and you will believe my co-operation advantageous enough for the N.B.C. . . . call me and I shall be glad to resume once more my work. [. . .]

Accordingly, NBC invited Leopold Stokowski to become the orchestra's music director, beginning with the 1941–42 season.

In the meantime, the 1940–41 season continued as planned. Wallenstein and George Szell each conducted four concerts, after which Toscanini returned to lead the final four programs, including an all-Wagner concert at Carnegie Hall to benefit the Lenox Hill Neighborhood Association for underprivileged families; the event included white-hot performances of the final scene of Act I of *Die Walküre* (with the aging Lauritz Melchior and the American soprano Helen Traubel, then in her prime) and the final scene of *Götterdämmerung* (Traubel).

Szell had been invited on the basis of the improvements that he had made in The Hague's Residentie Orchestra between Toscanini's 1937 and 1938 appearances with the ensemble. Now, however, Toscanini observed Szell constantly starting and stopping the orchestra during a rehearsal of the "Eroica" Symphony (Shulman counted fifty-four stops in the slow movement alone), and during the break the maestro verbally attacked his younger colleague for treating the NBC musicians like babies and wearing them out unnecessarily. Szell, a refugee from Europe who was still a largely unknown quantity in America, must have feared the consequences of Toscanini's negative impression. Within hours of the rehearsal incident, he wrote to thank the maestro "for the criticism and advice you gave me this afternoon. Your benevolent frankness is a great honor and privilege for me and what you said, of unique importance." There seems to have been no follow-up to the unpleasant incident, and five years later Szell would begin his long, remarkable tenure as music director of the Cleveland Orchestra.

Toscanini ended the NBC Symphony's regular season on 19 April at Carnegie Hall—another benefit concert (an all-Tchaikovsky program that featured Horowitz in the First Piano Concerto), for the Junior League's Welfare Fund. The maestro then went immediately to Chicago to conduct a special concert for the Chicago Symphony Orchestra's pension fund; this was his only appearance with that ensemble. In mid-May, he continued a series of NBC Symphony recording sessions that he had begun three months earlier; the repertoire included Brahms's First Symphony and shorter pieces by Wagner, Verdi, Johann Strauss II, and Tchaikovsky, plus an unissued take of Berlioz's "Rákóczy" March.

Toscanini had heard good things about Dean Dixon, a young African American conductor who had won the moral backing of Eleanor Roosevelt, among others. When Sarnoff and Chotzinoff approached Toscanini about allowing Dixon to conduct the NBC Symphony, he gave his approval. Despite the opposition of a few racially prejudiced players, Dixon successfully led two of the orchestra's weekly summer concerts, in June 1941, and was invited back for a regular-season concert the following year.

6.

FLORO UGARTE, THE MAN WHO HAD PERSUADED RCA AND NBC TO send their orchestra and Toscanini to Argentina in 1940, had in the meantime persuaded the maestro to return in 1941 for concerts with the Teatro Colón's orchestra, reinforced by six players imported from the United States. On 5 June 1941, Arturo and Carla flew to Miami, the first leg of a trip that would bring them to Buenos Aires four days later, and between 20 June and 24 July Toscanini led four wildly successful performances of Beethoven's Ninth Symphony and three of the Verdi *Requiem*.

In Buenos Aires, the Toscaninis were reunited with the twenty-one-year-old Friedelind ("Mausi") Wagner. At the outbreak of war in 1939, the composer's granddaughter had made her way from Switzerland to England, with the intention of immigrating to the United States. She had been corresponding with the maestro since his final departure from Lucerne, and he had encouraged her to live by her principles. "We rejoice you are in London," he and Carla cabled her on 28 March 1940. They paid all her legal and ancillary expenses during those first months, but in the late spring, when the "Phoney War" was heating up in Western Europe, Friedelind and thousands of other refugees from enemy nations were interned on the Isle of Man. "I'm worried over the fate of my dear Mausi," Toscanini wrote. "I've sent recommendations to Argentina's ambassador" (about using Argentina as a way station en route to the USA) "and to [Joseph] Kennedy, the United States' ambassador [to Britain]. Everyone knows the feelings of this girl, who is not only against Hitler but also against her mother"—Winifred Wagner—"and who refused to return to her country. I've done everything that was humanly possible for me to do for her; now *we must wait*. But this 22-year-old girl is marvelous; she has a *strong and loyal* character, and I love her like a daughter."

He continued to encourage Friedelind and to pay her expenses. "How should I be able to thank him?" she wrote. "What an angel he is to me. If I weren't sure of his friendship and affection, I don't know how I would have stood it for so many months." Finally, thanks largely to the maestro's influence, she boarded a ship that reached

Buenos Aires in mid-March 1941; the Toscaninis had paid her passage and had sent money for her other expenses.

The maestro and Carla's arrival in June initiated one of the happiest periods in Friedelind's life. Day after day, she spent time with them, and she sang in the chorus in the Beethoven Ninth and Verdi *Requiem*. "The performances are just wonderful," she wrote to Margherita De Vecchi. "I was the only member on that platform that was'nt [sic] scared to death when Maestro appeared the first time. [. . .] The occasional outbursts could'nt [sic] frighten me because I feel they just have to happen like a thunderstorm—afterwards everything is nice and quiet again."

Friedelind had finally obtained a US entry visa, and when Arturo and Carla departed Buenos Aires by plane, she flew with them. The journey, with multiple overnight stops, lasted five days; during a stopover in Rio, Toscanini delighted in hiring someone to drive them around, so that he could show Friedelind the sights of the city in which he had made his debut, and they had lunch with Miecio Horszowski, who had become involved in the city's musical life and who reported that the maestro "was in good humor and talked a lot."

Friedelind's filial feelings toward her benefactor—her senior by fifty-one years—began to take a more passionate turn, and Toscanini's antennae were quick to receive even the faintest erotic signals from female transmitters. In New York, where they arrived on 31 July, some tension developed between the two of them, but before the matter got out of hand they settled back into their old father-daughter relationship. Friedelind was a frequent dinner guest in Riverdale, and the Toscaninis paid for her studio apartment at the Ansonia. A standing order from their account at New York's National City Bank provided Friedelind with $150 per month—the equivalent of an average American family's monthly income at the time—for at least three whole years and probably longer. Like her famous grandfather, Friedelind often lived beyond her means: the Toscaninis sometimes found themselves paying her telephone bills and dentist's bills in addition to everything else, and in July 1944 her lawyer wrote directly to Toscanini to ask him to "lend" her $2,500 so that she could pay off some outstanding debts and reclaim some jewelry that she had pawned. She eventually managed to support herself with lectures and teaching.

—

DESPITE THE EXTRAORDINARY ENTHUSIASM of the audiences at Toscanini's Buenos Aires concerts, the maestro was unhappy with the musical results and had once again been feeling pain in his right arm and shoulder. Upon his return to New York, he was in a generally disgruntled state of mind, and late in August, while Carla visited Wanda and Volodya in Los Angeles, he stayed home and fretted. Although Walter Toscanini told Sarnoff that his father was determined not only to avoid returning to South America but also to stop conducting altogether, he knew that his father would not be able to bear idleness for long—and that he would torment everyone around him if he stopped making music. In collusion with Charles O'Connell, RCA's chief classical record producer, Walter persuaded his father to complete some recordings (Brahms's First Symphony and the *Tristan* Prelude) that he had begun with the NBC Symphony and to promise to make other records with the Philadelphia Orchestra while he was carrying out some already scheduled concerts with that ensemble during the forthcoming 1941–42 season. Once Toscanini's appetite for work had been whetted, he decided to return to both of his former New York orchestras, the Philharmonic and the NBC Symphony, as a guest conductor, although he took his time deciding exactly when and in what way. He also met with William Paley, head of NBC's rival Columbia Broadcasting System, but whatever proposals they may have discussed were never realized.

Toscanini conducted one program twice with the Philadelphia Orchestra in November, a second pair in January, and a third in February. B. H. Haggin, the *Nation*'s music critic, attended some of the performances; he had been told that Toscanini read his articles, and after one concert he asked Walter Toscanini to introduce him to the maestro, who smiled, shook hands with him, said something in Italian to Walter, then turned to the next visitor. Toscanini's comment, which Walter translated for Haggin: "He writes like God: he knows what is good music and what is bad music. *I* do not know what is good music and bad music; but *he* knows." And he echoed this sentiment some months later in a letter in which he asked the American composer Morton Gould for permission to perform his *Lincoln Legend*. "I don't know [. . .] if the music is beautiful or good—clever or well written," Toscanini admitted. "I leave these things to the sterile critics, incapable of procreation but never doubting about their wisdom!"

After the Japanese attack on Pearl Harbor on 7 December 1941, the United States entered the Allied war effort, and Toscanini, an Italian citizen, was officially an enemy alien. When he was to take the Philadelphia to Washington, to repeat one of the programs that they had given at home, he had to receive a special government travel permit, and even with it he was subjected to police examination every time he crossed state lines. Eleanor Roosevelt, who attended the concert in the capital, commented on the situation in her syndicated newspaper column, "My Day." "I must say this situation seems to me rather tragic. There is an element of comedy, however, in suggesting that Mr. Toscanini needs thus to be classified." The maestro's long opposition to Mussolini and Hitler was well-known to the president and his wife, and Toscanini was eventually provided with documents that eliminated the problem. His shortwave radio was confiscated— enemy aliens were to be prevented from listening to propaganda from their countries of origin—but Sarnoff quickly provided him with another one, and the authorities turned a blind eye.

Despite his age and his worries over the war, Toscanini was still working at the highest artistic level. His Philadelphia recording sessions, interlaced among some of their joint concerts, yielded outstanding versions of Schubert's "Great" C Major and Tchaikovsky's "Pathétique" Symphonies; Debussy's *La Mer* and *Ibéria*; the overture and seven pieces from Mendelssohn's *A Midsummer Night's Dream* incidental music; Strauss's *Death and Transfiguration*; Respighi's *Feste Romane*; and the "Queen Mab" Scherzo from Berlioz's *Roméo et Juliette*. For a complicated series of reasons—including a recording ban imposed by the musicians' union from August 1942 to November 1944—none of these outstanding examples of the maestro's art was released until after his death.

Those sessions, however, marked the beginning of a decline in relations between Toscanini and the producer Charles O'Connell, and eventually between O'Connell and RCA. Toscanini had initially trusted and consulted with O'Connell, a trained musician who also had some conducting experience, but in the spring of 1942 Zirato informed Walter Toscanini that O'Connell was using his position at RCA as bait for lining up conducting engagements with several

American orchestras: if they would give him some concerts, he would arrange for their orchestras to make recordings—a special privilege, in those days. Then Nora Shea, a Columbia Artists executive, told Walter that O'Connell was "better known as a drunkard than as a conductor." O'Connell also asked Walter to have his father put in a good word for him to conduct some NBC Symphony summer concerts; when this did not happen, O'Connell informed Toscanini père that he wanted him to record such works as the Sibelius Third Symphony and Beethoven's potboiler, *Wellington's Victory*, neither of which was in the maestro's repertoire.

O'Connell's job with RCA ended in March 1944; he retaliated with a venomous, error-ridden book, *The Other Side of the Record*, in which he wrote scathingly about Toscanini (among much else, O'Connell, a devout Catholic, was offended to discover that there were no religious images in the Toscanini household) and damned with faint praise not only many of the other celebrated musicians with whom he had worked but also Sarnoff and other RCA executives. The mud quickly washed off of O'Connell's victims—although their detractors have often made indiscriminate use of his accusations—but much of it stuck to his own reputation.

Toscanini's first concert as an NBC Symphony guest conductor took place on 6 December 1941, the eve of the attack on Pearl Harbor. At the request of Secretary of the Treasury Henry Morgenthau Jr., the maestro had already agreed to allow the government to use that broadcast and another, a week later, to advertise the sale of defense bonds and stamps. Once the war effort had begun in earnest, Toscanini decided to give three more NBC concerts to raise money for the Defense Savings Campaign. The broadcasts were now only one hour long; his first one included his only public performance of the "Blue Danube" Waltz, and on the fourth concert he gave his first and last performance of *El Salón México*, by Aaron Copland, whose musical idiom was so distant from Toscanini's usual realm that the maestro made a piano reduction of the score for himself, presumably to get used to the shifting rhythms and meters by playing them repeatedly.

To avoid any public fuss over his seventy-fifth birthday, Toscanini scheduled no rehearsal or concert on 25 March 1942 and escaped for three days—with Carla, Walter and family, and Wanda and family—to a small hotel in upstate New York. RCA Victor nevertheless celebrated the event by releasing his recording of the Brahms First Symphony, and the *Times* and other newspapers published tributes to him.

An invitation to participate in the New York Philharmonic's 1941–42 centennial season had reached him by the end of 1940. First he said no, then maybe, and only when Walter Price, a Philharmonic board member, upbraided him for unfairness toward an organization that had treated him generously for a decade did Toscanini finally write to Marshall Field, the board's president, to accept the invitation. He atoned by offering to conduct not merely one or two programs but a two-week-long, postseason, six-concert Beethoven festival, and he sealed the agreement by visiting the orchestra's offices at Steinway Hall, where he shook hands not only with the board members and executive staff but with every employee present, including the elevator operator. The orchestra musicians sent him an affectionate telegram welcoming him back, and he replied, through Maurice Van Praag, expressing his happiness "to be once more their leader *though for a short while*!!! [. . .] I am sure we will find in ourselves the enthusiasm of former times." The Philharmonic's subscribers were offered first choice of tickets to the festival, and by the time sales were opened to the general public—over four months before the first concert—only a few boxes in Carnegie Hall's lower tier remained unsold. The Philharmonic eventually had to return $15,000 in checks to people whose ticket requests arrived too late.

Haggin attended the first rehearsal and noted that the orchestra played for Toscanini as if "not six years but one day" had gone by since he had last stood before it. In addition to the nine symphonies, the concerts included the *Missa Solemnis*, four overtures, and the "Triple" Concerto, with the pianist Ania Dorfman and the Philharmonic's concertmaster, Mishel Piastro, and principal cellist, Joseph Schuster. "At my tender age, I conducted six concerts in two weeks with the Philharmonic," Toscanini boasted in a letter that was smuggled to Wally in Italy. "So you see that I'm in good health. My body doesn't suffer, but my soul, oh! the soul is something else!"

In February, he had been shocked to learn that Stefan Zweig, who had immigrated to Brazil, had committed suicide together with his second wife, in despair over the war and the future of humanity. "He was a friend and I loved him, but I've never been able to forgive him his suicide," Toscanini said of him years later. Yet he continued to treasure his memories of his old friend as well as Zweig's writings, which he described as "marvelous. He enters into the spirit [of a character] in such a way that you know that person." In an act of friendship toward Zweig's stepdaughter, the photographer Susanne Winternitz Hoeller, Toscanini gave her permission to publish a slender "photobiography" of him early in 1943—the same year in which two of Toscanini's other Austrian Jewish acquaintances, Max Reinhardt and Paul Stefan, died in New York. One of the latter's last projects had been a collaboration with the novelist Franz Werfel (who had also escaped to America, together with his wife, the former Alma Mahler) in compiling the book *Verdi, the Man in His Letters*; Toscanini later bought and inscribed a hundred copies and gave one to each member of the NBC Symphony, as a Christmas present in 1942.

Toscanini had offered to conduct, gratis, an extra Philharmonic performance of the Ninth Symphony, in May 1942, to benefit the Red Cross, but the event was canceled because the Philharmonic musicians' seasonal contract could not be further extended. He did, however, begin immediately to make other charitable, war-related contributions and gestures: he asked that his royalties from his NBC recording of "The Star-Spangled Banner" be turned over to the Red Cross; he signed an appeal for the arming of 200,000 Jews in Palestine who wished to form their own army to join the Allied war effort in North Africa; and he joined other well-known classical and popular musicians in authorizing some thirty of his recordings (short pieces, most of them recorded during live performances) to be released on twenty-five vinyl 78 rpm "V-Discs" (V for Victory) and given gratis to members of the Armed Forces. In addition, he participated in an initiative to create libraries of recordings for American troops scattered around the globe, by donating two 100-record units in 1942, two more in 1943, and a total of one hundred units by the end of the war; and he joined Eugene Ormandy and the members of the Philadelphia Orchestra in signing petitions to the US secretary of state Cordell Hull and the Spanish ambassador Juan Francisco de Cárdenas demanding "immediate amnesty or safe conduct to the Portuguese border" for the antifascist Pablo Casals, who was believed (incorrectly) to have been repatriated from occupied France to fascist

Spain, where he was a wanted man. He also sent many books from his own library—especially books that had been banned by the Fascists—to Italian prisoners of war who were being held in camps in the United States.

WHEN SARNOFF AND CHOTZINOFF asked Walter Toscanini to try to persuade his father to return to the NBC Symphony as principal conductor for the 1942–43 season, Walter did not have to exert much effort in his quest. Despite the maestro's occasional remarks to the contrary, he wanted to keep working as long as he felt up to the task—and where would he do that if not at NBC? He could not return to Europe; the NBC schedule was a relatively easy one; the fees he was paid were unmatchable; and he hated Stokowski's performances with what had been his own orchestra.* Stokowski, however, was under contract for two more seasons; thus, when Toscanini decided to return, the two men were billed as co-conductors in 1942–43 and 1943–44. Toscanini then became sole principal conductor.

In 1942, Dmitri Shostakovich completed a symphony that was described as having been inspired by the suffering and heroism of the people of Leningrad during the Germans' siege of the city—a siege that was still underway—and Stokowski had persuaded NBC to purchase the rights to the US premiere from the Am-Rus Music Corporation. The score was microfilmed in Russia and sent via a circuitous route to New York, by which time the executives of both NBC and Am-Rus had decided that they wanted Toscanini to conduct the premiere; he studied and quickly memorized the score and agreed to give the first performance. Stokowski, understandably piqued, asked him to cede the premiere to him, also because he, like Shostakovich, was of Slavic blood, but Toscanini replied that as one of the first artists "who strenuously fought against fascism" he felt that he could "conduct it simply with love and honesty" even though

---

* In October 1941, Toscanini had heard a radio broadcast of Franck's Symphony with the Philharmonic under Stokowski and had written a letter (in error-ridden English) to his colleague: "Never in my long life I have heard such a brutal, bestial, ignobil, unmusical performance like yours—not even from you. The Divine Art of Music too, has its own gangster like Hitler and Mussolini. . . . Believe me, you are ready for mad-house or for jail. . . . Hurry up!!!" The letter was never sent.

"I have not any drop of Slavonic blood into my veins." He was "deeply taken by [the symphony's] beauty" and "its antifascist meaning," he said.

Stokowski interpreted this in his own way: "I am glad you are willing for me to make the first radio broadcast," he wrote. Toscanini then pointed out that four years earlier he had "renounced to be the first interpreter [in America] of Shostakowitch 5th Symphony because of my scanty interest in it." (Stokowski had conducted the US premieres of the Fifth and Sixth Symphonies.) "Happily, you are much younger than me and Shostakowitch will not stop writing new symphonies," Toscanini wrote. "Be sure you will never find me again in your way." And he suggested that Stokowski let him know his programs for the forthcoming NBC season "so I shall adapt mine in accordance."

Amid great fanfare, Toscanini conducted the symphony's US premiere on 19 July 1942. A day earlier, he and various orchestra members had exchanged greetings with Shostakovich via radio and cable; the composer had expressed regret at not being present, and Toscanini had said, in what was obviously a statement prepared for him, "This glorious musical occasion guarantees the opening of new cultural relations between the United States and the U.S.S.R."* On the air, the performance of the symphony was preceded and followed by pleas for donations to the Russian War Relief organization.

Both Olin Downes in the *Times* and Virgil Thomson in the *Herald-Tribune* disliked the symphony. Toscanini would conduct it again in the fall, on a Philharmonic program, and then set it aside forever. Years later, after having listened to Steinberg's recording of the work, he asked himself, "How could I have conducted this *ugly* music?" Then he listened to his own recording "and I liked it again," he said. According to Solomon Volkov's book *Testimony*, which claims to contain Shostakovich's actual words, the composer hated Toscanini's recording of the Seventh Symphony and hated Toscanini's recordings of other repertoire as well. But Maxim Shostakovich, the composer's son, who at one point disputed the authenticity of

---

* A few weeks later, Toscanini sent Shostakovich an invitation, on behalf of the Philharmonic, to come to New York to guest conduct or appear as piano soloist with the orchestra, but the composer cabled his regrets.

Volkov's book, said specifically that those were not his father's opinions of Toscanini.

In an article in *Il Messaggero*, a Roman newspaper, Vittorio Mussolini, one of the Duce's sons, commented on Toscanini's contribution to the glorification of Shostakovich and the Russians: "Oh, you good Bolognese Fascist who, in days that have now been forgotten by too many people, gave him those sonorous slaps when he refused to play the national anthems, stirring up an enormous international clamor—why didn't you increase the dose that he so deserved, so as to render him permanently unable to work? You would have made it impossible for this Italian to debase Italy before the enemy today."

7.

DESPITE HIS SEVENTY-FIVE YEARS, TOSCANINI FELT THAT PREPARing and conducting twenty concerts, with fifteen different programs, during the 1941–42 season had not consumed enough of his energy, so between early October 1942 and mid-September 1943 he conducted thirty-four concerts—twenty-five different programs—with four different orchestras. He began the new season with his first performances, and the first complete performances in America during the twentieth century, of Berlioz's Dramatic Symphony, *Roméo et Juliette*, with the New York Philharmonic.* Horszowski described Toscanini at one performance as "a young man full of fire, ardor, wisdom, and experience." Later, in preparing an all-Wagner, Red Cross benefit program, also with the Philharmonic and with Helen Traubel as soloist, the maestro wanted to make sure that the event would raise at least $20,000, so he gave a blank check to Zirato to make up the difference, if necessary; in the end, he contributed about $1,000.

In a patriotic gesture, he initiated his 1942–43 NBC season on 1 November (the concerts now took place on Sundays, from 5:00 to 6:00 P.M.) with an all-American program—music by Charles Martin Loeffler, Paul Creston, Morton Gould, and George Gershwin (*Rhap-*

---

* The forty-two-year-old mezzo-soprano Jennie Tourel made her US debut with Toscanini in these performances. She had just arrived in New York, an unknown refugee from occupied France via Lisbon; this engagement launched her successful American career.

sody in Blue, with the renowned jazz clarinetist Benny Goodman and young American piano virtuoso Earl Wild). In a telegram to Deems Taylor, president of the American Society of Composers, Authors, and Publishers, Toscanini said that the program was "not only a gesture of friendship to this great country, but [. . .] a purely musical one, and I hope that younger conductors will continue to present more and more American music." Three months later, he led a second all-American program, with works by Henry F. Gilbert, Kent Kennan, Charles Tomlinson Griffes, and Ferde Grofé. Although his performances of music by American composers remained rare, he was awarded a citation by the National Association for American Composers and Conductors, for his "outstanding service to American music."

Other features of his NBC season included his first performance of Dmitri Kabalevsky's Symphony no. 2, a six-concert Brahms cycle that concluded with the *German Requiem*, two all-Verdi concerts, an all-Bizet concert, and three programs consisting of mainly short, light pieces. He ended the program of 31 January 1943 with Verdi's *Hymn of the Nations*, which he had conducted in Milan during the First World War; the piece included quotations of "God Save the King," "La Marseillaise," and the Italian "Mameli Hymn," and Toscanini now amended it to end with "The Star-Spangled Banner." He also caused a *Times* editorialist to comment, gleefully, that "Arturo Toscanini, beaten by Mussolini's blackguards in 1931 because he had disobeyed their master's order to play the Fascist hymn, took a neat and subtle revenge" by instructing the tenor Jan Peerce and the Westminster Choir to change the phrase "O Italia, o patria mia" (O Italy, o my country) to "O Italia, o patria mia tradita" (O Italy, o my betrayed country).

By chance, that concert was contemporaneous with the publication of *What to Do with Italy*, a short book by Salvemini and La Piana about the anticipated post-Fascist political struggle; it was dedicated "To Maestro Arturo Toscanini, who, in the darkest days of Fascist crimes, Italy's shame, and world madness, uncompromisingly clung to the ideals of Mazzini and Garibaldi and with tenacious faith anticipated the dawn of the second Italian Risorgimento."

The British conductor Eugene Goossens, music director of the Cincinnati Symphony Orchestra, had told Toscanini that his ensemble was in danger of collapsing for lack of money and had invited the maestro to conduct a pair of fund-raising concerts in the city on the Ohio River. Toscanini accepted the invitation, and despite having come down with the flu, he gamely made the trip by train, with Carla and Walter in tow. Goossens had drilled his troops in advance; they responded excellently, and the enthusiastically received performances helped to muster civic support for the orchestra.* Happiest of all, it seems, was the Sicilian chef at the city's Netherland Plaza Hotel, who was thrilled to prepare whatever foods the most famous Italian in America desired. To counterbalance the glasses of milk and orange juice that Dr. Howe had ordered for Toscanini, the chef also provided doses of red wine as medicine for the maestro's spirits.

It was no surprise, given Toscanini's punishing schedule and advancing age, that the flu did not quickly disappear. Late in February, he conducted a pair of concerts with the Philadelphia Orchestra, but by the end of the second evening he was feeling so ill that he canceled planned performances with the same orchestra in Washington and Baltimore as well as a special concert with the NBC Symphony at the Naval Air Training Base in Lakehurst, New Jersey. Late in March, however, he led his NBC musicians in a Beethoven-Brahms-Wagner concert at Carnegie Hall for the benefit of the National Foundation for Infantile Paralysis—a deed for which President Roosevelt, a victim of the disease, sent him a personal letter of thanks. "The crippled children for whose sake you gave us an evening of inspiring music shall never forget you," the president wrote. "The magnificent contributions you have made to the world of music have always been highlighted by your humanitarian and unyielding devotion to the cause of liberty." Toscanini replied that the president's words were "the highest recompense that we could have hoped for" and that he would "continue unabated on the same path that I have trod all my life for the cause of liberty."

Always eager to avoid fanfare, Toscanini spent his seventy-sixth birthday quietly at home with his family. Walter had just been pro-

---

* Toscanini had planned to return to Ohio the following December, to conduct a pair of concerts (including the premiere of a work by the Russian American Nikolai Lopatnikoff) with the Cleveland Orchestra, but in September he canceled the engagement, pleading ill health and depression over the war situation in Italy—neither of which prevented him from carrying out his regular duties in New York.

moted from RCA's press division to NBC's music division and had moved, with Cia and Walfredo, from Haddonfield, New Jersey, to a house in Riverdale, New York, near his parents. Arturo and Carla's unrenewable three-year lease on Villa Pauline had recently expired, and they had moved into the nearby Wave Hill house, which had been a residence of Theodore Roosevelt and, later, of Mark Twain. Carla's health was beginning to decline: although she was ten years younger than her husband, she was considerably overweight and suffered from high blood pressure and other ailments. Everyone who knew the family well realized that someone close to the maestro and his wife—preferably one of their children—would have to be available to assist them. Wally was caught in war-torn Europe, and Wanda was involved full-time with her self-absorbed husband. That left Walter, who had valued his independence while he was living at a safe remove from his father and mother but who understood that they would become increasingly dependent on him. A year earlier, his parents had given him power of attorney, and as time went by more and more responsibilities were loaded onto his shoulders.

Toscanini père resumed his NBC Symphony concerts on 4 April 1943. The following week, his program included the US premiere of the overture to Kabalevsky's opera *Colas Breugnon*, and on the twenty-fifth he gave another benefit concert at Carnegie: seats for the all-Tchaikovsky program could be obtained only by purchasing US government war bonds, of which over $10 million were sold. Toscanini went in person to the Fifth Avenue office of the War Savings Staff to buy $50,000 in bonds, with which he reserved a box for his family. During the intermission—between the "Pathétique" Symphony and the First Piano Concerto, with Horowitz as soloist—the manuscript of Toscanini's orchestration of "The Star-Spangled Banner" was sold at auction for another $1 million in war bonds. Then, between mid-June and mid-September, he conducted, gratis, the NBC Summer Symphony in four one-hour special broadcasts, to promote over-the-air war bonds sales; seats in Studio 8H were reserved entirely for men and women in uniform.

In preparing one of those broadcasts—an all-Verdi program—Toscanini had asked the mezzo-soprano Nan Merriman, whom he had heard in a short radio broadcast, to audition for him. She brought along a copy of "O don fatale," from *Don Carlo*, handed it to Artur

Balsam, the NBC Symphony's principal keyboard player, and began to sing. She did not know that her edition of the aria had been transposed down a tone and a half. After the first few notes had been played, Toscanini jumped up from his seat shouting, "Non è giusto!" (It's not right!). He pushed Balsam away and began to play the piece in the correct key. "Somehow or other I found the strength to sing the aria to the end," Merriman said. "The Maestro liked it and had enough faith in me to sign me up immediately for his Verdi program."

Merriman, only twenty-three at the time, became one of the singers Toscanini relied on most during the last decade of his career. "I don't understand why some people insist on saying that it was very difficult to work with Toscanini," she later said. "He was as solid and secure as a rock, patient with every singer who was willing to work seriously enough and long enough. He understood the voice better than any other conductor with whom I had occasion to work; he knew exactly when to leave time for the singers for issues of breath control, and he was extremely understanding of any momentary vocal difficulty."

That Verdi concert took place on 25 July 1943. Toscanini had just left the stage with the soprano Gertrude Ribla after a performance of the aria "Pace, pace, mio Dio," from *La Forza del Destino*, when an announcement was broadcast into the hall and over the air: Mussolini had been deposed, but King Victor Emanuel had declared that Italy would fight on and had appointed Marshal Pietro Badoglio prime minister. Toscanini was shaken; he appeared nervous as he stepped onto the podium to conduct the last excerpt on the program—the final act of *Rigoletto*—but at the end of the concert, the audience rose to applaud and cheer him.

8.

NO SOONER HAD MUSSOLINI'S FALL FROM POWER BEEN ANNOUNCED than printed posters appeared on La Scala's external signboards: "Evviva Toscanini, Ritorni Toscanini." Rome radio broadcast the maestro's recording of Beethoven's Fifth Symphony, and Italian newspapers published a cable from Italy's new minister of education, inviting Toscanini to come home.

The following day, Toscanini called a special NBC Symphony rehearsal. He wrongly assumed that Italy would immediately surrender to and then join the Allies, and he wanted to be ready with a special concert to mark "the beginning of the end" of the war. But disappointment quickly set in. While the king and Badoglio dithered over the terms of a possible armistice with the Allies, the Germans, who understood that their alliance with Italy was about to end, began to move massive forces into the country. At the same time, the Allies continued to exert pressure on the new Italian government by bombing the industrial cities of the north; one of the incendiary bombs went through La Scala's roof, leaving the stage area intact but half destroying the auditorium. Italy was about to enter the most difficult phase of the war and to suffer the greatest physical devastation in its turbulent history.

Toscanini and other leading Italian exiles considered the king, who had unresistingly left Italy in Mussolini's hands for over two decades, at least as guilty of Fascist crimes as the Fascists themselves, and they were distressed that the Allies had agreed to negotiate not only with Victor Emanuel but also with Badoglio, who had supported Mussolini's military adventures. In August, Salvemini and La Piana drafted a letter to Roosevelt and sent it to Walter Toscanini; they wanted the letter to be sent over Arturo Toscanini's prestigious signature. The maestro made many insertions and deletions, and a decision was made to transform the document into an open letter "To the People of America," to be printed in the 13 September 1943 issue of *Life*.

In the article, Toscanini described himself as "an old artist who has been among the first to denounce Fascism to the world. I feel and believe that I can act as interpreter of the soul of the Italian people—those people whose voice has been choked for more than 20 years [. . .]." He said that the king and Badoglio were "bound by the alliance with Germany, which they endorsed jointly with Mussolini. They cannot be dissociated in any way from the militarist and fascist clique." An Italian revolution was foreseen "as a result of the current war," and were the revolution to "result in an orderly democratic government, as we hope, it will be necessary for the Allies to support all democratic elements currently arrayed against the King and Badoglio."

On 8 September, just as the issue of *Life* was appearing on news-stands, Badoglio and his government signed an armistice with the Allies. At first, the anti-Fascist exiles hoped that the compromised politicians would be replaced by people who had opposed the regime, and on the day after the armistice Toscanini at last conducted the special, half-hour NBC Symphony broadcast that he had planned more than six weeks earlier. "Victory, Act I"—his name for it—consisted of the first movement of the Beethoven Fifth (he would conduct the whole symphony when Germany was defeated, he said) plus Rossini's *William Tell* Overture, the "Garibaldi Hymn," and "The Star-Spangled Banner." To the press the maestro declared that he was "overwhelmed with joy" that Italy was at last "free to join the Allies, who are struggling to keep alive the name of liberty in the world." But then the truth sank in: the Allied leaders, including Stalin, would continue to accept Badoglio and the king as interlocutors.

The Mazzini Society broke up: Count Sforza, Tarchiani, and their faction accepted the compromise, but Salvemini, Toscanini, and other hard-liners continued to protest. When Sforza, who would again become foreign minister in postwar Italy, wrote to Toscanini to explain why he believed that the Allies were right to deal with the powers already in place, Toscanini sent a typically unequivocal reply:

From this moment on you may consider me a traitor to my country! Not even to save Italy could I compromise with the people who have shamefully betrayed her for more than twenty years! [. . .] Your politics may be intelligent and shrewd, but I condemn them and despise them—and I declare myself against you and the Allied government, which has fully demonstrated its complete ignorance and ineptitude [. . .]. Their policy regarding Italy has been a shameful fiasco—and, as Dorothy Thompson* says, completely bankrupt. Their *"unconditional surrender"* is ridiculous. And now they want to put the anti-fascist forces into the hands of those who have betrayed them for long and, alas! such sorrowful years! [. . .] One must stand on one side of

---

* Thompson was an influential liberal American journalist and an early opponent of Nazism. She was a great Toscanini admirer, and he read her columns regularly.

the fence or the other! Either for the King and Badoglio or against them—there is no other way.

Armando Borghi, a leading Italian anarchist and anti-Fascist exile, who had been arrested in New York in 1940 but then released—thanks largely to the intervention of Salvemini and the Toscaninis, father and son—later commented on the maestro's 1943 stand against the compromisers: "He was a thousand times stronger than we others, who acted with 'political' preparation and premeditation. [. . .] In that hour Toscanini openly ranked himself against compromise and against the compromise brokers."*

Vito Marcantonio, an Italian American congressman from New York, wrote to Toscanini in June 1944, requesting that he testify before a subcommittee of the House of Representatives in favor of reestablishing normal diplomatic relations between the United States and Italy. Toscanini responded at length, stressing "in the strongest way possible that until now the Italian people have not been free to have a democratically chosen government representative of every political current in Italy. [. . .] I can stand as a witness that the monarchy in Italy has always tried to oppose any social reform or any progressive attempt to better and improve the life of the worker and farmer in Italy, and that all the progressive reforms that were introduced in Italy were always a conquest by the people after long struggles, fights, strikes and bloody repressions." Toscanini said that he would not support Marcantonio's proposal unless and until Italy's regime change was completed. And on 22 June, *Life* carried a long article, "An Italian Manifesto," cosigned by Salvemini, Toscanini, and four other leading Italian exiles, who once again urged the British and Americans to stop supporting the king and Badoglio.

The Allies, aided by Italian partisans, fought their way up the peninsula, against tremendous German resistance, and the country was "mishandled and massacred by enemies and friends alike," as Toscanini wrote to Wally. She and Emanuela, together with the Polos and

---

* Toscanini was impressed with Borghi's abilities as a public speaker. "Once he asked me: 'How are you able to speak while facing the audience?'" Borghi recalled. "I answered that without looking at the audience I wouldn't know how to open my mouth. He said to me: 'If I didn't show my tail to my audience, I couldn't conduct.'"

a few other family members and friends, had taken refuge on the Toscaninis' farm at Ripalta Guerina, but when the German army, abetted by Italian Fascists, moved into the area, an informer warned Wally that she would be arrested because she was Arturo Toscanini's daughter. Reports that she had been deported were published in some American newspapers, but in fact she and ten-year-old Emanuela had escaped on foot and by horse-drawn cart—hiding at times in ditches—across the border into Switzerland, where they remained for the duration of the war; fortunately, the US State Department had sent the maestro and Carla news of their loved ones' escape to safety before the incorrect newspaper reports appeared. Emanuela attended a Swiss boarding school for the duration, and Wally became involved in various refugee aid organizations.*

9.

TOSCANINI CONSIDERED RETURNING TO THE MIDDLE EAST IN JANU-ary 1944 to conduct the Palestine Orchestra in concerts for Allied troops in Egypt, but his family and Dr. Howe persuaded him not to undertake what would have been a long, exhausting, and risky trip. He would stay put until the war came to an end.

The regular portion of his 1943–44 NBC Symphony season consisted of six weekly concerts between late October and early December and six more in March and April. NBC was no longer financing the series as a "public service"; instead, General Motors sponsored the broadcasts, at the first of which a performance of Haydn's Symphony no. 104 ("London") was followed by a talk about the building of the Panama Canal, read to the studio audience and over the airwaves by someone sitting at a table in the middle of Studio 8H's

---

* Wally and Emanuele Castelbarco had separated before her flight to Switzerland with their daughter. Many years later Wally told this writer that when her father found out about the separation, he began to preach about having warned her not to become involved with an aristocrat who had left his wife and who, moreover, was blond! She replied that the relationship had endured for a quarter of a century, which seemed to demonstrate that it was not merely a superficial fling; Toscanini did not raise the subject again. But he probably never knew that in Switzerland his daughter had had an affair with Allen Dulles, part of the Allied team that was negotiating Germany's surrender, and future founding director of the CIA.

stage. The talk ran on at such length that the last piece on the program, Beethoven's Eighth Symphony, was cut off the air before it had ended. Subsequent programs were timed better. New to Toscanini's repertoire were Gershwin's *An American in Paris* and Piano Concerto in F (the latter with Oscar Levant as soloist), the Sixth Symphony of the Swedish composer Kurt Atterberg, and the Prelude to Mussorgsky's *Khovanshchina*. Horszowski played Mozart's Piano Concerto in B-flat Major, K. 595, on one concert; on another, Heifetz was the soloist in the Mendelssohn Violin Concerto. An all-Russian program on 7 November—another tribute to the Soviet ally—coincided with the anniversary of the Bolshevik Revolution: it began with "The Internationale," continued with Toscanini's first performances of Anatoly Liadov's *Kikimora* and Glinka's *Jota Aragonesa*, and concluded with his only performance of Vasily Kalinnikov's First Symphony.

The maestro conducted "The Internationale" again on 8 and 20 December 1943, when he made a film at the request of the US Office of War Information (OWI). *Hymn of the Nations*, a thirty-minute propaganda film, was to be sent to the liberated portions of Italy, to demonstrate how anti-Fascist exiles were living and working in America, planning for the day when democracy would return to their native country. It begins straightaway with Toscanini and the NBC Symphony performing the Overture to *La Forza del Destino*. Toscanini, who does not speak in the movie, is then seen at his Wave Hill home, playing a record of the "Garibaldi Hymn" for fourteen-year-old Walfredo. There are brief cuts of other Italian exiles—Salvemini, Borgese, Pacciardi, Giuseppe Lupis (editor of the New York–based newspaper *Il Mondo*), and Father Luigi Sturzo (founder of the liberal Catholic party that had been banned by Mussolini and that became the Christian Democratic Party after the war.)* There is a reenactment of the moment when the news of Mussolini's fall from power reached the NBC newsroom, and Toscanini is then shown at the piano, editing the score of Verdi's *Hymn of the Nations* to include "The Internationale" and "The Star-Spangled Banner." The film con-

---

* At war's end, Sturzo, who was respected even by anticlericalists like the Toscaninis, would carry on an intense correspondence with Walter Toscanini about organizing massive relief operations for the devastated population of Italy.

cludes with a performance of the entire cantata, with Jan Peerce as soloist and Toscanini conducting the Westminster Choir and the NBC Symphony. The actor Burgess Meredith narrated the English-language version of the soundtrack.

Both pieces of music were filmed several times as they were being played, until Toscanini approved a version of each. Then, for various close-ups of him, of Peerce, and of sections of the orchestra and chorus, he had to conduct to playback. He found that frustrating at first, but he gradually took an interest in the process. According to several people involved in the production, he asked questions of the technicians, chatted during breaks with them and with his musicians, watched attentively as a stand-in—a gray-haired man of similar height and build—stood on the podium so that the camera crew could prepare the various takes, and even appeared to enjoy himself. He was "a real trooper," one of the technicians claimed, and the producers were impressed that the maestro's complexion was so smooth that he required no makeup.

When Toscanini was given a private showing of the completed film, he covered his eyes every time a close-up of his face appeared on the screen. But *Hymn of the Nations* was shown with great success not only in Italy but also in England, Switzerland, and other countries. The composer Marc Blitzstein, who was in charge of the American Broadcasting Station in Europe as the Allies were preparing to invade German-occupied France, had the film's soundtrack transferred to discs and beamed into France, the Netherlands, Norway, Denmark, and even Germany; the music alternated with instructions from the Supreme Headquarters of the Allied Expeditionary Force "concerning the coming invasion and the role [citizens] were to play in it," Blitzstein reported. "By devious methods we learned that the response to the music was electric." The BBC then borrowed the recording, which "began a second war career. I say without fear of contradiction that the Toscanini sound track provided the most potent single musical weapon of World War II," Blitzstein declared.

After the war, the film was at first banned in France because Toscanini was Italian and Italy had stabbed France in the back in 1940. But the French press protested ("There are Italians and Italians," wrote *Le Franc-Tireur*), and the ban was lifted. In postwar

America, it was shown as a short in various commercial cinemas; at the Little Carnegie in New York, for instance, it ran for fifteen weeks in 1946. Today, it is significant as the oldest extant audiovisual example of Toscanini at work; although some of the footage was shot to playback, *Hymn of the Nations* provides a fine view of the maestro's intense but never flamboyant conducting style, which George Szell aptly described as "deceptively simple."[*]

In addition to working on the film, Toscanini, during the three-month break in his regular NBC season, joined the temporary board of trustees of a committee for war relief for Italy—part of the President's War Relief Control Board. Reports from northern Italy indicated that some anti-Fascist organizations intended to propose Toscanini for the first presidency of Italy if and when it became a republic, but the maestro told family and friends that he would never accept such a position.

He attended, on 11 January 1944, the American premiere of Prokofiev's Seventh Piano Sonata, played by Horowitz for an invited audience at the Soviet consulate in New York. On 6 February, Toscanini conducted an all-Beethoven concert for the Philadelphia Orchestra's pension fund—his only performance outside New York that season and his last concert with the Philadelphians.[†] But he never forgot that orchestra's fine players. Once, when he was having dinner at a New York restaurant, he noticed the principal trumpet, Saul Caston, sitting at another table, wolfing down his food. Caston was surprised when a waiter brought him a menu with some bars of the March from *Tannhäuser* written on it: he understood that someone had observed the velocity of his eating. He looked around and was astonished to see Toscanini laughing at him.

Following the regular NBC Symphony season, Toscanini conducted two benefit performances, for which he once again contributed his services gratis. The first—a huge program (the Brahms First, Tchaikovsky Sixth, and Beethoven Fifth Symphonies) with the NBC musicians at Carnegie Hall on 18 April 1944—raised over

---

[*] Upon viewing that film in 1976, Carlos Kleiber commented to this writer, "It's amazing how much he does, doing so little."

[†] He was to have conducted another pension fund concert with the orchestra in April 1945, but he canceled the appearance.

$6,400,000 in war bonds. The second, an extraordinary event to assist the Red Cross, took place on 25 May before an audience of 18,000 at Madison Square Garden. During the first half of the concert, the combined NBC Symphony and New York Philharmonic—the assemblage a spectacle in itself—performed pieces by Wagner, and in the second part the NBC players performed the final act of *Rigoletto*, with Milanov (Gilda), Merriman (Maddalena), Peerce (the Duke), Leonard Warren (Rigoletto), and Moscona (Sparafucile). This was followed by the *Hymn of the Nations*, performed by both orchestras, with Peerce and a 600-voice choral ensemble made up of 250 members of the All-City Chorus and 350 singers from eight New York City high school glee clubs. The moving event ended with "The Star-Spangled Banner" and Sousa's march "Stars and Stripes Forever."

Dr. Howe had made a thirty-six-inch-long baton for Toscanini to conduct the massed forces: he needed the special stick in order to be seen by all the musicians and to feel the weight of the ensemble, he said, but he also joked that he felt as if he were conducting with a tree trunk. At the end, Mayor La Guardia auctioned the baton; the highest bidder paid $11,000 for it. Ticket sales raised $100,000, and copies of the souvenir program autographed by the maestro were given to the first hundred people who donated $100 each to the Red Cross.*

DURING THE SUMMER OF 1944, while the fighting in Europe raged on, Toscanini once again conducted, gratis, four NBC Symphony broadcast concerts of relatively light repertoire, the first two in support of the war bonds drive, the others to be beamed to Allied servicemen overseas. On 22 October, he began his regular NBC season, during which he would once again lead sixteen concerts, as he had done in earlier seasons—although the programs were now only sixty minutes long, as opposed to the original ninety-minute format.

Apart from a special Rossini-Verdi concert, not broadcast, at New York's City Center on 31 October, the first half of the maestro's por-

---

* Why such a discrepancy between the thousands raised for the Red Cross and the millions raised for war bonds? Because money for the Red Cross was a donation; money for war bonds was an investment: a bond costing $18.75 would yield $25 in ten years.

tion of the season was entirely occupied by an eight-concert Beethoven series that ended with a two-part broadcast of *Fidelio*, with Rose Bampton in the title role, Jan Peerce as Florestan, and Eleanor Steber, Herbert Janssen, and Nicola Moscona in other key parts. This was the first of what would become a series of unstaged Toscanini-NBC opera broadcasts. During the Beethoven cycle, Toscanini had his sole professional encounter with Arthur Rubinstein when they performed the Third Piano Concerto together, and the maestro was so pleased with it that he insisted that RCA publish a live recording of it. Rubinstein said that during a first run-through of the piece with the orchestra, his interpretation and Toscanini's had been completely at odds, but that a second run-through had gone perfectly because during the first one Toscanini had memorized Rubinstein's every nuance. The recording does not seem to back up Rubinstein's rosy recollection; nevertheless, Toscanini gave his soloist an autographed photo "in remembrance of the unforgettable date (October 29 – 1944) of our first artistic meeting." Their first artistic meeting proved to be their last as well, although the esteem remained mutual.

In addition to conducting eight regular broadcasts and numerous recording sessions with the NBC Symphony during the first half of 1945, Toscanini also led the orchestra in a benefit concert for the National Foundation for Infantile Paralysis; conducted a pension fund concert for the New York Philharmonic (the program was an exact replica of the one he had conducted at his first appearance with the orchestra nineteen years earlier, and the concert would prove to be his last one with his old ensemble); and gave his only concert with a West Coast orchestra—the Los Angeles Philharmonic—to initiate a pension fund for the orchestra's musicians. During this last event, in the middle of the Weber-Berlioz *Invitation to the Dance*, a barefoot young woman dressed in black slacks and shirtwaist ran onto the stage and began to dance in front of the orchestra. Toscanini stopped the piece and looked on with surprise and amusement as the woman danced into the arms of a backstage policeman. The concert continued normally, and Helen Favill, who claimed to have studied dance with Ruth St. Denis and Ted Shawn, told doctors at a psychiatric hospital that she couldn't resist Toscanini's music and "needed only one invitation to the dance." She was released.

———

LATE IN APRIL 1945, Italian partisans shot and killed Mussolini near Lake Como, and Hitler committed suicide in his bunker in Berlin. On 8 May, the historic date of the end of the war in Europe, Toscanini conducted his "Victory, Part II" broadcast—a complete performance of the Beethoven Fifth with the NBC Symphony. A week earlier, he had received the transcript of a message broadcast from Milan on Italy's national radio network: "The Italians have not forgotten Toscanini. They are thankful to him for his noble work for Italian art. Maestro, you will not hear this broadcast, but an echo will certainly reach you. Do hear in it the loving appeal sent to you by all Italians to return to your Milan. This appeal is addressed to you firstly by all the members of the Scala orchestra."

Toscanini resisted. "I have been near you with all my heart throughout these sorrowful years of struggle, of mourning, and of despair," he replied. "But the tens of thousands of Italian patriots who fell heroically alongside the Allied soldiers in this war, the decisiveness and discipline demonstrated by you Milanese in the hour of revolt, the inexorable and rapid execution of the major Fascist criminals, make me certain that the republican ideals of Cattaneo, Garibaldi, and Mazzini will all be fully actuated by you and by the Italian people. Every vestige of the ignominious past and of betrayal must disappear. [. . .] I shall be happy to return among you as a citizen of a free Italy, but not as a subject of the degenerate king and the princes of the House of Savoy."

It was Walter Toscanini who, with considerable difficulty, had persuaded his seventy-eight-year-old father not to rush back to war-ravaged Italy. He had worked out a twofold plan that he hoped would keep his father safe and simultaneously resolve the mess that his mother had made, and that Walter had recently discovered, of his parents' finances. The elder Toscanini was still earning large sums of money from conducting, but there was no guarantee that he would be able to go on much longer. Walter reasoned that if he could bring his father around to the idea of making more records, now that the musicians' union's recording ban had ended, his parents would have a guaranteed average annual gross income from royalties of approximately $100,000—a deluxe life insurance policy.* At the same time, he wanted to create a Toscanini Foundation, Inc., into which his father would deposit substantial portions of his earnings, "not for profit but exclusively for educational, musical, literary, scientific, and charitable purposes," especially in Italy and other European countries. Walter explained to Margherita De Vecchi's lawyer,

> It is useless for him to return to Italy for benefit concerts which would only net a 1000 or a million Italian liras when the lira is worth nothing. [. . .] I continually restrained him from following his first impulse of returning to Italy. But I must give him a goal and a worthwhile reason for his remaining here. You know that father is not interested in money but in ideas. A Toscanini Foundation could be that idea which would anchor him to this country, or to bring him back here, if by any chance he decided to make a brief visit to Italy.
>
> [. . .] I have letters from English committees asking him to give concerts there for the benefit of Queens Hall in London, which was completely destroyed by bombs. Salzburg is expecting him; Holland is waiting for him to revamp their musical life; Paris is planning big things with his support; Switzerland wants to resume the [Lucerne] Festival to help refugees and revive their tourist trade. It is very difficult for him to refuse all this. It is harder for me to explain to him that a man 78 years old cannot suffer the hardships of traveling in Europe when everything has been wrecked [. . .].
>
> I have in mind something that would reflect the human side of my father's character which is, in my opinion, greater than his musicianship. I want this to be an American Foundation with a deep sense of understanding for the human problems that beset all the little people who have devoted their lives to music and who are now to be the first victims of the various political crises in their countries. [. . .]

---

* Toscanini's royalties on recordings had skyrocketed from less than $1,000 in 1939 to more than $87,000 in 1942; in 1944, as a result of the recording ban, they had dipped to under $54,000—still an enormous sum for the day—but Walter knew that with the recent lifting of the ban the earnings would rise again if his father would agree to make more records.

Despite Walter's good intentions, the foundation would never materialize, but in the course of the 1944–45 season, Toscanini and his orchestra spent a total of eleven days making recordings of a wide range of music. And when the maestro learned that Wally and Emanuela would soon be allowed to travel to the United States (they arrived at the end of July, after many delays), he confirmed his decision not to return to Italy while it was still a monarchy.

ON 1 SEPTEMBER 1945, the official end of the war with Japan, Toscanini conducted the "Eroica" Symphony as his "Victory, Part III" contribution, and the following day he opened his 1945–46 NBC season (the third to be sponsored by General Motors), which again consisted of sixteen regular broadcasts, but, this time, only two days of recordings sessions. A special, all-Beethoven benefit concert—including a performance of the Ninth Symphony—for the Italian Welfare League, to help Italian war orphans, took place at Carnegie Hall on 25 September. Mayor La Guardia and Alberto Tarchiani, who had become Italy's ambassador to the United States, went to visit Toscanini in his dressing room afterward, but he would not receive them: Tarchiani had compromised with the king and Badoglio.

That performance of the Ninth gave the twenty-nine-year-old, California-born Robert Shaw his first opportunity to prepare a chorus for Toscanini, who came to consider Shaw the finest choral director with whom he had ever collaborated. Shaw later told B. H. Haggin that he had gone to Riverdale beforehand to look over the score with Toscanini, and he had asked the maestro for permission to have some tenors beef up the lower alto parts. "He said: 'Will it make the score sound?'" Shaw recalled. "I said: 'Maestro, I think this is the only way it *can* be made to sound.' And he said: 'Anything which makes the score sound is right.' Then he said: 'You know, I have never had a good performance of this work. Sometimes the chorus is bad; sometimes the orchestra is bad; many times the soloists are bad. And many times *I* am terrible.'"

The only compositions new to Toscanini's repertoire that year were all performed on the concert of 25 November: two were by Italian Jewish émigrés in America (Castelnuovo-Tedesco's *Overture to a Fairy Tale* and Vittorio Rieti's *Sinfonia Tripartita*), and two others came from native New Yorkers (Paul Creston's *Frontiers* and Elie Siegmeister's "Western" Suite); all except the Creston piece were premieres. But each of the season's guest conductors led contemporary works that were not in Toscanini's repertoire: Erich Kleiber, for instance, conducted Stravinsky's recent *Scènes de Ballet* and Alberto Ginastera's *Panambí*; Dimitri Mitropoulos performed Prokofiev's Third Piano Concerto and Berg's Violin Concerto; and a young Leonard Bernstein conducted Marc Blitzstein's "Airborne" Symphony.

A major event was Toscanini's two-part NBC concert performance of *La Bohème* on 3 and 10 February 1946, for the fiftieth anniversary of the work's premiere; the cast included Licia Albanese (Mimì), Peerce (Rodolfo), Anne McKnight (Musetta), Francesco Valentino (Marcello), Moscona (Colline), and George Cehanovsky (Schaunard). The performance was recorded live and is the only extant Toscanini recording of a complete Puccini opera.* Concert versions of operas, in which the singers stand directly in front of the conductor, tend to be more tightly controlled than staged ones, in which there is more give-and-take between stage and pit, and that is certainly the case with this performance. Yet there can be little doubt that the recording gives the best extant idea of the work as Puccini had conceived it and as Toscanini conducted it many times in the composer's approving presence. The emotional significance of the event, too, affected Toscanini: during the performance, "tears were coming down his face," Peerce recalled; "it wasn't put on: nobody saw it, just us." More than one music critic commented on the sad fact that Toscanini had not conducted a staged opera performance in America since his departure from the Metropolitan thirty-one years earlier, and suggested, in vain, that the situation be rectified.

---

* The performance of the Intermezzo and complete third act of *Manon Lescaut* conducted by Toscanini at his first postwar concert at La Scala is equally valuable as a powerful lesson in the interpretation of Puccini's music (especially since Puccini's enthusiasm for Toscanini's performances of *Manon* is thoroughly documented), although the acoustic quality of the recording is execrable.

10.

BEFORE WALLY'S LONG-ANTICIPATED TRIP TO NEW YORK, WHERE she and Emanuela were able to embrace the rest of their family after a separation of six years, Toscanini had authorized his elder daughter to donate $10,000 toward the reconstruction of La Scala's auditorium. The maestro was so eager to get back to his homeland that late in August 1945, when word came that La Scala would be ready for concerts by the following February, he made up his mind to return. The news that Clement Attlee's Labour Party had ousted Churchill's Tories from power in Britain persuaded him that movements for social reform were sweeping across Europe, and the promise of a referendum in Italy on the fate of the monarchy caused him to decide that he could go home even though Victor Emanuel III was still on the throne.

So great were the complications involved in rebuilding the theater that the opening was postponed by three months.* But at last, on 21 April 1946, Arturo, Carla, and Walter Toscanini boarded a plane for Geneva, bringing along replacement strings for the entire Scala orchestra's string section and a trunk-load of printed music. From Geneva they traveled by train to the Swiss-Italian border at Ponte Chiasso, where they were met by Wally and Emanuela (who had since returned to Europe), some old friends, and Antonio Ghiringhelli, La Scala's special commissioner.

Escorted by US Army vehicles, the Toscaninis crossed into their native country for the first time since October 1938. They were driven quickly through Milan, where glimpses of the destruction shocked them: most of the rubble from the 1943 bombings and the 1944–45 street fighting had been cleared away, but nearly 75 percent of the buildings in the city's center had been damaged or destroyed.

---

* The Allied Military Government was providing moral and material assistance for the house's reconstruction, and Lieutenant Clement C. Petrillo, a thirty-one-year-old American who had been a piano teacher before the war, was put in charge. He had been the US Army's representative in negotiating the surrender of SS troops in Milan the previous spring, but, he told the *New York Times*, the intrigue in Italy's opera world was such that dealing with the Nazis had been "child's play compared with this La Scala assignment."

Although the house in Via Durini had been spared, it was not yet inhabitable; thus the Toscaninis proceeded to their farm at Ripalta Guerina. Ghiringhelli went with them, so that he and Toscanini could begin to discuss La Scala's reopening concert. The orchestra and chorus had to be partly reconstituted (Toscanini insisted that people who had been forced out on political or "racial" grounds— including the chorus's Jewish conductor, Vittore Veneziani—be reinstated), and decisions had to be made about programs and other conductors for the first series of concerts. On the twenty-seventh, Toscanini paid his first visit to La Scala in sixteen years. As he walked from the stage entrance into the auditorium, a staff member offered to hang up his hat for him. "Thank you," he replied, "but I'm not the prima donna—and I'm not even the baritone."

He pronounced the restoration excellent, although in reality some of the hastily done work was not as good as it ought to have been, to the detriment of the auditorium's acoustics, and would not be repaired for over half a century. Toscanini selected an all-Italian program for the opening concert, which would begin with Rossini (the Overture to *La Gazza Ladra*, three excerpts from *William Tell*, and the Prayer from Act III of *Mosè*); proceed with Verdi (the Overture and the "Va, pensiero" chorus from *Nabucco*, symbolic of Italy's release from oppression, as well as the *Te Deum* from the Four Sacred Pieces); continue, after the intermission, with Puccini (the Intermezzo and Act III from *Manon Lescaut*) and Verdi again (the Overture to *I Vespri Siciliani*); and conclude with Boito (the Prologue to *Mefistofele*). Four of his singers from the 1920s—the soprano Mafalda Favero, tenor Giuseppe Nessi, baritone Mariano Stabile, and bass Tancredi Pasero—were chosen to participate; for the role of Des Grieux in *Manon*, he selected Giovanni Malipiero; and for the Rossini Prayer, he auditioned and engaged a twenty-four-year-old soprano, Renata Tebaldi, who, he said, had "the voice of an angel"—a description that would be applied to her for the rest of her extraordinary career.

As parts of the theater were still unusable, Toscanini rehearsed the soloists at his home in Via Durini, which had been rendered livable, and at the Palazzo dello Sport. "I didn't have the nerve to walk along the streets of Milan!" he wrote a few months later. "The view was too sorrowful to bear." He called the first orchestra rehearsal for 2 May but then postponed it by a day: he wanted to meet first with his orchestra in La Scala's Sala Gialla (Yellow Hall), where he and his former players embraced and wept openly, and where he shook hands with the newer members.

Enrico Minetti, still the orchestra's concertmaster, later recalled that he and the other older players had described to their younger colleagues Toscanini's "artistic intransigence, inflexible will, faithful and pure dedication to music, and (why not?) his outbursts, his nerves, the scenes and—our fear!" The rehearsals began in a friendly atmosphere; Toscanini

> even smiled a few times. A real idyll! The young men, in ecstasy, looked at us almost with sympathy. Was this [. . .] the terror of orchestras? But it was a matter of time: little by little the Maestro's observations became rather more authoritative, more incisive, less kindly; the invitations to "make an effort," the exhortations to "sweat," were peremptory, accompanied by the well-known gesture of the accusatory index finger; and his glances began to delve again into our eyes and into our hearts. We again saw a few scores fly into the beautiful new auditorium, and (nothing new under the sun) more than one handkerchief was pitilessly torn up and many batons were broken and thrown to the winds! The youngsters [. . .] appeared rather stricken. It was our turn to smile then [. . .]. At last we had found "our" Maestro again, just as we remembered him from distant times, just as we had known, admired, feared, and loved him.

The inaugural concert of the restored, 168-year-old Teatro alla Scala began at nine on the evening of 11 May—the same day, by chance, on which Victor Emanuel III went into exile.* La Scala, still smelling of fresh paint, was filled beyond legal capacity: ten or even twelve people were jammed into boxes that normally held four or six, and standees massed dangerously in the galleries. At Toscanini's request, the House of Savoy's coat of arms had been removed from the royal box, which—also at Toscanini's request—was filled with

---

* In the hope of saving the monarchy, the king had abdicated two days earlier in favor of his son, who became Umberto II. The referendum that took place barely more than three weeks later abolished the monarchy, thus Umberto is often referred to, jokingly, as "il re di maggio"—the May-king.

retired singers and musicians from the rest home that Verdi had created; they had been given free admission. Tens of thousands had gathered in Piazza del Duomo and Piazza della Scala to hear the concert on loudspeakers, while millions of others throughout the country and around the world listened on the radio. When Toscanini walked onto the stage, the house audience sprang to its feet, shouting, applauding, cheering the man who, to the Milanese public, was a living symbol of musical excellence, of political (in the broadest sense) integrity, and of the mixture of severity and humanity that had given Italy a Dante, a Michelangelo, a Verdi.

Performers on the stage and people in the auditorium wept with emotion, and each piece was followed by unrestrained outbursts of enthusiasm. Toscanini was radiant, almost ecstatic, and he stopped to talk with some of his musicians and pat them on the back each time he walked off the stage. For Italy's music lovers, the concert was a symbol that the horrors of war were truly over and that life would go on; for Toscanini, it was the culminating moment of his life as a musician, and he could hardly believe that it had come to pass.

Backstage after the concert, Minetti, on behalf of the whole orchestra, and with Emanuela standing next to her grandfather, presented Toscanini with a gold medallion that bore the inscription "TO THE MAESTRO WHO WAS NEVER ABSENT—HIS ORCHESTRA."

XI

FINALE

1.
———

"I CAN'T DESCRIBE THE EMOTION I FELT AT MY FIRST CONCERT!" Toscanini admitted in a letter written a few months after the reopening of La Scala. "I was afraid of fainting onstage!"

But not all Italians were pleased by Toscanini's reappearance. The right-wing and neo-Fascist press accused him of having become an anti-Fascist only because Mussolini hadn't offered him a senatorship or other honors, and he was attacked for having contributed to the bombing of his country by conducting war bonds concerts in America. The former accusations were patently untrue: he had refused a senatorship even before it had been officially offered, and he had always turned down the offers of other honors and exalted positions with which Mussolini and other Fascist officials had tried to make him enter the fold. The war bonds concerts that he had conducted had indeed helped to buy Allied armaments, some of which might have been used in the attempt to bring down fascism; but it was Mussolini's government that had vaingloriously and fatally declared war, first on Britain and France and then on the United States. In 1946, however, the anti-Toscanini voices could barely be heard over the hosannas. And on 2 June 1946, Toscanini had the satisfaction of voting in the referendum that abolished the monarchy and made Italy a republic.

The inaugural concert program was repeated three days later, and Toscanini conducted three other programs (five more performances) at La Scala between 23 May and 26 June; ticket prices for all seven events were exceptionally high, but he took no fee for any of them: the roughly $120,000 in net profits went toward the ongoing restoration of the theater. Toscanini's programs included not only compositions familiar to Milan (music by Beethoven, Brahms, Respighi, Debussy, Wagner, and Richard Strauss) but also pieces by Kabalevsky, Shostakovich, and Gershwin, whose works the Fascists had banned during the war. It was a tough bill for a newly reconstituted orchestra to fill, and Toscanini's remarks at rehearsals were not always patient. An observer jotted down some of them:

> Make the bow jump a bit—separate those two damned notes.
>
> The whole crescendo, all of it, ALL of it! Put something into your work!
>
> Wake up! Let's go! Come on! I've had to conduct for sixty years to hear playing like this! It's shameful! What an awful day.
>
> Maybe you've played well, but you can still play badly—it's much easier.
>
> Fool that I am, I thought you'd understood for the next time as well, but you don't have it in your heads yet.
>
> Horn . . . I know you, Allegri, with that hand of yours. Play open, *open*, OPEN—and if you don't know how to play, change professions!—He wants to play the way *he* likes, but he drives me crazy.
>
> Don't ever think you've succeeded. Always try to do better—otherwise, drop dead.
>
> [Finale of Brahms's Fourth Symphony:] It says *Allegro energico e passionato. Energico*—you don't play with energy! *Passionato*—you don't play with passion!! It's written in Italian, but here are Italians who don't understand it.

At the end of Toscanini's final concert—Beethoven's First and Ninth Symphonies—the audience continued to shout, "Come back soon!"

"I'm still here!" he remarked, smiling, to the players nearest him. But he was disappointed when General Mark Clark and his wife, who had flown in from Vienna especially for the performance, had to leave immediately after having paid their respects to him. Clark had been responsible for part of the Allied campaign in Italy, and

Toscanini had wanted to ask him why the Italian mainland had been invaded at Salerno instead of Genoa.

He was scheduled to take the orchestra to Paris and London for concerts at the end of June, in part as a token of reconciliation between Italy and its former enemies. But on the scheduled departure day, word arrived that the Allied government had ceded to France a tiny piece of Italy—the border villages of Briga (La Brigue) and Tenda (Tende). All arrangements had been made and the train was ready to depart, but Toscanini decided to cancel the trip. Although Ghiringhelli and Franco Abbiati, the *Corriere della Sera*'s chief music critic, tried to change his mind, he remained adamant. Instead, all three men composed a statement to the press, in which they declared, with a bit of truth stretching, that the decision had been made "in complete agreement with the City Council and the entire Scala Administration. The cancellation of the [Paris] concert—the receipts from which were to have gone entirely to the French Red Cross—was not caused by injured nationalism; it merely confirms the Italians' state of mourning for these new humiliations."

The Lucerne Festival's organizers quickly took advantage of the situation and invited the Scala orchestra to give two concerts in their town. Recordings of those events, and especially of a charming reading of Beethoven's First Symphony, seem to testify to Toscanini's pleasure at being back in Europe and working again with his old orchestra. The eighty-two-year-old Richard Strauss, hearing that Toscanini had conducted his *Death and Transfiguration* at La Scala and would conduct it again at Lucerne, wrote to the "Most honored Maestro, dear Friend!" that he had had the "great joy of knowing that under your masterly baton one of my works made a small contribution to the rebuilding of the beautiful Scala." Had he not been ill, he would have gone to Lucerne to hear Toscanini and his "most excellent orchestra." But Toscanini had not forgotten that Strauss had replaced him at the Nazified Bayreuth Festival; he did not reply.

MARGHERITA DE VECCHI'S LEDGERS indicate that since the war's end the Toscanini family had been sending food and clothing—and money, when the US government permitted—to friends and relatives in Italy, as well as packages for general distribution. Now, following the Lucerne excursion, the maestro, Carla, and Walter, all of whom spent most of July and the first half of August in Milan, dedicated themselves to helping old friends and acquaintances in need. They gave money and provisions to nearly everyone who asked, and they sought out those who were ashamed to ask. "When I arrived in Milan three months ago, I asked many, many people [. . .] about you, but no one, no one at all was able to give me even the tiniest piece of news," the maestro wrote to the seventy-five-year-old retired soprano Angelica Pandolfini, who had worked with him half a century earlier. She had just written to ask for help, and he told her that "Carla will bring this letter to you, and you should tell her [. . .] everything that might be of use to you." There were many other such examples, and Toscanini's assistance to people continued for years. On three different occasions around 1950, for instance, he received letters from the former singer and actress Bianca Stagno Bellincioni, then in her early sixties, who thanked him for having sent her money; Toscanini had never worked with her, but he had worked briefly, in his early years, with her parents, Roberto Stagno and Gemma Bellincioni. Records in the New York Public Library demonstrate that between 1943 and 1953, Toscanini and his family contributed to more than seventy charitable organizations—most of them war-related, in one way or another—in the United States and Italy.

In August 1946, Walter wrote to Margherita, "We are at the end of this first adventure, and thank heaven Papà's health has been very good and this is the most important thing. [. . .] As was foreseeable, Papà's coming to Italy and to La Scala did NOT resolve any of Italy's or La Scala's problems—on the contrary I would almost say that it made them worse since after him none of the other conductors interest the public. This, too, is an old story. [The visit] didn't even have the merit of making a clean sweep of the fascists—because here everyone is pure and innocent like so many lambs, especially after the amnesty.* I can't tell you how disgusting it is."

Many people hoped that Toscanini would resume the directorship

---

* In June, as a move toward national reconciliation, Palmiro Togliatti, secretary of the Italian Communist Party and minister of justice in the government of national unity, had granted a highly controversial amnesty to those imprisoned Fascists who were not accused of violent crimes.

of La Scala, but he had no wish to take on such responsibilities. Together with Ghiringhelli, who would remain at the ensemble's helm for a quarter century, and with the set designer Nicola Benois, he began to plan a production of *Otello* for the tentatively scheduled opening, in December, of the renovated house's first opera season, and after his return to New York he coached the Chilean tenor Ramón Vinay in the title role. But disagreements with Ghiringhelli plus doubt whether the theater would really be ready in time led Toscanini to postpone and eventually abandon the *Otello* project; this was a great disappointment to him—the more so because the sixtieth anniversary of *Otello*'s premiere would fall on 5 February 1947. The theater's first postwar opera season took place without him, and he came to the conclusion that America would have to remain his base of operations for as long as he could remain active.

He and Walter arrived in New York by plane on 18 August; Carla stayed in Milan until the following February. The previous spring, before leaving for Italy, the Toscaninis had bought Villa Pauline, the house in Riverdale that they had rented from 1939 to 1942. But as Villa Pauline had to be thoroughly overhauled and the Wave Hill house was no longer available, the maestro moved temporarily into another Riverdale house. He was living alone, excepting the domestic help, but "fortunately, Walter, Cia, and Walfredo come every day for supper, and this is a great joy," he wrote to Carla. Cia was "a treasure," he said, because she organized his day-to-day existence for him. He complained that he couldn't see the Hudson from the temporary residence and that he was suffering from hay fever, but during the two months before the start of his NBC season he hosted the Horowitzes for a long stretch; paid a condolence call to the Busch-Serkin family in Vermont (Frieda, Adolf's wife, had died during the summer);* spent a few days with the Chotzinoffs at their country house in Ridgefield, Connecticut; sent suggestions to Milan about the reorganization of La Scala; and spent much time trying to catch up on contemporary Italian literature. He also wrote, once, to Ada Mainardi, gently remon-

---

* Toscanini was shocked by the family members' stoicism—their "putting a good face on things" mistakenly appeared to him as a lack of true grief—and when Adolf married a much younger woman only a year later, Toscanini brusquely and unjustly cut off his relationship with his old friend. To have young lovers was fine; to marry one of them was not, he believed.

strating with her for not having communicated with him while he was in Italy. She kept his letter but probably did not answer it, and there are no traces of further communication between them.

Toscanini worried that he would not be able to cope with another NBC season. "I think it's time to pull in my oars and begin to rest, so as not to *be too tired when I get to the opposite bank*," he wrote, in that final letter to Ada. But once rehearsals had begun he felt fine and couldn't imagine why he had been so preoccupied. General Motors had stopped sponsoring the symphony's broadcasts, and some network executives had suggested moving the program to a less desirable time slot; in the end, however, the 5 P.M. Sunday hour was maintained. Toscanini conducted seven broadcasts between late October and early December 1946 and nine between early February and early April 1947. The only pieces new to his repertoire were all classics: Mozart's Divertimento in B-flat Major, K. 287; Beethoven's *Consecration of the House* Overture; and Mendelssohn's Octet for strings, played with multiple instruments on each part.

He had programmed the Mozart piece to teach a lesson to Koussevitzky, whose performance of it he had heard over the radio. As he told B. H. Haggin,

"Koussevitzky use *celli* without *bassi; allora* sometimes violas play lower than bass part." Also, [Toscanini said,] Koussevitzky's tempo in the variation movement had been too slow for the prescribed Andante and for the character of the music. But most shocking of all had been what happened near the end of the Adagio, where Toscanini showed me in the score the usual indication [. . .] for the interpolation of a cadenza: the halt on an anticipatory six-four chord, followed by a rest for the interpolated cadenza, and a trill to conclude the cadenza and bring in the orchestra for the rest of the movement. And Toscanini's face now expressed the horror with which he had heard the Boston Symphony pause on the six-four chord, break off for the rest, and—without any cadenza [. . .]—play the trill and conclude the movement. "This man is no musician!" Toscanini exclaimed. "Is *ignorante!*" He had therefore played the Divertimento correctly for Koussevitzky's instruction: "I think maybe he listen."

His 1946–47 programs included a complete performance, in two parts, of Berlioz's *Roméo et Juliette,* plus an excerpt from *La Damnation de Faust* with the baritone Mack Harrell; in a poll of newspaper music editors across the United States and Canada, the *Roméo* broadcasts were voted the outstanding musical event on radio during the 1946–47 season. A performance of the same composer's *Harold in Italy,* with Primrose as soloist, also elicited special interest, as did broadcasts of Beethoven's Third Piano Concerto with Dame Myra Hess, whom Toscanini wished to thank for her bravery in performing in London during the Blitz. He also commemorated his old friend Leone Sinigaglia by conducting the composer's overture, *Le Baruffe Chiozzotte.* (Sinigaglia, who was Jewish, had died of a heart attack in 1944 when SS officers had arrived at his door to arrest and deport him.) On another concert, Toscanini presented excerpts from rarely performed operas by Humperdinck, Dukas, and Catalani. Most important, however, was a two-part performance of *La Traviata,* with Albanese, Peerce, and the young baritone Robert Merrill.

Unlike his *Bohème* broadcasts, recorded ten months earlier, Toscanini's *Traviata* performance was controversial when it was broadcast live and has been controversial ever since. Toscanini himself was not happy with the results: he regretted having chosen Albanese for the title role, and he admitted to Franco Mannino, a young Italian pianist and conductor, that some of the unusually fast tempi that he took in this performance would be impossible in staged performances. During an ensemble rehearsal of Violetta's cabaletta, "Sempre libera," which Toscanini conducted at an exhilarating pace, he cautioned the orchestra not to let the tempo flag, then joked with the players and with the thirty-seven-year-old soprano: "She'll come along with me, too, and if she doesn't come along with me she'll be left behind. But she'll come along because she loves me." She was not left behind, but she wasn't comfortable, either.

One problem with this recording, and with Toscanini's six other complete concert-opera-broadcast recordings, including the earlier *Fidelio* and *Bohème,* is that they were made under exceptionally tense conditions—one-shot performances aired live around the world. A recording of the *Traviata* dress rehearsal sounds much less overwrought than the final performance. Indeed, almost every NBC Symphony musician interviewed after Toscanini's death remarked that the orchestra's best performances took place at rehearsals, without the nervousness of a single-broadcast performance. And according to the RCA producer Richard Gardner, Toscanini lived in constant fear of having his broadcasts cut off if he ran over the time limit—a fact that occasionally accounted for sprints in performances that had not occurred in rehearsals.

Toscanini wished to make a studio recording of *La Traviata* under less tense conditions, with a different soprano, and restoring most or all of the segments that he had cut in order to accommodate radio airtime requirements.* On 3 March 1947, RCA announced that he would record *La Traviata* and another full-length opera—probably *La Bohème*—but the project was scrapped because (according to Gardner) the singers demanded to be paid for rehearsal time, and because Toscanini was told that the sessions would be held at the Manhattan Center, which he disliked. After his retirement, Toscanini said that he wished he had also made complete recordings of *Rigoletto* and *Il Trovatore*. He initially refused to release the recording of the *Traviata* broadcast, but when he learned that unauthorized copies were being sold illegally—and when he himself heard one such copy broadcast on the radio in Milan—he resignedly approved an official release by RCA.

And yet, the virtues of Toscanini's authorized *Traviata* recording far outweigh its flaws: the individualized character of each segment, the refinement of phrasing and bowings throughout, the attention to the meaning of the text, and the overall impact of the entire work present a uniquely valuable synthesis of midperiod Verdian musical drama.

2.

NBC'S OFFICES WERE OVERWHELMED WITH CONGRATULATORY LETTERS, cards, and telegrams for Toscanini's eightieth birthday, 25 March 1947. There was even a cablegram from the USSR, signed by a clutch of the country's most famous composers, Prokofiev, Shosta-

---

* The main cuts comprised the second verses of "Ah, fors'è lui" and "Addio del passato," the tenor and baritone cabalettas in Act II, and thirty-eight bars of the duet "Ah, gran Dio, morir sì giovane," in Act III—at least fifteen minutes of music in all.

kovich, Kabalevsky, Reinhold Glière, Aram Khachaturian, and Niko-lai Miaskovsky. But the maestro marked the occasion only by sending $8,000 to the Verdi rest home in Milan and by having dinner at home with his family and Margherita, who brought along a recording made especially for the occasion by the NBC Symphony's first-desk string players; it contained the minuet from Schubert's String Quartet in A minor plus spoken greetings from each musician. The eleventh annual Three Choir Festival, held that month at New York's Temple Emanu-El, was dedicated to Toscanini, as were two new compositions written for the event: Paul Creston's *Homage to an Apostle of Beauty*, for viola and organ, and Lazare Saminsky's *Sonnet of Petrarch*, for three singers, violin, piano, and organ.

In the course of that major birthday year, *Musical Quarterly*, a scholarly journal, published "Arturo Toscanini—The First Forty Years," the earliest attempt at a thorough account of the maestro's life prior to his arrival at the Metropolitan. The article's author, Walter Toscanini's friend Alfredo Segre, who had immigrated to the United States as a result of Italy's racial laws, had received from Walter the materials he needed for his essay.

Toscanini wrote to Elsa Kurzbauer that someone, in wishing him a happy birthday, had expressed the hope that he would live to be a hundred; he would be happy to reach that age, he said, but only if he were still sexually potent. Elsa and Arturo were continuing to meet for their mutual pleasure from time to time, but in his letters to her he occasionally touched on subjects other than sex. He told her, for instance, that he had "worked very hard on my new records." (During the 1946–47 season, he devoted eight days to recording works by nine composers.) "I've spent many hours downtown adding the Timpani that couldn't be heard in Tchaikovsky's Romeo and Juliet fantasy. I've approved [Wagner's] Faust Overture. I'm fighting to *persuade myself* that [Mozart's] Haffner Symphony is good, but I'm not succeeding." He admitted that he had been in such a vile mood at one of the recording sessions "that I think I even *disgusted* the members of my orchestra [. . .]. To such a point that I received an anonymous letter full of insolent remarks—*all of them just*—only the person who wrote was a coward because he didn't sign."

He was still carrying on from time to time with Marcia Davenport and other women, but his sexual relationship with Eleonora von Mendelssohn had come to an end by 1947. Earlier in the decade, he had seen her act in Elmer Rice's play *Flight to the West* and in an English version of Jean Cocteau's *La Voix Humaine*, and she had attended many of his concerts—at one of which she was observed sitting next to Friedelind Wagner, who thought highly of her; friends of each of the women were amused to observe Mendelssohn and Wagner together. Eleonora became obsessed with Toscanini, as she had earlier been obsessed with the German statesman Walther Rathenau, who was assassinated in 1922, and then with Max Reinhardt. During the war years, she would go to Riverdale late at night with Leo Lerman, a well-known writer and editor, and make him wait for her in Toscanini's garden while she entered the house, using a key she had somehow obtained, and stole up to the maestro's bedroom door, just to listen to him clear his throat or cough in his sleep; then, trembling and giggling, she would return to the garden. Lerman later claimed that Toscanini had mistreated her, but he also admitted that her eccentricities made her almost impossible to deal with. She became a drug addict, and she died at age fifty, in January 1951, probably from an overdose of sleeping pills, although Lerman thought that her husband might have killed her.*

Toscanini decided not to return to Italy during the summer of 1947, in part owing to his disappointment over La Scala's failure to bring the proposed *Otello* production to fruition during the season just ended. Instead, Wally and Emanuela flew to New York so that the whole family could be together at a family dinner in Riverdale on 21 June, Arturo and Carla's fiftieth wedding anniversary.

A concert broadcast scheduled for 31 August was postponed by three weeks because Toscanini was again suffering from hay fever, but on 6 September he was able to lead about thirty-five players from the NBC Symphony in a benefit concert for the Library and Historical Society of Ridgefield, Connecticut, where the Chotzinoffs had their summer home and where Geraldine Farrar lived full-time. The event took place in the town's 580-seat high school auditorium. Toscanini conducted gratis, but the orchestra members were paid

---

* There is much more information about the elusive Eleonora and her brother, Francesco, in Thomas Blubacher's *Gibt es etwas Schöneres als Sehnsucht? Die Geschwister Eleonora und Francesco von Mendelssohn* (Berlin: Insel Verlag, 2012), and in *The Grand Surprise: The Journals of Leo Lerman*, ed. Stephen Pascal (New York: Knopf, 2007).

for their services, although Carlton Cooley, the principal viola, sent his check back to the association, in care of the maestro, saying that he had enjoyed the concert so much that he could not accept money for it. "May God bless and keep you with us dear Maestro for a long, long time to come," he wrote. And Toscanini responded, saying that he was moved by Cooley's words, which "prove you are not yet bored with the old maestro," and thanking him for his "noble gesture, worthy only of a man and artist *like you.*" Toscanini also told Chotzinoff that he had "felt the unusual *charm* (not quality) of that evening" and the "warm atmosphere [. . .] because of the small theatre which helps performers and public to make and enjoy music."

Toscanini's portions of the 1947–48 NBC Symphony season ran from late October to mid-December and from mid-February to early April—sixteen concerts in all. The broadcasts had been switched from Sunday afternoons to Saturday evenings at six thirty, and his fee was now $6,000 for each non-commercially-sponsored concert and $7,500 for each concert that was commercially sponsored.* His far from adventurous programming nevertheless contained some special events: an all-Mendelssohn concert in November and an all-Debussy concert in March to commemorate the hundredth and the thirtieth anniversaries, respectively, of the composers' deaths; a Bach-Vivaldi-Handel program; the maestro's sole performance of the Suite from Kodály's opera *Háry János*; and, most important from today's point of view, a two-part concert performance of *Otello*.

James Levine, longtime music director of the Metropolitan Opera, has described the recording of Toscanini's live *Otello* broadcast as "an outstanding candidate for the title of Greatest Opera Recording Ever Made." Even Toscanini was reasonably happy when, six years later, RCA decided to issue the recording; after having listened to the playback, he remarked to his son, "This is *Otello.* That one could do better—of that I'm sure, but we did this without ever thinking that it would have to be a recording." And he commented that he had the original interpretation, by Verdi and Faccio, imprinted in his head. At the first rehearsal, he had been ready to scold the double basses for

---

* In 1947 Toscanini's total gross income was $197,223.85, of which $102,000 was from NBC, $81,107.31 from RCA (recording fees and royalties), $13,991.54 from the Gramophone Company, and $125 from interest.

playing their solo passage in the last act out of tune—as had always been his experience in the past—but the NBC basses had played the part so perfectly in tune that he had been disappointed, he joked. All three of the principal singers were performing with him for the first time. He described Ramón Vinay (Otello) as "an animal" with no real musical talent or excellent high notes, but nevertheless gifted with a magnificent voice. Giuseppe Valdengo (Iago) was an idiot who happened to have a fine voice but was incapable of either getting inside a character or singing musically unless he received strict instruction, Toscanini said. And Herva Nelli (Desdemona) had a sweet voice, "all of a piece," and excellent Florentine pronunciation but, according to Toscanini, she had never learned proper breath control.

Licia Albanese had recommended Nelli—thirty-eight, born in Florence but educated in America—as a possible Desdemona. Nelli had so far had a modest, ten-year-long career, but her success in *Otello* led to engagements at the Metropolitan, La Scala, and other major venues, and Toscanini would call on her to sing other roles during the remaining years of his career. He repeatedly told Dick Marzollo, the opera coach who helped him to prepare singers during those years, that Nelli had great potential but lacked understanding and was a slow learner. And he appreciated her physical attributes, with which he reportedly became intimately familiar. At one point, when Toscanini was spending a great deal of time with Nelli, Carla packed a suitcase and moved in with Lucilla De Vescovi Whitman; only when the octogenarian Arturo went to Lucilla's and apologized to his wife did Carla agree to return home.

THE ADVENT OF TELEVISION as a popular medium had been delayed by the war, but by 1948 TV sets were becoming affordable to middle-class Americans. The American Federation of Musicians had barred its members from appearing in telecasts until proper contractual perameters could be worked out, but on 20 March 1948, two days after the ban was lifted, Toscanini and the NBC Symphony appeared on television for the first time, performing an all-Wagner concert.

"Without a doubt it was the finest program yet offered by television, a superb and exciting demonstration of the medium's potentialities as an original art form," Jack Gould, the *Times*'s television critic declared. "As if by magic, television suddenly and truly came of age." President Harry S. Truman, in Washington, watched the performance and sent his congratulations to Toscanini, and even viewers who knew nothing at all about music could sense that there was something noteworthy about Toscanini: a customer in a Greenwich Street tavern watched the concert and commented, in pure Newyorkese: "He knows his onions, dat old boid. See the signals he got?"

Just as Toscanini, despite his technological ineptitude, had quickly grasped the possibilities offered by radio for the dissemination of great music, so he immediately understood television's potential for further broadening the audience.* In Studio 8H, three cameras had been set up for the concert: one behind the timpani and two in different parts of the balcony; there was a powerful floodlight next to each camera, but the maestro put up with the glare and the heat. Nine more Toscanini concerts would be shown, with gradually increasing technical finish, over the following four years; they were all preserved on kinescopes—precursors of videotape—and were later made available on videocassettes, videodiscs, and DVDs. Few of these performances are among Toscanini's best—his physical discomfort under the floodlights is almost palpable—but they are essential documents of his intensity, concentration, gestural technique, eye contact with his players, and absorption in the task at hand. And it is remarkable that a man who was already a professional conductor when Verdi and Brahms were still active was able to conduct their music on television.

Five days after his first telecast, Toscanini turned eighty-one, and he joked with his orchestra that he wanted no celebrations until his ninetieth birthday. Every player could save ten cents each year until then, he suggested, so that they could each give him a one-dollar present when the time came.

Within three weeks of NBC's announcement, in February, that Toscanini's season would end on 3 April 1948 with a performance of the Beethoven Ninth, the company received 11,000 requests from people seeking to fit into Studio 8H's 1,200 seats. There was a similar rush for tickets to a postseason benefit performance (for the Building

---

* Sarnoff had given a television to Toscanini, who occasionally enjoyed watching boxing and wrestling matches and the comedian Milton Berle.

Fund of the New York Infirmary for Women and Children) of Verdi's *Te Deum* and *Requiem*, at Carnegie Hall on 26 April. The maestro conducted without fee and paid $250 for a box for family and friends. Over $55,000 was raised.

Four days later Toscanini, accompanied by Walter, boarded the Italian liner *Saturnia*, bound for Italy; Carla had returned home earlier. In Milan on 10 June 1948, the thirtieth anniversary of Arrigo Boito's death, and again two nights later, the maestro entered La Scala's orchestra pit for the last times, to conduct fully staged performances of excerpts from *Mefistofele* and *Nerone*. Special police had been assigned to the theater that evening—there had been warnings that neo-Fascists would protest Toscanini's presence—but no such demonstrations took place. Giuseppe Nessi, who had sung the role of Gobrias at *Nerone*'s premiere in 1924, took the part again; Giacinto Prandelli sang the role of Faust in the earlier opera; Herva Nelli took the lead soprano parts in both works; and Toscanini worked for the first time with three young singers: the mezzo-soprano Giulietta Simionato, baritone Frank Guarrera, and bass Cesare Siepi, of whom the first and the last would become major stars, and Guarrera, too, would develop a fine, long career. In addition to coaching all the singers in their roles, the maestro had worked with them onstage, demonstrating gestures and movements. During a break in one rehearsal, he stood in an aisle in the auditorium and told the people near him, "I remember how [Boito] sat there—it was right in that seat—during a rehearsal for my first *Meistersinger*." Fifty years had passed since Boito had persuaded the Scala administration to engage the young Toscanini as principal conductor.

The maestro divided most of his vacation time between Via Durini and the Isolino, which he had once again begun to rent,* but he returned to La Scala in September to conduct a concert. During a rehearsal of Schubert's "Great" C Major Symphony, he had trouble getting the orchestra to begin the third movement with the quickness and lightness that he wanted. Finally, he said, "You must stop thinking of Schubert as a sad man, feeble, reduced by illness to groping his way desperately through the streets of Vienna. Schubert was

---

* According to a subsequent contract (30 June 1950), Toscanini paid the Borromeo family a monthly rent of 40,000 lire ($64 at the time) for the island and all of its structures.

young, he loved cheerful company, songs, wine, women. . . . Anyway, if he didn't like them, so much the worse for him." The musicians laughed, and the passage went more freely.

Carla had begun to have serious circulatory problems, and in the course of the summer she suffered an episode during which she spoke incoherently and walked into a wall, thinking it was a door. Walter, writing to Margherita, said that his father "understood for the first time that Mamma is really ill [. . .], and he was very upset." Carla was sent to a clinic at Luino, on Lake Maggiore, for therapy, and while she was there Walter began the unpleasant task of untangling his parents' Italian finances, as he had already been trying to do with their American assets.

He soon realized that over the years, a series of economic advisers had "eaten up a lot of money that Papà earned by the sweat of his brow, because no one ever really checked on them, because everything is in such a state of mental and material confusion"; so he wrote to Margherita. Walter could not even determine which stocks and bonds belonged to his parents and which ones to his sister Wally. "This isn't the time to talk about it with Mamma. Papà tells me that it doesn't interest him. Wally doesn't understand anything about it." A year later, Walter would learn that in 1925 Carla and the family's lawyers had created a corporation, Alba, probably as a tax shelter, and that under that name Carla had bought properties in Milan and the farm at Ripalta Guerina. Alba was so poorly defined and documented that Walter could barely figure out exactly what it was or—once again—who owned what. The family may have lost as much as 300,000,000 lire (about $480,000 at the time) in various holdings. Ottocaro Weiss, a family friend who directed the New York office of the Italian insurance giant Assicurazioni Generali, eventually helped Walter straighten out most of the Toscaninis' Italian economic mess.*

Walter accompanied his father back to New York by plane; Carla was not yet able to travel, and Wally, assisted by Fosca Leonardi,

---

* The Trieste-born Weiss (1896–1971), a friend of James Joyce's, had been codirector of the Assicurazioni Generali in Italy until the racial laws had forced him to emigrate with his wife—an orchestral violinist and a niece of the novelist Italo Svevo—and their son, Piero, who became a well-known pianist and musicologist. It was Ottocaro Weiss who recommended Richard Ellmann to the Joyce family as a potential biographer of their most famous member; the biography remains a classic in the genre.

Puccini's stepdaughter and a longtime friend of the Toscaninis, kept Carla company and sent frequent reports to the "Maestrino," as Fosca teasingly addressed Toscanini. Almost immediately upon his return to New York, Toscanini set to work rehearsing the first of six all-Brahms broadcasts. The fourth concert in the series was televised, as was the first concert that followed the Brahms series—a Mozart-Dvořák-Wagner program. Following Toscanini's first portion of the season, three concerts were conducted by Ernest Ansermet, who was succeeded in turn by a twenty-eight-year-old Italian conductor in his American debut.

In Milan the previous May, Toscanini had attended Guido Cantelli's rehearsals with the Scala orchestra, and he had been impressed with the young man's musicianship, seriousness, and intensity. He spoke at length with Cantelli on several occasions; became friendly in a paternal way with him and his wife, Iris; and arranged for the young man to conduct the NBC Symphony. Cantelli risked displeasing his mentor by including in his four programs works that Toscanini did not like—Hindemith's *Mathis der Maler* Symphony, Giorgio Federico Ghedini's *Pezzo Concertante*, Alfredo Casella's *Paganiniana*, and Bartók's Concerto for Orchestra—but, on the contrary, Toscanini was pleased by Cantelli's boldness as well as by his approach to more traditional repertoire.

When Guido was about to return to Italy, Toscanini gave him a letter to take to Iris: "I must personally tell you that it is the first time, during my long artistic career, that I find a young man truly endowed with those qualities that can't be debated but that are the real ones, those that carry an artist high up—*very high up*[.] I attended all of Guido's rehearsals with ever-growing interest, and the impression I had from the first rehearsal at La Scala was repeated, always increasing." Toscanini's high opinion of Cantelli would quickly bring the young conductor an international career that rivaled those of his somewhat older contemporaries Herbert von Karajan and Leonard Bernstein.

TOSCANINI'S SECOND BLOCK of eight concerts, from mid-February to early April 1949, contained no repertoire surprises until the last two weeks, when he conducted a two-part concert performance of *Aida*, with Nelli (Aida), Eva Gustavson (Amneris), the young and later celebrated Richard Tucker (Radamès), Valdengo (Amonasro), Norman Scott (Ramfis), and the twenty-one-year-old Teresa Stich-Randall (Priestess). With its dramatic sweep, intense lyricism, and overarching unity of concept, this performance is another of the essential Toscanini recordings, although it must be listened to with the same caveats that apply to his other live NBC opera ventures. It was broadcast on radio and television and eventually issued on records, albeit with parts of Nelli's arias redone later.*

Toscanini conducted a Beethoven-Wagner benefit concert at Carnegie Hall on 20 April, for the Centennial Fund of City College. He was to have sailed for Europe eight days later, but on the twenty-fifth he slipped while getting into his bathtub, pulled some ligaments in his chest, and was unable to leave until 17 May, when he and Walter boarded the *Vulcania*; Carla, who had traveled to New York during the course of the NBC season, had returned to Italy as soon as the season had ended. As in the previous year, Toscanini again spent the summer between Via Durini and the Isolino, but after a little persuasion he agreed to open Venice's twelfth Festival of Contemporary Music by conducting the Scala orchestra in a concert at the Teatro La Fenice on 3 September 1949; the most contemporary piece on his program was Strauss's *Don Juan*, written six decades earlier.

At the Fenice, he attended a rehearsal of Alban Berg's *Lulu*—still a radical, controversial work at the time—and someone brought the young, later revered director Giorgio Strehler, who was staging the opera, to Toscanini's box, to meet the maestro. Upon opening the door to the box and hearing Toscanini cursing the music and its composer, Strehler turned and fled. Toscanini had tried to memorize the score of *Wozzeck*, Berg's other opera, but he had given up "after a couple of pages," he told Minetti, because the music "isn't part of my spirit." (More to the point: it's harmonic language was foreign to him.) And he couldn't under-

---

* Of course the video version contains only the original, uncorrected performance. Toscanini would have liked to remake some of Gustavson's solo passages, too, but he said that her voice had been ruined in the interim. About Tucker's performance, he commented, "He sang the notes but seemed like a chorister"—in other words, without a strong personality—but he added that Tucker sang the duet in the last act beautifully.

stand how the conductor Dimitri Mitropoulos "is able to knock all that stuff into his head."

He conducted two concerts at La Scala early in September, after which he and Carla returned to New York aboard the *Atlantic*, arriving on the twenty-first. There was another benefit concert in Ridgefield, Connecticut, this time with some forty NBC Symphony members, and by the end of October Toscanini had resumed his weekly broadcasts. But before the series began, he received a visit from Leonard Bernstein, who wanted to consult with him about Berlioz's *Roméo et Juliette*. The thirty-one-year-old Bernstein was a rising podium star; at the time of the visit, the younger man, breathing with difficulty from asthma, envied his eighty-two-year-old colleague, who was running up and down stairs to find scores and other materials. Bernstein mentioned that he had noted a substantial variation in the basic tempo of the love scene between Toscanini's live broadcast of the complete work and his studio recording of the scene in question a few days later. After Bernstein left, Toscanini listened to both versions, then wrote to Bernstein to confirm that the studio recording was "much faster. And I confirmed also another fact—namely that every man [. . .] can be from time to time a little stupid. So is the case of the old Toscanini." Bernstein's visit had given him "a great amount of pleasure" and had made him feel forty years younger, he said. But there would be little contact between them in the following years: Toscanini recognized Bernstein's talent but disapproved of his emotive podium style.

Cantelli and Ansermet again took over NBC's eight midseason concerts, after which Toscanini's broadcasts continued from mid-February through early April 1950; he also dedicated nine days to recording sessions. And the season ended with a memorable two-part concert performance of *Falstaff*, with Valdengo (Falstaff), Nelli (Alice), Guarrera (Ford), Merriman (Meg), Cloe Elmo (Quickly), Stich-Randall (Nannetta), and Antonio Madasi (Fenton).[*]

Falstaff was the opera that Toscanini loved best and the one that

---

[*] Toscanini had wanted Jussi Björling for the role of Fenton, a relatively small part for a big star, but the Swedish tenor was unavailable.

he had conducted in more seasons (twenty-six) than any other opera and in more cities (sixteen) than any other opera except *Aida*. To this, his final performance of Verdi's final stage work, he brought fifty-seven years of familiarity with the score. Merriman recalled that the piano rehearsals averaged six hours a day for six weeks; although Dick Marzollo had been engaged to accompany the sessions, Toscanini did much of the playing himself, so that he could immediately indicate the dynamics and tempo inflections that he wanted. But he later told a friend that a successful performance of *Falstaff* depended, among other things, on "the conductor's ability to *not* bother the singers. I can feel when a singer will get ahead of me in ten bars, and I'm ready to catch up with him," he said. "It's always been said that I'm together with the singers, but it's because I take very good care of the singers."

Toscanini considered the recording of his NBC *Falstaff* performance the best of his Verdi opera recordings. "When I hear it, I can't believe that I did it," he commented, four years later. The unity of the singing impressed him, as a listener, and he even agreed to leave some of the audience's applause in the published recording, because it gave an idea of the spontaneity of the occasion. His 1937 Salzburg Festival *Falstaff* recording is more theatrical, less tightly controlled than the 1950 concert version, but the 1950 performance is extraordinary by any standards, and its acoustical quality is incomparably better than that of the Salzburg recording.

3.

ACCORDING TO ITALY'S NEW CONSTITUTION, THE PRESIDENT OF THE republic had the right to nominate as "senators for life" five Italian citizens who had "brought distinction to the Nation for their great merits in the social, scientific, artistic, or literary field." Twice—in 1947 and again in 1948—Toscanini had been told that he was under consideration for such an honor, and on both occasions he had let government exponents know that he would refuse it. But in December 1949, Luigi Einaudi, the country's first constitutionally elected president, had nominated Toscanini all the same.

Toscanini replied to Einaudi,

It is an old Italian artist, very much troubled by your unexpected telegram, who turns to you and asks you to understand that this announcement of his nomination as Senator for Life clashes profoundly with his sentiments and that he is forced to refuse this honor, with great sadness.

Averse to any sort of accumulation of honors, academic titles, and decorations, I wish to end my existence in the same simplicity with which I have always lived it.

Grateful and happy for the recognition that has been expressed toward me in the name of my Country, ready to serve it again in any eventuality, I ask you not to interpret this wish of mine as a rude or arrogant gesture, but rather in the spirit of simplicity and humility that inspires it. Accept my deferential greetings and respectful homage.

Ivanoe Bonomi, president of the senate and former prime minister, read Toscanini's message in the senate on 7 December; the following day numerous senators decried the refusal, describing it as a "public slap in the face." But Toscanini would not change his mind. He wanted to spend his last active years working with his orchestra, not expressing himself on political issues.

Another upset occurred two months later, in February 1950, when Carla suffered a stroke that left her partially, albeit temporarily, paralyzed, and she spent the following six weeks in New York's Mount Sinai Hospital. Wally flew in from Europe to assist Walter and Wanda; knowing that their father would fret and hover but be of little use in the situation, they easily persuaded him to proceed with his spring season. Less than a week after Carla was hospitalized, her husband was busy rehearsing his orchestra, and he was eagerly looking forward to the challenge of another major project: a six-week, twenty-one-concert NBC Symphony national tour, from the Atlantic to the Pacific and back again.

The undertaking was sponsored by RCA Victor. Over the prior two years, the use of magnetic tape and the introduction of long-playing vinyl records had revolutionized the recording industry: tape could be cut and spliced, thereby making the recording process incalculably easier and more flexible than the old master disc system; and vinyl made the finished product virtually unbreakable, and far less expensive than shellac discs.* Toscanini was the biggest-selling classical recording artist of his day, thus for RCA the tour was promotional; for Toscanini, it was a new adventure. Marks Levine, president of the National Concert and Artists Corporation, had booked all the concerts in four days, and a week after the tour had been announced, nearly all tickets had been sold.

Toscanini must have had memories of his marathon 1920–21 tour with the Scala orchestra when, on the morning of 17 April, a special thirteen-car "Toscanini Tour" train carrying 106 musicians, 19 other RCA/NBC employees, the train's crew, tons of instruments and printed music—in addition to himself and his son—departed from New York's grandiose Pennsylvania Station. They were seen off by Sarnoff, other company executives, members of the Toscanini family, and a bevy of journalists and photographers. From then until the end of May, the tour provided grist for American newspapers' mills: the *New York Times* alone carried more than two dozen articles charting the orchestra's progress, describing the reception given the musicians and their maestro, with special focus on the fact that great numbers of young people turned out for the concerts in every city and town.

The tour repertoire comprised five substantial programs' worth of music—twenty-eight works, all Toscanini standards, by sixteen composers. Baltimore was the first stop, followed by Richmond, Atlanta, and New Orleans, in all three of which Toscanini conducted "Dixie" as an encore. Only afterward was he informed that the piece was offensive to African Americans, and the *Times* reporter Howard Taubman, who joined the tour in New Orleans, described the maestro as "disturbed" when he learned that "Dixie" was connected with the old, slaveholding South. The maestro then refused to perform it in the three Texas cities (Houston, Austin, and Dallas) that came next on the tour or, later, in St. Louis. In some of the southern cities, where racial segregation was the norm, sections of the audito-

---

* In the 1930s, a five-disc 78 rpm set—Beethoven's "Pastoral" Symphony, for instance—retailed for $10, a prohibitive sum for most people. A work of similar length on a single 33⅓ rpm disc cost only about $1.25 in 1950, thus making classical recordings available to a mass audience.

riums in which the orchestra performed were reserved for black people, but in St. Louis people of color could not attend at all. One African American music lover wrote to express the "sincere desire that Mr. Toscanini's next concert in St. Louis will be given in a place where all people regardless of race may have the pleasure of listening." The message was not shown to Toscanini.

Most orchestra musicians hate tours: they are constantly on the road, checking into or out of hotels, and playing rehearsals and concerts, with little opportunity to explore the places they visit. The quality of playing worsens as the tour progresses, and the musicians return home exhausted. But this tour was different. The men had decent sleeping and dining accommodations aboard the train and in hotels, and there were usually two days—sometimes even three—between concerts. Most important, an orchestra that often had to give commercial performances with run-of-the-mill conductors now spent six solid weeks playing under Toscanini. The violinist Samuel Antek wrote, "The performances all along were undoubtedly the finest I ever heard our orchestra give. No wonder Toscanini was delighted and pleased as I had never seen him before." In fact, the maestro told NBC and RCA executives that he would like to do another tour the following year, but to different American cities—with more concerts per week! Walter teased his father, "We'll have to spend a whole year en route." To which his father replied, "Good." And since he was feeling particularly healthy and energetic, the eighty-three-year-old maestro optimistically decided during the tour to sign a new, five-year contract with RCA.

The Toscaninis, father and son, had their own private railroad car—a completely equipped suite—and Walter, together with Albert Walker, a former physical education teacher whom NBC had hired in 1938 as a combination bodyguard/briefcase-carrier/errand boy for the maestro, had their hands full trying to satisfy all of the old man's needs: hunting up celluloid tie clasps, snap-together cuff-links, and a new hat in Atlanta; having his glasses repaired in various cities (he was constantly sitting on them by accident); taking his sweat-drenched concert shirts to the airport to be flown to Forzia-ti's New Shirt Laundry in New York; and, above all, simply keeping up with him.

"He will kill us all yet with his energy," Walter exclaimed as the musical caravan was about to pull out of Richmond. "The moment we reached his car after the concert tonight, he insisted on walking through the train; said he wanted to see the musicians. 'Father,' I said, 'the musicians have not yet arrived at the train.' But no, he goes through every car, first one way, then the other. Then he had some soup and red wine, and *then* he said, 'Walter, I will show you a trick,' and he stood in front of a divan and jumped up on it backwards."

Grandson Walfredo Toscanini, who was twenty at the time and studying at Yale University, later recalled, "I flew down to go along on part of the tour, and after a few days I was sick and exhausted. And all *I* did was listen to the concerts and go sightseeing. Grandfather did the sightseeing *plus* conducting rehearsals and concerts."

When there were vast distances to cover between concerts—from Dallas to Pasadena, for instance—the three Toscaninis went by plane. Pasadena was the only city in which two concerts were given, to accommodate music lovers from nearby Los Angeles: that city's Shrine Auditorium had been reserved for other events before the NBC tour was arranged. From there, the orchestra traveled up the Pacific coast to San Francisco, then onward to Portland and Seattle. En route to Denver, the musicians enjoyed a free day at Sun Valley, Idaho. Antek recalled,

> At ten in the morning I came upon Toscanini, stretched out full length on the lawn, drinking a toast in champagne to the beautiful mountains! Later that day, [. . .] we were amazed to see him coming up the ski tow, and broke into a cheer as his chair swung into view. The jaunty beret on his head and his waving arms gave him the appearance of a happy boy playing hooky. [. . .] "Maestro," I said to him, "you are a brave man. Some of the boys were afraid to come up." He looked at me very earnestly and said, "I've never been afraid of anything in my life. I like to try everything." All through the day he was "one of the boys," joining us in a marvelous outdoor barbecue and applauding the buffoonery of the "Sad Symphony," performed with pots, pans, and kazoos by the men, who were burlesquing the numbers we had been playing on the tour. We cheered wildly as he rather dazedly accepted an invitation to lead us in the "Stars and Stripes Forever."

From Denver the tour proceeded to St. Louis, Chicago, Detroit, Cleveland, and Pittsburgh; then back to the East Coast. On 25 May, President Truman, together with his wife and daughter, attended the orchestra's concert at Constitution Hall. Before the performance, David Sarnoff introduced Truman and his party to Toscanini in a backstage reception room. According to an unofficial source, the maestro was so nervous that when Truman asked him what was on the program, he didn't remember; once he was on stage, however, his memory functioned normally. Truman and other government officials and diplomats stayed for the entire concert, and after an encore the president said that he would have liked a second one.

The final concert of the 8,600-mile tour took place two nights later before a cheering audience at Philadelphia's Academy of Music, after which the "Toscanini Train" made its final journey, back to New York. On the twenty-ninth, Toscanini gave a party at his home for the orchestra members, their wives, and the NBC staff; he greeted each of the three hundred guests personally and remained on his feet for four hours. Then, on 1 and 2 June, he led recording sessions that lasted nearly three hours each and produced fine versions of *La Mer* and *Ibéria*.

Full of undiminished energy, he flew into Milan on 17 June 1950 and almost immediately began to rehearse Verdi's *Te Deum* and *Requiem* for two performances at La Scala, with Tebaldi, Elmo, Prandelli, and Siepi as soloists. Afterward, however, he wrote to Maria Cecchini, a family friend,* that the concerts had "left a very bitter taste in my mouth" and that performances by Karajan and the Vienna Philharmonic of Beethoven's *Missa Solemnis* and Bach's Mass in B minor, which he had attended, had "bored" him. "Not even Bach's divine Kyrie moved me as it did in a long-ago performance with a Berlin chorus conducted by Georg Schumann. Maybe my advanced age has hardened my heart a little!" But then he went to the Isolino and felt refreshed. "This is truly an enchanting place!" he continued, in his letter to Cecchini. "I brought my piano, and I bang on it from time to time."

---

* Cecchini often accompanied and tutored Toscanini's granddaughter Emanuela during extended stays in America. She later became involved in a program for training young singers at La Scala, and she married one of them—the basso Paolo Montarsolo.

He would often listen to music on the radio, and he heard Furtwängler's broadcast of *La Damnation de Faust* from the Lucerne Festival; through a common acquaintance he let his German colleague
know that he had found the performance excellent. Toscanini has
been accused of involvement in the postwar campaign undertaken
by Heifetz, Horowitz, Rubinstein, and other musicians, most of them
Jewish, to keep Furtwängler out of America. (The boycott was more
than understandable: had Germany won the war, those musicians
would have been slaughtered.) Not only is there no documentation to
support this theory: Toscanini even refused requests to protest
against Furtwängler's appearance in Lucerne immediately after the
war, and he made no attempt to keep him away from La Scala.
Indeed, Furtwängler had conducted the entire *Ring* at La Scala only a
month before Toscanini conducted the Verdi *Requiem* at the theater.

Toscanini made a trip to Rome for a consultation with Dr. Cesare
Frugoni, a leading Italian pathologist and clinician. In New York, the
maestro had fallen and hit his knee, which was in mild but constant
pain; during the Scala concert, he had felt that his leg was like a dead
weight and had feared not being able to turn to thank the audience.
Whatever recommendations Frugoni made did not work, and by the
time Toscanini, accompanied by Walter, boarded the *Vulcania* in
Naples at the end of September, his condition was "going from bad to
worse," he wrote to Carla, who had remained in Milan. During the
twelve-day voyage to New York, he stopped drinking wine and coffee because they were upsetting his stomach, and the knee problem
spread through his whole right leg.

Toscanini was angered by NBC's decision to convert 8H into a
television studio. At first, he was told that his concerts would take
place at Carnegie Hall; then, after United States Steel withdrew its
sponsorship of the program, rumor had it that a potential new sponsor would want to have the concerts moved from their current time
slot—6:30 to 7:30 on Saturday evenings—to Monday evenings from
10:00 to 11:00, and that they might take place in Hunter College's
auditorium, on Manhattan's Upper East Side, or at the Manhattan
Center, on West Thirty-Fourth Street; in the latter, however, live
audiences could not be accommodated. Toscanini wrote to Carla
that he felt like catching a plane back to Milan immediately. After
thirteen years at NBC, he said, "I didn't intend to be sent away [from

8H] for any reason whatsoever, or at least I ought to have been treated as a man of my age and my artistic position deserves"—consulted on the matter, in other words. The press had printed "every sort of nonsense—even that CBS will *hire* me. Imagine! And those idiots Chotzinoff and Sarnoff of the NBC are asking Walter if there's any truth in this news."

For the time being, however, the venue crisis was overshadowed by the leg problem, which forced Toscanini to cancel his first three NBC concerts and to go to Philadelphia for treatment by Dr. Irvin Stein, an orthopedic surgeon who had relieved the maestro's recurrent shoulder problems a few years earlier. In the end, Toscanini canceled all of his concerts during the first half of the season.*

He wrote frequently to Carla, to try to boost her sagging morale; he told her to play cards, which she had always enjoyed (he did not), and not to think about herself all the time—to take an interest in what was going on around her. And he kept her informed of his therapy, so that she wouldn't be alarmed by false reports in the press. Then other physical problems began to afflict him: his ankles were swollen; for the first time in his life he had to have a tooth—or rather three teeth—extracted; and, worst of all, his vision was worsening.

"I'm *quite a mess*," he wrote. He said repeatedly that he had reached his eighty-third birthday without feeling his age, but that now, only a few months later, he truly felt old. In December, he was saddened by the deaths of his old friend Vincenzo Tommasini and of the thirty-three-year-old pianist Dinu Lipatti, whom he had heard, admired, and met at La Scala in 1946. "My God, so much sadness! And the [Korean] war! And the atomic bomb!" And again: "I'm very agitated, my brain is full of nasty thoughts and my heart full of bitterness." His family had always laughed at him for feeling sorry for himself and calling himself *il povero Toscanini* (poor Toscanini), and he had laughed with them; now he wrote to Carla, "Poor Toscanini!!!—but this time *for real*."

Toscanini was bored in Philadelphia, with no work to do, but one evening he attended a performance by I Virtuosi di Roma, one of the first Italian early music groups. "They played magnificently and with

---

* He was replaced by Reiner, Leinsdorf, the Romanian conductor Jonel Perlea, and Cantelli.

great success," he wrote. "I went to greet them after the concert. They went crazy!! They kissed me, embraced me, and wept with emotion." He returned to New York from time to time; one Sunday, Cesare Siepi, Renata Tebaldi and her mother, and the mezzo-soprano Fedora Barbieri and her husband had lunch with him in Riverdale; on another occasion, the Cantellis came for dinner, with Miecio Horszowski. But Cia was suffering from severe heart disease; she often had to stay in bed for weeks at a time and couldn't climb the stairs. "My heart aches for her, the poor thing!" Toscanini wrote to Wally. Cia and Walter had given up their own home and had moved to the Villa Pauline's spacious third floor, so that Walter could simultaneously look after his father and his mother, when she was there, as well as his ailing wife. There was plenty of domestic help, but everyone consulted Walter and depended on him for assistance.

By early January 1951, Toscanini felt well enough to stay in New York and even to lead a three-hour recording session that produced a stunning version of Strauss's *Don Juan*. And at Carnegie Hall on 27 January, the exact fiftieth anniversary of Verdi's death, he conducted the composer's *Te Deum* and *Requiem*—a benefit performance for Casa Verdi; Toscanini himself bought ten of the high-priced tickets and had them distributed to two honors students at each of five New York music schools. But the concert's outcome distressed him. "I don't deserve any praise," he wrote shortly afterward, in a draft of a response to a listener who had sent him a letter of thanks. "I did my best in order to reach a good performance worthy of the circumstance instead I failed entirely and I was so unhappy as I cant say but the performance of both Requ and Te Deum faild to be as good as I hoped and I felt unhappy and ashamed of myself."

He was still angry with Chotzinoff and Sarnoff for his forced removal from Studio 8H, but today's listeners can be grateful to them, since all of Toscanini's remaining American concerts and recording sessions took place at Carnegie Hall, with its much better acoustics. More generally, the rapidly increasing popularity of television[*] and the consequent decreasing popularity of radio were caus-

---

[*]   In 1948, when the first of Toscanini's telecasts took place, there were 35,000 television sets in the United States. By 1952, when he would appear on television for the last time, there were nearly 17,000,000 of them.

ing American radio networks, which were commercial enterprises, to spend less and less on classical music—a fact that was deplored in the daily newspapers. Toscanini, however, was by then a nearly mythical figure, and Sarnoff was determined to keep the NBC Symphony going as long as the maestro was willing and able to conduct, whether or not commercial sponsorship could be found every season. E. R. Squibb & Sons, manufacturers of dental products, sponsored the 1950–51 season and refrained from interrupting the concerts with advertising.

Toscanini gave three more concerts in February 1951, during which he was in fine shape, musically. He occasionally reached for the podium rail, but only for extra security, not to grasp it out of necessity. When, during a rehearsal of Elgar's "Enigma" Variations, he found the orchestra's playing too phlegmatic, he exclaimed, "Quando sarò morto, avrò più vita di voialtri tutti!" (When I'll be dead, I'll have more life than all of you!) But he assumed that the condition of his knee and leg would continue to worsen, and—as he refused to sit down when he conducted—he decided that his 17 February concert would be his last, at least for the time being. At a rehearsal on the fourteenth, Toscanini took the unusual step of explaining to the musicians that he felt obliged to cancel the two remaining concerts on his season's schedule because of his leg problem, and he added that he was sorry to stop because the concerts were a source of enjoyment to him. NBC's executives were informed that he wanted no applause at his final concert, and the small invited audience in Carnegie Hall respected his wishes.

At Dr. Stein's suggestion, Toscanini had a stationary bicycle set up at home in order to strengthen his knee, but during an exercise session on 1 March he pedaled too furiously and suddenly felt extremely ill. He dragged himself upstairs and sat down in the bathroom doorway, where a family member found him some time later: his pride had prevented him from calling for help. He recovered quickly from what had been a minor stroke, but his feeling that his performing career was over now seemed confirmed. He had previously agreed to conduct staged performances of *Falstaff* and possibly *Macbeth* at Busseto that summer, under La Scala's auspices, as part of the Verdi commemorations, and he had auditioned a twenty-seven-year-old Maria Callas for the role of Lady Macbeth.* But the project had to be canceled.

Toscanini had also promised to return to London to inaugurate the new Royal Festival Hall, which replaced the old Queen's Hall, destroyed in wartime bombing. Detailed arrangements had been made the preceding year: he would give two performances of the Beethoven Ninth and, in between, a mixed program, the centerpiece of which would be his first performance of Ralph Vaughan Williams's Sixth Symphony—all with the BBC Symphony Orchestra. He had studied the Vaughan Williams symphony thoroughly and had been looking forward to the event, but on 14 February Walter had to inform Owen Mase, "Doctors have ordered him to give up all his future engagements for an indefinite period."

The conductor Malcolm Sargent tried to persuade Toscanini to change his mind and to consider the possibility of sitting down when he conducted: "Toscanini sitting down is better than any other conductor standing up," Sargent cabled him. But in the end, Sargent himself led the inaugural concert. Toscanini sent a "good luck" telegram on the day of the inaugural performance; Sargent replied, "The hall is magnificent but I wish I were in the audience listening to you."

Dr. Stein suggested that Toscanini spend two weeks in Arizona's dry climate, but the maestro wanted either to stay in New York in the hope of working again or to go home to Milan. He made no public comment about the new biography of him that Howard Taubman published within a few days of Toscanini's eighty-fourth birthday— which he spent quietly at home with Wanda, Walter, and Cia—or about Filippo Sacchi's Italian biography of him, which appeared at almost the same time. Taubman's account of the first half of Toscanini's life was closely based on Segre's 1947 article, and he did the best he

---

* In a letter of 29 January 1951, Walter Toscanini wrote that his father wanted essentially the same *Falstaff* cast that he had had in New York for the previous year's broadcast, but with Tebaldi as Alice and Barbieri as Meg. For *Macbeth* he wanted Paolo Silveri in the title role and either Cesare Siepi or Nicola Rossi-Lemeni as Banquo. "In Milan he heard a certain soprano Calla [*sic*] who perhaps had the qualities for this part" of Lady Macbeth, Walter wrote. Two years later, Toscanini heard and did not like Callas in a recording of *I Puritani*: "It's not the right kind of voice for that music," he said. "It's a Verdi voice."

could with the following four decades of that life, given the paucity of documents available at the time; there is little in the book about Toscanini's personal life—not surprisingly, given that the maestro was still alive—and one senses a reluctance on the author's part to deal with the backstage aspects of the maestro's work at the Metropolitan, the New York Philharmonic, and the NBC Symphony: Taubman was, after all, the *Times*'s music editor, and he needed to maintain a good rapport with all of those organizations.

Sacchi's book, in both its original form and in the revised and expanded version that was published in Italy in 1960, is short on factual substance and gives relatively little attention to the vast non-Italian portions of the maestro's career, but it provides a charming and useful picture of the Italian musical environment of his youth and of the personal side of his early years.[*]

4.

TOSCANINI HAD PLANNED TO STAY IN NEW YORK UNTIL LATE APRIL 1951, allowing his leg to heal as well as possible before making his annual trip to Italy, but early in the month Carla, in Milan, suffered a serious heart attack. Her husband, accompanied by Wanda (Walter had to stay in New York with Cia), flew home immediately. At first, Carla's condition seemed to improve, and Wally later recalled that "Papà was very affectionate, full of tenderness" toward his wife. But she no longer believed him. "He's always been a liar," she sighed.

Carla's apparent partial recovery gave Arturo more time to fret over his own condition. According to an obscure Italian proverb, a man does not live longer than his mother lived to be, and Toscanini, who was always keenly aware of dates and numbers, calculated that since his mother had lived eighty-four years and twenty-four days, he might not live beyond 18 April 1951. But the date came and went, and he was still breathing. He even noticed, with some surprise, that his knee and leg were improving, and he began to take solitary strolls through the city late at night. A cellist from Parma once saw him

---

[*] An English translation, published in the United States and the United Kingdom in 1957 with the unfortunate title of *The Magic Baton*, is an abridgment of the first Italian edition.

walking in the rain without an umbrella; when Toscanini stopped to read an election poster in Piazza San Babila, the cellist summoned up his courage and approached him. "Maestro, you're getting wet," he said.

"And you aren't?" Toscanini replied. But he let his fellow townsman accompany him to his door.

Toscanini and Wally went together to vote in the regional and municipal elections on 27 May. "After the war he always voted for the Social Democrats, the party of Giuseppe Saragat," a future president, Wally later reported. She made sure that her father's old friends and colleagues visited frequently, to keep him from becoming depressed over Carla's condition and his own inactivity. The tenor Giacomo Lauri-Volpi dropped by one day and expressed the wish that the maestro live to be a hundred. "And what if I do?" said Toscanini—refusing, typically, to look on the bright side of a matter. "Sixteen years pass quickly. And then?"

Having heard and liked a radio broadcast of *La Mer* conducted by a thirty-seven-year-old former violist from the Santa Cecilia Orchestra, Toscanini went to the Milan Conservatory to observe the man— Carlo Maria Giulini—conducting a concert version of Haydn's rarely performed opera *Il Mondo della Luna*; again, Toscanini approved. Wally invited Giulini to meet her father, and thereafter the two musicians would occasionally get together when the older maestro was in Italy. "He was always extremely kind and pleasant with me," Giulini said. "People often talk about his outbursts of anger but hardly ever about this sweet, benevolent aspect of his character."

Another conductor, Gianandrea Gavazzeni, spent much of each summer in the town of Baveno, on the western shore of Lake Maggiore, a short boat ride from the Isolino; Toscanini enjoyed discussing music, musicians, and literature with him. A man of broad intellectual curiosity who was then in his early to middle forties, Gavazzeni kept diaries in which he made notes of his conversations with Toscanini, and he later published excerpts from the diaries.*

Around 12 June, Toscanini traveled to Rome, probably to visit Dr. Frugoni again, but on the fourteenth he suddenly flew back to Milan:

---

* In preparing the present book, this writer has drawn on some of those writings and on his own conversations with Gavazzeni.

Carla had suffered another major attack and had fallen into a coma. He stayed near her bedside day and night, and Walter flew in from New York to be present at the end, which came on 23 June, six weeks before Carla's seventy-fourth birthday and two days after the couple's fifty-fourth wedding anniversary. Friends reported that the weeping maestro refused to leave his wife's bedside for several hours after her death and that he was too grief stricken to attend her funeral. Carla's coffin was walled into the tomb that had been built for little Giorgio Toscanini forty years earlier, in Milan's Cimitero Monumentale.

SHORTLY BEFORE CARLA'S DEATH, Toscanini had sent an oddly phrased cablegram to Frank Folsom in response to the RCA president's good wishes for Signora Toscanini's recovery: "Unfortunately for my Carla there is no more hope of recovering and in these sad hours of despair the only hope is to look forward to my work with the NBC." In the midst of his worry, and after having nearly persuaded himself that he would never conduct again, Toscanini was already planning his 1951–52 season. Friends continued to report that the grieving maestro was eating and sleeping even less than usual and that his children were worried about him, but Sarnoff and his wife spent a "happy week-end" with Toscanini and his family on the Isolino and were "happy beyond words that you have decided to carry on—as always," Sarnoff wrote. Less than a month after Carla's funeral, NBC announced that Toscanini would return to his orchestra in the fall.

To test his stamina away from the public eye, he recorded three Verdi pieces—the Overture to *I Vespri Siciliani* and the two *Traviata* preludes—with the Scala orchestra over four days in early August. Although the *Vespri* recording was rejected altogether and the other pieces were released only in Brazil (Toscanini's royalties were donated to Casa Verdi), he had proved to himself that he had overcome the physical and emotional lows of the first half of the year.

He went to the island of Ischia in the Bay of Naples for a cure at the thermal baths at Casamicciola, but he spent most of the summer on the Isolino, and on 17 September he and Walter flew back to New York. "I'm homesick for my old house in Via Durini!" he wrote to

Wally, two weeks later, but "the atmosphere I need for working is only here. And work I must, otherwise life is *intolerable!!*"

NBC had arranged to make Toscanini's schedule somewhat lighter for the 1951–52 season: instead of sixteen weekly broadcasts he would conduct only twelve, split into three groups of four weeks each, with four weeks' rest after the first and second groups; the concerts would take place at Carnegie Hall on Saturdays from 6:30 to 7:30 P.M. Before the season began, he conducted five days of recording sessions, and by the season's end he would have dedicated a total of twenty-one days—his all-time high—to the process. Dr. Howe measured his blood pressure after the first session: 122 over 80. "I didn't feel tired," he wrote to Wally. "So you see that your old father has gotten down to work, and with enthusiasm."

The NBC musicians found Toscanini's condition little short of miraculous, given the setbacks he had suffered a few months earlier. Yet those setbacks, together with the widely held belief that the NBC Symphony would be disbanded when the maestro retired, had caused several musicians to look for jobs elsewhere. The concertmaster, Mischa Mischakoff, first and foremost, adored Toscanini but worried about what would happen when the end came. "If it was not for the uncertainty of the NBC job, I would not think of moving," he wrote to his wife. He was engaged as concertmaster of the Detroit Symphony Orchestra but completed the 1951–52 season with Toscanini. Daniel Guilet, who had already been in the orchestra for a decade, replaced him; Toscanini admired Guilet's musicianship but not the quality of his tone.[*]

Four of the season's concerts were televised and, like their six predecessors, they were preserved and have been commercially available in various formats since the early 1990s. Although Toscanini suffered under the extremely hot television lights and tended to take quicker tempi than he normally chose for some of the pieces, they make essential viewing for anyone interested in the art of conducting. Parts of the Wagner concert of 29 December are especially remarkable: one marvels at the breadth of the *Tristan* Prelude; at the

---

[*]   Guilet (originally Guilevich), like Mischakoff and many other members of the NBC Symphony's string section, was Russian-born, but he had grown up and studied in Paris. Toscanini preferred the generally more intense Russian-school violin sound to the generally more elegant French-school sound.

increasing intensity of the "Liebestod," in which Toscanini restrains the orchestra from making a series of climaxes and instead builds the tension to a single, *real* climax; at the flexibility of his control over the menacing triple-triplets in "Siegfried's Death" from *Götter-dämmerung*; and at the holding back of the Funeral Music's heart-stopping double chords.

Another example is visible in "Nuages" from Debussy's Three Nocturnes (15 March 1952). The tempo is much too fast, in this writer's opinion, but the close-ups show Toscanini providing the players with all the specific assistance they need, above all through eye contact. He makes no mood-painting gestures, nor does he conduct phrase by phrase, let alone bar by bar; instead, he reveals the piece's whole structure in a single, unbroken line. He pays the musicians the ultimate compliment by counting on their attention and unity of intention—which explains why, in rehearsal, he would become upset when they were not "with him" 100 percent.

A few months later, the British critic Neville Cardus, not always a Toscanini admirer, wondered how the maestro achieved his "changes of tone" and "flow of phrase" with "few and not demonstrative indications: a curve of the right hand which a child might observe and follow, a quite gentle pointing of the forefinger of the left hand[.] Toscanini makes conducting look so effortless that we are compelled more than ever to wonder why other conductors are obliged to indulge in such exhausting supplications." But by watching him face-on, as his orchestras did, one understands that Toscanini's secret lay in his complete security, his simultaneous awareness of what the music was doing and what it was about to do, and the exceptional degree of his mental and visual focus and intensity.

THE DEVASTATING FLOODS in Italy's Po River delta in November 1951, which left dozens of people dead and 180,000 homeless, prompted Toscanini to expand his fifth performance of the season, on 22 December, from a one-hour broadcast into a full-length benefit concert that netted $28,000 for the Italian Welfare League. And he ended the NBC Symphony's fifteenth season on 29 March 1952 with a performance of the Beethoven Ninth that raised over $66,000 for the New York Infirmary's Building Fund. He seemed to lose control during parts of the first movement, and there are rough passages throughout the rest of the symphony. But a few days later he made his only studio recording of the Ninth; the sessions went well, and Toscanini was reported to have said that he was "almost satisfied" with the results. The interpretation is somewhat mellower than some of its immediate predecessors, but it cannot be compared in either sweep or subtlety to the poorly recorded yet remarkable 1936 New York Philharmonic performance or to several other versions that have been preserved.

Isaiah Berlin attended the concert performance of the Ninth and found it wonderful. Admittedly, however, the liberal British philosopher's worship of Toscanini had been colored by the maestro's stand against fascism. "Now he *is* the greatest figure, to me, in the world," the philosopher had written a few months earlier, and he described Toscanini as "the last proud, noble, unbending representative (with Salvemini) of the Risorgimento & 19th century ideals of human liberty." Toscanini was "not just a great conductor, but a symbol of discipline & spontaneity in one—the most morally dignified & inspiring hero of our time—more than Einstein, (to me) more than even the superhuman Winston [Churchill]."

A few days before the performance of the Ninth, the *New York Times* had saluted Toscanini with an editorial, on the occasion of his eighty-fifth birthday. "The only way one can tell that Arturo Toscanini is 85 today is to check the calendar. No one could guess it from his music." The article went on to remind New Yorkers how lucky they were to have enjoyed his music making for so many years, and it concluded, "As in other years, the Maestro will wish the day to pass without fanfare or ceremony, but we hope he won't mind if we take a moment to wish him long life, good health and many more years of music making."*

Three weeks later, Toscanini gave the orchestra members and their spouses an end-of-season party at his home, and on 5–6 May he flew to Milan with Wally, who had been visiting him in New York. The previous year, Silvano Caselli, a Florentine painter, had begun a

---

* Toscanini did, however, receive at least one birthday present that delighted him: a copy of Wagner's piano-vocal reduction of Donizetti's *La Favorita*, sent to him by Alfred Wallenstein. He had never seen it before, and he wrote to Wallenstein that he was "crasy [*sic*] with joy!"

portrait of Toscanini;* now Toscanini agreed to pose for Renato Vernizzi, a Parmesan painter. One afternoon, Vernizzi came to Via Durini accompanied by the writer Ubaldo Bertoli, a former Resistance fighter and a noted character in Parma, who got Toscanini to reminisce about his childhood.

> There was a little church, Santa Teresa, where my mother used to go to mass, and there was a fat priest with a purplish nose. He was always agitated. In those days it was a peaceful street. A cart would pass by "every time a bishop died," as we used to say.
> I went to Parma recently. I got out in Piazza del Duomo to go and see again Antelami's "Deposition," the most beautiful sculpture in the world, a stupendous symphony of sorrow and serenity. On the steps, a little man came up to ask if I needed a guide. I told him that I knew the Duomo very well, but I said it in dialect. It was a big mistake! He stared at me and shouted: "Ma lu l'è al mestor Toscanen." [But he's Maestro Toscanini.] I begged him not to tell anyone, then I quickly got back into the car.

At some point during the summer, Toscanini returned to Ischia for a cure at the thermal baths, and on another occasion he went by car from Milan to Rome for a checkup with Dr. Frugoni; he had intended to sleep during the trip, but instead he enjoyed himself immensely, waking Wally occasionally to point out sights of interest. At the home of his Roman friend Mimy Finzi, he saw Raffaele Calzini, a journalist he had known for many years, who described their encounter:

> He looked at me: "You've put on weight! [. . .] Everybody's getting fat, by God! Look at me! [. . .] No stomach. You have to have fire inside to not get fat. You people don't have fire inside!" He was very cheerful, smiling, happy. I thought he would talk to me about Rome, or maybe some museum, or some lady admirer, or his future plans. No: he talked to me about music.

---

* Caselli's painting and the preliminary sketches for it were reproduced in Orio Vergani et al., *Toscanini nella pittura di Caselli* (Bergamo: Istituto Italiano d'Arti Grafiche, 1953).

"I'm enthusiastic: I'm just coming back from the RAI [Italian Radio] in Via Asiago where I heard twelve fine, excellent kids, a perfect chamber orchestra [I Musici]—twelve young people, you know, eighteen or twenty years old [. . .]. They play without a conductor. I told those kids—I applauded them and thanked them. No, music won't die. People study more these days. In my day there were many dilettantes and bohemians and drunkards. There are orchestral ensembles in Italy that do honor to the country, to our traditions—like the Roman Collegium [I Virtuosi di Roma]* that went to America and was very well received. [. . .]

"Smell that perfume? It's the perfume of Rome. I had never noticed it; I discovered it during my sleepless hours. Here I don't have music on the radio to keep me company at night, so I've analyzed the odors: jasmine, pittosporum, magnolia, and, above all, pine—pine resin. [. . .]

"I want to get back to Milan as soon as possible. I must, I must. My son Walter sent me the test pressing of the Ninth from America; I want to hear it and check how it came out, and possibly to correct it. These long-playing records often make me happy. [. . .] You've got to work, always work."

And work he did. He flew back to New York early in July to listen to test pressings of more of his recordings and to conduct two concerts of light classics. The air-conditioning system at Carnegie Hall failed at the first concert, and the *Times* reported that many of the men in the orchestra appeared to be on the verge of passing out; the maestro, however, seemed unfazed, and at the end he "spryly left the podium and then trotted out for a few bows, grinning hugely." Following each broadcast, he spent a day in the recording studio, committing to tape the pieces that he had just conducted on the radio. He flew back to Milan late in August and spent most of the rest of the summer on the Isolino.

On 19 September, Toscanini conducted an all-Wagner program at

---

* In recorded conversations, Toscanini praised not only I Musici and I Virtuosi di Roma but also the Quintetto Boccherini and, even more enthusiastically, the young Quartetto Italiano.

La Scala and donated his fee to Casa Verdi. This was his first concert in his native country in over two years, and the last one he would ever give there. After having corrected some rudimentary rhythmic problems at a rehearsal, he commented, "I'm embarrassed to have to make these remarks." And during the "Liebestod" from *Tristan*, he shouted, *"Crescendo, voce, voce!* For God's sake—what do you have where your hearts should be?" At the end of the concert, as Toscanini was walking to his dressing room, a famous foreign conductor approached him and said, unctuously, in French, "What a marvelous concert, marvelous, marvelous!" Toscanini glanced at him and exclaimed, "Asino!" (jackass). The visitor, who did not understand Italian, smiled delightedly and said, "Oh, how kind, how kind!"

Wally waited until after the concert to tell her father that a day earlier Frances Alda had died while visiting Venice. Alda was Toscanini's junior by a dozen years, and he still thought of her as the pretty, sharp-tongued young soprano who had auditioned for him at La Scala in 1908, sung with him many times thereafter at the Metropolitan, and probably slept with him as well. She adored him ("I don't know anyone in the world that Alda loved more than Maestro and his family," her husband wrote to Walter Toscanini after his wife's death), and he took her death badly. But five days after the Scala concert he arrived in London for a new engagement.

Toscanini had regretted the cancellation of his London concerts the previous year, and in the meantime Cantelli had been telling him good things about the prowess of the Philharmonia Orchestra, an ensemble founded in 1945 by the record producer Walter Legge, who had in the meantime become an influential figure in postwar European musical life. The Philharmonia gave some performances in Italy in the spring of 1952, and Legge, together with his fiancée, the already celebrated, thirty-six-year-old German soprano Elisabeth Schwarzkopf, paid a visit to Toscanini in Milan. Legge's bluntness in criticizing Toscanini's recording of *La Traviata* impressed the maestro, who began to consider a proposal that he give some concerts with the Philharmonia. In the end, negotiations were taken over by Owen Mase and the impresario S. A. Gorlinsky on behalf of the London County Council, which controlled the Royal Festival Hall; Toscanini decided to give two all-Brahms concerts: the "Tragic" Overture and first two symphonies on 29 September, and the

"Haydn" Variations and Third and Fourth Symphonies on 1 October. For each concert he was paid £1,786 plus £900 for broadcasting rights—much more, per performance, than had ever before been paid to any musician in Britain.

There were over 60,000 applications for the 6,500 seats available for both concerts, even though the top ticket prices were more than eight and a half times the normal rate. According to some sources, Karajan, who worked frequently with the Philharmonia Orchestra, had prerehearsed the musicians, but it was Cantelli who accompanied Toscanini to his first rehearsal and introduced him beforehand to the leader (concertmaster), Manoug Parikian.

Parikian noticed that the eighty-five-year-old maestro was nervous—as he had always been before working with an orchestra for the first time—but conductor and orchestra understood each other immediately; the Philharmonia's now legendary principal horn, Dennis Brain, even had the mysterious feeling that the maestro was helping him, personally, to play his solo passages well. "The Philharmonia is a very good orchestra," Toscanini commented to American friends a few months later. "I played the Second of Brahms—I start[ed] and I did not stop in the four movements! Not once—not at all!" Still, the other symphonies, especially the Third, required more work, and Toscanini requested and was given a few extra string players (among them the violinist and future conductor Neville Marriner), because he felt that there wasn't quite enough weight to the sound. But the rehearsals went smoothly, and he even took a moment to tell the orchestra about having heard Fritz Steinbach's ear-opening Brahms performances in Munich in 1909. Toscanini confessed to Legge that he had long "sought to emulate" Steinbach's interpretation of the exceptionally problematic Third Symphony but had never completely succeeded.

People queued for up to three days to try to obtain one or two of the hall's 295 standing places, and there was a lockdown situation outside and within the premises before and during the concerts. When Toscanini walked onto the stage to begin what was his first London concert in thirteen years, traditional English reserve gave way to tumultuous cheering and applause. Cardus noted that the greeting "seems almost to embarrass him; he acknowledges it by a few modest, impersonal bows, and soon puts an end to it. There is no intimate approach to the audience, only a polite recognition of our presence. He turns as though with relief to the musicians now in front of him. Here, as in greater matters, he is an example for the majority of his colleagues to follow—but they do not, or cannot."

Tension caused a few mistakes to occur during the first concert but did not affect the overall impact of the performances, and by the second concert the nervousness was no longer discernible. Hooligans or pranksters set off firecrackers on the Festival Hall's roof during the finale of the Fourth Symphony, but Toscanini, immersed in his work, either did not notice or paid no attention to the disturbance. Some thought that the perpetrators might have been neo-Fascists, and Isaiah Berlin suspected that they had been hired by an envious Sir Thomas Beecham; they were never identified.

After the second concert, Wally quickly arranged a dinner at the Savoy Hotel, where she and Emanuela were staying with the maestro; the invited guests included Legge and Schwarzkopf; the composer William Walton and his wife, Susanna; Laurence Olivier and Vivien Leigh; and Charlie Chaplin and Oona O'Neill. The Chaplins, who were also staying at the Savoy, had just left the United States, where the film star had been a victim of the infamous McCarthy-era anticommunist witch hunt.

Toscanini attended Cantelli's rehearsals with the Philharmonia Orchestra on the days immediately following his own final performance, and during the breaks he chatted with orchestra members. Although he was not happy with the Festival Hall's acoustics, he would have liked to return to give more concerts and make recordings with the ensemble. But when he departed for New York from Heathrow Airport on 4 October, England had seen the last of him.

5.

"I'M WELL—THAT'S WHAT THE DOCTORS SAY," TOSCANINI WROTE to Wally one day after the first concert of his sixteenth NBC Symphony season. "But there's a sadness that can't be healed." It was All Souls' Day, and he was "thinking of all my dead, who are many, from the eldest of my sisters to my adored Carla!!" His sister Narcisa had been dead for nearly seventy-five years, Carla for only sixteen months. He missed Wally, he said, and wished she were always near, "like Walter and Cia, who are so good to me—poor things!"

Yet despite the bouts of melancholy, he had plunged energetically into the 1952–53 season, which was even more demanding than its predecessor. There would be fourteen concerts instead of twelve, and some of the works scheduled were not staples of Toscanini's repertoire: Saint-Saëns's Third Symphony, for instance, he had not conducted since 1934, and the *Missa Solemnis* had been absent from his programs since the 1942 New York Philharmonic Beethoven cycle. In November, he performed the second act of Gluck's *Orfeo ed Euridice* after having rehearsed with Nan Merriman at intervals over a nine-month period—"the same amount of time that you need for making a baby," he quipped. He worked especially hard with her on the coloring of each phrase, just as he had done with Louise Homer more than forty years earlier. In March 1953, he conducted Schubert's Symphony no. 5 in B-flat Major, for the first time in his life, using only half of the orchestra's string players, to achieve a more intimate sound quality;* it was the last piece that he added to his lifetime performing repertoire of over six hundred works.

In the course of the season, Toscanini dedicated eleven days to making recordings, some of which—Schubert's "Great" C Major Symphony, *Till Eulenspiegel*, Beethoven's Eighth Symphony, Berlioz's *Roman Carnival* Overture, and Rossini's *William Tell* Overture, among others—were remarkable achievements not only for an eighty-five-year-old but by any standards.† As the season progressed, however, Toscanini became increasingly worried about the performance of the *Missa Solemnis* that he had scheduled for 28 March 1953, three days after his eighty-sixth birthday. This benefit concert for the Artists' Veterans Hospital Programs and the Hospitalized Veterans Music Service would also be the last performance of the season, and

---

* Toscanini regretted that he had not used a reduced string section also for the *Prelude to the Afternoon of a Faun*, which he performed and recorded that season. He rejected his recording of it.

† In August 1953, Walter Toscanini, on his father's behalf, signed a revised, ten-year agreement with RCA Victor: the company would pay an annual advance against royalties of $30,000, and Toscanini or his heirs would receive a basic royalty of 7 percent of the US retail price of each published record, reduced to 5 percent if there were soloists in the recording.

he was considering making it the last of his career. His memory was troubling him from time to time, his vision constantly, and his insomnia was worse than usual. He wondered whether he had the physical stamina necessary not only for the grueling rehearsals (careful preparation of the vocal soloists, separate orchestral and choral rehearsals, and ensemble rehearsals)* and the performance itself, but also for three subsequent days to be dedicated to recording Beethoven's great mass. "If, with my enthusiasm and adoration for that saint, I could achieve something worthy, it would be the greatest reward for my long, too long, artistic life," he wrote to Maria Cecchini. He began to listen to an off-the-air recording of his 1940 NBC *Missa* performance but stopped when he realized that his ideas about the work had changed in the interim.

In the end, he brought off the difficult task remarkably well, but a comparison of the finished recording with earlier recorded performances betrays a dramatic diminution in control and subtlety. Toscanini himself found Guilet's playing cold in the long violin solo in the *Benedictus*, and he described Conley's singing of the tenor part as both cold and expressionless. Nevertheless, he approved the recording, as it was put together from various takes.

For some time, the possibility of another NBC Symphony American spring tour had been under discussion, but after the exertions for the *Missa Solemnis* Toscanini decided against the adventure. Now, however, he had to decide whether or not to undertake another season of concerts. Two years earlier, when his health had seemed to be going rapidly downhill, he had thought seriously about stopping; since then, he had enjoyed a substantial resurgence of strength, but the *Missa* process had shaken his confidence. He had always criticized performers who went on too long, and he wrote melodramatically to Wally that he "would like to rest for what little time remains to me and enjoy a peaceful death," complaining, further, that his fate

---

* Apart from the trustworthy Merriman, the solo singers were new to him. He had wanted Elisabeth Schwarzkopf—whom he had heard and liked in Karajan's recording of Brahms's *German Requiem*, and whose beauty he admired—for the soprano part, but she was unavailable; the Canadian Lois Marshall took her place. Likewise, the American tenor Eugene Conley replaced an indisposed Jussi Björling; and another American, Jerome Hines, sang the bass part. Toscanini also attended Robert Shaw's rehearsals with his chorale.

was "to work until I close my eyes." But he boasted, in the same letter, that "work doesn't tire me! Twenty years ago, a doctor would
come to give me an injection after a rehearsal or a concert; these
days, he comes to see whether my blood pressure is still good. I feel
tired for an hour or two, but then I'm nimble again."

Yet by the spring of 1953 he knew that he should stop. "I am not well,
and no one believes me, the jackasses, but I'm not the same as I was,"
he wrote to Cecchini. "My eyes have worsened so much that I can no
longer find glasses that can help me. I sleep little and badly, tormented
by tragic, commonplace, or fearful dreams. [. . .] Excuse my horrible
writing, but I'm very agitated and my hand slides around on the paper.
That's how it goes! I'm old, very old, and I can't stand it anymore!"

Toscanini told Chotzinoff that although he could still read if he
wore his glasses and held a book or score close to his eyes, he sometimes saw double and couldn't always see all the letters in a word;
when he sat at the piano he could not read a score on the music
stand. Two years earlier, with eight-diopter-strength lenses, he had
been able to read everything, he said, but now those lenses didn't
work for him. What should he do? He had been making music for
seventy-seven years, since the day he had entered the Parma Conservatory. What would his life become if he stopped?

On 16 April 1953, two weeks after the final *Missa Solemnis* recording session, Sarnoff and Chotzinoff came to Villa Pauline to discuss,
over lunch, Toscanini's future plans. Afterward, he claimed that
they had made the decision for him: "they have had the bad taste to
force me to accept another year of concerts," he wrote to Cecchini.
"And I, imbecile that I am and tired of hearing myself pestered, have
given in. The American public will again have to [. . .] put up with
having an old man of eighty-six before its eyes." And to Wally he
went so far as to say that his "ferocious resistance" to undertaking
another season "was broken down by the most ferocious ball breakers" and by "their exhortations about my return."

But not only had he put up no ferocious resistance: he had sketched
out the programs of his first three concerts for the following season
even before Sarnoff and Chotzinoff had come to see him. During the
postlunch conversation, which was recorded, Chotzinoff told Toscanini that if he wanted to conduct only twelve concerts, that number
would be sufficient; Toscanini calmly replied that he would do four-

teen: six weekly concerts followed by a four-week break, then four followed by another four-week break, and then four more, with Cantelli filling in the two intervals. And he went on chatting, with no reference to having had any difficulty in making his decision.

Six days later, New York's newspapers announced that Toscanini had agreed to return to the NBC Symphony in the fall. And the maestro, with a mixture of conscientiousness and trepidation, began to prepare the orchestra's seventeenth season. He remained in New York well into June, studying as best he could, given his failing eyesight, spending evenings with family and friends, and continuing to listen to playbacks of recordings for possible release.

AS ALREADY NOTED, some of those family gatherings and playback sessions were recorded, thanks to Walter Toscanini. Although Walter had had no formal musical training, by the early 1950s he understood better than anyone else that his father's powers were gradually, inevitably declining, and he began to redouble the efforts he had begun in the 1920s to preserve whatever he could of the elder Toscanini's life and legacy. With the help of some engineers and high-fidelity enthusiasts—including the NBC Symphony violinist David Sarser and the writer Ralph Ellison, who was about to burst upon the literary scene with his novel *Invisible Man*—Walter set up a state-of-the-art sound laboratory in Villa Pauline's basement, so that his father could listen in his own home to playbacks and test pressings of his recordings. A battery of speakers was placed in the living room and a microphone was taped to the stem of a floor lamp next to the chair in which Toscanini customarily sat: he could listen in comfort and communicate with Walter or the engineers in the basement without having to go down there himself.

Walter soon realized that, given the presence of the microphone in the living room, he could tape his father's comments on the recordings, in case doubts were later to arise. Then Walter had another idea: since his father would neither write about his career nor relate the story of his life to others in any systematic way, Walter would record get-togethers at the house. His father was easily drawn out by family members and friends about music and musicians and about specific episodes in his life, which he related with gusto and humor; Walter had only to run down to the basement and press the "Record" button.

Some 103 tapes were eventually recorded, without Toscanini's knowledge, and were numbered, dated, and labeled by Walter. The earliest, a *Missa Solemnis* playback session, dates from 1 April 1953;[*] the last was recorded on 29 December 1956, less than three weeks before Toscanini's death. With Walter's encouragement, eighteen additional tapes were recorded in Milan by Sandro Cicogna, an engineer and family friend, between July 1954 and January 1955, during the maestro's last stay in Italy; Wally Toscanini and Anita Colombo served as Cicogna's accomplices. Of the eighteen, six appear to have been lost.[†]

The recordings vary greatly in length, quality, and content. Some of the shortest ones last only a few minutes, whereas the longest run to over two hours; some were recorded at a tape speed of seven and a half inches per second, others at three and three-quarters; some were put on new tapes, others on used or even spliced-together tapes. Sometimes Toscanini was sitting near the microphone and his words are clear; at other times he was off-microphone to varying degrees, and what he said is hard or impossible to make out. Some of the conversations are useless, either for their poor acoustical quality or for their content (idle chitchat by and/or about people no longer identifiable), but many others are full of illuminating information and insights. Most of the conversations were in Italian, but when non-Italian-speaking guests were present Toscanini spoke with them in his flawed, Italian-peppered English, and, occasionally, in fractured French.

Other people present at these gatherings usually included one or more of Toscanini's three children[‡] and occasionally one or more of his three grandchildren, as well as Horowitz and, in some of the

---

[*] The tape in box no. 1 was mistakenly labeled 6 February 1953; the correct date is 6 February 1954.

[†] The tapes made in Italy lay untouched for more than forty years until this writer borrowed them from Emanuela Castelbarco and had them transferred to compact discs. Another decade went by before Walfredo Toscanini had the American tapes, which he had kept in boxes under his bed, converted to WAV files. The contents of all of these recordings have contributed to every chapter of this book.

[‡] On one of the tapes, Wanda is heard trimming her father's mustache—a job he had always done himself, but which his failing eyesight no longer allowed him to carry out.

earlier tapes, Cia. Frequent guests included, among others, Margherita De Vecchi; Anita Colombo; the Canadian conductor Wilfrid Pelletier and his wife, the soprano Rose Bampton, who was Walter Toscanini's lover, apparently with her husband's knowledge; and the vocal coach and conductor Dick Marzollo. There were also conversations with the conductors Antonino Votto, Guido Cantelli, Carlo Maria Giulini, Milton Katims, and Alfred Wallenstein, and the wives of some of them; the art historian and critic Gillo Dorfles; the Belgian cellist Iwan d'Archambeau, a member of the celebrated but long-defunct Flonzaley Quartet; the stage and screen director Luchino Visconti; the painter Arturo Tosi; David Sarnoff, Samuel and Pauline Chotzinoff, and George Marek, another RCA executive and later Toscanini biographer; the RCA producers Jack Pfeiffer, Richard Mohr, and Richard Gardner; various singers and NBC Symphony musicians; the pianists Ania Dorfman and Mieczyslaw Horszowski; Enrico and Ida Polo's daughter, Anna, and her husband, Walter Marx; Sandro Cicogna; and the Toscaninis' secretary, Eugenia Gale.

In addition to their verbal content, the conversation tapes are valuable for what they reveal about Toscanini's condition before and during his final active concert season and in the remaining thirty-three months of his life. Through most of that period, his mental faculties were outstanding. Although he often had trouble remembering names of people, places, or even compositions, once the name in question came to mind, either on its own or because someone else reminded him of it, he could go into minute and highly accurate detail on the subject at hand. His hearing was still good, although imperfect: if people spoke to him very softly or unclearly he would not always understand what they had said, especially if there was background noise, but he had no trouble hearing people who spoke to him in a normal conversational tone under normal conditions.

There is much mirth in the recordings. Toscanini was no joke teller, but he was constantly chuckling at others' amusing stories or in recounting episodes from his own life, including some that did not show him in the best light. And he was a good listener, open-minded and curious about others' ideas and opinions, even, indeed especially, when they conflicted with his own. His tales of encounters with other musicians were fascinating, as were his descriptions and opinions of singers of the past. He was often brutally negative in talking about conductors, including himself: although he occasionally expressed pride in some of his specific achievements, he was devastatingly critical of many of his own performances and recordings, and he would tell people who praised him effusively that they were wrong or even crazy. Sometimes, when he vehemently expressed an opinion, he seemed to be hoping that someone would argue with him—as occasionally happened: some of his visitors were in awe of him, but others were not. Margherita De Vecchi, in particular, often teased him and argued with him, and on one occasion, when he described an acquaintance as having a difficult character, she commented, "Look who's talking!"

He invariably spoke affectionately to his children and grandchildren, all of whom were respectful toward him but by no means afraid to tease or argue with him. When Toscanini, during one of the *Missa Solemnis* playback sessions, asked to have part of a rehearsal recording patched in, Walter told him, "We would, but unfortunately there's this Maestro Toscanini who's shouting 'Porco Dio!' at the orchestra."

6.

"VERDI PASSED AWAY AT MY AGE, BUT YOU MUST REMEMBER THAT he ate a lot more," Toscanini told Enzo Biagi, a journalist, who spotted him strolling with Emanuela in Milan one afternoon in the summer of 1953. He had flown to Italy early in June, with Walter, Cia, and Walfredo, arriving in time to vote in the Italian election on the eighth, and he spent most of June and July at home in Via Durini. But there were occasional trips to the Isolino, a return to Ischia for the thermal baths, and a four-day stay in Rome to see Dr. Frugoni. An electrocardiogram showed mild sinus and extrasystolic arrhythmia but nothing particularly worrisome.

According to Friedelind Wagner, Toscanini had told her that he had thought about revisiting Bayreuth in 1952; now, in August 1953, Winifred and all four of her children signed a telegram asking him to return the following year to conduct either Beethoven's Ninth Symphony or a Wagner concert. Toscanini did not reply. Not long thereafter, Friedelind and her mother—who had made a fragile peace with each other—were visiting friends in northern Italy and tried to phone Toscanini, hoping to see him on the Isolino. Wally, who answered the phone, "reacted so furiously and was quite indignant—'how could I do this to her father,'" Friedelind reported to Margherita. He had not seen Winifred, an unregenerate Hitler admirer, since 1933, and he would not see her again.

Late in September, the old maestro was thrilled to take a fifty-mile-an-hour speedboat trip around the picturesque, mountain-surrounded Lake Maggiore; Walfredo later commented that his grandfather had done so much traveling over the decades that he always enjoyed the fastest possible means of transportation. But in mid-October, instead of catching a plane to New York, Toscanini sailed from Naples aboard the SS *Constitution*, which developed technical problems en route and did not arrive at its destination until the twenty-eighth—barely in time for him to start rehearsing for his first NBC concert on 8 November. Before he could get to work, however, he came down with the flu. NBC engaged Pierre Monteux—a mere seventy-eight-year-old—for the first two concerts; Toscanini listened to both broadcasts on the radio, described the first one—a Beethoven-Brahms program—as "marvelous," and invited Monteux to the house for dinner. But he could not understand why Monteux had founded a school for conductors. "I wouldn't know how to give lessons," he said to a friend. "Within a tempo, every beat has its own physiognomy. [. . .] I beat time, but I'm not aware of it. I speak within myself. [. . .] There are some things—if you feel them, you can do them; if you don't feel them, no teacher can teach them to you."*

Once Toscanini felt reasonably well, he invited his first-desk players to a convivial lunch at his home, and a few days later he began his rehearsals. He had initially planned to include Brahms's *German Requiem*, Kodály's *Psalmus Hungaricus*, and all-Sibelius and all-Mendelssohn programs in his season's schedule, but he had given up all four ideas: his failing eyesight did not permit direct contact

---

* Most conductors of Toscanini's generation thought as he did on this subject, but Monteux, who had conducted the world premiere of *The Rite of Spring* and had led many other avant-garde works, grasped the fact that new music required new techniques, and he believed that even in traditional repertoire an experienced conductor could help younger colleagues find their way.

with the printed page, which had always been part of his method of study, photographic memory notwithstanding. He had also wanted to perform Bach's Second "Brandenburg" Concerto but had dropped the proposal when the principal trumpet, Harry Glantz, told him that he did not feel able to tackle the high Baroque trumpet part.

Toscanini later said that when he had gone before the orchestra for his first rehearsal of the season, "I was ashamed of myself to go there. I thought, 'You are too old, too old, too old'—I must stay home." There were moments, he said, when he could still feel his blood rising when he conducted music or spoke about music, but at other times "non sono contento di me" (I am not satisfied with myself). Three days after his first concert (22 November), he wrote to Maria Cecchini's mother that he had conducted "as well as possible" but that he was "in such a depressed state that I didn't have the courage to get any news or to confront any work. . . A real wretch. . . I am having trouble writing. [. . .] I am so tired of being M . . . Arturo Toscanini that it bores me even to read my own name"—a phrase that Verdi had written to Boito many decades earlier.

The hour-long broadcasts had been moved from Saturdays to Sundays, at 6:30 P.M., and were now sponsored by the Socony-Vacuum Oil Company, which inserted spoken commercial announcements between the pieces on the program; these were heard in the auditorium and on the air. Toscanini seemed unfazed—at his first concert he was observed talking softly with a member of the orchestra while the speaker was having his say—but several commentators deplored the crass intervention.

The main work on Toscanini's second program was Berlioz's dramatic *Harold in Italy*, with Cooley as solo violist, but only in the exciting finale did the maestro seem to take full charge of the orchestra and set the proceedings on fire. An all-Beethoven program on 6 December, with fine performances of the *Coriolan* Overture and the "Eroica" Symphony, was followed a week later by a mixed program. With Toscanini's first scheduled break of the season came a serious attack of bronchitis; an upset over news of the death, on 3 December, of his brother-in-law and former conservatory classmate Enrico Polo; and a great deal of worry.

What most preoccupied Toscanini was a two-part concert performance of Verdi's *Un Ballo in Maschera*, scheduled for 17 and 24 January

1954. He had taught Herva Nelli her part (Amelia) the previous spring, accompanying her at the piano with absolute security, but conditions had changed. Fourteen of Walter's tapes contain parts of the rehearsals that Toscanini held at home, as often as his health permitted, from mid-December almost until the first of the two broadcasts; in many of the sessions Toscanini was in a pitiable state. He worked as best he could with Dick Marzollo to establish tempi and discuss phrasing and articulation, and then with Marzollo accompanying most of the singers: Nelli, Robert Merrill (Renato), Virginia Haskins (Oscar), Claramae Turner (Ulrica), Nicola Moscona (Samuele), and Norman Scott (Tommaso). But he often felt feverish, and he was sneezing and coughing.

Marzollo tried to reassure him, telling him that he was agitated only because he wasn't well. Toscanini protested: "But, my friend, I can't sit at the piano to read this opera! I can't *see*! I see all of you through a fog." Then, laughing at himself, he said that he felt as if he were in the steam room in the spa at Salsomaggiore. He should not have decided to conduct this season, he declared, and he admitted that for the prebreak concerts he had had to stimulate his memory of the scores by listening to recordings of his previous performances of the works. Worse: the medication the doctor had given him was making him hallucinate. He woke up one morning and thought that everything in the house had been rearranged, and on another occasion his mother appeared to him, not as in a dream but seemingly for real, telling him not to get dressed but to stay in bed. To Marzollo he said, softly, "I'm no longer the man I used to be."

And yet there are dozens of interesting details in the rehearsals. For instance, at rehearsal no. 18 in Act III ("Dunque l'onta di tutti"), there is a metronome indication of quarter note = 66, which seems much too slow. Toscanini compares it (from memory, because he can't read) to "Ora e per sempre addio" in Act II of *Otello*, which has a similar feel (including the use of the harp) and is in the same key, A-flat Major, but is indicated at quarter note = 88. He tells Marzollo that perhaps 76 would make more sense than 66. At one point, he criticizes Verdi for having given a cadenza to Renato, the baritone, at the end of his first aria ("Alla vita che t'arride"), whereas the cadenza for Amelia in her third-act aria ("Morrò, ma prima in grazia") is right: Amelia's aria stands outside the flow of the action, Toscanini says, but Renato is giving advice in his aria, thus the flow should not have been interrupted.

By Christmas Eve, Toscanini was feeling somewhat better; Marzollo was still playing the piano and would continue to do so, but Toscanini worked hard and in detail with the singers on the delivery of each phrase, reminding them that they must always keep the dramatic action in mind even though they would be standing still at this performance. He asked Merrill, for instance, not only to pronounce double consonants correctly but also to vary his tone more. The aria "Eri tu" goes through a wide range of emotions, the maestro told the thirty-five-year-old baritone, who was already a star at the Metropolitan; it should begin seriously but not yet angrily. Later in that scene, Toscanini asked Merrill to sing the phrase "Ogni disegno vostro m'è noto" quietly and to crescendo on "Voi di Riccardo la morte volete." Toscanini was insistent but always patient with the singers, and during the breaks—when coffee and sweets were served—there was much laughter as he recounted episodes from his past.

A few days later, however, Toscanini couldn't remember the words of the opera, and he told Walter to tell the people at NBC to find another conductor for the broadcasts. Miecio Horszowski visited him and noted in his diary, "The Maestro made a very sad impression on me." But Walter cleverly decided to wait before sounding the alarm, and sure enough, on New Year's Day 1954 his father saw a score of *Ballo* lying on the piano and suddenly realized that all the words had come back to him. He was relieved to learn that he had not been replaced.

On 12 January, only five days before the first *Ballo* broadcast, Jussi Björling, who was to have sung the lead tenor role (Riccardo), sent word that he would be unable to perform.[*] A month earlier, Björling had had a preliminary rehearsal (not taped) in Riverdale, during which Toscanini had given him a recording of Bonci singing "È scherzo od è follia," to teach him how to insert the "traditional" laughs. Toscanini and Marzollo agreed, at the time, that Björling had a beautiful voice, knew the part, and sang the notes and words correctly but needed to work on communicating the meaning of the

---

[*] Toscanini had heard Björling in the part at La Scala in 1951 and had evidently liked what he heard.

lines. In the meantime, however, the tenor had gone home to Sweden for the holidays, and had then announced that he was suffering from laryngitis and was canceling all of his appearances for the time being. There were unconfirmed rumors that he had been hospitalized because of his chronic alcoholism; but whatever the truth of the matter, Toscanini said, the tenor ought to have warned him immediately, not at the last minute. "He's a man who isn't well, and we were *stupid* to believe him," Toscanini commented, adding that he never wanted to see Björling again.

The New York newspapers were soon reporting that what was perhaps Toscanini's last opera performance was in jeopardy. Toscanini had once heard Jan Peerce sing the part in a Metropolitan radio broadcast and had not liked him in it, he told Marzollo, but Merrill pointed out that Peerce could be counted on to bring off the difficult task. Toscanini agreed: "I want to see if I can phone Peerce," he said. Peerce later claimed that he had been told, months earlier, that Toscanini had wanted him for the part, and he had been surprised and disappointed to learn that Björling had been chosen instead. At first he resisted the idea of being a last-minute replacement, and when Toscanini phoned him, he said, " 'But Maestro, I haven't done *Un Ballo in Maschera* in six or seven years, and I don't remember it.' 'Peerce, you will know it—you will know it,' " Toscanini told him.

Peerce, who owed much of his career to Toscanini, felt that he couldn't let the maestro down. He restudied his part with his accompanist but did not have even one piano rehearsal with Toscanini or Marzollo. When he arrived at Carnegie Hall for the first ensemble rehearsal, Toscanini told him, " 'Just sing. I follow,' " Peerce recalled. "We went through the first act without a mistake; and he called an intermission; but before that he jumped off the podium and threw his arms around me and kissed me. I felt just like a kid. And upstairs he said to me: 'You afraid? You afraid? I told you: you just sing.' "

In the meantime, Toscanini had rehearsed the orchestra separately. At the beginning of the first session, his voice sounded uncharacteristically soft and sluggish, and he explained to the musicians that he was wearing glasses because "My eyes are no good." But as soon as the music began he became alert, and he worked with them in detail on note durations, articulations, pulse, and dynamics. Later, in rehearsing the second act's dramatic opening, he stopped the orchestra and shouted, "Verdi vuol tutto! Non vuole la metà! Non battere la fiacca!" (Verdi wants everything! He doesn't want half! Don't slack off!) And then: "Mi piace da morire questa musica!" (I love this music to death!)

And yet, had the NBC Symphony not been made up of excellent, experienced musicians who loved their maestro and who probably also feared for him (rather than fearing him—a thing of the past) during what was clearly the coda of his career, the *Ballo* broadcasts could well have fallen apart at several points. Sometimes he was fully in charge, but there were weak moments as well. And if one compares this performance of the aria "Eri tu" with the one made during a concert of Verdi excerpts that Toscanini had conducted in 1943, with the baritone Francesco Valentino, the diminution in tempo flexibility is noteworthy.

Like Toscanini's other NBC opera recordings, this version of *Ballo* must not be taken as holy writ by his greatest fans or used by his severest detractors as a stick for beating him. Until someone invents a time machine, we can have no reliable notion of his performances of this opera when he was at the height of his powers—at the Metropolitan in 1913, for instance, or at La Scala in 1925.

HAVING SUCCESSFULLY BROUGHT OFF the much-feared *Ballo* project, after the second broadcast Toscanini gave a party for the cast members and their spouses in the Berkshire Hotel's Barberry Room. Then, following a four-week respite—during which he was visited by Luigi Dallapiccola*—Toscanini returned to the podium on 28 February to conduct a mixed concert that included a fine performance of Mendelssohn's "Italian" Symphony. He felt that he had previously taken too fast a tempo for the first movement—so he told Milton Katims beforehand—and that many conductors took the third movement too slowly. He also had a feeling, he said, that the main theme of the "Italian" Symphony's second movement, with its profound sadness, was Jewish in origin and ought to be understood

---

* Dallapiccola (1904–1975), one of the most significant Italian composers of his day, wrote twelve-tone music that Toscanini did not understand, but they enjoyed discussing music together on this and other occasions, and Dallapiccola repeatedly expressed the greatest admiration and respect for the old maestro.

as such. And he added that he did not like his own, sole performance of Mendelssohn's "Scottish" Symphony, which had been recorded during a 1941 broadcast, whereas he had recently heard a beautiful recording of it conducted by Georg Solti, who, he remembered, was from Budapest.

On 7 March, Toscanini conducted weak performances of Beethoven's *Leonore* Overture no. 2 and "Pastoral" Symphony, but the following week he accomplished the difficult task of performing Vivaldi's Concerto Grosso in D minor, op. 3, no. 11; Verdi's *Te Deum*; and the Prologue to Boito's *Mefistofele*, with Moscona as soloist. In the Verdi and Boito works, he seemed to be in control, and he later authorized their release on records, but at a postconcert dinner at home he told Pelletier that he had had a memory lapse during the Vivaldi piece and had made a tremendous effort to continue to conduct. He had no desire to conduct his three remaining concerts, he said, but, after all, he wanted to do the *Barber of Seville* Overture, which was to open the following week's program, because he felt that he had previously conducted it at too fast a tempo. (He quoted Bernard Shaw as having said that Toscanini's tempi in Rossini's overtures were too fast, and he said that he agreed with him.) Then, after taking the following week off, he would conduct an all-Wagner concert to close the season, although he hadn't yet decided on a program. Anna Polo Marx, his niece, asked him whether he felt tired; he replied that apart from his eyes, his back, and his legs . . . and then he laughed at himself.

On the twenty-first, he seemed to be only half present during performances of the Rossini overture and Tchaikovsky's "Pathétique" Symphony, and he did withdraw from the following week's concert, which was taken over by the Boston Symphony Orchestra's conductor, Charles Munch. In between those two events, Toscanini, with a shaky hand, signed a typewritten letter to Sarnoff, announcing his retirement; Walter and probably others, including Chotzinoff, had prepared the letter for him.

The letter was dated 25 March 1954, his eighty-seventh birthday. "My very dear David," it began, and it continued with Toscanini's thanks for having had the opportunity to work with the wonderful orchestra that Sarnoff had created for him seventeen years earlier. But the point of the letter was in this sentence: "And now the sad time has come when I must reluctantly lay aside my baton and say goodbye to my orchestra." Sarnoff replied four days later, regretfully accepting the maestro's resignation and thanking him for all he had done for music in general and the NBC Symphony in particular.

Much has been written and debated about the circumstances surrounding Toscanini's retirement and the NBC Symphony Orchestra's demise, but the story now seems clear. A year earlier, when he had decided to conduct the ensemble's 1953–54 season, Toscanini had declared that it would be his last one, and the orchestra's musicians knew that in all likelihood their jobs would be terminated when Toscanini retired. Alfred Wallenstein later claimed that, in the fall of 1953, Sarnoff and Chotzinoff had tried to offer the maestro a contract for the 1954–55 season but had been intercepted by Walter, who had asked them not to make the offer. This scenario seems extremely unlikely, inasmuch as Toscanini had never, in recent years, been asked to sign a contract for the following season or seasons until the preceding one was concluded. Haggin, on the contrary, heard at third hand that Chotzinoff had told Walter that NBC would in any case terminate the orchestra at the end of the 1953–54 season, and that this had provoked a violent reaction from the maestro, who did not wish to retire. But this bit of hearsay is contradicted by several taped conversations in which Toscanini matter-of-factly told people that he was going to stop and that the orchestra would be disbanded.

Wally Toscanini summed up her father's decision with simplicity: "He realized that he was very old and thought it was time to stop," she said. Indeed, no one would or could have forced Toscanini to stop had he wanted to go on—or, more precisely, had he been able to persuade himself that he ought to go on. And, given the fact that NBC had found sponsors for the orchestra as long as Toscanini was its conductor, there is no reason to believe that the orchestra would have been disbanded had he decided to continue. Sarnoff, whose own career had been gilded by his stewardship of Toscanini's NBC tenure, truly admired the maestro and was proud of the orchestra, which he kept going in the face of harsh criticism from many members of his board of directors—also from Haggin and other critics, who took verbal potshots at him for allowing commercial sponsors to replace public service backing for the orchestra, for changing the broadcasts' time slots, and for misusing the musicians when they were not playing as the NBC Symphony.

Sarnoff, a businessman, was a visionary in the realm of media technology but without cultural pretensions. Yet he understood that great music is one of civilization's crowning jewels and that being able to help keep it alive is a privilege, even when the corporate accountants' balance sheets show a loss. No doubt he took into consideration, in the orchestra's later years, two practical facts: the maestro's name continued to lend prestige to NBC and to sell classical records for RCA Victor; and putting the world's most famous classical performing musician to pasture against his will would have looked bad. But the fact remains that in the many decades that have gone by since the disbanding of Toscanini's orchestra, and in a country in which subsidization of the arts from public funds remains—absurdly—anathema, private enterprise has produced nothing comparable to Sarnoff's NBC Symphony Orchestra.

7.

TOSCANINI WAS IN FINE SPIRITS AT A FAMILY GATHERING AT VILLA Pauline on his birthday, despite having put his signature to the letter of resignation earlier in the day. He encouraged his granddaughter Sonia, now nineteen, to develop her talent for drawing and painting, and he told her that she should come to visit him in Italy, where he planned to spend most of his time, following his retirement: there was so much to see there, he said. Walfredo, twenty-four, read a telegram from the Socony-Vacuum Oil Company, wishing the maestro all the best for many years to come. Toscanini laughed: "Many years! I'll continue to break their balls!" Walfredo then read an affectionate telegram from Bruno Walter, and Toscanini commented, "We've known each other for many years; he's always been a good friend. There is much we don't agree about [musically], but he's very kind, truly a refined person."

There remained, however, a final concert to conduct—the all-Wagner program on Sunday, 4 April 1954. At the first rehearsal, on Thursday afternoon, Toscanini told the orchestra that he would beat *alla breve* (two beats to the bar) in the Prelude to Act I of *Lohengrin*, but he had trouble maintaining the slow legato and sometimes lapsed into four, following the orchestra instead of leading it, and confusing everyone. In the *Meistersinger* Prelude, which followed, Toscanini "did nothing about the nerveless, poor playing," Haggin reported. Then came "Dawn" and "Siegfried's Rhine Journey" from *Götterdämmerung*, and at the timpani's entrance immediately after the off-stage horn calls, "Toscanini contended that the timpanist had come in too soon," Haggin reported. "'It's the same part I always play,' said the timpanist. [. . .] Eventually the passage was played the way Toscanini considered correct, and the piece was completed."

The following morning's rehearsal went much better: Toscanini seemed to be his old self. The final rehearsal, on Saturday afternoon, went reasonably well in the straight-through performances of the *Lohengrin* Prelude, the "Forest Murmurs" from *Siegfried*, and the *Götterdämmerung* excerpt—"as far as Toscanini got in it," Haggin wrote. But just where he had stopped at the first rehearsal, he now stopped again, "in a fury" with poor Karl Glassman, the timpanist. "While Toscanini raged I heard Frank Miller call out to the timpanist: 'Make it thirteen measures' rest instead of twelve.' Twelve was right, and the timpanist had waited that number of measures; but Toscanini mistakenly thought it should be one more; and Miller was telling the timpanist to do what would seem right to Toscanini. *'È vergogna! Vergogna!'* [It's shameful! Shameful!] he shouted. And when the passage was repeated, as he thought, correctly, he stopped again and exclaimed: *'Finalmente!'* Then, in bitter anger: *'L'ultima prova!'* [The last rehearsal!]" And with that, Toscanini left the stage without completing the session. Worried that the maestro might withdraw, NBC's officials asked Erich Leinsdorf—conductor, at the time, of the Rochester Philharmonic Orchestra—to stand by in case a replacement was needed. But Toscanini decided to proceed.

The journalists who arrived at Carnegie Hall the following afternoon for the last concert of the orchestra's regular season received copies of Toscanini's letter to Sarnoff and Sarnoff's reply, but the audience was not informed of the maestro's decision. The orchestra members, on the other hand, knew not only about the decision but also that their contracts would be terminated—some within two months, others not until October. The program opened with the *Lohengrin* Prelude; it was followed by the "Forest Murmurs," during which Toscanini forgot to indicate some changes of meter, but the orchestra did not go astray. The *Götterdämmerung* excerpts came off without incident and were followed by the *Tannhäuser* Overture and Bacchanale, which Toscanini had programmed instead of the originally planned Prelude and "Liebestod" from *Tristan*, which he had not been able to remember.

In the middle of the Bacchanale, Toscanini, looking ashen, suddenly stopped conducting and put his left hand over his eyes. The musicians, worried about the maestro, began to make wrong entrances; chaos ensued until Miller began to give cues and the ensemble coalesced, however weakly. In the meantime, however, Cantelli, frightened as he sat in the radio control booth, had insisted that the concert be taken off the air. Technical difficulties were announced, and—just as Toscanini was beginning to regain a measure of self-control—the beginning of his recording of the Brahms First Symphony was incongruously heard over the radio. In the hall he began to beat time again, and the program was put back on the air.

At the end of the Bacchanale, Toscanini stepped off the podium and prepared to leave the stage, but Miller stopped him and reminded him that he still had to conduct the *Meistersinger* Prelude. Toscanini nodded, stepped back onto the podium, and beat numbly through the last piece. But while the last joyous, cascading C Major chords were still being played, he dropped his baton, stepped slowly off the podium, and made his way off the stage. The audience cheered and cheered, but Toscanini did not return to the platform.

AT DINNER IN RIVERDALE that evening, the Cantellis, the Pelletiers, Maria Da Zara (an old family friend), Horowitz, and all three of Toscanini's children were present. At first, in the buzz of chitchat, the maestro seemed barely aware of what was going on around him; then he revived and joined in the conversation. Everyone avoided the subject of what had happened at Carnegie Hall that afternoon. But after the guests had left, and after Walter had turned off the tape recorder, Toscanini reportedly said to his children, "I conducted as if it had been a dream. It almost seemed to me that I wasn't there."

Tributes to Toscanini appeared in newspapers and magazines worldwide. The *New York Times* printed an honest but sympathetic review of his last concert plus articles about his career* and an editorial that expressed the hope that the maestro would return to conduct occasional concerts from time to time. *Life* magazine, however, published photos of Toscanini holding his hand over his eyes and looking forlorn during his final concert; his family made sure that he was not informed of what would have seemed to him a humiliation.

He did learn about, and was terribly upset by, the interruption in the broadcast and the airing of the opening of Brahms's First Symphony. Since he could not contemplate blaming Cantelli, his musical heir, who had been responsible for the deed, he irrationally blamed Chotzinoff, who had had nothing to do with the decision. In a conversation with Anita Colombo and Wally, recorded the following summer, Toscanini inveighed against "those Jews" Chotzinoff and Sarnoff: the former had betrayed him and—the maestro incorrectly surmised—had killed the orchestra because he was turning sixty-five and would have to retire from NBC; and the latter—Toscanini now persuaded himself—had favored the orchestra's demise.

For Sarnoff, the maestro's ostracism must have seemed ungrateful but probably mattered little in other respects; for Chotzinoff, on the other hand, the sudden and total exclusion from his idol's world was a terrible blow. He retaliated by publishing a book, *Toscanini: An Intimate Portrait*, in which the maestro was caricatured as an infantile, uncultivated genius whose behavior toward the people around him was whimsical and sometimes heartless. The book came out a few months before Toscanini's death; Walfredo believed that his grandfather never knew about it.

Two months after his last NBC concert, Toscanini felt strong enough to return to Carnegie Hall to correct some flaws in two of his broadcast recordings of Verdi operas; the orchestra was reconvened especially for this purpose. At a four-hour session on 3 June 1954, he rerecorded about sixteen minutes of music from *Un Ballo in Maschera* (Nelli and Peerce's duet, "Teco io sto," from Act II; part of their final scene together in Act III; and Peerce's "Amici miei, soldati," from Act I), as well as Nelli's "O cieli azzurri," from Act III of

---

* One of the articles included the information that in thirty-three years, since the issuing of Toscanini's very first recordings, 20,000,000 copies of his records had been sold for a total of $33,000,000.

Aida. Two days later, Toscanini spent three and a half hours remaking some of Nelli's solo parts in *Aida* plus the Prelude to Act II of *Ballo* and Nelli's subsequent recitative and aria. After he got the soprano to sing in one breath the climactic phrase of "O cieli azzurri," with its high C, she put her arms around him and he gave her an affectionate whack on the behind.

About those final sessions, the NBC cellist Alan Shulman recalled that Toscanini "came in like a house afire. [. . .] We said, 'My God, he's a rejuvenated man!'" Friedelind Wagner, who was present, noted that at one point Toscanini lost his temper over a detail, picked up the heavy full score of one of the operas, and threw it with such force that it landed in the tenth row of the auditorium. But the sessions were a last hurrah. According to notes taken by Robert Hupka, a Toscanini admirer who also was present, the second session ended with a remake of the dramatic timpani strokes that follow the baritone's "V'ha tre nomi in quell'urna," in Act III of *Ballo*. Toscanini then laid down his baton for what would prove to be the last time. The first opera that he had heard, before his fourth birthday, was *Un Ballo in Maschera*; the first opera that he had conducted, at the age of nineteen, was *Aida*; and the last music that he conducted was from those two works. The symmetry was perfect.

A party at Toscanini's home had been organized for the orchestra members two days after the final recording session, and when he learned that about twenty of the musicians had a professional engagement that evening, he invited them to come over the previous evening. But at that first, smaller party, Toscanini did not appear to greet the guests, as he had always done in the past: he had locked himself in his room, weeping, because he felt guilty that so many musicians were losing their jobs as a result of his withdrawal from the orchestra. One of the musicians wrote a note, which they all signed, asking him to come down and telling him that not only did they not blame him for the disbandment of the orchestra but that they were grateful to him for having continued to keep the orchestra together for so long. But Toscanini failed to appear, and the rest of the orchestra was informed that the following night's party had been canceled because the maestro was not well. On 8 June, Toscanini, accompanied by Wanda, boarded a plane bound for Milan.

8.

TWO WEEKS AFTER TOSCANINI'S RETURN TO ITALY, THE MUSIC critic Beniamino Dal Fabbro saw him at La Scala, at a rehearsal of Beethoven's Fourth Piano Concerto with Arthur Rubinstein and Cantelli. "Rubinstein came off the stage [. . .] and Toscanini stood up," Dal Fabbro noted in his diary. "Rubinstein kissed his hand, and kissed it again before taking his leave. Everyone kisses his hand nowadays, men and women, as if he were a pope [. . .]. Faded, distracted, [. . .] he is venerated as a sort of living mummy of that which was the great Toscanini."

Dal Fabbro's description was excessively grim. For most of the remainder of Toscanini's life, periods of relative physical well-being were interrupted by ischemic and cardiac crises, and his state of mind changed accordingly. His poor vision prevented him from studying music, reading books, or contemplating in detail his favorite paintings, but when he had family and friends nearby, and especially when musicians came to talk shop with him, he was generally in good spirits. There were visits from Giulini, Cantelli, Votto, and others, and Votto later recalled listening with Toscanini to test pressings of the maestro's recordings—at ear-splitting volume, he said.

At this point Anita Colombo, now sixty-three years old, reentered Toscanini's life and the life of the whole Toscanini family. According to the journalist Orio Vergani, Colombo, following her nine years as administrative assistant to Toscanini and Scandiani at La Scala and her single season as the theater's general manager, had lived in reduced circumstances. Her acquiescence, however unenthusiastic, to the Fascist regime had kept her for years in Toscanini's bad graces, but following Carla's death there had been a gradual rapprochement. Whether or not she had been one of Toscanini's lovers in the 1920s—a "fact" that "everyone knew" but that most of the people close to the two parties in question seriously doubted—her devotion to and love for the maestro remained total and indestructible.* Wally understood better than anyone else that Anita's desire to assist the maestro

---

* In the conversation tapes, Colombo always addressed Toscanini as "Maestro" and used the formal *Lei*, even when they were alone together.

dovetailed with his need to have near him someone with musical knowledge and with whom he shared a history and many acquaintances. For the remaining months of the maestro's life, Anita would virtually, and often literally, live with the Toscaninis, who came to depend on her.

In 1951, Toscanini had worried that he would not live a day longer than his mother had lived; now, three years later, he thought that he might die on 12 July, at the exact age at which Verdi had died: eighty-seven years, three months, and seventeen days. The previous evening, Guido and Iris Cantelli, Sandro Cicogna, and Anita had persuaded him to take a drive with them to the nearby town of Vigevano, to see its Piazza Ducale, with its Lombard Renaissance architecture. On the landing outside his apartment, he tripped, rolled down a few steps, and banged his head against the wall. Surprised to find himself unhurt, he decided to make the short excursion anyway, and he and his friends walked all around Vigevano's illuminated piazza and peered into shop windows. He was preoccupied throughout the following day, but at midnight, finding himself still alive, he drank a glass of chilled champagne. When friends laughed at the story, he snapped, "You tell *me* what kind of risk it is for someone my age to bang his head like that!" Then he laughed at himself and muttered, "My God, how old I am!"

The conversations recorded in Via Durini, when he was with a few friends, are full of laughter and teasing. Once, he mentioned to the Cantellis and Anita that his father had danced the waltz beautifully. "And you, Maestro, didn't you ever dance?" Anita asked.

"I? No, no."

"And yet, I remember the *Meistersinger* rehearsal"—she sings the waltz from Act III and evidently shows how he danced to demonstrate the right movement to the Scala chorus.

"That's another kettle of fish," Toscanini says. "In the theater I can do anything at all, but never outside the theater."

Iris Cantelli orders him to smell something. "Good smell," he says. "What is it?"

"Grappa di Bassano—the dark kind."

"What a drunkard you are!"

Iris laughs: "I'm going to give a drop to the maestro."

"Just a little," Anita cautions. Iris gives him some grappa and says, "Now he's going to go around"—she makes the sound of someone gasping for breath. Then she mentions that she doesn't like the Dvořák Cello Concerto, and Toscanini concurs: "Ah, damn it, with the tuba!" he says. "Not only three trombones, but the tuba! Horrible!" But then he mentions that he has just heard a recording of the Glazunov Violin Concerto played by a Russian—Cantelli supplies the name of David Oistrakh—and that he was "left open-mouthed. Ah, by God! That man has harmonics—an intonation that seems impossible!"

In a subsequent conversation Toscanini says, "Sometimes I feel the desire even to conduct an opera. But then I reason—because I still can't see people, you know. Now I see you like ghosts." When he felt well, he regretted not having taken on another NBC season; then he would lapse into a bad spell and become sad and withdrawn. Late in June 1954, he received a cablegram from members of the defunct NBC Symphony, telling him that the orchestra "refuses to die" and that their "first thought—as always—is of you. It is our profound hope that you be willing to conduct your orchestra at any time you desire." Toscanini replied with thanks for the "touching cable," he said. "Greatly appreciate it but my age and my present feeling do not allow me to make plans for the future. Extend my best wishes to each member of the orchestra." Many of the musicians eventually regrouped as the Symphony of the Air, which managed to survive for nine years.

Early in August, Toscanini wrote to Maria Cecchini, "I stay riveted between my bedroom and my study. I work with my mind because I can't with my wretched eyes." But he went to the Isolino and stayed for more than a month; he enjoyed being there but decided not to renew his lease for the following year: he had trouble getting into and out of the boat and even more difficulty walking on the tiny island's hilly paths.

By the end of the summer, however, he had formulated a plan to conduct *Falstaff* the following spring at the Piccola Scala, a 400-seat theater, then under construction, that would adjoin the historic house. Was this a desire to demonstrate that if Verdi, as he approached his ninth decade, could create such a masterpiece, he, Toscanini, toward the end of his own ninth decade, ought to be able to undertake the lesser but still difficult task of performing that work? Probably not. It was more likely the simple wish to continue to work and to give of himself until he could no longer do so. Late in September, while he was taking a mud cure for his arm at Sirmione on Lake Garda, he encountered Natale Gallini, of the Scala administration, and told him of his *Falstaff* project. Gallini replied enthusiastically, although he could not promise that the new theater would be ready by the spring. But Toscanini's children worried that the strain of conducting a staged opera would be too great for their father.

Obstinately, the maestro proceeded with his plans, and by mid-November newspapers around the world had announced the *Falstaff* project. After having beaten a case of pneumonia later in the fall, he began to hold discussions with Luchino Visconti about how to stage the opera. Visconti, already a famous film director, was the grandson of Duke Guido Visconti di Modrone, president of La Scala's board of directors in 1898, when Toscanini was chosen as conductor; Luchino had been one of Wanda Toscanini's childhood playmates. "Why don't you young people try to think up something different and propose it to me?" Toscanini asked the forty-eight-year-old Visconti. "I can imagine only the old scenes—the usual tavern, the usual garden. Suggest something fresh, something nice."

"He wanted the real *Falstaff*, in which the characters would truly recite the comedy even more than singing it," Visconti later recalled. But Toscanini became increasingly worried as construction of the Piccola Scala dragged on longer than anticipated. "Now I'm all right, but in a few months—who knows?" he would tell people. The journalist Camilla Cederna sat next to him at dinner in Via Durini one evening; when she mentioned that some people believed that Chinese mushrooms had a salutary effect, Toscanini's eyes lit up. "Do you have any?" he asked. She did, and he begged her to send him some. "I've got to do everything to stay well," he said. He told her that he had managed to keep his good health because he had never had indigestion (patently untrue), never been drunk, and never smoked. "My mouth is always fresh—I don't stink like an old man." He had again given up coffee—a great sacrifice—in an unsuccessful attempt to persuade Walter to break his smoking habit. And he told Cederna that he generally slept poorly but occasionally had a "restful" dream in which he saw himself shut into a coffin and felt fine there.

Toscanini attended one of Visconti's rehearsals for Gaspare Spontini's early nineteenth-century opera *La Vestale*, which would open the Scala season in December, with Maria Callas in the title role. "'I find this Callas woman very good, a beautiful voice and an interesting artist, but her diction is unintelligible,'" the maestro told Visconti. "'Opera is theater, and the words are more important than the music.' I was stupefied," Visconti recalled; "surely Toscanini could not mean this—and I explained that Maria was a Greek American and did not speak perfect Italian. But Toscanini held to his point. 'No! No! You *must* hear every word, otherwise it's a concert.'"

Victor De Sabata, with whom Toscanini had not been on good terms for many years, was then La Scala's artistic director, and during a break he, Callas, and Votto, who was conducting the production, all came into the auditorium to greet the maestro. De Sabata later recalled, "Toscanini whispered to me, 'You know, it's useless to think about choosing the other singers [for *Falstaff*] since I won't be able to conduct it. I look fine, but actually. . . .' I almost felt my heart stop from anguish," De Sabata said.

On good days, however, Toscanini wanted to proceed with his plans. He sat in Ghiringhelli's box directly over the stage on *La Vestale*'s opening night, and the audience shouted its approval when Callas, after taking a bow, walked over to the box and graciously handed the maestro a bouquet of flowers that had been tossed at her. Docilely, he accepted them. Afterward, Toscanini, Wally, Giulini, Visconti, and a few others had dinner at a restaurant, and the old maestro, smiling at Visconti from across the table, proposed a toast: "*Al nostro* Falstaff."

In Via Durini a few evenings later, Toscanini and Ghiringhelli decided on the *Falstaff* cast. "That evening was one of Papà's happiest," Wally recalled. "He saw his dream becoming a reality. During the night, perhaps because of the sense of responsibility and the fear of having taken on too heavy a task for his age, he worked himself into such a state that in the end it caused a cardiac crisis. When it had passed, Papà immediately understood that he was forced to give up."

"Cardiogram shows noteworthy change without arousing immediate worry," Anita cabled Walter, who was in New York, on 21 December. "Need to avoid emotional apprehensions and displeasures[.]" Walter was alarmed, but he was also relieved "that at last the Falstaff idea has faded," he wrote to Sandro Cicogna. "It seemed to me an act of cruelty to let him delude himself in preparing a task that he can no longer do."

Toscanini recovered well, but friends were warned to avoid telling him anything potentially upsetting. The only work he was able to undertake was listening, with Cicogna's help, to playbacks of his live and studio recordings, for possible release. The first item he approved—albeit with many splices from rehearsal material—was the 1951 NBC Verdi *Requiem* performance. RCA had sent two engineers to Milan to assist in the process, and Cicogna mailed Walter a two-page letter with details of the splices and volume changes that the maestro had requested. At the bottom of the second page, Toscanini wrote, with great difficulty, because he could not see what he was writing, "The two engineers have worked with great ardor and intelligence. I am happy—super happy."

Work on other recordings went slowly forward. With much effort, Cicogna persuaded a reluctant Toscanini to listen to the final act of *Rigoletto* as it had been recorded live at Madison Square Garden in 1944. "I'm warning you, it will make me angry," the maestro had said. But "by the end of the performance Toscanini was in tears," Cicogna recalled. "He said: 'I don't know whether I would be able to conduct that as well today.' It was the closest I ever heard him come to praising himself or anything he had done." (Toscanini later commented that even "that stupid Milanov," who sang the role of Gilda with her face "in the score," sounded beautiful.)* At the bottom of the letter in which Cicogna informed Walter of his father's approval, Toscanini wrote in red ink, over his signature, *"Evviva Verdi!"*

The difficulty of sending tapes and test pressings of Toscanini's rehearsals, performances, and studio recordings back and forth between New York and Milan, and of requiring Cicogna to take notes on the maestro's comments and instructions—which sometimes changed from one listening session to the next—caused Walter to ask his father to return to Riverdale, where everything was simpler. Toscanini eventually acceded to his son's request, and not only for logistical reasons: he did not want old friends and former colleagues to observe him slipping into senility and physical decay.

---

* It is safe to say that Toscanini, who had engaged *lirico leggero* sopranos like Toti Dal Monte to sing complete performances of *Rigoletto*, would not have chosen a *lirico spinto* like Milanov to sing the whole opera: her voice would not have been right for the first act. But in the final act, she did indeed sound wonderful.

He was ashamed of his age, Wally later wrote, and he felt a need "to hide himself, to finish in exile, forgotten by all."

Before he left Milan, Toscanini overheard Wally answer a telephone call from Mike Todd, the American movie producer, who wanted to film the maestro conducting overtures with the Symphony of the Air, using the new Todd-AO cinematic technique. Toscanini showed interest—which alarmed both Wally and Walter—but the proposal remained unrealized.

In mid-February, he made a last visit to La Scala, to attend a rehearsal or performance of *Porgy and Bess*, with an all–African American cast under the baton of Alexander Smallens. He had heard Gershwin's opera performed more dramatically in America, he said, but he was nonetheless enthusiastic about the Milan performance. *Porgy* was a true American opera, Toscanini remarked, and he compared it favorably to the operas of Menotti, although he allowed that he had been moved by the latter's *Amahl and the Night Visitors*. Smallens and his wife came to dinner in Via Durini, and Toscanini, despite his poor eyesight, noted with interest and amusement that one of Mrs. Smallens's breasts popped out of her low-cut dress.

On the eve of his departure, a few friends and acquaintances visited him at his beloved home in Via Durini. Natale Gallini tried to persuade him to stay and head an institute for Verdi studies. "Maestro," he said, "bring me that plane ticket so I can tear it up!" Votto, who phoned to say goodbye, recalled, "I told him that La Scala had proposed that I conduct Donizetti's *Poliuto* with Callas, [Franco] Corelli, and [Ettore] Bastianini. He [. . .] said that it was a great opera, and right there on the phone he began to sing parts of it," although it was a rarely performed work that Toscanini had never conducted. "His memory was still formidable, incredible."

The following day, 27 February 1955, Wally, Emanuela, and Maria Cecchini saw him off at the airport. He would not see his native country again.

9.

VILLA PAULINE FELT EMPTIER THAN BEFORE: CIA HAD DIED THE previous August. She had run the household for years, despite her illness, and Toscanini had been grateful to and affectionate toward her.* Responsibility for looking after the eldest Toscanini now fell mainly on Walter's shoulders, with assistance from his sisters, when they could be present, but mostly from Anita Colombo, who had accompanied the maestro back to New York.

"My stay gives me moments of joy and sorrow," she wrote to Cicogna and his wife in May 1955: "Joy when our great friend is serene and sorrow when he becomes demoralized over the slow decline, which he recognizes without resigning himself."

> Fortunately there is so much musical material here that we often manage to create pleasant surprises for him, and music still has the power to bring him pleasant hours. From time to time something untoward happens and makes us apprehensive, which forces us to be continually on guard without appearing to be so. [. . .]
>
> There are three tape machines that are always working, as well as three machines with double tone-arms for records of every size, which can be operated remotely. I can't begin to tell you what the archive is like, what with records, tapes, not only of performances but also of rehearsals [. . .], thus we have been able to do much work, and more remains to be done.

Walter, too, wrote to Cicogna. He described his father's "drastic mood swings" and said that "when you think you've gotten past a crisis, something unforeseen happens that knocks you for a loop again! My father is obsessed with the idea of becoming completely blind, and none of the doctors' assurances calms him down. [. . .] [I]f he would resign himself to accepting the setbacks that are inevitable at his age, I'm certain that his whole organism would greatly benefit from this nervous distension. . . . Instead, there is great discontent and unhappiness—the incarnation of the drama of Faust!"

Still, when guests came to dinner Toscanini was usually in fine fettle, telling rollicking stories, bragging of never having had a head-

---

* In 1955, Walter presented the New York Public Library with much of his and Cia's vast collection of ballet-related scores, prints, rare books, manuscripts, and other items; this donation, in Cia's name, became an integral part of the library's Dance Division, now considered the largest and most complete repository of its kind in the world.

ache ("Never! I don't know whether I have a head attached to my neck."), teasing Margherita De Vecchi that she was jealous because he had looked at another woman, severely criticizing one of his own recordings, wondering why the conductor Jonel Perlea wasn't having a more successful career, blaming De Sabata for Tebaldi's too-slow tempi in *Otello*'s Willow Song, questioning Pelletier about the children's concerts that he conducted in Montreal, and inquiring about every other subject that arose. When someone told him that in the Metropolitan's current *Otello* production Desdemona went to bed while still singing the *Ave Maria*, Toscanini commented that soon they would show her going "to make pee-pee" as well.

Stokowski wrote to Toscanini in March 1955, inviting him to conduct two concerts with his Houston Symphony Orchestra; Toscanini wired his thanks, wished Stokowski and his orchestra the very best, but said that after sixty-eight years of conducting "last year I decided to retire forever."

A month later, he learned that his sister Ada, his junior by eight years, had died; he had helped support her to the end, but there seems to have been little contact between them. Arturo, the oldest of four siblings, was now the only one left.

Wally came to New York to spend the summer with her father, and while she was there he suffered what she described as a "collapse"—probably a nonparalyzing stroke—after which he easily became upset and often wept, which frightened everyone close to him. In September and again in December 1955, the former NBC concertmaster Daniel Guilet brought his string quartet to play for Toscanini; in January 1956, the newly formed Beaux Arts Trio—with Guilet, the cellist Bernard Greenhouse, and the pianist Menahem Pressler—also went to Riverdale to give him a private performance; and later still, in November 1956, Italy's Boccherini Quintet, led by the violinist Pina Carmirelli, came to Villa Pauline to perform for the maestro.

Occasionally, Toscanini would go to the piano and improvise harmonic sequences around fragments of well-known pieces: he would work his way into a key, and it would remind him of something written in that key. Walter surreptitiously recorded two of these sessions, in which his father embroidered on themes by Catalani (the piano piece "A Sera"), Wagner (excerpts from *Lohengrin*, *Tannhäuser*, and

Götterdämmerung), Chopin (the Etude op. 10, no. 3), and Bellini ("O rendetemi la speme," from *I Puritani*). Toscanini's mind remained sharp: When musicians visited, he discussed in detail virtually any piece he had ever performed, studied, or heard; talked about the acoustics, stages, and backstage facilities of various opera houses; gossiped about singers and other musicians; and commented on performances he had heard live seventy years earlier or on the radio the previous evening. When Dick Marzollo came to the house in October 1955, Toscanini took him to the piano and demonstrated "A Sera" for him; told him how pleased he was that Lotte Lehmann was coming to see him the following Sunday and that a Russian pianist would visit two days later; and even suggested that Marzollo advise his daughter to breast-feed her newborn son. He complained about his insomnia and inability to read, but he also made fun of himself, calling himself *orbo*—a literary Italian term for "blind," which he was not. And he worried about Horowitz, who had not played in public since 1953; Toscanini was convinced that his son-in-law only *thought* he was ill.

The conversation tapes also reveal Toscanini's genuinely empathetic interest in the lives of his orchestra musicians. He may not have remembered every single string player in all of his orchestras, but whenever Marzollo, Pelletier, or any of his other interlocutors mentioned a member of the Scala or Metropolitan orchestra who had died, or of someone from the Philharmonic or NBC Symphony who had changed jobs or retired, the maestro described him in detail—good and bad qualities as a person and as a musician, where he had played before he worked with Toscanini and where he went afterward. His memory for his players seemed nearly as encyclopedic as his memory for music.

As the months passed by, however, and as the sporadic health crises continued, he seemed to sink deeper into himself. His voice weakened, and he became more removed from what was going on around him, even when he had visitors. Sometimes he would sit by himself, dressed in suit and tie, in his living room, and doze off in an armchair. He listened to concerts and operas on the radio and continued, with Walter's help, to approve or reject his own recordings, but at an ever-diminishing pace. On March 25, 1956, his eighty-ninth birthday, his former NBC musicians sent him a case of champagne, but, according to Walter, there was no celebration at home. Toscanini slept fitfully and had dreams and nightmares that he would relate in detail the following morning: he was in a train that never emerged from a tunnel, or he and a friend were stowaways on a ship.

Wally was now spending most of her time in New York, to be near her father. Emanuela, who had married Duke Luigi Filippo D'Acquarone in Milan in April 1956, came over from Italy with her husband, and the couple traveled around America in a camper. By the fall, Toscanini rarely went outside, but there is a brief home movie of him on the terrace of Villa Pauline, walking with tiny steps and holding on to Walter. Milton Katims and his wife visited him one day, and when they greeted him, saying, "Hello, Maestro," he said, "Do not call me Maestro. I am no longer a maestro."

He had had a partial falling-out with Cantelli, who had chosen *Così Fan Tutte* as the first opera he would conduct at the Piccola Scala, which had finally opened: Toscanini—conveniently forgetting that the first opera he himself had conducted at La Scala was *Die Meistersinger*—thought that Cantelli ought to have begun with an opera by an Italian composer. Cantelli, writing to Walter, rightly defended his position; the damage was repaired, and the Cantellis visited Toscanini whenever they were in New York. "Lucky Guido, who is conducting and who has a whole life ahead of him," Toscanini would say. "But he is capable and good, he deserves all the best luck."

Cantelli was a leading candidate to succeed Mitropoulos as music director of the New York Philharmonic; in addition, on 16 November 1956 Ghiringhelli announced that the thirty-six-year-old conductor would become La Scala's new music director. Eight days later, Cantelli was killed in a New York–bound airplane that crashed immediately after taking off from Paris's Orly airport. Toscanini's family, believing that news of this tragedy would kill their father, had someone in Milan send him a fake cable: "Owing to unforeseen terrible attack lumbago forced to delay departure and put off joy re-embrace you[.] With all my affection Guido." Everyone who visited Toscanini during the following weeks was instructed not to mention Cantelli's death.

On 1 December, Toscanini listened to recordings of his live performances of Sibelius's Second Symphony (1940), which he approved for release, and Strauss's *Ein Heldenleben* (1941), which he did not. But by then he was speaking very little, barely reacting when people addressed him. Hugo Burghauser and Jonel Perlea visited him on or around Christmas, and Burghauser later claimed that Toscanini had reminisced about Salzburg, spoken about other conductors, and said that he was looking forward to his ninetieth birthday the following March. That conversation was not recorded, but others recorded around the same time make one surmise that Burghauser was either remembering an earlier encounter or inventing the story altogether. Marcia Davenport, who also visited during those weeks, rushed into the kitchen and burst into tears after having greeted Toscanini; Walfredo, recalling the episode many years later, commented that the family saw his grandfather's decline as gradual, whereas Davenport, who hadn't seen him in several months, was shocked. But Walfredo also recalled that when he introduced a girlfriend to his grandfather, the old man's spirits seemed to perk up and his eyesight seemed to improve.

Mario Delli Ponti, a twenty-five-year-old pianist from Milan, went to Villa Pauline on 29 December and played music by Frescobaldi, Michelangelo Rossi, Bach, and Domenico Scarlatti for Toscanini, Anita, and other guests. Delli Ponti later recalled having had a rather elaborate conversation with Toscanini, but much of the visit was recorded, and one hears only an occasional monosyllable from the maestro. It was the last gathering that Walter taped.

At a New Year's Eve party in Riverdale on the last night of 1956, Toscanini was relatively lively, pleased that all of his children and grandchildren were present and that Emanuela was expecting a baby—his first great-grandchild—within a month. Anita, Giovanni Martinelli, the Wallensteins, and several other friends were on hand, and Virginio Assandri, a tenor from Parma who had sung some minor roles with Toscanini, had managed to get an enormous *culatello* (the finest Parma ham) illegally through US customs, simply by telling the inspector that it was for Maestro Toscanini. At midnight, Toscanini embraced each guest as well as the cook, the maid, and the chauffeur. At about 1 A.M. Wanda said, "Papà, you must be tired. Do you want to go to bed?"

"I wouldn't dream of it! I'm just fine," he replied. More than an hour later, he accompanied his guests to the door, then went upstairs. Wally and Anita had been taking turns sleeping in Toscanini's room, so that he would not be alone. Since he could no longer climb onto his bed, he slept on a reclining chair; they used the bed. It was Anita's turn that night, and, according to information that she and Wally later supplied to a newspaper, Toscanini "awoke at about 7 A.M., put on his bathrobe, and went to the bathroom. When he reappeared in the doorway, he was very pale and tottering. He leaned against the doorpost and put his hand to his forehead. Anita ran to him, held him up, and got him to the bed with difficulty. [. . .] Walter was called from his room, and the doctor arrived soon after. It was a cerebral thrombosis."

Toscanini regained consciousness, and when Sonia came to see him that afternoon he whispered to her, "*Cara, cara*, you've come in time, because your grandfather is dying." But he recovered enough to try to walk: "That iron will of his helped him to conquer the pain," Wally said, "but he was no longer himself. For me, Papà died that New Year's morning."

Further strokes made Toscanini lose consciousness altogether. One morning, Wally saw him move his hands; he "opened his eyes and saw a male nurse whom they had hired on the doctor's advice," according to the same article. "Toscanini had never been able to abide nurses. 'Who is that man?' he asked. They made the nurse hide. [. . .] 'Once in a while, one had the impression that he heard voices,' Anita Colombo said. 'He would nod his head and say "Yes" or "Sì" or a word in Parmesan dialect. On one of the last days [. . .] he murmured, "*No, non così, più morbido, prego, più morbido. Ripetiamo. Più morbido. Ecco, bravi, così va bene.*"'" (No, not like that, more flexible, please, more flexible. Let's repeat. More flexible. That's it, good, it's good like that.)

Wally, the only family member with religious tendencies, had tried to persuade Don Carlo Gnocchi—a family friend who was the only priest Toscanini could abide—to come to America to take her father's confession, although her father had not confessed since his conservatory days more than seven decades earlier. Gnocchi, perhaps fearing the old maestro's reaction, had replied, "It's not necessary for me to go to America. Your father has done so much good in his life that he doesn't need my absolution." Now, when it was clear that Toscanini could not last much longer, a priest was called to administer the last rites. The maestro's eyes were closed; he opened them for an instant only when he heard his name pronounced during the recitation of the liturgical formula.

Arturo Toscanini died at 8:40 A.M. on Wednesday, 16 January 1957, two months and nine days before his ninetieth birthday.

AS SOON AS NEWS of Toscanini's death became public, the Italian flag was lowered to half-staff at La Scala, and the evening's performance was canceled. President Giovanni Gronchi of Italy and US President Dwight Eisenhower issued tributes, as did musicians around the globe. Bruno Walter declared that "the memory of his glorious activities [. . .] will live on in us all," and Pierre Monteux said, simply, "The world has lost its greatest conductor." Milan's evening tabloid, *La Notte*, announced the news in gigantic headlines, and the following day's *New York Times* dedicated part of its front page plus an editorial and nine other articles to Toscanini.

He had left no instructions in his will about a funeral or other postmortem rites. Walter, Wally, and Wanda presumably made their decisions on the matter together. From Thursday afternoon through early Saturday morning, some five thousand people filed past Toscanini's open coffin at the Frank E. Campbell Funeral Home, on Madison Avenue; those who paid tribute included David Sarnoff, Fritz Kreisler, Maria Callas, the Italian ambassador Manlio Brosio, and hundreds of singers and orchestra musicians. At Saint Patrick's Cathedral at 10 A.M. on the nineteenth, Francis Cardinal Spellman presided over a pontifical mass attended by various dignitaries, illustrious figures from the music world, and nearly a hundred orchestra musicians who had performed with Toscanini.

For bureaucratic reasons, the coffin was temporarily interred in the Gate of Heaven Cemetery in Pleasantville, New York. In mid-February it was flown to Milan, and on the morning of the eighteenth approximately 40,000 people filed past the bier in La Scala's foyer. After the benediction, the theater's inside doors were opened, and the Scala orchestra, conducted by De Sabata, played the Funeral March from Beethoven's "Eroica" Symphony in the otherwise empty auditorium; the music was broadcast into the jammed Piazza della Scala. An enormous crowd followed the hearse past Piazza San Babila to Via Durini, where there was a brief pause in front of the house that had been Toscanini's favorite home for nearly half a century; then the procession moved on to the cathedral, where Archbishop Giovanni

Montini, the future Pope Paul VI, officiated, and De Sabata led the Scala ensemble in the *Libera me* from the Verdi *Requiem*, with the soprano Leyla Gencer as soloist.* More than 250,000 people, nearly 20 percent of the city's population, stood in the rain to watch the hearse proceed to the Cimitero Monumentale. Before the coffin was placed in the family vault, the combined choruses of La Scala, the Radio Italiana, and the Milan Conservatory sang "Va, pensiero," from Verdi's *Nabucco*—the same piece that Toscanini had conducted in the same place fifty-six years earlier, in tribute to its composer.

---

* These tributes to Toscanini were the ailing De Sabata's last public performances.

*One of Robert Hupka's
classic photos of Toscanini
rehearsing the NBC
Symphony.*

CODA

WALTER TOSCANINI SPENT THE REST OF HIS LIFE TRYING TO assemble and preserve his father's legacy—not only the vast collection of recordings but also the documentation that was scattered over three continents. He invested most of his inheritance in what he called the Riverdale Project, out of devotion to his father, on the one hand, and on the other out of a legitimate hope to reap a return, for himself and his sisters, from the sale of recordings. In the basement of Villa Pauline, Walter and the sound engineer John Corbett carried forward the enormous task of transferring recordings from acetate discs to tapes, sending the best transfers to RCA, and providing radio stations across the United States and abroad with tapes that could be used for broadcasts dedicated to Toscanini.

Before long, however, Walter found himself in a doubly difficult situation. First, there was the advance of the stereophonic recording process: for casual listeners who were more interested in acoustic quality than in comparing the musical interpretations of one performer against those of another, Toscanini's recordings began to sound outdated, even obsolescent, and sales began to drop dramatically. And Walter and his sisters disagreed as to how this part of their father's estate ought to be handled.

At the time of Toscanini's death, his liquid assets, real estate properties, and other valuable possessions were divided equally among the three children. Royalties on the recordings were also to be split three ways, but Walter believed that he ought to be able to recoup what he had spent on preserving and promoting their father's recordings before the split took place. Wanda wanted to stick to the letter of the agreement; she was much more strong-willed than her older sister, and she often incited Wally to oppose their brother. Within a decade of Toscanini's death, Walter had spent nearly all of his inherited money on the Riverdale Project, which had to be terminated. In 1968, he suffered a stroke that left him partially paralyzed and barely able to speak. Walfredo—who by then was married, had three small daughters, and was trying to make a career as an architect in the New York area—had to try to resolve his father's messy affairs. Villa Pauline was sold (the buyers eventually had it demolished), and its vast contents of recordings and documents were put in storage in the basement of the New York Public Library's Performing Arts Division at Lincoln Center. Walter, who had relocated to an apartment, died in 1971, at the age of seventy-three, and Walfredo found himself in conflict with his aunts.

Any decision about Toscanini's recordings, authorized or unauthorized, now had to be made jointly by Walfredo, Wally (later Emanuela), and Wanda. Wanda, however, would not approve the release of any recordings of her father from which no profit could be made. The consequent unavailability of many of Toscanini's finest performances—contained in unauthorized "live" recordings—caused his posthumous reputation to decline among younger musicians. Nor would Wanda agree to any of the proposals for the permanent placement of the archives that Walter had assembled, because the potential financial gains always seemed to her inadequate. Her relations with Walfredo broke down completely over these issues. But late in 1986, when US laws about tax deductible donations were about to change, Wanda suddenly pushed for an agreement with the New York Public Library—a combination sale and donation of the archives. Walfredo believed that the agreement, made in haste, did not provide sufficient guarantees regarding the use of the archives, but he knew that if he did not sign it the material would continue to languish. All three parties signed, and the archives have since been safely housed in the library at Lincoln Center, available to scholars and other interested persons.

Wally lived on in Italy, a familiar figure in Milanese society and the unofficial First Lady of La Scala. She had her father's generous nature but also his financial insouciance: in the 1980s the family house in Via Durini had to be sold. By then, Wally was suffering from senile dementia, and Emanuela, who was living in Rome, brought her mother there. Wally died at the age of ninety-one on 8 May 1991—the same day, by a strange coincidence, on which Friedelind Wagner, who thought of herself as Toscanini's adoptive daughter, also died, as did Rudolf Serkin, who owed the launch of his American career in part to Toscanini.

Wanda lived out her difficult marriage until Horowitz's death, in 1989; she died in 1998, at the age of ninety. Sonia, their daughter, led a troubled adult life and died, likely as a suicide, in January 1975, when she was forty.

Walfredo Toscanini used to joke that he had two professions—architect and grandson—but he was also active in the Democratic Party in New Rochelle, New York, where he and his family lived for many years. He died at eighty-two in 2011. His encouragement and his contribution of a great deal of documentary material in his possession were major factors in this writer's decision to produce the present book.

In 2016, as this book is being completed, Emanuela Castelbarco is Toscanini's only surviving grandchild. She lives in southern Tuscany, and her documentary material also contributed greatly to this book's substance. Toscanini's other descendants currently consist of four great-grandchildren and three great-great-grandchildren.

Few if any of the orchestra musicians who worked with Toscanini are still alive, and Licia Albanese, the last surviving singer whom the maestro coached in a major role, died at the age of 105 in 2014, sixty years after the maestro's retirement. Today and in the future, the only direct bearers of testimony to his remarkable career are his recordings.

THE EXCEPTIONAL LENGTH of Toscanini's career proved to be his greatest fortune but also his greatest misfortune. On the one hand, it enabled a man who had made his conducting debut long before cinema, radio, and commercial phonographs were invented to be filmed, broadcast on radio and television, and abundantly recorded. On the other hand, it caused many critics, in his later years and after his death, to base their opinions of his interpretations almost entirely on the work of a man in his seventies and eighties and to attack him for his conservative repertoire, overlooking the fact that during the first half of his professional life he had been a key proselytizer for some of the most important composers of his day.

During the 1920s and 1930s, when Toscanini was at the height of his powers and of his fame, overwhelming numbers of musicians and serious listeners considered him to be in a class by himself. Musicians as diverse as Kreisler, Paderewski, Adolf Busch, Klemperer, and Monteux described him as a phenomenon, as someone who stood apart from his colleagues, as "the greatest of all" (Monteux's words) or "the king of conductors" (Klemperer). According to Bernard Shore, principal viola of the BBC Symphony Orchestra in the 1930s, Toscanini was "the one living conductor whom every single member of the orchestra approves." Some musicians disagreed with many or even most of Toscanini's interpretations, but they not only perceived his results as striking and stimulating: they also had the highest regard for his exceptional talents and for the passionate honesty of his approach to music making.

Toscanini's reputation changed dramatically during the three decades after his death. As early as the 1960s, two main cliques were doing battle over the "Toscanini Question": there were the hardcore fans, who seemed to think that a recording by the maestro of even the most insignificant piece of music was automatically better than any other conductor's performance of anything at all; and there were the equally hard-core detractors, who "knew" that Toscanini's performances were too fast and too rigid. The latter faction found a persuasive leader in Joseph Horowitz, an esteemed American cultural critic, who, in 1987, published *Understanding Toscanini*, in which he not only described Toscanini's recorded performances as "redundant" and "as instantly and effortlessly preoccupying as a drawn six-shooter at the movies or a three-and-two count, bases loaded, at the ballpark," but also interpreted the Toscanini phenomenon in the United States as having been deleterious to the development of the nation's musical life. The second of these hypotheses benefited from its connection to an earlier attack by the German sociocultural critic Theodor W. Adorno, who had demonized the Toscanini of the NBC years as an exponent of a capitalist enterprise (RCA) that was attempting to subvert High Culture. The fact that millions upon millions of people around the world were introduced to great music through Toscanini's broadcasts, or that Toscanini was one of the few non-Jewish "star" musicians to have strenuously opposed the regimes that forced people like Adorno into exile, carried no counterbalancing weight, in this critic's view of things.

These polemics have waned in the ensuing years, but for an unfortunate, albeit inevitable, reason: Toscanini, like other significant performing musicians of the first half of the twentieth century, has simply faded further into the past. Although the broad dissemination of compact discs in the 1990s and the proliferation of music on the Internet in the early twenty-first century have made available not only the recordings that Toscanini and other celebrated musicians authorized for release but also recordings of large swaths of their live broadcast performances, many of today's young musicians barely know the names of the conductors, instrumentalists, and singers who dominated the field only one or two generations ago.

The first forty-three years of Toscanini's sixty-eight-year-long career—up to his retirement from La Scala, in 1929—coincided with both the peak and the initial waning of opera as a popular and constantly self-regenerating art form in his native Italy; the remainder coincided with and helped to encourage the tremendous flowering of symphonic life in the United States, his last professional homeland. But the situation in both genres and in both countries (and others as well) has been altered nearly beyond recognition during the intervening years; thus, in the narrow sense, the Toscanini Story is inapplicable to today's musical world.

Yet in a broader sense, that story remains current, because it is the history of a man who spent his life working extremely hard at his art, which he loved profoundly, and who tried always to become better at his work. The conductor Gianandrea Gavazzeni, who heard most of Toscanini's opera and concert performances in Italy from the early 1920s to the end of the maestro's career, and who knew his recordings as well, referred to the "evolutionary quality of his operation, which was tireless, never sated, never still," and he described Toscanini's interpretations as having been "always in a state of flux, as a result of his conviction that a great musical text is never merely a substance to be poured out, but rather a living organism." Such an approach is as valid today as it was a century ago, and as nearly impossible to realize.

One hopes, too, that Toscanini's life story will continue to remain up-to-date because it tells of a person who, despite his overwhelming sense of dedication to his art, refused to ignore his civic responsibilities when the political conditions in Europe became oppressive. "I can't alienate myself from life," he wrote in 1938, in a private letter. "Everyone ought to express his own opinion honestly and courageously—then dictators, criminals, wouldn't last so long."

Anyone who has read this biography from beginning to end knows that Toscanini had several major character flaws: dishonesty in his relationships with some women, most notably, but also outspokenness that could be needlessly hurtful to others and excessive harshness toward musicians whom he rightly or wrongly believed to be insufficiently dedicated to their calling. At the same time, however, readers will have learned of Toscanini's boundless generosity toward other people and toward musical and charitable organizations that he believed needed his assistance, and of his love for his family, for Italy, and for human freedom. Walter Toscanini, who knew his father's personal failings intimately, and suffered from some of them, was yet able to declare that the "human side" of his father's character was even "greater than his musicianship."

Personally, I can still say, as I said at the end of my 1978 biography of Toscanini, that I find most of his recorded performances to be valuable and many of them—especially those recorded between the late 1920s and the early 1940s—to be uniquely beautiful. Even more important, however, is the lesson of his intense purposefulness, concentration, and self-dissatisfaction.

One could object that Toscanini's virtues were those of the Romantic age into which he was born, but surely some of them are worth emulating in any era. As he himself wrote, in the aftermath of the Fascists' attack on him in Bologna in 1931: "the conduct of my life has been, is, and will always be the echo and reflection of my conscience, which does not know dissimulation or deviations of any type—reinforced, I admit, by a proud and scornful character, but clear as crystal and just as cutting."

CREDITS

Selections from the book *Cadenza* by Erich Leinsdorf used with permission of Vera Leinsdorf.

Selections from the book *Ricordi scaligeri* by Enrico Minetti used with permission of Edizioni Curci.

Selections from the book *Les Balcons du ciel* by Margarita Wallmann used with permission of Editions Robert Laffont.

ILLUSTRATION CREDITS

All illustrations courtesy of the Toscanini family unless otherwise indicated.

CHAPTER-OPENERS

Chapter V (p. 208): Photograph courtesy of the Metropolitan Opera Archive.

Chapter VIII (p. 468): Photograph courtesy of the New York Philharmonic Archive.

Coda (p. 858): Permission granted by Arthur Fierro.

ILLUSTRATION GALLERIES

Caricature by Enrico Caruso of the first staging rehearsal (November 1910) for the world premiere of Puccini's La Fanciulla del West: Photograph courtesy of the Metropolitan Opera Archive.

Photographs taken by Robert Hupka during NBC Symphony rehearsals in the 1940s: Permission granted by the estate of Robert Hupka, courtesy of Arthur Fierro, executor.

INDEX

Note: Page numbers in italics indicate photographs.